An Episcopal Dictionary of the Church> A User-Friendly Reference for Episcopalians> edited by Don S. Armentrout and Robert Boak Slocum

 CHURCH

Church Publishing Incorporated, New York

Library of Congress Cataloging-in-Publication Data
        [on request]

Church Publishing Incorporated
445 Fifth Avenue
New York, NY 10016

5   4   3   2   1

For
Sue Armentrout
and
Sheryl Slocum

Contents

Acknowledgments

Literally hundreds of people assisted us in the preparation of this volume. We are profoundly grateful to all, even if many go unnamed. Financial assistance was absolutely essential in bringing this book to completion. We are especially grateful for publication grants from Christ Church Cathedral, Indianapolis, Indiana; the Conant Fund of the Episcopal Church, which is managed by the Ministry Development Office; the Research Grants Committee of the University of the South; and the Discretionary Fund of the University of the South's vice-chancellor, Samuel R. Williamson. We also thank the Very Rev. Guy Fitch Lytle III, dean of the School of Theology of the University of the South, for his financial support and encouragement.

A number of research institutions and persons assisted the editors in this project. We appreciate the helpful suggestions of the Rev. James B. Brown, Helen Depew, the Rev. Travis T. Du Priest, Jr., Richard A. Edwards, the Rt. Rev. Reginald H. Fuller, the Rev. Marion J. Hatchett, the Very Rev. Martha J. Horne, David A. Kalvelage, the Rev. Patrick Mauney, the Rev. William C. Noble, the Rev. Ormonde Plater, Sheryl S. Slocum, George H. Tavard, the Rt. Rev. William C. Wantland, the Rev. Louis Weil, the Rt. Rev. Roger J. White, the Rev. J. Robert Wright, and Rebecca A. Wright. James Dunkly and the Rev. John L. Janeway IV, of the Library of the School of Theology of the University of the South, provided outstanding assistance. Also deserving praise are the Archives of the Episcopal Church, Austin, Texas; the Reference Department, St. Mark's Library, General Theological Seminary; Julia Randle, archivist, the Bishop Payne Library, the Virginia Theological Seminary; and F. Garner Ranney, historian and archivist, the Diocese of Maryland. Three students at the University of the South's School of Theology, Samuel Lee Boyd, the Rev. Susan Pullen Sloan, and the Rev. Bruce Alan White, rendered invaluable assistance to the editors. Bruce W. Woodcock, former secretary for legislation for the General Convention, answered hundreds of questions and assisted in research at the Episcopal Church Center in New York.

Students at the School of Theology of the University of the South were invited to participate in the project. The following M.Div. students provided research assistance and some initial drafts of entries for this book: the Rev. John David Badders, the Rev. Charles Lee Barton, Amy Carol Bentley, the Rev.

Fiona Mabel Bergstrom, the Rev. Robert Lee Brown, the Rev. John Joseph Capellaro, the Rev. William Bernard Carlin II, the Rev. Katherine Corrine Calore, the Rev. Michael Gerard Dunnington, the Rev. Albert Edward Eaton, the Rev. Judith Ann Ferguson, the Rev. Reed Harlow Freeman, the Rev. Ronald Fred Kotre-French, the Rev. Ellen J. Hanckel, Alice Smith Haynes, the Rev. Kenneth Bernard Herzog, the Rev. Charleene Diane Hill, the Rev. Helen McLeroy Jenner, the Rev. Raymond Frederick Kasch, Harry Wilder Lore, the Rev. Reid Tate McCormick, the Rev. Frank Blalock McRight Jr., the Rev. Patricia Craig Moore, the Rev. Paul Henry Phillips, the Rev. Allen Bradford Purdom, the Rev. William Thomas Richter, the Rev. Alicia Dawn Schuster, the Rev. William Gridley Scrantom II, the Rev. Marc Patrick Vance, Robert Reed Van Deusen, the Rev. Erwin Olin Veale Jr., the Rev. Joan Christine Vella, the Rev. Kenneth Nelson Vinal, the Rev. Stephen Bruce Walker, the Rev. Frank Fenn Wilson, and the Rev. Andrew Ray Wright. The following advanced degrees program students also participated: the Rev. James Michael Barrett, the Rev. Stephen Gay Clifton, the Rev. Donald Allston Fishburne, the Rev. Malcolm Fraser Murchinson, the Rev. Robert George Nichols III, the Rev. Henry Keats Perrin, and Ms. Nancy Marie Turner.

The editors thank Deneen Patton for doing a large part of the typing needed to prepare this manuscript for publication, and Elizabeth Anderson, Kevin Greene, and Donn Mitchell, who assisted with the proofreading and final preparation of this book. The editors also thank Michael Altopp and Frank Tedeschi of Church Publishing Incorporated for their patient and careful work in the publication of the dictionary.

Finally, we want to offer our heartfelt thanks to our contributors. Their work constitutes a significant portion of the entries in this book.

D.S.A.
R.B.S.

Preface

The publication of this book has been as sizable challenge. When we began this project, we knew it would be a long, long process to completion. It has certainly proved demanding beyond our expectations. We have done our very best to be thorough, balanced, and comprehensive. As much as possible, we intend this work to be descriptive rather than interpretive. Not every possible term has been included, but we have drawn together terms of interest and importance from the history, liturgy, organizations, and theology of the Episcopal Church. We have included many terms that are important but not exclusive to the Episcopal Church (e.g., baptism). In these cases we have related the topic of the entry to the belief and practice of the Episcopal Church as appropriate. We have also included many entries concerning important people, places, and events from the history and life of the Episcopal Church. With very few exceptions, we have avoided entries on people who are still living at the time of our writing. Their stories are still unfolding, and will be better summarized at a later time. We were saddened by the deaths of two of our contributors, H. Boone Porter and Charles P. Price, who died while this dictionary was in the final stages of completion. Entries for them have been added to the dictionary.

We believe that this book should serve as an important starting point for people with questions about the Episcopal Church and its terminology. Obviously, these concise entries will not answer all questions. We have provided a bibliography of key reference works and additional background materials that may prove helpful and interesting.

Finally, a word about our invaluable contributors, who reflect in many ways the variety of perspectives in the Episcopal Church. Roughly one-third of the entries in this dictionary are attributable, partially or wholly, to their writing and research. However, in the last analysis, we the editors prepared and shaped all entries, and we take full responsibility for the book in its entirety. We hope it will be of service to the Episcopal Church.

Don S. Armentrout
Robert Boak Slocum
All Saints' Day, 1999

Key to Abbreviations

BCP	The Book of Common Prayer	Jl	Joel
BOS	*The Book of Occasional Services*	Am	Amos
LFF	*Lesser Feasts and Fasts*	Ob	Obadiah
		Jon	Jonah
Gn	Genesis	Mi	Micah
Ex	Exodus	Na	Nahum
Lv	Leviticus	Hb	Habakkuk
Nm	Numbers	Zep	Zephaniah
Dt	Deuteronomy	Hg	Haggai
Jos	Joshua	Zec	Zechariah
Jgs	Judges	Mal	Malachi
Ru	Ruth	Mt	Matthew
1 Sm	1 Samuel	Mk	Mark
2 Sm	2 Samuel	Lk	Luke
1 Kgs	1 Kings	Jn	John
2 Kgs	2 Kings	Acts	Acts of the Apostles
1 Chr	1 Chronicles	Rom	Romans
2 Chr	2 Chronicles	1 Cor	1 Corinthians
Ezr	Ezra	2 Cor	2 Corinthians
Neh	Nehemiah	Gal	Galatians
Tb	Tobit	Eph	Ephesians
Jdt	Judith	Phil	Philippians
Est	Esther	Col	Colossians
1 Mc	1 Maccabees	1 Thes	1 Thessalonians
2 Mc	2 Maccabees	2 Thes	2 Thessalonians
Jb	Job	1 Tm	1 Timothy
Ps(s)	Psalms	2 Tm	2 Timothy
Prv	Proverbs	Ti	Titus
Eccl	Ecclesiastes	Phlm	Philemon
Sg	Song of Songs	Heb	Hebrews
Wis	Wisdom	Jas	James
Sir	Sirach	1 Pt	1 Peter
Is	Isaiah	2 Pt	2 Peter
Jer	Jeremiah	1 Jn	1 John
Lam	Lamentations	2 Jn	2 John
Bar	Baruch	3 Jn	3 John
Ez	Ezekiel	Jude	Jude
Dn	Daniel	Rv	Revelation
Hos	Hosea		

Dictionary

A

Aaronic Blessing. Prayer of blessing drawn from Nm 6:24–26. An optional blessing at the close of An Order of Worship for the Evening (BCP, p. 114). The form of committal in the Burial of the Dead is an adaptation of the Aaronic Blessing (BCP, pp. 485, 501). It is provided as a Seasonal Blessing by the *BOS* for Trinity Sunday.

Abbess. Female leader or superior of a religious community, usually a community following the Benedictine Rule. In community matters, the abbess has the same authority as an abbot, but without the abbot's sacramental function. The abbess is the spiritual, administrative, and jurisdictional superior of the community.

Abbey. A monastic community of religious persons along with the buildings of the community. The abbey consists of monks ruled by an abbot, or of nuns under an abbess. Abbeys are independent of the jurisdiction of the local bishop. The traditional plan of the buildings included an oratory (chapel), a chapter room (for assemblies of the community in which a chapter of the rule is read), a refectory (dining area), and dormitories, all of which are arranged around a cloister or an open inner court.

Abbot. Male leader or superior of a religious community. The title is derived from the Latin *abbas* or the Aramaic *abba*, "Father." The abbot functions as the "father" of the community. He is elected for life and receives authority from a bishop. The role of the abbot is to regulate the life of the community in accordance with the rule of life of his community.

Abjuration. A solemn renunciation of any belief, thing, or person to which one was previously loyal. This formal retraction of errors, made before witnesses, often concerned matters of apostasy, heresy, or schism. Prior to 1972, this solemn disavowal was required of baptized Christians being received into the Roman Catholic Church. The Greek Church has required particular forms of abjuration by which former members of other churches must specifically disavow certain beliefs of their previous faith community.

The Episcopal Church has no such requirements for persons being received from other denominations. *See* Anathema; *see* Apostasy; *see* Reception (Christian Commitment).

Abjure. *See* Abjuration.

Ablutions. Liturgical and ceremonial cleaning of the paten and chalice with water, or with water and wine, following the communion of the people at the Holy Eucharist. If the consecrated bread and wine are not reserved for later use, they are consumed by the ordained and lay ministers of the eucharist either after the communion of the people or after the dismissal. The ablutions may also include the cleaning of the celebrant's fingers before and after communion, depending on the liturgical custom of the congregation.

Absalom Jones Theological Institute. A unit of the Interdenominational Theological Center, Atlanta, from 1972 to 1978. Named for the first African American priest in the Episcopal Church, it was to be a resource institution for Episcopal seminarians who wanted to serve African American communities. Its only dean was Quinland Reeves Gordon.

Absolution. The formal act by a bishop or priest of pronouncing God's forgiveness of sins through Jesus Christ. The absolution of sins reflects the ministry of reconciliation committed by Christ to the church. Absolution may be pronounced following private confession of sins, as provided for by the two forms for The Reconciliation of a Penitent in the BCP (pp. 447–452). Absolution may also be pronounced following a general confession of sin in the Holy Eucharist, the Daily Offices, the Ash Wednesday service, and the Penitential Order. The BCP provides that a deacon or lay person may make a "Declaration of Forgiveness" by God of the penitent's sins after private confession, and that a deacon or lay person may pray for God's forgiveness following the general confession in the Daily Offices.

Abstinence, Days of. *See* Days of Abstinence.

Acclamation. A salutation or greeting in the opening dialogue of the eucharistic liturgy arranged by versicle and response and varied according to the liturgical season. The memorial acclamation is a congregational response that may follow the institution narrative in the eucharistic prayers.

Acolyte. In contemporary Anglicanism, a general term which covers not only servers, torchbearers, and lighters of candles but also crucifers, thurifers, and banner-bearers. Acolytes are mentioned as a minor order (along with porters, lectors, and exorcists) as early as a letter of Pope Cornelius to Fabius of Antioch in 252. They were also mentioned in Cyprian's writings. They assisted deacons or subdeacons at the preparation of the table. Later they carried candles in processions. In Rome they carried fragments of the bread consecrated at the papal Mass to other churches. In the late middle ages, when candles began to appear upon altars, they lighted the altar candles. Eventually lay servers or sacristans performed duties earlier associated with acolytes, and the order of acolyte was normally conferred upon a candidate for priesthood in the course of his training. The minor orders were not perpetuated in Anglicanism. Some of the duties earlier performed by persons in the minor order of acolyte were taken over by lay clerks. In the later nineteenth century the clerks were suppressed and their duties were largely taken over by lay "acolytes" and sacristans or altar guilds. *See* Minor Orders.

Acts 29. See Episcopal Renewal Ministries (ERM).

Adams, William (July 3, 1813–Jan. 2, 1897). One of the founders of Nashotah House, he was born in Monaghan, Ireland, and received his B.A. in 1836 from Trinity College, Dublin. In 1838 he came to the United States and entered the General Theological Seminary, New York, graduating in 1841. He was ordained deacon on June 27, 1841, and in Sept. of that year went to Wisconsin with two of his classmates, James Lloyd Breck and John Henry Hobart Jr., to do missionary work under Bishop Jackson Kemper. They formed the Nashotah mission and founded Nashotah House. Adams was ordained priest on Oct. 9, 1842, and served as professor of systematic divinity at Nashotah House from 1843 until his retirement in 1893. He died at Nashotah House and is buried there. Among his published works are *Mercy to Babes* (1847) and *A New Treatise Upon Regeneration in Baptism* (1871).

Addison, James Thayer (Mar. 21, 1887–Feb. 13, 1953). A leader and authority in overseas missionary work, Addison was born in Fitchburg, Massachusetts, and received his B.A. from Harvard in 1909. He received his B.D. from the Episcopal Theological School in 1913. Addison was ordained deacon on June 7, 1913, and priest on Dec. 13, 1913. After serving as a missionary in Oklahoma, he joined the faculty of the Episcopal Theological School as a lecturer in the History of Religion and Missions, 1915–1918, and then professor of the same, 1919–1940. From 1940 until 1947, he was vice-president of the National Council of the Episcopal Church, with supervision of its overseas missionary work. Among his numerous books are *Our Expanding Church* (1930) and *The Episcopal Church in the United States, 1789–1931* (1951, reprinted 1969). He died in Boston.

Adiaphora. From the Greek, "things indifferent," matters which can be accepted or rejected without prejudice to belief. Such practices or beliefs may be tolerated or permitted, but may not be required of faithful members of the church. A sixteenth-century dispute among German Protestants over Roman Catholic practices such as Extreme Unction and Confirmation was finally resolved by the Formula of Concord (1577), which allowed individual churches to use or alter ceremonies not commanded or forbidden by scripture. During this controversy, the "*adiaphorists*" urged that the disputed rites and practices were matters of indifference. In Anglicanism, many practices are allowed but not required.

Administration, Sentences of. Words said by the ministers of the eucharist at the distribution of the consecrated bread and wine during the communion of the people.

Adonai. A Hebrew word literally meaning "my lord," or simply "lord." It is frequently used in the OT to refer to human lords. However, in the period following the Exile when the proper name for God, *Yahweh*, was understood to be too holy to pronounce, *Adonai* was substituted. In most English translations, following this tradition, the LORD in upper case is used rather than the name *Yahweh*, which stands in the original Hebrew.

Adoptionism. The teaching that Jesus was born an "ordinary man" who lived an exemplary life pleasing to God and was consequently "adopted" by God as the divine Son. The moment of adoption was usually considered to be his baptism. Jesus' resurrection was also considered by some the moment of his adoption. Adoptionism relaxes the paradoxical divine-human relationship in Jesus in the interest of emphasizing his independent humanity. The church has regularly found this teaching one-sided and heretical in its failure to give full expression to Jesus' divine nature. Anglican theology has characteristically avoided it. *See* Chalcedon, Council of.

Adoration. An expression of supreme love and worship for God alone. Adoration, one of the six principal kinds of prayer, "is the lifting up of the heart and mind to God, asking nothing but to enjoy God's presence." (BCP, p. 857).

Advent. The first season of the church year, beginning with the fourth Sunday before Christmas and continuing through the day before Christmas. The name is derived from a Latin word for "coming." The season is a time of preparation and expectation for the coming celebration of our Lord's nativity, and for the final coming of Christ "in power and glory."

Advent Festival of Lessons and Music. A service held during the pre-Christmas Advent season in which the reading of the scriptural history of salvation from the creation to the coming of Christ is interspersed with the singing of the great music of the season, including but not limited to carols. A traditional form of service is included in the *BOS*. The most popular forms of service are those based loosely on that used on Christmas Eve at King's College, Cambridge.

Advent Wreath. A circle of greenery, marked by four candles that represent the four Sundays of the season of Advent. An additional candle is lit as each new Sunday is celebrated in Advent. Advent wreaths are used both in churches and in homes for devotional purposes. The candles may be blue, purple, or lavender, depending on local custom. Some Advent wreaths include a white candle in the center known as the "Christ Candle," which is lit on Christmas Eve.

Adventures in Ministry, Inc. (AIM). On May 3–5, 1985, twenty-three concerned Episcopalians met in Orlando, Florida, to discuss issues of renewal and lay ministry. AIM was organized at that time, with Jack and Nancy Ousley of Pensacola, Florida, as the leaders. Its purpose is to assist priests and parishes to become equippers and enablers for lay ministry in the church and in the world.

Advowson. The right to appoint a member of the clergy to a parish or other ecclesiastical benefice. The term also means the patronage of a church living. The right of advowson is a property right under English law. Advowson reflects the control that was exercised by feudal lords over churches on their estates. It also reflects earlier pagan practice in Teutonic Europe. The right of advowson may be held by a bishop or by a lay patron. The patron may also be a university or corporation. The patron may nominate or present a candidate to the bishop or ecclesiastical superior, and this nomination cannot be refused without legal cause. Under English law, an advowson may be transferred by gift or sale. This practice led to abuses and scandals. There is no right of advowson in the Episcopal Church.

Aelred (1109–Jan. 12, 1167). The son of a Saxon priest in Hexham, Northumberland, England, Aelred was a Cistercian monk at the abbey of Rievaulx who became the abbot there in 1147. His two major writings are *Mirror of Charity* and *Spiritual Friendship*. A biography of Aelred was written by his pupil, Walter Daniel. His ministry is commemorated in the Episcopal calendar of the church year on Jan. 12.

"Affirmation of St. Louis, The." A statement adopted by the St. Louis Congress, called by the Fellowship of Concerned Churchmen, Sept. 14–16, 1977. The Affirmation stated the basis for the structure of continuing Anglicanism in the United States and Canada. It argued that the Episcopal Church had "departed from Christ's One, Holy, Catholic and Apostolic Church" and that the holy orders of bishops, priests, and deacons consist "exclusively of men in accordance with Christ's will and institution." It insisted that the only standard of worship for Episcopalians was the 1928 BCP. The Affirmation said that the World Council of Churches was non-Apostolic, humanist and secular in purpose and practice, and that the Consultation on Church Union was non-Apostolic and non-Catholic. "The Affirmation of St. Louis" was the theological and ecclesiological basis for a number of new churches which were formed later.

Affirming Anglican Catholicism. A loose association of members of the Episcopal Church in the United States and of the Anglican Church of Canada who affirm developments in the life of the church such as the ordination of women and Prayer Book revision. In England, Scotland, and Wales it is called Affirming Catholicism. In 1990 a group of laity and clergy of the Church of England and the Scottish Episcopal Church, led by Bishop Richard Holloway of Edinburgh, met to assess the state of the Catholic tradition within the Anglican Communion. In July 1991 an Affirming Anglicanism conference was held in York, and in Nov. 1991 a conference was held in Chicago, led by Bishop Frank T. Griswold III of Chicago. On June 1–4, 1994, the "Living the Catholic Mystery in the 21st Century" conference was held at the University of St. Mary of the Lake, Mundelein, Illinois, with Bishop Rowan Williams of Monmouth, Wales, as leader. The British group publishes *Affirming Catholicism* and the North American group publishes *The Anglican Catholic*.

Affusion. A method of administering baptism by pouring water over the head of the candidate. Baptism may also be administered by immersion of the candidate.

African Mission School. Mission school for training African American Episcopal clergy and laypersons for work in Africa, especially Liberia. It opened on Oct. 6, 1828, in Hartford, Connecticut. It was founded by the African Mission School Society, which was formed on Aug. 10, 1828. The rector of the school was the Rev. Nathaniel Sheldon Wheaton. Six students, Gaylord Jackson, William Johnson, Edward Jones, Gustavus V. Caesar, James Henry Franklin, and Henry Williams, eventually matriculated at the school. Of these six original students, Jones, Caesar, and Williams graduated. Jones was born in 1807 or 1808, in Charleston, South Carolina. He was ordained deacon on Aug. 6, 1830, and priest on Sept. 6, 1830. Jones was sent as a missionary to Sierra Leone, and in 1840 he became the principal of Fourah Bay College, Freetown, where he served until 1858. Later he moved to England and died in Chatham, Kent, on May 14, 1865. Caesar was ordained deacon on Aug. 6, 1830, and priest on Sept. 6, 1830. He and his wife, Elizabeth, went to Liberia. In 1834 he drowned in the St. Paul River, near Monrovia. Little is known about Williams. The first African American priest ordained in Connecticut was Jacob Oson, who was born around 1763. He was ordained deacon on Feb. 15, 1828, and priest the next day. He died on Sept. 8, 1828. The school closed during the nineteenth century.

African Orthodox Church. This church was founded by George Alexander McGuire, a priest of the Episcopal Church, at a time when American Negro self-consciousness was developing as a result of the activities of Marcus Garvey, who wanted to establish a nation in Africa for American Negroes. In 1919 McGuire founded the Independent Episcopal Church of the Good Shepherd, New York, for Negro Episcopalians dissatisfied with the Episcopal Church. On Sept. 2, 1921, the First General Synod of the African Orthodox Church was held in New York City. At that meeting McGuire was elected bishop and was ordained and consecrated on Sept. 28, 1921, by Joseph Rene Vilatte, exarch and metropolitan of the American Catholic Church, one of the *episcopi vaganti*. It has its headquarters at the Holy Cross Pro-Cathedral, New York.

Afro-American Churchman. This periodical was established by George F. Bragg in 1886 at Petersburg, Virginia. It was published from 1886 until 1888. Beginning in 1889 it became a monthly and was published at Norfolk, Virginia. It ceased publication in 1890.

Agape. Selfless Christian love. Agape reflects the love of God, and it is the kind of love that Christians are called to share with one another. The term is also used for a common meal or "Love Feast" of the early church, from which the eucharist developed as a separate rite.

Agape and Reconciliation, Order of (OAR). A contemplative, semi-monastic religious order for clergy and lay people, men and women, married and celibate. It is sponsored by Anglicans, but ecumenical in outreach. It includes Eastern Orthodox and Roman Catholic members. The Order seeks a modern adaptation of the eremitical life and the cultivation of higher consciousness. The Order is based at the Prince of Peace Priory in British Columbia, Canada.

Agnes (d. 304). A martyr for the faith, Agnes died at the age of twelve in Rome during the persecution under the Emperor Diocletian. She is said to have been tortured and executed after refusing to worship the heathen gods. Her name means "pure" in Greek and "lamb" in Latin. Her principal iconograph is a lamb. In Rome, her feast day has been an occasion for the blessing of two lambs whose wool is woven into a scarf, known as the pallium, which is used by the Pope to invest archbishops. Gregory the Great sent such a pallium to Augustine of Canterbury, the first Archbishop of Canterbury. The coat of arms of the Archbishops of Canterbury has a representation of the pall. Agnes is commemorated in the Episcopal calendar of the church year on Jan. 21.

Agnus Dei. Latin for "Lamb of God." The fraction anthem "Lamb of God" is based on Jn 1:29, and may be used in the celebration of the eucharist at the breaking of the bread (BCP, pp. 337, 407). The invocation is repeated three times, with the first two invocations followed by the phrase "Have mercy upon us." The third invocation is concluded by the phrase "Grant us thy peace." The text of the *Agnus Dei* is also used in the Great Litany (BCP, p. 152).

Aidan (d. Aug. 31, 651). A native of Ireland and a monk at Columba's monastery of Iona, Aidan is credited with restoring Christianity throughout northern England. Oswald, nephew of King Edwin, had been in exile at Iona, where he was converted and baptized. Edwin had been converted by a mission from Canterbury, but his death in 632 caused a pagan uprising. Oswald restored Northumbrian independence in 635 when he defeated Cadwalla, the Welsh tyrant, in battle. He sent to Iona for help in restoring the Christian mission. Aidan was sent after another monk gave up in despair. He was consecrated bishop before his departure. When he arrived in Northumbria he was given the Island of Lindisfarne, close to the royal palace at Bamburgh, as his see. He set up a monastery. Aidan took in twelve English boys to train, and began missionary journeys all over Northumbria. He enjoyed the support of Oswald, who often served as his interpreter. Oswald's successor, King Oswin, also supported Aidan. Aidan died in Bamburgh and was buried at Lindisfarne. He is commemorated in the Episcopal calendar of the church year on Aug. 31.

Aisle. Derived from the French for "wing," an aisle, historically, was an extension of a side or "wing" of the nave. It was built to enlarge the seating capacity of the church. This extension typically had a separate and lower roof. The aisle was separated from the central nave of the church by a passageway. The term was eventually applied to the passageways themselves, including the central passageway of the nave or "center aisle." Although the expression "center aisle" is technically a contradiction of terms, it is common usage in the church today.

Alabama, Diocese of. A diocese of the Episcopal Church which consists of all of Alabama except those counties in the Diocese of the Central Gulf Coast. The primary convention was at Christ Church, Mobile, on Jan. 25, 1830. From then until 1844, when its first bishop was consecrated, the diocese had four provisional bishops: Thomas Church Brownell, 1830–1835; James Hervey Otey, 1835–1836; Jackson Kemper, 1837–1838; and Leonidas Polk, 1838–1844. On Feb. 12, 1982, the Church of the Advent, Birmingham, became the Cathedral.

Alabama Plan, The. A diocesan stewardship education project, it was born through a conversation between the Rev. William A. Yon, program director for Alabama and the Rt. Rev. Furman C. Stough, then Bishop of Alabama, in the spring of 1969. Their task was to come up with a grass roots plan for increasing pledges in a continuing growth pattern for a sustained period of time. The Alabama Plan makes it clear that it is designed for the "Christians who wish to become tithers, but cannot do so immediately." It was begun with four pilot projects in 1969 and 1970. The foundation of the plan is a theological statement of stewardship worked through by the vestry and the diocesan council, upon which the following building blocks are laid: thorough plan of action, theological purpose, adequate and committed staff, a staff-training program, and a purposeful publicity and educational program. The history of the Alabama Plan indicates that any congregation which conscientiously involves itself in the process can expect an increase in the number of its pledges and an increase in the amount of its pledged income as well as other less tangible but not less positive effects. Two important factors for success are recognized: a congregation must provide strong, open, committed leadership; and it must be able to assure that at least one-fourth of its membership will actively participate in the process.

Alaska, Diocese of. The General Convention of 1892 formed the Missionary District of Alaska. Alaska was a missionary district until 1972. The primary Convention of the Diocese was held Apr. 21–25, 1972, at All Saints' Church, Anchorage. The diocese does not have a cathedral.

Alb. A long white garment with narrow sleeves, which is the basic garment worn by ordained and lay ministers at the eucharist and at other church services. The alb (from

Latin *alba*, meaning white) is derived from the undertunic of the Greeks and Romans of the fourth century. It may be girded at the waist.

Alban, St. (d. c. 304). First Christian martyr of Britain. The little known about him is from the Venerable Bede. Bede's story places Alban's martyrdom during the persecution of Diocletius (c. 304), but some scholars suggest that it may have occurred during the persecution of Decius (c. 254) or of Septimius Severus (c. 209). Bede writes that Alban was a soldier in the Roman army stationed at Verularnium, a Roman city northeast of London. It is now called St. Alban's. Alban gave shelter to a priest, traditionally known as Amphilalus, who was being persecuted. Alban was converted by the priest and baptized. Alban clothed himself in the priest's clothing, allowing the priest to escape when soldiers came to search the house. Alban was killed in place of the priest. His life is commemorated in the Episcopal calendar of the church year on June 22.

Alban Institute, Inc., The. The Institute, founded on Feb. 1, 1974, by the Rev. Loren Benjamin Mead, seeks to encourage vigorous, faithful congregations and their leadership. It gathers, generates, and shares practical knowledge across denominational lines through research, consulting, publications, and education. In Feb. 1975 it began publishing *Action Information*, which was published bimonthly. With the Sept./Oct. 1992 issue the name was changed to *Congregations: The Alban Journal*. Mead served as director until his retirement on Jan. 31, 1994.

Albany, Diocese of. Formed by the General Convention of 1868, it comprises the counties of Albany, Clinton, Columbia, Delaware, Essex, Franklin, Fulton, Greene, Hamilton, Herkimer, Montgomery, Otsego, Rensselaer, Saratoga, Schenectady, Schoharie, St. Lawrence, Warren, and Washington. It held its primary convention at St. Peter's Church, Albany, Dec. 2–3, 1868. On Nov. 20, 1881, All Saints' Cathedral, Albany, was dedicated.

Albright, Raymond Wolf (July 16, 1901–July 15, 1965). Church historian and seminary professor. He was a direct descendant of Jacob Albright, founder of the Evangelical Church, now a part of the United Methodist Church. He sustained a lively and internationally recognized scholarly interest in the sectarian movements of the Middle Atlantic states in both the eighteenth and nineteenth centuries.

He was ordained deacon on May 23, 1953, and priest on Nov. 28, 1953. Albright was William Reed Huntington Professor of Church History (1952–1965) in the Episcopal Theological School, Cambridge, Massachusetts. Of particular significance among his writings are *Focus on Infinity: A Life of Phillips Brooks* (1961) and *A History of the Protestant Episcopal Church* (1964).

Alcuin (d. May 19, 804). Religious advisor to the Emperor Charlemagne. He was born about 730 in York of a noble family related to Willibrord, the first missionary to the Netherlands. In Pavia, Italy, he met Charlemagne, who persuaded him to become his advisor in religious and educational affairs. Alcuin started a palace library for Charlemagne and the Palace School at Aachen. He was appointed abbot of Tours in 796, and he helped to preserve the classical texts of western civilization. Through his work many of the ancient collects have been preserved, including the collect for purity. He died in Tours. Alcuin's work is commemorated in the Episcopal calendar of the church year on May 20.

Alcuin Club. Organized on Jan. 12, 1897, by four Anglican laymen to promote the study of the history and use of the BCP. Membership is open to any person or institution paying the club's subscription. To date it has issued over 150 liturgical publications.

Alexander, Cecil Frances (Humphreys) (1818–Oct. 12, 1895). Composer of hymns. She was born at Ballykean House, Redcross, County Wicklow, Ireland, in 1818 (some older sources say 1823). In 1835 the family moved to Miltown House in County Tyrone. She and her sister founded a school for the deaf. She published nearly four hundred hymns and poems, most of which were written for children. Her most famous collection, *Hymns for Little Children*, was first published in 1848. It went through more than one hundred printings. In 1850 she married the Reverend William Alexander, then serving the remote parish of Trienamongan (or Termonamongan) in County Tyrone. He became Bishop of Derry and Raphoe, and later Archbishop of Armagh, and Primate of all Ireland. In later life she is said to have walked miles daily ministering to the sick and the poor. She died in Londonderry. *The Hymnal 1982* contains six of her original hymns including stanzas 1–2 and 4–6 of "Once in royal David's city" (102) and "All things bright and beautiful" (405), and one translation, "I bind unto myself today" (370).

Alexander, George Mayer (May 15, 1914–Jan. 9, 1983). Bishop and seminary dean. He was born in Jacksonville, Florida. He received his B.A. (1938) and his B.D. (1939) from the University of the South. He was ordained deacon on July 2, 1939, and priest on Jan. 14, 1940. From 1939 to 1945, he served several small churches in Florida and from 1945 to 1949 was rector of Holy Trinity Church, Gainesville. In 1949 he became rector of Trinity Church, Columbia, South Carolina. He was dean of the School of Theology, University of the South, Sept. 1, 1956–June 1972, when he resigned to become assistant to the vice-chancellor and director of church relations. He was elected Bishop of Upper South Carolina, and was consecrated on Jan. 5, 1973. He served as fifth Bishop of Upper South Carolina until his retirement on Oct. 5, 1979.

Alfred the Great (849–Oct. 26, 899). Saxon king and patron of the church. He was born in Wantage, Berkshire, England. He became King of Wessex in 871, and spent most of his time fighting the invading Danes. He was able to halt their invasion and secure the southern part of England for the English. Alfred defeated the Danish leader Guthrum in 878 and persuaded him to be baptized as a Christian. He and other scholars translated such Latin works as the "Dialogues" and "Pastoral Rule" of Pope Gregory the Great, the "Consolations" of Boethius, the "History" of Orosius, and the "Soliloquies" of Augustine. Alfred is remembered primarily for promoting ecclesiastical reform and for the revival of learning. He alone, of all the English rulers, has been called "the Great." Alfred died in Winchester. He is commemorated in the Episcopal calendar of the church year on Oct. 26.

All Faithful Departed, Commemoration of. This optional observance is an extension of All Saints' Day. While All Saints' is to remember all the saints, popular piety felt the need to distinguish between outstanding saints and those who are unknown in the wider fellowship of the church, especially family members and friends. Commemoration of All Faithful Departed did not appear in an American Prayer Book until 1979, and it is celebrated on Nov. 2. It is also known as All Souls' Day. Many churches now commemorate all the faithful departed in the context of the All Saints' Day celebration.

All Hallows' Eve. The evening of Oct. 31, which precedes the church's celebration of All Saints' Day on Nov. 1. The *BOS* provides a form for a service on All Hallows' Eve.

This service begins with the Prayer for Light, and it includes two or more readings from scripture. The options for the readings include the Witch of Endor (1 Sm 28:3–25), the Vision of Eliphaz the Temanite (Jb 4:12–21), the Valley of Dry Bones (Ez 37:1–14), and the War in Heaven (Rv 12:[1–6]7–12). The readings are followed by a psalm, canticle, or hymn, and a prayer. The *BOS* notes that "suitable festivities and entertainments" may precede or follow the service, and there may be a visit to a cemetery or burial place.

The popular name for this festival is Halloween. It was the eve of Samhain, a pagan Celtic celebration of the beginning of winter and the first day of the new year. This time of the ingathering of the harvest and the approach of winter apparently provided a reminder of human mortality. It was a time when the souls of the dead were said to return to their homes. Bonfires were set on hilltops to frighten away evil spirits. Samhain was a popular festival at the time when the British Isles were converted to Christianity. The church "adopted" this time of celebration for Christian use by observing All Saints' Day on Nov. 1, and All Hallows' Eve on the evening of Oct. 31.

All Saints' Day. Commemorates all saints, known and unknown, on Nov. 1. All Saints' Day is one of the seven principal feasts of the church year, and one of the four days recommended for the administration of baptism. All Saints' Day may also be celebrated on the Sunday following Nov. 1.

All Saints' Episcopal College, Vicksburg, Mississippi. The college was founded by Bishop Theodore DuBose Bratton and opened on Sept. 16, 1909. It was a junior college and high school for women. In 1943 the dioceses of Arkansas and Louisiana joined Mississippi in ownership, and in 1962 the name was changed from All Saints' Junior College to All Saints' School. Men have been admitted since 1970. The school serves boarding and day students, grades eight through twelve.

All Saints Sisters of the Poor. The Society of the All Saints Sisters of the Poor was founded in England in 1856 and opened a house in Baltimore, Maryland, in 1872. The order is now based at All Saints Convent in Catonsville, Maryland. This traditional order uses an Augustinian rule of life, with stress on prayer and liturgical worship. The motto of the community is, "As having nothing and yet possessing all things."

All Souls' Day. *See* All Faithful Departed, Commemoration of.

Alleluia. A liturgical expression of praise, "Praise ye the Lord," from the Hebrew *Hallelujah.* The BCP states that Alleluia is omitted during Lent. *See* Hallelujah.

Alleluia Verse. Alleluias or alleluia psalms that are said or sung immediately before the gospel at the eucharist.

Allen, Alexander Viets Griswold (May 4, 1841–July 1, 1908). Theologian and broad churchman. He was born in a vicarage in western Massachusetts to a family deeply rooted in the Episcopal Church of New England. Educated at Kenyon College, Bexley Hall, and Andover Theological Seminary, he was ordained deacon on July 5, 1865, and priest on June 24, 1866. He served St. John's Church, Lawrence, Massachusetts, before joining the inaugurating faculty of the Episcopal Theological School in Cambridge, Massachusetts, in 1867. His thought and broad church stance were substantially shaped by his attention to such English broad church leaders as Frederick William Robertson, Samuel Taylor Coleridge, and Frederick Denison Maurice. His two major works, *The Continuity of Christian Thought* (1884) and *Christian Institutions* (1897), represent his broad and spacious incarnational theology and his probing methodology. He once said of himself, "I am always moving, as it seems to me, underground, beneath institutions and customs and formulas of thought, and trying to get at some deeper meaning." He also wrote *Life and Letters of Phillips Brooks*, 2 vols. (1900).

Allen, Benjamin (Sept. 29, 1789–Jan. 13, 1829). Poet and publisher. Born in Hudson, New York, and raised a Presbyterian, he became an Episcopalian and moved to Virginia in 1814 where he worked among African Americans at Charlestown. In 1815 he founded and edited the weekly paper, *The Layman's Magazine*, which was published until Nov. 1816 at Martinsburg, Virginia. He was ordained deacon on Dec. 18, 1816, and priest on May 21, 1818. From 1821 until his death at sea, he was the rector of St. Paul's Church, Philadelphia.

Allen, Ethan (1796–Nov. 21, 1879). Church historian. He was born in Plymouth County, Massachusetts, and raised in the Congregational Church. Allen graduated from Middlebury College in 1818. He then went to Prince George County, Maryland, as a lay reader in the Episcopal Church.

He was ordained deacon on Mar. 7, 1819. He served parishes in Maryland, Washington, D.C., and Ohio. He also served as an assistant to Bishop Cobbs of Alabama from 1844 until 1847. He returned to Maryland in 1847, serving as rector of St. John's in the Valley, Baltimore County, Maryland, from 1847 until 1854. He served parishes in Maryland until 1874. From 1870 until 1879, Allen was the historiographer of the Diocese of Maryland. Among his many historical publications, one of the most helpful is *Clergy in Maryland in the Protestant Episcopal Church Since the Independence of 1783* (1860). He died in Newport, Kentucky.

Allen, Roland (Dec. 29, 1868–June 9, 1947). English missionary and writer. He was educated at Oxford and ordained deacon on Dec. 18, 1892, and priest on Dec. 21, 1893 in the Church of England. He went to North China as a missionary in 1895 but was sent home in 1903 because of poor health. He served briefly as a parish priest until he resigned in protest over what he saw as a disregard for the meaning of baptism. Thereafter he devoted his life mainly to research, visiting overseas missions, and writing. His book *Missionary Methods: St. Paul's or Ours?*, appeared in 1912. He describes the apostle as visiting a selected city, imparting the gospel to converts and, perhaps only two years later, ordaining leaders so that the eucharist could always be celebrated. St. Paul would then depart, leaving behind a complete self-supporting and self-governing church under the guidance of the Holy Spirit. *The Spontaneous Expansion of the Church and the Causes which Hinder It* (1927) summarized much of his teaching, presenting careful arguments for a truly indigenous ordained ministry of clergy with many remaining in secular work. Allen retired with his family to Kenya during the early 1930s. The local bishop permitted him to celebrate, but felt it was too dangerous to allow him to preach.

Allen, Sturges (June 25, 1850–Mar. 26, 1929). Founding member of the Order of the Holy Cross and missionary to Liberia. He was born in Hyde Park, New York. Allen received his B.S. from the City University of New York in 1869 and his B.D. from the General Theological Seminary in 1880. He was ordained deacon on May 17, 1880, and priest on June 15, 1882. Allen was assistant minister at St. Mary's Church, Kansas City, Missouri, 1880–1881; assistant minister at St. George's Church, Newburgh, New York, 1881–1884; and assistant minister at the Church of the

Holy Cross, New York City, 1884–1889. On Dec. 1, 1888, Allen became the second Life Professed member of the Order of the Holy Cross. He served as superior of the Order from Dec. 1, 1888 to June 16, 1894, and from Sept. 16, 1907 to Sept. 14, 1915. During his first term as superior, the Order was moved from New York to Westminster, Maryland. During his second term the Order began its missionary work in Liberia. Allen was a missionary priest in Liberia from 1921 until his death. He died in Bolahun, Liberia.

Allin, John Maury (Apr. 22, 1921–Mar. 6, 1998). Twenty-third Presiding Bishop of the Episcopal Church. He was the sixth Bishop of Mississippi from May 31, 1966 to June 1, 1974, and Presiding Bishop from June 1, 1974 to Dec. 31, 1985. He was born in Helena, Arkansas, and received his B.A. (1943) and B.D. (1945) from the University of the South. He was ordained deacon on June 6, 1944, and priest on May 10, 1945. He served churches in Arkansas and Louisiana before becoming rector of All Saints' Junior College, Vicksburg, Mississippi, 1958–1961. He was consecrated Bishop Coadjutor of Mississippi on Oct. 28, 1961. He was a member of the Board of Trustees and the Board of Regents of the University of the South, and was its seventeenth Chancellor, May 28, 1973–Apr. 27, 1979. While he was Presiding Bishop women were ordained to the priesthood for the first time, the Book of Common Prayer was revised, and the Venture in Mission campaign was conducted. He died in Jackson, Mississippi.

Alms. Offerings of money and other gifts at the eucharist and at other times intended to express Christian charity for the needs of the church and the world. *See* Offering, Offerings.

Alms Basin. A plate, basket, or other container used to collect and present the alms given by the congregation.

Alphege (954–Apr. 19, 1012). Also known as Aelfheah, Elphege, or Godwine. Alphege was an anchorite monk near Bath, England, until Nov. 19, 984, when he was consecrated Bishop of Winchester. In Nov. 1006, he was translated to the Archbishopric of Canterbury. He served there until he was murdered by the Danes during a drunken feast. Alphege is considered a martyr, and his life is commemorated in the Episcopal calendar of the church year on Apr. 19.

Altar. The structure, also known as "the Lord's Table," "the Holy Table," and "the Table," where the offerings are presented and the elements of bread and wine are consecrated in the eucharist.

Altar Book, The. The book containing prayers and music needed by the celebrant for the regular celebration of the eucharist. In addition to prayers and chants for the various eucharistic services, the Altar Book includes materials for Ash Wednesday and Holy Week services, along with a Musical Appendix that provides optional settings for parts of the service that may be sung.

Altar Cloth. *See* Fair Linen.

Altar Guild. A volunteer group of the parish whose ministry is to care for the altar, vestments, vessels, and altar linens of the parish. Altar Guild members prepare the sanctuary for services, and clean up afterwards. Altar Guild members frequently supervise the decoration of the sanctuary of the parish with flowers.

Altar Lights. "Lights" are candles or lamps used as a sign of festivity and solemnity in Christian worship. Altar lights are typically candles on an altar. *See* Candles in Worship. *See* Candles.

Altar Rails. Chest-high rails around the altar were used as early as the fifth century to prevent the people from interfering with the ministers of the eucharist. The people came to the altar rails to receive the sacrament, which meant that the altar rails served as communion rails. Some places continued the early church practice of administering communion by ministers who moved among the people. Standing was the normal posture for receiving communion until the thirteenth century, when kneeling to receive the sacrament became customary. This practice was related to the elevation of the host by the celebrant. Altar rails were first used in England during the reign of Queen Elizabeth I. The Puritans disliked altar rails. They often removed them from churches and moved the altar into the body of the church. William Laud (1573–1645), Archbishop of Canterbury, directed that altars be returned to the east wall of churches and fenced by altar rails for protection against desecration. The altar rails were latticed. Bishop Wren of Norwich noted that they were "so thick with pillars that doggs may not gett in." The English clergy continued to move among the people to administer the sacraments until the eighteenth century, when the altar rail came to be used as the communion rail. In the nineteenth century, the chancel was seen as the room for the sacrament and the nave was seen as the room for the liturgy of the word. Altar rails in the Episcopal Church are low, reflecting the assumption that the people will kneel to receive communion. Altar rails may be made of metal or wood. Current liturgical usage has emphasized the shared participation of celebrant and people in the eucharist, and tended to remove barriers between the altar and the congregation. Standing to receive the sacrament is practiced with increasing frequency, and altar rails have been removed from some churches. Altar rails may become obsolete as standing to receive communion becomes more widespread in the Episcopal Church.

Altar of Repose. An altar other than the main altar of the parish upon which the consecrated bread and wine from the Maundy Thursday eucharist are reserved for communion on Good Friday. The altar of repose may be in a chapel or a room away from the church. It is usually decorated with candles and flowers. Members of the congregation may participate in a watch or vigil at the altar of repose from the conclusion of the Maundy Thursday service until the beginning of the Good Friday service.

Altar Stone. *See* Mensa.

Ambo. A lectern, reading desk, or elevated platform from which the scripture lessons are read. The ambo may also serve as the pulpit for preaching.

Ambrose (c. 339–Apr. 4, 397). Bishop and theologian. The son of a Roman governor in Gaul, Ambrose was made governor in Upper Italy in 373. Although he was brought up in a Christian family, he had not been baptized when he became involved in the election of a Bishop of Milan. Ambrose served as mediator between the battling factions of Arians and orthodox Christians. The election was important because the victorious party would control the powerful See of Milan. While he was exhorting the nearly riotous mob to keep the peace and to obey the law, the crowd called out, "Ambrose shall be our bishop!" He protested, but the people persisted. Ambrose was baptized with haste, and subsequently ordained bishop on Dec. 7, 374. He rose rapidly to defend the orthodoxy of the church against Arianism. He introduced antiphonal chanting to enrich the liturgy. He wrote straightforward, practical discourses to educate his people in such matters of doctrine as baptism, the Trinity, the eucharist, and the Person of Christ. His persuasive preaching was an important factor in the conversion of Augustine of Hippo. Ambrose baptized Augustine in 387. Ambrose did not fear to rebuke emperors, including Theodosius, whom he forced to do public penance for the slaughter of several thousand citizens of Thessalonica. Among hymns in *The Hymnal 1982* attributed to Ambrose are "The eternal gifts of Christ the King" (233–234), "O Splendor of God's glory bright" (5), "O God, creation's secret force" (14–15), "Now Holy Spirit" (19–20), "O God of truth, O Lord of Might" (21–22), and "Redeemer of the nations come" (55). Ambrose is considered one of the four Fathers of the Western Church. He is commemorated in the Episcopal calendar of the church year on Dec. 7.

Ambulatory. A sheltered place in which to walk, such as a gallery of a cloister or the outside aisle of a church. It is sometimes called the apse aisle. It may also be a passageway in back of the altar used for a procession.

Amen. Congregational response of assent to liturgical prayers. Amen derives from a Hebrew word that means "truly" or "so be it."

AMERC. *See* Appalachian Ministries Educational Resource Center (AMERC).

American Anglican Congress. On Dec. 4–6, 1995, twenty bishops, clergy, and laity met in Briarwood, Texas, to discuss ways to advance the cause of biblical orthodoxy among Episcopalians. The meeting was called the Briarwood Consultation. The Consultation agreed to form a broad, working alliance of persons, parishes, and ministries that identify with historic biblical Anglicanism. They sought to work for an effective missionary strategy to engage twenty-first century American culture. The alliance was named the American Anglican Congress. The Consultation adopted the 1994 statement, *A Place to Stand—A Call to Mission*, as their working theological document and the vehicle by which parishes, dioceses, and persons may associate with ACC during its formative period.

American Bible Society (ABS). This society was organized on May 10, 1816, by 126 men from a variety of state, regional, and local Bible societies. One of the first proposers of such an organization was the Episcopal layman, William Jay. The chairman of the organizational meeting was the Hon. Joshua M. Wallace, a Manager of the New Jersey Bible Society and in 1816, the Senior Warden of St. Mary's Church, Burlington. In the early nineteenth century, Protestants in the United States began to form national voluntary societies to promote Christian evangelism. Within this period a number of important organizations were formed, including the American Board of Commissioners for Foreign Missions (1812), the American Tract Society (1825), and the American Home Missionary Society (1826). Although some Bibles were published in America prior to 1816, most came from the British and Foreign Bible Society. It circulated them through a network of more than one hundred regional organizations. High church Episcopalians such as John Henry Hobart distrusted interdenominational bodies like the ABS and urged church members to work only through Episcopal circles. However, leading evangelical Episcopalians joined the ABS and aided its ecumenical efforts throughout the nineteenth century. The ABS has now printed the scriptures in more than a thousand languages. It publishes millions of Bibles every year.

American Church Institute for Negroes. Founded on Feb. 12, 1906, to encourage the education and evangelization of African Americans. The Institute raised funds for African American Colleges, including St. Augustine's School, Raleigh, North Carolina; the Bishop Payne Divinity School, Petersburg, Virginia; the St. Paul Normal and Industrial School, Lawrenceville, Virginia; Fort Valley College Center, Fort Valley, Georgia; Voorhees Normal and Industrial School, Denmark, South Carolina; Gailor Industrial School, Okolona, Mississippi; St. Mark's Normal and Industrial School, Birmingham, Alabama; and Gaudet Normal and Industrial School, New Orleans, Louisiana. The Institute was disbanded in 1968.

American Church Missionary Society (ACMS). In May 1860 several evangelical leaders organized the American Church Missionary Society as an independent missions organization to "advance the mission work agreeably to the views of religious truth and obligation which distinguish our Evangelical Church, and occupy still more extended fields of labor." Patterned after the English Evangelical Church Pastoral Aid Society and named in imitation of the English Church Missionary Society, it did missionary work both at home and abroad. At the General Convention of 1877 the ACMS became an auxiliary of the Domestic and Foreign Missionary Society.

American Church Monthly. 1) The first *American Church Monthly* was published in New York from Jan. 1857 until June 1858. It was edited by the Rev. Henry Norman Hudson (1814–1886), a leading Shakespearean scholar. It continued *The True Catholic*. 2) The second *American Church Monthly* began publication in Mar. 1917. It was published until Dec. 1937. It was "A Magazine of comment, criticism and review dealing with questions confronting the Anglican Communion and more especially the Church in the United States." With the Jan. 1938 issue, the name was changed to *The New American Church Monthly*.

American Church Review. *See* Church Review and Ecclesiastical Register, The.

American Church Sunday School Institute. An organization formed to provide churchwide coordination of Christian education. The Institute was officially established in 1884 and was preceded by fourteen years of organized activity. George C. Thomas, Sunday School Superintendent at the Church of the Holy Apostles, Philadelphia, was an advocate for the centralization of Episcopal Sunday Schools. On Feb. 15, 1870, at the Church of the Holy Trinity, Philadelphia, the Sunday School Association of the Diocese of Pennsylvania was organized. Thomas was elected president in 1871. In 1875 the American Church Sunday School Institute was proposed under the presidency of Bishop William Bacon Stevens of Pennsylvania. In 1877 representatives of the Bishop of Long Island and the Sunday School societies of New York and Pennsylvania met to plan a series of Uniform Lessons to be introduced into the Sunday Schools of the entire Episcopal Church. Publication of the *American Church Sunday School Magazine*, the Institute's official organ, began in 1885. The Institute is no longer in existence.

American Church Union, Inc., The (ACU). Although this organization came into existence on May 31, 1936, the organizational meeting was delayed until Feb. 16, 1937, immediately after the election of the ACU Council by the membership of the former Catholic Congress of the Episcopal Church. The purposes of the Union were to uphold the doctrine, discipline, and worship of the Episcopal Church; to extend the knowledge of the Catholic faith and practice of the church; to seek to bring everyone to worship and serve our Lord Jesus Christ, Savior and King; to maintain unimpaired the position of the Episcopal Church as an integral part of the whole Catholic church of Christ; and to promote and encourage the practical application of Christian principles in all social relationships. Later it was added that "membership is open to any baptized person who states his/her belief that Anglicanism must remain part of the Catholic and historic church of Christ, believes *ex animo* (in its entirety, in its historic sense) the Nicene Creed, recognizes Baptism, Confirmation, Holy Eucharist, Penance, Holy Orders, Matrimony, and Unction as sacraments expressed in the *1928 Book of Common Prayer*." The membership splintered in several ways after the 1976 General Convention, which allowed the ordination of women as priests and bishops, and the latest revision of the BCP. It is no longer associated with the Episcopal Church. It began publishing the *American Church Union News* at Eastertide 1937. With vol. 44, Number 2, Feb. 1977, it became the *New Oxford Review*, which is no longer associated with the American Church Union.

American Churchman. This weekly periodical began publication at Chicago in 1861, and continued until June 22, 1871. It was absorbed by the *Churchman*.

American Episcopal Church (AEC). This body was formed during the tensions of the late 1960s. On May 18, 1968, delegates from six parishes, four of which had been in the Anglican Orthodox Church, met at St. Stephen's Church, Mobile, Alabama, and organized the American Episcopal Church. At a meeting on May 20–22, 1982, at the St. Thomas Center, Seattle, Washington, the American Episcopal Church merged with the Anglican Episcopal Church, and adopted the name, American Episcopal Church. The AEC uses the 1928 BCP and subscribes to the Thirty-Nine Articles. It publishes a newsletter, *Ecclesia*.

American Friends of the Episcopal Diocese of Jerusalem, Inc. This organization was formed on Dec. 19, 1988, at the request of Presiding Bishop Edmond Browning in response to the extraordinary needs of the church in the Holy Land. The only purpose of the American Friends is to create and sustain support for the Episcopal Diocese of Jerusalem, which includes Israel, the Occupied Territories, Jordan, Lebanon, and Syria. It is not an advocacy group, and does not participate in political discussions of Israel-Palestine issues. It is especially concerned with children's homes, hospitals, and schools. The first issue of its *Newsletter* was published in Nov., 1990. The first president of the board of directors was the Rt. Rev. Peter James Lee, Bishop of Virginia.

American Missal, The. *The American Missal: The Complete Liturgy of the American Book of Common Prayer with Additional Devotional Material Appropriate to the Same.* It was first published in 1931 by Morehouse Publishing Company. A revised edition appeared in 1951 with the copyright: Earle Hewitt Maddux, S.S.J.E. A note on page iv states: "this book can claim no authority from the Church and is not an authorized publication thereof; but is distinctly supplementary to, and not a substitute for, the authorized publication of the Book of Common Prayer." It was offered as a supplement to the BCP for voluntary consideration and use. It represents an Anglo-catholic tradition and includes collections from monastic offices, and reprinted materials from English missals and ceremonial manuals. Its expanded liturgical calendar included patron saints from various ethnic groups. *See* Missal Mass.

American Quarterly Church Review and Ecclesiastical Register, The. *See* Church Review and Ecclesiastical Register, The.

American Standard Version of the Bible (1901). On July 7, 1870, the Convocation of the Province of Canterbury, England, voted to invite some "American divines" to join in the work of revising the Bible. An American Revision Committee was organized on Dec. 7, 1871, and began work on Oct. 4, 1872. In 1901 their work was published as *The Holy Bible Containing the Old and New Testaments Translated Out of the Original Tongues, Being the Version Set Forth A.D. 1611 Compared with the Most Ancient Authorities and Revised A.D. 1881–1885. Newly Edited by the American Revision Committee A.D. 1901. Standard Edition.* This is one of the versions of the Bible authorized by the Episcopal Church for use in worship.

Amice. A rectangular piece of white cloth that may serve as a hood or be rolled down to serve as the collar of an alb. The amice is tied beneath the alb by attached strings. Many modern albs have replaced the amice with a collar or an attached hood.

Ampulla. A vessel or container for consecrated oils. *Ampullae* of clay or glass were found in the tomb walls of ancient Christian catacombs. They held oil or perfume for anointing the dead. *Ampullae* have also been used to hold oil for lamps at shrines of martyrs.

Anamnesis. This memorial prayer of remembrance recalls for the worshiping community past events in their tradition of faith that are formative for their identity and self-understanding. The prayers of *anamnesis* in the various eucharistic prayers emphasize and make present the saving events of Jesus' death and resurrection.

Anaphora. The central prayer of the Eucharist, also known as the Great Thanksgiving, including the consecration, the *Anamnesis*, and the communion. *Anaphora* is derived from the Greek, meaning a "lifting up" or "offering."

Anathema. The term is derived from the Greek word for "suspended," and it concerns the official separation from the church of members guilty of persistent heresy or grave moral offenses. St. Paul pronounces anathemas on those who do not love the Lord (1 Cor 16:22), or who preach a gospel other than his (Gal 1:8). The Council of Elvira (c. 306) is the earliest occasion of the anathematization of offenders by a church council. Anathemas have been distinguished from excommunication, which only excludes from the sacraments and worship of the church. Anathemas involve total exclusion from the Christian community.

Anchorite, Anchoress. A person under religious vows who generally does not leave his or her habitation. An anchorite lives enclosed in a room or cell, usually in very confined conditions. This kind of asceticism preceded organized monasticism. Simeon the Stylite, who lived on top of a pillar, was an anchorite. Julian of Norwich, an English mystic and anchoress, lived in a cell attached to her parish church in Norwich. *See* Hermit, Hermitess.

Andalusia College, Bucks County, Pennsylvania. About 1859, the Rev. Horatio Thomas Wells (1816–1871) bought the property in Bucks County where a Dr. William Chapman operated a school for boys with speech defects, known as a "stammering school." Here Wells opened a boarding school for boys, and in 1865–1866 the state legislature granted a charter naming the school Andalusia College. The school never granted degrees and did not long survive its founder.

Anderson, Charles Palmerton (Sept. 8, 1865–Jan. 30, 1930). Seventeenth Presiding Bishop of the Episcopal Church, and advocate for world peace and Christian unity. He was born in Kemptville, Ontario, Canada, and educated at Trinity College School, Port Hope, Ontario. He was ordained deacon on Dec. 11, 1887, and priest on Dec. 16, 1888. His first church was at Beachburg, Ontario, where he began to serve in 1887. In 1891 he was called to the rectorship of Grace Church, Oak Park, Illinois, remaining there until 1900, when he was elected Bishop Coadjutor of Chicago. He was consecrated on Feb. 24, 1900, and became bishop of the diocese on Feb. 19, 1905. At a special meeting of the House of Bishops, Nov. 13, 1929, Anderson was elected Presiding Bishop. He died in Chicago.

Andrew, St. The brother of Simon Peter. They were both fishermen. It was Andrew who brought the boy with the loaves and fishes to Jesus for the feeding of the multitude. The tradition claims that he was crucified on an X-shaped cross. Andrew has been the patron saint of Scotland since the middle of the eighth century. St. Andrew the Apostle is commemorated in the Episcopal calendar of the church year on Nov. 30.

Andrewes, Lancelot (1555–Sept. 26, 1626). Bishop and spiritual writer. He was born in Barking, England. He received his B.A. from Pembroke Hall in 1575, and was ordained in 1580. From 1589 until 1605 he was master of Pembroke, and in 1601 he became dean of Westminster. Andrewes was consecrated Bishop of Chichester on Nov. 3, 1605, and served there until Nov. 6, 1609, when he was translated to Ely. From Feb. 25, 1619, until his death he was Bishop of Winchester. *The Private Devotions of Lancelot Andrewes* is one of his most famous writings. His ministry is commemorated in the Episcopal calendar of the church year on Sept. 26.

Andros, Sir Edmond (Dec. 6, 1637–Feb. 27, 1714). He was governor of the province of New York, 1674–1681, and governor of the Dominion of New England, 1686–1689, where he was a supporter of the Anglican Church and an opponent of the Puritans. From 1692 to 1698 he was governor of the province of Virginia. He was associated with the founding of the College of William and Mary.

Andrus, Joseph Raphael (Apr. 3, 1791–July 28, 1821). The first Episcopal clergyman to serve as an overseas missionary. He was born in Cornwall, Vermont, and studied for the ministry under Bishop Alexander Viets Griswold of the Eastern Diocese. He was ordained deacon on June 19, 1816, and priest on Aug. 22, 1817. Andrus was rector for a time of St. Paul's Church, King County, Virginia, but decided that he wanted to do missionary work. In 1821, he and three other members of the American Colonization Society sailed for Liberia. He did not survive the year and died of yellow fever in Liberia.

Angel. Created spirits that are understood to be sent as messengers of God to human beings. Angels are spiritual beings of a different created order from humanity. They are "spirits in the divine service, sent to serve for the sake of those who are to inherit salvation" (Heb 1:14). Angels are pure spirits because they do not depend on bodiliness or matter for existence. Divine interaction with people is often heralded by angels in the Bible. For example, angels announce Jesus' Incarnation (Lk 1:26–38) and nativity (Lk 2:9–15). Angels minister to Jesus after his temptation in the wilderness (Mk 1:13) and before his arrest and crucifixion (Lk 22:43). An angel rolls back the stone after Jesus' resurrection (Mt 28:2–4). Angels herald Jesus' victory over death (Mt 28:5–7; Jn 20:12–13). Angels serve God's glory and power. Angels are involved in God's judgment by separating the wicked from the righteous (Mt 13:41, 13:49). However, angels are not to be worshiped (Col 2:18).

The angelic choirs are understood to sing God's praises. The celestial hierarchy of angels is understood to include nine orders of angels: seraphim, cherubim, thrones, dominions, virtues, powers, principalities, archangels, and angels. The seraphim are understood to be the highest order of angels. The name seraphim is associated with the Hebrew verb which means "to burn," suggesting that the seraphim burn with devotion for God. The seraphim have been termed "the burning ones." In the vision of Isaiah (6:2) they are described as having six wings. The vision of Isaiah (Chapter 6) describes the seraphim in attendance above the Lord's throne. They called to each other and said, "Holy, holy, holy is the Lord of hosts; the whole earth is full of his glory." The cherubim are the second order of angels. They are understood to be celestial attendants. The vision of Ezekiel (Chapter 10) provides a vivid description of the cherubim that emphasizes their wings and wheels. The canticle *Te Deum laudamus* ("You are God") praises God, saying, "To you all angels, all the powers of heaven, Cherubim and Seraphim, sing in endless praise: Holy, holy, holy Lord, God of power and might, heaven and earth are full of your glory" (BCP, p. 95). Archangels are understood to be messengers of God to humanity in matters of greater significance. The three archangels mentioned in scripture are Michael, Gabriel, and Raphael. Jewish apocryphal writings identify Uriel as one of the four chief archangels. Guardian angels are understood to be appointed by God to watch over and help each person. Angels are commemorated by the Episcopal Church at the Feast of St. Michael and All Angels (Sept. 29), and in hymns such as "Ye holy angels bright" (Hymn 625) and "Hark! the herald angels sing" (Hymn 87).

Angelic Salutation, The. *See* Hail Mary.

Angelus. Devotion in honor of the Incarnation, traditionally done three times a day and accompanied by the ringing of a bell. The devotion typically includes repetition of scriptural verses concerning the Incarnation, followed by the prayer "Hail Mary" (Ave), and concluding with the collect of the Annunciation from the BCP (p. 240).

Anglican, The. The first issue of this journal appeared at Easter 1945. It described itself as "A Quarterly News-Letter of the American Branch of the Anglican Society." The last issue was Winter 1969/1970. In the Spring of 1970 a new series began, and with the Fall and Winter 1993/1994 issue it became affiliated with the General Theological Seminary. The subtitle is "A Journal of Anglican Identity."

Anglican and Eastern Churches Association. This organization was founded in 1864 by John Mason Neale in England to pray and work for the reunion of the Orthodox, Oriental and Anglican communions. It sponsors lectures and pilgrimages, and publishes a newsletter.

Anglican and Episcopal History. The *Historical Magazine of the Protestant Episcopal Church* began publication in 1932. With the Mar. 1987 issue the name was changed to *Anglican and Episcopal History*. It began to cover all churches of the Anglican Communion. International members were added to the editorial board. With the new name the journal began publishing "church reviews," short descriptions of religious services in local parishes around the world.

Anglican and International Peace with Justice Concerns, Standing Commission on. The 1997 General Convention established this commission. Its purpose is to develop recommendations and strategies regarding common ministry opportunities with other provinces of the Anglican Communion and to make recommendations pertaining to issues of international peace with justice. The commission includes four bishops, four presbyters, and six lay persons.

Anglican Association of Biblical Scholars. This association was organized in Nov. 1992. It is dedicated to fostering greater involvement of the biblical studies profession in the corporate life of the Anglican churches, and promoting the development of resources for biblical studies in Anglican theological education.

Anglican Catholic, The. The quarterly journal of Affirming Anglican Catholicism in North America. It began publication in Autumn 1994.

Anglican Catholic Church. This group resulted from the theological controversies in the Episcopal Church in the 1970s, especially the ordination of women and Prayer Book revision. It grew out of the Church Congress at St. Louis, Sept. 14–16, 1977. The Congress was called "to continue the Catholic and Apostolic faith of Episcopalians in America and to establish a church structure to that end." The Congress established the provisional Anglican Church in North America. A constitutional assembly was called to meet in Dallas on Oct. 18–21, 1978. At the assembly the name was changed and the Anglican Catholic Church was organized. A constitution was submitted to seven dioceses for ratification. On May 26, 1979, five bishops met at Grand Rapids, Michigan, and announced the legal existence of the Anglican Catholic Church. It uses the 1928 BCP, considers itself the continuation of traditional Anglicanism, operates Holyrood Seminary in Liberty, New York, and publishes *The Trinitarian*.

Anglican Centre in Rome. It was founded in 1966, after the Second Vatican Council, to foster fellowship and cooperation between Anglicans and Roman Catholics. The Centre provides a meeting place for clergy and laity of the Anglican Communion and of the Roman Catholic Church to come together for discussion and prayer; a focal point for Anglican collaboration with the various agencies of the Roman Catholic Church; a library of Anglican history,

theology, and liturgy; and a base where appointees of the Anglican Churches may pursue coordinated discussions for promoting Christian unity, especially with the Roman Catholic Church. The Centre is supported by the Anglican Consultative Council. In Apr. 1993 it began publishing *ACR Centro*, which appears quarterly.

Anglican Chant. Chant in four-part harmony for psalms and canticles. Anglican chant reflects development and adaptation of medieval plainsong. Each half verse of the psalm or canticle begins with a reciting note, and concludes with a melodic ending.

Anglican Chant Psalter, The **(1987).** *The Anglican Chant Psalter* was edited by Alec Wyton under the supervision of the Standing Commission on Church Music. It was published by the Church Hymnal Corporation. It followed the *Oxford Anglican Psalter* (1949), which was largely the work of Ray Francis Brown of the General Theological Seminary. The *Oxford Anglican Psalter* was used from the time of its publication until the publication of the Book of Common Prayer (1979). *The Anglican Chant Psalter* (1987) follows Brown's principles in pointing the canticles and invitatory psalms. In *The Anglican Chant Psalter*, each psalm is given two chants. The first is intended for congregational use and the second for a trained choir. It has a section on "Performance Notes," and an index of composers. It is dedicated "To the memory of Ray Brown in gratitude for his great work at The General Theological Seminary and throughout the Church..."

Anglican Church of North America. This body traces its origins to the Independent Anglican Church that was founded in Canada in the 1930s. It changed its name to the North American Episcopal Church, and in June 1984 it became the Anglican Church of North America. The Rt. Rev. Robert T. Shepherd is Bishop for the United States. It considers itself a continuing Anglican body and uses the 1928 Book of Common Prayer and various Anglican Missals. It accepted the 1977 Affirmation of St. Louis, and published *Our Anglican Heritage*.

Anglican Communion Secretariat. The Anglican Consultative Council came into being on Oct. 31, 1969. In *The Episcopal Church Annual 1993*, the Council was listed as the Anglican Communion Secretariat. *The Church of England Year Book* continues to call it the Anglican Consultative Council. *See* Anglican Consultative Council.

Anglican Communion, The. Churches in communion with the See of Canterbury throughout the world. Member churches exercise jurisdictional independence but share a common heritage concerning Anglican identity and commitment to scripture, tradition, and reason as sources of authority. Churches in the Anglican Communion continue to reflect the balance of Protestant and Catholic principles that characterized the *via media* of the Elizabethan settlement. Unity and cooperation in the Anglican Communion are encouraged by the assembly of Anglican bishops every ten years at Lambeth Conferences. The work and vision of the Lambeth Conferences are continued between meetings by the Anglican Consultative Council, which includes representatives from Anglican churches throughout the world. *See* Elizabethan settlement; *see* Via Media.

Anglican Congress. On June 15–24, 1908, a Pan-Anglican Congress was held in London. On Aug. 4–13, 1954, the first Anglican Congress met at Minneapolis, in response to an invitation from the General Convention of 1949. The bishops of each diocese and missionary district of the Anglican Communion were invited to the Congress, along with a priest and lay delegate from each diocese and missionary district. This was the first representative gathering of the Anglican Church held outside the British Isles. The theme of the Congress was "The Call of God and the Mission of the Anglican Communion." The next Anglican Congress was held at Toronto, Canada, Aug. 13–23, 1963. The leader at this Congress was the Rt. Rev. Stephen Bayne, resigned Bishop of Olympia, and the first Executive Officer of the Anglican Communion. The Congress developed the program, Mutual Responsibility and Interdependence in the Body of Christ (MRI).

Anglican Consultative Council. The Lambeth Conference of 1968 proposed the formation of an Anglican Consultative Council. It continued the responsibilities previously entrusted to the Lambeth Consultative Body and the Advisory Council on Missionary Strategy. The office of the Anglican Executive Officer was replaced by a secretary general. The council came into existence on Oct. 31, 1969. The Rt. Rev. John William Alexander Howe, formerly Anglican Executive Officer, became the first general secretary on Mar. 1, 1971. He served until Dec. 31, 1982. The Rev. Samuel Van Culin, an Episcopal priest, was secretary general from Jan. 1, 1983, until Dec. 31, 1994. On

Jan. 1, 1995, the Rev. John Louis Peterson, another Episcopal priest, became secretary general. The purpose of the council is to provide consultation and guidance on policy issues, such as world mission and ecumenism, for the Anglican Communion.

The first meeting was held at Limuru, Kenya, Feb. 23–Mar. 5, 1971. Subsequent meetings have been held in various locations throughout the Anglican Communion, including Dublin, Ireland; Trinidad, West Indies; Badagry, Nigeria; and Singapore. The 1993 meeting at Cape Town, South Africa, was the first joint meeting with the Primates of the Anglican Communion. The president of the council is the Archbishop of Canterbury. From 1971 until 1992, the council published a newsletter, *Anglican Information*, which became *Compassrose* in 1992, and *Anglican World* in 1993. *See* Anglican Communion Secretariat.

Anglican Cycle of Prayer. A collection of intercessions for provinces, dioceses, and bishops throughout the Anglican Communion. The *Anglican Cycle of Prayer* is published annually by Forward Movement Publications. It also includes special requests for prayers and maps of most provinces.

Anglican Digest, The. A bi-monthly magazine that seeks to present "an Episcopal miscellany reflecting the ministry of the faithful throughout the Anglican communion." It is published by SPEAK, the Society for Promoting and Encouraging the Arts and Knowledge (of the Anglican Communion) at Eureka Springs, Arkansas.

Anglican Episcopal Church of North America. This body was founded on Oct. 10, 1972, in Fountain Valley, California. It was formed by a group of parishes which left the Anglican Orthodox Church and by dissatisfied Episcopalians. In a sense, it was the western counterpart of the American Episcopal Church, which believed in similar things. On May 20–22, 1982, this body merged with the American Episcopal Church, and the new body took the name American Episcopal Church. Some members of the Anglican Episcopal Church of North America refused to participate in this merger and continued this body until it merged with the Anglican Catholic Church. The Anglican Episcopal Church of North America used the 1928 BCP, opposed the ordination of women, and stressed the Bible as the Word of God. It published *Episcopal Tidings*, and operated a seminary, Laud Hall, in Tucson, Arizona.

Anglican Executive Officer. At the 1958 Lambeth Conference, the Committee on Missionary Appeal and Strategy recommended that a full-time secretary of the Advisory Council on Missionary Strategy be appointed by the Archbishop of Canterbury with the approval of the Advisory Council. This officer was to collect and disseminate information, and to keep open lines of communication within the Anglican Communion. This official became known as the Anglican Executive Officer. The Rt. Rev. Stephen F. Bayne, Jr., the resigned Bishop of Olympia, USA, was the first officer. He served from Jan. 1, 1960 until Oct. 31, 1964. He was succeeded by the Rt. Rev. Ralph S. Dean, who served from Nov. 1, 1964 until Apr. 30, 1969. While he was officer, Dean took a leave of absence from his position as Bishop of Cariboo, British Columbia, Canada. The last officer was the Rt. Rev. John William Alexander Howe, resigned Bishop of St. Andrews, Dunkeld and Dunblane, Scottish Episcopal Church. He served from May 1, 1969, until Dec. 31, 1982. The Anglican Executive Officer ceased to exist when the Anglican Consultative Council was created. A secretary general of the council was created at that time. *See* Anglican Consultative Council.

Anglican Fellowship of Prayer (AFP). AFP was founded by Helen Smith Shoemaker, Polly Wylie, and Bishop Austin Pardue in 1958 as a response to the Call to Prayer throughout the church by the bishops attending the 1958 Lambeth Conference. Helen Shoemaker wrote several books on prayer during the first years of the AFP. The AFP seeks to promote the life of prayer within the Anglican Communion. The work of the AFP is extended through diocesan representatives who seek to promote the life of prayer in their dioceses. *See* Shoemaker, Helen Smith.

Anglican Frontier Missions (AFM). On All Saints' Day, Nov. 1, 1990, the first month of the Decade of Evangelism, twenty-three mission leaders of the Episcopal Church met at the Baptist Foreign Mission Board, Richmond, Virginia, and decided to form an Episcopal missionary society to work in places where "the least evangelized live." AFM grew out of this meeting. On Sept. 1, 1993, the Rev. Ernest Auguste de Bordenave began his work as director. AFM concentrates its work where no church exists or where Christian involvement has been slight. Its newsletter was named *Out of Sight*.

Anglican Institute, The. It was founded in 1983 under the leadership of the Rev. Edward L. Salmon, Jr., rector of the Church of St. Michael and St. George in St. Louis, Missouri. When Salmon left St. Louis to become Bishop of South Carolina, the Institute moved to Colorado Springs where it became a ministry of Grace Church. It is the purpose of the Institute to offer a forum for significant theological reflection on topics of importance to the church.

Anglican-Lutheran International Commission (ALIC). Its purpose is to monitor regional and local developments involving the Anglican and Lutheran churches, and to facilitate Anglican-Lutheran relationships internationally. Its genesis was in the 1983 "Cold Ash Report," produced by the Anglican-Lutheran Joint Working Group, which called for coordination and information-gathering rather than theological dialogue. Accordingly, the Anglican Consultative Council and the Lutheran World Federation created the Anglican-Lutheran International Continuation Committee. At the 1988 Lambeth Conference, that name was thought to imply inferior status when compared with the Anglican-Roman Catholic International Commission. Thus the name was changed to the Anglican-Lutheran International Commission.

Anglican Missal. *See* Missal Mass.

Anglican Opinion. A quarterly publication of the Episcopal Committee on Religion and Freedom, an affiliate of the Institute on Religion and Freedom. The Rev. David Apker began publishing *Anglican Opinion* in 1985 as a newsletter to provide a forum for Episcopalians who disagreed with institutional leaders on matters of public policy. In 1987 the Episcopal Committee on Religion and Freedom took over publication of *Anglican Opinion*.

Anglican Orthodox Church. This body was organized on Nov. 16, 1963, by the Rev. James Parker Dees (1915–1990), who had been an Episcopal priest since 1950. He left the Episcopal ministry on Nov. 15, 1963, because he believed the Episcopal Church was guilty of socialism and appeasement of the Communists. He differed with the Episcopal Church concerning civil rights and believed that the church had rejected much that is fundamental to biblical faith. He was also opposed to the ordination of women and to homosexuality. The Anglican Orthodox Church uses the King James Bible, subscribes to the Thirty-Nine Articles, and uses the 1928 BCP. Its clergy are educated at Cranmer Seminary in Statesville, North Carolina.

Anglican-Orthodox Joint Doctrinal Commission. This international commission of some forty officially appointed members was established by the highest authorities of the Orthodox churches and the Anglican Communion. It met for the first time in 1973, building upon contacts between the Anglican and Orthodox traditions for more than a century. The commission meets to consider important theological questions of agreement or disagreement between the churches concerned. Its most important products have been the Moscow Agreed Statement of 1976 and the Dublin Agreed Statement of 1984, which have reached a measure of accord on such questions as ecclesiology, primacy, intercommunion, prayer, holiness, the *filioque* clause in the Nicene Creed, worship, the communion of saints, and the veneration of icons.

Anglican/Orthodox Pilgrimage, The (AOP). This fellowship was formed on Oct. 2, 1987, by Episcopal priests of three dioceses. Its purpose is to move deliberately towards union with the Orthodox Church. The group believes that the Episcopal Church has failed in many essential ways to remain true to the apostolic and catholic faith, and that the Orthodox Church has remained faithful in a unique way to apostolic and catholic Christianity. The fellowship teaches that visible union with Orthodoxy is the solution to the problems of Anglicanism and the only way to preserve what is good in the Anglican tradition. The Rev. William Olnhausen, rector of St. Boniface Episcopal Church, Mequon, Wisconsin, was named chairman of the group. On June 3, 1989, Olnhausen renounced the ministry of the Episcopal Church. On Sept. 16, 1989, he joined the Greek Orthodox Church. In Nov., 1988, the fellowship began publishing a newsletter called *The Anglican/Orthodox Pilgrim*.

Anglican-Orthodox Theological Consultation in the USA. The official body for theological dialogue between the Episcopal Church and the churches belonging to the Standing Conference of Canonical Orthodox Bishops in the Americas. It began in 1962, building upon contacts between the Anglican and Orthodox traditions stretching back over a century. The word "theological" was added to the title in 1974. It consists of about twenty officially appointed members. Episcopal members are appointed by the Standing Commission on Ecumenical Relations.

Anglican Priests' Eucharistic League. It was founded in late 1979, by the Rev. John Gregg Moser (1949–1981), a priest in the Diocese of Fond du Lac. The purpose of the League is the sanctification of the priests of the Anglican Communion through the renewal of their spiritual lives and ministries by focusing on the eucharist as the source and summit of their devotion, as the central element in their life of prayer, and as a sign and bond of fraternal love among themselves. Membership is open to male bishops and priests of the Episcopal Church and of other churches in full communion with the Archbishop of Canterbury. Male deacons may be Associates and male candidates for holy orders may be Probationers. Members are to make an hour's visit to the Blessed Sacrament at least once each week, and to celebrate Mass with special intention for the League on the feasts of its two patrons, St. Peter Julien Eymard, a French Roman Catholic priest, on Aug. 1, and Blessed James DeKoven, an American pioneer of the Oxford Movement, on Mar. 22. Members also are to work for an increased devotion to the Blessed Sacrament in their parishes and dioceses, and to exhort the faithful to visit Jesus in the Blessed Sacrament. The League also has a rule of life for Companions. *See* Holy Hour.

Anglican Rite Jurisdiction of the Americas. An "umbrella jurisdiction" of the Philippine Independent Church which uses the 1928 BCP and insists that the World Council of Churches, the National Council of Churches, and the Consultation on Church Union are non-apostolic and non-catholic. It was established in 1979 by Bishop Francisco J. Pagtakhan, secretary for foreign and local mission and internal and external relations within the Philippine Independent Church, and three former priests of the Episcopal Church for those persons dissatisfied with the Anglican Catholic Church and the proposed Anglican Church in America. The jurisdiction was first suggested at the Second Provincial Synod of the Anglican Catholic Church at Indianapolis, Oct. 18–20, 1979. It published the *Evangelical*. It merged with the American Anglican Church in 1993.

Anglican-Roman Catholic Consultation (ARC/USA). The official body for dialogue between the Roman Catholic Church and the Episcopal Church in the U.S.A., and one of several national ARC dialogues in different countries of the world. This consultation was established in 1965 in the first wave of Roman Catholic ecumenical enthusiasm following the Second Vatican Council. Its members are appointed equally by the Bishops' Committee on Ecumenical and Interreligious Affairs of the National Conference of Catholic Bishops and the Standing Commission on Ecumenical Relations of the General Convention of the Episcopal Church. Consultation members include bishops, presbyters, and laity. ARC/USA promotes practical and pastoral ecumenism between the two churches. It responded to the statements on eucharist, ministry, and authority of the Anglican-Roman Catholic International Commission. ARC/USA has issued agreed statements on the eucharist as sacrifice, doctrinal methodology, the church's purpose or mission, ordination of women, future proposals, and Christian anthropology. Many of its results have been published by the United States Catholic Conference in a series of booklets, *Documents on Anglican-Roman Catholic Relations*. Its goal was defined in 1969 as "full communion of the Roman Catholic Church with the Episcopal Church and the other churches of the Anglican Communion."

Anglican-Roman Catholic International Commission (ARCIC). ARCIC was founded in 1966 by Archbishop Michael Ramsey and Pope Paul VI to be "a serious dialogue which, founded on the gospels and on the ancient common traditions, may lead to that unity in truth, for which Christ prayed." The commission first met in 1970 to seek theological agreement on matters that previously separated the two bodies. *The Final Report* of ARCIC I, published in 1982, claimed to record "substantial agreement," "on essential matters where it considers that doctrine admits no divergence" regarding eucharistic doctrine, ministry, and ordination, as well as a "degree of agreement" on the question of authority (including primacy and infallibility). Other matters discussed included Anglican orders, academic freedom of theologians, and the ordination of women. The agreements claimed on eucharistic doctrine, ministry, and ordination were especially significant because they were the areas of conflict inherited from the sixteenth century that were the basis for the declaration of invalidity of Anglican orders by the papal document *Apostolicae Curae* in 1896. The Anglican Communion gave its judgment on *The Final Report* at the 1988 Lambeth Conference, which recognized the agreements on eucharist and ministry as "consonant in substance with the faith of Anglicans and . . . a sufficient basis for taking the next step forward towards the reconciliation of our churches grounded in agreement in faith," and the authority statement "as a firm basis for the direction and agenda of the continuing dialogue on authority." The Vatican's response to *The Final Report*, released in 1991, was somewhat ambiguous and much less positive. In the meantime, a second commission ("ARCIC II") was appointed and met over the years from 1983–1991, producing an agreed statement on the doctrine of justification entitled "Salvation and the Church" (1987) and another on "The Church as Communion" (1990). Its successor ("ARCIC IIb") published a statement on moral teaching entitled "Life in Christ" (1993) and also released in 1994 a list of "Clarifications" to some of the questions on eucharist and ministry that were raised by the Vatican response to *The Final Report*. The basic documents of ARCIC's earlier history, including the full text of *The Final Report*, are collected in *Called to Full Unity: Documents on Anglican-Roman Catholic Relations 1966–1983*, ed. Joseph W. Witmer and J. Robert Wright.

Anglican School of Theology and Institute of Contemplative Studies, Dallas. In 1971 the Diocese of Dallas began the Diocesan Ordination Course to prepare candidates for ordination who could not pursue training in a full-time residential seminary. In 1975 it was expanded to a five-year program of graduate study, and its name was changed to the Anglican School of Theology. It served exclusively as a diocesan ordination course until 1980, when it received students from the recently disbanded Lay School of Theology. The expanded program prepared students for a variety of lay and ordained ministries. In 1977 the school moved its programs to the campus of the University of Dallas. In 1987 the University started to accept some of the Anglican School courses for credit toward one of two Masters programs. In 1985 the Institute of Contemplative Studies was created to help students pursue the practice of Christian spirituality and to provide training for spiritual directors.

Anglican Society. Founded in 1932, this association of clergy and laity seeks to promote Prayer Book liturgy and loyalty, centrist Anglicanism, and the exploration and affirmation of Anglican identity and self-understanding within the Episcopal Church. It published a quarterly journal, *The Anglican*.

Anglican Theological Review (ATR). A general theological journal serving the seminaries and colleges of the Episcopal Church by providing a forum where issues may be discussed with a view to deeper understanding. The *ATR* was founded in 1918, and publishes articles concerning theology, history of religion, social sciences, philosophy, language studies, and other areas. Its articles and reviews cover the full range of theological topics. It promotes a continuing discussion of the basic issues of our time to increase understanding of the role and function of the church in society. The *ATR* also seeks to participate in the emerging movement toward the recovery of Christian tradition, which "remembers in order to begin again." The *ATR* is published quarterly.

Anglicanism. This way of life is the system of doctrine, and approach to polity of Christians in communion with the See of Canterbury. The term derives from the word which, in a variety of forms, refers to the people of the British Isles, and especially the English. Anglicanism reflects the balance and compromise of the *via media* of the Elizabethan settlement between Protestant and Catholic principles. Anglicanism also reflects balance in its devotion to scripture, tradition, and reason as sources of authority. The *via media* of Anglicanism is expressed frequently in terms of a "golden mean" between extreme positions on either side of various issues. Anglicanism is both traditional and dynamic in the discovery of new expressions. It retains the ancient authorities of scripture and tradition. It also allows for development of new understandings of Christian faith and practice in continuity with the historical church. Until the present century, Anglicanism was largely defined in terms of its English origins and preservation of the language and customs of English-speaking peoples. For example, the Episcopal Church and the various Anglican churches in the British colonies retained their English heritage through a common language, Prayer Book worship, and an episcopal polity. At the end of the nineteenth century, however, Anglicanism began to take on a new identity. The national churches which derived from the Church of England became more conscious of their own identity while remaining in communion with the See of Canterbury. They also retained a common Anglican theological and ecclesial identity. Anglicanism is now a worldwide family of churches which share a common theological heritage and polity. *See* Authority, Sources of (in Anglicanism); *see* Elizabethan Settlement; *see* Via Media.

Anglican World. 1) Published by the Anglican Consultative Council, this bi-monthly periodical provides news for the Anglican Communion. 2) A different periodical named *Anglican World* began publication in Nov. 1960 by Church Illustrated Limited, under the patronage of the Archbishops of Canterbury, York, and Dublin; the Primus of Scotland; and the Presiding Bishop of the Episcopal Church. The last issue was Trinity 1968. A total of thirty-six issues were published.

Anglicans United. This group was organized by the Rev. Canon Albert J. DuBois in Feb., 1977 in opposition to the ordination of women and the revision of the BCP. The goal of the organization was to create an Anglican Province of persons dissatisfied with the Episcopal Church. This province was to be taken as a whole into an already existing branch of the Holy Catholic Church, such as Roman Catholicism or Eastern Orthodoxy. Anglicans United and Canon DuBois led in the formation of the Pro-Diocese of St. Augustine of Canterbury on June 29, 1978. The Pro-Diocese never realized its intention to join another branch of the Holy Catholic Church.

Anglo-Catholic Movement, Anglo-Catholicism. The Anglo-catholic movement was mainly inspired by the nineteenth-century Tractarian emphasis on the identity of Anglicanism with the catholic tradition of the church prior to the Reformation. It has placed considerable emphasis upon the sacramental life of the church, especially the central importance of the Holy Eucharist, and the Apostolic succession of the episcopate. Anglo-catholics were concerned not only with doctrine but with restoring the liturgical and devotional expression of doctrine in the life of the Anglican Church. Some of these expressions, such as the use of eucharistic vestments, altar candles, and incense, led to the controversy over ritual in the later part of the nineteenth century in the Episcopal Church. From the 1860s onward, the movement advanced steadily in America, especially in urban areas and in the Midwest. Anglo-catholic leaders included James DeKoven, Ferdinand Ewer, Charles Grafton, and John Henry Hopkins, Jr. In the earlier part of the twentieth century, Anglo-catholicism was especially strong in Britain and the United States, and in some Anglican churches in Africa.

Anglo-catholics sponsored Congresses which produced serious theological essays on the pastoral ministry of the church and on social questions. In the United States and Britain, Anglo-catholics were frequently involved in ministry to the poor of the large cities. They were also active in ecumenical conversations with the Roman Catholic and Orthodox Churches. The liturgical and theological scholarship of Anglo-catholics had considerable influence upon the revisions of the BCP in the United States in 1928 and 1976, including the central importance attached to the eucharist.

Controversies within Anglicanism in recent decades over the meaning of doctrinal tradition, the ordination of women, ecumenical conversations with Protestant churches, and liturgical renewal have led to divisions among Anglo-catholics. Some have seen themselves as a party within the church who are called to defend what they believe to be the traditions of Anglicanism. Others have supported theological and liturgical developments because they believe these changes are consistent with the catholic heritage of Anglicanism.

Anking, Missionary District of. On Oct. 11, 1910, the House of Bishops voted to divide the Missionary District of Hankow in China and create the Missionary District of Wuhu. The name was changed to the Missionary District of Anking on Oct. 17, 1913. It went out of existence in 1949 when it became a part of the Holy Catholic Church in China.

Anne and Joachim. Legendary parents of the Blessed Virgin Mary. The NT does not mention Mary's parents. The apocryphal gospel known as the *Protoevangelium of James* provides legendary stories of Mary's parents, Anne and Joachim. It was probably written in the second century. According to this document, Anne and Joachim were devout and generous but childless. Joachim was not permitted to offer sacrifice because they had no child. They prayed for a child, and Anne vowed to dedicate the child to God's service. Mary's parents brought her to the Temple when she was three years old, and Mary remained in the Temple until her betrothal to Joseph at age 12. This legend also appears in the apocryphal *Gospel of Pseudo-Matthew*, an eighth-century Latin work, and resembles the OT account of Samuel's birth (1 Sm 1:1–28). Samuel's parents Elkanah and Hannah had no child. Hannah went to the Temple and prayed for help, promising to dedicate her child to God. After Samuel was weaned, Hannah brought her son to the Temple and presented him to God.

The name "Anne," Mary's legendary mother, may be derived from "Hannah." In 550, a church in honor of Anne was built in Constantinople. In 1378, under Pope Urban VI, July 26 was named the day of celebration for Anne. In 1584 Pope Gregory XIII extended her feast to the whole Latin Church. The feast of St. Joachim was introduced in the west in the fifteenth century and has been commemorated on different dates. Joachim's commemoration was joined with Anne in the 1969 Roman calendar. The Parents of the Blessed Virgin Mary are commemorated in the Episcopal calendar of the church year on July 26. The collect in *Lesser Feasts and Fasts* for this day asks God the Father that "we all may be made one in the heavenly family of your Son Jesus Christ our Lord."

Annunciation, The. The feast commemorating the announcement by the angel Gabriel to Mary that she would be the mother of God's Son, Jesus, and Mary's assent in faith to God's invitation (Lk 1:26–38). The Annunciation is celebrated on Mar. 25 (nine months before Christmas). The Annunciation is a Feast of our Lord in the BCP.

Anointing. Sacramental use of oil as an outward sign of God's active presence for healing, initiation, or ordination. Anointing with oil by smearing or pouring may accompany prayers for healing (unction) and the laying on of hands in the rite for Ministration to the Sick (BCP, p. 453). The signing with the cross of the newly baptized may be done by anointing with the oil of chrism, which signifies that the person is "sealed by the Holy Spirit in Baptism and marked as Christ's own for ever." (BCP, p. 308). The oil for anointing may be scented, with different fragrances used in services for healing, initiation, or ordination.

Anselm, St. (1033–Apr. 21, 1109). Archbishop of Canterbury and theologian. Anselm is often called the father of Scholasticism and "the second Augustine." He was born in Aosta, Piedmont, Italy, and took monastic vows at the Abbey of Bec in Normandy in 1060. In 1063 he succeeded Lanfranc as prior of Bec, and in 1078 he became abbot. On Dec. 4, 1093, he was consecrated Archbishop of Canterbury. His time as archbishop was most notable for his struggle with King William Rufus over property and privileges, and with King Henry I over lay investiture of the clergy. He was exiled twice, 1097–1100 and 1103–1106, but eventually he and King Henry I worked out a compromise. Two of his most celebrated books are

Monologium and *Proslogium*, in which he articulated a rational, ontological proof for the existence of God. His argument is that "God is that than which nothing greater can be conceived." In *Cur deus homo* Anselm presented his understanding of the Atonement. He argued that the God-man, Jesus Christ, who was sinless, died for sinful humanity and made satisfaction for humanity's debt to God. Anselm believed that reason supports faith, and that faith seeks understanding. He stated, "I do not seek to understand that I may believe, but I believe in order that I may understand. For this, too, I believe, that unless I first believe, I shall not understand." He was canonized in 1494. Anselm is commemorated in the Episcopal calendar of the church year on Apr. 21.

Anskar (801–Feb. 3, 865). Also known as Ansgar, which means "God's Spear," he is known as the Apostle to the Scandinavians and as the Apostle of the North. Born in Corbie, France, and educated at the monastery there, he went to Denmark as a missionary in 826 and established a school at Schleswig. From 829 to 831, he was a missionary in Sweden. In 831, Emperor Louis established a see at Hamburg, Germany, which was responsible for missionary work in Scandinavia and northern Germany. In 832, Pope Gregory IV appointed Anskar Bishop of Hamburg, and in 848 he became the first Archbishop of Bremen. Although there is some debate as to the long-term effectiveness of Anskar's work, he is the patron saint of Denmark. His life is commemorated in the Episcopal calendar of the church year on Feb. 3.

Ante-Communion. The liturgy of the word (*Pro-anaphora*) from the eucharist, without the Great Thanksgiving or communion of the people. Ante-Communion includes the first part of the eucharistic rite through the prayers of the people. It may begin with the Penitential Order if a confession of sin is desired. The BCP (pp. 406–407) provides that a hymn or anthem may be sung after the prayers of the people and the offerings of the people are received. The service may conclude with the Lord's Prayer and with the grace or a blessing or the peace. Ante-Communion (without the final blessing) may be led by a deacon or lay person if a priest is unavailable.

Antependium. See Frontal.

Anthem. Choral setting of sacred vocal music set to scriptural or liturgical texts, "or texts congruent with them."

(BCP, p. 14). "Anthem" is an Anglicized form of the word "antiphon."

Anthon, Henry (Mar. 11, 1795–Jan. 5, 1861). A founder of the Protestant Episcopal Society for the Promotion of Evangelical Knowledge (1847) and one of the leading protesters against the ordination of Arthur Carey, controversial disciple of the Oxford Movement. He was born in New York City and graduated from Columbia College in 1813. He studied for the ministry under Bishop John Henry Hobart. Anthon was ordained deacon on Sept. 29, 1816, and priest on May 27, 1819. He was rector of St. Paul's Church, Red Hook, New York, 1816–1819, but because of illness spent the next two years in South Carolina. He was rector of Trinity Church, Utica, New York, 1821–1829, and of St. Stephen's Church, New York, 1829–1831. From 1831 to 1837 he was assistant minister at Trinity Church, New York. His last and major ministry was as rector of St. Mark's Church, New York. He was the tenth secretary of the House of Deputies, serving the General Conventions of 1832, 1835, 1838, and 1841.

Antinomianism. From the Greek *anti*, "against," and *nomos*, "law," the term is given to teaching opposed to the binding character of moral law. In Christian theology it denotes the doctrine that grace frees believers from the Law. The word "antinomian" seems to have emerged in the sixteenth century when it was applied to the teaching of the Lutheran theologian, J. Agricola, as well as that of certain Anabaptist sects. Although the word antinomian was not used in earlier times, St. Paul himself was accused of setting aside the force of the Law because of his teaching about justification. Lutheranism is thought by some to have invited antinomianism because of its emphasis on justification by faith alone. Anglican opposition to antinomianism is indicated in Article XII of the Articles of Religion: "Good works . . . cannot put away our sins; . . . yet they are pleasing and acceptable to God in Christ" (BCP, p. 870).

Antiphon. A verse sung before and usually after a psalm, canticle, or hymn text. It is often drawn from scripture (especially the psalms) and is appropriate to the liturgical season or occasion. The BCP (p. 141) provides that antiphons may be used with the psalms of the Daily Office. These antiphons may be drawn from the psalms, or from the opening sentences in the Daily Offices, or from other passages of scripture. The *BOS* suggests antiphons for use on special occasions such as the Stripping of the Altar on Maundy Thursday, the last stage of a Candlemas procession, and the welcoming procession for the new bishop at the Recognition and Investiture of a Diocesan Bishop. Hymns such as "This is the feast of victory for our God" (417, 418), "Remember your servants, Lord" (560), and "Where true charity and love dwell" (606) are sung with antiphons.

Antiphonal. Verse-by-verse alternation between groups of singers or readers for the singing or recitation of the Psalter. This alternation may be between choir and congregation, or between one side of the congregation and the other (BCP, p. 582). The term is from the Greek, meaning "voice against voice."

Antiphonary. A collection of chants to be sung antiphonally by the choir in public worship. It is also known as an antiphonal. It originally provided chants for the eucharist and the Daily Offices of the church. The chants for the eucharist and for the Daily Offices were eventually separated. A chant-book for the eucharist is now typically known as a *graduale*, or book of graduals. An antiphonary or antiphonal typically refers to a chant-book for the Daily Offices.

Antony (c. 251–356). Early Christian desert hermit. He was raised in a Christian home. After his parents died he sold all his possessions and became a hermit or anchorite. He devoted himself to a life of asceticism. He retired to the desert where he lived in solitude, fasting, and prayer. Antony is said to have fought with demons under the guise of wild beasts. Athanasius wrote a *Life of Antony* (c. 357), which helped to spread the idea of anchorite monasticism. Antony is commemorated in the Episcopal calendar of the church year on Jan. 17.

Apocrypha. From the Greek word for "hidden." It normally refers to fifteen books not found in the Hebrew canon of the OT and includes the following: Tobit, Judith, Additions to the Book of Esther, the Wisdom of Solomon, Ecclesiasticus (the Wisdom of Jesus son of Sirach), Baruch, the Letter of Jeremiah, the Prayer of Azariah and the Song of the Three Children, Susanna, Bel and the Dragon, 1 Maccabees, 2 Maccabees, 1 Esdras, the Prayer of Manasseh, and 2 Esdras. Eastern Orthodox churches recognize other books in this category, including 1 Esdras,

Psalm 152, the Prayer of Manasseh, 3 Maccabees, and 4 Maccabees. All of these books, with the exception of 2 Esdras, are found in the Septuagint, the Greek version of the OT. However, most of them were almost certainly originally written in Hebrew or Aramaic by pious Jews in the period between c. 250 B.C. and 100 A.D. The Roman Catholic Church has traditionally included the fifteen books in their authoritative canon. These books are called deutero-canonical in the Roman Catholic Church, as distinguished from the thirty-nine proto-canonical books of the Hebrew Bible. Since the Reformation, Protestants have recognized only the proto-canonical books as belonging to the authoritative canon.

Apollinarianism. Christological heresy of the fourth century, based on the teaching of Apollinarius, Bishop of Laodicea (c. 310–c. 390). Apollinarius held that Christ had no human spirit. The Divine Logos was believed to take the place of the human spirit in Christ. Christ thus was understood to be fully divine but less than fully human. Apollinarianism was opposed by Gregory of Nazianzus and Gregory of Nyssa. It was condemned by the General Council of Constantinople I (381).

Apologetics, Apologists, Apology. The theological discipline of defending the Christian faith against attack, often by use of the thought-forms of the attacker. An apologist is one who defends the faith by making an apology. The terms are derived from the Greek *apologia*, a "defense," the reply to the speech of the prosecution.

Apophatic. A theological term which derives from a Greek word meaning a denial or negation. Its opposite is cataphatic, which means something that is made known or affirmed. As a theological term it has chiefly been used in the tradition of Byzantine or Eastern Orthodox theology to refer to the relation of human rationality to the knowledge of God, although it has clear equivalents in western Latin theology.

In the Greek theological tradition, the three theologians who are most commonly associated with the apophatic tradition are Gregory of Nyssa (fourth century), Maximus the Confessor (seventh century), and Gregory Palamas (fourteenth century). The doctrine in Greek theology is extremely complex and the source of much controversy. Basically, however, it is the assertion that human beings, because of their finitude and sinfulness, cannot comprehend God's essence or being. God "lies beyond" or transcends all human apprehension of God, except as God is revealed in the positive symbols of revelation and the knowledge of God which is possible through the positive categories of dogma (cataphatic theology). Ultimately, God is "unknowable," not as an absence of knowledge but as a knowledge of silence or negativity— the kind of knowledge which is possible in the silence of contemplation.

Western or Latin theology has generally been more positive (scientific) in its approach to human knowledge of God, but the apophatic is found in both the theological and the mystical tradition. Thomas Aquinas, for example, begins his Treatise on God with the statement, "Now we cannot know what God is, but only what God is not; we must therefore consider the ways in which God does not exist, rather than the ways in which God does." He then proceeds to discuss how God is known from the positive effects of God in creation. This tradition is also carried out in the mystical tradition of Meister Eckhart, John of the Cross, and many others. One of its chief contemporary exponents is Karl Rahner. *See* Cappadocians, or Cappadocian Fathers; *see* Cataphatic.

Apophthegm. A Greek word that, literally translated, means "a thing uttered" or "something said." The term is used by form critics who focus on the editing of the gospels. The English terms used include the words "paradigm," "pronouncement story," and "anecdote." An *apophthegm* or pronouncement story refers to units in the gospels where Jesus is quoted as saying something very important as a conclusion to a situation. The situation which precedes the pronouncement helps to clarify the meaning of the statement. It is one of the most important and most used forms in the form critical approach. It occurs a significant number of times in the gospels. Form criticism raises the question about the validity of the material that precedes the pronouncement. It raises the question whether this material was added later as a way of trying to explain to the listeners why Jesus would make such a statement. *See* Form Criticism.

Apophthegmata. From the Greek *apophthegm*, meaning a terse or pointed saying, this term now usually refers to sayings and maxims of the Desert Fathers and Mothers, mostly from fourth- and fifth-century Egypt. Abbas Poemen, Antony, and Arsenius and disciples are featured. The *apophthegmata* are found in several collections in different languages, arranged either by particular Fathers and Mothers, or systematically. These collections provide evidence for the origins of monasticism and classical Christian spirituality and convey the spirit of primitive desert spirituality.

Apostasy. From the Greek *apo*, "away from," and *stasis* "standing," literally meaning a "standing apart," apostasy is used in Christian theology to speak of total renunciation of faith in Christ and abandonment of Christianity. It has always been considered to be among the most serious sins. Apostasy was regarded as unforgivable in the post-apostolic church. However, the magnitude of defections during the Decian persecutions in 250 compelled the church to apply its gospel of forgiveness to apostates. Hippolytus and Tertullian were rigorists in the discussion, but Callistus advocated a more merciful course. Cyprian required rebaptism.

The Diocletian persecutions in 303 spawned the Donatist controversy. Donatists claimed that only the pure could remain in communion with the church. Optatus and Augustine framed the catholic response. They urged that the church is a *societas mixta*, saints and sinners mixed together, and that even apostates could be accepted back into the communion of the church after rigorous penance. They did not demand rebaptism. Their position continues to be upheld by the church.

One who commits apostasy is an apostate. *See* Abjuration.

Apostate. *See* Apostasy.

Apostle. A term based on the Greek word which means "someone sent out." It is used seventy-nine times in the NT. It often refers to the disciples. The primary NT meaning seems to refer to someone who is a personal messenger of Jesus. This is emphasized in Acts when Matthias is chosen to replace Judas, the betrayer, after he committed suicide. Although Paul was not a follower or disciple of Jesus before his death and resurrection, he does refer to himself as an apostle because he had seen the risen Lord and he was sent out to preach to the Gentiles. In Heb 3:1 Jesus is called an apostle because he is one who was sent by God.

Apostles' Creed, The. Ancient formula of Christian belief in three sections concerning God the Father, the Son, and the Holy Spirit. Although its authorship is attributed to the twelve apostles, opinions vary concerning its origin.

Its title dates from the late fourth century, and it may be based on a shorter form of the creed in use at Rome in the middle of the second century. The Apostles' Creed may be considered to be an authentic expression of the apostolic faith. It contains twelve articles, and is known as the baptismal creed because catechumens were traditionally required to recite it before baptism. It was the basis for the original baptismal formula. Candidates were baptized by immersion or affusion after their response of faith to each of the three questions concerning Father, Son, and Holy Spirit. The Apostles' Creed is the basis for the baptismal covenant in the BCP (p. 304), and it is used in the Daily Offices. It may be used at the Celebration and Blessing of a Marriage, at the Burial of the Dead, and at the Consecration of a Church.

Apostolic Blessing. Among Roman Catholics, a blessing given by the Pope. It may also be given by bishops or priests in the Roman Catholic Church under certain circumstances. It is not to be confused with the pontifical (or episcopal) blessing given by a bishop at the end of the eucharist.

Apostolic Constitutions. A document belonging to the genre of early Christian literature known as Church Orders. Contemporary scholarship generally recognizes that it was written in Antioch shortly before the Council of Constantinople in 381. It is dependent upon a number of earlier documents, including *Didache*, *Didascalia Apostolorum*, and *Apostolic Tradition*. Its compiler probably held semi-Arian theological views. The work purports to be the decrees of a council of the twelve apostles in Jerusalem. The seventh and eighth books contain important liturgical material: a baptismal rite in Book 7, and a eucharistic liturgy, frequently called the Clementine liturgy, in Book 8. The words of institution, the *anamnesis*, and the *epiclesis* follow each other in that order in the Great Thanksgiving in this liturgy. This structure profoundly influenced the liturgies of the English and Scottish Nonjurors in the eighteenth century, and through the Scots became the model for the prayer of consecration in the first American Prayer Book, the present Eucharistic Prayer I (BCP, pp. 333–336).

Apostolic Episcopal Church. This body was founded around 1932 by the Rev. Arthur Wolfort Brooks (1888–1948), who had been an Episcopal priest. Prior to organizing this body, Brooks had been the titular Bishop of Sardis in the Anglican Universal Church, about which little is known. Its full name is the Apostolic Episcopal Church (Holy Eastern Catholic and Apostolic Orthodox Church).

Apostolic Succession. The belief that bishops are the successors to the apostles and that episcopal authority is derived from the apostles by an unbroken succession in the ministry. This authority is specifically derived through the laying on of hands for the ordination of bishops in lineal sequence from the apostles, through their performing the ministry of the apostles, and through their succession in episcopal sees traced back to the apostles. The apostolic succession is continued in the bishops of the Episcopal Church, who seek to "carry on the apostolic work of leading, supervising, and uniting the Church" (BCP, p. 510). The apostolic succession may also be understood as a continuity in doctrinal teaching from the time of the apostles to the present. The apostolic succession is said to be a "sign, though not a guarantee" of the church's basic continuity with the apostles and their time. The meaning of the apostolic succession relative to the historic episcopate has been a significant issue in Lutheran-Episcopal dialogues. *See* Bishop.

Apostolic Tradition. The belief that the church continues the faith and work of the apostles. The apostles received the faith from Jesus Christ through his teaching as well as his death and resurrection. Their authority comes from Christ, who was sent by the Father. During their lifetime the apostles passed on the faith to communities of Christians, who preserved and delivered it to their descendants as oral and written tradition. Later generations relied on the scriptures and the writings and actions of early Christians as expressions of the authentic faith. In the church, the Spirit maintains the apostolic tradition as a living force through 1) worship, preaching, teaching, and a constantly renewed understanding and living of scripture; 2) a mission to the world to save and transform it; and 3) an unbroken continuity of faith and life, manifested in a particular way by the succession of bishops. The Anglican approach to apostolic tradition allows a great variety of attitudes and teaching. The churches of the Anglican Communion are committed to four basic elements, expressed by the Lambeth Conference of 1888: the scriptures, the creeds, baptism and eucharist, and the episcopate. *See* Authority, Sources of (in Anglicanism); *see* Chicago-Lambeth Quadrilateral.

Apostolic Tradition of Hippolytus (215). *See* Church Orders; *see* Hippolytus.

Apostolicae Curae. The Encyclical issued by Pope Leo XIII on Sept. 13, 1896, in which Anglican holy orders were condemned as invalid through defect of form and intention in the Ordinal of Edward VII. This ordinal was used for the consecration of Archbishop Matthew Parker on Dec. 17, 1559. The letter judged Anglican ordinations to be "absolutely null and void" because the Ordinal deliberately excluded all reference to the sacrificial nature of the eucharist and the priesthood. These charges were answered in a "Responsio" issued by the Archbishops of Canterbury and York on Mar. 31, 1897, but to no avail. The Roman Catholic position set forth by *Apostolicae Curae* has remained an obstacle between these two traditions. The Ordinal in the 1979 BCP includes a petition that the priest may "offer spiritual sacrifices acceptable to [God]."

Apostolicity. *See* Notes of the Church.

Apotheosis. The raising of an emperor or other special person to the status of a god in pagan religion. Though initially done after death, from the time of Domitian (81–96 A.D.) the emperors were deified even during their lifetime. This concept is not to be confused with Christian notions of sanctification and canonization. *See* Theosis.

Appalachian Ministries Educational Resource Center (AMERC). The largest consortium of seminaries in the history of theological education in the United States, specializing in training persons for ministry in small towns and rural communities. AMERC has several training programs which offer seminary students exposure to rural culture, economy, and religious traditions. It stresses contextualized theological education. AMERC was founded when representatives from some thirty theological institutions met at Berea College, Berea, Kentucky, on Apr. 12–13, 1985 to form the original AMERC Consortium. On Dec. 16, 1985, the AMERC board of directors met for the first time at the Virginia Theological Seminary in Alexandria, Virginia. The Virginia Theological Seminary and the School of Theology of the University of the South were founding members of the AMERC Consortium from the Episcopal Church.

Appalachian People's Service Organization (Appalachia South, Inc.) (APSO). *See* Episcopal Appalachian Ministries.

Appalachian South, Inc. *See* Episcopal Appalachian Ministries.

Apse. Semicircular or polyhedral construction at the end of the chancel, containing the altar and sanctuary, and roofed with a half dome. The apse was a standard feature of the architecture of the early church.

Apthorp, East (1733–Apr. 16, 1816). An early advocate for the episcopate in the colonies. He was part of a vigorous pamphlet war in the 1760s reflecting the tensions between the Church of England in the American colonies and the Congregational establishment, and the increasing confluence of anti-crown and anti-church sentiment in New England. Apthorp was born into a prominent Boston merchant family. He received his M.A. from Jesus College, Cambridge University, and was ordained deacon on Sept. 21, 1755, and priest on June 5, 1757. He was appointed an S.P.G. (Society for the Propagation of the Gospel) missionary at Cambridge, Massachusetts, and became the first rector of Christ Church, Cambridge. Made uncomfortable by the controversies of the times, he accepted appointment as vicar of Croydon, England, a position he held for twenty-eight years. He also devoted himself to classical and historical studies. He never returned to the New World.

Aquinas, Thomas (1225–Mar. 7, 1274). The leading theologian of the medieval church, Aquinas was given the title *doctor angelicus*. On July 18, 1323, he was pronounced a saint by Pope John XXII. His two major writings are the *Summa Theologica* and the *Summa Contra Gentiles*. The *Summa Theologica* is a systematization and summary of Christian revelation in terms of the philosophy of Aristotle. Aquinas insisted that faith and reason, or theology and philosophy, must be kept distinct, and that faith is dependent upon biblical revelation for the major Christian doctrines such as the Trinity and the Incarnation. He was born at his father's castle of Roccasecca in Italy. When he was five Aquinas was sent to study at the Benedictine monastery at Monte Cassino, but in 1244 he joined the Dominican order. He then studied at Paris and Cologne under Albertus Magnus, the most learned man of his age. Aquinas has four eucharistic hymns in *The Hymnal 1982*: "O saving Victim" (310, 311), "Humbly I adore thee" (314), "Zion praise thy Savior" (320), and "Now, my tongue, the mystery telling" (329, 330, 331). On Jan. 28, 1369, his remains were moved to Toulouse. He is commemorated in the Episcopal calendar of the church year on that date.

Arcae. See Pyx, or Pix.

Archangel. *See* Angel.

Archbishop. A bishop with administrative and disciplinary authority over other bishops. In the Anglican Communion, an archbishop is the chief bishop of a province. The term is not used by any bishop in the Episcopal Church, where the chief bishop is known as the "Presiding Bishop, Primate, and Chief Pastor," or simply as the "Presiding Bishop." Historically, from the fourth and fifth centuries, an archbishop was a patriarch or holder of another important see, later including those with broad regional jurisdiction such as metropolitans and primates.

Archbishop of Canterbury. *See* Canterbury, Archbishop of.

Archdeacon. A clergyperson with a defined administrative authority delegated by the diocesan bishop. Originally the chief of the deacons who assisted the bishop, the archdeacon is now typically a priest who serves as the bishop's administrative assistant. The title of an archdeacon is "The Venerable," which is abbreviated "The Ven."

Archives of the Episcopal Church. The archives preserve, arrange, and make available the records of the General Convention, the Executive Council, and other important records and memorabilia of the life and work of the Episcopal Church. The archives are located at the Episcopal Theological Seminary of the Southwest in Austin, Texas.

Archivist of the Episcopal Church. The General Convention of 1940 appointed and designated the Church Historical Society "an official agency of General Convention for the collection, preservation, and safekeeping of records and historical documents connected with the life and development of the [Episcopal Church] . . . and to foster as far as possible the investigation of its history and the development of interest in all relevant research." The Church Historical Society named Virginia Nelle Bellamy as archivist, and she served from June 1, 1959, until Dec. 31, 1985. The General Convention of 1985 passed a canon which established a Board of the Archives and Office of the Archivist.

Arculae. See Pyx, or Pix.

Area Cluster (Ministry). An effective and widely used mission strategy for ministry among small congregations unable to support a full-time priest. Churches "cluster" together to share ministry and resources. These clusters generally involve two to three congregations. Some of the benefits include: availability of special ministries (e.g., youth ministry, educational ministry) and the financial benefits of shared resources.

Area Mission. The 1973 General Convention changed the Canon "Of Missionary Jurisdictions," and created a new jurisdiction called an area mission. The House of Bishops may establish a mission in any area not included within the boundaries of a diocese of the Episcopal Church, or of a church in communion with the Episcopal Church. An area mission may be undertaken under the sole authority of the Episcopal Church or jointly with another Christian body or bodies. For every area mission, a bishop of the Episcopal Church, or of a church in communion with the Episcopal Church, shall be assigned by the House of Bishops. A bishop assigned to an area mission is a missionary bishop. An area mission may become a missionary diocese. In a general sense, the term can refer to a specific geographical area that is designated by a diocese for evangelization, congregational development, and ministry development.

Arianism. The teaching that the Son of God was a creature "of like substance" (*homoiousios*), though not identical with God. It is named for Arius, a fourth-century presbyter of Alexandria who made a highly influential (if not especially original) contribution to the discussion of the proper way to express the relationship between God and the Son within the divine life. Arius was not primarily interested in the relationship between the divinity and humanity of Jesus. He was concerned to preserve the unity, sole eternity, and self-existence of God. The famous epitome of Arius's position is, "There was when the Son was not."

Arius's determined opponent was Athanasius, who saw that if the Word were not fully God, then God's act in Christ was not fully a divine act and hence ultimately ineffectual. At the Council of Nicaea in 325, the Athanasian position prevailed. The Son was declared to be "of one Being with the Father" (*homoousios*) (Nicene Creed, BCP, p. 358). The full divinity of the Son was upheld. *See* Homoiousios; *see* Homoousios.

Arizona, Diocese of. On Oct. 19, 1859, the House of Bishops created the Missionary District of the Southwest, which included Arizona. On Oct. 21, 1865, it created the Missionary Bishopric of Nevada with jurisdiction in Arizona. The Missionary Bishopric of New Mexico and Arizona was created by the House of Bishops on Nov. 2, 1874. On Oct. 13, 1892, the House of Bishops formed the Missionary District of Arizona. It had the same bishops as New Mexico until 1911. On Mar. 5 in that same year, Trinity Church, Phoenix, became Trinity Pro-Cathedral. The primary Convention of the Diocese of Arizona was held at Grace Church, Tucson, Feb. 4–5, 1959. On Oct. 28, 1988, Trinity Pro-Cathedral, Phoenix, became Trinity Cathedral.

Arkansas, Diocese of. The House of Bishops nominated and the House of Deputies confirmed Leonidas Polk as Missionary Bishop of Arkansas and the Indian Territory. Polk was consecrated on Dec. 9, 1838, and served until Oct. 16, 1841, when he was elected Bishop of Louisiana. From Oct. 18, 1841, until Oct. 10, 1844, James Hervey Otey was Acting Missionary Bishop. In 1859 Arkansas became a part of the Missionary District of the South West. On Nov. 1–3, 1862, the primary convention of the Diocese was held at Christ Church, Little Rock, and the Diocese voted to join the Protestant Episcopal Church in the Confederate states. At the close of the Civil War Arkansas again became a part of the Missionary District of the South West. On Apr. 24–27, 1871, the primary convention was held at Christ Church, Little Rock, and on Oct. 19, 1884, Trinity Cathedral, Little Rock, was established. Arkansas was the second diocese to have an African American suffragan bishop, Edward Thomas Demby. The diocese includes the entire state.

Arkansas Theological Chautauqua School. In 1904 Bishop William Montgomery Brown of Arkansas called for an institution of higher learning to be known as the "School of Theology of the Diocese of Arkansas." It was to be established at the State University, Fayetteville, to educate a group of "competent men who can and will work at the beginning on small salaries." The school attracted men over thirty who were excused from the study of Latin and Greek. Bishop Brown described the school as "a kind of institution which has no fixed organization or name or laws. It simply exists, and does as it pleases. And yet it is one of the most interesting and variously useful things in the Diocese . . . It is, in fact, a kind of ecclesiastical hash made up of a good deal of the several things which usually bear these names. It meets once a year, not always at the same place or the same time, for it is in every sense of the term, a movable feast." There remain no existing records of the school, but it appears to have produced at least twenty-two men for the ordained ministry. It ceased to exist in 1913. It was also known as the "Arkansas Theological Chautauqua School" and "Bishop Brown's Pet."

Armed Forces Prayer Book. The title was given to the revision of the World War II *Prayer Book for Soldiers and Sailors* issued in 1951 at the time of the Korean War for the Armed Forces Division of the Episcopal Church. It contained many items not in the BCP, mostly of a devotional nature, including forms for emergency baptism and "The Way of Penitence." It was thoroughly revised in 1967 under the editorship of the Rev. H. Boone Porter and reissued as *A Prayer Book for the Armed Forces*. It was revised again in 1988 by Howard E. Galley and the Rev. Donald W. Beers to conform to the 1979 BCP and *The Hymnal 1982*, but it largely retains its 1967 format.

It contains personal prayers, a service of worship which may be led by a lay person, a short form of the Holy Eucharist, Baptism, Reconciliation, prayers for the wounded and the dying, burial, psalms, hymns, canticles, and biblical passages.

Armed Forces, Suffragan Bishop for. The Constitution of the Episcopal Church states that it is "lawful for the House of Bishops to elect a Suffragan Bishop who, under the direction of the Presiding Bishop, shall be in charge of the work of those chaplains in the Armed Forces of the United States, Veterans' Administration Medical Centers, and Federal Correction Institutions who are ordained Ministers of this Church." On Oct. 21, 1964, the General Convention elected Arnold Meredith Lewis (1904–1994), resigned Bishop of Western Kansas, to this position. At the consecration of Clarence Edward Hobgood as the second Suffragan Bishop on Feb. 2, 1971, at the Cathedral Church of St. Peter and St. Paul, Washington, the Episcopal Peace Fellowship staged a peaceful protest.

Army and Navy Commission. The General Convention of 1919 established a Commission on the Relation of the Church to the Army and Navy. It consisted of five bishops, five presbyters, and five laymen. It was "to press upon the attention of Congress the need for Army and Navy Chaplains in such a way as to secure for Chaplains that position and those facilities which will enable them to fulfill their difficult task effectively." On Dec. 31, 1945, it ceased to be a commission of the General Convention and became a division within the Home Department of the National Council of the Episcopal Church.

Articles of Religion. *See* Thirty-Nine Articles, or Articles of Religion.

Ascension of Christ, The, or Ascension Day. The occasion on which the risen Christ is taken into heaven after appearing to his followers for forty days (Acts 1:1–11, Mk 16:19). The Ascension marks the conclusion of Jesus' post-resurrection appearances. It is the final elevation of his human nature to divine glory and the near presence of God. The Ascension is affirmed by the Nicene and Apostles' Creeds. The Ascension is celebrated on Ascension Day, the Thursday that is the fortieth day of the Easter season. It is a principal feast of the church year in the Episcopal Church.

Ascension, Guild of the. A devotional society founded by a small group of priests and students at the General Theological Seminary. The society was founded at an early celebration of Holy Communion in Trinity Chapel on Ascension Day, May 29, 1919. It is a society to encourage the development of the spiritual life by cultivating systematic devotional habits. The membership includes clergy, theological students, and lay people who are communicants of the Episcopal Church. Each member lives by a simple rule of life.

Ascension, Order of the. The order was formally established on Jan. 8, 1983, at St. Helena's Convent, New York, New York. It is a dispersed Christian community of women and men who make promises of stability, obedience, and conversion of life. They also share a commitment to parish revitalization and justice in American society. The order desires to live within and advance Catholic faith and practice as received in the Anglican tradition. Professed members are priests who serve in pastoral ministry and

have oversight of a parish. The order has a special concern for parishes that are in poor, working class, and minority communities; those in urban, rural and isolated settings; and those that are small, have a history of instability, or have a desire for renewal as a Christian community. Corporate ministries include the Parish Development Institute, co-sponsored by the General Theological Seminary, and the Ascension Press. On Jan. 30, 1988, the first Professed Members and Companions took three year vows of stability, obedience, and conversion of life before Bishop Roger White of Milwaukee in the Chapel of the Good Shepherd at the General Theological Seminary.

Asceticism. The discipline of strict self control at all levels of body, feeling, thought, and imagination. Ascetic practices are not ends in themselves. Asceticism is best practiced as a way to overcome obstacles to the soul's love of God rather than self-denial for its own sake. Asceticism is intended to foster love and charity. The term is from the Greek for "exercise" or "training." In 1 Cor 9:25, St. Paul notes that Christians, like athletes, "exercise self-control in all things." Although it is sometimes confused with masochism or with false doctrine, asceticism is favored by some philosophies (stoicism) and most religions. It is reflected in the purity rules of Leviticus, in the Qumran writings, and in the NT statements that some demons are vanquished through "fasting and prayer" (Mk 9:29) and that there are eunuchs for the kingdom of heaven (Mt 19:12). Christians have practiced fasting and abstinence from meat on certain days. The monastic tradition identifies asceticism with patient bearing with one another, simplicity of life, and celibacy. A moderate asceticism is included in the rules of all religious communities. The vows of celibacy, poverty, and obedience subordinate asceticism to a life-long search for the kingdom. In the church at large asceticism is associated with the observance of Lent.

Ash Wednesday. The first of the forty days of Lent, named for the custom of placing blessed ashes on the foreheads of worshipers at Ash Wednesday services. The ashes are a sign of penitence and a reminder of mortality, and may be imposed with the sign of the cross. Ash Wednesday is observed as a fast in the church year of the Episcopal Church. The Ash Wednesday service is one of the Proper Liturgies for Special Days in the BCP (p. 264). Imposition of ashes at the Ash Wednesday service is optional.

Ashes, Blessed. Ashes blessed for use on Ash Wednesday as a sign of penitence and a reminder of mortality. The OT frequently mentions the use of ashes as an expression of humiliation and sorrow. Ashes for use on Ash Wednesday are made from burned palms from previous Palm Sunday services. Ashes are imposed on the penitent's forehead with the words, "Remember that you are dust, and to dust you shall return" (BCP, p. 265). The imposition of ashes on Ash Wednesday is optional.

Asheville, Missionary District of. *See* Western North Carolina, Diocese of.

Asperges. The liturgical practice of sprinkling with holy water as a reminder of baptism. The term comes from the Latin version of Ps 51, "Thou shalt sprinkle me with hyssop." The asperges may be done after the Renewal of Baptismal Vows at the Easter Vigil. It may also be done as a preparatory ceremony before the eucharist, with the altar, clergy, and people all sprinkled with holy water. Historically, it was performed as a kind of exorcism and cleansing of a building or other place for liturgical services. An aspergillum is used for sprinkling the holy water.

Aspergillum. Brush, branch, metal rod, or other instrument used to sprinkle holy water at the asperges.

Aspersion. A means of baptism in which the candidate is sprinkled with water. The BCP instead requires immersion (dipping most of the candidate's body in water) or affusion (pouring water on the candidate).

Aspirant. A person seeking ordination as a deacon or priest, or a person who desires to be admitted to a religious order. When an aspirant has received approval from the diocese to begin seminary or other required training, he or she becomes a postulant. An aspirant to a religious order is one who is preparing to test his or her vocation with the order. An aspirant may subsequently be admitted as a postulant and later as a novice with the approval of the community.

Assistant Bishop. A bishop who assists the diocesan bishop by providing additional episcopal services. An assistant bishop is appointed by the diocesan bishop, with the approval of the Standing Committee of the diocese. The assistant bishop must already be exercising episcopal jurisdiction as a diocesan bishop, or serving as a suffragan bishop, or a qualified bishop who has previously resigned all previous responsibilities, or a qualified bishop of a church in communion with the Episcopal Church. The assistant bishop serves under the direction of the diocesan bishop, and may not serve beyond the termination of the appointing bishop's jurisdiction. In the nineteenth century, bishops coadjutor in the Episcopal Church were known as assistant bishops.

Associate Mission. The name of a house of clergy and laity living under a common rule but no formal vows, subject to episcopal oversight, for evangelization and for educational and charitable enterprises. The first associate mission was Nashotah House, Wisconsin (1842), followed by other early foundations such as Valle Crucis, North Carolina (1847) and Seabury Mission, Faribault, Minnesota (1857).

Associated Parishes for Liturgy and Mission. This organization, first called Associated Parishes, had its beginnings in the spring or summer of 1946, when several priests met in Cincinnati, Ohio. According to one-time president Henry H. Bruel, they "were in despair over eleven o'clock Sunday morning." At this meeting it was agreed to contact others interested in liturgical revision and the centrality of the eucharist in the Christian life. On Nov. 4–8, 1946, twelve priests met in the common room of the College of Preachers, Washington, D.C. On Nov. 6, they organized Associated Parishes. Associated Parishes supported freestanding altars so that the celebrant could face the people. They also supported church art and architecture that was clean, joyful, and simple. They urged that daily Morning and Evening Prayer should be said publicly; baptisms, weddings, and funerals should be public services; and the eucharist should be the primary Sunday service. Associated Parishes supported the Standing Liturgical Commission and its work on the 1979 BCP. Until 1963, membership was closed and one could join only by invitation. Membership became open in 1963, and the name was changed to Associated Parishes for Liturgy and Mission. Associated Parishes has published numerous pamphlets on the liturgy, one of the most important of which is *The Parish Eucharist* (1951). It promotes the centrality of the eucharist as the norm for public worship on the Lord's Day, and stresses the essential unification of "The Proclamation of the Word" and "The Celebration of the Sacrament." From 1954 until Dec. 1962, it published the quarterly *Sharer's*. In 1968 it began publishing *Open*.

Association for Promoting the Interests of Church Schools, Colleges, and Seminaries. It was founded in 1933 to promote church schools, colleges, and seminaries. It went out of existence around 1955.

Association of Anglican Musicians (AAM). An organization of musicians and clergy in the Episcopal Church and throughout the Anglican Communion seeking to elevate, stimulate, and support music and the allied arts in the liturgy of the Episcopal Church and beyond. The idea for this organization was conceived in 1965 and realized in May 1966 when the American Cathedral Organists and Choirmasters Association, modeled after the Association of English Cathedral Organists, was founded in Indianapolis. In 1973 the name was changed to the Association of Anglican Musicians. Its publications include *Handbook for the Selection, Employment and Ministry of Church Musicians* (1990), and *A History of Music in the Episcopal Church* (1988). Its first regular publication was the *Association of Anglican Musicians Newsletter*. This publication became *The Journal of the Association of Anglican Musicians* in Oct. 1992 and is published ten times a year.

Association of Diocesan Liturgy and Music Commissions, The (ADLMC). A coalition of lay and ordained leaders in liturgy and music from throughout the Episcopal Church. It began as an organization of chairs of diocesan liturgy commissions in 1969 to assist the Standing Liturgical Commission with the task of evaluating trial use liturgies. The first meeting was convened by Associated Parishes at the request of the Standing Liturgical Commission. The Prayer Book was adopted by General Convention in 1979. In that year, the organization was expanded to include music commissions, and the name was changed to the Conference of Liturgical and Music Commissions to reflect this broadened mission. Individual memberships as well as diocesan representatives were allowed. The Rev. Vincent Pettit, later Suffragan Bishop of New Jersey, was chosen first president. Bylaws were adopted and the name was changed to the Association of Diocesan Worship Commissions at the 1982 meeting. The name was changed again to the Association of Diocesan Liturgy and Music Commissions (ADLMC) in 1983. ADLMC encourages communication, training, and education among its members through annual conferences and other activities. It seeks to promote better understanding of the contents of the Prayer Book, to advise and assist diocesan bishops at their request in implementation of the guidelines and other liturgical directions of General Convention or the House of Bishops, and to provide technical and monetary support to the Standing Commission on Liturgy and Music. It seeks to offer collegial support for chairs of diocesan liturgy and music commissions. ADLMC also provides updated information concerning the work of the Standing Commission on Liturgy and Music, and publishes a newsletter with discussions of topics related to worship. *See* Associated Parishes for Liturgy and Music; *see* Book of Common Prayer, The ("BCP"); *see* Standing Commission on Church Music.

Association of Diocesan Worship Commissions. *See* Association of Diocesan Liturgy and Music Commissions, The (ADLMC).

Association of Episcopal Colleges. An association of schools formed in 1962 as the Foundation of Episcopal Colleges by the presidents of eight colleges to work together on common issues. It is now called the Association of Episcopal Colleges and includes Bard College, Clarkson College, Cuttington University College, Hobart College, Kenyon College, St. Augustine College (Chicago), St. Augustine's College, St. Mary's College, St. Paul's College, Trinity College of Quezon City, the University of the South, and Voorhees College. The Association serves as a liaison between the twelve schools and the Episcopal Church, organizes learning through service programs in the United States and abroad, participates in joint efforts with the Colleges and Universities of the Anglican Communion, and engages in fund raising activities. It also sponsors Christian service intern programs, scholarships for needy Episcopalians, visiting fellows programs, chaplains' conferences, student/faculty exchanges, and faculty study grants. It began publication of *Views on Education & News of Episcopal Colleges* in the spring of 1986.

Association of Professional Women Church Workers (APW). This organization was formed by 100 women at the 1949 General Convention. It was formally organized in 1952. Its membership consisted chiefly of parish religious education directors and women employed on national and diocesan staffs. Among the founders were Marion Kelleran, Margaret Marston (Mrs. Arthur) Sherman, Mrs. Clifford Samuelson, Helen Turnbull, Ellen Gammack, Avis Harvey, Ruth Johnson, and Virginia (Mrs. Richard L.) Harbour. It worked to develop professional standards in performance and training, insure adequate salaries and benefits, recruit women church workers, and provide opportunities for study, spiritual refreshment, and fellowship. In 1964 the APW formulated two canons which defined the status of professional women workers. These canons were adopted by the 1964 General Convention. Three years later, decimated by widespread layoffs of women professionals, the association disbanded.

Association of Theological Schools in the United States and Canada (ATS). The accrediting and program agency for graduate theological education in North America. It began in 1918 as a conference of theological schools that met biennially. It became an Association in 1936, and adopted standards for judging the quality of theological schools. In 1938 it established the first list of accredited schools. In 1956 it was incorporated as the American Association of Theological Schools (AATS), and secured a full-time staff. In 1964 it began publication of the journal, *Theological Education*. The *Fact Book on Theological Education* was first published in 1969. There are eleven accredited Episcopal seminaries: Episcopal Divinity School, previously called Episcopal Theological School (1938); General Theological Seminary (1938); Protestant Episcopal Theological Seminary in Virginia (1938); Seabury-Western Theological Seminary (1938); Church Divinity School of the Pacific (1945); Bexley Hall (1952); Berkeley Divinity School (1954); Nashotah House (1954); Episcopal Theological Seminary of the Southwest (1958); University of the South, School of Theology (1958); and Trinity Episcopal School for Ministry (1985).

Assumption of Mary. The belief that the Mother of Jesus was taken up body and soul into heaven. Though not in scripture, it was described in apocryphal stories of the fifth century. It originated in the lack of scriptural data on Mary's death. It found support in the absence of bodily relics of the Virgin, in meditation on Jesus' filial love, and in a liturgical feast which dates from the fifth century. This feast was known as Memory of Mary in the fifth century and was celebrated as the Dormition in the sixth century on Aug. 15. In the seventh century it was called the Assumption in the west. It was universally accepted by

piety in Byzantium. It became a theological opinion in western theology. As the belief spread it was featured in iconography and gothic sculpture (as at Canterbury Cathedral). Though accepted by most Reformers, the feast was not included in the BCP. The belief was eventually abandoned in the churches of the Reformation. It was preserved in Orthodoxy and by some Anglicans as a pious belief. It became a dogma of the Roman Catholic Church in 1950.

Athanasian Creed. Statement of faith dating from the fourth or fifth centuries. It is also known by its opening Latin words as the *Quicunque Vult*, "Whosoever will be saved, before all things it is necessary that he hold the Catholic Faith." The creed is attributed to St. Athanasius (296–373), but this attribution has generally been discounted since the Athanasian Creed includes doctrinal expressions that appeared only in later theological controversies. It was considered to express the faith that Athanasius taught. It is unlike other standard creeds because of its length and its anathemas against those who would deny its doctrines. The creed emphasizes the triune nature of God and the Incarnation. Although it was used in the Church of England on certain principal feasts of the church year, the Athanasian Creed was never appointed for liturgical use in the Episcopal Church. It is published as one of the Historical Documents of the Church in the 1979 BCP (pp. 864–865).

Athanasius (c. 296–373). Bishop and theologian. He was born in Egypt and educated at the catechetical school in Alexandria, where he was profoundly influenced by Bishop Alexander. Athanasius was ordained deacon in 319, and immediately became an opponent of the presbyter Arius, who taught that the second person of the Trinity was not fully divine. Bishop Alexander took Athanasius as his secretary and adviser to the first Ecumenical Council at Nicaea in 325, which dealt with the Arian conflict. Athanasius defended the full divinity of the second person at Nicaea, insisting that the Son is "of one Being with the Father." When Bishop Alexander died in 328, Athanasius became Bishop of Alexandria. He spent the rest of his life defending the Nicene position and fighting the Arians. His major writing was *On the Incarnation of the Word of God*. Athanasius is recognized as "the theologian of the Incarnation." He wrote a biography of the monk Antony, which helped to spread monasticism in the west.

Athanasius is commemorated in the Episcopal calendar of the church year on May 2.

Atkinson, Thomas (Aug. 6, 1807–Jan. 4, 1881). Bishop and advocate of the religious education of African Americans. He was born on his father's plantation, Mansfield, Dinwiddie County, Virginia. He attended Yale and graduated from Hampden Sidney College. Atkinson prepared for the ministry after studying law and nine years of legal practice. He was ordained deacon on Nov. 18, 1836. From then until his ordination to the priesthood, May 7, 1837, he was an assistant at Christ Church, Norfolk, Virginia. When he was ordained priest he became rector of St. Paul's Church, Norfolk, where he stayed until 1843. In that year he was elected rector of St. Peter's Church, Baltimore. He and others from St. Peter's formed Grace Church, Baltimore, in 1850. Atkinson served there as rector until he was elected Bishop of North Carolina. He was consecrated bishop on Oct. 17, 1853. He supported the founding of the University of the South and later participated in organizing the Protestant Episcopal Church in the Confederate States. After the Civil War, Atkinson supported the reunion of the Episcopal Church. He was one of three southern bishops attending the General Convention of 1865. He died in Wilmington, North Carolina.

Atlanta, Diocese of. The General Convention of 1907 voted to divide the Diocese of Georgia, and the primary convention of the Diocese of Atlanta met at Christ Church, Macon, Dec. 4–5, 1907. The Diocese of Atlanta consists of the following counties: Baldwin, Banks, Barrow, Bartow, Bibb, Butts, Carroll, Catoosa, Chattahoochee, Chattooga, Cherokee, Clarke, Clayton, Cobb, Coweta, Crawford, Dade, Dawson, Dekalb, Douglas, Elbert, Fannin, Fayette, Floyd, Forsyth, Franklin, Fulton, Gilmer, Gordon, Greene, Gwinnett, Habersham, Hall, Hancock, Haralson, Harris, Hart, Heard, Henry, Houston, Jackson, Jasper, Jones, Lamar, Lincoln, Lumpkin, Macon, Madison, Marion, Meriwether, Monroe, Morgan, Murray, Muscogee, Newton, Oconee, Oglethorpe, Paulding, Peach, Pickens, Pike, Polk, Putnam, Rabun, Rockdale, Schley, Spaulding, Stephens, Talbot, Taliaferro, Taylor, Towns, Troup, Union, Upson, Walker, Walton, Warren, White, Whitfield, and Wilkes. On May 6, 1897, St. Philip's Church, Atlanta, was designated St. Philip's Cathedral. It was consecrated on the Feast of St. Philip and St. James, May 1, 1904. When the Diocese of Georgia split in two in 1907, St. Philip's became the cathedral for the new Diocese of Atlanta.

Atonement. The term (literally, "at + one + ment") has been applied since the earliest English translations of the Bible to the sacrificial ceremonies in the Hebrew temple on Yom Kippur (Day of Atonement). It has come to be applied universally to God's reconciling work accomplished by the death of Christ. This is supported by the treatment of Jesus' death in the epistle to the Hebrews as the fulfillment of the temple sacrifices. There is widespread agreement among contemporary theologians that God's reconciling work includes Christ's life as well as his death.

In the NT this work is described by an abundance of metaphors, some drawn from religious life (sacrifice and sanctification, Heb 9–10), some from legal life (justification, Rom 5), some from personal life (reconciliation and forgiveness, 2 Cor 5), and ransom and redemption from Satan (Mk 10:45). In his book *Christus Victor*, Gustaf Aulén identified three leading theories of atonement: 1) victory over Satan, which he regarded as the most adequate, the "classical" view; 2) sacrifice and satisfaction, the "Anselmian" view; 3) the "moral influence" theory, derived from Peter Abelard and used in much modern Protestant thought. The Episcopal theologian William Porcher DuBose emphasized an understanding of atonement as the fulfillment and intended end of humanity in union (at-one-ment) with God.

Atrium. The term indicated the main court of a Roman house. It was also used to describe the covered court in front of the main doors of a church or basilica. People entered the church through the atrium.

Attrition. Imperfect repentance for sin, possibly due to fear of punishment or displeasure at the sin itself. Attrition has been distinguished from contrition since the twelfth century. Contrition is motivated by love of God, causing the penitent to regret sin as evidence of a turning away from God who loves us. Attrition falls short of the firm intention for amendment of life that characterizes contrition. Attrition has been referred to as imperfect contrition. Nevertheless, moral theologians have generally held that attrition is sufficient for the forgiveness of sins by God in the context of sacramental reconciliation. *See* Contrition.

Auchmuty, Samuel (Jan. 26, 1722–Mar. 4, 1777). Early proponent of an American episcopate. He was born in Boston and graduated from Harvard in 1742. The Bishop of London ordained him deacon on Mar. 8, 1747, and priest on Mar. 15, 1747. In 1748 he became the assistant minister at Trinity Church, New York, and also catechist to the Negroes for the Society for the Propagation of the Gospel. He was rector of Trinity Church from Sept. 1, 1764, until his death. He was a high churchman and a strong Loyalist during the American Revolution.

Augustine of Canterbury (d. May 26, 604 or 605). First Archbishop of Canterbury. He began his career as prior of St. Andrew's monastery in Rome. Pope Gregory the Great sent Augustine and some other monks to England in 597 to refound the church in England. They arrived in Kent and began their missionary work. King Ethelbert, whose wife Bertha was already a Christian, adopted Christianity and was baptized by Augustine. He was the first Christian king in England. Augustine was consecrated an archbishop at Arles, in France. He rebuilt and reconsecrated an old church at Canterbury and founded a monastery in connection with it. One of Augustine's final acts, probably in 604, was to send Justus to preach west of the Medway, with the title of Bishop of Rochester, and Mellitus to preach among the East Saxons, with the title of Bishop of London. Augustine's missionary work is commemorated in the Episcopal calendar of the church year on May 26.

Augustine of Hippo (354–Aug. 28, 430). Bishop and theologian, widely regarded as the greatest of the Latin Fathers and one of the major theologians in the history of Christianity. He was born in Tagaste in North Africa and was influenced greatly by his Christian mother, Monica. He studied Manichaeism and Neoplatonism and struggled with his personal morals. In 384 he became the professor of rhetoric at Milan and came under the influence of the eloquent preacher, Ambrose, Bishop of Milan. In the summer of 386 he was converted to Christianity. He was baptized by Ambrose on Easter Eve 387. He returned to North Africa and was unexpectedly chosen by the people of Hippo to be a presbyter. In 395 he was consecrated Bishop of Hippo and turned the episcopal house into a monastic community. Among his many writings are *The Confessions* (c. 397–401), in which he interprets his life up until the death of Monica, *The Trinity* (399–419), which sums up Trinitarian theology in the west, and *The City of God* (c. 413–427), which interprets Christian history as a struggle between two cities, the city of God and the city of man. Augustine was an opponent of the Donatists, who insisted on the purity of the clergy. He also opposed the Pelagians, who taught that people can live a sinless life and thus be saved. He shaped western Christian thought with regard to the Fall, original sin, predestination, and the Trinity. His contributions are commemorated in the Episcopal calendar of the church year on Aug. 28.

Aumbry. A cupboard or secure receptacle in the side wall of the sanctuary or sacristy. Aumbries traditionally have been used to keep sacred vessels, books, reliquaries, and oils for anointing. Aumbries may also be used for the reservation of the Blessed Sacrament.

Auricular Confession. Verbalized confession of sin by a penitent to another Christian. Absolution may only be pronounced by a bishop or priest. The BCP provides two forms for the Reconciliation of a Penitent (pp. 447–452). *See* Reconciliation of a Penitent.

Authority, Sources of (in Anglicanism). The threefold sources of authority in Anglicanism are scripture, tradition, and reason. These three sources uphold and critique each other in a dynamic way. Scripture is the normative source for God's revelation and the source for all Christian teaching and reflection. Tradition passes down from generation to generation the church's ongoing experience of God's presence and activity. Reason is understood to include the human capacity to discern the truth in both rational and intuitive ways. It is not limited to logic as such. It takes into account and includes experience. Each of the three sources of authority must be perceived and interpreted in light of the other two.

The Anglican balance of authority has been characterized as a "three-legged stool" which falls if any one of the legs is not upright. It may be distinguished from a tendency in Roman Catholicism to overemphasize tradition relative to scripture and reason, and in certain Protestant churches to overemphasize scripture relative to tradition and reason. The Anglican balancing of the sources of authority has been criticized as clumsy or "muddy." It has been associated with the Anglican affinity for seeking the mean between extremes and living the *via media*. It has also been associated with the Anglican willingness to tolerate and comprehend opposing viewpoints instead of imposing tests of orthodoxy or resorting to heresy trials.

This balanced understanding of authority is based in the theology of Richard Hooker (c. 1554–1600). It may be further traced to the teaching of Thomas Aquinas (1225–

1274). Urban T. Holmes III (1930–1981) provided a thorough and helpful discussion of the sources of authority in his book *What is Anglicanism?* (1982).

Authorized Services (1973), or the "Zebra Book." Text of the proposed revisions for the BCP, as authorized by the 1973 General Convention in the last stages of the Prayer Book Revision process. The text included revised services of Baptism, Eucharist, and the Daily Offices; along with a complete revision of the Psalter. Its nickname, the "Zebra Book," refers to the zigzag pattern of blue and tan lines on its cover.

Autocephalic Churches. "Autocephalic" denotes independence or autonomy. Literally, it is "self-headed." The autocephalic churches are understood to be the fourteen autocephalic churches of the Byzantine or Eastern Rite which are not in communion with the Church of Rome.

AVE. 1) Bulletin of the Church of Saint Mary the Virgin in New York City. It was first published in Jan. 1932. 2) Newsletter of the Society of Mary.

Ave Maria. *See* Annunciation, The.

AWAKE. The full name of this organization is An Association of Concerned Episcopalians to Inform and Awaken Our Church. It was incorporated on Oct. 25, 1995, in Mobile, Alabama. Its purpose is to promote Christian religious ideals and to compile information and publish statements about what is happening in the Episcopal Church. Its first publication was *A Catalog of Concerns: The Episcopal Church in the U.S. under Edmond Lee Browning.*

Ayres, Anne (Jan. 3, 1816–Feb. 9, 1896). The first American nun in the Anglican tradition. She was born in London and came to the United States when she was twenty years old. She was deeply influenced by William Augustus Muhlenberg. At his Church of the Holy Communion, New York, she made monastic vows on Nov. 1, 1845. In 1852 the order was regularly organized as the Sisterhood of the Holy Communion. For most of her life she and her associates were in charge of nursing at St. Luke's Hospital, founded by Muhlenberg. Her major published work was *The Life and Work of William Augustus Muhlenberg* (1880). *See* Holy Communion, Sisterhood of the.

B

"Baby Bishop." An informal term that refers to a newly ordained bishop. It reflects the assumption that a period of time will be required for the newly ordained bishop to gain experience and grow into the new position.

Bach, Johann Sebastian (Mar. 21, 1685–July 28, 1750). Dominant figure in the history of church music whose output embraces practically every musical genre of his time except opera. His reputation during his lifetime was earned principally as organ virtuoso and expert in organ construction and design. Bach's musical production falls into three principal categories corresponding to the posts he held. He was born in Eisenach, Germany, and received his earliest musical training in choir schools in Ohrdruf and Luneburg. His early period consisted mainly of organ works while organist at Weimar. His next position, Kapellmeister to Prince Leopold of Cothen, produced works for instruments and orchestra including the Brandenburg Concertos. His prestigious post in Leipzig produced church works, a large output of cantatas, the St. John and St. Matthew passions, and the B minor Mass. Bach's association with the Lutheran chorale was not in composing new tunes but rather in harmonizing and embellishing the rich body of church song already in existence. Many of Bach's rich and ingenious harmonizations are included in today's hymnals, including *The Hymnal 1982*, which has twenty Bach chorale harmonizations. He died in Leipzig.

Baldachino (Baldaquin). A canopy used to cover an altar. It may be made of wood, stone, metal, or fabric. The term is also applied to the canopy over a bishop's throne, a canopy over statues, and the canopy carried in processions such as processions of the Blessed Sacrament. *See* Blessed Sacrament.

Baldwin, Mary Briscoe (May 20, 1811–June 1877). Missionary to Greece and Syria. She was born at Belle Grove, Frederick County, Virginia. When she was twenty-four, Baldwin went to Athens, Greece, to teach at the girls' school established by the Rev. and Mrs. John Hill. She was part of the Athens Episcopal Mission School family and its leadership from 1835 until 1852. From 1852 until 1866, Baldwin operated her own school in Athens. For the next several years, she ran an industrial mission where she provided sewing employment to needy Athenian women. In 1871 Baldwin moved to Jaffa, Syria, and established her own mission school. Her cousin, Mary Julia Baldwin, was the educator after whom Mary Baldwin College in Staunton, Virginia, was named. After Mary Briscoe's death, the school she founded in Jaffa was renamed the Mary Baldwin Memorial School. Baldwin died in Jaffa.

Baltimore Declaration. A manifesto issued on May 26, 1991, the Feast of the Holy Trinity, by six Episcopal priests in the Diocese of Maryland. It was patterned after the 1934 Barmen Declaration of the Confessing Church in Germany. The Baltimore Declaration charged that the leadership of the Episcopal Church was intent on abandoning the Christian faith. Alvin Frank Kimel, Jr., principal author of the Declaration, and five colleagues from the Baltimore area called Episcopalians to repentance for failing to uphold both "the doctrinal norms of the historic creeds and ecumenical councils" and "the formative and evangelical authority of the Holy Scriptures." The Baltimore Declaration was divided into seven articles, each of which contained a positive statement of belief and a repudiation of theological error. It affirmed such traditional doctrines as the Trinity, the Incarnation, salvation through the atoning work of Jesus Christ, and the divine inspiration of the Bible. The Declaration was distributed widely throughout the Episcopal Church. Its authors invited clergy and lay people to join them in affirming orthodox Christianity.

Banner of the Church. This journal first appeared on Sept. 3, 1831. It was published in Boston, and it represented high church views. Its motto was "In the Name of Our God We will Set Up Our Banner." It was edited by George Washington Doane and William Croswell. The last issue was published on Nov. 24, 1832. Its subscription list was given to *The Churchman*.

Banner of the Cross, The. This weekly publication continued the *Protestant Episcopalian* and had the Latin motto, *Pro Deo, Pro Ecclesia, Pro Hominum Salute*, and the English slogan, "Gospel Truth, and Primitive Ecclesiastical Order." It was published in Philadelphia. It began publication on Jan. 5, 1839. Its last issue was published on Oct. 31, 1861.

Banns of Marriage. Public announcement during a church service of an intended marriage. The Banns are "published"

on three occasions to determine if any matrimonial impediments exist. The practice is optional in the Episcopal Church. A form for publishing the Banns of Marriage is provided by the BCP (p. 437).

Baptism. This is full initiation by water and the Holy Spirit into Christ's Body, the church. God establishes an indissoluble bond with each person in baptism. God adopts us, making us members of the church and inheritors of the Kingdom of God (BCP, pp. 298, 858). In baptism we are made sharers in the new life of the Holy Spirit and the forgiveness of sins. Baptism is the foundation for all future church participation and ministry. Each candidate for baptism in the Episcopal Church is to be sponsored by one or more baptized persons. Sponsors (godparents) speak on behalf of candidates for baptism who are infants or younger children and cannot speak for themselves at the Presentation and Examination of the Candidates. During the baptismal rite the members of the congregation promise to do all they can to support the candidates for baptism in their life in Christ. They join with the candidates by renewing the baptismal covenant. The water of baptism may be administered by immersion or affusion (pouring) (BCP, p. 307). Candidates are baptized "in the Name of the Father, and of the Son, and of the Holy Spirit," and then marked on the forehead with the sign of the cross. Chrism may be used for this marking. The newly baptized is "sealed by the Holy Spirit in Baptism and marked as Christ's own for ever." When all baptisms have been completed, the celebrant and congregation welcome the newly baptized into the household of God. Baptism is normally administered within the eucharist as the chief service on a Sunday or another feast. The Catechism notes that "Infants are baptized so that they can share citizenship in the Covenant, membership in Christ, and redemption by God." The baptismal promises are made for infants by their parents and sponsors, "who guarantee that the infants will be brought up within the Church, to know Christ and be able to follow him" (BCP, pp. 858–859). Baptism is especially appropriate at the Easter Vigil, the Day of Pentecost, All Saints' Day or the Sunday following, and the Feast of the Baptism of our Lord (the First Sunday after the Epiphany).

Baptism, Eucharist, and Ministry (BEM). This is Faith and Order Paper No. 111, published by the World Council of Churches in 1982. It is sometimes referred to as the "Lima Report," since the 1982 meeting of the Faith and

Order Commission of the World Council of Churches was at Lima, Peru. *BEM* represents what divided Christians can affirm in common on baptism, the eucharist, and ministry, as formulated by the Faith and Order Commission. It is generally regarded as the most influential theological text of the modern ecumenical movement. Anglican, Orthodox, Protestant, and Roman Catholic communions participated in writing *BEM*.

Baptism in (of) the Spirit. John the Baptist baptized in water but announced also the coming of a "Strong One" who would baptize with the Holy Spirit (Mk 1:7–8). John focused primarily on the need for repentance and the importance of the future (eschatology). The early Christian community saw the fulfillment of John's promise in the Pentecost event (Acts 1:5). The gift of the Spirit was extended to converts through the response of faith, followed by baptism in the name of Jesus (Acts 2:38). While the reception of the Spirit is invariably associated with baptism, it occasionally precedes (Acts 10:44–48) or follows (Acts 8:14–17; 19:2–9) baptism. In holiness and Pentecostal traditions, "Spirit Baptism" or "Second Baptism" refers to an ecstatic experience distinct from conversion or justification in which the sanctification of the Spirit is bestowed. The Episcopal Church maintains that "Holy Baptism is full initiation by water and the Holy Spirit" into the church (BCP, p. 298). The Episcopal Church thus recognizes no baptism in or of the Spirit separate from or additional to sacramental initiation. *See* Baptism; *see* John the Baptist.

Baptismal Covenant. The rite of Christian initiation contains a series of vows, made by all present, called the "baptismal covenant" (BCP, pp. 304–305). After the candidates have renounced evil and committed themselves to Christ, the presider asks the congregation to join them and "renew our own baptismal covenant." Responding to a series of questions, the people affirm belief in the triune God (through the Apostles' Creed) and promise to continue in the Christian fellowship, resist evil and repent, proclaim the gospel, serve Christ in all persons, and strive for justice and peace. The BCP also suggests the covenant for use, in place of the Nicene Creed, on four days when there are no candidates for baptism: the Easter Vigil, the Day of Pentecost, All Saints' Day or the Sunday thereafter, and the feast of the Baptism of our Lord. In the Episcopal Church the baptismal covenant is widely regarded as the normative statement of what it means to follow Christ.

Baptismal Creed, The. The Apostles' Creed, which is stated by the people in the baptismal covenant (BCP, p. 304). The affirmations of the Apostles' Creed are made by the people in response to the celebrant's first three questions in the baptismal covenant. These questions and responses correspond to the three sections of the Apostles' Creed (see BCP, p. 96). The baptismal covenant then continues with five additional questions and responses concerning how the people will live the Christian life. The baptismal covenant is also used at Confirmation (BCP, pp. 416–417). The affirmations of the Apostles' Creed are also made by the people in the Renewal of Baptismal Vows at the Easter Vigil and other baptismal feasts (BCP, pp. 292–293, 312). The Nicene Creed is not used at Baptism, Confirmation, or the Easter Vigil (BCP, p. 312, 412, 295). The text used for the Apostles' Creed is based on the questions and responses of candidates for baptism at Rome in the late second century.

Baptismal Feasts. Baptism is especially appropriate at the Easter Vigil, the Day of Pentecost, All Saints' Day or the Sunday after All Saints' Day, and the Feast of the Baptism of our Lord (the First Sunday after the Epiphany). These feasts of the church year may be referred to as baptismal feasts. The BCP recommends that, as far as possible, baptism should be reserved for these feasts or occasions or when a bishop is present (p. 312).

Baptismal Regeneration. The doctrine that at baptism the candidates are not only initiated into the Christian community but are also "born again." That is, the Holy Spirit pours upon them the gift of new life. The doctrine is rooted in the NT. The Fourth Gospel states that "no one can enter the kingdom of God without being born of water and the Spirit . . . You must be born from above (or, born again)" (Jn 3:5–7). According to the BCP, candidates for Holy Baptism "receive the Sacrament of new birth" (p. 305), and are declared to have been "raised . . . to the new life of grace" (p. 308).

Like the transformation of bread into the body of Christ at the eucharist, baptismal new life is "spiritually" discerned. The transformation of the baptized persons into participants in the risen life of Christ is not seen with ordinary vision. This transformation is seen with eyes opened by the Spirit. Baptismal regeneration, however, does not immediately or necessarily result in moral betterment. Confusion on this point accounts for numerous controversies on this subject which have occurred in the history of the church. The Rev. Charles E. Cheney, rector of Christ Church, Chicago, refused to use the word "regeneration" in the baptismal service. He was brought to trial in 1869 and subsequently deposed from the ordained ministry. The Rt. Rev. George D. Cummins, Assistant Bishop of Kentucky, also opposed the use of the term. This was the main theological issue in the formation of the Reformed Episcopal Church.

Baptismal Vows, The Renewal of. *See* Renewal of Baptismal Vows.

Baptistry, or Baptistery. The liturgical space where the font is located for the celebration of baptism. The baptistry may be a portion of the church set aside for baptisms, a side chapel, or a separate building.

Bard College, Annandale-on-Hudson, New York. The Rt. Rev. Jonathan Mayhew Wainwright, Provisional Bishop of New York, and the Rev. John McVickar, superintendent of the Society for Promoting Religion and Learning, both urged the diocese to establish a church school to prepare young men for entrance to the General Theological Seminary, New York City. John Bard (1819–1899), president of the New York Life Insurance and Trust Company, and his wife, Margaret Johnston Bard (d. 1875), gave part of their estate in 1860 to establish a college in Annandale. On Mar. 20, 1860, St. Stephen's College was chartered by the New York state legislature. The school was established under the leadership of the Rt. Rev. Horatio Potter, Provisional Bishop of New York. On May 24, 1934, the name was changed to Bard College in honor of the original benefactors. It is a coeducational, liberal arts college, and a member of the Association of Episcopal Colleges.

Barnabas the Apostle, Saint. He was a Levite from Cyprus, and one of the leading members of the early church at Jerusalem. Originally named Joseph, the apostles gave him the Aramaic surname Barnabas, which means "son of consolation" or "son of encouragement." He introduced St. Paul to the apostles after Paul's conversion, and he worked with Paul as a missionary. At the Council of Jerusalem, he defended the rights of the Gentile Christians and argued that they did not have to be circumcised. He and Paul separated after they disagreed about the role of John Mark as a missionary. Barnabas continued as a missionary on his own. He is the traditional founder of the church in Cyprus. Legend claims that he was martyred at Salamis in Cyprus, in 61, during the persecution of Nero. Barnabas is commemorated in the Episcopal calendar of the church year on June 11.

Barnabas Ministries, Inc. This mission agency was founded on Sept. 25, 1980, by the Rev. Canon Philip Edward Phlegar Weeks. Its primary mission work is to provide support to the Philippine Episcopal Church, the Philippine Independent Church, the Christian Fellowship Church, the Charismatic Episcopal Church, and other Christian bodies in the Philippine Islands. It supports orphanages, child care programs, and educational scholarships in the Philippines. Barnabas Ministries publishes a newsletter, *Glad Tidings.*

Barnes, Calvin Rankin (Mar. 23, 1891–Mar. 26, 1976). Priest and national church leader. He was born in Manitowoc, Wisconsin. Barnes received his B.A. from the University of California in 1912, and his B.D. from the General Theological Seminary in 1915. He was ordained deacon on June 27, 1915, and priest on July 16, 1916. Barnes was vicar of the Imperial Valley Mission, El Centro, California, 1916–1918, rector of St. James' Church, South Pasadena, California, 1918–1931, and executive secretary of the Social Service Department of the Episcopal Church, 1931–1936. From 1936 until 1947, Barnes was rector of St. Paul's Church, San Diego, and from 1947 until 1961, he was secretary of the National Council of the Episcopal Church. Barnes served as secretary of the House of Deputies from Sept. 10, 1946, until Sept. 18, 1961. In 1937 he was named an honorary canon of St. Paul's Cathedral, Los Angeles. From 1939 until 1946, he was a Lecturer at the Church Divinity School of the Pacific. His major publication was *The General Convention: Offices and Officers, 1785–1950* (1951). Barnes died in San Diego.

Baroque Architecture. A florid, highly ornamented style of architectural decoration. It appeared in Italy in the late Renaissance and became prevalent on the continent of Europe in the late eighteenth century. It flourished at the same time that the Georgian style was most popular in England and America.

Barrett, Kate Harwood Waller (Jan. 24, 1858–Feb. 23, 1925). Pioneer in Progressive Era women's ministries. She was born in Falmouth, Virginia. She attended the Arlington Institute for Girls in Alexandria. On July 19, 1876, she married the Rev. Robert South Barrett, rector of the church at nearby Aquia, Virginia. The family moved to Henderson, Kentucky, where she helped her husband do pastoral work among prostitutes. When he became dean of St. Luke's Cathedral, Atlanta, in 1886, she enrolled in the Women's Medical College of Georgia and received her M.D. in 1892. The following year, with another woman, she opened a home for unwed mothers. She received $5,000 from Charles N. Crittenton, the "millionaire evangelist," who devoted himself to preaching and rescuing prostitutes. The Barrett family moved to Alexandria in 1894, and in 1895 the National Florence Crittenton Mission was established, with Charles Crittenton as president and Barrett as vice-president and general superintendent. On Charles Crittenton's death in 1909, Barrett became president of the National Florence Crittenton Mission. She belonged to a number of women's groups and was an advocate for women's suffrage. She died in Alexandria, Virginia.

Bartholomew the Apostle, Saint. One of the twelve apostles. His name appears only in the listings of the Twelve in Matthew, Mark, Luke, and Acts. Many believe he is the Nathanael mentioned in John. Tradition, based on the writings of Jerome and Eusebius, says that Bartholomew wrote a gospel, preached to the people of India, and died a martyr. Hippolytus claims that he was flayed (skinned) alive, then crucified, and finally decapitated for his Christian belief. Bartholomew is commemorated in the Episcopal calendar of the church year on Aug. 24.

Basil the Great (c. 330–Jan. 1, 379). Principal architect of monasticism in the east. He was born in Caesarea in Cappadocia. After his baptism in 357, Basil founded a monastery on a family estate in Pontus. His ascetical writings helped to promote monasticism in the east. The Rule of St. Basil, in two forms, shaped monasticism in Eastern Orthodoxy. In 370 Basil became Bishop of Caesarea. He spent the rest of his life opposing the Arians and the Macedonians in the east. Basil was one of the earliest theologians to insist on the divinity of the Holy Spirit. The Liturgy of St. Basil, which he either wrote or revised, is the source for Eucharistic Prayer D in Rite 2 of the BCP (p. 372). Basil, his brother, Gregory of Nyssa, and Gregory of Nazianzus are known as the "Cappadocian Fathers." Basil is commemorated in the Episcopal calendar of the church year on June 14.

Basilica. 1) Church building designed according to the architectural style of a Roman basilica, which served as a law court and commercial exchange. Roman basilicas were used for Christian worship after Constantine gave the church freedom to exist. This architectural style included an outer courtyard or atrium, a narrow porch or narthex, and a semi-circular apse at one end. The building was rectangular, with two rows of columns parallel with the longer side. The basilica had a broad nave, with two or more aisles. The entrance was through the narthex by three or more doorways into the basilica. 2) One of the seven principal Roman Catholic churches in Rome, or any Roman Catholic parish that has been given the privileged title of basilica by the Pope.

Bass, Edward (Nov. 23, 1726–Sept. 10, 1803). First Bishop of Massachusetts. He was born in Dorchester, Massachusetts, and graduated from Harvard in 1744. After graduation, Bass remained at Harvard for theological studies, but moved from the Congregational Church to the Episcopal Church. He went to England and was ordained deacon on May 17, 1752, and priest on May 24, 1752. He became a missionary of the Society for the Propagation of the Gospel (SPG), and served at St. Paul's Church, Newburyport, Massachusetts. Bass supported the colonists' cause during the American Revolution. This support for the American Revolution caused the SPG to dismiss him. On May 7, 1797, he was consecrated bishop. He also exercised episcopal functions in New Hampshire, Rhode Island, and Vermont. He died in Newburyport.

Batterson, Hermon Griswold (May 28, 1827–Mar. 9, 1903). Priest and prominent nineteenth-century Anglo-catholic. He was born at Marbledale, Litchfield County, Connecticut. Batterson was educated privately. He was ordained deacon on Nov. 17, 1861, and began his ministry at St. Mark's Church, San Antonio, Texas. From 1862 until 1866, he was rector of Grace Church, Wabasha, Minnesota. He was ordained priest on Dec. 19, 1865. Batterson moved to Philadelphia, where he was rector of St. Clement's Church, 1869–1872, and the Church of the Annunciation, 1880–1889. His last parochial work was as rector of the Church of the Redeemer, New York City. Batterson was a person of independent means. He was a generous contributor to the building of the Church of St. Mary the Virgin in New York City. His widow gave the building of Christ Church Cathedral, Salina, Kansas, in his memory. Batterson was an Anglo-catholic. Among his publications were *The Missionary Tune Book* (1868) and *A Sketch-Book of the American Episcopate* (1876). Batterson died in New York City.

Bayne, Stephen Fielding, Jr. (May 11, 1908–Jan. 18, 1974). Bishop and first executive of the Anglican Communion. He was born in New York City. Bayne received his B.A. from Amherst College in 1929 and his S.T.B. from the General Theological Seminary in 1933. He was ordained deacon on May 22, 1932, and priest on June 11, 1933. Bayne served as Fellow and Tutor at General Seminary, 1932–1934, rector of Trinity Church, St. Louis, Missouri, 1934–1939, and rector of St. John's Church, Northampton, Massachusetts, 1939–1942. From 1942 until 1947, Bayne was chaplain and chairman of the Department of Religion at Columbia University. On June 11, 1947, he was consecrated Bishop of Olympia and served in that position until he resigned on Dec. 31, 1959. From 1960 until 1964, Bayne was the first executive officer of the Anglican Communion, and from 1964 until 1968, he was the director of the Overseas Department of the Episcopal Church. In 1970 he returned to General Seminary as Professor of Christian Mission. In 1972–1973 he was dean of General Seminary. Bayne retired in 1973. One of the best known of his thirty-three major writings is *Christian Living* (1957), a volume in the first Church's Teaching Series. Bayne died in Santurce, Puerto Rico.

BCP. *See* Book of Common Prayer, The (BCP)

B.D. Bachelor of Divinity. The degree presupposes a first bachelor's degree and was designed to prepare persons for ministry in the church and synagogue. It has been supplanted by the M.Div. (Master of Divinity).

Beach, Abraham (Sept. 9, 1740–Sept. 14, 1828). Missionary and Loyalist. Born in Cheshire, Connecticut, Beach graduated from Yale in 1747, became an Episcopalian, and studied for the ministry under Samuel Johnson. He went to England and was ordained deacon on May 17, 1767, and priest on June 14, 1767. He served as a missionary for the Society for the Propagation of the Gospel (SPG) at New Brunswick and Piscataway, New Jersey, 1767–1784. He was a Loyalist during the American Revolution. He did not officiate and his church was closed. From 1784 to 1811, he was assistant minister at Trinity Church, New York City, and from 1811 to 1813, he was assistant rector there. Beach was elected president of the House of Deputies at the 1801, 1804, and 1808 General Conventions. He retired to New Brunswick in 1813 and died there.

Beardsley, Eben Edwards (Jan. 8, 1818–Dec. 21, 1891). Leading historian of the Episcopal Church. Born in Stepney, Connecticut, Beardsley graduated from Trinity College, Hartford, in 1832. He was ordained deacon on Aug. 11, 1835, and priest on Oct. 24, 1836. From 1835 until 1848, he was in charge of St. Peter's Church, Cheshire, Connecticut, and head of the Episcopal Academy of Connecticut at Cheshire. In 1848 he became the rector of St. Thomas' Church, New Haven, and remained there until his death. Beardsley was a clerical deputy to eight consecutive General Conventions, from 1868 to 1889. He was elected the president of the House of Deputies at the 1880 and 1883 General Conventions. His historical writings include *The History of the Episcopal Church in Connecticut*, Vol. I: *From the Settlement of the Colony to the Death of Bishop Seabury* (1865); Vol. II: *From the Death of Bishop Seabury to the Present Time* (1868); and *Life and Correspondence of the Right Reverend Samuel Seabury, D.D.* (1882). He died in New Haven.

Beatific Vision. The joy or blessedness given in the vision of God. It is reflected in the beatitude "blessed are the pure in heart, for they shall see God" (Mt 5:8) and Paul's confession that we shall see God "face to face" (1 Cor 13:12). The vision of God serves as the primary metaphor for the end of the Christian life in monastic traditions, mysticism, and Thomism. It has been understood as an immediate knowledge of God. It is not a theoretical knowledge but a personal knowledge of the incomprehensible mystery and love of God. The beatific vision may be understood as another expression for the highest good (or *summum bonum*), perfect fulfillment in God, and eternal life. Anglican Kenneth Kirk wrote what remains a classic study of moral theology based on the beatific vision in his 1931 book titled *The Vision of God*.

Beatitudes. From a Latin root that means "blessed" or "happy." It refers to statements in the OT and NT which begin with a similar form: "Blessed are . . ., for. . . ." Emphasis in the OT is on the present state of the person addressed who has earned this special blessed status in relation to God. In the NT beatitudes, the blessing is based in the future, usually indicated by the coming of the Kingdom of God. The most quoted beatitudes are at the beginning of the Sermon on the Mount in the Gospel of Matthew and in the Sermon on the Plain in Luke. These beatitudes are spoken by Jesus to his disciples. The beatitudes are usually interpreted as paradox, comparing the difference between present and future. Those who suffer or are poor now are blessed (or happy) because they are destined to be saved in the future when the Kingdom arrives. The mercifulness and goodness of God will be demonstrated in the future.

Becket, Thomas (c. 1118–Dec. 29, 1170). Archbishop of Canterbury and martyr for the church. He was born in London and educated at the University of Paris. After serving for a time as archdeacon of Canterbury, he became chancellor to King Henry II. He and Henry were friends and allies. When Archbishop Theobald died in 1161, Henry saw an opportunity to extend his authority over the church by having Becket become archbishop. Becket was consecrated Archbishop of Canterbury on June 3, 1162. He immediately became a great defender of the rights and liberties of the church. He and Henry disagreed over a number of church/state issues, and Becket fled to France. After a reconciliation with the King in 1170, he returned to Canterbury. But they were soon in conflict again. On Dec. 29, 1170, Becket was murdered by four overzealous knights who overheard the king murmur that someone should rid him of the archbishop. He was canonized by the Roman Catholic Church in 1173, and his shrine was a major pilgrimage destination until it was destroyed by King Henry VIII in 1538. Becket is commemorated in the Episcopal calendar of the church year on Dec. 29.

Bede the Venerable (673–May 25, 735). Monk, priest, theologian, chronologist, and historian. He was born in Northumbria and at the age of seven was entrusted into the charge of Benedict Biscop at St. Peter's monastery at Wearmouth. Later he moved to St. Paul's monastery at Jarrow where he spent the rest of his life. He was ordained deacon at nineteen and priest at thirty. His *Ecclesiastical History of the English People* is his major work. It is especially significant in recording the conversion of Celtic Christianity to Roman Christianity. This book is a primary source for the period 597 to 731 in English history. On Nov. 13, 1899, Pope Leo XIII declared him a Doctor of the Church. His ministry is commemorated in the Episcopal calendar of the church year on May 25.

Bedell, Gregory Thurston (Aug. 27, 1817–Mar. 11, 1892). Leading evangelical theologian and the third Bishop of

Ohio. He was born in Hudson, New York, and attended William Augustus Muhlenberg's famous school at Flushing, New York. He graduated from Bristol College, Pennsylvania, in 1836 and from Virginia Theological Seminary in 1840. Bedell was ordained deacon on July 19, 1840, and priest on Aug. 29, 1841. He was rector of Trinity Church, West Chester, Pennsylvania, 1840–1843, and of the Church of the Ascension, New York, 1843–1849. He was consecrated Assistant Bishop of Ohio on Oct. 13, 1859. Bedell was Bishop of Ohio from Mar. 13, 1873, until he retired on Oct. 18, 1889. He died in New York City.

Bedell, Gregory Townsend (Oct. 28, 1783–Aug. 30, 1834). A leading evangelical preacher, who wrote several poems and musical compositions. He was born in Fresh Kill, Staten Island, New York, and educated at the Episcopal Academy, Cheshire, Connecticut. He graduated from Columbia College in 1811 and then studied for the ordained ministry. He was ordained deacon on Nov. 4, 1814, and priest on June 28, 1818. From June 15, 1815, until late 1818, he was the pastor of Christ Church, Hudson, New York. He was rector of St. John's Church, Fayetteville, North Carolina, 1818–1822. In 1822 he moved to Philadelphia and established St. Andrew's Church. He died in Baltimore, Maryland. He was the editor, 1824–1827, of the *Philadelphia Recorder* (later the *Episcopal Recorder*), a periodical "standing for Low Church evangelical principles." He was the father of Gregory Thurston Bedell, the third Bishop of Ohio.

Bedell, Harriet (Mar. 19, 1875–Jan. 8, 1969). Missionary among indigenous peoples. She was born in Buffalo, New York, and graduated from the State Normal School in Buffalo in 1894. She taught in the Buffalo public schools, and then studied at the New York Training School for Deaconesses. In Dec. 1907, she began working as a missionary teacher among the Cheyenne Indians at Whirlwind Mission, Oklahoma. She provided Christian education and rudimentary medical care. In 1916 the Board of Missions transferred her to the Indian School in Nenana, Alaska. This school was accessible only by the Yukon River, which was frozen eight months of the year. The next year Bedell was transferred to Tanana, Alaska, as the sole missionary, teaching and nursing the entire community. On Sept. 14, 1922, during the General Convention, she was set apart as a deaconess by Bishop Peter Rowe of Alaska at St Mark's Church, Portland, Oregon. In 1931, when the Alaskan budget was cut, she reopened the Church's work among the

Mikasuki Indians in Florida. She created a ministry of economic empowerment, education, and health care for Indians of the Everglades. Though she officially retired in 1943, she continued diocesan missionary work until her death at Davenport, Florida.

Beecher, Catharine Esther (Sept. 6, 1800–May 12, 1878). Influential advocate of women's concerns. She was born in East Hampton, Long Island, New York, and was raised a Presbyterian. She was a daughter of Lyman Beecher, a leading clergyman who served Presbyterian and Congregational churches. Later in life she rejected the "soul-withering doctrines" of her family's Calvinistic background and converted to the Episcopal Church. She wrote extensively in defense of women's responsibilities in the home and of their family management skills. Among her many books are *A Treatise on Domestic Economy* (1841); *The Duty of American Women to their Country* (1845); *The Evils Suffered by American Women and Children: Causes and Remedy* (1846); and with her sister Harriett Beecher Stowe, *The American Woman's Home* (1869). In 1852 she organized the American Woman's Educational Association. Beecher had a major impact through her popular books on homemaking and on the role of women as shapers of moral and spiritual values for their families.

Believer's Baptism. A term describing the practice of baptizing only those who consciously and knowingly affirm their faith in Christ. The practice normally requires prior instruction and precludes infant baptism. In contrast, the Episcopal Church allows infants and younger children to be presented for baptism by their parents and sponsors who "make promises in their own names and also take vows on behalf of their candidates" (BCP, p. 298).

Bell, Bernard Iddings (Oct. 13, 1886–Sept. 5, 1958). A leading American educator. He was born in Dayton, Ohio. Bell received his B.A. from the University of Chicago in 1907 and his S.T.B. from the Western Theological Seminary in 1912. He was ordained deacon on May 29, 1910, and priest on Dec. 18, 1910. From 1910 until 1913, Bell was the vicar of St. Christopher's Church, Oak Park, Illinois. From 1913 until 1918, he was dean of St. Paul's Cathedral, Fond du Lac, Wisconsin. In 1919 he became Warden of St. Stephen's (Bard) College, and served in that position until 1933. When St. Stephen's became a branch of Columbia University in 1930, he was given a three-year appointment

as Professor of Religion at Columbia. From 1933 until 1946, Bell was preaching canon at St. John's Cathedral, Providence, Rhode Island. He later served as chaplain to Episcopalians at the University of Chicago. After his retirement in 1954, he continued to write and lecture. Bell published over twenty books and numerous articles and sermons. He was an Anglo-catholic and a very popular preacher on college campuses. He died in Chicago.

Bell, Wilbur Cosby (Apr. 1, 1881–Apr. 6, 1933). Theologian and Seminary Professor. He was born in Augusta County, Virginia. Bell received his B.A. from Hampden-Sydney College in 1900 and his M.Div. from the Virginia Theological Seminary in 1905. He was ordained deacon on June 16, 1905, and priest on Feb. 4, 1906. Bell began his ministry at Trinity Church, Onancock, Virginia. From 1906 until 1911, he was rector of Robert E. Lee Memorial Church, Lexington, Virginia. In 1911–1912, he was rector of St. Andrew's Church, Louisville, Virginia. In 1912 Bell became Professor of Systematic Divinity and Apologetics at the Virginia Theological Seminary, where he remained until his death. His major publications were *Sharing in Creation: Studies in the Christian View of the World* (1925), *The Making of Man* (1931), *If a Man Die* (1934), and *The Reasonableness of Faith in God* (1937). He stressed the theory of evolution and believed that creation is a process in which God is always involved. He was an optimistic, hopeful, forward-looking theologian of the 1920s. Bell died in Alexandria.

"Bells and Smells." Colloquial term for the elaborate ritual style common in many Anglo-catholic parishes. In this expression, "bells" refers to the ringing of bells at various points during the eucharist. "Smells" refers to the use of incense. This term is used pejoratively by some, playfully by others.

Bene Esse. *See* Esse, Bene Esse, Plene Esse.

Benedicite, omnia opera Domini. Canticle from the Apocryphal book, Song of the Three Young Men, verses 35–65. It is also known as the *"Benedicite."* It appears as Canticles 1 and 12 in the BCP (pp. 47–49, 88–90) and has been used at the morning office since the fourth century. The *Benedicite* is a continuation of the canticle *Benedictus es, Domine* (Canticles 2 and 13). The *Benedicite* and the *Benedictus es, Domine* form an extended paraphrase of Ps 148. The *Benedicite* begins with the invocation, "Glorify the Lord, all you works of the Lord," and concludes with a doxology. It summons all the cosmic order, the earth and its creatures, and all the living and departed people of God to "bless ye the Lord."

Benedict of Nursia (c. 480–c. 547). The "Patriarch of Western Monasticism." He was born in Nursia in Umbria, Italy, and then educated at Rome. He did not like the degenerate life of the city, and withdrew to the country, where he lived as a hermit in a cave at Subiaco. Gradually a community grew up around him. Sometime between 525 and 530 he moved south with some of his disciples to Monte Cassino, where he composed his Rule about 540. The Rule of St. Benedict shaped monasticism in western Christianity. His ministry is commemorated in the Episcopal calendar of the church year on July 11.

Benedictine Spirituality. Shaped by the Rule of St. Benedict (c. 540), Benedictine spirituality is essentially monastic. It focuses on the desire to seek God under the guidance of an abbot. The abbot was originally elected for life. The monks' chief work (*opus Dei*) is the praise of God, in the form of a community recitation or chanting of the Latin Psalter. The recitation of the Psalter is spread over several days at the rhythm of seven times a day. Each day is divided into three equal periods of prayer, work (manual or intellectual), and care of the body with food and rest. A meditative reading of scripture (*lectio divina*) is the common form of spiritual reflection, and eucharist is the central exercise of the day. Lay "oblates" living in the world share the monastic ideal. The shape of this spirituality was formative for the Daily Office of the BCP.

Benediction. A blessing pronounced by a bishop or priest at the conclusion of a worship service. In a general sense, it may refer to any prayer that closes a meeting or gathering. See Benediction of the Blessed Sacrament.

Benediction of the Blessed Sacrament. A service of devotion to the Blessed Sacrament. In this service a large Host is placed in the luna of a monstrance on the altar so that the Host is visible to the congregation. The Host is censed while it is in the monstrance and used to bless the congregation by making the sign of the cross over the people. This service includes prayers and one or more hymns that emphasize the Incarnation and Christ's real presence in the sacrament of the eucharist. The Host is returned to the tabernacle at the end of the service. The BCP makes no provision for Benediction of the Blessed Sacrament, but it may be seen in parishes with an Anglo-catholic piety. *See* Luna; *see* Monstrance.

Benedictus. *See* Benedictus Dominus Deus.

Benedictus Dominus Deus. Canticle based on Zechariah's hymn of thanksgiving at the circumcision of his son, John the Baptist (Lk 1:68–79). The hymn blesses God "who has come to his people and set them free," and celebrates the prophetic ministry that John the Baptist will have as forerunner of the Messiah. It is also known as "The Song of Zechariah," and it appears as Canticles 4 and 16 in the BCP (pp. 50, 92) for use at Morning Prayer. The table of Suggested Canticles at Morning Prayer (BCP, p. 144) lists it as the first option for use after the OT reading on Sundays as well as Feasts of our Lord and other major feasts. It is also one of three canticles that may be used at a burial as the body is carried from the church (BCP, pp. 484, 500). The ICET translation is used as the Rite 2 version of the canticle in the BCP. *See* John the Baptist; *see* International Consultation on English Texts (ICET).

Benedictus es, Domine. Canticle based on the Apocryphal Song of the Three Young Men, verses 29–34. The canticle offers glory and praise to God, and concludes with a doxology. It is also known as "A Song of Praise." It appears as Canticles 2 and 13 in the BCP (pp. 49, 90). It is recommended for use in the Daily Office on Tuesday mornings and Friday evenings by the table of suggested canticles (BCP, pp. 144–145).

Benedictus qui venit. The anthem "Blessed is he who comes in the name of the Lord. Hosanna in the highest," which follows the *Sanctus* in the eucharistic prayer. It may be sung or said. The term is from the Latin first words of the anthem. It is included in all Rite 2 eucharistic prayers of the BCP, and it is optional in Rite 1. The text is from the acclamation of the crowd at Jesus' triumphal entry into Jerusalem, described in Mt 21:9. It first appeared as an invitation to communion in the liturgy of the fourth-century Apostolic Constitutions. It was subsequently made an expansion of the *Sanctus*. It was included in the 1549 Prayer Book in a modified form but dropped in the 1552 Prayer Book. The 1979 BCP restored the anthem to its current use. Although its use is optional in Rite 1 eucharistic liturgies, it is included in all Rite 1 musical settings for the *Sanctus* in The Hymnal 1982 (S 113–S 117).

Bennett, Dennis Joseph (Oct. 28, 1917–Nov. 1, 1991). The "father of charismatic renewal in the Episcopal Church." He was born in London, England. His family moved to the United States when he was ten years old. He graduated from San Jose State College in 1944. Two years later he entered the University of Chicago Divinity School and received his M.Div. in 1949. Bennett was ordained a Congregational minister in 1949, and served Congregational churches in San Diego, California, from 1949 until 1950. He later became interested in the Episcopal Church and was appointed lay vicar of St. Paul's Church, Lancaster, California. He was ordained deacon on Feb. 21, 1952, and priest on Oct. 20, 1952. Bennett became the rector of St. Mark's Church, Van Nuys, California. Under his leadership its membership increased from approximately 500 to 2,500 by 1960. In 1959, he and some members of his congregation received "baptism in the Holy Spirit." On Apr. 3, 1960, Bennett preached a sermon in which he revealed to his congregation that he had experienced "baptism in the Holy Spirit" and had spoken in unknown tongues. This generated opposition to him and he resigned the parish. In 1960 he became the vicar of St. Luke's Church, Seattle, Washington, which was about to close. Under his leadership it grew to over 2,000 members. Bennett was one of the founders of the Episcopal Charismatic Fellowship, later called Episcopal Renewal Ministries. He resigned as rector of St. Luke's Church in 1981, and spent the rest of his life writing, speaking, and conducting seminars. With his second wife, Rita Marie Reed, he held renewal conferences and wrote the best seller, *The Holy Spirit and You* (1987). *Nine O'clock in the Morning*, which he published in 1970, was also very successful. He died in Seattle.

Benson, Richard Meux (July 6, 1824–Jan. 14, 1915). A founder of the Society of St. John the Evangelist. He was born in London. Benson received the M.A. at Christ Church, Oxford, in 1849. He was ordained deacon in 1848 and priest in 1849. In 1850 he became vicar of Cowley, two miles from Oxford. A sermon preached by John Keble at Wantage on July 22, 1863, moved him to think about founding a community for men. On Dec. 27, 1866, Benson, Simeon Wilberforce O'Neill, and Charles Chapman Grafton founded the Society of St. John the Evangelist. Each took a life vow of celibacy, poverty, and obedience. In Nov. 1870 Benson went to the United States and established a branch house in Boston. He served as superior of the order, 1866–1890.

***Berakoth* (singular *Berakah*).** The Hebrew word for blessings. Typically, they begin, "Blessed are you, Lord our God, King of the universe," followed by naming that for which God is blessed, such as "who brings forth bread from the earth." Scholars distinguish between *berakoth* and *hodayoth* prayers. The latter begin, "We give you thanks." Jewish liturgical prayers have tended to use the *berakoth* form and Christian prayers the *hodayoth*. These Jewish prayer forms lie behind the Christian Great Thanksgiving (BCP, pp. 333ff, 340ff, 361ff, 367–376). The Jewish thanksgiving after meals, which includes both forms, is almost certainly the ancestor of the Christian *eucharistia*, or eucharistic prayer.

Berkeley Divinity School. One of eleven Episcopal seminaries in the U.S. It was founded by Bishop John Williams of Connecticut. It began in 1849 as the theological department of Trinity College, Hartford, and opened as a divinity school on Oct. 2, 1854, at Middletown. In 1928 it moved to New Haven and was affiliated with Yale University. On June 30, 1971, it merged with the Yale Divinity School. The School is named for George Berkeley.

Berkeley, George (Mar. 12, 1684–Jan. 12, 1753). Priest and educator. He was born in Kilcrin, near Thomastown, Kilkenny, Ireland, and educated at Trinity College, Dublin. He was ordained in 1707, and in 1724 he became dean of Derry, where he became very interested in supporting the churches in colonial America and in converting the Native American tribes to Christianity. He persuaded the English government to give him a grant of money to establish the proposed college of St. Paul's in the Bermudas. In 1728 he sailed for America, and reached Newport, Rhode Island, on Jan. 23, 1729. Later he bought a farm which he named Whitehall. His plans for a college did not work out, so he returned to Ireland. He eventually gave Whitehall to Yale College, along with a fine collection of books. Berkeley College at Yale, the Berkeley Divinity School at Yale, and Berkeley, California, are named in his honor.

Berkeley, William (1606–July 9, 1677). Colonial governor of Virginia. He was born in or near London and educated at Queen's College and Merton College, Oxford University. He was governor of Virginia from 1642 until 1652, when he was forced out of office during the interregnum. When the English monarchy was restored in 1660 he became governor again and served until 1676. He agreed with the church policies of King Charles II. He was an opponent of Nonconformity, especially the Quakers and the Puritans. When he was governor, tithes were collected by law, and only members of the Church of England could vote. He died in England.

Bernard (1090–Aug. 20, 1153). Influential monk who was called the "Pope maker" and "the uncrowned emperor of Europe." He was born in Fontaines, France, and entered the Cistercian monastery at Citeaux, France, in 1113. In 1115 he established a Cistercian monastery at Clairvaux and became its abbot. In 1130 both Innocent II and Anacletus II claimed to be Pope, resulting in controversy. Bernard sided with Innocent II and became his confidant and advisor. His influence with the papacy increased even more when Eugenius III, a monk of Clairvaux, became the Pope. Bernard was a leading mystic of the period, and he had a great impact on medieval devotional life. His literary masterpiece was *On Loving God.* He also was called "The Mellifluous Doctor" because of his eloquence. His work as a monastic reformer earned him the title, "second founder of the Cistercian Order." He was declared a saint in 1174. He was named a Doctor of the Church in 1830. The hymn, "O Jesus, joy of loving hearts," numbers 649, 650, in *The Hymnal 1982*, is attributed to Bernard. He died in Clairvaux. Bernard is commemorated in the Episcopal calendar of the church year on Aug. 20.

Berry, Martha McChesney (Oct. 7, 1866–Feb. 27, 1942). Founder of Berry College. She was born and grew up at Oak Hill, a cotton plantation near Rome, Georgia. She inherited a substantial estate in her early twenties when her father died. In the 1890s she started a Sunday School in the Blue Ridge mountains north of Rome, where her family had a hunting lodge. In 1902 she opened the Boys' Industrial School, later the Mount Berry School for Boys, and in 1909 she opened the Martha Berry School for Girls. These were vocational boarding schools that taught the mountain children agricultural and domestic skills. In 1926 these schools became Berry College. In 1924 the Georgia legislators named her a "distinguished citizen." Berry died in Atlanta and is buried on the grounds of Berry College.

Bethany, College of the Sisters of, Topeka, Kansas. On Feb. 2, 1861, the Kansas legislature granted a charter for "The Episcopal Female Seminary of Topeka." On June 10, 1861, the school opened with thirty-three students. On July 9, 1872, Bishop Thomas Hubbard Vail obtained a new charter which changed the name to the College of the Sisters of Bethany. Vail named it in honor of the Sisters of Bethany, Mary and Martha, who represent "the two great classes of Christian womanhood, the contemplative and the active." In 1897 the first Bachelor of Arts degrees were awarded, and on July 2, 1924, the name was changed to Vail College. The school closed in 1928.

Bethlehem, Diocese of. The General Convention of 1871 voted to divide the Diocese of Pennsylvania. On Nov. 8–10, 1871, the primary convention of the Diocese of Central Pennsylvania met at St. Stephen's Church, Harrisburg. The 1904 General Convention voted to divide the diocese again. On May 26, 1909, the name was changed to the Diocese of Bethlehem. It consists of the following counties: Berks, Brandford, Carlson, Lackawanna, Lebanon, Lehigh, Luzerne, Monroe, Northampton, Pike, Schuylkill, Susquehanna, Wayne, and Wyoming. In Apr. 1900, Nativity Church, Bethlehem, became the Cathedral.

Betrothal. A free and faithful promise of future marriage between two persons. It was an ancient Roman custom for a man to give a woman a ring as a sign of betrothal. The usefulness of betrothal was associated with prenuptial arrangements involving the couple and their families, such as dowry. Mary was betrothed to Joseph, but she was found to be pregnant before they lived together. An angel of the Lord told Joseph in a dream not to be afraid to take Mary home as his wife because the child was conceived by the Holy Spirit (Mt 1:18–20). Betrothal is now archaic. The term does not appear in the BCP. However, the Declaration of Consent in the marriage service may be understood as a final ratification of the engagement (BCP, p. 424). These promises were originally made prior to the marriage. They are the couple's public acknowledgment of their free consent to the responsibilities of marriage.

Bexley Hall. It was founded on Nov. 4, 1824, by Bishop Philander Chase and the Diocese of Ohio as "The Theological Seminary of the Protestant Episcopal Church in the Diocese of Ohio." It was incorporated by the Ohio State Assembly on Dec. 29, 1824, and opened at Worthington. In 1828 it moved to Gambier as Kenyon College and Bexley Hall Theological Seminary, named in honor of Lord Bexley (Nicholas Vansittart, 1766–1851), a benefactor. On July 1, 1968, Bexley Hall was separated from Kenyon College and moved to Rochester, New York. It is part of Colgate Rochester Divinity School/Bexley Hall/ Crozer Theological Seminary and St. Bernard's Institute. *See* Chase, Philander; *see* Kenyon College, Gambier, Ohio.

Bible, The. Holy Scriptures of the OT and NT, written under the inspiration of the Holy Spirit, containing all things necessary to salvation. The OT reveals God's mighty acts in creation, the deliverance of the people of Israel from bondage in Egypt, and the making of the old covenant with the chosen people. God's saving will for his people is made known in the OT through the gift of the Law in the Ten Commandments and through the witness of the prophets. The OT is also known as the "Hebrew Scriptures." The NT describes the life, death, and resurrection of Jesus Christ, the Messiah, whose coming was foretold in the OT. It also tells the story of the creation of the Christian church through the gift of the Holy Spirit and presents the new covenant, based on love, which is the new relationship with God given by Jesus Christ to all who believe in him. (BCP, pp. 850–851). The additional books of the Apocrypha, written by people of the old covenant, are often included in the Bible. Although selections from the Apocrypha are used in the worship of the Episcopal Church, the Apocryphal books are not generally considered of equal scriptural authority in Anglicanism with the OT and NT. The translations of the Bible authorized for use in the worship of the Episcopal Church are the *King James (Authorized Version)*, together with the Marginal Readings authorized for use by the General Convention of 1901, the *English Revision* of 1881, the *American Revision* of 1901, the *Revised Standard Version* of 1952, the *Jerusalem Bible* of 1966, the *New English Bible with the Apocrypha* of 1970, the 1976 *Good News Bible* (*Today's English Version)*, the *New American Bible* (1970), the *Revised Standard Version, an Ecumenical Edition*, known as the *"R.S.V. Common Bible"* (1973), the *New International Version* (1978), the *New Jerusalem Bible* (1987), the *Revised English Bible* (1989), and the *New Revised Standard Version Bible* (1990). *See* Apocrypha.

Bible and Common Prayer Book Society. *See* New York Bible and Common Prayer Book Society.

Bible Reading Fellowship. This organization was founded in England in 1922 with the primary purpose of bringing people into a greater knowledge of God through systematic reading of the Bible. The Bible Reading Fellowship in the United States was established in 1971 to meet the need for daily Bible study material. These materials emphasize the spiritual message of the Bible and provide an incentive for daily meditation. Among its resources have been: *Salt*; *Pepper*; *Journey through the Word*; *Compass*; *Good News Daily*; *Path of Life*; and *This Week's Word*.

Bidding Prayer. An informal intercessory prayer, covering a wide variety of concerns such as the church, the state, the living and the dead, and public and private necessities. It followed the sermon and the dismissal of the catechumens in the early church. The celebrant bid a particular intention of prayer, and the congregation joined in silent prayer for a short time until the celebrant summed up the congregation's prayers with a collect. Another bidding would follow, until the bidding prayer was concluded. The bidding prayer is the oldest form of intercessory prayer and has traditionally been said in the language of the people. It was replaced by the litany in the sixth century, and the litany later fell into disuse. The bidding prayer subsequently appeared as an unofficial group of intercessions in the Latin Rite in the middle ages. It was known as the "bidding of the bedes," which means the praying of the prayers. The bidding prayer was flexible, and it could be adapted at the discretion of the celebrant. It was later formalized. In some places it preceded the sermon. Although the 1549 Prayer Book restored liturgical intercession, an Anglican canon of 1604 required a formal bidding prayer before the sermon. The 1928 BCP included a bidding prayer for use before sermons or on special occasions. The minister had discretion to shorten or lengthen the prayer. The ancient bidding prayer is reflected in the solemn collects of the Good Friday liturgy (BCP, pp. 278–280).

Bier. A stand or frame on which a corpse, or a coffin containing a corpse, rests during the burial rite. A bier may also be used to carry the corpse or coffin into the church building and to the grave.

Bilateral Dialogues. Ecumenical dialogues that are held between two churches ("two-sided"), rather than "multilateral" or between many churches. Typically, each of the two churches appoints about ten representatives to the dialogue, and it meets once or twice a year to consider past disagreements and seek ways toward unity. In recent years the Episcopal Church has participated in bilateral dialogues with the Lutherans, the Roman

Catholics, and the Eastern Orthodox. Bilateral dialogues characteristically produce agreed statements on particular points, which remain statements "to" the churches unless or until they are officially endorsed and become statements "of" the churches.

Bioethics. The ethics of life. As a field of study bioethics has expanded from an initial focus on medicine and health care to a focus on life itself. It includes both the goods of human life and the goods of the natural order. Bioethics was initially shaped by the discipline of ethics but has come to include disciplines ranging from the natural and social sciences to history, political science, law, and the humanities in general. This development has arisen in light of new technologies which have raised questions of treatment, development and availability, and questions of consequences for humanity and the environment. These questions concern the nature and meaning of human life, health, suffering, and death; the value of human life in relationship to the value of nature; the nature of technology and the place and responsibility for human action; the specific relationship and responsibilities between the individual and the community, including the extent to which persons should exercise autonomy over their lives; and social questions about the distribution of the goods and burdens of life to provide for the health of the whole community of human and non-human life.

Biretta. Stiff, brimless, three- or four-sided cap worn by clergy on ceremonial occasions. It is black if worn by a priest, and purple if worn by a bishop. The biretta may be ornamented by a pompon. It is rarely used in the Episcopal Church, except in some parishes with an Anglo-catholic piety.

"Biretta Belt." Slang expression for dioceses in the vicinity of the Great Lakes that were once considered to be characterized by Anglo-catholic practices. The term is derived from the traditional fondness of some Anglo-catholic clergy for wearing birettas. Use of this hat was considered by some to be an emblem of Anglo-catholicism. The term is dated and imprecise because few dioceses in this region are now characterized by distinctive Anglo-catholic practice. It is also misleading because Anglo-catholicism cannot be equated with use of a biretta. *See* Biretta.

Bishop. One of the three orders of ordained ministers in the church, bishops are charged with the apostolic work of leading, supervising, and uniting the church. Bishops represent Christ and his church, and they are called to provide Christian vision and leadership for their dioceses. The BCP (p. 855) notes that the bishop is "to act in Christ's name for the reconciliation of the world and the building up of the church; and to ordain others to continue Christ's ministry." Bishops stand in the apostolic succession, maintaining continuity in the present with the ministry of the Apostles. Bishops serve as chief pastors of the church, exercising a ministry of oversight and supervision. Diocesan bishops hold jurisdiction in their dioceses, with particular responsibility for the doctrine, discipline, and worship of the church. Bishops serve as the focus for diocesan unity and for the unity of their dioceses with the wider church. Since the bishop's ministry is a ministry of oversight, the term "episcopal" (derived from the Greek *episcopos*, "overseer") is applied to matters pertaining to bishops. An "episcopal" church is a church governed by bishops, and "episcopal" services are led by bishops. Episcopal services in the BCP include the services for the Ordination and Consecration of Bishops, Ordination of Priests, Ordination of Deacons, the Celebration of a New Ministry, and the Consecration of a Church or Chapel. Bishops also preside at services of Confirmation, Reception, or Reaffirmation. Bishops bless altars and fonts, and the blessing of chalices and patens and church bells are traditionally reserved for the bishop. In the Episcopal Church, diocesan and suffragan bishops are elected by Diocesan Convention. Bishops-elect are ordained and consecrated after consents have been received from a majority of the diocesan standing committees and from a majority of the bishops exercising jurisdiction in the Episcopal Church. If the episcopal election takes place within three months before General Convention, the consent of the House of Deputies is required instead of a majority of the standing committees. Three bishops are required to participate in the ordination and consecration of a bishop. Diocesan bishops may be succeeded by bishops-coadjutor upon resignation of diocesan jurisdiction. Diocesan bishops may also be assisted by suffragan and assistant bishops, who have no right of succession upon the resignation of the diocesan bishop. *See* Apostolic Succession.

Bishop and Council. In some dioceses, Bishop and Council is the group which exercises all powers of the diocesan convention between meetings of the convention. It consists of the bishop; bishop coadjutor, if there is one;

bishop suffragan, if there is one; and a designated number of clergy and lay persons. Bishop and Council may not elect a bishop, may not amend the constitution and canons of the diocese, may not take any action contrary to the actions of the convention, and may not elect any canonical officers of the diocese.

Bishop Coadjutor. Assistant bishop with the right of succession upon the resignation of the diocesan bishop. Before a bishop coadjutor is elected, the diocesan bishop must consent to such an election and state the duties which will be assigned to the bishop coadjutor when duly ordained and consecrated.

Bishop-elect. A presbyter elected to the episcopate but not yet ordained and consecrated. The term may also apply to a person who is already a bishop in one jurisdiction, who has been elected to another jurisdiction, but who has not yet been officially recognized and invested with authority in that diocese.

Bishop Payne Divinity School. A former seminary of the Episcopal Church to train African American men for the ministry. On Oct. 2, 1878, the Virginia Theological Seminary (VTS) opened a branch seminary for Negroes in connection with St. Stephen's Normal and Industrial School, Petersburg, Virginia, under the Rev. Thomas Spencer (1852–1904). In 1884 the name was changed to the Bishop Payne Divinity and Industrial School in honor of James Payne, the first Bishop of Liberia. In 1910 the name was changed to the Bishop Payne Divinity School, and it was empowered to confer the degree of Bachelor of Divinity. It closed on May 25, 1949. On June 3, 1953, it was merged with VTS. The library at VTS is the Bishop Payne Library.

Bishop Potter Memorial House. This training house for women church workers was opened in Philadelphia in 1867. Mr. and Mrs. William Welsh of St. Mark's Church, Philadelphia, were the leading founders. It was named after the Rt. Rev. Alonzo Potter, Bishop of Pennsylvania, 1845–1865. The women formed a sisterhood with a Protestant emphasis. In 1877 the name was changed to the Bishop Potter Memorial House for Deaconesses. It went out of existence in 1891.

Bishop, Provisional. A bishop authorized to serve a diocese whose own bishop is unable to fulfill that ministry due to disability or judicial sentence. The convention of a diocese may choose a bishop (or bishop coadjutor) of another diocese to take full episcopal authority until the disability or judicial sentence no longer exists or until the diocese elects and consecrates another bishop of its own. The convention may revoke such a provisional charge at any time.

Bishop Seabury University. Intended predecessor of the Seabury Divinity School. James Lloyd Breck went to Faribault, Minnesota, in 1858, with the desire to establish a university. It was to be called the Bishop Seabury University after the first bishop of the Episcopal Church. It was never realized, but the Seabury Divinity School, first called Seabury Divinity Hall, was established. *See* Seabury-Western Theological Seminary.

Bishop Visitor or Protector. The bishop named to have an official, canonical relationship with a religious order. Each order must designate a Bishop Visitor or Protector, who serves as guardian of the order's constitution and arbiter of last resort for issues of conflict in the community. The Visitor or Protector may be the bishop in whose jurisdiction the order is established. Another bishop may accept election to this role with the permission of the diocesan bishop.

Bishop White Parish Library Association. It provides grants for Episcopal clergy and parishes to buy theological books. The Association also provides grants to overseas parishes. It was founded in 1848 in honor of Bishop William White of Pennsylvania, first Presiding Bishop of the Episcopal Church.

Bishop White Prayer Book Society. It was founded in Philadelphia in 1833 in honor of William White, the first Bishop of Pennsylvania, and the first Presiding Bishop of the Episcopal Church. It sends copies of the BCP and hymnals to missions and parishes that cannot afford to buy them. The society sends these books to both domestic and foreign parishes.

Bishops' Bible. A revision of the Great Bible. This project was sponsored by Matthew Parker, Archbishop of Canterbury. The Bishops' Bible was published in 1568. The work of revision was assigned to several English bishops. They were directed to follow the Great Bible unless it clearly diverged from the Hebrew or Greek original. The initials of each translator were placed at the end of the translator's section of work. The Bishops' Bible countered the Calvinist bias of the Geneva Bible, but it was not generally as popular as the Geneva Bible. The Convocation of 1571 directed use of the Bishops' Bible in all the churches of England. It was the official English version of the Bible until publication of the Authorized Version in 1611. *See* Great Bible, The.

Bishops' Crusade. The Commission on Evangelism, in July, 1925, made an impassioned report to the National Council concerning evangelism and the church. It called for the Episcopal Church to make evangelism its top priority. It was decided that the initial step in a program of evangelism would take the form of a nationwide effort to rouse the people of the church to a sense of their responsibilities as Christians. The commission organized a movement known as the Bishops' Crusade to emphasize the essentials of the Christian gospel. It called the membership of the church to a rededication in life and service to the Lord Jesus Christ. The Crusade began on Jan. 9, 1927. Nearly three hundred bishops, priests, and lay persons were enlisted for special involvement and leadership. Between three and four million copies of printed matter of various kinds were sent out for the Crusade. Especially notable was *Evangelism in the Church: An Appeal to Christians* (1927), by the Rev. Julius Augustus Schaad (1866–1938), rector of St. Paul's Church, Augusta, Georgia. The book emphasized the quiet, personal work done by people in the regular program of the church rather than preaching to mass meetings. The commission also published and distributed *The Crusade Hymnal* (1927), a twenty-four page hymnal which provided the convenience of evangelistic hymn texts in one volume for preaching missions in diverse circumstances and locations.

Bishops' Executive Secretaries Together (BEST). This organization was founded by Marlene Elacqua, the Bishop's executive secretary of the Diocese of Albany. Elacqua, Sheila Lange of Central New York, Jerri Mead of New York, Cheryl Daves of Washington, Wanda Hollanbeck of Newark, and Karen Glover Glasco of Virginia, held an initial planning meeting in 1987. With the support of Presiding Bishop Edmond L. Browning, the first annual conference of BEST was held at San Francisco on Mar. 5, 1988. Whether called "Secretary," "Executive Secretary," "Assistant," "Executive Secretary," "Administrative Assistant," or "Administrator," that person is automatically a member of BEST. The members work to improve communication, work out problems, and develop continuing education programs. BEST holds a national meeting each year.

Bishops, House of. This second house, along with the House of Deputies, of the General Convention is composed of all bishops, active and retired, of the church. It meets concurrently with the House of Deputies during General Convention, and also holds yearly meetings between conventions.

Bishop's Staff. *See* Crozier, or Crosier.

Black Fast. The custom of observing the two great Prayer Book fast days, Ash Wednesday and Good Friday, by eating no food at all. This was observed as a pious custom by some devout church people in the nineteenth century in imitation of the fasting of the ancient church.

Black Letter Days. Lesser feasts of the church year. About sixty-seven lesser feasts were added to the calendar of the English Prayer Book in 1567. These lesser feasts became known as black-letter days. They were distinguished from the major feasts which were known as red-letter days. That term reflects the early practice of printing Prayer Book calendars in red. The major feasts were included in the Prayer Book calendar and printed with red letters. In Prayer Books with single-color printing, major feasts are printed in bold type and lesser feasts are printed in lightface type. See the calendar of the church year (BCP, pp. 19–30). *Lesser Feasts and Fasts* includes proper collects and lessons for these days of optional observance in the Episcopal calendar, along with biographical and historical information.

Black Ministries, Office of (OBM). The office of secretary for Negro Work was created by the 1940 General Convention, and later Bravid Washington Harris was soon named to the position. He was later elected the Missionary Bishop of Liberia, and the Rev. Tollie LeRoy Caution was named secretary. Caution served in that position until 1967. He was asked to retire and the Department of Negro Workers was closed. This resulted in the creation of the Union of Black Clergy and Laity, which evolved into the Union of Black Episcopalians (UBE). In conjunction with the African American bishops, the UBE successfully petitioned the 1973 General Convention for another office. The Office of Black Ministries was created. Presiding Bishop John Allin named the Rev. Franklin Delton Turner as Staff Officer for Black Ministries. Turner remained in the position until 1982. The Rev. Canon Harold Lewis served as Staff Officer of Black Ministries from 1983 until 1994. The Commission for the Office of Black Ministries was dissolved in 1994 due to reorganization and cutbacks at the national Episcopal Church. A combined Multi Cultural/Ethnic Committee was put in place. This Committee has a Staff Officer for the Office of Black Ministries.

Black Rubric, The. Name usually given to the "Declaration on Kneeling" that was printed at the end of the rite for Holy Communion in the 1552 BCP. The "Declaration" was understood to deny the real presence in the eucharistic elements. This statement was removed in the 1559 BCP, but replaced in the 1662 BCP in an altered version that denied only Christ's "corporal" presence in the eucharist. The term dates from nineteenth-century England. Prayer Book rubrics were printed in red, and the "Declaration" was therefore printed in black since it was not a rubric. The "Declaration" has never appeared in an American Prayer Book. *See* Receptionism.

Blair, James (c. 1656–Apr. 18, 1743). Commissary to Virginia and Founder of the College of William and Mary. He was born in Scotland. Blair received his M.A. from the University of Edinburgh in 1673. He was ordained in the Church of Scotland in late June or early July, 1679. He moved to England and was ordained in the Church of England. In 1685 the Bishop of London offered him the rectorship of the parish of Henrico, then called Varina, in the colony of Virginia. On Dec. 15, 1689, the Bishop of London named Blair the Commissary to Virginia. As Commissary he wielded little official authority within the colony, but he did have great influence upon several of the governors. He began the practice of calling the clergy of the colony together for conventions. Blair looked out for the interests of the clergy and churches in the colony, and worked successfully for better salaries for clergy. Blair also sought morally sound and reliable priests for the parishes, and he fought to retain the rights of the vestries to appoint their own clergy rather than submit to royal appointments. His greatest contribution was the founding of the College of William and Mary. In 1691 he went to England to petition the King and Queen for the college. On Feb. 8, 1693, the charter was granted. In the charter Blair was named president of the college "during his natural life." In 1694 he became the minister of the church in Jamestown. In 1710 he became the rector of Bruton Parish in Williamsburg, where he remained until his death. He was also the president of William and Mary until his death. Blair died in Williamsburg.

Blandina (d. 177). She was a virgin slave girl. Blandina was one of forty-eight Christians who were martyred at Lyons, France, during a persecution by the Emperor Marcus Aurelius. Her heroic courage is described in a "Letter of the Churches of Lyons and Vienne," which was preserved by Eusebius in his *Ecclesiastical History*. Blandina and the Bishop of Lyons, Pothinus, are among seven of the forty-eight martyrs who are mentioned by name. They are all known as "The Martyrs of Lyons." They are commemorated in the Episcopal calendar of the church year on June 2.

Blasphemy. An expression of contempt for God. A Scottish jurist in the seventeenth century characterized it as "treason against God." The term has been used differently in different eras. Understandings of what constitutes blasphemy have changed with changing sensibilities, social norms, and political considerations. The Judeo-Christian tradition rejects blasphemy on the basis of Ex 22:28, "You shall not revile God." The punishment for blasphemy in the OT was death by stoning. Blasphemy laws in England date from 1558.

Blessed Sacrament. The term may indicate the sacrament of the eucharist, or the consecrated eucharistic elements of bread and wine, or the reservation of the consecrated elements. Christ's body and blood are understood to be really present in the consecrated bread and wine. *See* Eucharistic Adoration.

Blessed Trinity Society. An organization founded in 1960 by Jean Stone Willans to promote and support charismatic renewal in the mainline Protestant churches. Willans was a member of St. Mark's Episcopal Church in Van Nuys, California, where the rector, the Rev. Dennis Joseph Bennett, received the baptism of the Holy Spirit. From 1961 until 1965, the society published a quarterly magazine, *Trinity*, to promote the Pentecostal experience.

Blessing. 1) A sacerdotal pronouncement of God's love and favor, addressed to one or more persons. The BCP prescribes forms of blessing to be used by a bishop or priest prior to the dismissal in Rite 1 eucharistic liturgies.

Although no form of blessing is required in the Rite 2 eucharistic liturgies, all four Rite 2 eucharistic prayers allow a blessing at the conclusion of the service. The *BOS* provides Seasonal Blessings, which may be used by a bishop or priest whenever a blessing is appropriate. A nuptial blessing of the husband and wife concludes the Celebration and Blessing of a Marriage (BCP, pp. 430–431). The Reconciliation of a Penitent, Form One, begins with a blessing of the penitent by the priest. The deacon may be blessed by the celebrant before reading or singing the gospel at the eucharist. Individuals may also be blessed by a bishop or priest outside the context of a liturgy for pastoral reasons. The *BOS* provides a form for the Blessing of a Pregnant Woman, which may be done privately. 2) A blessing may also be used to consecrate or dedicate something to holy use. The celebrant blesses the water to be used in baptism (BCP, pp. 306–307). The elements of the eucharist are blessed in the prayer of consecration. The BCP provides a form for the blessing of oil for the Anointing of the Sick (p. 455), and for the consecration by a bishop of the oil of chrism for use in baptism (p. 307). Wedding rings may be blessed at the Celebration and Blessing of a Marriage (p. 427). The new fire is blessed at the Lighting of the Paschal candle in the Great Vigil of Easter (BCP, p. 285). The *BOS* provides forms for the blessing of a home. Forms for the Dedication of Church Furnishings and Ornaments are provided in the *BOS*. Other items for use in or out of the church may be blessed for pastoral reasons.

Bliss, William Dwight Porter (Aug. 20, 1856–Oct. 8, 1926). Priest and social reformer. He was born in Constantinople, the son of missionaries. He received his B.A. from Amherst College in 1878 and his B.D. from the Hartford Theological Seminary in 1882. After several years as a Congregationalist minister, he became an Episcopalian. He was ordained deacon on June 16, 1886, and priest on June 8, 1887. Bliss was rector of Grace Church, Boston, 1887–1890. During this period he became very interested in the Christian Socialism of Charles Kingsley and F. D. Maurice. In 1889 he helped to organize the Christian Socialist Society. In 1890 he founded the Church of the Carpenter, Boston, an inner-city experimental center, of which he was rector for four years. He lectured widely in the United States, Canada, and England, on the responsibility of the church for social reform and its obligations to help the poor. He served churches in New York, New Jersey, and California. He was a pastor and YMCA worker in Switzerland, 1914–1921. Among his numerous publications was the *Encyclopedia of Social Reform*, first published in 1898. Bliss died in New York City.

Blood Theology. In the OT "blood" denotes life, especially the life of a sacrificial animal poured out in death. In the NT it denotes the sacrificial death of Christ inaugurating the new covenant in which the faithful partake in the Lord's Supper (1 Cor 11:25). Blood theology typically concerns the saving benefits of Christ's sacrifice on the cross.

Bloomer, Amelia Jenks (May 27, 1818–Dec. 30, 1894). Social reformer. She was born in Homer, Cortland County, New York. She married Dexter C. Bloomer, editor of the *Seneca County Courier*. With his encouragement, she began to publish articles in newspapers on moral and social issues. Bloomer was baptized at Trinity Episcopal Church, Seneca Falls. She attended the first women's rights meeting in Seneca Falls but was not an active participant. In Jan., 1849, she began publishing the *Lily*, probably the first paper published by a woman. She wrote about women's suffrage and worked in the temperance movement. She published a picture of herself in the *Lily* wearing trousers, which were later called "bloomers." After several years in Mt. Vernon, Ohio, the family moved to Council Bluffs, Iowa, where she continued to work on numerous reforms. Bloomer died in Council Bluffs. She is commemorated in the Episcopal calendar of the church year on July 20. *See* Stanton, Elizabeth Cady; *see* Truth, Sojourner; *see* Tubman, Harriet Ross.

Bloy House. *See* Episcopal Theological School at Claremont (Bloy House).

"Blue Book." A book containing reports from boards, committees, and commissions for the General Convention. It is distributed to delegates and other participants prior to General Convention. The first "Blue Book" was published for the sixty-fourth General Convention, Oct. 11–Oct. 29, 1973, which met at Louisville, Kentucky. It was entitled *The Blue Book: Supplement*. The name is associated with the color of the book's cover, although the 1973 edition was not blue. Future volumes were blue, and were entitled *The Blue Book: Reports of the Committees, Commissions, Boards, and Agencies of the General Convention of the Episcopal Church*. The 1997 edition was entitled *Report to the 72nd General Convention, Otherwise Known as The Blue Book. Reports and Resolutions of the Committees, Commissions, Boards and Agencies of the General Convention of the Protestant Episcopal Church, USA for Consideration in Philadelphia, Pennsylvania, July Sixteenth to Twenty-fifth, inclusive, in the Year of Our Lord 1997*. Its color was maroon. Earlier collections of documents for General Convention were also known by the color of the book cover. The "Blue Book" was preceded by *The Green Book*, which was preceded by *The Yellow Book*.

"Blue Box" (UTO). Also called "mite boxes," these small, blue, cardboard boxes are used to collect funds for the United Thank Offering, sponsored by the Episcopal Church Women. The name was first used at the General Convention of 1925. Mary Abbot Emery, first secretary of the Women's Auxiliary to the Board of Missions, and Mrs. Richard Soule of Pittsburgh, each claimed that the other began the offering to raise money for building churches and supporting missionaries. The date generally given for the beginning of these offerings is Oct. 3, 1889, at the Triennial Meeting of the churchwomen. The original name was the United Offering.

Blue Box (Bishop Gordon's Airplane in Alaska). In 1952 the United Thank Offering appropriated money to purchase a Cessna 170 airplane for Bishop William Gordon of Alaska. The plane was named after the "blue box" that the women used to raise funds for their projects. A replica of a "blue box" was painted on the plane. A year later, a second plane, a Cessna 180 (Blue Box II) was secured for the bishop after Blue Box I developed mechanical problems.

Board for Church Deployment. *See* Church Deployment Office.

Board for Theological Education (BTE). The BTE was formed by a resolution of the 1967 General Convention. The Board studied the needs and trends of theological education within the Episcopal Church. It made recommendations to the boards of trustees of the seminaries, the Executive Council, the House of Bishops and the General Convention. The BTE also served as a source of advice for the seminaries, and promoted cooperation among the seminaries. It maintained information about seminary enrollments, costs, and finances, and served as a focal point for discussions concerning theological education. The BTE also provided assistance in programs of lay theological education. It was merged into the Standing Commission on Ministry Development by the 1997 General Convention. *See* Ministry Development, Standing Commission on.

Board of Missions. A Board of thirty members that provided leadership for the Episcopal Church between General Conventions from 1835 to 1919. Its formation was recommended to the 1835 General Convention by a committee of the Domestic and Foreign Missionary Society. The Board held its first meeting on Sept. 1, 1835. Over time the Board began to be ineffective. It was stated at the 1877 General Convention that "the old Board of Missions is dead and buried." A new Board of Missions was organized and held its first meeting on Oct. 30, 1877. The 1919 General Convention reorganized the national church and established the National Council to administer and carry on the missionary, educational, and social service work of the church. On Dec. 10, 1919, the Board of Missions met for the last time.

Board of the Archives of the Episcopal Church. The Board of the Archives was established by the 1985 General Convention. It consists of the archivist (*ex officio*, with vote), the dean of the Episcopal Theological Seminary of the Southwest (*ex officio*, with vote), and nine appointed persons, three of whom shall be bishops and six shall be lay and clerical members. The bishops are appointed by the Presiding Bishop, and the six lay and clerical members are appointed by the president of the House of Bishops. All must be confirmed by the General Convention. All appointed members serve terms beginning with the close of the General Convention at which their appointments were confirmed and ending with the close of the second regular convention thereafter. The board sets the policy for the archives, elects the archivist, and meets at least once annually. The board selects its own officers, and reports to the General Convention and the Executive Council.

Boise, Missionary District of. The 1898 General Convention changed the name of the Missionary District of Wyoming and Idaho to the Missionary District of Boise. It was in existence until Oct. 10, 1907, when the General Convention formed the Missionary District of Wyoming and the Missionary District of Idaho.

Bonhoeffer, Dietrich (Feb. 4, 1906–Apr. 9, 1945). Pastor and theologian. He was born in Breslau, Germany. Bonhoeffer began his theological studies at Tübingen University but moved to Berlin University. In 1927 he received the licentiate in theology, *summa cum laude*, and defended his doctoral dissertation. It was published as *The Communion of Saints* (1927). In 1929 Bonhoeffer became assistant professor in systematic theology at Berlin University. The next year, he published his second dissertation, *Act and Being* (1930). On Sept. 5, 1930, he began a year of theological studies at Union Theological Seminary in New York City. In 1931 he was appointed youth secretary of the World Alliance for Promoting International Friendship through the Churches. On May 29–31, 1934, the Confessing Church, to which Bonhoeffer belonged, issued the Barmen Declaration, which repudiated the claims of National Socialism and upheld the lordship of Christ. In 1936 his authorization to teach at Berlin University was terminated because of his resistance to the powers of Nazi Germany. He was declared a "pacifist and enemy of the State." In 1939 he went to the United States again, but decided he must return to Germany and suffer with his people. On Sept. 9, 1940, Bonhoeffer was prohibited from public speaking and ordered to report regularly to the police. Because of his opposition to Hitler and the Nazi regime, he was arrested on Apr. 3, 1943, and held in Tegel Prison, Berlin. On Apr. 9, 1945, he was hanged with six other Hitler resisters. Among his most popular books are *The Cost of Discipleship* (1937), *Life Together* (1938), and *Letters & Papers from Prison* (1944). Bonhoeffer is commemorated in the Episcopal calendar of the church year on Apr. 9.

Boniface (c. 680–June 5, 754). The "Apostle of Germany," he was born near Crediton in Devonshire, England, and was originally named Winfred. He was educated in abbeys at Exeter and Nursling, near Winchester. Boniface spent most of his life doing missionary work in Frisia, Thuringia, Hesse, and Bavaria. He was consecrated bishop in 722, was made archbishop in 732 by Pope Gregory III, and named a papal legate in 739. Boniface established numerous Benedictine monasteries, of which Fulda was the most famous. Under papal authority, he established the archiepiscopal see at Mainz in about 743. In 752, with the consent of Pope Zecharias, Boniface anointed Pippin King of the Franks, which gave divine sanction to the change of rulers. After a few years at Mainz he resigned as archbishop to return to his missionary work in Frisia. On

June 5, 754, while on a mission to the Frisians, Boniface and some companions were killed by a band of pagans near Dokkum. His missionary work helped to spread papal influence north of the Alps. Boniface is commemorated in the Episcopal calendar of the church year on June 5.

Bonn Agreement. This agreement grew out of a meeting of representatives of the Old Catholic churches of Holland, Germany, and Switzerland, and of the Church of England, at Bonn, Germany, July 2, 1931. The Bonn Agreement states that 1) Each Communion recognizes the catholicity of the other and maintains its own; 2) Each Communion agrees to admit members of the other Communion to participate in the Sacrament; 3) Intercommunion does not require from either Communion the acceptance of all doctrinal opinion, sacramental devotion, or liturgical practice characteristic of the other but implies that each believes the other to hold all the essentials of the Christian faith. The 1934 General Convention accepted and ratified the terms of intercommunion agreed to by the Joint Commission of Old Catholics and Anglicans at Bonn, and also agreed to establishment of intercommunion between the Episcopal Church and the Old Catholics of the Utrecht Convention under the terms of the Bonn Agreement.

Book Annexed, The. A shortened form of the title of *The Book Annexed to the Report of the Joint Committee on the Book of Common Prayer Appointed by the General Convention of MDCCCLXXX* or of *The Book Annexed . . . As Modified by the Action of the General Convention of MDCCCLXXXIII.* These books were published in 1883 and 1885 in elegant quarto and octavo forms at the expense of J. P. Morgan for the use of deputies to the General Conventions of 1883 and 1886. They were complete Prayer Books which embodied the changes being proposed to the 1883 General Convention and those that were accepted at that convention. The later book was modified in the conventions of 1886 and 1889, but most of the changes that were accepted in the Prayer Book revision finalized in 1892 are changes that appeared in *The Book Annexed* published in 1883. Much of the new material in *The Book Annexed* of 1883 had been in William Reed Huntington's *Materia Ritualis*, An Appendix to a Paper on *"The Revision of the Common Prayer"* in *The American Church Review* for Apr. 1881 (Worcester, 1882).

Book of Common Prayer, The (BCP). Official book of worship of the Episcopal Church. The BCP provides liturgical forms, prayers, and instructions so that all members and orders of the Episcopal Church may appropriately share in common worship. Anglican liturgical piety has been rooted in the Prayer Book tradition since the publication of the first English Prayer Book in 1549. The first American BCP was ratified by the first General Convention of the Episcopal Church in 1789. It was based on the Proposed Book of 1786, and the 1662 English Book of Common Prayer, as well as the Scottish eucharistic rite of 1764. The BCP is ratified by General Convention, with alterations or additions requiring the approval of two successive General Conventions. The General Convention may also authorize services for trial use. The process of Prayer Book revision led to publication of editions of the BCP for the Episcopal Church in 1789, 1892, 1928, and 1979. The BCP notes that "The Holy Eucharist, the principal act of Christian worship on the Lord's Day and other major Feasts, and Daily Morning and Evening Prayer, as set forth in this Book, are the regular services appointed for public worship in this Church" (p. 13). The BCP includes the calendar of the church year, and it provides forms for the Daily Office, the Great Litany, the Collects, Proper Liturgies for Special Days, Holy Baptism, the Holy Eucharist, Pastoral Offices, and Episcopal Services. In addition to many forms for corporate worship, the BCP also provides forms for Daily Devotions for Individuals and Families (pp. 136–140). The BCP includes both contemporary language (Rite 2) and traditional language (Rite 1) versions of the forms for Morning and Evening Prayer, the Collects, the Eucharist, and the Burial of the Dead. The BCP also includes the Psalter, or Psalms of David; Prayers and Thanksgivings; An Outline of the Faith, or Catechism; Historical Documents of the Church (including the Articles of Religion); Tables for Finding the Date of Easter and other Holy Days; and lectionaries for the Holy Eucharist and the Daily Office.

Book of Homilies. In 1547, Thomas Cranmer, Archbishop of Canterbury (1533–1556), issued his *Book of Homilies.* This was a time when many clergy did not want to preach, and when they did, some preached inflammatory sermons. Readings from the *Book of Homilies* were intended to insure that congregations of the Church of England would hear only officially approved doctrine. Cranmer's book was a compilation of twelve sermons. Three sermons are known to have come from Cranmer's hand—*Of Salvation, Of Faith*, and *Of Good Works.* Those sermons cover matters of greatest concern to the reformers. The whole collection is a significant expression of Reformation doctrine. Rubrics in both the 1549 and 1552 Prayer Books called for one of the homilies if there were no sermon. A *Second Book of Homilies* was published some time prior to the Convocation of 1562, which issued the Thirty-Nine Articles of Religion. Article XXXV lists the twenty-one titles of the homilies found in the new edition (BCP, p. 875). Although the 1662 Prayer Book repeats the 1552 rubric, clergy increasingly took up the preacher's role again. The *Homilies* fell into disuse and are now rarely heard.

Book of Occasional Services, The (BOS). Book of optional services and texts prepared by the Standing Liturgical Commission in response to a directive from the General Convention of 1976 to replace *The Book of Offices* (third edition, 1960). The services and texts of the *BOS* are available for "occasional" pastoral and liturgical needs of congregations. The *BOS* includes special materials for the church year (such as forms for Seasonal Blessings, a Christmas Festival of Lessons and Music, and a service for All Hallows' Eve); Pastoral Services (such as forms for Welcoming New People to a Congregation, the rites of the Catechumenate, and a form for the Blessing of a Pregnant Woman); and Episcopal Services (such as forms for the Reaffirmation of Ordination Vows and the Welcoming and Seating of a Bishop in the Cathedral). The Preface to the *BOS* notes that "None of it is required, and no congregation is likely to make use of all of it."

Book of Offices, The. A collection of offices for specific purposes and occasions "which occur in the work of Bishops and other Clergy." It was first published in 1940. It includes forms for the dedication of various buildings and forms for the blessing of articles of church furniture. It was contrasted with *The Kingdom, the Power, and the Glory* (1933) which was a collection of services and prayers for devotional occasions. *The Book of Offices* was compiled by the Liturgical Commission in accordance with a resolution of the 1937 General Convention. Much of the material in *The Book of Offices* was taken from *Offices for Special Occasions* (1916), which also included a variety of occasional offices, devotions, and forms for dedication. Both books may be understood as precursors of the *Book of Occasional Services.*

Boone College, Wuchang, China. The Bishop Boone Memorial School, a boarding school, opened in Wuchang in Sept., 1871, with three students. It was named after

Bishop William Jones Boone, the first Episcopal Bishop of China. It was raised to the rank of college in 1905 and graduated its first class in 1906. It was incorporated as a university in 1909. At one time it had preparatory and college departments as well as a theological school and a medical school. It also published *The Boone Educational World*.

Boone, William Jones (July 1, 1811–July 17, 1874). First foreign Missionary Bishop of the Episcopal Church. He was born in Walterborough, South Carolina, and graduated from the College of South Carolina in 1829. He was admitted to the bar in 1833 but decided to enter the ordained ministry. After studying for a while at the Virginia Theological Seminary, Boone was ordained deacon on Sept. 18, 1836, and priest on Mar. 3, 1837. He was appointed a missionary to China on Jan. 17, 1837, by the Domestic and Foreign Missionary Society. He sailed for China on July 8, 1837. Boone was consecrated the first Missionary Bishop of China on Oct. 26, 1844, and served in that position until his death. He translated the BCP into the Chinese language and helped to translate the Bible. He died in Shanghai.

Boone, William Jones, Jr. (Apr. 17, 1846–Oct. 5, 1891). Missionary bishop. He was born in Shanghai, China. Boone graduated from Princeton in 1865. He then studied at the Philadelphia Divinity School and the Virginia Theological Seminary. He was ordained deacon on July 26, 1868, and priest on Oct. 28, 1870. Boone was appointed to the mission at Wuchang, China, and served there for ten years. He then became head and chaplain of the theological department of St. John's College, Shanghai. He was consecrated the fourth Missionary Bishop of China on Oct. 28, 1884, and served in that position until his death. He died in Shanghai.

BOS. *See* Book of Occasional Services, The (*BOS*).

Bosher, Robert Semple (May 27, 1911–Dec. 29, 1976). Priest and church historian. He was born in Richmond, Virginia. Bosher received his B.A. from the University of Virginia in 1932, his S.T.B. from General Theological Seminary in 1936, and his Ph.D. from Cambridge University in 1949. He was ordained deacon on Apr. 14, 1936, and priest on Oct. 28, 1936. Bosher was rector of Grace Church, Standardsville, Virginia, 1936–1940, and vicar of St. John's Church, Bernardsville, New Jersey, 1942–1945, before becoming a fellow and tutor at the General Theological

Seminary. From 1949 until 1951, he was instructor in Ecclesiastical History. He was associate professor from 1951 until 1954, and from 1954 until 1972, professor at the General Theological Seminary. While he was professor he was also Director of Graduate Studies. His major publication was *The Making of the Restoration Settlement* (1951). He died in Richmond, Virginia.

Boucher, Jonathan (Mar. 12, 1738–Apr. 27, 1804). Tory clergyman. He was born in Blencogo, parish of Bromfield, Cumberland County, England. He came to Virginia in 1759 to serve as tutor for two boys in Port Royal. Boucher felt called to ordained ministry while he was in Virginia, but he had to go to England for ordination because there was no bishop in the colonies. He was ordained deacon on Mar. 26, 1762, and priest on Mar. 31, 1762. Boucher returned to Virginia where he became rector of St. Mary's Parish, Caroline County. At St. Mary's he was a parish pastor, schoolmaster, and planter. Among his pupils was John Park Curtis, son of Martha Washington and step-son of George Washington. Boucher and Washington became friends and shared an extensive correspondence. On May 10, 1770, he became rector of St. Anne's Church, Anne Arundel County, Maryland, and in Nov. 1771 he became rector of Queen Anne's Parish, Prince George's County. Boucher was a forceful advocate for bishops in the colonies, and a firm supporter of the established order. To protect himself when he preached he carried a pair of loaded pistols into the pulpit. In 1775 he returned to England and served parishes there until his death at Carlisle.

Bowden, John (Jan. 7, 1751–July 31, 1817). Priest and educator. He was born in Ireland. Bowden came to the American colonies at an early age. For two years he was a student at the College of New Jersey (Princeton). He graduated from King's College, New York, in 1772. Bowden was ordained deacon on Apr. 25, 1774, and priest on May 29, 1774. He began his ministry as assistant minister at Trinity Church, New York. He left the city during the Revolution because he did not support the patriot cause. In 1784 he became the rector of St. Paul's Church, Norwalk, Connecticut. He remained there until 1789, when he went to the West Indies for his health. When he returned to the United States, he served as the first Principal of the Episcopal Academy of Connecticut at Cheshire from June 1796 until Apr. 1802. In 1802 he became Professor of Moral Philosophy and Logic at Columbia College. He served there until his death. Bowden died in Balston Spa, New York.

Bowie, Walter Russell (Oct. 8, 1882–Apr. 23, 1969). Seminary professor and renowned preacher. Born in Richmond, Virginia, Bowie received his B.A. in 1904 and his M.A. in 1905, both from Harvard. He received his B.D. from Virginia Theological Seminary in 1908. He was ordained deacon on June 19, 1908, and priest on June 18, 1909. He was rector of Emmanuel Church, Greenwood, Virginia, 1908–1911; of St. Paul's Church, Richmond, Virginia, 1911–1923; and of Grace Church, New York City, 1923–1939. From 1939 until 1950, he was professor of practical theology at Union Theological Seminary, New York, and from 1945 until 1950, he was dean of Students. In 1950 he became professor of homiletics at Virginia Theological Seminary, where he taught until his retirement in 1955. Bowie was one of the great preachers in the Episcopal Church. He is included in most histories of preaching. In 1935 he delivered the Lyman Beecher Lectures on Preaching at Yale Divinity School, and they were published under the title *The Renewing Gospel.* Bowie published numerous books and was an associate editor of exposition for the twelve volumes of *The Interpreter's Bible* (1951–1957). He died in Alexandria, Virginia.

Boyle, Sarah Patton (May 9, 1906–Feb. 21, 1994). Outstanding Episcopal opponent to segregation in the era of the civil rights movement. She was born in Albemarle County, Virginia. In the late 1940s she became aware of the evils of segregation and racism. In the 1950s she worked to increase public awareness of segregation's harm to people of all races. She is best known for *The Desegregated Heart*, published in 1962. Her last book, *The Desert Blooms: Creative Aging*, published in 1983, also received critical acclaim. She was honored for her public efforts against segregation by a Martin Luther King Jr. Award in 1963. Boyle was a life-long Episcopalian. She died in Arlington, Virginia.

Bragg, George Freeman, Jr. (Jan. 25, 1863–Mar. 12, 1940). African American civil rights leader, priest, editor, and author. He was born in Warrenton, North Carolina, and grew up in Petersburg, Virginia, where he studied at St. Stephen's Parish and Normal School. He entered the Theological School for Negroes in Petersburg in 1879, a branch of the Virginia Theological Seminary. Bragg was suspended the next year because the rector claimed he was "not humble enough." After a serious illness in 1883, he continued his theological studies under private tutors. In 1885 he reentered the theological school, which was renamed in 1886 the Bishop Payne Divinity School. He was ordained deacon on Jan. 12, 1887, and priest on Dec. 19, 1888. From 1891 until his death, he was the rector of St. James Church, Baltimore. In 1886 he founded the *Afro-American Churchman*, which became the *Church Advocate*. Bragg served as editor for thirty-four years. He was a pioneer writer on the history of African American Episcopalians, and his major work was *History of the Afro-American Groups of the Episcopal Church* (1922, reprinted in 1968). He died in Baltimore.

Bratton, Theodore DuBose (Nov. 11, 1862–June 26, 1944). Bishop and educator. Bratton was born near Winnsboro, South Carolina, and his mother was the sister of William Porcher DuBose. He studied at the Sewanee Grammar School. Bratton received his B.A. in 1887 and his B.D. in 1889 from the University of the South. He was ordained deacon on Sept. 25, 1887, and priest on Sept. 23, 1888. His first charge was in 1887 as missionary in York, Chester, and Lancaster counties, South Carolina. The next year he became rector of the Church of the Advent, Spartanburg, and from 1890 to 1899 he taught at Converse College. Bratton was head of St. Mary's Junior College, Raleigh, North Carolina, 1899–1903. He was consecrated Bishop of Mississippi on Sept. 29, 1903, and held that position until he retired on Nov. 2, 1938. While bishop he founded All Saints' Junior College for women. It opened on Sept. 16, 1907, and is now a private school for boys and girls, grades eight through twelve. He was the author of several books, including *An Apostle of Reality: The Life and Thought of the Reverend William Porcher DuBose* (1936). He died in Jackson, Mississippi.

Bray, Thomas (1656–Feb. 15, 1730). Commissary to Maryland and Founder of the Society for the Propagation of the Gospel and the Society for Promoting Christian Knowledge. He was born in Marton, Shropshire, England. Bray graduated from All Souls College, Oxford, in 1678, and then was ordained deacon and priest. He served as a country curate, chaplain, and vicar until 1690, when he became rector of Sheldon, Warwickshire. While at Sheldon he wrote his famous *Catechetical Lectures*. In 1696 the Bishop of London named Bray the first Commissary to Maryland. He served in that position until 1706. Before going to Maryland he founded the Society for Promoting

Christian Knowledge, which sent missionaries and libraries to the colonies, and provided charity schools in England. Bray arrived in Maryland on Mar. 12, 1700. He returned to England in early 1701. Bray also founded the Society for the Propagation of the Gospel, which sent 354 missionaries to the American colonies. In 1706 he became the rector of St. Botolph's Without, Aldgate, where he remained until his death. In 1723 the Associates of Dr. Bray was established. It was a trust to assist in converting Negroes and Indians. Bray was described as "a Great Small Man." He died in Aldgate.

Bray's Associates. Thomas Bray (1656–1730) was deeply interested in the English colonies. While visiting Holland, he met Monsieur Abel Tassin, who was commonly known as Sieur d'Allone. D'Allone provided in his will that the income from a fund that represented a significant portion of his estate would be used by Doctor Bray and his associates for erecting schools for the instruction of the young children of Negro slaves "& such of their Parents as show themselves inclineable." In 1723 Bray named trustees to execute the work made possible by D'Allone's benefactions, as well as other funds accumulated by him for the instruction of Indians and Negroes. Their authority was confirmed by a decree of chancery on June 24, 1730. The title "Doctor Bray's Associates," or "Bray's Associates" remained with them. The official name was the "Trustees for Mr. D'Allone's Charity for the Instruction of the Negroes in America." The organization used missionaries, books, and schools to educate and convert Negroes and Native Americans. Their activities in America were ended by the Revolutionary War.

Brazier. A metal bowl containing coals for burning incense. It is sometimes used in worship in place of the thurible, which is an incense bowl swinging from hand-held chains.

Brazil, Missionary District of. The mission to Brazil began on Aug. 31, 1889 when James Watson Morris (1859–1954) and Lucien Lee Kinsolving (1862–1929) sailed for Brazil as missionaries. On Oct. 20, 1898, the House of Bishops elected Kinsolving Bishop for the United States of Brazil. The General Convention of 1907 created the Missionary District of Brazil and elected Kinsolving Missionary Bishop. The same General Convention also changed the name to the Missionary District of Southern Brazil. On Sept. 30, 1949, the House of Bishops divided the Missionary District of Southern Brazil into three missionary districts—Southern Brazil, Southwestern Brazil, and Central Brazil. On Oct. 20, 1964, the House of Bishops voted for an independent Brazilian Church, and in 1965 the Episcopal Church of Brazil became an independent province of the Anglican Communion.

Bread. *See* Elements, Eucharistic.

Breaking of the Bread, The ("The Fraction"). The breaking of the consecrated bread for distribution by the celebrant at the eucharist. The fraction also recalls Christ's body as broken for us and our salvation. The breaking of the bread follows the eucharistic prayer and the Lord's Prayer and is accompanied by a period of silence. A fraction anthem, or *confractorium*, may also be sung or said after the breaking of the bread. The fraction is followed by the celebrant's invitation to communion and the administration of communion. The 1662 English Prayer Book directed the celebrant to break the bread at the words "he brake it" in the institution narrative of the eucharistic prayer. The direction of this rubric was continued by American Prayer Books through the 1928 BCP. The breaking of the bread was restored to its traditional place in the 1979 BCP, after the eucharistic prayer and immediately before the communion of the people.

Breastplate of St. Patrick. An ancient Irish hymn, "I bind unto myself today," which appears as Hymn 370 in *The Hymnal 1982*. It is a Celtic lorica, or breastplate prayer, which was recited while dressing or arming for physical or spiritual battle. The text invokes the Trinity, angels, apostles, patriarchs, prophets, the powers of heaven and earth, and Christ to be present for protection in all times and situations of life. The hymn strongly emphasizes personal commitment, awareness of God in everyday events "today," and Christ's pervasive presence. The text is ascribed to St. Patrick (c. 390–c. 460). It is very unlikely but not impossible that St. Patrick wrote it. The earliest copy of the text dates from the ninth century, and it may well have been written in the sixth century or earlier. Cecil Frances Alexander (1818–1895) translated the metrical English version of the text that appears in *The Hymnal 1982*. She originally prepared this expanded paraphrase of the text for the 1891 revision of the *Irish Church Hymnal*. The hymn was completed in time to be sung throughout Ireland on St. Patrick's Day, Mar. 17, 1889. It is now frequently used on Trinity Sunday because of its powerful invocation of the Trinity. *See* Celtic Spirituality; *see* Lorica (Celtic).

Breck, James Lloyd (June 27, 1818–Mar. 30, 1876). Founder of Nashotah House and Seabury Divinity School. He was born in Philadelphia County, Pennsylvania, and educated at Flushing Institute, Flushing, New York. He graduated from the University of Pennsylvania in 1838. He studied at the General Theological Seminary, 1838–1841, where he was influenced by the high church principles of the Oxford Movement. Breck was ordained deacon on July 4, 1841. Accompanied by two other graduates of General Seminary, William Adams and John Henry Hobart, Jr. (1817–1889), Breck headed west to establish a center of missionary activity in the newly opened Territory of Wisconsin. On Oct. 9, 1842, he was ordained priest. He and his associates established Nashotah House in that year. In 1850 Breck moved to Minnesota and worked among the Chippewa Indians. In 1858 he established the Seabury Divinity School at Faribault. After nine years at Faribault, the "apostle of the wilderness" moved to California and settled in Bernica, where he established St. Augustine's College with a grammar school and a divinity school attached. He died in Bernica. His life is commemorated on Apr. 2 in the Episcopal calendar of the church year.

Brent, Charles Henry (Apr. 9, 1862–Mar. 27, 1929). Bishop and ecumenist. He was born in Newcastle, Ontario. Brent graduated from Trinity College, University of Toronto, in 1884, and then spent two years studying for the ordained ministry. He was ordained deacon on Mar. 21, 1886, and priest on Mar. 6, 1887. Since no vacancy existed in the Diocese of Toronto, he accepted a position as organist and curate at St. Paul's Church, Buffalo, New York, in 1887, and then for about two years he served St. Andrew's Mission, Buffalo. From 1888 until 1891, Brent lived and worked with the Society of St. John the Evangelist, but he never took monastic vows. He served as assistant minister at St. Stephen's Church, Boston, from 1891 until 1901. Brent was consecrated the first Missionary Bishop of the Philippines on Dec. 19, 1901, and served in that position until Feb. 19, 1918. While Bishop of the Philippines, he worked against the illegal use of drugs and was president of the American delegation to the International Opium Commission at Shanghai in 1911. During World War I, Brent served as senior Chaplain of the American Expeditionary Forces. On Oct. 2, 1917, he was elected the fourth Bishop of Western New York, and he assumed that position on Feb. 19, 1918. Brent was deeply committed to the ecumenical movement. He led the Episcopal Church in the movement that resulted in the first World Conference on Faith and Order. He was a popular preacher and a widely published author. A prayer for mission in Morning Prayer, Rite 2 (BCP, p. 101) was written by Brent. He is commemorated in the Episcopal calendar of the church year on Mar. 27.

Breviary. A liturgical book used for recitation of the Divine Office (Canonical Hours). It includes psalms, lessons, hymns, prayers, antiphons, and readings from patristic sources and other Christian writers. The breviary provides in a single volume all materials needed for recitation of the Canonical Hours. The first breviaries began to appear as early as the eleventh century. Portable breviaries were spread throughout Europe during the expansion of the Franciscan Order in the thirteenth century. Several breviaries have been compiled for use by religious communities, parishes, and individuals in the Episcopal Church. *See* Canonical Hours.

Bridges, Robert Seymour (Oct. 23, 1844–Apr. 21, 1930). Poet and hymn composer. He was born in Walmer on the Island of Thanet, Kent. He was educated at Eton and Corpus Christi College, Oxford, and studied medicine at St. Bartholomew's Hospital, London. He gave up the practice of medicine in 1882 and settled at Yattendon, Berkshire, to devote himself to literature. His first volume, *Shorter Poems*, was published in 1873. He was made poet laureate in 1913. His most famous poem, *Testament of Beauty*, appeared in 1929. He sought to upgrade the quality of the poetry of hymnody and to bring into use some worthy continental tunes that were in meters not frequently used in English hymnody. He published, with the help of H. E. Woolridge, a small supplement of a hundred hymns, *The Yattendon Hymnal*, for use in his parish church. A number of these texts and tunes were published in *The English Hymnal* (1906), edited by Percy Dearmer and Ralph Vaughan Williams, and soon afterward in other hymnals. Seven of Bridges's translations are included in *The Hymnal 1982*, including "O gladsome Light" (36), "O sacred head, sore wounded" (168–169), and "All my hope on God is founded" (665).

Briggs, Charles Augustus (Jan. 15, 1841–June 8, 1913). OT scholar and biblical critic. He was born in New York

City, and studied at the University of Virginia, 1857–1860; Union Theological Seminary, New York, 1861–1863; and in Berlin, 1866–1869. After serving as pastor of the Presbyterian Church in Roselle, New Jersey, 1870–1874, he became the Professor of Hebrew and Cognate languages at Union Theological Seminary, New York, serving from 1874 to 1891. In 1891 he was transferred to the newly established Edwin Robinson Professorship of Biblical Theology, and gave his inaugural address on the authority of scripture. In the address he defended modern biblical scholarship and condemned the inerrancy dogma of Protestant orthodoxy, "superstitious Bibliolatry," verbal inspiration, and "predictive prophecy." He was accused of teaching heresy and suspended from the Presbyterian ministry by the General Assembly. Union Seminary severed relations with the General Assembly, and Briggs joined the Episcopal Church. He was ordained deacon on May 27, 1898, and priest on May 24, 1899. He died after nearly forty years as professor at Union seminary.

Brigid, or Bride (c. 453–c. 523). Very little is known about Brigid, except that she became a nun and founded the first nunnery in Ireland at the Church of the Oak, now Kildare. She is thus known as the Abbess of Kildare. She is also known as St. Bride, and "the Mary of the Gael." With Patrick and Columba she is a patron saint of Ireland. She is also patron of poets, blacksmiths, and healers. She was born at Fauchart in Leinster, Ireland, and died in Kildare. She is commemorated in the Episcopal calendar of the church year on Feb. 1.

Bristol College, Bristol, Pennsylvania. In 1825 the Rev. Drs. Gregory Townsend Bedell, James Milnor, and Stephen Higginson Tyng founded the Episcopal Education Society of Philadelphia. They began a manual labor college for prospective ministers near Wilmington, Delaware. It moved to Bristol, Bucks County, Pennsylvania, and reopened as Bristol College on Oct. 2, 1833. It promoted the idea of "uniting manual labor with mental improvement." The Rev. Chauncey Colton (d. 1876) was its only president. It closed in Feb. 1837 for lack of financial support.

Broad Church Movement. The term appeared in mid-nineteenth century theological discourse to describe an approach to the doctrine and worship of the Church of England which was more tolerant and liberal than the views of the existing low church and high church parties. Thomas Arnold, S. T. Coleridge, F. D. Maurice, A. P. Stanley, and Benjamin Jowett are associated with the early years of the broad church movement.

Some of the features of the broad church attitude were a desire that the church should contribute to the welfare of the life of the English nation, as opposed to the individualism of the low church party and the ecclesiastical emphasis of the high churchmen; an openness to reason as a mediator of religious truth, as opposed to the exclusive reliance on scripture and tradition in the other parties, with particular interest in the new teaching of the German idealist philosophers; and a passion for rigorous morality and social justice. The broad church movement desired the Church of England to be comprehensive rather than exclusive. Those identified with the broad church movement in its early years considered it to be above parties—hence "broad." Within a generation, the impossibility of such a view was commonly discerned. The broad church movement was ranked as a third party, the heir of the Elizabethan settlement and the latitudinarians.

Brooks, Phillips (Dec. 13, 1835–Jan. 23, 1893). Bishop and celebrated preacher. He was born in Boston and received his B.A. from Harvard in 1855. After receiving his B.D. from the Virginia Theological Seminary in 1859, he was ordained deacon on July 1, 1859, and priest on May 27, 1860. Brooks served two pastorates in Philadelphia, one at the Church of the Advent, 1859–1862, and the other at Holy Trinity Church, 1862–1869. While at Holy Trinity he wrote the Christmas carol, "O Little Town of Bethlehem," for the children in the Sunday School (see Hymns 78–79, *The Hymnal 1982*). On Oct. 31, 1869, he became rector of Trinity Church, Boston, and remained there until his consecration to the episcopate. While at Trinity he became recognized as one of the great preachers in American church history. In 1877 he delivered the Lyman Beecher Lectures on Preaching at the Yale Divinity School. In these lectures he described preaching as "the communication of truth through the personality of the preacher to his brother man." Brooks was the demonstration of that definition. The truth to be communicated was the Incarnation, that God was in Christ and that God is Christlike. Brooks was consecrated the sixth Bishop of Massachusetts on Oct. 14, 1891. He died in Boston in less than eighteen months. He was a broad church evangelical committed to liturgical openness and inclusivity.

Brother. The term has been applied to male Christians since the earliest NT times. The language of family kinship recalls the closeness of the bond that is shared by those who live in Christ. For example, the Gospel of Mark (3:35) records Jesus' statement that "Whoever does the will of God is my brother and sister and mother" (NRSV). The term has been used more specifically to indicate a man who is a member of a religious order or community. Historically, the term indicates a layman, but it is now also used by some priests in religious orders or communities as an expression of equality and community.

Brotherhood of the Carpenter. The Rev. William Dwight Porter Bliss, a leading Episcopal Social Gospel advocate, founded the Mission of the Carpenter in Boston. The first service was held on Apr. 13, 1890. The Mission was to cut across economic lines, to attract members of other churches, and to study methods of direct and practical social action. The mission was incorporated as a parish in 1892 and became the Church of the Carpenter with Bliss as the rector. When the church did not accomplish what Bliss wanted, he founded the Brotherhood of the Carpenter as a guild of the parish in 1892. The Brotherhood was not restricted to Episcopalians. It was an ecumenical "Brotherhood of Work" to spread the literature and ideas of Christian Socialism. The Brotherhood continued until 1896. The Church of the Carpenter went out of existence shortly thereafter.

Brotherhood of St. Andrew. The Brotherhood began on Nov. 30 (St. Andrew's Day), 1883, as a prayer and Bible study group of young men at St. James Church, Chicago. They agreed to follow the example set by St. Andrew in bringing his brother, Peter, to Christ. The leader of the group was James Lawrence Houghteling (1855–1910), a Chicago banker and YMCA leader. He was supported by the rector, William H. Vibbert (1840–1918). Houghteling was president of the Brotherhood from 1883 until 1900. The Brotherhood was incorporated by an Act of Congress signed by President Theodore Roosevelt on May 30, 1908. The Act states, "That the sole object of said corporation shall be the spread of Christ's Kingdom among men." The Brotherhood implements its program by forming chapters in parishes throughout the church. Chapter members are called Brothers Andrew, and are asked to accept the Brotherhood disciplines of prayer, study, and service. Where multiple chapters exist within a diocese, assemblies may be formed to further the work of the Brotherhood. It publishes a quarterly newsletter, *St. Andrew's Cross.* This newsletter began publication in Oct., 1886, with the motto, "For the Spread of Christ's Kingdom Among Young Men." In the 1970s the Brotherhood founded the Christian renewal program known as Faith Alive. It also founded the PEWSACTION program to bring together the work of all the renewal groups. It is an international organization today.

Brotherhood of St. Gregory (BSG). Religious order for men. The brotherhood was founded on Holy Cross Day, Sept. 14, 1969, when four brothers, including the founder, Richard Thomas Biernacki, made their professions in the Monastery Chapel of the Visitation at Riverdale, New York. It is a Christian Community of the Episcopal Church, and its members live under a common rule and serve the church on the parochial, diocesan, and national levels. Its membership is open to both clergy and laity, married and single. The brothers live individually, in small groups, or with their families. They support the community's activities from their secular or church-related employment. They seek to be witnesses to the Christian ideal of living in the world while not being of the world. The brotherhood was granted recognition as a Religious Community of the Episcopal Church in 1969. The habit of the brotherhood is a white, hooded tunic which is covered by a brown scapular with capuche. The motto is "To God Alone the Glory."

Brown, Daniel (Apr. 26, 1698–Apr. 13, 1723). One of the Yale converts. He was born in New Haven, Connecticut. Brown (sometimes Browne) graduated from Yale College in 1714. He was the rector of the Hopkins Grammar School in New Haven. In 1718 he was appointed tutor in Yale College and remained in that position until 1722. On Sept. 13, 1722, he, Samuel Johnson, Timothy Cutler, and James Wetmore announced that they questioned their ordinations in the Congregational Church. This announcement was known as the "Yale Apostasy." It is considered the birth of the high church party in the Episcopal Church. Brown resigned his tutorship on Oct. 17, 1722. On Dec. 5, 1722, he, Johnson, and Cutler sailed to England to obtain episcopal ordination. On Mar. 9, 1723, Brown received "private hypothetical baptism" at the Church of St. Sepulchre, London. On Mar. 22, 1723, he was confirmed and ordained deacon, and then on Mar. 31, 1723, he was ordained priest. He became ill on Apr. 4, 1723, and died in London. *See* Yale Converts.

Brown, Lelia Ann (Sister Anna Mary) (June 14, 1873–Jan. 2, 1967). Leading African American sister. She was born in Macon, North Carolina. Brown was left an orphan as a small child and brought up by a white Baptist minister. She was confirmed in the Episcopal Church in 1895, and in 1897 she entered the novitiate of the Community of All Saints. On Dec. 13, 1910, she was professed in the Community of St. Mary and All Saints, a Negro order affiliated with the Community of All Saints. When the Community of St. Mary and All Saints was later disbanded, Sister Anna Mary continued to keep her vows and wear her habit. Brown was a parish worker in St. Andrew's Church, Cleveland, and St. Monica's Church, Washington, D.C. In 1931 she became house mother and dietitian at St. Agnes' Hospital, Raleigh, North Carolina. She retired in 1941. During the next fourteen years she was a volunteer worker in East Orange, New Jersey. In 1955 she went to Glendale, Ohio, and in 1956 received the habit and became a full member of the Community of the Transfiguration. Brown died in Glendale.

Brown, Ray Francis (June 23, 1897–Mar. 23, 1964). Church musician and composer. He was born in Roxbury, Vermont. Brown was a graduate of Oberlin College and an associate of the American Guild of Organists. Upon graduation from college he became director of the Music School of Fisk University, Nashville. In 1935 he became instructor in church music and organist at the General Theological Seminary in New York, a post he held until his retirement in 1963. During those years he also served as organist and choirmaster of several New York area parishes. At General Seminary he was known as a person of great compassion. In 1949 Oxford University Press (New York) published *The Oxford American Psalter* in which his pointing of the psalms reflected his advocacy of "speech rhythm" chanting, a method of pointing developed in England earlier in the century. The principles established by Brown in his work in chant at General Seminary influenced the pointing of Anglican chant in *The Book of Canticles*, *The Hymnal 1982*, and *The Anglican Chant Psalter*. Brown served on the Tunes Committee for *The Hymnal* (1940). *The Hymnal 1982* contains one tune, "*Chelsea Square*" (521), which he harmonized and one Anglican chant (S 214) which he composed. Brown died

in New York City. *The Anglican Chant Psalter* was dedicated to his memory.

Brown, Robert Raymond (June 16, 1910–Feb. 5, 1994). Bishop and civil rights leader. He was born in Garden City, Kansas. Brown received his B.A. in 1933 from St. Mary's University and his B.D. in 1937 from the Virginia Theological Seminary. He was ordained deacon on June 20, 1937, and priest on Dec. 24, 1937. He was priest-in-charge of All Saints' Church, San Benito, and St. Alban's Church, Harlingen, Texas, 1937–1940, and associate rector of Trinity Church, Houston, 1940–1941. From 1941 until 1947, Brown was rector of St. Paul's Church, Waco, and from 1947 until 1955, he was rector of St. Paul's Church, Richmond, Virginia. Brown was consecrated Bishop Coadjutor of Arkansas on Oct. 5, 1955, and became the ninth Bishop of Arkansas on Oct. 5, 1956. He held this position until his retirement on Nov. 1, 1970. Brown was a civil rights advocate and a supporter of Negro causes. He served as a Trustee of the American Church Institute for Negroes. In 1957 Brown became involved in the integration of Central High School in Little Rock. His book, *Bigger Than Little Rock* (1958), is the story of reconciliation during that tumultuous period. He died in Little Rock.

Brown, William Montgomery (Nov. 6, 1855–Oct. 31, 1937). Deposed bishop. He was born in Wayne County, near Norville, Ohio. Brown attended Seabury Hall, Faribault, Minnesota, and then studied theology at Bexley Hall, Gambier, Ohio. He was ordained deacon on June 17, 1883, and priest on May 22, 1884. Brown served Grace Church, Galion, Ohio, from 1883 until 1891. He was then made general missionary of the Diocese of Ohio with the title of archdeacon. On June 24, 1898, he was consecrated Bishop Coadjutor of Arkansas, and he became the second Bishop of Arkansas on Sept. 5, 1899. Brown was given a leave of absence by the diocese on May 11, 1911, and on Apr. 11, 1912, he resigned as bishop of the diocese. Later he became a bishop in the Old Catholic Church. After his resignation as an Episcopal bishop, Brown became an advocate of communism and published books about it. On Oct. 12, 1925, Brown was deposed from the ordained ministry of the Episcopal Church by the House of Bishops. He died in Galion, Ohio.

Brownell, Thomas Church (Oct. 19, 1779–Jan. 13, 1865). Seventh Presiding Bishop of the Episcopal Church. He was born in Westport, Massachusetts. Brownell began his education at the College of Rhode Island, but transferred to Union College where he graduated in 1804. From 1805 until 1817, he taught at Union College, and during his last years there he studied theology. He was ordained deacon on Apr. 11, 1816, and priest on Aug. 4, 1816. After serving briefly as assistant minister at Trinity Church, New York, he was elected Bishop of Connecticut and was consecrated on Oct. 27, 1819. One of his major accomplishments was the founding of Washington College, Hartford, in 1824. He remained president of Washington College until 1831. While Bishop of Connecticut he made several missionary trips through Kentucky, Mississippi, Louisiana, and Alabama. On Sept. 20, 1852, he became Presiding Bishop and served until his death. Brownell published more than ten books, the most important being *Commentary on the Book of Common Prayer* (1843). He died in Hartford.

Browning, Edmond Lee (b. Mar. 11, 1929). Twenty-fourth Presiding Bishop of the Episcopal Church. He was born in Corpus Christi, Texas. Browning received his B.A. in 1952 and his B.D. in 1954 from the University of the South. He was ordained deacon on July 2, 1954, and priest on May 23, 1955. Browning was an assistant at the Church of the Good Shepherd, Corpus Christi, 1954–1956; rector of the Church of the Redeemer, Eagle Pass, Texas, 1956–1959; and priest-in-charge of All Souls Church, Okinawa, 1959–1963. From 1963 to 1965, he and his wife studied at the Language School in Kobe, Japan, before returning to Okinawa to serve St. Matthew's Church in Oruku until 1968. On Jan. 5, 1968, Browning was consecrated the first Missionary Bishop of Okinawa. He resigned on May 16, 1971, to become the Bishop-in-Charge of the Convocation of American Churches in Europe. He resigned this position on June 1, 1974, to return to the United States and become executive for national and world mission at the Episcopal Church Center. On Aug. 1, 1976, he became the sixth Bishop of Hawaii. At the General Convention of 1985 Browning was elected Presiding Bishop and assumed that office on Jan. 1, 1986. He resigned as Bishop of Hawaii to become Presiding Bishop. His tenure as Presiding Bishop was characterized by a very strong international dimension and by a commitment that the Episcopal Church would have no outcasts. Browning retired as Presiding Bishop on Dec. 31, 1997.

Bruton Parish, Williamsburg, Virginia. An important pre-Revolutionary parish. It had a strong association with both the College of William and Mary and the colonial government of Virginia. In 1632 or 1633, the parish of Middler Plantation was formed. In 1658 it was combined, by act of the Colonial Assembly, with Harrop Parish to form the new parish of Middletown. The first building was completed around 1660. In 1674 the parishes of Middletown and Marston were combined to form Bruton Parish, named for the town of Bruton in Sussex, England, the ancestral home of the governor, Sir William Berkeley. It is assumed that the 1660 structure was of wood, since in 1677, by order of the vestry, a brick structure was to be built. This building was completed on Nov. 29, 1683. In 1699 the colonial government of Virginia was moved from Jamestown to Williamsburg and Bruton Parish became the court church. Church and state were united in Virginia in colonial times and office holders were required to attend church regularly.

In 1706 the vestry again ordered a new, larger church to be built. It requested that the government contribute to defray costs. The governor, Alexander Spotswood, agreed to supply the bricks and to pay for twenty-two of the seventy-five feet length of the building. The building was completed in 1715. It has remained in continuous use. Other additions were made by 1769, but no subsequent additions have been made to the exterior. In 1744 the vestry suggested that the General Assembly purchase an organ for the church. In 1752 the church was enlarged and what is believed to be the first church organ in the colonies was installed. During the Civil War, the congregation went "underground" to avoid praying for the President of the United States, as ordered by the Federal commander. The building was used as a hospital. Restoration of the building was begun in 1905 and again in 1960.

Brydon, George MacLaren (June 27, 1875–Sept. 26, 1963). Priest and church historian. He was born in Danville, Virginia. Brydon received his B.A. from Roanoke College, Salem, Virginia, in 1896, and his B.D. from Virginia Theological Seminary in 1899. He was ordained deacon on June 23, 1899, and priest on May 31, 1900. Brydon was deacon-in-charge of Randolph Parish, Halifax County, 1899–1900; assistant at Emmanuel Church, Baltimore, 1900–1901, and again 1904–1907; rector of St. Paul's Church, Hamilton, as well as Mt. Calvary, Round Hill, and Christ Church, Lucketts, all in Loundon County, 1901–1904; rector of Trinity Church, Morgantown, West Virginia, 1907–1911; rector of St. Paul's and Hanover Parishes in King George County, 1911–1914; Richmond City Missionary, 1914–1917;

and rector of St. Mark's Church, Richmond, 1917–1919. He was executive secretary and treasurer of the Diocese of Virginia, 1919–1940, and the Archdeacon of Colored Work, 1914–1930 and 1937–1941. He made many of his most significant contributions as historiographer of the Diocese of Virginia. His major work was *Virginia's Mother Church and the Political Conditions Under Which It Grew*, 2 vols. (1947, 1952). He died in Richmond, Virginia.

BTE. *See* Board for Theological Education (BTE).

Bucer, or Butzer, Martin (Nov. 1, 1491–Feb. 28, 1551). Reformation leader. He was born in Schlettstadt, Alsace. Bucer came under the influence of Martin Luther, and from 1523 he worked as a reforming pastor in Strasbourg. After the death of Ulrich Zwingli in 1531, Bucer became the leader of the reformed churches in Switzerland and South Germany. He worked with Hermann von Weid, Archbishop of Cologne, to produce the Church Order known as *Hermann's Consultation* (1543), which had some influence on the 1549 Prayer Book. In 1548 he went to England at Thomas Cranmer's invitation and was appointed Regius Professor of Divinity at Cambridge University, a position he held until his death. Bucer's opinion of the 1549 Prayer Book was stated in his *Censura*, and some of his suggestions were incorporated into the 1552 Prayer Book. He also had an influence on the Ordinal of 1550.

Buck, or Bucke, Richard (c. 1582–c. 1642). Colonial clergyman. He studied at Caius College, Cambridge. He arrived at Jamestown, Virginia, on May 23, 1610, as the second minister at James City Parish. He succeeded Robert Hunt. Buck officiated at the marriage of John Rolfe and Pocahontas on Apr. 14, 1614. He opened with prayer the first General Assembly of Virginia on July 30, 1619. He died in Jamestown.

Burgess, John Melville (b. Mar. 11, 1909). First African American diocesan bishop. Burgess was born in Grand Rapids, Michigan. He received his B.A. and M.A. from the University of Michigan. In 1934 he received his B.D. from the Episcopal Theological School. Burgess was ordained deacon on July 29, 1934, and priest on Jan. 25, 1935. He served St. Philip's Church, Grand Rapids, 1934–1938, and St. Simon of Cyrene Church, Lincoln Heights, Ohio, 1938–1946, before becoming the Chaplain at Howard University in 1946. From 1951 until 1956, Burgess was Canon of the Cathedral of St. Peter and St. Paul, Washington, and from 1956 until 1962, he was Archdeacon of Boston. On Dec. 8, 1962, he was consecrated Suffragan Bishop of Massachusetts, and on June 7, 1969, he was elected Bishop Coadjutor of Massachusetts. On Jan. 11, 1970, Burgess became the Bishop of Massachusetts, the first African American diocesan bishop in the Episcopal Church. He retired on Jan. 1, 1976. During his episcopate he had an active ministry to college students and to the urban poor. After his retirement Burgess taught pastoral theology at Yale Divinity School and was active in programs for the welfare of the African American community.

Burial of the Dead. Funeral rite for burial of a baptized Christian, including anthems, psalms, scripture readings, and prayers. The BCP provides both traditional and contemporary liturgies (pp. 469–507). This rite may serve as the liturgy of the word at a Requiem Eucharist. When there is communion at the Burial of the Dead, the commendation and the committal follow the communion of the people and the postcommunion prayer (BCP, pp. 482, 498). The burial rites also include the Apostles' Creed, a special form of the prayers of the people, forms for the consecration of the grave, and additional prayers that may be added after the Lord's Prayer. The BCP also provides an Order for Burial which permits the composition of a rite to suit particular circumstances "when, for pastoral considerations, neither of the burial rites in this Book is deemed appropriate" (pp. 506–507). The *BOS* provides appropriate texts for the burial of a person who was not a baptized Christian or who rejected the Christian faith. The burial office is an Easter liturgy. The liturgical color is appropriately white, and the Paschal candle should be lighted as a visible reminder of Jesus' resurrection and our hope of life everlasting in Christ. At the Burial of the Dead those who mourn may express grief and sorrow as they share in the community's expression of faith, hope, and mutual support in Jesus Christ.

Burlington College. This school was granted a charter on Feb. 27, 1846. It was founded by Bishop George Washington Doane in Burlington, New Jersey. It was adjacent to and affiliated with St. Mary's Hall for girls, which was founded in 1837. During the 1870s the college had a Divinity Department. Burlington College closed around 1881, but it continued as Burlington Academy, a secondary school. It is now closed.

Burnham, Mary Douglass (May 13, 1832–Dec. 26, 1904). Leading deaconess and founder of the Dakota League. She was born in Quincy, Massachusetts. In 1852 she married Wesley Burnham. He spent most of his time working in the Sandwich Islands in the sugar cane industry. In 1864 she founded the Dakota League and served as its president until 1875. The Dakota League supported Indian mission work and was a predecessor organization for the Woman's Auxiliary to the Board of Missions, which was formed in 1871. She established the Woman's Auxiliary in the newly created Diocese of Central New York. Burnham was set apart as a deaconess there on Apr. 22, 1876. She served as head of the Diocesan Deaconess Order and Superintendent of the Hospital of the Good Shepherd at Syracuse. Following a winter holiday in St. Augustine, Florida, she persuaded Bishop Frederic Dan Huntington to seek the transfer of Cheyenne Indian David Oakerhater from the military prison in St. Augustine to Central New York. Oakerhater was educated in New York for what became his fifty-year ministry in Oklahoma. Burnham then went to Boston, where she became superintendent of the Home for Incurables and president of the Diocesan Woman's Auxiliary. In 1892 she moved to Yonkers, New York, where she became superintendent of St. John's Hospital. The last years of her life were spent as hostess of a home for visiting missionaries in New York City. She died in New York City.

Burr, Nelson Rollins (June 6, 1904–Jan. 10, 1994). Prominent historian of the Episcopal Church. He was born in West Hartford, Connecticut. Burr received his B.A. in 1927 and his Ph.D. in 1937 from Princeton University. His first position was supervisor of the Church Records Survey for the northeastern United States in the Works Progress Administration. In 1942 Burr became a research librarian at the Library of Congress. He held this position until his retirement in 1967. He wrote many parish histories in the dioceses of Massachusetts, New York, New Jersey, and Connecticut. Among his many major publications are *A Critical Bibliography of Religion in America*, 2 vols. (1961), *The Story of the Diocese of Connecticut: A New Branch of the Vine* (1962), and *The Anglican Church in New Jersey* (1954). He was a long-time member of Grace Church, Hartford, Connecticut. Burr died in Hartford.

Burse. A case of two squares of stiff material, hinged or bound together at one end, which contains the corporal and purificators for use at the celebration of the eucharist. The burse is covered in the liturgical color of the day, and placed on top of the veil which covers the chalice.

Butler, Joseph (May 18, 1692–June 16, 1752). Bishop and opponent of deism. He was born in Wantage, England, to Presbyterian parents. In 1714 he left the Presbyterians, joined the Church of England, and entered Oriel College, Oxford. Butler was ordained priest in 1718. From 1719 until 1726, he was the preacher at Rolls Chapel, London. From 1726 until 1738, he held a variety of positions, and on Dec. 3, 1738, he was consecrated Bishop of Bristol. On Oct. 16, 1750, he was translated to become Bishop of Durham and remained there until his death. Butler's major publication was *The Analogy of Religion, Natural and Revealed, to the Constitution and Course of Nature* (1736), which is the leading orthodox answer to the English deists. In the Advertisement to the book, he acknowledged that it is "taken for granted by many persons that Christianity is not so much as a subject of inquiry; but that it is, now at length, discovered to be fictitious," and "a principal subject of mirth and ridicule." Butler refuted this claim and argued that there are reliable grounds for not doubting Christianity. He insisted that nature is no more reliable than revelation, and that "probability is the very guide of life." Butler died in Bath. He is commemorated in the Episcopal calendar of the church year on June 16.

"BVM." These three letters stand for the Blessed Virgin Mary, the mother of Jesus.

Byzantine Rite. Principal liturgical tradition of the Orthodox and Eastern Catholic churches. It originated in Constantinople, which was the city of Byzantium in ancient times. The heritage of the liturgy is Syrian and Palestinian, going back to the two great Syrian centers of Antioch and Jerusalem. The Byzantine Rite was adopted by the patriarchates of Alexandria, Antioch, and Jerusalem during the middle ages. It was the rite of the ancient Byzantine Empire, and it displaced other eastern liturgies. It is characterized by grandeur, full ceremonial, and rich liturgical symbolism. The *Kontakion* and *Ikos* from the Byzantine Rite may be used for the anthem at the commendation in the BCP service for the Burial of the Dead, with the *Kontakion* repeated as an antiphon (pp. 482–483, 499).

C

Cadle, Richard Fish (Apr. 17, 1796–Nov. 9, 1857). One of the Episcopal Church's earliest and most active missionaries. Bishop Kemper called him "the real pioneer in the West." Cadle was born in New York City and graduated from Columbia College with a B.A. degree in 1813. He was influenced by Bishop John Henry Hobart. Cadle was ordained deacon on Apr. 27, 1817, and served St. James' Church, Goshen, New York, from 1817 until 1819. He was ordained priest before 1820 and was the rector of St. John's Church, Salem, New Jersey, from 1820 until 1823. On May 20, 1824, the Domestic and Foreign Missionary Society appointed its first three domestic missionaries, one of whom was Cadle. He was sent to Detroit, where he organized the first Episcopal church, St. Paul's Church, on Nov. 22, 1824. In 1829 he was made the superintendent of the Indian mission school at Green Bay, Wisconsin, then in the territory of Michigan. Disputes over his leadership led to his resignation in 1834. He later entered upon extensive missionary work in Wisconsin. In 1841 Bishop Jackson Kemper named Cadle superior of the religious brotherhood proposed by James Lloyd Breck and his companions. This brotherhood resulted in the Nashotah mission and Nashotah House. Finding himself unsuited to this task, he soon resumed his mission labors. Cadle retired from the western field in 1844. He became a missionary in Sodus, Pultneyville, and Point Sodus, New York. In 1849 he became the rector of Trinity Church, Shelburne, Vermont. In 1853 he became the rector of the parishes in Sussex County, Delaware. He died in Seaford, Delaware.

Calendar of the Church Year, The. The calendar (BCP, pp. 15–33) orders the liturgical year of the Episcopal Church by identifying two cycles of feasts and holy days—one dependent upon the movable date of Easter Day and the other dependent upon the fixed date of Christmas, Dec. 25. Easter Day is the first Sunday after the full moon that falls on or after Mar. 21. The sequence of all Sundays in the church year is based on the date of Easter. Tables and rules for finding the date of Easter Day, and other movable feasts and holy days are provided by the BCP, pp. 880–885. The date of Easter determines the beginning of the season of Lent on Ash Wednesday and the date of Pentecost on the fiftieth day of the Easter season. The Sundays of Advent are always the four Sundays before Christmas Day. The church year begins on the first Sunday of Advent. The calendar also identifies and provides directions concerning the precedence and observance of principal feasts, Sundays, holy days (including Feasts of our Lord, other major feasts, and fasts), Days of Special Devotion, and Days of Optional Observance. The calendar lists dates for celebration of major feasts and lesser feasts by month and date. Appropriate Sunday Letters and Golden Numbers are also provided. (see BCP, pp. 880–881). The calendar also lists the titles of the seasons, Sundays, and major holy days observed in the Episcopal Church throughout the church year, including Advent season, Christmas season, Epiphany season, Lenten season, Holy Week, Easter season, the season after Pentecost, holy days, and National Days.

California, Diocese of. The primary convention of the Diocese of California met at Trinity Church, San Francisco, June 24, 1850. The General Convention of 1853 elected William Ingraham Kip Missionary Bishop of California, and the diocese elected him Bishop on Feb. 5, 1857. Grace Cathedral, San Francisco, was established on Feb. 4, 1910, and consecrated on Nov. 20, 1964. The diocese was divided in 1874, 1879, 1895, and 1910. Today it consists of the following counties: Alameda, Contra Corta, Marine, San Francisco, and San Mateo.

Callings. This national newsletter for lay professions is published by the National Network of Lay Professionals in the Episcopal Church. It began publication in Oct. 1986. Its purpose is to provide news, features, and commentary on issues relating to the work and ministry of lay professionals in the Episcopal Church. Gail C. Jones was the first editor.

Calvin, John (1509–1564). Reformer and theologian. He was the leading figure in the sixteenth-century movement of reform in Switzerland. Calvin was born in Noyon, in Picardy, France. He was sent to Paris at about age fourteen to study in the university. He was apparently headed for an ecclesiastical career and the study of theology. Calvin received a Master of Arts degree in 1528. In that year his father ordered him to study law. Calvin studied civil law at Orléans and Bourges. After his father's death, Calvin returned to Paris for work in classical studies and Hebrew. By 1533 he was converted to Protestantism. He fled to Basle, Switzerland, from France in 1535. Calvin published the first edition of his *Institutes of the Christian Religion* in 1536. The last edition of the *Institutes* was published in

1559. His teaching emphasized the sovereignty of God, scripture as the supreme rule of faith and life, the total depravity of humanity after the Fall, the predestination of the elect to salvation and the reprobate to damnation, and the importance of the church as an ordered and disciplined community. The ministers or officers of the Reformed Church included pastors, teachers, elders, and deacons. Calvin's reform is especially associated with the city of Geneva, Switzerland. In July, 1536, Guillaume Farel (1489–1565) convinced Calvin to stay in Geneva to organize the Reformation. Calvin and Farel were expelled from Geneva in 1538, but the city council invited Calvin to return in 1541. Calvin worked to establish a theocracy in Geneva. He lived in Geneva and dominated the religious life of the city until his death. Calvinism influenced the French Huguenots, the Scottish Church reforms of John Knox (c. 1513–1572), the Puritans in England, and the reformed churches in the Netherlands. Calvinism came to dominate the Protestant movement of reform. Calvin's influence is also seen in the American Reformed, Congregational, and Presbyterian churches.

Calvinism. *See* Calvin, John; *see* Protestantism.

Cameron, James Gibbon (d. Nov. 22, 1928). Participant in founding of the Order of the Holy Cross. He was born in Oswego, New York. Cameron studied for the ordained ministry at St. Andrew's Divinity School, Syracuse, New York. He was ordained deacon on June 8, 1879, and priest on May 28, 1880. He served as the first missionary to the Onondaga Indians near Syracuse, 1879–1880. On Nov. 1, 1881, Cameron, James Otis Sargent Huntington, and Robert Stockton Dod, began to live the religious life together in New York City. He left the novitiate in early Oct., 1883, and became a diocesan priest. Cameron served churches in Pittsburgh, Philadelphia, New York, Baltimore, and Alaska. He died in Kingston, New York.

Camm, John (1718–1779). Commissary and president of the College of William and Mary. He was born in Yorkshire, England. Camm graduated from Trinity College, Cambridge University. He emigrated to Virginia. On Aug. 24, 1749, he became Professor of Divinity at the College of William and Mary. Camm served in this position from 1749 until 1757, and again from 1763 until 1772. Around 1749, he became rector of Yorkhampton Parish. In 1771 he began to call for the establishment of a bishopric in Virginia. This made him unpopular with many of the colonists. Also in 1771, he was named the commissary to Virginia and chosen the president of William and Mary. He was rector of Bruton Parish from 1771 until 1773. He was a staunch Tory and disapproved of Virginia separating from England. As a result of his Tory position, he was removed as president of William and Mary in 1776. Camm died in Hansford, six miles from Williamsburg.

Campbell, Robert Erskine (Aug. 13, 1884–Aug. 23, 1977). Bishop and superior of the Order of the Holy Cross. He was born in Florida, New York. Campbell received his B.A. from Columbia University in 1906 and graduated from the General Theological Seminary in 1909. He was ordained deacon on June 6, 1909, and priest on Dec. 7, 1909. Campbell began his ministry as a missionary in the mountains of Tennessee, 1909–1910. He was curate at St. Luke's Church, New York, 1910–1911. From 1911 until 1915, he was headmaster of St. Andrew's School, St. Andrews, Tennessee. He was a novice in the Order of the Holy Cross from 1915 until 1917. Campbell made his life profession on Dec. 21, 1917. He was prior of St. Michael's Monastery, St. Andrews, Tennessee, 1918–1922, and 1938–1947, and prior of St. Athanasius Monastery, Bolahun, Liberia, 1922–1925. On Nov. 30, 1925, he was consecrated the sixth Missionary Bishop of Liberia. He served until he resigned on Jan. 1, 1936. Campbell was the first monk in the Episcopal Church to be consecrated bishop. He was the superior of the order from Aug. 4, 1948, until Aug. 6, 1954. Campbell lived the last years of his life in retirement at Mount Calvary Retreat House, Santa Barbara, California, where he died.

Candidate. One who is to make a sacramental commitment. Those who are to be baptized and those who are to be confirmed, received, or reaffirmed are referred to as candidates in the BCP (pp. 301, 415). The term also indicates one who is in the final stage of the canonical process leading to ordination as a deacon or priest. After an applicant (aspirant) for holy orders has been admitted as a postulant for six months, the postulant may apply to the bishop for admission as a candidate for holy orders. Candidacy follows postulancy and precedes ordination. The time of candidacy is to be at least one year, although this may be shortened to not less than six months. During this time the candidate is to complete or satisfy the canonical requirements for ordination, including requirements concerning age, education, academic examination, practical training or experience in ministry, and medical and psychological examinations. Also during this time a certificate of the candidate's fitness for ordination is sent from the rector and vestry of the candidate's parish to the standing committee of the diocese. A similar certificate is then sent by the standing committee to the bishop. A report from the diocesan commission on ministry is also sent to the bishop. In the case of one who is to be ordained deacon and later ordained priest, a certificate concerning the candidate's scholastic record and an evaluation concerning the candidate's personal qualifications for holy orders is sent to the bishop by the candidate's theological school or those who have directed the candidate's studies. The candidate must also apply for ordination in writing. *See* Aspirant; *see* Postulant (Holy Orders, Monastic).

Candlemas. *See* Presentation of our Lord Jesus Christ in the Temple, The.

Candles. Candles have extensive ceremonial use in the Christian liturgical tradition. Lighted candles may be seen to symbolize the light of Christ, or the light of the gospel, or simply to remind the congregation that the time and space for worship are sacred. Candles provide illumination that enhances the beauty of the church, and may provide additional light for worship. Candles may be carried in procession by acolytes, and held as the gospel is said or sung. Candles may be placed on the altar, or on a reredos behind the altar, or on pavement lights beside the altar. The BCP provides for the lighting of the altar candles at certain times in special services. At the Easter Vigil, the altar candles are lighted after the Renewal of Baptismal Vows and before the Easter Acclamation, "Alleluia. Christ is risen" (BCP, p. 204). Candles are lighted after the dedication of the altar by the bishop at the Consecration of a Church (BCP, p. 574). At the Order of Worship for the Evening, the lighting of the altar candles and other candles follows the Prayer for Light and precedes the hymn "O Gracious Light" (*Phos hilaron*). (BCP, p. 112). The *BOS* provides a variety of anthems (*Lucernaria*) at the candle lighting for optional use at the Order of Worship for the Evening, including seasonal anthems. Certain candles have special liturgical uses. The Paschal candle is a large, decorated candle that symbolizes the light of Christ who was crucified, died, rose, and ascended into heaven. It is lighted at the Easter Vigil, and at all services during the season of Easter. The Advent Wreath has four candles that represent the four Sundays of the season of Advent, and may also include a "Christ candle" that is lighted on

Christmas Eve. A candle may be given to each of the newly baptized or a godparent after baptism. This candle may be lighted from the Paschal candle, and it serves as a reminder of baptism. Candles may be lighted and extinguished with a candle taper.

Candles are often used as a sign of festivity and solemnity in Christian worship. The use of such lights has a long and varied tradition. Acts 20 records that there were "many lights" at the service at Troas when Paul and other Christians gathered to break bread. Lamps and candles were in normal use in Christian worship by the fourth century, but for many years it was not customary to place candles on the altar. The first known mention of the use of altar lights was a twelfth-century report that two candles flanked an altar cross in the papal chapel. The injunction of Edward VI in 1547 called for there to be two lights on the high altar "for the signification that Christ is the very true light of the world." Candles have been used in some English cathedrals and churches since the seventeenth century. The use of candles at the eucharist was disputed in the Church of England and in the Episcopal Church during the nineteenth century. During the years of the ritualist controversy in the Episcopal Church, the General Conventions of 1868, 1871, and 1874 considered proposals to prohibit the use of altar candles. Use of candles in worship was strongly favored by Episcopalians of the catholic tradition and resisted by those of the evangelical tradition. The use of altar candles was never prohibited by General Convention. Use of altar lights and other candles in the worship of the church is now customary. Some BCP services make special provision for the use of candles in worship. The Easter Vigil service begins with the lighting of the Paschal candle, which is to burn at all services from Easter Day through Pentecost (BCP, pp. 285–287). In an Order of Worship for the Evening, the candle lighting follows the Prayer for Light (p. 112).

Caner, Henry (1700–Feb. 11, 1793). He was a missionary for the Society for the Propagation of the Gospel (SPG) in Connecticut. He worked with missionary zeal in Fairfield, Connecticut, among Native Americans and Negroes and with women and men alienated from their congregations by the excesses of the Great Awakening. In 1747 he was elected rector of King's Chapel, Boston, by the congregation which had been seeking an American in holy orders. This was an unprecedented procedure. The customary protocol directed application for a parson to the Bishop of London who had jurisdiction over the church in the colonies. When the British evacuated Boston in Mar. 1776, King's Chapel was closed and Caner moved to Halifax, Nova Scotia.

Cannon, Harriett Starr (May 7, 1823–Apr. 5, 1896). One of the first American nuns in the Anglican tradition. She was born in Charleston, South Carolina. When her parents died, she was raised by an aunt in Bridgeport, Connecticut. The order of the Sisterhood of the Holy Communion had been founded by Anne Ayres and William Augustus Muhlenberg at the Church of the Holy Communion, New York City, in 1852. On Feb. 6, 1856, Cannon was received by Muhlenberg as a candidate for the sisterhood in the Oratory of the Sisters' house. On the Feast of the Purification of the Virgin Mary, Feb. 2, 1857, Cannon was admitted into full membership in the sisterhood. Several of the sisters, led by Sister Harriett, wanted a more traditional monastic order. In 1863 they left the Sisterhood of the Holy Communion and St. Luke's Hospital, where they worked. On Feb. 2, 1865, Sister Harriett and several other women were received into the Sisterhood of St. Mary, now called the Community of St. Mary. Their service of religious profession was presided over by Bishop Horatio Potter of New York at St. Michael's Church, Manhattan. Sister Harriett was elected mother superior in Sept. 1865. She served in that position until her death. On Feb. 2, 1867, she made her formal life vows. She died in Peekskill, New York.

Canon. The word is derived from the Greek *kanon*, a "measuring rod or rule." It has several different meanings in the church. 1) [Scripture] The canon of scripture is the list of inspired books recognized by the church to constitute the Holy Scriptures. 2) [Church Law] Canons are the written rules that provide a code of laws for the governance of the church. The canons of the Episcopal Church are enacted by the General Convention. Canons of the Episcopal Church may only be enacted, amended, or repealed by concurrent resolution of the House of Deputies and the House of Bishops at General Convention. The canons of the Episcopal Church are organized by titles or sections concerning Organization and Administration, Worship, Ministry, Ecclesiastical Discipline, and General Provisions. 3) [Ecclesiastical Title] A canon may be a member of the clergy on the staff of a cathedral or diocese. A canon on a cathedral staff assists the dean, and a canon on a diocesan staff assists the bishop. Members of the clergy and laity have at times

been made honorary canons of a cathedral in recognition of significant service or achievement. Historically, canons were secular clergy who were connected to a cathedral or collegiate church, sharing the revenues and a common rule of life at the church. 4) [Liturgy] The canon designates the fixed portion of the Great Thanksgiving or the prayer of consecration at the Holy Eucharist, including the institution narrative. The canon does not vary with the liturgical season. 5) [Church Music] A musical composition, with a note-for-note imitation of one melodic line by another that begins one or more notes later than the first, also known as a round. *The Hymnal 1982* includes a section of rounds and canons (Hymns 710–715).

"Canon 9 Clergy." Priests and deacons ordained to serve in a particular location which is "small, isolated, remote, or distinct in respect of ethnic composition, language, or culture." These locations cannot otherwise be provided sufficiently with the sacraments and pastoral ministrations of the Episcopal Church through ordained ministry. The term refers to the canon by which such "local priests and deacons" are ordained. The canonical requirements concerning standards of learning and other canonical requirements for ordination are relaxed or modified for those ordained under this canon. Canon 9 clergy are to be recognized as leaders in their congregation and firmly rooted in the local community. Such clergy are typically called by their congregation, although a person from another community may be called if necessary. It is the normal expectation that persons ordained under this canon will not move from the congregation for which they were ordained.

Canonical Hours. In the monastic traditions of the western church, the appointed times for prayer throughout the day. Benedict (c. 480–c. 547) set the basis for this pattern of daily prayer in his *Rule for Monasteries.* The seven "hours" are: matins and lauds (usually counted as a single hour), in the middle of the night; prime, at sunrise; terce, 9 A.M.; sext, noon; none, 3 P.M.; vespers, sunset; and compline, bedtime. The Christian monastic Daily Office, with prayers or hours at seven times in each day, was based on the Jewish pattern of daily prayer at sunrise and at other times. Thomas Cranmer reduced the Daily Office to services for morning (matins) and evening (evensong or vespers) in the first English Prayer Book (1549). The BCP now includes services for the so-called minor hours:

An Order of Service for Noonday (p. 103) and An Order for Compline (p. 127).

Canonical Residence. Clergy serving under the jurisdiction of the ecclesiastical authority of a diocese (typically the diocesan bishop) are canonically resident in that diocese. Clergy may move from jurisdiction to jurisdiction by presenting Letters Dimissory, a testimonial by the ecclesiastical authority of the former diocese that the clergyperson has not "been justly liable to evil report, for error in religion or for viciousness of life, for the last three years." The transfer of canonical residence is dated from the acceptance of Letters Dimissory by the ecclesiastical authority.

Cantab. Pertaining to or belonging to Cambridge, England. It is a colloquial abbreviation of *Cantabrigian*, which comes from the Latin *Cantabrigiensis*. Usages include reference to degrees and diplomas conferred by the University of Cambridge. It usually follows nouns in titles, such as M.A. Cantab.

Cantate Domino. The Latin *incipit* or opening phrase for Ps 98 which in earlier Prayer Books began "O sing unto the Lord a new song." Objection was raised to use in the 1549 Prayer Book of the "Gospel canticles" (*Benedictus, Magnificat,* and *Nunc dimittis*) by some who believed that these songs of Zechariah, Mary, and Simeon could not properly be sung by others. In the 1552 revision of the Prayer Book, a psalm was provided as an alternative to each of these gospel canticles. Ps 98, *Cantate Domino,* was provided as the alternative to the *Magnificat* at Evening Prayer.

Cantemus Domino. *See* Song of Moses, The.

Canterbury. The city in southeastern England that became the ecclesiastical center for England and, eventually, the Anglican Communion. The Benedictine monk Augustine founded the church in Canterbury on his mission from Rome in 597. From there Christianity spread throughout England. Canterbury has had a preeminence from the beginning of the English church. The Archbishop of Canterbury is "Primate of All England" and head of the Church of England. The churches of the Anglican Communion may be defined as the churches in communion with the See of Canterbury. The Archbishop of Canterbury likewise holds a position of honor in the Anglican

Communion. The Archbishop of Canterbury convenes the bishops when they gather, especially at the Lambeth Conferences, and sits with them as "greatest among equals." Canterbury holds a position of honor and preeminence in the Anglican Communion but holds no official authority over the churches of the communion or its individual members. This may be contrasted with the Roman Catholic understanding of papal authority and the authority of the church.

Canterbury, Archbishop of. In the Church of England, the Archbishop of Canterbury is the "Primate of all England and Metropolitan" of the ecclesiastical province of Canterbury in southern England. In addition to a palace at Canterbury, the Archbishop of Canterbury also has a residence at Lambeth Palace in London. The history of the present see begins in 597, with the arrival of St. Augustine. However, Canterbury was the seat of a bishop named Liudhard, who had been sent by the King of the West Franks, prior to 597. Augustine was sent by Pope Gregory I to convert the Anglo-Saxons. He was well received by Ethelbert (Aethelbehrt), King of Kent. Ethelbert's wife, Bertha, was a Christian princess and the daughter of the King of the West Franks who had sent Liudhard.

There was no break in the continuity of the office with the sixteenth-century Reformation. Thomas Cranmer, Archbishop 1533–1556, accepted Henry VIII's Act of Supremacy, by which the English sovereign replaced the Pope as head of the Church of England. The sovereign's role was subsequently redefined by Queen Elizabeth I as "supreme governor" in recognition that Christ is the head of the church. No one is recognized as head of all the churches which make up the Anglican Communion. The Archbishop of Canterbury is regarded as its titular leader, and exercises considerable spiritual authority beyond the province of Canterbury. The Archbishop of Canterbury presides over the Lambeth Conferences, the decennial meeting of the bishops of the Anglican Communion, and is president of the Anglican Consultative Council.

"Canterbury Cap." A four-cornered cloth cap that is sometimes worn by Anglican clergy. It is soft, flat, and typically black in color. The Canterbury cap reflects a style of academic headgear that developed during the later middle ages. It served to keep the head warm in drafty lecture halls and churches. It is occasionally used by clergy today when ecclesiastical headgear is needed.

Canterbury College. This school was established in 1946 and closed in 1951. It was begun with the gift of the buildings and campus of Central Normal College, which was founded on Sept. 5, 1876. It was at Danville, Indiana.

Canterbury Guild, The. This organization was formed as an *ad hoc* way of getting quick publication of *A House Divided* by the Rev. Robert C. Harvey in 1976, "when it was imperative that it be gotten into the hands of bishops and deputies" for the 1976 General Convention. *A House Divided* was a 74-page booklet which criticized the liberal trends in the Episcopal Church. When it was written, Harvey was rector of All Saints Church, East Orange, New Jersey. On Apr. 18, 1980, he was consecrated Bishop of the Diocese of the Southwest of the Anglican Catholic Church. The main work of The Canterbury Guild was participation in the Fellowship of Concerned Churchmen.

Canterbury Statement. This agreed statement on Ministry and Ordination was finalized by the Anglican-Roman Catholic International Commission (ARCIC) at Canterbury in 1973. It was eventually included within the ARCIC *Final Report* (1982). It expressed agreement upon such matters as the origins of sacramental ordination, emergence of the threefold ministry, relationship of the ordained ministry to the laity, the concept of *episcope*, relationship of ordination to eucharistic presidency, evolution of priestly terminology, the meaning of ordination, indelibility of holy orders, and the nature of apostolic succession. The statement concluded that the negative judgment of the Roman Catholic Church on Anglican Orders (1896) was now placed in a new context and that the commission had reached consensus on essential matters. An "Elucidation" issued by the commission in 1979 considered that the principles upon which its doctrinal agreement rested were not affected by the ordination of women, since it had been "concerned with the origin and nature of the ordained ministry and not with the question of who can or cannot be ordained." The 1979 General Convention of the Episcopal Church went on to affirm that the Canterbury Statement "provide[s] a basis upon which to proceed in furthering the growth towards unity of the Episcopal Church with the Roman Catholic Church." The official response of the 1988 Lambeth Conference also found the Canterbury Statement, together with the Elucidation, to be "consonant in substance with the faith of Anglicans" and "a sufficient basis for taking the next step forward towards the reconciliation of our Churches grounded in agreement in faith." The Vatican's definitive response to the *Final Report*, however, finally released in 1991, raised a number of objections.

Canticle. A non-metrical song used in liturgical worship. Canticles are drawn from biblical texts other than the Psalter. The term is derived from the Latin *canticulum*, a "little song." In practice, canticles are sung or said in worship. The BCP provides contemporary and traditional language canticles. Contemporary language canticles may be used in traditional language services and vice versa. Many canticles are traditionally known by the opening words (*incipit*) of the canticle in Latin versions of the Bible or service books, such as the *Benedictus Dominus Deus* (Canticle 16, BCP, p. 92). The BCP provides a Table of Canticles suggested for use at Morning and Evening Prayer (pp. 144–145). Canticles serve as responses to the readings at the services of the Daily Office. Canticles may also be used at the Burial of the Dead after the OT and NT readings, at the Holy Eucharist on certain occasions as an alternative to the psalm appointed, at the Easter Vigil after certain OT readings in the liturgy of the word, in the Daily Devotions for Individuals and Families, and after the Bible reading in the Order for Evening.

Cantor. A singer who sets the pitch and leads the liturgical singing of psalms, canticles, anthems, and other sung texts. Cantors often lead unaccompanied singing. In responsorial recitation of the Psalter, the cantor sings the verses of the psalm and the congregation sings a refrain after each verse or group of verses. This was the traditional way of singing the *Venite* in the Daily Office, and it was also a traditional way of chanting the psalms between the lessons at the Holy Eucharist (BCP, p. 582).

Cantoris. The term is from Latin meaning "place of the cantor." Traditionally, the cantor sat on the north side of the cathedral. In antiphonal singing, the term *cantoris* indicates those who sit on the cantoral or cantor's side of the choir of a church or cathedral. The opposite side is known as "*decani*." The terms were used in *The Hymnal* (1940) version of "Ye watchers and ye holy ones" to designate different parts for singing the antiphonal alleluias.

Cantrix. A female cantor. *See* Cantor.

Canvass, Every Member. *See* Every Member Canvass.

Cape Palmas, Missionary District of. *See* Liberia, Diocese of.

Cappadocians, or Cappadocian Fathers. Three important theologians of the Patristic Era. Basil the Great of Caesarea (330–379), his brother Gregory of Nyssa (c. 330–395), and their friend Gregory of Nazianzus (329–389) all came from Cappadocia, a Roman province in what is now Turkey. In their lives and literary works, the three friends were largely responsible for extending the Nicene doctrine of the Trinity to the person of the Holy Spirit, and thus to the final defeat of the Arians, semi-Arians, and Macedonians at I Constantinople in 381. They also gave a final definitive shape to eastern monasticism, and contributed greatly to the formation of Orthodox theology, spirituality, and liturgy. In the calendar of the church year, Basil the Great is commemorated on June 14, Gregory of Nyssa is commemorated on Mar. 9, and Gregory of Nazianzus is commemorated on May 9.

"Cardinal Rector." An influential rector, usually of a large parish.

Cardinal Virtues. For Thomas Aquinas (1224–1274), the cardinal virtues form the basis for moral growth and development in all persons, although for Christians they can only be understood and fully achieved through God's grace as given in the theological virtues. Initially stated in Book Four of Plato's *Republic*, Aristotle develops the cardinal virtues in his *Ethics* as moral virtues, the perfection of human powers as they lead to happiness. Translating from the Greek, the cardinal virtues are referred to in English as wisdom, courage, temperance, and justice. Translating the equivalent English from Latin, they are referred to as prudence, fortitude, temperance, and justice. Prudence is the perfection of the intellect as a matter of practical wisdom. It concerns knowing what to do and when to do it. Fortitude is the perfection of the will in terms of being neither timid nor foolhardy but holding steadfast to what needs to be done. Temperance is the perfection of the appetites, seeking enough but not too much. Justice is the perfection of the whole in which the parts are fairly balanced in relationship to the whole. In the fourth century Ambrose assumed this understanding of the cardinal virtues in his instruction for the clergy in *De Officiis Ministrorum*. Other theologians, most notably Augustine in *On the Morals of the Catholic Church*, tie the human virtues to the ultimate end of the love of God.

Thomas draws this thought to its most systematic formulation in his *Summa Theologica*, which became the basis for subsequent Roman Catholic thought. It was also the source for much of Anglican thought at the time of the English Reformation and in Anglo-catholic moral theology arising from the Oxford Movement.

Carey, Arthur (June 26, 1822–Apr. 4, 1844). Controversial figure in the Oxford Movement. He was born in the vicinity of London, England. When he was eight years old, his father moved the family to New York City. In 1839 he graduated from Columbia College. Carey was considered "the most brilliant student in the [General] Seminary" in the early 1840s. He was profoundly influenced by the Oxford Movement. While at General Seminary, Carey was associated with St. Peter's Church, New York City. Carey taught in the Sunday School. The Rev. Hugh Smith was the rector of St. Peter's. When Carey's ordination to the diaconate approached, Smith refused to sign the canonical testimonies because he thought Carey was too sympathetic to Roman Catholicism. Carey then received the necessary testimonials from the Rev. William Berrian, rector of Trinity Church, New York. Meanwhile, Smith convinced the Rev. Henry Anthon, rector of St. Mark's Church, to join him in opposing Carey's ordination. Bishop Benjamin T. Onderdonk of New York arranged for Smith and Anthon to assist at an examination of Carey before him and six other presbyters of the diocese. After the examination, Smith and Anthon were still dissatisfied, but the other six said that Carey's answers were satisfactory. Carey was ordained deacon on July 2, 1843. Smith and Anthon read a formal protest at the ordination. Carey became an assistant at the Church of the Annunciation, New York. He died of tuberculosis soon thereafter on a voyage to Havana, where he was going in hope of recuperation. His memorial tablet is on the wall of the outer sacristy at the Chapel of the Good Shepherd of General Seminary.

Carillon. This musical instrument of twenty-three or more cast bronze bells ranges from two to six octaves, usually set in chromatic order like the keys of a piano. Instruments with fewer bells are called chimes. Unlike bells used in peals, carillon bells are stationary. Only the clappers move. They are activated by a carilloneur seated at the keyboard which is mechanically linked to the bells' clappers. The volume and character of the sound may be controlled by the force the carilloneur uses to strike the note. A few carillons are also linked to electrical activators which may be played from an organ console, but this is discouraged since touch control of the mechanism is lost. Carillon bells are tuned internally, usually in minor keys. The keyboard is played with hands and fists. There are more than 160 carillons in the United States, and many are in Episcopal churches. Those at the National Cathedral, Washington, D.C.; the University of the South, Sewanee, Tennessee; and Christ Church, Cranbrook, Michigan, are among the best known. Some churches use electronic instruments which simulate the sound of bells.

Carilloneur. A person who plays a musical instrument known as a carillon.

Carol. The term carol finds its origin in the French *carole*, a round dance in which the singers provide their own music by singing a refrain after uniform stanzas sung by a soloist. English medieval carols are poetic works in a similar form. Carols appear in a pattern of uniform stanzas, each with a burden, or refrain. The carol, "Nova, nova" (Hymn 266 in *The Hymnal 1982*) is an example of this early form of an English carol. See also Hymns 109, 110, and 192 in *The Hymnal 1982.*

Caroline Divines. This unorganized grouping of seventeenth-century churchmen and scholars flourished during the reign of King Charles I (d. 1649) and derived its name from him. They furthered the theological precepts established in the sixteenth century by Archbishop Thomas Cranmer (1489–1556); John Jewel (1522–1571), Bishop of Salisbury; and Richard Hooker (1554–1600), the great Elizabethan theologian. Taking strong positions against Puritanism, they developed a *via media* approach between Roman Catholic and Puritan extremes and set forth an Anglican "High" doctrine of the church and episcopacy based on teachings of the early church. Chief among the divines are Jeremy Taylor (1613–1667), Lancelot Andrewes (1555–1626), and William Laud (1573–1644). Others sometimes included are poet-priest George Herbert (1593–1633); Deacon Nicholas Ferrar (1593–1637), who formed the community at Little Gidding; Bishop John Cosin (1594–1672), who became Bishop of Durham at the Restoration (1660); and somewhat lesser-known figures such as Bishop Richard Montague and Thomas Fuller.

Case, Adelaide Teague (Jan. 10, 1887–June 19, 1948). The first woman to be appointed to full professional rank in an Anglican seminary. She was born in St. Louis, Missouri, and raised in New York City. She received her B.A. from Bryn Mawr College in 1908, her M.A. in 1919, and her Ph.D. in 1924 from Columbia University. From 1914 to 1916 she was librarian in the national headquarters of the Episcopal Church, New York, and from 1917 to 1919 she taught at the New York Training School for Deaconesses. From 1919 to 1941 she taught in the religious education department of Columbia University's Teachers College. On Sept. 22, 1941, Case became Professor of Christian Education in the Episcopal Theological School, Cambridge, Massachusetts. She served on a number of boards of national religious organizations, and was a liberal catholic in churchmanship. Her two major publications are *Liberal Christianity and Religious Education* (1924) and *As Modern Writers See Jesus: A Descriptive Bibliography of Books about Jesus* (1927). She died in Boston.

Casserley, Julian Victor Langmead (Nov. 28, 1909–Aug. 27, 1978). Theologian. He was born in London and educated at the London School of Economics and King's College, London. Casserley was ordained deacon on Sept. 24, 1933, and priest on Sept. 30, 1934, both by the Bishop of Southwark in England. He served various churches in England until 1952 when he came to the United States to be professor of dogmatic theology at General Theological Seminary. He remained there until 1959. In 1960 he became the professor of philosophy and theology at Seabury-Western Theological Seminary. On Apr. 18, 1960, Casserley was received as a priest in the Episcopal Church. He retired in 1975, and moved to Kittery, Maine. He was active at Christ Church, Portsmouth, New Hampshire, during his retirement. Among his numerous books are *The Christian in Philosophy* (1949), *The Retreat from Christianity in the Modern World* (1952), *No Faith of My Own* (1950), *Graceful Reason* (1954), and *Apologetics and Evangelism* (1962). Casserley died in Portsmouth, New Hampshire. After his death a number of his former friends and colleagues founded the Julian Casserley Research Center at the General Theological Seminary. The center sought to encourage scholarly research into Casserley's works and to make his thought more available to clergy and lay persons in the church. The center also published new editions of his writings. It is now inactive.

Cassock. A long, close-fitting garment with narrow sleeves worn by clergy and other ministers. Cassocks are typically black but also may be blue, gray, or red. Bishops may wear purple cassocks. It may be worn under a surplice. Historically, the cassock was the street garb of a person in clerical orders. It was part of the outdoor dress of Anglican clergy until the beginning of the nineteenth century.

Casuistry. The study of cases or situations in light of moral goods, principles, duties, and consequences. Casuistry arises from conflicts of conscience where in a particular situation more than one course of action appears good or bad, right or wrong. Called "cases of conscience," casuistry sees moral reasoning and judgment as evolving as new circumstances lead to new choices. The critique of the abuse of casuistry, most notably by Blaise Pascal in the seventeenth century, has given casuistry a negative connotation associated with subtle distinctions and twisted logic. But casuistry has a much broader tradition, including casuistic study of the *Talmud* by Jewish rabbis and Islamic application of the *Koran*. Christian casuistry began in the late sixth century with the development of penitentials and reached its culmination in moral theology as shaped by the thought of Thomas Aquinas. Protestants rejected penitential confession, given its abuse in a system of penances and indulgences, and they also rejected the Roman Catholic casuistic tradition. However, the English Puritans and the Anglicans of the seventeenth century developed a casuistic tradition. Most notable among Anglicans are Jeremy Taylor's *Ductor Dubitantium* (1660) and the work of twentieth-century Anglican moralist Kenneth Kirk. A contemporary renewal of casuistry began in the development of biomedical ethics. It has continued in other areas such as business ethics and professional ethics.

Caswall, Henry (May 11, 1810–Dec. 17, 1870). Educator and writer. He was born in Yateley, Hampshire, England. On Aug. 16, 1828, Caswall left England for the United States. In Nov., 1830, he received his B.A. from Kenyon College. He was ordained deacon on June 12, 1831, and began his ministry in Portsmouth, Ohio. After about two years, he moved to Andover, Massachusetts, to study Hebrew under Professor Moses Stuart of Andover Theological Seminary. In May, 1834, Caswall became the Professor of Sacred Literature at the new Theological Seminary of the Protestant Episcopal Church in Kentucky at Lexington. In 1837 he accepted the call to be rector of Christ Church, Madison, Indiana, and was ordained priest on July 2, 1837. In 1838 he settled in Brockville, Canada, for health reasons.

In 1841 Caswall became Professor of Theology at Kemper College. He returned to England in May, 1842. He served several churches in England. In 1854 he became proctor in the Convocation of Salisbury, and then in 1859 he became prebendary of Salisbury Cathedral. Caswall returned to the United States in 1868. He was the author of several books, including *America and the American Church* (1838), which is a primary resource for the early history of the Episcopal Church. Caswall died in Franklin, Pennsylvania.

Catafalque. Temporary structure used to receive the coffin of a dead person, or to simulate the coffin when the body is not in the church. It was treated with the same respect that would be accorded to the body of the deceased. The term is from the Italian for scaffold. It is placed immediately outside the sanctuary. The catafalque was used at requiem masses to represent the deceased. It was historically surrounded by lights, sprinkled with holy water, and censed by the celebrant. Many contemporary liturgists consider use of the catafalque to be inappropriate and obsolete.

Cataphatic. This term describes those forms of spirituality which advocate meditation "according to or with images." It emphasizes meditation on concrete symbols or biblical events using physical and spiritual senses. The Ignatian and Franciscan schools of spirituality are cataphatic. *See* Apophatic.

Catechesis. Systematic instruction and formation of adults for baptism, initiating them into the mysteries and life of Christian faith. This instruction is not merely informative but intended to form one's outlook on life, values, and identity as a Christian. The instruction takes place in the context of the prayers and life of the Christian community. It is based in the scriptures, creeds, and prayers of the church. The period of this instruction and formation is known as the catechumenate.

In the early church, the catechumenate lasted for a period of three years. Adults preparing for baptism were known as catechumens. They attended services of readings, instructions, and prayers. These services concluded with the laying on of hands by the teacher, even if the teacher was a lay person. The teacher was known as a catechist. Those who proved themselves worthy by their lives and understanding were admitted as candidates for baptism several weeks before Easter.

There is evidence for both pre- and post-baptismal instruction in the early church. The *Didache* includes teaching to precede baptism. Hippolytus's *Apostolic Tradition* indicates that an organized catechumenate was well developed in Rome by the early third century. The catechumenate declined in the fifth and sixth centuries with the spread of infant baptism. However, in recent years there has been a renewal of interest in the catechumenate. The *BOS* provides a form for the Preparation of Adults for Holy Baptism, along with a lengthy explanation Concerning the Catechumenate.

Catechism. Outline for instruction in the Christian faith presented in a question and answer format. The Catechism appears in the BCP as "An Outline of the Faith" (pp. 845–862). Although the Catechism serves as a commentary on the creeds, it is not intended to be a complete statement of belief and practice. It provides a brief summary of the church's teaching. The Catechism is intended to serve as a point of departure for discussion by the catechist (lay or ordained) with those who seek to understand the beliefs and practices of the Episcopal Church.

Catechist. A teacher, lay or ordained, who provides instruction in the Christian faith. The BCP (pp. 845–862) provides "An Outline of the Faith, commonly called the Catechism," as a point of departure for this process of instruction. A confirmed adult lay person may be licensed as a catechist by the bishop or ecclesiastical authority of the diocese. Catechists are licensed to prepare persons for Baptism, Confirmation, Reception, and the Reaffirmation of Baptismal Vows. Prior to licensing, catechists are trained, examined and found competent in the Holy Scriptures, the BCP and the Hymnal, church History, the church's Doctrine, and methods of catechesis.

Catechumen. An adult preparing for baptism who has been admitted to participation in the catechumenate.

Catechumenate. An organized time of Christian formation and education in preparation for baptism. The catechumenate is a time for training in Christian understandings about God, human relationships, and the meaning of life. According to Hippolytus's *Apostolic Tradition*, a third-century document, adult converts to the Christian faith were presented to teachers by those who could vouch for them, and entered into a three-year period of study and preparation in the catechumenate.

These "hearers," or catechumens, attended services of readings, instructions, and prayers which concluded with the laying on of hands by the teacher. They were trained in Christian doctrine and morals. Catechumens were admitted as candidates after three years in the catechumenate when their faith, life, and understanding indicated their readiness for baptism. Candidates were enrolled at the beginning of Lent and entered into an intense time of instruction in the gospel and of daily exorcisms prior to their baptism at Easter. The catechumenate is now being revived in the Episcopal church. It is marked by three stages: 1) During the Pre-catechumenal period, inquirers may test their desire for baptism. 2) Those desiring baptism may be admitted to the catechumenate. Entry into the catechumenate begins with a public liturgical act at the principal Sunday liturgy. Each catechumen is presented by a sponsor who normally accompanies the catechumen through the process of candidacy and serves as a sponsor at baptism. Catechumens participate in regular worship and Christian service and receive instruction in Christian faith and doctrine, including the scriptures. The instructional sessions are led by a catechist, and continue through the period of candidacy until baptism. These sessions conclude with a time of silence, prayers for the catechumens by other baptized persons who are present, and prayers and the laying of a hand on the head of each catechumen by the catechist. 3) Candidacy for baptism is normally a period of six weeks, marked by a series of liturgical acts on the Sundays leading up to the baptism. Candidates for baptism at the Great Vigil of Easter are normally enrolled on the First Sunday of Lent. Candidates to be baptized on the First Sunday after Epiphany are enrolled on the First Sunday of Advent. The *BOS* provides liturgical forms for the catechumenate, including a form for the admission of catechumens, prayers for use at the conclusion of sessions of instruction during the catechumenate and the period of candidacy, a form for the enrollment of candidates for baptism, and prayers and blessings for use before the prayers of the people during the period of candidacy. When candidates are enrolled, their names are written in a large book and the celebrant prays, "God grant that they may also be written in the Book of Life." *See* Apostolic Tradition; *see* Christian Formation; *see* Sponsor (at Baptism).

Cathedra. Official seat or throne of the bishop in the cathedral of the diocese. The *cathedra* is considered to be the oldest insignia of the bishop's authority to preside over the church in the diocese. Historically, the bishop preached the sermon and presided at the eucharist from the *cathedra*, which was located in the center of the apse behind the altar. *See* Cathedral.

Cathedral. A church that contains the diocesan bishop's seat, throne, or *cathedra*. The cathedral is the principal church of the diocese. As the symbol and center of diocesan ministry, the cathedral is an appropriate place for diocesan celebrations and episcopal services. The dean is the clergyperson with pastoral charge of the cathedral. The dean may be assisted by other clergy, known as canons. Some cathedrals also have honorary canons who do not share in the daily pastoral responsibilities of the cathedral parish. The cathedral chapter consists of members who serve as the vestry in all matters concerning the corporate property of the cathedral and the relations of the cathedral parish to its clergy. Not all Episcopal dioceses have cathedrals, and most cathedrals are parish churches used for diocesan purposes. The Cathedral of Our Merciful Saviour in Faribault, Minnesota, was one of the earliest cathedrals in the Episcopal Church. The Cathedral of St. John the Divine in New York City, the Cathedral of St. Peter and St. Paul in Washington, D.C., the Cathedral of St. Philip in Atlanta, and Grace Cathedral in San Francisco are among the best known Episcopal cathedrals. *See* Cathedra.

Cathedral Car. Bishop William D. Walker of North Dakota faced many difficulties in his missionary work. He conceived the idea of a traveling chapel which would carry the church to those outlying places where there were no facilities for services. In 1889 he approached friends in the east for money to build a railway chapel. The sixty-foot car was built by the Pullman Palace Car Company at a cost of $3,000. Eighty persons could be seated on portable chairs in the coach. Painted on the car were the words: "The Church of the Advent," and "The Cathedral Car of North Dakota." Bishop Walker sometimes referred to the car as the "Roaming Catholic Cathedral." The Cathedral Car was sold in 1901.

Cathedral Church of Saint Peter and Saint Paul in the City and Diocese of Washington, The. George Washington was the first person to suggest a "great church for national purposes in the capital city." In 1893 Congress granted a charter to the Protestant Episcopal Cathedral Foundation

of the District of Columbia that empowered it to establish a cathedral. In 1898 Bishop Henry Yates Satterlee arranged the purchase of fifty-seven acres, which is now Mount St. Alban. The cornerstone was laid on Sept. 29, 1907. The completed nave was dedicated in 1976. Philip Hubert Frohman was the main architect. He took over the design in 1921, and worked until his death in 1972. After eighty-three years of construction, the cathedral was consecrated on Sept. 30, 1990. Bishop Satterlee envisioned the cathedral as "a House of Prayer for All People," especially at times of significance for the nation such as crises, celebrations, and funerals. The cathedral is the seat of the Bishop of Washington. As it was being built and finished it also became "by custom and tradition" the seat of the Presiding Bishop. It is the sixth largest cathedral in the world. It is also known as the Washington Cathedral, the National Cathedral, and the Washington National Cathedral.

Cathedral of Our Merciful Saviour, Faribault, Minnesota. Pioneer cathedral. The cornerstone of a bishop's church was laid by Bishop Henry Benjamin Whipple of Minnesota on July 16, 1862. It was the first structure built solely as a cathedral in the Episcopal Church. Whipple envisioned the cathedral as the center of all diocesan missionary, educational, and charitable work. The cathedral was consecrated in 1869 by Bishop Jackson Kemper, first missionary bishop of the Episcopal Church.

Cathedral of St. John the Divine, New York City. The largest gothic cathedral in the world. It was incorporated in 1873. Its foundation was laid on Dec. 27, 1892, the Feast of St. John. The east end and crossing were opened in 1911 and its entire length (601 feet) was opened in 1941. The sanctuary and choir are of Romanesque style. The great nave was built in French Gothic according to the plans of Ralph Adams Cram. The height of the nave vault is 124 feet. After Our Lady at Yamasoukro in the Ivory Coast and St. Peter's in Rome (which are not cathedrals), it is the world's third largest church. It is said that if the Statue of Liberty were placed underneath the main dome, her torch would just graze the vault. Construction was halted in 1941 during World War II, but resumed in 1979.

Catherine of Siena, St. (1347–Apr. 29, 1380). Mystic and spiritual writer. Caterina Benincasa was born in Siena, Italy. She joined the Third Order of the Dominicans when she was sixteen. She gave her life to serving the poor and converting sinners. In 1376 she went to Avignon, where the papacy was in "Babylonian Captivity," and begged the Avignon Pope, Gregory XI, to return to Rome. She is recognized for her Christocentric spirituality. Catherine was especially devoted to the Precious Blood of the Lord Jesus Christ. She lived an extremely austere life and wore an iron chain around her waist. Catherine was especially gifted in reconciling opponents, including political leaders. Catherine wrote *The Dialogue* in 1377–1378. She died in Rome. She was canonized by Pope Pius II in 1461. In 1939 Pope Pius XII named her and St. Francis of Assisi the chief patron saints of Italy. In 1970 she was named a Doctor of the Church. Catherine is commemorated in the Episcopal calendar of the church year on Apr. 29.

Catholic. Derived from the Greek word meaning "general" or "universal," the phrase "the catholic church" was first used by Ignatius of Antioch in the early second century. The BCP Catechism states (p. 854) that "The Church is catholic, because it proclaims the whole Faith to all people, to the end of time." The catholicity of the church means the wholeness and universality of Christian doctrine in continuity with the undivided early church, the fullness of Christian life and worship, and the inclusion of all kinds of people in the church.

Catholic Champion. A monthly journal published by the Guild of St. Ignatius, New York, and edited by Arthur Ritchie. Its slogan was 1 Sm 17:50, "So David prevailed over the Philistine with a sling and with a stone." It was "to speak out fearlessly on behalf of every good cause no matter which Bishop, Standing Committee or Board of Missions shall assume the role of Goliath." It was nicknamed the "Catholic Scorpion." It merged with *The Living Church*. It began publication in Dec. 1888, and its last issue was published in Nov. 1901.

Catholic Clerical Union. This organization was formed in 1888, but the precise date is unclear. Its 100th anniversary celebration was held May 14, 1988, at the Church of St. Mary the Virgin, New York City. It was founded over the issue of baptismal regeneration and the teaching of the catholic faith concerning that issue. A preliminary meeting was held in New York City on Nov. 4, 1886. On Jan. 5, 1887, a platform for the New York Clerical Union was adopted. The first meeting of a Philadelphia Clerical Union was held in Dec. 1887. The Catholic Clerical Union was founded as the Clerical Union for the Maintenance and Defence of Catholic Principles. The objects of the union, called "the

Credenda," must be signed by the members. Among the tenets of the Credenda are affirmation of the catholic doctrine concerning the person of Jesus Christ as expressed in the creeds and the seven ecumenical councils of the undivided church; the doctrine of the Holy Catholic Church as the Body of Christ and the sacramental bearer of grace; the promotion of the Holy Eucharist as the principal act of worship, teaching that in the eucharist the sacrifice of Christ is represented, and that he is really and objectively present and therefore to be worshiped in the Blessed Sacrament of his Body and Blood; and the defense of the catholic doctrine on baptismal regeneration. On Oct. 28, 1976, the council of the union adopted a "Declaration of Conscience," repudiating the action of the General Convention endorsing the ordination of women to the priesthood and episcopate. The revised Credenda added a tenet affirming the maintenance of the traditional, threefold, apostolic ministry as received from the undivided church, and the affirmation of the continuing catholic consensus that only males may be validly ordained to the priesthood and episcopate.

Catholic Congress of the Episcopal Church, The. An Anglo-catholic organization inspired by the English Congress in London in 1923, it was organized under the auspices of the Central Conference of Associated Catholic Priests. The congress stressed that it wanted all members of the Episcopal Church to realize in faith and practice the heritage of the catholic church and to make America a catholic country. The congress met triennially after initial meetings in New Haven, Connecticut, in 1925 and in Milwaukee, Wisconsin, in 1926. The work of the Catholic Congress and the Central Association was continued by the American Church Union, which was organized in 1936. *See* Central Conference of Associated Catholic Priests.

Catholic Evangelical Orthodoxy. An activity of the Fellowship of St. James of Jerusalem, a society devoted to individualized pastoral attention to the spiritual needs of Episcopalians, Eastern Orthodox, and Polish National Catholics (Utrecht Union of Old Catholics). It grew out of a response to the report of the Episcopal Church's Army and Navy Commission to the 1943 General Convention. This report identified the problems encountered by service men and women with a catholic heritage whose classification as "Protestant" made it difficult for them to be ministered to in the military and receive the sacraments. The Eastern Orthodox and Polish National Catholics had been promised spiritual support from Episcopal chaplains since they had no chaplains in the U.S. Armed Services. The Eastern Orthodox and Polish National Catholics also had difficulty in being ministered to by chaplains and receiving the sacraments.

Catholic Fellowship of the Episcopal Church, The. This fellowship of laity and clergy was founded in 1983 by Br. Tobias S. Haller, B.S.G. It seeks to nurture the catholic tradition in Anglicanism. The fellowship advocates reverence, care and discipline in worship, support for the religious life, and concern for spiritual formation of laity and clergy. Unlike some other Anglo-catholic groups, it specifically recognizes the authority of the church in General Convention. It supports the authorized BCP and the ordination of women to all orders in the church.

Catholicity. *See* Notes of the Church.

Caution, Tollie LeRoy (Aug. 20, 1902–Aug. 31, 1987). Leading African American priest and national church executive. He was born in Baltimore. Caution received his B.A. in 1926 from Lincoln University, his M.A. in 1929 from the University of Pennsylvania, and his M.Div. in 1929 from the Philadelphia Divinity School. He was ordained deacon on June 8, 1929, and priest on Apr. 12, 1930. Caution served churches in Baltimore and Cumberland, Maryland; Meyersdale, Harrisburg, Altoona, and Philadelphia, Pennsylvania; and New York City. In 1945 Caution was named the second secretary for Negro work. He served in that position until asked by Presiding Bishop John Hines to retire in 1967. Caution served in numerous other national positions while he was secretary for Negro work. From 1968 until 1970 he was consultant to the Presiding Bishop on pastoral affairs. He was very active with students at the traditionally African American colleges, and he worked to recruit African American clergy. He was a member of the National Association for the Advancement of Colored People. He worked with the National Council of Churches, and he was a charter member of the Union of Black Episcopalians. Caution died in New York City.

CDO Personal Profile. A form that provides personal and professional information for deployment of Episcopal clergy and lay professionals. The profile is intended to present a concise summary of the skills and experience of each person registered in the deployment system. It is used to match individual skills and talents with opportunities for ministry in the Episcopal Church. The profile includes information concerning the registrant's education, work address, work history, current annual compensation, ministry specialties and skill/experience, and references. A short personal ministry statement by the registrant is also included, along with the registrant's responses to a leadership description survey that represents the registrant's style of ministry. This computerized form was prepared by the Church Deployment Office (CDO) of the Episcopal Church Center. A registration manual is completed and returned to the CDO by clergy and lay professionals who will be registered. The CDO maintains a computerized data bank of the completed profiles. Copies of the profiles are sent to the registrant and the registrant's diocesan office. When a parish needs a member of the clergy or a lay professional, the parish confers with the diocese concerning the qualifications required. The diocese asks the CDO to search its computerized files for the registrants best matching the parish's needs. The CDO sends lists of possible candidates with their profiles to the diocesan office, and the diocese submits lists of nominees with their profiles to the parish.

Celebrant. The bishop or priest who presides at the eucharist and at baptism, and at other sacramental and liturgical occasions such as the Celebration and Blessing of a Marriage, Ministration to the Sick, and Thanksgiving for the Birth or Adoption of a Child. The celebrant leads the community's celebration of these liturgies and rites.

Celebration and Blessing of a Marriage. Rite for holy matrimony in the Episcopal Church (BCP, p. 423). Marriage is a solemn public covenant between a man and a woman in the presence of God. At least one of the couple must be a baptized Christian. Prior to the marriage, the couple sign a declaration of intention. It states that they hold marriage to be a lifelong union of husband and wife; that they believe this union in heart, body, and mind is intended by God for their mutual joy, for help and comfort given one another in prosperity and adversity, and for the procreation (when it is God's will) of children and their Christian nurture. There must be at least two witnesses for the ceremony. A priest or bishop normally presides at the marriage. If no priest or bishop is available, a deacon can preside if permitted by civil law. A deacon presiding at the marriage would omit the nuptial blessing. The marriage may be celebrated and blessed in the context of a nuptial eucharist. The marriage service then replaces the ministry of the word, and the eucharist begins with the offertory. Any authorized liturgy for the eucharist may be used with the marriage service. Prior to the service, the Banns of Marriage may be posted to announce the upcoming marriage and insure that there is no impediment. The title "Celebration and Blessing of a Marriage" in the 1979 BCP replaces the earlier title, "The Form of Solemnization of Matrimony." *See* Marriage.

Celebration for a Home. The *BOS* provides a form for Celebration for a Home, which is also known as a house blessing. Members of the household and friends assemble in the living room of the home. The service includes a collect and one or more readings from scripture or other appropriate readings. A homily or brief address may follow. The service may include an invocation that God will be present in the home to banish every unclean spirit, and make it a secure habitation for those who dwell in it. A procession may go to the different rooms of the house. The *BOS* provides an antiphon, versicle and response, and prayer for use at the entrance; in an oratory, chapel, or shrine; in a study or library; in a bedroom; in a child's room; in a guest room; in a bathroom; in a workroom or workshop; in the kitchen; in a dining room or area; in a terrace or garden; and in the living room or family room. After the procession has returned to the living room, or immediately after the homily and invocation if there is no procession, the service continues with the Blessing of the Home. This blessing includes an antiphon, a versicle and response, a prayer of blessing, and the peace. The service may continue with the eucharist. Members of the household present the offerings of bread and wine at the eucharist. The *BOS* provides a proper preface and a postcommunion prayer. If there is no communion, the service concludes with the Lord's Prayer and a blessing. The service may conclude with a dismissal. Incense and holy water may be used to symbolize the purification and blessing of the home. The service may be followed by a party to continue the celebration. This service may be done shortly after a household moves to a new home, or at any appropriate time when a Celebration for a Home is desired.

Celebration of a New Ministry. Form for the institution or induction of a priest as the rector of a parish. It may be used for the installation of deans and canons of cathedrals, or the induction of other diocesan or parochial ministries, including assistant ministers and vicars of missions (BCP, p. 558). It may also be used for the institution of deacons and lay persons with pastoral responsibilities. The bishop is normally the chief minister, but a deputy may be appointed if necessary. The BCP provides a form for the Letter of Institution of a Minister (p. 557), which is appropriate for the induction of the rector of a parish, the dean of a cathedral, or a similar office. The Letter of Institution may be read by the bishop after the wardens state that the new minister is well qualified, and that he or she has been prayerfully and lawfully selected. The Litany for Ordinations or another appropriate litany precedes the collect and the liturgy of the word. This service includes an induction ceremony in which the bishop, representatives of the congregation, and representatives of the diocesan clergy present symbolic gifts to the new minister. The BCP calls for the presentations to include a Bible for proclaiming the Word, a vessel of water for baptizing, a stole or symbol of the new minister's order, a book of prayers, olive oil for healing and reconciliation, the keys of the church (if the new minister is a rector or vicar), the Constitution and Canons of the Church, and bread and wine for the eucharist (pp. 561–562). These presentations may be added to, omitted, or adapted in light of the order of the new minister and the nature of the new ministry. The priest's prayer (BCP, pp. 562–563) is appropriate only for rectors, deans, vicars, hospital chaplains, and other priests with similar canonical charge. The new ministry is celebrated in the context of a eucharist. The bishop is normally the chief celebrant. The new minister, if a priest, concelebrates the eucharist with the bishop and other clergy. This service takes the place of an earlier form in American Prayer Books titled "An Office of Institution of Ministers into Parishes or Churches."

Celibacy. Abstinence from marriage and from marital or sexual relations, especially for religious reasons. A person may vow to refrain from marriage and live as a celibate. Celibacy is not a requirement for ordination in the Episcopal Church. *See* Religious Order; *see* Vows.

Celibate. *See* Celibacy.

Cell. 1) The individual room or hut of a nun, monk, friar, or hermit. This room or dwelling is usually furnished in a very simple manner. The term is from the Latin *cella*, "little room" or "hut." 2) A religious house that is an offshoot from a large religious community. This cell or colony remains dependent on the mother house. This practice originated in the Benedictine order. 3) A small group of Christians who meet frequently for prayer, study, and mutual encouragement. Cell members are typically lay people who seek to share the Christian faith in the secular world.

Cella. A small memorial chapel built in early Christian cemeteries. It was used to commemorate those buried in the cemetery and for ordinary worship.

Celtic Spirituality. Little is known of the original form of Celtic spirituality (in Ireland, Scotland, Wales, England, and Brittany), which may have been influenced by druidic religion. It was dominated by a strict ascetic monasticism. Only an ordained monk in a monastery could become a bishop. An eclectic liturgy mixed Roman and Gallic rituals and kept the Jewish computation of Easter. Missionary zeal led to the founding of monasteries in continental Europe. Through the influence of Celtic spirituality, a monastic practice of individual confession and of satisfaction proportional to the offense became normative for the sacrament of penance in the whole western church. In 665 the Synod of Whitby abandoned Celtic customs for those of Rome. Yet great works of art (*The Book of Kells*, c. 775–800) testified to a persistent religious perception that was unique in Christendom. The monastic rule of St. Columba (c. 543–615) gave way gradually to the more moderate rule of St. Benedict.

Cense. To perfume with the smoke of aromatic incense. Censing may express honor, respect, blessing, and celebration in a liturgy. It may also express the lifting up of the prayers of the assembly, or the prayers of the saints. The thurifer or member of the clergy may dramatize the censing by swinging the thurible (censer) that contains burning incense. Puffs of incense smoke come from the thurible as it swings. People and symbolic objects may be censed. For example, it is customary for the deacon to cense the gospel book before proclaiming the gospel in some parishes with an Anglo-catholic piety. It is also customary for the celebrant to cense the altar and the elements of bread and wine on the altar before the eucharistic prayer. The clergy, the choir, and the congregation may also be censed. *See* Incense.

Censer. *See* Thurible.

Center for Jewish-Christian Studies and Relations. The center began in May 1986, when it was approved by the General Theological Seminary Board of Trustees as an official institute of the seminary. It drew its initial support and impetus from the Committee on Jewish-Christian Relations of the Diocese of New York, which was chaired by the Rev. Dr. James Anderson Carpenter. Carpenter, professor of dogmatic theology at General Seminary, was the founding director and served in that position until his retirement on Jan. 1, 1994. The center serves as an embodiment of Christian commitment to the furtherance of Jewish-Christian relations. It opposes Anti-Judaism, which is an impoverishment of Christianity and an injustice to Jews. The center's journal, *Dialogue*, began publication in Spring 1987.

Centering Prayer. A method of quiet meditation in which a single symbolic word is used as a sign of one's willingness to wait on God and be available to God's presence. This word is used as a point of focus. The discipline involves setting aside twenty minutes or so for quiet prayer. This apophatic method has been widely taught and practiced in the Episcopal Church since the early 1980s. Thomas Keating's *Finding Grace at the Center* (1978) encouraged the practice of centering prayer.

Central America, Missionary District of. On Nov. 13, 1956, the House of Bishops voted to divide the Missionary District of the Panama Canal Zone and create the Missionary District of Central America. It included the Republic of Costa Rica, Nicaragua, Honduras, Guatemala, and El Salvador. Jurisdiction for Guatemala, El Salvador, and Honduras was transferred to the Episcopal Church from the Diocese of British Honduras on June 5, 1957. The Missionary District of Central America ceased to exist on Sept. 18, 1967, when the House of Bishops divided it into the five Missionary Districts of Costa Rica, El Salvador, Guatemala, Honduras, and Nicaragua.

Central and South Mexico, Diocese of. The General Convention of 1904 established the Missionary District of Mexico. The 1972 General Convention divided the Missionary District of Mexico into the Missionary District of Central and South Mexico, the Missionary District of Western Mexico, and the Missionary District of Northern Mexico. All three of these Missionary Districts became dioceses. In 1988 the House of Bishops divided the Diocese of Central and South Mexico into the Diocese of Mexico, the Diocese of Cuernavaca, and the Diocese of Southeastern Mexico. The General Convention of 1994 granted the five Mexican dioceses permission to withdraw from the Episcopal Church and form an autonomous province. The Anglican Church of Mexico came into existence on Jan. 1, 1995.

Central Brazil, Missionary District of. On Sept. 30, 1949, the House of Bishops divided the Missionary District of Southern Brazil into three missionary districts—Central Brazil, Southern Brazil, and Southwestern Brazil. On Oct. 20, 1964, the House of Bishops voted for an independent Brazilian church, and in 1965 the Episcopal Church of Brazil became an independent province of the Anglican Communion.

Central Conference of Associated Catholic Priests. Organized in 1923 in New York City by Episcopalians who sought to convert America to the catholic religion as professed in the Apostles' Creed. It sponsored a conference of catholic-minded bishops and clergy in Philadelphia in 1924, with about 700 people in attendance. It also sponsored the Catholic Congresses in New Haven, Connecticut, in 1925, and in Milwaukee, Wisconsin, in 1926. The work of the Central Conference was continued by the American Church Union, which was organized in 1936.

Central Florida, Diocese of. The General Convention of 1969 voted to divide the Diocese of South Florida into three dioceses, one of which was temporarily called the Diocese of South Florida. The primary convention met at the Cathedral Church of St. Luke, Orlando, on Dec. 3, 1969, and changed the name to the Diocese of Central Florida. St. Luke's Church, Orlando, had been designated the Cathedral Church of the Diocese of South Florida on Mar. 31, 1902. Central Florida consists of the following counties: Brevard, Citrus, Hardee, Highlands, Indian River, Lake, Marion, Okeechobee, Orange, Osceola, Polk, St. Lucie, Seminole, Sumter, and Volusia.

Central Gulf Coast, Diocese of. The General Convention of 1970 approved the creation of the Diocese of South Alabama and Northwest Florida. It held its primary convention at Christ Church, Pensacola, Dec. 3–5, 1970, and changed the name to the Diocese of the Central Gulf Coast. It consists of the following counties: Alabama:

Baldwin, Barbour, Butler, Choctaw, Clark, Coffee, Conecuh, Covington, Crenshaw, Dale, Escambia, Geneva, Henry, Houston, Mobile, Monroe, Pike, Washington, Wilcox; Florida: Bay, Calhoun, Escambia, Gulf, Holmes, Jackson, Okaloosa, Santa Rosa, Walton, Washington. The diocese does not have a cathedral.

Central New York, Diocese of. The General Convention of 1868 voted to divide the Diocese of Western New York and create the Diocese of Central New York. Its primary convention met at Trinity Church, Utica, and Grace Church, Utica, on Nov. 10–12, 1868. On Nov. 13, 1971, St. Paul's Church, Syracuse, was set apart as St. Paul's Cathedral. The Cathedral Institutes were signed on Dec. 7, 1971, and the Service of Dedication was held on May 25, 1972. The Diocese consists of the following counties: Broome, Cayuga, Chemung, Chenango, Cortland, Jefferson, Lewis, Madison, Oneida, Onondaga, Oswego, Seneca, Tioga, and Tompkins.

Central Pennsylvania, Diocese of. 1) The General Convention of 1904 voted to divide the Diocese of Central Pennsylvania. The primary convention of the Diocese of Harrisburg met at St. James Church, Lancaster, on Nov. 29–30, 1904. On Jan. 27, 1932, St. Stephen's Church, Harrisburg, became St. Stephen's Cathedral. The name was changed to the Diocese of Central Pennsylvania on May 1, 1971. It consists of the following counties: Adams, Bedford, Blair, Centre, Clinton, Columbia, Cumberland, Dauphin, Franklin, Fulton, Huntingdon, Juniata, Lancaster, Lycoming, Mifflin, Montour, Northumberland, Perry, Potter, Snyder, Sullivan, Tioga, Union, and York. St. Stephen's Church, Harrisburg, became St. Stephen's Cathedral on Jan. 27, 1932. 2) The current Diocese of Bethlehem was known as the Diocese of Central Pennsylvania from Nov. 8, 1871, until May 26, 1909.

Central Philippines, Diocese of. The 1901 General Convention established the Missionary District of the Philippines. In 1973 the Diocese of the Philippines was divided into three missionary districts. One of these was the Central Missionary District. In 1985 it became the Diocese of Central Philippines. In July 1988, the House of Bishops voted to release the Philippine Episcopal Church to form a new province. On May 1, 1990, the Philippine Episcopal Church became autonomous as the twenty-eighth province of the Anglican Communion.

Ceremonial. The physical actions, gestures, and postures of public worship. Ceremonial may be distinguished from ritual, which concerns the prescribed words that are used in worship. The BCP rubrics provide directions and options concerning some matters of ceremonial. For example, the people may stand or kneel during the Eucharistic Prayer. The celebrant is directed to hold or lay a hand on the bread and the wine when those elements are mentioned in the institution narrative of the Great Thanksgiving. Similarly, the celebrant at baptism is directed to touch the water during the Thanksgiving over the Water. Ceremonial choices not directed by the rubrics are matters of tradition and custom. *See* Elements, Eucharistic; *see* Ritual.

Certain Trumpet, The. This journal was published at Norwalk, Connecticut, from Mar. 1972 until Feb. 1981. It was founded and edited by Perry Laukhuff, who wrote that "At Minneapolis [the 1976 General Convention], the Episcopal Church unilaterally altered the sacred Apostolic ministry by purporting to allow the ordination of women in the contravention of Christ's example, theological principle, and the entire history and practice of the Holy Catholic Church. The Episcopal Church also broke, for the first time, with the ancient, orthodox and beautiful Book of Common Prayer by introducing radical changes and dangerously unsound doctrine in a new book." After the 1976 General Convention, *The Certain Trumpet* devoted itself to the creation of a new church body. That goal was attained with the formation of the Anglican Catholic Church.

Certificate of Membership. Any member of a congregation in the Episcopal Church is entitled to a certificate of membership to indicate whether the member is a communicant and to indicate whether the member has been confirmed or received by a bishop. The member is enrolled in the new congregation upon presentation of this certificate, and removed from the rolls of the former congregation.

Chad, or Ceadda, Bishop of Lichfield (d. Mar. 2, 672). He was one of Aidan's students at Lindisfarne. Around 665 he was consecrated Bishop of Mercia, and in Sept. 669 he moved the see to Lichfield. Chad is one of the most popular saints in English history. He is remembered for his simplicity, piety, and devotion to duty. He is commemorated in the Episcopal calendar of the church year on Mar. 2.

Chalcedon, Council of. The fourth of the Ecumenical Councils, held in 451 at Chalcedon, a town near Constantinople. The council was held in the wake of the decision delivered by the so-called "Robber Synod" of Ephesus in 449 that upheld the "one-nature" Christology of Eutychianism. That synod adjourned without giving the Roman delegation an opportunity to make the opposite case by reading "Leo's Tome," a letter written by Pope Leo I which upheld a "two-nature" Christology. In 451 a new emperor, Marcian, anxious for the peace of the church, convened a new council at Leo's urging. After considerable discussion it produced the "Chalcedonian Definition," which is a summary of the christological decisions of three earlier Ecumenical Councils and a clear repudiation of Eutychianism. It upheld the understanding of "two natures, without confusion, without change. . . ." This delicately balanced statement has become the received Christology of the universal church, eastern and western, Catholic and Protestant. The Council of Chalcedon is the last Council which many Anglicans and most Protestants regard as ecumenical. *See* Chalcedonian Definition; *see* Ecumenical Councils.

Chalcedonian Definition. The Council of Chalcedon was summoned in 451 to consider the christological question in light of the "one-nature" picture of Christ proposed by Eutyches which prevailed at the "Robber Synod" of Ephesus in 449. The Council of Chalcedon promulgated the *Definition of the Union of the Divine and Human Natures in the Person of Christ*, which proved to be the touchstone of orthodox Christology (Text in BCP, p. 864). In carefully balanced phrases the Definition establishes that "one and the same Son, our Lord Jesus Christ" is "at once truly God and truly man (Latin, *vere deus, vere homo*), *homoousios* (of one substance) "with the Father as regards his Godhead" (against Arianism) and "with us as regards his humanity" (against Apollinarianism), in two natures— "without confusion, without change" (against Eutychianism), "without separation, without division" (against Nestorianism). Mary is recognized as *theotokos*, the God-bearer. *See* Christology; *see* Homoousios; *see* Monophysitism.

Chalice. The cup for the wine that is consecrated and administered at the eucharist. The chalice normally has a footed base. It is appropriate for only one chalice to be on the altar during the Eucharistic Prayer, but additional chalices may be filled with consecrated wine as needed after the breaking of the bread. The chalice usually matches the paten, which is the plate or dish for the consecrated bread. Chalices are typically made of silver, or other precious or semi-precious metals, and may be decorated by jewels or engraved designs. Pottery chalices are also used. A chalice and paten may be presented as symbols of office at the vesting of a newly ordained priest in the ordination service.

Chalice Bearer. *See* Lay Eucharistic Minister (LEM).

Chalice Veil. A square of material that covers the chalice and paten until they are needed for preparation of the altar at the eucharist. It typically matches the eucharistic vestments and the liturgical color of the day. The chalice veil is placed on top of the pall, which rests on top of the chalice and paten. A purificator rests between the chalice and paten. Additional purificators and the corporal may be kept in the burse. When the chalice and paten are completely prepared for the liturgy with chalice veil and burse, they may be referred to collectively as a "vested chalice."

Chancel. Area of the church set apart for the altar, lectern, pulpit, credence table, and seats for officiating and assisting ministers. It may also include the choir. The chancel is typically raised somewhat above the level of the nave, where the congregation gathers. The chancel may be separated from the nave by a low screen, rail, or open space. In some churches, the congregation may gather on three sides or in a semicircle around the chancel.

Chancel Rail. Low railing or lattice-work that separates the chancel from the nave in a traditionally designed church. The term "chancel," a liturgical space near the altar for clergy and choir, is from the Latin *cancellus*, "lattice." The chancel was separated from the nave in medieval churches by a rood screen or choir screen. Orthodox churches still use screens to separate the areas of chancel and nave. Many western churches have done away with the chancel rail to emphasize that clergy, choir, and people are one community of prayer.

Chancellor. In the Episcopal Church a chancellor is a legal adviser appointed by the Presiding Bishop or a diocesan bishop. A chancellor advises the bishop and diocese on matters of secular and ecclesiastical law. A chancellor is usually an attorney at law.

Chandler, Thomas Bradbury (Apr. 26, 1726–Apr. 20, 1790). An Anglican parson in New Jersey and a Loyalist at a time when adherence to the Church of England and the British Crown were increasingly attacked in the American Colonies. Chandler was a leading advocate of an American episcopacy. He memorialized the English archbishops on behalf of an American episcopacy at the request of the clergy of New Jersey, New York, and Pennsylvania. The events of July 1775 drove him to leave his parish, St. John's, Elizabethtown, New Jersey, and move to England. He returned to St. John's a decade later and served there for forty-three years in all. He was the first American chosen bishop by the English church (Nova Scotia in 1786), but he declined due to failing health.

Change Ringing. The ringing of tower bells of different tones in a precise relationship to each other in order to produce a pleasing cascade of sound. The sequence of bells is varied from "row" to "row" of bells, but the rhythm does not vary. Bells "change" places with adjacent bells in the sequence of the row to produce pleasing variations in the sound. A "ring" of bells has four to twelve bronze bells. These bells may vary in weight from a few hundred pounds to several tons. Each bell is attached to a wooden wheel and hung in a frame that allows the bell to swing through 360 degrees. There is one "ringer" for each bell. The ropes of the bells hang in a circle in the ringing chamber below the bells. The ringers typically stand in a circle to ring the bells. Peal ringing has 5,000 or more changes without a break or the repeating of a row. Peals usually last about three hours. Peal ringing dates from 1715 in England. In 1850 the first peal in North America was rung at Christ Church, Philadelphia.

Chant, Chanting. Singing liturgical prose texts to the rhythm of speech. The term is from the Latin *cantus*, "song." Since ancient times, psalms and canticles, prayers, dialogue, scripture, and other liturgical texts have been sung to many types of melodic formulas. For Anglicans, the most familiar types of chant until recent times were plainchant and Anglican chant. Since the 1950s many other chants have been introduced, based on the rhythms and stresses of modern speech. The most famous are the psalm tones composed by Joseph Gelineau for the Psalter in French, in the eight Gregorian modes. The twentieth century has also witnessed a revival of plainchant, including its Gregorian, Ambrosian, and Mozarabic families, and interest in Slavonic and other eastern chants.

Chantry. An endowment or foundation for the saying of masses and prayers for the founder. It is also the place where the endowed masses are said. This may be a chapel or a separate structure. Chantries were often educational centers. Priests appointed to chantries often conducted schools. Chantries were suppressed in the Church of England in 1547.

Chapel. A building or structure for worship that is not a church. Chapels may be found in public institutions, such as schools and hospitals. Chapels may also be found on private property in residences or estates. A chapel may be a separate building, a room within a larger building, or an area set apart in a larger church or cathedral. A chapel has its own altar.

Chapel of Ease. A chapel located at a distance from its mother church where services are held for the convenience of parishioners who live near it. Clergy leadership is usually provided by the mother church. The chapel is not an independent parochial entity with records or finances of its own. The term is therefore not correctly applied to a small mission or parish that is not attached to a larger church.

Chaplain. A person who serves a chapel, or exercises a nonparochial ministry. Chaplains serve in a variety of public institutions, including schools, hospitals, and prisons. Chaplains in special settings may or may not be members of the organization which they serve. Chaplains serve as military officers in the Armed Forces of the United States. Chaplains may serve a variety of other public institutions and organizations, ranging from police departments to legislatures. Chaplains may have special responsibilities, such as examining chaplains who examine candidates for ordained ministry. In some settings, such as military chaplaincies, chaplains must be priests or bishops. In other settings, such as many hospitals, chaplains may be lay or ordained persons. Historically, chaplains were appointed to serve monarchs, bishops, and the nobility. Some modern bishops, especially primates, have chaplains. Some bishops use a "bishop's chaplain" to assist with ceremonial at episcopal services.

Chaplaincy. *See* Chaplain.

Chaplet. *See* Rosary.

Chapter. A regular assembly of members of an ecclesiastical organization with responsibility for the organization's governance. For example, the meeting of those with the responsibilities of a vestry for a cathedral church, or the assembly of members of a religious house in their corporate capacity.

Chapter House. Building used for official meetings of those with responsibility for the governance of a religious house or cathedral. Separate buildings for this purpose date from the ninth century. The voting members of the religious community or the cathedral canons constituted the chapter, with corporate legal and moral responsibility for their ecclesiastical institution. The term "chapter" may be traced to the practice of daily monastic assembly for a reading of a chapter of the community's rule, for exhortation by the superior or abbot of the community, for announcements, and for discussion of community business. This meeting was known as "the chapter." Members of religious communities also met in the chapter house for public confession of their faults, which was known as the "chapter of faults."

Character (Sacramental). The term transliterates the Greek word which literally means an impress or impression, as on a coin or a seal. It is used metaphorically in Heb 1:3 to refer to Christ as having the "exact imprint" of God's very being (*hypostasis*). Clement of Alexandria, developing the thought of Eph 1:13, speaks of the "shining character of righteousness" imprinted on the soul of the Christian by Christ himself, a quality of life which participates in the Holy Spirit. This idea was amplified by St. Augustine. In medieval scholastic theology baptism was said to confer an indelible character upon those who received it. The BCP states that "The bond which God establishes in Baptism is indissoluble" (p. 298). It is this character, this indissoluble bond, which makes baptism unrepeatable. In the same way, medieval scholastics held that confirmation and ordination conferred indelible character. Contemporary Anglican theology appears to reject this view in the case of Confirmation, recognizing no separate character of Confirmation apart from the baptismal character. Although the Episcopal Church makes no such specific claim about ordination, it acts as though ordination were indelible. One who has abandoned or renounced the ordained ministry, or even been deposed from it, is not reordained if he or she is reinstated. Instead, the person is formally restored to the order already held.

Charismata, or Charismatic Gifts. The term is the plural form for the Greek *charisma*, "gift of grace." In a Christian context, it refers to divine gifts that enable the believer to fulfill his or her vocation. These gifts may be understood as outward signs of grace received through faith. Those who receive these gifts are to be "good stewards of God's varied grace" (1 Pt 4:10), especially in terms of their ministry and life as members of the Christian community. A variety of gifts are given to believers by the one Spirit. The gifts of the Spirit are for the upbuilding of the church and the spread of the gospel. The charismata include utterance of wisdom, utterance of knowledge, faith, gifts of healing, working miracles, prophecy, discernment of spirits, tongues, and interpretation of tongues (1 Cor 12:4–11). Certain gifts are specifically associated with offices or ministries in the church, including the charismata given to apostles, prophets, teachers, workers of miracles, healers, helpers, administrators, and those who speak in tongues (1 Cor 12:28). In view of the great and changing variety of ministries in the church, such lists of charismata must not be considered to be exhaustive. The term "charismata" is also used to indicate the remarkable signs of God's blessing that empowered the early church, beginning at Pentecost (Acts 2:1–4). It has also been applied to extraordinary or miraculous signs of God's favor at any time in the history of the church.

Charismatic. Concerning gifts of the Spirit. The term is derived from the Greek *charisma*, "gift." In 1 Cor 12, St. Paul describes a variety of gifts that are given to Christians as manifestations of the Spirit for the common good and the upbuilding of the faith community. The renewal movement in the Episcopal Church has come with increased attention for the gifts of the Spirit, and openness to the Spirit's activity. The gifts of the Spirit are for all Christians, regardless of piety or denomination. Some have associated the term "charismatic" more narrowly with the Pentecostal Movement. Pentecostalism began in the early twentieth century in the United States among Christians seeking a baptism in the Spirit, accompanied by speaking in tongues and other manifestations of the Spirit. *See* Pentecostalism.

Charismatic Episcopal Church of North America. It was founded on June 26, 1992, when the first synod met at St. Michael's Church, San Clemente, California. At that service, Austin Randolph Adler was ordained and consecrated bishop by Bishop Timothy M. Barker of the Church of Antioch and the International Free Catholic Communion. Adler is Presiding Bishop and Archbishop of the International Communion of the Charismatic Episcopal Church. The First National Convocation of the Charismatic Episcopal Church of North America was held at Kansas City, Missouri, Apr. 12–15, 1994. The church wants to bring "together the dignity, beauty, and liturgy of the ancient church and the life-giving, refreshing power of Pentecost." The church accepts the Chicago-Lambeth Quadrilateral (1888), the Thirty-Nine Articles of Religion (1801), and the Book of Common Prayer (1979). In 1993 it began publishing a newsletter called *Update*, which was renamed *Sursum Corda* in 1994.

Charismatic Renewal, or Neo-Pentecostalism. These terms describe the impact of Pentecostalism in the mainline churches such as the Episcopal Church. Pentecostalism refers to churches and movements that claim to re-experience the spiritual gifts associated with the outpouring of the Holy Spirit at Pentecost in Acts, especially the gift of tongues. The experience is usually referred to as "Baptism in the Holy Spirit." In 1953 Agnes Sanford was one of the first in the Episcopal Church to have such a Pentecostal experience. She was a noted healer and activist in the Order of Saint Luke. Richard Winkler, rector of Trinity Episcopal Church, Wheaton, Illinois, also had such an experience at about this time. He began holding meetings in his home and later in the parish. Winkler was also a member of the Order of Saint Luke. In 1959 several California parishes witnessed Pentecostal experiences, including St. Luke's, Monrovia, St. Mark's, Van Nuys, and Holy Spirit, Monterey Park. Dennis Bennet was at this time rector of St. Mark's, Van Nuys, and Frank Maguire was vicar of Holy Spirit, Monterey Park. Dennis Bennet and his wife Rita quickly emerged as leaders of the new movement, along with Jean Stone Willans of St. Mark's. Willans founded the Blessed Trinity Society in 1961 and its *Logos* magazine to promote charismatic renewal in mainline denominations. Also during this period the Cathedral of St. Paul in Detroit became involved in the charismatic movement under the leadership of Dean John Weaver. Episcopalians involved in the charismatic movement have often not shared the more fundamentalistic theology of those involved in classical Pentecostalism. By the 1990s, the charismatic movement in the Episcopal Church was largely organized through Episcopal Renewal Ministries.

Charisms. Gifts bestowed on believers and their communities by the Holy Spirit, from the Greek *charisma*, related to *charis*, "grace." They are subordinate to love (1 Cor 12:4–31) and the edification of the community (1 Pt 4:10). The gift of prophecy was notable for early Christians, along with "many wonders and signs" (Acts 2:43), including being understood simultaneously in several languages (Acts 2:6). Teaching, ministry, and administration necessary to the common life of the faithful are the primary charisms. Yet some happenings of religious revivals (like speaking in tongues) may also be due to genuine charisms. In their personal prayer many Christians receive interior charisms that transform their lives.

Charleston, College of, Charleston, South Carolina. This school was established by a group of Charleston citizens, including the Rev. Robert Smith, later the first Bishop of South Carolina. A charter was granted on Mar. 19, 1785, and classes began on July 3, 1785, in Smith's home. The college was officially opened in 1790, and Smith served as principal until 1797. While the school was not officially an Episcopal school, it did have three Episcopal priests as presidents.

Chase, Carlton (Feb. 20, 1794–Jan. 18, 1870). First Bishop of New Hampshire. He was born in Hopkinton, New Hampshire, and graduated from Dartmouth in 1817. Chase was ordained deacon on Dec. 9, 1818, and priest on Sept. 27, 1820. His sole parochial charge was the rectorship of Immanuel Church, Bellows Falls, Vermont. He was consecrated Bishop of New Hampshire on Oct. 20, 1844, and served in that position until his death at Claremont, New Hampshire.

Chase, Philander (Dec. 14, 1775–Sept. 20, 1852). Presiding Bishop, missionary, and founder of educational institutions. He was born in Cornish, New Hampshire, and graduated from Dartmouth College in 1796. Chase was ordained deacon on June 10, 1798, and priest on Nov. 10, 1799. He began his ministry with missionary work in northern and western New York. In 1805 he went to New Orleans where he organized and was rector of Christ Church. In 1811 he became the rector of Christ Church, Hartford, Connecticut, but before long he moved west of the Aileghenies to do mission work. In 1817 he organized a church in Salem, Ohio. He was elected the first Bishop of Ohio and was consecrated on Feb. 11, 1819. In 1821–1822 he was president of Cincinnati College, and in 1824 he founded Kenyon College and Bexley Theological Seminary at Gambier, Ohio. On Sept. 9, 1831, he resigned as president of Kenyon and as Bishop of Ohio. He moved to Michigan where he did missionary work for several years. On Mar. 9, 1835, he was elected the first Bishop of Illinois. While Bishop of Illinois he established Jubilee College in Peoria County. Chase was the sixth Presiding Bishop of the church, serving from Feb. 15, 1843, until Sept. 20, 1852. He died at Jubilee College. *See* Bexley Hall; *see* Jubilee College; *see* Kenyon College, Gambier, Ohio.

Chase, Salmon Portland (Jan. 13, 1808–May 7, 1873). Episcopal lay anti-slavery leader and Chief Justice of the United States Supreme Court. He was born in Cornish, New Hampshire, and raised by his uncle, Bishop Philander Chase of Ohio. He was admitted to the Ohio bar in 1829. From the beginning of his career he was unalterably opposed to slavery. In 1837 at Cincinnati, he defended a fugitive slave woman. Chase defended so many fugitive slaves that he was called "attorney-general for runaway Negroes." Chase was U.S. Senator from Ohio, 1849–1855 and 1860, and Governor of Ohio, 1855–1859. He was secretary of the treasury in President Lincoln's cabinet, 1861–1864, and Chief Justice of the U.S. Supreme Court, 1864–1873. Chase believed that he was called by God to work for the freedom of the Negro slaves. He died in New York City.

Chastity. The term literally means "purity" and usually refers to sexual purity. In the development of Christian sexual ethics this has meant virginity for the unmarried, fidelity for the married, and continence for the widowed. Under the influence of Augustine, chastity was a matter of true love rather than being understood narrowly as a matter of physical purity. Spiritual purity is therefore a matter of the full devotion of the self to the service of God.

Chasuble. The sleeveless outer vestment worn by the celebrant at the eucharist. The chasuble and cope are both derived from the outdoor cloak worn by all classes and both sexes in the Greco-Roman world. The chasuble may be oval or oblong, with an opening for the head. It typically reflects the liturgical color of the day. Chasubles vary widely in fabric and style. They may be plain cloth or decorated with orphreys or symbols. The chasuble is also known as a *planeta. See* Cope.

Checkley, John (1680–Feb. 15, 1754). An avid defender of the Church of England in New England. He was born in Boston and educated at Oxford. In 1723 in Boston, he published a pamphlet entitled *A Modest Proof of the Order and Government Settled by Christ and His Apostles, in the Church*, which was a defense of episcopacy. In 1724 he and other laymen founded the Episcopal Charitable Society in Boston. In May 1738, he was ordained deacon and priest, probably by the Bishop of Exeter. He was rector of King's Church, Providence, Rhode Island, until his death. He served there as a missionary of the Society for the Propagation of the Gospel (SPG).

Cheney, Charles Edward (Feb. 12, 1836–Nov. 15, 1916). A founder of the Reformed Episcopal Church. He was born in Canandaigua, New York. Cheney graduated from Hobart College in 1837, and studied at the Virginia Theological Seminary, 1857–1859. He was ordained deacon on Nov. 21, 1858, and priest on Mar. 4, 1860. Cheney was assistant rector of St. Luke's Church, Rochester, New York, 1858–1859, minister in charge of St. Paul's Church, Havana, New York, 1859–1860, and rector of Christ Church, Chicago, Illinois, from 1860 until his death. He was part of the evangelical movement in the Episcopal Church which objected to the use of the word "regenerate" in the baptismal liturgy of the Prayer Book. Cheney omitted the word "regenerate" at a baptism, and was brought to trial in 1869. He was deposed from the ministry but a civil court overturned that decision. On May 4, 1871, "the Canonical and Ecclesiastical Sentence of Degradation from the Ministry in the Church of God" was pronounced upon him by an ecclesiastical court and Bishop Henry John Whitehouse of Chicago. On Dec. 2, 1873, Cheney participated in the organization of the Reformed Episcopal Church. On Dec. 14, 1873, he was consecrated Missionary Bishop of the Northwest for the Reformed Episcopal Church. Christ Church, Chicago, became a parish in the Reformed Episcopal Church in 1874, and Cheney continued to serve as rector. From 1875 until his death he was Bishop of the Synod of Chicago. He was Presiding Bishop of the Reformed Episcopal Church, 1876–1877 and 1887–1889. He died in Chicago.

Cherubim. The plural form of the Hebrew word cherub, which refers to mythological creatures in the Bible. They appear in various passages, such as Gn 3:24, guarding the tree of life; Ex 25:18–22, in connection with the ark of the covenant; and Ez 1:10, in the visions of Ezekiel. The cherubim are depicted with wings, bodies of lions or bulls, and usually human faces. *See* Angel.

Cheshire, Joseph Blount, Jr. (Mar. 27, 1850–Dec. 27, 1932). Bishop and church historian. He was born in Tarborough, North Carolina. After graduating from Trinity College, Hartford, he studied law and was admitted to the bar in North Carolina in 1872. In 1876 he began to read theology. On Apr. 21, 1878, he was ordained deacon, and on May 30, 1880, he was ordained priest. Cheshire established St. Philip the Deacon Church at Durham, and from 1881 until 1893, he was rector of St. Peter's Church, Charlotte. On Oct. 15, 1893, he was consecrated Assistant Bishop of North Carolina, and on Dec. 13, 1893, he became the fifth Bishop of North Carolina. He served as Bishop of North Carolina until his death. Cheshire was a high churchman and insisted that his clergy follow the rubrics of the BCP. One of his most significant historical studies is *The Church in the Confederate States: A History of the Protestant Episcopal Church in the Confederate States* (1912). Cheshire died in Charlotte.

Chicago, Diocese of. The primary convention of the Diocese of Illinois met at the "Episcopal Hall of Worship" in Peoria, Mar. 9, 1835. The General Convention of 1877 voted to divide the Diocese of Illinois into three dioceses— Illinois, Quincy, and Springfield. The name was changed to the Diocese of Chicago on May 28, 1884. On Mar. 4, 1861, the Church of the Atonement, Chicago, became the Cathedral Church of St. Peter and St. Paul. It was destroyed by fire on Mar. 6, 1921. On Dec. 2, 1928, St. James' Church, Chicago, was designated as the Cathedral, but this arrangement was terminated in 1931. St. James' Church, Chicago, was again designated the Cathedral on May 3, 1955, and was formally set apart on June 4, 1955. The Diocese of Chicago consists of the following counties: Boone, Carroll, Cook, DeKalb, Dupage, Ford, Grundy, Iroquois, Jo Daviess, Kane, Kankakee, Kendall, Lake, LaSalle, Lee, Livingston, Marshall, McHenry, Ogle, Putnam, Stephenson, Whiteside, Will, and Winnebago.

Chicago-Lambeth Quadrilateral. Statement of the four Anglican essentials for a reunited Christian Church. It concerns the scriptures, creeds, sacraments, and the historic episcopate. It was approved by the House of Bishops at the 1886 General Convention in Chicago, and subsequently approved with modifications by the bishops of the Anglican Communion at the Lambeth Conference of 1888.

A primary source for the Quadrilateral was *The Church-Idea, An Essay Towards Unity* (1870) by William Reed Huntington (1838–1909), an Episcopal priest. He indicated the Anglican basis for an ecumenical "Church of the Reconciliation" in America should be acceptance of l) the Holy Scriptures as the Word of God; 2) the Nicene Creed as the rule of faith; 3) the two sacraments ordained by Christ himself (baptism and the eucharist); and 4) the episcopate as the keystone of governmental unity in the church. This "foursquare" approach became known as the "Quadrilateral." Huntington was the moving force behind its approval by the House of Bishops in Chicago.

The Chicago version of the Quadrilateral provides an ecumenical statement of purpose and introduction which states that the Episcopal Church is "ready in the spirit of love and humility to forego all preferences of her own" concerning things of human ordering or choice regarding modes of worship, discipline, and traditional customs. However, the statement of purpose warns that Christian unity "can be restored only by the return of all Christian communions to the principles of unity exemplified by the undivided Catholic Church during the first days of its existence."

The four points of the Quadrilateral were listed by the Chicago statement as "inherent parts" of the sacred deposit of Christian faith and order "committed by Christ and his Apostles to the Church unto the end of the world, and therefore incapable of compromise or surrender. . . ." The Chicago statement lists the Nicene Creed as the sufficient statement of the Christian faith. With respect to baptism and the eucharist, the Chicago statement calls for administration of these sacraments "with unfailing use of Christ's words of institution and of the elements ordained by Him." The Chicago version expressed the fourth part of the Quadrilateral in terms of "The Historic Episcopate, locally adapted in the methods of its administration to the varying needs of the nations and peoples called of God into the unity of His Church." Although the Quadrilateral was not enacted by the House of Deputies at the 1886 General Convention, it was incorporated in a general plan referred for study and action by the newly created Joint Commission on Christian Reunion.

The Quadrilateral was passed in a modified form as "Resolution II" of the Lambeth Conference of 1888. At Lambeth the four essential "parts" were termed "Articles." The introductory statement of purpose of the Chicago version of the Quadrilateral was deleted and replaced by a simple statement that the four Articles "supply a basis on which approach may be by God's blessing made towards Home Reunion. . . ." The Lambeth version states that the scriptures provide "the rule and ultimate standard of faith." The Lambeth text affirms the Nicene Creed as the "sufficient statement of the Christian faith" but also adds the "Apostles' Creed, as the Baptismal Symbol" to the creedal article of the Quadrilateral. The Lambeth version adds the statement that the dominical sacraments of Baptism and Eucharist were "instituted by Christ himself." The article concerning the historic episcopate was not changed at Lambeth.

At the 1895 General Convention of the Episcopal Church, the Commission on Christian Unity was continued with the goal of seeking Christian unity on the basis of the "principles enunciated throughout the Declaration of the house of Bishops made at Chicago in 1886, and as reaffirmed by the Lambeth Conference of 1888." Thus for the first time the entire General Convention of the Episcopal Church affirmed the Quadrilateral in its Lambeth form. The Chicago-Lambeth Quadrilateral has continued to serve as the primary Anglican working document and reference point for ecumenical Christian reunion. The Chicago and Lambeth versions of the Quadrilateral are included in the historical documents of the 1979 BCP (pp. 876–878).

Chimere. This robe without sleeves is worn over an alb or rochet as part of the vestments of a bishop. At first it was simply the outer garment in general use. It was of one piece with openings for head and arms. Not until the introduction of wigs did it open down center front. The chimere was usually of black or red silk when it was adopted for liturgical or ceremonial use. As an outer garment, the chimere is not usually appropriate when a chasuble or cope is worn.

China, Missionary District of. The General Convention of 1844 elected William Jones Boone the Missionary Bishop of China. He was consecrated on Oct. 26, 1844. The 1874 General Convention changed the name to "Missionary Bishop of Shanghai, with jurisdiction in China." The General Convention of 1901 voted to divide China into the Missionary District of Shanghai and the Missionary District of Hankow. On Oct. 11, 1910, the Missionary District of Hankow was divided and the Missionary District of Wuhu was created. Wuhu was changed to Anting in 1913. In 1949 the three American

Districts of Anting, Hankow and Shanghai became part of the Holy Catholic Church in China.

Chi-Rho. *See* Labarum.

Choir. A body of singers who provide musical leadership for congregational singing in the worship of the church. Choirs may also sing anthems or make other special musical offerings to beautify and enhance the experience of worship. The primary role of the choir is to lead and support the congregation's worship through singing, not to provide a musical performance. Choir members may wear a cassock and surplice, or an alb. Some choirs do not wear vestments. The choir may be placed in a section of the chancel (also known as the "choir" or "quire"), or the choir may sit together in a designated part of the nave.

Choir Loft. A gallery set aside for the seating of the choir and placement of an organ and other instruments. It is usually in the west end of the nave.

Choir Office. A service, typically one of the Daily Offices, which is sung or said in the choir space of the chancel.

Choir Stall. Seating for a choir, usually a row of benches with backs, kneelers, and a rack for music.

Choirmaster. A musician who provides training and leadership of a choir.

Choral Service. In a choral service, certain texts of the liturgy are sung rather than spoken by the officiant, choir, and people. A choral celebration of the Holy Eucharist is one in which portions of the ordinary and the propers are sung by the officiant, choir, and congregation. Choral Matins is a service of Morning Prayer in which the versicles and responses, invitatory, psalm(s), and proper collects are sung. "Choral" distinguishes music that is sung, rather than played on an instrument or instruments.

Choristers. Persons who sing in a choir.

Chorley, Edward Clowes (May 6, 1865–Nov. 2, 1949). Historiographer of the Episcopal Church, founder and editor of the *Historical Magazine.* He was born in Manchester, England. Chorley graduated from Richmond College in England in 1888, and served for a number of years in the Methodist ministry. He then came to the United States. Chorley was ordained deacon on Feb. 23, 1902, and priest on May 25, 1902. After serving as assistant to the rector of Christ Church, Yonkers, New York, 1901–1902, he became rector of Emmanuel Church, Great River, New York, 1902–1906, and assistant at Bethesda Church, Saratoga, New York, 1906–1908. From 1908 until his retirement in 1940, Chorley was rector of St. Philip's Church-in-the-Highlands, Garrison, New York. He served in many positions in the Diocese of New York. He was historiographer of the diocese from 1915 until his death. He served as the fifth historiographer of the Episcopal Church from Oct. 14, 1919, until Oct. l, 1949. He persuaded the General Convention of 1931 to authorize the publication of the *Historical Magazine of the Protestant Episcopal Church,* now called *Anglican and Episcopal History.* Chorley published many articles on the history of the Episcopal Church and six books. Among his books are *The New American Prayer Book—Its History and Contents* (1929), and *Quarter of a Millennium: Trinity Church in the City of New York, 1697–1947* (1947). His *magnum opus* was *Men and Movements in the American Episcopal Church* (1946), which were the Hale Lectures delivered at Seabury-Western Theological Seminary. Chorley died in Cold Spring, New York.

Chrism. Consecrated oil used for anointing the newly baptized person with the sign of the cross at baptism. At this consignation, the bishop or priest says to each newly baptized person that "you are sealed by the Holy Spirit in baptism and marked as Christ's own for ever" (BCP, p. 308). Chrism must be consecrated by a bishop. It may be consecrated immediately prior to the baptism. It may also be consecrated by the bishop on an episcopal visitation when there is no baptism, or at a diocesan service such as the Reaffirmation of Ordination Vows of the diocesan clergy. The *BOS* provides a form for the consecration of chrism apart from baptism. Chrism is olive oil mixed with a fragrant ointment, usually balsam.

Chrismation. Baptismal anointing that may be done when the bishop or priest marks the sign of the cross on the forehead of the newly baptized person, saying, "you are sealed by the Holy Spirit in Baptism and marked as Christ's own for ever" (BCP, p. 308). Use of chrism at baptism is optional in the Episcopal Church. The expression "to christen" is derived from this practice. The term "chrismation" is from the Greek for an anointing. The anointing is done with scented oil which is blessed by the bishop before use. A form for the consecration of chrism by the bishop is provided in the BCP (p. 307). Chrismation recalls the ancient anointing of kings and priests, and signifies the seal of baptism and incorporation into Christ, "The Anointed One." Use of chrism (which must be consecrated by the bishop) signifies the relationship of the episcopacy to baptism. In the eastern church, chrismation is always administered immediately after baptism, regardless of the age of those baptized. It is understood to give the "seal of the gift of the Holy Spirit" to the newly baptized, and it is understood as confirmation. There are varied understandings in the western church concerning the meaning of chrismation relative to confirmation.

Chrisom or chrysom or chrysome. A white baptismal gown or mantle worn by the newly baptized. The term is associated with the anointing of the newly baptized with chrism. It may be a remnant of the white garment worn by the newly baptized in the early church. It was also traditionally worn during Easter Week on liturgical occasions. This "chrism robe" symbolizes the cleansing of sin in baptism. Its use was ordered by the 1549 Prayer Book, but not required after 1552. A white baptismal gown is worn by some baptismal candidates today, but its use is not required.

Christ. *See* Jesus Christ; *see* Messiah.

Christ Candle. Large white candle that may be placed in the center of an Advent wreath to represent Christ. The Christ candle is lit at the beginning of the Christmas celebration. It may be lit throughout the Christmas season. It contrasts with the colored candles (which may be blue, or purple, or three purple and one rose-colored) that represent the four Sundays of Advent on the Advent wreath. *See* Advent Wreath.

Christ Centered Ministries, Order of (OCCM). A quasi-contemplative religious order for clergy and laypersons, married or celibate, seeking to live the baptismal covenant in the Benedictine tradition. Members are from the Anglican, Roman Catholic, and other communions and practice a life of prayer, study, eucharistic celebration, and ecumenical outreach. It also sponsors retreats, quiet days, contemplative outreach groups, and offers courses for centering prayer and contemplative living.

Christ Church, Alexandria, Virginia. The City of Alexandria was founded in 1749, and a chapel-of-ease, or branch church for the ease of parishioners distant from the main parish church at Falls Church, Virginia, was located there by 1753. In 1765 the growth of local population led the Virginia legislature to divide the parish, which included Alexandria, into two. A new parish was created out of the northern end of Truro Parish and named Fairfax Parish. The vestry of Truro Parish decided that the main church at Falls Church and the chapel-of-ease at Alexandria were inadequate and would be replaced. Two similar churches were built from one set of plans at those two locations. The church built at Alexandria is Christ Church today. The construction of the Georgian-style church began in 1767 and was completed in 1773. The first services in this building were celebrated on Feb. 27, 1773. The galleries were added in 1787. Virginia Theological Seminary used Christ Church buildings at first, as did Episcopal High School. George Washington was a parishioner at Christ Church. However, he served on the vestry of Truro Parish where his home, Mt. Vernon, was located. He once bought and then rented a pew in Christ Church. Washington attended services at Christ Church when he was in Alexandria. Robert E. Lee was confirmed at Christ Church and married Mary Custis, Washington's step-great granddaughter, at Christ Church. On Jan. 1, 1942, President Franklin Roosevelt and British Prime Minister Winston Churchill visited Christ Church for the World Day of Prayer for Peace during World War II.

Christ Church, Philadelphia. This church was founded on Nov. 15, 1695, with the assistance of Henry Compton, the Bishop of London, who had responsibility for the Church of England in the American colonies. It was the first Anglican church founded in the Pennsylvania colony. In 1758 St. Peter's Church was founded in the city, and in 1761 the "United Churches of Christ Church and St. Peter's" was established. In 1809 St. James' Church was founded and the parishes were known as the "United Churches of Christ Church, St. Peter's Church and St. James' Church." St. James' Church became a separate corporation in 1829, and St. Peter's in 1832. Christ Church has been called the Shrine of the Patriots. On June 25, 1775, members of the Constitutional Convention met at Christ Church to hear the Rev. William Smith preach a sermon on "The Present Situation in American Affairs." The General Convention of 1785 and the first session of the General Convention of 1786 met at Christ Church. The General Convention of

1789 also met there. During its second session the first House of Bishops met in a small room in the northeast corner of Christ Church. William White, rector of Christ Church from 1779 until 1836, presented plans to a vestry meeting on Nov. 3, 1788, for a Sunday School. From this developed one of the first Sunday Schools in the United States and the first in the Episcopal Church. At least eleven bishops have been consecrated at Christ Church.

Christ our Passover. *See* Pascha nostrum (Christ our Passover).

Christ School, Arden, North Carolina. This school was founded in 1900 by the Rev. and Mrs. Thomas C. Wetmore on land deeded to them by Mrs. Wetmore's family, the Robertsons. The school was established as a mission to the underprivileged children of western North Carolina. It began under the jurisdiction of the Missionary District of Asheville. It offered an education in all grade levels to any male or female student who wished to learn. Most of the work of operating the school, from shoveling coal for the furnaces to milking the cows on the associated farm, was done by the students. It was incorporated in 1907 as a private, self-supporting institution. Under headmaster Reuben R. Harris it became a boy's college preparatory school, and girls have not been admitted since 1928. It continues to be committed to the residential nature of its founding. It no longer has official connections with the Episcopal Church or the Diocese of Western North Carolina.

Christ the King, Diocese of. The Diocese of Christ the King was organized at Glendale, California, on Dec. 10, 1977, by clergy and lay persons disaffected from the Episcopal Church. At that meeting the delegates elected Robert S. Morse, rector of St. Peter's Episcopal Church, Oakland, California, as bishop of the diocese. He was consecrated with three others at Augustana Lutheran Church, Denver, Colorado, on Jan. 28, 1978. The Diocese of Christ the King, which is a non-geographical diocese, was one of seven newly formed dioceses which met at Dallas, Oct. 18–21, 1978, to organize the Anglican Catholic Church. When the Diocese met at Payson, Arizona, on Jan. 30–31, 1979, it refused to ratify the constitution of the Anglican Catholic Church. It has continued as a separate body. In Jan. 1978, it opened St. Joseph of Arimathea Anglican Theological Seminary in Berkeley, California. St. Peter's Anglican Church, Oakland, was consecrated as the pro-cathedral on Oct. 31, 1983. The Diocese adheres to the Affirmation of St. Louis and is in the Anglo-catholic tradition.

Christ the King Sunday. Feast celebrated in the Roman Catholic Church and the Lutheran Church on the last Sunday of the liturgical year. It celebrates Christ's messianic kingship and sovereign rule over all creation. The feast is unofficially celebrated in some Episcopal parishes, but it is not mentioned in the Episcopal calendar of the church year. Marion Hatchett notes that the Prayer Book collect for Proper 29, the last Sunday of the church year, is a "somewhat free" translation of the collect of the Feast of Christ the King in the Roman Missal. This collect prays that God, "whose will it is to restore all things in your well-beloved Son, the King of kings and Lord of lords," will "Mercifully grant that the peoples of the earth, divided and enslaved by sin, may be freed and brought together under his most gracious rule" (BCP, p. 236). The feast was originally instituted by Pope Pius XI in 1925 and celebrated on the last Sunday in Oct. It has been observed on the last Sunday before Advent since 1970.

Christen. The ceremony of baptizing and naming. The term has been used as a synonym for baptism, where the candidates for baptism are presented with their "Christian" names and made Christians.

Christendom. Christianity, or Christians collectively, or the regions where Christianity is the dominant faith ("the Christian world"). The term has been associated, at times pejoratively, with the concept of a "Christian state" or "Christian society" which can be traced to Constantine. The contemporary United States has been described in terms of a "post-Christendom" era.

Christian Challenge, The. The major publication of the traditionalist movement in Anglicanism. This periodical began publication in Jan. 1962, and was subtitled "A Newsletter for Episcopalians." The founding editor was Dorothy Allen Faber (1924–1982). She was nicknamed the "Dragon Lady." At first it was published by the Society of Fishermen, Inc., and then by the Anita Foundation. In Aug. 1966, it began to be published by the Foundation for Christian Theology. For a while its subtitle was "An Independent Witness in the Anglican/Episcopal Tradition," and later it was "The Only Worldwide Voice of Traditional Anglicanism." Some issues carry the slogan, "To Believe

What Is True, To Resist What Is Wrong, To Do What Is Right." *See* Foundation for Christian Theology, The.

Christian Communities. According to the canons of the Episcopal Church, a Christian Community is a society of Christians, in communion with the See of Canterbury, who voluntarily commit themselves for life, or a term of years, in obedience to their rule and constitution. To be officially recognized, a Christian Community must have at least six full members and be approved by the Standing Committee on Religious Communities of the House of Bishops. Each Christian Community must have a Bishop Visitor or Protector. A Christian Community may establish a house in a diocese only with the permission of the bishop of the diocese. The canons distinguish Christian communities from religious orders. The members of religious orders commit themselves for life or a term of years to hold their possessions in common or in trust, to live a celibate life in community, and to obey their rule and constitution.

Christian Education. A general term referring to all forms of education and training sponsored by the church. In more specific terms Christian education is understood as an aspect of catechesis. Along with Christian formation, Christian education is one of the two ways in which catechesis takes place in the life of the church. As Caroline and John Westerhoff write in their book, *On the Threshold of God's Future*, Christian education "includes those intentional, critical-reflection activities that provide the opportunity to consider life experience an activity in light of the community's story and tradition." Christian education also includes the knowledge and skills necessary for living the Christian life.

Christian Formation. The aspect of catechesis concerned with inculturation in the community of faith. Formation involves the ways in which we embrace what the scriptures refer to as "life in Christ." The principle modes of formation are our experiences of worship and the deepening of our inner life through greater openness to the Spirit.

Christian Foundations. The Fellowship of Witness (FOW) published this journal from the time of FOW's beginning in 1965. In 1976 Trinity Episcopal School for Ministry and the Rev. Professor Leslie Parke Fairfield assumed publication responsibilities and changed the name to *Kerygma*. Very few copies of *Christian Foundations* have been located.

Christian Initiation. The sacramental rites incorporating one into the life of the church. In the ancient church such initiation consisted of water baptism, anointing with oil and the laying on of hands, followed immediately by the reception of the Holy Eucharist. In later times this continuity of rites was broken. In the western church, what came to be known as Confirmation was administered separately from water baptism either by the laying on of hands and the invocation of the Spirit or by anointing and the invocation of the Spirit. The bishop was the minister for Confirmation. The BCP now states that Holy Baptism is "full initiation by water and the Holy Spirit into Christ's Body the Church" (BCP, p. 298). Confirmation follows a mature, public affirmation of faith and commitment to the responsibilities of baptism by the candidate (BCP, p. 413).

Christian Journal and Literary Register, The. This journal began publication on Jan. 22, 1817, in New York, "under the inspection of the Right Rev. Bishop Hobart." At first it was published every two weeks, but eventually became monthly. The last issue was published in Dec. 1830. It was "devoted to theological and miscellaneous subjects, and particularly to interesting religious and literary intelligence, and biographical and obituary notices."

Christian Ministry Among Jewish People (CMJ/USA). Christian Ministry among Jewish People (CMJ) was founded in London in 1809. It is the recognized agency in the Anglican Communion for work among Jewish people. CMJ/USA was incorporated in 1982. Its purpose is to provide an Episcopal ministry through which Jewish people can be encouraged to recognize Jesus as their Messiah and educate Christians in the Jewish origins of the church and their continuing obligations to the Jewish people.

Christian Nurture Series. A Sunday Church School curriculum for children and high school students designed to encourage growth in the Christian faith and tradition. Published in 1916, it continued in use until it began to be replaced by the Seabury Series in 1949. It had two essential elements: 1) a sequence of themes, one for each year of the growing pupil's life; and 2) the pedagogical principle that the pupil should be informed and at the same time trained through participation in the activities of worshiping God and serving other human beings. The leaders in establishing the series were the Rev. William Edward Gardner (1872–1965), and the Rev. Lester Bradner (d. 1929).

Christian Socialism. The beginnings of Christian socialism in the Church of England are associated with the work of J. M. Ludlow, Charles Kingsley, and F. D. Maurice. Maurice was its prophet and theologian whose influence continues today. But he was no Marxist, and with most Englishmen he was unsympathetic to revolution. But these leaders did see constructive forces at work in the revolutionary impulses. In assuming the name Christian socialism, they did not propose an economic doctrine nor a program of reform, but the "science of partnership." They held that Christianity looked to a society in which people would work cooperatively together. Competition was held to be a denial of what the church believed. Maurice proposed cooperative workers' unions and educational institutes. Maurice died in 1872, but his ideas continued to be influential. In June 1889, the Christian Social Union was formed to urge fundamental Christian social principles. Bishop B. F. Westcott was its first president, and its leaders included Henry Scott Holland and Bishop Charles Gore. In the twentieth century several successive Christian socialist groups were formed in the Church of England. In 1921 *The Return of Christendom* appeared, in which industrial capitalism was criticized in the light of catholic doctrine. In the United States, the American Church Socialist League and its successor, the Church League for Industrial Democracy, sought to further the Christian socialist agenda. The great figure of the twentieth century was William Temple (1881–1944), Archbishop of Canterbury, who urged that the church must choose between socialism and heresy. His *Christianity and Social Order* is a basic text for twentieth-century Christian socialism. The emphasis on theology and the gospel in Christian socialism rescues any effort to change social structures from simple expediency and avoids the separation of prayer and action.

Christian Social Service, Department of. It was established by the canons of the 1919 General Convention as one of the five departments acting under the Presiding Bishop and Council. It was one of the three major fields of church activity, along with the Department of Missions and Church Extension and the Department of Religious Education. Its job was to promote the witness of the church concerning social and industrial righteousness. It also had responsibility for coordinating and stimulating social service activities and agencies throughout the church. One of its major accomplishments was the organization of the National Conference of Social Service Workers in the Episcopal Church. In 1939 the name was changed to the Department of Christian Social Relations. This department went out of existence with organizational changes at the national level.

Christian Social Union. This organization was founded on Apr. 3, 1891, in New York City by William Dwight Porter Bliss, Richard Theodore Ely, Frederic Dan Huntington, and James Otis Sargent Huntington. It was an educational organization which taught that Christian law is the ultimate authority to rule social practice, and that the moral truths and principles of Christianity must be applied to the social and economic difficulties of the present time. In 1894 the name was changed to Church Social Union. In 1897 its name was changed back to Christian Social Union. It disbanded in 1912.

Christian Warrior, The. Described as a "militant Low Church publication," its first issue appeared on Jan. 2, 1828, in Philadelphia. It was founded and edited by the Rev. Benjamin Allen (1789–1829). Although it was intended to be a weekly, it soon became a monthly periodical. The name was changed to *Christian Magazine* after Allen bought the subscription list of the American edition of the *London Christian Review and Clerical Magazine*. It was discontinued shortly after Allen's death.

Christmas, or Christ's Mass. Christmas (in old English, *Cristes maesse*) is a festival celebrated on Dec. 25, commemorating the Incarnation of the Word of God in the birth of Jesus Christ. In the BCP it is also called The Nativity of Our Lord Jesus Christ. In the United States it is also a popular secular holiday.

According to the Philocalian calendar, Christmas was first celebrated in Rome in the year 336. It gradually spread to the churches of the east, which already had a festival on Jan. 6 commemorating the manifestation of God in both the birth and baptism of Jesus. The date, Dec. 25, rests on no historical foundation. It was probably chosen to oppose the feast *Natalis Solis Invicti*, the birthday of the "Unconquerable Sun God" (Saturn), which took place at the winter solstice to celebrate the birth of "the Sun of Righteousness."

The customs associated with Christmas have developed from many sources. From early days the popular observance of Christmas was marked by the joy and celebration characteristic of the Roman Saturnalia and the pagan festivals which it replaced. It came to include the decoration of houses with greenery and the giving of gifts to children and the poor. In Britain other observances were added including the Yule log and Yule cakes, fir trees, gifts, and greetings. Fires and lights (symbols of warmth and lasting life) and evergreens (symbols of survival) were traditionally associated with both pagan and Christian festivals. Their use developed considerably in England with the importation of German customs and through the influence of the writings of Charles Dickens.

In the BCP, Christmas Day is one of the seven principal feasts. The Christmas season lasts twelve days, from Christmas Day until Jan. 5, the day before the Epiphany. The season includes Christmas Day, the First Sunday after Christmas Day, the Holy Name of Our Lord Jesus Christ, and may include the Second Sunday after Christmas Day. In many parishes, the main liturgical celebrations of Christmas take place on Christmas Eve. The *BOS* includes a variety of resources for use during Christmas, including a form for a Station at a Christmas Crèche, a form for a Christmas Festival of Lessons and Music, and seasonal blessings for use during the Christmas season.

Christmas Festival of Lessons and Music. The *BOS* provides a form for this festival, including contemporary and traditional language versions of a bidding prayer and various scriptural options for use as the lessons. Nine readings are customarily used at this festival, but fewer may be used. The lessons are interspersed with carols, hymns, canticles, and anthems. If the festival is celebrated in the evening, it may be introduced by the Service of Light (BCP, p. 109). The service may conclude with an appropriate collect and a seasonal blessing for Christmas.

Christology. From the Greek *Christos*, "Christ," and *logia*, "doctrine." In Christian theology the word refers to the doctrine of Christ. It can be used in a broad sense to designate the whole body of teaching about Jesus the Christ, including both his person and his work. The traditional scope of Christology, however, is narrower. It covers only an exposition of the person of Christ, usually in terms of the Chalcedonian Definition, a carefully balanced formula designed to express both the full humanity of Jesus of Nazareth and his full divinity as the Son of God.

The work of Christ concerns the action of God in the Incarnation in "reconciling the world to himself" (2 Cor 5:19). Since the sixteenth century, many Protestant and some Anglican theologians have focused their discussion of Christ's work in the "three offices" of prophet, priest, and king. *See* Eutychianism; *see* Nestorianism; *see* Atonement.

Christus Rex. The earliest depictions of the crucifixion show Christ upon the cross, with body erect and with arms stretched straight out. He is clothed either in a long robe or with a loin cloth. There is no attempt to be realistic or to emphasize suffering or agony.

The modern "Christus Rex" crucifix is in the same tradition. Christ stands erect in front of a cross, with arms straight out. The body may be clothed in modern, western eucharistic vestments, and there may be a crown on the head.

The image portrays several concepts at the same time: the historic event of the crucifixion, Christ as the King in his kingdom, and Christ as the victorious sacrifice in the eucharistic feast.

Chronicle, The. A monthly journal first published and edited by Alexander Griswold Cummins (1868–1946), at Christ Church, Poughkeepsie, New York. Cummins was a consummate low churchman who refused to have a cross or candles on the altar. *The Chronicle* was referred to by moderates and Anglo-catholics as the "Chronic-hell." It began publication in 1900, and ceased publication with the June/July, 1947 issue.

Chronicle of the Church. This weekly journal was published in New Haven, Connecticut. The first issue appeared in Jan. 1837. In 1840 the name was changed to *Practical Christian and Church Chronicle.* It ceased publication in 1845.

Chronos. Measured quantitative time. *See* Kairos.

Chrysom. *See* Chrisom or chrysom or chrysome.

Chrysostom, John (c. 347–Sept. 14, 407). Eastern patriarch. He was born at Antioch in Syria. Early in life John became a monk. At times he lived as a hermit. He was soon recognized as a great preacher. Shortly after his death he was given the name Chrysostom, which means "golden-mouthed." In 397 he became the Patriarch of Constantinople. He served in that position until 404 when he was deposed and banished by Empress Eudoxia and Theophilus, Patriarch of Alexandria. Chrysostom was an opponent of the Arians. He placed great emphasis on the eucharist. The liturgy used by Orthodox Christians every Sunday, except in Lent, is attributed to him. He died in Comana in Pontus, now in northeast Turkey. His most significant writing was *On the Priesthood*, a manual for priests and bishops. Chrysostom is a Doctor of the Church. In 1908 Pope Pius X named him the patron saint of preachers. On Jan. 27, 438, Emperor Theodosius II moved his body to Constantinople and buried it under the altar of the Church of the Holy Apostles. His life and ministry are commemorated in the Episcopal calendar of the church year on Jan. 27.

Chung Hua Sheng Kung Hui. The Holy Catholic Church in China. The Episcopal Church had been active in China since 1844, when William Jones Boone was consecrated the Missionary Bishop of China. He was the first foreign Missionary Bishop of the Episcopal Church. English and Canadian Anglicans were also active in China. On Apr. 26, 1912, the American, Canadian and English jurisdictions united to form the *Chung Hua Sheng Kung Hui*. The last Episcopal Missionary Bishop to serve in the Holy Catholic Church in China was William Payne Roberts, who retired on Apr. 12, 1950.

Church. This weekly journal was published in Philadelphia from Nov. 29, 1884, until probably Nov. 20, 1886.

Church, The. The community of faith headed by Christ, the body of Christ in the world (see 1 Cor 12:12–27; Eph 1:22–23, 4:12, 5:29–30). Baptism is full initiation into the church, and all baptized persons are members of the church (BCP, pp. 299, 854). The church is the community of the New Covenant, the People of God, the New Israel, the Temple of the Holy Spirit, a holy nation, a royal priesthood, and the pillar and ground of truth (see BCP, p. 854). The church is described in the Nicene Creed as one, holy, catholic, and apostolic (see BCP, pp. 358–359). It is described as one because it is one body headed by Christ; holy because the Holy Spirit dwells in it, consecrating and guiding the members of the church; catholic because the church proclaims the whole Christian faith to all people, to the end of time; and apostolic because it continues in the teaching and fellowship of the apostles, and it is sent to fulfill Christ's mission to all people (BCP, p. 854). We believe that Christ's presence is available in the life and sacraments of the church for our salvation, even though the church does not yet embody or represent Christ in a perfect way,

and the four characteristics or "marks" of the church have not yet been perfectly realized. The fallibility of the church was recognized in Anglicanism by the Thirty-Nine Articles in the sixteenth century (see Articles XIX and XXI, BCP, pp. 871, 872).

The Episcopal theologian William Porcher DuBose noted that Christ in the NT frequently means humanity in Christ or humanity in the church, as Adam in the NT frequently means humanity or the human race. Christ is the head of the church, and we are to share Christ's salvation in and through the church. We are to be one in Christ and one with each other in Christ through the church. The mission of the church is to restore all people to unity with God and each other. The church pursues its mission through prayer and worship, proclaiming the gospel, and promoting justice, peace, and love. The church completes its mission through the ministry of all its members (BCP, p. 855).

The term "church" is from Greek words *kyriakon*, "belonging to the Lord," and *ekklesia*, "assembly." Church can also indicate a particular church body or denomination, such as the Episcopal Church; or a particular congregation or parish; or the building or place where a congregation gathers. *The Hymnal 1982* provides sections of hymns for "The Church" (Hymns 517–527) and "The Church's Mission" (Hymns 528–544), including "The Church's one foundation" (Hymn 525), "Let saints on earth in concert sing" (Hymn 526), and "Spread, O spread, thou mighty word" (Hymn 530).

Church Advocate **(Baltimore).** This periodical was published at Baltimore. It carried news for and about African American Episcopalians. It was published weekly from 1892 until 1898, and it was published monthly from 1899 until 1923. It ceased publication in 1923.

Church Advocate **(Lexington).** This periodical was published monthly in Lexington, Kentucky. It began publication early in 1835. It was the private venture of Dr. John E. Cooke, a prominent Kentucky lawyer. In Nov. 1835, the Rev. Henry Caswall became editor. Publication was suspended at the end of 1836.

Church and State. *See* Protestant Churchman, The.

Church and the World, The. This quarterly periodical began publication in Jan., 1872, and ceased publication in 1874. It was an Anglo-catholic publication.

Church Army. A society of lay evangelists in the Anglican Communion. It was founded in 1882 by Prebendary Wilson Carlile, a priest and evangelist of the Church of England. His vision was that the Church Army would be an evangelistic arm of the church, recruited from ordinary working men and women. It was to reach out to those outside the church, particularly to the most needy, through evangelism and practical programs of social aid. The Church Army came to the United States in 1925 at the invitation of Bishop William Manning of New York. It undertook an evangelistic tour which began with a march through New York City and New England to Canada. There was preaching at open air stations and churches along the way. In 1926 Carlile came to the United States at the invitation of Bishop Manning. Carlile and several Church Army captains conducted evangelistic programs. The first Church Army Center was opened in Providence, Rhode Island. By the 1970s, the Church Army had declined and almost ceased to exist. In 1984 Presiding Bishop John M. Allin called the Rev. Canon George Preble Pierce to head a task force to revitalize the Church Army. A new board was formed and Canon Pierce was installed as National Director in the presence of the House of Bishops at the 1985 General Convention. The purpose of the Army is "To so present the Gospel that others may be brought to a saving knowledge of Jesus Christ and be incorporated into His Body, the Church."

Church Association for the Advancement of the Interests of Labor (CAIL). This organization was formed on May 18, 1887, in New York City by James Otis Sargent Huntington and William Dwight Porter Bliss. It taught that the church has a genuine concern for the welfare of the workers in industry. It stressed that God is the sole owner of the earth and that people are God's stewards. CAIL used prayer, sermons on the relevance of the gospel to social problems, and printed addresses to convey its message. Bishops Frederic Dan Huntington and Henry Codman Potter were among its leaders. It had about fifty bishops as honorary vice-presidents. CAIL had special committees on sweatshops and slum tenements. It promoted remedial legislation and arbitrated strikes. In 1890 it instituted in Episcopal churches the first observance of Labor Sunday (the Sunday after Labor Day). This was the first observance of Labor Sunday in the United States. It published a quarterly magazine, *Hammer and Pen*, beginning in 1895. CAIL voluntarily disbanded in May,

1926, when the Joint Commission on Social Service formed its Division of Industrial Relations.

Church at Work, The. A publication of the Publicity Department of the Presiding Bishop and Council. It began publication in Sept. 1920. It is no longer in existence.

Church Congress. The Church Congress movement was a series of national conferences in which Episcopalians discussed a variety of pressing social and theological concerns. Organized along an English model in 1874, it was also the most visible institutional manifestation of the Episcopal broad church party at the end of the nineteenth century. Phillips Brooks, one of the founders of the Congress, observed that its leaders were all "broad churchmen" desiring to keep their denomination both "liberal and free."

Sponsors of the movement intended to instill tolerance for a diversity of thought in the Episcopal Church and provided a forum for discussion without any vote or official action being taken. In the late nineteenth century, Congress members debated such issues as the church's attitude toward industrialism and ecumenical cooperation. In the period around World War I, the Congress also fostered debate between modernist and fundamentalist positions on the interpretation of the Bible and the meaning of the Christian creeds. However, by the 1920s, participants began to lose confidence in their ability to find consensus within the church. The Congress eventually halted its regular meetings in 1934.

Church Deployment Board. *See* Church Deployment Office.

Church Deployment Office. At a special meeting of the House of Bishops in 1966 at Wheeling, West Virginia, Presiding Bishop John E. Hines appointed a committee to study the matter of clergy deployment, "giving special attention to the placement of clergy in parishes and the authority to remove ineffective clergy." By action of the General Convention meeting in Seattle in 1967, a Joint Commission on the Deployment of the Clergy was appointed by the Presiding Bishop to study deployment matters. This Joint Commission was chaired by the Rt. Rev. John H. Burt, Bishop of Ohio, and is sometimes known as the "Burt Commission." At the Special General Convention of 1969 at South Bend, Indiana, a resolution was adopted which created the Church Deployment Office (CDO). The 1970 General Convention at Houston established the Board for the Deployment of the Clergy. The 1979 General Convention changed the name to the Board for Church Deployment in recognition of the expanded role of lay people in professional ministry. The board is established by canon. Its primary duties are to oversee the CDO and to study deployment needs and trends in the Episcopal Church and other Christian bodies. The CDO office opened in space rented at the Episcopal Church Center on Apr. 1, 1970. It is now part of the Ministry Development Office. *See* CDO Personal Profile.

Church Deployment Office Personal Profile. *See* CDO Personal Profile.

Church Divinity School of the Pacific (CDSP). One of the eleven Episcopal seminaries accredited by the Association of Theological Schools, this school was founded by Bishop William Ford Nichols of California. It opened on Oct. 18, 1893, at San Mateo, California. In Apr., 1930, the school moved to Berkeley, its present location. One of its most significant faculty members was liturgical scholar Massey Hamilton Shepherd, Jr.

Church Eclectic, The. This journal began publication on Mar. 15, 1873, and carried the subtitle "A Magazine of Church Opinion, Religious Literature, and Ecclesiastical Miscellany." The first editor and proprietor was the Rev. William Thomas Gibson (1822–1896). In Apr. 1878 the subtitle was changed to "A Monthly Magazine of Church Literature and Church Work; With Notes and Summaries." The subtitle was changed to "An Anglo-Catholic Magazine of Church Literature with Notes and News Summaries" in Apr. 1892. The editor from 1896 to 1900 was Frederick Cook Morehouse (1868–1932). The Rev. Arthur Lowndes (1858–1917) was the editor from Apr. 1900 until Feb. 1908, when it ceased publication.

Church Historical Society. *See* Historical Society of the Episcopal Church.

Church Hymnal Corporation. *See* Church Publishing Incorporated (CPI).

Church in Japan, The. This journal was published six times a year to create interest among American Episcopalians in the Japan Mission. It first appeared in Dec. 1894, and in 1896 it became a monthly publication. The last issue was Dec. 1900.

Church in Metropolitan Areas, Standing Commission on the. This commission was originally organized as a Joint Commission following the 1973 General Convention. It was renewed by the General Convention of 1976, and created as a Standing Commission by the General Convention of 1979. Its primary purpose was to shape new patterns of ministry for the cities. The 1997 General Convention discontinued this commission and formed the Standing Commission on Domestic Mission and Evangelism. *See* Domestic Mission and Evangelism, Standing Commission on.

Church in Small Communities, Standing Commission on. The General Convention of 1976 established this Standing Commission. It has twelve members: three bishops, three presbyters or deacons, and six lay persons. The commission concerns itself with plans for new directions for churches in small communities.

Church Insurance Agency Company. A general agency of the Church Insurance Company. It was incorporated on Aug. 5, 1930. The Church Agency Company places types of insurance the company does not write with other insurance carriers.

Church Insurance Company, The. Affiliate of the Church Pension Group. It was incorporated on Apr. 16, 1929, and provides broad property and liability insurance at affordable rates for churches and clergy. It provides homeowner's and tenant's insurance for clergy at a reasonable cost. It also provides services to the Episcopal Church that are not within the charter of the Church Pension Fund itself but called for by the canons of the church.

Church Intelligencer, The. This weekly publication was the principal organ of the Protestant Episcopal Church in the Confederate States. It was published at Raleigh, North Carolina, from Mar. 14, 1860 until Apr. 8, 1864. On Sept. 14, 1864, publication was resumed at Charlotte under the direction of the Episcopal Publishing Association. It was published until May 4, 1865.

Church Journal, The. This periodical was published in New York City. It was a vigorous Anglo-catholic publication. It began publication on Feb. 5, 1853. Its leading editor was John Henry Hopkins, Jr. (1820–1891). It merged with the *Gospel Messenger*. With the Nov. 4, 1872, issue it carried the new title, *Church Journal and Gospel Messenger*. It ceased publication on Feb. 14, 1878, and was absorbed by *The Churchman*.

Church League for Industrial Democracy, or Episcopal League for Social Action. This social gospel agency was organized in May, 1919, by clergy and lay persons in New York. Later the name was changed to the Episcopal League for Social Action. Among its leaders were Vida Dutton Scudder and William Benjamin Spofford (1892–1972). Spofford was the executive secretary of the league for many years and an editor of *The Witness*. The league's original statement of principles declared, "only that social order can properly be called Christian which substitutes fraternal cooperation for mastership in industry and life." It worked to make the church aware of social evils and social issues, and to stimulate social action where needed. It is no longer in existence.

Church Life Insurance Corporation, The. Affiliate of the Church Pension Group. It was incorporated on June 24, 1922, and offers life insurance for clergy, lay employees of the church, and their families. The company also provides group life insurance, annuities, individual retirement accounts, and other investment plans for dioceses and church organizations. The Church Life Insurance Corporation administers pension plans for lay employees.

Church Mission to Deaf-Mutes. This group was organized in Oct. 1872, and Thomas Gallaudet was named general manager on Dec. 11, at the first meeting of the trustees. Its work was gradually confined to the dioceses of New York, Long Island, and Newark. Its major work was running the Gallaudet Home for Aged and Infirm Deaf near Poughkeepsie, New York. It was last listed in *The Episcopal Church Annual* in 1966.

Church Mission of Help. It was founded in 1911 by the Rev. James O. S. Huntington, Mr. and Mrs. John M. Glenn, and others. It sought to help adolescents, especially girls, faced with serious difficulties. The mission was committed to restoring broken lives. The 1919 General Convention recognized it as an official agency of the church. It grew into a national federation of Episcopal case work agencies which offered the services of trained and experienced case

workers, the counsel of clergy, and consultation with psychiatrists and other specialists. In 1947 the name was changed to Episcopal Service for Youth. *See* Episcopal Service for Youth, Inc.

Church Missions House. In Oct., 1836, a joint committee was formed to confer on securing a building for the work of the Domestic and Foreign Missionary Society. In 1888 the Rev. William Langford, general secretary of the Missionary Society, argued that the church needed a headquarters so that its missionary activities could be centrally administered. A site was secured in New York City in June, 1889, and the plans were approved by the Board of Missions in Oct. 1889. On Oct. 3, 1892, the cornerstone of the building was laid, and on Jan. 1, 1894, the Missionary Society moved into its new headquarters at 281 Fourth Avenue. The land and building cost $450,000. The Woman's Auxiliary was housed there, and space was rented to the American Church Missionary Society, the American Church Building Fund, the Society for Promoting Christianity Among the Jews, the Church Temperance Society, the Church Periodical Club, and the Brotherhood of St. Andrew. It was called the Church Missions House. It was also known as both the "Church Center" and "281" for its address. Later the Church Center moved to 815 Second Avenue in New York City.

Church Missions Publishing Company, The. This agency makes grants to members of the Anglican Communion to purchase or publish literature, such as Prayer Books, which are helpful in the missionary work of the church. It was founded in Hartford, Connecticut, on June 1, 1894, by Mary and Edith Beach to publish literature on the history of the church. It was modeled on the Society for Promoting Christian Knowledge. From its founding to 1939 it published sixteen books and over 300 pamphlets. The topics covered were biographies of famous church leaders and histories of institutions, particularly those with a missionary theme. Following World War II, publication was limited to historical monographs on the Diocese of Connecticut and the magazine *Pan Anglican*, which ceased publication in 1971. Since 1974, it has operated as a granting agency for missionary publications. It is under the office of the Bishop of Connecticut, who is president of the Board of Managers.

Church Monthly. This journal was published in Boston from Jan. 1861, until 1870. It was founded by Frederic Dan

Huntington and George Maxwell Randall (1810–1873). In 1870 it became the *Church Weekly*, of New York. However, it survived for only another year. *See* Huntington, Frederic Dan.

Church Music, Standing Commission on. Predecessor to the Standing Commission on Liturgy and Music. The 1832 General Convention passed a resolution to prevent "the scandalous performances of Church choirs." The 1874 General Convention made the resolution a canon that required the clergy to regulate the music of the church. The 1919 General Convention established the Joint Commission on Church Music. In 1973 the General Convention established the Standing Commission on Church Music to collaborate with the Standing Liturgical Commission concerning the musical setting of liturgical texts and rubrics, encourage the writing of new music for liturgical use, and collect and collate material bearing upon future revisions of the Hymnal. This commission produced *The Hymnal 1982*. The 1997 General Convention discontinued the Standing Commission on Church Music and consolidated it into a new Standing Commission on Liturgy and Music. *See* Hymnal, The.

Church of the Advent, Boston. It was founded by lay people in 1844 and has long been one of the leading Anglo-catholic parishes in the American Church. Its strong adherence to the principles of the Oxford Movement and the ritualist movement often has put it at odds with other Episcopalians. Innovative practices concerning liturgy and parish governance led to conflict with the Bishop of Massachusetts, Manton Eastburn. He refused to make a visitation to the parish. This refusal precipitated passage of a canon at the 1856 General Convention requiring bishops to visit each parish in their jurisdictions at least once every three years.

Church of the Advocate, Philadelphia. This parish was founded in 1886, and its first service was held on Nov. 28, 1886. Its building is modeled on the Cathedral of Amiens in France. It was constructed between 1890 and 1897. The cornerstone was laid on May 30, 1892, and the church was consecrated on Oct. 11, 1897. Although the church was designed to seat more than a thousand worshipers, the congregation began to decline in the 1950s as many of its white members left the inner city. The parish was revitalized under the leadership of Paul Matthews Washington, an African American priest who served as rector from 1962 until 1989. On July 29, 1974, the church was the site of the first ordination of eleven women deacons to the priesthood. This irregular action preceded the approval of women's ordination by General Convention. Today the Church of the Advocate is one of the premier African American parishes in the Episcopal Church.

Church of the Carpenter, Boston. Organized in 1890 by William Dwight Porter Bliss as an experiment in Christian Socialism, the notice announcing its formation declared that "the Church of Christ, in her true spirit, is a Christian Socialist Church." It attracted many Christian Socialists, including Wellesley professor and staunch churchwoman Vida Dutton Scudder. The church participated in the struggle for economic justice and the elimination of poverty. *See* Scudder, Vida Dutton.

Church of England. Before the sixteenth-century Reformation in western Europe, the Christian church in a given country or region was customarily described as the church of the region, such as the Gallican Church, the Spanish Church, the English Church (Lat. *ecclesia anglicana*), or the Church of England. After the Reformation, the English national church continued to be called the Church of England, but it repudiated the supremacy of the Pope. It retained, however, its ancient episcopal polity. By the 1534 Act of Supremacy, King Henry VIII became "Supreme Head of the Church of England," and by the 1559 Act of Supremacy, Elizabeth I became "Supreme Governor of the Church of England," supplanting the Pope. To this day the Church of England is episcopal in polity, with the sovereign, who still bears the Elizabethan title, as its legal administrative head. The Church of England is divided into the Province of Canterbury and the Province of York. The Archbishop of York is the Primate of England and Metropolitan, and the Archbishop of Canterbury is the Primate of all England and Metropolitan. The Province of Canterbury consists of thirty-one dioceses and the Province of York consists of fourteen dioceses. The Episcopal Church derives much of its doctrine, discipline, and worship from the Church of England.

Church of the Holy Communion, New York. The parish was founded in 1844 by William Augustus Muhlenberg. The cornerstone was laid on July 25, 1844. The church was built with funds from Muhlenberg's sister, Mary Anna C. Rogers, the widow of John Rogers. The church building was designed by Richard Upjohn and consecrated on Dec.

13, 1846. The parish's ministry took the shape of a community-wide program, which was a novel concept for its day. It was the first church in New York to have free pews. It was one of the first to have weekly communion. Its sisterhood of women church workers (1852) opened new fields of church social ministry for women. Muhlenberg served as rector until 1860. A dwindling congregation stayed on until the early 1970s. In 1975 it merged with Calvary Church and St. George's Church, combining into one parish with three congregations under one rector. Soon after the merger the Church of the Holy Communion property was desacralized. *See* Muhlenberg, William Augustus; *see* Holy Communion, Sisterhood of the.

Church Orders. Ancient church documents containing a variety of materials for the instruction and ordering of the church, including liturgical descriptions, models, and directions. Significant Church Orders included the *Didache* (second century), the *Apostolic Tradition* of Hippolytus (215), the *Didascalia Apostolorum* (third century), and the *Apostolic Constitutions* (late fourth century). These Church Orders were formative for the liturgical tradition of the church, including liturgies of the BCP. Church Orders also appeared in Germany during the time of the Reformation, including the Church Order of Johann Brenz and Andreas Osiander for Brandenburg-Nürnberg (1533); the Church Order of Electoral Brandenburg (1540); and the *Consultation* of Archbishop Hermann von Wied of Cologne (1543), which was translated into English in 1547. These German Church Orders also had a significant influence on the BCP. *Hermann's Consultation* may have been the most influential of the German Church Orders for the Anglican liturgical tradition. *See* Apostolic Constitutions; *see* Didache, The; *see* Hermann von Wied of Cologne; *see* Hippolytus.

Church Pension Fund, The. A corporation chartered in 1914 by the legislature of the state of New York. Its incorporators and their successors are broadly authorized, as trustees of the corporation, to establish and administer the clergy pension system of the church, including pensions, insurance, annuities, and other programs. The fund was established by the 1916 General Convention; the fund and its affiliates are official agencies of the church for these purposes and operate under the canons of the church.

The fund began its operations on March 1, 1917. Subsequently affiliates of the fund were formed as its activities expanded. Major affiliates and their years of formation include: Church Publishing Incorporated, 1918; Church Life Insurance Corporation, 1922; The Church Insurance Company, 1929; Church Insurance Agency Corporation, 1930; and The Medical Trust, 1978. All operations of the Church Pension Fund and Affiliates informally known as the Church Pension Group, are governed by the fund's board of trustees or by a subsidiary board including fund trustees.

The Clergy Pension Plan is a defined-benefit pension plan, the assets of which are pooled for the benefit of all participants.

Church Pension Group. *See* Church Pension Fund, The.

Church Periodical Club (CPC). It began in 1888, when missionaries asked for reading material to help convert Sioux Indians and western settlers. It started out as a club at the Church of the Holy Communion in New York City. Mary Ann Drake Fargo (d. 1892) and a small group of women began sending bundles of church periodicals, prayer books, and Bibles via the Wells Fargo Stage Coach Line to missionaries in the Dakotas. The stage coaches belonged to Mrs. Fargo's husband. In 1892, with forty-eight dioceses participating, CPC incorporated. The CPC now helps seminarians buy books, provides parochial reading matter, and distributes vital information about health and farming worldwide. It is the only Episcopal organization dedicated solely to providing religious and secular literature, tapes, and videos to those who could not normally afford them. CPC has two granting funds. The National Books Fund distributes printed materials to individuals, churches, and organizations affiliated with the Anglican Communion. The Miles of Pennies fund provides materials to children only, pre-school to grade 12.

Church Publishing Incorporated (CPI). The trustees of the Church Pension Fund established the Church Hymnal Corporation in 1918, and it became Church Publishing Incorporated in 1997. In addition to Prayer Books, hymnals, and other titles mandated by the General Convention through the Standing Commission on Liturgy and Music, CPI now publishes works on liturgy, music, homiletics, church history, theology, Anglican spirituality, contemporary global Anglicanism, significant emerging issues, liturgical and music software, recorded music, and electronic ecclesiastical data.

Church Record, The. *See* Episcopal Recorder, The.

Church Review, The. *See* Church Review and Ecclesiastical Register, The.

Church Review and Ecclesiastical Register, The. This periodical was published under five different titles. It was at various times quarterly, monthly, and bimonthly. From Apr. 1848 until Apr. 1858, and from Apr. until Oct. 1889, it was called *The Church Review and Ecclesiastical Register*. From July 1858 until Jan. 1870, it was *The American Quarterly Church Review and Ecclesiastical Register*. It was called *The American Quarterly Church Review* from Apr. 1870 until Oct. 1871; *The American Church Review* from Jan. 1872 until Apr. 1885; and finally *The Church Review* from July 1885 until Jan. 1889, and from Jan. 1890 until Oct. 1891. Its founder and first editor was Nathaniel Smith Richardson. He edited it from 1848 until 1868. Other editors were John McDowell Leavitt, 1868–1871, M. H. Mallory, 1872–1874, Edward B. Boggs, 1875–1880, and Henry Mason Baum, 1881–1891. It was one of the Episcopal Church's major publications in the nineteenth century. Later issues carried the statement, "Questions Are Discussed Falling Within The Province Of Religion, Ethics, Art and Literature."

Church of St. Mary the Virgin, New York City. Ritualistic parish. This parish was founded in 1868 by the Rev. Thomas McKee Brown to be a free church in the full tradition of catholic faith and worship. The original building, erected on West 45th Street on property given by John Jacob Astor, was dedicated on Dec. 8, 1870. The growth of the parish led to the building of the present church near Times Square on Broadway. The new church, one of the finest examples of thirteenth-century French Gothic in America, was dedicated on its patronal festival in 1895 by Bishop Grafton of Fond du Lac. From its foundation the parish enjoyed great celebrity for its ritual. It has been called "Smoky Mary's" because incense is used abundantly at certain services. The mission house of the parish has maintained a vital ministry to the surrounding urban community.

Church of the Transfiguration, New York. A pioneer Anglo-catholic parish of the Episcopal Church. It was organized in 1849. The founder and first rector was the Rev. George H. Houghton. Confessions were heard there, and it had altar candles and a processional cross, which were rare and controversial for the time. This parish claims to have had the first vested choir in America. The Transfiguration was considered a peculiar place by some people. In 1870 a neighboring rector directed an actor to see the rector of "the little church around the corner" about burial arrangements for another actor since, "they do that sort of thing there." Since then the Transfiguration has been known as "The Little Church around the Corner." It was an important station of the underground railway and a refuge for African Americans during the Civil War. In 1863 Houghton brandished a cross to repel white lynch-mobs who were angry over the parish's abolitionist stance. A parishioner who was conspicuous for her involvement in this movement was the mother of President Theodore Roosevelt. The parish is the headquarters of the Episcopal Actors' Guild. It also has the oldest boys' choir in New York City, dating from 1881.

Church Scholarship Society. It was founded in 1827 and incorporated in 1874. In 1831 the board of directors issued an "Appeal" to the church for funds. It stated that the purpose of the society was "to render just so much assistance as will serve to prevent discouragement at the same time that it leaves the motives to personal exertion in full exercise." The current purpose of the society is to lend money to candidates who are studying for holy orders. Loans may be made to a person who is studying for the ordained ministry under the direction of the Bishop of Connecticut and to persons who are attending a graduate school in Connecticut under the direction of a bishop outside the Diocese of Connecticut.

Church Scholiast. With the Oct. 1885 issue, the *Nashotah Scholiast* was changed to the *Church Scholiast*. The *Church Scholiast* was published by the Bishop Welles Brotherhood at Nashotah House until Sept. 1888.

Church Socialist League. It was founded in 1911 to promote socialist ideals. It was founded by Bernard Iddings Bell, Vida Dutton Scudder, Bishop Franklin Spencer Spalding of Utah, and Missionary Bishop Benjamin

Brewster (1860–1941) of Western Colorado. In 1913 it began publishing the quarterly, *The Social Preparation for the Kingdom of God*. It disbanded in 1924.

Church Society for Promoting Christianity Among the Jews (CSPCJ). It was organized in Jan. 1878. The Bishop of New York was president of the board of directors and the Presiding Bishop was the patron. Its primary effort to reach the Jews was the establishment of schools. At one time the CSPCJ had missions in sixteen cities across the United States. It went out of existence in 1904.

Church Standard, The. The weekly *Standard of the Cross* merged with *The Church* in 1892 to become *The Church Standard*. It was a weekly periodical published in Philadelphia. The first issue was published on May 14, 1892, and in July 1908, it was absorbed by *The Churchman*.

Church Temperance Society of the Protestant Episcopal Church. This society was organized in New York City on Mar. 14, 1881, by a group of clergy and laity. The first "mission" was organized and conducted by R. Graham, special organizing secretary and one of the general secretaries of the Church of England Temperance Society, at St. Augustine's Chapel, New York, on Dec. 5, 1881. *The Manual of the Church Temperance Society of the Protestant Episcopal Church* was first published in May, 1881. It included a list of officers, the organization's constitution, rules and regulations pertaining to the operation of diocesan and parochial societies, sample forms of pledges, and prayers for private and public use as well as prayers of intercession. The constitution stated "that Temperance is the Law of the Gospel, and imperatively demanded by the Baptismal Vow." Total abstinence was seen as a rule of expediency in certain cases. The objects of the society were the promotion of temperance, the removal of the causes which lead to intemperance, and the reformation of the intemperate. The Presiding Bishop was the *ex officio* president. The founding president was Bishop Benjamin Bosworth Smith. He was Bishop of Kentucky and Presiding Bishop. Thirty-two bishops were listed as charter vice-presidents. Membership was open to anyone willing to sign the pledge of the society and pay $2 per year. A member was never permitted to drink in "public houses or bar-rooms," nor was "solitary drinking" permitted. The society is no longer in existence.

Church Training and Deaconess House of the Diocese of Pennsylvania. The second training school for deaconesses in the Episcopal Church. It opened in Jan., 1891, in Philadelphia. It had a two-year course of study for women desiring to be deaconesses. In 1939 the school became the Department of Women of the Divinity School in Philadelphia. As the Department of Women, it trained women as deaconesses, directors of religious education, missionaries, and parish workers. It offered a two-year program leading to a certificate and a three-year program leading to a Th.B. degree. The Department of Women went out of existence in 1950.

Church University Board of Regents. An agency established by the 1889 General Convention. Its purpose was to promote the general welfare of the church's schools, colleges, and institutions of higher learning, and to award scholarships. It accomplished little, and was dissolved by the General Convention on Oct. 11, 1898.

Church Weekly. In 1870 the *Church Monthly* of Boston became the *Church Weekly* of New York. It survived for only about one year.

Church Work. This journal was founded and edited by Mary Abbot Emery Twing to promote communication among women church workers. Its sub-title was "A Monthly Magazine for Church Workers," and it was published from Nov. 1885 until Oct. 1889. Twing used the journal to promote the deaconess movement. The General Convention passed a Canon on Deaconesses in 1889. This action had been urged by Twing in *Church Work*.

Church Year. The liturgical year has two significant parts: 1) the week, based on the seven days of creation, with the Lord's Day or Sunday as both the first and the eighth days, the beginning and completion of God's work; 2) the cycles of Easter and Christmas, resurrection and incarnation. The resurrection cycle includes Lent through the fifty days of Easter, the incarnation cycle includes Advent through the Epiphany. The rest of the year is commonly known as "ordinary time," from the Latin *tempus ordinarii*, "numbered time," our countdown until the Lord comes again. Saints' days and other occasional feasts are scattered throughout the year. As Thomas J. Talley has shown in *The Origins of the Liturgical Year* (1986), church seasons originated and developed in many ways in many places. The two cycles, he argues, have a common origin in the primitive observance of Pascha. Early Christians believed that the death of Christ on 14 Nisan (estimated as Mar. 25 that year on the Julian calendar) occurred on the same date as his conception in the womb of Mary. The day of his coming and passion will also be the day of his coming again. Thus Pascha, origin and hinge of the church year, celebrates the entire mystery of Christ.

Churching of Women. A liturgy for the purification or "churching" of women after childbirth, together with the presentation in church of the child. The rite is based on scriptural sources, especially the ritual purification of Mary and Presentation of Christ in Lk 2: 22–38. Following the title in the Sarum use, Cranmer called the 1549 rite "The Order of the Purification of Women." In 1552 and later it became "The Thanksgiving of Women after Childbirth," commonly called the "Churching of Women." The 1979 BCP, avoiding any hint of ritual impurity, replaces the older rite with "A Thanksgiving for the Birth or Adoption of a Child." The rite is to take place within the Sunday liturgy, after the intercessions, soon after the birth or adoption. In this service, parents and other family members come to the church with the newly born or adopted child "to be welcomed by the congregation and to give thanks to Almighty God" (BCP, p. 439). *See* Thanksgiving for the Birth or Adoption of a Child.

Churchman, Churchmanship. Before the sixteenth-century Reformation, when there was only one Christian church in England, the word "churchman" designated an ecclesiastic or clergyman. After the establishment of religious toleration in England by the Act of Toleration in 1689, it came to designate any person, whether cleric or lay, who is a member of the established church—the Church of England in England or the (Presbyterian) Church of Scotland in Scotland. A churchman is the opposite of a dissenter. In imitation of English usage, Episcopalians in the United States and members of other Anglican churches sometimes refer to themselves as churchmen. With the development of parties in the Church of England, the manner of thought and especially the style of worship of a churchman was called churchmanship. Varieties of churchmanship include broad church, low church, and high church. In an increasingly secular society, the word "churchman" is occasionally used to denote one who attends any church as opposed to a non-churchgoer.

Churchman, The. This weekly journal began publication on Mar. 26, 1831. It carried the slogan, "The Church of the Living God, the Pillar and Ground of the Truth." In Nov. 1833, it absorbed the *Episcopal Watchman.* It suspended publication with the May 2, 1861 issue because of the Civil War, and then resumed publication in 1867. It absorbed several other church-related publications including the *American Churchman* (1871), the *Church Journal* (1878), the *Guardian* (1883), the *Church Magazine* (1887), the *Church Press* (1888), the *Church Year* (1891), and the *Church Standard* (1908). In Mar. 1933 it moved from a weekly to a semi-monthly publication. Its name was changed to *The Churchman's Human Quest* with the Dec.–Jan. 1986 issue. It became *The Human Quest* with the Jan.–Feb. 1990 issue, but returned to the title *The Churchman's Human Quest* with the Sept.–Oct. 1995 issue. It described itself as "An independent journal of religious humanism."

Churchman's Human Quest, The. *See* Churchman, The.

Churchman's Magazine, The. The first regular periodical in the Episcopal Church. It began publication in Jan. 1804, at New Haven, Connecticut. Its full title was *The Churchman's Monthly Magazine, or Treasury of Divine and Useful Knowledge.* In Apr. 1808 it began to be published in New York. John Henry Hobart served as Editor until 1811. It was not published in 1812, but it began publication again with the Jan.–Feb. 1813 issue. It ceased publication in 1815. It was published again from 1821 until 1827, with the exception of 1824. It was succeeded by the *Episcopal Watchman.*

Churchman's Monthly Magazine, The. This journal described itself as a repository of religious, literary, and entertaining knowledge for the Christian family. It was published in New York from Jan. 1854, until Dec. 1861.

Church's Teaching Series, The. The Church's Teaching Series is a series of volumes written to provide adults with the basic content teaching of the Episcopal Church. The first series was done by an author's committee under the chairmanship of John Heuss, the director of the Department of Christian Education of the National Council. The first series had six volumes: Robert C. Denton, *The Holy Scripture* (1949); Powel Mills Dawley, *Chapters in Church History* (1951); James A. Pike and W. Norman Pittenger, *The Faith of the Church* (1951); Massey H.

Shepherd, Jr., *The Worship of the Church* (1952); Powel Mills Dawley, *The Episcopal Church and Its Work* (1955); and Stephen F. Bayne, Jr., *Christian Living* (1957). A new Church's Teaching Series was published in 1979 with Alan Jones as chair of the committee. This new official series had seven volumes: Urban T. Holmes, III, and John H. Westerhoff, III, *Christian Believing* (1979); Robert A. Bennett and O. C. Edwards, *The Bible for Today's Church* (1979); John E, Booty, *The Church in History* (1979); Richard A. Norris, *Understanding the Faith of the Church* (1979); Charles P. Price and Louis Weil, *Liturgy for Living* (1979); Earl H. Brill, *The Christian Moral Vision* (1979); and Rachel Hosmer and Alan Jones, *Living in the Spirit* (1979). Gary T. Evans and Richard E. Hayes, *Equipping God's People: Basic Concepts for Adult Education* (1979) is a guide to the use of the series.

Ciborium. l) A container or box with a lid for eucharistic wafer bread. It is usually of silver or another precious metal. The ciborium, which may resemble a chalice or cup, has been used instead of the plate-like paten for the administration of the consecrated bread at the eucharist. Unfortunately, the chalice-like ciborium was lacking in symbolic relation to the bread, and the character of the eucharist as meal was obscured. The ciborium is now more typically used as a container for bread wafers that will be consecrated at the eucharist. It may be one of the vessels placed on the credence table for use in the service. A ciborium may be used when the people's offerings of bread and wine are presented and placed on the altar prior to the Great Thanksgiving. A ciborium may also be used as a container for consecrated bread and placed in the tabernacle for the reservation of the Blessed Sacrament. 2) A ciborium is also a canopy of stone, wood, metal, or fabric that is suspended over the altar. This canopy, also known as a *baldachino*, rests on four pillars or columns. *See* Baldachino (Baldaquin).

Cincinnati Summer School. Founded in 1923, the school was a joint project of the Department of Social Service of the National Council of the Episcopal Church and the Social Service Department of the Diocese of Southern Ohio. It was called the Cincinnati Summer School in Social Work and sometimes the Cincinnati Summer School in Social Service. Its work was to give a select group of candidates for ordination and junior clergy a first-hand knowledge of social case work and the methods of social agencies through clinical experience under supervision. It was designed to increase the effectiveness of the clergy's pastoral care. Joseph Fletcher served for a time as the school's co-director. In 1944 the Cincinnati Summer School merged with the Episcopal Theological School in Cambridge, Massachusetts.

Cincture. A cord or sash that serves as a belt for an alb or cassock. Also called a girdle.

Circumcision, Feast of the. *See* Holy Name of Our Lord Jesus Christ, The.

Claggett, Thomas John (Oct. 2, 1743–Aug. 2, 1816). The first Bishop of Maryland and the first Episcopal bishop consecrated on American soil. He was born in Prince George's County, Maryland, and graduated from the College of New Jersey (now Princeton University) in 1762. He pursued theological studies under the tutelage of his uncle, a priest. He was ordained deacon on Sept. 20, 1767, and priest on Oct. 11, 1767, by the Bishop of London. Claggett served at All Saints' Church, Calvert County, Maryland, until the beginning of the American Revolution. Although the war caused a two-year hiatus, he returned to ministerial duties at St. Paul's Church, Prince George's County, in 1779. He was consecrated at Trinity Church, New York City, on Sept. 17, 1792, by Samuel Provoost, Samuel Seabury, William White, and James Madison. Since Provoost, White, and Madison were consecrated in England, while Seabury was consecrated in Scotland, Claggett's consecration united both the English and Scottish episcopal lines of succession in the Episcopal Church. During his episcopate, Claggett also served as chaplain of the United States Senate and, later, as rector of Trinity Church, Upper Marlborough. He died in Croom, Maryland.

Clare (July 16, 1194–Aug. 11, 1253). She was born in Assisi, Italy. Clare came under the influence of St. Francis. On Mar. 18, 1212, she took the three monastic vows of poverty, chastity, and obedience, and went to reside in the Benedictine convent of St. Paul in Assisi. Soon she was joined by her sister Agnes, and Francis made a cloister for them near the Church of St. Damian. This was the beginning of the order of Poor Clares, and Clare became the abbess in 1215. The rule of the order was one of extreme poverty and austerity. She was canonized by Pope Alexander IV in 1255. There is an order of the Poor Clares of Reparation in the Episcopal Church. Clare died in Assisi.

She is commemorated in the Episcopal calendar of the church year on Aug. 11.

Clark, Lois Carter (1910–Nov. 19, 1985). Leading Native American churchwoman. She was born in Council Hill, Oklahoma. Clark was a member of the Creek Nation and a longtime English teacher. She was a leader at every level of the church from her parish, St. John's Church, Brookline, Oklahoma, to the diocesan Episcopal Church Women, the National Committee for Native Americans, Church Women United in Oklahoma, and the Presiding Bishop's Committee for World Relief. She was active in the founding of the Council for Women's Ministries. One of her major accomplishments was her involvement in the inclusion of Deacon David Oakerhater in the Episcopal calendar of the church year. Oakerhater, a Cheyenne deacon, was added to the calendar at the 1985 General Convention. Clark wrote *David Pendleton Oakerhater: God's Warrior* (1985). She died in Oklahoma City, Oklahoma.

Clark, Thomas March (July 4, 1812–Sept. 7, 1903). Twelfth Presiding Bishop. He was born in Newburyport, Massachusetts. He graduated from Yale College in 1831 and worked for two years as a teacher. Clark was raised a Presbyterian. He studied at Princeton Theological Seminary and was licensed as a preacher after his graduation in 1835. He soon applied for ordination in the Episcopal Church. Clark was ordained deacon on Feb. 3, 1836, and priest on Nov. 6, 1836. He served parishes in Boston, Philadelphia, and Hartford, Connecticut, prior to his election as the fifth Bishop of Rhode Island. He was consecrated in Grace Church, Providence, on Dec. 6, 1854. Clark was rector of Grace Church between 1854 and 1866, but then resigned to devote himself full-time to episcopal duties. He served as Presiding Bishop from Feb. 7, 1899, until his death. Clark was an active supporter of the Union cause during the Civil War, and he was committed to the theological and social liberalism of the broad church party. He died in Newport, Rhode Island.

Clarkson College, Omaha, Nebraska. The Bishop Clarkson School of Nursing was founded in 1888 in memory of Bishop Robert Harper Clarkson (1826–1884), the first Bishop of Nebraska. In 1981 it became the Bishop Clarkson College of Nursing and became a degree-granting institution. In 1993 it became a comprehensive, four-year college offering the bachelor's degree. It is a member of the Association of Episcopal Colleges.

Clebsch, William Anthony (July 27, 1923–June 12, 1984). Church historian. He was born in Clarksville, Tennessee. Clebsch received his B.A. from the University of Tennessee in 1946 and his B.D. in the same year from the Virginia Theological Seminary. He was ordained deacon on July 26, 1946, and priest on Sept. 28, 1947. From 1946 until 1949, Clebsch was Episcopal chaplain and lecturer in religion at Michigan State University. From 1949 until 1956, he was instructor and then assistant professor of church history at the Virginia Theological Seminary. He received his Th.D. from Union Theological Seminary, New York, in 1957, and then studied at Clare College, Cambridge University. From 1956 until 1964, Clebsch taught church history at the Episcopal Theological Seminary of the Southwest. From 1964 until 1984, he taught religion and humanities at Sanford University. In 1980 Clebsch was named the George Edwin Burnell Professor of Religious Studies at Sanford. Among his many publications are: with C. R. Jaekle, *Pastoral Care in Historical Perspective* (1964); Clebsch also wrote *England's Earliest Protestants, 1520–1535* (1964), *From Sacred to Profane America: The Role of Religion in American History* (1968), *Christian Interpretations of the Civil War* (1969), *American Religious Thought: A History* (1973), and *Christianity in European History* (1979). Clebsch was involved in numerous academic organizations and projects. He renounced the ordained ministry of the Episcopal Church and was deposed on Jan. 7, 1969. Clebsch died in Sanford, California.

Clement of Alexandria (c. 150–215). Early church theologian. Titus Flavius Clemens was probably born in Athens. In 190 he succeeded his teacher, Pantaenus, as the head of the Catechetical School in Alexandria. In 202 he fled to Jerusalem because of the persecution of Emperor Severus. He was welcomed to Jerusalem by Bishop Alexander, a former student. Clement remained in Jerusalem until his death. The primary contribution of his writings was to combine Greek philosophy with the Christian faith, harmonizing faith and reason. Clement was one of the earliest Christian scholars, and a leading opponent of gnosticism. *The Hymnal 1982* includes two of his hymn texts, "Sunset to sunrise changes now" (Hymn 163) and "Jesus, our mighty Lord" (Hymn 478). His feast day was celebrated on Dec. 4 in some early martyrologies. Pope Sixtus V removed it in 1586 because he questioned the orthodoxy of some of Clement's writings. Clement is commemorated in the Episcopal calendar of the church year on Dec. 5.

Clement of Rome (d. c. 101). Usually considered the fourth Bishop of Rome, after Peter, Linus, and Anacletus, he is noted for his "The Letter of the Church of Rome to the Church of Corinth, Commonly Called Clement's First Letter." It was written around 96. The letter urges the Corinthian Church to restore the duly chosen leaders to their offices. He claims that the apostles had appointed the bishops and deacons. Neither they nor their successors were to be deprived of their offices. This is the seed of the theology of apostolic succession. However, Clement does not mention the single episcopate. A later writing, "An Anonymous Sermon, Commonly Called Clement's Second Letter," was not written by him. His "Letter" to the Corinthian Church was treated by some as scripture as late as 170. He is commemorated in the Episcopal calendar of the church year on Nov. 23.

Clerestory, or clearstory. The upper part of a church building with windows for interior lighting. It rises above and "clears" the rest of the building.

Clergy, Members of the. Persons in holy orders, ordained for the ministry of bishop, priest, or deacon. The Episcopal Church canons concerning ordination for these ministries are equally applicable to men and women.

Clergy as Recorded on Special List by the Secretary of the House of Bishops. The list of clergy whose whereabouts are unknown. Prior to 1934, the list was kept by the Presiding Bishop. The General Convention of 1934 changed the canon so that whenever a member of the clergy of the Episcopal Church shall have been absent from the diocese or missionary district for a period of more than two years and has failed to make the annual report so that his or her whereabouts are unknown, the bishop may send his or her name to the secretary of the House of Bishops. The list was first published in *The Living Church Annual 1936*. It was later published in *The Episcopal Church Annual*.

Cleric. A member of the clergy.

Clerical. Of or concerning the clergy. For example, a clerical collar is a collar worn by a member of the clergy.

Clericalism. A pejorative term that indicates a condescending attitude by one or more members of the clergy, an exaggerated deference to the clergy, or an inappropriate concentration of power in the clergy. It also can indicate inappropriate influence of the clergy in secular matters.

Clericals. Distinctive clothes worn by clergy that make the wearer identifiable as a member of the clergy. For example, a black shirt with a white clerical collar identifies the wearer as a member of the clergy. Clericals are clothes that may be worn in secular contexts, unlike vestments.

Clerical Union for the Maintenance and Defense of Catholic Principles. *See* Catholic Clerical Union.

Clericus. A meeting of clergy. It is often a meeting of clergy in a locality or deanery.

Clerk (Singer). A church official who makes the people's responses in liturgy. The term is from the Latin *clericus*, "cleric." Clerks were originally ordained, but they are now usually lay people. The clerk sometimes reads the epistle, and helps in the general care of the church. The office has existed since the time of Augustine of Canterbury. It has lost most of its original purpose in places where the people take an active part in liturgy.

Clerk (Vestry). The clerk or secretary of the parish vestry records minutes of the vestry meetings. These minutes are approved by the vestry and kept in the permanent records of the parish. The clerk may or may not be a member of the vestry. The parish by-laws typically include provisions concerning selection and duties of the clerk. The Episcopal Church canons require the clerk's attestation for the rector and vestry's certificates of a candidate's fitness for ordination.

Cloister. 1) Covered walk attached to a monastery, church, or collegiate building. 2) The term may indicate a monastery or convent, or refer generally to the religious life. 3) It may also indicate an enclosed area or "close" in connection with monastic, church, or collegiate buildings. *See* Close.

Close. An enclosed space in connection with monastic, church, or collegiate buildings. The enclosed space may be surrounded by a cloister, or covered walk. A close may also indicate an area of land around a cathedral or church. *See* Cloister.

"Clothing Day." Christians who feel called to the religious life under vows normally pass through a period of testing known as the novitiate. In traditional orders where habits are worn by the members, the novice receives the habit as part of the ceremony. The new novice is said to be "clothed" on this day. In many traditional religious orders, "clothing day" refers to this day of commitment and clothing in the habit. After the novitiate, there is typically a period in which the vows of poverty, chastity, and obedience are taken on a temporary or annual basis, followed by a time when final or life vows may be made. Depending on the rules and customs of the community, distinctive clothing may be given to one who enters the novitiate or to one making temporary or final vows. Any of these days of commitment, accompanied by the presentation of distinctive clothing and other symbols of special vocation, could be referred to as one's "clothing day." The *BOS* includes a form for Setting Apart for a Special Vocation. Many religious communities have their own forms for admitting members.

Coalition 14. A coalition of aided dioceses, established in 1970–71, to receive block grants from the Episcopal Church. The coalition originally consisted of fourteen aided dioceses, hence "Coalition 14." The members agreed to pay full apportionment to the National Church and make full disclosure of financial matters to each other. The coalition consisted of up to sixteen members in the 1980s. At first, a diocese left the coalition as it became financially self-supporting. However, other dioceses elected to stay with the coalition after becoming self-supporting because of program and insurance benefits. Aided dioceses with major Indian work began to receive funding from the Episcopal Council of Indian Ministries in the late 1980s.

Coalition for the Apostolic Ministry. Late in 1972 the Committee for the Apostolic Ministry was organized by the Rev. John L. Scott, Jr., of Norwalk, Connecticut. It later changed its name to the Coalition for the Apostolic Ministry. The Coalition insisted that the scriptures and the Christian tradition reveal only a male priesthood and episcopate. It gradually dissolved after the General Convention of 1976 voted to ordain women to these orders of ministry.

Cobbs, Nicholas Hamner (Feb. 5, 1796–Jan. 11, 1861). Bishop and evangelist. He was born in Bedford County, Virginia. He was raised a Presbyterian and educated privately. He was subsequently confirmed an Episcopalian and ordained a deacon on the same day, May 23, 1824. Cobbs was ordained to the priesthood on May 23, 1825. He served for several years as a schoolteacher and missionary in southwestern Virginia. He later held positions as the Episcopal chaplain at the University of Virginia (1837–1839); as rector of St. Paul's Church, Petersburg, Virginia (1839–1843); and as rector of St. Paul's Church, Cincinnati, Ohio (1843–1844). He was consecrated Bishop of Alabama on Oct. 20, 1844. Cobbs was a determined evangelist who helped to guide the new Diocese of Alabama into a period of tremendous growth in the mid-nineteenth century. He died in Montgomery on the day of his state's secession from the Union on the eve of the Civil War.

Coffin, Margaret (Apr. 16, 1769–Nov. 21, 1855). First person confirmed in Massachusetts. She was born in Boston and confirmed in 1786 at Christ Church, better known as Old North Church by Bishop Samuel Seabury. She loved the Prayer Book, which she called "the second greatest book in the world," and distributed three thousand of them during the last years of her life. This work was made permanent by provision in her will, and the Margaret Coffin Prayer Book Society held its first meeting on July 19, 1856. The society continues to provide Prayer Books and hymnals to missions and institutions.

Coit, Henry Augustus (Jan. 20, 1830–Feb. 5, 1895). First rector of St. Paul's School, Concord, New Hampshire. He was born in Wilmington, Delaware. At the age of fifteen he entered St. Paul's College, College Point, Flushing, New York, where he studied under William Augustus Muhlenberg. In 1847 he entered the University of Pennsylvania but had to withdraw because of poor health. Coit then served as tutor to the family of Bishop Stephen Elliott of Georgia. After this, he taught at St. James College, Hagerstown, Maryland, and then at a parish school in Lancaster, Pennsylvania. Coit was ordained deacon on Jan. 22, 1854, and priest on Dec. 3, 1854. He was the rector of St. Paul's School from 1856 until his death. He instituted many of Muhlenberg's educational ideas at St. Paul's. Coit died in Concord.

Coit, Thomas Winthrop (June 28, 1803–June 21, 1885). Biblical scholar, liturgics scholar, student of church history, and educator. He was born in New London, Connecticut. Coit graduated from Yale College in 1821. He studied at Andover Theological Seminary, 1823–1824, and Princeton Theological Seminary, 1824–1825. His studies led him away from the Congregational Church and into the Episcopal Church. He was ordained deacon on June 7, 1826, and priest on Nov. 15, 1827. Coit was rector of St. Peter's Church, Salem, Massachusetts, until 1829, and rector of Christ Church, Cambridge, until 1835. From 1835 until 1837, he was president of Transylvania University, Lexington, Kentucky, and from 1839 until 1854, he was professor of church history at Trinity College, Hartford, Connecticut. He was rector of St. Paul's Church, Troy, New York, 1854–1872, and professor of church history at the Berkeley Divinity School, Middletown, Connecticut, from 1872 until his death. Coit was a biblical scholar and a liturgics scholar, as well as a student of church history. He left his library of 14,000 volumes to the Berkeley Divinity School. Coit died in Middletown, Connecticut.

Cole, Azel Dow (Dec. 1, 1818–Oct. 15, 1885). Second dean of Nashotah House. He was born in Sterling, Connecticut. Cole received his B.A. from Brown University in 1838, and graduated from the General Theological Seminary in 1841. At General he was a classmate of the future founders of Nashotah House. Cole was ordained deacon on July 22, 1841, and priest in 1842. Cole began his ministry at St. James Church, Woodsocket, Rhode Island. In 1845 he became rector of St. Luke's Church, Kalamazoo, Michigan, and moved in 1849 to St. Luke's Church, Racine, Wisconsin. From Sept. 1, 1850, until his death he was dean of Nashotah House. He deserves great credit for the lasting foundation of Nashotah as a center for education and missionary training in the catholic tradition. While at Nashotah he served as Peter Hubbell Professor of Pastoral Theology. Cole died at Nashotah.

Coleman, Leighton (May 3, 1837–Dec. 14, 1907). Bishop and church historian. He was born in Philadelphia. Coleman was ordained deacon on July 1, 1860. He graduated from the General Theological Seminary in 1861. From 1860 until 1862, he was a missionary at Randall's and Blackwell's Islands, New York. On May 15, 1862, Coleman was ordained priest. From 1862 until 1863, he was rector of St. Luke's Church, Bustleton, Pennsylvania. He was rector of St. John's Church, Wilmington, Delaware, 1863–1866; St.

Mark's Church, Mauch Chunk, Pennsylvania, 1866–1874; and Trinity Church, Toledo, Ohio, 1874–1879. Coleman lived and worked in England from 1879 until 1887, and then was rector of the Church of the Redeemer, Sayre, Pennsylvania, 1887–1888. He was consecrated the second Bishop of Delaware on Oct. 18, 1888, and served in that position until his death. He wrote several books, of which the most significant was *The Church in America* (1895). It was issued in a second edition in 1906 with the title, *A History of the American Church to the Close of the Nineteenth Century.* He died in Wilmington, Delaware.

Collect. A short liturgical prayer, variable according to the day, the season of the church year, and the occasion. It is typically a single sentence. Collects appear in all the BCP services, and may "collect" and draw together the themes appropriate to the day. Collects have a consistent form, including an invocation to God, a petition, and a conclusion. The invocation, or preamble, may mention divine attributes or acts that are grounds for the petition. For example, the collect for the Second Sunday of Advent begins with the invocation, "Merciful God, who sent your messengers the prophets to preach repentance and prepare the way for our salvation. . . ." (BCP, p. 211). The petition may be modified by a result or consequence clause that states the intended outcome of the petition. For example, the collect for the Fifth Sunday of Easter includes the petition with consequence clause, "Grant us so perfectly to know your Son Jesus Christ to be the way, the truth, and the life, that we may steadfastly follow his steps in the way that leads to eternal life. . . ." (BCP, p. 225). The conclusion typically gives glory to God, and is in the formula of a doxology. The collect of the day precedes the lessons at baptism and the eucharist. A collect typically concludes the prayers of the people at the eucharist. The Daily Offices conclude with one or more collects. The BCP provides contemporary and traditional language collects for all Sundays of the church year and holy days, as well as common collects for categories of saints (e.g., "Of a Martyr," "Of a Missionary"), and collects for various occasions and observances (e.g., "For all Baptized Christians," "For a Church Convention").

Collect for Purity, The. Collect following the opening acclamation at the eucharist that asks God to "Cleanse the thoughts of our hearts by the inspiration of your Holy Spirit, that we may perfectly love you, and worthily magnify your holy Name. . . ." (BCP, pp. 355, 323). This collect is required in Rite 1, but optional in Rite 2. Its omission is especially appropriate during festal seasons, when it may seem to interrupt the movement of the liturgy from the opening acclamation to the song of praise.

Collect of the Day, The. Collect appointed for use on the day of the service. The collect of the day precedes the lessons at baptism and the eucharist and may be used as one of the collects that follow the suffrages in the Daily Office. The collect of the day is drawn from the collects appointed by the BCP for use on the Sundays, holy days, and other occasions of the church year (pp. 159–261).

Collect Tones. The *Altar Book* of the Episcopal Church gives two tones, derived from Gregorian chant, for singing the collect of the day and similar presidential prayers. Tone I is a modern adaptation of an ancient melody, related to the tone sung at the *Sursum corda* and eucharistic prayer. Tone II is more recent in origin. When the prayers of the people are sung, either tone may be used for the concluding collect. The intercessory collects of Good Friday are set to Tone I. The original Gregorian versions of the two chants are found in *The Choral Service* (1927), a guide to singing liturgies in the 1928 BCP, and in the *Missale Romanum* of Paul VI. Since the use of ministerial music in the *Altar Book* is not required, presiders may use other chants, ancient or modern, or sing prayers to a monotone.

College of Philadelphia. In 1740 a charity school was founded in Philadelphia by George Whitefield. Trustees for an academy were named on Nov. 13, 1749. In Dec., 1749, the trustees of the academy bought the Charity School building. Classes began on Sept. 16, 1751. On July 16, 1755, a new charter was granted and the school was named "The Trustees of the College, Academy, and Charitable School of Philadelphia." The Rev. William Smith was named provost of the school in 1755. The first commencement was held on May 17, 1757. On Nov. 27, 1779, the legislature voided the charter of the college and created the Trustees of the University of the State of Pennsylvania. Smith resigned as provost. Thus there were two institutions. On Sept. 30, 1791, an act of the state legislature united the University of the State of Pennsylvania and the College of Philadelphia as the University of Pennsylvania. Although this school was not exclusively a church institution, the Anglican influence dominated until the Revolution. Episcopal leaders included two presidents of the board of trustees and five provosts.

College of Preachers. In the summer of 1925, retired Bishop Philip Mercer Rhinelander (1869–1939) of Pennsylvania convened a "School of the Prophets" at the Washington Cathedral. In 1927 Alexander Smith Cochran made a gift for the construction of a College of Preachers and promised to endow the program. In 1929 Cochran's bequest of $1,000,000 endowed the College of Preachers. The College, on the grounds of the Cathedral Church of St. Peter and St. Paul, Washington, was dedicated on Nov. 14, 1929. In 1931 the first College of Preachers Fellows were selected. It was originally conceived as a center for the renewal of preaching for Episcopal clergy. The College now serves clergy and laity of all denominations as a center for continuing education. It is dedicated to strengthening, sustaining and nourishing those who are called to the ministry of preaching. It also serves as a major conference center for the Episcopal Church. The College publishes the *College of Preachers Newsletter.*

Colleges and Universities of the Anglican Communion (CUAC). This group was inaugurated at a meeting at Canterbury, England, Mar. 26–29, 1993, with the official inauguration on Saturday, Mar. 27, in the Great Quire of Canterbury Cathedral. Support emerged between 1988 and 1993 for an international organization of colleges and universities with ties to the Anglican Communion. Representatives from forty institutions from Australia, Canada, England, Hong Kong, India, Ireland, Jamaica, Japan, Jerusalem, Korea, Liberia, New Zealand, Philippines, Republic of China, United States, and Wales were present at the inaugural meeting. This worldwide association works together to develop programs of exchanges of students, faculty, chaplains and administrators, and to foster the development of programs of both traditional and non-traditional modes of learning. The initial headquarters of CUAC was the office of the Association of Episcopal Colleges. Dr. Linda A. Chisholm, president of the Association, was first general secretary of CUAC.

Collegiality. The principle that bishops are ordained (consecrated) into a college. It is based on the assumption that bishops succeed the apostles collectively, not individually. As a consequence each bishop is responsible not only for a diocese but also for the universal church. The mode of exercise of this responsibility varies with circumstances. While bishops are equal within the episcopal college, the principle respects the traditional primacies, as of the Bishop of Rome, the oriental patriarchs, regional and provincial primates, and notably, in the Anglican Communion, the Archbishop of Canterbury. By extension, collegiality is a principle at work in the college of presbyters (*presbyterium*) within a diocese, and among ministers and people in a local parish.

Colloquium of Episcopal Professional and Vocational Associations (CEPVA). The Professional Ministry Cluster of the Episcopal Church Center held a conference on May 2–4, 1996, at the Bishop Mason Center in Dallas, Texas. The title for the meeting was "Strengthening Working Relationships in the Church Conference." It was at this meeting that CEPVA was organized, and a set of "Principles Of Justice And Accountability In The Church Workplace" was adopted. The group is committed to working for the just treatment and pastoral care of those who work for the church.

Colombia, Diocese of. The House of Bishops established the Missionary District of Colombia on Nov. 12, 1963. In 1970 it became the Missionary Diocese of Colombia and later the Diocese of Colombia. The first indigenous bishop was the Rt. Rev. Bernardo Merino-Botero, who was consecrated on June 29, 1979.

Colorado, Diocese of. The state of Colorado was part of the Missionary District of the Northwest from Oct. 19, 1859, until Oct. 21, 1865, when the House of Bishops established the Missionary District of Colorado and Parts Adjacent with jurisdiction in Colorado, Idaho, Montana, and Wyoming. On Oct. 4, 1866, the House of Bishops changed the Missionary District of Colorado and Parts Adjacent to include Colorado, New Mexico, and Wyoming. Montana and Idaho were detached from Colorado. On Oct. 30, 1874, it was changed by the House of Bishops to the Missionary District of Colorado with jurisdiction in Wyoming. New Mexico was detached from Colorado. The Missionary District of Colorado was established by the House of Bishops on Oct. 15, 1883, when Wyoming was made a separate missionary district. The primary council of the Diocese of Colorado was held at St. John's Cathedral, Denver, June 9–10, 1887. On June 28, 1880, St. John's Church, Denver, was set apart as St. John's Cathedral, and the building was consecrated on June 11, 1925.

"Colorado Curriculum." *See* Living the Good News ("Colorado Curriculum").

Colorado School of Mines. The Rt. Rev. George Maxwell Randall (1810–1873), the first Bishop of Colorado, received a gift of $5,000 in 1868 from a Brooklyn, New York, merchant, George A. Jarvis, to establish a school. With this gift plus ten acres of land in Golden, Colorado, he laid the cornerstone of Jarvis Hall, on Aug. 25, 1869. It was named for the Rt. Rev. Abraham Jarvis, the second Bishop of Connecticut. This was to be a School of Mines, and the school was known as Jarvis Hall. On Nov. 17, 1869, a storm destroyed Jarvis Hall. On Oct. 19, 1870, Jarvis Hall reopened. On Feb. 9, 1874, the School of Mines was deeded to the Territory of Colorado.

Colors, Liturgical. Although early Christians preferred white for liturgical dress, other colors gradually came into use. Patterns of colors designating seasons and feasts date from the twelfth century in western Europe, with many regional variations. A fixed scheme came into being with the 1570 missal of Pius V. In reaction against medieval practices, Anglicans at the Reformation abandoned liturgical colors. Anglican Prayer Books have never designated a liturgical color scheme. Under the influence of the Oxford Movement and as part of a revival of medieval customs, Anglicans began to restore the use of colors in the nineteenth century. Most Anglicans today follow modern Roman Catholic practice, sometimes mixed with medieval Sarum use. Liturgical colors include white or gold for Christmas, Easter, other feasts (except those of martyrs), marriages, and funerals; blue or violet for Advent; violet or Lenten array for Lent; red for Holy Week, martyrs, the Day of Pentecost, and ordinations; green for the ordinary time after the Epiphany and after the Day of Pentecost. Some use rose for Advent 3 and Lent 4. Many Anglican parishes use combinations of fabrics and colors, and some have returned to the old custom of wearing the best dress for the best occasions.

Columba, St. (c. 521–June 9, 597). Founder of many churches and monasteries in Ireland. He was born in Gartan, County Donegal, Ireland. Columba was trained in several Irish monasteries. He was ordained priest around 551. In 563 Columba left Ireland with twelve companions and went to the Isle of Hy or Ioua, now called Iona. He founded a monastery and school at Iona to train missionaries for the evangelization of the Northern Picts. He spent the remaining thirty-four years of his life at Iona. His greatest triumph was the conversion of King Brude of the Picts at Inverness. Columba was a scholar, a preacher, and a courageous leader. He is commemorated in the Episcopal calendar of the church year on June 9.

Columbarium. A vault or structure with niches (openings) for the burial of urns or other containers of ashes of the dead. Many parishes have a columbarium. It may be located in an undercroft or chapel or elsewhere on the church grounds. The BCP service of committal (p. 501) allows the celebrant to state that the deceased person's body is committed to "its resting place." *See* Cremation.

Come Celebrate! A Hymnal Supplement. This volume consists of "Service Music," and "Songs and Hymns." It represents the results of the life of worship of the Community of Celebration. Its contents are eclectic: international, intergenerational, and sacramental. *Come Celebrate!* was designed to be a supplement to *The Hymnal 1982*. It was commended by the 1991 General Convention. It includes "Performance Notes," and has several indices. It was edited by Betty Pulkingham, Mimi Farra, and Kevin Hackett, and published by Cathedral Music Press in 1990.

"Comfortable Words." A series of sentences from scripture that provide encouragement for penitent sinners. The term "comfortable" originally meant "strengthening." The sentences appear after the confession and absolution in the Rite 1 Eucharist (BCP, p. 332), and in the Reconciliation of a Penitent, Form Two, prior to the bidding to confession and the confession of sins by the penitent (BCP, pp. 449–450). Use of the comfortable words is optional in both cases. All previous editions required that all four sentences be said at every eucharist. One or more of the sentences may be said. The comfortable words date from the 1548 Order of the Communion. The BCP introduces the sentences with the statement, "Hear the Word of God to all who truly turn to him." The sentences are based on Mt 11:28, Jn 3:16, 1 Tm 1:15, and 1 Jn 2:1–2.

Commendation, The. Concluding portion of the burial rite prior to the committal at the grave or other place of final repose. The commendation is typically said in the church building. After the post-communion prayer, or the prayers if there is no eucharist, the celebrant and other ministers take their places at the body. The anthem, "Give rest, O Christ, to your servant(s) with your saints," based on the *Kontakion* and *Ikos* of the Byzantine Rite, may be sung or

said. Another suitable anthem or hymn may also be used at this time. After the anthem, the celebrant says the prayer of commendation, commending the deceased to our merciful Savior (BCP, p. 499). A blessing and dismissal may follow the prayer of commendation. As the body is borne from the church, an appropriate hymn, anthem, or canticle may be sung or said. The commendation was added to the 1979 BCP burial rite in response to the pastoral reality that many attending the burial service do not go to the grave for the committal of the body. *See* Committal.

Commination. A "threatening of punishment." A service for Ash Wednesday drawn up for the first English Prayer Book of 1549 to replace the blessing of ashes. It included an exhortation on God's judgment, the solemn cursing of those who have committed various sins, Ps 51, suffrages, and a collect. It has remained in the English Prayer Book, but is not in the English *Alternative Service Book*. The American Prayer Book never included it. Ps 51 is the only feature of the commination service that is used in the Prayer Book service for Ash Wednesday. *See* Ash Wednesday.

Commissary. Representatives of the Bishop of London appointed to oversee the work of the Church of England in the American colonies during the late seventeenth and early eighteenth centuries. By the time of the Glorious Revolution (1688), the Bishop of London held responsibility for control over Anglican affairs in America. Since commissaries already performed functions for bishops in distant areas of dioceses in England, the Rt. Rev. Henry Compton, Bishop of London, decided in 1689 to appoint James Blair as the first American commissary. Blair served in Virginia for fifty-seven years. He established order over the church, enforced morality laws, and in 1693 founded the College of William and Mary, the first Anglican college in America. Blair's success demonstrated the usefulness of Compton's plan. Commissaries were soon designated for other colonies, including most notably Thomas Bray in Maryland. The system reached its peak of influence in the 1740s, when commissaries were active in nine of the thirteen colonies. However, the canonical powers of the commissary were limited, and the need for Anglican bishops resident in America gradually became apparent. As a result, the commissary system fell into disuse everywhere except in Virginia in the decade prior to the American Revolution. At least sixteen commissaries were sent to the American colonies.

Commission on Home Missions to Colored People (1865). *See* Freedman's Commission.

Commission on Ministry. In 1970 the General Convention of the Episcopal Church passed a new canon, Canon III.1, which required each diocese to establish a Commission on Ministry. The number of members, their selection, and their terms of office are to be determined by diocesan canons.

The functions of Commissions on Ministry specified in the canon are to assist the bishop "in determining present and future needs for ministry in the diocese" and to assist "in enlisting and selecting persons for Holy Orders." Commissions are to develop, train, and affirm lay ministries. They interview candidates prior to their ordination as deacons and may interview candidates prior to their ordination as priests, if requested by the bishop, reporting to the bishop in each case. They assist the bishop in guiding and counseling deacons and other ministers, and they assist in matters pertaining to the continuing education of the clergy.

The creation of Commissions on Ministry reflects the growing sense of the church that broad participation in decisions about all types of ministry is desirable and necessary.

Commission on Work Among Colored People. This commission was formed by the General Convention of 1898 to support African American clergy. It was the successor to the Commission of Home Missions to Colored People which went out of existence in 1878. It helped to support the operation of several schools for Negroes through private philanthropy and some diocesan support. The commission supported St. Augustine's School in Raleigh, North Carolina, St. Paul's School in Lawrenceville, Virginia, and the Bishop Payne Divinity School in Petersberg, Virginia. The commission was discontinued in 1904, and its work was transferred to the Board of Missions. *See* Freedman's Commission.

Commissions of the General Convention. The General Convention may establish Standing Commissions and Joint Commissions. A Standing Commission is to study and make recommendations to the General Convention on major subjects considered to be of continuing concern to the church. Members of the Standing Commissions have a six-year term, serving until the adjournment of the second General Convention following their appointment. A Joint Commission is to study and make recommendations to the General Convention on specific matters of concern between regular meetings of General Convention. This is a three-year term. Joint Commissions cease to exist at the end of the single interval for which they were created unless extended by action of the General Convention. The Presiding Bishop appoints the Episcopal members and the president of the House of Deputies appoints the clerical and lay members. The Presiding Bishop and the president of the House of Deputies are members *ex officiis* of every commission. They have the right to attend meetings with seat and vote. Every commission must elect a chair, a vice-chair, and a secretary.

Committal. The portion of the burial rite that is said at the graveside or other place of final repose. The committal typically concludes the burial rite, but it may also take place before the service in the church or prior to cremation. The committal includes an anthem, a prayer of committal with the Aaronic blessing (Nm 6:24–26), a salutation, the Lord's Prayer, and a concluding dismissal or blessing. Earth may be cast upon the coffin as the celebrant says the prayer of committal (BCP, p. 501). *See* Commendation, The.

Commixture. The placing of a small fragment of consecrated bread in the chalice of consecrated wine at the time of the fraction at the eucharist. It is also known as commingling. The origin of this custom seems to be the ancient practice of the *fermentum*, which was a fragment of consecrated bread from the bishop's celebration of the eucharist. This fragment was taken to a presbyter celebrating the eucharist and added to the chalice after the fraction. It symbolized the unity of the church, and the unity of the presbyter's celebration and ministry with that of the bishop. At times, a portion of consecrated bread has also been reserved to be placed in the chalice at a later eucharist. This symbolized the unity of the later eucharist with the earlier one. In the Syrian Church, the commixture was understood as a reuniting of Christ's body and blood, symbolizing his resurrection. The commixture was not retained in the Anglican Prayer Book tradition, but it is occasionally done as an act of personal piety.

Common Collects. Collects occurring in the various liturgical Commons, such as the Common of Saints or the Common of Martyrs. Liturgical books distinguish between

Propers, which contain collects, psalms and readings, prefaces, and other particular elements of a service which are proper to a particular feast or seasonal celebration, and Commons, which contain the same elements for common (generic) use on a number of similar occasions. The BCP contains common collects and indicates readings for a number of categories of lesser feasts, such as martyr, missionary, pastor, theologian, and "a saint." These may be used to observe any lesser feast in the calendar, or a local feast not in the calendar. The collects frequently contain the letter "N.," to permit the inclusion of the saint's name. Proper collects for many of these lesser feasts may be found in *Lesser Feasts and Fasts*, but the common collects (and readings) from the BCP may always be used instead.

Common Lectionary. A number of North American churches, beginning with the Episcopal Church, adopted the Roman Catholic three-year lectionary after Vatican II, but with varying modifications. An ecumenical committee was set up in the 1980s to bring order into these variations. This led to the formulation of the *Common Lectionary*. Its most notable feature is an attempt to allow the OT to speak for itself instead of being subordinated to the gospel reading. This has been achieved through a series of mini-courses on OT persons and themes during ordinary time.

Common of Saints, The. *See* Common Collects.

Common Worship, Standing Commission on. The 1997 General Convention discontinued the Standing Liturgical Commission and the Standing Commission on Church Music and formed the Standing Commission on Common Worship. This commission consists of sixteen members: four bishops, four presbyters or deacons, and eight lay persons. The Custodian of the Standard Book of Common Prayer is a member *ex officio* with voice, but without vote. The commission is to collect, collate, and catalogue material bearing upon possible future revisions of the BCP and *The Hymnal 1982*. It will make recommendations to General Convention concerning the musical settings of liturgical texts and rubrics. It will also present to General Convention recommendations concerning the Lectionary, Psalter, and Daily Offices for special occasions as authorized or directed by the General Convention or House of Bishops.

Communicant. One who receives Holy Communion. In the BCP the term refers to those receiving communion at a

particular service. Communicants are defined in the canons as all members of this church who have received Holy Communion at least three times in the past year. They further define "communicants in good standing" as communicants who " . . . for the previous year have been faithful in working, praying, and giving for the spread of the Kingdom of God."

Communicate. To receive Holy Communion. The verb may also be used with an object, meaning to minister the eucharistic elements to someone.

Communion. The term means "union with." It is used in phrases such as "the Anglican Communion" and "the communion of saints." It is also used to mean Holy Communion, union with one another in Christ in the Sacrament of His Body and Blood. In this sense it is used 1) as a title for the entire service of the Holy Eucharist, 2) as a title for the Great Thanksgiving, beginning with the offertory, and 3) to mean the ministration or reception of the consecrated Bread and Wine. The term is used to translate the Greek *koinonia*.

Communion in Both Kinds. Reception of both the consecrated bread and wine in Holy Communion. It is the normal Anglican method of receiving communion, although communion in one kind is permitted. Each communicant is given the opportunity to receive the consecrated bread and wine separately. However, the Sacrament may be received in both kinds simultaneously, in a manner approved by the bishop (BCP, pp. 407–408). The restoration of the chalice to the laity was avidly sought by the Reformers. It was accomplished in the Church of England in 1548.

Communion in One Kind. Reception of Holy Communion under the form of bread (or wine) only. It was the regular method by which lay people received communion in the western church from the twelfth century to the Reformation. There is evidence as early as the third century that lay people took the consecrated bread home with them to receive during the week. The communion of the sick in one kind became common, apparently for practical reasons. Between the seventh and eleventh centuries the practice of intinction, dipping the consecrated bread in the consecrated wine, became popular. By the thirteenth century, intinction had been replaced almost universally by communion in one kind. The Reformers were strong advocates for the restoration of the chalice to the laity. It was restored in the Church of England in 1548. In the Byzantine Church, infants at their baptisms were usually communicated under the form of wine only, since they were unable to swallow bread. This was also true of the Latin Church in the first millennium. The BCP allows for administration of the Sacrament to the sick in one kind if the sick person is unable to receive either the consecrated bread or wine (p. 457). *See* Concomitance.

Communion of Saints, The. The union and shared life of all Christians in Christ, including those who now live in the world and those whose mortal lives have ended. The collect for All Saints' Day states, "Almighty God, you have knit together your elect in one communion and fellowship in the mystical body of your Son Christ our Lord" (BCP, p. 245). The Apostles' Creed affirms the communion of saints, and the Catechism explains that it is "the whole family of God, the living and the dead, those whom we love and those whom we hurt, bound together in Christ by sacrament, prayer, and praise" (BCP, pp. 96, 862). A hymn text by Charles Wesley (526 in *The Hymnal 1982*) prays, "Let saints on earth in concert sing with those whose work is done; for all the servants of our King in heaven and earth are one."

Communion Rails. *See* Altar Rails.

Communion Table, or Holy Table. A name for the altar, the table on which the eucharistic gifts of bread and wine are placed for the celebration of the Holy Eucharist. Also known as the Lord's table. The name is intended to emphasize that the eucharist is a meal, while the term "altar" suggests offering and sacrifice. The term was popular among sixteenth-century Reformers and widely used in the reformed churches for that reason. The name was frequently used in the sixteenth century to distinguish a wooden table with legs from a solid stone altar.

Community of All Angels. An order for women, no longer in existence. It was founded around 1895 in Wilmington, Delaware. Its ministries included St. Michael's Hospital for Babies and St. Matthew's Colored Mission. The nuns also did parish work.

Community of Celebration, Aliquippa, Pennsylvania. A religious order in the Diocese of Pittsburgh. It is part of the Society of the Community of Celebration, established in the Anglican Communion in England and Scotland. Its roots in the United States go back to the Church of the Redeemer, Houston, in the 1960s. The community is not typical of traditional religious orders. They do not wear habits. The membership includes men and women, married and single, adults and children, clergy and laity. Members take the traditional vows of poverty, chastity, and obedience. At the center of the community's life is the daily discipline of worship as prescribed in the BCP. The mission of the community is to offer itself in service to the church and to the world. A primary work of the community is the ministry of music. The members have recorded and published many musical works. One significant publication is *Come Celebrate!* (1990), which is a supplement to *The Hymnal 1982*. The only active community in the United States is at Aliquippa, Pennsylvania. It began in 1985.

The Companions of Celebration are men, women, and children, who have a formal relationship with the community to support its work by prayer and gifts. Companions follow a simple rule of life.

Community of Christian Family Ministry (CCFM). This community began in 1971 as a parish extension of St. Elizabeth's Episcopal Church in San Diego, California. It was then known as the "Mustard Tree." It was an extended family household ministering to drug-afflicted teenagers. The Mustard Tree later moved to the oceanfront area of Newport Beach, California, where its ministry included counseling and intensive care for persons in need. It was there that the nucleus of the community took definite form. In 1974 the community moved to Vista, California. The rule of life is to live out the gospel as an intentional family, applying the principle of J.O.Y., that is, putting Jesus First; Others Second; Yourself Last. The community has professed members, oblates, companions, associates, and junior associates. It ministers through evangelical outreach, such as hospital visitation, preaching, music, drama, retreats, Bible studies, counseling, creative writing, and prayer groups. The community was recognized as an official community of the Episcopal Church on Mar. 27, 1977. It publishes *Religious Renewal Quarterly*.

Community of the Cross of Nails. The Community of the Cross of Nails (CCN) is an ecumenical international fellowship of individuals, communities, and centers dedicated to the ministry of reconciliation. The CCN was founded in 1967 by the Very Reverend H. C. N. (Bill) Williams at Saint Michael's Cathedral in Coventry, England.

Provost Williams had been inspired to create a ministry of reconciliation after the medieval Saint Michael's Cathedral in Coventry was destroyed by German Bombers in 1940. A priest going through the ruins put together three nails in the form of a cross; this cross was to become the unifying symbol of the Community of the Cross of Nails. CCN Centers have been established in cathedrals, churches, hospitals, and religious communities throughout the world. They display a silver cross of nails, work on projects of reconciliation, meet in foyer groups, and pray according to a Common Discipline developed in conjunction with the Benedictine Roman Catholic Monastery in Ottobeuren, Germany. Although the CCN is ecumenical, many centers in the United States are found in Episcopal churches and cathedrals. CCN-USA publishes *Crossroads*, a newsletter, and organizes conferences and pilgrimages.

Companion Diocese. A diocese of the Episcopal Church may enter into a companion relationship with an overseas diocese of the Anglican Communion. The mission of the dioceses in the companion relationship includes mutual encouragement and prayer, intensified understanding and concern, and the exchange of both spiritual and material resources. Companion relationships are to strengthen the Anglican Communion through the direct experience of interdependence across cultural and geographical boundaries. Each partner in the companion relationship is to be both a giver and a receiver.

Companion diocese relationships are formally recognized by the Executive Council of the Episcopal Church at the request of the dioceses involved, on the basis of a resolution by both partners proposing the companion relationship. The companion dioceses usually commit to the relationship for a fixed period of years, but this commitment is renewable. A companion relationship may be shared as long as the dioceses wish to continue the relationship.

Companion Sisterhood of St. Gregory (CSSG). A religious community for women formed at the Little Flower Chapel, Graymoor, Garrison, New York, on July 24, 1999. It was originally the Companion Sisterhood of St. Gregory, which was founded by the Chapter of the Brotherhood of St. Gregory on Mar. 15, 1987, as a "community in formation." During the years of community formation, the sisterhood followed the rule and constitution of the brotherhood. They were trained in the brotherhood's novitiate program and governed by the brotherhood's existing structure.

The sisterhood became autonomous when the initial community formation was complete. The sisterhood is open to women, clergy or lay, married or single. The members of the community follow a common rule but live individually, in small groups, or with their families. *See* Brotherhood of St. Gregory (BSG).

Compasrose, The. This journal had the subtitle, *News of the Anglican Communion*. It was published four times a year by the Anglican Consultative Council. It is continued by *Anglican World. See* Anglican Consultative Council.

Compass Rose. The emblem of the Anglican Communion. It was designed by Canon Edward West of the Cathedral of St. John the Divine in New York City. It has a stylized compass in which the center holds the Cross of St. George, surrounded by the Greek inscription "The truth shall make you free." It symbolizes the spread of the Anglican Communion around the world. A bishop's mitre atop the northern arrow of the compass emphasizes the centrality of the episcopate and apostolic order in the Anglican Communion. The symbol was set in the nave of Canterbury Cathedral and dedicated at the final eucharist of the 1988 Lambeth Conference. A similar symbol was placed in the Cathedral of St. Peter and St. Paul, Washington, in 1990, and the Cathedral of St. John the Divine, New York City, in 1992. *See* West, Edward Nason.

Compline. The last of the four services in the Daily Office (BCP, p. 127). It is descended from the night prayers said before bed at the end of the monastic round of daily prayer. Compline is a simple office including a confession of sins, one or more psalms, a short reading from scripture, versicles and responses, the Lord's Prayer, collects which ask for God's protection during the night to come, and the canticle *Nunc dimittis*. A hymn for the evening may follow the short reading from scripture. The collects may be followed by a time of silence, along with free intercessions and thanksgivings.

Compton, Henry (1632–July 7, 1713). He was consecrated Bishop of Oxford on Dec. 6, 1674, and was the ninety-fourth Bishop of London from Feb. 6, 1676, until his death. As Bishop of London he had responsibility for the Church of England in the American colonies. He was the first Bishop of London to send or name commissaries for the colonies. On Dec. 15, 1689, Compton appointed James Blair as Commissary to Virginia, and in

1696 he appointed Thomas Bray as Commissary to Maryland. *See* Commissary.

Concelebration. Joint celebration of the eucharist by a chief celebrant and one or more concelebrants. Concelebration may or may not include recitation of all or part of the eucharistic prayer by the concelebrants. In the early church, the bishop typically served as chief celebrant and was flanked by priests who joined in the celebration. The bishop alone spoke the eucharistic prayer, which did not have a fixed form. The concelebrants extended their hands over the oblations and prayed silently. This pattern of concelebration is described in the *Apostolic Tradition* of Hippolytus (c. 225). The practice of verbal concelebration developed in Rome in the seventh century. The necessity of verbal participation by the concelebrants has been a subject of dispute. Concelebration may express the unity of the church and the collegiality of the ordained ministries represented in the celebration of the eucharist.

Concelebrants may wear matching or similar chasubles and stand in a semicircle with the chief celebrant in the center. At times, concelebrants have alternated in pronouncing sections of the eucharistic prayer. Concelebrants may extend their hands toward the bread and wine and may join the chief celebrant in reading the institution narrative and the invocation of the Holy Spirit. Concelebrants should share in the breaking of the bread at the fraction.

The BCP notes that it is appropriate for other priests to stand with the celebrant at the altar, joining in the consecration of the gifts, breaking the bread, and distributing communion (p. 354). At the Ordination of a Bishop, the new bishop serves as chief celebrant while other bishops and presbyters serve as concelebrants (p. 522). At the Ordination of a Priest, the bishop serves as chief celebrant while the newly ordained priest and other presbyters serve as concelebrants (p. 535). The bishop also serves as chief celebrant at a Celebration of New Ministry, joined by the new priest and other priests of the diocese "as an expression of the collegiality of the ministry in which they share" (p. 558).

Concerned Clergy and Laity of the Episcopal Church (CCLEC). This group was organized on Nov. 13, 1994, at Atlanta, Georgia. It was a lay-led movement concerned with biblical faith and moral standards. It was conservative in outlook, and called for the resignation of Presiding Bishop Edmond L. Browning in 1995.

Concomitance. Eucharistic doctrine that affirms the simultaneous presence of Christ's body and blood in each of the eucharistic elements. It contradicts a narrow identification of Christ's body with the bread and Christ's blood with the wine. The doctrine of concomitance upholds the truth that the fullness of communion is available by receiving either the consecrated bread or wine. A Prayer Book rubric concerning the administration of Holy Communion to the sick states that "it is suitable to administer the Sacrament in one kind only" if the sick person is unable to receive either the consecrated bread or wine (BCP, p. 457). The doctrine of concomitance affirms that the communicant receives Christ's body and blood in this situation. The doctrine of concomitance was used in the Roman Catholic Church to justify the withdrawal of the chalice from the laity, thereby allowing their communion in one kind only. The term is from the Latin, "to accompany."

Concordat. A term originally used to describe an agreement between civil and ecclesiastical authorities. It is also now used to describe an agreement between churches governing sacramental communion. The Anglican Communion has such a concordat with the Old Catholic churches in Europe, and the Episcopal Church has additional concordats with the Philippine Independent Church and the Polish National Catholic Church.

Concordat of Agreement. The *Concordat of Agreement Between The Episcopal Church And The Evangelical Lutheran Church in America* was issued on the Feast of the Epiphany, Jan. 6, 1991. It is the conclusion of a series of three Lutheran-Episcopal Dialogues which began on Oct. 14, 1969, and concluded on Jan. 6, 1991. From Jan. 1991, until 1996, the *Concordat* was discussed, and in late 1996 some revisions were made to it which were approved by the Church Council of the Evangelical Lutheran Church in America and the Standing Commission on Ecumenical Relations of the Episcopal Church. The purpose of the *Concordat of Agreement* is to achieve full communion between the Evangelical Lutheran Church in America (ELCA) and the Episcopal Church. Full communion means that members of one body may receive the sacraments of the other; that bishops of one church may take part in the consecration of bishops of the other; and that a bishop, pastor/priest or deacon of one ecclesial body may exercise liturgical functions in a congregation of the other body, if invited. The *Concordat* was approved by the 1997 General

Convention, but it failed to pass by six votes at the 1997 Churchwide Assembly of the ELCA. The *Concordat of Agreement* was rewritten and named *Called To Common Mission: A Lutheran Proposal For a Revision Of the Concordat of Agreement*. The ELCA Churchwide Assembly passed *Called to Common Mission* in Aug. 1999 by a vote of 716 to 317. It was submitted to the 2000 General Convention of the Episcopal Church for approval.

Conditional Baptism. When there is "reasonable doubt" that a person has been baptized, or baptized validly (with water and a trinitarian formula), baptism takes place with a special form of words beginning, "If you are not already baptized. . . ." (BCP, p. 313).

Conference of Anglican Church Historians (COACH). This organization was planned during the first half of 1975 and held its first meeting at the General Theological Seminary, Oct. 17–19, 1975. Its purpose is to discuss and reflect on the place of church history within the whole context of theological education and to improve the historical skills and knowledge of theological students. Members of COACH teach church history in the seminaries of the Episcopal Church. It normally meets every two years at one of the Episcopal seminaries.

Conference of Anglican Theologians. It is an organization of Anglican/Episcopal theological scholars from the United States and Canada. It was formed in the early 1960s following two meetings at the Church Divinity School of the Pacific. At first it was composed largely of persons teaching systematic theology in the seminaries, including Shunji Nishi, Langmead Casserley, Owen Thomas, David Scott, and others. Today membership is more than one hundred. It is open to persons of any denomination teaching a theological discipline in an Anglican institution and to all Anglicans with an earned doctorate in a theological discipline, or teaching a theological discipline in any institution of higher learning. On Sept. 28, 1997, at the Lutheran Theological Seminary at Gettysburg, Pennsylvania, the Conference's name was changed to the Society of Anglican and Lutheran Theologians (SALT) in support of ecumenical relations between the Episcopal Church and the Evangelical Lutheran Church of America. *See* Society of Anglican and Lutheran Theologians (SALT).

Conference of Church Workers Among Colored People (CCWACP). In 1883 a number of southern bishops, clergy and lay persons met at Sewanee, Tennessee, to discuss a plan to segregate Negroes into a racial diocese. In response to the "Sewanee Plan," John Peterson, a deacon at St. Philip's Church, New York, called the African American clergy together, and they organized the Convocation of Colored Clergy in 1883. Alexander Crummell of St. Luke's Church, Washington, was chosen the first president. At the fourth annual Convocation in St. Luke's Church, Washington, on Sept. 22, 1886, it changed its name to the Conference of Church Workers Among Colored People since several African American lay persons and two white priests had joined it. The Conference met every year, and every third year it met at the site of the General Convention. It published a monthly newspaper, *The Afro-American Churchman*, and later *The Church Advocate*, edited by George Freeman Bragg, Jr. The conference was an advocate for African Americans in the Episcopal Church. CCWACP went out of existence in the mid–1960s. Many of its concerns were taken up by the Episcopal Society for Cultural and Racial Unity, which was formed in 1957.

Conference of Church Workers Among the Deaf. *See* Episcopal Conference of the Deaf.

Conference of Diocesan Executives (CODE). An organization seeking to promote the development of effective organizational and executive procedures, and to serve as a primary vehicle for communication among the members and with the Episcopal Church for planning, program, and administration. It includes diocesan executives from the Episcopal Church and the Anglican Church of Canada. CODE was started in the mid-1980s.

Conference of Liturgical and Musical Commissions. *See* Association of Diocesan Liturgy and Music Commissions.

Conference on the Religious Life in the Anglican Communion in the Americas, The. An association of religious communities under vows of poverty, chastity, and obedience who live in community. The conference, whose official name is the Conference on the Religious Life in the Anglican Communion in the United States and Canada, was organized on Nov. 4, 1949, when delegates representing the chapters of religious communities in the United States and Canada signed the constitution of the conference. The initial membership comprised nineteen communities. Every three years delegates convene to transact business and to elect an advisory council, which meets as often as necessary between triennial meetings. The advisory council is composed of six delegates representing three men's and three women's communities. The conference serves as a vehicle of support by providing mutual advice and encouragement to the member communities. It also provides information to the church about the religious life.

Confession of Faith. A declaration of belief in the triune God, after the example of the Christian martyrs and confessors of faith. In Christian liturgy, this confession is expressed through the recitation of the ancient ecumenical creeds—the Apostles' Creed and the Nicene Creed—and through the eucharistic prayer. At every baptism in the Episcopal Church, the congregation welcomes the newly baptized by urging: "Confess the faith of Christ crucified, proclaim his resurrection, and share with us in his eternal priesthood" (BCP, p. 308).

Confession of Saint Peter the Apostle, The. The confession of Peter is recorded in the Gospel According to Matthew (16:16), "You are the Christ, the Son of the living God." The liturgical celebration of Peter's confession is celebrated on Jan. 18. It is a major feast in the Prayer Book calendar. This observance was first included in the 1979 BCP. The date is that of an ancient Gallican feast called "the Chair of Saint Peter." It honored Peter as the head of the Roman Catholic Church as well as his chair of episcopal authority. Contemporary observance of the Confession of Saint Peter the Apostle marks the beginning of the Week of Prayer for Christian Unity. The martyrdom of St. Peter and St. Paul is commemorated on June 29.

Confession of Sin. An acknowledgment of sin, as in Ps 51: "Against you only have I sinned and done what is evil in your sight." Confessions of sin during the liturgy are general, made by all the people. The church also provides for confessions of sin by individual penitents, and for their absolution, pronounced by a bishop or priest. A declaration of forgiveness may be stated by a deacon or lay person who hears a confession. The BCP provides two forms of service for the Reconciliation of a Penitent (p. 447, 449). The Reconciliation of a Penitent is one of the sacramental rites of the church (p. 861). The secrecy of the confession is morally absolute for those who hear a private confession. *See* Reconciliation of a Penitent.

Confessional. An enclosed place in a church building where a bishop or priest hears confessions. The older type was a darkened box, much like a double telephone booth, in which the confessor on one side and the penitent on the other talked through a screened partition. Many Anglican priests sit in a chair at the altar rail or in a pew, facing away from the penitent. A more recent style of confessional uses a larger but still private space, such as a room, in which the two can face each other. *See* Reconciliation of a Penitent.

Confessionalism. Adherence of a church or denomination to particular standards, expressions, confessions, doctrines, or symbols of faith. Confessional statements focus and codify the beliefs of a church or denomination, and distinguish the church's beliefs from the beliefs of others outside the church. Many confessional statements were made during the era of reformation and counter-reformation, including the Augsburg Confession (Lutheran), the Westminster Confession (Presbyterian), the Thirty-Nine Articles (Anglican), and the canons and decrees of the Council of Trent (Roman Catholic). Confessional statements were the basis for catechetical training by each church. For some, the term "confessionalism" has a pejorative meaning that suggests narrowness and exclusivity on the part of the confessional church. This may result from a stance by church authorities that a particular confession or statement of faith is necessary for salvation or church membership.

Confessor. The term has two meanings: 1) One who suffers greatly for confessing the faith, without being martyred, and 2) the bishop or priest who hears a private confession of sin. *See* Reconciliation of a Penitent.

Confirmation. The sacramental rite in which the candidates "express a mature commitment to Christ, and receive strength from the Holy Spirit through prayer and the laying on of hands by a bishop" (BCP, p. 860). Those who were baptized at an early age and those baptized as adults without laying on of hands by a bishop are expected to make a mature public affirmation of their faith, recommit themselves to the responsibilities of their baptism, and receive laying on of hands by a bishop (BCP, p. 412). Adults baptized with the laying on of hands by a bishop are considered to be confirmed.

The Prayer Book rite for Confirmation includes forms for Reception and the Reaffirmation of Baptismal Vows. In some dioceses, those who have already made a mature Christian commitment in another denomination are recognized as members of the one holy catholic and apostolic church, and received into the fellowship of the Episcopal Church and the Anglican Communion. In other dioceses, those who have been sacramentally confirmed in the Roman Catholic or Orthodox churches are received and others are confirmed. Those who have returned from a time of religious inactivity to an active practice of faith may publicly reaffirm their baptismal vows. Others who have experienced a renewal of faith or desire to renew their Christian commitment may also reaffirm their baptismal vows. Reaffirmation may be repeated, depending on the pastoral needs of the person. Preparation for Confirmation/Reception/Reaffirmation should help the candidates discover the meaning of Christian commitment in their lives, and explore ways that their Christian commitment can be lived. This preparation may draw upon the baptismal covenant (BCP, pp. 416–417) and An Outline of the Faith (BCP, pp. 845–862).

Confirmation, Reception, and Reaffirmation are rooted in the baptismal covenant. Confirmation/Reception/Reaffirmation may be done at the service of Holy Baptism or at the Easter Vigil when a bishop is present (BCP, pp. 292, 309–310). When there is no baptism, the entrance rite for Confirmation/Reception/Reaffirmation follows the entrance rite for baptism (BCP, p. 413). Candidates for Confirmation, Reception, and Reaffirmation are presented in separate groups by their presenters. Candidates may have individual presenters who will support them in their Christian life by prayer and example. It is not necessary that the presenters be members of the clergy. The candidates reaffirm their renunciation of evil, and renew their commitment to Jesus Christ. They reaffirm the promises made by them or for them at the time of baptism. Those present in the congregation promise to do all in their power to support the candidates in their life in Christ. The bishop leads the congregation in renewing the baptismal covenant. The Prayers for the Candidates from the baptismal liturgy may be used as the Prayers for the Candidates for Confirmation/Reception/Reaffirmation (BCP, p. 417). The bishop lays hands on each candidate for Confirmation. The BCP provides specific prayers to be said by the bishop for Confirmation, for Reception, and for Reaffirmation. The bishop may shake hands with those who are being received to welcome them into this communion; and the bishop may lay hands on them in blessing. The bishop may also bless those who reaffirm their baptismal vows.

The Episcopal Church's theology of Confirmation has continued to evolve along with its understanding of baptism. Confirmation is no longer seen as the completion of Christian initiation, nor is Confirmation a prerequisite for receiving communion. Baptism is full initiation by water and the Holy Spirit into Christ's body the church (BCP, p. 298). Accordingly, Confirmation has been increasingly understood in terms of a mature, public reaffirmation of the Christian faith and the baptismal promises. Some dioceses require that candidates for Confirmation be at least sixteen years old to insure that the candidates are making a mature and independent affirmation of their faith. There is considerable diversity of understanding and practice concerning Confirmation in the Episcopal Church. Confirmation has been characterized as "a rite seeking a theology."

When Confirmation/Reception/Reaffirmation is celebrated on Sunday or a major feast, the propers (collect and readings) for that day are used. The BCP also provides special propers for Confirmation at other times.

Confiteor. The Latin word for "I confess." In the late medieval period a form of confession in the first person singular was used in the Roman rite by the priest and the server before Mass. Some Episcopal parishes with an Anglo-catholic piety continue this practice.

Confractoria. The Latin word is used in earlier liturgies and in the current *BOS* for anthems sung at the fraction or breaking of the bread in the eucharistic rite. Psalms such as 23, 34, 148–150 were used as confractoria in various rites. Some books included anthems proper to the days, which covered a wide range of eucharistic imagery. Such eucharistic imagery included various OT meals; the wedding at Cana; feedings of the multitudes; meals shared with publicans and sinners; post-resurrection meals; the eschatological banquet; and Paul's imagery of one bread, one body. In the Roman rite "Lamb of God, who takes away the sins of the world, have mercy on us" came into use in the late seventh century. At first the one line was repeated as long as necessary for the Breaking of Bread for the communion of the people. The anthem "Christ our Passover is sacrificed for us" is based on a text which replaced "Behold the Lamb of God who takes away the sins of the world" in the 1549 BCP. The *BOS* and *The*

Hymnal 1982 include additional anthems with a broader range of imagery.

Confraternity of the Blessed Sacrament of the Body and Blood of Christ. It was founded in 1862 in England. The American branch was founded at St. Paul's Chapel, New York City, on Sept. 11, 1867. It is for adult communicants of the Episcopal Church, both lay and clergy. Members honor the person of Jesus Christ in the Blessed Sacrament of his Body and Blood. They make mutual and special intercession at the time of, and in union with, the Eucharistic Sacrifice. They promote the practice of receiving the Holy Communion after fasting.

Congregant. A member of a congregation.

Congregation. 1) A gathering of people for worship. The term may also refer to a parish church, or the people who participate in the life of the parish. 2) In the Roman Catholic Church, the term is applied to religious societies with simple vows. The term is not used in the Episcopal canons concerning religious orders and other Christian communities.

Congregation of the Companions of the Holy Saviour (CSSS). Seven young clergymen, William McGarvey (1861–1924), William Walker Webb (1857–1933), Walter Clayton Clapp (d. 1915), Frederick Danforth Lobdell (d. 1930), Maurice Ludlum Cowl (deposed 1908), James Gibbon Cameron (d. 1928), and George Weed Barhydt (d. 1930), met at the Church of the Evangelists, Philadelphia, to form a religious society. On Sept. 15, 1891, with four others, Alexander Irenee duPont Coleman (deposed 1897), George Barker Stone (1862–1939), Lawson Carter Rich (d. 1942), and William Wirt Mills (deposed 1897), they met at the Church of the Evangelists and adopted a rule and the name Community of the Companions of the Holy Saviour. The next day McGarvey was elected master. The rule stated that they would recite the Offices daily, celebrate the eucharist at least twice a week, fast before communion, go to confession at least one a month, and make a yearly retreat. Although not stated, the real object of the companions was to encourage clerical celibacy. On Oct. 8, 1895, eleven members of the companions founded the religious community, the Congregation of the Companions of the Holy Saviour (*Congregatio Sociorum Sancti Salvatoris*), CSSS. McGarvey was elected superior. Most members of the congregation became convinced that reunion with the Roman Catholic Church should be their goal. After the General Convention of 1907 passed the "Open Pulpit Canon," which allowed Christians who are not members of the Episcopal Church to make addresses in the church on special occasions, some of the members of the congregation joined the Roman Catholic Church. At a meeting of the chapter on Mar. 12, 1908, two members decided to continue the congregation. It exists today as a Christian community for ordained celibate men in the Episcopal Church who live a common rule but not in community. Most members of the congregation are involved in parochial ministry. The companions' life is one of ordered prayer, study, service, and mutual support which affirms the religious life centered in the eucharist and the Daily Office. Membership is open to celibate male bishops, priests, deacons, and candidates for holy orders in the Anglican Communion. *See* McGarvey, William Ignatius Loyola.

Congregation of St. Augustine. This monastic order was organized by the Rev. Michael (William) Wesley Adams and the Rev. William King Hart at St. John's Church, Chula Vista, California, in 1964. In 1966 it moved to All Saints' School, San Diego. On Sept. 14, 1966, Bishop Francis E. Bloy of Los Angeles received the first vows of the founders, and a novitiate was established. On July 1, 1970, the Congregation moved to Picayune, Mississippi, where Hart became the president and Adams the assistant director of St. Michael's Farm for Boys, which had been founded in 1954. After the 1976 General Convention voted to ordain women to the priesthood and episcopate, Adams and Hart stated that the Episcopal Church had "abrogated its heritage as a member of the One, Holy, Catholic and Apostolic Church and repudiated the Ecumenical Councils, the Church's Tradition, and the Church's Liturgy." On Aug. 9, 1977, they renounced the ministry of the Episcopal Church and were received into the Orthodox Church of America.

Connecticut, Diocese of. On Mar. 25, 1783, Samuel Seabury and Jeremiah Leaming were elected as candidates for Bishop of Connecticut. Seabury accepted the election, and was consecrated Bishop of Connecticut on Nov. 14, 1784, by nonjuring bishops at Aberdeen, Scotland. The Diocese of Connecticut was organized at Christ Church, Middletown, on Aug. 3, 1785. On June 15, 1919, Christ

Church, Hartford, was set apart as Christ Church Cathedral. *See* Consecration of Samuel Seabury, First American Bishop, Feast of; *see* Seabury, Samuel.

Conscience. A person's moral judgment upon himself or herself. It often indicates the sense of judgment of right or wrong regarding what has been done. For Thomas Aquinas, for example, conscience is the mind of the human person making moral judgments. In moral theology, conscience is the basis of moral action. A primary moral obligation is always to obey one's own conscience. Acting against conscience violates one's own self-identity. Historically, in Anglicanism, the most significant contribution to understanding conscience was made by Joseph Butler in his *Fifteen Sermons* (1726). Butler developed the view that conscience was a power arising from affective sensibilities and rational judgment.

"Conscience Clause." This clause, otherwise known as "A Statement of Conscience," was a response by the House of Bishops to the 1976 General Convention approval of a canonical change that allowed for the ordination of women to the priesthood and episcopate. It was initiated by Presiding Bishop John Allin's opening remarks to the Oct. 1977, meeting of the House of Bishops at Port St. Lucie, Florida. Bishop Allin stated that he did not think "that women can be priests any more than they can become fathers or husbands," and he offered to resign as Presiding Bishop. The House of Bishops passed a resolution affirming Allin's leadership. The bishops also responded by adopting a "conscience clause" designed to appease the episcopal opponents of the ordination of women. This clause affirmed that "No Bishop, Priest, or Lay Person should be coerced or penalized in any manner, nor suffer any canonical disabilities as a result of his or her conscientious objection to or support of the sixty-fifth General Convention's actions with regard to the ordination of women to the priesthood or episcopate." Since the clause was adopted by the House of Bishops only, and not also by the House of Deputies, it had no canonical authority. The clause insured that no bishop could be punished for opposing the ordination of women in the Episcopal Church. The Lambeth Conference of 1978 also adopted a similar resolution. It stated that the conference accepts those member churches which ordain women, and declared "its acceptance of those member churches which do not ordain women."

Consecration. To set something or someone apart for a sacred purpose. The bread and wine of the Eucharist are consecrated at the Great Thanksgiving, and "the consecration" often means the consecration of the eucharistic gifts. The central prayer accompanying the laying on of hands in the ordination of bishops, priests, and deacons is called the prayer of consecration. The prayer, the action, and the accompanying ceremonies are called "the consecration" in the BCP. The Prayer Book also speaks of the consecration of chrism by the bishop, the consecration of a grave, and the consecration of a church.

Consecration of Samuel Seabury, First American Bishop, Feast of. On Mar. 25, 1783, ten clergy met at the home of the Rev. John Rutgers Marshall in Woodbury, Connecticut, and elected Samuel Seabury and Jeremiah Leaming as candidates for Bishop of Connecticut. Seabury accepted the election and sailed for England to be consecrated. He arrived in England on July 7, 1783, and spent over a year trying to get consecrated by English bishops. For a number of reasons, including the need to take the oath of allegiance to the King of England, no bishops would consecrate Seabury. He then went to Scotland, where he was consecrated at Aberdeen on Nov. 14, 1784, at the chapel in the home of John Skinner, Bishop Coadjutor of Aberdeen. The consecrator was Robert Kilgour, Bishop of Aberdeen and Primus of the Nonjuring Episcopal Church in Scotland. Kilgour was assisted by Arthur Petrie, Bishop of Ross and Murray, and John Skinner. On Aug. 3, 1785, the clergy of the Connecticut convocation elected Seabury their bishop. The consecration of Samuel Seabury and the bringing of the historic episcopate to the Episcopal Church is commemorated on Nov. 14 in the Episcopal calendar of the church year.

Consensus Tigurinus. *See* Protestantism.

Consents for Ordination. After the election of a bishop, if the date of the election is more than three months before the next meeting of the General Convention, the Standing Committee of the electing diocese shall send a certificate of election to the standing committees of all the dioceses of the Episcopal Church for their consent to the ordination of the bishop-elect. If a majority of the standing committees consent, evidence of the consents shall be forwarded by the Standing Committee of the electing diocese to the

Presiding Bishop, who communicates this to the bishops of the Episcopal Church exercising jurisdiction. If a majority of those bishops consent, the Presiding Bishop then notifies the Standing Committee of the electing diocese and the bishop-elect of the church's consent. If the election of a bishop takes place within three months of the General Convention, consent must be given by the House of Deputies at Convention. If the House of Deputies consent, notice is sent to the House of Bishops. If a majority of bishops exercising jurisdiction consent to the ordination, the Presiding Bishop notifies the Standing Committee of the electing diocese and the bishop-elect of the church's consent. There have been occasions when the granting of consent has been more than a formality, especially when the bishop-elect was a controversial figure in the Episcopal Church. For example, James DeKoven (1831–1879) was elected to be Bishop of Illinois in 1875, but the consents were not given because of his controversial reputation as a ritualist.

Consignation. Marking the sign of the cross on the forehead of the newly baptized person by the bishop or priest at baptism, with the statement that "you are sealed by the Holy Spirit in Baptism and marked as Christ's own for ever." (BCP, p. 308). Chrism may be used for marking the sign of the cross. *See* Seal of Baptism.

Consortium of Endowed Episcopal Churches, The. The consortium was initiated through conversations among clergy and laity from endowed Episcopal parishes in the early eighties. It was formally organized in 1985, and the first executive director was the Rev. Robert Ayres MacGill, who served 1985–1988. It is a parish-based, collegial organization working to enhance the ministry and mission of endowed parishes. Three primary areas are emphasized: stewardship, grant making and outreach ministries, and investment and endowment structure. The consortium sponsors an annual conference and publishes a newsletter, *Issues and Trends*. It also participates in the production of the *Episcopal Mission Resource Information Service* (*EMRIS*), a comprehensive directory of Episcopal Church funders and a grants index. Membership is based on a parish endowment of at least one million dollars.

Constance, Nun, and her Companions, Commonly Called "The Martyrs of Memphis." In 1873 a group of sisters of the Sisterhood of St. Mary went to Memphis, Tennessee, at the request of Bishop Charles T. Quintard, to establish a school for girls adjacent to the Cathedral of St. Mary. They were confronted by an epidemic of yellow fever and began to care for the sick. Yellow fever returned in 1878. The sisters stayed in Memphis to continue to minister to the sick while others fled the city. Sister Constance and six other Sisters of St. Mary, Sister Clare of the Society of St. Margaret in Boston, and a number of Memphis clergy ministered to the victims of the deadly disease. More than 5,000 people died, including Sister Constance on Sept. 9, 1878, Sister Thecla on Sept. 12, Sister Ruth on Sept. 17, and Sister Francis on Oct. 4. The high altar at the Cathedral of St. Mary is a memorial to the four martyred sisters. These martyrs are commemorated in the Episcopal calendar of the church year on Sept. 9.

Constantine I (c. 285–337). Roman emperor from 306 to 337. On the night before battle with an imperial rival at the Milvian Bridge near Rome in 312, Constantine had a vision that apparently led to his conversion to Christianity. He saw a fiery cross in the heavens above the statement written in Greek, "In this sign you will conquer." According to Lactantius (c. 250–c. 325), Constantine had a dream telling him to place on the shields of his soldiers a monogram of the Greek letters Chi (X) and Rho (P), which begin the word "Christ." Under Constantine the *labarum* or military standard of the imperial Roman legions featured the Chi-Rho monogram. Slightly different accounts of this story are provided by Lactantius and Eusebius of Caesarea (c. 260–c. 339). After Constantine's victory at the Milvian Bridge, he and Licinius, emperor of the eastern empire, published the Edict of Milan in 313. It granted religious freedom throughout the Roman Empire. Constantine was a strong supporter of Christianity and sought to build a Christian empire. The concept of a Christian state can be traced to Constantine. He defeated Licinius in 324 and rebuilt Byzantium as his new capital. He renamed the city Constantinople. He convened and presided over the First Council of Nicaea (325). Constantine was baptized shortly before his death. He is celebrated as a saint in the eastern church. He was buried in the Church of the Twelve Apostles at Constantinople.

Constitution and Canons, Standing Commission on. The General Convention of 1976 established the Joint Commission on Constitution and Canons. This became the Standing Commission on Constitution and Canons. It has twelve members: three bishops, three presbyters or deacons, and six lay persons. The Commission is to review the Constitution and Canons for internal consistency and clarity.

Constitution of the Episcopal Church. This document of church government was first adopted by the General Convention of the Church in 1789. The Constitution contains regulations for General Convention, election and jurisdiction of bishops, Standing Committees, the formation of new jurisdictions, the establishment of provinces, ordinations, ecclesiastical courts, and the BCP.

Constructive Quarterly, The. This quarterly was published from Mar. 1913, until June 1922. Its sub-title was *A Journal of the Faith, Work, and Thought of Christendom*. It served as a "forum where the isolated Churches of Christendom may introduce themselves to one another." The editor was Silas McBee (1853–1924), a close friend and former student of William Porcher DuBose. DuBose published eleven articles in the *Quarterly*, including "A Constructive Treatment of Christianity," which was the lead article in the first issue of *The Constructive Quarterly*. *See* DuBose, William Porcher.

Consubstantial. The term means "of the same substance." In Trinitarian theology, one divine substance exists fully and equally, or consubstantially, in three Persons. Bitter controversies arose in early Christianity concerning the divinity of the Son. The councils determined that the fullness of divinity exists not only in the Father but also in the Son and the Holy Spirit. Jesus is consubstantial with the Father and the Holy Spirit in respect to his divinity. Jesus is also consubstantial with humanity in respect to his humanity. See the Nicene Creed (BCP, p. 358) and the decree of the Council of Chalcedon (BCP, p. 864).

Consubstantiation. Doctrine of the Real Presence of Christ in the Eucharist associated with the theology of Martin Luther. It teaches that after the consecration the substance of the Body and Blood of Christ and the substance of the bread and wine coexist in union with each other. The doctrine was formulated in opposition to the doctrine of transubstantiation, which held that the substance of the consecrated bread and wine no longer existed, but their accidents (external form) were sacramentally united to the substance of the Body and Blood of Christ. This doctrine was condemned by Luther in *The Babylonian Captivity.*

Transubstantiation was believed by the Reformers generally to overthrow the nature of a sacrament by denying the reality of the external sign.

Consultation on Church Union (COCU). The Consultation on Church Union (COCU) is an ecumenical organization founded in 1962 with the intention of uniting the major American Protestant denominations. In Dec. 1960, Eugene Carson Blake, Stated Clerk of the United Presbyterian Church in the United States of America, and James Pike, Bishop of the Episcopal Diocese of California, challenged the United Methodist Church, the United Church of Christ, and their own denominations to work toward overcoming the differences separating them. The proposal that led to the formation of COCU was first made by Blake in a sermon at Grace Cathedral, San Francisco, on Dec. 4, 1960. The Blake-Pike proposal inspired the first COCU gathering in 1962, when representatives of the four denominations met and discussed issues relating to Christian reunion. In 1966 COCU produced a document, *Proposals of Church Union*, that outlined teachings common to all mainline churches on the Bible, theology, the ordained ministry, and the sacraments.

The 1994 General Convention affirmed the Episcopal Church's participation in COCU as a symbol of its continuing commitment to the ideal of Christian unity. The African Methodist Episcopal Church, the African Methodist Episcopal Zion Church, the Christian Church (Disciples of Christ), the Christian Methodist Episcopal Church, the International Council of Community Churches, the Presbyterian Church (U.S.A.), the United Church of Christ, the United Methodist Church, and the Episcopal Church are currently COCU members. "COCU" now stands for Church of Christ Uniting.

Contemplation. A form of mental prayer in which meditation and petition give way to quiet adoration of the mysteries of God. Contemplation is the fruit of divine grace. It comes after a period of recollection and self-abandonment. Daily concerns vanish and exclusive attention is given to the mysteries of the Trinity, the Incarnation, and Redemption. Active imagination gives way to waiting and listening. God is sought and found within the self as divine dwelling-place. The contemplative way may lead through phases of spiritual dryness, often called "nights." Its summit is conscious participation in the very life of God, metaphorically called the state of "spiritual marriage." Forms of contemplation are found in all great religions. It is described in the Upanishads and by the sûfîs of Islam. The experience of contemplation does not guarantee the orthodoxy of its expression. Yet the great Christian contemplatives remain within the parameters of faith as their experience rests upon the mediation of Christ and is nurtured by the gifts of the Spirit. While contemplation is not experienced by all believers, it may be desired by all, and such a desire is already God's grace.

Contemplative Order. A religious community that is primarily devoted to the contemplative life. The Benedictine Order exists in the Anglican Communion, including St. Gregory's Abbey ("Three Rivers") in the Episcopal Church. Contemplative orders in the Episcopal Church also include the Order of Julian of Norwich in Waukesha, Wisconsin, and the Order of Poor Clares of Reparation in Mount Sinai, New York.

Contrition. Full repentance for sin and a firm intention for amendment of life. Contrition is motivated by love of God, causing the penitent to regret sin as evidence of a turning away from God who loves us. Contrition has been distinguished from attrition since the twelfth century. Attrition has been referred to as imperfect contrition. Attrition is imperfect repentance for sin, possibly owing to fear of punishment or displeasure at the sin itself. *See* Attrition.

Convent. The term may refer either to a religious community or the building where the community lives. The term is most frequently applied to a community of nuns, although it may refer to a religious community of men or women. The term is from the Latin, *con* and *venire*, "to come together."

Conversion. An experience or process whereby an individual comes to belief in Christ as Savior and Lord. In Protestant Christianity, conversion usually emphasizes an adult experience of sudden or dramatic change. Nevertheless, many Christians are brought to belief in Christ as Lord through a gradual process of growth in the Christian life.

In Benedictine monasticism, conversion (with stability and obedience) is one of the three vows guiding the religious life. It implies that one "puts on Christ" through work, worship, study, and cultivation of relationships with other people. One's response and commitment to God may gradually deepen as conversion continues.

Conversion of Saint Paul the Apostle, The. The conversion of Paul to Christianity is so important that the story is told three times in Acts, and Paul mentions the experience three times in his letters. An observance of Paul's conversion is mentioned in some calendars from the eighth and ninth centuries. Pope Innocent III (1198–1216) ordered that it be observed with great solemnity. After his conversion, Paul devoted his life completely to Christ. He was the leading missionary to the Gentiles in the early church. The Conversion of Saint Paul is commemorated on Jan. 25 in the Episcopal calendar of the church year. This observance concludes the Week of Prayer for Christian Unity. *See* Paul, Saint.

Convocation. 1) In the Episcopal Church, a meeting of clergy and lay representatives from a section or area of a diocese. The term may also indicate the section or area of the diocese that is represented by the assembly. The name may be used by other church gatherings or assemblies. 2) In the Church of England, a provincial assembly of the clergy. There are two ancient convocations in the two provinces of the Church of England. The Convocation of Canterbury dates from the ecclesiastical reforms of Theodore of Tarsus, Archbishop of Canterbury, 668 to 690. The Convocation of York dates from 733. Convocation has met in two houses since the fifteenth century, with the bishops in the Upper House, and other clergy in the Lower House. Convocation is an exclusively clerical assembly, but a House of Laymen has been associated with the convocation in each province since 1885.

Convocation of American Churches in Europe. The convocation is under the jurisdiction of the Presiding Bishop. Its history goes back to 1859, when an American Episcopal congregation in Paris, France, was recognized by the Episcopal Church as a parish. Over the years the number of Episcopal parishes in Europe increased. At various times the American churches in Europe were assigned to the foreign missionary field and then to the domestic missionary field. The American churches in Europe were under the particular responsibility of the Presiding Bishop, who named a Bishop-in-Charge. The first full-time Bishop-in-Charge of the convocation was the Rt. Rev. Edmond L. Browning, the resigned Bishop of Okinawa. He became Bishop-in-Charge on May 16, 1971. The member churches include the Cathedral of the Holy Trinity (the American Cathedral), Paris; St. Paul's Within-the-Walls, Rome, Italy; St. James Church, Florence, Italy; Emmanuel Church, Geneva, Switzerland; the Church of the Ascension, Munich, Germany; the Church of Christ the King, Frankfurt-am-Main, Germany; St. Augustine of Canterbury, Wiesbaden, Germany; All Saints' Church, Waterloo, Belgium; and Christ Church, Royat, France (a mission station of the cathedral in Paris).

Convocation of Colored Clergy. *See* Conference of Church Workers Among Colored People (CCWACP).

Cooper, Susan Augusta Fenimore (Apr. 17, 1813–Dec. 31, 1894). Author and churchwoman. She was born in Heathcote Hill, Mamaroneck, New York, and privately educated. She was the daughter of the novelist James Fenimore Cooper, who wrote *The Last of the Mohicans* (1826) and *The Deerslayer* (1841). In 1850 she published *Rural Hours*, which was a very successful nature diary, and in 1890 she published *William West Skiles, a Sketch of Missionary Life in Valle Crucis in Western North Carolina, 1842–1862*. In 1873 Cooper founded the Orphan House of the Holy Savior in Cooperstown, New York, a village founded by her family. She is commemorated in a stained-glass window in Christ Church, Cooperstown. She died in Cooperstown.

Cope. A ceremonial cloak, semicircular, richly ornamented, with a clasp in front and a hood or hood-like appendage in back, worn over the alb (or rochet) and stole. It is based on the *cappa*, an outdoor overcoat worn in the Roman empire. The presider wears a cope usually at non-eucharistic liturgies in place of the chasuble. Several Anglican practices dating from the sixteenth century have extended usage of the cope. Presiders sometimes wear a cope at the eucharist during the entrance procession and even during the liturgy of the word. Bishops sometimes wear it when performing episcopal functions such as ordinations and confirmations. Deacons, cantors, and others may also wear a cope since its use is not restricted to bishops and priests.

Cornelius the Centurion. He and his household were the first known Gentile converts to the Christian faith. Cornelius was stationed at Caesarea in Palestine. The story of the conversion and baptism of Cornelius and his household is recorded in Acts 10:1–11:18. Their conversion and baptism served as a precedent in resolving the question whether a Gentile must first become a Jew to become a Christian. Cornelius, "a devout man who feared God," was commanded in a vision by an angel to send for Peter at Joppa. Before those sent by Cornelius arrived, Peter was told while in a trance, "What God has made clean, you must not call profane." Peter subsequently visited Cornelius's home, and proclaimed the Christian faith to them. While Peter was speaking, the Holy Spirit came down on Cornelius and his household. They spoke in tongues. This event was like the gift of the Holy Spirit to the apostles at Pentecost. Peter directed that Cornelius and his household should be baptized. Circumcision was not required by Peter for baptism.

Peter was criticized by the Judaistic Christian church in Jerusalem for visiting the uncircumcised and eating with them. He defended himself by recalling the story of the baptism of Cornelius and his household. He noted that "God gave them the same gift that he gave us when we believed in the Lord Jesus Christ." This silenced Peter's critics, who praised God and proclaimed that "God has given even to the Gentiles the repentance that leads to life." This issue was later resolved more fully by an apostolic council in Jerusalem which determined that "we should not trouble those Gentiles who are turning to God" (Acts 15). Gentiles were admitted into the Christian church on an equal basis with Jewish converts.

According to tradition, Cornelius became Bishop of Caesarea. His life is commemorated on Feb. 4 in the Episcopal calendar of the church year.

Cornerstone Project, The. Since its inception in 1987, the Cornerstone Project has been committed to strengthening and sustaining the ordained leadership of the Episcopal Church. It is a partnership initiative of the Episcopal Church Foundation. Some of its programs are: clergy-laity dialogues; being well in Christ; priestly leadership conference—looking at ministry three to seven years after ordination; transition support program—beginning of a new pastoral relationship; mutual ministry review; and deepening the spiritual life. From Sept. 1, 1992, to Dec. 31, 1994, the Rev. James C. Fenhagen was the project director. He published a newsletter called *A Cornerstone Reflection*. On Jan. 1, 1995, William S. Craddock, Jr., director of the Clergy Leadership Project, became the project director.

Corporal. A square of white linen, spread on the altar during the preparation of the altar, on which the bread and wine are placed. The term is from the Latin *corpus*, "body." It originally covered the entire altar. By the ninth century the cloth had become an additional, smaller cloth with a special name, corporal. Its specific purpose was to sustain and protect the body and blood of Christ. The BCP simply directs: "The Holy Table is spread with a clean white cloth during the Celebration."

Corporeal Presence. A term stating that Christ is *physically* present in the consecrated elements of the eucharist. It is not to be confused with the doctrine of the "real presence," which holds that Christ is truly present in the consecrated elements but in a spiritual, nonphysical manner.

Corpus Christi, Feast of. This feast commemorates the institution of the eucharist by Jesus on the night of his betrayal and arrest. It is often associated with a festive procession that follows the celebration of the eucharist. A consecrated host in a monstrance is prominently displayed in this procession. It is treated as the triumphant Christ the King. This feast is observed in the Roman Catholic Church on the Thursday after Trinity Sunday. Emphasis on Jesus' Passion in the Maundy Thursday service led to selection of another day for celebration of the Feast of Corpus Christi, even though the eucharist was instituted by Jesus on the Thursday before his death. The Feast of Corpus Christi is not included in the feasts of our Lord or other feasts of the Episcopal calendar of the church year. However, it is celebrated by some Episcopal parishes, especially those with an Anglo-catholic piety.

The BCP provides a proper collect and readings for the celebration "Of the Holy Eucharist" among the "Various Occasions" for optional use. This service is a commemoration of the institution of the eucharist. It may be celebrated at any time, subject to the rules set forth in the calendar of the church year. A Prayer Book rubric notes that this celebration is especially suitable for Thursdays. The collect for this celebration is a revised version of the collect composed by St. Thomas Aquinas (c. 1225–1274) for the Feast of Corpus Christi (BCP, p. 252). The BCP provides another version of this prayer for use "After Receiving Communion" (p. 834).

Observance of this feast dates from the thirteenth century. The nun Juliana of Liège (d. 1258), in Belgium, became an advocate for such a feast in response to a vision. The first Feast of Corpus Christi was celebrated at Liège around 1247. Its observance by the western church was commanded by Pope Urban IV in 1264.

A procession of the host has been a prominent part of the celebration since the fourteenth century. Historically, in medieval times, cycles of mystery plays were performed around the time of the Feast of Corpus Christi in France, Germany, and England. These plays dramatized salvation history with stories from the OT and NT.

Anglican and Episcopal ambivalence about the Feast of Corpus Christi is likely related to its historic association with the Roman Catholic dogma of transubstantiation. Urban IV commissioned Aquinas to compose the special Mass and offices for the feast. Aquinas also composed hymns for this celebration. Aquinas's hymn, "Lauda Sion," was originally composed as the sequence hymn for the eucharist on the Feast of Corpus Christi. The "Tantum ergo" was originally Aquinas's hymn for vespers on the Feast of Corpus Christi. *The Hymnal 1982* includes both the "Lauda Sion" (Hymn 320) and the "Tantum ergo" (Hymn 330; Hymns 329/331, stanzas 5–6), but with Aquinas's original references to transubstantiation omitted.

Corrigan, Daniel (Oct. 25, 1900–Sept. 21, 1994). One of three bishops who first ordained women. He was born in Rochester, Minnesota, and received his B.D. from Nashotah House in 1925. He was ordained deacon on June 1, 1924, and priest on May 21, 1925. He was rector of St. John the Baptist Church, Portage, Wisconsin, 1925–1931; Zion Church, Oconomowoc, Wisconsin, 1931–1944; Grace and St. Peter's Church, Baltimore; and St. Paul's Church, St. Paul, Minnesota. He was consecrated Suffragan Bishop of Colorado on May 1, 1958. He resigned on June 1, 1960, to become director of the Home Department of the Executive Council of the Episcopal Church, where he served until 1968. In 1969–1970 he was acting dean of Bexley Hall. Corrigan was one of three bishops who ordained eleven women to the priesthood on July 29, 1974, two years before General Convention voted to ordain women to the priesthood. He was known as an advocate for peace and human rights. He demonstrated against the Vietnam War and participated in AIDS ministry in Los Angeles. He died in Santa Barbara, California.

Costa Rica, Missionary District of. The House of Bishops created the Missionary District of Costa Rica on Sept. 18, 1967. It was a Missionary District of the Episcopal Church until Sept. 1976, when the General Convention voted to make it an Extra-Provincial Diocese related to Province 9.

Cotta. A white vestment that typically reaches to the hips. It has a square-yoke neck, and sleeves that are less ample than the surplice. The cotta is a shorter version of the surplice. The cotta is seldom worn today, except by young members of the choir or acolytes. *See* Surplice.

Council for the Development of Ministry (CDM). On Dec. 4, 1970, representatives of the Board for Church Deployment, the Standing Commission on Structure, the Board for Theological Education, the House of Bishops Committee on Pastoral Development, and Consultation/Search, Inc., met at the Episcopal Church Center to form what would be called the Ad Hoc Ministry Council. At the first meeting of the Ministry Council on Mar. 1, 1971, representatives from the General Board of Examining Chaplains and the Executive Council's program "Professional and Ordained Ministry" were added to the Council. The General Convention of 1973 established the Ministry Council and removed the "Ad Hoc" from its name. The Ministry Council proposed to the 1976 General Convention that "a national instrumentality" be established to strengthen the ministry of the church. The 1976 General Convention responded by creating the Council for the Development of Ministry. The agency membership of the CDM established by the General Convention included the Board for Theological Education, the Church Pension Fund, the Church Deployment Board and Office, the Council of Seminary Deans, the Standing Committee of Education for Ministry of the Executive Council, the General Board of Examining Chaplains, the House of Bishops Committee on Pastoral Development, the National Institute for Lay Training, and the National Network of Episcopal Clergy Associations. The Council provided services to help the church recognize its ministry needs and better utilize its resources. It was merged into the Standing Commission on Ministry Development by the 1997 General Convention. *See* Ministry Development, Standing Commission on.

Council for Women's Ministries (CWM). CWM is a body composed of representatives of over twenty women's organizations within the Episcopal Church. It seeks to increase the effectiveness of women's ministries and it works to advance the roles of women in the mission of the church. This group was organized on Apr. 19–20, 1983, in New York City by representatives from Episcopal Church Women, Episcopal Women's Task Force, Episcopal Women's History Project, National Altar Guild Association, and Episcopal Women's Caucus. It represents women's organizations and concerns within the Episcopal Church. CWM publishes the *Journal of Women's Ministries*, which is described as "a Christian journal published by women and dedicated to bringing wholeness to the church through personal and corporate transformation." It began publication in the Winter of 1984. *See* Women in Mission and Ministry (WIMM).

Council of Advice, House of Bishops. Common name given for the Advisory Committee of the House of Bishops. The Advisory Committee includes a bishop from each province of the Episcopal Church who has been elected president or vice-president of that province. The nine bishops act as advisory council to the Presiding Bishop between meetings of the House of Bishops.

Council of Seminary Deans. The 1967 General Convention created the Board for Theological Education. Shortly afterwards the deans of the accredited Episcopal seminaries began meeting together to discuss common issues and concerns. The council also works to insure that the concerns of the theological seminaries come before the General Conventions. The president of the council is the senior dean and the secretary is the newest dean. The council has no canonical standing.

"Course of Ecclesiastical Studies." As early as 1801, the House of Deputies had tried to standardize the academic preparation of candidates for ordination by requesting the House of Bishops to prepare an official course of theological studies. This was necessary since there were no Episcopal theological seminaries at the time. Presiding Bishop William White drew up such a course. It was approved by the House of Bishops in 1804. The list contained about fifty books divided into seven categories: apologetics or Christian evidences; scripture; church history; systematic theology; homiletics; liturgics; and pastoral theology. It remained unchanged until 1889. Even after theological seminaries were established, the course list was used as the reading for courses in the seminaries.

Court for the Trial of a Bishop. It has original jurisdiction to try all Presentments made against a bishop which have been approved for trial by the Board of Inquiry, which is a body serving to conduct a Preliminary Hearing on charges. The court consists of nine bishops, three of whom shall be elected at each General Convention by the House of Bishops for a nine-year term.

Court of Review of the Trial of a Bishop. The court has appellate jurisdiction to hear all appeals from a convicted bishop. In cases involving holding and teaching doctrine contrary to that of the church, it may hear appeals from the church attorney in cases of acquittal. In the latter case, the appeal is only as to questions of law and cannot reverse a finding of "not guilty." It consists of nine bishops, three of whom shall be elected at each General Convention by the House of Bishops for a nine-year term.

Covenant. A binding agreement that is freely entered into by two or more parties. The parties to this solemn agreement may be individuals or groups of people. They may be of equal or unequal status. A covenant also typically includes terms, oaths, and a ritual enactment (possibly a sacrifice, a meal, an exchange, or even a handshake). A covenant with God is a relationship initiated by God for salvation and responded to in faith. The old covenant was given by God to the Hebrew people. The story of this covenant is revealed in the OT (see BCP, pp. 846–847). It was by covenant that the Hebrew people entered into special relationship with God and became the people of God.

The OT tells many stories of God's covenant with the people of Israel. God made a covenant with Noah and his descendants that there will never again be a flood to destroy the earth. Noah serves as mediator of this covenant between God and all that lives on the earth. God's bow in the clouds was the sign of this covenant (Gn 9: 8–17). God also made a covenant with Abraham, in which God promised Abraham that his posterity would be as numerous as the stars and that Abraham's descendants would have the promised land (Gn 15: 1–21). God made a covenant with Moses that the people of Israel would be God's people, and God would be their God. God also promised to free them from the burdens of the Egyptians and to bring them to the land that God covenanted to give to Abraham, Isaac, and Jacob (Ex 6: 2–8). God's covenant with Moses and the people of Israel was to be lived out by them in terms of the Ten Commandments (see Ex 20: 1–17, Ex 34, Dt 5: 6–21).

The new covenant is the new relationship with God given by Jesus to the apostles and through them to all who believe in Jesus (see BCP, pp. 850–851). At the Last Supper, Jesus shared the cup of wine with the apostles, saying, "This cup that is poured out for you is the new covenant in my blood" (Lk 22:20). We share in the new covenant as participants in Christ's life, death, and resurrection. Jesus' Summary of the Law was that we are to love God with all our heart, soul, and mind; and we are to love our neighbor as we love ourselves (Mt 22:37–40; see BCP, p. 851). We live out our participation in the new covenant in terms of the new commandment that we love one another as Christ loved us (Jn 13: 34–35; see BCP, p. 851). The new covenant is a life of love that we share with Christ and with each other in Christ's name. Christian initiation takes place in terms of the baptismal covenant (BCP, pp. 304–305), which is renewed at Confirmation (BCP, pp. 416–417).

Coverdale, Miles (1488–Jan. 20, 1569). Reformation-era Bible translator. He was probably born in what is called Cover-dale in that part of Yorkshire known as Richmondshire. He studied at Cambridge and was ordained priest in 1514. He joined the Augustinian Friars at Cambridge, where Robert Barnes, later a Protestant, was the prior. Coverdale left the monastery in 1526. From 1528 until 1535, he lived on the Continent. His translation of the Bible was published in 1535. It was the first complete Bible in English. He revised this 1535 translation, and in 1539 it was issued as the "Great Bible." The Psalter of the Great Bible was the Psalter of the 1549 BCP. In 1540 he edited "Cranmer's Bible." Coverdale returned to England in 1539, but he was forced into exile again in 1540. He lived for a time at Tübingen. From 1543 until 1547 he was the Lutheran pastor at Bergzabern, Germany. He returned to England. On Aug. 30, 1551, he was consecrated Bishop of Exeter. He was deprived of this office on Sept. 28, 1553, after Mary became Queen. Again he went into exile, but he returned to England in 1559. Coverdale is recognized as an outstanding preacher, and a faithful Bible translator. Later in life he was a Puritan leader. He died in London.

Coverdale's Bible. The first completed Bible printed in English, translated by Miles Coverdale. It was produced on the Continent and issued in 1535. This translation was based on the Vulgate, Luther's German translation of the Bible, and William Tyndale's translations of the Pentateuch, Jonah, and the NT. This Bible provided a basis for the Great Bible (1539), which was subsequently prepared by Coverdale.

Cowl. A hooded garment worn by a monk. The term may also refer to a hooded cloak or cape.

"Cowley Fathers." *See* Society of St. John the Evangelist, The (SSJE) (Cowley Fathers).

Cowley Publications. The publishing ministry of the Society of St. John the Evangelist (SSJE), an Anglican religious order for men. Cowley Publications was founded in 1979 by M. Thomas Shaw, SSJE, and James Madden, SSJE, to revive the educational work of their order, which was then widely known as the Cowley Fathers. Cynthia Shattuck, a seminary-educated lay woman, was chosen to serve as editor of the press, and she was named director of the organization in 1994. Cowley publishes books that reflect the tradition of prayer, spiritual direction, and intellectual reflection nurtured by SSJE. In 1997 Cowley inaugurated the multi-volume New Church's Teaching Series as a successor to the earlier denominational teaching series of the 1950s and 1970s. James E. Griffiss is the series editor. *See* Society of St. John the Evangelist, The (SSJE) (Cowley Fathers).

Cowper, William (Nov. 15, 1731–Apr. 25, 1800). British poet and hymn-writer. His life was marred by deep melancholy which began in his school days at Westminster School and oppressed him until his death. During Cowper's residency at Olney he established a creative, strong friendship with the Rev. John Newton who encouraged his hymn writing. Sixty-eight of his finest hymns were included in the *Olney Hymns* published with Newton in 1770. His last years were marked by periods of insanity. Three of his texts are included in *The Hymnal 1982*, including "Sometimes a light surprises" (667) and "O for a closer walk with God" (683–684).

Coxe, Arthur Cleveland (May 10, 1818–July 20, 1896). Leading figure of the high church party. He was born in Mendham, New Jersey. He graduated from the University of New York in 1838 and then from General Theological Seminary in 1841. He was ordained deacon on June 27, 1841, and priest on Sept. 25, 1842. He was rector of St. John's Church, Hartford, Connecticut, 1842–1854, Grace Church, Baltimore, 1854–1863, and Calvary Church, New York, 1863–1865. Coxe was consecrated Assistant Bishop of Western New York on Jan. 4, 1865, and became Bishop of Western New York on Apr. 5, 1865. He published several volumes of ecclesiastical poetry.

Cram, Ralph Adams (Dec. 16, 1863–Sept. 22, 1942). Church architect. He was born in Hampton Falls, New Hampshire. After completing high school in 1880, he studied for five years in an architectural firm in Boston. Although he abandoned architecture for a time, he returned to that profession in 1890 and formed a partnership with Charles Francis Wentworth. Cram's firm (later known as Cram, Goodhue and Ferguson) soon began to specialize in the design of churches. Cram identified himself at this time with the Anglo-catholic party of the Episcopal Church. His interest in medievalism and religious ritual inspired his efforts to make gothic the preeminent style for the construction of American church buildings in his day. Among Cram's most famous designs are the Cathedral of St. John the Divine and St. Thomas Church in New York City, and the chapel of the United States Military Academy at West Point, New York. Cram was also instrumental in the founding of the Medieval Academy of America in 1925. He died in Boston.

Cranmer, Thomas (July 2, 1489–Mar. 21, 1556). First Protestant Archbishop of Canterbury and leader of the Anglican Reformation. He was born in Aslockton, Nottinghamshire, England. Cranmer received his B.A. from Jesus College, Cambridge University, in 1511. In 1520 he was ordained priest and selected as one of the university preachers. Around 1521 he began to be influenced by Lutheran ideas and became antipapal. When King Henry VIII was seeking the annulment of his marriage to Catherine of Aragon, Cranmer suggested that the king refer the issue to the professors at the universities. Henry was impressed with this idea. In 1531 Cranmer was named ambassador to the imperial court of Charles V with the task of making contact with the German Lutherans and getting their support for the annulment. While in Germany he met the Lutheran theologian Andreas Osiander and married Osiander's niece, Margaret. Henry named Cranmer Archbishop of Canterbury, and Pope Clement VII consented. Cranmer was consecrated Archbishop of Canterbury on Mar. 30, 1533. One of Cranmer's first official acts came on May 25, 1533, when he formally stated that Henry's marriage to Catherine was null and void. As archbishop he was the author of the first Anglican Prayer Book (1549). He was the leader in moderate doctrinal reform as expressed in the Ten Articles of 1536 and the *Bishops' Book* of 1537. Under King Edward VI (1547–1553), he continued as a leader of the Reformation. With the accession of Queen Mary in 1553, Cranmer's Protestant policies fell into disfavor. On Nov. 13, 1553, he was deprived of his office as archbishop. In 1556 he was accused of high treason and handed over to the state for execution. He recanted, but the prospect of death restored both his faith and his dignity. He renounced his recantation and reaffirmed his opposition to papal power and the doctrine of transubstantiation. At the stake he steadfastly held his right hand in the fire until it was consumed. He did this because his right hand "had offended" by signing the recantation. The BCP of 1549, revised in 1552, stands as the greatest achievement of his genius. Cranmer is commemorated along with Hugh Latimer and Nicholas Ridley in the Episcopal calendar of the church year on Oct. 16.

Crapsey, Algernon Sidney (June 28, 1847–Dec. 31, 1927). Priest deposed for heresy. He was born in Fairmount, Ohio. He studied at St. Stephen's College (now Bard College) from 1867 to 1869 and received a B.D. from the General Theological Seminary in 1872. He was ordained deacon on June 30, 1872 and priest on Oct. 5, 1873. Crapsey served as assistant minister at St. Paul's Chapel of Trinity Church, New York City. In 1879 he was called as rector of St. Andrew's Church, Rochester, New York, a position he held for the next twenty-eight years. Crapsey was a colleague of Social Gospel theologian Walter Rauschenbusch. In 1905 Crapsey published a series of lectures entitled *Religion and Politics*. In this book he advocated that the church become involved in social reform. He also argued for the reinterpretation of traditional doctrines such as the Trinity and the Virgin Birth. Crapsey was tried for heresy. He was convicted and deposed by William Walker, Bishop of Western New York, on Dec. 4, 1906. Crapsey continued to write and lecture on his religious ideas for the next two decades. He died in Rochester, New York.

Creationism. 1) Understanding that God creates and directly infuses a new soul in every person at conception. The soul is understood to be created by God out of nothing. Creationism denies the pre-existence of the soul (Pre-existentialism), and it denies that the soul is transmitted by the parents or generated with the body (Traducianism). 2) Understanding that God created the universe out of nothing by a free act of will. Creationism denies that creation is identical with God, or an emanation from God, or an illusion. 3) Creationism also refers to an understanding that God created the universe without employing an evolutionary process. Many creationists believe that biblical faith is contradicted by scientific theories of evolution. This understanding is associated with a literal reading of the Book of Genesis. On the other hand, many Christian theologians, including William Porcher DuBose of the Episcopal Church, understand evolutionary theory to be compatible with God's continuous process of saving activity in the world. *See* Fundamentalism; *see* Process Theology.

Crèche. A representation of a nativity scene. It typically includes a figure of the infant Jesus in a manger, along with Mary, Joseph, shepherds, angels, and animals. It is usually displayed from Christmas Eve until Epiphany Day. Figures of the Wise Men may be added on Epiphany Day. The term is also used occasionally for a nursery.

Credence. A small table or shelf, sometimes called a credence table. It is typically located near the altar. It may hold the elements and vessels that are used in the eucharist, including the bread, the cruets with wine and water, the chalice and paten, and the offering plates or basins. It is customary in many parishes for the credence to be covered with a white cloth. The term is derived from the Latin for "belief" or "trust." It reflects the historic use of such a table to hold food for sampling to detect poison.

Creed. A concise and formal statement of basic beliefs about God. The term is derived from the Latin *credo*, "I believe." Creeds are usually authorized by a faith community and state important points of doctrine. Creeds do not provide an exhaustive statement of all points of belief shared by the community. The language of a creed may require interpretation as the creed is passed on from generation to generation in the church. Confessions of faith were not in fixed form in the first 150 years of the church. The text of the Apostles' Creed can be traced to the set of questions that were asked of candidates for baptism at Rome around the end of the second century. The historic creeds of Christendom include the Apostles' Creed and the Nicene Creed, which are both used by the Episcopal Church in worship. The Apostles' Creed is used in the Daily Offices, the baptismal covenant, and the Renewal of Baptismal Vows (BCP, pp. 304, 292). The Nicene Creed is used at the eucharist. The Athanasian Creed is not typically used for worship in the Episcopal Church, but it is included among the Historical Documents of the Church in the BCP (pp. 864–865). *See* Apostles' Creed; *see* Athanasian Creed; *see* Deposit of Faith, The; *see* Nicene Creed.

Cremation. The reducing by fire of a dead body to ashes. The ashes may be placed in an urn or other container and interred in a niche of a columbarium. The ashes may also be buried or scattered in a memorial garden on church grounds or in a cemetery. The ashes may be referred to as "cremains." The early Christians considered cremation inappropriate because the body was to be resurrected. Early Christians followed the Jewish practice of burial. Cremation largely ceased in the Roman empire by the fifth century. However, several cremation societies were organized in Europe during the nineteenth century. Cremation was urged by some because of concern for public hygiene and conservation of land. The practice became more widespread, and was no longer understood to deny the resurrection of the body. The 1979 BCP is the first American Prayer Book to recognize cremation. The BCP states (p. 490) that the committal service may precede cremation. The legitimacy of cremation in the Church of England is recognized by the 1969 Canons which state that the ashes of a cremated person should be interred or deposited in consecrated ground. The Roman Catholic Church resisted the practice of cremation in the nineteenth century because it was associated with anti-Catholic sentiments and materialism. The Roman Catholic penalties for cremation were withdrawn by a decree of the Holy Office (July 5, 1963), unless there is evidence of bad faith. *See* Columbarium.

Croes, John (June 1, 1762–July 26, 1832). First Bishop of the Diocese of New Jersey. He was born in Elizabethtown, New Jersey. He pursued a brief career as a teacher and served in the Continental Army during the American Revolution. After the war, he received theological instruction from Bishop William White of Philadelphia, who ordained him deacon on Feb. 28, 1790, and priest on Mar. 4, 1792. He was rector of Trinity Church, Swedesborough, New Jersey from 1790 to 1801, and of Christ Church, New Brunswick, New Jersey from 1801 until his death. He was consecrated at St. Peter's Church, Philadelphia, on Nov. 19, 1815. Croes helped strengthen and expand the Diocese of New Jersey over the course of his seventeen-year episcopate.

Cross. The instrument of Jesus' death and the central symbol of the Christian faith. It represents Jesus' offering and sacrifice of his life in love for us and our salvation. The cross thus symbolizes the Christian life, especially in terms of love, generosity, and sacrifice.

The cross itself was a vertical stake in the ground which often had a horizontal piece attached at the top or just below the top of the vertical piece. Death on a cross was both execution and extreme torture. The victim to be executed on the cross would be attached to it until death. At times an inscription would be attached to the cross to state the victim's crime. Crucifixion was a shameful death that carried with it a considerable stigma in Jesus' day. Jesus' death on a cross is described in the NT gospels (Mt 27, Mk 15, Lk 23, Jn 19).

The cross has been the traditional focus of Christian piety. The practice of making the sign of the cross on the forehead dates from the second century. Devotion to the cross was spurred by the alleged finding of the true cross of Jesus' crucifixion in the fourth century. Use of altar crosses dates from the fifth century, and use of processional crosses dates from the sixth century. During the middle ages, large crosses, or roods, were placed on beams at the dividing point between the chancel and nave of the church. Designs for crosses became very ornate, and some crosses were decorated with jewels.

Crosses are used in Christian art and architecture, and worn as an expression of personal piety. Crosses are found in a variety of shapes and sizes. A crucifix is a cross with a figure of the crucified Christ. A Christus Rex is a cross with a figure of the risen Christ in glory. A Jerusalem cross is a cross with four small crosses in between the arms of the larger cross.

The Prayer Book Good Friday service allows a wooden cross to be brought into the church after the solemn collects. The cross is placed in the sight of the people, and appropriate devotions may follow (BCP, pp. 281–282). Hymns in *The Hymnal 1982* that express devotion to the cross include "When I survey the wondrous cross" (474), "In the cross of Christ I glory" (441–442), and "Lift high the cross" (473).

Cross, Wilford Oakland (July 26, 1903–Sept. 12, 1978). Priest and theologian. He was born in Nottinghamshire, England. His family moved to the United States when he was nine years old. Cross received his B.A. from the University of Illinois in 1926, a Certificate in Theology from the Berkeley Divinity School in 1929, and his M.A. from Columbia University in 1931. He taught English at Long Island University, 1929–1931, and was Assistant Professor of English at Washington and Jefferson College, 1931–1934. Cross was ordained deacon on Apr. 8, 1934, and priest on Nov. 1, 1934. He was vicar of St. Clement's Church, Harvey, Illinois, 1934–1937; rector of the Church of the Good Shepherd, Norwood, Ohio, 1937–1941; rector of St. Paul's Church, Kittanning, Pennsylvania, 1941–1947; and rector of Trinity Church, Washington, Pennsylvania, 1947–1949. In 1950 Cross went to Daniel Baker College as professor of philosophy and religion. He was president of Daniel Baker from 1951 until it closed in 1953. From 1953 until 1961, he was professor of the philosophy of religion and ethics at the School of Theology, University of the South. From 1961 until 1969, he was professor of ethics and moral theology at Nashotah House. Cross retired in 1969. He died in Madison, Connecticut.

Crossroads: The Journal of the Rural Workers' Fellowship. *See* Rural Workers' Fellowship.

Croswell, William (Nov. 7, 1804–Nov. 9, 1851). Leading Anglo-catholic. He was born in Hudson, New York. Croswell graduated from Yale College in 1822, and for the next two years was an assistant teacher in a private school in New Haven. He then studied at the General Theological Seminary and graduated in 1826. Croswell also studied with Bishop Thomas Brownell of Connecticut. He was ordained deacon on Jan. 25, 1829, and priest on June 24, 1829. Croswell served Christ Church, Boston, and a church in Auburn, New York, before becoming rector of the Church of the Advent, Boston, in 1844. The Church of the Advent has many claims to be the first Anglo-catholic church in the Episcopal Church. Feasts and fasts were observed, the Daily Office was used, and the altar was placed within the rail. Some of Croswell's practices offended Bishop Manton Eastburn of Massachusetts, an evangelical, and Eastburn refused to visit the parish for Confirmation. General Convention subsequently passed a canon requiring diocesan bishops to visit each parish in their jurisdictions at least once in every three years. Croswell died in Boston. He was described by Phillips Brooks as "a man of most attractive character and beautiful purity of life."

Crozier, or Crosier. The pastoral staff of a bishop. It was originally a walking stick and later acquired the symbolism of a shepherd's crook. It is a sign of pastoral authority. It may also be carried by abbots and abbesses. In liturgy the diocesan bishop carries the crozier in the left hand, with the crook facing outward. Although the crozier was originally part of the insignia of all bishops, it is now used mainly by diocesans in their own jurisdictions. Its use dates from the seventh century. In the Eastern Orthodox Church the staff is surmounted by a cross between two serpents. A crozier is not the same as the archiepiscopal cross, carried before archbishops in procession.

Crucifer. The acolyte who carries the cross in processions. The crucifer often assists in other ways, such as holding the altar book for the presider and serving at the altar. *See* Acolyte.

Crucifix. A cross bearing the image of Christ crucified, either in agony or in triumph (Christus Rex).

Crucifixion. Death by nailing or binding to a wooden cross. The practice began in the ancient east and was common among the Romans as punishment inflicted on slaves and certain non-Romans. It was abolished by Constantine. The crucifixion of Christ is recorded by all four evangelists. Crosses used for execution are either *crux commissa* (in the form of the letter T) or *crux immissa* (the upright extending above the cross bar). *See* Cross.

Cruciform. In the shape of a cross.

Cruet. A vessel of glass, precious metal, or pottery, in which the wine or water for the eucharist is brought to the altar. The term is from the medieval French *cruette* "little jug."

Crummell, Alexander (1819–Sept. 12, 1898). African American priest, missionary, and educator. He was born in New York City. Crummell completed a course of study at the Oneida Institute, Whitesboro, New York, in 1839. However, he was denied entrance to the General Theological Seminary because of his color. He then studied for the ordained ministry on his own and was ordained deacon on Mar. 30, 1842. He worked first among African Americans in Providence, Rhode Island. He then moved to Philadelphia, where he was ordained priest in Nov. 1844. From 1848 until 1853, Crummell lived in England. In 1853 he received his B.A. from Queen's College, Cambridge University. From 1853 until 1873, he was a missionary for the Episcopal Church in Liberia. He was professor of intellectual and moral science in the College of Liberia, 1853–1866. In 1873 Crummell settled in Washington, D.C. He later founded St. Luke's Church, Washington, D.C., and served as rector of St. Luke's until 1894. In 1883 he organized the Conference of Church Workers Among Colored People, an Episcopal organization. In 1897 he founded the American Negro Academy, a group limited to forty members which encouraged intellectual excellence among African Americans. Crummell worked for the education of African Americans and supported their full participation in the cultural life of the United States. He died in Point Pleasant, New Jersey. Crummell is commemorated in the Episcopal calendar of the church year on Sept. 10. *See* Conference of Church Workers Among Colored People (CCWACP).

Cry Hosanna. This volume of 142 songs and hymns with music was edited by Betty Pulkingham and Mimi Farra and published by Hope Publishing in 1980. Its predecessors were *Sound of Living Waters* and *Fresh Sounds.* It contains hymns from various traditions and countries. It is a collection of traditional hymns and celebrative songs.

Crypt. An underground chamber, vault, or complex of rooms. A crypt is often used as a burial place or chapel and located beneath the main floor of a church. The term was applied by early Christians to their places of worship and burial below the ground in the Roman catacombs.

Cuba, Missionary District of. On Oct. 17, 1901, the House of Bishops established the Missionary District of Cuba. At first it was placed under the jurisdiction of the Presiding Bishop. In 1904 the first Missionary Bishop was consecrated. On Oct. 27, 1966, the House of Bishops made the Missionary District of Cuba the autonomous Diocese of Cuba within the Anglican Communion. The Episcopal Church of Cuba is under a Metropolitan Council composed of the Primate of Canada, the Archbishop of the West Indies, and the president of Province 9 of the Episcopal Church.

Cuernavaca, Diocese of. This diocese was established in 1989. Jose Guadalupe Saucedo, Bishop of Central and South Mexico, became its first bishop. The General Convention of 1994 granted the five Mexican dioceses, including Cuernavaca, permission to withdraw from the Episcopal Church and constitute themselves an autonomous province. The Anglican Church of Mexico came into existence on Jan. 1, 1995. On Feb. 25–26, 1995, the first General Synod of the Anglican Church of Mexico met at Mexico City. Bishop Saucedo of Cuernavaca was elected Primate.

Cully, Kendig Brubaker (Nov. 30, 1913–Mar. 29, 1987). Leading Christian educator, editor, and seminary administrator. He was born in Millersville, Pennsylvania,

and received his B.A. from American International College in 1934; and his B.D. in 1937, his M.R.E. in 1938, and his Ph.D. in 1939 from the Hartford Seminary Foundation. He was ordained deacon on May 20, 1955, and priest on Dec. 12, 1955. He held posts and conducted research in religious education in parish churches and theological seminaries. He taught Christian Education at Seabury-Western Theological Seminary, 1953–1964 and at the New York Theological Seminary, 1964–1971, where he also served as dean, 1965–1971. Cully was rector and dean of the Episcopal Theological Seminary in Kentucky, 1980–1985. He was a founding co-editor of *The Review of Books and Religion* from 1971 to 1984. Among his publications are *Confirmation: History, Doctrine, and Practice* (1962), *The Episcopal Church and Education* (1966), and *Confirmation Re-Examined* (1982). He and Iris V. Cully were the general editors of *Harper's Encyclopedia of Religious Education* (1990), and he edited *The Westminster Dictionary of Christian Education* (1963). Cully died in Claremont, California.

Cummings, Archibald (d. Apr. 19, 1741). Commissary to Pennsylvania. He arrived in Philadelphia from England on Sept. 8, 1726. The next day he began his ministry as fifth rector of Christ Church and first Commissary to Pennsylvania. He served in those positions until his death.

Cummins, George David (Dec. 11, 1822–June 26, 1876). First Presiding Bishop of the Reformed Episcopal Church. He was born near Smyrna, Delaware. Cummins received his B.A. from Dickinson College in 1841. From 1842 until 1845, he was a Methodist circuit rider in Maryland and West Virginia. He became interested in the Episcopal Church deacon and was ordained on Oct. 26, 1845. He began his ministry as assistant minister at Christ Church, Baltimore. He was ordained priest on July 6, 1847. From 1847 until 1853, he was the rector of Christ Church, Norfolk, Virginia. He was rector of St. James's Church, Richmond, Virginia, 1853–1854; rector of Trinity Church, Washington, D.C., 1855–1858; rector of St. Peter's Church, Baltimore, 1858–1863; and rector of Trinity Church, Chicago, 1863–1866. Cummins was consecrated Assistant Bishop of Kentucky on Nov. 15, 1866. He was a leading evangelical, and was opposed to both the Oxford Movement and ritualism. Cummins resigned from the Episcopal ministry on Nov. 10, 1873. He drafted the call to organize the Reformed Episcopal Church, which was issued on Nov. 15, 1873. He presided at the organization and First General Council of the Reformed

Episcopal Church in New York City on Dec. 2, 1873. He served as Presiding Bishop of that church from its organization until his death. Cummins died in Lutherville, Maryland. *See* Reformed Episcopal Church.

Curate. The term typically refers to an assisting priest in a parish. It is from the Latin *curatus*, "entrusted with the care" of something. It was originally used to describe a priest entrusted with the care (or "cure") of souls in a particular area or parish. The term is not used in the BCP or the Constitution and Canons of the Episcopal Church. *See* Cure.

Cure. The pastoral responsibility and charge of a member of the clergy. A cure is often a parish, but that pastoral responsibility may take other forms such as a specialized ministry or chaplaincy. In this regard, the member of the clergy has responsibility for the "cure of souls" of those entrusted to his or her pastoral care. The term "cure" is related in derivation to the word "care." *See* Pastoral Care.

Cursillista. One who has participated in a three-day Cursillo weekend. *See* Cursillo

Cursillo. The Spanish word means "little course" (in Christian life). It is identified with a Roman Catholic movement that was begun in Spain after World War II with the specific intention of bringing men back into the church. By 1949 the movement had largely taken its present form. The Cursillo is normally a three-day weekend. It includes fifteen talks on Christian faith and living by laity and clergy, along with a variety of shared prayer activities and celebrations. The movement and its method quickly spread around the world, becoming a major contributor to the renewal movement. The first Cursillos were held in the United States in the 1950s, and English language events began around 1961. The term itself is a registered trademark of the National Cursillo Secretariat (Roman Catholic) and may not be used without permission. Episcopal Cursillo was founded in 1978, and in 1980 it received a license from the Roman Catholic body to conduct similar weekends for Episcopalians. Similar movements have sprung up for other denominations, such as Emmaus Walk in the United Methodist Church, but not all are chartered or recognized by the National Cursillo Secretariat. Despite a national board to set policies, Episcopal Cursillo is typically diocesan in its organization. It is open to men and women. The character of the Cursillo weekend may vary greatly

from diocese to diocese. Many Episcopalians have experienced a renewal of active faith on these weekends.

Custodian of the Standard Book of Common Prayer. The first custodian was appointed by the 1868 General Convention to keep the plates and a copy of the Standard Book for General Convention. The 1871 General Convention granted the custodian the responsibility for recording any alterations made by General Convention in the BCP. The custodian is nominated by the House of Bishops and confirmed by the House of Deputies, and serves until a successor is appointed. The Custodians have included Benjamin Isaac Haight, 1868–1879; Francis Harrison, 1880–1885; Samuel Hart, 1886–1917; Lucien Moore Robinson, 1917–1932; John Wallace Suter, 1932–1942; John Wallace Suter, Jr., 1942–1962; and Charles Mortimer Guilbert, 1963–1998.

Customary. This book contains rules and directions for ceremonies, and may contain the ceremonies. Customaries are usually designed for a particular place, such as a cathedral, monastery, or religious order. In the Episcopal Church several customaries were published in the 1970s to help clergy and congregations use revised liturgies.

Cuthbert (c. 625–Mar. 20, 687). Bishop and hermit. He was born on Farne Island, near Bamborough, Northumberland, England. In 651 Cuthbert went to the monastery at Old Melrose and became a monk, where he received the Celtic tonsure. He was prior of Melrose Abbey from 661 until 664 when he moved to Lindisfarne. Under the influence of Wilfrid he changed his tonsure to the Roman pattern. On Mar. 26, 685, Cuthbert was consecrated Bishop of Lindisfarne. He resigned that position in 686 and became a hermit. One of his major contributions was to help reconcile the Roman and Celtic factions in the Church of England after the Synod of Whitby in 664. He died in Lindisfarne. Cuthbert is commemorated in the Episcopal calendar of the church year on Mar. 20.

Cutler, Timothy (May 31, 1684–Aug. 17, 1765). Participant in the "Yale Apostasy." He was born in Charlestown, Massachusetts, and graduated from Harvard College in 1701. From 1710 to 1719, he was the Congregational minister at Stratford, Connecticut. He was chosen rector of Yale College in 1719. On Sept. 13, 1722, Cutler, tutor Daniel Brown, and several other Congregational ministers met with the trustees of Yale

College and stated: "Some of us doubt of the validity, and the rest are more fully persuaded of the invalidity, of Presbyterian ordination, in opposition to Episcopal." On Oct. 27, 1722, the trustees voted to "excuse the Rev. Mr. Cutler from all further service, as rector of Yale College." This conversion to episcopacy was known as the "Yale Apostasy" or the "Dark Day" at Yale. Cutler, Brown, and Samuel Johnson went to England where they were rebaptized, and on Mar. 22, 1723, they were confirmed and ordained deacons. On Mar. 31, 1723, they were ordained priests. Cutler became the rector of the newly formed Christ Church, Boston, which opened on Dec. 29, 1723. He served there as a missionary of the Society for the Propagation of the Gospel until his death. He was a high churchman and an advocate for episcopacy in the colonies.

Cuttington University College, Liberia. It was founded on Feb. 22, 1889, as Hoffman Institute at Harper, Liberia, by Bishop Samuel David Ferguson (1842–1916). In 1897 a divinity school was added and the name was changed to Cuttington Collegiate and Divinity School in honor of its first donor, R. Fulton Cutting. The school closed in 1929 and was reopened in 1949 at Suacoco by Bishop Bravid Washington Harris (1895–1965). In 1976 the name was changed to Cuttington University College.

Cuttington University College-in-Exile (Lawrenceville, Virginia). Cuttington University College in Suacoco, Liberia, was forced to close in 1989 because of the civil war in Liberia. The college president, Dr. Melvin J. Mason, and many friends of Cuttington, including alumni, former Fulbright scholars, and Peace Corps volunteers, established Cuttington-in-Exile to keep hope alive for Liberia and students displaced by the war. Cuttington's supporters recognized its importance to Liberia and realized the role it could have in rebuilding the country. At first, Cuttington operated in the office of the Association of Episcopal Colleges in New York. Cuttington-in-Exile was subsequently relocated to St. Paul's College in Lawrenceville, Virginia. Many Cuttington students then gained admission to colleges and universities in the United States and abroad. Some received Cuttington degrees through joint programs. The office at St. Paul's College closed early in 1996 in anticipation of returning to Liberia, but hostilities prevented the move. The office of Cuttington-in-Exile returned to the office of the Association of Episcopal Colleges. *See* Cuttington University College, Liberia.

Cyprian (200–Sept. 14, 258). Martyr and theologian of church unity. Also known as Thascius Caecilianus Cyprianus, he was converted to Christianity in 245 or 246. He was ordained a presbyter and in 248 was consecrated Bishop of Carthage. During the Decian persecution of 249, he was forced to flee from Carthage and did not return until 251. During the persecution many Christians lapsed from their faith. When Cyprian returned to Carthage he insisted that they be reconciled to the church only after appropriate penance. In a heated controversy with Pope Stephen, Cyprian insisted that schismatics had to be rebaptized on the ground that no one outside of the church could administer the sacraments. Cyprian's major writing was *De ecclesiae catholicae unitate* ("On the Unity of the Catholic Church"), written in 251, in which he argued that the unity of the church is based on the unity of equal bishops. He insisted that *extra ecclesiam nulla salus*, "outside of the Church there is no salvation." He is known as "the apostle of unity," and as the classical representative of the episcopal form of church government. There is a hymn about Cyprian in *Lift Every Voice and Sing II: An African American Hymnal* (1993). He was martyred at Carthage during the persecution of Emperor Valerian. His life is commemorated in the Episcopal calendar of the church year on Sept. 13.

Cyril (826–869) and Methodius (c. 815–885). Known as the "Apostles of the Slavs," these two brothers were from Thessalonica. After their ordinations to the priesthood they went to Constantinople. Cyril was named Constantine until he became a monk. He was the librarian at St. Sophia Church in Constantinople. Around 863 Emperor Michael III and Patriarch Photius sent them to Moravia as missionaries. In Moravia they translated some of the Bible and some of the liturgy into Slavonic and invented the Glagolithic alphabet from which the Cyrillic alphabet was derived. In 868 Cyril entered a monastery in Rome and died there the next year. Methodius was consecrated Bishop by Pope Adrian II and returned to Moravia as Metropolitan of Sirmium (Pannonia). Methodius died in Velehrad in Czechoslovakia. The missionary work of Cyril and Methodius is commemorated in the Episcopal calendar of the church year on Feb. 14.

Cyril of Jerusalem (c. 315–c. 386). Bishop and Doctor of the Church. He was probably ordained deacon around 330 and priest about 343. From 348 until 386, Cyril was the Bishop of Jerusalem. While he was bishop he wrote his

Catechetical Lectures on the Christian faith, which were given to candidates for baptism. In these lectures he explained the liturgical practices of Lent and Holy Week in fourth-century Palestinian Christianity. The *Mystagogical Catecheses*, which were lectures given to the newly baptized after Easter, are ascribed to Cyril, but were probably written by his successor, John. Cyril attended the Council of Constantinople in 381, accepted its conclusions, and was a defender of the Nicene faith. He was made a Doctor of the Church by the Roman Catholic Church in 1882. He is commemorated in the Episcopal calendar of the church year on Mar. 18.

D

Daily Evening Prayer. *See* Evening Prayer.

Daily Morning Prayer. *See* Morning Prayer.

Daily Office. Use of daily prayers to mark the times of the day and to express the traditions of the praying community is traditional in Judaism and in Christianity. The third, sixth, and ninth hours (9 A.M., 12 noon, and 3 P.M.) were times of private prayer in Judaism. The congregational or cathedral form of office developed in Christianity under Constantine (274 or 288–337) with the principal morning and evening services of lauds and vespers. The people participated in the cathedral form of office. The monastic form of office also developed at this time. In addition to lauds and vespers, the monastic form included matins (at midnight or cockcrow), prime (the first hour), terce (the third hour), sext (the sixth hour), none (the ninth hour), and compline (at bedtime). By the late middle ages, the Daily Office was seen as the responsibility of the monks and clergy rather than an occasion for participation by all in the prayers of the community throughout the day.

After the Anglican Reformation, Archbishop Thomas Cranmer (1489–1556) reduced the eight monastic offices to the two services of Morning and Evening Prayer. These services were printed in vernacular English and intended for use by all members of the church. Participation in the Daily Office is at the heart of Anglican spirituality. It is the proper form of daily public worship in the church. In addition to forms for Daily Morning Prayer and Daily Evening Prayer in contemporary and traditional language, the BCP section for the Daily Office includes forms for Noonday Prayer, Order of Worship for the Evening,

Compline, and Daily Devotions for Individuals and Families. These offices include prayers, a selection from the Psalter, readings from the Holy Scriptures, one or more canticles, and the Lord's Prayer. Forms for Morning and Evening Prayer include an optional confession of sin. The BCP provides a Daily Office Lectionary that identifies readings and psalm choices for Morning and Evening Prayer (pp. 936–1001), and a Table of Canticles with suggested canticles for use at Morning Prayer and Evening Prayer (pp. 144–145). The officiant in the Daily Office may be a member of the clergy or a lay person.

Dakota, Missionary District of. On Oct. 21, 1865, the House of Bishops created the Missionary District of Nebraska and Dakota. The House of Bishops divided this District on Oct. 28, 1868, and established the Missionary District of Dakota. The Missionary District of Dakota existed until 1883, when on Oct. 13, the House of Bishops divided it and created the Missionary District of North Dakota and the Missionary District of South Dakota.

Dalcho, Frederick (1770–Nov. 24, 1836). Church historian. He was born in London, England, and was baptized on Oct. 15, 1770. Dalcho came to Baltimore, Maryland, studied medicine, and became a surgeon's mate in the United States Army in Apr. 1792. In 1799 he settled in Charleston, South Carolina, where he practiced medicine. In 1807 he became one of the two editors of the *Charleston Courier*, a Federalist daily newspaper. Dalcho began to study theology in 1811. He was ordained deacon on Feb. 15, 1814, and priest on June 12, 1818. On Feb. 23, 1819, he became assistant minister at St. Michael's Church, Charleston, where he remained until his death. In 1820 Dalcho published *An Historical Account of the Protestant Episcopal Church, in South-Carolina, from The First Settlement of the Province, to The War of the Revolution; with Notices of the Present State of the Church in each Parish; and some Account of the Early Civil History of Carolina, never before published. To which are added; The laws relating to religious worship; the Journals and rules of the Convention of South-Carolina; the Constitution and Canons of the Protestant Episcopal Church, and the course of ecclesiastical studies: with An Index, and List of Subscribers.* This was the first diocesan history. In 1824 he with others established *The Charleston Gospel Messenger and Protestant Episcopal Register*, a monthly journal of church affairs, which was published until 1853. The Dalcho Historical Society of the Diocese of South Carolina, named in honor of Dalcho, was organized on Apr. 23, 1945. It was organized at St. Philip's Church Home, Charleston, for the "study and preservation of the history of the Diocese of South Carolina, its origin and development, and the stimulation of interest in the same." Dalcho died in Charleston.

Dale, Thomas (d. Aug. 9, 1619). Public official in colonial Virginia. He was born in England. On June 19, 1606, he was knighted Sir Thomas Dale of Surrey. Dale entered the service of the Virginia Company of London, which appointed him marshal of Virginia. When he arrived in Virginia on May 19, 1611, the Governor of Virginia, Lord De la Warr, was away, and Dale served as deputy governor of the colony. He was noted for his discipline. At one time he placed the colonists under martial law for insubordination. Sir Thomas Gates became governor in Aug., 1611. When Gates left in Mar. 1614, Dale again became deputy governor. While Gates was governor he issued stringent regulations for the colony. Gates's regulations were enlarged by Dale and published as "Articles, Lawes, and Orders, Divine, Politique, and Martial for the Colony in Virginia. ..." This is frequently referred to as "Dale's Laws," but that is a misnomer. These laws were very strict with regard to religious matters. For example, one could be put to death for speaking "impiously or maliciously, against the holy and blessed Trinitie," or for blaspheming God's Holy Name. Dale returned to England in 1616. He died in Masulipatam, India, while serving with the London East India Company.

Dallas, Diocese of. The General Convention of 1874 voted to divide the Diocese of Texas and create the Missionary District of Northern Texas and the Missionary District of Western Texas. At the primary convention on Dec. 19–20, 1895, at St. Matthew's Cathedral, Dallas, the Missionary District of Northern Texas became the Diocese of Dallas. The Diocese of Dallas was divided in 1910 and again in 1982. It includes the following counties: Bowie, Camp, Cass, Collin, Cooke, Dallas, Delta, Denton, Ellis, Fannin, Franklin, Grayson, Hopkins, Hunt, Kaufman, Lamar, Morris, Navarro, Rains, Red River, Rockwall, Titus, Upshur, Van Zandt, and Wood. On Feb. 5, 1875, Bishop Alexander Charles Garrett named St. Matthew's, Dallas, the Cathedral of the Missionary District.

Dalmatic. The distinctive vestment of deacons in the western church. It may be worn at any liturgy in any season.

The term is derived from a white tunic worn in second-century Dalmatia. The dalmatic was an ample white tunic with wide sleeves, bands about the cuffs, and *clavi*, or colored bands, descending from the shoulders to the hem. Historically, it was worn over an alb by both bishops and deacons by the fourth century, but it did not become a vestment until around the ninth century. The dalmatic was accepted as the vestment worn by the deacon at the eucharist by the ninth century. Eventually deacons adopted the eastern *orarion* or stole, worn on top and hanging straight down from the left shoulder. Over the centuries the dalmatic, like other vestments, lost its full shape. The stole disappeared beneath the outer garment. By the late middle ages, deacons (or, more commonly, priests acting as liturgical deacons) were wearing a short dalmatic in the color of the day, ornate in fabric, adorned with orphreys (two vertical and two horizontal), with narrow sleeves, and open at the sides. The dalmatic has varied widely in appearance, and this variety continues in the Episcopal Church today. In many places the medieval dalmatic has given way to a full-length white or off-white tunic which is simple and functional. It is worn sometimes over an alb, sometimes by itself (as a combination cassock-alb-dalmatic). Deacons often wear the stole on top, placed over the left shoulder and tied under the right arm or hanging straight down.

Daniel Baker College. The Presbyterians established Daniel Baker College in 1888 at Brownwood, Texas. In 1930 the school became an independent, self-supporting institution. On June 1, 1950, the Rt. Rev. Charles Avery Mason, Bishop of Dallas, took over the school. Daniel Baker College was also called "The Episcopal College of the Southwest." When Canterbury College in Danville, Indiana, closed in 1951 some of its students transferred to Daniel Baker. The last class graduated in June 1953, and the school closed. *See* Canterbury College.

Daniels, Jonathan Myrick (Mar. 20, 1939–Aug. 20, 1965). An Episcopal seminarian killed while working in the civil rights movement in Hayneville, near Selma, Alabama. Daniels was born in Keene, New Hampshire. He had a profound conversion experience on Easter Day, 1962, at the Church of the Advent, Boston. He entered the Episcopal Theological School in Cambridge, Massachusetts. In Mar. 1965 Martin Luther King, Jr. made a televised appeal for people to come to Selma to seek voting rights for all citizens. King's appeal persuaded

Daniels to work in Selma under the sponsorship of the Episcopal Society for Cultural and Racial Unity (ESCRU). Daniels and three companions were arrested and imprisoned on Aug. 14, 1965, for joining a picket line. They were unexpectedly released six days later. They walked to a small store. As Ruby Sales, a sixteen-year-old African American woman, approached the entrance of the store, a deputy sheriff appeared with a shotgun and cursed her. Daniels pulled her to one side and was killed by a single blast from the shotgun. His life and witness are commemorated in the Episcopal calendar of the church year on Aug. 14.

Dare, Virginia (b. Aug. 18, 1587). The first child born of English parents in America. She was the granddaughter of Governor John White of Virginia and the child of his daughter Ellinor and her husband Ananias Dare. She was baptized on Aug. 20, 1587, on Roanoke Island. She was probably the first person baptized in America in the English language. Governor White sailed for England on Aug. 27, 1587, and little is known about Virginia Dare's life after her family's departure from Virginia.

Dashiell, George (1780–Apr. 1852). Priest who sought to found an evangelical Episcopal Church. He was born in Stepney, Maryland. Dashiell was licensed as a lay reader at the age of twenty. He was ordained deacon on June 9, 1805, and subsequently ordained priest (date unavailable). He served churches in Maryland and Delaware. He later became the rector of St. Peter's Church, Baltimore. He served on the Standing Committee of the Diocese of Maryland, and he was a deputy to four General Conventions. Dashiell was strongly opposed to the election of James Kemp as Suffragan Bishop of Maryland in 1814. He led a small group of followers out of the Episcopal Church to make, as he said, "the evangelical part of the church a distinct body, and to enlarge its boundaries by admitting faithful men to labor in the work of the Lord." He was unable to get any bishop to consecrate him, but he began to ordain men for what he called the Evangelical Episcopal Church. Dashiell was deposed from the ministry of the Episcopal Church on Dec. 8, 1815. His movement died out when he moved from Maryland in 1826. Dashiell's actions were a forerunner of the Reformed Episcopal Church. It was founded in 1873 by Assistant Bishop of Kentucky George David Cummins, also a former rector of St. Peter's, Baltimore. Dashiell died in New York City. *See* Reformed Episcopal Church.

Daughters of the King, Junior Division. The Daughters of the King was founded on Apr. 4, 1885, in New York City. In Jan. 1896, after the organization of Emmanuel Chapter, No. 28, Daughters of the King in Emmanuel Church, Anacostia, Maryland, Mrs. Williard G. Davenport, wife of the rector, selected a number of young girls of appropriate age from her children's guild and formed them into a chapter on the pattern of the Daughters of the King. She called them her "Junior Daughters," and gave them little silver crosses to wear. She sent them to check on absentees from the Sunday School, and to look after girls their own age. They also visited the sick, the aged and the afflicted, and read to them. After several years, the example of her Junior Daughters inspired chapters in the Diocese of Washington to organize Junior Daughters. The Junior Daughters of Emmanuel Church, Anacostia, are known as the "Alpha Chapter." Junior Daughters are girls and young women between the ages of seven and twenty. Junior Daughters pledge to pray daily for the spread of Christ's Kingdom, to take part regularly in the worship, study and lay ministry of the church, to make a constant effort to bring others to Christ, and to serve in the church and community. *See* Daughters of the King, Order of.

Daughters of the King, Order of the. A lay order for women in the Episcopal Church. Its objective is to bring women and girls into a personal relationship with Jesus Christ through his church. It was organized on Apr. 4, 1885, Easter Even, when Margaret J. Franklin taught a Bible Class named Daughters of the King in Holy Sepulchre Church, now the Church of the Resurrection, New York City. The Daughters of the King's first members pledged themselves to daily prayer and to spread the Kingdom of Christ among young women. By 1889, the order had become national with the addition of six affiliated chapters. A quarterly, *The Royal Cross*, began publication in 1891. The order's first convention was held in Baltimore, Maryland, in Oct. 1893, with members from fourteen states attending. In 1896 a Junior Division was established with a chapter in Washington, D.C. The first missionary supported by the order founded a chapter in Shanghai in 1900. Beginning in 1907, the order began meeting in conjunction with the women's Triennial and General Convention. The emblem of the order is a silver cross inscribed with Latin words which translate, "With heart, mind and spirit uphold and bear the cross." At the base of the cross are the letters "FHS," which stand for the motto of the order, "For His Sake." *See* Daughters of the King, Junior Division.

David (d. c. 601). A saint and founder of monasteries. Although little is known about David, he remains one of the most popular British saints. He became the Bishop of Menevia in southwest Wales, and was also the abbot of a monastery in Menevia which practiced an extreme form of monasticism in the tradition of Antony of Egypt. Legend claims that he was consecrated the Metropolitan Archbishop of Wales by the Bishop of Jerusalem. It is certain that during the time of the invasions of the Angles, Saxons, and Jutes, a pocket of Britons retained the Christian faith in Wales. David was one of them. He is the patron saint of Wales. David is commemorated in the Episcopal calendar of the church year on Mar. 1.

Davis, Jefferson (June 3, 1808–Dec. 6, 1889). Episcopal layman and president of the Confederate States of America. He was born in Fairview, Kentucky. Davis graduated from the United States Military Academy at West Point, New York, in 1828. He commanded a regiment of the U.S. Army during the Mexican War. Davis also served as Secretary of War during the presidency of Franklin Pierce. Davis represented the State of Mississippi in the United States Senate. After the secession of the southern states and the formation of the Confederacy in 1861, he was elected its first and only president. Davis was raised a Baptist, but he chose to join the Episcopal Church at the urging of his second wife, Varina. They attended St. Paul's Episcopal Church, Richmond, where Charles Minnegerode was the rector. On May 6, 1862, Minnegerode came to the executive mansion and baptized Davis "hypothetically," or conditionally, uncertain if there had been a previous baptism. At noon that same day, Davis went to St. Paul's Church, where Bishop John Johns confirmed him. After the collapse of the Confederacy in 1865, Davis was captured and imprisoned without trial for two years. He was released in 1867. He spent the rest of his life attempting to justify his efforts as the South's political leader during the Civil War. Davis died in New Orleans.

Dawley, Powel Mills (Mar. 1, 1907–July 10, 1985). Church historian. He was born in Newport, Rhode Island. Dawley received his Ph.B. in 1929 and his M.A. in 1931 from Brown University. He received his B.D. in 1936 from the Episcopal Theological School and remained there for two additional years as Phillips Brooks Fellow. Dawley received his Ph.D. from Cambridge University in 1938. He was ordained deacon on June 27, 1935, and priest on May 21, 1936. Dawley

began his ministry as curate and then as associate rector of St. David's Church, Baltimore, Maryland. From 1942 until 1945, he was dean of St. Luke's Cathedral, Portland, Maine. In 1945 he became the St. Mark's-in-the-Bowery Professor of Ecclesiastical History at the General Theological Seminary. He remained there until his retirement in 1971. From 1954 until 1971, he was sub-dean of the Seminary. Upon his retirement, he became canon to the Bishop of Maine. Dawley was active in the ecumenical movement. He lectured at numerous American and English colleges. Among his many publications are *John Whitgift and the English Reformation* (1953); *Chapters in Church History* (1950), Vol. 2 of the first "Church's Teaching Series"; *The Episcopal Church and Its Work* (1955), Vol. 6 of the first "Church's Teaching Series"; *The Religion of the Prayer Book* (1943); and *The Story of the General Theological Seminary: A Sesquicentennial History, 1817–1967* (1969). He edited *Report of the Anglican Congress 1954* (1954). Dawley died in Brunswick, Maine. There is a bibliography of his published writings in *Anglican and Episcopal History* 54 (Sept. 1987).

Dawson, Thomas (d. Dec. 5, 1761). Commissary to Virginia and president of William and Mary College. Dawson came to Virginia at an early age. He was educated at William and Mary College. Dawson served as master of the Indian School at William and Mary College from 1738 until 1755. At this time he also studied for the ordained ministry under the guidance of his brother, William Dawson. In 1740 he went to England for ordination. When James Blair died in 1743, Dawson became the rector of Bruton Parish in Williamsburg, Virginia. In 1752, after the death of his brother, he became the third Commissary to Virginia and served until his death. Dawson was the fourth president of William and Mary College, 1755–1761. He died in Williamsburg.

Dawson, William (1704–July 24, 1752). Commissary and president of William and Mary College. Dawson was born in Aspatria, Cumberland County, England. He received his B.A. in 1725 and his M.A. in 1728 from Queens' College, Oxford University. He was ordained deacon and priest, and in 1729 came to Virginia to be professor of moral philosophy in William and Mary College. Soon after coming to Williamsburg, he became curate at Bruton Parish and served there until 1741. From 1741 until his death, Dawson was the rector of James City Parish. He was the second president of William and Mary College, 1743–1752. On

July 18, 1743, he was appointed the second Commissary to Virginia. He served in that position until his death. Dawson died in Williamsburg.

Day Hours. Canonical offices other than matins, including lauds, prime, terce, sext, none, vespers, and compline. These day hours of the church are traditionally included in an office book known as the Diurnal. Matins was the traditional night office. By the fourth century, the monks were joined by the secular clergy and laity for the principal morning and evening offices of lauds and vespers. The other offices were said by the monks. Matins and the day hours were consolidated by Archbishop Thomas Cranmer (1489–1556) into Matins and Evensong in the 1549 Prayer Book. The little offices of terce, sext, and none were not included in the Prayer Book until the twentieth century. The Order of Service for Noonday in the 1979 BCP (pp. 103–107) contains elements of the little offices of terce, sext, and none. It may be adapted for use at any or all of the traditional times of prayer for these three little offices. Similarly, Compline was not included in the 1549 Prayer Book, but elements from Compline were adapted into the Prayer Book service for Evensong. The 1979 BCP provides An Order for Compline (pp. 127–135). *See* Little Hours of the Divine Office; *see* Terce, Sext, None.

Day, Peter Morton (Aug. 1, 1914–May 5, 1984). Editor and ecumenist. After graduating from Dartmouth College in 1935, he was employed in Milwaukee by *The Living Church* magazine. He soon became managing editor and then acting editor in the frequent absence of the editor, Clifford P. Morehouse. In 1941 Day married the former Lorraine Kirschnick, the copy editor of the magazine, and the couple had two children. In 1952 the magazine became independent of the Morehouse Corporation, and Day became editor. He called attention to many issues such as civil rights, Christian education, and ecumenical relations. He shared Morehouse's vision of an Anglican catholicism seeking unity with other Christians. He served as president of the Associated Church Press, and was involved in charities and church activities in Milwaukee. Day resigned from *The Living Church* in 1964 at the time of his appointment as the first national ecumenical officer of the Episcopal Church. He served as ecumenical officer until 1981. *See* Living Church, The.

Days of Abstinence. Days when Christians traditionally abstained from eating meat. Roman Catholics prior to Vatican Council II distinguished fast days on which the quantity of food consumed was reduced (e.g., the weekdays of Lent), and days of abstinence on which meat was not eaten (e.g., Fridays). The 1928 BCP in its table of fasts listed "other days of fasting on which the Church requires such a measure of abstinence as is more especially suited to extraordinary acts and exercises of devotion." These included the forty days of Lent, the ember days, and Fridays. No distinction was made between fasting and abstinence. The 1979 BCP dropped the ember days from the list and refers to both Lenten weekdays and Fridays outside of the Christmas and Easter seasons as Days of Special Devotion "observed by special acts of discipline and self-denial" (p. 17). While this permits the traditional observance of Days of Abstinence, it clearly leaves the nature of the special acts of discipline and self-denial to the individual *See* Black Fast.

Days of Optional Observance. Days in the calendar of the church year for which a liturgical observance is allowed but not required (BCP, pp. 17–18). Sundays, principal feasts, and other holy days always take precedence over any optional days or festivals. Days of optional observance include the various commemorations in the calendar (that is, the "lesser feasts"), other commemorations—not in the calendar—that would use the common of saints, ember days, rogation days, and the "various occasions" for which propers are provided. The days of optional observance, the "lesser feasts," are sometimes called "Black Letter Days," from the English Prayer Book style of listing principal festivals in red and lesser festivals in black.

Days of Special Devotion. Term used in the table of precedence in the BCP to describe the weekdays of Lent and Holy Week (except the feast of the Annunciation) and the Fridays of the year, except for Fridays in Christmas and Easter seasons, and any Feasts of our Lord which occur on a Friday. They are observed by "special acts of discipline and self denial" (BCP, p. 17). The term "fasts," formerly used to describe these days, is now reserved for Ash Wednesday and Good Friday. At the time of the Reformation, these days, as well as the Ember Days and the vigils of certain feasts, were observed by abstinence from meat. The BCP has never specifically stated exactly what "special acts of discipline and self denial" were expected.

D.C.M. The Doctor of Church Music degree. It presupposes a master's degree in church music from a school that follows the guidelines of the National Association of Schools of Music.

D.D. Doctor of Divinity. An honorary degree that may be awarded by a seminary to a member of the clergy or laity in recognition of significant contributions to the church. Seminaries frequently confer the degree on their alumni who are consecrated bishops.

Deacon. Deacons are members of one of three distinct orders of ordained ministry (with bishops and presbyters). In the Episcopal Church a deacon exercises "a special ministry of servanthood" directly under the deacon's bishop, serving all people and especially those in need (BCP, p. 543). This definition reflects the practice of the early church, in which deacons were ordained "not to the priesthood but to the servanthood [*diakonia,* "ministry"] of the bishop" (Hippolytus, *Apostolic Tradition*). In the ancient Greek-speaking world the term *diakonos* meant an intermediary who acted or spoke for a superior. Christian deacons were agents of the bishop, often with oversight of charity. Since ancient times the liturgical functions of deacons have suggested the activity of angels. As they proclaim the gospel, lead intercessions, wait at the eucharistic table, and direct the order of the assembly, deacons act as sacred messengers, agents, and attendants. The revival of the order of deacons in the twentieth century has emphasized social care and service. Many bishops in the Episcopal Church expect their deacons to promote care of the needy outside the church. In addition to those ordained deacon as a permanent vocation, there are also "transitional deacons" who are ordained deacon as a preliminary step toward ordination as a priest. This practice is required by the canons of the Episcopal Church, but its theology and usefulness has been questioned by those who favor direct ordination to the order for which one is chosen. *See* Direct Ordination.

Deaconess. Following the example of German Lutherans in the early nineteenth century, and later of English Anglicans, during 1885–1970 almost five hundred Episcopal women were "set apart" as deaconesses to care for "the sick, the afflicted, and the poor." The 1889 General Convention passed a canon on deaconesses that recognized their ministry. This canon reflected the influence of Mary Abbot Emery and William Reed Huntington. It set standards and qualifications for the deaconesses. Wearing blue habits that often caused them to be mistaken for nuns, they served in places of poverty ranging from the inner city to swamps and mountains. Their work included instructing in the faith, preparing candidates for baptism and confirmation, caring for women and children, and organizing and carrying on social work. There were training schools for deaconesses in New York and Philadelphia. Although deaconesses were more purely diaconal than their male counterparts (missionary and indigenous deacons) in care of the needy, the church did not allow them to function liturgically. In 1970 women were allowed to be ordained as deacons. All deaconesses were automatically assumed into the diaconate, although a few refused to be called deacons.

"Deacon's Mass." A communion service led by a deacon. After the liturgy of the word, the deacon administers communion to a congregation from the reserved sacrament. The service became popular in the Episcopal Church in the 1950s and 1960s. Because the 1928 BCP did not provide for this service, many deacons made up their own liturgies. The 1979 BCP is the first Prayer Book to provide for such a service. An outline for the service is included in the Additional Directions for the Celebration of the Eucharist (BCP, p. 408). The directions make clear that the service is not one of the ordinary liturgies of the church, since its use is limited to occasions "when the services of a priest cannot be obtained." Other preferred titles, suggested by liturgical scholar Howard E. Galley, are "Liturgy of the Presanctified" and "Liturgy of the Word and Holy Communion." The service may be used only when a priest is unavailable and when the bishop authorizes it. Even if a priest is unavailable, the authorization is entirely in the bishop's discretion. Many Episcopal bishops forbid the service or restrict its use to emergencies because it misrepresents the shape of the church, the eucharist, and the ordained ministry.

Dean (Cathedral, Seminary, College, Deanery). At a cathedral, the dean is the member of the clergy in charge, although the cathedral is the official headquarters of the bishop. Assisting clergy at a cathedral have the title "Canon." At a seminary, the dean's function is like that of the president of a college or university. The dean is responsible for spiritual, academic, and fiscal aspects of the seminary's mission. The title is sometimes "Dean and President." The dean of a college is responsible for curriculum as well as securing and supervising faculty. The dean of a deanery is a priest, usually rector of one of the deanery parishes, who is elected or appointed to oversee the work of the deanery. The dean is responsible for convening the clergy and at times the lay representatives of the congregations of the deanery.

Clergy who serve as deans use the title "The Very Reverend." They may wear a distinctive piping (colored trim) on the cassock.

Deanery. 1) Geographical section or area within a diocese. A dean presides at meetings of the lay representatives and clergy of the deanery. 2) House where a dean lives. *See* Dean (Cathedral, Seminary, College, Deanery).

Dearmer, Percy (Feb. 27, 1867–May 29, 1936). Liturgical scholar and hymn composer. He was born in London, England. Dearmer was educated at Westminster and at Christ Church, Oxford. He was one of the early members of the Christian Social Union, which was established in 1889. After he was ordained deacon and priest, he began a systematic and life-long study of liturgics and liturgical ceremonial. In 1899 he published *The Parson's Handbook*, in which he demonstrated that it is possible to be a ritualist without being a Romanist. He put his ideas into practice as vicar of St. Mary's Church, Primrose Hill, Hampstead, 1901–1915. From 1919 until 1936, he was professor of ecclesiastical arts at King's College, London. In 1931 he became a Canon of Westminster Cathedral. Dearmer was a co-editor of the *English Hymnal* (1906), *Songs of Praise* (1925), and the *Oxford Book of Carols* (1928). In the 1920s, he published a five-volume work, *Lessons on the Way*. It was to form the basis for a course of lay education which would take five years to complete. Dearmer contributed to eight hymns in *The Hymnal 1982*, including his translation of the Latin text "Father, we praise thee" (Hymns 1–2), his text "Now quit your care and anxious fear and worry" (Hymn 145), his alteration of "Strengthen for service, Lord" (Hymn 312), and his text "He who would valiant be," after John Bunyan (Hymns 564–565). Dearmer died in Westminster.

Decade of Evangelism. The decade of the 1990s was declared the Decade of Evangelism by resolution of the Lambeth Conference of 1988. It called the provinces and dioceses of the Anglican Communion, in cooperation with other Christians, to make this a time of "renewed emphasis on making Christ known to the people of his world." A. Wayne

Schwab, Evangelism Officer of the Episcopal Church in the early 1990s, and the Standing Committee on Evangelism, initiated several programs to implement the Decade of Evangelism. The programs included the Partners in Evangelism training and the E-Share publications.

Decalogue. *See* Ten Commandments, The.

Decani. The term is derived from Latin, meaning "place of the dean." Traditionally, the dean sat on the south side of the cathedral. In antiphonal singing, the term *decani* indicated those who sit on the *decanal* or dean's side of the choir of a church or cathedral. The opposite side is known as "*cantoris.*" The terms were used in *The Hymnal* (1940) version of "Ye watchers and ye holy ones" to designate different parts for singing the antiphonal alleluias.

Declaration of Consent. Statement of belief in the scriptures and conformity to the doctrine, discipline, and worship of the Episcopal Church by an ordinand in the ordination service. The Declaration of Consent is stated by the ordinand and then a written version of the Declaration of Consent is signed by the ordinand in the sight of all present. Although the statement made by a bishop-elect is somewhat more elaborate than the statements made by those being ordained priest or deacon, all state "I solemnly declare that I do believe the Holy Scriptures of the Old and New Testaments to be the Word of God, and to contain all things necessary to salvation; and I do solemnly engage to conform to the doctrine, discipline, and worship of The Episcopal Church" (BCP, pp. 513, 526, 538).

Dedication and Consecration of a Church, The. The BCP provides a form for the Dedication and Consecration of a Church (pp. 567–574). The bishop presides at this service. The church may be consecrated at any time after it is ready for regular use as a place of worship. The building does not have to be debt-free or owned (see BCP, p. 575). All participants typically assemble near the church before the service begins. They process to the main door of the church after prayers by the bishop. Sacred vessels, ornaments, and decorations may be carried into the building in the procession. Blueprints, keys, and tools used in building the church may also be carried in procession (BCP, p. 575). The bishop uses the pastoral staff to mark the threshold with the sign of the cross. Sections of the prayer for the consecration of the church are said by the bishop, by a warden or other representative of the congregation, and by the rector or minister in charge. The bishop then dedicates the font, the lectern, and (or) the pulpit. After the liturgy of the word, with sermon or address, other pastoral offices (possibly including Blessing of Oil for the Sick or Commitment to Christian Service), the Nicene Creed, and the prayers of the people, the bishop consecrates the altar. After the altar is consecrated, bells may be rung. Members of the congregation vest the altar, place the vessels on it, and light the candles (BCP, p. 574). The service continues with the eucharist. Appropriate portions of this form may be used or adapted to dedicate parts of a building or furnishings that have been added or renovated, or to dedicate a chapel or oratory in another building.

The consecration of a church building was traditionally associated with its first use. This connection was broken by a canon enacted in 1868. It required the building and its ground to be fully paid for and free of debt or legal encumbrances when consecrated. The 1979 BCP once again connects first use of the church building and consecration. As a practical reality, depending on the bishop's schedule, the service of consecration may not be the very first service in the new building.

The BCP provides an order of service for use when a church or chapel has long been used for worship without formal consecration by a bishop. This form provides an opportunity for the congregation to reaffirm its commitment to mission and ministry. This order is especially appropriate on occasions such as recognition of the congregation as an independent parish, a major anniversary, or paying off a debt. It recognizes that the church building has already been consecrated by prayerful use.

Dehon, Theodore (Dec. 8, 1776–Aug. 6, 1817). High church bishop. He was born in Boston. He graduated from Harvard College in 1795 and received his theological education from Samuel Parker, later Bishop of Massachusetts. He was ordained to the diaconate on Dec. 24, 1797, and to the priesthood on Oct. 9, 1800. Dehon served as rector of Trinity Church, Newport, Rhode Island from 1797 until 1810, when he accepted charge of St. Michael's Church, Charleston, South Carolina. A highly respected pastor at St. Michael's, he was soon chosen bishop and consecrated on Oct. 15, 1812. He served as Bishop of South Carolina until his death. Dehon worked diligently to revive the spiritual life of the diocese. He stressed the value of the sacraments and conformity to the Prayer Book, introduced

weekday feasts and fasts, and urged a special reverence for Lent and Holy Week. Dehon remained rector of St. Michael's during his episcopate. He died in Charleston.

Deification. *See* Apotheosis; *see* Theosis.

Deism. A teaching about God which appeared in both Christian and non-Christian forms during the seventeenth and eighteenth centuries in England and France, under the influence of rationalism and the rise of natural science. Lord Herbert of Cherbury (1580–1630) introduced deist thought to England. It was developed by Matthew Tindal (1653–1733) and John Toland (1670–1722), among others. The title of Toland's book, *Christianity Not Mysterious*, expresses the tone of this body of thought.

Deists used the cosmological argument to prove the existence of God, who created the universe and governed it through natural law. Natural laws were discoverable by reason, according to this "natural religion." Teachers, among whom Jesus was regarded as definitive, taught humans the divinely inspired moral law to keep their behavior in harmony with the divine plan. People were to be moved to obey the moral law by the expectation of future rewards and punishments. Some Deists viewed God as an original architect and initial mover of creation. Deism denied that God exercises providential care for humanity or the universe. It believed in a "divine clock-maker" who merely set the universe in motion. Deism also denied our need of special revelation, holding that human reason alone leads to the principles of natural reason and morality. Matthew Tindal, whose *Christianity as Old as the Creation* (1730) became known as the "Bible" of Deism, held that the gospel added nothing to the law of nature, that true religion was a "republication" of the law, and that God's design was to free humanity from superstition. A number of eighteenth-century Anglican theologians endeavored to show that Christianity did not contradict natural religion (Joseph Butler's *Analogy of Religion*), or that it could be understood in deistic terms (William Paley's *Natural Religion*). Deistic works were produced in America by Ethan Allen and Thomas Paine.

The mechanical, astronomical model of the universe which informed deistic thought remained theologically influential until supplanted by biological models in the nineteenth century. *See* Rationalism; *see* Evolution.

DeKoven Center, The, Racine, Wisconsin. Located on the campus of the former Racine College (1852–1933), it was named for the Rev. James DeKoven, warden of Racine College, 1859–1879. The DeKoven Center is a complex that includes the Collegiate Chapel of St. John; the shrine of James DeKoven; gardens and a nature trail; a gym and pool; and Taylor Hall. The five National Historic Register buildings on the campus are owned by the DeKoven Foundation for Church Work, a retreat and conference ministry that is an entity of the Episcopal Diocese of Milwaukee. Taylor Hall houses the offices of the DeKoven Foundation for Church Work; St. Mary's Chapel; and a large collection of books, antiques, and paintings. The DeKoven Center sponsors retreats, quiet days, conferences, continuing education and aquatic courses, and also makes its facilities available to the public for meetings, seminars, and conferences. The center was operated by the Community of St. Mary for more than fifty years. *See* DeKoven, James.

DeKoven, James (Sept. 19, 1831–Mar. 19, 1879). DeKoven was born in Middletown, Connecticut. He graduated from Columbia College in 1851 and as valedictorian at the General Theological Seminary in 1854. DeKoven was ordained deacon on Aug. 6, 1854, and priest on Sept. 23, 1855. In 1854 he became professor of ecclesiastical history at Nashotah House and rector of St. John Chrysostom at nearby Delafield, Wisconsin. In 1858 he became warden of St. John's Hall, a preparatory school in Delafield. DeKoven became warden of Racine College in 1859 and served there until his death. DeKoven was the most widely known and respected leader of the Anglo-catholic movement of the nineteenth century. DeKoven was known as the "American Keble." He was influenced by the Oxford Movement (Tractarians) and brought many of their principles, especially the doctrine of the Real Presence in the Holy Eucharist, to the attention of the Episcopal Church. DeKoven was also a ritualist, and under his leadership, the choir at Racine College was vested. He allowed lights (candles) on the altar of St. John's Chapel. At the General Conventions of 1871 and 1874 he defended eucharistic adoration and pleaded for comprehensiveness in doctrine and worship. His addresses to General Convention on these occasions are considered to be some of the most significant moments of oratory in the history of General Convention. A stringent canon on ritual was avoided through DeKoven's advocacy. But his defense of ritualism caused many in the Episcopal Church of his day to be suspicious of him. He was nominated Bishop of

Massachusetts in 1872 and of Milwaukee in 1874. He was elected but not consecrated Bishop of Illinois in 1875 because he did not receive the necessary consents from a sufficient number of diocesan standing committees in the Episcopal Church. He was never made a bishop. DeKoven died in Racine. His shrine is on the grounds of the DeKoven Center, Racine, Wisconsin. His life is commemorated in the Episcopal calendar of the church year on Mar. 22.

DeLancey Divinity School. William Heathcote DeLancey (1797–1865), the first Bishop of Western New York, opened a diocesan school of divinity at Geneva, New York, in 1850. The Rev. Dr. William Dexter Wilson (1816–1900) was in charge of it. It operated until 1858. On Feb. 1, 1861, DeLancey opened the Diocesan Training School at Geneva, under the direction of the Rev. James Rankine (1827–1896). In 1866, after the death of Bishop DeLancey, it was named the DeLancey Divinity School. In 1920 it moved from Geneva to Buffalo. It closed in 1935.

Delaney, Henry Beard (Feb. 5, 1858–Apr. 14, 1928). Second African American bishop in the Episcopal Church. He was born a slave in St. Mary's, Georgia. Delaney was raised in Fernandina, Florida. He was a grown man when he entered St. Augustine's College at Raleigh, North Carolina, from which he graduated in 1885. Upon graduation he became a teacher at St. Augustine's. He was later vice-principal of St. Augustine's. On June 7, 1889, he was ordained deacon, and on May 2, 1892, he was ordained priest. From 1889 until 1904, Delaney was a member of the Commission for Work Among Colored People, assistant minister of St. Augustine's Chapel, Raleigh, and priest-in-charge of All Saints Mission, Warrenton, North Carolina. In 1908 he became Archdeacon of the Convocation for Work Among Colored People in the Diocese of North Carolina. On Nov. 21, 1918, Delaney was consecrated Suffragan Bishop for Colored Work in the Diocese of North Carolina. The African American Episcopalians in the dioceses of South Carolina and East Carolina were also under his jurisdiction, and these two dioceses participated in his support. Along with Bishop Edward T. Demby of Arkansas, the first African American Suffragan Episcopal bishop, Delaney was charged with the supervision of African American clergy and parishes within the racially segregated ecclesiastical system of the South. Delaney died at St. Augustine's College, Raleigh. *See* Delaney Sisters.

Delaney Sisters. Annie Elizabeth (Bessie) (1891–1995), and Sarah Louise (Sadie) Delaney (1889–1999), were the daughters of Henry Beard Delaney and Nancy Logan Delaney. Henry Delaney was a Suffragan Bishop of North Carolina and the second African American bishop in the Episcopal Church. Annie and Sarah and their siblings were raised on the campus of St. Augustine's College, Raleigh, North Carolina. In 1919 they moved to Harlem in New York City where they continued their education. Both of them received degrees from Columbia University. Bessie Delaney became the second African American female dentist in the state of New York, and Sadie Delaney became the first African American home economics teacher in New York City. The Delaney sisters lived very private lives until 1993 when they published *Having Our Say: The Delaney Sisters' First Hundred Years*, which was based on recollections and anecdotes of their long lives. Later the book was made into a Broadway play. In 1994 they published *The Delaney Sisters' Book of Everyday Wisdom.* Bessie Delaney died in Mt. Vernon, New York. *See* Delaney, Henry Beard.

Delaware, Diocese of. It was organized on Sept. 26–27, 1786, at Dover. The first bishop was not consecrated until 1841. On May 14, 1935, St. John's Church, Wilmington, was set apart as St. John's Cathedral.

Demby, Edward Thomas (Feb. 13, 1869–Oct. 14, 1957). First African American Episcopal bishop in the United States. He was born in Wilmington, Delaware. Demby studied at Howard University, and in 1893 received his B.D. from Wilberforce University. He was dean of Paul Quinn College in Texas between 1894 and 1896. Demby was ordained deacon on Mar. 16, 1898, and priest on May 8, 1899. He served churches in Tennessee, Missouri, and Florida. In 1907 he became the rector of Emmanuel Church, Memphis, Tennessee. From 1912 until 1917, he was Archdeacon for Colored Work in the Diocese of Tennessee. The 1916 General Convention opened the way for African Americans to become suffragan bishops with responsibilities over African American churches in the racially segregated South. Demby was elected "Negro Suffragan Bishop of the Diocese of Arkansas and other Dioceses and Missionary Jurisdictions of the Seventh Province where he may be asked to officiate by the respective Bishops." He was consecrated on Sept. 29, 1918. He served until his retirement on Feb. 1, 1939. Demby died in Cleveland, Ohio.

Demythologize. A twentieth-century theological term that was used extensively by Rudolph Bultmann. He understood the word "myth" to be a way to communicate one's faith to others in a time- and culturally-dependent way. For example, in the NT, the writers used the language and specific terminology of their own time to communicate their faith. But it is difficult for us, in a different time and place, to comprehend the message which is presented. To demythologize, Bultmann argued, is to recognize the existential character of the faith and rephrase it in a contemporary form that will be easier for people of our day to comprehend. Some critics have argued that the term "demythologize" should be changed to "remythologize," admitting that any interpretation today is just as limited and time-constrained as an interpretation from an earlier century in the history of the church.

Denver Theological School and the College of St. John the Evangelist. These related educational institutions in Colorado were for the education of clergy. Theological education began at Matthews Hall, Golden, and then moved to Denver in 1879 as the Denver Theological School. The College of St. John the Evangelist, "a theological school for the education of clergy for the West," operated at Greeley from 1910 until 1937.

Depose, Sentence of Deposition. Sentence of ecclesiastical discipline pronounced by a bishop that permanently excludes the exercise of ordained ministry by the bishop, priest, or deacon who is deposed. Conditions for deposition are prescribed by the Constitution and Canons of the Episcopal Church.

Deposit of Faith, The. The saving revelation of Christ that has been given to the church, especially as known through biblical witness and tradition. The deposit of faith is to be upheld and proclaimed by the church. This requires fidelity to the received tradition, willingness to rediscover continually the truth of the Christian faith in each time and situation of the Church's life, and evangelical zeal to share the faith with others. *See* Salvation; *see* Tradition.

Deposition. 1) In canon law, a deposition is a sentence that removes or deposes a bishop, priest, or deacon from the ordained ministry. A member of the clergy who is deposed is entirely banned from the sacred ministry, and not merely changed from one order to another. For example, a deposed bishop could not serve as a priest or a deacon.

A sentence of deposition may be imposed after final conviction by an ecclesiastical trial court; after an accused presbyter or deacon confesses the truth of the charges made, waives in writing the right to a trial, and submits to disciplinary action; after a renunciation of the ministry when there may be a question of prior misconduct or irregularity by the member of the clergy; or after an abandonment of the communion of the church by the member of the clergy. 2) In terms of Christian history, the Deposition refers to the taking down of Jesus' body from the cross. The Deposition also indicates an artistic representation of this event.

Depravity. A state of corruption that is believed to affect the unredeemed human nature. The doctrine of original sin affirms that the first human beings sinned against the Creator in such a way that their descendants inherit a corrupt nature. It derives by contrast from the scriptural teaching that the divine Word took flesh to redeem the human race. Theological schools differ as to the extent of inherited depravity. The extremes are found in Calvinism, including Puritanism, on the pessimistic side; and Eastern Orthodoxy, along with the Jesuit school in Roman Catholicism, on the optimistic side. A certain depravity of human nature is assumed in the Thirty-Nine Articles (Art. XIII: "Of Works before Justification"). However, the Caroline Divines were not over-concerned with the question of depravity, and most Anglican authors follow a middle way.

Deprecation. Prayer for deliverance. Deprecations in the Great Litany include petitions for deliverance from all evil and wickedness, all blindness of heart, all inordinate and sinful affections, all false doctrine, lightning and tempest, and all oppression. Deprecations in the Great Litany ask for deliverance by the mystery of Christ's holy Incarnation, by Christ's agony and bloody sweat, in all times of tribulation and prosperity, in the hour of death and in the day of judgment. Each deprecation in the Great Litany is addressed to Christ, and followed by the response *"Good Lord, deliver us"* (BCP, pp. 148–149). Similarly, deprecations in the Litany at the Time of Death include intercessions that the dying person will be delivered from all evil, sin, and tribulation by Christ's holy Incarnation, by his cross and passion, and by the coming of the Holy Spirit. These deprecations are followed by the response *"Good Lord, deliver him (or her)"* (BCP, p. 463).

Deputies, House of. The House of Deputies is the oldest of the two Houses of General Convention. It has equal numbers of clergy and lay deputies selected by the dioceses of the church. The first session of the first General Convention, held in 1789, consisted only of the House of Deputies. It adopted a constitutional provision establishing a separate House of Bishops, which joined the Convention at its second session in 1789.

Deputy. Each diocese, area mission, and the Convocation of the American Churches in Europe is entitled to not more than four ordained representatives in the House of Deputies. They must be presbyters or deacons, and canonically resident in the diocese. Each diocese, area mission, and the Convocation of the American Churches in Europe is also entitled to not more than four lay persons in the House of Deputies. These lay persons must be confirmed adult communicants in good standing in the diocese, but not necessarily domiciled in the diocese. These clergy and lay representatives are called deputies. The General Convention may by canon reduce the number of representatives in each delegation to not fewer than two deputies in each order. Each diocese, area mission, and the Convocation of the American Churches in Europe prescribes the manner in which its deputies are chosen.

Descant. Harmony with a fixed theme in music. It is usually a higher soprano part sung to complement one or more verses of a hymn. For example, "While shepherds watched their flocks" (Hymn 94) has descants on the second and sixth verses, and "Praise to the Lord, the Almighty" (Hymn 390) has a descant on the fourth verse.

"Desks." These "desks," sometimes called "ethnic desks," refer to the staff at the Episcopal Church Center in New York who have networks, or commissions and committees, whom they represent at Episcopal or ecumenical meetings. These "desks" may also provide program services if funded in the general church program budget. These have included American Indian/Alaska Native Ministries, Asiamerican Ministries, Black Ministries, and Hispanic Ministries.

De Veaux College. Judge Samuel De Veaux (De Voe) (1789–1852) left a bequest of all his residuary estate for the foundation of "a benevolent institution under the supervision of the Convention" of the Diocese of Western New York. Under the provisions of this will De Veaux College was founded in Niagara Falls, New York. It was incorporated on Apr. 15, 1853. Bishop William Heathcote DeLancey (1797–1865) of Western New York was chairman of the board of trustees. The school opened on May 20, 1857, with thirty pupils. It had a domain of 300 acres. Four Episcopal priests were presidents of the school. Gradually the college curriculum was dropped and the president was listed as headmaster. The preparatory school closed in 1973.

D.H.L. The Doctor of Hebrew Letters presupposes a first theological degree and is to equip persons for teaching and research in theological seminaries, colleges, and universities.

Diaconate. Once fallen into disuse as an inferior order used mainly as a stepping stone to the priesthood, the diaconate (order of deacons) has been restored in the Anglican, Roman Catholic, and several Protestant churches. In the Episcopal Church the diaconate is a full order equal to the presbyterate and the episcopate, and it plays an important role in many dioceses and congregations. As commonly used, the term refers to those ordained deacon as a permanent vocation. Those ordained deacon as a preliminary step toward ordination as a priest, as required by canon law, are called "transitional deacons." Many persons in the Episcopal Church question the theology and usefulness of the transitional diaconate, and want to restore direct ordination. *See* Deacon; *see* Direct Ordination.

Dialogue, Opening (Eucharist). The practice of opening the eucharistic prayer with a dialogue between presider and people dates from the early church, as recorded in the *Apostolic Tradition* of Hippolytus in about the year 215. The dialogue consists of three exchanges: the salutation, "The Lord be with you," the command, "Lift up your hearts," and the request, "Let us give thanks to the Lord our God." The people express their agreement or consent in each exchange. Anglican Prayer Books from 1552 until recent revisions omitted the salutation.

Didache, The. This document, also known as *The Teaching of the Twelve Apostles*, and sometimes called *The Teaching of the Lord to the Heathen by the Twelve Apostles*, dates from the early second century. Its author, date, and place of writing are unknown. "Didache" is Greek for "teaching." The document, an early church order, is essentially a manual of instruction for the early Christian community. The first part provides moral instruction for adherents of the faith

and for catechumens. It describes the "Two Ways," the "Way of Life" and the "Way of Death." The second part is a manual of instructions about baptism, the eucharist, fasting, and prayer. Baptism is to be by immersion. Baptism can be done by threefold affusion if immersion is impossible. This is the first reference to baptism other than by immersion. *See* Church Orders.

Dignus es. Canticle based on Rv 4:11; 5:9–10, 13, which describes hymns sung before the One seated on the heavenly throne and to the Lamb in the heavenly vision. These may be drawn from early Christian hymns. *Dignus es* is also known as A Song to the Lamb. It identifies Christ as the "Lamb that was slain," who redeemed with his blood for God "From every family, language, people, and nation, a kingdom of priests to serve our God." It appears as Canticle 18 in Morning Prayer, Rite 2 (BCP, pp. 93–94). The BCP suggests its use after the NT Reading at Morning Prayer on Tuesday and Friday (p. 144). It may be used in either Rite 2 or Rite 1 services. *The Hymnal 1982 Accompaniment Edition, Vol. 1*, provides a variety of musical settings for the *Dignus es* (S 261–S 266). *Dignus es* would be appropriate for use as the song of praise in the eucharistic entrance rite during Easter.

Diocesan Directors of Diaconate Formation. This group was organized on Jan. 31–Feb. 2, 1997, at the Dominican Conference Center in New Orleans. The fifty participants were from twenty-two dioceses, and included twenty-seven deacons, nineteen presbyters, one bishop, and three lay persons. At the meeting, the directors drafted a vision statement as a guide for the formation of deacons and adopted a definition of a deacon. This definition states that "A deacon is a baptized person called and empowered by God and the Christian community to be an icon illuminating Christ as a model of servanthood for all people. The role of the deacon in the liturgy mirrors the role of the deacon in church and world." This organizational meeting was sponsored by the North American Association for the Diaconate (NAAD), an unofficial Anglican organization. The directors discussed the possible certification of formation programs and instructors.

Diocese. The territorial jurisdiction of a diocesan bishop. The term also refers to the congregations and church members of the diocese. Before the church adopted the word it had a long secular usage. It was originally used in the Roman Empire for an administrative subdivision. A diocese was a division of a prefecture of the Roman Empire. In the reorganization of Diocletian and Constantine, the Roman Empire was divided into twelve dioceses. As the church expanded out from the cities, it adopted the use of the word "diocese," and ecclesiastical dioceses tended to correspond to civil units. For example, at first the Diocese of Georgia corresponded with the State of Georgia. Later, many statewide dioceses were divided into smaller dioceses for pastoral and practical reasons. For example, the State of New York includes six dioceses. In more recent years, some dioceses have been formed from portions of more than one state. The Diocese of the Rio Grande includes all of New Mexico and part of west Texas, and the Diocese of the Central Gulf Coast includes portions of southern Alabama and western Florida. In England, the diocese is the territory of the bishop and the parish is a subdivision of it. Every diocese in the Episcopal Church has a Standing Committee. When there is a bishop in charge of the diocese, the Standing Committee is the bishop's council of advice. When there is no bishop, bishop coadjutor or suffragan bishop, the Standing Committee is the ecclesiastical authority of the diocese. A diocese usually meets annually in a diocesan convention. Each diocese is entitled to representation in the House of Deputies by not more than four ordained persons, presbyters or deacons, canonically resident in the diocese, and not more than four lay persons, who are confirmed adult communicants of the Episcopal Church and in good standing in the diocese. Dioceses also elect clerical and lay deputies to the Provincial Synod. The Constitution and Canons of the Episcopal Church provide guidelines for the division of a diocese. Some persons insist that the diocese is the primary unit in the Episcopal Church.

Diptych. A set of two tablets, made of wood or metal, and bound together by rings. The names of saints, bishops, rulers, and the faithful departed were inscribed on the inner surfaces. These names were read out by the deacon during the eucharistic liturgy.

Direct Ordination. Sometimes called *per saltum* (by a leap), it is ordination directly to the order for which one is chosen. In the early church those elected presbyter or bishop were commonly ordained directly to that order. Although direct ordination continued in Rome and elsewhere until the eleventh century, notably in the elevation of archdeacons as popes, after the fourth century ordination gradually became sequential. One was expected to pass through a sequence of orders to get experience in leadership and ministry. By the late middle ages, under the influence of Augustine's teaching about the Donatist heresy, orders were considered indelible and therefore cumulative. One was understood to remain in a "lower" order even after being ordained to a "higher" order. In the Episcopal Church in recent years there have been efforts to allow direct ordination. Although there is no historical or theological barrier, the restoration of direct ordination has been deferred for study and dialogue with Anglican and ecumenical partners.

Dirge. A mournful hymn. It can be a hymn that expresses grief, and it may be a lament for the dead. The term comes from the Latin *Dirige*, the first word of the antiphon *Dirige, Dominus Deus*, "Lead me, O Lord God" (Ps 5:8). This antiphon preceded the first psalm in the Office of the Dead in medieval breviaries and in early English primers. A dirge came to mean a burial hymn.

Disciple, Discipleship. A follower or pupil of a great master. A disciple is a learner who follows a movement or teacher and helps to spread the master's teaching. The term is used in various senses and contexts in the NT to indicate the followers of Jesus. Although it is used at times relative to the Twelve, it is more frequently used as a general term for the first followers of Jesus. Lk 14:27 (NRSV) records Jesus' statement that "Whoever does not carry the cross and follow me cannot be my disciple." The term is also used in Acts to describe those who were Christian believers after Jesus' death and resurrection. At Antioch the disciples were first called Christians (Acts 11:26). The term "Christian" came to be the usual term for a Christian believer. The term "disciple" does not appear in the epistles. However, the concept of discipleship (being a Christian disciple) continues to be an important part of the Christian life. For example, Dietrich Bonhoeffer (1906–1945) considered discipleship in *Die Nachfolge*, or *The Cost of Discipleship* (1937, trans. by Reginald H. Fuller, 1948). Bonhoeffer urged that grace without discipleship is "cheap grace," and that faith must be expressed in obedience.

Disciples of Christ in Community (DOCC). This program of basic catechesis and parish community-building uses a combination of content presentations and small group process. DOCC is led by clergy and laity in a trained parish team. It was begun in 1975 at Trinity Church, New Orleans, by the Rev. John Stone Jenkins, rector of Trinity. DOCC spread to many other congregations. It was originally named "DOC." In 1989 the School of Theology, University of the South (Sewanee) was asked to assume management and development of the program, and the name was changed to avoid confusion with the denomination Christian Church/Disciples of Christ.

Disciplina Arcani. The term is from Latin for the "discipline of secrecy." It concerns the secrecy practiced by the early church so that certain teachings and practices were not shared with converts until they were initiated and had begun full participation in the life of the Christian community. Catechumens in the early church were dismissed from the Sunday service before the prayers of the faithful, the peace, and eucharistic sharing. Some have noted parallels of the *Disciplina Arcani* to the secrecy of mystery religions. But the main reasons for the *Disciplina Arcani* were to protect the church during times of active persecution or marginal toleration, and a catechetical approach that emphasized experiencing the initiatory sacraments (including baptism, anointing, laying on of hands, and first communion) before learning about them. After the sixth century the need for secrecy had passed, but there was continuing catechetical emphasis on experience and participation. The *BOS* explains that "The catechetical methodology of the catechumenal and baptismal rites is: experience first, then reflect." *See* Mystagogy.

Disciplinary Rubrics. These rubrics are found among "Additional Directions" at the end of the eucharistic services in the 1979 BCP. The rubrics derive from the 1549 Prayer Book and involve the prohibition of communion to those known to be living in major contradiction to the Christian life. The rubrics require notification of the bishop within fourteen days of such disciplinary action. *See* Discipline.

Discipline. 1) In a general sense, the right ordering of Christian life and community. The Constitution, Canons, Prayer Book rubrics, and rules of the church are meant to govern the proper conduct, responsibilities, services, and actions of church life. At the time of ordination, all persons being ordained bishop, priest, or deacon state that "I do solemnly engage to conform to the Doctrine, Discipline, and Worship of the Episcopal Church" (Art. VIII of the Constitution of the Episcopal Church).

2) In a specific sense, ecclesiastical discipline refers to the canonical provisions for presentment and trial of a member of the clergy. Grounds for presentment and trial of a member of the clergy include crime; immorality; holding and teaching any doctrine contrary to the doctrine of the Episcopal Church; violation of the rubrics of the Prayer Book; violation of the Constitution or Canons of the General Convention; violation of the Constitution or Canons of the diocese of canonical residence; violation of the Constitution or Canons of a diocese in which one was located temporarily; any act involving a violation of ordination vows (including, under certain circumstances, disregard or disobedience of a Pastoral Direction); habitual neglect of the exercise of the ministerial office without cause, or habitual neglect of public worship and Holy Communion, according to the order and use of the Episcopal Church; or conduct unbecoming a member of the clergy.

The bishop may authorize a temporary inhibition of a priest or deacon who is charged with an offense or serious acts that would constitute grounds for a canonical Charge of an Offense. After allegations of the commission of an offense have been made to the ecclesiastical authority, or after Charges of an Offense have been filed, the accused member of the clergy may voluntarily submit to the discipline of the church prior to an ecclesiastical trial. The consent of the ecclesiastical authority is required. The canons also include provisions for renunciation of the ordained ministry by members of the clergy who may be charged with an offense. The canons make detailed provisions concerning ecclesiastical presentments, courts, trials, appeals, and remissions or modifications of judicial sentences. The three sentences that may be adjudged by an ecclesiastical trial court and imposed by the bishop are admonition, suspension, or deposition.

The Prayer Book rites for Holy Eucharist include Disciplinary Rubrics authorizing the priest to bar from communion those who are living a notoriously evil life, those who have done wrong to their neighbors and are a scandal to others of the congregation, and those who hate other members of the congregation and refuse to forgive them. A priest who bars a person from communion must notify the bishop within fourteen days and explain the reasons for refusing communion (BCP, p. 409).

3) The term "discipline" also may indicate a whip or scourge of knotted cords that is used as an instrument of penance.

Dismissal. A deacon, or the presider if no deacon is present, ends the eucharistic liturgy by dismissing the people. The term comes from the Latin *Ite, missa est*, "Go, it is the sending." The Episcopal Church allows the dismissal in Rite 1 and requires it in Rite 2. There are four alternate texts: 1) "Let us go forth in the name of Christ"; 2) "Go in peace to love and serve the Lord"; 3) "Let us go forth into the world, rejoicing in the power of the Spirit"; and 4) "Let us bless the Lord." To each the people respond: "Thanks be to God." During the fifty days of Easter, "alleluia, alleluia" is added to the dismissal and its response. The *Altar Book* and *The Hymnal 1982* provide music for the dismissal. It is part of the deacon's angelic function of making announcements, exhorting, and aiding the active participation of the people.

Dispensation. (1) The exceptional relaxation of a church law or penalty by the canonical authority owing to the needs of a special case or occasion. The dispensation must be for good cause. The church law remains valid despite the dispensation, but it is not applied to the case or situation specified by the dispensation. Members of the church not included in the dispensation continue to be bound by the church law as they were before the dispensation. The church can only dispense its own laws, not natural or divine law. Dispensations have often concerned the church's requirements concerning ordination, marriage, religious vows, and disciplines such as fasting.

2) The term "dispensation" may also refer to systems or periods of time that are relevant for salvation. The New and Old Covenants may be referred to as the New and Old Dispensations. Dispensationalism refers to a system of biblical interpretation which identifies seven periods or eras of God's relationship with humanity. These dispensations extend from the time of Innocence in the Garden of Eden to the coming of the Kingdom, the time when God's promises are fulfilled with Christ as King. The term "dispensation" may also refer generally to the divine ordering of worldly affairs or a divinely revealed religious system or code of commands.

Diurnal. A Prayer Book containing the monastic Daily Office, except for the night hour of matins. Anglican versions include *The Monastic Diurnal* (1932, rev. 1963), with relevant material adapted from the English and American Prayer Books, and *The Monastic Diurnal Noted* (1952), a plainchant version edited by Winfred Douglas.

The term is derived from the Latin for "daily," or "of a day."

Divine Liturgy. A title for the eucharistic liturgy, used primarily by Eastern Orthodox. It is one of six names for the Eucharist given in the Catechism (BCP, p. 859).

Divine Office. *See* Daily Office.

Divinization. *See* Apotheosis; *see* Theosis.

Dix, Morgan (Nov. 1, 1827–Apr. 29, 1908). Long-time rector of Trinity Church, New York City, and General Convention leader. He was born in New York City. Dix graduated from Columbia College in 1848 and from General Theological Seminary in 1852. He was ordained deacon on Sept. 19, 1852, and priest on May 22, 1853. He began his ministry as assistant minister at St. Mark's Church, Philadelphia, where he served from 1852 until 1855. At Trinity Church Dix served as assistant minister from 1855 to 1859, and assistant rector from 1859 to 1862. On Nov. 10, 1862, he was elected the ninth rector of Trinity Church. He served in that position until his death. Dix was the sixteenth president of the House of Deputies, serving five terms in that capacity, 1886–1898. For many years he was president of the Standing Committee of the Diocese of New York and a clerical deputy from New York to eight consecutive General Conventions, 1877–1898. Dix was a leader of catholic churchmanship. He was the author of many devotional works as well as the monumental *History of the Parish of Trinity Church in the City of New York*, 4 vols. (1898–1906). It treated the history of Trinity Church from its founding in 1697 until 1862. He died in New York City. Dix is commemorated by a monument in All Saints Chapel, Trinity Church.

D.M.A. The Doctor of Musical Arts degree presupposes a master's degree in church music from a school that follows the guidelines of the National Association of Schools of Music.

D.Min. The Doctor of Ministry degree presupposes the M. Div. degree and constitutes an advanced professional degree at the doctoral level with an emphasis on the profession and practice of ministry.

D.Miss. The Doctor of Missiology degree is a two-year, part M. Div. professional degree for missionaries interested in advanced training in cross-cultural ministries. It was first developed by Roman Catholic schools.

Doane College. This school in Crete, Nebraska, had extremely tenuous Episcopal connections. It was founded in 1872. It was not endorsed by the Diocese of Nebraska until 1931, when Bishop Ernest Vincent Shayler (1868–1947) was elected to its board of trustees. It was related in this superficial way to the diocese for twenty years, until Mar. 15, 1951, when Bishop Howard Rasmus Brinker (1893–1965) resigned from the board.

Doane, George Washington (May 27, 1799–Apr. 27, 1859). High church bishop. He was born in Trenton, New Jersey, and graduated from Union College, Schenectady, New York, in 1818. In 1820 he entered the General Theological Seminary, New York, where he came under the influence of Bishop John Henry Hobart, the leader of the high church party in the Episcopal Church. Doane was ordained deacon on Apr. 19, 1821, and became Hobart's assistant at Trinity Church, New York. He was ordained priest on Aug. 6, 1823, and in 1825 he became professor of *belles-lettres* at Washington College, Hartford, Connecticut. Doane and William Croswell began editing and publishing the *Episcopal Watchman* on Mar. 26, 1827, to defend high church principles. In 1828 Doane became assistant minister at Trinity Church, Boston, and in 1830 he became the rector. While in Boston he and Croswell edited the *Banner of the Cross*, which used as its motto Bishop Hobart's watchword, "Evangelical Truth and Apostolic Order." Doane was consecrated the second Bishop of New Jersey on Oct. 31, 1832. Shortly after his consecration he became the rector of St. Mary's Church, Burlington, and served there until his death. He opened St. Mary's Hall for girls on May 1, 1837, in Burlington, New Jersey, and in 1846 he founded Burlington College for boys. He wrote "Thou art the Way," used as Hymn 457 in *The Hymnal 1982*. On Sept. 25, 1835, Doane preached the sermon at the consecration of Jackson Kemper as the first missionary bishop of the Episcopal Church. He emphasized that bishops are "*sent out* by Christ himself to preach the Gospel." Doane died in Burlington.

Doane, William Croswell (Mar. 2, 1832–May 17, 1913). Leader of the high church party. He was born in Boston, Massachusetts. Doane graduated from Burlington College in 1850. He studied for the ordained ministry under his father, George Washington Doane, the second Bishop of

New Jersey. He was ordained deacon on Mar. 6, 1853, and began his ministry as assistant to his father at St. Mary's Church, Burlington. Doane was ordained priest on Mar. 16, 1856. He founded St. Barnabas Free Church in northern Burlington, where he was rector from 1856 until 1860. He succeeded his father as rector of St. Mary's and served there from 1860 until 1863. While in Burlington he taught English literature at Burlington College. Doane was rector of St. John's Church, Hartford, Connecticut, from 1863 until 1867. On Feb. 2, 1869, he was consecrated the first Bishop of Albany. He served in that position until his death. He founded the Cathedral of All Saints, Albany, in 1872, and the Sisterhood of the Holy Child Jesus in 1873. Doane was a leader of the high church party. He insisted on a weekly eucharist. He was a poet. *The Hymnal 1982* includes his hymn text, "Ancient of Days," (Hymn 363). Doane died in New York City.

Docetism. A heretical teaching about the person of Christ which holds that Christ, the divine Word, only seemed to assume the flesh of Jesus. The term is from the Greek *dokein*, "to seem." Jesus' life, suffering, death, and bodily resurrection were considered unreal. It thus undermines belief in the reality of the Incarnation as a doctrine of Christian faith. The roots of docetism lie in the pervasive Greek understanding of matter as evil and of God as incapable of suffering or "impassive."

As early as the mid-second century, Justin Martyr identified "some who declare that Jesus Christ did not come in flesh but only as spirit." Serapion of Antioch first called such teachers "docetists" about 200 A.D. Other opponents of Docetism included Polycarp, Irenaeus, and Tertullian. Docetism was contradicted by the Council of Chalcedon (451).

Any extreme emphasis on the divinity of Christ at the expense of his humanity has docetic implications. Docetism continues to be a temptation to those who idealize the figure of Jesus. It was found in Gnosticism, and it has reappeared from time to time in the history of the church. *See* Chalcedonian Definition; *see* Eutychianism; *see* Gnosticism.

Doctors of the Church. *See* Patristics.

Doctrine. The term is from the Latin *docere*, "to teach." It means teaching or instruction in the most general sense. In a theological context the word carries the implication of belonging to a school of thought or a body of believers.

Christian doctrine is the rational exposition and illumination of the affirmations of the Christian faith as made, for example, in the Apostles' and Nicene creeds. It is also possible to consider the doctrine of a particular theologian or theological issue. For example, one may speak of the Anselmian doctrine of the atonement, indicating the particular development of this question associated with Anselm of Canterbury. The body of teaching put forward by any influential teacher of the church also may be described as doctrine. Doctrine is distinguished from dogma because, unlike dogma, it is not officially promulgated.

Dod, Robert Stockton (Jan. 13, 1855–Aug. 27, 1924). One of three founders of the Order of the Holy Cross. He studied at General Theological Seminary. Dod was ordained deacon on June 9, 1878, and priest on Aug. 24, 1880. He and James Otis Sargent Huntington attended a retreat in Philadelphia on Nov. 8–13, 1880, led by the Rev. William John Knox-Little, a leading English ritualist. Here they decided to form an American religious order for men. Dod then went to England where he was received as a postulant of the Society of St. John the Evangelist at Cowley on Feb. 1, 1881. In Apr. 1881, he left Cowley and went to the Mother House of St. John the Baptist at Clewer, Windsor. At Clewer, Dod wrote the preliminary notes for the rule and constitution of the proposed order. On Aug. 27, 1881, Dod returned to the United States. On Oct. 1, 1881, he and Huntington moved into the first house of the Order of the Holy Cross. Dod served as superior of the developing order. The Order of the Holy Cross was officially formed on Nov. 25, 1884, when Huntington took his vows. Dod never made a monastic profession, but Huntington called him the "founding father" of the order. He lived much of the rest of his life as an invalid. Dod died in Alpine, Texas.

Doddridge, Philip (June 26, 1702–Oct. 26, 1751). English independent theologian, writer, and poet. He was born in London and educated at Kingston Grammar School at the Rev. John Jenning's Dissenting Academy, Kibworth, Leicestershire. Doddridge served as minister at the Dissenting Academy after Jenning's death in 1723. The academy was reconstituted at Northampton in 1729 under Doddridge, who also became minister of an important Dissenting congregation there. He was a pioneer in missionary efforts of Independent Churches. Doddridge received a D.D. from the University of Aberdeen in 1736. Respected by many Independents, Anglicans, and

Methodists, his hymns, written primarily between 1735 and 1740, were published posthumously as *Hymns Founded on Various Texts in Holy Scriptures* (1755). Six of his texts are found in *The Hymnal 1982*, including "Hark! the glad sound! the Savior comes" (71–72), and "Awake, my soul, stretch every nerve (546). He died in Lisbon, Portugal.

Dogma. Definitive teaching of the church which is to be believed by the members of the church. The term is from the Greek *dokein*, "to seem." It designates doctrine which has been considered by an authoritative body and promulgated as officially established teaching. It "appears to be good" to that body, and there "seems" to be no objection to it. Dogma is, hence, definitive and normative for future thought. The chief matters so approved in the church include the doctrines of the Trinity and the Incarnation, which were defined by the first four general councils. Virtually all Anglicans recognize these councils as ecumenical and authoritative, and most Anglicans recognize the first seven general councils. The judgments of these councils consequently rank as dogma. There is no authoritative Anglican pronouncement as to the number of authoritative councils. The Roman Catholic Church regards all councils summoned by the Pope as authoritative, and their pronouncements count as dogma. The Eastern Orthodox Church similarly regards all synods convened by the Ecumenical Patriarch. Thus the scope of dogma varies in different Christian bodies. Heresy may be understood as the formal and deliberate rejection of a dogma. *See* Ecumenical Councils.

"Dom." An abbreviated form of *Dominus*, which means "master." This title is given to some professed Benedictine monks and to some monks in other monastic orders.

Domestic and Foreign Missionary Society. The missionary organization and corporate body of the Episcopal Church. The constitution of the missionary society was first adopted by the special General Convention of 1821 and incorporated by the New York State legislature. In 1835 the General Convention adopted a new constitution which made membership in the society no longer voluntary but inclusive of all the baptized in the Episcopal Church. The constitution further declared the world to be the missionary field of the church and entrusted general missionary work to a reorganized board of missions. In 1877 the constitution of the society was enacted as a canon of the General Convention. This canon was amended in 1919 to provide for the Presiding Bishop and Council (now Executive Council) to be the directors of the society and to administer its work.

Domestic Mission and Evangelism, Standing Commission on. The 1997 General Convention established this commission. Its purpose is to identify, study, and consider major policies, priorities, and concerns as to the domestic mission of the church. Its primary purpose is to review the shaping of new directions for evangelism, particularly in rural and metropolitan areas. The commission consists of two bishops, six presbyters, and eight lay persons.

Domestic Missionary Partnership. Coalition 14 changed its name to the Domestic Missionary Partnership at a meeting at Mercy Center in Burlingame, California, on Feb. 6–9, 1997. The Partnership will continue to promote ministry in small and rural dioceses. *See* Coalition 14.

Dominic (c. 1170–Aug. 6, 1221). Dominic de Guzman was born in Calaruega, Castile, Spain. He studied at the University of Palencia, in the Kingdom of Leon. In 1216 Pope Honorius III granted Dominic the right to establish a new religious order. This new order was to preach the gospel, convert heretics, defend the faith, and propagate Christianity. It was named the Order of Friars Preachers (OP). Members of the order are sometimes called Dominicans, in honor of their founder. In England the members of the order are sometimes called Black Friars because of the black mantle or *cappa* which they wore over their white habits and scapulars. The first Dominican monastery was established at Toulouse. The order followed the rule of St. Augustine, and was known for a while as the "regular canons of St. Augustine." The Dominicans were dedicated to refuting heresy by intellectual argument and the example of a holy life. They frequently founded their houses in university cities. The greatest Dominican teacher is St. Thomas Aquinas. Dominic was canonized by Pope Gregory IX on July 13, 1234. Dominic died in Bologna. He is commemorated in the Episcopal calendar of the church year on Aug. 8. *See* Aquinas, Thomas.

Dominical Letter. *See* Sunday Letter.

Dominical Sacraments. Sacraments associated with the Lord Jesus Christ. The two great sacraments given by Christ to his church are Baptism and Eucharist (BCP, p. 858). The term "dominical" is from Latin words meaning "of a lord," and "lord."

Dominican Republic, Diocese of the. Anglicanism was brought to the Dominican Republic in 1897 when Benjamin Isaac Wilson migrated from the Virgin Islands. Wilson was a teacher of the Christian faith, and was ordained priest in 1898 by the Bishop of the Independent Haitian Episcopal Church. His primary mission was to serve the English-speaking community in the Dominican Republic. The work of the Episcopal Church began in the Dominican Republic during the occupation of the United States Marine Corps. The Rev. William Wyllie arrived in 1918, and the Rev. Archibald Beer came in 1920. From 1918 until 1960, the supervision of the church was assumed by the Bishops of Puerto Rico and Haiti. In 1940 the General Convention established the Missionary District of the Dominican Republic. The first resident Bishop of the Dominican Republic was the Rt. Rev. Paul Axtell Kellogg, who was consecrated on Mar. 9, 1960. In 1970 it became a missionary diocese, and on Jan. 1, 1986, it became the Diocese of the Dominican Republic.

"Don." This term comes from "Dominus." In Spain it was a title given to a nobleman. It is now used for the head of a college and for fellows in English universities, such as an "Oxford Don."

Donatism. Rigorist schism. Donatists were the followers of Donatus Magnus, a schismatic bishop of Carthage in the mid-fourth century, who believed that the validity of a sacrament depended on the personal virtue of the celebrant. Many other North African Christians shared this view. In particular this group of rigorists rejected the ordination of Caecilian as Bishop of Carthage by a neighboring bishop, who was falsely believed to have betrayed the church during the Diocletian persecutions earlier in the fourth century. Caecilian was excommunicated and Majorinus ordained in his stead. Caecilian was confirmed in his position by the Council of Arles in 314, but a flourishing schismatic church sprang up around Majorinus and his able and aggressive successor, Donatus. Imperial force was used for several decades to suppress the schism, and was met with widespread violent resistance. The Donatist sect survived for several centuries. Augustine engaged in a celebrated and extensive controversy with the Donatists. He established the catholic teaching that the validity of sacramental action depends upon the power of the Holy Spirit in the church, and not the personal character of the celebrant. Augustine argued that the catholic church is a mixed society in the process of salvation rather than a perfect society in itself. This view is shared by the Articles of Religion (Art. XXVI, BCP, p. 873).

Donne, John (1572–Mar. 31, 1631). Noted preacher and poet. He was born in London, sometime between Jan. 24 and June 19, 1572. Donne studied at Hart Hall, Oxford. In 1592 he was admitted to Lincoln's Inn to study law. At about the same time, he had a gradual conversion from Roman Catholicism to the Church of England. In 1615 Donne was ordained priest, and King James I made him his royal chaplain. He continued to live in London, where he was appointed divinity reader of Lincoln's Inn. Donne soon became recognized as one of the leading preachers of the time. In 1621 he was appointed dean of St. Paul's Cathedral, London. His major publications were his sermons and his poetry. He is recognized as a great "metaphysical poet" in English literature. His sonnet, "Batter my heart, three person'd God," is one of his classics. Two of his hymns are in *The Hymnal 1982*: "Wilt thou forgive that sin, where I begun" (140, 141), and "When Jesus died to save us" (322). He died in London. Donne's ministry is commemorated in the Episcopal calendar of the church year on Mar. 31.

Door Keeper. *See* Minor Orders.

Dort, Synod of. Assembly of the Dutch Reformed Church convened at Dordrecht, near Rotterdam, from Nov. 1618 to May 1619, to deal with the Arminian Controversy. The Arminians (Remonstrants) opposed the Calvinist doctrine of absolute predestination. The synod was strongly biased in favor of the strict Calvinist position from the beginning. The Arminians were treated as defendants on trial and were not admitted to the sessions of the first weeks of the synod. They were found guilty of heresy by the synod. The synod made a positive statement of its Calvinistic views through its canons. These canons are based on the principle of the absolute sovereignty of God and the basis for the five points of Calvinism: 1) total depravity, 2) unconditional election, 3) limited atonement, 4) irresistibility of grace, and 5) the perseverance of the saints. *See* Protestantism.

Dossal. A large cloth or piece of fabric that is hung on the wall behind the altar. Its color may match the liturgical color of the day, and it may be decorated with religious symbols.

Double Procession. *See* Processions (Trinitarian).

Douglas, Charles Winfred (Feb. 15, 1867–Jan. 18, 1944). Church musician and editor. He was born in Oswego, New York, and received his Bachelor in Music degree from Syracuse University in 1891. He also studied at St. Andrew's Divinity School, Syracuse; Matthew's Hall, Denver; and in England, France, and Germany, particularly with the Benedictines of Solesmes. He was ordained deacon on Oct. 15, 1893, and began his ministry as curate at the Church of the Redeemer, New York, but he moved to Denver in 1894 for health reasons. He was Canon Minor at St. John's Cathedral, Denver, 1894–1897. From 1897 until 1907, he was associate missionary at Evergreen, Colorado, and established the Church of the Transfiguration. He was ordained priest on Aug. 6, 1899. Douglas was canon residentiary at St. Paul's Cathedral, Fond du Lac, Wisconsin, 1907–1934. In 1923 he was largely responsible for the founding of the Evergreen Conference. Douglas assumed a leading role in conference planning, especially the School of Music. He had a life-long relationship as musical and liturgical leader with the Sisters of the Community of St. Mary, in both Peekskill, New York, and Kenosha, Wisconsin. In 1934 he was made honorary canon of St. John's Cathedral, Denver. He was musical editor of *The Hymnal* (1916), and served on the Joint Commission of the Revision of the Hymnal which produced *The Hymnal* (1940). He delivered the Hale Lectures at Seabury-Western Theological Seminary in 1935 with the title "The Praise of God," which were published in 1937 under the title *Church Music in History and Practice*. His catalogue of publications as an editor of chant is vast. Douglas translated texts or stanzas that are used in six hymns in *The Hymnal 1982*, including "On Jordan's Bank" (76), "Give praise and glory unto God" (375), and "Spread, O spread, thou mighty word" (530). He died in Santa Rosa, California.

Doxology. Words of glory (from the Greek *doxa logos*) or praise to God, usually in a trinitarian form. Christian tradition contains three main forms of doxology: 1) the Greater Doxology, the hymn "Glory to God in the highest," originally sung at Morning Prayer in the eastern church and now, in the west, used in the entrance rite of the Eucharist on many Sundays and other festal occasions; 2) the Lesser Doxology, the verse beginning "Glory to the Father," sung at the opening and at the end of psalms and canticles in the Daily Office; and 3) metrical doxologies, such as the familiar verse beginning "Praise God from whom all blessings flow," sometimes used at the presentation of offerings.

Dozier, Verna J. (b. Oct. 9, 1917). Leading African American female lay theologian. She was born in Washington, D.C. Dozier received her B.A. and M.A. from Harvard University. She taught English in the Washington public schools for more than thirty years, and from 1968 until 1972, was the curriculum specialist for the Urban Teachers Corps. From 1972 until 1975, when she retired, she was the assistant director of the English Department of the Washington public schools. She was a member of the vestry and senior warden of St. Mark's Church, Washington, 1970–1972. Dozier was an adjunct instructor in NT at the Virginia Theological Seminary and adjunct staff for the College of Preachers. She served on the Board of Examining Chaplains and the Board of the Alban Institute. Dozier was chairperson of the Commission on Ministry and a member of the Standing Committee of the Diocese of Washington. She was a freelance consultant in Bible study and the ministry of the laity. She was a popular retreat leader and made presentations in every state in the United States. Among her books are *Equipping the Saints: A Method of Self-Directed Bible Study for Lay Groups* (1981); with Celia A. Hahn, *The Authority of the Laity* (1982); *The Calling of the Laity: Verna Dozier's Anthology* (1988); and *The Dream of God: A Call to Return* (1991).

Drake, Sir Francis (c. 1540–Jan. 28, 1596). Celebrated navigator. He was born near Tavistock, Devonshire, England. He probably anchored at San Francisco Bay on June 17, 1579. On June 21, 1579, Francis Fletcher, Drake's chaplain, celebrated the eucharist at Drake's Bay, near San Francisco, for the crew of the *Pelican*. This may have been the first BCP service in what is now the continental United States. Drake died near Portobelo, Venezuela.

D.S.M. Sometimes referred to as S.M.D., the Doctor of Sacred Music degree presupposes a master's degree in church music from a school that follows the guidelines of the National Association of Schools of Music.

Dublin Agreed Statement. A statement issued in Aug. 1984 by the Anglican-Orthodox Joint Doctrinal Commission after the Episcopal Church began to ordain women to the priesthood. The Orthodox opposed the ordination of women, and there was considerable concern about the future of the consultation before the meeting. General agreement was noted in eucharistic doctrine, but differences in the two faith communities concerning the oneness of the church, the presence of sin and division in the church, and the understanding of Ecumenical Councils were also noted. The statement clearly presented problems and differences, but it also stated that none were insoluble and that tradition must be seen in dynamic terms.

duBois, Albert Julius (June 9, 1906–June 6, 1980). Influential opponent of the ordination of women and a leader of splinter groups. He was born in Neenah, Wisconsin. DuBois received his B.A. from Lawrence College in 1928 and his S.T.B. from the General Theological Seminary in 1931. He was ordained deacon on Apr. 12, 1931, and priest on Nov. 1, 1931. From 1931 until 1935, he was rector of St. Mark's Church in Waupaca, and vicar of St. Olaf's Mission Church, both in Wisconsin. He was Canon Pastor of St. Paul's Cathedral, Fond du Lac, 1935–1938. During the years 1938–1941, and again from 1946–1950, he was rector of Ascension and St. Agnes Parish in Washington, D.C. During World War II, 1942–1946, duBois served as a chaplain in the army. In 1950 he became the first executive director of the American Church Union. He held that position until 1974. During those twenty-four years, duBois served as editor of the *American Church News*. From 1974 until 1977, he served as professor of liturgics and church history at the Episcopal Theological Seminary in Kentucky. In 1976 duBois became president of Episcopalians United, which was opposed to Prayer Book revision and the ordination of women. In 1977 he founded Anglicans United and became its first president. After renouncing the ordained ministry of the Episcopal Church, he was deposed on Sept. 28, 1977. DuBois supported and joined the Anglican Church of North America. On Jan. 7, 1978, the Convocation of the West Coast of the Diocese of the Holy Trinity in the Anglican Church of North America voted to leave the Diocese of the Holy Trinity and form a new diocese. It was opposed to both the Episcopal Church and the Anglican Church of North America. On that same day, duBois was elected Bishop Designate of the proposed new diocese. He was never consecrated. On June 29, 1978, the Pro-Diocese of

St. Augustine of Canterbury was formed to restore unity between the Roman Catholic Church and the Anglicans. DuBois was the senior priest in the Pro-Diocese. He died in Long Beach, California.

DuBose Memorial Church Training School, Monteagle, Tennessee. This school was one of the recognized theological seminaries of the Episcopal Church. It operated from Sept. 21, 1921, until Aug. 1944. It was founded by the Rev. William Sterling Claiborne (1877–1933) to train men for ordained ministry in rural areas. It was named in honor of William Porcher DuBose, late dean and professor at the School of Theology of the University of the South. The campus of Fairmont College, a school for young ladies that closed in 1917, was purchased and remodeled. The DuBose School concentrated on practical training among the mountain people of Tennessee but also taught church history, scripture, doctrine, worship, sociology, Christian education, and church administration. Tuition was kept low because the students did all the work on the campus and ran a farm. About 275 students from at least seventy-five dioceses in the United States and the Caribbean attended the school before World War II caused a declining enrollment. After the school closed, the property was sold to the Diocese of Tennessee and turned into the DuBose Conference Center. The assets were made into a scholarship fund for candidates thirty-two years and older to attend an Episcopal seminary. *See* DuBose, William Porcher.

DuBose, William Porcher (Apr. 11, 1836–Aug. 18, 1918). Theologian and educator. He was born in Winnsboro, South Carolina. He graduated from The Citadel in 1855, and received his M.A. from the University of Virginia in 1859. His study for the ordained ministry at the Theological Seminary of the Protestant Episcopal Church in the Diocese of South Carolina at Camden was interrupted in 1861 by the Civil War. DuBose served as an adjutant in the Confederate Army. He was wounded in action and taken as a prisoner of war. After his release, he was ordained deacon on Dec. 13, 1863. He began his ministry as a chaplain to Confederate soldiers. After the war, he was rector of St. John's Church, Fairfield, South Carolina. He was ordained priest on Sept. 9, 1866. DuBose served as rector of Trinity Church, Abbeville, from 1868 until 1871. He was chaplain at the University of the South, Sewanee, Tennessee, from July 17, 1871, until June 30, 1883. He helped to establish the School of Theology at the University of

the South. DuBose taught in both the College of Arts and Sciences and the School of Theology. He was the second dean of the School of Theology from July 31, 1894, until June 24, 1901.

DuBose is recognized as a major theologian in the history of the Episcopal Church. He published seven books, the first of which was *The Soteriology of the New Testament* (1892), which presented his systematic approach to theology. He then applied this theological system to the history of the early church in *The Ecumenical Councils* (1896), and to the NT. DuBose worked out his theological system relative to the synoptic gospels in *The Gospel in the Gospels* (1906), the Pauline literature in *The Gospel According to Saint Paul* (1907), the Letter to the Hebrews in *High Priesthood and Sacrifice* (1908), and the Johannine writings in *The Reason of Life* (1911).

DuBose's theology was deeply rooted in the lessons of his experience. He discussed his experience and theology in his autobiographical *Turning Points in My Life* (1912). In this book he described a powerful experience of conversion he had while he was a cadet at The Citadel. This experience was formative for the rest of his life and ministry. DuBose came to understand salvation in terms of a continuing process by which the objective truth of God's grace may become increasingly a subjective reality for the believer. DuBose's experiences of loss, poverty, and suffering—during the Civil War and afterwards—were formative for his understanding of the role of the cross in the life of Christ and in the Christian life.

DuBose's experiences of discovery in education as a teacher and student were formative for his understanding of the needed openness of the church. He was ecumenical in outlook and wary of the claims of ultimate truth held by any faction of the church in isolation. He believed in the working out of extremes and the unmasking of errors through open discussion. He was a frequent contributor to the ecumenical journal *The Constructive Quarterly.* DuBose believed in the continuity of church tradition, but he also believed that the truth must be discovered anew in each time and situation. He died in Sewanee. He is commemorated in the Episcopal calendar of the church year on Aug. 18.

Dudley, Helena Stuart (Aug. 31, 1858–Sept. 29, 1932). Peace and labor activist. She was born in Nebraska, probably in Florence. Dudley graduated with the first class of Bryn Mawr College in 1889. She was acquainted with the founders of the settlement house movement. She participated in the establishment of the College Settlements Association in 1890. She became head worker at the College Settlement House in Philadelphia. Dudley moved to Boston where she held a similar post at Denison House. She arrived in the middle of the financial crisis of 1893 and reorganized the settlement house as a relief agency. Dudley thought that the greatest need of the neighborhood residents was a living wage. This cause led her to become very active in organized labor. Dudley repudiated violence, but she was very supportive of the strikes and protests of the early twentieth century in New England. She resigned as head resident of Denison House in 1912 to avoid jeopardizing the fund-raising efforts. Dudley devoted herself next to the world peace movement. She joined other prominent Americans in maintaining a pacifist stance as the United States entered World War I in 1917. An active Episcopalian, Dudley was a member of the Society of the Companions of the Holy Cross. She spent many years working for Adelynrood, the Society's home in South Byfield, Massachusetts. She lived the last years of her life with fellow Companion Vida Scudder in Wellesley, Massachusetts. She died in Geneva, Switzerland, after attending the Congress of the Women's International League at Grenoble, France, in 1932.

Dulia. A term used in medieval theology to distinguish the reverence which may legitimately be paid to the saints from the worship (*latria*) which is paid only to God. Since both words can be translated as worship in English and most other languages, the distinction was important in the controversies concerning the veneration of saints, icons, and things other than God. *See* Latria.

Duluth, Diocese of. The General Convention of 1895 voted to divide the Diocese of Minnesota and created the Missionary Diocese of Duluth. It consisted of the following counties: Aitken, Becker, Beltram, Benson, Big Stone, Carlton, Cass, Clay, Clearwater, Cook, Crow Wing, Douglas, Grant, Hahnomen, Hubbard, Itasca, Kanabec, Kittson, Koochiching, Lake, Lake of the Woods, Marshall, Mille Lacs, Morrison, Norman, Otter Tail, Pennington, Pine, Polk, Pope, Red Lake, Roseau, St. Louis, Sterns, Stevens, Todd, Traverse, Wadena, and Wilkin. On Dec. 4–5, 1895, the primary convention of the Missionary District was held at St. Paul's Church, Brainerd. On May 26, 1907, Trinity Cathedral, Duluth, was dedicated. The primary convention of the Diocese of Duluth was held at Trinity Cathedral, Duluth, on June 19, 1907. On Jan. 14, 1944, the Diocese of

Duluth was reunited with the Diocese of Minnesota. Trinity Cathedral was sold to the Lutherans in 1956.

Dun, Angus (May 4, 1892–Aug. 12, 1971). Bishop and leading ecumenist. He was born in New York City. Dun received his B.A. from Yale University in 1914 and his B.D. from the Episcopal Theological School in 1917. He was ordained deacon on May 17, 1917, and priest on Nov. 20, 1917. Dun was vicar of St. Andrew's Church, Ayer, Massachusetts, 1917–1919. From 1920 until 1940, he taught theology at the Episcopal Theological School (ETS). From 1940 until 1944, he was dean of ETS. On Apr. 19, 1944, Dun was consecrated Bishop of Washington. He served in that position until he retired on May 6, 1962. He helped to lay the groundwork for the World Council of Churches, which was founded in 1948. Dun served as chairman of the Joint Commission on Ecumenical Relations of the Episcopal Church. He was a member of the Central Committee of the World Council of Churches. He repudiated the Senate investigations of alleged Communist activities led by Joseph McCarthy, and denounced segregation. Among his major publications were *The King's Cross* (1926), *We Believe* (1934), and *Not by Bread Alone* (1942). Dun died in Washington.

Dunblane Consultations. A series of annual consultations on church music and hymnody sponsored by the Scottish Churches. The consultations were held at the Scottish Churches House, Dunblane, Scotland, from 1962 to 1969. The consultations were very important for the contemporary development of English hymnody, even though relatively few of the Dunblane hymns have continued in use. Poets involved in the consultations whose work appears in *The Hymnal 1982* include John B. Geyer, Caryl Micklem, and Erik Routley. Composers whose work appears include Peter Cutts, Christopher Dearnley, and Eric Routley.

Dunstan (c. 909–May 19, 988). Monk, statesman, educator, Benedictine monastic reformer, and Archbishop of Canterbury. In 943 he became the Abbot of Glastonbury. He made Glastonbury famous for its asceticism and scholarship. In 957 he became the Bishop of Worcester. In 959 he became Bishop of London. That same year King Edgar of Mercia and Northumbria became King of all England and appointed Dunstan the twenty-third Archbishop of Canterbury. He served as archbishop from Oct. 21, 960, until his death. Dunstan has been called "the patron and father of the monks of medieval England." He died at Canterbury. Dunstan is commemorated in the Episcopal calendar of the church year on May 19.

"D.V." *Deo Volente*, Latin for "God willing." This abbreviation sometimes appears on formal announcements for celebrations and events such as an ordination.

Dyer, Herman (Sept. 24, 1810–July 29, 1900). Nineteenth-century leader of the evangelical party. He was born in Shaftesbury, Vermont. Dyer graduated from Kenyon College in 1833 and studied at Bexley Hall. He was ordained deacon on Sept. 7, 1834, and priest on Sept. 11, 1836. Dyer taught school for a while. In 1840 he became a professor at the Western University of Pennsylvania in Pittsburgh; and from 1844 until 1849 he was president of the university. In 1849 he moved to Philadelphia where he worked for the American Sunday School Union. Later he became secretary and general manager of the Evangelical Knowledge Society. In 1854 he moved to New York to edit the *Episcopal Quarterly Review*. Dyer was critical of those evangelicals who left the Episcopal Church and organized the Reformed Episcopal Church. *Records of an Active Life* (1886), his autobiography, went through numerous editions. He died in New York.

Dykman, Jackson Annan (July 11, 1887–Feb. 7, 1983). Canon lawyer. He was born in Brooklyn, New York. Dykman received his B.A. from Yale University in 1909, and his LL.B. from Harvard Law School in 1912. He was admitted to the New York bar in 1913. Dykman was chancellor of the Diocese of Long Island, 1925–1952, and a member of its Standing Committee, 1922–1962. He was a member of the National Council of the Episcopal Church from 1943 until 1949. In 1924 Edwin Augustine White wrote *Constitution and Canons for the Government of the Protestant Episcopal Church in the United States of America, Adopted in General Conventions, 1789–1922, Annotated, with an Exposition of the Same, and Reports of Such Cases as Have Arisen and Been Decided Thereunder*. The General Convention of 1949 added Dykman to the Joint Committee to Supervise Publication of a New Annotated Edition of the Constitution and Canons. Dykman took the lead revising White's volume. The new edition was published in 1954 with the title *Annotated Constitution and Canons for the Government of the Protestant Episcopal Church in the United States*

of America, Adopted in General Conventions, 1789–1952, 2d ed., 2 vols. Dykman died in Jacksonville, Illinois.

E

East Carolina, Diocese of. The 1883 General Convention voted to divide the Diocese of North Carolina. The primary convention of the new diocese met Dec. 12–13, 1883, at Christ Church, New Bern, and chose the name the Diocese of East Carolina. It includes the following counties: Beaufort, Bertie, Bladen, Brunswick, Camden, Carteret, Chowan, Columbus, Craven, Cumberland, Currituck, Dare, Duplin, Gates, Greene, Hereford, Hoke, Hyde, Jones, Lenoir, Martin, New Hanover, Onslow, Pamlico, Pasquotank, Pender, Perquimans, Pitt, Robeson, Sampson, Tyrell, Washington, and Wayne. The Diocese of East Carolina does not have a cathedral.

East Tennessee, Diocese of. The General Convention of 1982 voted to divide the Diocese of Tennessee into three Dioceses—Tennessee, East Tennessee, and West Tennessee. The Diocese of East Tennessee held its primary convention on Oct. 5–6, 1984, in Knoxville. The diocese includes the following counties: Anderson, Bledsoe, Blount, Bradley, Campbell, Carter, Claiborne, Cocke, Cumberland, Grainger, Greene, Hamblen, Hamilton, Hancock, Hawkins, Jefferson, Johnson, Knox, Loudon, Marion, McMinn, Meigs, Morgan, Monroe, Polk, Rhea, Roane, Scott, Sequatchie, Sevier, Sullivan, Unicoi, Union, and Washington. It also has three counties in Georgia: Catoosa, Dade, and Walker.

Easter. The feast of Christ's resurrection. According to Bede, the word derives from the Anglo-Saxon spring goddess Eostre. Christians in England applied the word to the principal festival of the church year, both day and season. 1) Easter Day is the annual feast of the resurrection, the *pascha* or Christian Passover, and the eighth day of cosmic creation. Faith in Jesus' resurrection on the Sunday or third day following his crucifixion is at the heart of Christian belief. Easter sets the experience of springtime next to the ancient stories of deliverance and the proclamation of the risen Christ. In the west, Easter occurs on the first Sunday after the full moon on or after the vernal equinox. Easter always falls between Mar. 22 and Apr. 25 inclusive. Following Jewish custom, the feast begins at sunset on Easter Eve with the Great Vigil of Easter. The Eastern Orthodox Church celebrates Easter on the first Sunday after the Jewish *pesach* or Passover (which follows the spring full moon). Although the two dates sometimes coincide, the eastern date is often one or more weeks later. 2) Easter Season. *See* Great Fifty Days.

Easter Eve, Easter Even. The Saturday before Easter. In the early church it was a day of fasting and preparation for the Easter Vigil. There is no celebration of the eucharist on this day, in accordance with church tradition. The term "Easter Even" was used by the 1549 Prayer Book. The 1979 BCP uses the title "Holy Saturday" for the Saturday before Easter (p. 283). The title distinguishes this day and its proper liturgy from the Easter Vigil. *See* Holy Saturday.

Easter Vigil. The liturgy intended as the first (and arguably, the primary) celebration of Easter in the BCP (pp. 284–95). It is also known as the Great Vigil. The service begins in darkness, sometime between sunset on Holy Saturday and sunrise on Easter, and consists of four parts: The Service of Light (kindling of new fire, lighting the Paschal candle, the Exsultet); The Service of Lessons (readings from the Hebrew Scriptures interspersed with psalms, canticles, and prayers); Christian Initiation (Holy Baptism) or the Renewal of Baptismal Vows; and the Eucharist. Through this liturgy, the BCP recovers an ancient practice of keeping the Easter feast. Believers would gather in the hours of darkness ending at dawn on Easter to hear scripture and offer prayer. This night-long service of prayerful watching anticipated the baptisms that would come at first light and the Easter Eucharist. Easter was the primary baptismal occasion for the early church to the practical exclusion of all others. This practice linked the meanings of Christ's dying and rising to the understanding of baptism.

Eastern Catholic Churches. Byzantine or Eastern Rite churches which retain their rites, canons, customs, and national language, but are in full communion with the Roman Catholic Church. They include Albanian, Armenian, Bulgarian, Chaldean, Coptic, Ethiopian, Georgian, Greek, Hungarian, Italo-Albanian, Malabarese, Malankarese, Maronite, Melkite, Romanian, Russian, Ruthenian, Slovak, Syrian, Ukrainian, and Yugoslavian churches. The largest group is the Ukrainian. During the 1940s the Ukrainian and Romanian Catholic churches were officially suppressed under communism and forced into Orthodoxy. These Eastern Catholic churches continued underground until religious freedom was restored in the former Soviet bloc. The Ukrainian Church was legalized in 1989, and the Romanian Church was legalized in 1990. The Eastern Catholic churches have been called "Uniate" by the Orthodox, but this term is considered derogatory and not acknowledged by these churches. The issue of the Eastern Catholic churches has strained ecumenical relations between the Orthodox and the Roman Catholic Church, especially in places such as Ukraine and Romania where the Orthodox are perceived to have collaborated with the communists in the persecution of these churches.

Eastern Diocese. On May 29, 1810, representatives from New Hampshire, Vermont, Rhode Island, and Massachusetts (at that time including Maine) met at Boston and organized the Eastern Diocese. This was not a diocese in the regular sense, but an arrangement whereby four weak dioceses could work together. On May 29, 1811, Alexander Viets Griswold was consecrated Bishop of the Eastern Diocese. The four constituting dioceses held their own annual conventions and each sent deputies to the General Convention. In 1820 the Diocese of Maine was organized and joined the Eastern Diocese. When Bishop Griswold died on Feb. 15, 1843, the Eastern Diocese ceased to exist.

Eastern Michigan, Diocese of. The General Convention of 1994 voted to divide the Diocese of Michigan. The new diocese consists of the following counties: Alcona, Alpena, Arenac, Bay, Cheboygan, Crawford, Genesee, Gladwin, Gratiot, Huron, Iosco, Lapeer, Midland, Montmorency, Ogemaw, Osconda, Otsego, Presque Isle, Roscommon, Saginaw, St. Clair, Salinac, Shiawassee, Tuscola, that part of Oakland County comprising Holly Township, and that part of Clinton County north of Price Road. The primary convention of the new diocese was held at Grace Church, Port Huron, Oct. 28–29, 1994.

Eastern Oklahoma, Missionary District of. On Oct. 11, 1910, the General Convention formed this missionary district. It consisted of the counties lying east of the west line of the counties of Creek, Johnston, Marshall, Okfuskee, Osage, Pontotoc, and Seminole. It had only one bishop. On Oct. 10, 1919, the House of Bishops reunited it with the Missionary District of Oklahoma.

Eastern Oregon, Diocese of. The General Convention of 1907 voted to divide the Diocese of Oregon and form the Missionary District of Eastern Oregon. It was a missionary district from 1907 to 1971. The primary convention of the Diocese of Eastern Oregon met at the Church of the

Redeemer, Pendleton, Nov. 19–21, 1971. It includes the following Oregon counties: Baker, Crook, Deschutes, Gilliam, Grant, Harney, Hood River, Jefferson, Klamath, Lake Malheur, Morrow, Sherman, Umatilla, Union, Wallowa, Wasco, Wheeler; and Klickitat County in the state of Washington.

Eastertide. Another term for Easter season, the Great Fifty Days. As used in English-speaking churches, "tide" is an old word meaning a festival and its season.

Easton, Burton Scott (Dec. 4, 1877–Mar. 7, 1950). Seminary professor and NT scholar. He was born in Hartford, Connecticut. Easton studied first at the University of Göttingen in Germany. He subsequently received his B.S. in 1898 and his Ph.D. in 1901, both from the University of Pennsylvania. While teaching mathematics at the University of Pennsylvania, 1901–1905, he studied at the Philadelphia Divinity School, where he received his B.D. in 1906. Easton was ordained deacon on May 26, 1905, and priest on Dec. 17, 1905. From 1905 until 1911, he taught NT at Nashotah House. From 1911 until 1919, he taught NT at Western Theological Seminary in Chicago. Easton was professor of NT at the General Theological Seminary from 1919 until 1948, when he became Professor Emeritus. He served as Associate Editor of the *Anglican Theological Review* from 1923 until his death. Easton became a NT scholar of international repute with his commentary on *The Gospel of St. Luke* (1926). Among his many other publications were *The Gospel Before the Gospels* (1928), *Christ in the Gospels* (1930), and *The Pastoral Epistles* (1947). He also published a translation and edition of the *Apostolic Tradition* of Hippolytus (1934). Easton died in New York City.

Easton, Diocese of. The General Convention of 1868 voted to divide the Diocese of Maryland and form a new diocese. The primary convention of the new diocese met at Christ Church, Easton, on Nov. 19–20, 1868, and adopted the name Diocese of Easton. On May 25, 1894, Trinity Church, Easton, was set apart as Trinity Cathedral.

Eastward Position. The posture of the presider who stands at the altar with his or her back to the people. In churches oriented with the altar at the east end, as was once customary, the presider would thus be facing east. The practice originated in Rome in the eighth or ninth century. It replaced the ancient westward position, with the presider behind the altar and facing the people. In contemporary usage the westward position has been reintroduced and become common.

Eau Claire, Diocese of. The 1928 General Convention voted to create a new diocese from the dioceses of Fond du Lac and Milwaukee. The primary convention of the Diocese of Eau Claire was held at Christ Church, Eau Claire. It consists of the following counties: Ashland, Barron, Bayfield, Buffalo, Burnett, Chippewa, Clark, Douglas, Dunn, Eau Claire, Iron, Jackson, Juneau, Lacrosse, Monroe, Pepin, Pierce, Polk, Price, Rusk, Sawyer, St. Croix, Taylor, Trempealeau, Vernon, and Washington. On May 27, 1931, Christ Church, Eau Claire, became the cathedral of the diocese.

"E & B." Evensong and Benediction. These services are sometimes scheduled consecutively in parishes with an Anglo-catholic piety. *See* Benediction of the Blessed Sacrament; *see* Evensong.

Ebionites. The term (Hebrew *ebion,* "poor") refers to a sect of Jewish Christians who upheld the Jewish law and rejected Paul's teaching and ministry to the uncircumcised. They lived an ascetic, communal life east of the Jordan in the early centuries of the Christian era. They regarded Jesus as the Messiah who would come to establish God's kingdom on earth. They rejected the virginal conception of Jesus, believing that he had a normal birth and was adopted as the divine Son at his baptism. They were thus the first adoptionists. *See* Adoptionism.

Ecce, Deus. Canticle based on Is 12:2–6, which celebrates the return of Israel from exile. It begins, "Surely it is God who saves me; I will trust in him and not be afraid." Isaiah 12:1–6 presents two songs: Is 12:1–3 is a song of deliverance, and Is 12:4–6 is a song of thanksgiving. The canticle *Ecce, Deus* is also known as the First Song of Isaiah. It appears as Canticle 9 in Morning Prayer, Rite 2 (BCP, p. 86). It may be used in either Rite 2 or Rite 1 services. The BCP suggests its use at Morning Prayer after the OT reading on Monday, and at Evening Prayer after the OT reading on Saturday (pp. 144–145). *The Hymnal 1982 Accompaniment Edition, Vol. 1,* provides a variety of musical settings for the *Ecce, Deus* (S 213–S 216).

Ecclesia. The term is the Latin transliteration of the Greek *ekklesia,* which indicated a civic assembly. The word was

159

derived from the Greek for "call out" or "summon," so it was a "called assembly." In biblical usage it meant the assembly called by God, the church. Because of the Incarnation, in which the Word of God is united to humanity, the entire human family—past, present, future—is called into union with God in the Body of Christ. More specifically, the *ecclesia* is the body of those who are made members of His Body through baptism. They are sustained in that membership through participation in the eucharist. Samuel John Stone's hymn, "The Church's one foundation" (Hymn 525) has been a favorite Anglican expression of the meaning of *ecclesia*. *See* Church, The.

Ecclesiastical. Of or pertaining to the church.

Ecclesiology. From the Greek *ekklesia*, "church," and *logia*, "doctrine," the term refers to the doctrine of the church. The Greek word *ekklesia* (from *ek*, "out of," and *kalein*, "to call") describes the church as those "called out" by God from worldly existence to a new life in Christ. The account of the origin of the church on Pentecost (Acts 2) emphasizes the gift of the Holy Spirit to all the disciples. The church is described in Paul's Letter to the Ephesians as the body of Christ, with Christ as the head. The Johannine image of "vine and branches" (Jn 15:5) shows that life for the Christian is participation in the life of Christ. In the *Treatise on the Laws of Ecclesiastical Polity, Book V*, Richard Hooker emphasizes the importance of participation in the life of Christ through participation in the life of the church (especially the sacraments). The church is described in the creeds as one, holy, catholic, and apostolic. The mission of the church is to restore all people to unity with God and each other in Christ. The church carries out its mission through the ministry of all its members, including lay persons, bishops, priests, and deacons. A doctrine of ministry is usually included in ecclesiology. Recognition of the importance of the ministries of all baptized persons has led to a renewal of interest in ecclesiology. See the Catechism, BCP, pp. 854–855.

Economic Trinity. *See* Trinity.

Ecuador, Central Diocese of. The House of Bishops established the Missionary District of Ecuador on Oct. 27, 1966. It became the Diocese of Ecuador on Jan. 1, 1980. The General Convention of 1985 voted to divide the Diocese of Ecuador and established the Central Diocese

of Ecuador and the Litoral Diocese of Ecuador. The Central Diocese is the continuation of the Diocese of Ecuador.

Ecuador, Litoral Diocese of. The House of Bishops established the Missionary District of Ecuador on Oct. 27, 1966. It became the Diocese of Ecuador on Jan. 1, 1980. The General Convention of 1985 voted to divide the Diocese of Ecuador and established the Central Diocese of Ecuador, which is the continuation of the Diocese of Ecuador, and the new Litoral Diocese of Ecuador.

Ecumenical, Ecumenical Theology. The term is derived from the Greek *oikoumenē*, "inhabited world." Ecumenical refers to the wholeness of the church. Ecumenical theology is theology especially concerned to recover visible unity for the whole church in the world.

Ecumenical Bulletin. This journal began publication in Winter 1965/1966. It was originally published by the Executive Council of the Episcopal Church. After Mar./ Apr. 1976, it was issued in cooperation with the Episcopal Diocesan Ecumenical Officers. *The Handbook for Ecumenism*, which was prepared by the Episcopal Diocesan Ecumenical Officers, was issued as a number of the *Ecumenical Bulletin*. The journal seeks to exchange information and to stimulate dialogue and action concerning ecumenical issues.

Ecumenical Councils. From NT times the church has relied on the decisions of councils called by recognized authority to settle disputes over doctrine and discipline. When a council involves representative bishops from the whole church, it is called "general." When the decisions of a council are recognized by the whole church, it is called "ecumenical" (from the Greek *oikoumenē*, "inhabited world"). The terms "general" and "ecumenical" are not quite synonymous. Seven councils are recognized as ecumenical by both eastern and western churches: Nicaea (325), which dealt centrally with the divinity of the Logos; Constantinople (381), which established the formula for expressing the Trinity and dealt with the divinity of the Holy Spirit; Ephesus (431), which decided against Nestorianism and promulgated a definition of the person of Christ; Constantinople II (553); Constantinople III (680–681); and Nicaea II (787). The latter three councils did refining work on the person of Christ and defined the role of images in worship.

Because of their crucial role in defining the doctrine of the Trinity and Incarnation, Anglicans often regard the first four councils as the most important. *See* Chalcedonian Definition; *see* Monothelitism.

Ecumenical Movement. Inspired in part by the Chicago-Lambeth Quadrilateral (1880), the ecumenical movement was born at the International Missionary Conference of Edinburgh (1910) as a search for the reunion of Christians. Two organizations were formed: Life and Work, and Faith and Order, which joined together in 1948 as the World Council of Churches (WCC). The Anglican Communion is part of the WCC along with most Protestant and some Orthodox churches. Through plenary meetings in Amsterdam (1948), Evanston (1954), New Delhi (1961), Upsala (1968), Nairobi (1975), Vancouver (1983), and Canberra (1994), along with meetings of its Faith and Order Commission in Lund (1950), Montreal (1963), and Compostella (1993), the WCC has assisted the churches in working together toward the reunion of Christians and better stewardship of creation. Vatican Council II (1962–1965) gave further impetus to the movement by involving the Roman Catholic Church through its Pontifical Council for the Unity of Christians.

Ecumenical Relations, Standing Commission on. The 1976 General Convention established this Standing Commission. It includes 18 members: six bishops; six presbyters or deacons; and six lay persons. Its work is to develop a comprehensive and coordinated policy and strategy on relations between the Episcopal Church and other churches, to make recommendations to General Convention concerning interchurch cooperation and unity, and to carry out such instructions on ecumenical matters as may be given it by the General Convention. It also nominates for appointment by the Presiding Bishop, with the advice and consent of the Executive Council, persons to serve on the governing bodies of ecumenical organizations to which the Episcopal Church belongs, such as the World Council of Churches and the National Council of Churches.

Ecumenical Theological Seminary. An association of schools, religious denominations, and other educational institutions. In the early 1950s, the Rev. Dr. Reuel Howe concluded from his years of teaching at Virginia Theological Seminary that clergy were not fully prepared in seminary for ministry. Using the new idea of continuing education for professionals, Howe founded the Institute for Advanced Pastoral Studies in 1957, located at Cranbrook House in Bloomfield Hills, Michigan. The institute was the first ecumenical facility for the continuing education of clergy in the United States. In 1973 the Rev. John Biersdorf succeeded Howe as director of the institute. Biersdorf stressed the life of prayer as the basis and foundation for ministry. The institute focused on the integration of social action with the life of prayer. The institute's mission was expressed in the motto, "Inner Growth and Outer Change." In 1978 a pilot project was begun for developing a Doctor of Ministry program. It was decided that instead of building a new school, they would initiate cooperation among the resources already existing in the area. This resulted in the establishment in 1980 of the Ecumenical Theological Center. The institute and the center relocated to the Convent at St. Bede's Roman Catholic Church in Southfield, Michigan. Following another relocation to the Marygrove College campus in Detroit, the institute and the center merged into a new organization in 1986, also called the Ecumenical Theological Center. Beginning in 1988, a number of seminaries entered into cooperative affiliation with the center. It offered the Master of Divinity degree. One of the schools which joined the center was Seabury-Western Theological Seminary. In June, 1990, the Association of Theological Schools accredited the cooperative Master of Divinity program. In Sept., 1992, the center moved to First Presbyterian Church in Detroit. In 1994 the name was changed from the Ecumenical Theological Center to the Ecumenical Theological Seminary. The Episcopal Diocese of Michigan is an institutional member of the seminary.

Ed.D. The Doctor of Education degree is for those persons who desire leadership positions in the field of education.

Edmund of East Anglia (c. 840–Nov. 20, 870). Christian martyr and King of East Anglia. He became king at the age of fifteen. Edmund was subsequently defeated and captured by an army of invading Danes. The invaders offered to spare his life if he would share his kingdom with a Danish leader. As a Christian, Edmund refused to collaborate in this way with a pagan or compromise the faith. He was tortured, used as a target for the Danes' archery practice, and finally beheaded. A cult of the martyr developed immediately, and Edmund was declared a saint. He is commemorated in the Episcopal calendar of the church year on Nov. 20.

Education, Evangelism and Ministry Development. This division of the executive staff of the Episcopal Church Center focuses its work in the areas of education, evangelism, and ministry development.

Education for Ministry (EFM). This four-year program of theological education for the laity began in 1974 under the direction of the Rev. Dr. Charles L. Winters, Jr., at the School of Theology of the University of the South, Sewanee, Tennessee. EFM is a non-degree program that exists primarily for the development of lay ministry and provides the laity with the basics of theological education. The program was revised between 1983 and 1989. The contents of the four years proceed chronologically. The program begins with Genesis, includes two years of biblical studies, a year of church history, and concludes with modern theologians and theological questions.

Educational Center, The, St. Louis, Missouri. An organization that seeks to promote the transformation of the learning experience in both religious and secular settings through issue-centered, story-based education. The Education Center developed from the Episcopal Home for Children, which was started by the women of St. John's Church, St. Louis, in 1843. Its charter was amended in 1939 to allow more flexibility in its work with young people. In 1940 Dr. Adelaide Chase recommended that religious education research was needed to strengthen the educational ministry of the Diocese of Missouri. The energies of the Episcopal Home for Children were directed to religious education research. The Rev. Matthew Warren became the first director of The Educational Center, where he served from 1941–1945. It was housed in the orphanage infirmary. Warren established a demonstration center at Emmanuel Church, Webster Groves, Missouri, to develop and test curriculum.

The Rev. Dr. Charles Penniman served as director, 1945–1957. He encouraged students to discover the religious dimensions of life as they experienced it. Instead of offering a predetermined curriculum, Penniman urged that "the student is the curriculum." He listened to individual churches in the "clinical" setting of parish Christian education. After recording transcripts of Christian education classes, or after receiving these transcripts, Penniman would use these materials to help church staffs with creative planning for the next session. Penniman sought to identify points in the class discussions where the teacher could engage a life issue with the students.

After Penniman's retirement, Elsom Eldridge became director and Chandler Brown became associate director. They served from 1958–1979, and infused the center's course materials with the perspectives of C. G. Jung's analytical psychology. The Rev. Dr. William Dols became Director in 1987. The center's three branches are Centerquest, the Bible Workbench, and Centerpoint. Centerquest makes use of story in literature, film, myth, and sacred writings to explore issues. Centerquest provides skills training, experiential workshops, and support materials for religious, secular, and adult classes (K-adult). The Bible Workbench uses self-guided small group or individual study to focus on a lectionary text selected for each Sunday of the year. The materials examine a biblical passage through questions, exegetical and historical background, and related readings. Centerpoint uses self-guided small group study to explore Jung's concepts and archetypal patterns. These self-guided, multi-session courses are recorded on cassette tapes and accompanied by written transcripts. *See* Penniman, Charles Frederic.

Efficacious Grace. This is grace that accomplishes its intended result in the human soul, especially in terms of a saving work or salvation. The English reformers affirmed the efficacious nature of the sacraments, urging that they are not mere "badges or tokens of Christian men's profession," but "they be certain sure witnesses, and effectual signs of grace" (Art. XXV, Articles of Religion, BCP, p. 872). The grace conveyed by the sacraments invariably affects the human soul, working to the soul's good. Richard Hooker stated in his *Of the Laws of Ecclesiastical Polity* that the sacraments convey the "grace which worketh salvation," which he called a "saving efficacy."

Egeria (or Etheria or Aetheria), Pilgrim. Egeria's personal account of her journey to holy places in the Sinai, Palestine, Egypt, Mesopotamia, and Asia Minor around the end of the fourth or the beginning of the fifth century. She was likely an abbess or nun from northern Spain or southern Gaul. An incomplete copy of Egeria's chronicle of her pilgrimage was discovered in 1884 in an eleventh-century manuscript. It was written in a curious Latin dialect.

Egeria was a keen observer. She provided a detailed account of what she saw. The last half of the *Peregrinatio Aetheriae* describes the liturgical celebrations in and around Jerusalem. Her work is especially prized by liturgists for her descriptions of the daily and weekly services at

Jerusalem and for her chronicle of the major celebrations of the church year. She describes the Palm Sunday procession to the top of the Mount of Olives and a later procession down from the Mount of Olives into the city of Jerusalem. The people waved palms as they walked. They also sang psalms, including Ps 118, and shouted the antiphon, "Blessed is he who comes in the name of the Lord!" Egeria recalls that on Maundy Thursday the Eucharist was celebrated at 2 P.M. in the Martyrium. This church was a large basilica built by Helena, the mother of Constantine. After the Eucharist, a cross was erected in the courtyard of the church at the supposed site of Jesus' crucifixion. Egeria also describes the veneration of the supposed true cross in the courtyard behind the Martyrium during the morning of Good Friday. A service of psalms, readings, hymns, and prayers lasted from noon until three o'clock in the courtyard. Marion J. Hatchett dates Egeria's accounts of the Palm Sunday, Maundy Thursday, and Good Friday celebrations in Jerusalem at about 381–384. Egeria's account has also been useful in the study of the architecture of the early church.

Eighth Day. Sunday, the Lord's Day. Sunday is both the First Day and the Eighth Day of the liturgical week. The Christian week has been ordered around the Sunday Eucharist since the days of the early church. Sunday is the day of Christ's resurrection and the day of the gift of the Holy Spirit. The number eight breaks the closed seven-day cycle of the week. It surpasses the weekly cycle of chronological time. The number eight has been associated with resurrection, the eschatological fulfillment of time, new life, redemption, and baptism. Octagonal baptisteries and fonts reflect this symbolism of the number eight, and faith that in baptism we share the new life of Christ's resurrection and rebirth by the Holy Spirit. *See* Lord's Day, The; *see* Sunday.

Ekklesia Nika Guild. A league of prayer among those devoted to the Catholic Faith and Apostolic Order for the restoration of the ancient undivided church. It was organized as a devotional organization in the combat area of the South Pacific in 1942 by Anglican and Orthodox servicemen in the American and New Zealand forces. The Guild promotes daily prayer for the unity of the church, works to keep Christianity in the Holy Land, and binds together in catholic love those devoted to catholic faith and apostolic order. It also stresses that the church is the Body of Christ.

Ekklesia Society, The. A fellowship committed to the historic, creedal, and biblical faith of the Anglican Communion. It was chartered on Apr. 12, 1996. The society is made up of parishes, individuals, seminaries, dioceses, ministries, missionary societies, clergy, and lay associates who affirm their commitment to the faith received from the Apostles and summarized in the Chicago-Lambeth Quadrilateral. Members also affirm their commitment to the Great Commission, "To make disciples of Jesus Christ." Members follow ministry commitments to pray faithfully, bear witness regularly, cooperate readily, and contribute generously. There is an American office in Carrollton, Texas, as well as a Caribbean office in Nassau, Bahamas, and an African office in Enugu, Nigeria.

El Camino Real, Diocese of. The 1979 General Convention voted to divide the Diocese of California and create a new diocese called El Camino Real. The primary convention of the Diocese of El Camino Real was held at St. Paul's Church, Salinas, on June 20–21, 1980. It includes the following counties: Monterey, San Benito, San Luis Obispo, Santa Clara (except St. Mark's Church, Palo Alto, and Christ Church, Los Altos), and Santa Cruz. On June 18, 1989, Trinity Church, San Jose, became Trinity Cathedral.

Elder. *See* Presbyter, Presbyterate.

Elements, Eucharistic. Bread and wine that are consecrated in the eucharist. The bread recalls the work of human hands required to harvest the wheat and make the bread, and the companionship of sharing. The wine recalls festivity and celebration, along with sacrifice. These elements of the communal meal are offered by the congregation and blessed during the Great Thanksgiving. The bread and wine of the eucharist are commonly called "elements" or "species." The elements are the outward and visible sign in the sacrament of the eucharist and the matter of the sacrament. The body and blood of Christ are understood to be really present in the eucharistic elements after consecration. They represent the inward and spiritual grace of Christ's Body and Blood that is given to his people and received by faith (BCP, p. 859).

Following a widespread and ancient tradition, congregations of the Episcopal Church use bread made from wheat and wine made from grapes. Other sources of bread and wine may be more appropriate in other cultures. The bread may be leavened or unleavened. It may be in the form of wafers or a loaf that is broken for distribution.

No particular kind or color of wine is required, although many prefer red wine as a symbol of sacrifice and Christ's blood. It is an increasingly common practice to use loaf bread made by members of the congregation. Homemade or local wine may also be used. The BCP makes no provision for the replacement of bread and wine with other eucharistic elements. For example, unfermented grape juice is not used for the eucharist in the Episcopal Church. *See* Matter (Sacramental).

Elevation of the Elements. The lifting up of the eucharistic elements for adoration at the concluding doxology of the eucharistic prayer. This gesture identifies the bread and wine with the sacrifice of Christ. The presider lifts the bread and the deacon lifts the cup, replacing them after the people respond "Amen." The presider lifts both bread and cup if there is no deacon. Historically, the bread and cup have also been lifted up at the words of institution or at the oblation (offering) of the elements in the eucharistic prayer. The BCP rubrics direct that at the words of institution the celebrant will hold or lay a hand on the bread and vessels of wine to be consecrated. Elevation of the elements at this time is permissible but not required. The bread and wine may also be lifted up at the time of the presentation of the gifts, prior to the eucharistic prayer.

El Himnario. A hymnal for Hispanic congregations prepared by the Hispanic Ministry Office of the Episcopal Church Center. It was published in 1998 as an ecumenical effort of the Episcopal Church, the Presbyterian Church (USA), and the United Church of Christ. It has more than 500 hymns, songs, choruses, psalms, and service music selections from throughout the Spanish-speaking world. It was published for the Episcopal Church by Church Publishing Incorporated.

Eliot, Thomas Stearns (T. S.) (Sept. 26, 1888–Jan. 4, 1965). Poet and literary critic. He was an American, born in St. Louis and educated at Harvard, the Sorbonne, and Merton College, Oxford. He became a British citizen. He worked and wrote in London most of his life. After being raised in the Unitarian tradition and going through a time of agnosticism, Eliot was baptized in the parish church at Finstock, Oxfordshire, in 1927. He subsequently declared his perspective in religion to be Anglo-catholic. His poetry reflected his intense faith, as his poem *The Waste Land* (1922) and *The Hollow Men* (1925) had expressed his earlier experience of meaninglessness. His religious poems include

Journey of the Magi (1927) and *Ash Wednesday* (1930). Eliot was responsible to a large extent for the revival of interest in the so-called metaphysical poets, several of whom were Anglican priests, including John Donne, George Herbert, and Thomas Traherne. He also used Little Gidding, the religious house founded by Nicholas Ferrar, as the inspiration and title of one of his *Four Quartets* (1935–1942). Eliot wrote the play *Murder in the Cathedral* (1935), which deals with the martyrdom of Archbishop Thomas Becket in Canterbury Cathedral. In 1948 Eliot received the Nobel Prize for literature and the Order of Merit.

Elizabeth, Princess of Hungary (1207–Nov. 16, 1231). Medieval saint. She was born at Pressburg (Bratislava), Hungary, the daughter of King Andrew II of Hungary and his queen, Gertrude. In 1221 she married Louis IV, the Landgrave of Thuringia. Elizabeth came under the influence of the Franciscans. After the death of her husband on Sept. 11, 1229, she joined the Tertiaries (Third Order) of the Franciscans at Marburg, Germany. She lived a most austere life, wore the poorest of clothes, existed on the scantiest food, gave all her income to charity, and took care of the sick. She died at Marburg, and was canonized by Pope Gregory IX on May 27, 1235. Many hospitals throughout the world are named in her honor. Elizabeth and King Louis IX of France are the patron saints of the Third Order of Franciscans. Her life is commemorated in the Episcopal calendar of the church year on Nov. 19.

Elizabethan Settlement. Religious and political arrangements worked out during the reign of Elizabeth I in England. Elizabeth I (1533–1603), daughter of Henry VIII and Anne Boleyn, became Queen of England in 1558. Religious differences threatened the stability of England at that time. England had been officially Protestant under the rule of Edward VI from 1547 to 1553 and Roman Catholic under the rule of Mary Tudor from 1553 to 1558. Elizabeth's subjects included both Catholics and Calvinists. Elizabeth faced the religious question squarely at the beginning of her reign. The year 1559 was crucial for the future of Anglicanism.

The Elizabethan settlement sought to be an inclusive middle course between divergent religious positions in English Christianity. Much of traditional Catholic faith and practice was retained, but without submission to papal authority. Much latitude for individual conscience was allowed, but uniformity of worship was required. Faithful

Christians with differing theological convictions could find a home in a comprehensive English church.

The Act of Supremacy of 1559 proclaimed Elizabeth to be the "supreme governor of this realm" in all spiritual, ecclesiastical, and temporal matters. Elizabeth's assertion of power over the English church was not as sweeping as that of Henry VIII, who was proclaimed the only supreme head on earth of the English church. The Act of Supremacy of 1559 included an oath of obedience to the Crown that was imposed on all clergy and public officials. Elizabeth exercised royal power concerning the church within the provisions of religious legislation, and she protected the church from attempts by Parliament to meddle.

An amended version of the 1552 Prayer Book was reissued under the Act of Uniformity of 1559. The revised Prayer Book included the Ornaments Rubric, which was inserted before the services of Morning and Evening Prayer. It declared that the ornaments of churches and clergy should be those in use in the second year of the reign of Edward VI, a time when traditional vestments and church furnishings were used. The Ornaments Rubric reversed a rubric in the 1552 Prayer Book that prohibited clergy from wearing albs, vestments, or copes.

The Elizabethan edition of 1559 deleted the "Black Rubric" from the 1552 BCP, which stated that no adoration of any real presence was intended by kneeling at communion. It retained the receptionistic formula of administration of communion from the 1552 BCP ("Take and eat this in remembrance . . . "), but this was preceded by the more traditional sentence of administration from the 1549 BCP ("The Body of our Lord Jesus Christ which was given for thee. . . ."). This combination of sentences of administration allowed considerable latitude of belief concerning the eucharist. The Elizabethan edition of 1559 also dropped from the litany a petition for deliverance from the tyranny of the Bishop of Rome and all his detestable enormities. This petition was understandably offensive to Elizabeth's Roman Catholic subjects.

The continuity of the Church of England in apostolic succession was strongly upheld under Elizabeth. The consecration of Matthew Parker (1504–1575) as Archbishop of Canterbury in 1559 was done with great care to make sure that the line of English bishops in apostolic succession was unbroken. Although Elizabeth would have preferred a celibate clergy, clerical marriage was permitted as an indulgence. The Elizabethan settlement was foundational for the *via media* that has become characteristic of Anglicanism. Through this settlement the English church was comprehensive and inclusive, catholic and protestant, but neither Roman Catholic nor Genevan Protestant. *See* Receptionism; *see* Via Media.

Ellerton, John (Dec. 16, 1826–June 15, 1893). Hymn writer. He was born in London. He was educated at King William's College on the Isle of Man, and at Trinity College, Cambridge. Shortly after his ordination he began writing hymns for the children of St. Nicholas' Church, Brighton, where he was curate. While vicar of Grewe Green, Cheshire, he brought out *Hymns for Schools and Bible Classes* (1859). From 1876 to 1884 he was at Barnes, Surrey. While there he compiled *Church Hymns with Notes and Illustrations* (1881), *The Children's Hymn Book* (with Mrs. Carey Brock) (1881), and *London Mission Hymn Book* (1884). Ellerton made many contributions to the 1889 edition of *Hymns Ancient and Modern*. He died in Torquay. *John Ellerton: Being a Collection of His Writings on Hymnology, Together with a Sketch of His Life and Works* (1896) was edited by Henry Hausman, who had been his curate at Barnes. Seven of his original hymn texts appear in *The Hymnal 1982*, including "The day thou gavest, Lord, is ended" (24), and "Sing, ye faithful, sing with gladness" (492). He was also translator for two hymn texts in *The Hymnal 1982*, including "'Welcome, happy morning!' age to age shall say" (179).

Ellinwood, Leonard Webster (Feb. 13, 1905–July 8, 1994). Hymnal editor and music historian. He was born in Thomaston, Connecticut, and received his B.A. from Aurora College in 1926. He received his Master of Music degree in 1934 and his Doctor of Philosophy degree in 1936 from the Eastman School of Music. He taught at Michigan State University before joining the Library of Congress Music Division in 1940. Ellinwood was ordained deacon on June 17, 1948, and retired in 1975 as Head of the Humanities Section of the Library of Congress Subject Cataloguing Division. He edited *The Hymnal 1940 Companion* (1949) and compiled the *Dictionary of American Hymnology* (1984). He wrote *The History of American Church Music* (1953).

Elliott, Stephen (Aug. 31, 1806–Dec. 21, 1866). Bishop and educator. He was born in Beaufort, South Carolina. In the fall of 1822 he entered the sophomore class at Harvard, and the next year he transferred to Carolina College in Charleston. After studying law for two years, he was admitted to the bar in 1827. In 1830 he assumed the editorship of *The Southern Review*, but after a few months he moved to Beaufort to practice law. In Beaufort he was converted to evangelical Christianity and became a "new creature in Christ." He studied for the ordained ministry on his own. Elliott was ordained deacon on Nov. 8, 1835. He served a church in Wilton, South Carolina, for about a month and then became the professor of the evidences of Christianity and sacred literature at Carolina College. He was ordained priest on June 22, 1838. On Feb. 28, 1841, he was consecrated the first Bishop of Georgia and served in that position until his death. From 1845 until 1852 he was the head of the Montpelier Institute, and from 1852 until 1866 he was the rector of Christ Church, Savannah. Elliott presided at three of the General Councils of the Protestant Episcopal Church in the Confederate States of America. He was a founder of the University of the South and served as its third Chancellor from June 14, 1864, until his death. He died in Savannah.

Elohim. A Hebrew word in the plural which occasionally means pagan gods, superhuman creatures, or earthly judges in the OT; but the term usually refers to Israel's one God, Yahweh. Although the word is plural, it typically appears with singular verbs when the term refers to God. The use of the plural form may be explained as a "plural of majesty" rather than an indication of polytheism.

Elohist, The. One of four sources for the composition of the Pentateuch, according to a theory accepted by many biblical scholars. Known as Documentary Theology, the theory assigns the name Elohist to the source that consistently uses the Hebrew word *Elohim* for God until the call of Moses in Ex 3, when the proper name Yahweh is first revealed. It is found in the books of Genesis, Exodus, Numbers and perhaps in Joshua, chs. 2–11, 24. It begins with a narrative of the ancestors, then recounts the call of Moses, the Exodus, the covenant at Sinai, the wilderness wanderings and perhaps the conquest and assembly at Shechem under Joshua. It may have been written in northern Israel around 850 B.C.

El Salvador, Diocese of. The House of Bishops created the Missionary District of El Salvador on Sept. 18, 1967, and assigned jurisdiction to the Missionary Bishop of Guatemala. It became the Diocese of El Salvador on Jan. 1, 1980. On Mar. 28, 1992, the Rt. Rev. Martin de Jesus

Barahona was consecrated bishop. He was the first native of El Salvador to be bishop of the diocese.

Ely, Richard Theodore (Apr. 13, 1854–Oct. 4, 1943). Social Gospel advocate. He was born in Ripley, New York. He received a B.A. from Columbia University in 1876 and a Ph.D. from Heidelberg University in Germany in 1879. He taught economics at Johns Hopkins University (1881–1892) and at the University of Wisconsin (1892–1925). He also directed research institutes at Northwestern University (1925–1932) and at Columbia University (1937–1943). Ely believed that God called Christians to work for the salvation of their society and culture as well as the salvation of individual souls. He devoted himself to the promotion of social reform throughout his lifetime. Ely wrote a number of books on the relationship of economics and Christian faith, including *The Social Aspects of Christianity* (1889). He helped found the American Economics Association in 1885. He also helped found the Episcopal Social Union along with Social Gospel advocate William D. P. Bliss in 1891. Ely died in Old Lyme, Connecticut.

Emancipation, African American, and the Episcopal Church. The freeing of slaves after the Civil War had a negative effect on the institutional strength of the Episcopal Church in the South. Episcopalians experienced "a wholesale exodus" of African Americans from their denomination in the late 1860s.

Beginning with the founding of the Society for the Propagation of the Gospel in Foreign Parts in 1701, Anglican slave holders sought to incorporate African Americans within the traditions of Anglicanism. In the nineteenth century, evangelicals developed an active, paternalistic ministry among slaves. White Episcopalians encouraged household servants to sit in special sections in their churches and occasionally allowed separate African American congregations (guided by white clergy) to be formed. But when emancipation came, most ex-slaves chose the Baptist and Methodist denominations instead of the Episcopal Church. At the 1868 General Convention, all southern dioceses reported major losses of African Americans. South Carolina had the most dramatic decline, with a reduction of nearly ninety percent of its African American membership. The Episcopal Church had limited appeal in the African American community. Most southern dioceses refused to grant equal status to African American communicants, and most African American parishes were led by white clergy. The 1865 General Convention attempted to address this problem by creating the Protestant Episcopal Freedman's Commission as an agency for the evangelization and education of ex-slaves. But the commission often lacked funding and was eventually dissolved in 1878. A report to the 1877 General Convention noted that there were only thirty-seven congregations and fifteen African American Episcopal clergy among the four million African Americans in the southern states.

Ember Day Letter. Every postulant or candidate for holy orders in the Episcopal Church is required by canon to report to the bishop four times a year, during the Ember Weeks. The report must be made in person or by letter, and must include reflection on the person's academic experience as well as personal and spiritual development. *See* Ember Days.

Ember Days. Three days which occur four times a year: the Wednesday, Friday, and Saturday after St. Lucy's Day (Dec. 13), Ash Wednesday, the Day of Pentecost, and Holy Cross Day (Sept. 14). The name comes from the Latin title *Quattuor tempora*, meaning "four times." In ancient Italy the times (originally three) were associated with sowing, harvest, and vintage, for which one prayed, fasted, and gave alms. Later the four times became occasions for ordination, for which the Christian community prayed and the candidates prepared themselves by prayer and retreat. The BCP appoints proper collects and readings for this observance under the title "For the Ministry (Ember Days), including propers "For those to be ordained," "For the choice of fit persons for the ministry," and "For all Christians in their vocation" (BCP, pp. 256–257, 929).

Ember Weeks. The four weeks in each year during which the Ember Days occur. *See* Ember Days.

Emery, Julia Chester (Sept. 26, 1846–Jan. 9, 1922). Leader of women's ministry. She came to New York in 1874 to edit *The Young Christian Soldier.* In 1876 she was appointed secretary of the Woman's Auxiliary to the Board of Missions (WA). Emery held that position for the next forty years, resigning in 1916. She directed the expansion of the WA into every domestic and missionary diocese of the Episcopal Church and was key to the founding and growth of the United Offering (now the United Thank Offering). To promote the Auxiliary, she visited churches

and missionaries throughout the United States. In 1897 she addressed the woman's missionary congress held in London in conjunction with the Lambeth Conference. In 1908 she represented the Diocese of New York at the Pan-Anglican Congress in London. She then continued around the world, visiting mission stations in Europe and Asia. She was the author of A *Century of Endeavor* (1921), the centennial history of the Domestic and Foreign Missionary Society, and biographies of John Henry Hobart and Alexander Viets Griswold. Emery is commemorated in the Episcopal calendar of the church year on Jan. 9. Mary Abbot Emery, Susan Lavinia Emery, and Margaret Theresa Emery were her sisters.

Emery, Margaret Theresa (Aug. 3, 1849–July 20, 1925). She worked in the national office of the Woman's Auxiliary of the Episcopal Church from 1876 until 1919. She edited *The Young Christian Soldier* and directed the Auxiliary's program to provide supplies for foreign and domestic missionaries in "mission boxes" provided by local chapters. Julia Chester Emery, Mary Abbot Emery, and Susan Lavinia Emery were her sisters.

Emery, Mary Abbot (Mrs. Alvi Tabor Twing) (Feb. 23, 1843–Oct. 14, 1901). The oldest daughter of Charles and Susan Hilton Emery, she was appointed secretary of the newly formed Woman's Auxiliary to the Board of Missions in 1871. She was chiefly responsible for the early development of that organization. Though she resigned as secretary in 1876 to marry the Rev. Dr. Alvi T. Twing, she continued to be actively involved. After her husband died in 1882, she was appointed honorary secretary of the Woman's Auxiliary. Emery founded the periodical *Church Work* 1885. She was influential in the passage of the canon on deaconesses by the 1889 General Convention, which recognized the ministry of deaconesses. The canon set standards and qualifications for deaconesses. Emery then served on the faculty of the newly created New York Training School for Deaconesses, teaching the course in church missions. She traveled twice around the world, visiting missionaries and reporting on their work in articles that she later assembled in the book, *Twice Around the World* (1898). Julia Chester Emery, Susan Lavinia Emery, and Margaret Theresa Emery were her sisters. *See* Deaconess.

Emery, Susan Lavinia (Sept. 26, 1846–Mar. 1, 1914). She wrote children's stories and edited *The Young Christian*

Soldier, the Episcopal Church's missionary magazine for children, from 1871 until 1875. Julia Chester Emery, Margaret Theresa Emery, and Mary Abbot Emery were her sisters.

Emma of Hawaii. *See* Kamehameha and Emma, King and Queen of Hawaii.

Emmanuel. A Hebrew word that means "God is with us." It is mentioned in Is 7:14 as a sign from the Lord and the name of a child to be born. In the NT it is used only in Matthew at the beginning of his gospel as a way of understanding the significance of Jesus. Many scholars have suggested that its mention at the beginning of Matthew is directly connected with Jesus' concluding statement in Matthew: "I will be with you to the end." The meaning of the term is vividly recalled in the Advent hymn, "O Come, O Come, Emmanuel" (Hymn 56).

Emmanuel Movement. The Rev. Dr. Elwood Worcester became the rector of Emmanuel Church, Boston, in 1904, and served there until his retirement in 1929. While at Emmanuel Church he worked on combining religion and science, resulting in a healing ministry which lasted until his retirement. The movement began when Worcester developed a program for the treatment of tuberculosis patients under the auspices of Emmanuel Church. The plan included health education for patients and their families as well as in-home medical care. Gradually the plan was expanded to include the treatment of nervous and psychic disorders. In Nov. 1906, Emmanuel Church held a series of four lectures about health and healing, culminating with the offer of treatment beginning the next day. On the next day, approximately 200 persons arrived at Emmanuel Church for healing prayer and treatment by physicians. This ministry expanded and grew into the Emmanuel Movement. It spread from its New England base. It was aided by stories in *Good Housekeeping* and *Ladies' Home Journal*, as well as books such as *Religion and Medicine: The Moral Control of Nervous Disorders*. The movement stressed the cooperation of clergy and medical professionals in the ministry of healing. The movement declined after Worcester retired.

Empie, Adam (Sept. 5, 1785–Nov. 6, 1860). College president and rector. He was born in Schenectady, New York. Empie was educated at Union College, Schenectady, and decided to enter the ordained ministry of the Episcopal

Church. He was ordained deacon on July 30, 1809, and began his ministry as assistant at St. George's Church, Hempstead, Long Island. He was later ordained priest (date unavailable). From 1811 until 1814, he was rector of St. James' Church, Wilmington, North Carolina. From 1814 until 1816, he was professor and chaplain at the United States Military Academy, West Point, New York. He returned to St. James' Church in 1816. He remained there until 1827 when we became the twelfth president of the College of William and Mary. Under his leadership, the enrollment of the college increased from about twelve students to sixty-nine students. Empie resigned as president of William and Mary on July 6, 1836, to become the rector of St. James' Church, Richmond, Virginia. He served there until 1853, when he had a stroke and retired. He spent the last seven years of his life in retirement in Wilmington, North Carolina, where he died.

Enablement, Inc. This ecumenical agency was incorporated in Oct. 1971 at Boston, Massachusetts. It was a not-for-profit organization which provided research, management, and consultation services to personnel-support people, groups, and structures from a variety of denominations. It did most of its business with Episcopalians. It published *Enablement Newsletter* ten times a year, which provided "news, analysis, and opinion concerning tested alternatives for present and future clergy ministry development." Enablement's primary purpose was "the betterment of the ordained ministry," and it published numerous studies of the ordained ministry. The Rev. James Lincoln Lowery, Jr., served as its executive director and editor of the newsletter. Enablement went out of business on Sept. 1, 1993.

English Hymnal, The. A British hymnal published in 1906 under the leadership of Percy Dearmer as general editor and Ralph Vaughan Williams as musical editor. A second edition including minor but important changes was published in 1933, and a more comprehensive revision, *The New English Hymnal*, was published in 1986. The first two editions had a strong influence on the form and content of *The Hymnal* (1940).

Enlightenment, The. An intellectual and cultural development which emphasized the ability of human reason to grasp the ultimate meaning of life and creation in terms of self-evident truths. It was widespread in western Europe during the seventeenth and eighteenth centuries.

The Enlightenment upheld the autonomy of human reason and reason's adequacy to grasp and shape the world by its own power. In Enlightenment terms, truth was self-authenticating by virtue of its inherent reasonableness. This differed from orthodox Christian theology, which held that truth came from beyond reason by revelation.

The Enlightenment understanding of reason was based in the natural sciences, and it was characterized by skepticism concerning the NT miracles. This skepticism concerning the miracles was expressed in David Hume's *Essay on Miracles* (1748), which noted the absence of contemporary analogs of miracles, and concluded that no human testimony could establish the reality of such events without analogs. The Enlightenment was critical of the idea of supernatural revelation, and viewed the contingent truths of history as much less significant than the necessary truths of reason. The Bible was not distinguished from other literary forms on the basis of divine revelation, and it was considered in light of the same forms of textual analysis as other works of literature. Jesus was understood as merely different in degree from other human beings relative to certain qualities. He was understood to be a great moral teacher of enlightened truths, not a supernatural redeemer. Jesus' death was understood as a supreme moral example of self-giving. His death and resurrection were minimized in importance relative to his teaching and example. The Enlightenment understanding of Jesus inspired the "quest" for the historical Jesus who was believed to be concealed behind the NT accounts. The Enlightenment also rejected the doctrine of original sin, and the Christian doctrine of redemption.

The inductive method of Francis Bacon, the empiricism of John Locke, and the mathematical cosmology of Isaac Newton were formative for the English Enlightenment. The purest example of Enlightenment theology in England is afforded by the Deists, who were hostile to revealed religion. Deism was opposed by, among others, Locke and Joseph Butler. Locke understood Christianity as a reasonable supplement to natural religion, which maintained a place for divine revelation. Butler's elaborate work *The Analogy of Reason* (1736) argued for both natural and revealed religion on the basis of ingenious analogies from nature itself. The Enlightenment ideal of a universal rationality proved elusive to discover as many perspectives appeared concerning the meaning of self-evident truths and principles. *See* Deism.

Enmegahbowh (c. 1813–June 11, 1902). American Indian priest and missionary. He was born on the north shore of Rice Lake, Ontario, Canada, and was a member of the Chippewas (Ojibbewas). His name means "one-who-stands-before-his-people." After he was baptized by a Methodist preacher he took the name John Johnson. Some time before 1850 he was given a Prayer Book. Through the influence of James Lloyd Breck he became a candidate for ordination in the Episcopal Church. He was ordained deacon on July 3, 1859, and priest on June 2, 1867. Enmegahbowh and Bishop Henry Benjamin Whipple of Minnesota worked together among the Indians until Enmegahbowh's death at White Earth, Minnesota.

Enriching Our Worship. A collection of supplemental liturgical materials prepared by the Standing Liturgical Commission (1997) and published by Church Publishing Incorporated. It includes resources and forms for Morning and Evening Prayer, Order of Worship for the Evening, the Great Litany, and the Holy Eucharist. The canticles and prayers represent the recovery of ancient biblical and patristic images, including the identification of Christ with Wisdom and language for God that does not use familiar masculine terms. The liturgical texts reflect the influence of the prayer experience of women, and a desire to honor that experience while remaining faithful to the norms of liturgical prayer as received by the Episcopal Church. Supplemental liturgical texts may only be used with the permission of the diocesan bishop, or the appropriate ecclesiastical authority in the absence of the diocesan bishop. These texts may be used in conjunction with Rite 2 liturgies of the BCP, or supplemental texts may be used to develop an entire liturgy. Copyright is extended to congregations for reproduction of texts included in *Enriching Our Worship.*

Entrance Rite. The liturgical gathering of the people as the worshiping community at the beginning of the eucharist. The entrance rite prepares the congregation for the liturgy of the word. Until the fourth or fifth centuries, the eucharistic liturgy typically began with the celebrant's salutation and the first reading. As Christian worship became more formalized, entrance rites became more elaborate. The ministers entered in procession, with the gospel book carried in procession. The entrance rite has at times become cumbersome with too many additions, which can distract instead of preparing the people to hear the Word of God.

The entrance rite of the 1979 BCP includes the entrance of the ministers and may begin with a hymn, psalm, or anthem. A seasonal acclamation follows. The collect for purity is optional in Rite 2 eucharistic liturgies but is required in Rite 1. Then may follow the *Gloria in excelsis* or another song of praise, or the *Kyrie eleison*, or the *Trisagion*. The *Gloria in excelsis* or other hymn of praise is to be used from Christmas Day through the Feast of Epiphany and throughout the Easter season. The salutation is followed by the collect of the day. The BCP provides special entrance rites for the Proper Liturgies for Special Days such as Palm Sunday and the Easter Vigil, for Baptism, for pastoral offices such as Marriage and Burial, and for episcopal services such as Ordination and the Consecration of a Church. Other options for the entrance rite include A Penitential Order (BCP, p. 351), which is especially appropriate for Lent or other penitential occasions; the Great Litany (p. 148); and the Order of Worship for Evening (p. 109). The BCP prescribes use of the Order of Worship for Evening as the entrance rite for the Vigil of Pentecost (p. 227). The *BOS* calls for its use at the Vigil Eucharist of other baptismal feasts, the First Sunday after the Epiphany, and All Saints' Day or the Sunday after All Saints' Day. *See* Liturgy of the Word.

Ephrem (Ephraem) of Edessa (d. June 373). Early church theologian. He was born at or near Nisibis, in modern-day Turkey. Ephrem lived at Nisibis until 363, when he moved to Edessa. He lived there as an anchorite or hermit. He is remembered for his exegetical, theological, and especially poetic writings. Ephrem has been called the "Lyre of the Holy Ghost" and the "Prophet of the Syrians." He may have attended the Council of Nicaea in 325. His hymn, "From God Christ's deity came forth," is Hymn 443 in *The Hymnal 1982*. Ephrem is commemorated in the Episcopal calendar of the church year on June 10.

Epiclesis. The invocation of the active presence of the Holy Spirit in the eucharistic prayer so that the bread and wine may become the body and blood of Christ. The presider at the eucharist may extend his or her hands over the gifts at the *epiclesis*. The term is based on the Greek word that means "to call upon," "to invoke." The *epiclesis* typically follows the institution narrative (see eucharistic prayers A, B, and D, BCP, pp. 363, 369, 375), but it precedes the institution narrative in eucharistic prayer C (BCP, p. 371). The Roman Mass did not have an explicit *epiclesis*, although recent reforms in the Roman Church have added

prayers of *epiclesis*. Thomas Cranmer placed the *epiclesis* prior to the institution narrative in the 1549 Prayer Book, but he replaced it with a prayer for worthy reception of communion in the 1552 BCP. The *epiclesis* was not reintroduced in the 1662 BCP. Scottish reformers restored the *epiclesis*, and the Scottish Book of 1637 included the petition that God the Father would "vouchsafe to bless and sanctify with thy word and Holy Spirit these thy gifts and creatures of bread and wine, that they may be unto us the body and blood of thy most dearly beloved Son. . . ." The Episcopal Church followed the Scottish rather than the English model with respect to the *epiclesis*. An *epiclesis* in some form has been included in the eucharistic prayers of the Episcopal Church since the 1789 BCP. The *epiclesis* of Prayer I in Rite 1 of the BCP is substantially the same as that in the 1789 BCP. *See* Holy Spirit.

Epiphany, The. The manifestation of Christ to the peoples of the earth. The winter solstice was kept on Jan. 6 at some places during the first centuries of the Christian Era. In opposition to pagan festivals, Christians chose this day to celebrate the various manifestations, or "epiphanies," of Jesus' divinity. These showings of his divinity included his birth, the coming of the Magi, his baptism, and the Wedding at Cana where he miraculously changed water into wine. The day was called "The Feast of Lights." Celebration of the Son of God replaced celebration of the sun. Baptisms were done, and a season of preparation was instituted. It was later called Advent.

The solstice was kept on Dec. 25 by the fourth century. Jesus' birth was celebrated on this day in both eastern and western churches. The western church commemorated the coming of the Magi on Jan. 6. The eastern church continued to celebrate the Baptism of our Lord and the Wedding at Cana on Jan. 6. In the east the day was called "Theophany" (manifestation of God).

The coming of the Magi is celebrated on the Feast of the Epiphany, Jan. 6, in the BCP. The Baptism of our Lord is celebrated on the First Sunday after the Epiphany.

Epiphany Season. A season of four to nine weeks, from the Feast of the Epiphany (Jan. 6) through the Tuesday before Ash Wednesday. The length of the season varies according to the date of Easter. The gospel stories of this season describe various events that manifest the divinity of Jesus. The coming of the Magi is celebrated on the Epiphany. The Baptism of our Lord is observed on the Sunday after Epiphany. The gospels for the other Sundays of the Epiphany season describe the wedding at Cana, the calling of the disciples, and various miracles and teachings of Jesus. The Last Sunday after the Epiphany is always devoted to the Transfiguration. Jesus' identity as the Son of God is dramatically revealed in the Transfiguration gospel, as well as the gospel of the baptism of Christ. We are called to respond to Christ in faith through the showings of his divinity recorded in the gospels of the Epiphany season.

Episcopal. 1) Concerning the Episcopal Church. Used in this sense, the adjective "Episcopal" is always capitalized. For example, "The Episcopal liturgy will be used at the wedding." Similarly, "The Episcopal priest attended the ecumenical gathering." 2) Concerning a bishop or bishops. Used in this sense, the adjective "episcopal" is not always capitalized. For example, an episcopal ring is a ring worn by a bishop as a sign of the bishop's office. *See* Episcopalian.

Episcopal Academy, Merion, Pennsylvania, The. The vestry of Christ Church in Philadelphia, Pennsylvania, founded The Episcopal Academy on Jan. 1, 1785. It opened on Apr. 4, 1785. The president of the board of trustees was the rector of Christ Church, the Rev. William White. Among the founders were Robert Morris and Francis Hopkinson, signers of the Declaration of Independence, Edwin Shippen, later Chief Justice of Pennsylvania, and Richard Peters, a federal judge. In 1787 the academy's trustees laid the cornerstone of a new school building two doors from Independence Hall. The faculty included the Rev. John Andrews (1746–1813), later provost of the University of Pennsylvania. The most notable faculty member in 1787 was Noah Webster, editor of *Webster's Dictionary*. The academy was established to teach Anglican doctrine. In 1789 the trustees set up free schools for 80 boys and 40 girls. In 1921 after merging with two other schools, the academy sold its building and purchased property in Merion, just west of Philadelphia's city limits. In 1970 the trustees decided to make the academy coeducational. It has campuses in Merion and in Devon, Pennsylvania.

Episcopal Academy of Connecticut. This school was founded at Cheshire, Connecticut, in 1794 to "serve the double purpose of a preparatory school and a university." Sometimes it was referred to as "Seabury University." The academy opened in 1796 and admitted boys and girls until

1836, when it became a boys' school. It never developed into a college. It closed in 1917.

Episcopal Ad Project. This ministry was started at St. Luke's Episcopal Church, Minneapolis, in 1978. The Rev. Dr. George Harvey Martin, the rector, asked for help from advertising professionals to write ads which would invite people into the Episcopal Church. Martin asked for help from Tom McElligott, Jr., the son of an Episcopal priest in the Diocese of Minnesota. McElligott agreed to participate. In 1978 six ads were created using line drawings and simple headlines. One of the most familiar ads presented a picture of Christ with the words, "He died to take away your sins, not your mind." In 1991 the name for the ministry was changed to The Church Ad Project. The Ad Project has created more than 90 black and white ads. Many of the ads have been turned into posters, which have been used in hundreds of churches and conference centers. The Church Ad Project is an independent, interdenominational ministry.

Episcopal Appalachian Ministries. Successor to Appalachian South, Inc., and Appalachian People's Service Organization. Appalachian South was organized in Dec. 1964. It began in the same year as the United States' War on Poverty. Its name was later changed to Appalachian People's Service Organization, Inc. (APSO). APSO's newsletters were *APSOlution* and *APSOlution Spotlights*. On Apr. 25, 1995, the board of governors changed the name to Episcopal Appalachian Ministries. It is a coalition of fourteen dioceses in the states of Georgia, Tennessee, North Carolina, Kentucky, Virginia, West Virginia, Ohio, Maryland, and Pennsylvania. It attempts to meet the challenge presented to the church by the economic, social, and cultural problems inherent in Appalachia. Eleven percent of American Episcopalians live in this region. APSO coordinates its efforts with seventeen other denominations and ten state councils of churches through the Commission on Religion in Appalachia (CORA). It has four ministry units: Intramont, Social and Specialized Ministries, Urban, and Youth. Intramont helps indigenous congregations to be faithful to their Appalachian culture and customs. Social and Specialized Ministries focuses on research and education. The Urban Ministry Unit works for innovative change on behalf of the poor in the cities of Appalachia. The Youth Unit works to utilize young people in shared ministry with the need in Appalachia. Episcopal

Appalachian Ministries publishes the newsletter *Mountain Echoes*.

Episcopal Asiamerica Ministry. It was established at the 1973 General Convention to support the development of Asian and Pacific Island ministries in partnership with the dioceses of the Episcopal Church, and to be a missionary program of evangelism and service to people of Asian and Pacific Island background.

Episcopal Book Club (EBC). EBC was founded in 1953 by the Rev. Howard Lane Foland at All Saints' Parish, Nevada, Missouri, to provide lay persons with books about the Episcopal Church. When new and larger accommodations were needed, the EBC purchased a 1,124-acre ranch in Eureka Springs, Arkansas. It was named Hillspeak. The EBC was incorporated on June 22, 1960. The Book Club provides its members four "Books of the Season" each year. Titles selected reflect the mainstream teachings and latest books on the Anglican tradition and faith. *See* Society for Promoting and Encouraging Arts and Knowledge (SPEAK); *see* Hillspeak.

Episcopal Cathedral Teleconferencing Network (ECTN). An association formed in late 1992 to incorporate satellite broadcast technology into the educational mission of Episcopal cathedrals. The Rev. Clement Lee of the Electronic Media Department of the Episcopal Church Center and the Rev. Dr. Frederic Burham and the Rev. Dr. Daniel Matthews, both of Trinity Church, New York, proposed the idea of a network of affiliated downlink sites located primarily at Episcopal cathedrals. Their proposal was made to the North American Cathedral Deans Conference. Downlink sites have been established in nearly half of the cathedrals of the Episcopal Church. ECTN draws its name and purpose from the cathedral's traditional role as a center for education and information, and extends that mission to today's broadcast technology. ECTN seeks to reach out and attract audiences for a wide variety of programs. ECTN bases its work on three principles: high-quality programming, user-friendly broadcast technology, and a high love of service and support. ECTN programming covers such subjects as spiritual formation, contemporary social issues, and continuing education for clergy and laity.

Episcopal Center for Evangelism. The first National Episcopal Conference on Evangelism was held at Grace-St. Luke's Church, Memphis, Tennessee, on Oct. 4–7, 1972. This conference was organized by the Rev. Robert Benjamin Hall. It was the beginning of the Episcopal Center for Evangelism. The primary work of the center was organizing evangelism and renewal conferences in the church. The center served in a consultant relationship with parishes to teach the principles of church growth and how to structure for evangelism. It published a newsletter, *Refreshment*, five times a year. It also published a number of books, most written by Robert Hall. It was located in Live Oak, Florida. The center went out of existence on Dec. 31, 1993.

Episcopal Charismatic Fellowship. *See* Episcopal Renewal Ministries (ERM).

Episcopal Church, The. A conference of three clergy and twenty-four lay delegates met at Chestertown, Kent County, Maryland, on Nov. 9, 1780, and resolved that "the Church formerly known in the Province as the Church of England should now be called the Protestant Episcopal Church." On Aug. 13, 1783, the Maryland clergy met at Annapolis and adopted the name "Protestant Episcopal Church." At the second session of the 1789 General Convention, Sept. 29–Oct. 16, 1789, a Constitution of nine articles was adopted. William White was one of the chief architects of the new church. He was Presiding Bishop from July 28, 1789 to Oct. 3, 1789, and from Sept. 8, 1795 until his death on July 17, 1836. White had previously served as chaplain to the Continental and Constitutional Congresses and the United States Senate from 1777 until 1801. The new church was called the "Protestant Episcopal Church in the United States of America" (PECUSA). The word "Protestant" noted that this was a church in the reformation tradition, and the word "Episcopal" noted a characteristic of catholicity, the historic episcopate. The first American BCP was based on the Proposed Book of 1786 and the 1662 English BCP. It was ratified by the 1789 General Convention. Alterations or additions to the BCP require the approval of two successive General Conventions. BCP revisions were ratified in 1892, 1928, and 1979.

The church has grown from thirteen dioceses to more than one hundred dioceses. It is divided into nine geographical provinces. It is governed by a bicameral General Convention, which meets every three years, and by an Executive Council during interim years. The General Convention consists of the House of Bishops and the

House of Deputies. The House of Bishops is composed of every bishop with jurisdiction, every bishop coadjutor, every suffragan bishop, every retired bishop, every bishop elected to an office created by General Convention, and every bishop who has resigned because of missionary strategy. All members of the House of Bishops have seat and voice in the House of Bishops. The House of Deputies is composed of up to four lay and four clerical deputies from each of the dioceses. The two top leaders of the church are the Presiding Bishop, who is also called Primate and Chief Pastor, and the president of the House of Deputies.

Over the years there were numerous efforts to change the name of the church and to drop the word "Protestant." Among the names suggested were "The Reformed Catholic Church," "The American Catholic Church," "The American Church," and "The American Anglican Church." The 1967 General Convention voted to add a preamble to the Constitution, which states, "The Protestant Episcopal Church in the United States of America, otherwise known as The Episcopal Church (which name is hereby recognized as also designating the Church)...." The title page of the 1979 BCP states that the Book of Common Prayer is "According to the use of The Episcopal Church." The Episcopal Church in the United States of America is sometimes called ECUSA. The Episcopal Church is a province of the Anglican Communion.

Episcopal Church Annual, The. An annual directory of the Episcopal Church. It contains the names and addresses of all parishes and diocesan offices, bishops, priests and deacons, seminaries, publications, conference centers, social agencies, religious orders, and other agencies. It also contains national church statistics and information on all the provinces in the Anglican Communion. Its historical predecessors go back to 1830. The *Churchman's Almanack* was published from 1830 until 1840. From 1841 until 1892 it was called *The Church Almanack*, and from 1893 until 1917 it was called the *American Church Almanac and Year Book.* From 1918 until 1921 the name was the *Churchman's Year Book and American Church Almanac. Whittaker's Churchman's Almanac* was published from 1854 until 1908. *The Living Church Annual* began publication in 1882. In 1885 its name was changed to *The Living Church Annual and Clergy List Quarterly.* In 1890 it was renamed *The Living Church Quarterly*, and in 1903 it once again became *The Living Church Annual.* In 1909 *The Living Church Annual* and *Whittaker's Churchman's*

Almanac merged to create *The Living Church Annual and Whittaker's Churchman's Almanac.* In 1915 *Whittaker's* was dropped from the title. This publication continued until 1921. In 1922 *The Living Church Annual* absorbed *The Churchman's Year Book and American Church Almanac.* In 1953 *The Living Church Annual* became *The Episcopal Church Annual.*

Episcopal Church Building Fund (ECBF). A self-supporting agency established by General Convention in 1880 as the American Church Building Fund Commission. In 1974 the name was changed to the Episcopal Church Building Fund. It assists financing of construction, purchase, improvement, and repair of churches, rectories, and other parochial buildings. ECBF also conducts workshops and provides consultation services on planning, designing, and financing building projects. The Fund has produced a workbook for congregations entitled *Church Sites and Buildings*, and *The Church for Common Prayer, A Statement on Worship Space for the Episcopal Church.* The second volume sets the theological principles for worship space. It also publishes *The Builder*, a newsletter which focuses on practical issues for parishes concerned with how their buildings serve as tools for ministry.

Episcopal Church Center. The national headquarters for the Episcopal Church, located in New York City. It includes the executive offices of the Presiding Bishop. It is the place where the fiduciary responsibilities for the Domestic and Foreign Missionary Society are carried out; a focal point for the work of General Convention; a center for ecumenical and interfaith engagement; and a contact point for international and national agencies. The 1889 General Convention authorized the managers of the Domestic and Foreign Missionary Society to build quarters for the international missionary work of the Board of Missions and its Woman's Auxiliary. In Dec. 1893, the Church Missions House was completed in New York City. In 1919 General Convention "nationalized" great portions of the missionary, educational, and social work of the church under one body. More space was needed by 1926, but serious work was not begun until 1958. On Feb. 21, 1963, Bishop Fred J. Warnecke of Bethlehem, chairman of the committee on housing the business operations of the National Council, handed the master keys of the new twelve-story building to Presiding Bishop Arthur Lichtenberger. The dedication of the church center on Apr.

29, 1963, was the culmination of this work. In 1970 General Convention called for a study on the location of the Church Center. The possibility of relocation of the Church Center continues to be considered from time to time.

Episcopal Church Clergy and Employees' Benefits Trust ("The Medical Trust"). This trust was founded on Sept. 28, 1978, to provide medical and dental insurance coverage for employees of the Episcopal Church. From 1971 until 1978, medical insurance was provided by the Church Life Insurance Corporation. The Medical Trust provides programs for employees of dioceses, seminaries, and other Episcopal agencies.

Episcopal Church Flag and Seal. On Oct. 16, 1940, the House of Bishops and the House of Deputies adopted an official flag for the Episcopal Church. This was the 251st anniversary of the day the General Convention ratified the Constitution and Canons and adopted the BCP. It was designed by William M. Baldwin (d. 1942), a member of the Cathedral of the Incarnation, Long Island, New York. The symbolism of the flag has been explained as follows: The white field represents the purity of the Christian religion. The red cross represents the sacrifice of Jesus and the blood of the martyrs. The red cross on a white field is the cross of Saint George, the patron saint of England, indicating our descent from the Church of England. The blue in the upper left-hand corner is the light blue of the sky, often used by artists for the clothing of the Blessed Virgin. It is called Madonna blue and represents the human nature of our Lord, which he received from his mother. The nine white crosslets on the blue field represent the nine original dioceses of the Episcopal Church in America in 1789: Massachusetts, Connecticut, New York, New Jersey, Pennsylvania, Maryland, Virginia, Delaware, and South Carolina. They are arranged in the form of a St. Andrew's Cross to commemorate the fact that Samuel Seabury, the first American bishop, was consecrated in Aberdeen, Scotland, on Nov. 14, 1784. The colors red, white, and blue represent the United States and stand for the American branch of the Anglican Communion. The same design is incorporated in the Episcopal Church seal, which was also adopted by the 1940 General Convention. The seal and flag serve as emblems of the Episcopal Church. The design is seen on signs, publications, decals, letterheads, pins, and many other places. Some congregations display the Episcopal Church flag and the American flag in the church or parish hall.

Episcopal Church Foundation. Philanthropic organization formed by Presiding Bishop Henry Knox Sherrill and endorsed by the 1949 General Convention. Its goal is to strengthen the mission and ministry of the Episcopal Church. The mission of the foundation is to support ministry projects throughout the United States, to fund research and development programs, and to underwrite educational efforts. It is supported through contributions and investment income. The Presiding Bishop serves as chairman of the board of directors, who determine policy and raise funds. An administrative staff at the foundation's New York office processes applications.

In the 1950s, the foundation originally served as a funding agency for the construction of new churches through its Revolving Loan Fund. The foundation provides fellowships for doctoral students who are committed to teaching in Episcopal seminaries. The foundation also sponsors the Cornerstone Project to strengthen ordained leadership and nurture congregational wholeness and holiness, and supports the *Anglican Theological Review*. It publishes *Response* to keep the church aware of its ministries. The foundation operates the planned giving program for the national church.

Episcopal Church Lay Employees' Defined Contribution Retirement Plan. This program began on Jan. 1, 1992. It is a defined-contribution retirement plan for lay employees of the Episcopal Church and its institutions.

Episcopal Church Lay Employees' Retirement Plans. This program began operation on Jan. 1, 1980, to provide a choice of defined-benefit or defined-contribution retirement plans for lay employees of the Episcopal Church and its institutions.

Episcopal Church Missionary Community (ECMC). An autonomous, voluntary society dedicated to helping Episcopalians in missionary work. It seeks to develop an informed, active, and effective concern for missions at all levels of the Episcopal Church. It offers courses on world mission at Trinity Episcopal School for Ministry, orientation courses for missionaries of the South American Missionary Society and for other missionaries, one-day Mission Awareness Seminars, and scholarships for advanced training for returning missionaries. It also trains and encourages "tentmakers," people who hold professional positions overseas as a way of bringing the Christian faith to countries that are less receptive to missionaries. ECMC is directed by the Rev. Walter W. Hannum and Louise Hannum. They have trained more than 300 missionaries. It also sponsors an annual Day of Prayer for World Missions.

Episcopal Church Public Policy Network. An advocacy group established at the 1982 General Convention. It is a grassroots network of Episcopalians who bring the social policies of the Episcopal Church to the nation's lawmakers. It also equips members of the network with background on issues, church policies targeted for action, legislative updates and alerts, information on advocacy techniques, and sample letters to send to members of Congress. It seeks to bring a Christian view of public policy to the nation's leaders.

Episcopal Church Publishing Company (ECPC). It publishes *The Witness*, and it has also been involved in a variety of social justice causes. The first issue of *The Witness* was dated Jan. 6, 1917. The Rt. Rev. Irving Peake Johnson, Bishop of Colorado, was the first editor-in-chief. *The Witness* sought to address the problems of the people and the social mission of the church. Johnson formed the first board of directors for the publication. In later years, William Spofford, an Episcopal priest, produced *The Witness*. He served in a variety of roles, including reporter, secretary, treasurer, managing editor, editor and chairman of the board of editors. A corporation was formed in Illinois with Johnson, Spofford, Frank A. Clarke, and Benjamin Clarke as stockholders. This corporation was Episcopal Church Publishing Company. Johnson died in 1947, and Spofford eventually held all the capital stock of the corporation in his name. Spofford died on Oct. 19, 1972, and *The Witness* temporarily ceased publication. Spofford's family assigned the stock of the corporation to a board of seven trustees/directors. The trustees/directors were Presiding Bishop John E. Hines; Bishops Morris Arnold, Robert L. DeWitt, Lloyd E. Gressle, John B. Krumm, and J. Brooke Mosley; and Joseph Fletcher, a priest. They decided that *The Witness* should resume publication. The first issue of *The Witness* after Spofford's death was dated Aug. 25, 1974. This issue featured the irregular ordination to the priesthood of 11 women deacons in Philadelphia on July 29, 1974.

The assets of The Episcopal Church Publishing Company have also been used to assist in organizing a network of church people concerned with the social mission of the church and to support special projects. Special projects supported by ECPC have included publication of a study/action guide titled *Struggling with the System, Probing Alternatives*; joining with other members of the Interfaith Center for Corporate Responsibility in waging proxy fights and filing shareholder resolutions; providing special funds to enable *The Witness* to cover the story about two Episcopal Church staff members, Maria Cueto and Raisa Nemikin, who were jailed in 1977 for refusing to testify before a federal grand jury investigating a militant Puerto Rican group; and support for meetings in the 1970s such as the Urban Crisis Conference of 1978, the public hearings of the Urban Bishops' Coalition of 1978, and a meeting in 1976 of editors of 16 small periodicals to discuss the role of religious journals in social change. *See* Philadelphia Eleven, The.

Episcopal Church Seal. *See* Episcopal Church Flag and Seal.

Episcopal Church Women (ECW). This organization is a descendant of the Woman's Auxiliary to the Board of Missions which was founded in 1871. In 1919 it became the Woman's Auxiliary to the National Council of the Episcopal Church. In 1958 the Woman's Auxiliary became the General Division of Women's Work of the Executive Council. With this change came the transfer of several former members of the auxiliary staff to other departments of the Executive Council. The General Division of Women's Work was abolished in the 1960s, and the remaining few officers assigned to other departments. Women were encouraged at the diocesan and parish levels to rename themselves "Episcopal Church Women." Many chose to discontinue their organizations as some of their members moved into larger leadership roles and men were integrated into a few of their functions. An administrative structure was required for the Triennial Meetings of women, which had occurred concurrently with General Convention and continued to take place. This provided the core of a partial reconstruction of women's organizations at the national level. The Triennial Planning Committee of the National Board of Episcopal Church Women organizes and administers Triennial Meetings. These meetings are attended by provincial and diocesan delegates along with representatives of other women's groups. The national board administers a program of partnerships between Anglican women around the world. It sponsors training programs designed to help women develop the skills which will enable them to carry out their ministries in the church and in the world. It also publishes a newsletter, *ECW Communique*. In the early 1980s, the Triennial Planning Committee proposed that a new Coordinator of Women's Ministries be requested to call together representatives of several women's organizations to discuss ways of working together. This led to the formation of the Council of Women's Ministries. *See* Woman's Auxiliary to the Board of Missions; *see* Woman's Auxiliary to the National Council.

Episcopal Churchnews (Jan. 27, 1952–Aug. 18, 1957). This journal continued *The Southern Churchman*, which began publication in 1835. The first volume of *Episcopal Churchnews* was published on Jan. 27, 1952. It was weekly until Sept. 20, 1953, when it became bi-weekly. It carried the motto "Catholic for every Truth of God, Protestant against every error of man." It was a news magazine with articles. The last issue was on Aug. 18, 1957.

Episcopal Churchpeople for a Free Southern Africa. This organization was formed on June 12, 1956. It supports those within and outside the churches struggling for freedom in South Africa and Namibia. It works to provide accurate information about the events which take place in Southern Africa. The group also collates and publishes news articles about Southern Africa for the education of citizens in the United States.

Episcopal Clerical Directory. A compilation of clergy biographies was first published in 1898. Over the years it was variously called *Lloyd's Clerical Directory*, *The American Church Directory*, and *Stowe's Clerical Directory*. In 1956 the name was changed to *The Clergy Directory*. In 1972 it was changed to *The Episcopal Clergy Directory*. Since 1974 the title has been *Episcopal Clerical Directory*. Beginning in 1956 *The Clergy Directory* was revised and published every three years following General Convention. Since 1977 the *Directory* has been published every two years by Church Publishing Incorporated.

Episcopal Committee on Religion and Freedom. Founded on Dec. 10, 1984, as a committee of the Institute on Religion and Democracy to support religious freedom, freedom of conscience, and recognition of the importance of democratic government and the limited nature of the state. Members receive the quarterly, *Anglican Opinion*, and the monthly newsletter, *Religion and Democracy*, published by the Institute on Religion and Democracy.

Episcopal Communicators. The descendant of an informal group of diocesan editors who met in New York in May, 1971, at the invitation of the Episcopal Church Center's management team. The topic of discussion was the appearance of a "credibility gap" between the church's leadership and its membership. The eleven editors decided to form a network called Net-11. By 1973, the group had grown, and it became necessary to adopt a name more reflective of the membership. Episcopal Communicators was born at that time. The organization includes persons with communications responsibilities in the Episcopal Church at parish, diocesan, provincial, and national levels in both print and electronic media. The Polly Bond Awards were established in the mid-1970s to acknowledge excellence and achievement in the ministry of church communications. The Janette Pierce Award, established in 1988 to honor the memory of one of the Episcopal Church's outstanding journalists, recognizes exceptional contributions to the ministry of communications and recipients who exemplify the ideals and goals of Janette Pierce. Episcopal Communicators publishes a newsletter, *The Communicator*.

Episcopal Conference of the Deaf. The Conference of Church Workers Among the Deaf was organized on Oct. 4–5, 1881, at St. Ann's Church for the Deaf, New York. At the thirty-ninth convention of the conference in July 1970 at Albion College, Albion, Michigan, the name was changed to the Episcopal Conference of the Deaf. The Rev. Oliver John Whildin (1869–1943), missioner to the deaf in the Diocese of Maryland, published a newsletter called *The Silent News-Letter*. After he became the president of the Conference of Church Workers Among the Deaf in 1926, it became the official organ of the conference. In 1928 the name was changed to *The Silent Missionary*, and in Sept. 1946 it became *The Deaf Churchman*. In July 1977 the name was changed to *The Deaf Episcopalian*.

Episcopal Consortium for Theological Education in the North East (ECTENE). This consortium was formed by the Episcopal Theological School, the Philadelphia Divinity School, and the General Theological Seminary in Oct. 1971. It was funded for three years by the Episcopal Church Foundation to carry out common policies, standards, and practices including curriculum planning and faculty and student exchange, and the formation of a corporate entity in anticipation that the functions of all three seminaries may one day be merged. ECTENE was a response to the efforts of the Board for Theological Education to foster joint national planning for Episcopal theological seminaries. Although ECTENE did not achieve all its goals, one result was the merger of the Philadelphia Divinity School and the Episcopal Theological School on the Cambridge, Massachusetts, campus. The new school is the Episcopal Divinity School.

Episcopal Council for Global Mission (ECGM). The council was created June 14–16, 1990, in St. Louis, Missouri, by persons representing mission organizations that participated in the World Mission Conference at the University of the South, Sewanee, Tennessee, July 19–23, 1989. It was the culmination of several years of work to create a sense of community rather than competition among the many Episcopal entities engaged in international mission activities. It was created to constitute a network of Episcopal organizations involved in global mission. These organizations are committed to meet and communicate in dialogue with Anglican partners and each other to promote the unity and effectiveness of the mission of the Body of Christ. Thirty groups participated in the founding of the council. All members subscribe to four covenants: theology, unreached people, partnership in mission, and information sharing. The covenants recognize the religious pluralism of the world and focus on partnership and sharing. ECGM was affirmed by the Executive Council of the Episcopal Church in Nov. 1990. It met concurrently with the Standing Commission on World Mission of the General Convention in Santo Domingo in Mar. 1993.

Episcopal Council on Indian Ministry (ECIM). The council which coordinates ministries among Native Americans. Presiding Bishop Edmond L. Browning was especially interested in Native American ministry. In 1988 the Executive Council met in South Dakota and focused on Native American Ministry. The outcome of this meeting was a charge from Bishop Browning to his Blue Ribbon Task Force on Indian Affairs to develop a comprehensive and coordinated model for Native American ministries. The Episcopal Council on Indian Ministry was established at the Nov. 1989 meeting of the Executive Council. The General Convention of 1991 affirmed the creation of ECIM. The founding chairperson of ECIM was the Ven. Philip Allen of the Oglala Sioux, then-Archdeacon for Indian

work in the Diocese of Minnesota. He was succeeded by Owanah Anderson, a Choctaw Indian.

Episcopal Diocesan Ecumenical Officers (EDEO). The national network of diocesan ecumenical officers. Late in the 1950s the Joint Commission on Ecumenical Relations suggested that each diocese appoint an ecumenical officer. In 1964 Peter Day was appointed the first Ecumenical Officer of the Episcopal Church. By 1966 many diocesan officers had been appointed, and their first national meeting was held in Chicago in 1966. In 1969, in response to an invitation from Roman Catholics, Episcopal ecumenical officers began to meet in conjunction with what became the National Workshop on Christian Unity. The Episcopal ecumenical officers began to recognize the need for their own national organization. On Mar. 13–14, 1974, the EDEO was organized at Charleston, South Carolina. It works with the Ecumenical Officer of the Episcopal Church and the Standing Commission on Ecumenical Relations to encourage the wider visible unity of the church and to implement actions adopted by the General Convention. It has also published a number of studies focused on the ecumenical commitment of the Episcopal Church.

Episcopal Divinity School (EDS). EDS was established at Cambridge, Massachusetts, on June 6, 1974, by the merger of the Philadelphia Divinity School and the Episcopal Theological School, Cambridge, with the encouragement of the Episcopal Church's Board for Theological Education. The faculty and student body are mostly Christians, but other faith communities are represented as well. The mission of EDS is to prepare women and men for ministry, lay or ordained, in the church and the world. Feminist liberation theology and feminist biblical studies are important aspects of the curriculum.

Episcopal Education Society. It was organized in 1825 by the Revs. Gregory Townsend Bedell, James Milnor, and Stephen Higginson Tyng, all three Episcopal priests in Philadelphia. Around 1826 the society began a manual labor college for prospective clergy near Wilmington, Delaware. It was to be "under Evangelical auspices." It later moved to Bristol, Pennsylvania, but went out of existence in 1837. In 1828 the society took over the publication of *The Philadelphia Record*, an evangelical journal. The society is no longer in existence. *See* Bristol College, Bristol, Pennsylvania.

Episcopal Election Leadership Project (EELP). This project began in May 1993 to examine and review episcopal search processes, elections of bishops, and diocesan transitions of episcopal leadership.

Episcopal Engaged Encounter. A diocesan service within the church offering a weekend that calls engaged couples to a sacramental way of life through the vocation of marriage. A team of two trained Episcopal married couples and an Episcopal priest and his or her spouse present talks and guide the three-day weekend. All team members are volunteers. In 1969 the General Convention endorsed Episcopal Engaged Encounter as a "comprehensive method of sacramental marriage preparation. . . ."

Episcopal Evangelical Journal, The. It is published by the Fellowship of Witness, the American branch of the Evangelical Fellowship of the Anglican Communion. The first issue appeared in July 1994.

Episcopal Evangelism Foundation, Inc. *See* Episcopal Preaching Foundation, Inc., The.

Episcopal Female Tract Societies. In the second decade of the nineteenth century, women in several cities formed tract societies that raised funds for the publication and distribution of the Bible, the BCP, and religious tracts. Many of these associations participated in the founding of the Domestic and Foreign Missionary Society. Among these societies were: Elizabethtown (New Jersey) Female Bible and Common Prayer Book Society, 1816; Newark (New Jersey) Female Bible and Common Prayer Book Society, 1816; Female Society of Shrewsbury and Middletown (New Jersey) for Promoting Christian Knowledge and Piety, 1817; Protestant Episcopal Female Society of Baltimore, 1817; Albany (New York) Prayer Book and Tract Society, 1817; Episcopal Female Tract Society of Philadelphia, 1818; Female Auxiliary Bible and Common Prayer Book Society of St. Andrew's Church, Orange County, 1819; Female Tract Society of Washington (Ohio), 1819; Female Bible and Prayer Book Society of Guilford (Vermont), 1820; Episcopal Bible, Prayer Book and Tract Society of South Carolina, 1827.

Episcopal Guild for the Blind. The full title of this group, which was rarely used, was the Episcopal Guild for the Blind of the Diocese of Long Island. Its director was the Rev. Harry Julius Sutcliffe (1925–1987). He and the guild

were among the founders of the Fellowship of Concerned Churchmen. At the time of his death, Sutcliffe was listed as president and executive director of the Episcopal Guild of the Blind of the American Church Union (ACU), even though the ACU no longer existed in the Episcopal Church.

Episcopal Healing Ministry Foundation (EHMF). A clearing house and resource center for information on the healing ministry. The foundation was established in 1987 to promote teaching and training of clergy and laity to encourage the practice of the sacramental healing ministry. The founding of EHMF commemorated the ten-year healing ministry at St. Thomas' Episcopal Church, Terrace Park, Ohio, where Deacon Emily Gardiner Neal led weekly healing services. Neal also served as president of EHMF. The Rt. Rev. Donald M. Hultstrand, Bishop of Springfield, served as chair of the Bishops' Advisory Council of EHMF.

EHMF seeks to aid in restoring the ministry of healing as part of the congregational life of the church. The foundation sponsored five conferences between its founding and 1992 to address the theoretical and practical aspects of the healing ministry. The conferences encouraged spiritual counseling in cooperation with medical care for those who suffer in body, mind, or spirit. Neal presented some 1,800 meditations and homilies during 30 years of healing mission talks throughout the United States and abroad. All her correspondence, papers, and writings were left to EHMF at the time of her death in 1988. Volunteers have catalogued and cross-referenced these materials. The foundation produced a video of Neal speaking on the church's healing ministry, and published an anthology of her works, *Celebration of Healing*. The collection of Neal's papers, meditations, homilies, audio cassettes, and her personal library are housed at the Marion B. Wade Collection at Wheaton College in Wheaton, Illinois. EHMF retains all rights to this material, and its publication will be subject to the approval of the foundation. The foundation and others contributed to defray the costs for Wheaton graduate students to enter Neal's materials on computer disks. Copies of these disks will be stored in the foundation office.

Episcopal High School, Alexandria, Virginia. In 1831 the widow of William Holland Wilmer opened a school adjacent to Virginia Theological Seminary in Alexandria, Virginia. The school was in a house called Howard, and it was known as the Howard School for Boys. It closed in 1834. At the 1837 Convention of the Diocese of Virginia, it was proposed that a school be established. The trustees of Virginia Seminary assumed responsibility for it. The Episcopal High School began operation on Oct. 15, 1839, but closed in 1844 for financial reasons. It reopened again in 1845. The school has operated continuously since 1845, with the exception of the Civil War years. It separated from Virginia Seminary and became an independent school in 1923.

Episcopal Hospitals and Chaplains, Assembly of. A professional organization of Episcopal chaplains and health care institutions. The assembly was organized in Chicago in Mar. 1950, when fifteen hospital administrators and chaplains met the day before the meeting of the American Protestant Hospitals Association. It promotes communication, cooperation, education, and mutual support among members as well as advocacy for chaplaincy. The assembly is an affiliate of the College of Chaplains and the Congress on Ministry in Specialized Settings (COMISS). It also serves as a facilitating agency for ecclesiastical endorsement of specialized ministers. The organization's title represents the Episcopal Church's long-standing tradition of ministry in hospitals. It teaches that chaplaincy is sacramental and healing to those who suffer in body, mind, or spirit.

Episcopal Lay-Leadership Directory. Conceived as the lay ministry companion volume to the *Episcopal Clerical Directory*, this resource contained detailed biographical information about lay leaders in the Episcopal Church. First published in 1980 by Church Publishing Incorporated, it was produced every two years until 1998, the last of the series in its biographical format. As its replacement, a more comprehensive electronic directory of both lay and ordained leaders is being developed.

Episcopal League for Social Action. *See* Church League for Industrial Democracy, or Episcopal League for Social Action.

Episcopal Life. This monthly journal is an official publication of the Episcopal Church "that seeks faithfully and fully to support the whole life of the Church and its mission, encouraging all people in their commitment to Jesus Christ." It began publication in Apr. 1990, and replaced *The Episcopalian.* It is primarily a news journal. *See* Episcopalian, The.

Episcopal Marriage Encounter. The Marriage Encounter movement was born in Spain in the 1960s to enable couples with basically good marriages to enrich the quality of their lives. Marriage Encounter came to the United States in 1967. The Episcopal Marriage Encounter was formed in 1971, when it was licensed by Worldwide Marriage Encounter. A Marriage Encounter Weekend includes a series of presentations by trained teams of two or three lay couples and a clergy couple. Each presentation involves a sharing of some aspect of the presenting couple's own relationship, and concludes with a question for personal reflection and discussion by the participants. The weekend is a private experience, and there are no group discussions. The weekends are focused on teaching a technique of communication which may be used after the weekend. It is directed by a national board, which is chaired by the National Executive Couple. Episcopal Marriage Encounter is a completely volunteer organization.

Episcopal Media Center, The. The center produces, distributes, and promotes television and radio programs designed for the mass audience, as well as audio-visual productions designed for personal in-home and group in-church use. It is located in Atlanta. This ministry began informally in 1945 under the leadership of the Rt. Rev. John Moore Walker, Jr., Bishop of Atlanta. The charter of the Episcopal Radio-TV Foundation, Inc., was granted on Dec. 8, 1954. One of its most successful productions was the filming of the C. S. Lewis classics, *The Chronicles of Narnia*. On May 8, 1997, the name of the foundation was changed to The Episcopal Media Center. It is self-supporting. The Center depends on voluntary contributions and income from the sale of materials to fund its programs.

Episcopal Medical Missions Foundation (EMMF). This organization was founded in Jan. 1992 to promote the mission program of the Episcopal Church with special emphasis on medical missions. It is an independent organization, not an office of the national church. It is an organization of health professionals, lay persons, and clergy who work to promote and support medical missions in the Episcopal Church. EMMF proclaims the story of missions, recruits volunteers for short term mission service, seeks donations of equipment and supplies, and raises funds to answer the needs of medical missionaries. The founding director was Keith McCaffety, who was succeeded by Dr. Thomas E. Williams.

Episcopal Mental Illness Network (EMIN). The network endeavors to support families and service providers in the Episcopal Church whose lives are affected by major psychiatric illness. It seeks to remove barriers which prevent persons with psychiatric illnesses and their families from participating in the total life of the church. It publishes *EMIN News*, which first appeared in Dec. 1991. In 1983 the Episcopal Church established the Presiding Bishop's Task Force on Accessibility for Persons with Disabilities. This task force was formed within the Office of Social Welfare. On Oct. 12, 1990, the task force passed the resolution which established the Episcopal Mental Illness Network.

Episcopal Migration Ministries (EMM). Through EMM the Episcopal Church provides a variety of services to refugees and immigrants. Nationally and locally, it offers assistance in sponsorship, advocates on national refugee and migration issues, and provides immigration counseling services. It also participates in international relief and development programs for refugees. Bishop Robert Clarkson of Nebraska first petitioned the General Convention in 1883 to establish a "Committee for the Spiritual Care of Immigrants." Soon after that a port chaplaincy was established in New York City. After World War I the newly created Bureau of Immigration of the Episcopal Board of Missions was specifically charged with ministry to new arrivals. In 1942 the Presiding Bishop's Fund for World Relief was founded to respond to the needs of refugees, especially war victims and displaced persons. In 1946 the Episcopal Church and sixteen Protestant denominations founded Church World Service, the overseas relief and service arm of the National Council of Churches of Christ. The Presiding Bishop's Fund for World Relief continued to resettle refugees through Church World Service until 1981. In 1988 the refugee ministry was separated from the Presiding Bishop's Fund for World Relief. In 1989 Episcopal Migration Ministries was established as a distinct program within the national church structure. In 1991, following another reconfiguration of the national church, EMM became part of the Advocacy, Witness, and Justice Ministries.

Episcopal Missionary Association for the West. Organized in 1851 by a group of Philadelphia churchmen because of the rapid increase of population in the west, it was an unofficial missionary society which wanted to secure appointment of evangelical missionaries for the west. The association began its work in Iowa. In 1877 it became an auxiliary to the Board of Missions.

Episcopal Missionary Church (EMC). In 1990 the Episcopal Synod of America (ESA) called for a non-geographical diocese for traditionalists in the Episcopal Church. On Nov. 8, 1991, the ESA voted to form such a diocese, and named it the Missionary Diocese of the Americas. On Nov. 18–20, 1992, the Missionary Diocese of the Americas met at Houston and voted to become the Episcopal Missionary Church. The EMC affirms the principles of the undivided catholic church and the Lambeth Quadrilateral. It uses the 1928 BCP and *The Hymnal* (1940), and does not ordain women. The Rt. Rev. A. Donald Davies, former Bishop of Dallas and Bishop of Fort Worth, is the Presiding Bishop. Its two newsletters are *The Missioner* and *International Missioner.*

Episcopal Network for Economic Justice (ENEJ). An association of individuals and organizations affiliated with the Episcopal Church who are engaged in economic justice ministry. The 1988 General Convention called for a ministry of community investment and economic justice. An Economic Justice Implementation Committee (EJIC) was formed to implement this program at the national level. However, EJIC was phased out at the end of 1995. This decision reflected budget cuts and a reconceptualizing of how the church would organize and fund its justice ministries. Aware that the EJIC was to be phased out, a national conference met in Chicago in 1993 with the theme, "Do Justice, Justice Due," sponsored by the Province V Task Force on Economic Justice and EJIC. This conference called for an economic justice network. ENEJ was officially organized on Feb. 1, 1996.

Episcopal Network for Stewardship, The (TENS). A voluntary network of people who want to grow in their understanding of Christian stewardship theology and in their skill in teaching it. Its purpose is to provide stewardship program assistance to congregations and members of the Episcopal Church. Program resources include print, video, and electronic media resources, as well as personal consultation services. TENS has published *A Manual for Stewardship Development Programs in the Congregation*, and two workbooks, *A Personal Note Commitment Program* and *The Festive Meal Commitment Program*. It also publishes a newsletter, *Networking*. The seed for this organization was planted in Aug. 1994 at a meeting of diocesan stewardship leaders. It began functioning in Jan. 1996.

Episcopal News Service (ENS). Diocesan Press Service (DPS) became the Episcopal News Service in the fall of 1989. It seeks to provide timely and accurate news to diocesan-level communicators, to religion writers for secular publications, to select radio/television outlets, as well as the bishops and elected leaders of the Episcopal Church. ENS covers the decision-making bodies of the church, especially at the national level. It also includes extensive coverage of the church's international and ecumenical commitments, especially with the rest of the Anglican Communion and ecumenical partners. It often chooses stories which illustrate the life of the church at all levels. ENS also releases statements from Episcopal leaders and texts of major documents. The audience has expanded considerably with access to the World Wide Web so that ENS is posted through the Internet and the church's home page, while continuing its printed format. Photographs are also sent electronically by ENS.

Episcopal Peace Fellowship, The (EPF). Founded in 1939 as the Episcopal Pacifist Fellowship, EPF seeks to support and interpret to the church and the world the right of conscientious objection to war and to support Episcopalians who seek exemption from armed service and alternative service in war time as conscientious objectors. It was called together by John Nevin Sayre (1884–1977) in June 1939. Sayre was an Episcopal priest and chair of the International Fellowship of Reconciliation (FOR) at the time of the founding of EPF. The co-founders were Walter Russell Bowie, Elmore McKee, Eric M. Tasman, Luke White, and Katharine Pierce. In addition, Bishops W. Appleton Lawrence, Walter Mitchell, and Paul Jones were central to its formation. The formal organization came on Armistice Day 1939 at a meeting in the Church of the Incarnation, New York City. In 1965 the name of the organization was changed to the "Episcopal Peace Fellowship." During the Vietnam War, the EPF provided literature on conscientious objection to war and extensive draft counseling services. The EPF has been continuously involved in the anti-war movement by means of symbolic and direct action on the part of its members. It urged the adoption of anti-war resolutions by General Convention, and the establishment of the Joint Commission on Peace in 1978. EPF has steadily promoted the gospel imperative to speak for peace and peacemaking. A comprehensive history of the organization was written in 1989 by Nathaniel Pierce and Paul Ward, *The Voice of Conscience: A Loud and Unusual Noise.*

Episcopal Peace and Justice Network, The (EPJN). The EPJN is a coalition of all in the church who work for justice and peace. It brings together such groups as the General Convention's Standing Committee on Peace with Justice, the Executive Council's Committee on Justice, Peace and Integrity of Creation, and the Episcopal Peace Fellowship. The network operates under an executive committee which includes representatives from each of the nine provinces of the Episcopal Church. It has a convenor who acts as an executive officer. It publishes a newsletter, *Episcopax.*

Episcopal Preaching Foundation, Inc., The. At a May 1998 meeting of the Episcopal Evangelism Foundation, the board of directors changed its name to the Episcopal Preaching Foundation, Inc. Its purpose is to promote and support excellence in preaching for the Episcopal Church. The Episcopal Evangelism Foundation was incorporated in the State of Indiana in 1981 in response to a challenge by Presiding Bishop John M. Allin. Its original mission was to provide supplementary education for seminarians in the area of parish-based evangelism ministry. In the early 1980s, the foundation provided summer programs in parishes for selected students interested in the ministry of evangelism. Interest in and support for this program waned after three summers. For several years the foundation was inactive. In 1988 Dr. A. Gary Shilling, the Very Rev. James Fenhagen, and the Rev. Roger Alling conferred on the possibility of using the foundation as a means to provide supplementary education in preaching for Episcopal seminarians. This resulted in the Preaching Excellence Program, the first of which was held in the winter of 1988 at the General Theological Seminary. These conferences for select seminarians from all eleven accredited Episcopal seminaries have been held each summer. The foundation also conducts the Best Sermon Competition. Sermons are solicited from parishes across the nation, evaluated by the board of directors, and published in conjunction with sermons and addresses from the Preaching Excellence Programs. They are published under the title *Sermons That Work.*

Episcopal Radio-TV Foundation, Inc. *See* Episcopal Media Center, The.

Episcopal Recorder, The. This weekly publication was a leading periodical standing for low church evangelical principles. It began publication on June 22, 1822, in Philadelphia, under the name *The Church Record*. With the Apr. 5, 1823, issue the name was changed to *The Philadelphia Recorder*. On Apr. 2, 1831, the name was changed to *The Episcopal Recorder*. It absorbed *The Washington Theological Repertory* in Dec. 1830, and *The Western Episcopalian* in Sept. 1859. It continued publication until Dec. 1919. An editorial in the May 6, 1865, issue demanded that some of the leading bishops and clergy of the South be hanged by the government on the grounds that they had been leaders in the original movement for secession.

Episcopal Renaissance of Pennsylvania. This group in the Diocese of Pennsylvania was organized in 1967 "in an effort to rescue the Episcopal Church from spiritual treason and to stem the tide that was pulling the Episcopal Church into a position of surrender to secular humanism, the prevailing neurosis of the day." It was opposed to the ordination of women to the priesthood and episcopate, and it supported "biblical morality and Apostolic Church Order." From 1972 until 1979, it published a newsletter, *Shield and Sword*. On Jan. 15, 1980, it dissolved and became the Church of the Holy Sacraments in the Diocese of the Resurrection of the Anglican Catholic Church, Narberth, Pennsylvania.

Episcopal Renewal Ministries (ERM). Successor to the Episcopal Charismatic Fellowship (ECF). ECF was organized at a meeting at St. Matthew's Cathedral, Dallas, Texas, on Feb. 12–14, 1973. On Dec. 1, 1972, a letter was sent to every Episcopal priest in the United States inviting them to attend "A National Conference For Episcopal Clergy Involved In The Charismatic Movement." More than 300 clergy attended this conference called by the Rev. Dennis Bennett and the Rev. Wesley Theodore (Ted) Nelson. Soon after its founding, the Fellowship began publishing *Acts 29*, a newsletter which evolved into a bimonthly magazine. The first issue was published in Jan.–Feb. 1982. In 1978 the name of the organization was changed to Episcopal Renewal Ministries to avoid misunderstandings associated with the word "charismatic." ERM stresses that it is "Dedicated to the Renewal of the People and Parishes Through: Apostolic Teaching, Biblical Preaching, Historic Worship, Charismatic Experience." The vision statement slogan is "Releasing the Holy Spirit's life and power in the Church." In addition to Bennett and Nelson, the leaders of ERM included William Graham Pulkingham, Robert Harold Hawn, Todd Wilford Ewald, Everett Leslie (Terry) Fullam, Charles Manning (Chuck) Irish, Carl Eugene Buffington, Jr., Charles Britton Fulton, Jr., and Frederick Llewellyn Goodwin, Jr. ERM publishes *On Line*, an ERM ministry to clergy, and *Insights*, "the Inside story of Episcopal Renewal Ministries."

Episcopal Ring. A ring worn by a bishop as a sign of the bishop's office. It is worn on the third finger of the right hand. It is one of the traditional symbols of episcopal office. It may be given to a newly ordained bishop after the presentation of the Bible and the formula "Receive the Holy Scriptures" at the ordination service (BCP, pp. 521, 553). Early episcopal rings were engraved with a signet and used as a seal. Some episcopal rings enclosed relics. These rings are often gold and may contain an amethyst. They were once seen to represent the bishop's marriage to the diocese.

Episcopal Schools, National Association of. *See* National Association of Episcopal Schools (NAES).

Episcopal Service for Youth, Inc. A ministry to young people during the first half of the twentieth century. The Church Mission of Help was formed in 1911. In 1947 the name was changed to Episcopal Service for Youth, Inc. It was designed to meet the problems of young people, especially girls. In 1966 the services provided by the Episcopal Service for Youth were transferred to the Division of Community Services of the Department of Christian Social Relations of the Executive Council, and Episcopal Service for Youth went out of existence. *See* Church Mission of Help.

Episcopal Services. Services in which a bishop presides. A bishop presides at Confirmation/Reception/Reaffirmation (BCP, p. 413), and a bishop may preside or officiate at any service. A section of the BCP is designated Episcopal Services. This section includes Ordination of a Bishop (p. 512), a Priest (p. 525), or a Deacon (p. 537), with the Litany for Ordinations (p. 548); Celebration of a New Ministry (p. 559); and Consecration of a Church or Chapel (p. 567). It also provides a format for a Letter of Institution of a Minister by the bishop (p. 557). Although a bishop normally presides at a Celebration of a New Ministry, the priest being inducted may serve as chief celebrant in the bishop's absence (p. 558). A bishop must preside at all the other episcopal services in the BCP. The *BOS* also has a section of episcopal services, including Consecration of Chrism apart from Baptism, with a Proper for the Consecration of Chrism; Reaffirmation of Ordination Vows (which may also be used for Reception of a Priest into this Communion, and Restoration of a Deposed Priest or Deacon); Recognition and Investiture of a Diocesan Bishop; Welcoming and Seating of a Bishop in the Cathedral; and Setting Apart for a Special Vocation. A bishop must preside at all the episcopal services listed in the *BOS*. The dedication of altars, fonts, and bells is also reserved to the bishop, and the dedication of chalices and patens is traditionally reserved to the bishop. The *BOS* provides forms for these dedications.

Episcopal Society for Cultural and Racial Unity (ESCRU). ESCRU was a short-lived organization of Episcopalians committed to the ideal of interracial harmony within their denomination and American society.

On Dec. 28–30, 1959, approximately one hundred Episcopalians who supported the civil rights movement gathered at St. Augustine's College in Raleigh, North Carolina, and established ESCRU. That meeting resolved to press for the participation in church life of all people regardless of their race or social class. A national office was soon opened in Atlanta with John Morris, a non-parochial priest, as the organization's executive director. One of ESCRU's initial activities was the Prayer Pilgrimage to the Detroit General Convention of 1961. The "prayer pilgrims" were a group of white and African American clergy who rode together on buses from New Orleans to Detroit in order to protest the existence of racially-segregated church institutions. ESCRU also sponsored Jonathan Daniels, the seminarian and civil rights worker who was martyred in Alabama in Aug. 1965.

Declining cooperation between African American militants and white liberals in the late 1960s eventually undermined the work of ESCRU. With membership dwindling, ESCRU's leaders disbanded the organization in Nov. 1970.

Episcopal Society for Ministry on Aging (ESMA). The nationally affiliated agency of the Episcopal Church responsible for the development and support of ministries on aging. Since its inauguration by the 1964 General Convention, it has worked to serve the spiritual, mental, and physical needs of older persons and to maximize the use of their unique gifts and talents in continuing contributions to church and society. It is a volunteer organization of clergy and lay persons working or interested in the field of aging. An integral part of ESMA's structure is its national network of bishop-appointed coordinators and diocesan designees who help implement ESMA's goals and objectives. ESMA has provided resource materials such as *Affirmative Aging* and *Older Adult Ministry*, as well as an extensive bibliography of religious and secular sources on aging. ESMA publishes a newsletter entitled *Aging Accent*.

Episcopal Society for Ministry in Higher Education (ESMHE). ESMHE was organized on June 21, 1968, at a time when the Executive Council of the Episcopal Church was drastically reducing the church's national programs and staff. These changes and diocesan cutbacks threatened to diminish the church's ministry in higher education. Full-time chaplaincy positions were lost or reduced to part-time positions. ESMHE brought together college chaplains and others interested in campus ministry. These meetings provided continuing education opportunities, orientation for new chaplains, and helpful exchanges of ideas among colleagues. ESMHE seeks to provide advocacy for ministry in higher education, and encouragement for theological reflection, continuing education, and fellowship for chaplains and others involved in ministry in higher education. It publishes *Plumbline* jointly with the Higher Education Ministry Arena, an ecumenical organization.

Episcopal Society of New Jersey for the Promotion of Christian Knowledge and Piety. The major organization in establishing the Episcopal Church in New Jersey. It was formed on Oct. 12, 1810, and sometimes known as the Christian Knowledge Society.

Episcopal Special Interest Group (SIG) of American Mensa. Mensa is an international group that was founded in England in 1946. The only qualification for membership is that a person score in the top 2% of the population on a standardized IQ test. American Mensa was established in 1961, and the Episcopal Special Interest Group was founded in July 1979 at the annual gathering of American Mensa at Kansas City. Mensa has three purposes: to identify and foster human intelligence for the benefit of humanity; to encourage research into the nature, characteristics and uses of intelligence; and to promote intellectual and social opportunities for its members. The Episcopal SIG is for mensas who follow the Anglican tradition. *ANGELOS* is the newsletter of the group, published three times a year. It began publication in Sept. 1979.

Episcopal Synod of America (ESA). An association of chapters and institutions, clergy and laity, who embrace the gospel of Jesus Christ and who "seek a way in which faithful witness to Apostolic Faith and Catholic Order may be continued in the [Episcopal] Church." Membership is open to clergy and laity of the Episcopal Church who subscribe to the ESA Declaration. The Declaration affirms the Chicago-Lambeth Quadrilateral and adds that no church can "change the historic tradition of the Church that the Christian ministerial priesthood is male." The ESA affirms the doctrines of the Trinity, the Virginal Conception of Jesus, and his bodily resurrection. It also stands against euthanasia, homosexual intercourse, adultery, fornication, and abortion as inconsistent with Christianity. The ESA was born in the wake of the first election of a woman to the episcopate. On Nov. 11, 1988, the Bishops of the Evangelical and Catholic Mission issued "A Pastoral Letter Convoking A Synod," to address "the final crisis" in the Episcopal Church. The crisis was the election of the Rev. Barbara Harris as Suffragan Bishop of Massachusetts. The synod met at Fort Worth, Texas, June 1–3, 1989, and organized the Episcopal Synod of America. At the meeting in Fort Worth, Bishop Clarence C. Pope of Fort Worth was elected the first president. On Nov. 8, 1991, the Synod voted to begin the development of a non-geographic missionary diocese for traditionalist individuals, congregations, and institutions, and called it the Missionary Diocese of the Americas. Later some of these persons organized the Missionary Episcopal Church. ESA is the continuation of the Evangelical and Catholic Mission, and continues to publish *The Evangelical Catholic*. It also publishes a newsletter, *Foundations*.

Episcopal Theological School (ETS). Predecessor to Episcopal Divinity School. The school was founded at Cambridge, Massachusetts, by a group of prominent Boston businessmen in 1867 to be a place of preparation for holy orders and an Episcopal presence at Harvard University. It provided a place of worship for Episcopal undergraduates. All Harvard undergraduates were required to attend Sunday worship in either the Harvard Chapel or their church of choice. The board of trustees was limited to lay persons. The faculty were required to assert belief in justification by faith upon assuming their teaching duties. It was the first Episcopal theological seminary to welcome modern biblical scholarship. It was also the first Episcopal seminary to introduce into the curriculum courses in sociology taught by a professor of sociology, the first Episcopal seminary to establish a chair in the history of religion and mission, and the first Episcopal seminary to appoint a woman to a full-time faculty position (Professor Adelaide Teague Case in 1941). ETS has been associated with controversy at various times. *Creeds and Loyalty*, a collection of seven faculty essays on the issue of creedal literalism, was published in 1924. Professor Joseph Fletcher's exposition of situation ethics in the 1960s was also controversial. In 1974 the school merged with the Philadelphia Divinity School (1857) to form Episcopal Divinity School (EDS), Cambridge. *See* Case, Adelaide Teague; *see* Situation Ethics; *see* Fletcher, Joseph Francis.

Episcopal Theological School at Claremont (Bloy House). A diocesan seminary which was originally begun in 1958 as an extension program through the Church Divinity School of the Pacific (CDSP) in the Diocese of Los Angeles. CDSP intended the school to serve students who were not able to study at their Berkeley campus. In 1962 CDSP could no longer maintain the Los Angeles campus because of financial problems. The Diocese of Los Angeles took over full operation of the seminary and named it "Bloy House" after Bishop Francis Eric Irving Bloy (1904–1993). In 1970 the diocese agreed to combine their resources with the Claremont School of Theology. The school moved to the Claremont, California, campus. The move occasioned a name change to Episcopal Theological School at Claremont. The school is affiliated with the Diocese of Los Angeles, and the Bishop serves on its board. The school offers a joint M.Div. program with the School of Theology at Claremont.

Episcopal Theological Seminary in Kentucky. Former diocesan seminary. It was founded in 1834 at Lexington by Bishop Benjamin Bosworth Smith to educate clergy for the western frontier. The school was granted a charter on Feb. 24, 1834. It went into a quick decline because of financial troubles in 1837 and controversy between the diocese and Bishop Smith. After 1840, for a short time, it had a nominal existence as a department of Shelby College in Shelbyville, Kentucky. Bishop William Robert Moody reopened the seminary in Sept. 1951 with four students. In its last years it trained students for the diaconate. The final graduation service for the remaining diaconal students was on June 9, 1990.

Episcopal Theological Seminary of the Caribbean, San Juan, Puerto Rico. The seminary was founded in 1961, and its chapel was dedicated on Jan. 11, 1962, by Presiding Bishop Arthur Lichtenberger. The seminary trained more than seventy persons for ministry. It closed in 1976.

Episcopal Theological Seminary of the Southwest (ETSS). The idea for a seminary in Austin, Texas, was initiated in 1945. The Rt. Rev. Clinton S. Quinn, Bishop of Texas, approached the Board of Trustees of the Austin Presbyterian Theological Seminary about training Episcopal students at the Presbyterian seminary in a cooperative program. Nothing came of this first effort. However, in 1951 three Episcopal students enrolled at the Austin Presbyterian Seminary, under the leadership of the Rt. Rev. John E. Hines, Bishop Coadjutor of Texas. They were taught at an off-campus location by an Episcopal faculty. The diocesan council of the Diocese of Texas approved the school in Jan. 1952. Five acres of land, located near the University of Texas and the Austin Presbyterian Seminary, were given to the school. In Jan. 1954, ground was broken for the new campus. The Lutheran Seminary Program in the Southwest is located on the ETSS campus. The school has a program of Theological Studies for Hispanic Ministry and Intercultural Understanding. The Archives of the Episcopal Church are located in the ETSS Library. ETSS publishes *Ratherview*.

Episcopal Urban Caucus (EUC). This organization was founded in Indianapolis in mid-Feb. 1980. It is a group of Episcopalians who study, work, pray, and give to improve the quality of life for all people. At the third national assembly of EUC, Feb. 12, 1982, the members adopted "A Rule of Life," which affirmed belief "in God, and the reign of God on earth as in Heaven, a kingdom of justice and peace; in Jesus Christ, the eternal Word of God made flesh for our salvation, and the Good News which he proclaimed to the poor and the oppressed, the year of the Lord's jubilee; in the Holy Spirit and in the holy Church, God's power to reconcile and to liberate us as individuals and as a community." "A Rule of Life" calls the members to a daily recognition of society's sicknesses, and commits them to the mission of the church with the poor. It holds an Annual Assembly at which issues such as disarmament

are studied and discussed. Since the General Convention of 1991, EUC has made anti-racism its principal ministry. It stresses "A Church for all races . . . a Church to end racism."

Episcopal Visitation. A bishop's official pastoral visit to a congregation of the diocese. Canon law requires every diocesan bishop to visit every congregation in his or her diocese at least once every three years. The canonical purposes of a visitation are for the bishop to examine the condition of the congregation, oversee the clergy, preach, confirm, preside at the eucharist, and examine parochial records. The BCP also assumes that the bishop's visitation will be an occasion for baptism, and that the bishop will preside.

Episcopal Visitors. The 1988 General Convention passed the legislation which created Episcopal Visitors. This legislation was to deal pastorally with those bishops, priests, deacons, and lay persons who were unable to accept women bishops. It allowed the Presiding Bishop to designate members of the House of Bishops to act as Episcopal Visitors. They were to provide episcopal sacramental acts for Episcopal congregations upon the request and under the authority of the Ecclesiastical Authority of a diocese. This provision was only to be used for the time of transition as women were incorporated into all ordained ministries. This legislation expired upon adjournment of the 1994 General Convention on Sept. 2, 1994.

The term may be distinguished from a bishop visitor or protector, who serves as the guardian of the constitution of a religious order and as an arbiter in matters that the order or its members cannot resolve through its normal processes.

Episcopal Watchman. This journal was published at Hartford, Connecticut, from Mar. 26, 1827, until Nov. 2, 1833, when it was absorbed by the *Churchman.* Its motto was "the Gospel of Christ in the Church of Christ." It was founded and at first edited and published by George Washington Doane and William Croswell (1804–1851).

Episcopal Women's Caucus. The caucus works to enable the church to free itself from racism, sexism, clericalism, heterosexism, and from technologies and practices that sustain power inequities. It was organized on Oct. 30–31, 1971, when a group of women met at Virginia Theological Seminary to discuss and assess the role of professional women workers in the Episcopal Church. Just prior to this meeting, the House of Bishops had voted to refer the question of the ordination of women to another study committee. The women at the Alexandria meeting were dismayed that the bishops did not take a position on this issue, and they sent a letter to the Presiding Bishop that expressed their disappointment. All 60 women present signed the letter. In signing the letter of protest, the group constituted the Episcopal Women's Caucus. In Apr. 1974 the steering committee appointed an editor for a publication to be called *Ruach*, which became a monthly newsletter. The caucus continues to advocate for full implementation of the baptismal covenant for women and men.

Episcopal Women's History Project (EWHP). The purpose of EWHP is to research, write, publish, and celebrate the contributions made by Episcopal women to both church and society. It is independently incorporated and run by a volunteer Executive Board with the assistance of an Advisory Committee of historians and scholars. In Aug. 1980 a group of women met in New York City under the leadership of Mary Sudman Donovan and Joanna Bowen Gillespie to discuss the establishment of an organization devoted to the history of women in the Episcopal Church. This was the beginning of EWHP. On June 1–3, 1982, the first National Conference of the Episcopal Women's History Project met at Austin, Texas, with the theme, "Notable Episcopal Women: The Feminine Dimension of Church History." Several of these papers were published in the Dec. 1982 issue of the *Historical Magazine of the Protestant Episcopal Church*, which carried the subtitle, *Special Issue: Episcopal Women's History I.* In addition to serving as co-sponsor for several conferences of Episcopal historians, EWHP's other activities have included the Deaconess History Project, an oral history project, and the publication of a handbook on women's church history, *Cultivating our Roots* (1984). The quarterly *Episcopal Women's History Project Newsletter* began publication in Fall 1981. With the Spring 1996 issue, the name was changed to *Timelines*. In 1997 EWHP established the Frank Sugeno Research Award, which was a grant of $1,000 for a current research project on the history of Episcopal women and a program of Travel/ Research Awards to support work on the history of Episcopal women.

Episcopal World Mission, Inc. (EWM). A voluntary missionary society of the Episcopal Church. It was founded in 1982 when Dr. Paul Walter asked James Martin and Edgar Tetrick to pray with him about starting a new mission society in the Episcopal Church. Walter had been Executive Director of the South American Missionary Society (SAMS). Since the ministry of SAMS was limited to South and Central America, there was a clear need to send evangelical Episcopal missionaries to the rest of the world. Walter and the others did not want to interfere with the ministry of SAMS. They requested and received permission from the SAMS Board of Trustees to undertake the venture. EWM was incorporated on July 19, 1982. The corporate creed was adopted on Aug. 20, 1982, by the initial board of trustees. The first EWM missionary was appointed during the board meeting at Oral Roberts University, Feb. 17–18, 1983. John Suann was posted to Singapore. In Sept. 1983, Todd Hicks was appointed the first long-term missionary. He was sent to the Occupied West Bank in response to a request from the Bishop of Jerusalem. The distinctive character of the organization is its foreign mission focus on Africa, Asia, and Europe.

Episcopal Young Church People (EYC). This group serves the needs of young people, usually between the ages of thirteen and eighteen. EYC members may also participate in regional, diocesan, and national gatherings. These groups normally meet under the sponsorship and supervision of adults who may be professional youth workers. Such groups are usually granted recognition at church meetings but have no official or canonical standing. These groups meet socially and usually participate in educational, worship, and social service activities. Such groups have also been known as YPF (Young People's Fellowship).

Episcopal Youth Event, The (EYE). A national gathering of young people and adult sponsors from throughout the Episcopal Church. The participants are to reflect the ethnic, cultural, and racial diversity of each diocese. It is sponsored by the Youth Ministries Office of the Episcopal Church. The first EYE was in 1982, with subsequent gatherings in 1984 and afterwards at three-year intervals. A design team of young people and adults from all the provinces of the church is responsible for planning the programs and worship.

Episcopalian. A member of the Episcopal Church. The term is used as a noun, not as an adjective. The term can be applied to a member of any church under the leadership of bishops. *See* Episcopal.

Episcopalian, The. Predecessor to *Episcopal Life*. This monthly journal began publication in Apr. 1960, and continued *Forth* and *The Spirit of Missions*. The first issue stated that it was published by the Church Magazine Advisory Board by authority of the General Convention. It continued the numbering of *The Spirit of Missions*, which meant that the Apr. 1960 issue was vol. 125, number 4. The last issue was published in Mar. 1990, and described itself as an independently edited, officially sponsored monthly published by the Domestic and Foreign Missionary Society of the Episcopal Church/The Episcopalian, Inc., by authority of the General Convention. *See* Spirit of Missions, The.

Episcopalian Harmony, The. A collection of hymns that was approved by General Convention and published in 1811 by John Cole in Baltimore. It was reprinted in 1817. The layout of text and music employed by Cole in this collection was adopted in Episcopal chant collections for the next several decades.

Episcopalians United. Late in 1975 this group was organized by the Rev. Canon Albert J. duBois, president of the American Church Union at the time. Episcopalians United was organized to present a solid front against the ordination of women and the adoption of a new Prayer Book. Its motto was "No Surrender—No Desertion." This meant no surrender of the apostolic heritage of the Episcopal Church as set forth in its constitution and the Book of Common Prayer, and no desertion of the Episcopal Church as presently constituted. Episcopalians United was a part of the Fellowship of Concerned Churchmen. It is no longer in existence. *See* duBois, Albert Julius.

Episcopalians United for Revelation, Renewal and Reformation. This organization grew out of a meeting on Jan. 7–10, 1986, in Winter Park, Florida. The meeting was called the 3Rs Conference and focused on the revelation of God, the renewal of the church, and the reformation of society. Nearly 100 leaders of the Episcopal Church from the catholic, evangelical, and charismatic traditions met there to seek God's guidance for the church's future. In Apr. 1987, many of these same people met in Pittsburgh, Pennsylvania, to discuss the direction of the church as the 1988 General Convention approached. The movement, known simply as Episcopalians United, was incorporated on June 14, 1987. Its mission is to influence the structures of the Episcopal Church so that they may reflect the lordship of Jesus Christ more faithfully. It holds scripture as the primary source for doctrine, discipline, and worship. Episcopalians United teaches that sexual relations are a gift of God to be celebrated only by a man and a woman who have been united in the bonds of holy matrimony. It also affirms the sanctity of human life and the ordination of persons who by their lives and teachings proclaim the biblical standards of holiness. In Apr. 1988 Episcopalians United began the publication of *Advocate*. The name was changed to *United Voice* at the time of the 1991 General Convention. Publication frequency has been sporadic, but the norm is a bimonthly schedule.

Episcopate, Episcopacy, *Episcopos.* Church governance under the leadership of bishops. The term is from the Greek for "overseer." The Prayer Book service for the ordination of a bishop states that a bishop "is called to be one with the apostles in proclaiming Christ's resurrection and interpreting the Gospel, and to testify to Christ's sovereignty as Lord of lords and King of kings." A bishop is called to guard the faith, unity, and discipline of the church, to celebrate and provide for the administration of the sacraments, to ordain priests and deacons and join in ordaining bishops, and to be a faithful pastor and wholesome example for the whole church. Bishops share in the leadership of the church throughout the world (BCP, p. 517).

The terms may refer to the collective role of the order or office of bishops in the church. The "Historic Episcopate, locally adapted in the methods of its administration to the varying needs of the nations and peoples called of God into the unity of His Church" is one of the four points of the Chicago-Lambeth Quadrilateral. The 1886 General Convention of the Episcopal Church in Chicago identified the historic episcopate as an inherent part of the sacred deposit of Christian faith and order committed by Christ and his apostles to the church until the end of the world. The Convention accounted the historic episcopate to be one of four essentials for the restoration of unity among the divided branches of Christendom (BCP, p. 877). The Lambeth Conference of 1888 included the historic episcopate as one of the four points that supply a basis on which approach may be made towards Home Reunion (BCP, pp. 877–878).

Episcopate or episcopacy may also indicate the body or college of bishops in a church or region, or the tenure or office of a bishop. *See* Chicago-Lambeth Quadrilateral; *see* Historic Episcopate.

Episcopi Vaganti. "Wandering bishops" who acquired episcopal orders in an irregular or surreptitious manner. They are unaffiliated with any historic Christian body or jurisdiction. Their episcopal acts have questionable validity. *See* Jurisdiction (episcopal); *see* Independent Bishops.

Epistle. Literally, a letter, the name was given to the first of the two NT readings in the eucharist. The majority of these passages were taken from the epistolary literature of the NT, such as the letters of Paul to communities of Christians in various places. On occasion, other books (Acts, Revelation, or OT readings) were substituted. In such cases the 1662 BCP prescribed the introduction: "The portion of Scripture appointed for the Epistle is written in . . . ." The Prayer Book permits the reader of the second lection to conclude with the formula "Here ends the Epistle," which is appropriate only when the reading is actually taken from the epistolary literature.

"Epistle Side." *See* Gospel Side.

Epistoler. The lector who reads the epistle in the liturgy of the word at the eucharist. The term "epistle" may be applied to any NT reading at the eucharist, including a selection from the epistles, Acts, or Revelation. The epistoler may be vested, depending on local custom.

Eremitic. Concerning the solitary life of a hermit. In Christianity, the earliest hermits were the Desert Fathers of third-century Egypt. Some religious orders, like the Carthusians, retain elements of the eremitic lifestyle in their rule. They live in separate dwellings but gather for meals and worship. *See* Hermit, Hermitess.

Erie, Diocese of. When the Diocese of Northwestern Pennsylvania was organized in 1910, it was called the Diocese of Erie. It used that name until Nov. 14, 1981, when the name was changed to the Diocese of Northwestern Pennsylvania.

Eschatology. Theology of the last things, the end of time and history, the coming of the Kingdom of God. Use of the term dates from the nineteenth century. It is from the Greek, *eschatos*, "last." Eschatology concerns the final end and meaning of all things, but it is possible to distinguish individual, social, and universal aspects of eschatology.

The Christian hope is centered in the victorious Christ, who will come again in glory to judge the living and the dead and whose kingdom will have no end (see the Nicene Creed, BCP, p. 359; and the Apostles' Creed, BCP, p. 96). Some approaches to eschatology emphasize the coming of the Kingdom of God as a radical break from the existence of creation as we know it, or a breaking into time from the future. Other approaches emphasize that the power of God's Kingdom was inaugurated in Christ's life, death, and resurrection, and that God's power for salvation and the fulfillment of all things is currently active in history. Thomas Aquinas understood the ultimate end and perfect happiness of humanity in terms of union with God, which may be described as the beatific vision. He also held that each thing intends as its ultimate end to be united to God as closely as possible for it. The NT scholar C.H. Dodd presented a "realized eschatology" in which the perfect fulfillment of the messianic hope is realized in Jesus' incarnate life and earthly ministry. The Kingdom of God may be understood as already present through Christ's resurrection and yet to be fulfilled perfectly when Christ returns at the end of time. The theme of Christian expectation for the coming of Christ in power and glory is given liturgical expression in the season of Advent. The Prayer Book Catechism states that "the Christian hope is to live with confidence in newness and fullness of life, and to await the coming of Christ in glory, and the completion of God's purpose for the world" (BCP, p. 861). The Catechism section on the Christian Hope considers such eschatological themes as the meaning of the coming of Christ in glory, the meaning of heaven and hell, prayers for the dead, the meaning of the last judgment, the meaning of the resurrection of the body, the communion of saints, the meaning of everlasting life, and the Christian assurance (BCP, p. 862).

Eschaton. The term (from the Greek, *eschaton*, "last") denotes the end of history when God will act decisively to establish the divine rule of justice and peace throughout the created order. Jesus refers to the eschaton as "the Kingdom of God," which he proclaimed to have "come near" (Mk 1:15). In Christian understanding, the resurrection of Jesus was the anticipation of the eschaton. The resurrection signals a preliminary victory over sin and death and points to the final victory. The quality of life in the eschaton is shown to Christian believers by the love, justice, and peace that marked Jesus' life and death.

Essays and Reviews. This volume, published in England in 1860, was a significant collection of essays advocating a free and open interpretation of Holy Scripture. It included essays by Mark Pattison, Benjamin Jowett, and Frederick Temple. The collection was condemned in 1861 by the bishops of the Church of England because several of the essays were thought to deny the inspiration of scripture.

Essays Catholic and Critical. This collection of fifteen essays by liberal catholics of the Church of England was edited by Edward Gordon Selwyn. It was published in 1926. It was an effort to take seriously both the catholic tradition and critical scholarship. The contributors felt compelled to "think out afresh the content and the grounds of their religion." They believed that two factors necessitated rethinking the Christian faith. These factors were the renewed interest in catholic unity and authority, and the increasing information being discovered by the critical movement in biblical studies. Among the contributors were Alfred Edward John Rawlinson, Lionel Spencer Thorton, Edwyn C. Hoskyns, John Kenneth Mozley, and Will Spens. This volume inspired a group of Episcopal priests to publish a similar collection of essays entitled *Liberal Catholicism and the Modern World* (1934).

Esse, Bene Esse, Plene Esse. Terms for characterizing the significance of a doctrine or practice for the church. *Esse* indicates that which is of the essence of the very existence of the life of the church. *Bene esse* indicates that which is of benefit for the life of the church. *Plene esse* indicates that which is of the fullness of the Church's life. These terms have been frequently used with respect to the role of the historic episcopate in the life of the church. This question has often been raised in the context of ecumenical discussions, especially with churches that do not have an episcopal ministry and do not require episcopal ordination of clergy. The statement "No bishop, no Church" would reflect the position that the historic episcopate is of the *esse* of the church. This view, strictly applied, serves to "unchurch" Protestant denominations that do not have the episcopate. It also serves to restrict severely the possibilities for Anglican ecumenical relations with these churches.

The historic episcopate (as locally adapted) was identified by the Quadrilateral adopted by the House of Bishops in 1886 as one of the four parts of the sacred deposit of the faith that are "essential to the restoration of unity among the divided branches of Christendom." The historic episcopate was likewise identified by the Lambeth Conference of 1888 as one of the four bases for Home Reunion. See the Chicago-Lambeth Quadrilateral 1886, 1888 (BCP, pp. 876–878). The other three "essential" parts identified by the House of Bishops in 1886 were the Holy Scriptures of the OT and NT as the revealed Word of God; the Nicene Creed as the sufficient statement of Christian faith; and the two sacraments of Baptism and the Supper of the Lord, ministered with unfailing use of Christ's words of institution and of the elements ordained by Christ. The other three elements of the Lambeth Conference Resolution of 1888 are similar to the Chicago declaration, except that the Apostles' Creed as the Baptismal Symbol is mentioned along with the Nicene Creed as the sufficient statement of Christian faith.

The distinction of *esse* and *bene esse* with respect to the episcopate can be traced to the thought of Richard Hooker (c. 1554–1600). He believed that the apostles left bishops with authority above other pastors and that the church has power to determine its own positive law and governance. But Hooker also believed that episcopacy does not belong to "the essence of Christianity." On the other hand, nineteenth-century Tractarians took the position that Christ created the apostolic order. For example, in Tract 4, John Keble (1792–1866) doubted that there was assurance and safety for salvation except in the sacraments of the apostolic Church of England. Keble and other Tractarians believed that episcopacy was of the *esse* of the church.

The term *plene esse* was used in essays by H. W. Montefiore and Kenneth M. Carey in *The Historic Episcopate* (1954), edited by Carey. This collection of essays was published in response to the controversy concerning whether the Church of England should enter into full communion with the Church of South India. In the Church of South India, episcopal and non-episcopal churches came together on an episcopal basis. Clergy who had not been episcopally ordained were not reordained by bishops. But all future ordinands were to be episcopally ordained, so that the Church of South India would eventually be an episcopal church whose clergy were all episcopally ordained. Carey admits that the interim presence of nonepiscopally ordained clergy was an admitted "anomaly" for an episcopal church. Nevertheless, the essays by Montefiore and Carey support full communion with the Church of South India because the episcopate is of the *plene esse*, or fullness, of the church— not the essence. In 1955 the Convocations of Canterbury and York approved limited inter-communion between the Church of England and the Church of South India. A similar plan and understanding of episcopacy was the basis of the proposed Lutheran-Episcopal Concordat (1991). *See* Historic Episcopate; *see* Chicago-Lambeth Quadrilateral.

Establishment of Religion. An arrangement in which a religion or a particular religious institution enjoys official status and the state may enforce conformity. The establishment of Christianity began with Constantine the Great (d. 337) who first tolerated Christianity instead of persecuting it, and then later actively sought to make it the official religion of the Roman Empire. Established Christianity was understood as ordering the ends of the state as well as providing for the salvation of individuals. It was expected to legitimate the authority and actions of the state. This was expressed in the duty of Christians to fight for the preservation and ends of the state and in the duty of the state to suppress and punish false religion and doctrine. In terms of faith, Christianity became less a matter of conscious decision and commitment and more a matter of birth and assimilation into the surrounding culture. No longer was there a process of initiation (the catechumenate) in preparation for adult baptism. Instead, all citizens were baptized at birth so that "Christian" became just another word for citizen. In this context, religious orders became "a higher way" which transcended the roles and relations of citizen to state and thereby at times challenged the authority of the state. With the Protestant Reformation and a renewed sense of the individual decision of faith, the increase of religious bodies, and the rise of the nation-state seeking to secure itself amidst competing religious bodies, establishment of religion gave way to religious freedom. This change ultimately led, in fact if not in principle, to the secular state. Anglicanism follows this development, moving from exclusive establishment at the time of the English Reformation, to increased religious toleration, to an established church in a secular state. Although the Church of England continues as an established church, the Anglican Communion worldwide is seen as a denomination whose churches are spread throughout the world by voluntary membership apart from the efforts of the state.

Etheria. *See* Egeria (or Etheria or Aetheria), Pilgrim.

Ethics. As a field of study, the subject matter of ethics is the moral life. The moral life itself has been variously understood, although two approaches have most fundamentally defined ethics. One approach emphasizes human fulfillment and happiness and results in a teleological ethic focusing on ends. The other approach emphasizes moral duty and results in a deontological ethic focusing on moral obligations apart from ends. Since Aristotle, three questions have shaped the discipline of ethics: 1) What is the nature of what is good or right? 2) What is the nature of human understanding and action, or how do you come to know and do the good or right? 3) What are the criteria for judging actions? Christian ethics considers the moral life with primary reference to understanding God through Jesus Christ. Scripture is a primary source for this understanding.

Eucharist. The sacrament of Christ's body and blood, and the principal act of Christian worship. The term is from the Greek, "thanksgiving." Jesus instituted the eucharist "on the night when he was betrayed." At the Last Supper he shared the bread and cup of wine at a sacred meal with his disciples. He identified the bread with his body and the wine with his blood of the new covenant. Jesus commanded his disciples to "do this" in remembrance of him (see 1 Cor 11:23–26; Mk 14:22–25; Mt 26:26–29; Lk 22:14–20). Christ's sacrifice is made present by the eucharist, and in it we are united to his one self-offering (BCP, p. 859). The Last Supper provides the basis for the fourfold eucharistic action of taking, blessing, breaking, and sharing. Christ's body and blood are really present in the sacrament of the eucharist and received by faith. Christ's presence is also known in the gathered eucharistic community.

In the BCP, the whole service is entitled the Holy Eucharist. The first part of the service is designated the Word of God. It usually includes the entrance rite, the lessons and gradual psalm, the gospel, the sermon, the Nicene Creed, the prayers of the people, the confession of sin and absolution, and the peace. The second portion of the service is designated the Holy Communion. It includes the offertory, the consecration of the bread and wine in the Great Thanksgiving, the communion of the people, and the concluding prayers of thanksgiving and dismissal. A blessing may be given prior to the dismissal.

The eucharist is also called the Lord's Supper, Holy Communion, the Divine Liturgy, the Mass, and the Great Offertory (BCP, p. 859). *The Hymnal 1982* includes a section with a variety of hymns for the Holy Eucharist (300–347), including "Come, risen Lord, and deign to be our guest" (305–306), "My God, thy table now is spread" (321), "Now, my tongue, the mystery telling" (329–331), and "I am the bread of life" (335).

Eucharistic Adoration. Adoration of God in prayer "is the lifting up of the heart and mind to God, asking nothing but to enjoy God's presence" (BCP, p. 857). Eucharistic adoration is devotional adoration of the real presence of Christ in the consecrated bread and wine of the eucharist. Private eucharistic adoration often involves prayer near the tabernacle or aumbry where the sacrament is reserved. Corporate acts of adoration include Benediction of the Blessed Sacrament and Exposition of the Blessed Sacrament. Article XXV of the Articles of Religion protested against eucharistic adoration, stating that "The Sacraments were not ordained of Christ to be gazed upon, or to be carried about, but that we should duly use them" (BCP, p. 872). The BCP does not include forms for the services of Benediction or Exposition. But forms for these services are found in some devotional books such as *Saint Augustine's Prayer Book*. Eucharistic adoration is an important aspect of the prayer life of some members of the Episcopal Church, especially those with an Anglo-catholic piety. James DeKoven, the most widely known and respected leader of the Anglo-catholic movement in the nineteenth century, defended eucharistic adoration at the General Conventions of 1871 and 1874. He urged that "to adore Christ's person in His Sacrament, is the inalienable privilege of every Christian and Catholic heart."

Eucharistic Canon. The fixed portion of the eucharistic prayer which does not vary with the liturgical season or occasion. *See* Canon.

Eucharistic Elements. *See* Elements, Eucharistic.

Eucharistic Prayer. This prayer over the bread and wine at communion begins with the Sursum Corda dialogue and concludes with the doxology and the Great Amen. The prayer is also called The Great Thanksgiving, the *anaphora*, the prayer of consecration, and the canon of the Mass. The BCP includes eight eucharistic prayers: two for Rite 1 (pp. 333–343), four for Rite 2 (pp. 361–375), and two shortened forms in An Order for Celebrating the Holy Eucharist (pp. 402–404). The booklet *Supplemental Liturgical Materials* includes two additional eucharistic prayers. The diversity and variety of eucharistic prayers in the BCP can be contrasted with earlier Prayer Books

which had only one eucharistic prayer. In some parishes, eucharistic prayers are chosen in light of the seasons or occasions of the church year. *See* Great Amen.

Eucharistic Sacrifice. That which is offered to God in the Holy Communion. The identification of Jesus' sacrifice with the eucharist is derived from the Last Supper, when Jesus identified the bread with his body and the wine with his blood of the new covenant (see 1 Cor 11:23–26; Mk 14:22–25). The Letter to the Hebrews describes Christ as the high priest who is the mediator of the new covenant through his once-for-all sacrifice (see Heb 9). Identification of the eucharist as a sacrificial action has been dated from the early third century. However, abuses and exaggerations had become associated with the eucharist by the Reformation era, including the popular concept of the Mass as a repetition of Jesus' death on Calvary. Reactions against this understanding were reflected in the sixteenth-century liturgies of the Lutheran and Anglican churches. Article XXXI of the Articles of Religion denied the efficacy of sacrifice other than Christ's (BCP, p. 874). Anglicans in the Puritan, low-church, and evangelical traditions have closely followed Article XXXI, spurning mention of any sacrifice other than the "full, perfect, and sufficient sacrifice, oblation, and satisfaction" of Jesus' death. Eucharist is not sacrifice in these traditions, and eucharist can only recollect the one sacrifice of Christ. On the other hand, Anglicans in the high church and catholic traditions have taught that eucharist always involves sacrifice. These traditions typically hold that eucharist requires believers to join their lives with Christ's one sacrifice. The eucharistic prayers in the BCP reflect our sacramental participation in the once-for-all sacrifice of our Lord. Eucharistic Prayer B states that "we offer our sacrifice of praise and thanksgiving to you, O Lord of all; presenting to you, from your creation, this bread and this wine," and asks that God may "Unite us to your Son in his sacrifice, that we may be acceptable through him, being sanctified by the Holy Spirit" (BCP, p. 369). *See* Oblation.

Eucharistic Sharing. The sharing of the Holy Communion among members of different churches. Conditions for such admission are defined and stated by each church for itself. *See* Ecumenical Movement.

Eucharistic Vestments. Traditional liturgical garments worn at the celebration of the eucharist. In medieval times in the western church, priests officiating at the altar wore six garments over the cassock. These were the amice (a loose collar or hood), the alb (a full-length sleeved gown), and girdle. Over them was the stole, the maniple on the left wrist, and most conspicuously the chasuble (a robe covering front, back, and shoulders). These three were usually of fine fabric with ornamental needlework, with different liturgical colors being used for different days. In medieval times, symbolic meanings were attached to each item. Although they were disallowed in England in the sixteenth century, they were revived in the nineteenth century following the Oxford Movement. Evangelicals opposed them, preferring the customary Anglican surplice with tippet or stole. Today, with less polemical associations, eucharistic vestments are widely used in most Episcopal parishes. The maniple and amice are now typically omitted. The amice may be replaced by a hood attached to the alb. The girdle may be omitted.

Eutychianism. Heretical teaching about the person of Christ associated with Eutyches (c. 378–454). He was the archimandrite (monastic superior) of a large monastery in Constantinople, and influential at the imperial court in Constantinople in the middle of the fifth century. Eutyches was caught up in the controversy then raging over the relationship between the humanity and divinity of Christ. He opposed Nestorianism, a heretical teaching which held that Christ was two persons, one divine and one human, as well as two natures in moral union. Eutyches taught that Christ was one person (*hypostasis* or *prosopon*) with just one nature. Hence, Eutychianism is also called *monophysitism*. It is not clear whether Eutyches held the one nature of Christ to be simply divine, or whether it was a "third thing" between divinity and humanity. He taught that Christ's one nature was not consubstantial with our humanity. His Christology was unbalanced because he did not uphold the full humanity of Christ. This teaching led his followers toward Docetism. Eutychianism was condemned by the Council of Chalcedon. Eutychianism has been characterized as the opposite and symmetrical error of Nestorianism. *See* Docetism; *see* Nestorianism.

Evangelical. Formed from the noun *evangel* (from the Greek *euanggelion*, "good news"), it means simply "pertaining to the gospel." Hooker referred to the *Magnificat*, *Benedictus*, and *Nunc Dimittis* as "Evangelical Hymns" since their texts come from the Gospel of Luke.

During the intra-Protestant controversies in Germany and Switzerland in the sixteenth and seventeenth centuries, Lutherans were called evangelical and Calvinists were called reformed. The Evangelical Church is the official name of the church formed in Germany by the union of Lutherans and Calvinists. In England a movement in the eighteenth century formed under the leadership of John and Charles Wesley and George Whitfield was called indiscriminately "methodist" or "evangelical." English evangelical teaching was characterized by emphasis on atoning sanctification and marked by "enthusiasm." Evangelicals who remained within the Church of England formed an evangelical or low church party, often at odds with the Laudian, catholic, or high church party.

The evangelical movement in the Episcopal Church was influenced strongly by the Great Awakening in America during the mid-eighteenth century. Episcopal evangelicals reflected American evangelicalism in many ways, including a characteristic emphasis on personal religion and religious emotion, personal conversion, the authority of the Bible as centered in the revelation of God in Christ, the importance of justification by faith, the preaching of the Word and the study of the gospel, the centrality of the cross for salvation, the importance of the believer's direct relationship with God, and a desire for pure and undefiled religion which included a strong aversion to worldliness and threats to public morals. Episcopal evangelicals attended prayer meetings which included informal prayers and enthusiastic singing of hymns. Evangelicals wrote many of the hymns that were used in the first years of the Episcopal Church. Evangelicals in the Episcopal Church used the Prayer Book and participated in the sacraments, but they did not emphasize the importance of sacramental form or the importance of apostolic succession. They saw much value in the less liturgical style of other Protestant churches and were impatient with canonical restrictions that prevented their participation in the services of other Protestant denominations or the participation of other Protestant ministers in Episcopal services. They were opposed to ritual excess, which they associated with the Roman Catholic Church. Bishop Charles P. McIlvaine of Ohio challenged the theology of the Oxford Movement in his *Oxford Divinity* (1841), which identified Oxford divinity with the Roman Catholic Church and urged that both served to undermine the Protestant doctrine of justification by faith. The evangelicals gave rise to the low church party in the Episcopal Church. Evangelicals have been at the center of the overseas missionary work of the Episcopal Church since the 1830s. Noted evangelicals in the Episcopal Church included Bishops Richard Channing

Moore and William Meade of Virginia; Philander Chase, Gregory T. Bedell, McIlvaine of Ohio; Alexander Viets Griswold of the Eastern Diocese, who later served as Presiding Bishop; and Alonzo Potter of Pennsylvania. Other notable evangelicals were Elizabeth Channing Moore, and the Rev. William H. Wilmer, who served as president of William and Mary College; and Francis Scott Key, author of "The Star-Spangled Banner." Evangelical principles guided the founding of the Virginia Theological Seminary in Alexandria, Virginia, by Meade, Wilmer, and others; and the founding by Chase of Kenyon College and Gambier Theological Seminary (later Bexley Hall) in Ohio.

Evangelical and Catholic Mission (ECM). At a meeting in Chicago on Dec. 1–2, 1976, several hundred clergy and laity from the United States and Canada considered the future of the Episcopal Church in light of the decision by the 1976 General Convention to allow the ordination of women to the priesthood and the episcopate. In 1977 some of them organized the Evangelical and Catholic Mission under the leadership of Bishop Stanley H. Atkins of Eau Claire. ECM later inaugurated a series of national congresses. It claimed to be evangelical because it affirmed the faith which is grounded in the authority of the Bible, and it claimed to be catholic because it adhered to the faith of the ancient, undivided, apostolic church. It was opposed to the ordination of women to the priesthood and the episcopate. At the June 1–3, 1989, ECM meeting at Fort Worth, Texas, the members voted to become the Episcopal Synod of America. On Sept. 15, 1977, ECM began publication of *The Evangelical Catholic*, using the name of a journal edited by William Augustus Muhlenberg and published in the 1850s.

Evangelical Catholic, The. This journal was published biweekly and then weekly from Sept. 13, 1851, until Dec. 30, 1852. It was founded and edited by William Augustus Muhlenberg. It was intended to be above the party divisions of the Episcopal Church at the time. Muhlenberg wanted to unite evangelical and catholic in the church. Its subtitle called it "A Paper Devoted Chiefly to Matters of Practical Christianity." *See* Muhlenberg, William Augustus.

Evangelical Catholics. This was a party or style of churchmanship which was advocated primarily by William Augustus Muhlenberg. Muhlenberg developed its ideas in his publication *The Evangelical Catholic*. An evangelical catholic is *evangelical* in stressing a personal faith in Jesus Christ and the role of the emotions in the Christian life. An evangelical catholic is *catholic* by adhering to the ancient documents of the faith, such as the Nicene and Athanasian Creeds and the Chalcedonian Definition of the Person of Christ, and by being "liberal, comprehensive, large-minded." *See* Muhlenberg, William Augustus.

Evangelical Education Society. This Society was founded on Nov. 3, 1862, under the leadership of the Rt. Rev. Alonzo Potter, Bishop of Pennsylvania, and incorporated on Nov. 1, 1869. It was "founded to educate for the Ministry of the Protestant Episcopal Church young men, who are in hearty sympathy with the Evangelical teaching of this Church as set forth in the Book of Common Prayer." As evangelicals, the members of the society believe in the elevation of the ministry of the word, and teach that the Bible is the "'Word of God written' as the Prayer Book says." The meaning of the biblical text is reliable when it tells us about God and the truth of God, and authoritative when it calls men and women to obedience. The society supports simplicity in the use of ceremonial so that no "human deportment" may interfere when the Word of God speaks to the heart and conscience of believers. The primary purpose of the society is to help qualified men and women to study in accredited seminaries of the Episcopal Church. It has helped more than 2,000 students in its history. It publishes *The Evangelical Outlook.* In 1981 the society published *A Prayer Book Manual*, "explaining in clear language the 1979 Book of Common Prayer."

Evangelical Episcopal Church. The Rev. George Dashiell, rector of St. Peter's Church, Baltimore, Maryland, was strongly opposed to the election of James Kemp, a high churchman, as Suffragan Bishop of Maryland. Kemp was elected and consecrated in 1814. Dashiell led seven or eight of the low church evangelicals in opposition to receiving Kemp as bishop. Dashiell renounced the ministry of the Episcopal Church and was deposed. He then organized the Evangelical Episcopal Church and assumed its leadership. The Evangelical Episcopal Church died out when Dashiell left Baltimore in 1826. *See* Dashiell, George.

Evangelical Fellowship in the Anglican Communion–USA (EFAC–USA). The American branch of the Evangelical Fellowship in the Anglican Communion, which the Rev. John R. Stott began after World War II. It was incorporated in the United States as the Fellowship of Witness. In 1996 it refocused on the links with the worldwide parent body by changing the name to EFAC–USA. It works to foster fellowship among evangelical Episcopalians, to practice evangelism as a biblical priority, and to provide training for biblical preaching in the Episcopal Church. The Fellowship publishes the *Episcopal Evangelical Journal. See* Fellowship of Witness.

Evangelical Knowledge Society. *See* Protestant Episcopal Society for the Promotion of Evangelical Knowledge.

Evangelical Movement, Evangelicalism. Evangelicalism first expressed itself in the Episcopal Church during the Great Awakening. From 1811 until 1873, there was a very significant evangelical movement or party within the Episcopal Church. The beginning of the movement can be dated from the consecration of Alexander Viets Griswold as Bishop of the Eastern Diocese on May 29, 1811. The evangelical party stressed adult renewal, whereas the Hobartian high church party stressed the baptismal covenant. Evangelicals stressed the absolute supremacy of the Bible as the only rule of faith and practice, the corruption of human nature by sin, the centrality of the atoning death of Jesus Christ, an experiential knowledge of Christ, a conversion experience, holiness of life, and a deep commitment to the work of mission and evangelism. In 1873 a number of evangelicals left the Episcopal Church and formed the Reformed Episcopal Church. In the twentieth century a liberal evangelical movement emerged. It retained evangelical principles, but combined them with new intellectual ideas such as Darwinism and higher criticism. In the 1970s a conservative evangelicalism emerged in the Episcopal Church. The founding of Trinity Episcopal School for Ministry in 1976 was an expression of that conservative evangelicalism. *See* Evangelical; *see* Reformed Episcopal Church; *see* Trinity Episcopal School for Ministry.

Evangelical Quarterly, The. It was published by the Protestant Episcopal Society for the Promotion of Christian Knowledge, also known as the Evangelical Knowledge Society. It was published in Philadelphia from Jan. 1860, until Sept. 1862.

Evangelism, Evangelist. From the Greek *euangelion*, "good news." An evangelist is one who tells the story of Jesus. The epistle to the Ephesians (4:11) names evangelists after apostles and prophets in the list of ministers in the NT church. Little else is said about evangelists or evangelism except that Philip was an evangelist (Acts 21:8), and Paul urged Timothy to "do the work of an evangelist" (2 Tm 4:5).

Later, in the early church, the word "evangelist" was used to describe the writer of a gospel and eventually considered an office. An evangelist is primarily someone who presents God's message to make known the good news of the life, suffering, and death of Jesus. The evangelist presents the importance and significance of the good news for the people of the evangelist's own time and cultural situation. Therefore, the message of specific evangelists can differ from what others have said, even though they are all presenting the good news. The term "evangelist" is now often used to refer to someone who is dedicated to evangelism or missionary work. The 1988 Lambeth Conference summarized evangelism simply as "the making of new Christians." It also asked each province and diocese of the Anglican Communion to make the closing years of this millennium a "Decade of Evangelism" with a renewed and united emphasis on making Christ known to the people of his world. The General Convention of 1991 designated the 1990s a "'Decade of Evangelism,' during which we will reclaim and affirm our baptismal call to evangelism and will endeavor, with other Christian denominations, to reach every unchurched person in the nine Provinces of the Episcopal Church with the Gospel of Jesus Christ." Evangelism is virtually synonymous with mission.

Evangelism, Standing Commission on. The General Convention of 1988 established this commission. It held up before the church the needs and opportunities for the exercise of the church's ministry of evangelism. It also had responsibility to develop policy and recommend appropriate action to the General Convention, the Executive Council and the dioceses. The 1997 General Convention discontinued this commission and formed the Standing Commission on Domestic Mission and Evangelism. *See* Domestic Mission and Evangelism, Standing Commission on.

Evans, Hugh Davey (Apr. 26, 1792–July 16, 1868). Lay theologian and defender of high church principles. He was born in Baltimore, Maryland. Evans began to study law when he was eighteen, and entered practice on Aug. 19, 1815. Throughout his life, Evans was a widely published author and an editor of church journals. From 1843 until 1856, he edited *The True Catholic*, a high church journal under the patronage of Bishop William Whittingham of Maryland. He also published articles in the *Protestant Episcopalian*, *The Register* (Philadelphia), *The Churchman*, and *The American Church Monthly*. Evans was a leader in conventions of the Diocese of Maryland, a deputy to the General Conventions, 1847–1859, and a defender of the Union. He was a lecturer on civil and ecclesiastical law at St. James College, Washington County, Maryland, 1852–1864. Evans died in Baltimore.

Eve (liturgical). The evening or day before a feast or other important celebration. Depending on local customs and practice, the celebration of a feast may begin on the eve of the feast. In many parishes, the principal Christmas services take place on Christmas Eve. The BCP provides directions for a Vigil of Pentecost (pp. 175, 227). The *BOS* provides forms for a Vigil for Christmas Eve, a Service for New Year's Eve (Eve of the Feast of the Holy Name), a Vigil for the Eve of All Saints' Day or the Sunday after All Saints' Day, a Service for All Hallows' Eve (Oct. 31), and a Vigil on the Eve of Baptism.

Evening Prayer. One of the principal Daily Offices. Evening Prayer has been the title for the Evening Office in Anglican worship since the 1552 revision of the Prayer Book. The BCP provides forms for Daily Evening Prayer in traditional and contemporary language (pp. 61, 115). Evening Prayer may begin with an opening sentence of scripture and with the confession of sin. The Invitatory may include the canticle *Phos Hilaron*, an ancient hymn praising Christ at the lighting of lamps at sunset. The office continues with a selection from the Psalter, readings from scripture followed by canticles (typically the *Magnificat* and *Nunc dimittis*), the Apostles' Creed, the Lord's Prayer, a set of suffrages, one or more collects, and the dismissal. One of the two suffrages is a version of the litany in the Evening Office of Eastern Orthodox churches with images of evening and death. Evening Prayer may also include an office hymn or anthem, the General Thanksgiving, a Prayer of St. Chrysostom, and a concluding sentence of scripture. *See* Daily Office.

Evensong. Since the late middle ages "evensong" has been the popular name for vespers (from the Latin *vesperis*, "evening"), the Evening Office of the western church. Cranmer used it in the 1549 BCP. Although in 1552 he replaced it with "Evening Prayer," the common name remains "evensong." In many Anglican cathedrals and other large churches, especially in England, evensong is sung by clergy and choir as a choral liturgy. *See* Evening Prayer.

Every Member Canvass. A parochial stewardship campaign that invites every member of the parish to make a pledge for the upcoming year. The campaign may urge the parishioners to offer their time, talent, and treasure. Members of the parish pledge to give a certain amount of money to the church. The campaign may encourage parishioners to tithe as an expression of Christian generosity and commitment. Parishioners may also pledge to participate in specific forms of Christian service and ministry. The campaign emphasizes the importance of inviting each member to make a pledge to the parish. Members of the stewardship or every member canvass committee may seek to contact all parish members by home visits or telephone. All members of the parish are urged to participate in stewardship as an expression of Christian generosity. *See* Stewardship.

Evolution. A process of development or unfolding. A dynamic "evolutionary" understanding of the development of the cosmos and the forms of life within it appeared in European thought before the nineteenth century. The theory of evolution was forcefully introduced into the English scene by Charles Darwin's *Origin of Species* (1859). Darwin argued that new species of animal life evolved over long periods of time from earlier species by wholly natural processes. The theory of evolution was subsequently applied to social as well as natural processes, perhaps without as much empirical foundation.

The church reacted at first with great hostility because the theory of evolution contradicted biblical teaching concerning the age of the world and the creation of the world in six days.

Anglican approaches to the theory of evolution were set by *Lux Mundi* (1883), a collection of essays edited by Bishop Charles Gore. Its contributors presented evolution as an intelligible account of the way God works creatively and continually within natural and historical process. *Lux Mundi* provided a helpful corrective to deism. The Episcopal theologian William Porcher DuBose (1836–1918) also viewed the theory of evolution sympathetically in his book *High Priesthood and Sacrifice* (1908), in which he considered atonement with God to be the ultimate evolution of humanity. *See* DuBose, William Porcher; *see* Gore, Charles.

Ewer. A pitcher for pouring water. It is typically made of silver or another precious metal, or pottery. A ewer may be used to pour water into the font before the prayer of thanksgiving over the water at baptism, or to fill basins for the washing of feet on Maundy Thursday. Images of a ewer and basin are commonly used to denote the servant ministry of the church and may therefore symbolize the diaconate.

Ewer, Ferdinand Cartwright (May 22, 1826–Oct. 10, 1883). Priest and leading nineteenth-century Anglo-catholic. He was born on Nantucket Island, Massachusetts. He graduated from Harvard College in 1849, and joined the California gold rush. In California he worked as an engineer and a newspaper editor. Ewer was a self-proclaimed agnostic, but he returned to the Episcopal Church in the mid-1850s. He was ordained deacon on Apr. 5, 1857, and priest on Jan. 26, 1858. Ewer served briefly at Grace Church, San Francisco, and at St. Ann's Church in New York City. He was called to be rector of Christ Church, New York City, in 1862. Ewer believed that Christians could be catholic without being Roman Catholic. He advocated the reunion of the Roman Catholic, Orthodox, and Episcopal communions in a series of sermons published in 1869. These ideas, along with the ritualist liturgical practices he introduced at Christ Church, led to his resignation from the parish in 1871. A number of supporters left with him and organized the Church of St. Ignatius, New York City, where Ewer served as rector for the rest of his life. He died during a preaching mission in Montreal, Canada.

Ex Opere Operantis. From the Latin, meaning "by the work of the doer." In sacramental theology, the phrase concerns the proper disposition of the minister or recipient of a sacrament. It does not deny the objective reality of the sacraments, but it indicates that the proper disposition is needed for the sacrament's full effectiveness in the life of the participant. For example, lack of faith can block or hinder the effectiveness of a sacrament in a person's life.

Ex Opere Operato. From the Latin, meaning "by the work done." In sacramental theology, the objective reality and effectiveness of the sacraments when validly celebrated, regardless of the subjective attitudes or qualities of the ministers or recipients. For example, the real presence of Christ in the eucharist is not diminished by the lack of faith of one who receives the eucharist. Similarly, the validity of sacraments does not depend on the worthiness of the ministers. *See* Donatism.

Exaltation of the Cross. *See* Holy Cross Day.

Examining Chaplains, General Board of. *See* General Board of Examining Chaplains (GBEC).

Excommunication. The disciplinary exclusion of a person from receiving communion by competent religious authority. It represents exclusion from the corporate life of the church. Excommunication was intended to encourage repentance and not meant to be a punishment. The Prayer Book Disciplinary Rubrics for the Holy Eucharist provide that if the priest "knows that a person who is living a notoriously evil life intends to come to Communion," the priest shall tell the person not to come to communion until the person "has given clear proof of repentance and amendment of life." Similarly, the priest shall not allow those who have wronged their neighbors and are a scandal to the other members of the congregation to receive communion "until they have made restitution for the wrong they have done, or have at least promised to do so." When there is hatred between members of the congregation, the priest shall deny communion to those who refuse to forgive. If one side is open to forgiveness and the other refuses forgiveness, the priest shall allow those who "desire and promise to make up for their faults" to receive communion. The priest shall refuse to allow "those who are stubborn" (BCP, p. 409). These rubrics are a modern language version of disciplinary rubrics in the 1549 Prayer Book. The 1662 BCP added the requirement that the Bishop be notified within 14 days of an excommunication. This safeguard against unwarranted excommunication is continued in the 1979 BCP. It states that in all cases of excommunication the priest must notify the bishop within 14 days, "giving the reasons for refusing Communion." In pastoral practice, the disciplinary rubric for excommunication is rarely used. Penitent persons at the point of death may not be refused communion.

Executive Council of the Episcopal Church. The national body that administers the program and policies adopted by the General Convention. It was called the National Council from 1919–1964. It is currently composed of twenty members elected by General Convention, eighteen members elected by the Provincial Synods, and the following *ex officio* members: the presiding bishop, the president of the House of Deputies, and the vice president, secretary, and treasurer of the Executive Council. Members are elected to six-year terms with half the membership elected each triennium. The body must have specified numbers of bishops, presbyters, and lay persons. The council meets at least three times each year.

Exegesis. Literally a "leading out." The term is used in biblical studies to signify the drawing out of the meaning of the texts of Holy Scripture. Some biblical scholars, notably Rudolf Bultmann, use the term to indicate what the text means to the contemporary reader or hearer. Others, such as Krister Stendahl, use the term for the meaning of the text as intended by the original author. Having discovered what the text *meant*, a further step of exposition is necessary to discover what the text now *means* to the contemporary reader or hearer.

Exhortation. An earnest admonishment. Two exhortations to prepare the congregation for communion were published in the 1548 Order for Communion, and these were included in the 1549 BCP. A third exhortation was added in the 1552 BCP. The 1928 BCP also included three exhortations, but the 1979 BCP has only one, a conflation of prior material (pp. 316-317). The exhortation is not printed with the Rite 2 eucharistic liturgy. The BCP allows the exhortation to be used in whole or in part during the liturgy or at other times. The exhortation recalls the institution of the eucharist and its benefits for a spiritual sharing in Christ's risen life and for making us one with Christ and members one of another. It also gives thanks to God for the creation of the world, for God's continual providence and love for us, for the Incarnation and our redemption through Christ, who died to "make us the children of God by the power of the Holy Spirit, and exalt us to everlasting life." As a public spiritual direction, the exhortation calls on the people to make a worthy approach to the eucharist, including examination of their lives and conduct. It advises those who "need help and counsel" to seek a suitable priest and make a sacramental confession of sin. The final paragraph is new to this revision, with allusions to the oblation of various eucharistic prayers in the 1979 BCP. *See* Oblation.

Exorcism. The driving out of evil spirits from persons or places with authority derived from Christ. The NT records exorcisms performed by Jesus, e.g., Mk 5:1–13, and by the apostles, e.g., Acts 16:18. The *BOS* does not provide a rite of exorcism, but it gives these guidelines: "Those who find themselves in need of such a ministry should make the fact known to the bishop, through their parish priest, in order that the bishop may determine whether exorcism is needed, who is to perform the rite, and what prayers or other formularies are to be used." Liturgies of the Episcopal Church retain elements of exorcism. Following an ancient tradition, several prayers of the catechumenate call for release from the powers of evil. More commonly, spiritual cleansing and deliverance is the practice of those who pray, "Deliver us from evil."

Exorcist. From early times certain Christians with charismatic gifts have been recognized to have the power to exorcise. Exorcist was also one of the old minor orders. Originally it designated a person whose liturgical duties included laying hands on catechumens (those preparing for baptism) and energumens (those possessed by unclean spirits). It was later one of the orders through which one passed on the way to priesthood. The Church of England abandoned minor orders at the Reformation, and the Roman Catholic Church suppressed them in 1972. Today an exorcist is a person appointed by the bishop to perform a rite of exorcism. An exorcist is usually but not necessarily a priest. *See* Minor Orders.

Exposition (Sacramental). Exhibition of the consecrated eucharistic bread for the purpose of devotion. The practice became common in the fourteenth century. It is an extension of the practice of the elevation of the host to be seen by the people during the words of institution in the eucharist. Popular devotion to the sacrament and the desire to see, rather than to receive, was characteristic of the late middle ages. Exposition was a method of extending this time. A monstrance may be used for exhibition of the Host. A monstrance is a gold or silver frame, usually in the form of a cross or a sunburst, with a glass case through which the host may be seen in the center. Exposition can also form the focus of a service of Benediction of the Blessed Sacrament, an extra-liturgical devotion, in which hymns (usually the eucharistic hymns of Thomas Aquinas) are sung and the priest blesses the people with the sacrament. Exposition ceased in the Church of England at the Reformation but was reintroduced by Anglo-catholics in the late nineteenth century. The BCP makes no provision for exposition, but it may be seen in parishes with an Anglo-catholic piety. The significance of exposition may be questioned relative to the proper use of the sacrament for the communion of the people of God.

Extempore Prayer. A free-form prayer without text. It may or may not reflect a stream of consciousness of prayer by the one who prays. Considerable preparation may have taken place before the prayer was offered, or the prayer may be a spontaneous expression. Extempore prayer is distinguished from prayers which are read or memorized.

Extreme Unction. Use of oil for the anointing of the sick at the time of death. After the seventh century, western Christianity associated the rites of anointing with penitence and death. This differed from the earlier practice of anointing for healing and recovery from illness. Unction became a rite reserved for situations *in extremis*, near death. The various movements of liturgical renewal in the twentieth century have recovered the anointing of the sick in its ancient sense as a rite of healing. Anointing may also be done at the time of death. *See* Anointing.

"EYC." *See* Episcopal Young Church People (EYC).

F

Fabian (d. Jan. 20, 250). Early Pope and martyr. According to the early church historian Eusebius of Caesarea, the Roman-born Fabian was chosen to succeed Pope Anterus when a dove descended from heaven and lighted on his head. He was Pope from Jan. 10, 236, until his death. Fabian was an opponent of the Gnostic heresies and a very effective administrator. Under his leadership the Roman church was strengthened, and its temporal power was increased. When the Emperor Decius began a persecution in the year 250, Fabian was arrested. He was treated brutally and among the first to die. He is commemorated in the Episcopal calendar of the church year on Jan. 20.

Faculty. 1) Authority or license from an ecclesiastical superior to perform an action. 2) A branch of instruction at a college, school, or university. The traditional university faculties were theology, canon and civil law, medicine, and arts. The term may also refer to the instructors in a branch of instruction at a school, a body of teachers, or the members of a learned profession.

Fair Linen. A long white cloth that covers the top of the altar. It typically hangs down some distance over the ends of the altar. The BCP directs that at the eucharist the altar "is spread with a clean white cloth during the celebration" (p. 406). Historically, in the early church, a small table was brought out and put in place for the liturgy of the table. A white cloth was spread on the table at this time. As late as the eighth century, a white cloth was spread upon the holy table during the eucharist by deacons after the liturgy of the word. It is appropriate for the altar cloth to be spread on the altar before the service or at the offertory. It may be embroidered with five crosses, one on each corner and one in the center. References to the fair linen date from the 1552 BCP.

Fairfield Academy. This school was opened in 1803 by the Rev. Caleb Alexander, a Presbyterian minister. In 1813 an Episcopalian, the Rev. Bethel Judd, became the Principal. Trinity Church, New York City, gave it a grant of $750 provided it should give free tuition to four divinity students of the Episcopal Church. As a result it was sometimes called a "Divinity School." When the third Episcopal principal, the Rev. Daniel McDonald, left in 1821 to become principal of the Geneva Academy, Trinity Church transferred its patronage to the Geneva Academy, and Fairfield Academy ceased to be an Episcopal institution.

Faith Alive. A weekend format for congregational renewal in the Episcopal Church. It focuses reflection on the baptismal covenant, lay faith sharing, and prayer. It was organized in Jan. 1970, at the annual meeting of the Brotherhood of St. Andrew, after a number of men and women shared their experiences on Lay Renewal Weekends in Methodist churches. The Methodist program is called Lay Witness Mission. Fred Gore, a Delaware layman, and others decided to adapt that program to an Episcopal format. It was named for a series of taped personal testimonies that had been circulated by the Brotherhood entitled "Faith Alive." The weekends are coordinated by clergy and laity of the congregation sponsoring the weekend. They are assisted by a team of visiting laity with experience in the Faith Alive format. Weekends begin on Thursday evening and culminate in the congregation's worship on Sunday. There are large and small group gatherings throughout the weekend, both in the church buildings and in private homes. Components for children and youth are included. Faith Alive is designed to build strong small groups and to reach those on the periphery of church membership.

Faith and Order. The Faith and Order Movement was an early attempt to reunite the divided Christian churches by means of dialogue and analysis of divisive issues of doctrine (faith) and polity (order). The 1910 General Convention passed a resolution to appoint a joint commission to bring about a conference to consider questions concerning faith and order, and to invite all Christian communions to join in arranging and conducting the conference. The joint commission was continued by the General Conventions of 1913, 1916, 1919, and 1922, and a preliminary meeting was held at Geneva in Aug. 1920. The first World Conference on Faith and Order was held at Lausanne, Aug. 3–21, 1927, with the Episcopal Church as one of the convening churches. The Episcopal Church was represented and the president of the conference was Charles Henry Brent, Bishop of Western New York. The second World Conference was held at Edinburgh, Aug. 3–18, 1937, and the Episcopal Church sent ten delegates. When the World Council of Churches was formed in 1948, Faith and Order became a commission of the council. The 1982 meeting of the Faith and Order Commission issued *Baptism, Eucharist, and Ministry*, which represented an unprecedented convergence among the Christian churches of the world on these topics. *See* Brent, Charles Henry; *see* Life and Work; *see* World Conference on Faith and Order.

Faldstool. Backless chair with arms or stool that can be used for sitting or as a prayer desk. The term is from the Latin, "folding stool." It is portable, and it may or may not fold. It was historically used by a bishop or prelate who does not occupy the episcopal throne in the sanctuary. The term may indicate a prie-dieu or litany desk.

Fanfare. A brief composition, usually for brass instruments or organ trumpet stops. A fanfare is often in a martial style used to proclaim important events, such as the moment a new bishop is presented to a congregation following ordination and consecration.

Fast. Fasting is abstaining wholly or partially from all or certain foods, for physical or spiritual health. The extent and rigor of abstinence depends largely on custom and circumstance. Ancient Jews used fasting extensively. Christ taught it and practiced it. Early Christians fasted on specific days of the week, especially Wednesday and Friday. Baptismal candidates fasted for up to two days before their baptism. By the late middle ages abstinence from food was required before the reception of communion, and western Christians also fasted during Lent by abstaining from meat. As a spiritual discipline, fasting is an act of contrition, cleansing, and preparation. The BCP recommends fasting for the season of Lent, which Christians should observe "by self-examination and repentance; by prayer, fasting, and self-denial; and by reading and meditating on God's Word" (BCP, p. 265). The BCP designates the weekdays of Lent and Holy Week and all Fridays except in the seasons of Christmas and Easter as days of "special devotion" with "special acts of discipline and self-denial" (which normally include fasting). An exception is made for the feast of the Annunciation in Lent and feasts of our Lord on Friday. Although modern social habits have led to a decline in fasting on Fridays, and in Lent and Holy Week, the BCP calls for fasting, discipline, and self-denial on those days.

"Father." Honorific title used by some male priests. Anglican usage of the title dates from the ritual revival of the Anglo-catholic movement of the nineteenth century. It was borrowed from Roman Catholic practice, and it spread to widespread acceptance among Anglo-catholics. By the late twentieth century, the title was used widely by male priests in the Episcopal Church, including many who were not Anglo-catholics. Its counterpart, "Mother," is sometimes used by female priests. The BCP does not require the use of any title by priests.

Fauxbourdon, or Faburden. From the French, meaning "false bass," this fifteenth-century term is used to describe a style of composition in which the melody, usually a plainsong tune, is moved to a lower voice, often the tenor. Since much early chant-based music found the melody in the lower or bass voice, music in this style was given the name "fauxbourdon." Early examples of what later became known as Anglican chant were written as fauxbourdon.

Feast of the Tabernacles (Booths). One of three great festivals of Israel requiring attendance of all males. Also called Ingathering (in Hebrew, Sukkoth), Tabernacles was an autumn feast observed at the time of the full moon of the seventh month. It continued for eight days (Ex 23:16; 34:22; Lv 23:33–36; Dt. 16:13–17). The Feast of the Tabernacles came at the conclusion of the harvests of grapes, olives, and fruits. During its course the participants lived in tents or booths covered with branches, and thus remembered the forty years when their ancestors did the same as they wandered in the wilderness after the Exodus. It was such an important observance that it came to be referred to as *the* feast. It is referred to in Jn 7:10. The Feast of Tabernacles is a festival that has continued to be observed by Jewish people into the present. Passover/ Leaven and Weeks/Pentecost are the other two great festivals of Israel at which the attendance of all males is required.

Feasts of the Church Year. The calendar of the church year includes two cycles of feasts and holy days. One cycle is based on the movable date of Easter Day, and the other is based on the fixed date of Christmas Day, Dec. 25. Easter Day is the first Sunday after the full moon that falls on or after Mar. 21. The four Sundays of Advent are the four Sundays before Christmas Day (BCP, p. 15). The principal feasts of the church year are Easter Day, Ascension Day, the Day of Pentecost, Trinity Sunday, All Saints' Day (Nov. 1), Christmas Day, and the Epiphany (Jan. 6). Ascension Day is celebrated on the Thursday forty days after Easter. The Day of Pentecost is the eighth Sunday after Easter, the fiftieth day of the Easter season. Trinity Sunday is the Sunday after the Day of Pentecost, nine Sundays after Easter. All Saints' Sunday is the Sunday following All Saints' Day, Nov. 1, and the feast may be observed on either day. The principal feasts take precedence over any other observance.

The feasts of the Holy Name (Jan. 1), the Presentation (Feb. 2), and the Transfiguration (Aug. 6) also take precedence over the usual Sunday observance if they fall on a Sunday. These are Feasts of our Lord. Other Feasts of our Lord include the Annunciation (Mar. 25), the Visitation (May 31), St. John the Baptist (June 24), and Holy Cross Day (Sept. 14). Other major feasts include all feasts of Apostles, all feasts of Evangelists, St. Stephen (Dec. 26), the Holy Innocents (Dec. 28), St. Joseph (Mar. 19), St. Mary Magdalene (July 22), St. Mary the Virgin (Aug. 15), St. Michael and All Angels (Sept. 29), St. James of Jerusalem (Oct. 23), Independence Day (July 4), and Thanksgiving Day.

There are other days of optional observance, including the commemorations listed in the calendar of the church year. The BCP provides proper readings and collects for the major feasts. Propers for the lesser feasts and fixed holy days are published in *Lesser Feasts and Fasts.* The BCP also provides the Common of Saints, which are propers for general categories of lesser saints such as martyrs, missionaries, pastors, theologians and teachers, and monastics.

Federal Council of Churches of Christ in America (FCC). FCC was a Protestant ecumenical organization founded in 1908 to coordinate the social action programs of its member denominations. In Nov. 1905, the Interchurch Conference on Federation assembled at Carnegie Hall in New York City. The Carnegie Hall conference approved a plan that intended both "to manifest the essential oneness of the Christian churches of America" and "to promote the application of the law of Christ in every relation of human life." Delegates from thirty-three denominations formally brought the FCC into being at a meeting in Philadelphia in Dec. 1908. They also established a Commission on Church and Social Service at the 1908 meeting. In 1912 the FCC adopted the Social Creed of the Churches, which became a classic statement of the ideals of the Social Gospel. The initial membership of the FCC represented approximately eighteen million American Protestants. Although the Episcopal Church did not join, it established a cooperative relationship with the FCC. The FCC merged in 1950 with several other interdenominational groups to form the National Council of Churches, of which the Episcopal Church is a member. *See* Social Gospel.

Federation of Episcopal Priests. This group, first called the Federation of Independent Episcopal Priests, was organized in July 1978 by three priests. The convenor of the group was the Rev. Roy Benton Davis, Jr., rector of Grace Church, Louisville, Kentucky. He later renounced the ordained ministry of the Episcopal Church and was deposed on Feb. 2, 1986. The group wanted to be loyal to the doctrine, discipline, and worship "of the 1928 Prayer Book—or actually, 1549 through 1928." On Apr. 27, 1979, a number of sympathetic clergy met at St. John's Church, Kansas City, Missouri, and issued "A Statement of Conscience." Their primary purpose was to have the right to continue using the 1928 BCP. The Federation was opposed to the ordination of women, and insisted that at the "official seminaries . . . the theology is very liberal, the moral theology is relativistic." The Federation is no longer in existence.

Felicitas, or St. Felicity. One of the martyrs at Carthage. She was the slave of St. Perpetua when Perpetua and other African catechumens were arrested in the persecution of the Emperor Septimius Severus (193–211). They were put in prison. A number of Carthaginians were martyred in 202, including Felicitas. A contemporary account of the martyrdoms is in *The Martyrdom of Perpetua and Felicity*. Felicitas is commemorated on Mar. 7, the feast of Perpetua and her Companions, Martyrs at Carthage. *See* Perpetua and her Companions.

Fellowship of Concerned Churchmen. This group was founded in the summer of 1973 as the Coalition of Concerned Churchmen. It was a leading organization for those dissatisfied with developments in the Episcopal Church in the 1970s. At its peak it included the following groups: The American Church Union, *The Anglican Digest*, The Canterbury Guild, *The Certain Trumpet*, Congregation of St. Augustine (CSA), Council for the Faith (Canada), The Episcopal Guild for the Blind, Episcopal Renaissance of Pennsylvania, Episcopalians United, The Foundation for Christian Theology, *The Living Church*, The Society of the Holy Cross (SSC), SPEAK, and the Society for the Preservation of the Book of Common Prayer. After the General Convention of 1976 voted to allow the ordination of women to the priesthood and the episcopate, the Fellowship called a church Congress. The congress met at St. Louis on Sept. 14–16, 1977, to discuss the "ecclesiastical structure of the continuing Episcopal Church." The congress adopted the "Affirmation of St. Louis" which was basic to a number of new churches with an Anglican heritage. It laid the groundwork for a new church with the provisional title, "Anglican Church of North America." The fellowship then went out of existence.

Fellowship of Contemplative Prayer. It was organized in England in 1946 by the Rev. Robert G. Coulson. He was on a committee appointed by the Archbishop of Canterbury during World War II which produced a report entitled "Toward the Conversion of England." Coulson was convinced that England could be reclaimed for Christ and the church after the war through a great deepening of its collective life of prayer. Coulson gathered a small group of clergy for a retreat, and the fellowship was born. The Rev. Richard Lyon Stinson established the fellowship in the United States in 1971. The founding retreat of the American fellowship was held in Sept. 1971 at a Trappist monastery in Berryville, Virginia. Members of the fellowship follow a simple rule stressing daily contemplation of the scriptures. They attend an annual retreat. Coulson's books include *On Prayer* (n.d.), *I Am: The Exercise of Supreme Sovereignty* (n.d.), and *Into God: An Exercise in Contemplation* (1956). His writings were formative for the fellowship.

Fellowship of Reconciliation, The (FOR). The FOR seeks to address violence, racism, and economic injustice on the local level. It opposes militarism and war. The FOR was founded in Cambridge, England, in 1914 when Henry Hodgkin, an English Quaker, and Friedrich Sigmund-Schultze, a German Lutheran pastor, pledged to remain friends and to continue to work for peace even though their countries were at war. In 1915 it was established in the United States. Important leadership in the American branch of the FOR was provided by two Episcopal clergy, Bishop Paul Jones and the Rev. John Nevin Sayre. The FOR is now organized in twenty-seven countries. It has an international secretariat in Holland. The FOR is comprised of persons who recognize the essential unity of all humanity and who have joined together to explore the power of love and truth for resolving human conflict. As a pacifist organization, it has always vigorously opposed war. As a peace and justice community, it has sought to achieve a world order upholding the full dignity and freedom of every human being. The FOR offers itself as a resource for local communities who seek alternatives to violence and injustice. The Episcopal Peace Fellowship is a member of the FOR. The headquarters of the American branch is in Nyack, New York.

Fellowship of St. Alban and St. Sergius. This ecumenical group developed from the British Student Christian Movement and the Russian Student Christian Movement in Exile during the post-World War I period. It was founded at a meeting of English and Russian students and theologians at St. Alban's Retreat House, England, Dec. 28, 1927–Jan. 2, 1928. Its purpose is to further mutual understanding and cooperation among Christians of east and west. The fellowship promotes friendship, study, dialogue, prayer, common work, increased understanding, and unity. It is named for national patron saints in England and Russia. It is more active in England than in the United States. The fellowship has operated the study centers known as St. Basil's House in London and the House of St. Gregory and St. Macrina in Oxford. The first issue of its quarterly, *The Journal of St. Alban and St. Sergius*, was published in June 1928. In the Mar. 1935 issue, the name was changed to *Sobornost*, which means conciliatory, charitable collaboration. In England it sponsors an annual conference for worship but not intercommunion, although the sharing of eucharistic worship is a goal. There are chapters of the fellowship in various countries. Membership is open to Christians of any denomination. Most of the participants in the fellowship have been Anglican or Russian Orthodox.

Fellowship of St. Gregory and St. Augustine, The. *See* St. Gregory and St. Augustine, Fellowship of.

Fellowship of Witness (FOW). Predecessor of the Evangelical Fellowship of the Anglican Communion-USA. It was founded in May 1965 at Carroll Lodge, Pawling, New York, by Philip Edgcombe Hughes and Peter Childress Moore. Hughes and Moore were both priests in the Episcopal Church. It is the American branch of the Evangelical Fellowship in the Anglican Communion, founded by John R. W. Stott in 1961. It took its current name at the May 2–4, 1996, meeting of the Episcopal Evangelical Assembly at Sewickley, Pennsylvania. It is frequently referred to as EFAC-USA. It is committed to historic, biblical Christianity and seeks to preserve the evangelical heritage of the Anglican tradition. FOW was the founder of Trinity Episcopal School for Ministry in 1976. It sponsors the Episcopal Evangelical Assembly and the Expository Preaching Workshop. FOW began publishing a journal called *Christian Foundations* in 1965. This journal was later taken over by Trinity Episcopal School for Ministry. EFAC-USA began publishing *The Episcopal Evangelical Journal* in July 1994. *See* Evangelical Fellowship in the Anglican Communion (EFAC-USA).

Feria, or Ferial Day. An ordinary weekday in the liturgical calendar, a day that is neither a feast nor a fast. A ferial day is understood as an extension of the preceding Sunday. The collect and proper readings for the Sunday eucharist are used in weekday celebrations of the eucharist unless otherwise provided. Ferial days became important in the western church in the early middle ages as daily Mass became customary. The term originally meant "holiday" or "day of rest" in Latin.

Fermentum. Small pieces of the consecrated bread from the episcopal Mass, called fermentum (leaven), were sent to parish churches and placed in the consecrated wine at the eucharist to signify the unity of the Christian assembly with their bishop. This practice dates from the fifth century in Rome. It continues today in some dioceses of the

Episcopal Church on Maundy Thursday. A fragment of bread from a eucharist celebrated by the bishop during Holy Week is placed in the cup after the eucharistic prayer at the evening parish liturgy. A related custom is called commixture, in which the presider places a fragment of consecrated bread in the cup at every eucharist. It is infrequently practiced in the Episcopal Church today. *See* Commixture.

Ferrar, Nicholas (Feb. 22, 1592–Dec. 4, 1637). Priest and founder of Little Gidding. He was born in London. Ferrar received his B.A. in 1610 and his M.A. in 1613, both from Clare College, Cambridge. In 1626 Ferrar, his widowed mother, and the families of his brother and brother-in-law established a religious community at Little Gidding, Huntingdonshire, England. They said the Daily Offices, kept vigils throughout the night, and practiced meditation. Every person there was to learn a trade. The Puritans called Little Gidding a "Protestant nunnery," and in 1641 it was attacked in a pamphlet entitled *The Arminian Nunnery.* Early in 1647 the manor house and the chapel were destroyed by the Parliamentary army. Ferrar died at Little Gidding. The poet T. S. Eliot used Little Gidding as the inspiration and title of one of his *Four Quartets* (1935–1942). Ferrar is commemorated in the Episcopal calendar of the church year on Dec. 1. *See* Little Gidding.

Ferris, Theodore Parker (Dec. 23, 1908–Nov. 26, 1972). Seminary professor and ecumenist. He was born in Port Chester, New York. Ferris received his B.A. from Harvard University in 1929 and his B.D. from General Theological Seminary in 1933. He was ordained deacon on June 11, 1933, and priest on May 27, 1934. From 1933 until 1937, Ferris was assistant to the rector of Grace Church, New York, and at the same time served as fellow and tutor at General Seminary. From 1937 until 1942, he was rector of Emmanuel Church, Baltimore, and from 1942 until his death, he was the fourteenth rector of Trinity Church, Boston, Massachusetts. Many of his publications were books of sermons. He published a book on preaching, *Go Tell the People* (1951), in which he stated that "A sermon is by nature a disclosure, an unveiling, a revelation . . . to preach is to draw the curtain aside from the figure of Christ and to lose oneself in the folds of it." From 1943 until 1963, Ferris was instructor in homiletics at the Episcopal Theological School, Cambridge, Massachusetts. He was active in the ecumenical movement and an alternate delegate to the first assembly of the World Council of Churches at Amsterdam in 1948. Ferris died in Boston.

Festal. Concerning a feast day or festivity. Something that is joyous and festive.

Festivals (Ecclesiastical). *See* Feasts of the Church Year.

Filioque. Latin for "and the Son." The words were added to the Nicene Creed at the Council of Toledo in 589 and gradually grew in acceptance in the west. The *filioque* states that the Holy Spirit proceeds not only from the Father, but from the Father *and* the Son. The Eastern Orthodox churches condemn the addition as contrary to the admonition of the Council of Chalcedon (451) that no change be made in the faith expressed in the Nicene Creed. Disagreement over the *filioque* was a major cause of conflict between the eastern and western churches. The Lambeth Conference of 1988 recommended that the phrase be dropped from the Nicene Creed in Anglican churches. The 1994 General Convention of the Episcopal Church resolved to delete the *filioque* from the Nicene Creed in the next edition of the Prayer Book. *See* Pneumatology.

Findings in Religious Education. This periodical was published by the Department of Religious Education of the National Council of the Episcopal Church from Mar. 1927 until Oct. 1932. It was for leaders in Christian education.

First Day. *See* Sunday.

First Promise, The. On Sept. 9, 1997, twenty-six clergy met at All Saints' Church, Waccamaw, Pawley's Island, South Carolina, and organized The First Promise. The First Promise refers to a statement in the BCP services for ordination of priests and deacons, whose "first promise" is "to be loyal to the doctrine, discipline, and worship of Christ as this Church has received them" (pp. 526, 538). The document, "The First Promise," states that many of the leaders of the Episcopal Church have abandoned "the faith once delivered to the saints." The document also states that there were three actions of the 1997 General Convention which demonstrate this alleged defection from the faith: the election of a primate (Frank Griswold) who has departed from the teaching of the apostles; the mandatory and coercive enforcement of the ordination of women; and the failure to uphold and require a biblical sexual ethic for the Episcopal Church's clergy and people. The document further states that "the Domestic and Foreign Missionary Society, headquartered at 815 Second Avenue in New York City, and the present structures of the General Convention have departed from 'the doctrine, discipline, and worship of Christ as this Church has received them,' and we declare their authority to be fundamentally impaired, and that they are not upholding the truth of the gospel."

Fish (Christian Symbol). *See* ICHTHUS (ICHTHS).

Flagon. A large vessel with handle and spout, shaped like a pitcher. It is used as a container for wine or water at the eucharist. It may be made of metal, pottery, or glass. The Prayer Book directs that only one chalice is to be on the altar during the Great Thanksgiving. This emphasizes the symbolism of the common cup. If more wine is needed, a flagon of wine may be consecrated at the eucharist. Additional chalices may be filled from the flagon after the breaking of the bread (BCP, p. 407).

Fletcher, Joseph Francis (Apr. 10, 1905–Oct. 28, 1991). Leading proponent of situation ethics. He was born in Newark, New Jersey. He received his B.A. from the University of West Virginia in 1929 and his B.D. from the Berkeley Divinity School in the same year. He was ordained deacon on June 23, 1929, and priest on Sept. 7, 1930. He taught at St. Mary's College, Raleigh, 1932–1935, and was acting dean of St. Paul's Cathedral, Cincinnati. He was dean of the Graduate School of Applied Religion in Cincinnati from 1936 to 1944 and subsequently called to the Episcopal Theological School, Cambridge. While at ETS he was successively assistant professor of pastoral theology and social studies, 1944–1953; professor of Christian ethics, 1953–1955; and professor of social ethics, 1955–1970. Following his retirement from ETS in 1987, he was appointed professor of medical ethics in the University of Virginia Medical School. His major publications are *Morals and Medicine* (1954), *William Temple, Twentieth Century Christian* (1963), *Situation Ethics: The New Morality* (1966), and *Moral Responsibility: Situation Ethics at Work* (1967). *Morals and Medicine* was a series of discussions of critical ethical issues in health care. It was the basis for his utilitarian ethical theory which he expanded in his later two books on situation ethics. His critics accused him of destroying all ethics by relativizing principles for the guidance of conduct. Fletcher was a significant figure in the post-World War II ethical debates on the roles of deeds and rules in the moral life. He exerted a widespread influence in the medical and ethical community. Fletcher died in Charlottesville, Virginia.

Florida, Diocese of. The primary convention of this diocese met at St. John's Church, Tallahassee, on Jan. 17, 1838. However, the diocese did not consecrate a bishop until Oct. 15, 1851. On May 2, 1861, the diocese voted to send delegates to the first preliminary meeting of the dioceses of the Confederate States which met July 3–6, 1861, at Montgomery, Alabama. On Feb. 22, 1866, the diocese voted to rejoin the Protestant Episcopal Church. The General Convention of 1892 divided the diocese and created the Missionary Jurisdiction of Southern Florida. The General Convention of 1970 voted to divide the Diocese of Florida again and created a new diocese from Northwest Florida and South Alabama. The Diocese of Florida consists of the following counties: Alachua, Baker, Bradford, Clay, Columbia, Dixie, Duval, Flagler, Franklin (except the city of Apalachicola), Gadsden, Gilchrist, Hamilton, Jefferson, Lafayette, Leon, Levy, Liberty, Madison, Nassau, Putnam, St. John's, Suwannee, Taylor, Union, and Wakulla. On May 4, 1951, St. John's Church, Jacksonville, was set apart as St. John's Cathedral.

Flushing Institute. A school for boys founded by William Augustus Muhlenberg. Muhlenberg resigned as rector of St. James' Church, Lancaster, Pennsylvania, in 1826, and moved to Flushing, Long Island. He became supply priest at St. George's Church in Flushing, and later became the rector. Several men in Flushing wanted to establish an academy for boys and asked Muhlenberg to be the head instructor. He accepted, and the school opened in the spring of 1828. Muhlenberg served in this position for eighteen years. He made the school the model for other church schools in the United States. Flushing Institute stressed the ideals of a Christian atmosphere, the role of the Bible in the curriculum, physical education, and a sense of family life. One of the most famous schools influenced by Flushing is St. Paul's School, Concord, New Hampshire. Flushing Institute closed in 1848. *See* Muhlenberg, William Augustus; *see* St. Paul's School, Concord, New Hampshire.

"Fond du Lac Circus." Pejorative name given to the ceremony in which Reginald Heber Weller was consecrated Bishop Coadjutor of the Diocese of Fond du Lac on Nov. 8, 1900. Charles C. Grafton was the Bishop of Fond du Lac

at the time and a leading proponent of Anglo-catholicism. Grafton's bishop coadjutor was consecrated with a fullness of ceremonial that was unprecedented in the Episcopal Church. All officiating bishops wore copes and miters. Chrism was used in the consecration, and the newly ordained bishop was given an episcopal ring and a pastoral staff. Bishops from the Russian Orthodox Church and the Polish National (Old) Catholic Church were also present and fully vested in accordance with their traditions. Considerable uproar resulted in some parts of the Episcopal Church when a picture of the assembled bishops was published in *The Living Church*. Weller's consecration, known through this controversial photograph, was referred to as the "Fond du Lac Circus." The ordinations of bishops now routinely include many of the liturgical practices and customs that led to controversy over the "Fond du Lac Circus." *See* Anglo-Catholic Movement, Anglo-Catholicism; *see* Grafton, Charles Chapman.

Fond du Lac, Diocese of. The General Convention of 1874 voted to divide the Diocese of Wisconsin. The primary convention of the Diocese of Fond du Lac met at St. Paul's Church, Fond du Lac, on Jan. 7, 1875. On Jan. 11, 1877, St. Paul's Church, Fond du Lac, was set apart as St. Paul's Cathedral. The General Convention of 1928 voted to create a new diocese from the dioceses of Fond du Lac and Milwaukee. The new diocese was the Diocese of Eau Claire. The Diocese of Fond du Lac consists of the following counties: Adams (eastern part), Brown, Calumet, Door, Florence, Fond du Lac, Forest, Green Lake, Kewaunee, Langdale, Lincoln, Manitowoc, Marathon, Marinette, Menominee, Oconto, Oneida, Outagamie, Portage, Shawano, Sheboygan, Vilas, Waupaca, Waushara, Winnebago, and Wood. *See* Grafton, Charles Chapman.

Font. The term comes from the Latin *fons*, "spring of water," and designates a receptacle for baptismal water. Fonts in the early church were pools or sunken basins, often in the shape of a cross, in which candidates were immersed in running water. Many fonts remained large even after infant baptism became the norm, but they were raised above ground for convenience. Eventually the typical font was the size of a wash basin, and even adult candidates were baptized by pouring a little water on their heads. The ancient practice never died out, however, and the BCP lists immersion as a method of baptizing. Today some new or renovated church buildings have a large font, suitable for immersion, located where the people can easily see it or gather around it.

Footpace, or Foot-Pace. *See* Predella.

Foot Washing. The washing of feet was a menial act of hospitality in the OT (see Gn 18:4, 19:2). It was often performed for guests by a servant or the wife of the host. The Gospel of John (13:1–17) records that Jesus washed the feet of the disciples at the Last Supper. Jesus urged the disciples to follow his example of generous and humble service. They should wash one another's feet, as their feet had been washed by Jesus, their Lord and Teacher. Jesus' washing of the disciples' feet was a lived expression of his teaching that "whoever wishes to be first among you must be slave of all" (Mk 10:43–44). The foot-washing also expressed Jesus' "new commandment" for his disciples to love one another, as he had loved them (Jn 13:34). The washing of feet continued in the early Christian church. The requirements for enrollment on the list of widows includes the expectation that a widow would have "washed the saints' feet" (1 Tm 4:9–10). The ceremonial washing of feet is mentioned by Augustine of Hippo (354–430). The foot-washing has been associated with the Maundy Thursday liturgy since the seventh century in Spain. The name "Maundy" is from the Latin antiphon that was used on this day, based on Jesus' "new commandment" of love on the Thursday before his death. The foot-washing has also been associated with baptism. In the ancient Gallican rites, the feet of the newly baptized were washed by the ranking prelate after baptism.

The early editions of the Prayer Book did not provide for the foot-washing. The 1979 BCP restored the washing of feet as an option for the Maundy Thursday service. The foot-washing follows the gospel and homily. Representatives of the congregation may be appointed to have their feet washed by the celebrant. The celebrant may be assisted by other ministers or acolytes. The BCP provides anthems that may be sung or said during the ceremony (pp. 274–275). Musical settings for these anthems are available in the Appendix of *The Hymnal 1982 Accompaniment Edition, Vol. 1* (S 344–S 347). It is also traditional to use the hymn "*Ubi Caritas*" at the foot-washing (see Hymns 576, 577, 581, 606). The *BOS* provides a brief address that may be used by the celebrant to introduce the ceremony of foot-washing. This statement recalls Jesus' teaching that "strength and growth in the life of the Kingdom of God come not by power, authority, or even miracle, but by such lowly service" as the washing of feet.

Forbes, John Murray (May 5, 1807–Oct. 11, 1885). Controversial priest and seminary dean. He was born in New York City. Forbes graduated from Columbia College in 1827 and from the General Theological Seminary in 1830. He was ordained deacon on Aug. 1, 1830, and priest on May 24, 1831. Forbes began his ordained ministry as a tutor at Trinity College, Hartford, Connecticut. He resigned that position in 1835 to become the rector of St. Luke's Church, New York City. While there he was influenced by the Tractarians. On Nov. 21, 1849, he renounced the ordained ministry of the Episcopal Church. He joined the Roman Catholic Church, and on Feb. 27, 1850, he was deposed from the ordained ministry of the Episcopal Church. Forbes was ordained a Roman Catholic priest on Nov. 16, 1850. In 1855 he was awarded a papal doctorate by Pius IX but on Oct. 17, 1859, he left the Roman Catholic Church. He was restored to the Episcopal priesthood on Nov. 20, 1862. Upon his return to the Episcopal Church, Forbes became the associate rector of St. Luke's, his former parish. Forbes was the first person elected dean of the General Theological Seminary by the Board of Trustees under the revised statutes of 1867. Prior to his election as dean, resident professors at General Seminary served as dean in annual rotation. Forbes returned to the Episcopal Church a firm Protestant, militantly anti-Roman and anti-ritualist. He resigned as dean on Nov. 1, 1872, and retired. Forbes died in Elizabeth, New Jersey.

Forgiveness. To forgive is to give up or absolve legitimate claims upon another, as when a debt is forgiven. In forgiveness, a relationship is restored or renewed. Central to Christian faith is the forgiveness of sins, understood as an action of God. God is understood to be forgiving, a God of love, mercy, and grace.

Form (Sacramental). In sacramental theology, the words of prayer that express the meaning of the sacrament and the matter used in the sacrament. The words and the matter of the sacrament constitute a valid sacrament when used with appropriate intent by an appropriate minister. At the eucharist the form is the Great Thanksgiving that is said in the consecration of the bread and wine. The BCP notes that in an emergency any baptized person may administer baptism according to the following form, "I baptize you in the Name of the Father, and of the Son, and of the Holy

Spirit." This form is joined to the ministration of water (BCP, p. 313). The sacramental form may be understood in terms of the minimum words required for the sacrament to be valid. It is not a particular verbal formula as such. For example, the BCP provides a variety of forms for the Great Thanksgiving at the eucharist. *See* Matter (Sacramental).

Form Criticism. A scholarly method used for the interpretation of biblical texts. A form is a passage or unit of biblical material. It has a structure that is considered self-consistent. Units include miracle story, pronouncement story, legend, and saying. Herman Gunkel is an important OT form critic; Martin Dibelius and Rudolf Bultmann are two of the most important NT form critics. Form criticism assumes that a unit was transmitted orally before being written. Form criticism is often described as a search for the "history of the tradition." Form criticism considers how the forms were transmitted orally before they were written in the document where they now exist. Since the material in the Bible represents a later written stage, this method works backward from the complex written form toward the much simpler oral form. It is assumed that the forms were modified or edited as they were transmitted. The goal is to reconstruct a hypothetical, earlier, oral tradition. Some "form critics," such as Vincent Taylor, do not emphasize the importance of the history of the tradition. Their analysis of the form is simply a recognition of its literary features. Most form critics seek to understand the "situation of life" (*Sitz im Leben*) of the early church and gospel writers or editors when they wrote down the modified material. Form criticism evolved into redaction criticism, the search for the theology of an editor, such as Matthew or Mark, and the rationale for their own distinctive gospel forms and stories. *See* Apophthegm.

Fort Valley College, Georgia. Predecessor to Fort Valley State College. The Fort Valley High and Industrial School at Fort Valley, Georgia, was chartered in 1895. Under its second principal, Henry A. Hunt (d. 1938), the trustees voted on Nov. 11, 1918, to place the school under the auspices of the Diocese of Atlanta, with the Bishop of Atlanta as chairman of the board of trustees. In 1919 the school affiliated with the American Church Institute for Negroes of the Episcopal Church. The Diocese of Georgia joined the Diocese of Atlanta in 1928 in partial support of the school. Affiliation with the American Church Institute was discontinued in 1939 when the school passed from

church to state control. On July 1, 1939, the State Teachers and Agricultural College at Forsyth, Georgia, merged with the Fort Valley High and Industrial School to create Fort Valley State College.

Fort Worth, Diocese of. The General Convention of 1982 voted to divide the Diocese of Dallas and establish a new diocese. At that time it was named the Western Diocese. The primary convention met at All Saints' Church, Fort Worth, on Nov. 13, 1982, and changed the name to the Diocese of Fort Worth. On Sept. 1, 1986, All Saints' Church, Fort Worth, became All Saints' Cathedral. However, on Oct. 3, 1991, it reverted to All Saints' Church. On Jan. 9, 1995, Bishop Jack Iker designated St. Vincent's Church, Bedford, the pro-cathedral of the diocese. The Diocese of Fort Worth consists of the following counties: Archer, Bosque, Brown, Clay, Comanche, Cooke, Eastland, Erath, Hamilton, Hill, Hood, Jack, Johnson, Mills, Montague, Palo Pinto, Parker, Somervell, Stephens, Tarrant, Wichita, Wise, Young, and the portion of the city of Grand Prairie located in Dallas County.

Forth. This publication began in Jan. 1940 and continued until Mar. 1960. It was published by the National Council of the Episcopal Church and described itself as the "official organ of the Protestant Episcopal Church." It continued *The Spirit of Missions* and was replaced by *The Episcopalian.* It was published monthly, with a combined July–Aug. issue.

Fortunatus, Venantius Honorius (c. 535–c. 600). Latin poet born near Trevisco, Italy. Fortunatus received a classic education in rhetoric, grammar, and law at Ravenna. About 565 he went to Tours to give thanks at the tomb of St. Martin for healing from an eye disease. He settled in Poitiers, where he became acquainted with the former Queen Radegunde, a nun and widow of Clothar, King of the Franks, and Agnes, the abbess of her community. Fortunatus entered the service of the community, first as steward and later as chaplain after his ordination. Fortunatus was encouraged to publish his hymns by his friend, St. Gregory of Tours. Shortly before his death he became Bishop of Poitiers. He was a prolific writer. His true genius is found in his hymns, including "Sing, my tongue, the glorious battle" (Hymns 165–166), "Hail thee, festival day" (Hymns 175, 216, 225), and "'Welcome, happy morning!' age to age shall say" (Hymn 179).

Forward Movement. The General Convention of 1934 appointed a Joint Commission on a Forward Movement "to prepare and carry out definite plans for an organized effort to reinvigorate the life of the Church and to rehabilitate its General, Diocesan, and Parochial work." Gradually, the work of the commission became a movement, and the commission came to an end in 1940. Its work continues in Forward Movement Publications, the major one being *Forward Day by Day* (Spanish edition, *Día a Día*), a manual of daily Bible readings and devotions. It has published thousands of books and tracts over the years. The chair of Forward Movement Publications is the Presiding Bishop.

Forward Movement Publications. *See* Forward Movement.

Fosbroke, Hughell Edgar Woodall (Apr. 5, 1875–Oct. 18, 1957). Biblical scholar and seminary professor. He was born in Netherton, Worcestershire, England. His family came to the United States in 1890. He was a student at Harvard University from 1893 to 1895. He received his B.D. from Nashotah House in 1901. Fosbroke was ordained deacon on June 3, 1900, and priest on Dec. 23, 1900. Fosbroke was Professor of Old Testament at Nashotah House, 1902–1908, and Professor of the History and Religion of Israel at the Episcopal Theological School, Cambridge, 1908–1916. From Sept. 29, 1916, until May 27, 1947, he was dean of the General Theological Seminary. Under his leadership the faculty and curriculum were reinvigorated. The tutorial system was established in 1926. A number of his essays were published posthumously as *God in the Heart of Things* (1962). Fosbroke died at Winchester Center, Connecticut.

Foundation for Anglican Tradition, The. It was founded in 1983 to restore, defend, and promote traditional Christianity as received by the Anglican Church. It held the essential elements of traditional Anglicanism to be the apostolic succession of bishops, an all-male priesthood, and traditional worship. It was committed to the restoration of traditional Anglicanism in the Episcopal Church, in other Anglican churches throughout the world, and its continuation in the churches of Anglicans who left the Episcopal Church. The foundation began publication of *The Seabury Journal* in Apr./May 1983. It was last listed in *The Episcopal Church Annual 1986*. The founder and president, the Rev. Ross Bryant Baxter, renounced the ordained ministry of the Episcopal Church on Mar. 2, 1987.

Foundation for Christian Theology, The. The foundation was established in 1966 as the sponsoring corporation for *The Christian Challenge*. The foundation seeks to defend the Christian Faith as embodied in traditional Anglicanism, defined in Holy Scripture, and enshrined in the historic Book of Common Prayer; to work for the unity of the church under Christ, based on sound doctrine and discipline, as exemplified by the Chicago-Lambeth Quadrilateral of 1886–1888; to resist false teaching in the church; and to restore the church to her primary mission of proclaiming the gospel. At first the foundation was based in Victoria, Texas, but it is now located in Washington, DC. *See* Christian Challenge, The.

Founding of a Church, The. The *BOS* provides a form for the Founding of a Church. It includes prayers for the ground breaking, collects, a reading from scripture (Gn 28:10–17, Jacob's dream at Bethel), antiphons and psalms, the Lord's Prayer, and prayers for the laying of a cornerstone. Before the service, stakes are set in the ground at the corners of the proposed church building. During the service, persons appointed stretch two cords diagonally across the stakes, from the northeast to the southwest and from the southeast to the northwest. These cords are secured to the stakes, forming the Greek letter Chi (X), symbolizing the cross and the name of Christ. A third cord is stretched completely around the four stakes to enclose the area. Antiphons and psalms accompany the placement of the cords. The ministers and people may follow in procession. Ground is broken with a spade by the celebrant at the site of the altar. If the laying of the cornerstone is done after the church is built, the ceremony appropriately takes place in the context of a eucharist. The ceremony follows the homily.

"Fourth Day." The day after a three-day Cursillo weekend is completed. The "fourth day" is a symbol for the rest of one's life. The "fourth-day community" is the larger body of all who have completed a Cursillo weekend. Cursillo participants join the "fourth-day community" on completion of the weekend. *See* Cursillista.

Fraction. The breaking of one bread into many pieces for communion. Christ broke the bread at the Last Supper, and "the breaking of the bread" became a name for the entire liturgy (Acts 2:42). Throughout the history of the church the manner and location of the fraction have varied. The 1662 Prayer Book directed that the fraction take place at the words "he brake" in the institution narrative of the eucharistic prayer, thereby emphasizing its relation to Christ's action at the Last Supper. This practice continued through the 1928 BCP. Marion Hatchett notes that the fraction is returned to its traditional place in the 1979 BCP, which places the fraction immediately after the Lord's Prayer (p. 364). The fraction should not be hurried, or cluttered with allegorical gestures. The BCP calls for silence at the initial breaking of the bread. This silence should continue as the celebrant replaces the bread on the paten. The celebrant then breaks the bread for distribution. This may be accompanied by a fraction anthem, also known as the *confractorium*, which may be sung or said. Other priests may assist the celebrant in breaking the bread, and deacons may also assist in the absence of a sufficient number of priests. The pouring of consecrated wine into additional chalices may also be done during the fraction anthem, prior to the celebrant's invitation for the people to receive communion. The breaking of bread for distribution is emphasized by use of one loaf or a few large wafers. *See* Fraction Anthem.

Fraction Anthem. The anthem at the fraction, sometimes called the *confractorium*, a term borrowed from the Ambrosian rite. The BCP prints two anthems but permits others. Rite 1 prints both *Pascha nostrum* (Christ our Passover) (adapted from a similar anthem in the 1549 Prayer Book) and *Agnus Dei* (O Lamb of God). It allows either or both or another suitable anthem. Rite 2 prints only "Christ our Passover" (BCP, p. 364). Another suitable anthem may be used in place of or in addition to the printed one. The *BOS* gives fifteen anthems for various seasons and occasions. Several of these anthems are set to music in *The Hymnal 1982*. The *confractoria* may be said or sung, responsively or in unison. In many places the choir or a cantor sings the anthem, sometimes responsively with the people, while the presider breaks the bread.

Francis of Assisi (1181 or 1182–Oct. 3, 1226). Thirteenth-century saint and founder of the Franciscan order. He was born in Assisi in central Italy and named Giovanni Bernardone. His father changed his name to Francesco, "the Frenchman," after a visit to France. Francis's gradual conversion began in the spring of 1205. He gave generously to the poor and became devoted to "Lady Poverty." Francis stressed absolute simplicity of life marked by poverty, humility, and contemplation of Christ.

Others gathered around him, and on Feb. 24, 1209, the Order of Friars Minor (*Fratres minores*), sometimes called Minorites, was founded. In England they were popularly called Grey Friars because of the color of their habit. The Second Order of St. Francis, known as the Poor Clares, was established for nuns in 1219. The Third Order for lay men and women was founded in 1221. Francis is especially remembered for his writing, "The Canticle of Brother Sun." *The Hymnal 1982* includes two hymn texts written by Francis, "All creatures of our God and King" (400) and "Most High, omnipotent, good Lord" (406–407). The hymn text "Lord make us servants of your peace" (593) is based on a prayer attributed to Francis. He died in Assisi. Francis is commemorated in the Episcopal calendar of the church year on Oct. 4. *See* Clare; *see* Franciscan Spirituality.

Franciscan Friars of the Atonement—Graymoor. This Roman Catholic Order operates the Graymoor Ecumenical and Interreligious Institute at Garrison, New York. The Institute is an information and service organization serving primarily, but not exclusively, the Roman Catholic Church in the United States in its mission of Christian unity and interreligious dialogue. It sponsors the Week of Prayer for Christian Unity, Jan. 18–25, and publishes *Ecumenical Trends* and *At.One.Ment*.

Franciscan Spirituality. St. Francis of Assisi (1181 or 1182–1226) initiated a form of life centered on the practice of evangelical poverty as a means and sign of a spiritual poverty that can be filled only by divine grace. Franciscan spirituality is also characterized by an attitude of reverence for God in all things and a deep appreciation of the goodness of creation as a reflection of God's love. All creatures are worthy of our respect as sisters and brothers. Francis's disciples, the Mendicant Friars (Franciscans, or First Order of St. Francis), owned no property, lived from alms, and were devoted to itinerant popular preaching. The Sisters of St. Clare (Clarists, or Second Order) practice Franciscan poverty in a cloistered life. A Third Order associates lay people in the same ideal. St. Francis's primitive rule (1210) had to be relaxed as more candidates joined the order. St. Bonaventure deepened the contemplative dimension of Franciscan spirituality in *The Journey of the Mind to God* (1259). Francis's "Most High, omnipotent, good Lord" (Hymns 406–407) provides a beautiful expression of Franciscan spirituality. *See* Francis of Assisi.

Free African Society. This society was organized on Apr. 12, 1787, by Absalom Jones and Richard Allen. It was the first religious organization of freed African Americans in the United States. It was not a church but a benevolent and reform society for freed Africans. In Nov. 1787 a group of African American Philadelphia Methodists, led by Jones and Allen, left St. George's Methodist Church after they were pulled from their knees during a worship service and ordered to leave the gallery where they were seated. After this incident, the Free African Society assumed more religious functions. At first it met in a rented storeroom. The society met at the Friends Free African School House from 1788 until 1791. Allen went on to found the African Methodist Episcopal Church. The Free African Society was at times referred to as the "African Church." The Free African Society erected its own building, and it was dedicated as St. Thomas African Episcopal Church on July 17, 1794. Absalom Jones eventually became its pastor. This was the first African American congregation in the Episcopal Church, and the first African American congregation of any American denomination. On Oct. 12, 1794, it was formally received into the Diocese of Pennsylvania. *See* Jones, Absalom.

Free Church. A church that is not an established church or a state church, and in that sense it is "free" from governmental control. The term emphasizes the contrast or distinction relative to the established church. In England, those who did not conform to the doctrine, discipline, and polity of the established Church of England were known as nonconformists or dissenters, and their churches were known as Free churches. In England, the term has been applied to Presbyterians, Congregationalists, Methodists, Quakers, and Baptists. There has also been a Free church tradition in Scotland relative to the established Church of Scotland, which is Presbyterian; and in Sweden, Norway, and Denmark relative to the established Lutheran churches in those countries. Free church ideals may be seen in the American Constitutional principle of separation of church and state. *See* Establishment of Religion.

Free Pew. The renting of pews was the primary way that churches of many denominations collected funds. Pew renting persisted into the nineteenth century. The use of free pews began first in city missions for work among the poor in the larger cities. These missions were supported by dioceses and missionary societies. It appears that the first self-supporting Episcopal churches without pew rents

were the Church of the Holy Communion, New York, and the Church of the Advent, Boston.

Freedman's Commission. A commission established by the General Convention of 1865 to provide schools and teachers for African Americans in the South. The General Convention of 1868 changed the name to the Home Missionary Commission to the Colored People, sometimes shortened to Home Missions to Colored People. It went out of existence on Feb. 12, 1878. The four secretaries and general agents of the commission were the Rev. Francis Wharton (1820–1889), 1865–1866; Joseph Brinton Smith (1822–1872), 1866–1867; the Rev. Charles Gillette (1813–1869), 1867–1869; and the Rev. Wellington Edwin Webb (d. 1890), 1869–1878.

Freeman, George Washington (June 13, 1789–Apr. 29, 1858). Missionary Bishop. He was born in Sandwich, Massachusetts. After Freeman moved to North Carolina around 1822, he studied for the ordained ministry. He was ordained deacon on Oct. 8, 1826, and priest on May 20, 1827. For two years, 1827–1829, he was a missionary in North Carolina. In 1829 he became the rector of Christ Church, Raleigh, where he remained until 1840. In 1840 he became rector of St. Peter's Church, Columbia, Tennessee, and in 1841–1842, he served as rector of Trinity Church, Swedesborough, New Jersey. After two years as rector of Immanuel Church, Newcastle, Delaware, he was consecrated the second Missionary Bishop of Arkansas and the Indian Territory on Oct. 26, 1844. As Missionary Bishop of Arkansas, Freeman "exercised Episcopal functions" over the Episcopal missions in the Republic of Texas. Freeman died in Little Rock, Arkansas.

Frensdorff, Wesley (July 22, 1926–May 17, 1988). Bishop and advocate of "total ministry." He was born in Hanover, Germany. He received his B.A. from Columbia University in 1948 and his S.T.B. from the General Theological Seminary in 1951. He was ordained deacon on Mar. 31, 1951, and priest on Nov. 3, 1951. He had an extensive ministry in Nevada and Washington and was dean of St. Marks' Cathedral, Salt Lake City, Utah, 1962–1971. He was consecrated Bishop of Nevada on Mar. 4, 1972, and served until his resignation on Sept. 30, 1985. Frensdorff was Interim Bishop of the Navajoland Area Mission from Jan. 2, 1983, until his death, and Assistant Bishop of Arizona from Sept. 1, 1985, until his death. He is best known for his emphasis on local ministry following the model offered by

Roland Allen. The phrase "total ministry" is associated with his vision of all church people, lay and ordained, as involved in the total and complete ministry of the church. He believed "total ministry" to be an effective way to serve in largely rural and sparsely populated regions such as Nevada. He died in an airplane accident.

Friar. The term is from the French, *frère*, and the Latin, *frater*, both meaning "brother." Friars were members of mendicant (begging) orders that were founded in and after the thirteenth century. The mendicant friars wandered freely. They were not bound to a particular monastery or abbey by a vow of stability. This mobility freed them for a direct apostolate and active ministry of preaching, teaching, and service to the needy. Their active and contemplative life was a departure from previous monastic practice in which the community's life was in many ways enclosed within the monastery. They depended on begging or their own work to survive. Mendicant orders did not hold corporate possessions. The absolute ban on corporate ownership of property proved impractical. Most mendicant orders relaxed this rule in favor of community control of the order's resources and individual poverty. The four great mendicant orders in England were the Black Friars (Dominicans), the Grey Friars (Franciscans), the White Friars (Carmelites), and the Austin Friars (Augustinians).

Front Row/Back Row. A newsletter published by the Committee on Pastoral Development of the House of Bishops. It was originally called *The Front Row*. It began publication in Nov. 1979. It was started by the Rt. Rev. John Raymond Wyatt, the retired Bishop of Spokane. Wyatt wanted the newsletter to maintain contact among retired bishops after they stopped attending meetings of the House of Bishops. Shortly thereafter, his wife began enclosing her letter to the spouses of retired bishops. Wyatt called his letter *The Front Row* because bishops move forward in the House of Bishops so that the longest in membership sit on the first rows. Mrs. Wyatt called her letter *The Back Row* because spouses usually sit in the visitors' gallery at the rear of the house. The letter is now called *Front Row/Back Row*. For a while the letter was called *Front and Back Row*.

Frontal. Covering for the front of an altar, often made of silk or brocade cloth and matching the liturgical color of the season of the church year. Altar hangings were once on all sides of the altar. As altars were placed against back walls of churches in the later middle ages, only the front of the altar was visible to the congregation. Its covering was known as the frontal or *antependium*. Frontals may also be panels of precious metal or decorated wood. They may be hung, suspended, or attached to the altar. An additional covering, known as a frontlet or superfrontal, may hang down from the top front edge of the altar. It is usually long horizontally and narrow vertically and may be used with or without the frontal.

Frontlet. *See* Frontal.

Full Communion. The mutual recognition of the members and ministry of two or more churches and the common recognition of the validity of the sacraments of the churches. Churches so related remain canonically distinct and need not assent to all the doctrines, customs, and practices of each other. Such communion is found among the churches of the Anglican Communion and between the Anglican and Old Catholic churches.

Fulton, John (Apr. 2, 1834–Apr. 24, 1907). Editor and church historian. He was born in Glasgow, Scotland. Fulton studied at Aberdeen, Scotland, and came to the United States in 1853. He was ordained deacon on May 27, 1857, and priest on May 23, 1858. He was successively rector of Christ Church, Mobile, Alabama; St. Paul's Church, Indianapolis; and St. George's Church, St. Louis. From May 17, 1879, until Jan. 27, 1900, he was editor of the *Layman's Magazine of the Living Church.* In 1892 Fulton became the editor of *The Church Standard* in Philadelphia, a post he held until his death. He was a student of canon law and in 1872 published *Index Canonum*, a study of the canons of the general and provincial councils of the church in Greek and Latin. He also wrote "The Church in the Confederate States," in *The History of the American Episcopal Church, 1587–1883*, edited by William Stevens Perry, vol. 2, pp. 560–592. Fulton died in Philadelphia.

Fundamentalism. A movement of Christian thought which arose during the late nineteenth and early twentieth centuries in response to a growing liberal and modernist accommodation to evolution and other scientific advances which some perceived as a threat to Christian faith. Fundamentalism aimed to protect the essentials (or fundamentals) of faith from rationalism which seemed to make the Bible a record of developing ideas of God, and from psychology which seemed to reduce God to feelings of awe, and from a "social gospel" which seemed to make Christianity into a program for the reform of society.

The term "fundamentalism" was introduced by Carl Laws, editor of the *Watchman-Examiner*, who proposed five central and non-negotiable doctrines: 1) biblical inerrancy; 2) the divinity of Christ; 3) the Virgin Birth; 4) the substitutionary theory of the Atonement; and 5) the resurrection and second coming of Christ literally interpreted.

Laws put forward these fundamentals as moderately conservative proposals, in a spirit which today might be called "evangelical" or "neo-evangelical." In the course of time, however, the word has come to describe the most extreme, closed-minded, militant opposition to a changing liberal theology. By extension, the term has also been applied to militant or extreme movements in other nations and religious traditions.

Funeral. Ceremony or service for the burial of the dead. The term may be used as an adjective to indicate something that concerns the burial of the dead, such as a funeral procession. *See* Burial of the Dead.

G

Gablet. A small gable or gable-shaped canopy over a tabernacle.

Gabriel the Archangel. Archangel accorded the highest rank after Michael the Archangel in Jewish theology. The Book of Daniel (chs. 8 and 9) records that Gabriel helped Daniel to understand his visions. Gabriel tells Zechariah of the coming birth of his son John the Baptist and announces the conception of Jesus to Mary (Lk 1). In the 1549 BCP the feast of St. Michael the Archangel was expanded to include all angels. *See* Angel; *see* Annunciation, The.

Gadsden, Christopher Edwards (Nov. 25, 1785–June 24, 1852). Bishop and early advocate of a general seminary to educate clergy. He was born in Charleston, South Carolina. Gadsden graduated from Yale College in 1804, and then returned to South Carolina to study theology. He was ordained deacon on July 25, 1807. He began his ministry at St. John's Church, Berkeley, South Carolina. In Feb. 1810 he became assistant minister at St. Philip's Church, Charleston, and was ordained priest on Apr. 14, 1810. Gadsden became rector of St. Philip's Church in 1814 and served there until his death. Gadsden was a clerical deputy to the 1814 General Convention. He presented a resolution asking the General Convention to appoint a joint committee "to take into consideration the institution of a theological seminary." The resolution was defeated, but this initiative eventually resulted in the establishment of the General Theological Seminary. Gadsden was consecrated the fourth Bishop of South Carolina on June 21, 1840, and served until his death. He died in Charleston.

Gailor, Thomas Frank (Sept. 17, 1856–Oct. 3, 1935). Educator and Presiding Bishop. He was born in Jackson, Mississippi. Gailor received his B.A. in 1876 from Racine College, where he was the valedictorian, and his S.T.B. from the General Theological Seminary in 1879. He was ordained deacon on May 15, 1879, and priest on Sept. 17, 1880. Gailor began his ordained ministry at Messiah Church, Pulaski, Tennessee. On May 15, 1882, he became the professor of ecclesiastical history and polity at the School of Theology of the University of the South in Sewanee, Tennessee, a position he held until 1893. While teaching at the School of Theology he also taught English literature, political economy, and history in the College of Arts and Sciences. From 1883 until 1893, he was the chaplain of the University of the South, succeeding William Porcher DuBose. From Aug. 6, 1890, until July 27, 1893, he was the fourth vice-chancellor of the University. Gailor was consecrated the first Assistant Bishop of Tennessee on July 25, 1893. He became the third Bishop of Tennessee on Feb. 15, 1898, serving until his death. He served as the eighth chancellor of the University from June 23, 1908, until his death. In 1916 Gailor was elected president of the House of Bishops, and at the 1919 General Convention he was elected president of the National Council of the Episcopal Church. He served in this position until 1925, when a Presiding Bishop was elected for a six-year term. Gailor also wrote the "Sewanee Hymn." He died in Sewanee.

Gallaudet, Thomas (June 3, 1822–Aug. 27, 1902). Father of Episcopal missionary work among the hearing impaired. He was born in Hartford, Connecticut. He received his B.A. in 1842 and his M.A. in 1845 from Washington College (Trinity), Hartford. From Sept. 1843 until Oct. 1, 1858, he taught in the New York Institution for Deaf-Mutes. He was ordained deacon on June 16, 1850, and priest on June 29, 1851. On Oct. 2, 1852, he founded St. Anne's Church for Deaf-Mutes, New York City. In Oct. 1872, he founded the Church Mission to the Deaf, and in 1885 he founded the Gallaudet Home for Deaf Mutes near Poughkeepsie, New York. Gallaudet College in Washington, D.C., was named for him. The ministry of Gallaudet and Henry Syle with the hearing impaired is commemorated in the Episcopal calendar of the church year on Aug. 27. *See* Syle, Henry Winter.

Galley, Howard Evans, Jr. (Apr. 24, 1929–May 20, 1993). Author, editor, musician, and lay leader of the liturgical movement in the Episcopal Church. He was born in Lawrence, Massachusetts. He received his B.A. from the University of Massachusetts and his M.A. from New York University. Galley was a member of the Church Army from 1951 to 1981. His ministry included missionary work among the Lakota Indians. From 1961 until 1981 he served as assistant to the Coordinator of Prayer Book Revision as an editor for the Trial Rites of the BCP and *BOS.* He was an editor of Seabury Press, 1980–1985. Galley had a vast and technical knowledge of both liturgy and language. He was a valuable resource in the 1979 revision process. He was the author of Eucharistic Prayer C, the reviser and translator of much of the catechumenal material in the *BOS*, and many other prayers and rubrics in both the *BOS* and the BCP.

He produced two widely-used adaptations of the Daily Offices, *The Prayer Book Office* and *Morning and Evening Prayer*, and a ceremonial guide, *Ceremonies of the Eucharist.* He also edited the 1981 edition of White and Dykman, *The Annotated Constitution and Canons*, and the annual *Episcopal Church Lesson Calendar.*

He worked as a free-lance editor after the closing of the Prayer Book Revision Office. He worked on *The Hymnal 1982.* He gave lectures and workshops, and served on the council of Associated Parishes for Liturgy and Mission. Galley died in Jersey City, New Jersey.

Gambier Observer. The first periodical published by the Episcopal Church in the Midwest. Its founder and sponsor was Bishop Philander Chase, the first Bishop of Ohio. When it was first published on May 28, 1830, it was called the *Gambier Observer: Devoted to the Interests of Religion in the Protestant Episcopal Church.* It was published under this title until Nov. 8, 1837. The first editor was Professor William Sparrow of Kenyon College, later of the Virginia Theological Seminary. With the first issue of vol. 8 in 1837 the name was expanded to the *Gambier Observer and Western Church Journal.* In 1840 it was moved from Gambier, Ohio, to Cincinnati, and the name

was changed to the *Western Episcopal Observer.* It ceased publication in the fall of 1842. Its tradition was carried on by the *Western Episcopalian*, which began publication in Aug. 1843.

Gantt, Edward (1746–c. 1837). Gantt and Mason Locke Weems were the first two persons ordained in England after Parliament passed an act which allowed the ordination of deacons and priests without the requirement of an oath of allegiance to the English monarch. He was born in Prince George County, Maryland, and practiced medicine in Somerset County. He was ordained deacon on Sept. 5, 1784, and priest on Sept. 12, 1784, in England. In 1795 he moved to Georgetown, District of Columbia. After 1800 he was repeatedly chosen chaplain of the United States Senate. About 1807 he moved to Kentucky and died near Louisville.

Garden, Alexander (1685–Sept. 27, 1756). Third Commissary to North and South Carolina. He was born and educated in Scotland. Garden became a priest in the Church of England. He came to the American colonies in 1719. Shortly after his arrival, he became rector of St. Philip's Church, Charleston, South Carolina. In 1729 the Bishop of London named him the third Commissary to North and South Carolina. He served in that position until 1749. As Commissary he began annual meetings of the clergy to regularize church life in the province. While Commissary, Garden had a controversial correspondence with George Whitefield, the Church of England evangelical preacher. When Whitefield was in South Carolina, he did not follow the Prayer Book and made derogatory remarks about the colonial clergy. Whitefield was brought to trial and suspended from his office as a priest, but he continued to preach. Garden retired as rector of St. Philip's Church in 1754. While rector he did extensive missionary and educational work among African Americans. Garden died in Charleston.

Gardiner, Robert Hallowell (Nov. 5, 1882–Sept. 16, 1944). Lay ecumenical leader. He was born in Newton, Massachusetts. Gardiner received his B.A. in 1903, his M.A. in 1904, and his law degree in 1907 from Harvard University. He was a major in World War I, commanding the 3rd Battalion, 303rd Field Artillery in France. In 1928 Gardiner organized the Fiduciary Trust Company of Boston and served as its president until his death. He was a member of the National Council of the Episcopal Church and attended every General Convention from 1926 until his death. He was a warden of Christ Church, Gardiner, Maine, and a trustee of the Church Pension Fund. Gardiner was secretary of the Episcopal Joint Commission on Faith and Order. He and Bishop Charles Henry Brent were the Episcopal founders of the ecumenical Faith and Order Movement. Gardiner died in Gardiner, Maine.

Gargoyle. The term is from the Old French for "throat" or "gullet" and related to the word for "gargle." It was originally a projecting waterspout used in gothic architecture to throw water from the roof gutter or upper part of a building or tower. It protected the building by throwing water away from the walls or foundations. The spouts eventually became known by their decorative figures. By the thirteenth century they were made of stone instead of wood. Gargoyles were soon built for decoration only and not for drainage. These carvings are usually fanciful and often grotesque. Gargoyles may represent wildly imaginative animal or human-like forms. The largest gargoyles project as much as three feet from their building. Gargoyles are found on many gothic cathedrals throughout Europe and on neo-gothic cathedrals of the Episcopal Church such as the Cathedral of St. John the Divine in New York City and the Cathedral of St. Peter and St. Paul in Washington, D.C.

Garrett, Alexander Charles (Nov. 4, 1832–Feb. 19, 1924). Presiding Bishop and missionary. He was born in Ballymot, County Sligo, Ireland. Garrett received his B.A. from Trinity College, Dublin, in 1855. He was ordained deacon on July 6, 1856, and priest on July 5, 1857. He held the curacy of East Worldham, Hampshire, until Sept. 1859. He went to British Columbia as a missionary to the Indians, chaplain at the naval station at Esquimalt, rector of St. Paul's Church, Nanaims, and minister to the gold miners at Cariboo. In 1869 he moved to San Francisco, California, where he was rector of St. James' Church until 1872. From 1872 until 1874, he was dean of Trinity Cathedral, Omaha, Nebraska. On Dec. 20, 1874, Garrett was consecrated the first Missionary Bishop of Northern Texas (Dallas). He was an active supporter of a School of Theology at the University of the South. He gave the opening address when St. Luke's Hall was opened on Mar. 25, 1879, in which he called the School of Theology a "General Theological Seminary for the South." He was the leader in building St. Matthew's Cathedral, Dallas. He founded St. Mary's College for women at Dallas. It opened on Sept. 10, 1889, and operated

until 1930. At one time, Bishop Garrett said that he needed clergy who could "ride like a cow-boy, pray like a saint, preach like an apostle, and having food and raiment be therewith content." He was the fourteenth Presiding Bishop from Apr. 17, 1923, until his death. He died in Dallas.

Garth. A grassy quadrangle or garden surrounded by a cloister walk in a monastery, church, seminary, or college.

Gather the Family Institute for Evangelism and Congregational Development. Founded by the Rev. Robert Darrell Noble (1929–1998) as Noble Ventures in Faith, a ministry dedicated to church growth and mission, it later grew into the Gather the Family Institute. It provides consultants, training workshops, and workbooks to help congregations and dioceses learn the concepts and skills to develop individualized programs for evangelism and assimilation of new members.

Gaudete Sunday. The third Sunday of Advent in the Roman Catholic calendar of the church year. The term is derived from the Latin opening words of the introit antiphon, "Rejoice (*Gaudete*) in the Lord always." The theme of the day expresses the joy of anticipation at the approach of the Christmas celebration. This theme reflects a lightening of the tone of the traditional Advent observance. It was appropriate for the celebrant of the Mass to wear rose-colored vestments on this day instead of the deeper violet vestments that were typically used in Advent. This Sunday was also known as "Rose Sunday." This custom is not required in the Episcopal Church, but it is observed by some parishes with a traditional Anglo-catholic piety. This custom is reflected by the practice of including a pink or rose-colored candle among the four candles of an Advent wreath. *See* Laetare Sunday.

Gavin, Frank Stanton Burns (Oct. 31, 1890–Mar. 20, 1938). He was born in Cincinnati, Ohio. Gavin received his A.B. from Cincinnati University in 1912; and his M.A. in 1914 and Ph.D. in 1922 from Columbia University. In 1915 he received his S.T.B. from the General Theological Seminary. He was ordained deacon on May 15, 1914, and priest on Apr. 7, 1915. Gavin also received the B.H.L. from Hebrew Union College, Cincinnati, in 1918. After ordination to the priesthood, he served a year at St. Luke's Church, Cincinnati. Gavin then entered the novitiate of the Society of St. John the Evangelist at Cambridge, Massachusetts. He never took permanent vows. While at Cambridge he received the S.T.M. in 1917 and the Th.D. in 1919 from Harvard University. In 1919–1920 he taught in the preparatory department at Nashotah House. In 1920–1921 he studied Greek theology in Athens, and in 1921–1923 he was professor of NT at Nashotah House. In 1923 Gavin joined the faculty of the General Theological Seminary, where he was professor of ecclesiastical history until his death. He wrote numerous books about Eastern Orthodoxy and was a leader in the Episcopal Church in the ecumenical movement. He edited *Liberal Catholicism and the Modern World* (1934), which described the liberal catholic position in the Episcopal Church. Gavin died in New York City.

Gelasian Sacramentary. The earliest source of a number of collects and other forms in the BCP. A sacramentary is a liturgical book which contains those parts of the rites (Daily Offices, Eucharist, and Pastoral Offices) read by the celebrant. The oldest known Roman Sacramentary is the Leonine or Verona Sacramentary which exists in a manuscript from about 600. It contains materials from the fifth and sixth centuries. The next oldest is the so-called Gelasian Sacramentary which exists in an eighth-century manuscript but represents a time slightly later than the Leonine or Verona Sacramentary. It was for a long time incorrectly attributed to Pope Gelasius I (d. 496).

General Board of Examining Chaplains (GBEC). The General Convention of 1970 created this board to standardize the process of canonical examination for ordination. The GBEC includes four bishops, six clergy with pastoral cures or in specialized ministries, six members of accredited seminary faculties or of other educational institutions, and six lay persons. The members of the board are elected by the House of Bishops and confirmed by the House of Deputies for six-year terms. Each member has a special competence in one or more of the seven areas of canonical examination. The seven areas are: 1) the Holy Scriptures; 2) church history, including the ecumenical movement; 3) Christian theology; 4) Christian ethics, and moral theology; 5) studies in contemporary society, including racial and minority groups; 6) liturgics and church music; and 7) theory and practice of ministry. The GBEC is charged with preparing and administering an examination for the entire church. The first meeting of the GBEC was at Trinity Church, New York City, Dec. 1970. *See* General Ordination Examination (GOE).

General Board of Religious Education. The General Convention of 1910 established this General Board for "the unification and development of the Church's work of religious instruction . . . especially through the Sunday School." The board consisted of the Presiding Bishop, seven other bishops, seven presbyters, and seven laymen, together with two members from each of the missionary departments, later called provinces. The board worked through four departments: parochial education, secondary education, collegiate education, and theological education. The board published *The Christian Nurture Series* of textbooks. In 1919 the board's duties were assumed by the Department of Religious Education of the National Council of the Episcopal Church.

General Clergy Relief Fund. The 1853 General Convention passed a resolution authorizing the incorporation of a fund for the relief of aged, infirm, and disabled clergy, and the widows and orphans of deceased clergy. Unfortunately, it did not materialize. The 1871 General Convention directed that the royalties of *The Hymnal* (1871) go to this fund, which became the General Clergy Relief Fund. The 1907 General Convention appointed a Joint Commission to raise $5,000,000 for the fund. Little happened until Bishop William Lawrence of Massachusetts assumed leadership of the campaign. Under his leadership the General Clergy Relief Fund evolved into the Church Pension Fund. *See* Church Pension Fund.

General Convention. The national legislative body of the Episcopal Church. It consists of a House of Bishops, which includes all active and retired bishops, and a House of Deputies, which includes four lay persons and four clergy from each diocese, each area mission, and the Convocation of the American Churches in Europe. The Convention meets every three years. The Houses meet and act separately, and both must concur to adopt legislation. The General Convention alone has authority to amend the Prayer Book and the church's Constitution, to amend the canons (laws) of the church, and to determine the program and budget of the General Convention, including the missionary, educational, and social programs it authorizes. A majority of bishops may request the Presiding Bishop to call a Special General Convention. Special General Conventions met in 1821 and in 1969. The General Convention elects twenty of the forty members of the Executive Council, which administers policy and program between the triennial meetings of the General Convention.

General Convention Special Program (GCSP). At the 1967 General Convention in Seattle, Washington, Presiding Bishop John E. Hines called on the Episcopal Church to "take its place humbly and boldly alongside of, and in support of, the dispossessed and oppressed peoples of this country for the healing of our national life." In response to Hines's leadership, the General Convention adopted a $9,000,000 fund and set up the Special Program. GCSP was given top priority for the church's use of personnel, time, and money for the years 1968–1970. In Nov. 1967, following the General Convention, Bishop Hines, in consultation with the elected members of the Executive Council, set up a special staff unit of the council to carry out this GCSP. Hines named Leon Modeste, an Episcopal layman, to direct the program and administer the funds. Some grants were made to organizations outside the Episcopal Church, some of which were perceived by some Episcopalians as supporters of violence. By 1969, some Episcopal clergy and laity were calling for the end of GCSP. Over the next few years opposition to GCSP continued to grow and restrictions were placed on the recipients of grants. At the 1973 General Convention it was decided to place all minority organizations of the Episcopal Church under one funding program, and the name of GCSP was changed to the Commission on Community Action and Human Development. Modeste's position was abolished on Dec. 31, 1973.

General Ordination Examination (GOE). The General Convention of 1970 created the General Board of Examining Chaplains (GBEC), with responsibility to prepare at least annually a General Ordination Examination covering 1) The Holy Scriptures; 2) church history, including the ecumenical movement; 3) Christian theology; 4) Christian ethics and moral theology; 5) studies in contemporary society, including racial and minority groups; 6) liturgics and church music; Christian worship and music according to the contents and use of the Prayer Book and *The Hymnal*; and 7) theory and practice of ministry. Candidates are examined in these seven areas before ordination to the diaconate. The GBEC conducts, administers, and evaluates these examinations. The first General Ordination Examinations (GOEs) were administered Jan. 31–Feb. 5, 1972. The exams are read by readers chosen by the administrator of the GOE from names suggested to GBEC members. The purpose of the GOE is advisory. It offers assistance to diocesan authorities in determining a candidate's readiness for ordination. It also provides guidance to the candidate and his or her mentors in planning future continuing education. *See* General Board of Examining Chaplains (GBEC).

General Protestant Episcopal Sunday School Union (GPESSU). A committee was formed at the 1826 General Convention to consider the formation of an American Society for the Promotion of Christian Knowledge. This plan was modified, and the General Protestant Episcopal Sunday School Union was organized under the leadership of bishop William White. It had no official connection to the General Convention. Bishop John Henry Hobart was also a leader in its organization. The union was a private association with only voluntary membership. The object of the union was "to combine the resources of Episcopalians into one great whole, which, by its concentration of power, may be enabled to give life and vigour to the multitude of branches which now pine in solitude and neglect." In 1827 the union issued its handbook, *System of Instruction, for the Use of Protestant Episcopal Sunday Schools in the United States*, which supplied a curriculum, rules for the government of Sunday Schools, record-keeping materials, and periodical material for instruction. The materials for instruction were the Bible, the Prayer Book, and the Catechism. The classroom method was memorization followed by recitation. In 1829 it issued *Catechism on the Evidences of the Bible; In Easy Rhyme. Intended for the Young to Commit to Memory*. In 1829 it also began the publication of two periodicals: *The Family Visiter and Sunday School Magazine*, for adults, and the *Children's Magazine*. In 1835 the union revived its adult magazine under the name *The Sunday School Visiter*. The formation of the union marked the end of the evolution of the Sunday School from a charitable lay enterprise for the instruction of needy children in reading and writing to a recognized church institution for the training of children in the parish. The General Convention gradually took over the work of the union.

General Thanksgiving. The BCP includes two prayers of General Thanksgiving. The traditional prayer of General Thanksgiving was composed by Edward Reynolds (1599–1676), Bishop of Norwich. It was possibly inspired by a private prayer of Queen Elizabeth that was issued in 1596. Prior to the 1604 revision of the Prayer Book, Puritans complained that there were not enough prayers of thanksgiving in the Prayer Book. This prayer was added to the Prayer Book in 1662 under the heading, "A General

Thanksgiving." It preceded other prayers of thanksgiving for particular benefits. This prayer asks God to "give us such an awareness of your mercies, that with truly thankful hearts we may show forth your praise, not only with our lips, but in our lives, by giving up our selves to your service, and by walking before you in holiness and righteousness all our days" (BCP, p. 101). The first American Prayer Book (1789) required use of this prayer at every Daily Office. In 1892 its use became optional, except on Sundays when the litany or eucharist did not follow immediately. The prayer appears as "The General Thanksgiving" in the 1979 BCP. It precedes "A Prayer of St. Chrysostom" and the dismissal at the close of Morning Prayer and Evening Prayer (BCP, pp. 58–59, 71–72, 101, 125). Its use is optional. The General Thanksgiving is said by the officiant and the people.

The 1979 BCP also includes "A General Thanksgiving" among the Prayers and Thanksgivings found near the end of the BCP (p. 836). This new occasional prayer of thanksgiving was composed by the Rev. Charles P. Price. It thanks God for the splendor of creation, for the blessing of family and friends, for tasks which demand our best efforts, for disappointments that lead us to acknowledge our dependence on God, for Jesus, and for his resurrection that raises us to the life of God's kingdom, and for the gift of the Spirit through whom we give thanks to God in all things.

General Theological Seminary, The. The oldest seminary of the Episcopal Church, founded by the 1817 General Convention. By 1827 it was located at "Chelsea Square," in New York City, part of the family estate of Clement Clarke Moore. He was the author of "A Visit from St. Nicholas" ("'Twas the night before Christmas") and the seminary's first professor of biblical languages. Its first class graduated in 1822. It was an American center of the Oxford Movement. The General Seminary received authority to grant degrees in 1869 and conferred its first Bachelor of Sacred Theology in 1876. Under its third dean and "most munificent benefactor," Eugene Augustus Hoffman, most of the seminary's present quadrangle and grounds, buildings, professorships, endowments, and customs were established. The first earned doctoral degree was awarded in 1881, the first honorary doctorate in 1885. By the end of Hoffman's tenure there were nearly 150 students and thirteen full-time faculty members. The Chapel of the Good Shepherd was consecrated in 1888 by Presiding Bishop John Williams and placed under the spiritual jurisdiction of the Bishops of the Episcopal Church. The St. Mark's Library, founded in 1820 by John Pintard, also the founder of the New York Historical Society, was from the later nineteenth to the later twentieth century regarded as the finest theological library in the Episcopal Church. Women were first admitted as regular full-time degree students in the fall of 1971. Students were first allowed to marry during the academic term in the fall of 1972.

Geneva Bible. English translation of the Bible published at Geneva, Switzerland, in 1560. Based on translations by William Tyndale and Miles Coverdale, it was the work of Protestant exiles in Geneva. Its notes reflect Calvinist influence. The Geneva Bible was the first English edition with verse numeration. It is known as the "Breeches Bible" because its translation of Gn 3:7 states that Adam and Eve made "breeches" for themselves. It was the most widely read English version of the Bible until publication of the Authorized Version.

Geneva College. *See* Hobart College, Geneva, New York.

Genuflection, or Genuflexion. A gesture of reverence in worship. It involves touching a knee briefly to the floor while holding the upper body upright, and then returning to a standing position. It is not required by the Prayer Book at any time. In some parishes it is a customary gesture of reverence for Christ's real presence in the consecrated eucharistic elements of bread and wine. Genuflections are often customary in parishes with an Anglo-catholic piety. Genuflections may be seen as people enter or leave a church, or the seating area of a church, or the vicinity of a tabernacle where the Blessed Sacrament is reserved. The celebrant and assisting ministers may genuflect at the end of the eucharistic prayer or after the words of institution concerning each element in the eucharistic prayer. Genuflection has also been associated with veneration of the cross at the Good Friday liturgy and with the affirming of the Incarnation in the Nicene Creed. The genuflection is from imperial and feudal ceremonial. The custom of genuflecting to the Blessed Sacrament dates from the eleventh century, and it was introduced into the Mass in the fourteenth century. Some prefer the profound bow as a more ancient gesture of reverence in worship.

George Mercer, Jr., Memorial School of Theology. In Feb. 1955, Bishop James P. DeWolfe initiated a new form for alternative theological training by establishing the School of Theology of the Diocese of Long Island. It was a program designed for training older men for the ministry. The school met regularly at St. Paul's Boys School and in the Cathedral House in Garden City, New York. When this project ended, it was succeeded by the George Mercer, Jr., Memorial School of Theology. It was incorporated in Feb. 1961. It is the primary adult educational ministry of the Diocese of Long Island. The School offers courses in Christian education, preparation for licensed lay ministries, and a curriculum for persons preparing for ordained ministry. Classes at Mercer are held at times which are convenient for persons who are employed on a full-time basis. It is not a seminary accredited by the Association of Theological Schools (ATS).

Georgia, Diocese of. The primary convention of the Diocese of Georgia was held Feb. 24–28, 1823, at St. Paul's Church, Augusta. The first bishop of the diocese was not consecrated until 1841. The diocese left the Protestant Episcopal Church on July 3, 1861, and joined the Protestant Episcopal Church in the Confederate States of America. It reunited with the Protestant Episcopal Church on Aug. 12, 1865. The General Convention of 1907 voted to divide the Diocese of Georgia and establish the Diocese of Atlanta. The Diocese of Georgia includes the following counties: Appling, Atkinson, Bacon, Baker, Ben Hill, Berrien, Bleckley, Brantley, Brooks, Bryan, Bulloch, Burke, Calhoun, Camden, Candler, Charlton, Chatham, Clay, Clinch, Coffee, Colquitt, Columbia, Cook, Crisp, Decatur, Dodge, Dooly, Dougherty, Early, Echols, Effingham, Emanuel, Evans, Glascock, Glynn, Grady, Irwin, Jeff Davis, Jefferson, Jenkins, Johnson, Lanier, Laurens, Lee, Liberty, Long, Lowndes, McDuffie, McIntosh, Miller, Mitchell, Montgomery, Pierce, Pulaski, Quitman, Randolph, Richmond, Screven, Seminole, Stewart, Sumter, Tattnall, Telfair, Terrell, Thomas, Tift, Toombs, Treutlen, Turner, Twiggs, Ware, Washington, Wayne, Webster, Wheeler, Wilcox, Wilkinson, and Worth. On Nov. 14, 1993, St. Paul's Church, Savannah, was set apart as the pro-cathedral of the diocese.

Gesture. Stylized motions of the body, especially the arms and hands, during worship. Along with postures, these natural and instinctive motions express in a nonverbal, kinetic way the meaning of the action. Over the centuries many gestures once made by all the people came to be made only by the presider. Liturgical reform has included the tendency to restore these gestures to all. Principal gestures and postures in Christian liturgy are: 1) *Orans*, lifting hands in prayer; 2) sign of the cross, made especially with the right thumb on the forehead or with the right hand on the forehead, chest, and shoulders; 3) standing for praise and kneeling for confession; 4) bowing in reverence; 5) genuflection, or bending the knee, in reverence; 6) kiss of peace, sign of greeting and reconciliation; 7) elevation of the elements, offering them to God or showing them to the people; 8) extending the hands in greeting, as at "The Lord be with you"; 9) laying on of hands (or extending them over persons), a sign of blessing and authorization, as in Baptism, Confirmation, Ordination, and other sacramental acts.

Gifts of the Spirit. Five NT texts form the basis for understanding the gifts of the Spirit, known as the *charismata* in Greek. These texts include 1 Cor 12:1–14:40, Rom 12:8, Eph 4:11–12, Rom 1:11, and 1 Cor 2:14. The lists of gifts in the NT passages are neither exhaustive nor entirely consistent. Apostles, prophets, and teachers are mentioned in 1 Cor 12:28–30. Those who exhort, give, preside, and show mercy are mentioned in Rom 12:6–8. Evangelists and pastors are mentioned in Eph 4:11. These gifts may be understood as charismatic ministries rather than offices. Some gifts, on the other hand, refer to functions or activities. Knowledge, healing, working of miracles, prophecy, tongues, and interpretation of tongues are mentioned in 1 Cor 12:7–10. Some contemporary charismatics consider tongues to be the essential gift of the Spirit, despite Paul's statement in 1 Cor 14:18–19 that he would rather speak five words with his mind in church to instruct others than ten thousand words in a tongue. Paul declares that he intends to share his gifts with the Christian church in Rome (Rom 1:11), indicating that gifts can be shared with others. In 1 Cor 12:7, each believer is said to have a gift, which suggests that there are many gifts. These points are prominent in contemporary discussion of the gifts of the Spirit.

At baptism, at the sanctifying of the water, the celebrant prays that by the power of the Holy Spirit "those who here are cleansed from sin and born again may continue for ever in the risen life of Jesus Christ our Savior" (BCP, p. 307). In a general sense, the life of faith—including forgiveness and renewal—can be understood as a gift of the Spirit. After the action of baptizing with water, the celebrant prays for specific gifts for the newly baptized from the Lord in the Spirit, including an inquiring and discerning heart, the courage to will and to persevere, a spirit to know and love God, and the gift of joy and wonder in all God's works (BCP, p. 308). The "sevenfold gifts" imparted to all by the Holy Spirit are mentioned by the hymns *Veni Creator Spiritus* (Hymns 503–504) and *Veni Sancte Spiritus* (Hymns 226–227), one of which is sung prior to the prayer of consecration at ordinations of bishops, priests, and deacons. *See* Charismata, or Charismatic Gifts; *see* Charismatic; *see* Charisms.

Girdle. *See* Cincture.

Girls' Friendly Society (GFS). This society was founded in England in 1875, and it spread to many churches of the Anglican Communion. The first branch of the GFS in the United States was organized in 1877 by Emily M. Edson in Lowell, Massachusetts, to "promote the welfare of underprivileged factory girls." The early focus of GFS work was to provide wholesome social and religious programs for young working women, particularly those who were living away from their families' homes for the first time. Many branches operated vacation lodges where women could enjoy a short, inexpensive respite from urban life. GFS spread across the United States by the early 1920s. It gradually became the primary organization for Episcopal girls and young women. Its mission came to be focused on worship, service to others, study, and recreation. GFS chapters developed a wide range of missionary projects. Many units trained young women as volunteer church workers who assisted in service projects in domestic and foreign missions. Though membership in the organization began to decrease in the 1960s, it continues to be active in many parishes.

Glebe. The term is derived from a Latin word meaning "clod" or "soil." Glebes were farm lands set aside for the support of the clergy in American colonies where the Church of England was established. These glebes sometimes included homes, barns, and slaves. Glebes were usually two hundred or more acres. It could be farmed to supplement the rector's salary, or it could be leased to others. After the American Revolution, most of the glebes were transferred to the newly organized Protestant Episcopal Church. The Baptists led an effort in Virginia to seize the glebe lands. In Jan. 1802 the Virginia Assembly passed the *Act Concerning the Glebe Lands and Churches within this Commonwealth.* It provided that each county would have a group called the Overseers of the Poor, which would seize the glebes purchased prior to 1777 upon the death or resignation of the parish's present rector. This Act contributed to the decline of the Episcopal Church in Virginia after the Revolution.

Glebe House, Woodbury, Connecticut. Site of the first episcopal election in the United States. Built around 1750, Glebe House was the rectory for St. Paul's Church, Woodbury. The Rev. John Rutgers Marshall lived there from 1771 until 1785. On Mar. 25, 1783, ten clergy met there and selected Samuel Seabury and Jeremiah Leaming as candidates for Bishop of Connecticut. Eventually Glebe House was privately owned. In 1892 three Connecticut clergy bought it for $500 as a gift for their bishop, John Williams. In 1923 Edward C. Acheson, Bishop Coadjutor of Connecticut, formed the Seabury Society for the Preservation of Glebe House. It is now the Glebe House Museum. *See* Consecration of Samuel Seabury, First American Bishop, Feast of.

Global Episcopal Mission Network (GEM). The network seeks to be a vehicle for involving dioceses and their congregations directly in global mission. At the House of Bishops meeting in Mar. 1994, Bishop Richard F. Grein of New York and Bishop Herbert T. Thompson, Jr., of Southern Ohio proposed a network structure aimed at enabling dioceses to become the primary sending and receiving mission entities of the Episcopal Church. The organizing meeting of the GEM Network was held in Cincinnati on Apr. 18–20, 1995.

Gloria in Excelsis. "Glory in the highest," a short hymn of praise to the Trinity. Its opening verse is based on the song of the angels to the shepherds at the time of Jesus' birth, as reported in Lk 2:14. It is known as the "Angelic Hymn." It is also known as the "Greater Doxology," distinguishing it from the *Gloria Patri*, the "Lesser Doxology." It dates from the fourth century, and was the canticle for the morning office in the Apostolic Constitutions. It continues to be used in the morning office by the eastern churches. The *Gloria* became a part of the entrance rite of the Roman Mass in the twelfth century and was dropped from the Daily Office in the west. The *Gloria* was also used in the eucharistic entrance rite of the 1549 BCP, but later editions used the *Gloria* as a postcommunion prayer. This reflected the penitential emphasis of those editions of the Prayer Book. The 1789 American Prayer Book allowed the use of the *Gloria* instead of the *Gloria Patri* as an option at the end of the psalmody in the Daily Office, but that option is no longer allowed. The 1979 BCP restored the *Gloria* to its place in the eucharistic entrance rite (pp. 324–325, 356). The *Gloria* may be used from Christmas Day through the Feast of the Epiphany, on Sundays in Easter season, on all the days of Easter Week, on Ascension Day, and at other times. The *Gloria* is not used at the eucharist on the Sundays or ordinary weekdays of Advent or Lent (BCP, p. 406). The 1979 BCP uses the *Gloria* as canticle 20, "Glory to God." It is printed in the Rite 2 service for Morning Prayer, it may be used for Morning Prayer or Evening Prayer, and it is suggested for use at Morning Prayer on Thursday except in Advent and Lent. *The Hymnal 1982* provides various musical settings for the *Gloria* (S 272–S 281), including those by William Mathias (S 278) and Robert Powell (S 280).

Gloria Patri. A short acclamation of praise to the Trinity. "Glory to the Father, and to the Son, and to the Holy Spirit: as it was in the beginning, is now, and will be for ever. Amen." The term is from the opening words of the acclamation in Latin. *Gloria Patri* is also known as the "Lesser Doxology," distinguishing it from the *Gloria in excelsis*, the "Greater Doxology." It may have been influenced by the trinitarian baptismal formula of Mt 28:19.

Gloria Patri is always sung or said at the conclusion of the entire portion of the Psalter at Morning Prayer, Noonday Prayer, Evening Prayer, and Compline. It may be used after the invitatory psalm or the canticle "Christ our Passover" at Morning Prayer; and after each psalm, and after each section of Ps 119 at Morning and Evening Prayer (BCP, p. 141). *Gloria Patri* is used in the BCP to conclude Canticles 3, 4, 5, 8, 9, 10, 11, 15, 16, 17, and 19. It is also used to conclude the *Magnificat* and the *Nunc dimittis* in Evening Prayer. *Gloria Patri* may be omitted after these canticles. It follows the opening versicle and response at Morning Prayer, Noonday Prayer, and Evening Prayer. It follows the confession of sin and a versicle and response from Ps 70:1 at Compline. This pattern of versicle and response is based on the model for the beginning of the Daily Offices prescribed by St. Benedict of Nursia (c. 480–c. 550). *Gloria Patri* is also used with verses from Ps 44 at the opening of the Supplication. An alternative pointing of the *Gloria Patri* is provided by the BCP (p. 141). In Rite 1 services of Morning Prayer and Evening Prayer, it is permissible to use the form "Glory be to the Father, and to the Son, and to the Holy Ghost: As it was in the beginning, is now, and ever shall be, world without end. Amen."

Gloria Patri was traditionally used to provide a climax and cut-off for psalms that "covered" liturgical actions such as the procession at the entrance of the clergy, the presentation of the oblations, and the communion of the people. A signal would be given when the liturgical action was completed, and the psalm would then end with *Gloria Patri*. It was not used with gradual psalms or tracts, since these texts were understood to have their own integrity in the service. This tradition continues in modern practice. *Gloria Patri* is seldom used after the gradual psalm at the eucharist.

Gloria Tibi. "Glory to you, Lord Christ." The term is from the opening words of the statement in Latin. It is the people's response to the announcement of the gospel at the eucharist (BCP, p. 357). It precedes the reading of the gospel. This response at the announcement of the gospel in the Roman rite was retained by the 1549 BCP. It is omitted before the Passion gospel on Palm Sunday (the Sunday of the Passion), and Good Friday (BCP, pp. 272, 277).

Glossolalia. Ecstatic utterance as an expression of faith and praise for God. This Greek term designates the phenomenon of "speaking in new tongues" promised in Mk 16:17. For Paul (1 Cor 14:1–20), speaking in tongues is praise of God. It is not edification of the faithful unless an inspired interpreter is available. In Pentecostal churches and the charismatic movement, *glossolalia* is seen as the fruit of baptism by the Holy Spirit. But Paul was ambivalent about the importance of speaking in tongues for the church (see 1 Cor 14), and the main line of Christianity has always denied that it is a necessary mark of authentic Christian experience.

Gnosticism. The term (from the Greek *gnosis*, "knowledge") refers to a loosely defined group of religious sects which flourished near the beginning of the Christian era. They were all syncretistic, incorporating elaborate myths, elements of Hellenistic mystery cults, Greek philosophy and mythology, and features of Christian and Jewish faith. Some gnostic teachers regarded themselves as Christians, but theologians like Irenaeus and Tertullian denounced them as heretical. They were called gnostics because they consistently understood salvation as a deliverance from the material world and held that salvation came through knowledge of "otherworldly things." This knowledge was usually secret.

The features which most gnostic systems share are 1) spirit-matter dualism, with matter regarded as evil; 2) a creation understood as botched, not effected by the supreme God but by a lower "demiurge"; and 3) the existence of an elite group, the "spirituals" (*pneumatikoi*), who possess a divine spark which longs to be released from the body and return to heaven. This deliverance was to be accomplished through the *gnosis* offered by the sect.

The NT insistence on the goodness of creation and salvation by the Cross alone stands as the bulwark of Christian orthodoxy against gnosticism.

Godparent. *See* Sponsor (at Baptism).

Godwin, Morgan (1640–c. 1690). Missionary and author. He was baptized at Bicknor, Gloucestershire, England, on Dec. 2, 1640. Godwin (sometimes spelled Godwyn) studied at Christ Church, Oxford, and graduated in 1664. He was ordained deacon and priest and began his ministry in Virginia in 1666. Godwin returned to England around 1670 and served several cures before his death. In 1680 he published a book in which he argued for the Christianizing of the African Americans and American Indians. It was called *The Negro's and Indian's Advocate suing for their Admission into the Church; or a Persuasive to the instructing and baptising of the Negros and Indians in our Plantations; shewing that as the Compliance therewith can prejudice no Man's just Interest, so the wilful neglecting and opposing of it is no less than a manifest Apostasy from the Christian Faith. To which is added, A brief Account of Religion in Virginia.* Like many missionaries of the time, he argued that baptism did not imply manumission and that Christianizing the slaves would help against insurrection. He died near London.

Gold, William Jason (June 17, 1845–Jan. 11, 1903). Theologian, liturgist, and seminary professor. He was born in Washington, D.C. Gold studied first at Columbia College and graduated from Harvard College in 1865. He attended General Seminary for two years, 1865–1867, and then Seabury Hall from 1867 until 1868. Gold was ordained deacon on June 7, 1868, and priest on June 25, 1869. He began his ordained ministry as rector of the Church of the Holy Communion, Dundas, Minnesota. Gold was professor of exegesis at Seabury Hall, 1873–1876, and instructor in classical languages at Racine College, 1877–1880. He was professor of Greek at Racine, 1880–1885. In 1885 Gold joined the faculty of Western Theological Seminary as professor of exegesis and liturgics. He remained there the rest of his life. He attended the General Conventions of 1886, 1889, and 1892. Gold exercised a significant influence on the 1892 BCP. He died in Chicago.

Golden Number. An indication of the date of the full moon which follows the spring equinox (Mar. 21) in a nineteen-year cycle, used in finding the date of Easter Day. The Golden Number is printed before the Sunday Letter in the calendar of the BCP, pp. 21–22, for the dates from Mar. 22 through Apr. 18. The Golden Number is calculated by taking the number of the year, adding 1, and then dividing the sum by 19. The remainder, if any, is the Golden Number. If there is no remainder, 19 is the Golden Number. The Golden Number and the Sunday Letter provide the points of reference necessary to find the date of Easter Day according to the Tables and Rules for Finding the Date of Easter Day, BCP, pp. 880–885.

"Golden Rule." Maxim based on Jesus' teaching in the Sermon on the Mount, Mt 7:12 (NRSV), "In everything do to others as you would have them do to you; for this is the law and the prophets." (see also Lk 6:31.) It is frequently expressed, "Do unto others as you would have them do unto you."

"Golden Sequence, The." The sequence hymn for the Day of Pentecost, *Veni Sancte Spiritus* (Hymns 226–227), is sometimes called the Golden Sequence. The BCP rubrics direct that the *Veni Sancte Spiritus* or the *Veni Creator Spiritus* (Hymns 503–504) is to be sung before the prayer of consecration at the ordination of bishops, priests, and deacons (BCP, pp. 520, 533, 544). The hymn has been attributed to various writers, including Stephen Langton, Archbishop of Canterbury (d. 1228), and Pope Innocent III (1160–1216). It was probably written about 1200.

Good Friday. The Friday before Easter Day, on which the church commemorates the crucifixion of Jesus. It is a day of fasting and special acts of discipline and self-denial. In the early church candidates for baptism, joined by others, fasted for a day or two before the Paschal feast. In the west the first of those days eventually acquired the character of historical reenactment of the passion and death of Christ. The liturgy of the day includes John's account of the Passion gospel, a solemn form of intercession known as the solemn collects (dating from ancient Rome), and optional devotions before the cross (commonly known as the veneration of the cross). The eucharist is not celebrated in the Episcopal Church on

Good Friday, but Holy Communion may be administered from the reserved sacrament at the Good Friday service. The BCP appoints readings for Morning Prayer and Evening Prayer on Good Friday. *See* Altar of Repose; *see* Bidding Prayer; *see* Cross.

Good News Bible (The Bible in Today's English Version). An English translation of the Bible, published by the American Bible Society. The NT translation was published in 1966, and the OT translation was published in 1976. This Bible translation is presented in contemporary style and language. The *Good News Bible* does not always seek to have an exact, word-by-word translation. A modern term may be substituted to express the correct meaning of the original text. For example, "the heavens and the earth" is at times translated as "the universe." Some have described it as a paraphrase rather than a precise translation. It includes an introduction to each book and notes which often indicate other possible translations of a word or phrase. The *Good News Bible* is authorized for use in the worship of the Episcopal Church.

Good Shepherd, Oratory of the. A society of unmarried priests and laymen in the Anglican Communion who live under a rule for a life of service and devotion. It was founded in 1913 at Cambridge University. The Oratorians' Rule requires celibacy, the Daily Offices, a daily eucharist, and the "Labor of the Mind," that is, time for study. Members are grouped into colleges. There are colleges in England, the United States, Canada, Africa, and Australia. The North American Province was established in 1942, when Robert Casey made his profession before Bishop James DeWolfe Perry of Rhode Island. The North American Province is divided between the Canadian College and the U.S. College. The oratory has a strong tradition of scholarship, pastoral work and spiritual direction. Also attached to the oratory are Companions who keep a rule of life. They may be lay or ordained, married or single.

Good Shepherd, Sisterhood of. This sisterhood was founded on Apr. 6, 1869, when Bishop Horatio Potter of New York received three sisters at St. Anne's Church for the Deaf, New York City. It was in charge of St. Barnabas' House, New York; Christ Hospital, Jersey City; and St. James' Parish Home and Day School, Wilmington, North Carolina. Thomas Gallaudet was their first pastor. It was last listed in the *Living Church Quarterly 1901.*

Goodwin, William Archer Rutherfoord (June 18, 1869–Sept. 7, 1939). Historian and priest. He was born in Richmond, Virginia. Goodwin received his B.A. and M.A. from Roanoke College in 1889. In 1890 he studied at Richmond College. He received his B.D. from Virginia Theological Seminary in 1893. Goodwin was ordained deacon on June 23, 1893, and priest on July 1, 1894. He was rector of St. John's Church, Petersburg, Virginia, 1893–1903, and while there taught at the Bishop Payne Divinity School in Petersburg. From 1903 until 1909, he was rector of Bruton Parish, Williamsburg. From 1909 until 1923, he was rector of St. Paul's Church, Rochester, New York. In 1923 he became head of the Department of Biblical Literature and Religious Education at the College of William and Mary. He served a second time as rector of Bruton Parish, 1923–1937. Goodwin was a leader in the restoration of Bruton Parish Church. He also directed the Rockefeller restoration of historic Williamsburg. Goodwin was the author of numerous books, including several studies of Bruton Parish. He also edited *History of the Theological Seminary in Virginia and Its Historical Background*, 2 vols. (1923–1924). Goodwin died in Williamsburg.

Gordon, Patrick (d. July 1702). One of the first missionaries to colonial America. Gordon was the first missionary sent by the Society for the Propagation of the Gospel (SPG) to the province of New York. He died in New York shortly after his arrival.

Gordon, Quinland Reeves (June 6, 1925–Jan. 3, 1990). African American theological educator. He was born in Greenwich, Connecticut. He graduated from Wilberforce University in 1945 and from the Episcopal Theological School in 1947. He was ordained deacon on Mar. 31, 1949, and priest on Oct. 31, 1949. He was rector of the Church of the Atonement, Washington, D.C., 1949–1965, and associate secretary of the Division of Christian Citizenship of the Executive Council of the Episcopal Church. From 1971 to 1978, he was the first and only dean of the Absalom Jones Theological Institute, Atlanta. Gordon was vicar of St. Luke's Church, Fort Valley, Georgia, 1978–1980. Gordon served as canon for outreach at St. Philip's Cathedral, Atlanta, 1981–1985. He died in Atlanta.

Gordon, William Jones, Jr. (May 6, 1918–Jan. 4, 1994). Bishop of Alaska. He was born in Spray, North Carolina. Gordon received his B.A. in 1940 from the University of North Carolina and his B.D. from the Virginia Theological

Seminary in 1943. He was ordained deacon on Jan. 24, 1943, and priest on July 25, 1943. Gordon was deacon-in-charge of St. Peter's Church, Steward, Arkansas, in 1943, and priest-in-charge of St. Thomas Mission, Point Hope, Arkansas, 1943–1948. He was consecrated the third Bishop of Alaska on May 18, 1948. He served in that position until his retirement on Aug. 28, 1974. From 1976 until 1986, he was Assistant Bishop of Michigan. Gordon learned to fly when he became Bishop of Alaska, and spent about six months a year traveling among the Indian and Eskimo villages in his single-engine plane. He was called "Alaska's Flying Bishop." The United Thank Offering purchased airplanes for his use. These planes were called the "Blue Box," because UTO offerings were received in small blue boxes. He crashed at least six times. He was described as a "dynamic and unorthodox leader." Gordon died in Midland, Michigan. *See* Blue Box (Bishop Gordon's Airplane in Alaska); *see* Blue Box (UTO).

Gore, Charles (Jan. 22, 1853–Jan. 17, 1932). Theologian and bishop. He was a prolific writer, producing during his lifetime major studies in theology which had an influence far beyond the Church of England. He was also Bishop of Worcester, Birmingham, and Oxford. Gore first came to public attention when he edited *Lux Mundi: A Series of Studies in the Religion of the Incarnation* (1889), to which he also contributed a major essay on the inspiration of Holy Scripture. The volume itself, which included essays by other members of the University of Oxford, was responsible for the development of what came to be known as liberal catholicism.

He continued to develop an incarnational theology in his Bampton Lectures, *The Incarnation of the Son of God* (1891), *The Body of Christ* (1901), and, after his retirement as Bishop of Oxford, his trilogy *Reconstruction of Belief* (1921–1924). He also edited *A New Commentary on Holy Scripture* (1928), which drew together the theology and biblical critical scholarship which *Lux Mundi* had begun. He was one of the most significant theologians of his era. Gore was also a leading figure in the Christian socialist movement in the Church of England and in the revival of the religious life in the Anglican Communion.

Gore's incarnational theology was influential in the United States. William Porcher DuBose, at the University of the South, and Marshal B. Stewart, at the General Theological Seminary, shared many of the concerns found in Gore's theology. DuBose and Stewart had considerable influence upon generations of Episcopal clergy. *See* Lux Mundi; *see* Oxford Movement, The.

Gore's contribution to Anglican theology derived from the Tractarian movement in the Church of England, which sought to revive the Catholic tradition in Anglicanism. The central theme of his extensive theological writing was the Incarnation which, he believed, provided a means for putting the Catholic faith "in a right relation to modern intellectual and moral problems," chief among those being the Darwinian theory of evolution and the critical and historical analysis of Holy Scripture, both of which were a major concern in the nineteenth and early twentieth centuries.

Gospel. The English word "gospel" (from Anglo-Saxon *godspel*) or "good news" translates the Greek *euangelion*. Originally in Christian usage it meant the good news of God's saving act in Jesus Christ, focused on the cross and resurrection (1 Cor. 15:1–11). The term was used in the opening verse of the Gospel of Mark. It signified that the prefacing of the account of Jesus' death and resurrection with a string of passages or pericopes covering his earlier ministry was a way of proclaiming the good news. The unintended result was that the term became a designation for the literary genre which was created by Mark's gospel, and it came to be applied to other works of the same genre. The NT contains four gospels—Matthew, Mark, Luke, and John. Other apocryphal writings, mostly heretical, have been designated as gospels.

The gospel in the Episcopal liturgy is the final reading from Holy Scriptures taken from the canonical gospels at the eucharist (BCP, pp. 326, 357). It marks the climax of the liturgy of the word. The gospel may include elaborate ceremonial, such as a gospel procession with two candle bearers and a thurifer. The congregation stands for the gospel, which may be read or sung from the midst of the congregation. The proclamation of the gospel is properly done by a deacon, and in the Episcopal Church the gospel must be proclaimed by a gospeler in holy orders. Acclamations normally precede and follow the gospel. In the Episcopal Church, the Sunday gospel is drawn from the three-year cycle of the lectionary (BCP, pp. 889–921). The gospel may also be read at the Blessing of a Marriage (BCP, p. 426), and at the Burial of the Dead (BCP, pp. 479, 495).

A gospel reading is appointed for each day of the church year by the Daily Office lectionary (BCP, pp. 936–1001). The gospel reading may be used at Morning Prayer or Evening Prayer, and it is the last reading of the lessons. It may be read by a lay person or a member of the clergy. *See* Gospel Acclamation; *see* Gospel Book; *see* Gospel Procession.

Gospel Acclamation. Before and after a gospel reading, the people acclaim Christ present in the sacred word. The acclamations of the Episcopal Church are translations of the Latin *Gloria tibi, Domine* and *Laus tibi, Christe.* They are, in Rite 1, "Glory be to thee, O Lord" and "Praise be to thee, O Christ"; and in Rite 2, "Glory to you, Lord Christ" and "Praise to you, Lord Christ." The acclamations may be sung when the gospel is sung. The customary acclamations are omitted for the Passion gospel on the Sunday of the Passion, Palm Sunday, and Good Friday.

Gospel Advocate, The. A monthly periodical published at Newburyport, Massachusetts, beginning with the issue of Jan. 1821. It was a continuation of the *Churchman's Repository for the Eastern Diocese.* In Jan. 1822, it moved to Boston. It was published until Dec. 1826, when its subscription list was turned over to the *Episcopal Watchman.*

Gospel Book. From ancient times the gospel pericopes have been collected in a large book with an ornate cover, often illustrated and adorned with icons and jewels. This practice was recovered with the 1979 BCP, which suggests that the lessons and gospel "be read from a book or books of appropriate size and dignity" (BCP, p. 406). Following this advice, several publishers have produced gospel books for use in the Episcopal Church, and other books have been privately compiled. A deacon or server usually carries the gospel book in the entrance procession and places it on the altar until time for the gospel proclamation. Afterward, it may be returned to the altar or placed on a side table or a stand. The Second Council of Nicaea in 787 decreed that icons, crosses, and gospel books may be venerated as sacred images, just as the incarnate Christ is the image of the invisible God.

Gospel Messenger. This weekly periodical began publication on Jan. 20, 1827, at Auburn, New York. In 1835 it was moved to Utica, New York. The last issue was published in Nov. 1872.

Gospel Messenger and Southern Episcopal Register. This periodical was published at Charleston, South Carolina. The initial issue was dated Jan. 1824, and it

continued until 1853. It was for years the most influential publication of the Episcopal Church in the South. It was also called the *Charleston Gospel Messenger and Protestant Episcopal Register.*

Gospel Procession. In many places it is customary to have a gospel procession to the place of reading. A procession may include several persons—the reader, two candle bearers, a thurifer, and, if needed, someone to hold the gospel book. Incense may be used to honor the gospel book. The presider blesses the deacon or other gospeler. The gospeler takes up the gospel book from the altar and follows the others to a lectern, ambo, pulpit, or into the midst of the congregation. Afterward, the reader leads the way back and places the altar book either on the altar or on a side table. If the gospeler is to preach, someone else may return the book to the altar.

"Gospel Side." An archaic term referring to the left side of the altar, and that side of the church building, as viewed by the congregation from the nave. The gospel was read from this side of the altar in the low mass of the Roman Rite. The epistle was read from the opposite side of the altar, which was known as the "Epistle Side." This usage made its way into widespread Anglican practice after the revival of ceremonial in the second half of the nineteenth century. The BCP discourages this practice, stating "it is desirable that the lessons be read from a lectern or pulpit, and that the Gospel be read from the same lectern, or from the pulpit, or from the midst of the congregation" (p. 406).

Gospeler (or Gospeller). The term names a liturgical function, referring to a member of the clergy who reads the gospel. A deacon normally reads the gospel when present at the eucharist. *See* Deacon.

Gothic Architecture. The style of architecture prevalent in Europe from the twelfth to the sixteenth centuries. The chief distinguishing feature is the pointed arch. A revival of gothic architecture began in England in the last half of the eighteenth century, but it did not achieve popularity until the nineteenth century. An early advocate of the gothic revival was Augustus Welby Northmore Pugin (1812–1852). The Cambridge Camden Society, founded in May 1839, quickly popularized the movement through its monthly periodical, *The Ecclesiologist.* In the mid-nineteenth century most new Anglican churches were built in the gothic style.

Gown. A long, loose-fitting garment that is distinctive for students, graduates, or officers of a university or college. It is an academic insignia. The wearer's academic degree may be indicated by the trim material or the cut of the gown. Gowns are typically black, but some schools use a distinctive color. Use of the gown in academic dress dates from the middle ages. The term has been used to refer in a collective way to an academic community or its members as distinguished from the nonacademic community or other people in an area. This distinction has been referred to as "town and gown."

The gown has also been used in the liturgy. It was worn with bands. Anglican preachers have worn the gown with hood and scarf for the sermon. This use could be seen as a display of academic credentials by the preacher. Some members of the clergy (especially with a low-church piety) wore the gown throughout the service, following the Genevan practice. Liturgical use of the gown continued into the late nineteenth century. E. Clowes Chorley credited the influence of the catholic movement in the Episcopal Church with the gradual substitution of the surplice for the black preaching gown during the nineteenth century.

Grace. God's love freely given to humanity for salvation. The term is from the Latin *gratia*, a "gift or favor freely given," translating the Greek NT *charis.* Various themes concerning grace have been emphasized since the NT. The Pauline epistles present grace as unmerited and effective as God's forgiving love for humanity. The Johannine scriptures present grace as God's indwelling of humanity. The western church has generally followed the Pauline emphasis in terms of grace as God's forgiveness of sin and healing of humanity for salvation. The eastern church has generally followed the Johannine emphasis of grace as bringing about divinization and human participation in the divine life for salvation.

Augustine urged that grace is necessary to free the human will from bondage to sin, making it possible to choose the good. Augustine's teaching contradicted Pelagianism, which considered human nature to be able to achieve salvation without special divine assistance, and Semi-Pelagianism, which considered humanity to be capable of initiating the process of salvation that would subsequently be perfected by grace. Aquinas also urged that union with God is impossible for humanity without the help of divine grace. He noted that grace is inwardly received and transformative for new life. Luther emphasized that grace is God's absolutely free gift, and not the result of human works. Lutheran thought came to understand justification in terms of imputed righteousness in which the person remains inherently sinful. Calvinist understandings of grace minimized the role of human freedom, emphasizing God's predestination of the elect for salvation and the irresistibility of grace. In the Roman Catholic Church, the Council of Trent emphasized the transforming effect of grace in human life and the important role of active human cooperation in salvation.

Anglican theology, notably represented by Richard Hooker, has emphasized the gratuitous nature of grace and the importance of participation in the economy of God's salvation, especially as known in the life of the church where grace is sacramentally represented and made known. The Catechism notes that grace is "God's favor towards us, unearned and undeserved." By grace God "forgives our sins, enlightens our minds, stirs our hearts, and strengthens our wills." The Catechism also states that the sacraments and other sacramental rites of the church are means of grace (BCP, pp. 857–860).

The term can also refer to a concluding prayer at the Daily Office, or a prayer of thanksgiving or blessing before a meal. *See* Grace, The.

"Grace, The." Prayer based on 2 Cor 13:13, "The grace of the Lord Jesus Christ and the love of God and the fellowship of the Holy Spirit be with you all" (RSV). It is named for the opening words of the prayer. The words of St. Paul's trinitarian benediction are modified in the Prayer Book version, "The grace of our Lord Jesus Christ, and the love of God, and the fellowship of the Holy Spirit, be with us all evermore" (BCP, p. 102). The grace was printed at the conclusion of the Daily Offices and the litany in the 1559 Prayer Book. It continues to be the first of the concluding sentences in Morning Prayer and Evening Prayer (BCP, pp. 59, 72, 102, 126). Although the grace was dropped from the litany in the 1928 BCP, it appears as an option at the end of the litany in the 1979 BCP (p. 154). It concludes the Prayer Book service for Holy Saturday (p. 283). The grace also introduces the *Sursum corda* at the beginning of the Great Thanksgiving, Form 2, in An Order for Celebrating the Holy Eucharist (p. 404). When A Penitential Order is used as a separate service, it may be concluded with the grace (p. 353). Similarly, the eucharistic liturgy of the word may be used without communion and conclude with the Lord's Prayer and the grace (p. 407). A musical setting of the grace is at S 67 in *The Hymnal 1982*

Accompaniment Edition, Vol. 1, at the end of the music for the Great Litany.

Grace Cathedral, San Francisco. The seat of the Bishop of California. It was organized on Apr. 28, 1850, by the Rev. Jean Leonard ver Mehr (1809–1886), the first priest appointed to San Francisco. It was the second Episcopal parish in San Francisco. The first church building opened for services on July 20, 1850. On Jan. 24, 1910, the cornerstone for a new building was laid, and on Feb. 4, 1910, Grace Parish merged with the newly formed Grace Cathedral Corporation. The Cathedral was consecrated on Nov. 20, 1964.

Gradine. A raised shelf or ledge behind the altar. The altar cross, altar lights, and vases of flowers may be placed on it. The tabernacle may also be placed on it. *See* Retable.

Gradual. A psalm, hymn, or anthem that is sung or read between the OT reading and the epistle at the eucharist. The term comes from the Latin *gradus*, "step," on which cantors stood. The gradual serves as a meditation or response to the reading, and the gradual psalm has sometimes been called the "responsorial psalm." Although the gradual is optional in the Episcopal Church, it is considered by many to be an essential part of the liturgy of the word. It dates from the mid-fourth century, representing the oldest regular liturgical use of psalmody in the eucharistic liturgy. It may be a chant setting of the psalm appointed for the day. The choir or a cantor may sing the psalm to an elaborate chant, or the choir may sing an anthem based on the psalm, or all may sing the psalm to a simple chant. It may also be a metrical setting or hymn based on the appointed psalm. In the early church, a cantor sang the psalm from a lectern or ambo, and the congregation sang a refrain after each verse or group of verses while seated. The gradual was at times sung between the epistle and the gospel after the OT lesson was dropped from certain rites. Traditionally, the gradual is not concluded with a doxology. Many musical settings are available, including a plainchant version published by Church Publishing Incorporated.

Grafton, Charles Chapman (Apr. 12, 1830–Aug. 30. 1912). Co-founder of the Society of St. John the Evangelist and Anglo-catholic bishop. He was born in Boston. Grafton came under the influence of William Croswell, the founder of the Church of the Advent, Boston, which was a leading Anglo-catholic parish. He was confirmed in the Episcopal Church in 1851. In 1853 he graduated from Harvard with a degree in law but found himself drawn toward the ordained ministry. Grafton studied theology under Bishop William Whittingham of Maryland and was ordained deacon on Dec. 23, 1855. He began his ordained ministry as assistant at Reisterstown, Maryland. On May 30, 1858, he was ordained priest and served as curate at St. Paul's Church, Baltimore, and chaplain of the deaconesses of the Diocese of Maryland. At the close of the Civil War he went to England and with Richard Meux Benson and Simeon Wilberforce O'Neill founded the Society of St. John the Evangelist (SSJE), also known as the Cowley Fathers. SSJE is the oldest Anglican monastic order for men. Grafton returned to the United States, and in 1872 became the head of the American Province of SSJE as well as the rector of the Church of the Advent, Boston. A jurisdictional dispute concerning Grafton's overseas religious superior led to his withdrawal from SSJE. In 1888 he was a founder of the Sisterhood of the Holy Nativity, along with Mother Ruth Margaret. On Apr. 25, 1889, Grafton was consecrated Bishop of Fond du Lac, where he served until his death. Grafton's publications included *Plain Suggestions for a Reverent Celebration of the Holy Communion* (2d ed., 1898), and *A Journey Godward of a Servant of Jesus Christ* (1910). The fullness of ceremonial accompanying the consecration of Grafton's bishop coadjutor led to a controversy known as the "Fond du Lac Circus." Grafton died in Fond du Lac. *See* Church of the Advent, Boston; *see* Society of St. John the Evangelist, The (SSJE) (Cowley Fathers); *see* Fond du Lac Circus.

Grant, Frederick Clifton (Feb. 2, 1891–July 11, 1954). Scholar and theologian. He was born in Beloit, Wisconsin. Grant was ordained deacon on June 6, 1912, and received his B.D. from the General Theological Seminary in 1913. He was ordained priest on June 22, 1913, and served parishes in Michigan and Illinois before becoming professor of systematic theology at the Berkeley Divinity School in 1926. From 1927 until 1938, he was president of Seabury-Western Theological Seminary and presided over the merger of Western Seminary and Seabury in 1933. Grant was professor of biblical theology at Union Theological Seminary, New York, from 1938 until his retirement in 1959. He was editor-in-chief of the *Anglican Theological Review* from 1924 until 1955. In 1962–1963 he was an Anglican Observer at Vatican Council II. Grant wrote thirty-one books, including *An Introduction to New Testament*

Thought (1950) and *Ancient Judaism and the New Testament*. He is notable for introducing form criticism to America and for pioneering the use of insights from sociology for the interpretation of early Christianity. He died in New York City.

Gray, Walter Henry (Aug. 20, 1898–Dec. 4, 1973). Ecumenical leader and eighth Bishop of Connecticut. Gray was born in Richmond, Virginia. He studied at the College of William and Mary and the Law School of the University of Richmond before receiving his B.D. from the Virginia Theological Seminary in 1928. Gray was ordained deacon on June 8, 1928, and priest on Feb. 17, 1929. He was assistant rector of St. John's Church, West Hartford, Connecticut, 1928–1932, and dean of the Pro-Cathedral of the Nativity, Bethlehem, Pennsylvania, 1932–1936. Gray was dean of Christ Church Cathedral, Hartford, 1937–1940. He was consecrated Suffragan Bishop of Connecticut on Nov. 12, 1940. He was elected Bishop Coadjutor on Oct. 2, 1945, and became Bishop of Connecticut on Jan. 15, 1951. Gray served in this position until he retired on Apr. 30, 1969. While Bishop of Connecticut he was devoted to the development of church homes and a leader in religious education. He did pioneer work for the Interracial Commission and for Interfaith Housing. He was one of the leaders at the Lambeth Conferences of 1948, 1958, and 1968. He wrote the famous "Gray Report" on overseas missions. Gray helped to organize the Pan-Anglican Congress at Minneapolis in 1954, and was the editor of *Pan-Anglican.* He died in Hartford.

Graymoor. *See* Franciscan Friars of the Atonement—Graymoor.

Great Amen. The response of assent by the congregation at the conclusion of the eucharistic prayer. As the eucharistic celebration is shared by the congregation and the presider, the Great Amen emphasizes the assent of the people to the words spoken on their behalf by the presider. The Great Amen is the "people's prayer" that concludes the eucharistic prayer. The Great Amen is printed in all capital letters in the BCP to emphasize the importance of this moment in the liturgy. Historically, the "moment of consecration" at the eucharist was considered to be the institution narrative in the western church. Some eastern churches understood the *epiclesis* (invocation of the Holy Spirit) to be the moment of consecration. However, the eucharistic prayer (including institution narrative and

epiclesis) is now understood to be a single text, with the consecration completed as the eucharistic prayer concludes with the people's Great Amen.

Great Awakening. A religious revival in the American colonies in the eighteenth century. It occurred episodically from about 1720 until about 1770. It was part of the religious fervor which swept western Europe during the latter part of the seventeenth century and most of the eighteenth century. This movement was called pietism in Germany and evangelicalism in England. In the New World the Great Awakening was one of the first great movements to give the colonists a feeling of unity and sense of special purpose in God's providential plan. It was a reaction against arid rationalism in New England, formalism in liturgical practices among the Dutch Reformed in the Middle Colonies, and neglect of pastoral supervision in the South. Because the revival took place especially among the Dutch Reformed, the Congregationalists, the Presbyterians, the Baptists, and some Anglicans, it was largely a development toward evangelical Calvinism. Revival preachers tended to emphasize the "terrors of the law" to sinners, the unmerited grace of God, and a "new birth" in Jesus Christ. One of the movement's great figures was George Whitefield, an Anglican priest who was influenced first by John Wesley and then by Calvinists. Jonathan Edwards (1703–1758), the great apologist of the movement, was a strong Calvinist and preached a doctrine of justification by faith. His chief opponent was Charles Chauncy (1704–1787), a Congregational minister of Boston. Chauncy preached against the revival, which he considered an outbreak of extravagant emotion. The Great Awakening was responsible for stemming the tide of Enlightenment rationalism in the colonies. It also led to divisions in some of the denominations between those who supported and those who rejected its tenets. It was responsible for stimulating missions to the Native Americans and the slaves, and for the establishment and growth of several educational institutions, including Princeton, Dartmouth, and Brown. The itinerant preaching associated with the Great Awakening helped to break up the old parish system in which everyone in an area belonged to a single church. It also led to a broader religious toleration and the democratization of religious experience. It contributed to the fervor that resulted in the American Revolution. Although the Anglican Church in America was not strongly affected by the Great Awakening, there was significant participation in this revival by individual Anglican clergy and laity. *See* Jarratt, Devereux; *see* Wesley, John; *see* Whitefield, George.

Great Bible, The. English Bible prepared by Miles Coverdale. The term is based on the size of the Bible. It was printed by Richard Grafton and Edward Whitchurch. It has been called "Whitchurch's Bible." The printing was begun in Paris but later continued in London owing to the hostility of the Sorbonne. In Sept. 1538, Thomas Cromwell had ordered this Bible to be placed in every parish church. The Great Bible was finally issued in the early summer of 1539. It was based on Coverdale's Bible (1535), Matthew's Bible (1537), and the work of William Tyndale. The title page of the Great Bible depicts God blessing the King, who is handing out copies of the Bible to Thomas Cranmer and Thomas Cromwell. This artwork is generally attributed to Hans Holbein. Coverdale later revised the Great Bible, which was reissued with a preface by Thomas Cranmer in 1540. This version has been known as "Cranmer's Bible." The Great Bible is also known as the "Treacle Bible," due to Coverdale's distinctive rendering of Jer 8:22, in which he mentions "treacle in Gilead" instead of "balm in Gilead." The Great Bible influenced the Geneva Bible (1560) and the Bishops' Bible (1568). The Convocation of 1571 ordered the Bishops' Bible to be used in all the churches of England. The Psalter of the Great Bible became the Psalter of the 1549 Prayer Book. Coverdale's Psalter in the Great Bible has been carefully preserved in subsequent Prayer Book revisions, including the 1979 BCP, although some archaic words and inaccurate renderings have been changed.

Great Commission Alliance. A movement of Episcopalians working to fulfill the commission of Jesus Christ to "go and make disciples of all nations." It was formed in Oct. 1995. The three fundamental principles of the Alliance are: 1) a commitment to put Jesus first; 2) the affirmation that God's way of salvation is through Jesus Christ; and 3) a pledge to radical cooperation. The three sending agencies of the Alliance are the North American Missionary Society, the South American Missionary Society, and Anglican Frontiers Mission. The Alliance also cooperates with the Episcopal Church Missionary Community, SOMA (Sharing of Ministries Abroad), and the Church Army. In 1995 the Alliance identified a ten-year goal of planting 1,000 new churches in North America.

Great Fifty Days. The feast of Easter is a season of fifty days, from Easter Eve through the Day of Pentecost. From early times the Greek word *pentecost* (fiftieth day) was used also for the whole Paschal season. During this season there is no fasting. The Council of Nicaea (325) directed that Christians are to pray standing. The word "alleluia" (praise the Lord) is said or sung repeatedly, which contrasts sharply with the season of Lent when the alleluia is omitted. The color of liturgical vestments and hangings is white or gold. The BCP notes that it is customary for the Paschal candle to burn at all services of the Easter season. The "Alleluia, alleluia" may be added to the dismissals and their responses during the Great Fifty Days. The traditional Christian Easter greeting (see Lk 24:34) serves as the opening acclamation at the eucharist during the Easter season. *See* Easter.

Great Litany, The. An intercessory prayer including various petitions that are said or sung by the leader, with fixed responses by the congregation. It was used as early as the fifth century in Rome. It was led by a deacon, with the collects led by a bishop or priest. The Litany was the first English language rite prepared by Archbishop Thomas Cranmer. It was first published in 1544. Cranmer modified an earlier litany form by consolidating certain groups of petitions into single prayers with response. The Litany's use in church processions was ordered by Henry VIII when England was at war with Scotland and France. It was printed as an appendix to the eucharist in the 1549 BCP. The Litany was used in each of the three ordination rites of the 1550 ordinal, with a special petition and concluding collect. The 1552 BCP called for use of the Litany after the fixed collects of Morning Prayer on Sundays, Wednesdays, and Fridays. The 1928 BCP allowed the Litany to be used after the fixed collects of Morning or Evening Prayer, or before the Eucharist, or separately. The 1928 BCP included a short Litany for Ordinations as an alternative to the Litany. The 1979 BCP titled the Litany "The Great Litany" (p. 148), distinguishing it from other litanies in the Prayer Book.

The Great Litany may be said or sung. The officiant and people may kneel or stand, or it may be done in procession. The Great Litany may be done before the Eucharist, or after the collects of Morning or Evening Prayer, or separately. Because of its penitential tone, it is especially appropriate during Lent. The Great Litany includes an invocation of the Trinity; a series of deprecations which seek deliverance from evil, spiritual harm, and natural calamities; a series of obsecrations which plead the power of Christ's Incarnation, life, death, and resurrection for deliverance; prayers of general intercession; the *Agnus Dei*; the *Kyrie*; the Lord's Prayer; a versicle and response based on Ps 33:22; a concluding collect; and the grace (BCP, pp.148–154). The Supplication (BCP, p. 154) may be used at the conclusion of the Great Litany, taking the place of all that follows the Lord's Prayer.

When the Great Litany precedes the eucharist, the Litany concludes with the *Kyrie* and the eucharist begins with the salutation and the collect of the day (BCP, p. 153). The Great Litany should not be preceded by a hymn, psalm, or anthem when it is used as an entrance rite at the eucharist. The Great Litany takes the place of the prayers of the people at the eucharist. The confession may also be omitted.

The Great Litany is also especially appropriate on Rogation Days. The *BOS* order for a Rogation Procession calls for the Great Litany to begin as the procession enters the church. It adds petitions for favorable weather, productive lands and waters, and God's favor for all who care for the earth, the water, and the air. The Great Litany may also conclude the *BOS* Service for New Year's Eve.

Great O Antiphons of Advent. Antiphons sung before and after the *Magnificat* at vespers on the seven days before Christmas. The texts are of unknown origin and date at least from the ninth century. Each antiphon begins with the letter "O" and a name or attribute of God from the Hebrew Scriptures: *O Sapientia*, "O Wisdom"; *O Adonai*, "O Sacred Lord"; *O Radix Jesse*, "O Root of Jesse"; *O Clavis David*, "O Key of David"; *O Oriens*, "O Rising Sun"; *O Rex gentium*, "O King of nations"; and *O Emmanuel*, "O Emmanuel." In the Roman rite the antiphons are sung from Dec. 17–23, but in the medieval Sarum use they began on Dec. 16, adding on Dec. 23, *O Virgo virginum* (O Virgin of virgins). The Great O Antiphons have been adapted as a popular Advent hymn, "O come, O come, Emmanuel" (Hymn 56), whose verses may be used as antiphons for the *Magnificat* on the appropriate days.

Great Silence. In religious communities, the time between the last common prayer at night (compline or evensong) and the first common prayer in the morning (laud, prime, or morning prayer). Typically a period of solemn silence and quiet before and after sleep, it may be used for private reading and meditation. During this time one should avoid disturbing noises and speak only in emergencies.

Great Thanksgiving. Title used by the BCP for the eucharistic prayer, the central prayer of the Eucharist. It is also known as the prayer of consecration. It begins with the dialogue called *Sursum corda* and continues through the Great Amen at the end of its doxology. It gives thanks for creation, redemption, and sanctification. The bread and wine are consecrated in the context of giving thanks over them in the eucharistic prayer. The institution narrative, oblation (*anamnesis*), invocation of the Holy Spirit (*epiclesis*), intercessions, and the angelic hymn *Sanctus* are included in the eucharistic prayers of Rite 1 and Rite 2.

Eucharistia is Greek for "thanksgiving," and the Great Thanksgiving distinguishes the thanksgiving over the bread and wine from other thanksgivings, such as that over the baptismal font or the chrism. This ancient title was restored in *Prayer Book Studies 19* and succeeding trial rites leading up to the 1979 BCP. The Greeks call this prayer *anaphora* (offering), and the traditional Latin title is *Prex* (Prayer). *Canon* is not a generic name for the eucharistic prayer, but the proper name of the *canon Romanus*, also called the *canon missae*, or *canon actionis*, the present Eucharistic Prayer 1 of the Roman Sacramentary. It was so called because, unlike the eucharistic prayers of other rites, it was always the same, an inflexible rule, or canon. The eucharistic prayer had no title in the 1549 BCP. The Scottish Prayer Book of 1637 introduced the title "Prayer of Consecration," which was used through the 1967 *Liturgy of the Lord's Supper*. This focuses on the consecration of the bread and wine but neglects the wider eucharistic aspects of the prayer.

Great Vigil of Easter. *See* Easter Vigil.

Greek Mission. This was the name of the Episcopal mission to Constantinople. It was also called the Constantinople Mission. After Greece's war of independence from Turkey in 1829, the Episcopal Church sent five missionaries to Greece in 1830. They were to help rebuild the Christian church in Greece after centuries of Muslim occupation. The Greek Mission focused on education and did not attempt to proselytize. In 1844 Horatio Southgate was consecrated Missionary Bishop in the Dominions and Dependencies of the Sultan of Turkey. Southgate resigned Oct. 12, 1850, and the Greek Mission ended with his resignation.

"Green Book." *See* Proposed Book of Common Prayer.

"Green Season." *See* Ordinary Time.

Green, Fred Pratt (b. Sept. 2, 1903). British Methodist minister and hymn writer. He was born near Liverpool, England, and educated at Huyton High School, Wallasey Grammar School, Rydal School, and Didsbury College, Manchester. From the time of his ordination in 1925 until his retirement, Green wrote plays, hymns, and poems. After retirement in the late 1960s, he devoted much of his time to writing hymns. As a founder and leader of the British "Hymn Explosion," his hymns were among the finest composed in the last third of the twentieth century. They are included in most major English language hymnals. *The Hymnal 1982* uses six of his original hymn texts, including "When in our music God is glorified" (420) and "For the fruit of all creation" (424). Another of these original texts, "By gracious powers" (695), is based on the writings of Dietrich Bonhoeffer (1906–1945). *The Hymnal 1982* also includes one hymn text translated by Green, "Blest be the King whose coming" (74).

Green, William Mercer (May 2, 1798–Feb. 13, 1887). Bishop and educator. He was born in Wilmington, North Carolina. Green received his B.A. from the University of North Carolina in 1818. After reading theology he was ordained deacon on Apr. 29, 1821, and priest on Apr. 23, 1823. He was the rector of St. John's Church, Williamsboro, 1823–1826, and then rector of St. Matthew's Church, Hillsborough, 1826–1836, both in North Carolina. In 1837 he joined the faculty of the University of North Carolina. He was also rector of the Chapel of the Holy Cross, Chapel Hill, which he helped to found. On Feb. 24, 1850, he was consecrated the first Bishop of Mississippi, and served in that position until his death. Green was a great proponent of education as a function of the church. He founded three schools before the Civil War: St. Andrew's College, Jackson; Rose Gates, Okolona; and Trinity School, Pass Christian. He was also involved in the founding of the University of the South and served as its fourth Chancellor from Dec. 21, 1866, until his death. In 1873 he helped found the Bishop Green Training School in Dry Cove, Mississippi, to train African American men for ordained ministry. Green died in Sewanee, Tennessee.

Greenfield, Robert Harvie (Feb. 11, 1925–Apr. 23, 1999). Priest, monk, and Prayer Book reviser. Greenfield was born in Portland, Oregon. He received the B.A. from Reed College in 1949, the M.Litt. from Oxford University in 1951, and the D.Phil from Oxford in 1956. Greenfield was ordained deacon on Oct. 18, 1951, and priest on Apr. 23, 1952. He served a number of parishes in the Diocese of Oregon and the Diocese of Oxford. In 1973 he became the dean of the Cathedral of St. John the Baptist, Portland, Oregon. He held that position until 1980, when he went to the Society of St. John the Evangelist in Cambridge, Massachusetts, to test his vocation. He was life professed on Apr. 15, 1986. Greenfield was a member of the Standing Liturgical Commission and made numerous contributions to its work. He wrote the second Eucharistic Prayer in Rite 1 and the prayers of the people for the Rite 1 Burial Office. His most significant contribution to Prayer Book revision was An Outline of the Faith, or Catechism (pp. 845–862), which was almost entirely his work. Greenfield died in Boston.

Greer, David Hummel (Mar. 20, 1844–May 19, 1919). Bishop and opponent of war. He was born in Wheeling, West Virginia. Greer graduated from Washington College, Washington, Pennsylvania, in 1862. From 1863 until 1866, he studied at the Bexley Hall Divinity School. He was ordained deacon on June 27, 1866, and began his ordained ministry at Christ Church, Clarksburg, West Virginia. On May 19, 1868, he was ordained priest. From 1868 until 1871, he was rector of Trinity Church, Covington, Kentucky. He was rector of Grace Church, Providence, Rhode Island, 1872–1888, and later rector of St. Bartholomew's Church, New York City, 1888–1904. On Jan. 26, 1904, Greer was consecrated Bishop Coadjutor of New York, and he became the eighth Bishop of New York on July 21, 1908. He served in that position until his death. During his episcopate he supported the continuing construction of the Cathedral of St. John the Divine, and he opposed the entrance of the United States into World War I. Greer died in New York City.

Gregg, Alexander (Oct. 8, 1819–July 11, 1893). Bishop and leading supporter of the University of the South. He was born in Society Hill, Darlington District, South Carolina. Gregg received his B.A. from South Carolina College in 1838 and then studied law. He practiced law in Cheraw, South Carolina. He was attracted to St. David's Church in Cheraw, where he was baptized and confirmed in 1843. Gregg was ordained deacon on June 10, 1846, and priest on Dec. 19, 1847. His entire parochial ministry was spent as rector of St. David's Church, Cheraw. On Oct. 13, 1859, he was consecrated the first Bishop of Texas and served in that position until his death. As bishop of the largest geographical diocese in the Episcopal Church, Gregg was an inveterate traveler. Under his leadership the

Diocese of Texas was divided into three dioceses in 1874. He was the fourth Chancellor of the University of the South, serving from Aug. 1, 1887, until his death. He was the first elected Chancellor of the University. His three predecessors served by virtue of their seniority in terms of the date of their consecration as bishops. Gregg has been called "the John Henry Hobart of Texas." He died in Austin, Texas.

Gregorian Chant. *See* Plainsong.

Gregory the Great (c. 540–Mar. 12, 604). Sixth-century Pope and Doctor of the Church. He was born in Rome. After serving as prefect of Rome, c. 572–574, Gregory entered the monastery of St. Andrew on the Caelian Hill around 575. He was consecrated Bishop of Rome on Sept. 3, 590, and served until his death. He was very successful in the struggle against the Lombards in Italy and in the administration of the church and its benevolent activities. He was also very active in extending papal authority. Gregory is remembered for sending Augustine to Canterbury in 597 to do missionary work among the Anglo-Saxons. Gregory's book, *Pastoral Care* (c. 591), is one of the classics of pastoral theology and sets out his view of the bishop as the shepherd of souls. He described himself as "servant of God's servants." Gregory is one of only two popes to be given the title, "the Great," and is one of the four great Doctors of the Western Church. He died in Rome. Gregory is commemorated in the Episcopal calendar of the church year on Oct. 12.

Gregory the Illuminator (c. 257–c. 332). Bishop and missionary to Armenia. He was born in Valarshapat or possibly Caesarea in Cappadocia. After studying at Caesarea in Cappadocia, he returned to Armenia and converted King Tiridates. With the help of the king he converted the nation to Christianity. He was consecrated bishop around 315, and he baptized the kings of Caucasian Iberia, Lazes, and Albania. Sometime before his death he retired as a hermit in the wilderness. By his missionary work Armenia was the first country to become officially Christian. Gregory died in Armenia. He is commemorated in the Episcopal calendar of the church year on Mar. 23.

Gregory of Nazianzus (c. 329–389 or 390). Leading trinitarian theologian. He was born at Arianzus in Cappadocia. Gregory succeeded his father as Bishop of Nazianzus and in 379 was elected Bishop of Constantinople. He was a great defender of the Nicene Faith and played a leading role at the Second Ecumenical Council in Constantinople in 381. He insisted that the only distinctions that can be established between the three Persons of the Trinity are those which refer to the origin of each of them. The Father is unbegotten, the Son is begotten, and the Holy Spirit proceeds. He was an opponent of Apollinaris and taught the complete humanity and the complete divinity of Jesus Christ. Gregory has been called "the Theologian," "the Divine," and the "Christian Demosthenes." He and Basil of Caesarea, along with Basil's brother, Gregory of Nyssa, are known as the "Cappadocian Fathers." His works include *Five Orations on the Divinity of the Word*; and the *Philocalia*, a collection of Origen's writings that he compiled with Basil. Gregory is commemorated in the Episcopal calendar of the church year on May 9.

Gregory of Nyssa (c. 335–c. 395). Theologian and leading defender of the Nicene faith. He was consecrated Bishop of Nyssa in 372. Gregory attended the Second Ecumenical Council at Constantinople in 381, where he asserted the unity of the three Persons in the one Godhead. With regard to the Trinity, Gregory taught a doctrine of coinherence or *perichoresis*, that the three Persons of the Trinity are equally involved in all the operations of the Godhead and do not act independently. He is remembered for his mysticism, his asceticism, and his understanding of salvation as deification. Gregory of Nyssa is recognized as a leading Greek theologian of the fourth century. He, his brother, Basil of Caesarea, and Gregory of Nazianzus, are known as the "Cappadocian Fathers." Gregory is commemorated in the Episcopal calendar of the church year on Mar. 9. *See* Theosis.

Grey Book, The. See Kingdom, the Power and the Glory, The.

Griffith, David (1742–Aug. 3, 1789). Missionary and early leader of the Diocese of Virginia. He was born in New York City. Griffith went to England to study medicine and returned to New York to begin his practice in 1763. He went to England to be ordained. Griffith was ordained deacon on Aug. 19, 1770, and priest on Aug. 24, 1770. The Society for the Propagation of the Gospel (SPG) appointed him missionary to Gloucester County, New Jersey. At the end of 1771, he took charge of Shelburne Parish, Loudon County, Virginia. He continued at Shelburne Parish until May 1776, when he entered the Army as Chaplain to the Third Virginia Regiment. He resigned his Chaplaincy in 1779, and became the rector of Christ Church, Alexandria, in 1780. He served there until his death. Griffith was instrumental in organizing the Diocese of Virginia in 1785. He was a clerical deputy to the 1786 General Convention. He was president of the House of Deputies, June 22–Oct. 11, 1786. On May 31, 1786, Griffith was elected the first Bishop of Virginia. It was expected that he would go with William White and Samuel Provoost to England for consecration. Monetary difficulties made this impossible, and he resigned as bishop-elect on May 6, 1789. Griffith died in Philadelphia while attending the third General Convention.

Griswold, Alexander Viets (Apr. 22, 1766–Feb. 15, 1843). Bishop and evangelist. He was born in Simsbury, Connecticut. He was educated privately by his uncle, a priest. Although he cultivated a small farm as a young man, he decided in 1794 to study for ordination. He was ordained deacon on June 7, 1795, and priest on Oct. 1, 1795. He served three small churches in Litchfield County. Griswold was chosen rector of St. Michael's Church, Bristol, Rhode Island, in 1804. Following the organization of the Eastern Diocese, a jurisdiction that included all of New England except Connecticut, he was elected bishop and consecrated on May 31, 1811. He remained in parishes until 1835 when he devoted himself wholly to episcopal duties. He also served as the Episcopal Church's fifth Presiding Bishop from July 17, 1836, until his death. After being elected bishop, Griswold underwent a conversion experience. His preaching and piety became markedly evangelical. A tremendous spiritual awakening occurred throughout his diocese. Church membership increased approximately tenfold between 1790 and 1840. Griswold died in Boston, and the Eastern Diocese ceased to exist shortly thereafter.

Griswold College, Davenport, Iowa. Around 1858 the Rt. Rev. Henry Washington Lee, first Bishop of Iowa, bought the property of Iowa College, Davenport. In 1859 he secured a charter for Griswold College, named for Bishop Alexander Viets Griswold of the Eastern Diocese. This venture was to be "the college of the Trans Mississippi bishops and sees," but this interdiocesan aspect was never realized. A theological department opened in 1861, which was called Lee Hall after Bishop Lee's death in 1874. Kemper Hall for boys served as a preparatory department until it closed in 1895. St Katherine's School for Girls was established under Bishop William Stevens Perry. The college, the boy's school, and the theological department closed in the 1890s.

Griswold, Frank Tracy, III (b. Sept. 18, 1937). Twenty-fifth Presiding Bishop of the Episcopal Church. He was born in Bryn Mawr, Pennsylvania. Griswold received the A.B. at Harvard in 1959, and he attended the General Theological Seminary, 1959–1960. He received the B.A. in 1962 and the M.A. in 1966 from Oxford University. He was ordained deacon on Dec. 15, 1962, and priest on June 23, 1963. He served as curate at the Church of the Redeemer, Bryn Mawr, 1963–1967. He was rector, St. Andrew, Yardley, Pennsylvania, 1967–1974; and rector, St. Martin-in-the-Fields, Philadelphia, Pennsylvania, 1974–1985. He was also an instructor in Anglican liturgical prayer and spirituality at the Lutheran Seminary in Philadelphia. On Mar. 2, 1985, he was consecrated Bishop Coadjutor of the Diocese of Chicago. He served as Bishop of Chicago, 1987–1998, and was invested as Presiding Bishop on Jan. 10, 1998. He served as co-chair of the Anglican-Roman Catholic dialogue in the United States, and chair of the Standing Liturgical Commission. He contributed to writing Eucharistic Prayer "B" in the 1979 BCP.

Grosseteste, Robert (c. 1175–Oct. 1253). Reforming bishop. Very little is known about his early life, except that he had a great interest in science. Later in life he studied theology. On June 17, 1235, he was consecrated Bishop of Lincoln. He held this position until his death. He was conscientious and regular in visiting his diocese, which was a departure from the usual practice of his day. During a visitation of his diocese he deposed those abbots and priors who did not adequately staff the parish churches in their care. He was a Greek scholar and translated the *Nicomachean Ethics* of Aristotle. Grosseteste was also a supporter of the Franciscans. His life is commemorated in the Episcopal calendar of the church year on Oct. 9.

Groton School. A five-year, coeducational boarding school located forty miles northwest of Boston at Groton, Massachusetts. It was founded in 1884 by Endicott Peabody, an Episcopal priest who wished to imbue Christian values in young men and prepare them both for college and leadership in American society. Students and faculty worshiped together twice a day, and at the turn of the century a large gothic-style chapel was erected at the heart of the campus. Peabody considered Groton a family. He and his wife said good night to students daily with a handshake. He served as headmaster until 1940. The school's bylaws stated that the headmaster must be an ordained Episcopalian. John Crocker, an Episcopal priest, was headmaster between 1940 and 1965. The original bylaws have been changed, and the chaplain now bears the primary responsibility of overseeing the school's spiritual life.

Grotto. A natural or artificial cave. The term is from the Italian for "cavern." Grottos from natural caves were once seen as dwelling places for gods. A tradition from the second century holds that Jesus was born in a cave at Bethlehem, known as the Grotto of the Nativity. A basilica was built over this cave in 325. Many Roman Catholic churches and retreat centers have reproduced the cave at Lourdes, France, where the Virgin Mary is said to have appeared to Bernadette Soubirous in 1858.

Guardian Angel. *See* Angel.

Guatemala, Diocese of. The House of Bishops created the Missionary District of Guatemala on Sept. 18, 1967. On Nov. 26, 1967, William Carl Frey was consecrated the first Missionary Bishop. On Jan. 20, 1973, Anselmo Carral-Solar was consecrated the first native Bishop of Guatemala. It became the Diocese of Guatemala on Jan. 1, 1980.

Guerry, William Alexander (July 7, 1861–June 9, 1928). Bishop assassinated by a priest. He was born in Clarendon County, South Carolina. Guerry received his B.A. in 1884, his M.A. in 1884, and his B.D. in 1891, all from the University of the South. He was ordained deacon on Sept. 23, 1888, and priest on Dec. 22, 1889. After serving as rector of St. John's Church, Florence, South Carolina, 1888–1893, he became chaplain of the University of the South, where he was also professor of homiletics and pastoral theology at the School of Theology. While at Sewanee, he was influential in the building of All Saints' Chapel. On Sept. 15, 1907, Guerry was consecrated Bishop Coadjutor of South Carolina, and became the eighth Bishop of South Carolina on Apr. 22, 1908. He was one of the few southern bishops who supported the Social Gospel. On June 5, 1928, Guerry was shot in his office in St. Philip's Church, Charleston, by a mentally disturbed priest who was one of his clergy, and died four days later.

Guidelines and Procedures for Continuing Alteration of the Calendar. *See* Lesser Feasts and Fasts, The (LFF).

Guild of All Souls. The objects of the guild are intercessory prayer for the dying and the repose of the souls of the departed, to encourage Christian customs at burial, especially the celebration of the eucharist, and to promote the Christian doctrines of the communion of saints and the resurrection from the dead. Guild members are encouraged to pray for the dying and the dead, to participate in a requiem on All Souls' Day and say a Litany of the Faithful Departed at least once a month. Members of the Guild are prayed for on the date of death for 25 years. The guild had its beginnings when the Rev. Arthur Tooth, vicar of St. James's Church, Hatcham, England, held a preliminary meeting with two laymen on Mar. 15, 1873, to form a "Burial Guild." On Apr. 26, 1873, the guild prayers were said publicly for the first time in the Lady Chapel of St. James', Hatcham. Its purpose was to pray for the dead. This became the Guild of All Souls. The first known reference to praying for the dead in the United States occurred in a sermon at St. Clement's Church, Philadelphia, Pennsylvania, on Nov. 1, 1869. It is not recorded who preached the sermon, but the Rev. Herman Griswold Batterson was rector at the time. The annual meeting of the guild in England on May 14, 1889, granted independence to the American branch of the guild.

Guild of the Holy Cross. A society for invalids founded by the Rev. James A. Bolles around 1892. It sought to provide mutual support and useful employment for invalids so that they did not feel themselves cut off from the church. The guild encouraged its members to use their leisure as given them by God for the work of intercession to the benefit of others who, like them, suffered bodily pain and weariness. The guild consisted of invalids who were called members, and persons in health who were called associates. It went out of existence around 1949.

Guild of the Iron Cross. A society of men for the promotion of temperance, reverence, and chastity by the use of prayer, sacramental grace, and the exercise of works of mercy. It was organized in 1883, and it appears to have gone out of existence around 1900. The founders chose the name "Iron Cross" because it reminded them of the cross of Christ and the nails by which he was fastened there, and because it was the sign of a holy war, like a crusade. The guild worked with boys in the inner city, helped with the burial of poor Christians, and participated in the flood rescue effort in Johnstown, Pennsylvania. It published *The Iron Cross*.

Guild of Scholars of the Episcopal Church. An unofficial organization of about sixty Episcopal lay men and women who are, for the most part, professors in American colleges and universities. The guild meets annually to present and share papers relating the academic interests of the members to their Christian faith commitment within the Episcopal Church. It was founded in 1938 with the encouragement of the Rev. Norman Pittenger who was its first chaplain. Well-known members have included John Wild, W. H. Auden, Charles Lawrence, and Cleanth Brooks. Membership is restricted to those not ordained, and it is voted following nomination by members of the guild.

Guild of St. Barnabas for Nurses. An international, ecumenical organization of nurses, those working in fields related to nursing, and others interested in nursing. The guild seeks to provide deeper spiritual meaning for the lives of its members in their several vocations and to offer further enrichment by shared education and fellowship. The rule of life of the guild requires members to pray for their patients and read a few verses of the Bible each day. In the early years of its existence, it often met in conjunction with the Woman's Auxiliary to the Board of Missions of the Episcopal Church. The guild was founded on June 11 (St. Barnabas Day), 1886, in Boston, Massachusetts. On this day three nurses were admitted as probationers of the guild by the Rev. Edward Osborne, mission priest of St. John the Evangelist Church, Boston, who served as the guild's first chaplain. On Oct. 28, 1886, the guild was organized when ten nurses were admitted to membership.

H

Habit. The garment worn by members of classical religious communities. It derives from various forms of male or female dress in the middle ages. Later communities adopted a variant of the clerical black cassock. In recent years many religious communities have simplified the habit, stopped wearing it in public, or abolished it.

Hagiography. The writing of the lives of the saints. It involves studying and comparing the sources, assessing their historical validity and importance, and relating them to their context in contemporary secular history. The primary sources for hagiography include martyrologies, calendars, biographies, prose and verse literary compositions, and liturgical texts. Eusebius (260–340) compiled the first hagiography. The term often means an uncritical appreciation of the life of a saint and is used pejoratively in this sense.

Hail Mary. Prayer addressed to the Blessed Virgin Mary. The first two of its three parts are drawn from the salutation of the Archangel Gabriel to Mary at the Annunciation, "Hail, O favored one, the Lord is with you!" (Lk 1:28, RSV); and Elizabeth's words to Mary at the Visitation, "Blessed are you among women, and blessed is the fruit of your womb!" (Lk 1:42, RSV). These verses have been used as a single formula in Christian liturgy since the sixth century. They were used in the Roman antiphonary in the seventh century as an offertory text for the feast of the Annunciation, for the Ember Wednesday of Advent, and for the Fourth Sunday of Advent. The two verses were a popular devotion by the eleventh century. The third part of the Hail Mary is the concluding petition, "Holy Mary, Mother of God, pray for us sinners now and at the hour of our death. Amen." Various concluding prayers for this devotion were added in the fifteenth century. The concluding petition in its present form has been dated from the sixteenth century. The Hail Mary is also known as the Angelic Salutation. Its Latin form is *Ave Maria*. The Hail Mary is used in other Christian devotions, such as the *Angelus* and the Rosary.

Haiti, Diocese of. On Nov. 3, 1874, the House of Bishops gave its consent to the consecration of James Theodore Holly as Bishop of Haiti and signed a covenant with the Protestant Episcopal Church in Haiti. Holly served as Bishop until his death in 1911. On Oct. 4, 1913, the House of Bishops created the Missionary District of Haiti. Holy Trinity Cathedral, Port-au-Prince, was dedicated on Jan. 2, 1919. In 1985 it became the Diocese of Haiti.

Hakluyt, Richard (c. 1552–Nov. 23, 1616). Priest who developed the theoretical rationale for British colonization of America. He was born in Herefordshire, England. Hakluyt received his B.A. in 1574, and his M.A. in 1577, both from Christ Church, Oxford. Although he was a priest, he was most interested in geography and cosmography. Hakluyt was an authority on maritime affairs and colonization. He was a member of the Virginia Company of London. He helped organize and strongly supported the colonization of North America, especially the Virginia colony. Sir Walter Raleigh asked Hakluyt to write a treatise on the advantages of planting colonies in America to encourage Queen

Elizabeth's support for colonization. Hakluyt wrote *A Discourse on Western Planting* in 1584 as a treatise for the Queen only. It was not intended for public reading, and it was not published until 1877. In this treatise Hakluyt presented the spiritual and temporal reasons for colonization in America. He noted the potential of colonization for missions and the expansion of Protestantism against Roman Catholicism. He also observed that colonization could shift attention from ecclesiastical problems in England at the time, encourage trade and investments, and provide jobs and training for sailors as well as a place for sending criminals and rebels. Hakluyt died in London.

Hale, Sarah Josepha (Oct. 24, 1788–Apr. 30, 1879). Editor, poet, and advocate for social justice. She was born in Newport, New Hampshire. In 1813 she married a lawyer, David Hale, and they had five children. He died in 1822, and she supported the children by writing. Her poem, "Mary Had a Little Lamb," published in her *Poems For Our Children* (1830), became a favorite nursery rhyme. Hale edited the *Ladies Magazine*, later the *American Ladies Magazine*, 1828–1837, and *Godey's Lady's Book*, 1837–1857. She advocated "female improvement," the kindergarten movement, education for the deaf, charitable organizations, the movement to win property rights for women, the deaconess movement being imported from Germany, and the foreign mission field for women. Hale campaigned for funds to complete the Bunker Hill monument, to have Thanksgiving Day declared a national holiday, and to have Mount Vernon named a national shrine. She was converted to the Episcopal Church and was an active member at Holy Trinity, Philadelphia. Hale died in Philadelphia.

Hall, Arthur Crawshay Alliston (Apr. 12, 1847–Feb. 26, 1930). Leader of Anglo-catholicism, committed ecumenist, and author of twenty books, including *The Virgin Mother* (1894) and *The Doctrine of the Church* (1909). He was born in Binfield, Berkshire, England. He received his B.A. in 1869 and his M.A. in 1872 from Christ Church, Oxford. At Oxford he came under the influence of the Tractarians, and entered the Society of St. John the Evangelist as a lay brother. He was ordained deacon on Dec. 18, 1870, and priest on Dec. 21, 1871. In 1874 he was sent to the American branch of the society and became associate priest at the Church of the Advent, Boston, where he remained until 1882. From 1882 until 1891, when he was recalled to

England, he served the Church of St. John the Evangelist, Boston. He was consecrated the third Bishop of Vermont on Feb. 2, 1894, and served in that capacity until his death.

Hall, Francis Joseph (Dec. 24, 1857–Mar. 12, 1932). Called the "most notable of Anglo-Catholic theologians" in the Episcopal Church, he was born in Ashtabula, Ohio. Hall received his B.A. in 1882 and his M.A. in 1885, both from Racine College. He then studied for the ordained ministry at the General Theological Seminary and Western Theological Seminary. He was ordained deacon on July 1, 1885 and priest on Feb. 21, 1886. From 1886 until 1913, Hall taught dogmatic theology at Western Theological Seminary. From 1913 until his retirement in 1928, he was professor of dogmatic theology at the General Theological Seminary. He was the author of several works, including the three-volume *Theological Outlines* (1892–1895) that established his reputation as a scholar. His ten-volume *Dogmatic Theology* (1907–1922) remains a valuable exposition of traditional catholic theology. Hall was deeply interested in church unity and participated in organizing the World Conference on Faith and Order. He died in Baldwinsville, New York.

Hallelujah. Ancient Hebrew praise-shout. It means "Praise Yah," which is a shortened form of the word "Yahweh." It is translated into Latin as "Alleluia," and translated into English as "Praise the Lord." It appears in Psalms 106, 111–113, 135, and 146–150. With one exception (Ps 135:3), it is always found at the beginning and/or end of the psalms in which it appears. Its imperative form suggests that it may have been a call to praise in post-exilic temple worship. The 1979 BCP restored "Hallelujah" to the Psalter, unlike earlier Prayer Books which used the translated form "Praise (ye) the Lord." The BCP explains that the Hebrew form was considered more appropriate than the Latin "Alleluia" for the context of the Psalter (p. 584). This use of Hallelujah also regains for Episcopal liturgy a word that is found in many well-known anthems, such as the "Hallelujah chorus" of George Frederick Handel's *Messiah*. If desired, Hallelujah may be omitted from the Psalter during Lent. *See* Alleluia.

Halloween. *See* All Hallows' Eve.

Hankow, Missionary District of. The General Convention of 1901 voted to divide China into the Missionary District of Shanghai and the Missionary District of Hankow. On

Oct. 11, 1910, the House of Bishops voted to divide the Missionary District of Hankow and create the Missionary District of Wuhu. The Missionary District of Hankow became a part of the Holy Catholic Church in China in 1949.

Hannington, James (Sept. 3, 1847–Oct. 29, 1885). Missionary bishop and martyr. He was born in Hurstpierpoint, England. Hannington received his B.A. in 1873 and his M.A. in 1875, both from St. Mary's Hall, Oxford. Six years after his ordination to the priesthood in 1876, he volunteered to be a Church Missionary Society missionary at Rubaga in Central Africa. On June 24, 1884, he was consecrated Missionary Bishop of Eastern Equatorial Africa. Some of the natives feared encroachment from Europeans. Hannington and his companions were seized by Chief Mwanga of Uganda on Oct. 21, 1885. They were tortured and put to death eight days later. Hannington and his companions are commemorated in the Episcopal calendar of the church year on Oct. 29.

Hanson, Francis R. (Mar. 27, 1807–Oct. 21, 1873). One of the first two Episcopal missionaries to China. He was born in Durham, Charles County, Maryland. Hanson graduated from the Virginia Theological Seminary in 1833. He was ordained deacon on May 19, 1833, and priest on May 30, 1834. On June 1, 1835, he and the Rev. Henry Lockwood set sail from New York to Canton. When they arrived in Canton they found China closed to foreigners. They took up residence in Batavia (Jakarta), Java, an island of the Malay Archipelago, to study Chinese. The tropical weather was too extreme for them, and in 1838, Hanson returned to the United States. In 1839 Hanson became rector of Trinity Church, Demopolis, Alabama, and served there until 1851. From 1851 until 1873, he was rector of St. Andrew's Church, Macon Station, Alabama. Hanson died in Baltimore, Maryland.

Happening. A renewal weekend for youth in high school. In some places, early college youth and/or adults who work with youth may attend. It was created in the Diocese of Dallas in the early 1970s, based on the Cursillo model for adults and a Roman Catholic derivative of Cursillo for teens called Search. The Rev. Pat Hutton and lay youth workers are credited with its initial development. Happening is designed to provide an opportunity for participants to encounter Christ in the midst of an intentional Christian community. Features of the weekend include teen leadership with support from clergy and lay adults, talks, songs, worship, and small group activities. Happening is a diocesan event under the authority of the diocesan bishop. The Happening National Committee (HNC), formed in 1983, provides information to dioceses concerning the program. It sponsors a biennial National Leadership Conference in even-numbered years. *See* Cursillo; *see* New Beginnings; *see* Vocare.

Hardy, Edward Rochie (June 17, 1908–May 26, 1981). Church historian. He was born in New York City. Hardy received his B.A. in 1923, his M.A. in 1924, and his Ph.D. in 1931, all from Columbia University. In 1933 he received his S.T.B. from General Theological Seminary. He was ordained deacon on Dec. 21, 1929, and priest on June 18, 1932. From 1929 until 1945, he was fellow, tutor, and instructor at General Seminary. In 1945 he joined the faculty of the Berkeley Divinity School as associate professor of church history. From 1947 until 1969, Hardy was professor of church history at Berkeley, and from 1969 to 1975, he was lecturer in early church history at Cambridge University. He served on a number of ecumenical commissions, and in 1942 he was president of the American Society of Church History. He was also a leading specialist on Eastern Orthodoxy, and a widely published scholar. Hardy died in Cambridge, England.

Hare, William Hobart (May 16, 1838–Oct. 23, 1909). Bishop and missionary to American Indians. He was born in Princeton, New Jersey. Hare studied at the University of Pennsylvania but never graduated. He studied for the ordained ministry on his own, while teaching at St. Mark's Academy, Philadelphia. Hare was ordained deacon on June 19, 1859, and served as an assistant at St. Luke's Church, Philadelphia. In May 1861 he became rector of St. Paul's Church, Chestnut Hill, Pennsylvania. He was ordained priest on May 25, 1862. Because of his wife's failing health, he took her to Minnesota in Sept. 1863 for a change of climate to help her. In Minnesota, Hare met some Indians and this awakened in him the interest which would dominate the rest of his life. In 1867 he became the rector of the Church of the Ascension, Philadelphia. Hare was appointed secretary and general agent of the Foreign Committee of the Board of Missions in 1871, and moved to New York. On Oct. 24, 1871, the House of Bishops created the Missionary District of Niobrara, and on Nov. 1, 1872, elected Hare the Missionary Bishop. Hare was consecrated Missionary Bishop on Jan. 9, 1873. The missionary district was named for the Niobrara River, which runs along the border between Nebraska and South Dakota. He worked only among the American Indians. In a sense, he was bishop for a race of people rather than a particular place. On Oct. 11, 1883, the House of Bishops divided the Missionary District of Dakota into the Missionary Districts of North Dakota and South Dakota, and the Missionary District of Niobrara was abolished. Hare became the Missionary Bishop of South Dakota. He served in this position until his death in Atlantic City, New Jersey.

Harris, Barbara Clementine (b. June 12, 1930). First female bishop in the Anglican Communion. She was born in Philadelphia. Harris studied at the Charles Morris Price School of Advertising and Journalism at Villanova University, and at the Urban Theology Unit in Sheffield, England. Harris worked for 14 years with the Sun Oil Company. She was a member of the Church of the Advocate in Philadelphia, and led the procession on July 29, 1974, when eleven Episcopal female deacons were irregularly ordained to the priesthood. She was ordained deacon on Sept. 29, 1979, and priest on Oct. 18, 1980. Harris was priest-in-charge of St. Augustine of Hippo Church, Norristown, Pennsylvania, 1980–1984, and also worked as a prison chaplain. She was executive director of the Episcopal Church Publishing Company, 1984–1988. On Feb. 11, 1989, Harris was consecrated Suffragan Bishop of Massachusetts. She has been an advocate for the dispossessed, the poor, and those on the margins of society.

Harrisburg, Diocese of. The Diocese of Central Pennsylvania was named the Diocese of Harrisburg from Nov. 29, 1904, until Apr. 30, 1971.

Harrowing of Hell. The medieval English term for Christ's descent to hell and victory over Satan. Christ's descent to hell or the place of the dead after his death on the cross is mentioned or suggested by several NT sources, including Mt 12:40; Acts 2:24, 31; Rom 10:7; Eph 4:9; Col 1:18; and possibly 1 Pt 3:18–19, 4:6. The traditional language version of the Apostles' Creed affirms that Jesus "descended into hell," and the contemporary version states that Jesus "descended to the dead" (BCP, pp. 53, 96). The story was a favorite theme for English mystery plays and art in the middle ages. Christ was portrayed as conquering Satan, and then victoriously leading out Adam and Eve, the prophets, and the patriarchs. The gates of hell cannot withstand Christ's power. Christ's victory was expressed

in terms of words from Ps 24, "Lift up your heads, O gates; lift them high, O everlasting doors; and the King of glory shall come in." This language dramatizes the power of Christ's resurrection and shows Christ's ultimate victory over death. It also portrays the fulfillment of the theme of Christ as second Adam who reverses the tragedy of Adam's fall.

Hart, Samuel (June 4, 1845–Feb. 25, 1917). Secretary of the House of Bishops and dean of the Berkeley Divinity School. He was born in Saybrook, Connecticut. Hart received his B.A. from Trinity College, Hartford, Connecticut, in 1866, and his B.D. from the Berkeley Divinity School in 1869. He was ordained deacon on June 2, 1869, and priest on June 28, 1870. From 1870 until 1873, he was tutor at Trinity College. From 1873 until 1899, he was a professor at Trinity where he taught almost all the courses in the curriculum. In 1899 he became vice-dean and professor of doctrinal theology at Berkeley. From 1908 until his death he was the third dean of Berkeley. Hart became the third custodian of the Standard Book of Common Prayer in 1886, secretary of the House of Bishops on Oct. 24, 1892, and the fourth historiographer of the Episcopal Church on Oct. 17, 1898. He served in all three positions until his death. His major book was a *History of the American Book of Common Prayer* (1910). Hart died in Middletown, Connecticut.

Hatchett, Marion Josiah (b. July 19, 1927). A leading liturgical scholar of the twentieth century. He was born in Monroe, South Carolina. His father was a Methodist pastor. Hatchett was confirmed in the Episcopal Church in Dec. 1946 while a student at Wofford College, where he received his B.A. in 1947. He received his B.D. in 1951 from the School of Theology, University of the South. He was ordained deacon on June 13, 1951, and priest on June 25, 1952. Hatchett began his ministry as curate at the Church of the Advent, Spartanburg, South Carolina, and deacon-in-charge of the Church of the Incarnation, Gaffney, and the Church of the Atonement, Blacksburg. In 1957 he became the rector of St. Peter's Church, Charleston, and Chaplain to Episcopal students at the Citadel. He remained there until 1965 when he began his graduate studies at the General Theological Seminary. He received his S.T.M. from General Seminary in 1967 and his Th.D. in 1972. Hatchett taught liturgics and church music at the School of Theology from Feb. 1, 1969, until his retirement on May 16, 1999. On Jan. 15, 1991, he was named the Cleveland

Keith Benedict Professor of Pastoral Theology. He was a member of the Standing Commission on Church Music, 1974–1985; the Standing Liturgical Commission, 1977–1982; and the General Board of Examining Chaplains, 1988–1994. He was Chair of the Text Committee for *The Hymnal 1982*, and Chair of the Committee for the *BOS*. Among his many publications are *Sanctifying Life, Time and Space: An Introduction to Liturgical Study* (1976), *A Manual for Clergy and Church Musicians* (1980), *Commentary on the American Prayer Book* (1981), and *The Making of the First American Book of Common Prayer* (1982).

Haven, Emily Bradley Neal (Sept. 13, 1827–Aug. 23, 1863). One of the best known popular Episcopal writers of morally instructive novellas in the nineteenth century. She was born in Hudson, New York. She married Joseph C. Neal of Philadelphia on Dec. 12, 1846. He was editor of *Neal's Saturday Gazette* and *Lady's Literary Museum.* He published her stories in the *Gazette.* Neal died in 1847, but she remained in Philadelphia and helped to edit the *Gazette.* She took a special interest in the children's section and wrote under the pseudonym "Cousin Alice."

She had been raised a Baptist, but in 1849 she was confirmed at St. Peter's Church, Philadelphia. In that same year the General Protestant Episcopal Sunday School Union published the first of her books in a series called "Home Books for Children." These were novels with minimal plot and major emphasis on character formation. On Jan. 1, 1853, she married Samuel L. Haven. They moved to Mamaroneck, New York, where she continued her writing. She died at 35 of tuberculosis in Mamaroneck.

Hawaii, Diocese of. The 1901 General Convention formed the Missionary District of Honolulu, and on Mar. 9, 1902, St. Andrew's Cathedral, Honolulu, was consecrated. On Sept. 4, 1969, the General Convention voted to reconstitute the Missionary District of Honolulu as the Diocese of Hawaii. The primary convention of the Diocese of Hawaii met at St. Andrew's Cathedral, Honolulu, on Oct. 24–25, 1969.

Hawks, Francis Lister (June 10, 1798–Sept. 27, 1866). Early historian of the Episcopal Church, and a popular preacher. He was born in New Bern, North Carolina. Hawks graduated from the University of North Carolina in 1815, and then studied law. After practicing law for a while, he studied under William Mercer Green. Hawks was ordained deacon on Nov. 18, 1827, and priest on Jan. 25, 1828. In 1829 he served as an assistant at Trinity Church, New Haven, and in 1830 he was an assistant at St. James' Church in Philadelphia. For a while he was professor of divinity at Washington College, Hartford, Connecticut. From 1831 until 1843, he was rector of St. Stephen's Church and then St. Thomas Church, both in New York City. From 1833 until 1835, Hawks was professor of ecclesiastical history at the General Theological Seminary. In 1844 he was rector of Christ Church, New Orleans, and from 1844 until 1849, he was president of the University of Louisiana. In 1853 he helped to establish the *Church Journal* in New York City. From around 1851 until his death, Hawks was the historiographer of the Episcopal Church. His major publications were *Contributions to the Ecclesiastical History of the United States*, 2 vols. (1836 and 1839), and (with William Stevens Perry) *Documentary History of the Protestant Episcopal Church in the United States of America*, 2 vols. (1863 and 1864). He died in New York City.

Haywood Collection of Negro Spirituals, The. A collection of seventeen Negro spirituals collected by Carl W. Haywood (b. 1949). It was published in 1992. These Negro spirituals were all included in *Lift Every Voice and Sing II, An African American Hymnal* (1993). *The Haywood Collection of Negro Spirituals* was a continuation of the work of musicians such as R. Nathaniel Dett and John Work, who collected simple spirituals for use in college chapels and university choirs. Haywood served as a professor of music at Norfolk State University, Norfolk, Virginia, and as organist and choir master at Grace Episcopal Church, Norfolk.

Heathcote, Caleb (Mar. 6, 1666–Mar. 1, 1720). Leading churchman in New York. He was born in Chesterfield, Derbyshire, England. Heathcote came to New York in 1691 and soon became a wealthy merchant and a councilor of the province. In 1692 he became a colonel in the militia. He was the leading layman in the establishment of Trinity Parish, New York. He served as a warden and member of the vestry of Trinity Parish from 1697 until 1714. In 1701 his large estate in Westchester County became the city of Scarsdale. Heathcote also helped to establish the Episcopal Church in Rye, New York. He was the mayor of New York City from 1711 until 1713. Heathcote was a leading supporter of the Society for the Propagation of the Gospel (SPG) and was its first American member. He helped to found churches in New Rochelle, Eastchester, and Yonkers. Heathcote died in New York City.

Heaven. Eternal life in our enjoyment of God (BCP, p. 862). The unending fulfillment of salvation and happiness in relationship with God. Heaven has been equated with the beatific vision, and described in terms of perfect bliss and union with God. Many Christians emphasize heaven as a state of completed and eternal relationship with God, rather than a "place." However, belief in heaven in terms of a place beyond known spatial limits is important in light of belief in the resurrection of the body. God is certainly not contained by any place.

The term "heaven" or "the heavens" has been applied to the sky, outer space, and the place where God lives with the angels and those who share God's life. Although heaven is not understood to be "up" in spatial terms, scripture records that Jesus looked up to heaven when he blessed and broke the bread to feed the five thousand (Mk 6:41), and that Jesus "was carried up into heaven" at the Ascension (Lk 24:51). The Book of Revelation provides a vision of the glory of God in heaven. A vivid and detailed poetic description of heaven is provided by Dante Alighieri's *Divine Comedy*.

Christian worship includes many expressions of faith concerning heaven. The Lord's Prayer is addressed to "Our Father in heaven," and prays for God's will to be done "on earth as in heaven" (BCP, p. 364). The Nicene Creed affirms that Jesus Christ "came down from heaven" for our salvation (BCP, p. 358). The Apostles' Creed and the Nicene Creed affirm that Jesus "rose again" on the third day after his death, and that he ascended into heaven and is seated at the right hand of the Father (BCP, pp. 96, 358). The *Sanctus* in the eucharistic prayer, based on Is 6:3, proclaims that heaven and earth are full of God's glory (BCP, p. 362). We are to share the joy of heaven with God. Collect 8 from the prayers of the people states that God by the Holy Spirit has made us one with the saints in heaven and on earth (BCP, p. 395). The first of the additional prayers from the Burial of the Dead states that the spirits of those who die in the Lord still live with God, and that the "souls of the faithful are in joy and felicity" with God (BCP, p. 503). The liturgy expresses Christian belief that heaven is not just a remote place, but a relationship of love with God that can be known in daily life and especially in the church. The postcommunion prayer at the Burial of the Dead thanks God for having "given us a foretaste of your heavenly banquet" (BCP, p. 498). Similarly, one of the sentences of administration for the Eucharist is "The Body of Christ, the bread of heaven" (BCP, p. 365). As we can know (at least in part) the heavenly joy of God's love in the present

moment, we can also anticipate the eternal perfection of sharing God's love which is yet to come.

Heber, Reginald (Apr. 21, 1783–Apr. 3, 1826). British bishop and hymn writer. He was born in Malpas, Cheshire, England. He was educated at Brasenose College, Oxford, and a Fellow of All Souls. After his ordination in 1807, Heber served in parishes in England. In 1815 he delivered the noted Bampton Lectures. In 1823 he became Bishop of Calcutta. He was a fervent missionary. Heber is best remembered for his hymns. He envisioned a collection of texts connected with the epistles and gospels for each Sunday and feast day of the church year. Along with his own poems he solicited works from others. The collection, *Hymns written and adapted to the Weekly Church Service of the Year* (1827), was published by his wife after his death. Heber wrote several hymn texts that are used in *The Hymnal 1982*, including "Brightest and best of the stars of the morning" (Hymns 117–118), "Holy, holy, holy! Lord God Almighty!" (Hymn 362), and "Hosanna to the living Lord!" (Hymn 486). He died in Trichinopoly, India.

Hell. Eternal death in our rejection of God (BCP, p. 862). This state or place of separation from God is closely related to the concept of human free will. We may choose to accept or reject God. We will not be forced by God to receive God's love. Hell is a permanent state of separation from God that can be freely chosen, not God's angry punishment for misdeeds.

The concept of hell can be traced to the OT belief that the dead continued to live a shadowy life in a nether region of darkness and silence known as Sheol. However, it was not a place of torment or retribution. In later Judaism, at the end of the OT period, concepts of final judgment and retribution led to belief that the righteous were separated from the unrighteous in Sheol. Belief in Gehenna, a blazing hell of punishment, likely reflects the influence of Iranian ideas of punitive judgment by God for the wicked.

In the NT and Apocrypha, Hades is mentioned as the place of all the dead (Lk 10:15; Acts 2:31; Rv 20:13; Bar 2:17). Gehenna, the "hell of fire," is where the wicked are punished (Mt 5:22, 10:28, 18:9; Mk 9:43; Lk 12:5; 2 Esd 2:29). NT concepts of hell reflect the darkness of Sheol (Mt 8:12, 22:13, 25:30), and the fire of Gehenna (Mt 3:12; Mk 9:43; Lk 3:17; Rv 20:14–15). Vivid poetic descriptions of hell are provided by Dante Alighieri's *Divine Comedy* and John Milton's *Paradise Lost*. Jesus foretold the coming judgment in which the Son of Man will come in glory and separate the righteous from the unrighteous as the shepherd separates the sheep from the goats. The Son of Man will send the unrighteous to eternal punishment and the righteous to eternal life (Mt 25:31–46). In the parable of the talents, the Master commands that the "worthless" servant who buried his talent is to be thrown into the outer darkness where there will be weeping and gnashing of teeth (Mt 25:14–30).

The traditional language version of the Apostles' Creed affirms that Jesus "descended into hell," and the contemporary version states that Jesus "descended to the dead" (BCP, pp. 53, 96). Canticle 14, A Song Of Penitence, based on The Prayer of Manasseh, prays that God will "not let me perish in my sin, nor condemn me to the depths of the earth" (BCP, pp. 90–91). Belief in the reality of hell or the pain of separation from God should never lead to despair that God's mercy is measured or limited. God's mercy and power to save exceed our understanding. *See* Harrowing of Hell.

Henderson, Jacob (1681–Aug. 27, 1751). Commissary to Maryland. He was born in Ireland. Henderson was ordained by the Bishop of London in 1710 and appointed to a mission in Dover, Kent County, Maryland. He returned to England in 1711 and was appointed in 1712 to the mission on the western shore of Maryland in Queen Anne Parish, Prince George County. In 1716 the Bishop of London named Henderson the Commissary of the Western Shore of Maryland, and in 1730 he was named the Commissary of Maryland. He served until 1734. Henderson died in Queen Anne Parish.

Henrico College, Virginia. In 1618 the London Company ratified a former grant whereby a suitable place at Henrico, Virginia, was set aside to establish a university. Ten thousand acres were allotted for endowing the university. George Thorpe was sent from England to supervise the construction. The Rev. Thomas Bargrave (d. 1621), rector of the Henrico parish, donated his library. On Mar. 22, 1622 (Good Friday), Chief Openchancanough and his Indians killed Thorpe and about 400 colonists. The charter for the school was revoked on June 16, 1624. This would have been the first college in the American colonies.

Heraldry, Ecclesiastical. Heraldry is the science of devising appropriate "bearings" (emblems) for military armor and determining the right of persons to certain arms or bearings through genealogical study. Heraldry has also been applied to the seals and coats-of-arms of religious organizations. In 1307 religious houses in England were ordered to have a common seal. The miter, the crozier, and the ecclesiastical hat appeared as emblems in the fourteenth century.

Ecclesiastical heraldry is visible today in the seals of many dioceses. It is interesting to note that the seal of some dioceses has a cartouche or oval design, while other dioceses employ a shield design for the seal. The shield is a military symbol, and its appropriateness for use as a diocesan symbol may be questioned. Many diocesan seals include a cross, or other religious symbols. Some diocesan seals incorporate one or more symbols that are associated with the location of the diocese. For example, the seal of the Diocese of Milwaukee displays a badger, which is associated with Wisconsin, "the badger state." Some parishes and other church organizations also have seals.

Herbert, George (Apr. 3, 1593–Mar. 1, 1633). A priest considered to be one of the chief devotional poets of the Anglican Communion. Herbert was educated at Westminster School and Trinity College, Cambridge. He was public orator at Cambridge in 1620. This position could have led to high public office. However, he subsequently studied divinity and was ordained priest in 1630. His turning away from a secular career followed the death of James I, who had shown him favor. His new direction in life may also have reflected the influence of his friend, Nicholas Ferrar, the founder of the religious community at Little Gidding. Herbert ended his days as priest at Bemberton (1630-1633), outside Salisbury, England. He was devoted to his parish work and came to be known as the "holy Mr. Herbert."

Herbert's poems reflect a faith that is heartfelt, passionate, and expressed with grace. His collection of poems, *The Temple* (1633), includes his most beloved poems such as "Prayer," "Love III," "The Altar," and "Easter Wings" in the section called "The Church." Several of Herbert's poems have been set to music and are included in *The Hymnal 1982*, including "King of glory, King of peace" (382), "Let all the world in every corner sing" (402-403), and "Come, my Way, my Truth, my Life" (487). Shortly before his death, Herbert sent his English poems to Ferrar to be published or burned. Herbert's best known prose work is *A Priest to the Temple; or the Country Parson* (1652). His life is commemorated in the Episcopal calendar of the church year on Feb. 27. Herbert's mother, Lady Herbert, was John Donne's patron.

Heresy. The term is derived from the Greek *hairesis*, which means "choice" or "thing chosen." Traditionally, heresy was the sin of a baptized and professing Christian who denied a defined doctrine of the faith. Heresy is distinguished from apostasy, the abandonment of the church by one who denies the church's teaching; and from schism, the fracturing of the church's unity for reasons other than disagreement in basic doctrine. Many of the classical formulations of the Christian faith were made by the ecumenical councils in response to beliefs that were later judged to be heretical.

Hermann von Wied of Cologne (1477–1552). He was Archbishop-elector of Cologne, and he called a provincial council in 1536 to institute reforms. The canons enacted there were published in 1538 with an *Encheridion* (handbook or manual) based on the Apostles' Creed, the seven sacraments, the Lord's Prayer, and the decalogue. Martin Bucer, who had worked on various German church orders, was brought to Cologne by Hermann in Feb. 1542. Bucer began work on a church order based largely on the 1533 Brandenburg-Nuremberg Order of Andreas Osiander and Johann Brenz. Philipp Melancthon, brought to Cologne in May 1543, revised and enlarged the doctrinal portion. The order, adopted in July, was published in October. A slightly revised German version was published in Nov. 1544. An amended Latin version was published in 1545. An English translation of the Latin version, *A Simple, and Religious Consultation*, was published in London on Oct. 30, 1547, and an amended edition was published in 1548. Various sections were printed separately. The 1549 BCP is indebted to this book in its calendar and in almost every rite. The Cologne chapter published a rejoinder, first in German and then in Latin, *Antididagma*, which supplied a few phrases in the first Prayer Book. Hermann was excommunicated and deposed by Pope Paul III in 1546.

Hermit, Hermitess. A person who lives alone for religious reasons. The term is from the Greek for "wilderness" or "uninhabited regions." Hermits often live in a place that is remote from others. They may be distinguished from anchorites who live in a cell near a community. Hermits typically live contemplative lives devoted to meditation, prayer, manual work, and reading. Hermits may be called eremites or solitaries. *See* Anchorite, Anchoress.

Hesychasm. A style of piety associated with the eastern church and ascribed to the monks of Mt. Athos in the fourteenth century. The word means "quiet." The monks of Mt. Athos developed a method of prayer and contemplation which included a continuous repetition of the "Jesus Prayer" while controlling the breath, resting the chin upon the chest, and focusing the eyes upon the navel. These practices were believed to lead the participant to perceive the Divine Light with the senses. This light was identified with God and with the light that surrounded Jesus at the Transfiguration. Hesychasm was controversial. Gregory Palamas was a principal defender of hesychasm in the fourteenth century, and its supporters have been known as "Palamites." Hesychasm has been a point of division between eastern and western churches. It led to the expression "navel gazing." *See* Jesus Prayer, The.

Heuss, John (July 30, 1908–Mar. 20, 1966). Leader in the post-World War II development of Christian education in the Episcopal Church. He was born in Hastings-on-Hudson, New York, and received his B.A. from St. Stephen's College (Bard) in 1929 and his B.D. from Seabury-Western Theological Seminary in 1931. He was ordained deacon on Sept. 13, 1931, and priest on Nov. 13, 1932. He was assistant at St. Luke's Pro-Cathedral, Evanston, 1932–1937; chaplain to Episcopal students at Northwestern University, 1937–1943; and rector of St. Matthew's Church, Evanston, 1937–1947. He became director of the Department of Christian Education of the National Council of the Episcopal Church in 1947. He served in that position until he became rector of Trinity Church, New York, in 1952, where he served until his death. While director he served as editor of the first Church's Teaching Series. The post-war period was an exciting era in Christian education, including the development of the Seabury Series for theological education of the laity and various programs to invigorate parish life. Heuss died in New York City.

Hie Hill Community, The. A religious community for men and women at Westbrook, Connecticut. With the Anglican tradition of Christianity as its particular inspiration, it seeks to encourage and maintain a way of life incorporating worship, study, and care for the creation. The community grew out of an Education for Ministry group meeting at the home of Richard and Olive Brose from 1980 until 1984, and in response to Olive Brose's vision for a community. It operates on a non-residential basis. The members share a Benedictine Rule of life and meet monthly in a chapel and library on the Brose's property for worship, study, and fellowship.

Higgins, John Seville (Apr. 14, 1904–Dec. 28, 1992).
Bishop and ecumenist. He was born in London, England.
He graduated from Oberlin College in 1928 and Western
Theological Seminary in Chicago in 1931. He was ordained
deacon on May 1, 1931, and priest on Nov. 1, 1931. Higgins
served parishes in Nevada, Illinois, and Minnesota before
becoming rector of St. Martin's Church, Providence, Rhode
Island, in 1948. He was elected Bishop Coadjutor of Rhode
Island in Nov. 1952 and consecrated on Feb. 4, 1953. He
became Bishop of Rhode Island on Jan. 1, 1955. Higgins's
episcopate coincided with a period of rapid growth in the
1950s, and he provided critical leadership in the rebuilding
of the diocesan headquarters in Providence in the mid–
1960s. He was also a committed ecumenist who was
instrumental in the formation of the Rhode Island State
Council of Churches. Higgins retired in 1972, but he
remained active in local and national church affairs until
his death.

High Altar. The main altar for eucharistic celebration in a
church. In medieval and gothic revival churches, the high
altar stands centered, near or placed against the east wall.
The high altar is typically on a platform some steps higher
than the rest of the church. This position of prominence
distinguishes the high altar from the other altars in the
church, a common design in medieval and Anglo-catholic
styles. Current architectural conventions for the liturgy
emphasize a single altar, prominently placed and not remote
from the people, as a practical sign of unity for the
eucharistic gathering.

High Church. The terms "high church" and "high
churchman" began to appear in the late seventeenth
century to describe those who opposed the Calvinist-
Puritan wing of the Church of England. In colonial America
a high church party emerged in Connecticut when four
Congregationalist ministers decided their ordinations were
invalid, and went to England to be ordained deacons and
priests. After the American Revolution, a new high church
party emerged under the leadership of John Henry Hobart
of New York. This party stressed adherence to the doctrine,
discipline, and worship of the Episcopal Church. They
stressed the necessity of the historic episcopate as the
primary guarantee of apostolic succession; the threefold
order of ministry—bishops, priests, and deacons; the
careful and faithful use of the Prayer Book; and the two
dominical sacraments of Baptism and Eucharist. They
emphasized the spiritual presence of Christ in the meal,

and insisted that baptisms should be done in the church
and not in the home. Most high churchmen did not
participate in ecumenical activities or organizations. high
churchmen stressed the ministry and sacraments of the
church as the primary means of grace. *See* Hobart, John
Henry; *see* Low Church; *see* Yale Converts.

"High and Dry." The term generally indicates a high
church Anglican or Episcopalian who precedes or is not
strongly influenced by the Oxford Movement, especially
the advanced catholic ritual practices that came to be
associated with the Oxford Movement. In this case, a
"high" theology of the church is associated with the less
elaborate ("dry") ritual practices that preceded the Oxford
Movement. *See* High Church; *see* Oxford Movement, The;
see Ritualism.

High Mass. This is a term used, mostly in Anglo-catholic
parishes, to describe a celebration of the eucharist
characterized by multiple ministers (a priest- or bishop-
celebrant, deacon, "subdeacon," acolytes, choir, and
possibly others) and a rich ceremonial (incense, candles,
processions, stylized movements and gestures), and a
preference for singing rather than saying the various texts
of the eucharist. A eucharist in which the celebrant is
assisted by a deacon and a layperson serving as a liturgical
subdeacon may be known as a Solemn Eucharist. The
contrasting low mass is characterized by its requirements
of a single minister (a priest-celebrant) and a strictly
restrained ceremonial. The high mass was recognized as
the eucharistic norm in the Roman rites of the middle ages,
although the low mass was by far the more common
celebration. The eucharistic rite in the 1549 BCP drew on a
style similar to the normative high mass. But the 1552 BCP,
alert to popular sensibilities favoring the more familiar low
mass, used that style as the basis for its communion service.
Subsequent Prayer Books followed the pattern of the 1552
BCP, which presupposed the priest-celebrant as the single
liturgical leader at the eucharist. This tendency was
somewhat reversed by the 1979 BCP, which calls for a
variety of ministers—ordained and lay—in roles of
liturgical leadership at the eucharist.

Higher Criticism. This method of scriptural interpretation
was considered a step beyond text criticism (lower
criticism) because it was dealing with larger historical
problems. Source criticism, form criticism, redaction
criticism, and narrative criticism are the most widely used

"higher" methods. All these methods assume that the biblical texts have developed over time within various specific Christian communities, and that the biblical material must be understood in its cultural and historical context. *See* Lower Criticism.

Hilary, Bishop of Poitiers (c. 315–c. 367). Bishop and theologian. He was born in Poitiers, Gaul (France). Around 353 he was consecrated Bishop of Poitiers and spent most of his episcopal life fighting the Arians and defending the great Nicene theologian, Athanasius. Hilary also promoted the work of Martin of Tours, who introduced monasticism into Gaul. His most significant writing was *De Trinitate* (*On the Trinity*), the first extensive study of this doctrine in the west, which was written against the Arians. Jerome called him "the trumpet of the Latins against the Arians," and he also was called "the Athanasius of the West." In 1851 Pope Pius IX named him a Doctor of the Church. He is commemorated in the Episcopal calendar of the church year on Jan. 13.

Hilda (c. 614–Nov. 17, 680). Abbess and saint. She was baptized at Easter 627 by Paulinus, Bishop of York. When she was thirty-three she entered the monastic life, and Bishop Aidan placed her in a small monastery in East Anglia. After about a year she became the abbess at Hartlepool. In 657 Hilda founded a monastery at Streanaeshalch, later called Whitby, where she presided over a community of men and women. At the Synod of Whitby she sided with the Celtic Colman against Wilfrid who supported the Roman customs. But she loyally accepted the decision made at Whitby to follow Rome. She was known for her prudence and good sense. Under her rule at Whitby several of the monks were ordained, and some became bishops. Her life is commemorated in the Episcopal calendar of the church year on Nov. 18.

Hildegard, Abbess of Bingen (1098–1179). Abbess, mystic, scholar, composer, scientist, and physician. She was born in the Rhineland Valley of Germany and raised by the anchoress Jutta in a cottage near the Benedictine monastery of Disibodenberg. Hildegard experienced spiritual visions from early childhood. Other women came to live with Jutta and Hildegard, and a convent was organized with Jutta as abbess under the authority of the abbot of Disibodenberg. Hildegard became abbess in 1136 after Jutta's death. Hildegard later founded independent convents at Bingen and Eibingen, under the authority of the Archbishop of Mainz. Hildegard described her visions in *Scivias*. Music was essential to worship for Hildegard. The devil was condemned to live without music in Hildegard's *The Play of the Virtues*. Hildegard's influence and talents were wide-ranging. She was widely sought for her counsel, and she went on preaching missions in northern Europe. She corresponded with rulers and church leaders. Her writings included scientific and theological works. Hildegard is commemorated on Sept. 17 in the Episcopal calendar of the church year.

Hill, Frances Maria Mulligan (July 10, 1799–Aug. 5, 1884). Episcopal missionary and pioneer woman educator. She was born Francis Maria Mulligan in New York City. She married John Henry Hill, a banker and graduate of Columbia College, on Apr. 26, 1821. He then attended the Virginia Theological Seminary. On Oct. 1, 1830, after his ordination, he, Mrs. Hill, and the Rev. John J. Robertson and his wife sailed to Greece to do missionary work. This was the first foreign mission from the Episcopal Church. They went as educational missionaries. They did not seek to convert students from Greek Orthodoxy to Anglicanism. Robertson set up a printing press, and the Hills started a school for poor children in Athens. After five years, they had 650 pupils in five groups. Frances Hill was in charge of the children aged four to eight. She was also responsible for the girls' elementary school and a "school for industry," training destitute girls to be teachers and seamstresses. In 1834 the schools were recognized officially by the Greek ecclesiastical and civil authorities. In 1837 a wing of the school was opened for paying students. However, local opposition closed the mission in 1882–1883. It reopened with only the infants' and girls' schools. In 1869 she opened a private school, the Hill Institute. As recently as 1970 it was known as the Hill Memorial School. It remained one of the leading schools in Athens. She died in Athens. *See* Hill, John Henry.

Hill, John Henry (Sept. 11, 1791–July 1, 1882). Foreign missionary and educator. He was born in New York City. Hill graduated from Columbia College when he was sixteen and entered the mercantile business. He then studied at the Virginia Theological Seminary. Hill was ordained deacon on May 23, 1830, and priest on June 20, 1830. He and his wife, Frances Maria Mulligan Hill, went to Greece in late 1830 as missionaries. They opened schools for both boys and girls. When the Greek government began to provide education for boys, the Hills concentrated on the education of girls. Their school became the best educational institution for girls in the Greek-speaking world. They did not try to convert the Greeks to the Episcopal Church, but concentrated on education. They gave advice to the government on the development of national schools. Hill served for fifty years in Greece and is recognized as a major American missionary. Hill died in Athens, Greece. *See* Hill, Frances Maria Mulligan.

Hillspeak. Hillspeak in Eureka Springs, Arkansas, is the headquarters of SPEAK, the Society for Promoting and Encouraging Arts and Knowledge (of the Church). SPEAK began with the founding of the Episcopal Book Club in 1953. The Episcopal Book Club was founded by the Rev. Howard Lane Foland at All Saints' Parish, Nevada, Missouri. When Foland resigned as rector of All Saints in 1957, it was recognized that the club needed new and larger accommodations. The club bought a 1,124-acre ranch at Eureka Springs. On St. Mark's Day, Apr. 25, 1960, EBC moved to what is known as Hillspeak. It is atop Grindstone Mountain in the Ozarks. Hillspeak is the home for all five of SPEAK's ministries, *The Anglican Digest*, The Anglican Bookstore, Episcopal Book Club, the Howard Lane Foland Library, and Operation Pass Along. *See* Episcopal Book Club (EBC).

Hines, John Elbridge (Oct. 3, 1910–July 19, 1997). Twenty-second Presiding Bishop. He was born in Seneca, South Carolina. Hines received his B.A. from the University of the South in 1930 and his B.D. from the Virginia Theological Seminary in 1933. He was ordained deacon on Aug. 31, 1933, and priest on Oct. 28, 1934. Hines was assistant rector of St. Stephen and St. George Church, St. Louis, Missouri, 1933–1935; rector of Holy Trinity Church, Hannibal, Missouri, 1935–1937; and rector of St. Paul's Church, Augusta, Georgia, 1937–1941. From 1941 until 1945, he was rector of Christ Church, Houston, Texas. On Oct. 18, 1945, Hines was consecrated Bishop Coadjutor of Texas. He became the fourth Bishop of Texas on Nov. 1, 1955. While Bishop of Texas he was one of the founders of the Episcopal Theological Seminary of the Southwest at Austin, which opened in 1951. Hines was elected Presiding Bishop at the age of 54, the youngest in the history of the church at that time. He served in that capacity from Jan. 1, 1965, until May 31, 1974. Hines was committed to racial and social justice. He was the architect of the General Convention Special Program, which was established by the General Convention of 1967 to encourage the use of political and economic power by and for the dispossessed and oppressed people of the United States. While he was Presiding Bishop, women were seated as deputies at General Convention and allowed to be ordained deacons. Hines died in Austin, Texas.

Hinman, Samuel Dutton (1839–Mar. 24, 1890). Missionary to the Dakota Indians. He was born in Pittsburgh, Pennsylvania, and orphaned at an early age. Hinman studied at Cheshire Academy in Connecticut and graduated from the Seabury Divinity School in 1860. He was ordained deacon on Sept. 20, 1860, and priest on Mar. 8, 1863. Hinman began his missionary work in Redwood County, Minnesota. He established a mission to the Dakotas at the Lower Sioux Agency. In 1864 he translated most of the BCP into the Dakota language. It was published in 1865. He then worked at the Santee mission at the mouth of the Niobrara River in Nebraska. Under William Hobart Hare, Missionary Bishop of Niobrara in the Dakotas, Hinman served as Archdeacon of the Nebraska and Dakota Indian work. Bishop Hare heard rumors of Hinman's "immorality," alleging that Hinman misused church funds and consorted with a native prostitute. On Mar. 25, 1878, Bishop Hare severed Hinman's connection with the Santee mission, and suspended him from the exercise of the active ordained ministry. Hinman refused to renounce his ministry. He demanded a trial, which was held in July 1878. Hinman was found guilty, but continued to fight with Bishop Hare. During this period Hinman worked for the Bureau of Indian Affairs. In 1886 he moved to the Birch Coulee Mission in Minnesota. In 1887 his suspension was lifted. Bishop Henry Benjamin Whipple received him into the Diocese of Minnesota. During his ministry he worked among the Dakota Indians in Minnesota, Nebraska, and South Dakota. Hinman died in Birch Coulee, Minnesota.

Hippolytus (c. 170–c. 236). Theologian of the Roman Church, presbyter, antipope, and martyr. Hippolytus strongly resisted Popes Zephyrinus, Callistus, Urban, and Pontianus. Hippolytus was zealous for orthodoxy and a rigorist concerning penitential discipline. He wanted a church of the pure. He accused Callistus of heresy and laxity. Hippolytus was apparently made antipope of a schismatic Christian community in Rome when Callistus was Pope. Hippolytus's schism continued under Callistus's successors Urban and Pontianus. Hippolytus and Pontianus were both exiled to Sardinia during the persecution of Emperor Maximinus Thrax. Hippolytus and Pontianus apparently reconciled before they died. Pope Fabian brought both bodies back to Rome for burial on the same day, Aug. 13. Although Hippolytus is not included in the Episcopal calendar of the church year, his feast day has traditionally been celebrated on Aug. 13 in the western church and on Jan. 30 in the eastern church.

Hippolytus has been described as the most important third-century Roman theologian. He was the last significant Roman theologian to write in Greek. He wrote at a time when Greek was not generally understood by the Christian community in Rome. His *Philosophumena*, or *Refutation of all Heresies*, was recovered and published in 1851. Hippolytus believed that all heresies were derived from ancient philosophies. Hippolytus wrote exegetical treatises and the *Commentary on Daniel*. One of Hippolytus's best known works is the *Apostolic Tradition*. It was written about 215 in Rome. It was one of the earliest church orders, which provided norms for church life including the liturgy. The *Apostolic Tradition* has detailed information concerning the rites and practices of the church in Rome in the early third century, including descriptions of Baptism, Eucharist, and the Easter Vigil. Hippolytus's *Apostolic Tradition* continues to be highly valued and influential in contemporary liturgical studies. It is frequently cited in Marion J. Hatchett's *Commentary on the American Prayer Book* (1980). *See* Church Orders.

Historic Episcopate. The succession of bishops in the history of the church from the apostles until the present. During the colonial period there were several efforts to bring the historic episcopate to America, but none succeeded. Samuel Seabury went to England in 1783 to receive the historic episcopate. It proved impossible for Seabury to be ordained and consecrated a bishop in England because English law required all ordinands to swear an oath of loyalty to the English sovereign. Seabury was ordained and consecrated into the historic episcopate by nonjuring bishops of the Episcopal Church in Scotland on Nov. 14, 1784. On June 26, 1786, Parliament passed an act which granted the Archbishop of Canterbury the right to consecrate three bishops who would not be required to take the oath of loyalty to the sovereign. William White and Samuel Provoost were consecrated Bishops of Pennsylvania and New York, respectively, on Feb. 4, 1787, and James Madison was consecrated Bishop of Virginia on Sept. 19, 1790. On Sept. 17, 1792, Thomas Claggett was consecrated Bishop of Maryland by Bishop Provoost,

assisted by Bishops Seabury, White, and Madison. This combined the lines of succession of the historic episcopate in the Episcopal Church. The fourth point of the Chicago-Lambeth Quadrilateral states that one of the "inherent parts" of the sacred deposit of the Christian faith is "The Historic Episcopate, locally adapted in the methods of its administration to the varying needs of the nations and peoples called of God into the Unity of His Church" (BCP, pp. 876–878).

Historical Criticism. This term refers to the kind of scriptural interpretation which developed after the study of the texts or manuscripts of these writings. It is clear that we do not have any of the original documents, merely copies of copies. Because questions were raised about their validity, scholars began to question the significance of the different gospels and other biblical stories. The historical approach was an attempt to understand each writing in its historical context. Historical criticism seeks to explain the difference between various scriptural passages in terms of the different times of writing, the different locations of the authors, and the way earlier writings were used by later authors. If the specific details of a writing are primarily determined by its time, place, author, and situation, it is easier to understand its distinctiveness using these historical contexts. This approach also makes it easier for us to find a significant understanding for our time and place. We should analyze the text not primarily on the basis of timeless ideas or themes but in light of the cultural context of the author and the intended audience. We need to learn as much as possible about the other writings, philosophy, and language-usage of the time in which the text was created to discover its basic meaning.

Historical Documents of the Church. This is a collection of five documents in the 1979 BCP (pp. 863–878), the first Prayer Book to have and use the title Historical Documents. The five documents are the "Definition of the Union of the Divine and Human Natures in the Person of Christ," which was adopted by the Council of Chalcedon in 451; the "*Quicunque Vult*," commonly called "The Creed of Saint Athanasius"; the "Preface: The Book of Common Prayer (1549);" the "Articles of Religion"; and "The Chicago-Lambeth Quadrilateral 1886, 1888," as adopted by the House of Bishops in Chicago, 1886; and Resolution II of the Lambeth Conference of 1888.

Historical Magazine of the Protestant Episcopal Church. Predecessor to *Anglican and Episcopal History*. This journal began publication in Mar. 1932, and for years carried the statement, "Published With The Approval Of A Joint Committee Of The General Convention And Under The Auspices Of The Church Historical Society." The last issue with this title was Dec. 1986. With the Mar. 1987 issue the title was changed to *Anglican and Episcopal History.* The founder and first editor, 1932–1949, was E. Clowes Chorley, followed by Walter Herbert Stowe, 1950–1961, and Lawrence Lord Brown, 1962–1977. *See* Anglican and Episcopal History.

Historical Society of the Episcopal Church. The Church Historical Society was founded on May 7, 1910, by a group of laymen in Philadelphia. The leader of the group was William Ives Rutter, Jr. (1871–1951). It is now called the Historical Society of the Episcopal Church. The society serves the church by adding a historical dimension to discussions of contemporary significance. It publishes the journal, *Anglican and Episcopal History*, holds conferences on church history for the general public, publishes a series called *Studies in Anglican History* in conjunction with the University of Illinois Press, and supports special projects in historical research. The society encourages the constant reexamination of the church's tradition using the tools of criticism and evaluation.

Historical Theology. The study of theology in light of historical periods, movements, events, trends, or figures. For example, Arthur Michael Ramsey's *An Era in Anglican Theology, From Gore to Temple, The Development of Anglican Theology between* Lux Mundi *and the Second World War, 1889–1939* (1960) is a work of historical theology.

Historiographer of the Episcopal Church. The General Convention of 1838 established this office. The historiographer collects documents related to the Episcopal Church and sees that they are transmitted to the Archives of the Church in Austin, Texas. The historiographers of the church have included Samuel Farmar Jarvis (1838–1851), Francis Lister Hawks (?–1866), William Stevens Perry (1868–1898), Samuel Hart (1898–1917), Edward Clowes Chorley (1919–1949), Edgar Legare Pennington (1949–1951), and Walter Herbert Stowe (1952–1967). From 1976 until 1989, the Church Historical Society was the historiographer. On Mar. 22, 1989, John Everett Booty became the historiographer.

Historiography. Discipline which deals with the methods of writing history and with the techniques of historical investigation. Historiography seeks to reconstruct an accurate record of human activities and to achieve a deeper understanding of them. Until the nineteenth century, the interpretation of human life as a whole was more properly the function of the theologian, the philosopher, or the poet.

Historiographical traditions developed slowly in the ancient world. In Greece and Rome the writing of history was a branch of literature. The most appreciated historians were those who, like Thucydides, touched on universal problems or, like Tacitus, wrote in a dramatic way about important events. Their works were judged more on their stylistic methods than on their accuracy. Christian historiography in medieval Europe emphasized divine influence in human affairs. The fascination with pagan antiquity which characterized the Renaissance led to the development of philological studies and textual criticism, a renewed emphasis on style, and a gradual awareness of the process of historical change, along with a desire to recapture the rational causes of events. With the Reformation, the starting point for a Protestant rewriting of history was the idea that the "true Church" always existed. The "true Church" was understood to have been at times overshadowed by the enemies of the divine order, including the upholders of papal authority as well as pagans and heretics. Historians writing in this tradition were uninterested in objectivity, but they gathered masses of documentary sources to support their arguments. The Enlightenment introduced new impulses in historiography: a sense of the unity of human history, including an interest in continents outside Europe; a capacity for bold generalizations about the important features of particular periods or societies; and a preference for topics connected with the progress of human civilization. In the nineteenth century historiography emerged as a distinct discipline. It was practiced mainly by professional academicians.

HIV/AIDS, Commission on. This commission of one bishop, two presbyters or deacons, and three lay persons was established by the 1988 General Convention. It studies the theological, ethical, and pastoral questions of the AIDS crisis and develops strategies to increase awareness of this crisis throughout the church.

"Hobart Chancel." An arrangement of church interiors that was favored in the late eighteenth and early nineteenth centuries by John Henry Hobart, Assistant Bishop of New York, 1811–1816, and diocesan bishop, 1816–1830, and others of pre-Oxford Movement high church principles. The design called for the pulpit to be placed against the east wall. The holy table was in front of the pulpit, and the baptismal font was nearby, all within the altar rails. All three liturgical centers were before the people throughout the rites. The term is something of a misnomer. The arrangement was also favored by leading evangelicals, and it can be traced to late eighteenth-century churches in England, Scotland, and Ireland, and even earlier German Lutheran churches. New churches were built in America, and old churches were renovated to conform to this design. Several examples still exist. St. Luke's Church, Rochester, New York, and St. Matthew's Church, Brewster, New York, are examples of churches built according to this scheme. Christ Church, Alexandria, Virginia, and St. James Church, Goose Creek, South Carolina, are examples of older churches that were renovated in the early nineteenth century to conform to this design.

Hobart College, Geneva, New York. Hobart College, first called Geneva College, grew out of the Geneva Academy which was in operation prior to 1800. The Rt. Rev. John Henry Hobart, third Bishop of New York, was the primary founder. A provisional charter was granted on Apr. 10, 1822, and the school's existence dates from that year. On Aug. 5, 1822, ten students began their studies in Geneva Hall. The first commencement was on Aug. 1, 1826. A medical college opened in 1835. On Jan. 23, 1849, Elizabeth Blackwell (1821–1910) graduated from the medical college, the first woman in the United States to receive the Doctor of Medicine degree. In 1882 the name was changed to Hobart College.

Hobart, John Henry (Sept. 14, 1775–Sept. 12, 1830). Bishop, high church leader, and author. His famous phrase describing his position was "Evangelical Truth and Apostolic Order." He was born in Philadelphia. He studied two years at the College of Philadelphia before transferring to the College of New Jersey, Princeton, where he received his B.A. in 1793. He studied theology under Bishop William White of Pennsylvania. Hobart was ordained deacon on June 3, 1798, and priest on Apr. 5, 1801. He served parishes in Pennsylvania, New Jersey, and New York from 1798 to 1830. He was rector of Trinity Church, New York City, 1816–1830. Hobart was consecrated Assistant Bishop of New York on May 29, 1811. He became Bishop of New York on Feb. 27, 1816, and served in that ministry until his death. He was secretary of the House of Bishops at the 1799 General Convention, and secretary of the House of Deputies at the 1804 and 1808 General Conventions. He was one of the leaders in the revival of the Episcopal Church in the first two decades following the American Revolution. Hobart was the leader of the early high church party and a founder of the General Theological Seminary in New York City. He strongly influenced General Seminary to reflect his high church principles. He died in Auburn, New York. His life is commemorated in the Episcopal calendar of the church year on Sept. 12.

Hobson, Henry Wise (May 16, 1891–Feb. 9, 1983). Bishop and publisher. He was born in Denver, Colorado. Hobson graduated from Yale University in 1914. After two years in the Army, he graduated from the Episcopal Theological School in 1920. He was ordained deacon on Dec. 5, 1919, and priest on June 15, 1920. He was assistant minister at St. John's Church, Waterbury, Connecticut, 1920–1921; and rector of All Saints' Church, Worcester, Massachusetts, 1921–1930. On May 1, 1930, Hobson was consecrated Bishop Coadjutor of Southern Ohio. On Oct. 13, 1931, he became the fourth Bishop of Southern Ohio. He served in that position until his retirement on June 30, 1959. He was committed to the ministry of publications. Hobson served as chairman of the Forward Movement, 1934–1937, and of its executive committee from 1937 to 1959. Hobson founded the "Wayside Cathedral" program, a church-on-wheels to visit and minister to persons in rural and isolated areas. He supported the School for Social Work in Cincinnati, later known as the Graduate School of Applied Religion, which exposed seminarians to the work of social service agencies. After his retirement, he declined to continue voting in the House of Bishops. Hobson died in Cincinnati.

Hodges, George (Oct. 6, 1856–May 27, 1919). A leading proponent of the opportunities for ministry in urban churches. He was born in Rome, New York. Hodges graduated from Hamilton College in 1877. He began his theological studies at St. Andrew's Divinity School, Syracuse, New York. He transferred to the Berkeley Divinity School, where he graduated in 1881. He was ordained deacon on June 5, 1881, and priest on June 4, 1882. Hodges was Stone Professor of Homiletics and Pastoral Theology and dean (1894–1919) at the Episcopal Theological School, Cambridge, Massachusetts. His *The Administration of an Institutional Church* (1906) urged appropriate attention to the social, economic, and recreational needs as well as the spiritual needs of the members of a congregation. Hodges served as an assistant minister at Calvary Church, Pittsburgh, 1881–1887; associate minister, 1887–1889; and rector, 1889–1894. Under his leadership in Pittsburgh, members of Calvary Church worked effectively for social betterment and governmental reform. As dean of the Episcopal Theological School, he was the first to introduce into the curriculum of an Episcopal seminary courses in sociology taught by a sociology professor. He died in Cambridge, Massachusetts.

Hoffman, Cadwallader Colden (Dec. 15, 1819–Nov. 25, 1865). Missionary to Liberia. He was born in New York City and graduated from the Virginia Theological Seminary in 1848. He was ordained deacon on July 30, 1848, and priest on May 21, 1849. In 1849 he and a classmate, Jacob Rambo, sailed for Cape Palmas, Liberia. Under Hoffman's leadership St. Mark's Church, Fishtown, was established and the building was consecrated on Dec. 21, 1853. He also established an Orphan Asylum, a Girl's School, St. Mark's Hospital, and a Home for the Blind. Hoffman was called "the Henry Martyn of our American Church." He married Virginia Haviside Hale on Sept. 5, 1850, and she also served as a missionary at Cape Palmas. He died in Cape Palmas. *See* Hoffman, Virginia Haviside Hale.

Hoffman, Eugene Augustus (Mar. 21, 1829–June 17, 1902). Third dean of the General Theological Seminary. He was born in New York City. Hoffman studied first at Rutgers College and then received his B.A. from Harvard College in 1848. He received his B.D. from the General Theological Seminary in 1851. Hoffman was ordained deacon on June 29, 1851, and priest on Apr. 28, 1853. As a deacon he was in charge of Grace Church, Elizabeth Port, New Jersey, and from 1853 until 1863, he was rector of Christ Church, Elizabeth, New Jersey. He served one year, 1863–1864, as rector of St. Mary's Church, Burlington, New Jersey, and then from 1864 until 1869, he was rector of Grace Church, Brooklyn Heights, New York. His last parish was St. Mark's Church, Philadelphia, where he was rector from 1869 until 1879. Hoffman was dean of General Seminary from June 15, 1879, until his death. Hoffman is remembered as General Seminary's "most munificent benefactor," and under him most of its present quadrangle and grounds, buildings, professorships, endowments, and customs were established. The deanship and the chairs of pastoral theology, NT, and dogmatic theology all received their endowments from him or his family. The seminary's Gutenberg Bible, sold by the trustees at public auction in 1978, was the gift of Dean Hoffman. The Chapel of the Good Shepherd, completed 1885–1888 in English collegiate gothic with a 161-foot bell tower, is a gift of Hoffman's mother in memory of her husband. Hoffman made the chapel the vital center of the seminary's life. Under his leadership the vested faculty evensong procession was instituted, as well as the wearing of academic gowns by students and faculty. He also established the custom of conferring the honorary doctorate upon graduates of the seminary who became bishops. Hoffman was a high churchman, an avid collector of rare books, chairman of the building committee for the Cathedral of St. John the Divine, and president of the New York Historical Society. Hoffman died on a train returning to New York from Canada.

Hoffman Hall, Fisk University. A seminary to train "colored men for the work of the ministry." On July 15, 1889, Bishop Charles Todd Quintard of Tennessee laid the cornerstone for Hoffman Hall on land adjoining Fisk University. The building was named for the Rev. Dr. Charles Frederick Hoffman. He was a friend of Bishop Quintard. Hoffman gave $6,000 for a lot and a building. The school opened in June 1890 and trained some African American clergy. On Oct. 19, 1901, the School of St. Mary the Virgin for Colored Girls was founded in Nashville near Hoffman Hall. Hoffman-St. Mary operated for eight years. In 1911 the Hoffman property was sold and the money was used to buy one hundred acres of land in Mason, Tennessee. The new Hoffman-St. Mary School was very successful in educating African American boys and girls. After the death of Bishop Thomas Frank Gailor, the school was renamed the Gailor Industrial School. It was sold in 1965.

Hoffman, Virginia Haviside Hale (Oct. 14, 1832–Mar. 23, 1855). One of the earliest Episcopal missionaries to Liberia. She was born in Glastonbury, Connecticut. Early in life she became interested in missions to foreign unbelievers. She was an evangelical. On Sept. 5, 1850, she married Cadwallader Colden Hoffman. They served at Cape Palmas, West Africa, as missionaries. She died in Cape Palmas.

Holiness. *See* Notes of the Church.

Holiness, Code of. The name scholars have given to the collection of cultic and moral laws in Lv 17–26. It was apparently one of the sources used by the authors of the priestly source of the Pentateuch. It may have reached its final form in Jerusalem around 650 B.C. It is distinguished by the divine admonition: "You shall be holy to me; for I the LORD am holy" (Lv 20:26).

Holly, James Theodore (Oct. 3, 1829–Mar. 13, 1911). Missionary to Haiti and first Bishop of Haiti. He was born in Washington, D.C. Holly was raised a Roman Catholic but became an Episcopalian. He was ordained deacon on June 17, 1855, and priest on Jan. 3, 1856. He then went to Haiti to establish the Episcopal Church there. Upon his return to the United States he was the rector of St. Luke's Church, New Haven, Connecticut. In 1861 he returned to Haiti and worked there as a missionary. In 1874 the House of Bishops signed a covenant between the Protestant Episcopal Church in the United States and the Protestant Episcopal Church in Haiti. Holly was consecrated the first Bishop of Haiti on Nov. 8, 1874. He served in that capacity until his death.

Holmes, Urban Tigner, III (June 12, 1930–Aug. 6, 1981). Priest, seminary dean, teacher, and writer. He was born in Durham, North Carolina. Holmes received his B.A. in 1950 and his M.A. in 1954, both from the University of North Carolina. He received his M.Div. from the Philadelphia Divinity School in 1954. He was ordained deacon on June 26, 1954, and priest on Dec. 27, 1954. From 1954 until 1956, he was curate at St. Luke's Church, Salisbury, North Carolina, and chaplain at Catawba College. He was Episcopal chaplain at Louisiana State University from 1956 until 1966, and from 1959 until 1966, he was lecturer in Greek. Holmes received his S.T.M. from the Graduate School of Theology at the University of the South in 1962. In 1966 he became professor of pastoral theology at Nashotah House, and in 1973 he received his Ph.D. from Marquette University. From Aug. 1, 1973, until his death, Holmes was the ninth dean of the School of Theology at the University of the South. In 1975 he was elected to the Executive Council of the Episcopal Church. Holmes was a prolific writer. His major publications include *Turning to Christ: A Theology of Renewal and Evangelization* (1981), and (with John H. Westerhoff III) *Christian*

Believing (1979, vol. 1 of the new *Church's Teaching Series*). He died in Atlanta, Georgia.

Holy Communion. *See* Eucharist.

Holy Communion, Sisterhood of the. On Nov. 1, 1845, William Augustus Muhlenberg, rector of the Church of the Holy Communion, New York City, heard Anne Ayres take her monastic vows. The service was held in secret, the only witness being the sexton who was waiting to extinguish the lights. By taking monastic vows, she became the first nun in the Episcopal Church, although Muhlenberg referred to her as a "deaconess." The Sisterhood of the Holy Communion was officially organized in 1852. It was not really a religious order. There were no lifetime vows, and the sisters wore ordinary clothes. It helped to prepare the Episcopal Church for the more traditional orders for women that appeared later. The primary focus of the Sisterhood of the Holy Communion was St. Luke's Hospital, New York. It was a pioneer in the development of the nursing profession in the United States. In 1863 Ayres resigned as "First Sister," and the Sisterhood dissolved. Muhlenberg revived it in 1873 as the Sisterhood of St. Luke and St. John, which dissolved in 1934. *See* Ayres, Anne; *see* Muhlenberg, William Augustus.

Holy Cross Day. A major feast observed on Sept. 14 in honor of Christ's self-offering on the cross for our salvation. The collect for Holy Cross Day recalls that Christ "was lifted high upon the cross that he might draw the whole world unto himself," and prays that "we, who glory in the mystery of our redemption, may have grace to take up our cross and follow him" (BCP, p. 192). The themes of Holy Cross Day are powerfully expressed by the hymn "Lift high the cross" (Hymn 473).

This feast is known as "The Exaltation of the Holy Cross" in the eastern church and in missals and sacramentaries of the western church, and it is known as "The Triumph of the Cross" in the Roman Catholic Church. It was one of the 12 great feasts in the Byzantine liturgy. The 1979 BCP is the first American Prayer Book to include Holy Cross Day.

Historically, the feast has been associated with the dedication on Sept. 14, 335, of a complex of buildings built by the Emperor Constantine (c. 285–337) in Jerusalem on the sites of the crucifixion and Christ's tomb. This shrine included a large basilica and a circular church. Constantine's mother, Helena (c. 255–c. 330), supervised the construction of the shrine, and a relic believed to be the cross was discovered during the work of excavation. Claims by the Church of Jerusalem to have the cross date from the mid-fourth century, and the pilgrim Egeria mentions a feast commemorating the discovery of the cross in Jerusalem in the late-fourth-century. This feast has also been associated with the exposition at Jerusalem of the cross by the Byzantine Emperor Heraclius (575–641). He recovered the relic from the Persians who took it from Jerusalem in 614 when they destroyed the Church of the Holy Sepulchre. Although the authenticity of alleged relics of the cross may be questionable, Holy Cross Day provides an opportunity for a joyous celebration of Christ's redeeming death on a cross. *See* Cross; *see* Relics.

Holy Cross, Order of the (OHC). The oldest American Episcopal monastic order for men. It was founded by James Otis Sargent Huntington, Robert Stockton Dod, and James Gibbon Cameron. It began on Nov. 25, 1884, when Huntington took vows of poverty, chastity, and obedience before Henry Codman Potter, Assistant Bishop of New York, at the Chapel of the Sisters of St. John the Baptist, New York City. OHC follows the Benedictine Rule and lives according to Benedictine spiritual traditions. The primary work of the order has been in the Lower East Side of New York City, in West Africa, and at St. Andrew's School in Tennessee. Members include both clergy and laity, who take a threefold vow of poverty, chastity, and obedience. The Holy Eucharist and the fourfold Divine Office are central to the life of the order. The brothers engage in teaching, preaching, counseling, spiritual direction, parish ministry, and community service. There are several groups for lay and clerics who are associated with the order: the Oblates of Mt. Calvary, Associates of the Holy Cross, Oblates of the Holy Cross, and the Confraternity of the Christian Life. The brothers wear white tunics and a scapular with a hood. The symbol of the OHC is a plain ebony cross. It is headed by a superior who is elected by the membership. OHC publishes *The Holy Cross Magazine. See* Benedictine Spirituality.

Holy Cross, Society of the. The oldest catholic clerical society in the Anglican Communion. It is known by its Latin initials, S. S. C., *Societas Sanctae Crucis*. It was founded at the House of Charity in Soho, London, on Feb. 28, 1855, by Father Charles Fuge Lowder and five other London priests. Lowder was vicar at St. Peter's, London Docks. S. S. C. exists to strengthen and consolidate priestly

spirituality, to maintain and extend catholic faith and discipline, and to unite its membership in a special bond of mutual charity. Membership is open to male priests and bishops by invitation only. The original rule, which remains substantially unchanged to this day, was written by Edward B. Pusey, one of the leaders of the Oxford Movement. The society was involved in the revival of the practice of reserving the Blessed Sacrament and for having regular eucharistic devotions, including Benediction. It was also involved in the restoration of retreats, religious communities, the sacraments of Holy Unction and Penance (Reconciliation), and the cultus of the saints, including particular devotion to the Blessed Virgin Mary. The first meeting of the American chapter of the society was held on Sept. 14, Holy Cross Day, 1972. The society is opposed to the ordination of women to any clerical order. A major objective of the society is the reunion of Christendom, with the Roman Catholic Church in particular, which they consider the center of western Christianity.

Holy Days. In a general sense, a holy day is any day set apart for special observance because of its significance for faith. The BCP Calendar of the church year specifically lists as holy days the Feasts of our Lord (such as the Presentation, and the Transfiguration), other major feasts (such as all feasts of Apostles and all feasts of Evangelists), and fasts (such as Ash Wednesday and Good Friday). In this sense, holy days are distinguished from principal feasts (such as Christmas Day and Easter Day), Sundays, and Days of Optional Observance (such as the Ember Days and the Rogation Days) (BCP, pp. 15–18). The Calendar also lists major holy days at pp. 32–33. The BCP Lectionary provides a proper collect and readings for all holy days. *See* Calendar of the Church Year, The.

Holy Eucharist. *See* Eucharist.

Holy Family, Order of the. A double monastery of monks and nuns, clergy and laity, living under the Familian Rule that combines Benedictine and Franciscan elements. It was founded by the Rt. Rev. Jon Aidan on June 29, 1969. Members live under the three vows of stability, conversion of life, and obedience. The order has oblates who live under one vow (either poverty, obedience, or chastity) and associates who follow a spiritual rule of life. It is committed to the pursuit of world peace and personal holiness. The order began in Denver, Colorado, then moved to Abbot Galisteo Priory in Santa Fe, New Mexico. It is now located in Lumberton, New Jersey.

Holy Hour. Devotion in the presence of the Blessed Sacrament of the Eucharist for an hour. *See* Eucharistic Adoration.

Holy Innocents, The. Male infants slaughtered by King Herod the Great in Bethlehem in an unsuccessful attempt to kill the "king of the Jews." The Gospel of Matthew, ch. 2, records that the wise men, or Magi, from the east were seeking the child who was born king of the Jews. They had "observed his star at its rising," and came to pay him homage. They told this to Herod, which frightened him "and all Jerusalem with him." Herod feared that the young "king" would threaten his throne. The chief priests and scribes told Herod that the Messiah was to be born in Bethlehem. They also told him when the star had appeared. Herod told the wise men to search diligently for the child in Bethlehem and tell him when they found the child. He said he wanted to go to the child and pay him homage. The wise men found the child Jesus and offered him gifts of gold, frankincense, and myrrh. But the wise men were warned in a dream not to return to Herod, and "they left for their own country by another road." Herod was furious when he realized that he had been tricked by the wise men. He ordered the death of all male children in and around Bethlehem who were two years old and under. The child Jesus was not harmed because Joseph had been warned in a dream to escape to Egypt with Jesus and Mary. The feast of the Holy Innocents has been dated from the fourth century in Bethlehem and from the fifth century in North Africa and Rome. It is a major feast of the Episcopal calendar of the church year, observed on Dec. 28. The collect for this feast prays that God will receive "into the arms of your mercy all innocent victims; and by your great might frustrate the designs of evil tyrants and establish your rule of justice, love, and peace" (BCP, p. 238). The hymns "In Bethlehem a newborn boy" (Hymn 246) and "Lully, lullay, thou little tiny child" (Hymn 247) are especially appropriate for the feast of the Holy Innocents.

Holy Matrimony. *See* Celebration and Blessing of a Marriage.

Holy Mysteries. An early name for the eucharistic liturgy. The term has several overlapping meanings: the mystery of Christ's death and resurrection, the mystery of faith, the sacraments, and the truth that passes all rational understanding.

Holy Name of Our Lord Jesus Christ, The. Celebration on Jan. 1, the eighth day after the birth of Jesus, when he was named and circumcised. He was "called Jesus, the name given by the angel before he was conceived in the womb" (Lk 2:21). Under the Law of Moses, all male infants were to be circumcised on the eighth day after birth (Lv 12:3). It was also customary at this time for family and friends to witness the naming of the child. This major feast is celebrated on Jan. 1, the eighth day of the Christmas season. The designation of the feast in honor of Jesus' Holy Name is new to the 1979 BCP. It was traditionally celebrated as the Feast of the Circumcision. Celebration of the Holy Name reflects the significance of the Holy Name of Jesus, and the emphasis of the Gospel of Luke on the naming of Jesus rather than his circumcision.

Liturgical celebration of Jesus' circumcision began in the Gallican Church. The Council of Tours (567) called for Jan. 1 to be observed as a fast day to counter pagan celebrations of the beginning of the new year. This day was also traditionally associated with devotion to the Virgin Mary. Celebration of the Feast of the Name of Jesus dates from the end of the middle ages. In the fifteenth century, the Franciscans Bernardino of Siena (1380–1444) and Giovanni Capistrano (1386–1456) encouraged devotion to the name of Jesus. This celebration was officially granted to the Franciscans in 1530 for observance on Jan. 14. In 1721 Innocent XIII called for the whole Roman Catholic Church to observe the feast on the Second Sunday after Epiphany. This feast was introduced into England in 1489 and celebrated on Aug. 7. It was included as a black letter day in the Elizabethan Calendar of the church year in 1561.

The name "Jesus" is from the Hebrew *Joshua*, or *Yehoshuah*, "Yahweh is salvation" or "Yahweh will save." Devotion to the Holy Name of Jesus is particularly derived from Phil 2:9–11, which states that God highly exalted Jesus "and gave him the name that is above every name, so that at the name of Jesus every knee should bend, in heaven and on earth and under the earth." This scriptural devotion is paraphrased by the hymn "At the name of Jesus" (Hymn 435) in *The Hymnal 1982*. Other hymns that express devotion to the Holy Name of Jesus include "To the name of our salvation" (Hymns 248–249) and "Jesus! Name of wondrous love!" (Hymn 252).

Holy Nativity, Sisterhood of the (SHN). This sisterhood was founded on Nov. 1, 1882, by the Rev. Charles Chapman Grafton and Mother Ruth Margaret Vose on Brimer Street in Boston, Massachusetts. In 1884 the sisterhood moved to Providence, Rhode Island. In 1889 Grafton was consecrated the second Bishop of Fond du Lac. In 1894 the sisterhood moved to Fond du Lac, Wisconsin. The sisterhood was a parochial mission society, having as its primary work the teaching of the catholic faith and winning souls to Christ. This was the first Episcopal sisterhood to work among Native Americans. The sisterhood was founded to embrace both an active and a contemplative lifestyle. Its primary work and first obligation is prayer, the personal relationship between Christ and the individual. The sisters' lives are centered around the daily celebration of the eucharist and the praying of the fourfold divine office. The sisterhood expresses its active life through such ministries as leading retreats and quiet days, preaching and teaching missions, teaching church school, visiting the sick and shut-in, and providing spiritual direction to those who request it. At one time it had branch houses in Providence, Rhode Island; New York City; Milwaukee; Oneida, Wisconsin; Baltimore; Bay Shore, New York; Los Angeles; Philadelphia; Santa Barbara, California; and Fond du Lac. The two remaining houses are in Fond du Lac and Santa Barbara. In the late 1990s, the sisterhood was planning to close its house in Fond du Lac and open a house in Green Lake, Wisconsin, in the Diocese of Fond du Lac. It was also beginning a new mission work in the Diocese of West Virginia. The community offers a rule of life for lay and clerical associates; as well as one for companions, young people from ages 12 to 21. The motto of the order is "Press on the Kingdom." *See* Grafton, Charles Chapman.

Holy Oil. *See* Chrism; *see* Oil, Holy.

Holy Orders. The ordained ministries of bishops, priests (presbyters), and deacons. Canonical provisions concerning ordination to these three orders are equally applicable to men and women in the Episcopal Church.

Holy Redeemer, Order of the. This order for men and women was founded on Sept. 24, 1967, by Brother William Mitzenus in Keansburg, New Jersey. The work of the order is parish-centered and pragmatic, with an emphasis on serving the poor, the homeless, and the hungry. The novitiate is two years in length. After completion of the

novitiate and manifestation of suitable spiritual and academic formation, the novice is invited to profess the vows of simplicity, chastity, and obedience. An oblate may hold a secular occupation in addition to the monastic commitments. Its one house is Holy Redeemer Abbey in Keansburg.

Holy Saturday. The Saturday after Good Friday, which recalls the day when the crucified Christ visited among the dead while his body lay in the tomb of Joseph of Arimathea. In the Episcopal Church there is no eucharist on Holy Saturday. The BCP provides a simple liturgy of the word with collect and readings for the Holy Saturday service. The funeral anthem "In the midst of life" (BCP, pp. 484 or 492) is used instead of the prayers of the people (BCP, p. 283). In the ancient church, those preparing for baptism and perhaps others continued the fast they began on Good Friday. Holy Saturday ends at sunset. Fasting and other preparations end at sunset or with the Easter Vigil, which begins the celebration of Easter. *See* Triduum; *see* Easter Vigil.

Holy Spirit. The third person of the Trinity. In the OT, "spirit" was primarily used to express God's power in the world. In the NT, Jesus is called the Christ because he is the one anointed by the Spirit. The gift of the Spirit to Jesus' disciples after the crucifixion is associated with the post-resurrection appearances of Jesus in Jn 20:19–23 and with the Day of Pentecost in Acts 2. The Catechism states that the church is holy "because the Holy Spirit dwells in it, consecrates its members, and guides them to do God's will" (BCP, p. 854). The Council of Constantinople in 381 stated that the Holy Spirit is as truly God as the Son, both being of "one substance" with the Father. The Nicene Creed states belief "in the Holy Spirit, the Lord, the giver of life, who proceeds from the Father and the Son. With the Father and the Son he is worshiped and glorified. He has spoken through the prophets" (BCP, p. 359). In the relations of the persons of the Trinity, the Spirit is said to proceed from the Father by the mode of "spiration" or "breathing," while the Son is said to proceed from the Father by the mode of "generation." Western theology came to speak of the Spirit proceeding "from the Father and the Son." The Episcopal theologian William Porcher DuBose stated in *The Soteriology of the New Testament* (1892) that "*all* God's operations in us as spiritual beings are by the word through the spirit" (p. 56). Pneumatology is the theological study of the Holy Spirit. *The Hymnal*

1982 provides a section of hymns on the Holy Spirit (Hymns 500–516), including "Come, Holy Ghost, our souls inspire" (Hymns 503–504) and "Breathe on me, Breath of God" (Hymn 508). *See* Filioque; *see* Trinity.

Holy Spirit, Community of the (CHS). In 1949 Sister Ruth E. Younger (1897–1986) and Sister Edith Margaret Brown (1905–1988), of the Sisterhood of St. John the Divine in Toronto, were granted a leave of absence to test a vision about establishing a settlement house in New York City. When they got to New York they discovered that a settlement house was not needed. Some persons in New York encouraged them to establish a school. On Feb. 2, 1950, they opened St. Hilda's School, later named St. Hilda's and St. Hugh's School. However, the Sisterhood of St. John the Divine did not want to support a school in the United States. Sister Ruth began to lay the foundations for a new community. On Aug. 27, 1952, in the Cathedral of St. John the Divine, Bishop Horace W. B. Donegan received the transfers of Sr. Ruth and Sr. Edith Margaret, and professed the first two sisters of the Community of the Holy Spirit. At the first chapter held on the same day, Sr. Ruth was elected the first Mother. In 1963 the community established the Melrose School in Brewster, New York. The Fellowship of the Community of the Holy Spirit are men and women who offer their prayers and means for the development of the community. The Associates of the Community of the Holy Spirit under the Rule of St. Augustine's Chapter are men and women who are in association with the sisters and seek to bring their lives under the guidance of the Holy Spirit.

Holy Spirit, Gifts of. *See* Gifts of the Spirit.

Holy Table. The altar, also known as the Lord's table. The term "holy table" has been used by those seeking to emphasize the eucharist as a shared meal. All three terms are used with the same meaning in the Prayer Book (see BCP, pp. 354, 361).

Holy Water. Water that has been blessed for religious and devotional use. It may symbolize purification, blessing, dedication, and renewal of the baptismal covenant. An aspergillum (tube with holes) or a small branch of a tree or shrub may be used to sprinkle holy water during a church service or at other times. It is especially appropriate to sprinkle the congregation with holy water at the Renewal of Baptismal Vows at the Easter Vigil (BCP, p. 292) and at other times of renewal of the baptismal covenant. The asperges is the ceremony of sprinkling holy water over the altar, clergy, and people before the eucharist. Some parishes use a stoup, basin, or font to make holy water available to those who enter the church. Those who wish to participate in the pious custom of "taking holy water" may touch it with the fingers, placing a drop of it on the forehead while making the sign of the cross on the forehead, chest, and shoulders. The early origin of this custom is evidenced by the presence of stoups for holy water in ancient basilicas. Holy water has been known as "lustral water," reflecting its symbolic role in purification. A rubric in the service for Restoring of Things Profaned in the *BOS* notes that each profaned object may be symbolically cleansed by use of water or incense as signs of purification.

Holy Week. From early times Christians have observed the week before Easter as a time of special devotion. As the pilgrim Egeria recorded in the late fourth century, Jerusalem contained many sacred places that were sites for devotion and liturgy. Numerous pilgrims to the holy city followed the path of Jesus in his last days. They formed processions, worshipped where Christ suffered and died, and venerated relics. From this beginning evolved the rites we observe today on Palm Sunday, Maundy Thursday, Good Friday, and Holy Saturday. These services provide a liturgical experience of the last days of Jesus' earthly life, as well as the time and events leading up to his resurrection. The BCP provides special liturgies for each of these days. The eucharistic lectionary also provides proper readings for Monday, Tuesday, and Wednesday in Holy Week. Some parishes observe the service of *Tenebrae* on one of these days in Holy Week. In many dioceses, the diocesan clergy will make a reaffirmation of ordination vows in the context of a eucharist during Holy Week, usually before Maundy Thursday. The three holy days, or *Triduum*, of Maundy Thursday, Good Friday, and Holy Saturday are at the heart of the Holy Week observance. In many Episcopal parishes, the liturgical color for Holy Week from Palm Sunday through Maundy Thursday is red. Holy Week ends at sundown on the Saturday before Easter, or with the celebration of the Easter Vigil.

Homilist. The person who preaches the homily or sermon.

Homily. *See* Sermon.

Homoiousios. The term is from the Greek *homoi*, "similar," and *ousia* "being," meaning "of similar being." It is associated with the Arian understanding of the relation between the Father and the Son (or Word). Arius understood Father and Son to be of similar—but not identical—being or essence. Although Father and Son were considered to be in some sense similar, they were also considered in some sense dissimilar. Arius regarded the Son or Word to be a created being, as a boat is created by a shipbuilder. For Arius, Father and Son could not be said to be of one substance. The Council of Nicaea in 325 declared such an understanding of the relationship between Father and Son to be inadequate to provide for the divine salvation of the world through the Son. It insisted that Father and Son are not merely similar but are of one substance, one being, *homoousios*. *See* Homoousios; *see* Arianism; *see* Ecumenical Councils.

Homoousios. This term is from the Greek *homo* (same or identical), and *ousia* (being or essence). It is the word translated in the English version of the Nicene Creed as "being of one substance" (BCP, p. 327, Rite 1) or "of one Being" (BCP, p. 358, Rite 2). After lengthy debate at the Council of Nicaea in 325, *homoousios* became the approved, orthodox way to express the relationship between the first and second persons of the Trinity. This understanding contradicted Arius, who conceived the Word to be a creature of God, similar but in some respects unlike the first person of the Godhead (*homoiousios*). However, orthodox dogma insisted that Father and Son were of identical substance or being (*homoousios*), and that the Son was "begotten, not made" (BCP, pp. 327, 358). *See* Homoiousios; *see* Arianism; *see* Ecumenical Councils.

Honduras, Diocese of. The General Convention of 1967 divided the Missionary District of Central America into five Missionary Districts: Costa Rica, El Salvador, Guatemala, Honduras, and Nicaragua. Honduras became a diocese in 1985.

Honolulu, Missionary District of. It was formed by the General Convention on Oct. 15, 1901, and reconstituted by the General Convention as the Diocese of Hawaii on Sept. 4, 1969.

Hood, Academic. A flowing, stylized hood that drapes over the shoulders and back of the wearer. It is an academic insignia. The wearer's academic degree and institution are indicated by the size, cut, and trim material of the hood. It was worn over the gown in medieval academic dress. Anglican preachers have worn the hood with scarf and gown for the sermon. This use could be seen as a display of academic credentials by the preacher. Some members of the clergy (especially with a low church piety) wore the hood, scarf, and gown throughout the service, following the Genevan practice. This practice continued into the late nineteenth century in the Episcopal Church. Although liturgical use of the academic gown is now rare, the academic hood (possibly with the tippet) is at times worn over the surplice for the Daily Office.

Hooker, Richard (c. 1554–Nov. 2, 1600). Theologian and leading advocate of Anglicanism. Hooker was born in Heavitree, Devonshire, near Exeter. In 1568 Hooker entered Corpus Christi College, Oxford. He received his B.A. in 1574 and his M.A. in 1577. In 1577 he was chosen fellow of his college. In 1579 he was named reader in Hebrew for the University. He was ordained deacon in 1582, and priest in the same year. On Mar. 17, 1585, Hooker was appointed Master of the Temple in London. He encountered Walter Travers, a leading Calvinist Puritan, at the Temple. Thomas Fuller said, "the pulpit spake pure Canterbury in the morning and Geneva in the afternoon until Travers was silenced." In 1591 Hooker left the Temple and became the rector at Boscombe in Wiltshire. In July, 1595, he became rector of Bishopsbourne in Kent, where he died.

Hooker's major contribution was his monumental *Of the Lawes of Ecclesiastical Polity.* The first four books of the *Lawes* were published in 1594, the fifth book was published in 1597, and the last three books were published much later after his death. With the *Lawes*, Hooker became the great apologist of the Elizabethan Settlement. In the *Lawes* he created both a distinctive philosophy of constitutional government and an Anglican theology that remains congenial to modern thought. He provided the classical Anglican answer to the Puritan criticisms of episcopacy and the Prayer Book. Hooker affirmed the threefold Anglican sources of authority—scripture, tradition, and reason. He countered the Roman Catholic argument which treated the Bible and tradition as equally authoritative for belief. He also countered the Puritans whose literal obedience to scripture was so absolute that they considered unlawful whatever scripture did not command. He recognized the absolute authority of scripture where it spoke plainly. Reason was to be used in reading scripture. If scripture were silent or ambiguous, wisdom would consult the tradition of the church. On this foundation Hooker built an elaborate theory based on the "absolute fundamental of natural law," the expression of God's supreme wisdom which governs the universe and to which both ecclesiastical and civil polity must yield. Hooker saw the church not as a static but as an organic institution whose methods of government change according to circumstances. He understood the Church of England, though reformed, to be in continuity with historic Christianity. He is commemorated in the Episcopal calendar of the church year on Nov. 3.

Hopkins, John Henry (Jan. 30, 1792–Jan. 9, 1868). Eighth Presiding Bishop. He was born in Dublin, Ireland, and came to the United States in 1800. Educated privately, he began work in 1813 as a superintendent of ironworks near Pittsburgh. Although not yet ordained, he was called in 1823 as rector of Calvary Church, Pittsburgh, where he was temporary organist. He was ordained deacon on Dec. 14, 1823, and priest on May 12, 1824. Hopkins became assistant minister at Trinity Church, Boston, in 1831, and was elected the first Bishop of Vermont. He served as bishop from his consecration on Oct. 31, 1832, until his death. He served as Presiding Bishop from Jan. 13, 1865, until he died. Hopkins was a prolific writer and controversialist. In *Slavery: Its Religious Sanction* (1851) he argued that slavery had a divine warrant. After the Civil War, Hopkins as Presiding Bishop welcomed the return of the southern dioceses and helped to end the division that was caused by the war. *The Law of Ritualism* (1866) was influential in the eventual acceptance in most Episcopal parishes of such liturgical customs as eucharistic vestments and altar candles. He died in Burlington.

Horrocks, James (c. 1734–Nov. 20, 1772). Commissary to Virginia and sixth president of the College of William and Mary. He was probably born in Wakefield, Yorkshire, England. Horrocks received his B.A. in 1755 and his M.A. in 1758 from Trinity College, Cambridge University. After his ordination he was licensed to preach in Virginia in 1761. In 1762 he became the master of the grammar school connected with the College of William and Mary. From 1764 until 1771, he was president of William and Mary and rector of Bruton Parish. In 1768 the Bishop of London appointed Horrocks the fifth Commissary to Virginia. In 1771 he returned to England. Horrocks died in Oporto, Portugal.

Hosmer, Rachel Elizabeth (May 15, 1908–Dec. 23, 1988). Educator and founder of the Order of St. Helena. She was born in Everett, Massachusetts. Hosmer attended Smith College, 1926–1927, and the Boston Museum School of Fine Arts, 1927–1928. In Aug. 1928 she entered the Convent of St. Anne, Boston, and took the name Rachel. In 1933 she received her B.A. in ancient languages from Boston University. That same year, with four other sisters, Hosmer reopened Margaret Hall School in Versailles, Kentucky, and in 1934 she became the principal. She professed life vows on July 26, 1936. In 1938 she became reverend mother of the Convent of St. Anne in Versailles. On Nov. 8, 1945, nine sisters of the Order of St. Anne at Margaret Hall School, led by the superior, Mother Rachel, formed the Order of St. Helena. Sister Rachel served from 1962 to 1971 at various mission schools in Liberia, West Africa. She taught at several schools after returning to the United States. In 1976 she became the associate director of the Center for Christian Spirituality at the General Theological Seminary. Hosmer was ordained deacon on June 14, 1975, and priest on Apr. 25, 1977. In 1979 she joined the faculty of the School of Theology at the University of the South as lecturer in spiritual theology. In 1979 she coauthored (with Alan Jones) *Living in the Spirit*, a volume in the second Church's Teaching Series. She died in Vails Gate, New York. *See* St. Helena, Order of (OSH).

Host (Eucharistic). The consecrated bread of the eucharist. The term is from the Latin *hostia*, "victim." Use of the term reflects an understanding of the eucharist in sacrificial terms relative to Christ's death on the cross. The term is also extended to mean the bread or wafers to be consecrated at the eucharist. The individual wafers of the eucharist may be referred to as "hosts." Many parishes use a large host that is broken by the celebrant at the fraction. This "Priest's Host" may be decorated with Christian symbols that are pressed into the large wafer. It is typically placed on the paten prior to the service when the chalice is vested. The smaller "hosts" that will be distributed to the people are placed in a ciborium and placed on the paten with the "Priest's Host" when the altar is prepared before the Great Thanksgiving at the eucharist.

"Hound of Heaven." This image for God who loves us persistently is from the poem "The Hound of Heaven" by the English poet Francis Thompson (1859–1907). The poem recalls how one fled God, even "in the mist of tears," but eventually fell into God's loving embrace. This image reminds us that God's love is not deterred by our fears or imperfections, and that God steadfastly seeks our salvation.

House of Bishops' Committee on Pastoral Development. This committee of the House of Bishops serves as a support to the director of the Office of Pastoral Development and to the Presiding Bishop. The committee is appointed by the Presiding Bishop and normally meets twice a year. The committee serves as a council of advice and a sounding board for the director of the Office of Pastoral Development. It seeks to discern the pastoral needs of the larger church.

House Blessing. *See* Celebration for a Home.

Hugh of Lincoln (c. 1140–Nov. 16, 1200). Friend of the oppressed, especially lepers and Jews. He was born at Avalon in Burgundy. With his father, he entered a priory of Austin Canons at Villarbenoit, where he received his education. In 1160 he became a monk in the strict Carthusian Order at Grande Chartreuse. Hugh became the procurator of the monastery in 1170. In 1175 King Henry II of England invited him to come to Witham, Somersetshire, to establish the first Carthusian house in England. Hugh was chosen Bishop of Lincoln in an open election. He was consecrated on Sept. 21, 1186. He remained in this position until his death. He never permitted encroachments upon his ecclesiastical rights and consistently refused the demands of Kings Henry II, Richard, and John. Hugh was canonized in 1220, the first Carthusian to receive this honor. His tomb was an important pilgrimage site until it was dismantled during the Reformation. He is commemorated in the Episcopal calendar of the church year on Nov. 17.

Hughson, Shirley Carter (Feb. 15, 1867–Nov. 16, 1949). Superior of the Order of the Holy Cross, educator, spiritual director, and Anglo-catholic theologian. He was born in Camden, South Carolina. Hughson was educated at the University of South Carolina, Johns Hopkins University, and received his B.D. from the General Theological Seminary in 1896. He was ordained deacon on June 11, 1896, and priest on June 13, 1897. Hughson began his ministry as rector of St. Mark's Church, Philadelphia. He soon became interested in the monastic life. He was life professed in the Order of the Holy Cross on May 3, 1902. He was prior of the community at St. Andrew's, Tennessee

from 1906 until 1914. He was also head of the St. Andrew's Industrial and Training School for Boys, which the order took over in Apr. 1906. He was superior of the order, Aug. 6, 1918–Aug. 11, 1921, and Aug. 5, 1930–Aug. 4, 1936. Hughson was novice master of the order, 1903–1906, 1914–1921, 1924–1925, and 1945. He was a chaplain to the Community of St. Mary from 1906 until 1943, and chaplain general from 1908 until 1918. Hughson was a prolific writer. He published more than 25 books. His *The Warfare of the Soul, Practical Studies in the Life of Temptation* (1910), led him to be recognized as an authority on prayer and spiritual direction. His *The Fundamentals of the Religious State* (1915) became the basic text on the theology of the religious life. He died at the Holy Cross Monastery, West Park, New York.

Human Affairs and Health, Standing Commission on. The 1976 General Convention established this commission. It replaced and combined the Joint Commission on the Church in Human Affairs and the Joint Commission on Religion and Health. The commission studied the theological, ethical and pastoral questions inherent in such aspects of human affairs as health, sexuality, and bioethical problems. The 1997 General Convention discontinued this commission.

Human Quest, The. *See* Churchman, The.

Humble Access, Prayer of. A prayer for worthy reception of communion that begins with the statement, "We do not presume to come to this thy Table, O merciful Lord, trusting in our own righteousness" (BCP, p. 337). It is optional in Rite 1, and not used in Rite 2. It may be said by the celebrant and people after the fraction (and fraction anthem), before the invitation to communion. This prayer first appeared in the 1548 Order of Holy Communion. Its name is from the Scottish Prayer Book of 1637, where it was known as the "Collect of Humble Access to the Holy Communion." It has a strong penitential emphasis, stating that "We are not worthy so much as to gather up the crumbs under thy Table."

Humeral Veil. This large scarf or shawl is worn over the shoulders and covers the hands. It may be used when carrying the vessels containing the consecrated elements of the eucharist, as in processions of the Blessed Sacrament and Benediction. *See* Benediction of the Blessed Sacrament.

Hunt, Robert (c. 1568–1608). First chaplain to Jamestown, Virginia. He was appointed vicar of Reculver in Kent, England on Jan. 18, 1594. On Oct. 5, 1602, he became vicar of Heathfield in the Diocese of Chichester. From 1603 until 1606, Hunt was a student at Trinity Hall, Cambridge University. He was the chaplain for the colonists who came to Virginia in 1607. He may have celebrated the first Anglican eucharist in America on May 24, 1607. Captain John Smith recorded in his journal that the eucharist was celebrated on June 21, 1607, and Hunt would have presided. Hunt died some time prior to Apr. 10, 1608.

Huntington, Frederic Dan (May 28, 1819–July 11, 1904). Bishop and editor. He was born in Hadley, Hampshire County, Massachusetts. Huntington graduated from Amherst College in 1839 and from the Divinity School of Harvard University in 1842. He was ordained minister of the South Congregational Church (Unitarian), Boston, on Oct. 19, 1842, and served as a Unitarian minister in Boston until 1855, when he went to Harvard as preacher to the college and Plummer Professor of Christian Morals. From 1845 until 1858, Huntington edited the *Monthly Religious Magazine*. While at Harvard he struggled with the Unitarian faith. In 1859 he decided to join the Episcopal Church. He left his positions at Harvard in 1860 and was confirmed in the Episcopal Church on Mar. 25, 1860. Huntington was ordained deacon on Sept. 12, 1860, and priest on Mar. 19, 1861. He organized Emmanuel Church, Boston, and served there until he was elected bishop. Huntington was consecrated the first Bishop of Central New York on Apr. 8, 1869, and remained in that position until his death. In 1861 he and George Maxwell Randall, later the first Missionary Bishop of Colorado, founded the *Church Monthly*. It was published until 1870. Huntington was supportive of the Social Gospel and committed to the ecumenical movement. He was also an opponent of extremes in ritual observances. He was the father of James Otis Sargent Huntington, one of the founders of the Order of the Holy Cross. Huntington died in Hadley, Massachusetts.

Huntington, James Otis Sargent (July 23, 1854–June 29, 1935). One of the founders of the Order of the Holy Cross. He was the son of Frederic Dan Huntington, Bishop of Central New York. He was born in Boston, Massachusetts. Huntington received his B.A. from Harvard in 1875. He studied at St. Andrew's Divinity School, Syracuse, 1876–1879. He was ordained deacon on Sept. 21, 1878, and priest on May 30, 1880. From 1875 until 1881, Huntington was assistant at Calvary Mission, Syracuse, and from 1881 until 1889, he was at Holy Cross Mission, New York City. On Nov. 1, 1881, Huntington, Robert Stockton Dod, and James Gibbon Cameron began to live the religious life together. On Nov. 25, 1884, at the Chapel of the Sisters of St. John the Baptist, New York City, Huntington made his life profession as the first monk in the Order of the Holy Cross. Henry Codman Potter, Assistant Bishop of New York, received Huntington's vows of poverty, chastity, and obedience. Huntington was superior of the order, 1884–1888, 1897–1907, 1915–1918, and 1921–1930. Huntington was a social reformer who worked to improve the lives of his poor parishioners. As a ritualist priest he brought beauty into the lives of those who lived in drab environments. His most radical activity was to support the single tax advocated by Henry George. This was a single tax on unearned increment (increased value) of real property, which would have been the only tax. He was also the author of several books. Huntington died at Holy Cross Monastery, West Park, New York. *See* Holy Cross, Order of the (OHC).

Huntington, William Reed (Sept. 20, 1838–July 26, 1909). Ecumenical leader and liturgical reformer. He was known as the "First Presbyter of the Church." Huntington was born in Lowell, Massachusetts. He received his A.B. from Harvard in 1859. He studied for the ordained ministry of the Episcopal Church under the direction of Frederic Dan Huntington, who was later Bishop of Central New York. He was ordained deacon on Oct. 1, 1861, and priest on Dec. 3, 1862. He was rector of All Saints Church, Worcester, Massachusetts, 1862–1883; and rector of Grace Church, New York City, 1883–1909. Huntington was a member of the House of Deputies of the General Convention, 1871–1907.

In *The Church Idea* (1870), Huntington presented the Anglican basis for an ecumenical "Church of the Reconciliation" in America in terms of acceptance of the Holy Scriptures as the Word of God; the Nicene Creed as the rule of faith; Baptism and Eucharist, the two sacraments ordained by Christ; and the episcopate as the keystone of church unity. This "foursquare" basis for church unity came to be known as the "Quadrilateral." Huntington's efforts led to the adoption of the Quadrilateral by the House of Bishops at the 1886 General Convention of the Episcopal Church in Chicago. It was not enacted by the House of Deputies at the 1886 Convention. However, the

Quadrilateral was passed in a modified form as a resolution at the Lambeth Conference of 1888. The Chicago-Lambeth Quadrilateral continues to be the primary Anglican ecumenical statement and standard.

Huntington also sought greater flexibility and accessibility in the worship of the Episcopal Church. He sought to modernize Prayer Book worship in light of the needs of the American people. He called for a complete revision of the BCP at the 1874 General Convention. His *Materia Ritualis* was the working paper of the joint committee on Prayer Book revision prior to the 1883 General Convention. Huntington was a leader in proposing *The Book Annexed to the Report of the Joint Committee* (1883), which was a significant revision of the BCP. *The Book Annexed* was not accepted, but this Prayer Book revision process ultimately resulted in the 1892 BCP. Some of the prayers of *The Book Annexed* were later incorporated into the worship of the church, such as the prayer For the Poor and Neglected (BCP, p. 826). Huntington also had an important role in the canonical authorization of the order of deaconesses in the Episcopal Church. He died in Nahant, Massachusetts. His life is commemorated in the Episcopal calendar of the church year on July 27. *See* Chicago-Lambeth Quadrilateral.

Hymn. A form of congregational song in praise of God, using metrical poetic texts set to tunes which are repeated for each stanza of the text. Hymns authorized for use in the Episcopal Church are collected in *The Hymnal 1982.* Other collections of hymns used in the Episcopal Church include *Wonder, Love, and Praise*, *Lift Every Voice and Sing II*, *El Himnario*, *Songs for Celebration*, and *Come Celebrate! A Hymnal Supplement.*

Hymnal, The. The collection of hymns, tunes, and service music authorized for use in the Episcopal Church by General Convention. It is published by Church Publishing Incorporated, formerly Church Hymnal Corporation, a subsidiary of the Church Pension Fund. Hymnals have been authorized for the Episcopal Church by General Convention in 1789, 1826, 1871, 1892, 1916, 1940, and 1982. Only hymn texts were authorized for the first four hymnals. Unauthorized editions of these hymnals with tunes were published privately. The 1916 *Hymnal* was the first to be published with an authorized musical edition. The music edition was prepared by the Joint Commission on Church Music, with final editing of the volume by Canon Charles Winfred Douglas (1867–1944). It was published in 1918,

and also known as the *New Hymnal.* Profits from its sale were designated to benefit the Church Pension Fund. *The Hymnal* (1940) drew on a variety of sources for hymn texts in addition to British and American authors. It included a significant representation of texts translated from Latin, Greek, and German, in addition to some representation of texts translated from Dutch, Italian, French, Hebrew, Danish, Irish, Swahili, Syriac, and Welsh. The music edition for *The Hymnal* (1940) was prepared by the Joint Commission on Church Music, with Douglas as musical editor. It was published in 1943. Prior to the 1982 revision of the *Hymnal*, the Standing Commission on Church Music adopted a statement of philosophy in 1981 for hymnal revision. This statement agreed that the *Hymnal* should be a companion for the new 1979 BCP, supporting its changes and areas of emphasis such as the expanded Lectionary, the revised Calendar, and the renewed emphasis on baptism as a public rite; the *Hymnal* should retain classic texts but also present a prophetic vision, speaking to the church of the future as well as the present; hymn texts should authentically and fully present the church's teaching, with the *Hymnal* serving as a practical book of theology for the people of God; the *Hymnal* should be comprehensive in its coverage of all major historic periods, reflecting and speaking to a variety of cultures and races; hymn texts should use inclusive language whenever possible; obscure language should be clarified for contemporary use; the *Hymnal* should be ecumenical in nature, although it is prepared for use in the Episcopal Church; the *Hymnal* should be a practical collection, with keyboard settings that can be used by a performer with average skills; the *Hymnal* should present various musical possibilities when tunes are used more than once; and the *Hymnal* should present a variety of musical styles that represent the best expressive artistic creativity of musicians. Music for *The Hymnal 1982* was prepared by the Standing Commission on Church Music. This edition was published in 1985. *The Hymnal 1982* provides a major section of Service Music for the Daily Office, the Great Litany, Proper Liturgies for Special Days, Baptism, Eucharist, and Canticles; Hymns for the Daily Office, the Church Year, Baptism, Eucharist, Confirmation, Marriage, Burial of the Dead, Ordination, Consecration of a Church, General Hymns (arranged by thematic categories such as "Praise to God," "Christian Vocation and Pilgrimage," and "The Church Triumphant"), the Christian Life, Rounds and Canons, and National Songs; along with Indexes for the volume. *The Hymnal 1982* includes 720 hymns.

Raymond F. Glover served as general editor. The Episcopal tradition of an official hymnal differs from the Church of England, which has never published an authorized collection of hymns. Background information concerning the *Hymnal* has been compiled and published as *Hymnal Companions* for the 1940 and 1982 editions of the *Hymnal*. *See* Hymnal Companion, The.

Hymnal Companion, The. Historical and background information on the words, music, and sources of the selections in the *Hymnal*, essays on church music, biographical information on authors and composers, and indexes for the collection have been published as *Hymnal Companions* for the 1940 and 1982 editions of the *Hymnal*. During the work of preparing *The Hymnal* (1940), the Joint Commission on the Revision of the *Hymnal* realized that a historical handbook for the *Hymnal* would be an important resource for the church. In 1939 Canon Charles Winfred Douglas was appointed as chair of the committee to compile *The Hymnal 1940 Companion*. He was replaced in 1941 by the Rev. Arthur Farlander. The Rev. Dr. Leonard Ellinwood contributed extensive original research to complete *The Hymnal 1940 Companion*. It was first published in 1949. A second edition was published in 1951, and a third edition was published in 1956. *The Hymnal 1982 Companion* has three volumes and includes four books. Volume 1, including a variety of scholarly essays on hymns, service music, and the liturgical and pastoral context of hymnody, was published in 1990. Volumes 2, 3A, and 3B were all published in 1994. Volume 2 includes background on the service music in *The Hymnal 1982* and biographies. Volumes 3A and 3B include background on the hymns. *The Hymnal 1982 Companion* also has indexes, glossaries, and bibliographies for further study. It was edited by Raymond F. Glover, general editor of *The Hymnal 1982*. It is published by Church Publishing Incorporated, formerly Church Hymnal Corporation, a subsidiary of the Church Pension Fund. Other hymnal companions published outside the Episcopal Church include the *Historical Companion to Hymns Ancient & Modern* (1962), and the *Hymnal Companion to the Lutheran Book of Worship* (1981). *See* Hymnal, The.

Hymnal Studies. A series of studies published by the Church Hymnal Corporation (now Church Publishing Incorporated), to assist clergy and laity in using *The Hymnal 1982*. The volumes are: *Hymnal Studies One: Perspectives on the New Edition* (1981); *Hymnal Studies Two: Introducing The Hymnal 1982* (1982); Marilyn J. Keiser, *Hymnal Studies Three: Teaching Music in the Small Church* (1983); John Fesperman, *Hymnal Studies Four: Organ Planning: Asking the Right Questions* (1984); Marion J. Hatchett, *Hymnal Studies Five: A Liturgical Index to The Hymnal 1982* (1986); Ray F. Glover, *Hymnal Studies Six: A Commentary on New Hymns* (1987); Dennis Schmidt, *Hymnal Studies Seven: An Organist's Guide to Resources for The Hymnal 1982* (*1987);* and Marion J. Hatchett, *Hymnal Studies Eight: A Scriptural Index to The Hymnal 1982* (1988).

Hymnody. A term used to refer to bodies or collections of hymns. For example, the hymnody of the Episcopal Church is collected in *The Hymnal 1982*.

***Hymns Ancient and Modern,* or "*Hymns A & M*".** Published in 1860, it was the first popular hymnal designed for the Church of England that was arranged largely according to the church year and intermixed metrical psalms and hymns. It included translations from Latin, Greek, and German and new hymns propagating principles of the Oxford Movement. It furnished more than twenty of the sixty-five hymns added to the "Prayer Book Collection" in 1865. The first Episcopal hymnal not bound with the Prayer Book (1871) drew heavily upon it for texts and tunes and was organized according to the same principles. This book also had great influence on hymnals for other Anglican provinces and other denominations. Early Anglican metrical psalters typically contained metrical versions of several Prayer Book texts and a few hymns. Eighteenth-century nonconformists and Methodists embraced hymns of Watts, the Wesleys, and others. From the mid-eighteenth century various English parishes published hymn supplements. The first American Prayer Book (1789) contained the Tate and Brady psalter and twenty-seven other paraphrases or hymns. This number grew to fifty-seven in 1808, and 212 in 1826. Hymnals arranged by subject and with metrical psalms intermixed were being published at this time by other denominations in England and America.

Hymns III. A 1979 publication in the Church Hymnal Corporation series of 150 hymns created by the Hymn Committee of the Standing Commission on Church Music. It was edited by Raymond F. Glover, Marion Hatchett, and Russell Schulz-Widmar.

I

ICHTHUS (ICHTHS). An early Christian symbol, the transliteration of the Greek word *ixous*, "fish." The letters are the initial letters of the Greek words for Jesus Christ, Son of God, Savior. This acrostic was used as a confession of faith. The fish was also an iconographic Christian symbol and identified with Christ. In early Christianity a representation of a fish frequently appeared in catacomb paintings and on seals, rings, urns, and tombstones. It is unknown whether the acrostic or the iconographic symbol was first used. Fish are associated with miraculous feedings by Jesus (Mk 6:35–44, 8:1–8) and post-resurrection meals (Lk 24:41–43, Jn 21:1–14). The fish symbol came to be associated with the eucharist, and fish have been shown on the table in artistic portrayals of the Last Supper.

Icon. The traditional icon is a stylized religious picture that is usually painted on a wood panel in egg tempera. Icons depict Christ, the Trinity, St. Mary, other saints, and events in the gospels and lives of the saints. Icons have been used in both eastern and western churches. Icons were painted or placed on the walls of churches and on interior beams and screens. They were also displayed in private houses and at wayside shrines.

The oldest extant icons date from the fifth century. The Seventh Ecumenical Council of 787 determined that the use of icons is supported by the Incarnation, in which the Word of God united to created human nature and thus to matter in general. That Council also taught that the honor given to an icon passes to that which it represents. The eastern churches developed the icon tradition extensively. In the west the tradition was eclipsed by the Renaissance and other artistic movements. However, offshoots of the icon tradition in the west include the use of stained glass windows and the illustrations in manuscripts and liturgical books. Today there is a revival of the use of icons in the western churches, including the Episcopal Church.

Iconoclasm. The term means "the smashing of icons." The most important iconoclastic controversies occurred in the seventh and eighth centuries. These controversies led to the Seventh Ecumenical Council of 787. The orthodox party urged that in the Incarnation deity was united to created human nature, so it is appropriate to make material images of Christ. There have been other iconoclastic movements in Christian history, notably during the Protestant Reformation. For example, English Puritans attacked the use of church ornaments and vestments. *See* Icon.

Iconography. The art of making icons. An iconographer who aspires to make a theological statement may be said to "write" an icon. The term also refers to the whole history and tradition of the Christian use of icons. A number of conventions of iconography have been maintained, such as the frontal position, inverse perspective, and elongated and somber features. This is the style of iconography defended by the Seventh Ecumenical Council of 787. The term also refers to the entire planned scheme of pictorial representations in a church building. In this sense, it is possible to consider the iconography of a cathedral or a great chapel.

Iconostasis. A wall of icons placed between the nave and sanctuary in an Eastern Orthodox church. It developed from the older custom of placing or painting icons on interior beams and low screens of ancient church buildings. The iconostasis became popular after the thirteenth century, especially in Russia. At the height of its development, the iconostasis had a number of rows of icons. The modern iconostasis is usually much simpler, with the icons arranged so that the view into the sanctuary is not completely obstructed.

Idaho, Diocese of. The state of Idaho was part of the Missionary District of the Northwest, which was established in 1859. The 1865 General Convention established the Missionary District of Colorado and Parts Adjacent, including Idaho. In 1866 the House of Bishops created the Missionary District of Montana, Idaho and Utah, and in 1880, it created the Missionary District of Idaho and Utah. In 1886 the House of Bishops established the Missionary District of Wyoming and Idaho. The 1898 General Convention changed the Missionary District of Wyoming and Idaho to the Missionary District of Boise. The 1907 General Convention created the Missionary District of Idaho. At the 1967 General Convention the Missionary District of Idaho became the Diocese of Idaho. The primary convention of the Diocese was held at St. Michael's Cathedral, Boise, on Dec. 9, 1967. St. Michael's Cathedral, Boise, was dedicated on May 25, 1902.

Ignatius (c. 35–c. 115). Bishop, patristic theologian, and martyr. Very little is known about the life of Ignatius. He was the second, or possibly third, Bishop of Antioch. He was serving as Bishop of Antioch by the year 100. Ignatius is the most significant of the Apostolic Fathers. He is remembered for his contributions to the development of the episcopate and the threefold orders of deacon, presbyter, and bishop; his contributions to the development of the eucharist; his orthodox defenses against heresies, especially Ebionism and Docetism; and his enthusiastic martyrdom. He is one of the most important figures in the early church, a period when the church was developing from its infant NT roots and moving in the direction of an organized, defined, and catholic religion. Ignatius was the first person to use the term "Catholic Church" and the first advocate of episcopacy. More than any other person he stressed the role of a single bishop, or monoepiscopacy. Prior to his time, each church was governed by groups of bishops or elders (presbyters), terms which were virtually synonymous. He insisted that there should be one bishop who presided over presbyters and deacons. Ignatius argued that a strong episcopate was needed for the order and unity of the church, and for the defense and continuity of church doctrine. He was arrested and taken to Rome for execution. On the way he wrote seven letters, which contain much information about the early church. He died in Rome. Ignatius is commemorated in the Episcopal calendar of the church year on Oct. 17. *See* Ebionites; *see* Docetism.

Ignatius of Loyola (1491–July 31, 1556). Founder of the Jesuits. He was born in the Basque province of Guipuzcoa, Spain. Ignatius was a soldier who underwent a conversion on May 20, 1520, while he was recuperating from a leg wound. With six companions he founded the Society of Jesus (Jesuits) in Paris on Aug. 15, 1534, to work for the conversion of heretics. In Nov. 1538 the society placed itself at the service of the Pope. The motto of the society is, "For the greater glory of God." Ignatius has influenced most forms of modern Christian spirituality through the *Spiritual Exercises.* Ignatius composed this work to guide retreatants through a thirty-day process in which they choose between God and evil. They also learn to meditate on the life of Christ and to imitate him. The society specializes in education in the spirit of the Counter-Reformation, with a generous opening to classical and humanistic studies. Ignatian spirituality has an Incarnational emphasis that seeks "to find God in all things," serving God and humanity. Ignatius died in Rome. He was canonized on May 22, 1622. Ignatius is commemorated in the Episcopal calendar of the church year on July 31.

IHS. Monogram of the Holy Name of Jesus. It is taken from the first three letters of Jesus' name in Greek, which have been latinized to "IHS." The monogram appears in liturgical art and architecture, especially vestments. Devotion to the Holy Name of Jesus was popularized by the Franciscans in the fifteenth century. Bernardino of Siena (1380–1444) displayed the monogram on a tablet at the end of his sermons to encourage devotion to the Holy Name of Jesus. *See* Holy Name of our Lord Jesus Christ, The.

IKHANA. This newsletter of American Indian/Alaska native ministry of the Episcopal Church began publication in Spring 1987. *IKHANA* is a Choctaw word which means "to teach, to inform."

Illinois, Diocese of. The Diocese of Chicago was named the Diocese of Illinois from Mar. 9, 1835, until May 28, 1884.

Immaculate Conception. This dogma of the Roman Catholic Church is that the Virgin Mary was kept free from original sin from the first moment of her conception. Mary is understood to be kept free from original sin by the grace of God and the merits of Christ. This dogma was defined in the bull *Ineffabilis Deus* of Pope Pius IX on Dec. 8, 1854. Belief in the Immaculate Conception was defined by the Pope in the same bull as being infallible and binding on all faithful Roman Catholics. *The Final Report* of the Anglican-Roman Catholic International Commission (ARCIC) recorded the disagreement of Anglicans, although some individuals may hold it as a pious, optional belief. This statement noted that Anglicans question the scriptural basis for such claims. The papal proclamation of the Immaculate Conception and the Assumption as dogmas binding on the faithful has prompted many Anglicans to question the teaching authority of the Bishop of Rome. Article XV of the Articles of Religion holds that Christ alone was without sin (BCP, p. 870). The Roman Catholic dogma of the Immaculate Conception remains a stumbling block in Anglican-Roman Catholic ecumenical relations.

Immanent Trinity. *See* Trinity.

Immersion. Mode of baptism in which the candidate's entire body is introduced into the water. The term "baptize" is from the Greek, "to dip." Immersion was the normal way of baptism in the early church. Questions concerning the candidate's belief in the Father, the Son, and the Holy Spirit were answered in the affirmative, and each followed by an immersion of the candidate. Christian creeds developed from these questions and answers at baptism. The candidate's immersion and emergence from the water of baptism is sharing in Christ's death and resurrection (Rom 6:1–11, Col 2:12). Scripture also describes baptism as a cleansing bath of spiritual renewal (Eph 5:26, Ti 3:5, Heb 10:22). In the early church, candidates were baptized by immersion in natural or existing sources of water such as rivers, fountains, pools, and the sea. The *Didache* permits pouring water over the head of the candidate three times in the name of the Father, Son, and Holy Spirit if there is insufficient water for immersion. Water and the trinitarian formula are essential for baptism, but there is flexibility concerning the mode and place of baptism.

By the third century baptisms were being done in pools or baths in a special room or area of a church known as a baptistery. The shallowness and size of some baptisteries has led some to question whether baptisms involved complete submersions. Immersion has been distinguished from submersion. The evidence of early baptisteries and Christian art has been interpreted to indicate that the candidate stood in a pool of water while water was poured over the candidate's head. Others have interpreted the architectural evidence of early baptisteries to argue that the candidate bent over to be completely immersed. Patristic writings indicate that the candidate for baptism stood about waist deep in water and was immersed by bowing forward with the celebrant's hand on the candidate's head. The Orthodox and some Protestant churches have generally insisted that immersion is required for baptism. Luther favored baptism by immersion to signify the drowning of sin, but he did not insist on immersion.

The 1549 BCP called for a threefold immersion and the trinitarian baptismal formula. The celebrant was to dip the child "discreetly and warily." Infant baptism was typical in the Anglican Church at that time. The 1552 BCP did not require a threefold immersion. The 1979 BCP directs (p. 307) that the celebrant or an assisting priest or deacon shall immerse or pour water upon each candidate and say the trinitarian formula of baptism. In practice, most Episcopal churches baptize by pouring (affusion). However, the renewal of the catechumenate and the Christian formation of adults has been accompanied by appreciation for the symbolic power and appropriateness of baptism by immersion.

Impetrate. To petition or beseech; to obtain by entreaty. Impetrative prayer asks God to accomplish what has been requested. Impetration relies on God's loving generosity and willingness to answer prayer. In eucharistic theology, impetrative sacrifice entreats God's favor, and impetration is one of the purposes of the celebration of the eucharistic sacrifice.

Imposition of Ashes. Ashes may be imposed on the heads of participants in the Ash Wednesday service as a sign of mortality and penitence. The ashes are imposed with the words, "Remember that you are dust, and to dust you shall return" (BCP, p. 265). Ashes are typically imposed by inscribing a cross on the forehead. The imposition of ashes has been practiced on Ash Wednesday since the ninth century.

Improperia. See Reproaches, The.

Incardination. The formal acceptance of a member of the clergy by the ecclesiastical authority of a new diocesan jurisdiction. In the Episcopal Church, such transfers of clergy from jurisdiction to jurisdiction are governed by the canon concerning Letters Dimissory.

Incarnation. The term, from the Latin *carnis* ("flesh") literally means "enfleshment." It reflects the christological doctrine that Jesus was fully human and fully divine, the Son of God "in the flesh." It is based on Jn 1:14, "And the Word became flesh and lived among us."

During the first four centuries of the church, the nature of the relationship of divine and human in Jesus was hotly contested. The notion that Jesus, a mere human being, was "adopted" by God (Adoptionism); or that Jesus was purely God and merely seemed to have human form (Docetism); or that Jesus had two completely distinct natures, divine and human (Nestorianism); or that Jesus had a single divine nature (Monophysitism) were all rejected by general councils of the church. In contrast, the orthodox doctrine of the Incarnation recognized Jesus to be "truly God and truly man . . . in two natures, without confusion, without change, without division, without separation," as noted by the Council of Chalcedon (451) (BCP, p. 864).

Incarnatus. Latin term translated into English as Incarnation. It refers to the christological assertion that Jesus was fully human and fully divine, the Son of God or Word in the flesh. The specific term *Incarnatus* refers to the assertion in the Nicene Creed that Jesus "became incarnate from the Virgin Mary and was made man" (BCP, p. 358).

Incense. When burned or heated, usually over charcoal, certain woods and solidified resins give off a fragrant smoke. Both the materials and the smoke are called incense. Incense was widely used in Judaism and other cultures of the ancient world as a means of sacrifice, purification, and veneration. Frankincense or pure incense, the resin of certain trees, was among the gifts brought by the Magi to the young child Christ (Mt 2:11). Despite this scriptural precedent, early Christians avoided incense as a pagan practice connected with sacrifice and emperor worship, and churches did not begin to use it until the fourth century. Thereafter incense was burned at several points in the Daily Office and the Eucharist, and extensively in eastern churches. For Christians today, incense is associated mainly with prayer, as Rv 8:3–4 suggests. Many Anglicans feel free to use it as a sacred symbol and aid to worship. The first option in the BCP for an opening sentence at Evening Prayer is "Let my prayer be set forth in your sight as incense, the lifting up of my hands as the evening sacrifice" (Ps 141:2) (BCP, pp. 61, 115). The BCP states that incense may be used during the singing of *Phos hilaron* in the "Order of Worship for the Evening" (p. 143), and during the covering of the altar in the "Consecration of a Church." There are congregations where incense is used at the Easter Vigil and other major feasts, and some parishes use it regularly on Sunday.

Incipit. The opening phrase or word of a text. The term is from the Latin, "it begins." It may refer to the opening words of the text of a psalm or to the introductory words of a medieval manuscript or early printed book. The *incipit* may also serve as the title of the text. The BCP publishes the Latin *incipit* for all psalms and Prayer Book canticles. For example, Ps 133 is published with its *incipit*, *Ecce, quam bonum!* (BCP, p. 787). Canticle 16, "The Song of Zechariah," is often known by its *incipit*, *Benedictus Dominus Deus*

(BCP, p. 92), and Canticle 21, "You are God," is often known by its *incipit*, *Te Deum laudamus* (BCP, p. 95).

Inclusive Language. Spoken and written language that intentionally avoids word use that is needlessly gender-specific or exclusive. Inclusive language also means the use of male and female imagery and metaphors in a balanced way to express the truths we know of God. Inclusive language may challenge the church to discover new depths of meaning and possibility in the words of faith that we use.

Traditional English usage referred to God and humanity with male pronouns. A male pronoun was often used "generically" when the pronoun could refer to either a woman or a man. This traditional English usage came to be perceived as demeaning and exclusive of women. It was judged to be offensive by women and men who called for a more inclusive use of language, especially in the life and worship of the church. This call for inclusive language was rooted in the theological understanding that God includes and transcends human masculinity and femininity. God is neither male nor female. Both women and men are equally loved and included by God and should be valued and shown respect in the church's language.

With the exception of Rite 1 services, the 1979 BCP uses inclusive language when speaking of people. For example, one version of the Nicene Creed in the Rite 1 Eucharist affirms that Jesus Christ came down from heaven "for us men and for our salvation" (BCP, p. 328). Although the clear intent is to include all humanity, only men are mentioned in this version of the Nicene Creed. In contrast, the first version of the Nicene Creed in the Rite 1 Eucharist and the Nicene Creed in the Rite 2 Eucharist use more inclusive language to state that Jesus Christ came down from heaven "For us and for our salvation" (BCP, pp. 326, 358). Such use of inclusive language is found in contemporary biblical translation. The Revised Standard Version (1952) renders Jesus' statement recorded in Jn 6:35, "I am the bread of life; he who comes to me shall not hunger, and he who believes in me shall never thirst." In contrast, the New Revised Standard Version (1989) renders the same statement in more inclusive language, "I am the bread of life. Whoever comes to me will never be hungry, and whoever believes in me will never be thirsty."

Supplemental liturgical texts and materials have been developed with sensitivity for inclusive language. A resolution of the 1985 General Convention called for the Standing Liturgical Commission to prepare inclusive language liturgies for the regular services of the church. This resolution and subsequent legislation by General Convention led to the publication of *Liturgical Texts for Evaluation* (1987), *Prayer Book Studies 30—Supplemental Liturgical Texts* (1989), and *Supplemental Liturgical Materials* (1991). These resources include liturgies for Morning Prayer, Order for Evening, Evening Prayer, and Holy Eucharist, as well as supplemental musical materials for use in these services. The First Supplemental Eucharistic Prayer in *Prayer Book Studies 30* prays to God who "remembered us from our beginning and fed us with your constant love," and "redeemed us in Jesus Christ and knit us into one body." The Second Supplemental Eucharistic Prayer prays to God who "took us by the hand, and taught us to walk in your ways." Even though we wandered away, God would not forget us, "as a mother cares for her children."

Concerns for inclusive language have been raised with respect to issues other than gender. There have been calls for language in the life of the church that includes and welcomes all people, whatever their race, age, ethnic or regional background, or sexual orientation.

Incumbent. The member of the clergy, typically a priest, who holds and has pastoral responsibility for a parochial charge. The incumbent may be a rector, a vicar, or a priest-in-charge.

Independence Day. Commemoration of the signing of the Declaration of Independence on July 4, 1776. It is a legal holiday in the United States. The 1785 General Convention directed that a service be drawn up for this day, and "That the said form of prayer be used in this Church, on the fourth of July, for ever." The Proposed Book of 1786 contained "A Form of Prayer and Thanksgiving to Almighty God for the inestimable Blessings of Religious and Civil Liberty" to be used on the Fourth of July. The presiding officer, William White, was opposed to the service since many of the clergy had been Loyalists and were against the Revolution. The General Convention of 1789 supported White, and the service was withdrawn from the 1789 BCP. Propers for this day were published in the 1928 Book of Common Prayer, but it was not a major feast. The 1979 BCP (p. 17), lists Independence Day as one of the "Other Major Feasts," and provides a collect for the day (pp. 190, 242). Eucharistic propers are provided as well as propers for the Daily Office. The collect "For the Nation" may be substituted for the collect for the day.

Independent Bishops. Independent bishops are those persons who hold the title bishop or archbishop in an irregular manner. Although they derive their authority through the traditional lineage of bishops reaching back through the ancient patriarchical sees of Rome, Jerusalem, Alexandria, Antioch, Canterbury, and Constantinople to the Apostles, they have neither organizational connection nor intercommunion with these traditional centers of Christianity. They are also called "bishops irregular," "bishops at large," and "*episcopi vagantes.*" See Episcopi Vaganti.

Indianapolis, Diocese of. Jackson Kemper was consecrated the Missionary Bishop of Indiana and Missouri on Sept. 25, 1835. On Aug. 24–27, 1838, the Diocese of Indiana was organized at Christ Church, Madison, Indiana. The General Convention of 1898 voted to divide the diocese. On Sept. 1, 1902, the name was changed to the Diocese of Indianapolis. The Diocese of Indianapolis consists of the following counties: Bartholomew, Boone, Brown, Clark, Clay, Clinton, Crawford, Daviess, Dearborn, Decatur, Delaware, Dubois, Fayette, Floyd, Fountain, Franklin, Gibson, Greene, Hamilton, Hancock, Harrison, Hendricks, Henry, Jackson, Jefferson, Jennings, Johnson, Knox, Lawrence, Madison, Marion, Martin, Monroe, Montgomery, Morgan, Ohio, Orange, Owen, Parke, Perry, Pike, Posey, Putnam, Randolph, Ripley, Rush, Scott, Shelby, Spencer, Sullivan, Switzerland, Tippecanoe, Tipton, Union, Vanderburgh, Vermillion, Vigo, Warren, Warrick, Washington, and Wayne. On Oct. 10, 1954, Christ Church, Indianapolis, became Christ Church Cathedral.

Induction. *See* Celebration of a New Ministry.

Inerrancy, Biblical. The belief that the Bible contains no errors, whether theological, moral, historical, or scientific. Sophisticated holders of this theory, however, stress that the biblical manuscripts as originally written in Hebrew, Aramaic, and Greek were inerrant, but not those that are presently available. Some more conservative scholars are reluctant to speak of inerrancy, but choose to speak of biblical infallibility. They mean that the Bible is completely infallible in what it teaches about God and God's will for human salvation, but not necessarily in all its historical or scientific statements. Biblical inerrancy and infallibility are not accepted by the Episcopal Church. *See* Fundamentalism.

Infallibility, Papal. The dogma of the Roman Catholic Church that the Pope is preserved from error in the teaching of revealed truth. This dogma was formulated in the decree *Pastor Aeternus* of Vatican Council I (1870). It was slightly reformulated at Vatican II in its dogmatic constitution on the church, *Lumen Gentium*, which stated that when the Pope proclaims by a definitive act some doctrine of faith or morals, his definitions need no approval of others and do not allow an appeal to any other judgment. No other church has accepted this teaching. *The Final Report* of the Anglican-Roman Catholic International Commission (1982) indicates Anglican agreement that an ecumenical council or universal primate could make a decisive judgment in matters of faith, excluding error, provided that the decision were "manifestly a legitimate interpretation of biblical faith and in line with orthodox tradition." Otherwise, the reception (acceptance) of the church would be required for the definition to be authoritative. Anglicans do not accept the guaranteed possession of a "gift of divine assistance in judgment" of the Bishop of Rome that would assure the infallibility of any formal papal decision before its reception by the faithful. The Roman Catholic dogma of papal infallibility remains a major stumbling block in Anglican-Roman Catholic ecumenical relations. *See* Reception (of Doctrine).

Infant Communion. Receiving communion was the climax of the baptismal rite for infants as well as adults until the thirteenth century in the west. Canon law asserted that infants should not die without having received communion. Withholding communion from infants was not a reasoned decision but the result of efforts to protect the eucharistic elements from desecration or from superstitious uses. As early as the twelfth century in some areas infants received only the consecrated wine, for concern had arisen because infants had on occasion regurgitated the bread. In the thirteenth century increased scrupulosity led to withholding the chalice from the laity, which had the effect of excommunicating small children because they had already been denied the bread. In some areas, however, infants and small children continued to communicate until the Council of Trent declared that those lacking use of reason were under no obligation to receive the eucharist. Reformation churches were united in not communicating those who had not reached the age of reason and been catechized. In recent decades, it has been reasserted in various provinces of Anglicanism, and in other churches as well, that baptism is full initiation into the church and the only prerequisite for communion. The eastern church has an unbroken tradition of infant communion after baptism.

Infusion of Grace. The grace of God may be understood to be "poured into" the human soul. Grace is said to come to us by infusion (from the Latin *in* and *fundere*, "to pour"). Although the BCP does not refer to infused grace, the collect for Proper 22, which asks God to "pour upon us the abundance of your mercy," reflects the doctrine of the infusion of grace (p. 234).

Inglis, Charles (1734–Feb. 24, 1816). Church of England clergyman and Loyalist. He was born in Ireland, probably at Glencolumbkille, County Donegal. Inglis came to the American colonies around 1755 and taught in the Free School at Lancaster, Pennsylvania. He went to England in 1758. He was ordained deacon on Sept. 24, 1758, and priest on Dec. 24, 1758. Inglis was appointed a Society for the Propagation of the Gospel (SPG) missionary at Dover, Delaware, with responsibility for the entire county of Kent. After six years at Dover, he went to New York to be the assistant minister at Trinity Church. He began his duties there on June 7, 1765. In New York he became friends with Thomas Bradbury Chandler, rector of St. John's Church, Elizabethtown, New Jersey. They were leaders in calling for the Episcopate for the American colonies. Inglis became rector of Trinity Church when his predecessor, Samuel Auchmuty, died in 1777. Inglis was a leading Loyalist and very much opposed to the Revolution. Opposition against him mounted. On Nov. 1, 1783, he resigned as rector of Trinity Church and went to England. On Aug. 12, 1787, at Lambeth Palace, he was consecrated the Bishop of Nova Scotia for what was to become the Anglican Church of Canada. He was the first overseas bishop of the Church of England. He died in Halifax.

Inquirers' Class. Class for newcomers or visitors who "inquire" about the Episcopal Church. Instruction typically includes information concerning the beliefs, history, worship, and practices of the Episcopal Church. Participants in the class may be known as inquirers. Those who wish to become members of the Episcopal Church may be presented for Confirmation or Reception if they have already been baptized. Inquirers who have not yet been baptized may be prepared for baptism through the catechumenate. The *BOS* notes that inquirers' classes belong to the "Pre-catechumenal Period," or first stage of the catechumenate, by providing "sufficient preparation to enable persons to determine that they wish to become Christians."

INRI. The initial letters of the inscription in Latin, "Iesus Nazarenus Rex Iudaeorum," which means "Jesus of Nazareth, the King of the Jews." When Jesus was crucified, Pilate had this inscription placed on the cross. It was written in Hebrew, Latin, and Greek (Jn 19:19–20). *INRI* is frequently used in depictions of the crucifixion.

Installation. *See* Celebration of a New Ministry.

Institute for Professional Youth Ministry (IPYM). IPYM was organized in 1991 to train, equip, and support people in youth ministry in the church. Its work was begun in 1981 by the Rev. John Palarine in the Diocese of Central Florida. IPYM oversaw a variety of programs and services, including a youth ministry intern program; training and consultation with individuals, congregations, and dioceses; networking, certification, and associations for those involved in professional youth ministry; placement services for linking youth ministers and congregations; and distribution of youth ministry resources. IPYM is no longer in existence.

Institution. *See* Celebration of a New Ministry.

Institution Narrative. Narration in a eucharistic prayer of Jesus' institution of the eucharist at the Last Supper, based on 1 Cor 11:23–26 (see Mt 26:26–29; Mk 14:22–25; Lk 22:14–20). The wording of the institution narrative varies slightly in different eucharistic prayers. The institution narrative states that Jesus gave thanks to God, broke the bread, gave it to his disciples, and said the words of institution concerning the bread, "Take eat: This is my Body, which is given for you. Do this for the remembrance of me" (BCP, p. 362). The institution narrative likewise states that after supper Jesus took the cup of wine, gave thanks, shared the cup with his disciples, and said the words of institution concerning the wine, "Drink this, all of you: This is my Blood of the new Covenant, which is shed for you and for many for the forgiveness of sins. Whenever you drink it, do this for the remembrance of me" (BCP, p. 363). Jesus' words of institution identify the

eucharistic bread and wine with his body and blood, and direct his followers to continue this sharing in remembrance of him. Jesus' words thus "instituted" the eucharist, and the eucharistic narration of this event is the institution narrative.

The words of institution are the same in all Rite 2 eucharistic prayers, and appear in a somewhat different form in Rite 1. The BCP directs that the celebrant is to hold the bread, or lay a hand upon it, at the words concerning the bread. At the words concerning the cup, the celebrant is to hold the cup, or place a hand on it, and any other vessel containing wine to be consecrated (BCP, p. 362). Institution narratives also include brief statements of context concerning the institution of the eucharist at the Last Supper. Prayer A states that the Last Supper was on the night Jesus was handed over to suffering and death (BCP, p. 362); Prayer B states that it was on the night before he died for us (BCP, p. 368); Prayer C and the Rite 1 prayers state that it was on the night he was betrayed (BCP, pp. 334, 342, 371); and Prayer D states that when the hour had come for Jesus to be glorified by God the Father, Jesus loved his own who were in the world, and loved them to the end (BCP, p. 374).

An institution narrative was included in the third-century eucharistic prayer of Hippolytus's *Apostolic Tradition*. Institution narratives were regularly included in eucharistic prayers after the fourth century. The medieval church came to understand the words of institution as the "moment of consecration" of the eucharist, instead of the warrant or basis for the entire eucharistic rite. This emphasis on the words of institution came to be expressed through dramatic elevations of the elements and the ringing of bells. Sacramental theology has once again emphasized the consecration in terms of the entire prayer of eucharistic thanksgiving. However, a vestige of the medieval emphasis on the words of institution can be found in a form for consecrating additional bread or wine at the eucharist. This form combines a brief invocation of the Holy Spirit and a short version of the appropriate words of institution (BCP, p. 408). *See* Eucharist.

Institution of a Minister, Letter of. During feudal times in England, a Letter of Institution from the bishop was part of the legal process of induction of a priest to a parish. This letter authorized the priest to exercise ministry in the parish. Ceremonies of institution and induction continued in the Anglican Church after the Reformation. In the Episcopal Church, Prayer Books included "An Office of

Institution of Ministers into Parishes or Churches." The bishop's Letter of Institution was read at this service. The 1979 BCP provides a form for the Celebration of a New Ministry (pp. 559–564). A format for the bishop's Letter of Institution of a Minister precedes this service (BCP, p. 557). It is addressed to the presbyter being inducted in the new ministry. The name and place of the church or place of ministry are stated in the Letter of Institution. The Letter of Institution is appropriate for the induction of a rector of a parish, a cathedral dean, or others with similar tenure of office (BCP, p. 564). The Celebration of a New Ministry begins with the institution. The bishop may read the Letter of Institution at the opening of the service, after the wardens have stated that the new minister is well qualified and properly selected (BCP, p. 559). The Letter of Institution is a sign that the presbyter is "fully empowered and authorized to exercise this ministry."

Institution, Office of. *See* Office of Institution.

Institution, Words of. *See* Institution Narrative.

Insufflation. Ancient liturgical practice of "blowing in" the Holy Spirit to the mouth of the candidate for baptism by the celebrant. It was preparatory to the baptism itself. The term is from the Latin *in* and *sufflare*, "to blow." It was the counterpart to the "exsufflation," or exorcism of evil spirits by the action of the celebrant, "blowing" the evil spirits "out of" the candidates. The distinction between "insufflation" and "exsufflation" has not always been preserved. Insufflation was also used to refer to the action of the priest during the blessing of the font, where the ancient rubric read, "let the priest breathe three times into the font in the form of a cross . . . ." Neither insufflation nor exsufflation appears in any English or American Book of Common Prayer. The action is optional in post-Vatican II Roman Catholic liturgies. The biblical roots of the insufflation ceremonies are found in such passages as the second creation story in Genesis which describes God breathing the breath of life into the first human being (Gn 2:7), and the account of Jesus' breathing upon the disciples and imparting to them the Holy Spirit (Jn 20:22). The term can also be used to describe these events.

Integrity, Inc. A national organization of gay and lesbian Episcopalians and others supportive of its causes and ministries. It publishes *Ex Umbris*, a monthly newsletter, and *The Voice of Integrity*, a quarterly journal. Sometimes subtitled "The Episcopal Lesbigay Ministry," Integrity dates its beginning from the first appearance of an advertisement in the Oct. 6, 1974, issue of *The Episcopalian*. This advertisement invited persons to subscribe to a publication called *Integrity: Gay Episcopal Forum*, edited by Dr. Louie Crew of Fort Valley, Georgia. In Oct. the first people signed on as subscribers/members. In Nov. 1974 the first issue of *Integrity Forum* was published. In Dec. 1974 the first local chapter of Integrity was organized in Chicago. The first national convention of Integrity, Inc. met at the Cathedral of St. James, Chicago, on Aug. 8–10, 1975. At this meeting James Wickliff of Chicago and Ellen Marie Barrett of New York were elected the first co-presidents of Integrity.

Intention. Conscious or willful purpose to do something. One's intention is freely chosen and not forced. In terms of moral theology, intention is associated with moral responsibility for an action. For example, a person who intentionally destroys a vase by knocking it off a table is responsible for the damage. But a person suffering from an unexpected seizure is not responsible for the damage if an involuntary movement knocks the vase off the table and breaks it. The outward actions and results may be much the same, but the difference of intent distinguishes these two cases. However, a degree of intent may be found in actions involving negligence or recklessness. For example, a driver who intentionally exceeds the speed limit may not intend to hurt anyone. But the driver has a degree of moral responsibility if others are hurt in an accident caused by the driver's excessive speed. Of course, that driver's responsibility is not the same as one who intended to hurt others by causing an accident.

In terms of sacramental theology, proper intention is required on the part of the minister of the sacrament or sacramental rite. If the proper intention is lacking, the sacrament or sacramental rite is not understood to be valid. For the minister of the sacrament, the minimal intent is "to do what the Church does" in terms of the particular rite. For example, a priest might go through the motions of a baptism for a dramatic production or demonstration but lack the intention to baptize anyone. Such a dramatic portrayal of a baptism without the intent to baptize would not be a valid sacrament. Similarly, a couple who exchange marriage vows at a wedding rehearsal are not understood to be married. At that moment their intent is to rehearse a ceremony that will happen in the future, not to make the vows of marriage. Proper intent might also be lacking at a marriage due to insanity, intoxication, mistake, or force. Lack of proper intent on the part of one or both of the couple in the wedding would be grounds for annulment of the marriage. A sacrament or sacramental rite would not be valid if the recipient had reached the age of reason and intended *not* to receive it. A valid sacrament or sacramental rite is not received against one's will. Proper intention is essential for sacramental validity. *See* Sacramental Rites; *see* Sacraments; *see* Validity (Sacramental).

Inter/Met. The term stands for Inter-faith Metropolitan Theological Education, Inc. This experiment in theological education was conceived by John Caldwell Fletcher, an Episcopal priest and associate professor of church and society at Virginia Theological Seminary. Inter/Met began its pilot year in 1970–1971. Fletcher served as director. Inter/Met's vision was that the best place to learn pastoral ministry was in the place of ministry, that is, the churches, and not in the cloister of a seminary. It stressed residentiary theological education, but resident in the place of ministry. Fletcher served as director from 1970 until 1977, and was assisted in his work by the Rev. Tilden Hampton Edwards III, director of the Washington Metropolitan Ecumenical Training Center. It ceased to exist on June 30, 1977, because of lack of funding.

Intercession. Prayer for another or others. Intercession "brings before God the needs of others" (BCP, p. 857). Intercession is one of the seven principal kinds of prayer (BCP, p. 856). An intercessor is one who prays an intercessory prayer. *See* Intercessor.

Intercessor. One who prays on behalf of another or others. An intercessor is one who prays an intercessory prayer. The term may indicate one who leads the prayers of the people, which are prayers of intercession (BCP, pp. 383–395). Jesus is known as the heavenly intercessor who prays for us. The hymn "Alleluia! sing to Jesus!" includes the phrase, "Intercessor, friend of sinners, earth's Redeemer, plead for me" (Hymns 460–461). *See* Intercession.

Interim Bodies. A term of convenience used to described the committees, commissions, boards, and agencies of the General Convention. It is not a canonically defined term. If a group was created by General Convention resolution, or if a group is constituted by Canon, Rule of Order, or Joint Rule, or if it is funded within the canonical

section of the budget, then it is an Interim Body. The interim period is the time between General Conventions. The Interim Bodies of the General Convention were first listed in *The Episcopal Church Annual 1997*.

Interment. Burial, the placing of the body of a deceased person in a grave. From the Latin, meaning "in earth" or "in the ground," the verb form of this term is "to inter." It is not used in the BCP. *See* Burial of the Dead.

International Commission on English in the Liturgy (ICEL). An organization formed by Roman Catholic bishops in English-speaking parts of the world to prepare English translations of the Latin liturgical texts of the Roman rite. ICEL was formed in 1963, following the Second Vatican Council of the Roman Catholic Church. ICEL's executive secretariat was located in Washington, D.C. The first translation by ICEL was the Roman missal in 1969. The ICEL translation is used for the memorial acclamation of Eucharistic Prayer A, "Christ has died./ Christ is risen./ Christ will come again." This memorial acclamation is a translation of one of the most frequently used memorial acclamations of the eastern church. It proclaims the "mystery of faith" in Christ (see BCP, p. 363).

International Consultation on English Texts (ICET) (1969). An international ecumenical body that produced revised English translations of liturgical texts in the years following the Second Vatican Council. Most of the major English-speaking denominations were represented in the preparation of the ICET texts. These texts were published as *Prayers We Have in Common: Agreed Liturgical Texts Prepared by the International Consultation on English Texts* (1970, 1971, and 1975). These texts were incorporated into modern English rites in the liturgical books of many Protestant and Anglican churches, including the 1979 BCP. For example, the Rite 2 translations of The Song of Mary: *Magnificat* (Canticle 15, pp. 91–92), The Song of Zechariah: *Benedictus Dominus Deus* (Canticle 16, pp. 92–93), and Glory to God: *Gloria in excelsis* (Canticle 20, pp. 94–95) are ICET translations. The contemporary language translations of the *Kyrie* and the Lord's Prayer are also ICET texts (see BCP, p. 106).

Intinction. Administration of the consecrated bread and wine of the eucharist at the same time, typically by dipping the bread in the wine and placing the moistened host in the mouth. Depending on local practice, this may be done by the communicant or the one who administers the wine. Historically, intinction has also been done by dropping the bread into the wine and administering the moistened host with a spoon. The term is from the Latin for "dip in." The BCP directs that opportunity always be given to every communicant to receive the consecrated bread and wine separately. However, the eucharist may be received in both kinds simultaneously, in a manner approved by the bishop (pp. 407–408). Some communicants prefer intinction because of concerns about contagious diseases or alcohol consumption. Separate intinction cups are to be avoided because they contradict the symbolism of the common cup.

Intinction was practiced in the east and west by the seventh century. The practice was also motivated by concern that the sacrament might be carried away for superstitious use. Intinction was opposed by the Council of Braga in Spain in the seventh century, and by Pope Paschal II in the twelfth century because it differed from Christ's action at the Last Supper. Intinction has been historically associated with giving communion to the sick.

Intone. Reciting or chanting to begin a psalm, antiphon, canticle, or hymn. The intonation is done by a cantor who sets the pitch and leads the singing, which is often unaccompanied by musical instruments. *See* Cantor.

Introit. A hymn, psalm, or anthem that is sung as the ministers enter to begin the eucharist. The term is from Latin, "to go in" or "enter." The use of an introit psalm at the entrance of the clergy was introduced into the Roman liturgy by Pope Celestine I (d. 432). The choir sang the psalm text, and the congregation repeated an antiphon after each psalm verse or group of verses. The antiphon for the introit was typically a verse of scripture. The theme of the introit was suited to gathering the congregation for worship, or possibly the season, feast, or occasion of the day. The introit continued as long as needed to accompany the entrance procession. After reaching the altar, the presider would signal the choir to stop the introit. The entrance psalm would then conclude with the *Gloria Patri*, which resolved the introit and focused attention on the salutation and readings that followed. By the late middle ages, the introit was reduced to an antiphon, the first verse of the chosen psalm, and the *Gloria Patri*. Luther preferred use of whole psalms for the introit instead of just one verse. The 1549 BCP used short psalms and sections of Ps 119 for the introit. The 1552 BCP did not include entrance psalms, but permission was given during the rule of Queen Elizabeth for a metrical psalm or hymn to precede the liturgy. The 1979 BCP provides that a hymn, psalm, or anthem may be sung before the opening acclamation of the eucharist (pp. 323, 355).

Investiture Struggle. Controversy in the latter part of the eleventh century and the early decades of the twelfth century between spiritual and temporal authorities over the installation of bishops. Feudal practice allowed kings to install bishops. In some places this led to disappointing and even scandalous appointments. This practice was challenged by Pope Gregory VII (c. 1021–1085) as a usurpation of the church's authority. Gregory's struggle with the German King Henry IV eventually led to Gregory's excommunication of Henry in 1076 and Henry's submission to the Pope at Canossa in 1077. Henry subsequently set up an antipope after a siege of Rome. Gregory was forced to escape from Rome and died in exile. However, Gregory's effort to free the church from feudal control eventually was followed by the Concordat of Worms (1122), which represented a workable compromise between ecclesiastical and feudal interests.

One of the issues in the investiture struggle was the actual ceremony of investiture of bishops. The land holding of the bishop was conferred by the feudal lord. The symbols of investiture were the bishop's crozier and ring. These symbols also suggested that the feudal overlord was conferring the power of ecclesiastical jurisdiction on the bishop. The Councils of Clermont (1095) and Rome (1099) forbade bishops to take the feudal oath. The problem was addressed at different times by Guido of Ferrara, Ivo of Chartres, and Hugh of Fleury. They distinguished the spiritual jurisdiction of the church (which was not under feudal control) from the temporal holdings of the bishopric which were under lay control. Negotiations between Anselm of Canterbury and Henry I of England led to the Concordat of London in 1107. This settlement eliminated lay investiture of bishops with the crozier and ring, but called for the bishop to take the oath of vassalage to the feudal overlord in return for the temporal holdings of the bishopric. The Concordat of Worms, a settlement between the church and Emperor Henry V of the Holy Roman Empire, called for free episcopal elections and provided for a "dual investiture." The crozier and ring, symbolizing ecclesiastical jurisdiction, were conferred at consecration. There was also a temporal investiture with a scepter, representing the temporal holdings of the bishopric.

Episcopal elections were to take place in the presence of the Emperor, who had the right to settle disputed cases. Although this controversy was settled in principle by the Concordat of Worms, the struggles of the Papacy and the Holy Roman Empire continued into the thirteenth century. The investiture struggle represented the church's efforts to disentangle itself from the lay dominance of feudal times. It led to the expanded political power of the medieval papacy.

Invitatory. *See* Invitatory Psalm.

Invitatory Antiphon. *See* Invitatory Psalm.

Invitatory Psalm. The Venite (Ps 95:1–7), or the entire Ps 95, or the Jubilate (Ps 100), which precedes the appointed selection of Psalmody at Morning Prayer (BCP, pp. 82–83). The Rule of St. Benedict of Nursia (c. 480–c. 540) called for Ps 95 and an antiphon to be sung daily as the first psalm of Matins. The Jubilate was used as an invitatory psalm in the medieval office of lauds, and in the Jerusalem temple.

An invitatory antiphon is used with the invitatory psalm to "invite" the congregation to prayer. The invitatory antiphon gives emphasis to the season or day. The invitatory antiphons may be said or sung before, or before and after the invitatory psalm. The invitatory antiphons may be used with either the Venite or the Jubilate. Responsorial recitation was traditionally used for the Venite. This method calls for the invitatory antiphon to be sung after each verse or group of verses of the invitatory psalm (BCP, p. 582).

The complete Ps 95 is appointed to take the place of the Venite on Ash Wednesday, Holy Saturday, and all the Fridays in Lent, including Good Friday. The canticle *Pascha nostrum* takes the place of the invitatory psalm in Easter Week, and it may be used throughout Easter season. An invitatory psalm may be substituted for the *Phos hilaron* at Evening Prayer.

The Hymnal 1982 provides musical settings for the Venite (S 2–S 7, S 35), for Ps 95 (S 8–S 10), for the Venite/Psalm 95 (S 34, S 36–S 40), and for the Jubilate (S 11–S 15, S 41–S 45). *The Hymnal 1982 Accompaniment Edition, Vol. 1*, also makes available the invitatory antiphons pointed for Anglican Chant (S 289, S 293), plainsong settings of invitatory antiphons (S 290– S 292, S 294), and a plainsong setting of the Jubilate (S 295).

Invocation. Among Anglicans the term "invocation" may refer to the epiclesis of the eucharistic rites, in which the presence of the Holy Spirit is invoked at the eucharist to bless and sanctify the eucharistic elements and the participants. More generally, it may simply refer to a prayer such as those commonly offered at the beginning of a meeting, banquet, or other public gathering. *See* Epiclesis.

Iowa, Diocese of. The primary convention of this diocese was held Aug. 17–18, 1853, at Trinity Church, Muscatine. The diocese has been in existence since then. On June 18, 1873, Grace Church Cathedral, Davenport, was consecrated. In 1909 Trinity Church, Davenport, merged with Grace Cathedral and the name was changed to Trinity Cathedral. The diocese includes the entire state of Iowa.

Irenaeus (c. 130–c. 202). Bishop and patristic theologian. He was probably from Smyrna in Asia Minor. When Pothinus, the Bishop of Lyons in Gaul died in 177, Irenaeus was chosen to succeed him. His two greatest theological works are *The Refutation and Overthrow of the Knowledge Falsely So-Called*, or *Five Books Against Heresies* written around 189, and *The Demonstration of the Apostolic Preaching*, written after the *Refutation*. In the *Five Books Against Heresy*, Irenaeus described and attacked the various Gnostic systems of his time. Against the Gnostics, who despised the flesh and exalted the spirit, he stressed two doctrines: the goodness of creation and the material world, and the resurrection of the body. His major contribution to the understanding of the Incarnation and the Atonement is his doctrine of "recapitulation." Irenaeus contrasted the First Adam and the Second Adam, Christ. He argued that God in Christ makes good all that was done wrong by Adam. He stresses a parallelism between Adam and Christ: Adam was disobedient, Christ was obedient. Christ was victorious over sin, death, and the devil by his obedience, making him *Christus Victor*. Irenaeus also stressed the importance of the tradition and role of the episcopate. Irenaeus died in Lyons. He may have been martyred. He is commemorated in the Episcopal calendar of the church year on June 28.

Irenaeus Fellowship. A loosely organized group of bishops concerned over uncertainty and confusion in faith and morals in the Episcopal Church. The fellowship first began meeting during the 1988 General Convention. On Mar. 6–8, 1990, twenty-seven bishops met at the St. Christopher Conference Center near Charleston, South Carolina, and adopted the Statement of Belief and Purpose of the Irenaeus Fellowship. An additional thirty-three bishops eventually signed the statement. They call themselves the Irenaeus Fellowship after the second-century Bishop Irenaeus, who was a champion of orthodoxy and an opponent of heresy. The members of the fellowship seek the highest standards of faith and practice for the Episcopal Church. Those standards must be based on the primacy of Holy Scripture, consistent with the historic traditions of the church, and interpreted by the best use of reason informed by the Holy Spirit. The Statement of Belief and Purpose affirms that Christ's tomb was empty on the first Easter Day, and it affirms the virginal conception of Jesus. Bishop Alex D. Dickson, Jr., of West Tennessee, and Bishop Mark J. M. Dyer of Bethlehem, were the original spokesmen for the group. The fellowship has no officers or offices.

Ives, Levi Silliman (Sept. 16, 1797–Oct. 13, 1867). Bishop of North Carolina and convert to Roman Catholicism. He was born in Meriden, Connecticut. In 1816 Ives entered Hamilton College to prepare for the Presbyterian ministry. He did not graduate because of ill health. In 1819 he joined the Episcopal Church because of its uninterrupted succession of apostolic ministry and its primitive worship. Ives studied theology under Bishop John Henry Hobart of New York and at the General Theological Seminary. He was ordained deacon on Aug. 4, 1822. He began his ministry at St. James' Church, Batavia, New York. In June 1823 he became rector of Trinity Church (Southwark), Philadelphia. He was ordained priest on Dec. 14, 1823. In 1826 Ives became co-rector of St. James' Church, Philadelphia, and in Sept. 1827 he moved to New York City to become assistant minister at Christ Church. In Mar. 1828 he became rector of St. Luke's Church, New York City. Ives was consecrated the second Bishop of North Carolina on Sept. 22, 1831.

As Bishop, Ives supported the founding of the Episcopal School of North Carolina for boys and St. Mary's School for girls. In 1842 he established a mountain mission in Western North Carolina, which he named Valle Crucis. This developed into a monastic community. Opposition formed against Valle Crucis and Bishop Ives. He was accused of promoting Roman Catholic practices, such as the reservation and adoration of the sacrament, monasticism, and auricular confession. On Oct. 1, 1852, Ives began a six-month leave of absence. He and Mrs. Ives traveled in Europe. On Dec. 22, 1852, he resigned as

Bishop of North Carolina, and on Dec. 25, 1852, he joined the Roman Catholic Church. The House of Bishops deposed him on Oct. 14, 1853. He returned to New York in 1854 and spent the remainder of his life as a Roman Catholic layman. Ives was the only Bishop to abandon the Episcopal Church over the Oxford Movement controversy. He died in Manhattanville, New York. *See* Valle Crucis.

J

James the Apostle, Saint (the Greater). James and John, sons of Zebedee, are mentioned frequently in the gospels. James is usually mentioned first. He is sometimes called "the elder" or "the greater," to distinguish him from the other apostle James, the son of Alphaeus, who is called James the Less. James was a fisherman by trade. James and John left their father and their work as fishermen when called by Jesus. They became apostles, and with Peter formed an inner circle in the apostolic group. They witnessed the Transfiguration, the healing of Peter's mother-in-law, the raising of the daughter of Jairus, and the agony at Gethsemane. Jesus nicknamed the brothers James and John "sons of thunder." Legend claims that James was a great traveler and carried the gospel to Spain. He is the patron saint of that country where he is called Santiago. His work for the Lord in Jerusalem angered Herod, who had him killed about the year 42. He was the first of the apostles to be martyred and the only one whose martyrdom is mentioned in the Bible (Acts 12:1–2). James's life is commemorated in the Episcopal calendar of the church year on July 25.

James, Fleming (Jan. 11, 1877–Sept. 11, 1959). Seminary dean and OT scholar. He was born in Gambier, Ohio. James received his B.A. in 1895, his M.A. in 1896, and his Ph.D. in 1899, all from the University of Pennsylvania. He graduated from the Philadelphia Divinity School, where his father was professor of homiletics, in 1901. He was ordained deacon on June 2, 1901. James began his ministry as minister-in-charge of St. Andrew's Church, Philadelphia. On May 25, 1902, he was ordained priest. He then became missionary-in-charge of the American Congregation of the Church of Our Saviour in Shanghai. In 1906 he returned to the United States and served as minister-in-charge of St. Anne's mission, Philadelphia, until 1912. From 1912 until 1921, James was rector of St. Paul's Church, Englewood, New Jersey. In 1921 he became professor of Old Testament at the Berkeley Divinity School, where he remained until

1940. From Sept. 1, 1940, until his retirement on Feb. 1, 1947, James was professor of Old Testament and dean at the School of Theology, University of the South. He moved to North Haven, Connecticut, and served as executive secretary of the OT section of the Revised Standard Version Bible Committee. His last position was as visiting professor of OT at the Yale Divinity School. His major publication was *Personalities of the Old Testament* (1939). James died in Hamden, Connecticut.

James of Jerusalem, Brother of Our Lord Jesus Christ, Saint (James the Just). In the gospels according to Matthew and Mark, and in the epistle to the Galatians, James of Jerusalem is referred to as the brother of Jesus. According to 1 Cor 15:7, he witnessed an appearance of Christ after the resurrection. Some scholars argue that he is a cousin or half-brother of Jesus, and that the word "brother" is used in a generic sense to describe his relationship to Jesus. Roman Catholics who uphold the perpetual virginity of Mary do not acknowledge that James was the son of Mary and Joseph. James was clearly a leader of the church at Jerusalem. He presided at the Council of Jerusalem which dealt with issues that divided Jewish and Gentile Christians. James was put to death in Jerusalem by the Sanhedrin in 62. James is traditionally acknowledged as the author of the epistle of James in the NT. James's authorship of this epistle has been challenged, but not conclusively refuted. Hegesippus, an early church historian, referred to James as "the Just" for his piety, and claimed "that he was holy from his mother's womb." James is commemorated in the Episcopal calendar of the church year on Oct. 23.

James the Less, Saint. Very little is known about this apostle. He was the son of Alphaeus. He is called "the Less" to distinguish him from James, the son of Zebedee, and from James, the brother of Jesus. It is also possible that he was small physically or younger than the other two. James labored diligently in and around Jerusalem until he was martyred when he was 96 years old. A saw is used as a symbol for James, recalling the story that he was thrown down from the top of the temple, stoned, beaten, and then cut into pieces with a saw. James the Less is commemorated in the Episcopal calendar of the church year on May 1, along with St. Philip.

Jamestown, Virginia. A royal charter was granted on Apr. 10, 1606, for a settlement in Virginia. On Dec. 20, 1606,

three ships, *Goodspeed*, *Discovery*, and *Susan Constance*, sailed from the Thames River. They reached Virginia on Apr. 26, 1607. The ships entered the Chesapeake Bay and disembarked at Jamestown. It was first called James Fort, after James I, King of England at the time. The chaplain on board was Robert Hunt. Captain John Smith led the expedition. They had a church service on their first Sunday in Jamestown. Six weeks later, on June 21, 1607, there was the first recorded Holy Communion at Jamestown. They had Morning and Evening Prayer every day, two sermons on each Sunday, and the Holy Communion every three months. It was here in 1613 that the Indian Princess Pocahontas was baptized and married to John Rolfe. The fifth church structure, the Brick Church, was destroyed by fire, but the tower, built in 1647, is still standing. This tower is now the entrance to the present church, built in 1907 by the Colonial Dames of America.

Janette Pierce Award, The. This award was established by the Episcopal Communicators at their Apr. 18–21, 1988 meeting to honor the memory of Janette Gayley Skerrett Pierce (1931–1988), one of the Episcopal Church's outstanding journalists. Pierce joined the staff of *The Episcopalian* as news editor. She was managing editor at the time of her death. The award is given occasionally in recognition of a person who has made exceptional contributions to the ministry of communications and who exemplifies the ideals of Janette Pierce.

Japan Mission. Channing Moore Williams, a priest of the Episcopal Mission in China, landed at Nagasaki on July 1, 1859, and the Japan Mission began. On Oct. 3, 1866, Williams was consecrated Missionary Bishop of China with jurisdiction over Japan. The 1874 General Convention constituted Japan a missionary district and named it the Missionary District of Yedo. At the same time, Williams relinquished jurisdiction over China and became the Missionary Bishop of Yedo. The Holy Catholic Church in Japan was organized in 1887 by uniting the work of the Church Missionary Society, the Society for the Propagation of the Gospel, and the Episcopal Church. Its Japanese name is *Nippon Sei Ko Kai* (also written *Nippon Seikokai*).

Jarratt, Devereux (Jan. 17, 1733–Jan. 29, 1801). Leading American Anglican priest during the Great Awakening. He was born in New Kent County, Virginia. Jarratt was first influenced by the Presbyterians and became a rigid Calvinist. He later entered the Church of England and was ordained deacon on Dec. 25, 1762, and priest on Jan. 1, 1763. He returned to Virginia and on Aug. 29, 1763, became the rector of Bath Parish, Dinwiddie County, where he remained the rest of his life. Jarratt was influenced by the Great Awakening and the preaching of George Whitefield and John Wesley. In his preaching he stressed the need for personal conversion and new birth. He formed religious societies in his parish and in neighboring areas, including North Carolina. He was a close friend of the Methodist Francis Asbury, who preached at his funeral. He was deeply hurt when the Methodists separated from the Church of England in the colonies in 1784 and formed their own independent church. In 1776 he wrote *A Brief Narrative of the Revival of Religion in Virginia. In a Letter to a Friend*, which he sent to John Wesley and which was published in London. His autobiography, *The Life of the Reverend Devereux Jarratt, Written by Himself, in a Series of Letters Addressed to the Rev. John Coleman* (1806), has much information about the church and the Great Awakening in Virginia. He died in Dinwiddie County.

Jarvis, Abraham (May 5, 1739–May 3, 1813). Bishop and high church Tory. He was born in Norwalk, Connecticut. Jarvis graduated from Yale College in 1761. For a short time he studied theology with the Rev. Thomas Bradbury Chandler, rector of St. John's Church, Elizabeth Town, New Jersey, where he learned strict high church principles. He went to England and was ordained deacon on Feb. 5, 1764, and priest on Feb. 19, 1764. Upon his return to America, Jarvis served as rector of Christ Church, Middletown, Connecticut, from 1764 until 1799. During the American Revolution he was a Loyalist and a chaplain to Tories who were imprisoned. He was secretary of the secret meeting on Mar. 25, 1783, at Woodbury, Connecticut, at which Samuel Seabury was chosen to go to England to be consecrated bishop. Jarvis was consecrated the second Bishop of Connecticut on Oct. 18, 1797, and served in that position until his death. Samuel Farmar Jarvis was his son. He died in New Haven, Connecticut.

Jarvis, Samuel Farmar (Jan. 20, 1786–Mar. 26, 1851). First historiographer of the Episcopal Church. He was the son of Bishop Abraham Jarvis of Connecticut. Born in Middletown, Connecticut, Jarvis graduated from Yale College in 1805. He was ordained deacon on Mar. 18, 1810, and priest on Apr. 5, 1811. From 1811 to 1813, he served St. Michael's Church, Bloomingdale, New York, and from 1813 until 1819, he was the rector of St. James' Church, New York City. In 1819 he became the first professor of biblical learning at the newly established General Theological Seminary. Jarvis left that position in 1820 over a disagreement with Bishop John Henry Hobart. From 1820 until 1826, Jarvis was the first rector of St. Paul's Church, Boston. For the next nine years he traveled in Europe, visiting its most important libraries. In 1835 he returned to the United States, and for two years was the professor of oriental literature at Washington (now Trinity) College. From 1837 until 1842, Jarvis was rector of Christ Church, Middletown. On Sept. 16, 1838, the General Convention named him historiographer of the Episcopal Church, with the directive to prepare "from the most original sources now extant, a faithful Ecclesiastical History, reaching from the Apostles' times, to the formation of the Protestant Episcopal Church in the United States." Only one volume, *The Church of the Redeemed*, was published, in 1850. Jarvis died in Middletown, Connecticut.

Jay, William (June 16, 1789–Oct. 14, 1858). Episcopal lay anti-slavery leader. He was born in New York, the son of John Jay, the first Chief Justice of the United States Supreme Court. William Jay graduated from Yale College in 1807 and then studied law. From 1818 until 1843, with one short interruption, he was judge of the court of Westchester County, New York. In the years before the Civil War, many Christians continued the campaign against slavery given impetus by the Revolution. Among them were a few white Episcopalians, most notably the Jay family of New York. William Jay contributed an article to the first issue of the *Emancipator*, which was published on May 1, 1833. In that same year he participated in the founding of the New York City Anti-Slavery Society. He was opposed to the plan of the American Colonization Society to send free African slaves to Africa. He also opposed Episcopal bishops who used the Bible to justify slavery. Jay was one of the founders of the American Bible Society in 1816, and this brought him into conflict with Bishop John Henry Hobart. Hobart wanted to delay emancipation, and limit the evangelicals and their American Bible Society. Hobart criticized inter-denominational societies because he thought they minimized the distinctive characteristics of the denominations and thus weakened the commitment of Episcopalians to their own church. Jay defended the evangelicals and their inter-denominational societies. He was opposed to war as a means to settle international disputes and argued for arbitration. Jay died in Bedford, New York.

Jefferson College, Washington, Mississippi. The first chartered college in Mississippi. The charter was granted on May 13, 1802. It began operation as an academy. It operated as a college, 1816–1821, and then reverted to academy status. Three Episcopal priests served as its president. It is no longer in existence.

Jehovah. A hybrid name for God, resulting from an erroneous combination of other names. In the period after the Exile, the proper name for God, Yahweh, was believed by Jewish people to be too holy to pronounce. The title *Adonai*, Lord, was spoken instead. In written texts the vowels of *Adonai* were combined with the consonants *YHWH* as a reminder to readers that they were to read *Adonai* rather than Yahweh. In the middle ages, Christians misunderstood this practice and simplistically combined the vowels of *Adonai* with the consonants of *YHWH*, which resulted in the erroneous hybrid "Jehovah." The name Jehovah has been used in a few translations of the Bible and also in some hymns. However, "the LORD" is found in the King James Version, as well as most modern translations.

Jenney or Jenny, Robert (1687–Jan. 5, 1762). Commissary for Pennsylvania and missionary. He was born in Ireland. Jenney received his B.A. from Trinity College, Dublin, and served as a chaplain in the Royal Navy, 1710–1714. On June 27, 1714, he was licensed by the Bishop of London as lecturer (catechist) and schoolmaster for Christ Church, Philadelphia. He served at Christ Church from 1714 to 1715. From 1715 until 1722, Jenney was the assistant minister at Trinity Church, New York City, and from 1717 until 1722, he was chaplain to the English forces in New York City. Jenney was the Society for the Propagation of the Gospel (SPG) missionary at Rye, New York, 1722–1724, and at Hempstead, Long Island, 1724–1742. In 1742 he resigned from the SPG to become rector of Christ Church, Philadelphia, and the second Commissary for Pennsylvania. He served in those positions until his death. Jenney died in Philadelphia.

Jerome (c. 347–Sept. 30, 420). One of the four great Doctors of the Western Church. He was born in Stridon, Italy. His full name was Eusebius Sophronius Hieronymus. He studied Hebrew and Greek and became the leading biblical scholar of the early church. In 382 Pope Damasus I commissioned Jerome to translate the scriptures into Latin, the "vulgar" or common tongue. This translation was therefore known as the Vulgate. The Vulgate played a large role in shaping western Christianity and in extending Jerome's influence. After the Pope's death in 384, Jerome went to Bethlehem and established a monastery where he lived until his death. He was the most learned of the Western Fathers and a promoter of monasticism. He is commemorated in the Episcopal calendar of the church year on Sept. 30.

Jerusalem Bible, The (1966). An English version of the Dominican Order's *La Bible de Jérusalem*. The work was done by the Dominicans of the École Biblique in Jerusalem. It was translated from the original Hebrew and Greek. It is distinguished by the use of the name Yahweh for God rather than "the LORD."

Jesse Tree. The depiction of the genealogy of Jesus in the form of a tree, springing from Jesse, the father of King David of Israel (see Is 11:1). It typically shows intermediary descendants on the foliage of the tree, which ends with Jesus or with the Virgin Mary and the baby Jesus. Its purpose is to stress the royal lineage of Jesus as the anointed king in the line of David. It is normally either painted on the glass or carved on the mullions of a window of a church or cathedral. Thus arose the term "Jesse Window." This practice began as early as the twelfth century. Examples are to be found in the cathedrals of Wells and Chartres. Some parishes decorate a tree with symbols appropriate for a Jesse Tree as an Advent devotion.

Jesus Christ. The Son of God, the second person of the Trinity, the savior and redeemer of humanity, the Word of God who was made flesh and dwelt among us in the world (see Jn 1:1–18). Jesus was the Messiah, the promised king and ancestor of David who was expected from OT times to deliver the people (see Is 9:6–7; Ez 34:23–24, 37:24–25). His name means "anointed one," as anointed kings and anointed priests were understood to have been given special powers and functions by God. Christ is also known as "Second Adam," who reverses the consequences of disobedience by Adam and humanity. St. Paul explains that "as in Adam all die, so also in Christ shall all be made alive" (1 Cor 15:22, RSV). The Episcopal theologian William Porcher DuBose emphasized that Jesus' sinlessness was "His own," and not the result of a human nature that was somehow incapable of sin or invulnerable to temptation.

By God's grace, through faith, Jesus humanly revealed the obedient righteousness that is the way of salvation.

The Nicene Creed affirms that Jesus Christ was eternally begotten and the only Son of God the Father, and is of one being with the Father, "God from God, Light from Light, true God from true God." All things were made through him; he came down from heaven for us and for our salvation; he became incarnate from the Virgin Mary by the power of the Holy Spirit; he died and was buried after being crucified under Pontius Pilate; and he rose on the third day after his death and ascended into heaven, where he is seated at the right hand of God the Father (see BCP, p. 358). The Apostles' Creed also states that Jesus descended to the dead, or hell, after his crucifixion and before the resurrection (see BCP, pp. 66, 120). The Council of Chalcedon (451) affirmed that the one person of Christ has two natures, divine and human, which are "in no way annulled by the union," and that Christ's divine and human natures are "without confusion, without change, without division, without separation." The Chalcedonian Definition also held that Christ is of one substance (*homoousios*) with God the Father concerning his divinity and of one substance with us concerning his humanity (see BCP, p. 864). The Christian hope is centered in the victorious Christ, who will come again in glory to judge the living and the dead, and whose kingdom will have no end (see BCP, pp. 120, 359). The Athanasian Creed states that at Jesus' coming all humanity "shall rise again with their bodies and shall give account for their own works" (BCP, p. 865). The Christian assurance is that nothing, not even death, will separate us from the love of God in Christ Jesus our Lord (Rom 8:38–39; BCP, p. 862).

The Prayer Book Catechism affirms that Jesus is the only perfect image of God the Father, and he reveals God's loving nature. Jesus received our human nature from the Virgin Mary, his mother, by God's own act. The divine Son became human so that we might be adopted as children of God and made heirs of God's kingdom. We are freed from the power of sin and reconciled to God by Jesus' obedience, which included suffering and death. Jesus overcame death and opened for us the way of eternal life by his resurrection. We share in his victory over sin, suffering, and death when we are baptized into the new covenant and become living members of Christ (see BCP, pp. 849–850). Major events in Jesus' life are recalled in the celebrations and observances of the church year, including his birth (Christmas); his circumcision and naming (Holy Name); the visitation of the Magi (Epiphany); his baptism by John the Baptist (First Sunday after the Epiphany); his Presentation in the Temple (Feast of the Presentation); his Transfiguration (Last Sunday after the Epiphany, and the Feast of the Transfiguration); his triumphal entry into Jerusalem (Palm Sunday); his institution of the eucharist and washing of the disciples' feet (Maundy Thursday); his crucifixion (Passion Sunday, Good Friday); his resurrection (Easter); and his Ascension (Feast of the Ascension). Christ's triumphal coming again is anticipated in the season of Advent. *The Hymnal 1982* provides a section of hymns on Jesus Christ our Lord (Hymns 434–499), including "O love, how deep, how broad, how high" (Hymns 448–449), "My song is love unknown" (Hymn 458), and "The head that once was crowned with thorns" (Hymn 483). The theological study of Jesus Christ is known as Christology. *See* Incarnation; *see* Messiah.

"Jesus Prayer, The." Repetitive prayer, often in the form "Lord Jesus Christ, Son of the living God, have mercy on me, a sinner," or variations of that form. It is associated with the spirituality of the eastern church. Early ascetics prayed the name "Jesus" and added to it the prayer of the publican, "God be merciful to me, a sinner" (Lk 18:13). The fourteenth-century hesychasts of Mt. Athos sought to follow literally St. Paul's injunction to "pray without ceasing" (1 Thes 5:17), praying the Jesus Prayer continuously. These monks developed the use of the Jesus Prayer as we know it. *See* Hesychasm.

Jesus Seminar, The. A group consisting mainly of NT scholars who discussed and decided by majority vote which sayings and incidents involving Jesus in the NT and other early literature were authentic reports of the historical Jesus. It was established in 1985. In reaching their decisions the members of the Jesus Seminar interpreted Jesus as a wisdom teacher in the Hellenistic-Cynic tradition rather than as an eschatological prophet in the Old Testament-Jewish tradition. There was disagreement on the validity of the decisions of the Jesus Seminar concerning authenticity.

Jewell, John (May 24, 1522–Sept. 23, 1571). English reformer, apologist, and Bishop of Salisbury. He was born at Buden in the parish of Berimber, Devonshire, England. Jewell received his B.A. in 1540, and his M.A. in 1545, both from Corpus Christi College, Oxford. He was a fellow at Corpus Christi College, 1542–1553, and vicar of Sunningwell, 1551–1553. When Queen Mary came to the throne in 1553, Jewell fled to the continent where he was an exile from 1553 until the death of Mary in 1558. While on the continent he lived and worked at Frankfurt, Strassburg, and Zurich. He was influenced by the Calvinism of those places. After returning to England, he was consecrated Bishop of Salisbury on Jan. 21, 1560, and served in that position until his death. In 1562 Jewell wrote *An Apology of the Church of England*, which was a defense of the Church of England and of the Elizabethan Settlement against the accusations of Roman Catholic critics. Jewell led the literary offensive against the Roman Church, and denounced transubstantiation, purgatory, celibacy of clergy, and the worship of saints and images as "trifles, follies, and baubles." He defended the Church of England as the true church and insisted that the English Reformation was the restoration of the true church in England. He claimed that the practices of the Church of England were older and thus better than the Church of Rome. Jewell and Richard Hooker are recognized as the two great apologists of the Church of England and of sixteenth-century Anglicanism.

Joachim. *See* Anne and Joachim.

John, Apostle and Evangelist, Saint. John was the son of Zebedee and the brother of James the Apostle, who is also called James the Greater. He was a fisherman. John is often assumed to be the "disciple whom Jesus loved," as stated by the Gospel According to John. He took Mary into his home after Jesus' crucifixion (Jn 19:26–27). John, his brother James, and Peter formed the inner circle in the apostolic group. With Peter and James, he witnessed the Transfiguration, the healing of Peter's mother-in-law, the raising of the daughter of Jairus, and the agony at Gethsemane. Jesus nicknamed the brothers John and James "sons of thunder." John is traditionally regarded as the author of the Fourth Gospel, the three epistles that bear his name, and the Book of Revelation. In connection with Revelation, he is called John "the Divine," and John "the Theologian." After a period of exile on the isle of Patmos under the emperor Domitian, he went to Asia Minor and settled at Ephesus. According to tradition, John wrote Revelation while on the isle of Patmos. He probably died in Ephesus. John is believed to be the only apostle who was not martyred. Some consider him the patron of theologians, writers, and those who produce books. John is commemorated in the Episcopal calendar of the church year on Dec. 27.

John the Baptist. Prophetic forerunner of Jesus. John preached conversion and proclaimed a baptism of repentance. Jesus and many others were baptized by John. John is called "the Baptist" because he was willing to baptize people if they repented to God for their sins. He urged people to repent and be baptized in preparation for a renewal of Israel through God's eschatological intervention. John is portrayed as focusing on the importance of the future and the possibility of imminent destruction. Many believe that John had been a member of the Qumran community or at least influenced by the thought and practice of Qumran prior to his public appearance.

John was the son of Zechariah and Elizabeth. Zechariah was a priest of the Jerusalem Temple. Elizabeth was a kinswoman of the Virgin Mary, and believed to be barren. Zechariah was told by an angel that his son was to be called John. Zechariah responded with unbelief to this news and was made unable to speak by the angel until John's birth. The child John leaped for joy in Elizabeth's womb when Elizabeth was visited by Mary (Lk 1:39–44). At that time Mary was pregnant with the child Jesus. On the eighth day after John's birth, Zechariah insisted that the child's name was John. Zechariah regained his speech, and uttered the hymn known as the *Benedictus Dominus Deus* or the Song of Zechariah (Lk 1:68–79; BCP, pp. 92–93).

Luke's gospel begins with a detailed account of John's birth and his relation to Jesus. Luke, Mark, and Matthew all give a summary of John's teaching and mention his baptism of Jesus. Matthew is the only one who reports that John questioned whether Jesus should baptize him. Matthew also indicates that when John was in prison he raised a question about whether Jesus was the "one who is to come." Jesus' reply indicates that he viewed John most favorably but that John is less than anyone who has become a member of the Kingdom of Heaven. According to the Fourth Gospel (Jn 3:25–30), John the Baptist denied that he was the Messiah. John the Baptist likened Jesus to the bridegroom and himself to the bridegroom's friend. He said that his joy was fulfilled hearing the bridegroom's voice, and that "He must increase, but I must decrease." John was imprisoned by Herod Antipas and later executed. John's birth is celebrated on June 24 in the Episcopal calendar of the church year. John is the focus of the liturgical readings for Advent II and III. His ministry is also recalled by several Advent hymns, including Hymn 76, "On Jordan's bank the Baptist's cry." *See* Nativity of St. John the Baptist, The.

John of the Cross (1542–1591). Known as the Doctor of Mystical Theology, Juan de Yepes was born in Fontiveros, Spain. He joined the Carmelites in 1563 and took the name John of St. Matthias. John studied at the University of Salamanca, 1564–1568, and was ordained priest in 1567. In that same year he met Teresa of Avila and joined with her in the reform of the Carmelite Order. On Nov. 11, 1568, he changed his name to John of the Cross. John and Teresa restored the austere Carmelite Primitive Rule which stressed the contemplative life. The friars of this reformed order wore sandals and were soon referred to as Discalced (unshod, no shoes) Carmelites. Those who opposed the reform of the order imprisoned him. For nine months, John lived in a cell six feet by ten feet with very little light. While imprisoned he wrote some of his greatest poetry. He escaped in Aug. 1578 and spent the rest of his life as a leader of the order and a spiritual writer. His major writings were *The Ascent of Mount Carmel, The Dark Night of the Soul, The Spiritual Canticle,* and *The Living Flame of Love.* These writings stressed how one reaches perfection or union with God. John was beatified by Pope Clement X in 1675, canonized by Pope Benedict XIII in 1726, and named a Doctor of the Church in 1926. John is commemorated in the Roman Catholic Calendar of the church year on Dec. 14.

John of Damascus (c. 650–c. 749). Monk and theologian. There is little known of his life, and the available sources are in conflict. He was called John Damascene. John was the son of a Christian tax collector for the Islamic Caliph of Damascus. He succeeded his father as the chief representative of the Christians to the Caliph. In 716 he became a monk and later a priest at the abbey of St. Sabas, near Jerusalem. The most important of his theological writings is *The Fount of Knowledge* or *The Fount of Wisdom.* The most significant part of this work is "On the Orthodox Faith," a summary and systematizing of previous eastern theology. During the iconoclastic controversy, which reached its climax in 787 at the Second Council of Nicaea, John was a leading defender of the use of icons. He was an opponent of the Monophysite heresy and of Manichaeism, both of which denied the completeness of the Incarnation. John was the last of the great eastern Fathers of the Church. Three of John's Easter hymns are in *The Hymnal 1982* : "Thou hallowed chosen morn of praise" (Hymn 198); "Come, ye faithful, raise the strain" (Hymns 199–200); and "The day of resurrection" (Hymn 210). He was declared a Doctor of the Church by Pope Leo III in 1890. John's life is commemorated in the Episcopal calendar of the church year on Dec. 4.

John Milton Society for the Blind. One of the agencies through which the Episcopal Church ministers to the blind. It is named for John Milton (1608–1674), the great English poet who wrote *Paradise Lost* (1667) and *Paradise Regained* (1671). Milton became totally blind in 1651.

Around 1872, William Waite, Frank Battles, and others in the Philadelphia area formed the Society for Providing Evangelical Religious Literature (SPERL). It was incorporated by the Commonwealth of Pennsylvania on May 28, 1879. In the 1920s, Helen Keller, Dr. Lewis Chamberlain of the American Bible Society, and others established the John Milton Foundation. It was incorporated on Mar. 17, 1928. In 1932 the name was changed to the John Milton Society. Chamberlain left the American Bible Society to head the John Milton Society. Frank Battles was the first president. He was succeeded by Helen Keller, who presided until her retirement in 1960. On Sept. 1, 1960, SPERL and the John Milton Society merged. In 1979 the Plymouth Braille Group of the Plymouth Church of The Pilgrims in Brooklyn, New York, also merged with the John Milton Society. The mission of the society is to provide Christian literature free of cost. Publications are in braille, large type, and talking book cassettes. A scholarship program underwrites the cost of education of blind persons and other people whose life vocations are to work with blind persons.

John Nevin Sayre Award. This peacemaker's award was established by the Episcopal Peace Fellowship (EPF) in 1979 to honor the Rev. John Nevin Sayre for his lifetime of service in the cause of peace. It is conferred every three years for "courageous witness in the cause of peace and justice" to a recipient chosen by the EPF Executive Committee. It is awarded during the time of the General Convention. *See* Episcopal Peace Fellowship, The (EPF).

Johns, John (July 10, 1796–Apr. 5, 1876). Bishop, college president, and evangelical leader. He was born in New Castle, Delaware. Johns graduated from the College of New Jersey in 1815, and then studied for two years at Princeton Theological Seminary. He was ordained deacon on May 6, 1819, and priest on July 26, 1820. Johns was rector of All Saints' Church, Fredericktown, Maryland, 1819–1829, and then rector of Christ Church, Baltimore, 1829–1842. He was consecrated Assistant Bishop of

Virginia on Oct. 13, 1842, and became the fourth Bishop of Virginia on Mar. 14, 1862. Johns was president of the College of William and Mary, 1849–1854. He was a leading evangelical and president of the Board of Trustees of the Virginia Theological Seminary, 1862–1876. His major published work was *Memoir of the Life of the Right Rev. William Meade* (1867), his predecessor as Bishop of Virginia. Johns died in Alexandria, Virginia.

Johnson, Samuel (Oct. 14, 1696–Jan. 6, 1772). One of the Yale converts. He was born in Guildford, Connecticut. He graduated from Yale College in 1714 and worked as a teacher. He was ordained a Congregational minister in 1720 and undertook a pastorate in West Haven, Connecticut. However, in Sept. 1722 Johnson and a group of other Congregational clergy shocked the Connecticut religious establishment by announcing their intention to seek Anglican ordination. Johnson was ordained in England. He returned home as a missionary of the Society for the Propagation of the Gospel. He served as rector of the parish in Stratford, Connecticut, for the next thirty-one years. He accepted the presidency of King's College (now Columbia University) in New York City on July 17, 1754. He resigned on Mar. 1, 1763. In 1764 he returned to the rectorship at Stratford, where he remained until his death. A theological rationalist, Johnson was renowned both as an opponent of strict Calvinism and as an advocate of idealist philosophy. His *Elementa Philosophica* (1752) was also the first philosophy textbook published in America. His conversion from Congregationalism to Anglicanism was a critical factor in strengthening the Anglican presence in New England during the colonial period.

Johnson, Samuel Roosevelt (Nov. 18, 1802–Aug. 13, 1873). Priest and seminary professor. He was born in Newton, Long Island, New York. Johnson graduated from Columbia College in 1820, and from the General Theological Seminary in 1823. He was ordained deacon on Jan. 6, 1824, and priest on Aug. 1, 1827. From 1824 until 1834 he was rector of St. James' Church, Hyde Park, New York. After a brief period as rector of St. George's Church, Flushing, Long Island, he traveled with Missionary Bishop Jackson Kemper in the Northwest. In 1837 Johnson moved to Lafayette, Indiana, where he founded St. John's Parish, and served as rector. In 1847 he moved to Brooklyn and served as rector of St. John's Church. On Nov. 5, 1850, he was elected professor of systematic divinity at the General Theological Seminary and served there until his retirement

in June 1870. Johnson was a high churchman in the tradition of John Henry Hobart. He argued for an early, daily celebration of the Holy Eucharist at General Seminary. After his retirement he served St. Thomas' Church, Amenia Union, New York, where he died.

Johnson, Sherman Elbridge (Mar. 7, 1908–Mar. 23, 1993). NT scholar and seminary dean. He was born in Hutchinson, Kansas. Johnson received his B.A. in 1933 from Northwestern University. He received his B.D. in 1933, and his S.T.M. in 1934, both from Seabury-Western Theological Seminary. He was ordained deacon on Apr. 30, 1933, and priest on Nov. 1, 1933. In 1933–1934, he was a tutor at Seabury-Western, and in 1934–1936, he was a lecturer there. In 1936 Johnson received his Ph.D. from the University of Chicago. He taught NT at Nashotah House, 1936–1940, and then at the Episcopal Theological School, 1940–1951. Johnson served as dean and president of the Church Divinity School of the Pacific from 1951 until 1972. After 1972 he served as visiting professor at several theological seminaries. Johnson supported an ecumenical consortium in Berkeley, California, which became a reality in 1962 as the Graduate Theological Union. He was the author of more than 150 books and articles, including *A Commentary on the Gospel According to St. Mark.* Johnson died in Holly, Vallejo, California.

Johnston, Gideon (c. 1671–Apr. 23, 1716). First Commissary to South Carolina. He was born in Tuam, Ireland. On Sept. 19, 1707, the Society for the Propagation of the Gospel informed Johnston that the Bishop of London had appointed him Commissary to South Carolina. On Mar. 2, 1708, the ship bearing Johnston and his family arrived off the coast of Charleston. While in South Carolina, Johnston did extensive missionary work among African Americans and Indians. He died in a shipwreck.

Joint Commission. *See* Commission of the General Convention.

Joint Commission on Christian Unity. The House of Bishops at the 1886 General Convention adopted the "Chicago Quadrilateral," which after the 1888 Lambeth Conference became the "Chicago-Lambeth Quadrilateral." In response to the "Chicago Quadrilateral," the 1886 General Convention established the Joint Commission on Christian Unity, sometimes called the Joint Commission on Church Unity. The Joint Commission was directed to send the "Chicago Quadrilateral" to all Protestant churches in the United States. By 1892 the Joint Commission had communicated the document to eighteen Protestant communions. It had some conversations with Presbyterians and Lutherans. The Joint Commission went out of existence around 1925.

Joint Commission on Church Music. The 1919 General Convention created the Joint Commission on Church Music. It included six bishops, six presbyters, and six laymen. It was to make recommendations concerning the character and form of music to be used in the services of the church and in schools and colleges. It also was to make recommendations about the methods of instruction in theological schools in the history and practice of church music. In 1973 the Joint Commission was replaced by the Standing Commission on Church Music. The 1997 General Convention established the Standing Commission on Liturgy and Music to replace the Standing Liturgical Commission and the Standing Commission on Church Music.

Joint Commission on Ecumenical Relations. The Joint Commission on Faith and Order was changed to the Joint Commission on Ecumenical Relations by the 1949 General Convention. The 1976 General Convention made the Joint Commission on Ecumenical Relations the Standing Commission on Ecumenical Relations. *See* Ecumenical Relations, Standing Commission on.

Joint Commission on Faith and Order. The General Convention of 1910 established this commission to bring about a conference for consideration of Faith and Order issues. All Christian communions throughout the world which confessed Jesus Christ as God and Savior were to be invited to participate in arranging for and conducting a conference. The conference would have no legislative power but would study and discuss the next step toward unity. The leading Episcopalians in this work were Bishop Charles Henry Brent and Robert H. Gardiner, a layman from the Diocese of Maine. The commission was given $100,000 by J. P. Morgan to help with expenses. This commission helped arrange the two World Conferences on Faith and Order, which led to the organization of the World Council of Churches in 1948. The commission was also called the Joint Commission on the World Conference on Faith and Order. The 1949 General Convention abolished this commission of the Episcopal Church and established in its place the Joint Commission on Ecumenical Relations.

Joint Commission on the Relations of Capital and Labor. The General Convention of 1901 appointed this commission. It was "to study carefully the aims and purposes of the labor organizations of our country; in particular to investigate the causes of industrial disturbances as these arise; and to hold themselves in readiness to act as arbitrators, should their services be desired, between the men and their employees, with a view to bring about mutual conciliation and harmony in the spirit of the Prince of Peace." This commission led the Episcopal Church in supporting the cause of labor and labor unions. It was discharged by the 1910 General Convention and replaced by the Joint Commission on Social Service.

Joint Commission on Rural Work. The 1928 General Convention established the joint commission "for fostering of the church's work in village and country life." As early as 1922 the National Council of the Episcopal Church had been asked to consider the conditions of the rural districts in their relation to the church. The national council was asked to make recommendations for reconstruction of the country church so that it could reassume its work of ministry to the whole of rural life. The commission submitted a report, "National Program of Village and Country Work," to the 1931 General Convention. It presented definite plans to meet such needs as adequate salaries and necessary equipment for rural workers. The economic depression of the 1930s forced the national council to reduce its budget. In 1934 the Joint Commission on Rural Work was abolished. Its work was assumed by the executive secretary of the Department of Christian Social Service.

Joint Commission on Social Service. The 1910 General Convention discharged the Joint Commission on the Relations of Capital and Labor, and appointed the Joint Commission on Social Service. Its purpose was "to study and report upon social and industrial conditions; to coordinate the activities of the various organizations existing within the church in the interests of social service; to cooperate with similar bodies in other communions; to encourage sympathetic relations between capital and labor; and to deal according to their discretion with these and kindred matters." The commission of five bishops, five presbyters, and five laymen existed until 1919. It was the main national authority of the church serving the cause of social justice. It went out of existence in 1919 with the creation of the Presiding Bishop and Council.

Jones, Bayard Hale (July 23, 1887–Apr. 27, 1957). Liturgical scholar. He was born in Golden, Colorado. He studied at the University of California, Harvard, Church Divinity School of the Pacific, General Theological Seminary, and Oxford. Jones was ordained deacon on June 11, 1913, and priest on Mar. 25, 1914. He served parishes in California and Reno, Nevada. With Bishop Edward Lambe Parsons, he produced *The American Prayer Book: Its Origins and Principles* (1937), one of the first Anglican publications that reflected current liturgical scholarship and movements. In 1939 he joined the faculty of the School of Theology, Sewanee, Tennessee. He was a member of the Liturgical Commission from 1934 until his death. Committee members gave him principal credit for the 1943 Daily Office Lectionary, for which he published the rationale in *The American Lectionary* (1944). In 1950 he became editor of the Prayer Book Studies of the Liturgical Commission. Later volumes give him principal credit for the following five studies: Prayer Book Studies II (*The Liturgical Lectionary*), IV (*The Eucharistic Liturgy*), IX (*The Calendar*), X (*The Solemnization of Matrimony*), and XII (*The Prayers for the Minor Holy Days*). A series of essays, *Dynamic Redemption* (1961), was published posthumously, and chapters from a projected book on origins of Christian liturgies appeared in the *Anglican Theological Review*. Some of his proposals for revision were incorporated in the 1979 BCP and in later editions of *Lesser Feasts and Fasts*. He died in Sewanee.

Jones, Paul (Nov. 24, 1880–Sept. 4, 1941). Socialist and pacifist bishop. He was born in Wilkes-Barre, Pennsylvania. He received his B.A. from Yale in 1902 and his B.D. from the Episcopal Theological School in 1906. He was ordained deacon on June 17, 1906, and priest on Dec. 16, 1906. From 1906 to 1914 he served St. John's Church, Logan, Utah, and in Sept. 1914 he was appointed archdeacon of the diocese. The House of Bishops elected him the fourth Missionary Bishop of Utah, and he was consecrated at St. Mark's Cathedral, Salt Lake City, on Dec. 16, 1914. He was a socialist and an ardent pacifist. He opposed American participation in World War I, which proved to be a very unpopular position in some sectors of the Episcopal Church at the time. The House of Bishops forced him to resign, and he submitted his resignation on Apr. 11, 1918. Later in 1918 he served a mission in Brownsville Junction, Maine, and from 1919 to 1929 he was secretary of the Fellowship of Reconciliation. From 1930 until his death he was student pastor at Antioch College, Ohio.

Joseph of Arimathea. After the death of Jesus, Joseph asked Pilate for the body of Jesus and buried it in a tomb newly hewn out of a rock (Mk 15:43–46). Joseph was a wealthy Jew, and a member of the Sanhedrin. He may have been a secret disciple of Jesus. The Gospel of Mark records that Joseph was "looking for the kingdom of God." Joseph is commemorated in the Episcopal calendar of the church year on Aug. 1.

Joseph, Saint. The husband of Mary. A pious Jew, a carpenter from Nazareth, and a descendant of King David, Joseph is also known as the "Guardian of Our Lord." Joseph was faced with an awkward situation when he learned that his betrothed wife was pregnant, and he knew he was not the father. He made plans to divorce her quietly, but when an angel of God came to him in a dream and revealed God's plans for him, Joseph took Mary as his wife without further hesitation. He traveled with Mary to Bethlehem, assumed legal responsibility for the child Jesus, and saw that the religious obligations were met through the circumcision of the child and the purification of the mother. Because of the silence of the gospels, and because Jesus entrusted Mary to the care of John, it is generally believed that Joseph died a natural death after the visit to Jerusalem when Jesus was twelve, but before the baptism of Jesus when he was thirty. Some believe that Joseph was much older than Mary. Joseph is considered the patron saint of the working person. His life is commemorated on Mar. 19 in the Episcopal calendar of the church year.

Jottings. A periodic publication of the Episcopal Church's Rural and Small Community Ministries Office. It began publication in Dec. 1992.

Journal of Women's Ministries. See Council for Women's Ministries (CWM).

Jubilate Deo. Invitatory psalm based on Ps 100. It begins, "Be joyful in the Lord, all you lands; serve the Lord with gladness and come before his presence with a song" (BCP, p. 82). *See* Invitatory Psalm.

Jubilee. The OT Year of Jubilee was the fiftieth year, the seventh sabbath year, in which debts were forgiven, Hebrew slaves were set free, and alienated lands were returned to their former owners. The name is from the Hebrew *yobhel*, "ram's horn," which was blown to proclaim the beginning of this special year. The Jubilee is mentioned in Leviticus (Chapters 25 and 27) and Numbers (Chapter 36). This year of liberty and release expresses God's sovereignty over creation, and provides a reminder that human beings are stewards of creation who must live justly. The directions for the Year of Jubilee in Leviticus include the repeated instruction, "you shall not wrong one another." Although the Year of Jubilee may not have been actually practiced, it upholds personal rights, human dignity, and family responsibility as ideals. The Year of Jubilee was to be a time of equality and justice for all. The OT Year of Jubilee also provided a biblical image of freedom and equality for African American slaves who yearned for liberty prior to emancipation.

In the Roman Catholic Church, the Jubilee Year is a "Holy Year" in which a special indulgence is granted to Roman Catholics who visit Rome and fulfill certain conditions. In 1300 Pope Boniface VIII made the first year of each century a year of special indulgence. The intervals between Jubilee years in the Roman Catholic Church was gradually reduced to twenty-five. The year 2000 was a Holy Year in the Roman Catholic Church. *See* Jubilee Ministry.

Jubilee College. No longer in existence, this college near Peoria was founded in 1839 by Philander Chase, the first Bishop of Illinois. The cornerstone of the chapel and schoolhouse was laid on Apr. 3, 1839, and the school opened in 1840. The charter of Jan. 22, 1847, stated that the institution was to consist of a theological department, the college proper, a classical preparatory school, and a female seminary. The first commencement was held on July 7, 1847. The school was continued by a distant relative, Samuel Chase (d. 1878). After Bishop Chase's death, the school closed in 1862 because of indebtedness. In 1933 the property was given to the State of Illinois for a park.

Jubilee Ministry. A social justice ministry of advocacy and service for the poor and oppressed. It is a network of parish and diocesan Jubilee Centers throughout the Episcopal Church. It was established by an act of the 1982 General Convention as "a ministry of joint discipleship in Christ with poor and oppressed people, wherever they are found, to meet basic human needs and to build a just society." The term "Jubilee" means the fiftieth year. It is derived from Lv 25:10, which says that the fiftieth year shall be a jubilee: "you shall return, every one of you, to your property and every one of you to your family." One of its major ministries is to locate and affirm as Jubilee Centers those congregations, including ecumenical clusters, already directly engaged in mission and ministry with poor people. The experience of ministry with poor people is used to help other parishes become Jubilee centers. It has a variety of other advocacy programs, and publishes a quarterly called *Jubilee Journal.* The Jubilee officer of the diocese is appointed by the diocesan bishop. Jubilee programs vary according to the needs of the local community. *See* Jubilee.

Jude the Apostle, Saint. *See* Simon and Jude, Saints and Apostles.

Julian of Norwich (c. 1342–c. 1413). English female mystic and anchoress. Almost nothing is known about Julian's life, not even her real name. As was the custom of anchoresses and anchorites in the fourteenth century, she took the name Julian from the name of the church where she lived in a cell. The Norwich church was named for St. Julian, probably named after Pope Julian (337–352). The information we have about her is in her writing, *The Revelations of Divine Love*, also known as the *Book of Showings*. In this volume she explains that she was thirty years old when at the end of a grave illness she received fourteen revelations or "showings." Later two other visions followed. In her fifties, Lady or Dame Julian wrote about the meaning of these showings. She described her struggles with sin as well as sin's effect on humanity and on personal relationship with God. The theme of her writings is the great love and compassion of God. She refers to God the Creator as father and mother and refers to the second person of the Trinity as mother. In the *Revelations*, Julian presents a vision of God in the feminine maternal role. She says God *is* mother, not simply *like* a mother. Julian has been called the first English woman of letters and the first English theologian to write in English. She reflects Christian optimism which is not dominated by sin and the Fall. Her spirituality is animated by grace and love. Julian is commemorated in the Episcopal calendar of the church year on May 8.

Julian of Norwich, Order of (OJN). A traditional, contemplative, semi-enclosed religious order in the Episcopal Church, located in Waukesha, Wisconsin. Its main purpose is to maintain a life of deep liturgical and silent prayer and intercession in the tradition of the great Christian mystics and contemplatives of past ages. It is named for Julian of Norwich, an English female mystic and anchoress. The order continues the medieval practice of including both monks and nuns with equal status in the same order. The order also has affiliated oblates and associates who follow a rule of life and live outside the community. The order publishes *Julian News*, which began publication in 1983. It was incorporated on July 12, 1982, and on Dec. 30, 1985, Father John-Julian Swanson took his life vows. In July 1986 full community life began when Sister Scholastica Marie Burton joined the order. *See* Julian of Norwich.

Junior Warden. *See* Wardens of a Parish.

Jurisdiction (episcopal). A bishop's canonical authority over an area, typically a diocese. The diocesan bishop has jurisdiction in his or her diocese. Jurisdiction is not held by bishops coadjutor, suffragan bishops, assisting bishops, resigned bishops, or retired bishops, although they may exercise other episcopal ministries. *See* Bishop.

Just War Theory. Proponents of just war theory claim that violent force should be used to protect innocent persons from attack. In contrast, pacifists maintain that war can never be just. Just war theory concerns the moral principles that indicate the justification and limitation of violent force. Drawing upon Roman ideas of just war, Ambrose and Augustine in the fourth and fifth centuries were the first Christian writers to develop a just war theory. A coherent theory based on cases that had been considered was first developed by Gratian in the twelfth century. This theory became the basis for international law. The criteria for going to war (*jus ad bellum)* include just cause, just authority, right intention, last resort, public declaration, probability of success, and proportionality. A favorable evaluation of proportionality means that the good to be achieved is greater than the evil to be suffered and inflicted. In addition, justice in the waging of war (*jus in bello)* has focused on two principles: proportionality in regard to the means of warfare rather than the ends; and discrimination or noncombatant immunity in regard to the damage to be caused by warfare. Contemporary Christian pacifism, including much pacifism in the Anglican Communion, comes not from absolute pacifism but from the judgment that modern warfare necessarily violates just war principles, particularly those of proportionality and noncombatant immunity.

Justice, Peace and the Integrity of Creation (JPIC). This program was mandated by the 1994 General Convention. The Justice, Peace and the Integrity of Creation Committee of the Executive Council was established at the Feb. 11–15, 1995, meeting of the Executive Council at Providence, Rhode Island. According to the enabling resolution, JPIC's mandate is "to facilitate communication and collaboration between the Executive Council and ministries throughout the Episcopal Church and Church Center units which address issues of peace, social and economic justice, and the environment." It carries on the work of the Jubilee Ministry program established by the 1982 General Convention; the Economic Justice Implementation Committee, which was created by the Executive Council after the 1988 General Convention; and the work of the Environmental Stewardship Team, which was created by action of the 1991 General Convention. During 1995–1997, the Racism Commission and the Global Peace with Justice initiative were added to the JPIC Committee. The committee is divided into five subcommittees: Anti-Racism, Global Peace and Justice, Economic Justice, Environmental Stewardship, and Jubilee Ministries. The Justice, Peace and the Integrity of Creation network met for the first time in Columbus, Ohio, Nov. 2–4, 1995.

Justification. The word (from the Latin *justus*, meaning "righteous," and *facere*, meaning "to make") is used in both the OT and NT to mean "being set in a right relation to another person or to God within the covenant. The Psalmist, realizing the weight of sin, acknowledged that God was "justified" in pronouncing judgment (Ps. 51:5). God was faithful to the old covenant, which required the Israelites to be morally righteous. St. Paul expressed the heart of the new covenant by the claim that Christians are "justified" by faith (trust) in the death of Christ, while nevertheless still sinners (Rom 5:1–11). Christians knew that they had been set in right relation to God in a new covenant although they were not morally righteous. They were justified by grace through faith (Eph 2.8). Justification became the Protestant cry against the medieval penitential system in the sixteenth-century Reformation. The penitential system was felt to require that penitents *make* themselves just by good works. Luther claimed that a believer was "*simul justus et peccator*" (at once in a right covenant relation and also sinner). Article XI of the Articles of Religion stated, "We are accounted righteous before God, only for the merit of our Lord and Savior Jesus Christ by faith and not for our work or deservings" (BCP, p. 870). An Agreed Statement by the second Anglican-Roman Catholic International Commission (ARCIC-II), *Salvation and the Church* (1987), noted that "the act of God in bringing salvation to the human race and summoning individuals into a community to serve him is due solely to the mercy and grace of God, mediated and manifested through Jesus Christ in his ministry, atoning death and rising again."

Justin the Martyr (c. 100–c. 165). Leading apologist, who has been called "one of the most original thinkers Christianity produced." He was born to Greek-speaking, pagan parents at Flavia Neapolis (Nablus), the ancient city of Shechem in Samaria. After a long search for the truth in pagan philosophies, he embraced Christianity around 130. Justin taught at Ephesus for awhile, where he disputed with Trypho the Jew. Later he moved to Rome, where he taught for the rest of his life. His *First* and *Second Apologies* were defenses of Christianity against charges of atheism, immorality, and disloyalty to the Roman Empire. He defended Christians on the basis of their superior moral lives, and he defended Christianity as the oldest monotheistic religion and the true philosophy. In his *Dialogue with Trypho the Jew*, Justin argued that the church is the true Israel and that only Christians can interpret the OT correctly. He provides considerable information about the celebration of baptism and the eucharist in the early church. Justin and six other Christians were arrested and then condemned to die by the prefect Junius Rusticus. They confessed the Christian faith and refused to sacrifice to the gods. They were scourged and beheaded at Rome. Justin is commemorated in the Episcopal calendar of the church year on June 1.

K

Kairos. 1) *Kairos* refers to a time of crisis and decision. The concept is drawn from Greek philosophy. The Christian *kairos* reflects the availability of salvation in Christ, which calls for a life-changing response of faith by the believer. This turning point or moment of decision takes place in chronological (clock) time, which is also known as *chronos*. But it also transcends the moment in time. God's dominion over time is implicit in the availability of salvation. Paul Tillich distinguished *chronos*, or mere measured quantitative time, from *kairos*, qualitative time as in "time of fulfillment." *Kairos* is time that is understood qualitatively in terms of moments of transcendence or redemption. *See* Chronos. 2) *Kairos* is the name for a movement of evangelism and conversion for prisoners. It is modeled on Cursillo, but adapted to the needs and requirements of the situation in prison. *Kairos* prefers to work with long-term prison residents, and seeks to christianize the prison environment. It provides an intense weekend of prayer, instruction, penitence, and celebration. *Kairos* seeks to bring Christ's love into the prison environment and to encourage conversion to Christ. *See* Cursillo.

Kamehameha (Feb. 9, 1834–Nov. 30, 1863) and Emma (Jan. 2, 1836–Apr. 25, 1885), King and Queen of Hawaii. Kamehameha IV became the King of Hawaii on Jan. 11, 1855. On June 19, 1856, he married Emma Rooke and she became queen. In 1860 they asked the Bishop of Oxford to send missionaries to Hawaii to establish the Anglican Church. On Oct. 11, 1862, Bishop Thomas N. Staley and two priests arrived in Hawaii. The king and queen were confirmed on Nov. 28, 1862. Their son and only child was born on May 20, 1858, but died on Aug. 27, 1862. This tragic death broke the king's heart, and he died shortly thereafter. Queen Emma declined to continue to rule and devoted herself to good works. It was under these two sovereigns that Anglicanism was established in Hawaii. They are commemorated in the Episcopal calendar of the church year on Nov. 28.

Kansas City, Diocese of. The Diocese of West Missouri was known as the Diocese of Kansas City from June 17, 1904, until May 13, 1914.

Kansas, Diocese of. The primary convention of the Diocese of Kansas met at St. Paul's Church, Wyandotte (now Kansas City), Aug. 11–12, 1859. On June 5, 1879, Grace Church, Topeka, was set apart as Grace Cathedral. The 1901 General Convention voted to divide the diocese and create a Missionary District in the western part of the state. The Diocese of Kansas includes the following counties: Allen, Anderson, Atchison, Bourbon, Brown, Butler, Chase, Chautauqua, Cherokee, Clay, Coffey, Cowley, Crawford, Dickinson, Doniphan, Douglas, Elk, Franklin,

Geary, Greenwood, Harvey, Jackson, Jefferson, Johnson, Labette, Leavenworth, Linn, Lyon, Marion, Marshall, Miami, Montgomery, Morris, Nemaha, Neosho, Osage, Pottawatomie, Riley, Sedgwick, Shawnee, Sumner, Wabaunsee, Washington, Wilson, Woodson, and Wyandotte.

Kansas Theological School, Topeka. This theological school operated from 1876 until 1918. In 1892 the charter was amended to permit the school to grant the degree of Bachelor of Divinity. The number of students varied from two to 26.

Kanuga Conference Center. The conference center is a mountain resort area, located at Kanuga, North Carolina. It is near Hendersonville. The idea of a summer conference center developed in 1923 and property was acquired shortly thereafter. It is now a large conference center that serves as a national center for major conferences, including meetings of the House of Bishops. The facilities are available throughout the year for conferences, retreats, and family outings.

Kataphatic. *See* Cataphatic.

Kearney, Missionary District of. The 1889 General Convention voted to divide the Diocese of Nebraska and create the Missionary District of The Platte. It was in existence from 1889 until 1946. From Oct. 10, 1907, until Oct. 14, 1913, it was known as the Missionary District of Kearney.

Keble College, Pass Christian, Mississippi. This school, named after John Keble, opened in 1951. The Rev. Hewitt Breneman Vinnedge (1898–1957) was its first president. It was to be a co-educational, liberal arts, pre-professional school. Vinnedge resigned as president in 1952 and the school closed.

Keble, John (Apr. 25, 1792–Mar. 29, 1866). One of the initiators of the Oxford (Tractarian) Movement in England. He was an Anglican priest and professor of poetry at Oriel College, Oxford. In 1833 he preached the sermon on "National Apostasy" before the Judges of Assize in the Church of St. Mary the Virgin, Oxford. This sermon defended the church, especially in view of the proposed suppression of ten Irish bishoprics by the civil government. This sermon by Keble is generally regarded as the beginning of the Oxford Movement. Keble wrote seven of the "Tracts for the Times." He also published *The Christian Year* (1827), a collection of poems for the Sundays and holy days of the year. This collection was the source of several popular hymn texts. *The Hymnal 1982* has two texts by Keble, including stanzas one and three of "Blest are the pure in heart" (Hymn 656) and "New every morning" (Hymn 10). Keble College, Oxford, was founded in his memory in 1870. Keble's life is commemorated in the Episcopal calendar of the church year on Mar. 29.

KEEP (Kiyosato Educational Experiment Project), American Committee for. Founded by American missionary Paul Rusch to bring food, health, faith, and hope for the youth of Kiyosato, an impoverished rural area in Japan. Rusch brought agricultural development, improvements in health care and hygiene, advances in education, and the Anglican tradition to this Japanese region. KEEP seeks to be an example of applied Christianity in action. The American Committee for KEEP supports the activities of KEEP in Japan. The Committee's theme is "Connecting the Separated: A Lasting Partnership of Americans & Japanese." Since there is not a precise date of founding, KEEP celebrates Rusch's birthday as Founder's Day. Rusch (1897–1979) first went to Japan in 1925 to help rebuild the Yokohama YMCA following the earthquake of 1923. He stayed as a lay missionary of the Episcopal Church and taught economics at St. Paul's University in Tokyo. On Nov. 30, 1927, he formed a Japanese branch of the Brotherhood of St. Andrew as a youth group for his students. With support from the Brotherhood, he formed a youth retreat in Kiyosato, a small rural village in the highlands of the Yatsugatake Mountain region. In 1938 he built Seisen-Ryo, a permanent lodge for residents and visitors of the camp. He was forced to leave Japan when war broke out at Pearl Harbor. Rusch returned to the United States, but went back to Kiyosato in 1945.

Keith, George (c. 1638–Mar. 27, 1716). First missionary for the Society for the Propagation of the Gospel. He was born in Aberdeen, Scotland. Keith was educated for the Presbyterian ministry of the Church of Scotland at Marischal College and received his M.A. degree from Aberdeen University in 1658. He joined the Quakers in 1662. Keith was harassed and imprisoned for his preaching. He came to the American colonies in 1668 and settled in

Philadelphia. Keith had theological controversies with the other Quaker leaders. After 1691 he organized his supporters as the "Christian Quakers," sometimes called "Keithians." He converted to Anglicanism in 1700 and joined the Church of England. Keith was ordained deacon in May of 1700, and priest in Mar. 1702. On Feb. 27, 1702, he was named the first missionary for the SPG and returned to America. From 1702 to 1704 he made an extensive missionary tour urging Quakers to join the Church of England. His work was especially effective in New Jersey. In 1705 he returned to England and served the remainder of his life as rector of Edburton in West Sussex. Keith died in Edburton. *See* Society for the Propagation of the Gospel in Foreign Parts.

Keith, Reuel (June 26, 1792–Sept. 1, 1842). Seminary professor and prominent low churchman. He was born in Pittsford, Vermont, and educated at Middlebury College in Vermont. He studied for the ordained ministry under John Prentiss Kewly Henshaw, later Bishop of Rhode Island, and at the Andover Theological Seminary. He was ordained deacon on May 10, 1817, and became assistant to the rector at St. John's Parish, Georgetown, Washington, D.C. While at St. John's he helped to establish Christ Church, Washington, and served as its rector, 1817–1820. He was ordained priest on May 24, 1818. He then moved to Williamsburg, Virginia, where he was professor of theology at the College of William and Mary and rector of Bruton Parish. The Virginia Theological Seminary opened in Oct. 1823, and Keith was professor of Old Testament literature, biblical criticism and evidence, as well as professor of pulpit eloquence and pastoral theology. He continued in this position until 1840. He has been described as a decided Calvinist and "the lowest of low churchmen." Keith died in Sheldon, Vermont. *See* Low Church.

Kelleran, Marion Macdonald (Apr. 20, 1905–June 27, 1985). Leader of the Anglican Communion and seminary professor. She was born in Byng Inlet, Ontario, Canada. Kelleran received her B.A. in 1926 from the University of Buffalo and did graduate study at Union Theological Seminary, New York, Harvard University, and the Episcopal Divinity School. She married the Rev. Harold C. Kelleran in 1934. She was director of Christian education for the Diocese of Washington, 1946–1962; and associate professor and then professor of Christian education and pastoral theology at Virginia Theological Seminary, 1963–1973. She was a founding member of the Anglican

Consultative Council, and became chairwoman of the council in 1973. She was also a member of the Executive Council of the Episcopal Church. As council chairwoman, she was the only woman among more than 440 men at the 1978 Lambeth Conference. Kelleran was recognized as an innovative educator, a missionary, and a leader of international Anglicanism. She retired from the Virginia Seminary faculty in 1973. Kelleran died in Alexandria, Virginia.

Kemp, James (May 20, 1764–Oct. 28, 1827). Second Bishop of Maryland. He was born in the parish of Keith Hall, Aberdeenshire, Scotland, and raised a Presbyterian. Kemp graduated from Marischal College, Aberdeen, in 1786, and came to America in the next year. He was attracted to the Episcopal Church and read for holy orders under the Rev. John Bowie, rector of Great Choptank Parish on the Eastern Shore of Maryland. He was ordained deacon on Dec. 26, 1789, and priest on Dec. 27, 1789. From 1790 until 1813, Kemp was rector of Great Choptank Parish, and in 1813–1814, he was associate rector of St. Paul's Church, Baltimore. On Sept. 1, 1814, he was consecrated Suffragan Bishop of Maryland, with the intention of succeeding the diocesan bishop. He became the second Bishop of Maryland on Aug. 2, 1816, and held that position until his death. Kemp was a high churchman. His election and consecration caused a minor schism in the church when some of his opponents formed the Evangelical Episcopal Church. Kemp died in New Castle, Delaware. *See* Evangelical Episcopal Church.

Kempe, Margery (c. 1373–d. after 1433). English mystic of the medieval period. She was born in Lynn, Norfolk, England. She was the wife of John Kempe, burgess of Lynn, by whom she had 14 children. After a period of mental illness, she received several visions. She and her husband went on a pilgrimage to Canterbury. In 1413 she began a series of pilgrimages. She went first to the Holy Land, Rome, and Germany. In 1417 she went to Compostela, Spain. In 1422 she went to Norway and Danzig. She describes her travels and her religious ecstasies in *The Booke of Margery Kempe*, which provides almost all the information we have on her life, her travels, and her mystical experiences. It is written in an unaffected prose style which uses such contemporary expressions as "thou wost no more what thou blabest than Balamis asse." She believed herself to be favored with singular signs of Christ's love, whereby for long periods she was conscious of her close connection with him. During these times she developed a strong compassion for the sins of the world. Apparently illiterate, she dictated her *Booke* to two clerks. The location of her death is not known. She has been considered for inclusion in the Episcopal calendar of the church year.

Kemper College. Nineteenth-century college named for the Rt. Rev. Jackson Kemper, the first Missionary Bishop of the Episcopal Church. Kemper had concluded that the only hope for supplying the west with clergy was to train westerners in the west. On Jan. 13, 1837, a charter for a college was granted with the qualification that the trustees would not use the name Missouri College, which had been agreed upon by the trustees and Bishop Kemper. In Kemper's absence, the trustees named the school Kemper College. In Apr. 1837 a 125-acre site was purchased. It was five miles from St. Louis. The college opened its doors on Oct. 15, 1838. In 1840 a medical school was opened. The school closed on Apr. 1, 1845, because of indebtedness.

Kemper, Jackson (Dec. 24, 1789–May 24, 1870). First missionary bishop of the Episcopal Church. He was born in Pleasant Valley, New York. He graduated from Columbia College in 1809 and studied for the ordained ministry under Bishop John Henry Hobart of New York. Kemper was ordained deacon on Mar. 10, 1811, and priest on Jan. 23, 1814. For twenty years he was assistant to Bishop William White in the United Parishes of Christ Church, St. Peter's, and St. James', Philadelphia. From the beginning of his ministry, Kemper championed western missions. He promoted a diocesan missionary society in Pennsylvania and was its first missionary. He was a prominent leader in the formation of the Domestic and Foreign Missionary Society in 1820 and 1821. He became the rector of St. Paul's Church, Norwalk, Connecticut, in 1831. On Sept. 25, 1835, he was consecrated Missionary Bishop of Indiana and Missouri. His jurisdiction grew to include Wisconsin, Iowa, Minnesota, Kansas, and Nebraska. Kemper visited General Theological Seminary in 1840 and inspired James Lloyd Breck, William Adams, and John Henry Hobart, Jr., to offer themselves for missionary work in the west. The following year they went to Wisconsin and founded Nashotah House. On Oct. 8, 1859, Kemper resigned his missionary jurisdictions and became the first Bishop of Wisconsin, where he remained until his death. A major result of his episcopate was seven organized dioceses, each with its own bishop. Kemper died in Delafield, Wisconsin, near Nashotah House. He is commemorated in the Episcopal calendar of the church year on May 24.

Kempis, Thomas (c. 1380–July 25, 1471). *See* Thomas à Kempis.

Ken, Thomas (July 1637–Mar. 19, 1711). Bishop of Bath and Wells, 1685–1691, Ken wrote devotional literature still popular among Anglicans, especially *The Practice of Divine Love* (1685). He was an important figure in early English hymnody, and two of his hymns are in *The Hymnal 1982*: "Awake, my soul, and with the sun" (Hymn 11), and "All praise to thee, my God, this night" (Hymn 43). The popular verse "Praise God, from whom all blessings flow," used in *The Hymnal* as the third verse of Hymn 380, "From all that dwell below the skies," was written by Ken. His dying words provide a succinct statement of the beliefs of the Caroline Divines: "I die in the Holy, Catholic and Apostolic Faith, professed by the whole Church before the division of east and west. More particularly I die in the Communion of the Church of England as it stands distinguished from all Papal and Puritan Innovations. . . ." His life is commemorated in the Episcopal calendar of the church year on Mar. 21. *See* Caroline Divines.

Kenosis. A Greek term which means "emptying." It appears in the christological hymn of Phil 2:6–11, where it means the giving up of divine glory by the eternal Son of God when he became incarnate. The Anglican theologian Charles Gore (1853–1932) popularized the term in Anglican theology as an explanation of the limitations of our Lord's human knowledge. Theologians had become acutely aware of these limitations through biblical criticism. Gore suggested that in the Incarnation the eternal Son of God voluntarily abandoned or emptied himself of certain divine attributes such as omnipotence and omniscience. This view was originally outlined in *Lux Mundi*, which Gore edited in 1889. Later, in response to criticism, Gore modified his position to say that the Son restrained his use of certain divine attributes. Arthur Michael Ramsey (1904–1988) noted that the real source of the kenotic doctrine of Christ's self-emptying is not the Philippians passage but consideration of the historical data of Jesus' life, considered along with belief in his deity. Although the doctrine of *kenosis* was helpful at the time in enabling Anglicans to come to terms with biblical criticism, it is less favored today. We accept the full humanity of Jesus, with its limitations. Jesus' embracing the fullness of our human nature did not compromise his divinity. We confess that God was uniquely and salvifically present and active in Jesus' humanity.

Kent School. Founded in 1906 by Frederick Herbert Sill of the Order of the Holy Cross, it is a coeducational Episcopal secondary school located in Kent, Connecticut. Sill envisioned the school as integral to the mission of his order and dedicated to the education of boys from families with modest financial means. He began classes at Kent in Sept. 1906 with a student body of seventeen young men. The school grew rapidly, and by 1916 it had more than 160 students. Known affectionately as "Pater," Sill served as headmaster for almost thirty-five years. He expressed his educational philosophy in words that became the school's motto: Simplicity of Life, Directness of Purpose, and Self-Reliance. William S. Chalmers, also a member of the Order of the Holy Cross, became headmaster in 1941. Conflict with the Order, however, led to the ending of its relationship with Kent in Sept. 1943. Chalmers was dispensed from monastic vows in 1945. He was succeeded in 1949 by John O. Patterson, also a priest. Under Patterson's direction a girls' division was opened on a separate campus in 1960. The two campuses were consolidated at the present site in 1992.

Kentucky, Diocese of. The Diocese of Kentucky was organized on July 8, 1829, at Christ Church, Lexington. The General Convention of 1895 divided the Diocese and created the Diocese of Lexington. The Diocese of Kentucky covers the western half of the state, including the following counties: Adair, Allen, Ballard, Barren, Breckinridge, Bullitt, Butler, Caldwell, Calloway, Carlisle, Carroll, Christian, Clinton, Crittenden, Cumberland, Daviess, Edmonson, Fulton, Graves, Grayson, Green, Hancock, Hardin, Hart, Henderson, Henry, Hickman, Hopkins, Jefferson, Larue, Livingston, Logan, Lyon, Marion, Marshall, McCracken, McLeane, Meade, Metcalfe, Monroe, Muhlenberg, Nelson, Ohio, Oldham, Russell, Shelby, Simpson, Spencer, Taylor, Todd, Trigg, Trimble, Union, Warren, Washington, and Webster. On May 24, 1894, Christ Church, Louisville, was set apart as Christ Church Cathedral.

Kenyon College, Gambier, Ohio. A coeducational, four-year liberal arts college founded by the Rt. Rev. Philander Chase, the first Bishop of Ohio, who wanted to establish "a school for the education of young men for the ministry."

He went to England to raise money for the project and met two of his greatest benefactors, Lord Kenyon and Lord Bexley. On Nov. 3, 1824, Bishop Chase and the diocese founded "The Theological Seminary of the Protestant Episcopal Church in the Diocese of Ohio" at Worthington. The school received its charter on Dec. 29, 1824. In 1828 the school was moved to Gambier as Kenyon College and Bexley Hall Theological Seminary. Bexley is no longer associated with Kenyon College. Kenyon is a member of the Association of Episcopal Colleges. *See* Bexley Hall; *see* Chase, Philander.

Kerygma. 1) A Greek term used in the NT to mean either the content or act of proclamation or preaching. The term began to be used in English and other modern western languages early in the twentieth century to signify the core of the Christian gospel. C. H. Dodd's *The Apostolic Preaching and Its Developments* (1936) helped to bring the word into common use among clergy, particularly as referring to the characteristic evangelistic formulations of the early church. In this usage, *kerygma* was to be distinguished from *didache*, a NT word for "teaching" that refers to the later elaboration of *kerygma*. 2) Predecessor to *Mission and Ministry*, published by Trinity Episcopal School for Ministry since 1982. Originally named *Christian Foundations*, this journal was published by the Fellowship of Witness beginning in 1965. The name was changed to *Kerygma* in 1976 when the Rev. Professor Leslie Parke Fairfield assumed responsibility for its publication.

Key, Francis Scott (Aug. 1, 1779–Jan. 11, 1843). Episcopal layman and author of "The Star Spangled Banner." He was born in Frederick, now Carroll, County, Maryland. Key studied at St. John's College, Annapolis, 1789–1796. After graduation he studied law in Annapolis. On Sept. 13–14, 1814, the British were firing on Fort McHenry in the Chesapeake Bay. Key was watching the fight in suspense during the night bombardment. At daybreak he was overjoyed to see the "Stars and Stripes" still flying over the fort. He wrote the poem, "The Star Spangled Banner." He also wrote a hymn, "Lord, with Glowing Heart I'd Praise Thee." Key was a religious person, and at one time he considered entering the ordained ministry. For many years he was a lay reader at St. John's Church, Georgetown. He was a deputy to six General Conventions from 1814 until 1826. Key died in Baltimore.

Keyser, Harriette Amelia (July 27, 1841–Oct. 9, 1936). Social reformer who lived and worked in New York City for almost a century. She was active in the labor movement and the campaign for women's suffrage. From 1896–1926 she served as executive secretary of the Church Association for the Interests of Labor (CAIL), at times also editing its journal, *Hammer and Pen*. She published her investigations of the working conditions and labor practices of industries ranging from New England fisheries to New York garment factories. Keyser led numerous reforms. She championed tenement house regulation and prohibition of child labor. Her books included two novels— *On the Borderland*, which featured the use of music as therapy for mentally ill patients, and *Thorns in Your Side*, which highlighted unfair labor practices. She also wrote *Bishop Potter, the People's Friend*, a biography of Bishop Henry Codman Potter of New York. An active member of the Society of the Companions of the Holy Cross, she joined other members of that society in petitioning the 1907 General Convention to involve the church more effectively in issues of social justice. This led to the appointment of the Joint Commission on Social Service.

King Charles the Martyr, Society of. Founded in England on Mar. 27, 1894, by the Hon. Mrs. Patrick (Ermengarda) Greville-Nugent, it works for the reinstatement of the Feast of King Charles the Martyr on Jan. 30 in the calendar of the church year throughout the Anglican Communion. Charles I (1600–1649) was king of Great Britain and Ireland from 1625 until his death. His ecclesiastical policies led to his defeat in the Civil War. He was a strong supporter of the catholic tradition, and he refused to sacrifice episcopacy in England after his defeat. Charles was executed by his enemies. His death has been seen as a martyrdom in defense of the church. From 1662 to 1859 Charles was commemorated in the calendar of the English Prayer Book. The society seeks to win recognition for Charles's defense of the Stuart Church and the apostolic ministry. It also encourages efforts to build churches and erect shrines dedicated to King Charles.

King Hall, Howard University (Washington, D.C.). From its beginning, Howard University in Washington, D.C., had a Theological Department to train African American ministers. On Jan. 15, 1889, the Board of the University resolved that the University would be glad to associate with denominations that might desire to establish divinity schools under their auspices and cooperate with them in giving the "colored population an educated minority in every branch of the Christian Church." King Hall, a building across the street from the campus, was purchased by the Episcopal Missionary Society in 1889. Professor William V. Tunnel of Howard University, an Episcopal priest, became the Warden (rector) of the new school. King Hall trained African American clergy for the Episcopal Church from 1889 until 1908.

King James (Authorized Version of the) Bible (KJV). This English translation of the Holy Scriptures of the Old Testament and New Testament, including the Apocrypha, was produced by Anglican bishops and other divines in 1611. It was undertaken in response to a request at the Hampton Court Conference, which was summoned by King James I of England and VI of Scotland in an attempt to reconcile Anglicans and Puritans. The KJV was a revision of earlier English versions, especially the so-called Bishops' Bible of 1568, which was based on the earlier translation by William Tyndale. The canons of the Episcopal Church recognize the KJV as "the historic Bible of this Church." However, it is also generally recognized today that the KJV has serious defects, especially in its use of inferior Hebrew and Greek texts. Although classic in its beauty, the language of the KJV is often difficult or misleading today.

King, Martin Luther, Jr. (Jan. 15, 1929–Apr. 4, 1968). Civil rights leader. He was born in Atlanta, Georgia, the son and grandson of African American Baptist preachers. He received his B.A. from Morehouse College in 1948 and was ordained a Baptist minister on Feb. 25, 1948. King received his M.Div. from the Crozer Theological Seminary, Philadelphia, in 1951. While a student at Crozer, he was exposed to the writings of Mohandas K. Gandhi. He was deeply impressed by Gandhi's faith in nonviolent protest. In 1955 King received his Ph.D. in Systematic Theology from Boston University. On Oct. 31, 1954, he was installed as the twentieth pastor of the Dexter Avenue Baptist Church in Montgomery, Alabama, where he stayed until 1960. On Dec. 1, 1955, Rosa Parks, an African American woman, refused to give up her seat on a bus to a white person. She was arrested. The African American community organized a bus boycott, and King became its leader. He soon became the leader of the civil rights movement in the United States and the nation's most ardent exponent of nonviolent social reform. The theme of the bus boycott was "We must stand up together so that we can sit down wherever we please." In Jan. 1957 the Southern Christian Leadership Conference was organized. King was its first president. Its motto was "To redeem the soul of America." On Jan. 24, 1960, King became the co-pastor with his father of Ebenezer Baptist Church in Atlanta, and stayed there until his death. King was frequently harassed and arrested. On Apr. 16, 1963, he published his well-known "Letter from Birmingham City Jail." In this letter he explained that Christian discipleship is at the heart of the African American struggle for justice. On Aug. 28, 1963, he gave the speech, "I Have a Dream," as the keynote address of the March on Washington for Civil Rights. King was given the Nobel Peace Prize on Dec. 10, 1964, for his efforts in getting the Civil Rights Act of 1964 passed. In the last several years before his death, he was a leader of the opposition to the war in Vietnam. At the beginning of Apr. 1968 he went to Memphis to participate in a sanitation workers' strike. On Apr. 3, the night before he was assassinated at the Lorraine Motel, he gave his "Mountain-top" speech at the Masonic Temple in Memphis. In this speech he said that he dreamed of an America free of racism and full of freedom. His ministry and witness are commemorated in the Episcopal calendar of the church year on Apr. 4.

Kingdom, the Power and the Glory, The. A collection of services and prayers for devotional occasions. It was first published in 1933 by Oxford University Press. It was subtitled "Services of Praise and Prayer for occasional Use in Churches." It was an American edition of the third volume of *The Grey Book*, a proposed revision of the English Prayer Book which was never adopted. Its occasional devotions include sections for acts of adoration, acts of recollection and self-examination, short services for the church year, litanies of intercession, acts of praise and thanksgiving, and prayers. It was recommended for use by the 1934 General Convention. It may be understood to be a precursor of the *BOS*. The section of prayers includes numbered prayers for special gifts and graces, for use on special occasions, intercessions, and commendations and benedictions. This section may be likened to the collection of occasional prayers in the BCP (pp. 814–835).

King's Chapel, Boston. The first Anglican church in Massachusetts, it also became the earliest recognized Unitarian congregation in America after the Revolution. The parish was organized on June 15, 1686, and the church building was opened for worship on June 30, 1689. King's Chapel remained an Anglican stronghold in Puritan New England throughout the colonial period. When British military forces abandoned Boston in 1776, the rector and many of the parish's Loyalist members fled to Nova Scotia. Although the church was reactivated under the leadership of lay reader James Freeman a few years later, the congregation held unorthodox theological views. They prepared their own edition of the Prayer Book with all references to the Trinity removed. Bishop Samuel Seabury refused to ordain Freeman because of his Unitarian beliefs. Freeman was ordained by the senior warden of the parish on Nov. 18, 1787. With Freeman's ordination, King's Chapel ceased to be an Anglican Church and became in effect the first Unitarian Church in America.

King's College, New York City. On Oct. 31, 1754, King George II of England granted the charter for King's College. On Nov. 22, 1753, the trustees invited the Rev. Samuel Johnson, rector of Stratford Parish in Connecticut, to be president. On July 17, 1754, Johnson began instruction in the vestry room of the schoolhouse of Trinity Church, New York City. On May 13, 1755, the corporation of Trinity Church conveyed to the trustees of the college a piece of land with the express condition that the president of the College be a member and communicant of the Church of England, and that the Prayer Book services of Morning and Evening Prayer be used for worship in the college. The first commencement was held on June 21, 1758. Several Episcopal clergy were presidents of the college. On May 1, 1784, the name was changed to Columbia College. In 1896 it was changed to Columbia University of the City of New York. Columbia no longer has any connection with the Episcopal Church.

Kiosk, The. "A Newsletter of The Anglican Academy, The Episcopal Diocese of Southern Ohio." A kiosk is used as a place to post items of interest about activities, events, and ideas.

Kip, William Ingraham (Oct. 3, 1811–Apr. 7, 1893). First Bishop of California. Born in New York City, Kip began his education at Rutgers and received his B.A. from Yale in 1831. He studied at the Virginia Theological Seminary, 1832–1833, and graduated from the General Theological Seminary in 1835. Kip was ordained deacon on June 28, 1835, and priest on Oct. 20, 1835. He was rector of St. Peter's Church, Morristown, New Jersey, 1835–1836, assistant rector of Grace Church, New York, 1836–1837, and rector of St. Paul's Church, Albany, New York, 1837–1853. On Oct. 28, 1853, Kip was consecrated Missionary Bishop of California. After California became a diocese, he was elected Bishop of California on Feb. 5, 1877. He served as bishop until his death. Kip was in the high church tradition. He wrote *The Double Witness of the Church* (1843), which stressed both the scriptures and catholic tradition, over against the evangelicals who stressed the Bible as the only rule of faith. He was the author of a number of other books. Kip died in San Francisco.

Kirk, Kenneth Escott (Feb. 21, 1866–June 8, 1954). A moral philosopher, he became Bishop of Oxford in 1937. The study of moral theology, which had been neglected after the seventeenth century in England, was revived by three pioneering works of Kirk: *Some Principles of Moral Theology* (1920), *Ignorance, Faith and Conformity* (1925), and *Conscience and its Problems* (1927). His monumental and enduring work came out of his 1928 Bampton Lectures, published in 1931 as *The Vision of God*. Kirk also wrote theological essays and contributed to *Essays Catholic and Critical* (1926) and *Essays on the Trinity and the Incarnation* (1928). He was an able administrator and a skillful pastor. During his episcopate he was able to integrate several English religious communities into the general life of the Church of England. He was known as an Anglo-catholic, but he was trusted by both Anglo-catholics and evangelicals in the church.

Kiss of Peace. A sign of peace which the people offer in the midst of the eucharistic liturgy. The practice of saluting one another with a kiss dates from ancient times and is recorded in several places in the NT. In the second century Justin wrote: "At the end of the prayers we greet one another with a kiss." Over the centuries the kiss, once exchanged by all, degenerated into a slight bow among the ministers at the altar. In the late middle ages a *pax brede* (peace board) was also passed among the people, who kissed it. The kiss of peace has two meanings, existing in tension: 1) the greeting of holy people, who love one another and share the peace of the risen Christ, and 2) the reconciliation of sinful people, who seek forgiveness before they share the sacred meal. In the Episcopal Church, consistent with ancient practice, the sign of peace occurs between the intercessions and the preparation of the bread and wine. It may also take place before or after the invitation to communion. The form varies from culture to culture—a kiss on the cheek, a hug, a handshake, hands placed between hands, a bow. The sign is accompanied by "any appropriate words of greeting" (BCP, p. 407). *See* Peace, The.

Klein, Walter Conrad (May 28, 1904–Mar. 1, 1980). Bishop and OT scholar. Klein was born in Brooklyn, New York. He graduated from Lehigh University in 1924 and from the General Theological Seminary in 1929. He was ordained deacon on May 17, 1927, and priest on June 24, 1928. From 1930 to 1943, he held parochial charges successively in New York, New Jersey, and Pennsylvania. He also served as lecturer at the Philadelphia Divinity School, and earned a Ph.D. from Columbia University in 1940. Following duty as a naval chaplain, he joined the staff of the Anglican Bishop of Jerusalem in 1946 and was a canon of St. George's Cathedral. From 1950 until 1959, Klein was professor of Old Testament Literature and Languages at Seabury-Western Theological Seminary. From July 1, 1959, until 1963, he was the dean of Nashotah House. On June 29, 1963, he was consecrated Bishop Coadjutor of Northern Indiana. He became Bishop of Northern Indiana on Nov. 1, 1963. Klein retired on June 23, 1972. He died in LaPorte, Indiana.

Knapp, Susan Trevor (Aug. 10, 1862–Nov. 21, 1941). A key architect of the deaconess movement in the United States, she graduated from the New York Training School for Deaconesses in 1894, worked for a year in Christian education, and then returned to the school to teach courses in NT and church history. She was set apart as a deaconess in 1899. Knapp traveled to England and met many of the founders of the English deaconess movement, including Randall Davidson who later became Archbishop of Canterbury. Their friendship forged an important link between the Episcopal Church and the Church of England. Knapp was appointed dean of the Training School for Deaconesses in 1903. She oversaw the development of curriculum as well as the transfer of the school from its original site at Grace Church to its new building on the grounds of the Cathedral of St. John the Divine. She visited deaconesses at work in the Far East in 1916 and returned to create better training programs for missionaries. She abruptly resigned her position as dean because the board of the school was suggesting an administrative reorganization. Knapp retired to Japan where she tutored students in Bible and English at St. Paul's University in Tokyo. She died in Los Angeles, California.

Kneel. A traditional posture of prayer in which one's weight rests on the knees. The pews of many churches have "kneelers" or cushions to protect the knees of those who kneel to pray. Kneeling to pray may express penitence, supplication, and humility. Depending on local custom and personal piety, worshipers may kneel to offer private prayer, during the prayers of the people, while saying the general confession and receiving absolution, during the Great Thanksgiving, to receive communion at the altar rail, during the prayer of thanksgiving after communion, and to receive the blessing. The more traditional of the two invitations to the confession of sin in the Rite 1 eucharistic liturgy (BCP, p. 330) includes a direction for the congregation to make their "humble confession to Almighty God, devoutly kneeling."

Recent liturgical reforms, following the ancient practice of the church, encourage the congregation to stand for prayer during most of the times of the service when kneeling has been customary. For example, the rubric in the Rite 2 eucharistic liturgy directs that the people may "stand or kneel" after the *Sanctus* (BCP, p. 362). This emphasis is reversed in the Rite 1 eucharistic liturgy, which states that the people may "kneel or stand" (BCP, p. 334). Many believe that standing for the eucharistic prayer emphasizes the eucharist to be a celebration in community rather than an expression of penitence by individuals.

Koinonia. The common life and fellowship of love shared by Christians with Christ and with each other in Christ. It is a Greek term for "communion" or "participation." A rich theology of *koinonia* is found in the Pauline letters and elsewhere in the NT. This saving fellowship with Christ is made possible through the Holy Spirit (Phil 2:1; 2 Cor 13:13). Paul's collection for the relief of the church in Jerusalem was an expression of *koinonia* (Rom 15:26, 2 Cor 8–9). *Koinonia* with Christ was the basis of Paul's appeal for love and harmony in the chaotic Christian community at Corinth (1 Cor 1:9–10). The reality of this *koinonia* is expressed in the sacrament of the eucharist (1 Cor 10:16–17). We may share in the community and fellowship of Christ's sufferings and thereby share in the power and glory of Christ's resurrection (Phil 3:10–11). *Koinonia* is listed as one of the four features of Christian community in Acts, expressed concretely in the sharing of goods (2:42). In 1 Jn 1:3, fellowship with the original eyewitnesses in the Christian community is understood in terms of fellowship with the Father and with Christ.

Kontakion. In Orthodox worship, a short hymn in honor of a saint or the departed. A *Kontakion*, "Give rest, O Christ, to your servant," is used in the Burial Office of the BCP as an anthem at the commendation. It is repeated as an antiphon at the commendation (p. 499). *The Hymnal 1982* provides a musical setting of this *Kontakion* (Hymn 355).

Kyoto, Missionary District of. The 1898 General Convention voted to divide the Missionary District of Tokyo and erect the Missionary District of Kyoto. This missionary district existed until 1941, when it was transferred to the Holy Catholic Church in Japan. The last Episcopal Missionary Bishop of Kyoto resigned on Feb. 4, 1942.

Kyrie eleison. In the early church, in the east, the Greek supplication *Kyrie eleison* ("Lord, have mercy") was the common response to intercessory biddings addressed to the people. It is now used in the eucharist at the entrance rite and the general intercessions. 1) In the Episcopal Church, *Kyrie eleison* may be sung or said in place of the *Gloria in excelsis* in the entrance rite in seasons other than Christmas and Easter in Rite 2 services. It may be sung or said in place of or in addition to the *Gloria in excelsis* in Rite 1 services. Some parishes use it during the penitential season of Lent. *Kyrie eleison* alternates with *Christe eleison* ("Christ have mercy"). The chant may be sung or said threefold, sixfold, or ninefold, in Greek or in English (BCP, p. 406). 2) *Kyrie eleison* is the response in intercessory litanies such as Forms I and V of the prayers of the people, which are based on early eastern prayers (BCP, pp. 383, 389).

Kyrie Pantokrator. The canticle *Kyrie Pantokrator* or "A Song of Penitence" appears as Canticle 14 in Morning Prayer, Rite 2, of the BCP (pp. 90–91). It is compiled from several verses of the Prayer of Manasseh, included in some Greek versions of the Hebrew Scriptures. The BCP suggests it for use in Lent at Morning Prayer on Sunday, Wednesday, and Friday and at Evening Prayer on Monday. It is also a Lenten song in the Byzantine and Mozarabic rites. It is especially suitable for use in Lent and other penitential occasions.

L

Labarum. Military standard of the imperial Roman legions from the time of Constantine I (c. 285–337). It featured the Christian monogram of the Greek letters Chi (X) and Rho

(P), which begin the word "Christ." Constantine was Roman emperor from 306 to 337. Prior to battle with an imperial rival at the Milvian Bridge near Rome in 312, Constantine had a vision that apparently led to his conversion to Christianity. He saw a fiery cross in the heavens above the statement written in Greek, "In this sign you will conquer." According to Lactantius, Constantine had a dream telling him to place the Chi-Rho monogram on the shields of his soldiers. Slightly different accounts of this story are provided by Lactantius and Eusebius of Caesarea. After Constantine's victory at the Milvian Bridge, he and the emperor Licinius published the Edict of Milan in 313. It granted religious freedom throughout the Roman Empire. Constantine was a strong supporter of Christianity, and sought to build a Christian empire. The labarum was widely used as a Constantinian insignia. The Chi-Rho is an ancient Christian symbol that is still used as a sacred monogram today.

Ladd, William Palmer (May 13, 1870–July 1, 1941). Church historian and seminary dean. Ladd was born in Lancester, New Hampshire. He received his B.A. from Dartmouth in 1891 and his B.D. from the General Theological Seminary in 1897. He also studied at the University of Paris, Oxford University, and the University of Leipzig. Ladd was ordained deacon on June 11, 1897, and priest on June 11, 1898. He was the rector of St. Barnabas Church, Berlin, New Hampshire, 1897–1902. Ladd was professor of church history (1904–1941) and dean (1918–1941) at Berkeley Divinity School, New Haven, Connecticut. During the early years of his deanship at Berkeley his progressive views on economic and justice issues caused him to be branded a "Bolshevist." He was responsible for the removal of Berkeley from Middletown, Connecticut, where it had been founded, to New Haven. Berkeley was later affiliated with Yale University. Ladd's major publication was *Prayer Book Interleaves* (1943). He died in New Haven. *See* Berkeley Divinity School.

Lady Chapel. A side chapel dedicated to "Our Lady," the Blessed Virgin Mary. It was often an addition that was constructed directly behind (east of) the high altar of the larger church building.

Laetare Sunday. The fourth Sunday of Lent in the Roman Catholic liturgical calendar. The term is derived from the opening words of the Latin Mass, "Rejoice (*Laetare*) Jerusalem" (Is 66:10). The church is called to joyful anticipation of the victory to be won. This joyful theme provides lightening from the penitential emphasis of Lent. Since the thirteenth century the celebrant of the eucharist has been permitted to wear rose-colored vestments which express the change of tone in the Lenten observance. Laetare Sunday therefore may be called "Rose Sunday." This custom is not required in the Episcopal Church, but it is observed by some parishes with a traditional Anglo-catholic piety. *See* Gaudete Sunday.

Laity. The people of God. The term is from the Greek *laos*, "the people." The laity has been defined negatively to indicate Christians who have not been ordained. However, all baptized Christians are the people of God, the church, a royal priesthood, a holy nation (1 Pt 2:9–10). All baptized persons are members of the Body of Christ, the church, but with different functions and ministries (Rom 12:4–8; 1 Cor 12:12). All Christian ministries and vocations represent specific ways of living out the baptismal covenant (see BCP, pp. 304–305). The ministers of the church are lay persons, bishops, priests, and deacons (BCP, p. 855). The ministry of the laity is "to represent Christ and his Church; to bear witness to him wherever they may be; and, according to the gifts given them, to carry on Christ's work of reconciliation in the world; and to take their place in the life, worship, and governance of the Church" (BCP, p. 855). Clericalism unfortunately caused some to view the ordained as the only real ministers of the church and to regard the laity as inferior to the clergy. Increasing appreciation of lay ministry has accompanied a renewed emphasis on the significance of baptism, and a growing understanding that the various ministries of the church can support and uphold one another. The ministries and orders of the church are to be complementary, and not mutually exclusive. Accordingly, the 1979 BCP encourages the participation of all orders of ministry in the worship of the church.

Lambeth College, Kittanning, Pennsylvania. This school, first known as Kittanning Collegiate School, was granted a charter on Sept. 7, 1868. The nine trustees were Episcopalians and the Bishop of Pittsburgh was *ex officio* chancellor of the corporation. It was named after the first Lambeth Conference which met Sept. 24–28, 1867. The college never awarded any degrees and closed in 1876.

Lambeth Conference. The first Lambeth Conference met in 1867, marking the occasion when the various churches of the Anglican Communion began to be conscious of themselves as a single family of churches.

The immediate cause of the first gathering was an effort on the part of several bishops to respond to the unsettling effects of the publication of *Essays and Reviews* and the "Colenso controversy." The "Colenso controversy" followed the arraignment of John Colenso, Bishop of Natal, on charges of heresy for holding "advanced" views of the creation stories in the OT. The debate aroused intense feelings. A jurisdictional dispute between two bishops in South Africa regarding the controversy became a matter of concern for all the colonial churches of England.

In 1867 Charles Thomas Longley, Archbishop of Canterbury, responding to an appeal from Canada, invited Anglican bishops from all over the world to Lambeth for the purposes of mutual discussion and consultation. The meeting, neither a synod nor general council, was a purely informal gathering of bishops meeting at the invitation of the Archbishop of Canterbury. The informal gathering continues to have no power to make binding decisions. The Conference has met at ten-year intervals, except during time of war. Its deliberations command considerable moral authority. From time to time it has made significant pronouncements, notably its *Appeal to All Christian People* (1920), a major ecumenical document.

Lambeth Palace. The London residence of the Archbishop of Canterbury for seven centuries. It is located on the Thames Embankment opposite the Houses of Parliament, and it has been the location of many historic events. The followers of Wycliffe were imprisoned and tortured at the Lollard's Tower (erected 1320). The English archbishops consecrated William White and Samuel Provoost as the first American bishops in the English succession in the chapel (built 1245). In 1867 in the Hall (built in the seventeenth century), the bishops of the Anglican Communion met for the first of a series of Lambeth Conferences.

Lambeth Quadrilateral. *See* Chicago-Lambeth Quadrilateral.

Lamp, The. First published on Feb. 2, 1903, by the Rev. Paul James Francis Wattson of the Society of the Atonement, it was the voice of the pro-Roman high church party of the Episcopal Church. When Wattson and 15 other members of the society joined the Roman Catholic Church in 1909, they took *The Lamp* with them.

Lappets. In ecclesiastical usage, these are the pendant bands or flaps on a clerical vestment or headdress, especially a mitre.

Laramie, Missionary District of. The 1889 General Convention voted to divide the Diocese of Nebraska and create the Missionary District of The Platte. From Oct. 20, 1898, until Oct. 10, 1907, it was known as the Missionary District of Laramie. It included not only the western counties of Nebraska but also that portion of Wyoming lying east of the west line of the counties of Sheridan, Johnson, Latrona, and Carbon.

"Last Gospel, The." The reading of a gospel passage, typically the prologue to the Gospel of John (1:1–18), at the end of the Latin Mass. The practice dates from medieval times. It originally was said as a private devotion by the priest on returning to the sacristy at the end of the service. It was later read aloud by the priest at the altar. This became general practice with the *Missale Romanum* of Pius V, published in 1570. The reading of the last gospel was suppressed in 1964 as part of the liturgical reform of Vatican II. The reading of the last gospel has never been a general practice in Anglican worship, although it has been done in some Anglo-catholic parishes.

Last Rites. Sacramental ministry to a dying Christian, which may include confession and absolution, laying on of hands, anointing (extreme unction), and communion. The dying received communion as *viaticum*, or sustenance for a journey, in accordance with ancient custom. The BCP provides forms for the Reconciliation of a Penitent (pp. 447–452), an order for Ministration to the Sick that includes the ministry of the word, laying on of hands and anointing, and Holy Communion (pp. 453–457). If communion is administered from the reserved sacrament, the form for Communion under Special Circumstances (pp. 396–399) is used. The BCP also provides a form for Ministration at the Time of Death, which includes a Litany at the Time of Death and prayers for a vigil (pp. 462–467). Prayers of commendation for the departed have been dated from the fourth century.

Last Supper. The term "Last Supper" does not appear in the NT. It is used to refer to the supper which Jesus ate with his disciples on the evening before his crucifixion. It is described somewhat differently in the gospel accounts (see Mt 26:17–29; Mk 14:12–16; Lk 22:7–23), and in Paul's reference to it in 1 Cor 11:23–26. The phrase "Lord's Supper" could be based on Paul's use of the term "Lord" in his description of the meal. This dinner is described as a Passover meal in the synoptic gospels but as a pre-Passover meal in John. Jesus instituted the eucharist at the Last Supper when he identified the bread with his body and the wine with his blood of the new covenant. Jesus commanded his disciples to "do this" in remembrance of him. Christian understanding of the Last Supper has also emphasized table fellowship shared by Jesus with his disciples and its eschatological implications. *See* Eucharist.

Latimer, Hugh (1490–Oct. 16, 1555). Bishop and Reformation leader. He was born in Thurcaston, Leicestershire, England, and studied at Cambridge University. At first he was a bitter opponent of the Reformation. Consecrated Bishop of Worcester on Sept. 26, 1535, he quickly became one of the Reform leaders. Although he supported Henry VIII in the dissolution of the monasteries, he played little part in various attempts to introduce changes in church doctrine. His sermons stimulated interest in reform by attacking the superstitions of the clergy and the poverty of those whom they served. He had his greatest fame as a preacher. His career came to an abrupt end when he opposed the Six Articles of Henry VIII. Latimer's stand was in accordance with his Protestant beliefs. He resigned his see on July 1, 1539. For the remainder of Henry's reign, Latimer was in the shadow of virtual exile. When Edward VI came to the throne in 1547, Latimer again became a popular preacher. He denounced social and ecclesiastical abuse. His views were suspect when Queen Mary came to power in 1553. On Sept. 13, 1553, he was imprisoned in the Tower and placed in the same room with Thomas Cranmer and Nicholas Ridley. He was burned at the stake in front of Balliol College, Oxford. He exhorted Nicholas Ridley, his fellow victim, with the famous words, "Be of good comfort, Master Ridley, and play the man; we shall this day light such a candle by God's grace in England as I trust shall never be put out." Latimer, along with Ridley and Cranmer, is commemorated in the Episcopal calendar of the church year on Oct. 16.

Latitudinarian, Latitudinarianism. Spiritual descendants of sixteenth-century humanists like Erasmus and the ancestors of the nineteenth-century broad church party. The middle years of the seventeenth century in England were marked by religious civil war, with royalists (Episcopalians) pitted against Puritans who had left the national church. Those outside the national church included Presbyterians, independents, and sectarians. Oliver Cromwell died in 1658, and his Puritan Commonwealth ended in great disillusionment and unpopularity. In 1660 the Stuart monarchy was restored under Charles II. The restored Stuart kings, however, flirted with Roman Catholicism. This was equally unpalatable to a vast majority of the English. After 1688, the latitudinarians sought to end religious controversy, to make the established church as inclusive as possible, to provide toleration for dissent, and to minimize the importance of doctrine and forms of worship in the interests of "reasonableness."

Although many of the "latitude men," like the Cambridge Platonists and their intellectual successor, John Locke, possessed a deep personal piety, some latitudinarians tended toward deism in religion. They saw the church as a department of the state. They considered the church to be necessary to preserve and encourage morality and to support a Protestant monarchy. Gilbert Burnet's *Exposition of the Thirty-Nine Articles* (1699) was written from this point of view.

Latria. This technical term is for the worship which is rightfully given to God alone, as distinguished from the appropriate veneration of the saints (*dulia*) or of images such as icons or relics. *See* Dulia.

Laud, William (Oct. 6, 1573–Jan. 10, 1645). Archbishop of Canterbury and the chief theological advisor of kings Charles I and Charles II of England. Laud was born in Reading, England. He studied at St. John's College, Oxford University. In his dissertation he stressed the divine right of episcopacy. He was ordained deacon and priest in 1601. In 1611 he became president of St. John's College and in that position was a leading opponent of Calvinism. Laud became dean of Gloucester in 1616. On Nov. 18, 1621, he was consecrated Bishop of St. David's in Wales. On Sept. 18, 1626, he became Bishop of Bath and Wells, and on July 15, 1628, he became Bishop of London. He was named Archbishop of Canterbury in 1633. Laud was a practical reformer. He enforced the canons of the church and restored the dignity of public worship. Laud encouraged the use of the surplice, kneeling to receive Holy Communion, bowing at the name of Jesus, placing the altar at the east end of the church, railed altars, and making the sign of the cross. He became one of the most unpopular statesmen of his day. He was unsuccessful in his attempt to enforce liturgical reform in Scotland. His attempts to tighten church organization and impose uniformity of ritual made him the object of intense popular hatred. His policies toward religious dissidents in England and Scotland was a major cause of the outbreak of the English Civil War. He was accused and found guilty of treason by the House of Commons and beheaded on Tower Hill. Laud is commemorated in the Episcopal calendar of the church year on Jan. 10.

Lauds. The ancient service at daybreak in the monastic round of daily prayer. This morning service of praise always included Psalms 148–150, in which the Latin word *"laudate"* (praise) is frequently emphasized. The name of this morning office is derived from the Latin term. The services of matins, lauds, and prime formed the basis of Cranmer's office of Matins in the 1549 Prayer Book, which became Morning Prayer in the 1552 BCP.

Laurence (or Lawrence), Saint (d. Aug. 10, 258). Deacon and martyr. Laurence was ordained a deacon by Pope Sixtus II. He was made chief of the seven deacons in Rome. When asked by the Roman governor during the persecution under emperor Valerian to surrender the church's riches, Laurence gathered together a large number of the blind, the lame, the maimed, lepers, orphans, and widows. Laurence said, "Here is the treasure of the Church." According to tradition, he was roasted alive on an iron grill, and is reported to have said to his executioners, "I am done on this side. Turn me over." More probably he was beheaded on Aug. 10, 258. In Rome the basilica of St. Laurence-Outside-the-Walls (San Lorenzo fuori de Mura) is dedicated to him. His martyrdom was one of the first to be commemorated by the church. Laurence's witness is commemorated in the Episcopal calendar of the church year on Aug. 10.

Laus tibi. "Praise to you, Lord Christ." The term is from the opening words of the statement in Latin. It is the people's response to the gospel at the eucharist (BCP, p. 358). It follows the concluding statement by the gospeler, "The Gospel of the Lord." This response was included in the 1928 BCP on an optional basis. It is no longer optional. It is omitted before the Passion gospel on the Sunday of the Passion (Palm Sunday), and Good Friday (BCP, pp. 272, 277).

Lavabo. Ceremonial cleansing of the celebrant's hands at the offertory of the eucharist. The term is from the Latin, "I will wash," taken from the opening of Ps 26:6, "I will wash my hands in innocence, O Lord, that I may go in procession round your altar." This verse was traditionally recited by the celebrant during the lavabo ceremony.

After the altar is prepared, and before the Great Thanksgiving, the celebrant may wash his or her hands in a small bowl called a lavabo bowl. An acolyte or server assists by holding the bowl and pouring water over the celebrant's hands. The celebrant's hands are dried on a lavabo towel which hangs over a wrist of the server at the lavabo ceremony. The lavabo is not mentioned by the Prayer Book, but it is practiced in many parishes.

Law, William (1686–Apr. 9, 1761). Spiritual writer, priest, and Non-Juror. Law is most famous as the author of *A Serious Call to a Devout and Holy Life* (1728), which is a call to a life of piety and devotion. A holy life is devotion to God and a regular method of daily prayer. *A Serious Call*, which was inspired by the teachings of such spiritual writers as Thomas à Kempis, is a forceful exhortation to embrace the Christian life in its moral and ascetical fullness. His major thesis was the unalterable love of God as expressed in Jesus Christ. *A Serious Call* had a profound impact on Charles and John Wesley. Law was born in King's Cliffe, Northamptonshire, England. He received his B.A. from Emmanuel College, Cambridge University, in 1708, and was ordained priest in 1711. When Queen Anne died in 1714, he was unable to take the oath of allegiance to King George I and the House of Hanover, and thus became a nonjuror. For 12 years he was a tutor at Putney. In 1740 he retired to his native village where he eventually died. He is commemorated in the Episcopal calendar of the church year on Apr. 9.

Lawrence, Charles Radford II (May 2, 1915–Apr. 3, 1986). The first African American president of the House of Deputies. He was born in Boston, Massachusetts. Lawrence received his B.A. from Morehouse College in 1936, his M.A. from Atlanta University in 1938, and his Ph.D. from Columbia University in 1952. Lawrence taught in the Atlanta public schools, 1936–1939. He was the student YMCA secretary of the Southeast Region, 1941–1942. From 1943 until 1947, he was an instructor and then research associate at Fisk University. In 1948 Lawrence joined the faculty of Brooklyn College and became chairman of the Sociology Department in 1966. He retired in 1977. Lawrence was the twenty-eighth president of the House of Deputies. He served from Sept. 20, 1976, until Sept. 14, 1985. He was elected in 1976, 1979, and 1982. He was senior warden at Trinity Church, New York City, and vice-chairman of the Executive Council of the Episcopal Church. He also served on the Board of Trustees of General Theological Seminary, and was a member of the Anglican Consultative Council. Lawrence died in Pomona, New York.

Lawrence, William (May 30, 1850– Nov. 6, 1941). Bishop, educator, fund-raiser, and primary founder of the Church Pension Fund. He articulated a theology of Christian stewardship known as the "Gospel of Wealth." In an article entitled "The Relation of Wealth to Morals" (1901), he argued that God gives wealth only to those who are moral. The wealthy in return bear the responsibility of serving their communities so that their prosperity can help uplift others. Born in Boston, Lawrence graduated from Harvard College in 1871, and received a B.D. from the Episcopal Theological School (ETS.) in 1875. He was ordained deacon on June 20, 1875, and priest on June 11, 1876. He served at Grace Church, Lawrence, Massachusetts, between 1876 and 1883. In Jan. 1884 he returned to ETS as professor of homiletics and pastoral care, and later served as dean of ETS from 1889 to 1893. Lawrence was consecrated Bishop of Massachusetts on Oct. 5, 1893. Although he retired in 1927, he maintained an active presence in educational and social affairs. He died in Milton, Massachusetts.

Lay Eucharistic Minister (LEM). Lay person licensed by the bishop to administer the consecrated elements of the eucharist. Lay eucharistic ministers may be licensed to administer the consecrated bread and wine at any celebration of the eucharist in the absence of a sufficient number of priests and deacons to assist the celebrant. They may also be licensed to go from a Sunday eucharist or other principal celebrations of the eucharist to share the sacrament with members of the congregation who were unable to be present at the celebration because of illness or infirmity. Lay eucharistic ministers may be licensed for either or both ministries. This ministry is understood to be an extraordinary ministry, and is not to take the place of the ministry of priests and deacons concerning the administration of the eucharist. Prior to the current lay ministry canons, specially licensed lay readers administered the chalice at the eucharist and were known as "chalice bearers."

Lay, Henry Champlin (Dec. 6, 1823–Sept. 17, 1885). Bishop of the Southwest, Arkansas, and Easton. He was born in Richmond, Virginia. Lay graduated from the University of Virginia in 1842, and from the Virginia Theological Seminary in 1846. He was ordained deacon on July 10, 1846, and began his ministry at Lynnhaven Parish in Virginia. Lay was ordained priest on July 12, 1848, and served as rector of the Church of the Nativity, Huntsville, Alabama, until 1859. On Oct. 23, 1859, he was consecrated Missionary Bishop of the Southwest, sometimes called Arkansas and the Indian Territory. At the primary convention of the Diocese of Arkansas in Nov. 1862 he was elected the third Bishop of Arkansas. Lay was one of the first southern bishops to advocate reunion with the Episcopal Church at the end of the Civil War. He and Bishop Thomas Atkinson of North Carolina were the only two southern bishops to attend the 1865 General Convention at which Presiding Bishop John Henry Hopkins offered them a "cordial welcome." On Apr. 1, 1869, he became the first Bishop of Easton. Lay died in Baltimore.

Lay Ministry. The term refers to the many ways the laity of the church live out their baptismal covenant. The laity are the people of the church, those who have been baptized. It generally refers to those who have not been ordained. The term "laity" is derived from the Greek word for "people." Lay ministry is exercised in the "gathered" church through the organizations of the church (e.g., vestry, Christian education, parish programs, etc.) and in the "scattered" church as the ministry of the baptized is expressed in the home, in the marketplace, and in the many places where there are opportunities to live the Christian faith. The ministry of lay persons includes bearing witness to Christ wherever they may be. The Catechism notes that "the ministers of the Church are lay persons, bishops, priests, and deacons" (BCP, p. 855). The laity is also know as the Lay Order. The various ministries of the church are complementary, not mutually exclusive or competitive. *See* Lay Order.

Lay Order. The laity are the people of the church, those who have been baptized. The term "laity" generally refers to those who have not been ordained. In a vote "by orders" at a church convention, clergy and laity vote separately.

An affirmative decision requires a majority of votes in each order to pass. *See* Lay Ministry.

Lay Preacher. A lay person licensed by the bishop to preach. This ministry is licensed under the provisions of the canon for licensed lay persons. The lay preacher must be a confirmed adult communicant in good standing, and recommended by the member of the clergy in charge of the congregation. Guidelines for training and selection of lay preachers are established by the bishop. A lay preacher is to be trained, examined, and found competent in the Holy Scriptures, the BCP and *The Hymnal*, the conduct of public worship, use of the voice, church history, Christian ethics and moral theology, the church's doctrine as set forth in the creeds and An Outline of the Faith (BCP, pp. 845–862), appropriate canons, pastoral care, and homiletics. A licensed lay preacher is to preach only upon the initiative and under the supervision of the member of the clergy in charge. Lay preachers may be commissioned for this ministry with a form adapted from the Commissioning for Lay Ministries in the Church in the *BOS*.

Lay Professional. Lay people employed in the mission and ministry of the church who regard their work as a vocation. These lay professionals see their work as their response to God's call in their lives and have acquired appropriate preparation and training for their work. They are committed to continuing education to improve their skills and to enhance their performance. They hold themselves accountable to the particular institutional structure within which they work and to the wider community of the faithful.

Lay Reader. A lay person licensed by the bishop to lead public worship under the direction of the member of the clergy in charge of the congregation. This ministry is licensed under the provisions of the canon for licensed lay persons. The lay reader must be a confirmed adult communicant in good standing and recommended by the member of the clergy in charge of the congregation. Guidelines for training and licensing of lay readers are established by the bishop. Licensed lay readers may be commissioned for this ministry with a form provided by the *BOS*. Lay readers have traditionally held an important place in the American church, dating from colonial times when clergy were scarce. The first American Prayer Book (1789) used the word "Minister" instead of "Priest" in rubrics in various places to allow greater participation of lay readers in the worship of the church.

A lay reader may lead the Daily Offices of the church. If needed, a lay reader may lead the liturgy for the Holy Eucharist through the prayers of the people, concluding with the Lord's Prayer and the grace, or with the exchange of the peace (BCP, p. 407). A lay reader may also lead the Burial Office (BCP, p. 490), as well as the Ash Wednesday liturgy (BCP, p. 269), the Palm liturgy (BCP, p. 272), and the Good Friday liturgy (BCP, p. 282). However, certain modifications in these services are required when led by a lay reader. There is no blessing of the people by a lay reader. A lay reader who leads the confession of sin at Morning or Evening Prayer is to use a modified form for the absolution that asks for God to "have mercy on *us*, forgive *us* all our sins," to "strengthen *us* in all goodness," and to "keep *us* in eternal life" (BCP, p. 80, emphasis added). A similar modification in the absolution is made by a lay reader who leads the penitential order at the beginning of the eucharist (BCP, p. 353). A lay reader who leads the Ash Wednesday service is to remain kneeling after the Litany of Penitence and substitute the prayer for forgiveness appointed at Morning Prayer. The Good Friday service concludes with the Lord's Prayer and a final prayer when the service is led by a lay reader.

Laying on of Hands. A significant ritual action in several sacramental rites. It is an external sign of the bestowal of God's grace through the prayer or the ministry of the one laying on hands, whether for spiritual growth or ministry or forgiveness or healing. It is the action which accompanies the prayer of consecration in ordination rites. It is a prominent action in the Ministration to the Sick. It accompanies the baptismal signing with the cross, and the pronouncing of the priestly absolution in the Reconciliation of Penitents. It may also accompany the nuptial blessing or other blessings. The term may be used as a synonym for confirmation.

Layman's Magazine. The first weekly publication in the Episcopal Church, this periodical was edited by the Rev. Benjamin Allen (1789–1829) from 1815 through 1816. It carried church news and stories for lay persons. The last issue available is dated Nov. 7, 1816.

Layman's Magazine of the Living Church. This journal was published as one of the weekly issues of *The Living*

Church. It was also published as a separate monthly periodical from Feb. 1940 until Sept. 1941.

Leadership Academy for New Directions (LAND). A mission development program for the church in small communities. It is primarily designed to serve archdeacons, rural deans, rectors of cluster parishes, members of diocesan boards or commissions, or others concerned with planning, training, coordination, or supervision in areas having small communities and (usually) small churches. In contrast to the usual demeaning status of mission congregations, LAND bases its vision on "New Directions," a set of principles distilled from the teaching of Roland Allen. This involves a systemic change to lay responsibility, regional coordination of small congregations, and a theological and biblical view of the church. The ordination of respected local leaders who continue to support themselves by secular work is seen as a successful and desirable mission strategy for many situations. The LAND classes begin with an intensive two-week training session held each year in a conference center in a different part of the country. Participants return home to carry out a project implementing some aspect of New Directions in their own area of responsibility. The following year there is a one-week session in which projects are compared, critiqued, and analyzed. Qualified persons from different parts of the church are engaged as faculty. LAND began at Roanridge, Kansas City, Missouri, in 1975. *See* Allen, Roland; *see* Porter, Harry Boone; *see* Roanridge Training Conference Center.

Leadership Program for Musicians Serving Small Churches. A joint venture of the Standing Commission on Church Music and the Virginia Theological Seminary. The goal of the program's work is to discover and implement ways to help small parishes in church music endeavors which might lead to more effective, inclusive, and inspirational worship. The Presiding Bishop's Diploma in Church Music is awarded to participants who complete six areas of study: basic church music; teaching new music to the congregation; service playing and accompaniment (for keyboard players and guitar players); survey of *The Hymnal 1982*; liturgy planning; and fresh approaches to developing an effective music program. In 1994 the program achieved its present structure. The first Leadership Training Conference was held at the Virginia Theological Seminary, July 2–8, 1995. The 1998 conference included persons from the Evangelical Lutheran Church in America.

The program was developed by the Standing Commission on Church Music's subcommittee on Music in Small Churches.

Leaming, Jeremiah (1717–Sept. 15, 1804). The first person elected Bishop in Connecticut, Leaming declined to be consecrated because of age and infirmities. Born in Middletown, Connecticut, Leaming was baptized on May 12, 1717, at Durham, Connecticut, as a Congregationalist. He graduated from Yale College in 1745. While at Yale, Leaming left Congregationalism and joined the Church of England under the influence of Samuel Johnson of Stratford, Connecticut. He was sent to England at the expense of Trinity Church, Newport, Rhode Island, to be ordained. He was ordained deacon and priest in England in 1748. He returned to Newport to be the head of the parochial school and assistant to the rector. From 1758 until 1779, Leaming was rector of St. Paul's Church, Norwalk, Connecticut. During the Revolution he was a Loyalist. He was once imprisoned for his views. In 1779 he went with the British troops to New York, where he remained until 1784. In Mar. 1783 the Connecticut clergy met at Woodbury to elect a bishop. They chose Leaming, but he declined the election, and Samuel Seabury was then elected. From 1784 until 1790 Leaming was rector of the church in Stratford, Connecticut. He spent his retirement in New York and New Haven. He died in New Haven.

Lectern. A book stand or reading desk that holds the book used for reading scripture in public worship. It may also be used for preaching the Word, and it may hold the preacher's notes or sermon text. The lectern where the Word is read and preached is the focal point for attention during the liturgy of the word at the eucharist. The term "lectern" is from the Latin, "to read." Lecterns vary in design from plain stands to ornate representations of an eagle or a pelican with outstretched wings. The Prayer Book service for the Dedication and Consecration of a Church includes a form for the dedication of a lectern. The prayer for this dedication begins, "Father, your eternal Word speaks to us through the words of Holy Scripture. Here we read about your mighty acts and purposes in history, and about those whom you chose as the agents of your will" (BCP, pp. 570–571). Another term for a lectern is an ambo.

Lectio Continua. The liturgical reading of selections of scripture by starting at the beginning of a particular book and working through consecutive readings to the end. This contrasts with selective readings ("propers") which are chosen for each particular occasion. At the time of the early church, readings in the services of the Jewish synagogue were chosen at the reader's discretion, from a fixed lectionary, or from a sequence of "in course" readings (*lectio continua*). Christian lectionaries developed with fixed patterns of readings. Marion Hatchett notes in his *Commentary on the American Prayer Book* that there was a system for reading the entire Bible at Matins in the church, but this system did not continue in use past the ninth century. The orderly sequence of readings was disrupted in the middle ages by the increased number of saints' days and their octaves, and the readings of the lives of the saints. The Preface of the 1549 Prayer Book states that "here is drawn out a Kalendar. . . wherein (so much as may be) the reading of Holy Scripture is so set forth, that all things shall be done in order, without breaking one piece thereof from another" (BCP, p. 866). The entire NT with the exception of Revelation was read three times in a year by following the Daily Office lectionary of the 1549 Prayer Book. The Daily Office lectionary of the 1979 BCP is arranged so that the NT is read twice and the OT is read once in a two-year cycle of readings (see pp. 936–995). The new eucharistic lectionary of the 1979 BCP provides for the reading of almost the entire NT and a significant part of the OT over a three-year cycle of readings (see pp. 889–921). Sequences of in course readings are frequently provided in the selections of the Daily Office lectionary and the eucharistic lectionary.

Lectio Divina. The term means, at root, the "reading of Holy Scripture." In Jerome and in the Rule of St. Benedict, it meant the scriptural text itself, the *lectio*, the "lesson" or reading. In the middle ages it came to refer to the act of reading the Bible, the sacred text, for a sacred purpose. It was a principal ingredient of monastic spirituality. This monastic reading led to meditation and prayer, with wisdom and appreciation as its goals. It was distinguished from a scholastic reading, which led to questions and disputations, with science and knowledge as objectives. The ultimate end of *lectio divina* is compunction, the desire for heaven. The term is still used to mean the meditative and prayerful reading of the Bible for purposes of devotion, rather than for scholarly study.

Lection. *See* Lesson.

Lectionary. An ordered system for reading the Holy Scriptures at the eucharist and the Daily Offices. It is usually presented in the form of a table of references for the psalms and readings for the various days of the liturgical year, although it may be a separate book containing the actual texts of the readings. The BCP contains two lectionaries: The eucharistic lectionary (BCP, pp. 887–931), and the Daily Office lectionary (BCP, pp. 933–1001*). Lesser Feasts and Fasts* contains a lectionary for weekdays in Advent, Christmastide, Lent, and Easter; and for lesser feasts during the church year. The Prayer Book lectionary is based on the lectionary developed in the Roman Catholic Church following Vatican Council II.

Lectionary Cycle. The Lectionary in the BCP and other contemporary lectionaries use a three-year cycle, referred to as Years A, B, and C. Year A begins on the First Sunday in Advent in years evenly divisible by three (e.g., 2001). The Daily Office lectionary follows a two-year cycle. Year One begins on the First Sunday in Advent preceding odd-numbered years and Year Two even-numbered years. In the eucharistic lectionary the Gospel According to Matthew is read in Year A, Mark in Year B, and Luke in Year C. The Gospel According to John is used during Lent and Easter, and on some Sundays in Year B, since Mark is shorter than the other gospels.

Lector. A lay person trained in reading scripture who is appointed by the clergy person in charge of the congregation to read lessons or lead the prayers of the people. The term is from the Latin, "to read." There is no license required for this lay ministry. A lector may also be known as a reader. Lay persons served as readers in the early church. However, by the third century this ministry was performed by those ordained to the minor order of lector (reader). The minor orders became steps leading to ordination to the priesthood. The reading of the gospel at the eucharist was the responsibility of the deacon by the fourth century. The lector read from the ambo (lectern) in the basilicas of the fourth and fifth century. Minor orders were not continued in Anglicanism. *See* Lesson.

Lee, Alfred (Sept. 9, 1807–Apr. 12, 1887). Tenth Presiding Bishop. Lee was born in Cambridge, Massachusetts. He graduated from Harvard University in 1827 and then studied law. He later studied for ordained ministry and graduated from the General Theological Seminary in 1837.

Lee was ordained deacon on May 21, 1837, and priest on June 12, 1838. He served as rector of Calvary Church, Rockdale, Pennsylvania, 1838–1841. Lee was consecrated the first Bishop of Delaware on Oct. 12, 1841, and served in that position until his death. He was rector of St. Andrew's Church, Wilmington, during his episcopate. In 1863 he worked in Haiti and helped to start a mission there under the care of the American Church Missionary Society. In 1875 he performed episcopal duties in Mexico. He served as Presiding Bishop from May 31, 1884, until Apr. 12, 1887. He died in Wilmington.

Lee, Robert Edward (Jan. 19, 1807–Oct. 12, 1870). Considered the premier Confederate general in the Civil War, Lee was an active Episcopal layman. Throughout the conflict he was noted not only for his skill as a soldier, but also for the piety he fostered among troops in his army. He was born at Stratford, his family's plantation on the Potomac river in Virginia. After graduating from the Military Academy at West Point in 1829, he began a distinguished military career that included service in the Mexican War (1846–1848) and a term as Superintendent at West Point from 1852 to 1856. Following the outbreak of war in Apr. 1861, Lee resigned from the United States Army and joined the military forces of Virginia. In June 1862 he received command of the Confederate Army of Northern Virginia, a position he held until the Civil War ended in 1865. Lee assumed the presidency of Washington College (later Washington and Lee University) in Lexington, Virginia, in Aug. 1865. He also served on the vestry of Grace Church, Lexington. By the end of the nineteenth century many southerners portrayed Lee as an exemplar of the moral and religious ideals of their society.

Lehigh University, Bethlehem, Pennsylvania. In 1865 Judge Asa Packer (1805–1879) asked the Rt. Rev. William Bacon Stevens (1815–1887), the fourth Bishop of Pennsylvania, to help him plan a university. On Feb. 9, 1866, a charter was granted, and the school opened on Sept. 1, 1866, with 40 students. The first four presidents of Lehigh University were Episcopalians, one of whom was a priest. The Bishop of Pennsylvania, and later, after the division of the diocese, the Bishop of Bethlehem, served as presidents of the board of trustees until 1907.

Le Jau, Francis (1665–Sept. 10, 1717). Colonial rector and missionary. He was born in Algiers, France, of Huguenot parents. Le Jau fled France when the Edict of Nantes was revoked in 1685. The Edict of Nantes had given freedom to the French Huguenots. He went to England. At some time before 1700 he was a Canon in St. Paul's Cathedral, London. Le Jau was sent to the colony of South Carolina in 1706 by the Society for the Propagation of the Gospel. He remained there until his death. Le Jau spent much of his time working as a missionary among the Indians and African Americans at Goose Creek, South Carolina, about 18 miles from Charles Town (Charleston). He taught them the Catechism and prepared them for baptism. When Commissary William Bull was absent, Le Jau served St. Philip's Church, Charles Town. On July 31, 1717, the Bishop of London appointed him rector of St. Philip's Church, but Le Jau died before he could assume the position. He died in Goose Creek.

Lent. Early Christians observed "a season of penitence and fasting" in preparation for the Paschal feast, or Pascha (BCP, pp. 264–265). The season now known as Lent (from an Old English word meaning "spring," the time of lengthening days) has a long history. Originally, in places where Pascha was celebrated on a Sunday, the Paschal feast followed a fast of up to two days. In the third century this fast was lengthened to six days. Eventually this fast became attached to, or overlapped, another fast of forty days, in imitation of Christ's fasting in the wilderness. The forty-day fast was especially important for converts to the faith who were preparing for baptism, and for those guilty of notorious sins who were being restored to the Christian assembly. In the western church the forty days of Lent extend from Ash Wednesday through Holy Saturday, omitting Sundays. The last three days of Lent are the sacred *Triduum* of Maundy Thursday, Good Friday, and Holy Saturday. Today Lent has reacquired its significance as the final preparation of adult candidates for baptism. Joining with them, all Christians are invited "to the observance of a holy Lent, by self-examination and repentance; by prayer, fasting, and self-denial; and by reading and meditating on God's holy Word" (BCP, p. 265).

Lenten Array. Lenten array usually refers to a rough or homespun fabric. It may have an off-white color or it may be made without any dye. Lenten array may be decorated with purple or dark orpheys and Lenten designs. Use of Lenten array follows the custom from the late middle ages of using dark or drab colors during penitential seasons. Many Anglican parishes use Lenten array instead of violet or purple for vestments and liturgical hangings during Lent.

Leo the Great (d. Nov. 10, 461). Defender of orthodox Christology and pope. On Sept. 29, 440, he was consecrated Bishop of Rome. He was a great opponent of heresy, and his major accomplishment was his condemnation of Eutyches and Monophysitism and his defense of the permanent distinction of Christ's two natures in his one person. Leo's letter, called a *Tome*, was read at the Fourth Ecumenical Council at Chalcedon in 451. It stated clearly that Jesus Christ was one person in two natures. This was a great victory for Rome, for Leo, and for western theology. At Chalcedon the papal legate said, "Peter has spoken through the mouth of Leo." *The Definition of the Union of the Divine and Human Natures in the Person of Christ*, adopted at Chalcedon, evolved from Leo's *Tome*. It is among the historical documents in the BCP (p. 864). Leo extended papal authority and advanced papal doctrine. He was declared a Doctor of the Church by Pope Benedict XIV. Leo is one of only two popes who are called "the Great." He died in Rome. Leo is commemorated in the Episcopal calendar of the church year on Nov. 10.

Lesser Feasts and Fasts, The (LFF). A collection of proper collects, lessons, and psalms for the eucharist on each of the weekdays of Lent, weekdays of Easter season, and each of the lesser feasts of the church year. It also includes a biographical or historical sketch for the lesser feasts and fixed holy days. The General Convention of the Episcopal Church may amend the calendar of the church year by adding or deleting lesser feasts from the calendar (see BCP, pp. 19–30). Commemorations may be added or deleted with the concurrence of two consecutive General Conventions. Successive editions of *Lesser Feasts and Fasts* are published as changes are made to the calendar. Each new edition bears in its title the date of the General Convention that determined its listing of commemorations. *Lesser Feasts and Fasts* was first published for trial use in 1964, with a second edition published in 1973. The third edition, published in 1980, was authorized by General Convention for optional use instead of trial use. The fourth edition, published in 1988, reflected the addition by General Convention of eight commemorations, and six more commemorations that were proposed by General Convention for trial use for a period of three years. Subsequent editions have reflected further amendments to the calendar by General Convention. The 1994 edition included Guidelines and Procedures for Continuing Alteration of the Calendar in the Episcopal Church, as adopted by the 1994 General Convention. The Guidelines identify qualities or traits that will be sought with respect to those who may be added to the list of commemorations in the calendar. Personal qualities or traits include heroic faith, love, goodness of life, joyousness, service to others for Christ's sake, and devotion. The Guidelines also call for recognition by the faithful at local and regional levels; and widespread support for the person's inclusion over a reasonable period of time ("historical perspective"), generally two generations or 50 years. *Lesser Feasts and Fasts* is published by Church Publishing Incorporated.

Lesser Silence (Little or Simple Silence). In monastic and religious communities, the silence that should be kept in working hours. Local regulations may tie it to specific times and places. It is generally less absolute than the Great Silence of evening and night hours. It is most complete among Trappists (Reformed Cistercians), who traditionally use sign language to communicate noiselessly. Its purpose is to help brothers or sisters keep internal peace while performing their daily tasks.

Lesson. A selection of scripture that serves as a reading for a church service. It is also known as a lection or a reading. The BCP appoints lessons for the eucharist in the Lectionary (pp. 889–931), and it appoints lessons for Morning and Evening Prayer in the Daily Office Lectionary (pp. 936–1001). Appropriate lessons for other services, such as An Order of Service for Noonday and Compline, are provided in those services. The gospel at the eucharist is to be read by a deacon, or by a priest or bishop if a deacon is unavailable. All other lessons may be read by lay people. The NT lesson at the eucharist is also known as the epistle. A lay person who reads a lesson is known as a lector. Lessons may be said or sung. Lessons have been announced since the twelfth century. The 1549 Prayer Book required the announcement of the lesson to include the citation of the chapter from scripture, and the 1662 BCP required citation of the verse. The 1979 BCP makes citation of the chapter and verse optional. The lector need only say "A reading (or lesson) from _____," and name the scriptural book which is the source of the lesson.

Similarly, the deacon who announces the gospel need only say "The Holy Gospel of our Lord Jesus Christ according to _____." After each lesson at Morning and Evening Prayer and after the lessons other than the gospel at the eucharist, the lector may say "The Word of the Lord," to which the congregation responds "Thanks be to God." Alternatively, the lector may also conclude the lesson by saying "Here ends the lesson (reading)." No congregational response follows this statement. Silence may follow each lesson at Morning and Evening Prayer. Silence may also follow each lesson at the eucharist other than the gospel. *See* Lectionary.

Letter of Agreement. A written agreement concerning terms of employment, either for a priest in charge of a congregation or a member of a diocesan staff. Several dioceses provide for Letters of Agreement to specify terms of a call to serve as rector or vicar of a congregation, and for other positions within a diocese. The phrase is not used in the BCP or the canons of the church.

Letter of Transfer. This term was previously used for a certificate of membership, typically used when a member of a congregation in the Episcopal Church moves to another congregation.

Letters Dimissory. Clergy may transfer canonical residence from one diocesan jurisdiction to another by presentation of Letters Dimissory from the ecclesiastical authority of the former diocese to the ecclesiastical authority of the new diocese. It is a testimonial by the ecclesiastical authority of the former diocese (typically a bishop) that the clergyperson has not "been justly liable to evil report, for error in religion or for viciousness of life, for the last three years." The transfer of canonical residence is dated from the acceptance of Letters Dimissory by the ecclesiastical authority. Letters Dimissory shall be presented if a member of the clergy has been called to a cure in another diocese and shall be accepted unless credible information is received concerning the character of the clergyperson that would call for a canonical inquiry and presentment.

Lewis, Clive Staples (C. S.) (Nov. 29, 1898–Nov. 22, 1963). Author and one of the best-known Christian apologists in the Anglican Communion. Lewis's works included literary history, criticism, essays, three science fiction novels with spiritual themes, speeches, and the well-known children's stories, *The Chronicles of Narnia*. Attractive to almost all Christian denominations, Lewis's writings have achieved an enthusiastic following. Much attention has been given both to his ideas and his personal life, especially his late-in-life marriage to Joy Davidson. The story of their marriage was made into the movie *Shadowlands*. Lewis taught Medieval and Renaissance literature at both Oxford and Cambridge. He was a member of a literary group called "The Inklings" which included J.R.R. Tolkien and Dorothy Sayers. His most beloved books include *The Pilgrim's Regress* (1933); *Mere Christianity* (1952); *Surprised by Joy* (1955), the story of his own conversion to Christianity; and *The Screwtape Letters* (1942). In *A Grief Observed* (1961) he reflected on his wife's death and the meaning of human loss. Lewis is appreciated as a leading "literary saint" of the Episcopal Church.

Lex Orandi, Lex Credendi. A Latin phrase often used in the study of liturgy, it means "the rule of prayer [is] the rule of belief." The phrase describes the pervasive pastoral reality that habits of prayer shape Christian belief. Official provisions for worship can thus have a determinative role in shaping Christian doctrine.

Lexington, Diocese of. The General Convention of 1895 voted to divide the Diocese of Kentucky to create a new diocese in the eastern half of the state. The Diocese of Lexington held its primary convention at Christ Church, Lexington, Dec. 4–5, 1895. Christ Church, Lexington, was dedicated as Christ Church Cathedral on Mar. 21, 1897 but was disestablished in 1933. On Apr. 28, 1963, the Cathedral Church of St. George the Martyr, the Cathedral Domain, Crystal, was consecrated. On Nov. 26, 1989, Christ Church, Lexington, was again consecrated as Christ Church Cathedral. The diocese has two cathedrals. The Diocese of Lexington includes the following counties: Anderson, Bath, Bell, Boone, Boyle, Bracken, Breathitt, Campbell, Carter, Casey, Clark, Clay, Elliott, Estill, Fayette, Fleming, Floyd, Franklin, Gallatin, Garrard, Grant, Greenup, Harlan, Harrison, Jackson, Jessamine, Johnson, Kenton, Knott, Laurel, Lawrence, Lee, Leslie, Letcher, Lewis, Lincoln, Madison, Magoffin, Martin, Mason, McCreary, Menifee, Mercer, Montgomery, Morgan, Nicholas, Owen, Owsley, Pendleton, Perry, Pike, Powell, Pulaski, Robertson, Rockcastle, Rowan, Scott, Wayne, Whitley, Wolfe, and Woodford.

Liberal Catholicism, Liberal Catholic Movement. Liberal catholicism, as a theological development in Anglicanism, had its beginnings in the publication of *Lux Mundi* (1889), a collection of essays written by Oxford Anglican teachers and edited by Charles Gore. *Lux Mundi* took the doctrine of the Incarnation as a central theme for interpreting Christian faith in light of the conflicts which were of great importance at the end of the nineteenth century: evolution and the historical criticism of the Bible. Liberal catholicism was a movement which also sought to integrate the sacramental and ritualistic aspects of the Tractarian movement with such social concerns as urban poverty, industrialism, war, and the development of a Christian socialism.

Theologically, the best exposition of the concerns of liberal catholicism can be found in *Essays Catholic and Critical* (1926) and in the writings of William Temple, Archbishop of York and later of Canterbury. The movement received its final, official expression in *Doctrine in the Church of England* (1937). Certain themes predominate in all the writings which represent the liberal catholic movement: revelation and history in the Bible, religious experience, the uniqueness of Christ and the Christian revelation, the synthesis of religious belief and intellectual integrity, and the relationship of the church to the political and social order. In all these concerns the authority of Christian belief in the rapidly changing social, scientific, and philosophical culture of the European world between the first and second World Wars was fundamental to liberal catholicism.

The influence of liberal catholicism upon the Episcopal Church in the United States can be seen in various statements and papers of General Convention on ecumenism and the authority of scripture, as well as social and moral questions. The fundamental concern with the authority of Christian belief in those documents reflects the liberal catholic concern for accepting the genuine historical development of cultures in the light of the Incarnation. Episcopal theologian William Porcher DuBose (1836–1918) reflected liberal catholic influence in his concern to rediscover the tradition of the church in new ways and contexts. *See* Essays Catholic and Critical; *see* Lux Mundi; *see* Temple, William.

Liberal Catholicism and the Modern World. This volume, published in 1934, was inspired by the English publication, *Essays Catholic and Critical* (1926). The volume stressed the Catholic tradition and a liberal, critical approach to biblical and historical studies. Liberal catholics wanted "to preserve the best of the past in the light of the best of the present so as to build for the best future." Liberal catholics encouraged the use of literary and historical criticism. The editor and guiding spirit of the book was Frank Gavin, then Professor of Ecclesiastical History at General Theological Seminary. Among the contributors were Frederick C. Grant, Wilbur M. Urban, Granville M. Williams, and Cuthbert A. Simpson.

Liberal Evangelicalism. Within Anglican churches evangelicalism is the name given to the movement founded and fostered by John Wesley. Those followers of Wesley who did not stay inside the Church of England became known as Methodists. Those who remained in the Church of England formed the evangelical party, which took shape during the latter years of the eighteenth century. The evangelical party flowered in the nineteenth century and still continues to be influential. A crisis of faith was created during the nineteenth century by the rise of new historical and scientific methods and the widespread replacement of the Platonic and Aristotelian philosophies by the new thought of Kant, Hegel, John Stuart Mill, and others. Liberal evangelicals sought to incorporate the new learning in a reformulated evangelical theology which retained its loyalty to the gospel and its emphasis on atonement and sanctification while at the same time accepting a critical stance toward the biblical text, the evolutionary account of creation, a scientific attitude toward miracles, a morally based criticism of doctrines like predestination, and a commitment to social justice as a major Christian obligation. Liberal evangelicalism has had a stronger influence on the Episcopal Church than on the Church of England, where its counterpart has been modernism.

Liberation Theology. Gustavo Gutiérrez notes in *A Theology of Liberation* (1973) that the problem which liberation theology seeks to address is "what relation is there between salvation and the historical process in the liberation of man?" This distinguishes liberation theology from any attempt at making human liberation a "spiritual matter." Gutierrez urged that "the work of salvation is a reality which occurs in history." Liberation theology is a Latin American response both to the fresh winds of Vatican II and to the crushing political and economic oppression experienced by the poor of Latin America. Although liberation theology has been centered in Latin America, its growth may be seen in theological calls for liberation of oppressed people in a variety of contexts and places. Its influence may be seen in the related movements of African American theology and feminist theology. Certain themes are characteristic of liberation theology: 1) Conscientization, or bringing into awareness one's own situation and its causes; 2) The use of Marxist analysis as a discriminate social analysis concerning the present historical situation of oppression; 3) The insistence of the union of thought and praxis; 4) The recovery of biblical themes as a basis for reflection; and 5) The condemnation of "development" in capitalist terms as a solution to poverty. Such development is understood as a cover for the benefit of the powerful. The answer to oppression in liberation theology is not development but the participation of the poor in the struggle for justice.

Liberia, Diocese of. The 1844 General Convention established the Missionary District of Cape Palmas and Parts Adjacent. The first Missionary Bishop of the District was John Payne, after whom the Bishop Payne Divinity School for African Americans in Petersburg was named. In 1884 the House of Bishops elected Samuel David Ferguson Missionary Bishop. He was the first African American man elected bishop in the Episcopal Church and was the first Liberian bishop. On Oct. 17, 1913, the name of the jurisdiction was changed to the Missionary District of Liberia. Cuttington College was incorporated on Dec. 18, 1923. Robert Erskine Campbell of the Order of the Holy Cross was elected Missionary Bishop on Oct. 17, 1925, by the House of Bishops. Campbell was the first monk elected and consecrated bishop in the Episcopal Church. Dillard Houston Brown, Jr., the ninth Missionary Bishop of Liberia, was assassinated on Nov. 19, 1969, by a Nigerian nationalist. On Jan. 1, 1970, the Missionary District of Liberia became the Diocese of Liberia. On Mar. 18, 1982, the Diocese of Liberia became a full member of the Church of the Province of West Africa and was no longer a part of the Episcopal Church.

Licentiate in Theology. This serves as a certificate of successfully completed study by a seminarian, but it is not an academic degree. A student without a bachelor's degree or equivalent who has fulfilled all the requirements for the M.Div. degree is eligible for the Licentiate in Theology. Many seminaries no longer award it.

Lichtenberger, Arthur (Jan. 8, 1900–Sept. 3, 1968). Twenty-first Presiding Bishop. Lichtenberger was a leading ecumenical churchman. He was a member of the General Board of the National Council of Churches and a member of the Central Committee of the World Council of Churches. In 1961 he made an unofficial visit to Pope John XXIII. In that same year he helped to lead the Episcopal Church into the Consultation on Church Union. Under his leadership the construction of the Episcopal Church Center in New York was completed. He was born in Oshkosh, Wisconsin. Lichtenberger received his Ph.B. from Kenyon College in 1923, and his B.D. from the Episcopal Theological School in 1925. He was ordained deacon on Mar. 21, 1925, and priest on Nov. 21, 1926. From 1925 to 1927, he was professor of NT at St. Paul's Divinity School, Wuchang, China. Lichtenberger did postgraduate study at Harvard University in 1927–1928. From 1928 until 1933 he was rector of Grace Church, Cincinnati, and from 1933 until 1941 he was rector of St. Paul's Church, Brookline, Massachusetts. He was also lecturer in Pastoral Care at the Episcopal Theological School from 1938 until 1941. Lichtenberger was dean of Trinity Cathedral, Newark, 1941–1948. From 1948 to 1950, he was professor of Pastoral Theology at the General Theological Seminary. On Apr. 5, 1951, he was consecrated Bishop Coadjutor of Missouri and was Bishop from Nov. 1, 1952, until May 15, 1959. He was Presiding Bishop from Nov. 15, 1958, until Oct. 12, 1964, when he retired because of ill health. From 1964 until 1968 he was visiting professor of Pastoral Theology at the Episcopal Theological School. Lichtenberger died in Bethel, Vermont.

Life and Work. An early ecumenical movement seeking, along with the Faith and Order Movement, the reunion of the separated Christian churches. Unlike the Faith and Order Movement, whose principal concern was theological, Life and Work emphasized the practical cooperation of separated churches in the moral, ethical, and social application of Christian faith in the world. It stressed the relation of the Christian faith to society, politics, and economics. Doctrinal differences between the churches were minimized. The earliest and chief proponent of the movement was Archbishop Nathan Söderblom of Uppsala, of the Swedish Lutheran Church. The first Universal Christian Conference on Life and Work met at Stockholm, Aug. 19–30, 1925. The second meeting, which was called the World Conference on Church, Community, and State, met at Oxford, July 12–

26, 1937. The Episcopal Church sent seven delegates to the second meeting. Life and Work became a commission of the World Council of Churches when the WCC was founded in 1948. *See* World Council of Churches (WCC); *see* Faith and Order.

Life in Jesus Community, The. Founded on Sept. 23, 1984, when the Rev. Philip Charles Zampino, his wife Jean, and others made covenant promises before Bishop David Keller Leighton of Maryland. On Nov. 15, 1986, five covenant members took vows of profession before Bishop Leighton. It is located at Libertytown, Maryland, and is a covenant community for clergy and laity, male and female, married and single. It is committed to a ministry of healing, evangelism, and missions. Members follow a single rule of life. On July 22, 1994, the entire community was received into the Charismatic Episcopal Church.

Life in the Lamb Community. A Christian Community of men and women within the Episcopal Church. They live in the world to serve the church. It was founded on June 18, 1987. The Community is dedicated to the Paschal Lamb, and its symbol is the Lamb Victorious. The feast day of the Community is Corpus Christi, which in the Roman Catholic calendar is the Sunday following Trinity Sunday. Members make promises of charity, purity, and obedience.

Lifeline. The educational and fundraising publication of the Presiding Bishop's Fund for World Relief. It began publication in Dec. 1988.

Lift Every Voice and Sing: A Collection of Afro-American Spirituals and Other Songs. This collection was published in 1981 by the Church Hymnal Corporation as a supplement to *The Hymnal* (1940). The project was conceived by the Rev. Franklin D. Turner, staff officer for Black Ministries at the time, and later Suffragan Bishop of Pennsylvania. The volume contains 151 selections and reflects the religious musical heritage of African Americans. The themes of personal assurance, comfort, and hope are often emphasized by the selections in the collection. The compiler and general editor was Irene V. Jackson, who also wrote the essay at the back of the collection, "Music Among Blacks in the Episcopal Church: Some Preliminary Considerations."

Lift Every Voice and Sing II: An African American Hymnal. This collection was published in 1993 by the Church Hymnal Corporation as a supplement to *The Hymnal 1982*. It contains 234 hymns and songs, and thirty-six selections of service music for the Holy Eucharist. The music is drawn from the following genres: Negro spirituals, traditional and contemporary gospel songs, adapted Protestant hymns, missionary and evangelistic hymns, and service music and Mass settings in both traditional and gospel styles. The Episcopal Commission for Black Ministries developed the book with the Rt. Rev. Arthur B. Williams, Jr., former Suffragan Bishop of Ohio, as chair of the editorial board. Dr. Horace Clarence Boyer was general editor, and Dr. Carl Haywood was service music editor. The volume was dedicated to the Rev. Curtis Winfield Sisco, Jr. (1958–1992), who was liturgical editor.

Lima Document. *See* Baptism, Eucharist, and Ministry (BEM).

Lima Eucharistic Liturgy, The. A liturgy developed by Max Thurion of the Taizé community. At the meeting of the Faith and Order Commission in Lima, Peru, in 1982, some revisions were made, and the liturgy was used for the first time on Jan. 15, 1982, with J. Robert Wright, an Episcopal priest, as the celebrant. It embodies the eucharistic theology of *Baptism, Eucharist, and Ministry* (1982). The General Convention of 1985 authorized its use provided an ordained priest of the Episcopal Church is the celebrant, or one of the celebrants at a concelebrated service of ecumenical worship.

"Lima Report." *See* Baptism, Eucharist, and Ministry (BEM).

Linkage. The newsletter of the Office of Black Ministries. It began publication in Feb. 1984. The first issue was called the Premier Absalom Jones Issue.

Litany. An intercessory prayer including various petitions that are said or sung by the leader and fixed responses by the congregation. It was used as early as the fifth century in Rome. It was led by a deacon, with the collects led by a bishop or priest. The litany was the first English language rite that was prepared by Archbishop Thomas Cranmer (1489–1556). It was first published in 1544. The 1979 BCP titled the litany "The Great Litany" (pp. 148–154), distinguishing it from other litanies in the BCP. The Great Litany may be done before the eucharist, or after the collects of Morning or Evening Prayer, or separately. The

BCP also includes a Litany of Penitence in the Ash Wednesday service (pp. 267–269); a Litany at the Time of Death (pp. 462–464); a Litany for Ordinations, which is also used in the Celebration of a New Ministry (pp. 548–551, 560); a Litany of Thanksgiving for a Church, which may be used for reaffirmation of mission and ministry when a building has been used for an extended time without consecration, or on the anniversary of the dedication or consecration of a church, or at other times (pp. 577–579); and a general thanksgiving in the form of a Litany of Thanksgiving (pp. 836–837). The *BOS* includes a Litany of Healing in a public service of healing, and a Litany for the Church in the service for the founding of a church. *See* Great Litany, The.

Litany Desk. A low kneeling desk for prayer. Historically it was placed in the midst of the church for use by the leader of the litany. It is also known as a faldstool and a *prie-dieu*.

"Little Church Around the Corner, The," New York. *See* Church of the Transfiguration, New York.

Little Gidding. The home of the community and household of prayer founded by Nicholas Ferrar (Feb, 22, 1592–Dec. 4, 1637) in Huntingdonshire, England, about 18 miles from Cambridge. Ferrar and his mother and some 40 members of his extended family and household retired to this deserted estate in 1625 and dedicated themselves to a life of prayer and Christian ministry. The mansion house was repaired and the little church, which had been used as a barn, was restored. Ferrar, a celibate, was ordained deacon in 1626. The community lived under a systematic rule of life based on the principles of the Church of England and the Prayer Book. Little Gidding was more a household and family with a shared life of prayer, charity, and work than a monastic community, but it has been seen as an experiment in family monastic living. Ferrar led the community in the Daily Offices of the church, the daily singing of the entire Psalter, hourly prayer offices throughout the day, and nightly vigils. The local vicar led the community in the celebration of Holy Communion on the first Sunday of every month. The Little Gidding community was quite generous in charity. They visited and helped the poor and sick and operated a dispensary. They also established a small academy for the education of children. Members of the community were involved in writing stories to illustrate themes of Christian faith and morality. The community

was also involved in bookbinding and produced illustrated harmonies of the gospels. Ferrar died in 1637. He is commemorated in the Episcopal calendar of the church year on Dec. 1. The Puritans opposed the Little Gidding community. A pamphlet titled *The Arminian Nunnery* (1646) criticized Little Gidding for attempting to introduce Roman Catholic practices in England. The community continued until 1646 when it was raided by Oliver Cromwell's soldiers and dispersed. "Little Gidding" is the title of the last of the *Four Quartets* (1935–1942) by the poet T. S. Eliot, who describes a place "Where prayer has been valid. And prayer is more/ Than an order of words." *See* Ferrar, Nicholas.

Little Hours of the Divine Office. The canonical hours of prime, terce, sext, and none. Prime was said at 6 A.M., the traditional "first hour" of prayer; terce was said at 9 A.M., the "third hour"; sext was said at 12 noon, the "sixth hour"; and none was said at 3 P.M., the "ninth hour." These offices make up the traditional day hours, along with lauds, vespers, and compline. Matins was the traditional night office. The times for the "little offices" of terce, sext, and none were associated by early Christians with the events of Jesus' Passion. By the fourth century, the monks were joined by the secular clergy and laity for the principal morning and evening offices of lauds and vespers. The other offices were said by the monks. Archbishop Thomas Cranmer (1489–1556) consolidated the Daily Office to the Prayer Book services of Matins and Evensong. The little offices of terce, sext, and none were not included in the BCP until the twentieth century. The Order of Service for Noonday in the 1979 BCP (pp. 103–107) contains elements of the little offices of terce, sext, and none. It may be adapted for use at any or all of the traditional times of prayer for these three little offices. *See* Day Hours; *see* Terce, Sext, None.

Little Offices. *See* Little Hours of the Divine Office.

Liturgical Movement, The. A movement of liturgical renewal and reform, rooted in new discoveries concerning the Christian liturgical tradition and new insights into the experience of common worship. The liturgical movement was encouraged by new developments and insights in the fields of biblical studies, patristic studies, and ecumenism during the nineteenth and twentieth centuries. The liturgical movement emphasized the active participation of all Christians in the liturgy. It also sought to view the prevailing practice of liturgy in light of the witness of the early church and to recover certain liturgical expressions from the early Christian tradition.

The liturgical movement originated in the Roman Catholic Church, especially in the Benedictine Order. In 1833 the ancient monastery at Solesmes, France, was re-established under the leadership of Dom Prosper Guéranger (1805–1875). The Benedictine community at Solesmes became a major center for research concerning chant in the 1870s. This community founded or influenced many Benedictine foundations during the period from 1833 to 1900. The Benedictine or monastic phase of the liturgical movement was followed by further research and scholarship concerning Christian liturgy. Liturgical scholarship concerned important documents such as the *Didache* (discovered in 1875 and published in 1883), and the publication of other sources such as the *Canons of Hippolytus* and the *Apostolic Constitutions*. Scholars came to approach liturgy in light of historical critical methods. The popular liturgical movement has been dated from an address by Dom Lambert Beauduin (1873–1960) at the National Congress of Catholic Action at Malines, Belgium, in 1909. Beauduin's address, "The Full Prayer of the Church," called for the active participation of the people in the church's work, especially in the liturgy. Beauduin's approach was based in parochial ministry, and it expressed theoretical concepts in popular language. The popular liturgical movement was advanced through publications, conferences, and the media. An important aspect of the liturgical movement was its intentional drawing together of the liturgy and the social issues facing the church's people. The popular liturgical movement in America has been dated from the travels and work of Dom Virgil Michel (1890–1938), a monk of St. John's Abbey, Collegeville, Minnesota, who visited Benedictine monasteries and Beauduin in Europe, 1924–1925. After Michel returned, the American liturgical movement began at St. John's with the founding of *Orate Fratres* (which later became *Worship*) and the Liturgical Press under Michel's leadership. In the Roman Catholic Church, the liturgical movement culminated in the reforms of the Second Vatican Council's *Constitution on the Sacred Liturgy* (1963). The liturgical movement spread beyond the Roman Catholic Church and led to the reform of the books and forms of worship of many churches during the later twentieth century, including the Anglican Communion and the Episcopal Church.

The Anglican Communion began to feel the influence of the liturgical movement in the 1920s and 1930s. A. G. Hebert wrote *Liturgy and Society* in England (1935). The advance of the English liturgical movement was encouraged by the Parish and People Movement. In the Episcopal Church, Dean William Palmer Ladd of Berkeley Divinity School helped to introduce the liturgical movement to the Episcopal Church. Massey H. Shepherd, Jr., and Bayard Hale Jones, both seminary professors associated with the Church Divinity School of the Pacific and the University of the South, were leaders in the work of liturgical revision. Walter Lowrie also encouraged the advance of the liturgical movement in the Episcopal Church. Shepherd helped to found the Associated Parishes in 1946. Associated Parishes' tracts and conferences helped to educate the membership of the Episcopal Church concerning liturgical reform. Shepherd's *Oxford American Prayer Book Commentary* was published in 1950. It reflected many of the concerns of the liturgical movement and the discoveries of liturgical scholarship. Also in 1950 the Standing Liturgical Commission began publishing a series of Prayer Book Studies. The 1958 Lambeth Conference set forth guidelines for Prayer Book revision in the Anglican Communion, and these guidelines were further developed by the 1963 Anglican Congress.

The eucharistic rite of the 1928 BCP was criticized in light of the principles of the liturgical movement. The relative lack of opportunity for congregational participation was one of the issues of concern, along with the penitential tone of the rite. The process of Prayer Book revision and trial use took place in the Episcopal Church during the 1960s and 1970s. A revised BCP was given final approval in 1979. The liturgies of the 1979 BCP reflect many of the concerns of the liturgical movement, including a strong emphasis on participation of the laity, the recovery of ancient forms such as the Easter Vigil, and renewed emphasis on the importance of baptism. These concerns are fully discussed in Marion J. Hatchett's *Commentary on the American Prayer Book* (1981).

Liturgical Studies. Collections of essays issued from time to time under the direction of the Standing Liturgical Commission. Liturgical Studies are designed to help the commission carry out its canonical mandate "to collect and collate material bearing upon further revisions of The Book of Common Prayer." The first two studies were edited by Ruth A. Meyers. Liturgical Studies One is entitled *Baptism and Ministry* (1994), and Liturgical Studies Two is entitled *How Shall We Pray? Expanding Our Language about God* (1994).

Liturgical Texts for Evaluation. A booklet containing adapted liturgical texts for the Daily Office and the Holy Eucharist, along with a musical supplement. These adapted texts reflect concern for use of liturgical language that is widely inclusive and representative of the variety of the human community. References to the human community are inclusive in all instances. Masculine pronouns are not used for general human reference. Two canticles drawn from Wisdom literature use feminine imagery for God, and an alternative form for the *Gloria Patri* was provided for optional use. The alternative form of the *Gloria Patri* states, "Honor and glory to God, and to God's eternal Word, and to God's Holy Spirit: As it was in the beginning, is now, and will be for ever. Amen." The term "Lord" is retained but used with less frequency than in previous liturgical texts because "it is often seen as a term of masculine domination in our society." This booklet was printed by the Church Hymnal Corporation for the Standing Liturgical Commission in 1987. It was intended for use in worship in selected evaluation centers from Sept. 20 through Oct. 14, 1987. Evaluation of these liturgical texts was considered in subsequent preparation of liturgical texts for use in the Episcopal Church.

Liturgics. The study of liturgy, including the rites, forms, texts, symbols, and theology of worship. It is also known as liturgiology. Candidates for ordination to the transitional diaconate and priesthood must be examined and show proficiency in liturgics concerning Christian worship according to the contents and use of the Book of Common Prayer. Similarly, candidates for ordination to the diaconate must complete a course of study that includes liturgics. *See* Liturgy.

Liturgiology. *See* Liturgics.

Liturgy. The church's public worship of God. The term is derived from Greek words for "people" and "work." The church's public worship of God is the work of the Christian people. The life of Christ active in the church by the Spirit is expressed through liturgy.

In ancient Greece, liturgy indicated work done for the public at private expense. Such public works were not necessarily religious in nature. The Septuagint uses the term for divine worship. In the NT, the term is identified with an act of service or ministry (Phil 2:30).

The unity of the members of the church in Christ is expressed most fully in liturgy. Liturgy expresses the church's identity and mission, including the church's calling to invite others and to serve with concern for the needs of the world. Whether the liturgy is done by many or few, it is the corporate liturgy of the whole church. Liturgy does not include private devotions or acts of piety by individuals and groups. For example, saying the Rosary is not a liturgy.

Liturgy is sacramental. Outward and visible realities are used to express the inward and spiritual realities of God's presence in our lives. Liturgy reflects the belief of incarnational theology that tangible and finite things may reveal divine grace and glory. By the Spirit, through liturgy, the church manifests the love of God and the unity we share in Christ. This loving unity was shared by the Father and the Son, and it is offered to all Christian believers. Liturgy is a public and social event. It engages our lives and faith, our thoughts, feelings, hopes, and needs—especially our need for salvation in Christ. Liturgy includes actions and words, symbols and ritual, scriptures and liturgical texts, gestures and vestments, prayers that are spoken or sung. It is also shaped by the seasons, feasts, and fasts of the calendar of the church year and the lectionaries for the Holy Eucharist and the Daily Office (BCP, pp. 15–33, 888–1001). Liturgy is to involve the various members and ministries of the church so that all are drawn together into one living expression of divine worship. It expresses what we believe and know about God, including belief and knowledge that cannot be completely stated in words.

The term "liturgy" may refer to the rites or texts that order the church's worship. It may indicate in particular the eucharist, which is also known as the Divine Liturgy (BCP, p. 859). In eastern Christianity, the term is applied more narrowly to the eucharist and not to other rites of divine worship. In the west, it includes all public rites and offices of the church.

Liturgy and Music, Standing Commission on. An interim body of the General Convention created in 1997. This commission combines the work and responsibilities of two previous bodies, the Standing Liturgical Commission and the Standing Commission on Church Music.

Liturgy of the Eucharist. The second half of the eucharistic service, from the offertory to the end of the eucharistic rite. It is also known as the liturgy of the table. It is named the Holy Communion in the BCP (p. 361). It follows the liturgy of the word. The liturgy of the eucharist includes the Great Thanksgiving, the breaking of the bread, the ministration of communion, the postcommunion prayer, the blessing (if used), and the dismissal. The term may also be applied loosely to the entire eucharistic service.

***Liturgy of the Lord's Supper, The* (1966).** A book containing a eucharistic rite for trial use, along with study materials concerning the process of liturgical revision, the problem of liturgical norms, new perspectives in liturgical renewal, and a detailed rationale for the proposed revision of the eucharistic rite. Its appendices included a document of an Inter-Anglican Committee on the structure and contents of the eucharistic liturgy, prayers of eucharistic consecration from a variety of traditions, and a bibliography. It was published by the Standing Liturgical Commission in 1966 as *Prayer Book Studies XVII*. It was a revision of *Prayer Book Studies IV*, which was issued by the Standing Liturgical Commission in 1953. *The Liturgy of the Lord's Supper* reflected current liturgical scholarship and communications sent to the Standing Liturgical Commission concerning *Prayer Book Studies IV* on the eucharist. It placed the *Gloria in excelsis* at the beginning of the ministry of the word. The Nicene Creed was followed by the penitential order, the peace, and the prayer of intercession. The eucharistic rite of this publication, titled the Liturgy of the Lord's Supper, included both traditional and contemporary language. God was addressed with traditional language, but the priest or minister and congregation were addressed with contemporary language. *The Liturgy of the Lord's Supper* was presented to the 1967 General Convention and approved for trial use. It was also in 1967 that the General Convention approved the constitutional change allowing trial use for liturgical revision. Responses to this eucharistic rite influenced *Services for Trial Use*, a series of rites authorized by the 1970 General Convention. Subsequent publications in the process of trial use for Prayer Book revision included *Authorized Services 1973* and the *Draft Proposed Book of Common Prayer*, which was approved by the 1976 General Convention. The final revised version of the BCP was approved in 1979. *The Liturgy of the Lord's Supper* was an integral part of the process of trial use and Prayer Book revision. *See* Prayer Book Studies.

Liturgy of the Table. A convenient, frequently used term for the portion of the eucharistic rite which is celebrated at the altar (holy table), titled "The Holy Communion" in the BCP. It consists of four basic actions: preparation of the table, the eucharistic prayer or Great Thanksgiving, the breaking of the bread, and the ministration of communion. These actions are followed by a postcommunion prayer. A blessing and/or dismissal may also follow. The postcommunion prayer may be preceded or followed by a hymn.

Liturgy of the Word. The first part of the eucharist, centered upon the proclamation of the Word of God, preceding the Great Thanksgiving. The BCP identifies this part of the eucharist as the Word of God (p. 355). Since it precedes the Great Thanksgiving (the *anaphora*), it is known as the *Pro-anaphora*. It is also known as the ministry of the word. In a standard eucharistic rite, it includes the entrance rite (with salutation and collect of the day), the lessons, the sermon, the prayers of the people, the confession and absolution, and the peace. The entrance rite may be preceded by a hymn. Morning Prayer or Evening Prayer may be used for the liturgy of the word at the eucharist. A lesson from the gospel is always used when Morning or Evening Prayer is the liturgy of the word. The Nicene Creed may take the place of the Apostles' Creed, and the officiant may pass directly from the salutation and response to the collect of the day (BCP, p. 142). There are various liturgies for special days or occasions that may serve as the liturgy of the word, including, for example, the proper liturgies for Ash Wednesday (BCP, p. 264), the Great Vigil of Easter (BCP, p. 285), Holy Baptism (BCP, p. 299), Confirmation (BCP, p. 413), the Celebration and Blessing of a Marriage (BCP, p. 423), and the Burial of the Dead (BCP, p. 491). *See* Entrance Rite.

Living Church, The. A weekly magazine dedicated to serving the Episcopal Church, *The Living Church* was founded in 1878 and published in Chicago under the editorship of the Rev. Charles W. Leffingwell. It soon achieved nationwide readership. Leffingwell established the policy still followed of providing honest news and articles on church-related topics for the entire Episcopal Church, while giving editorial support to catholic Anglican principles. In 1899 the magazine was acquired by the Young Churchman Co., the Morehouse publishing enterprise in Milwaukee. Frederic C. Morehouse, editor 1890–1932, and his son, Clifford P. Morehouse, editor 1932–1952, were widely known and respected Anglo-catholic lay leaders. The business ultimately moved to New York, leaving the magazine in Milwaukee. In 1952 it became an independent publication owned by a small non-profit foundation, with

Peter Day as editor. *See* Day, Peter Morton; *see* Porter, Harry Boone.

Living Church Annual, The. *See* Episcopal Church Annual, The.

Living Rosary of Our Lady & S. Dominic. A sodality of Anglo-catholics. It was founded at St. Mary Magdalene's Church, Paddington, London, in Oct., 1905, by William Henry Martin Havergal (1863–1948). He was in the Tractarian tradition. Because God became man in the Incarnation, this group stresses giving the Blessed Virgin Mary reverence and praise. "Hail Mary" is said as a daily memorial of the Incarnation. Mary should be saluted because it was by her obedience that *Emmanuel* (God with us) came to earth. The group stresses that the prayers of the person closest to the King of all should be sought first and frequently. Mary is the *theotokos*, the "God Bearer," the "Mother of God." It is called the Living Rosary of Our Lady and S. Dominic, since Dominic is traditionally associated with instituting the use of the Rosary. The American Branch was granted autonomy in Oct. 1927. In 1997 the Living Rosary in the United States officially came under the umbrella of the Society of Mary.

Living Stones Diocesan Partnership. A coalition of dioceses established in Feb. 1994 to promote mutual ministry. Living Stones was formed for reflection, mutual sharing, and ongoing biblical and theological reflection. The members encourage new ways of engaging in ministry. The Living Stones Covenant stresses that all Christian ministry is rooted in baptism and that the church is a ministering community. It began as a coalition of eight Anglican dioceses, both American and Canadian, working together to renew and revitalize ministry at the local level. Participating dioceses have included Indianapolis, Iowa, Kansas, Kootenay, Minnesota, Nebraska, Nevada, North Dakota, Northern Michigan, Nova Scotia, Ohio, Olympia, Qu'Appelle, Rupert's Land, and South Dakota.

Living the Good News, **or "Colorado Curriculum".** A Christian education curriculum based on the common lectionary. It was begun in the Diocese of Colorado in 1976 as a six-week program. It is sometimes referred to as the "Colorado Curriculum." *Living the Good News* emphasizes the heritage of the Episcopal Church, the sacraments, and the Prayer Book. The curriculum also emphasizes the liturgical seasons of the year. It is based on scripture, tradition, and reason. A goal of *Living the Good News* is discovering God in the liturgy and symbols of the church as well as in the people of God. The lessons are developed at six levels plus an inter-age edition, giving the opportunity for intergenerational events. The program also publishes *Celebrate the Good News*, which is designed for Children's Chapel.

Lloyd, Arthur Selden (May 3, 1857–July 22, 1936). Bishop and president of the Board of Missions. He was born in Mt. Ada, Alexandria County, Virginia. Lloyd received his B.A. in 1877 from the University of Virginia, and his B.D. from Virginia Theological Seminary in 1880. He was ordained deacon on June 25, 1880, and priest on June 24, 1881. He served five years as a missionary in Prince Edward County, Virginia. From 1885 until 1899, he was rector of St. Luke's Church, Norfolk. From 1900 until 1909, Lloyd was general secretary of the Domestic and Foreign Missionary Society. On Oct. 20, 1909, he was consecrated Bishop Coadjutor of Virginia. Lloyd left that position when he was elected president of the Board of Missions on Oct. 20, 1910. He resigned this position in 1919, and became the rector of St. Bartholomew's Church, White Plains, New York. He became Suffragan Bishop of New York on Aug. 4, 1921, and he served there until his death. Lloyd edited *The Spirit of Missions*, 1917–1919, and was the author of *Christianity and the Religions* (1909). He died in Darien, Connecticut.

Lloyd's Clerical Directory. In 1898 the Rev. Frederick Ebenezer John Lloyd, rector of Trinity Church, Hamilton, Ohio, published a volume patterned on the English *Crockford's Clerical Directory*. It was entitled *Lloyd's Clerical Directory for 1898: Being a Statistical Book of Reference for Facts Relating to the Clergy, Parishes and Missions of the Protestant Episcopal Church in the United States of America*. Editions were published in 1903 and 1905 under the title *The American Church Clergy and Parish Directory*. The last three editions, 1910, 1911, and 1913, were called *Lloyd's Clerical Directory*. It was continued by *Stowe's Clerical Directory*.

Local priest. *See* Canon 9 clergy.

Locum tenens. A member of the clergy who temporarily fills the office of another. From the Latin, "to hold a place." A substitute or deputy. The position may be known as a *locum tenency*.

Logos. Greek for "word," used in various senses. The term is used for the Christian message or *kerygma*, which is the proclamation of God's saving act in Jesus Christ. It is also used as a christological term, which is believed to have originated from use in Hellenistic Judaism as a synonym for the divine wisdom. In this sense it designates God's self-communication. This communication takes place in the act of creation, in the providential government of creation, in human religious experience, and in the calling of Israel to be God's people and in its subsequent history. This self-communication of God reaches its climax in the Christ event, the Word made flesh (Jn 1:1–14). In the early period of the Church Fathers, logos became a designation for the second person of the Trinity. In time it was generally replaced by the title "Son," which seemed to preserve more faithfully the personal relationship between the second person and God the Father. In the Episcopal eucharistic lectionary, Jn 1:1–14 is the gospel for the third eucharist of Christmas Day, and for the first Sunday after Christmas, with the addition of verses 15–18. The collect for Christmas I celebrates the fact that in the Incarnation, God the Father has "poured upon us the new light of (his) incarnate Word." (BCP, p. 213).

London, Bishop of. From the earliest days of the Virginia colony the Bishop of London had a vague responsibility for the Church of England in the American colonies. This may have been because Bishop John King of London was a member of the first Council of the Virginia Company. William Laud was Bishop of London from 1628 until 1633. In 1632 Laud sent a suggestion to the Privy Council "for the purpose of extending conformity to the national church to the English subjects beyond the sea." On Oct. 1, 1633, the Privy Council ordered with regard to the colonies that ". . . in all things concerning their church government they should be under the jurisdiction of the Lord Bishop of London." In 1638, when Laud was Archbishop of Canterbury, he proposed sending a bishop to New England. Lord Thomas Culpeper became Governor of Virginia in 1679. His instructions permitted appointment to cures of only those clergy who had certificates of conformity from the Bishop of London. This was the first specific reference to the traditional jurisdiction of the Bishop of London over the colonies. The American Revolution ended any jurisdiction held by the Bishop of London over the former American colonies. *See* Laud, William.

London Company. *See* Virginia Company of London.

Long Island, Diocese of. The 1868 General Convention voted to divide the Diocese of New York and establish a new diocese. The new diocese included the following counties: Brooklyn, Nassau, Queens, and Suffolk. The primary convention of the new diocese met at the Church of the Holy Trinity, Brooklyn, on Nov. 18–19, 1868, and adopted the name the Diocese of Long Island. On Feb. 9, 1877, the Cathedral of the Incarnation, Garden City, was incorporated. The cornerstone for the cathedral was laid on June 28, 1877, and it opened on Apr. 9, 1885.

Lord, The. The term is an English translation of several words from Hebrew, Aramaic, and Greek indicating a person or deity with power and authority. The Hebrew *Adon* indicates a superior or human master, with *Adonai* used almost exclusively for divine lordship. The BCP notes that *Adonai* is used in the Psalms with reference to God, and translated "Lord" (p. 583). The personal name YHWH, the "Four-letter Name" (*Tetragrammaton*), was the Hebrew special name for God. It was probably vocalized "Yahweh," but by around the third century B.C. it was considered too sacred to be pronounced. *Adonai* was most frequently substituted for it. This reverence and reticence concerning the name of God was also seen in the classical English of the Prayer Book Psalter and the OT of the King James Version, which regularly rendered the name of God as "Lord." This usage continues in the Psalter of the 1979 BCP. When LORD is used to translate YHWH, it is represented in capital and small capital letters (see Ps 150, v. 6, BCP, p. 808); but Lord is represented in capital and lower case letters when it translates *Adonai* (see Ps 37, v. 14, BCP, p. 634). Greek translations from the second century B.C. used *kyrios* for the Hebrew YHWH, and this Greek usage continued in the NT. During his earthly ministry, Jesus may have been called "lord" as a title of respect. However, after the resurrection, the title was applied absolutely by the Christian community to Jesus Christ as the Lord, so that *kyrios* became a confessional title for Jesus Christ in the NT (see Acts 2:36; Rom 10:9–13; 1 Cor 12:3; Phil 2:11). The full divinity of Jesus was subsequently affirmed by the Councils of Nicaea (325) and Chalcedon (451). The word "Lord" is frequently used throughout the liturgies of the Episcopal Church. For example, at the eucharist the celebrant begins the salutation by saying, "The Lord be with you." After the reading of each lesson, the reader may say, "The Word of the Lord"; and the gospeler says "The Gospel of the Lord" after the gospel (see BCP, pp. 357–358). However, the appropriateness of the term "Lord" for contemporary liturgical use has been questioned because it has been seen as a term of masculine domination. *See* Jehovah; *see* Liturgical Texts for Evaluation.

Lord's Day, The. Sunday, the day of Jesus Christ's resurrection, the first day of the week. The term was used in early Christian literature for the Christian observance of Sunday. Each Sunday was celebrated as an Easter festival. For Christians, the Lord's Day took the place of the Jewish Sabbath as the weekly day of rest appointed by God. The term is used in Rv 1:10. The BCP states that the eucharist is "the principal act of Christian worship on the Lord's Day" (p. 13). The Prayer Book also notes that baptism is appropriately administered on Sunday or other feasts (p. 298), emphasizing the primacy of Sunday, the Lord's Day, in the liturgical week.

Lord's Prayer, The. This prayer of Jesus was given to his disciples as an example of how they should pray. The phrase "Lord's Prayer" is not used in the NT. The prayer is found in Mt 6:9–13 as part of the Sermon on the Mount and in Lk 11:2–4 when Jesus and the disciples are on the road to Jerusalem. Luke's version is shorter and more compact than Matthew's. Scholars have argued that the Lord's Prayer was originally part of the "Q" source and that Luke's version is probably closer to the original. As a prayer, the Lord's Prayer is similar to Jewish prayers. It begins with an address to God the Father, continues with petitions which ask God to act in a way which would achieve his purposes, and then has petitions which ask for God's help. The traditional closing, the doxology, is probably a later addition. It is not found in Luke nor in all the manuscripts of Matthew's gospel. The Lord's Prayer is said at Baptism, Eucharist, the Daily Offices, and other services of the Episcopal Church. The BCP includes both contemporary and traditional language versions of the Lord's Prayer (see BCP, p. 364). It is also known as the "Our Father" and the "Pater Noster."

Lord's Supper. *See* Eucharist.

Lord's Table. The altar, also known as the holy table. The term "Lord's table" has been used by those seeking to emphasize the eucharist as a shared meal rather than a sacrifice. All three terms are used with the same meaning in the BCP (see pp. 354, 361).

Lorica (Celtic). Prayer to be chanted while dressing or arming for battle. It is also known as a breastplate prayer. It is recited for protection while one prepares for physical or spiritual battle. *The Hymnal 1982* includes two Celtic loricas, "I bind unto myself today" (Hymn 370) and "Be thou my vision, O Lord of my heart" (Hymn 488). *See* Breastplate of St. Patrick.

Los Angeles, Diocese of. The General Convention of 1895 voted to divide the Diocese of California and establish a new diocese. The new diocese consisted of the following counties: Los Angeles, Orange, Riverside, San Bernardino, San Diego, Santa Barbara, and Ventura. The primary convention of the new diocese met at St. Paul's Church, Los Angeles, Dec. 3–4, 1895, and chose the name the Diocese of Los Angeles. The General Convention of 1973 voted to divide the Diocese of Los Angeles and establish the Diocese of San Diego. The Diocese of Los Angeles now consists of the following counties: Los Angeles, Orange, Santa Barbara, and Ventura. The Cathedral Center of St. Paul, Los Angeles, was dedicated on Oct. 22, 1994.

Louis IX, King of France (Apr. 25, 1214–Aug. 25, 1270). The patron saint for the Third Order of St. Francis. Born in Poissy, Louis IX became King of France on Nov. 29, 1226, and ruled until his death. He lived an austere and prayerful life, and embodied the highest ideals of medieval kingship. He sought to live a Franciscan life of poverty and self-denial in the midst of royal splendor. Louis built the Sainte-Chapelle in Paris as a reliquary for the Crown of Thorns which he acquired in 1239. He participated in crusades in 1248 and 1270. Louis endowed a number of religious houses and supported the theological college founded by Robert de Sorbon in 1257. While on crusade in 1270 he urged the Greek ambassadors to seek reunion with the Church of Rome. He was canonized by Pope Boniface VIII in 1297. Louis died in Tunis while on crusade. He is commemorated in the Episcopal calendar of the church year on Aug. 25.

Louisiana, Diocese of. The Diocese of Louisiana was organized on Apr. 28, 1838, at Christ Church, New Orleans. Philander Chase (1775–1852) organized Christ Church, New Orleans, after a group of Protestants in New Orleans asked Bishop Benjamin Moore in 1805 to send a member of the clergy to start a church. The 1979 General Convention voted to divide the diocese. The continuing Diocese of Louisiana includes the following parishes: Ascension, Assumption, East Baton Rouge, East Feliciana, Iberville, Jefferson, Lafourche, Livingston, Orleans, Pointe Coupee, Plaquemines, St. Bernard, St. Charles, St. Helena, St. James, St. John the Baptist, St. Mary, the southeast portion of St. Martin, St. Tammany, Tangipahoa, Terrebonne, Washington, West Baton Rouge, and West Feliciana. On May 18, 1891, Christ Church, New Orleans, was set apart as Christ Church Cathedral.

Louttit, Henry Irving (Jan. 1, 1903–July 24, 1984). Bishop of South Florida and a key figure in the effort to try Bishop James A. Pike of California for heresy in the mid-1960s. He was born in Buffalo, New York. Louttit received his B.A. from Hobart College in 1925, and his B.D. from the Virginia Theological Seminary in 1929. He was ordained deacon on July 15, 1928, and priest on June 23, 1929. Louttit began his ministry at All Saints' Church, Tarpon Springs, Florida. He soon moved to his home parish, Trinity Church, Miami, as curate. From 1930 until 1933, he was rector of Holy Cross Church, Sanford, Florida. In 1933 he became the rector of Holy Trinity Church, West Palm Beach. During World War II, Louttit was a chaplain in the United States Army with the 31st Infantry Division in the Dutch East Indies. On May 23, 1945, he was consecrated the first Suffragan Bishop of South Florida. On Apr. 14, 1948, he was elected Bishop Coadjutor. On Jan. 1, 1951, he became the fourth Bishop of South Florida. Louttit retired on Dec. 31, 1969. During his episcopate he worked for integration and supported migrant ministries. The confrontation with Bishop James A. Pike was a major episode in his episcopate. Louttit and eleven other bishops formed a "Committee of Bishops to Defend the Faith" and prepared a presentment which charged Pike with several heresies. Eventually the presentment was dropped in exchange for a resolution of censure which was adopted by the House of Bishops at its meeting in Wheeling, West Virginia, in Sept. 1966. Louttit died in Orlando.

"Love Feast." *See* Agape.

Low Church. The term was apparently invented to describe churchmen whose principles were the opposite of "high church." The term "low church" emerged in England in the early eighteenth century. During this period, it was virtually synonymous with "latitudinarian." Low church teaching minimized the authority of the episcopate and tended to exalt royal supremacy. This loyalty to the throne was not because of the divine right of kings. It reflected a convenient anti-Roman Catholic political arrangement, since the Hanoverians were safely Protestant. The low church party stressed the importance of preaching as moral discourse and tended to assign sacraments to a subordinate place in church life. In this sense, they had a "low" doctrine of the church.

In the nineteenth century the term was used in contrast to the high church position of the Oxford reformers. In this case, "low church" designated the evangelicals. They were followers of the Wesleys who remained in the Church of England. Thus in this period, low church teaching became associated with individualism, personal religious experience, dislike of ritual, conversion by the power of the Holy Spirit, a strong emphasis on the authority of scripture, and evangelistic preaching. The term "low church" continues to carry these connotations in the early twenty-first century. *See* High Church.

Low Mass. A simple celebration of the eucharist in which the celebrant was typically assisted by only one server. The entire liturgy was said, not sung. The priest typically read all the lections and led all the prayers. The celebrant thus took over the prior liturgical roles of the deacon, lector, cantor, and choir in the eucharist. The priest alone said certain texts that were previously said with the congregation. Low mass dates from the late middle ages in the western church. All priests were expected to celebrate the Mass daily, and the traditional fullness of celebration was compromised. It became the most frequent celebration of the eucharist in the west. Low mass was never allowed in the east.

The congregation at low mass was relatively passive as the service was done for them by the celebrant. However, this tendency was countered by the Anglican Prayer Book tradition. The eucharistic liturgy of the 1549 Prayer Book was in the vernacular. It included responses that were made by the congregation. The 1789 American Prayer Book encouraged participation of lay readers by using the word "Minister" instead of "Priest" in certain directions. The 1979 BCP calls for lay persons to read the lessons other than the gospel at the eucharist. The eucharistic gospel is to be read by the deacon if a deacon is present. A deacon or lay person is to lead the prayers of the people. Representatives of the congregation are to present the people's offerings of bread and wine, and money or other gifts (BCP, p. 361). Various eucharistic texts are reserved for the congregation, or appointed to be said by the celebrant and congregation together. In these ways the liturgical roles of the eucharist are once again shared by the congregation and ministers other than the celebrant. Although the term "low mass" is obsolete, it is sometimes used loosely to indicate a simple eucharist that is said.

Low Sunday. The Sunday after Easter, the Second Sunday of Easter. The term may reflect the somewhat less intense celebration of the day relative to the great feast of Easter on the preceding Sunday. Many parishes experience lower attendance on Low Sunday than on Easter Day.

Low, Juliette Magill Kinzie Gordon (Oct. 31, 1860–Jan. 18, 1927). Founder of the Girl Scouts. She was born in Savannah, Georgia. Low was educated at Stuart Hall and Edge Hill in Virginia, and at the Mesdemoiselles Charbonnier's in New York City. She was a lifelong member of Christ Church, Savannah. In 1911 Low met the founder of the Boy Scouts, Sir Robert Baden-Powell, in England, where she was living at the time. Following his example, she organized Girl Guide troops in England and Scotland. On Mar. 12, 1912, Low formed the first Girl Guide units in Savannah, enrolling sixteen girls in two patrols. Interest in Girl Guide units increased around the country, following a tour of the United States by Sir Baden-Powell. In 1913 she worked in Washington to establish a national organization. She hoped to unite her organization with the Campfire Girls, which was organized in 1910, but this did not happen. In 1915 the Girl Scouts of America was formed with Low as president. In 1919 the first International Council of Girl Guides and Girl Scouts met in London. She resigned as president of the Girl Scouts in 1920. Low died in Savannah.

Lower Criticism. This method of scriptural analysis, most often called text criticism, focuses on the Hebrew, Greek, or Aramaic text of a particular portion of scripture. It works from the conclusion that we do not have any original copies of any scriptural material. When one manuscript is not exactly the same as another, it is necessary to find a way to determine which text is closest to the original. Because there are many scriptural manuscripts from different times and places, most of the arguments are based on how and why scribes might be the cause of the differences. The primary principle is the assumption that the text which is hardest to explain is likely to be the earliest. If we can explain why a scribe at a certain time and place might have caused a specific reading, then it is likely that the particular reading is non-original. Many scholarly Hebrew and Greek texts print a revision of the material which the critics have argued is the most original, with the significant manuscript variations listed at the bottom of the page. *See* Higher Criticism.

Lowrie, Walter (Apr. 26, 1868–Aug. 12, 1959). Kierkegaardian theologian and translator. He was born in Philadelphia. Lowrie received his B.A. in 1890, and his M.A. in 1893, both from Princeton University. He studied in Germany, Italy, and Switzerland in 1893–1894. Upon his return home he joined the Episcopal Church. Lowrie was ordained deacon on June 9, 1895, and priest on Dec. 27, 1896. From 1896 until 1898, he was curate at St. James Church, Philadelphia. In 1898–1899, and 1900–1903, he was with the City Mission in Philadelphia. He then served churches in Southwark, Pennsylvania; Boston, Massachusetts; and Newport, Rhode Island. From 1907 until 1930, Lowrie was rector of St. Paul's American Church in Rome. When he retired in 1930, he returned to Princeton and began what he called an "itinerant ministry." He published 39 books and numerous articles, including *The Short Story of Jesus* (1943) and *Kierkegaard* (1938). *A Complete Bibliography of Walter Lowrie* was compiled by Donald M. Fox, and published in 1979. From his retirement in 1930 until his death, Lowrie studied and translated the works of Søren Kierkegaard, the Danish nineteenth-century theologian. From 1939 until 1945, he published 12 volumes of Kierkegaard translations. During his retirement, he traveled and lectured throughout the world. Lowrie died in Princeton.

Loyalists. "Toryism" in the American colonies at the time of the American Revolution was virtually synonymous with "Loyalism." The term described those who were critical of colonial resistance to British imperial authority and remained loyal to the Crown. Evidences of such "loyalty" appeared tentatively in the pre-Revolutionary crises. After the Revolution, the term embraced those who supported the British imperial cause, the idea of colonial subordination, or who regarded all colonial remonstrance and resistance as morally wrong. Some 80,000 Loyalists and their dependents, including a large number of Anglican clergy, went into exile after the Revolution. They went to Great Britain, Canada, or the West Indies. *See* Loyalty Oath to the English Sovereign.

Loyalty Oath to the English Sovereign. Beginning in 1549, a person ordained in the Church of England was required to swear an Oath of Loyalty to the sovereign. In the liturgy for ordaining deacons, the ordinand had to say: "I, *A. B.*, utterly testify and declare in my conscience, That the King's Highness is the only Supream Governour of this Realm, and of all other his Highnesses Dominions and Countries, as well in all Spiritual or Ecclesiastical things or causes, as Temporal: And that no foreign Prince, Person, Prelate, State, or Potentate hath or ought to have any jurisdiction, power, superiority, pre-eminence or authority Ecclesiastical or Spiritual within this Realm. And therefore I do utterly denounce and forsake all foreign jurisdictions, powers, superiorities and authorities; and do promise, That from henceforth I shall bear faith and true allegiance to the King's Highness, His Heirs and Successors, and to my power shall assist and defend all jurisdictions, priviledges, pre-eminences and authorities granted or belonging to the King's Highness, His Heirs and Successors, or united and annexed to the Imperial Crown of this Realm. So help me God." All Church of England clergy in the American colonies had taken this oath of allegiance to the King. When the colonies declared independence from England, Loyalist clergy who believed this oath was binding fled the country. After American independence, the requirement for the loyalty oath delayed the ordination of Samuel Seabury as first Bishop of Connecticut and the first bishop in the Episcopal Church. Seabury was finally ordained bishop in Scotland by nonjuring bishops of the Episcopal Church in Scotland in 1784, with no loyalty oath to the English sovereign required. *See* Loyalists.

Lucernaria, Lucernarium. Lucernarium is the singular form and *Lucernaria* the plural of the Latin word for "light." In the *BOS* and *The Hymnal 1982* (S 305–S 320 in the *Accompaniment Edition, Vol. 1*), the term is used for the optional anthems which may be sung during the lighting of candles in the Order of Worship for the Evening (BCP, p. 109). These anthems, which vary with the season, were used at the lighting of the evening light in old Gallican liturgies.

Luke the Evangelist, Saint. St. Luke was a Gentile, and the traditional author of the Gospel According to Luke and the Acts of the Apostles. He was a physician and is identified with the church's ministry of healing. In Col 4:14, he is described as "the beloved physician." Many Episcopal hospitals have the name of St. Luke because he is the patron saint of healing and the healing professions. His uniqueness is seen in his detailed description of the birth of Jesus, possibly deriving from information given him by Mary, the Lord's mother. It is in the Gospel According to Luke that we have the texts of the earliest Christian hymns, *Magnificat*, *Benedictus*, and *Nunc dimittis*. Only this gospel has the parables about the Good Samaritan and the Prodigal Son. Luke gives special emphasis to the worth and status of women. He stresses the inclusivity of the compassion and love of God. Luke is often symbolized as a winged sacrificial ox holding a gospel book. This symbolism is taken from the Gospel According to Luke, which begins with Zechariah sacrificing in the temple and which describes the sacrifice of Christ. Luke is sometimes pictured as a painter making Christ known through art. Luke accompanied Paul on his second missionary trip from Troas to Philippi, and on the third missionary trip from Philippi to Jerusalem. He also went with Paul to Rome. Luke's life and work as a physician, historian, and evangelist is commemorated in the Episcopal calendar of the church year on Oct. 18.

Luna. A holder for the consecrated host in a monstrance, typically used for the service of Benediction. It is also known as a lunette. The luna fits into the back of the monstrance and holds the host in an upright and visible position. The host is seen through the transparent glass, but it does not touch the glass of the monstrance. *See* Benediction of the Blessed Sacrament; *see* Monstrance.

Lund Principle. An ecumenical principle set forth by the 1952 Faith and Order Conference of the World Council of Churches held at Lund, Sweden, and officially endorsed by Lambeth in 1968. This ecumenical principle was given specific shape for the Episcopal Church by the 1976 General Convention: "that the Episcopal Church at every level of its life be urged to act together and in concert with other churches of Jesus Christ in all matters except those in which deep differences of conviction or church order compel us to act separately."

Lunette. *See* Luna.

Lustral Water. *See* Holy Water.

Lustration. This purificatory rite or sacrifice may involve the ceremonial cleansing of a person, a house, a city, an army, or a whole people. The *BOS* provides a form for the Restoring of Things Profaned.

Luther, Martin (Nov. 10, 1483–Feb. 18, 1546). Founder of the sixteenth-century Reformation in Germany. He was born in Eisleben, Thuringia, Germany. Luther was baptized on Nov. 11, 1483, the Feast of St. Martin of Tours, and named after the saint. He received his M.A. in Feb. 1505 from the University of Erfurt. On July 17, 1505, he entered the cloister of the Order of St. Augustine in Erfurt. He was ordained priest on Apr. 4, 1507. In 1511 Luther transferred to the monastery in Wittenberg. In the next year he was named Professor of Holy Scripture at the University of Wittenberg. In 1514 he had an experience which enabled him to understand the righteousness of God in a totally new way. He came to believe that righteousness is a gift of God and that a merciful God justifies us by grace through faith. On Oct. 31, 1517, Luther posted his 95 Theses on the door of the Castle Church in Wittenberg. This date is regarded as the beginning of the Reformation. On June 15, 1520, Pope Leo X signed the papal bull, *Exsurge Domine*, condemning 41 of Luther's teachings. One of Luther's major contributions was translating the Bible into German. He was a musician and wrote numerous hymns. Seven of Luther's hymns are used in *The Hymnal 1982*, including "Savior of the nations come!" (Hymn 54), "When Jesus went to Jordan's stream" (Hymn 139), and "A Mighty Fortress is our God"(Hymn 687). He wrote the music used in "Before thy throne, O God, we kneel" (Hymn 575) and the musical setting that was the basis for S 283, *Te Deum laudamus*. Luther died in Eisleben. He is commemorated in the Episcopal calendar of the church year on Feb. 18.

Lux Mundi. A volume of theological essays edited by Charles Gore, principal of Pusey House, Oxford. It was published in 1889 in England. The collection was subtitled *A Series of Studies in the Religion of the Incarnation*, and it sought to interpret the doctrinal tradition of the church so that Christians could affirm new developments in scientific and historical studies. The purpose of the essays was expressed in the preface to the first edition which noted that the real development of theology is "the process in which the Church, standing firm in her old truths, enters into the apprehension of the new social and intellectual movements of each age."

Essays in the volume were written by young theologians associated with Oxford University, many of whom made significant contributions to theological scholarship later in their lives, including Gore himself, Henry Scott Holland, J. R. Illingworth, R. C. Moberly, and F. Paget. The volume provoked much protest, especially the essay by Gore on the inspiration of Holy Scripture. But for many *Lux Mundi* began a new theological

development in Anglicanism, subsequently known as liberal catholicism. *See* Gore, Charles; *see* Liberal Catholicism, Liberal Catholic Movement.

LXX. *See* Septuagint.

Lych-Gate. A covered gateway to a church yard or church property where a coffin containing a corpse is set down prior to burial to await the assembly of the mourners, the pall bearers, and the officiating minister. The formation of the funeral procession and the funeral service will follow this gathering at the lych-gate. The term is derived from an Old English word for "corpse."

M

M.A. Master of Arts. The degree requires a bachelor's degree and can be either a research program or a general academic program.

Mace. *See* Virge.

Macrina the Younger (c. 327–c. 379). Superior of a religious community of women, ascetic, spiritual director, and older sister of the Cappadocians Basil of Caesarea (c. 330–379) and Gregory of Nyssa (c. 331–c. 395). She was strongly influenced by Macrina the Elder (d. 340), her paternal grandmother. After the death of Macrina the Younger's fiancé when she was 12 years old, she decided to remain a virgin and stay with her mother, Emmelia. Their household at Annesi in Pontus, Asia Minor, became a religious community of women, with Macrina as superior. She was very influential in the education and spiritual development of Basil and Gregory. Much of what is known of her comes from Gregory's writings, including his *Life of Macrina*. She was a person of great spiritual depth. She was well educated, and a competent theologian. Macrina influenced Basil to receive holy orders instead of pursuing a secular career. When she was on her deathbed, she taught Gregory concerning the nature and destiny of the human soul. Macrina's life is commemorated in the Episcopal calendar of the church year on July 19. *See* Cappadocians, or Cappadocian Fathers.

Madison, James (Aug. 27, 1749–Mar. 6, 1812). The first Bishop of Virginia. He was born in Staunton, Virginia. Madison graduated from William and Mary College in 1771 and studied law for two years before becoming professor of natural philosophy and mathematics at William and Mary in 1773. During the American Revolution he supported the Patriots. He studied theology on his own. Madison went to England where he was ordained deacon on Sept. 29, 1775, and priest on Oct. 1, 1775. Upon his return to the United States, he served as president of William and Mary College from 1777 until his death. On Sept. 19, 1790, Madison was consecrated at Lambeth Palace, the last bishop of the Episcopal Church to be consecrated abroad. He died in Williamsburg, Virginia.

Madonna. The Blessed Virgin Mary. The term is from the Italian, "my lady." It also indicates artistic representations of Mary in portraits or statues. The Madonna Lily is the plant *Lilium candidum*, which is also called the White Lily and the Annunciation Lily. It has white flowers that are trumpet-shaped. The Madonna Lily has been used as a symbol of Mary.

Magna et mirabilia. Canticle 19 in the 1979 BCP (p. 94), based on Rv 15:3–4. It begins, "O ruler of the universe, Lord God, great deeds are they that you have done, surpassing human understanding." It is also known as the Song of the Redeemed. In this heavenly vision, the victorious faithful sing the Song of Moses and the Song of the Lamb. The Song of Moses was the celebration of Moses and the people of Israel after they crossed the Red Sea and escaped from bondage in Egypt (Ex 15:1–18; See Canticle 8, *Cantemus Domino*, BCP, p. 85). The Song of the Redeemed reflects a vision of the completion of salvation for the faithful in heaven, as the Song of Moses was a great event in the history of God's mighty acts in the world for human salvation. *Magna et mirabilia* draws together several OT passages. It may have been an early Christian hymn. It first appeared as a Prayer Book canticle in the 1979 BCP. It concludes with a doxology. *Magna et mirabilia* is recommended for use at Morning Prayer after the NT reading on Mondays and Saturdays and after the NT reading at Morning Prayer on Thursdays in Advent and Lent (BCP, p. 144). *The Hymnal 1982 Accompaniment Edition, Vol. 1*, provides several musical settings for *Magna et mirabilia* (S 267–S 271). The hymn "How wondrous and great thy works, God of praise" (Hymns 532/533 in *The Hymnal 1982*) by Henry Ustick Onderdonk (1759–1858), Bishop of Pennsylvania, is a metrical (poetic) version of *Magna et mirabilia*. The metrical version of the canticle may be used at Morning or Evening Prayer instead of *Magna et mirabilia* (BCP, p. 141).

Magnificat. This song of praise, also known as "The Song of Mary," is from the account in Lk 1:46–55 of Mary's visit to her relative Elizabeth when Mary was pregnant with Jesus and Elizabeth was pregnant with John the Baptist. It is attributed to Mary in the Lucan narrative, but a minority of ancient authorities attributed it to Elizabeth. The term is from the opening words of the passage in the Latin Vulgate, *Magnificat anima mea Dominum* ("My soul magnifies the Lord"). The *Magnificat* strongly resembles and may have been modeled after the Song of Hannah (1 Sm 2:1–10), which is quite similar in its structure and themes. Both songs emphasize God's holiness and power, God's option for the poor and judgment on the rich, the fulfillment of God's promises, and the redemption of God's people.

The *Magnificat* is the traditional canticle of vespers. It was the only canticle for use after the first lesson of Evensong in the 1549 BCP. It was not used in the 1789 American BCP, but it was restored in the 1892 BCP. The 1928 BCP allowed its use as the only canticle at Evening Prayer when one lesson was read. The 1979 BCP permits use of the *Magnificat* at both Morning Prayer and Evening Prayer. It appears as Canticles 3 and 15 in the BCP, and it is printed in both the Rite 1 and Rite 2 forms for Evening Prayer. It may also be used at the Act of Thanksgiving in the Thanksgiving for the Birth or Adoption of a Child (BCP, pp. 441–442).

The Hymnal 1982 has a variety of settings for the *Magnificat* (S 242–S 247), including Plainsong, Tonus Peregrinus, adapted by Bruce E. Ford (S 242) and the setting *Cathedral of the Isles* by Betty Carr Pulkingham (S 247). The hymn text "Tell out, my soul" by Timothy Dudley-Smith (Hymns 437–438) is based on the Song of Mary.

Mahan, Milo (May 24, 1819–Sept. 3, 1870). Historian, educator, and high churchman. He was born in Suffolk, Virginia. Mahan studied at the Flushing Institute, Long Island, and then taught Greek at the Episcopal High School in Alexandria, Virginia. His admiration of the Oxford Movement displeased Bishop William Meade. Mahan went back to Flushing where he taught at St. Paul's College. He studied privately for the ordained ministry and was ordained deacon on Oct. 27, 1845, and priest on Dec. 14, 1846. He began his ministry as an assistant at the Church of the Annunciation, New York. In Nov. 1848 he became rector of Grace Church, Jersey City, New Jersey. In 1850 he became the assistant at St. Mark's Church, Philadelphia. Mahan was Professor of Ecclesiastical History at the

General Theological Seminary from 1851 until 1864. He resigned at General Seminary because of his southern sympathies during the Civil War. He became rector of St. Paul's Church, Baltimore. On June 30, 1870, Mahan was called back to General Seminary to be Professor of Systematic Divinity, but died before he began his duties. His two major historical works were *A Church History of the First Three Centuries, from the Thirtieth to the Three Hundred and Twenty-third Year of the Christian Era* (1860), and *Church History of the First Seven Centuries* (1872). Mahan died in Baltimore.

Maine, Diocese of. This diocese was organized on May 3, 1820, at Brunswick. From 1811 until 1820 Maine was in the Diocese of Massachusetts, which was in the Eastern Diocese. On Sept. 5, 1820, the newly formed Diocese of Maine joined the Eastern Diocese and remained in it until Bishop Alexander Griswold's death in 1843. The Eastern Diocese was not a diocese in the usual sense, but an arrangement whereby several weak dioceses could work together. From Aug. 11, 1843 until Oct. 31, 1847, Bishop John P. K. Henshaw of Rhode Island had episcopal oversight of Maine. Since Oct. 31, 1847, Maine has had its own bishop. On Aug. 15, 1867, the cornerstone was laid for St. Luke's Cathedral, Portland, and the first service was held there on Dec. 25, 1868. It was consecrated on Oct. 18, 1877. The Diocese of Maine includes the entire state. *See* Eastern Diocese.

Major Feasts. Major celebrations of the church year for which the Prayer Book appoints proper collects, psalms, and lessons. They include the seven principal feasts (Easter Day, Ascension Day, Pentecost, Trinity Sunday, All Saints' Day, Christmas Day, and the Epiphany), Sundays, and major holy days (including feasts of our Lord, all feasts of apostles, all feasts of evangelists, and other designated feasts [see BCP, pp. 15–17, 31–33]). *See* Lesser Feasts and Fasts.

Major Orders. The term traditionally refers to the holy orders of bishop, priest, and deacon. The major orders were distinguished from minor orders such as porter (doorkeeper), lector, exorcist, and acolyte. The subdiaconate was considered a minor order until it was included among the major orders by Pope Innocent III in 1207. The subdiaconate was suppressed in the Roman Catholic Church in 1972. A few Episcopal churches continue to allow a liturgical role for a "subdeacon" at the

eucharist. The minor orders were transitory steps that led to the major orders. This hierarchical understanding of ministry is also reflected in the requirement that all candidates for the priesthood must first be ordained as deacons before ordination as priests. This requirement dates from the ninth century. It led to decreased appreciation for the significance of the diaconate. Since all Christian ministry is "major" and rooted in baptism and the promises of the baptismal covenant, the term "major orders" can be misleading. The Catechism states that "the ministers of the Church are lay persons, bishops, priests, and deacons" (BCP, p. 855). However, the Preface to the Ordination Rites does acknowledge the ancient origin of the "three distinct orders of ordained ministers" of bishops, priests, and deacons which "have been characteristic of Christ's holy catholic church." This Preface adds that it is "the intention and purpose" of the Episcopal Church to "maintain and continue" the three orders. Candidates for these ordained ministries are "admitted to these sacred orders by solemn prayer and the laying on of episcopal hands" (BCP, p. 510). *See* Minor Orders.

Malania, Leo (May 21, 1911–Sept. 1, 1983). Prayer Book revision coordinator. He was born in Tiflis, in the Russian province of Georgia. Malania received his B.A. from the University of Toronto in 1934. He studied at the George Mercer School of Theology. Malania was ordained deacon on Feb. 27, 1965, and priest on Dec. 21, 1965. Before ordination, he was special assistant executive officer for the secretary general of the United Nations. After his ordination, he taught liturgics and homiletics at the Mercer School of Theology. He was a fellow of the North American Academy of Liturgy, and a member of the council of the Associated Parishes. From 1968 until 1980, Malania was the Coordinator of the Book of Common Prayer Revision, which resulted in the 1979 BCP. He died in Cooperstown, New York.

Malines Conversations. A series of conversations between prominent Roman Catholic and Anglican figures. The conversations were held between 1921 and 1925 in Malines, Belgium, under the presidency of its Cardinal Archbishop, D. J. Mercier, at the instigation of Charles Lindley Wood, Second Viscount Halifax. Wood published the results in 1928 and 1930. All the conversations after the first took place with the knowledge of the Pope and the Archbishop of Canterbury. Anglican participants included Bishops Charles Gore and W. H. Frere. A wide range of agreements was reached on papal primacy of honor, real presence, eucharistic sacrifice, episcopacy, etc., which foreshadow the current discussions of the Anglican-Roman Catholic International Commission (ARCIC). The movement was temporarily set back by evangelical opposition in the Church of England and by the subsequent divergence of Anglican and Roman Catholic positions concerning birth control. *See* Anglican-Roman Catholic International Commission (ARCIC).

Mandate. *See* Prayer Book Society.

Manicheism, Manichaeism. This dualistic heresy was named after Manes, a third-century Babylonian. He taught that matter is evil and salvation consists in freeing the human soul from its commingling with the physical body. The soul was understood to return to an original state of separation from everything material in a purely spiritual realm of light. The movement emphasized self-knowledge and strict ascetical discipline.

Maniple. A eucharistic vestment, typically an oblong band of silk or linen, worn above the left wrist. The maniple is usually of the same color and material as the eucharistic stole. Its earliest use was as a handkerchief held in the left hand. It later became an ornament of secular rank. Although it may have had practical uses at one time, it also came to be a symbol of rank in the church. It was associated with subdeacons and higher orders of clergy. The maniple is seldom used in the Episcopal Church.

Manning, William Thomas (May 12, 1866–Nov. 18, 1949). Tenth Bishop of New York. Manning was born in Northampton, England. In 1882 his family came to the United States, and in 1888 Manning entered the College of the University of the South and enrolled in its School of Theology at the same time. In 1894 he was granted the B.D. degree. While at the University of the South he was greatly influenced by William Porcher DuBose and assisted DuBose in writing *The Soteriology of the New Testament* (1892). Manning was ordained deacon on Dec. 12, 1889, and priest on Dec. 12, 1891. From 1891 until 1893 he was rector of Trinity Church, Redlands, California. From 1893 until 1895 he was Professor of Systematic Divinity at the School of Theology of the University of the South. After serving as rector of St. John's Church, Lansdowne, Pennsylvania, 1896–1898, he was rector of Christ Church,

Nashville, 1898–1903. Manning then served as vicar of St. Agnes', New York, 1903–1904, assistant rector of Trinity Church, New York, 1904–1908, and rector from 1908 until 1921. On May 11, 1921, he was consecrated Bishop of New York and served in that position until he retired on Dec. 31, 1946. One of his major accomplishments was the building of the nave of the Cathedral of St. John the Divine, which was completed in 1939. Manning died in New York City.

Manross, William Wilson (Feb. 21, 1905–July 5, 1987). Episcopal Church historian, author, and seminary professor. He was born in Syracuse, New York. Manross received his B.A. from Hobart College in 1926; his S.T.B. from the General Theological Seminary in 1931; and his M.A. in 1930 and his Ph.D. in 1938, both from Columbia University. He was ordained deacon on June 4, 1929, and priest on June 11, 1930. From 1929 until 1939, Manross was fellow and tutor at the General Theological Seminary. Manross was librarian of the Church Historical Society from 1948 until 1956. He was professor of church history and librarian at the Philadelphia Divinity School from 1958 until his retirement in 1973. For thirty-five years Manross was a member of the editorial board of the *Historical Magazine of the Protestant Episcopal Church*. His two major books are *A History of the American Episcopal Church* (1935), and *The Episcopal Church in the United States, 1800–1840: A Study in Church Life* (1938). He also compiled *The Fulham Papers in the Lambeth Palace Library: American Colonial Section Calendar and Indexes* (1965). Manross died in Havertown, Pennsylvania.

Manteo. An American Indian whose baptism on Aug. 13, 1587 is regarded as the first recorded Anglican baptism in the American colonies. Manteo was among a group of Indians captured by English navigators Philip Amadas and Arthur Barlowe at Roanoke Island off the coast of North Carolina. Sir Walter Raleigh had sent the navigators to find a site for a colony in the new world. Manteo was given the title Lord of Roanoke and Dasmonguepeuk.

Manual Acts. Any gestures made by the presider or other ministers during a religious service. The term is used specifically to refer to the manual acts required by the rubrics of the BCP during the words of institution in the eucharistic Prayer (e.g., p. 362–363). More extensive manual acts were required by earlier editions of the Prayer Book. Other gestures not mentioned by the rubrics are frequently included, such as raising the bread and wine in offering at the words "we offer you these gifts" (BCP, p. 363).

M.A.R. Master of Arts in Religion. The degree requires a bachelor's degree and can be either a research program or a general academic program.

Maranatha, or Marana tha. An Aramaic liturgical exclamation, *marana tha,* used by Paul at 1 Cor 16:22, translated as an eschatological prayer, "Our Lord, come!" (NRSV). It is part of Paul's closing greeting at the end of his First Letter to the Corinthians. It could be read *maran atha,* and translated as a creedal statement, "Our Lord has come." The translation "Our Lord, come!" is preferred. It expresses yearning for Christ's return in glory and the eschatological hope of the early church. It has been likened to Rv 22:20, "Come, Lord Jesus!" (NRSV). Paul's use of an Aramaic expression in a letter to Gentile Christians at Corinth indicates that it was a familiar expression of hope and expectation of Christ's return that was shared by Christians. It is still used at times to express Christian hope, especially among charismatic Christians.

Marbeck, John (d. c. 1585). *See* Merbecke or Marbeck, John.

Marcionism. Name given to theological doctrines developed and advocated by the second-century Bithynian teacher, Marcion (d. c. 160). He was a Christian by upbringing, but he fell under gnostic influences. In 144 Marcion broke with the Christian church because he could not reconcile the Old and New Testaments. He argued that the God of the OT was a God of legalism and strict justice. In contrast, the God of the NT was a God of grace and love. For Marcion, the OT God who created the world was a lower deity, subordinate to the God revealed in Jesus Christ.

This dualism led Marcion to reject the OT as inspired writing. He acknowledged a severely truncated NT, consisting of the Gospel According to Luke and the ten genuine Pauline epistles all purged of what Marcion regarded as judaizing material. The church declared Marcion's teaching heretical. But the widespread popularity of his teaching forced orthodox Christianity to develop and defend its own list of canonical books. The popularity of Marcionism also prompted Christianity to

assert the goodness of creation by the one God of both Testaments.

M.A.R.E. Master of Arts in Religious Education. The degree requires a bachelor's degree and equips persons for competent leadership in educational ministry.

Margaret (c. 1045–Nov. 16, 1093). Queen of Scotland and reformer credited with removing Celtic influences in the Scottish Church. She was born in Hungary and came to England in 1057. Margaret married King Malcolm III of Scotland around 1067. They had eight children. She used her influence to bring Scotland under Roman obedience and remove what was left of Celtic Church life and practice. Margaret is remembered for her austere and ascetic life, her reformation of the Scottish Church, her founding of schools, orphanages, and hospitals, and her generosity. She was canonized in 1250. Margaret is commemorated in the Episcopal calendar of the church year on Nov. 16.

Margaret Coffin Prayer Book Society. *See* Coffin, Margaret.

Mark the Evangelist, Saint. Author of the second gospel. He was also known as John Mark. He was the son of Mary of Jerusalem. Although she was a widow, she was a woman of means. She owned a house which was large enough to hold a large Christian gathering, and she had at least one maid. The Last Supper of Jesus and his disciples may have been in her house. Mark may have witnessed some of the final events in Jesus' life. It is believed that Mark was in the Garden of Gethsemane when Jesus was taken captive. The young man was noticed and about to be questioned. Apparently he lost his nerve and ran away, leaving his clothes in the hands of Christ's captors. Later on, Mark went to Antioch with his cousin Barnabas. He accompanied Paul and Barnabas on part of their first missionary journey, but "ran away" again for some unknown reason. His action angered Paul. When Mark asked to go along on the second journey, Paul flatly refused. Mark seems to have been close to Peter. It is believed that Mark was Peter's secretary and wrote down many of the things Peter remembered about Jesus. The gospel which bears Mark's name may be based on the eye-witness reports of Peter. Mark is supposed to have taken Christianity to Alexandria. The church in Alexandria claims Mark as its first bishop. One ancient account states that he suffered a martyr's death there. Mark's life is commemorated in the Episcopal calendar of the church year on Apr. 25.

Marks of the Church. *See* Notes of the Church.

Marquette, Diocese of. The Diocese of Northern Michigan was known as the Diocese of Marquette from Nov. 14, 1895, until June 2, 1937.

Marriage. The sacramental rite of the church in which a woman and a man "enter into a life-long union, make their vows before God and the Church, and receive the grace and blessing of God to help them fulfill their vows" (BCP, p. 861). The union of husband and wife is understood to be intended by God for their mutual joy; for the help and comfort given one another in prosperity and adversity; and, when it is God's will, for the procreation of children and their nurture in the knowledge and love of the Lord (BCP, p. 423). At the Declaration of Consent, both the woman and the man promise to love, comfort, honor, and keep their spouse, in sickness and in health, and, forsaking all others, to be faithful to their spouse as long as they both live (BCP, p. 424). The congregation witnesses the couple's promises, and the members of the congregation promise to do all in their power to uphold the couple in their marriage. At the Marriage, the couple may pledge their lives to each other by the giving and receiving of rings as symbols of their vows. When desired, other appropriate symbols of their vows may be used instead of rings. In the Episcopal Church it is required that at least one of the parties be a baptized Christian, that the ceremony be attested by at least two witnesses, and that the marriage conform to the laws of the state and the canons of the church. The member of the clergy who will solemnize the marriage typically meets with the couple on several occasions prior to the service to discuss the meaning of Christian marriage in the couple's life. When one of the parties has been previously married and divorced, the consent of the diocesan bishop must be obtained prior to solemnization of the marriage. *See* Celebration and Blessing of a Marriage.

Marshall, John (Sept. 24, 1755–July 6, 1835). Third Chief Justice of the United States Supreme Court. He was born in Germantown, now Midland, Virginia. Marshall participated in the American Revolution and was part of the Minute Men at the siege of Norfolk. In 1780 he attended a course of lectures on law at William and Mary College,

and in August of that year he was admitted to the bar. He began his practice in Fauquier County and then moved to Richmond. Marshall served in the Virginia Assembly, 1782–1791 and 1795–1797, and was a delegate to the state convention which ratified the Federal Constitution in 1788. From Jan. 31, 1801, until his death, he was the third Chief Justice of the Supreme Court. His father, Thomas, was a vestryman; and his grandfather, William Keith, was a clergyman of the Church of England. John Marshall attended Monumental Church, Richmond. He was a delegate to the 1813 General Convention. Marshall's beliefs were primarily Unitarian. He never became a member of the Episcopal Church, which he attended "to set an example." His daughter, however, wrote in her journal that Marshall was converted late in life to a belief in the divinity by reading a book written by his grandfather. Marshall determined to become a member, but he died before this wish could be realized. He died in Philadelphia.

Martin of Tours (c. 330–Nov. 11, 397). The primary molder of Frankish Christianity and one of the patron saints of France. He was born in Sabaria, the modern Szombathely, in Hungary. After serving in the military, he came under the influence of Hilary of Poitiers. He became a defender of Nicene orthodoxy against the Arians. Around 370 he gathered a group of monks at Poitiers and established what was probably the first monastery in the west. In 372 he was elected Bishop of Tours and established a second monastery at Marmoutier. Martin was renowned as a miracle worker, a missionary, and a doer of good deeds. The most famous story about him is that while he was a catechumen and young soldier, a poor man without clothes encountered him on a cold winter day. Martin cut his cloak in two and gave half of it to the beggar. The next night Christ appeared to Martin in the half cloak and said to the attendant angels, "Martin, a simple catechumen, gave me this cloak." He is commemorated in the Episcopal calendar of the church year on Nov. 11.

Martyn, Henry (Feb. 18, 1781–Oct. 16, 1812). One of the founders of the Christian church in India and Iran. He was born in Truro, Cornwall, England. Martyn received his B.A. in 1801, his M.A. in 1804, and his B.D. in 1805, all from St. John's College, Cambridge. In 1803 he became the curate of Charles Simeon at Cambridge. He served there until July 17, 1805, when he sailed for India as a chaplain of the East India Company. While in India he translated the NT into Hindustani, Persian, and Arabic, the Psalms into

Persian, and the BCP into Hindustani. He died in Tokat, Armenia. Martyn is commemorated in the Episcopal calendar of the church year on Oct. 19.

Martyr. The term comes from the Greek word meaning "witness," which referred originally to the disciples and apostles who "witnessed" the life, ministry, death, and resurrection of Jesus Christ. Later it came to mean those who had witnessed to their faith in Jesus by their suffering and those who died during persecution since it meant witnessing to the greatest degree possible. Some regard the Holy Innocents of Bethlehem as the first Christian martyrs. Their martyrdom is commemorated on Dec. 28 in the Episcopal calendar of the church year. Others argue that Stephen was the first Christian martyr. Stephen's witness is commemorated on Dec. 26 in the Episcopal calendar of the church year. Clement of Rome wrote of witness in the sense of giving one's life for the faith. Tertullian wrote of martyrdom as a second baptism because it removed all sin and assured going to heaven. He urged that the blood of the martyrs is the seed of the church.

Martyrium. A church built over a martyr's tomb or relics. The term may also indicate a church built in honor of a martyr. *See* Relics; *see* Reliquary.

Martyrs of Japan, The. Francis Xavier, a Jesuit, first brought Christianity to Japan in 1549. Christianity spread rapidly, causing resentment and leading to persecution. On Feb. 5, 1597, twenty-six Christians—six European Franciscans, three Japanese Jesuits, and seventeen Japanese laymen, including three young boys, were crucified at Nagasaki. They were put on crosses and then stabbed with spears. Persecutions broke out again in the early seventeenth century. Christianity was driven underground around 1630. The leader of those martyred in 1597 was Paul Miki, a Japanese Jesuit priest. The Roman Catholic Church calls this commemoration "Paul Miki and Companions." These martyrs were canonized by the Roman Church in 1862. In 1959 they were added to the calendar of the Holy Catholic Church in Japan (Nippon Sei Ko Kai), which is the Anglican Church in Japan. These martyrs are commemorated in the Episcopal calendar of the church year on Feb. 5.

Martyrs of Lyons. In 177 a persecution of the Christians in Gaul (France) took place. The five persons most savagely persecuted were Attalus, Blandina, Maturus, Sanctus, and Pothinus, the first Bishop of Lyons. Nothing is known about Attalus. Blandina was a virgin slave girl, Maturus a recent convert, and Sanctus a deacon. Pothinus is believed to have been a disciple of Polycarp. Eusebius, the first church historian, has a "Letter of the Churches of Lyons and Vienne" in his *Ecclesiastical History* which describes in detail the horrible suffering and the heroic courage of these martyrs. They are commemorated in the Episcopal calendar of the church year on June 2.

Martyrs of New Guinea. Eight missionaries and two Papuan martyrs who died at the hands of Japanese invaders in 1942. The first Protestant missionaries to Papua New Guinea were sent by the London Missionary Society in 1870. Anglican missionaries reached New Guinea in 1891. In 1898 the Anglican Diocese of Papua New Guinea was established and remained a missionary diocese of the Church of England in Australia until 1977, when an autonomous Anglican province, the Church of the Province of Papua New Guinea, was established. During World War II Christian missionaries and the natives of New Guinea suffered greatly from the Japanese invaders. The martyrs of New Guinea are commemorated in the Episcopal calendar of the church year on Sept. 2.

Martyrs of Uganda. The Church Missionary Society began work in Uganda in 1877. At the end of the twentieth century the Anglican Church accounted for about 25% of the population of Uganda. On June 3, 1886, 32 young men, pages in the court of King Mwanga of Buganda, were burned to death on a large single pyre at the execution ground at Namugongo. These court pages were usually from the upper ranks of the culture. They cared for the king and his living quarters. King Mwanga's court was a place of considerable homosexual activity. The king liked handsome young men, and his position gave him access to many of them at court. The boys and young men who became Christians refused his homosexual advances, and he viewed their refusals as insubordination. When none of his pages greeted him upon his return home from a hunting trip on May 25, 1886, Mwanga was furious. The next day all the pages were summoned before the king. He demanded that those who were Christians renounce Christ. None of them did. He then pronounced the death sentence on a large number of them, and those not condemned to death were taken away and castrated. On Ascension Day, June 3, 1886, 32 of them were killed. Among the martyrs were Anglicans and Roman Catholics. The martyrdoms continued under Mwanga. The total number of martyrs is not known, but at least 23 were Anglicans and 22 were Roman Catholics. A leader among the Roman Catholics was Charles Lwanga, who was singled out for special cruelty. The 22 Roman Catholics were canonized in 1964, and are honored as the "proto-Martyrs" of African American Africa. The martyrs of Uganda are commemorated in the Episcopal calendar of the church year on June 3.

M.A.R.Y. *See* My Angelus-Rosary Yeomen (M.A.R.Y.).

Mary and Martha of Bethany. Mary, Martha, and Lazarus of Bethany were a family and very close friends of Jesus. Mary and Martha were disciples of Jesus who offered him hospitality. Martha provided him food and other courtesies. Mary, who chose the "better part," sat at Jesus' feet and listened to his teaching. The story shows clearly that these two women were disciples of Jesus (see Lk 10:38–42). The Gospel of John (11:1–44) records that Jesus restored Lazarus to life after Lazarus had died and been in the tomb for four days. Prior to this miracle, Martha states her belief that Jesus is "the Messiah, the Son of God, the one coming into the world" (Jn 11:27). In some traditions, Mary is identified with Mary Magdalene. Very little is known about the family outside the biblical stories. The Lutheran calendar includes Lazarus in this commemoration. The two sisters are commemorated in the Episcopal calendar of the church year on July 29.

Mary Magdalene, Saint. A disciple of Jesus, she was from the city of Magdala in Judea, hence the surname Magdalene. She was the woman Jesus delivered from evil spirits. Mary was among the women who accompanied and supported Jesus and the apostles. She was present at the crucifixion. Mary was also the first to witness the resurrection, which Jesus told her to announce to his disciples. Some traditions identify her with Mary of Bethany. Since she witnessed the resurrection, she has been called "equal to the Apostles." Bernard of Clairvaux called her the "apostle to the Apostles." Later tradition identified Mary Magdalene with Mary the Sinner, the penitent prostitute who anointed Jesus' feet. Mary Magdalene is commemorated in the Episcopal calendar of the church year on July 22.

Mary the Virgin, Mother of Our Lord Jesus Christ, Saint. Mary the mother of Jesus has been an object of veneration in the church since the apostolic age. She has been a favorite subject in art, music, and literature. Her humility and obedience to the message of God at the time of the Incarnation have made her an example for all ages of Christians. The following events of her life are in the NT: her betrothal to Joseph; the annunciation by the angel that she would be the mother of the Messiah; her visit to Elizabeth, the mother of John the Baptist; the birth of Jesus; the visits of the shepherds and the wise men; the presentation of Jesus in the temple; the flight into Egypt; the visit to Jerusalem when Jesus was twelve years old; the wedding at Cana; an occasion when Mary and Jesus' brothers asked to speak to him while he was speaking to the people; the crucifixion when Jesus commended her to John; and the meeting with the apostles in the upper room after the Ascension. Early in church history she was honored and esteemed. Irenaeus called her the New Eve, Athanasius taught her perpetual virginity, and the Council of Ephesus in 431 declared her *Theotokos*, Mother of God, because of the hypostatic union of divinity and humanity in the one person Jesus Christ. Anglicanism has not generally accepted beliefs concerning Mary's perpetual virginity or bodily assumption to heaven after her death, but some hold these views as pious opinions. In addition to Christmas, feasts associated with Mary include the Presentation, the Annunciation, and the Visitation. Mary the Virgin is commemorated in the Episcopal calendar of the church year on Aug. 15. *See* Hail Mary.

Mary, Society of. A devotional society to honor the Blessed Virgin Mary. It was formed in 1931 in England by the union of the Confraternity of Our Lady (founded in 1880) and the League of Our Lady (founded in 1902). In 1962 a regional organization was established in the United States. Members in an area form a ward with a priest as the superior. The society publishes *AVE*.

Maryland, Diocese of. This diocese was organized on Aug. 13, 1783, at Annapolis. On Oct. 12, 1868, the General Convention voted to divide the diocese and place some of the Maryland counties in the new Diocese of Easton. The 1895 General Convention created the Diocese of Washington and placed four Maryland counties in it. The Diocese of Maryland includes the following counties: Allegany, Ann Arundel, Calvert, Carroll, Frederick, Garrett, Hartford, Howard, and Washington. The city of Baltimore, which is not in a county, is also part of the diocese. On Feb. 1, 1955, the diocese passed a resolution establishing the Cathedral of the Incarnation, Baltimore, which was consecrated on Nov. 6, 1955.

Mason, Lowell (Jan. 8, 1792–Aug. 11, 1872). An American educator, composer, and hymnal editor. He was born in Medfield, Massachusetts. Mason was a very gifted and energetic person, and his work as a compiler of hymn books began while he was organist and choirmaster of the First Presbyterian Church, Savannah, Georgia. The *Boston Handel & Haydn Society Collection of Church Music* (1821) went through twenty-two editions. Mason often based his work on European collections, including pieces from Haydn, Mozart, Beethoven, and other German composers. He was able to further his goal of reform by improving the standards of church music in America. He transformed the music publishing business, and by 1872 he had produced almost sixty different church music collections. Many of these collections went through multiple editions. *Selected Chants, Doxologies etc. Adapted to the use of the Protestant Episcopal Church in the United States of America* (1824) represents his effort to serve the need for chant in the Episcopal Church. Mason also excelled as an educator. Through his work at his Boston Academy of Music, music education became part of the curriculum of Boston public schools, the first public school music program in the United States. Mason was a leader in the teacher-training movement and the first to publish a Sunday School hymnal with music. Many of his hymns remain in use today. *The Hymnal 1982* has several hymns that were harmonized or arranged by Mason, including *Antioch* (Hymn 100) from Handel, *Azmon* (Hymn 493) by Carl Glaser, *Mannheim* (Hymn 595), *Mendon* (Hymns 419, 512), and *Truro* (Hymns 182, 436). *The Hymnal 1982* also includes one original tune by Mason, *Olivet* (Hymn 691). He died in Orange, New Jersey.

Mason, Lucy Randolph (July 26, 1882–May 6, 1959). Labor activist and suffragette. She was born in Clarens, Virginia, and grew up in Richmond, where her father was an Episcopal priest. In 1914 Mason was appointed industrial secretary of the Richmond YMCA where she worked to get protective labor legislation for women and children and for workmen's compensation. When her mother died in 1918, Mason resigned from her job to take care of her aging father. She continued, however, to volunteer as a member of the Union Label League. She served as president of both the Richmond Equal Suffrage League and the Richmond League of Women Voters. In 1923 her father died and from then until 1932 she was general secretary of the Richmond YMCA. In this capacity she worked for social and industrial reform in the African American community. From 1932 until 1937, she worked in New York City as executive secretary of the National Consumers' League. In 1937 John L. Lewis invited her to join the Textile Workers Organizing Committee, and she used this position to promote the need for unions in southern industry. She moved to Atlanta where she worked as Southeastern public relations officer for the Congress of Industrial Organizations (CIO). Called "Miss Lucy," by the 1940s she was a legend in the labor movement. Mason retired in 1951. In 1952 she published her autobiography, *To Win These Rights*. Also in 1952 she received the Social Justice Award of the National Religion and Labor Foundation. She died in Atlanta.

Mass. A term for the Holy Eucharist. It is primarily used by Anglicans, Roman Catholics, and Lutherans. It appeared as a part of the title of the service in the first BCP of 1549. It is included by the Catechism in a list of names by which the eucharist is known (BCP, p. 859). It is derived from the Latin *missa*, which is from *mittere*, "to send." It was a part of the dismissal in the medieval Latin Mass, *Ite, missa est* ("Go, it is finished").

Mass of the Pre-Sanctified. *See* Pre-Sanctified, Mass of the.

Massachusetts, Diocese of. The Diocese of Massachusetts was organized at Boston on Sept. 8, 1784. The 1901 General Convention voted to divide the diocese and established the Diocese of Western Massachusetts. The Diocese of Massachusetts consists of the following counties: Barnstable, Bristol, Dukes, Essex, Middlesex, Nantucket, Norfolk, Plymouth, and Suffolk, and the township of Southborough in Worcester County. On Oct. 7, 1912, Bishop William Lawrence named St. Paul's Church, Boston, St. Paul's Cathedral.

Master of Ceremonies, or M. C. The person present in the liturgy to direct the movements of the various ministers and people involved and to coordinate a sustained ceremonial style throughout. A master of ceremonies, when designated, also takes responsibility for any rehearsals of the liturgy. The term "minister of ceremonies" (not gender-specific or hierarchical in its connotations) may be used instead of the customary term "master of ceremonies."

Master (or Mistress) of Novices. *See* Novice Guardian or Novice Master or Novice Mistress.

Matins. An early morning worship service, the first of the canonical hours. The name comes from the Latin *matutinus*, "pertaining to the morning." It is one of the canonical hours, which developed as special times or hours for prayer and devotion. Matins, sometimes spelled "mattins," was the longest of the services of the breviary. It consisted chiefly of three sets of psalms and lessons. It was a "vigil" service, begun several hours before dawn. In the Rule of St. Benedict of Nursia, matins was typically at 2 A.M. Thomas Cranmer combined portions of matins, lauds, and prime to form his English Mattins in the 1549 BCP. This service became Morning Prayer. *See* Breviary; *see* Canonical Hours; *see* Morning Prayer.

Matter (Sacramental). The material or gesture constituting the outward and visible sign of a sacrament. A valid sacrament also requires the appropriate form, minister, and intent. In this sacramental context, form refers to the words of prayer that express the meaning of the sacrament and the matter used in the sacrament. In baptism, the matter is water; and in the eucharist, it is the bread and wine. In the sacramental rite of Ordination, the matter is the imposition of hands. Contemporary theology has been willing to see ritual acts, such as the exchange of vows in marriage, or the confessing of sins in reconciliation, as the matter. *See* Form (Sacramental).

Matthew, Apostle and Evangelist. According to Mark, he was the son of Alphaeus. He was a Jewish tax collector working for the Roman government at Capernaum. Matthew is called Levi in the accounts of his call to discipleship in Mark and Luke, but he is always referred to as Matthew in the lists of the apostles. It is possible that Levi was his original name and that Matthew, which means "gift from God," was given to him after he became a disciple. Since the second century the authorship of the first gospel has been attributed to St. Matthew, but it is considered unlikely by most scholars that the present Gospel of Matthew was written by a Galilean tax collector. In Christian art he is pictured at a desk writing his gospel, as a winged man in his role as an evangelist, and sometimes with a spear, the legendary instrument of his death. We know nothing about his death, but he is venerated as a martyr. Matthew is commemorated in the Episcopal calendar of the church year on Sept. 21.

Matthew's Bible. English Bible issued in 1537. It was based on the work of William Tyndale, Miles Coverdale's Old Testament, and the work of Conrad Pellican. It was edited by John Rogers (c. 1500–1555), who used the alias "Thomas Matthew." This Bible was printed at Antwerp. It was dedicated to Henry VIII, and licensed by him for general reading. It provided a basis for the Great Bible (1539).

Matthews, Sister Eva Mary (Feb. 9, 1862–July 6, 1928). Founder of the Community of the Transfiguration. She was born in Oakencroft, near Glendale, Ohio, and raised a Presbyterian. Matthews studied at Wellesley College in 1880–1881. She decided to follow her clergyman brother Paul into the Episcopal Church during a visit to Oxford University in 1890. Shortly after her confirmation, she and Paul went to Omaha where he joined a group of young clergy living in community and serving as urban missioners. Eva kept house for the men, established women's guilds, did parish visiting, and taught Sunday School and parochial school. Early in 1893 Eva experienced a "personal revival" and recognized her calling to the religious life. She opened a community house for women, whose inhabitants continued the mission work she had begun. In 1896 Eva and Paul returned to Cincinnati. Eva and a friend established Bethany Mission House and began to live by a rule and wear a distinctive dress. On Aug. 6, 1898, the Feast of the Transfiguration, Eva and her companion, Beatrice Henderson, made their profession in St. Luke's Church, Cincinnati, before Assistant Bishop Boyd Vincent of Southern Ohio. This was the founding of the Community of the Transfiguration. On Aug. 6, 1903, Sister Eva took her life vows. Paul became Bishop of New Jersey in 1915. Mother Eva Mary died in Denver. *See* Transfiguration, Community of.

Matthias the Apostle, Saint. Nothing is known about the life of Matthias except the one mention of him in the Book of Acts. After the Ascension of Christ and the death of Judas, when some followers of Jesus met in the Upper Room, Peter asked the group to choose a replacement for Judas. Joseph called Barsabbas, and Matthias were nominated. They were witnesses to the resurrection who had been with the disciples from the beginning. After prayer, those present cast lots. Matthias was chosen to replace Judas among the Twelve (Acts 1:12–26). Matthias· is commemorated in the Episcopal calendar of the church year on Feb. 24.

Maundy Thursday. The Thursday in Holy Week. It is part of the *Triduum*, or three holy days before Easter. It comes from the Latin *mandatum novum*, "new commandment," from Jn 13:34. The ceremony of washing feet was also referred to as "the Maundy." Maundy Thursday celebrations also commemorate the institution of the eucharist by Jesus "on the night he was betrayed." Egeria, a fourth-century pilgrim to Jerusalem, describes elaborate celebrations and observances in that city on Maundy Thursday. Special celebration of the institution of the eucharist on Maundy Thursday is attested by the Council of Hippo in 381. The Prayer Book liturgy for Maundy Thursday provides for celebration of the eucharist and a ceremony of the washing of feet which follows the gospel and homily. There is also provision for the consecration of the bread and wine for administering Holy Communion from the reserved sacrament on Good Friday. Following this, the altar is stripped and all decorative furnishings are removed from the church. *See* Eucharist; *see* Foot Washing.

Maurice, Frederick Denison (Aug. 29, 1805–Apr. 1, 1872). English theologian and proponent of Christian Socialism. He was born in Normanstone, England, the son of a Unitarian clergyman. In 1823 Maurice entered Trinity College, Cambridge University, to study law. However, he was denied his degree because as a Nonconformist he refused to subscribe to the Thirty-Nine Articles of Religion. After several religious crises, he decided to enter the Church of England. He was ordained priest in 1834. From 1840 until 1846, Maurice was Professor of English Literature and Modern History at King's College, London. In 1846 he was appointed Professor of Theology at the same school. From 1848 until 1854, he was a leader of the Christian Socialist Movement. He insisted that "Christianity is the only foundation of Socialism, and that a true Socialism is the necessary result of a sound Christianity." In 1853 he published *Theological Essays*, in which he criticized the popular view of eternal punishment. He was dismissed from his position at King's College for teaching opinions "calculated to unsettle the minds of the theological students." His major publication was *The Kingdom of Christ* (1838). He urged that the church must

be a united body, transcending the diversities and partialities of its individual members, factions, and sects. He insisted that the true church had six signs: baptism, creeds, set forms of worship, the eucharist, an ordained ministry, and the Bible. These ideas may have influenced William Reed Huntington and the Chicago-Lambeth Quadrilateral. In 1854 he helped to establish the first Working Men's College in London. It provided a platform for his radical social reform. In 1866 he was elected to the Knightsbridge Professorship of Moral Theology at Cambridge, where he lectured on ethical subjects. He died in Cambridge. Maurice had a significant influence on the founders of the Episcopal Theological School. Since World War II there has been a revival of interest in Maurice as a theologian. He is commemorated in the Episcopal calendar of the church year on Apr. 1.

May, James (Oct. 1, 1805–Dec. 18, 1863). Seminary professor. He was born in Chester County, Pennsylvania. May received his B.A. in 1823 from Jefferson College. He entered Virginia Theological Seminary in 1826, and left in that same year to finish his theological studies with the Rev. George Boyd in Philadelphia. May was ordained deacon on Dec. 24, 1826, and priest on Oct. 11, 1829. He was rector of St. Stephen's Church, Wilkes-Barre, Pennsylvania, 1827–1836, and rector of St. Paul's Church, Philadelphia, 1836–1840. In 1842 May became Professor of Ecclesiastical History at Virginia Theological Seminary. He remained there until 1861, when he was driven from the seminary by the Civil War. From 1861 until 1863 he taught at the Philadelphia Divinity School. May was Editor of the *Philadelphia Recorder* and the *Protestant Episcopal Review*. He was noted for his evangelical character and piety. May died in Philadelphia.

M. C. *See* Master of Ceremonies, or M.C.

McCarty, John (June 7, 1789–May 10, 1881). First Episcopal priest in the Washington Territory. He was born in Rhinebeck, New York. He practiced law for three years and then decided to enter the ordained ministry of the Episcopal Church. McCarty was ordained deacon on Dec. 23, 1825, and priest on Oct. 26, 1827. He was a chaplain in the United States Navy from Mar. 3, 1825, until Apr. 21, 1826. On Dec. 29, 1826, he began his work as a missionary in Oswego County, New York, where he remained until 1845. During the Mexican War he was a chaplain. McCarty was stationed at Jefferson Barracks, Missouri, from 1848 until 1852. The Domestic and Foreign Missionary Society appointed him a missionary in 1852. He reached Portland, Oregon, on Jan. 19, 1853, to begin his ministry. McCarty did extensive missionary work throughout the Pacific Northwest until his death. He died in Washington, D. C.

McClenachan, William (c. 1710–1766). Church of England leader in the American Great Awakening. McClenachan (sometimes spelled Mcclenachan or Macclenaghan) was born in Armagh, Ireland. He was ordained in the Presbyterian Church. He settled in Georgetown, Maine, in 1734, and officiated there until 1744, when he moved to Chelsea, Massachusetts. While in Boston, he was attracted to the Church of England. McClenachan went to England where he was ordained deacon and priest by the Bishop of London in 1755. On Mar. 31, 1755, the Bishop of London appointed him a missionary of the Society for the Propagation of the Gospel in Foreign Parts (SPG), and he returned to Georgetown, Maine. After a trip to Virginia on his way back to Maine, McClenachan stopped in Philadelphia. He preached at Christ Church at the invitation of the rector, Robert Jenney. He made such an impression in the pulpit that he was asked to remain as the third assistant at Christ Church. In his preaching he stressed conversion. It seems that "his Railings and Revilings in the Pulpit" and "his extemporaneous Prayers and Preachings" offended the rector. McClenachan's preaching reflected his Presbyterian upbringing. On June 18, 1760, McClenachan was denied further use of the pulpit of Christ Church. Four days later, those members of Christ Church who supported McClenachan withdrew from Christ Church and established St. Paul's Church, which became a center of the evangelical movement. McClenachan was rector of St. Paul's until 1765. He went to Maryland in 1765 and died the next year.

McConnell, Samuel David (Aug. 1, 1845–Jan. 11, 1939). Church historian. He was born in West Moreland County, Pennsylvania. McConnell received his B.A. from Washington and Jefferson College in 1869. He was ordained deacon on June 18, 1871, and priest on June 12, 1872. McConnell was rector of Christ Church, Watertown, Connecticut, 1873–1876; of Holy Trinity Church, Middletown, Connecticut, 1876–1882; and of St. Stephen's Church, Philadelphia, 1882–1896. From 1896 until 1902, he was rector of Holy Trinity Church, Brooklyn. He served as rector of All Souls Church, New York City, from 1902 until

his retirement in 1905. In 1890 McConnell published *History of the American Episcopal Church*. This was one of the earliest histories of the Episcopal Church. It appeared in at least eleven editions. He died in Easton, Maryland.

McGarvey, William Ignatius Loyola (Aug. 14, 1861–Feb. 27, 1824). Episcopal priest and later a Roman Catholic priest. Born in Philadelphia, Pennsylvania, McGarvey studied at the General Theological Seminary and then Nashotah House. He was ordained deacon on June 20, 1886, and priest on Aug. 22, 1886. He began his ordained ministry as a curate at the Church of the Evangelists and then became rector of St. Elizabeth's Church, both ritualistic churches in Philadelphia. On June 15, 1891, seven young clergymen in Philadelphia, including McGarvey, met at the Church of the Evangelists to form a religious society. On Sept. 15, 1891, they met with four others at the same place and adopted a rule and the name Community of the Companions of the Holy Saviour. On the next day, McGarvey was elected Master. On Oct. 8, 1895, eleven members, including McGarvey, of the Community of the Companions of the Holy Saviour founded the Congregation of the Companions of the Holy Saviour (*Congregatio Sociorum Sancti Salvatoris*), C.S.S.S. The last meeting of the Chapter of the Congregation of the Companions of the Holy Saviour was held on Mar. 12, 1908. On May 19, 1908, McGarvey renounced the ordained ministry of the Episcopal Church. On May 27, 1908, McGarvey and several other former members of the Congregation of the Companions of the Holy Saviour were received into the Roman Catholic Church. McGarvey was ordained priest in the Roman Catholic Church on Dec. 17, 1910. He served parishes in Philadelphia. His last ministry was as rector of the Church of the Holy Infancy, Bethlehem, Pennsylvania. McGarvey died in San Diego, California. *See* Congregation of the Companions of the Holy Saviour (C.S.S.S.).

McGuire, George Alexander (Mar. 26, 1866–Nov. 10, 1924). Founder of the African Orthodox Church, a body for Negro Episcopalians dissatisfied with the Episcopal Church. He was born in Antigua, British West Indies, and graduated from the Moravian Theological Seminary, St. Thomas Island. He came to the United States in 1894, and was ordained deacon on June 29, 1896, and priest on Oct. 22, 1897. After ministries in Cincinnati, Richmond, and Philadelphia, he became archdeacon of the Convocation of Arkansas, a convocation for African American Episcopalians. He served as field secretary for the American

Church Institute for Negroes. In 1919 he joined the work of Marcus Garvey and the United Negro Improvement Association of the World. On Sept. 2, 1921, he organized the African Orthodox Church, and on Sept. 28, 1921, he was ordained and consecrated bishop by Joseph Rene Vilatte, an *episcopi vaganti*. He died in New York City.

McIlvaine, Charles Pettit (Jan. 18, 1799–Mar. 13, 1873). Bishop and foremost leader of the evangelical party in the Episcopal Church during the mid-nineteenth century. He was born in Burlington, New Jersey. McIlvaine graduated from the College of New Jersey (now Princeton University) in 1816 and studied theology at Princeton Seminary privately between 1816 and 1820. After being ordained deacon on June 18, 1820, he served as rector of Christ Church, Georgetown in the District of Columbia until 1824. He was ordained priest on Mar. 20, 1821, and was appointed chaplain of the Military Academy at West Point, where he helped spark a dramatic religious revival among the cadets. He later served as rector of St. Ann's Church, Brooklyn, New York, from 1827 until his election as Bishop of Ohio. He was consecrated on Oct. 31, 1832. McIlvaine was a staunch advocate of evangelical theological principles. His *Oxford Divinity* (1841) condemned Tractarianism as unscriptural and contrary to the Protestant roots of Anglicanism. During the Civil War, McIlvaine won political acclaim for his service as a special emissary of the Union government in England. He died in Florence, Italy.

M.C.M. The Master of Church Music degree presupposes a bachelor's degree and is designed to develop leaders of musical activities in the church.

M.Div. Master of Divinity. The degree presupposes a bachelor's degree and is designed to prepare persons for ministry in the church and synagogue. It has replaced the B.D. (Bachelor of Divinity) degree.

Meade, William (Nov. 11, 1789–Mar. 14, 1862). Presiding Bishop of the Confederate Church during the Civil War. Born in Frederick County, Virginia, Meade entered the junior class of the College of New Jersey (Princeton) in 1806, and graduated in 1808 as valedictorian. He studied for the ordained ministry under the Rev. Walter Addison of Maryland. He was ordained deacon on Feb. 24, 1811, and priest on Jan. 29, 1814. He was influential in the election of Richard Channing Moore as Bishop of Virginia in 1814, who began the work that revived the Episcopal Church in Virginia from the disorganization that followed the American Revolution. Meade served several churches in Virginia on a temporary basis and was rector of Christ Church, Winchester. On Aug. 19, 1829, he was consecrated Assistant Bishop of Virginia. He held this position until the death of Bishop Moore on Nov. 12, 1841. Meade then became the third Bishop of Virginia and served until his death. He was one of the leaders of the Evangelical Party in the Episcopal Church before the Civil War. Meade helped to found the American Colonization Society and to establish the nation of Liberia for freed Negro slaves. He was active in christianizing Negro slaves. One of his major accomplishments was the founding of the Virginia Theological Seminary. When the Civil War broke out, he was a defender of the South and a leader in the formation of the Protestant Episcopal Church in the Confederate States of America. He presided at the second preliminary meeting of the dioceses in the Confederate States at Columbia, South Carolina, Oct. 16–21, 1861, which adopted the constitution for the Confederate Church. He served as Presiding Bishop until his death. Meade presided at the consecration of Richard Hooker Wilmer as Bishop of Alabama, the only Bishop consecrated by the Confederate Church. He died in Richmond, Virginia.

Mealy, Norman Carleton (June 22, 1923–Mar. 12, 1987). Church musician, editor, and educator. Born in Troy, New York, Mealy received his B.S. in 1946 from the State University of New York at Potsdam. He studied at the Episcopal Theological School, 1957–1958. He was ordained deacon on Nov. 28, 1959, and priest on May 28, 1960. He was director of music at St. Mark's Church, Berkeley, 1948–1960, and he taught church music at the Church Divinity School of the Pacific, 1952–1964. From 1961 to 1976 he was a member of the Standing Commission on Church Music, and from 1967 to 1976 served as chairman of its Service Music Committee. With his wife, Margaret Williams Mealy, he co-edited *Sing for Joy: A Song Book for Young Children* (1967). He was general editor of *Songs for Liturgy* and *More Hymns and Spiritual Songs* (1971), a supplement to *The Hymnal* (1940). With Judith Rock he wrote *Performer as Priest and Prophet: Restoring the Intuitive in Worship Through Music and Dance* (1988). He wrote stanza five of Hymn 205, "Good Christians all, rejoice and sing!", and made several contributions to the Service Music section of *The Hymnal 1982* (S 46, S 208, S 222). Mealy died in Berkeley, California.

Meditation. The practice, usually in silence, of fixing attention on a specific word, phrase, image, sound, or text. Some meditative practices produce an emptying of thoughts and emotions. Meditation may lead to an experience of union between the one who meditates and the object of meditation. Meditation practices are known in most of the major religious traditions of the world. Meditation is a mainstay in the prayer life of many Episcopalians. The BCP allows times for silent meditation on the scriptural readings of the eucharist and the Daily Offices, and during the prayers of the people. *See* Centering Prayer.

Melisma. A series of notes in plainchant assigned to one syllable of the text.

Memorial (to General Convention). A written statement submitted by individuals or organizations that urges action by the General Convention. A memorial is not a resolution, even if it includes a suggested form of resolution. Memorials are referred to appropriate legislative committees for information by the president of the House of Bishops or the president of the House of Deputies. A legislative committee may consider the memorial and submit a resolution that embodies the substance of the memorial. However, the memorial itself is never the subject of a report from a committee to which it was referred. The legislative committee may also take no action on the memorial. Memorials have frequently been submitted to General Convention by dioceses.

Memorial Acclamations. An acclamation of the people after the institution narrative in the eucharist. For example, in Prayer B, the memorial acclamation is "We remember his death/ We proclaim his resurrection/ We await his coming in glory" (BCP, p. 368). All four Rite 2 eucharistic prayers include a memorial acclamation. In Eucharistic Prayers A, B, and D, the memorial acclamation is made by the celebrant and people together. In Eucharistic Prayer C, the memorial acclamation is stated in the people's response that follows soon after the institution narrative. Inclusion of the memorial acclamations reflects the emphasis on congregational participation of the 1979 BCP.

Memorial acclamations were common in the eucharistic liturgies of the east. The memorial acclamations of Eucharistic Prayers A, B, and C are based on the same text, which was the most commonly used acclamation at this place in the eastern liturgies. These prayers also may anticipate or serve as prayers of *anamnesis*, which recall the past and future completion of salvation history in the present moment. The memorial acclamation may be said or sung. *The Hymnal 1982* provides musical settings for the memorial acclamation of Eucharistic Prayers A (S 132–S 135), B (S 136–S 138), and D (S 139–S 141). *The Hymnal 1982 Accompaniment Edition, Vol. 1* also provides additional musical settings for the memorial acclamation of Eucharistic Prayers A (S 366), B (S 367–S 368), and D (S 371–S 372). The people's response following the institution narrative in Eucharistic Prayer C is included in the musical setting of S 370.

Mendicant, Mendicant Friar. *See* Friar.

Mensa. A flat stone inlay or other solid material that forms the top of an altar. The term is from the Latin for "table."

Mensa. *See* Episcopal Special Interest Group (SIG) of American Mensa.

Merbecke or Marbeck, John (c. 1510–c. 1585). English composer and theologian. He is best known as the composer of *The booke of Common praier noted* (1550) in which he set Prayer Book services to plainsong-like melodies in strict acknowledgment of Archbishop Cranmer's admonition, "for every syllable a note" (see *The Hymnal 1982*, S 67, S 90, S 113, S 157, S 201; and S 375–S 379 in *The Hymnal 1982 Accompaniment Edition, Vol. 1.*). His concordance to the Bible (third version) was also published in 1550. The first records concerning Merbecke appeared in 1541 and list him as a lay clerk and organist of St. George's Chapel, Windsor. In 1543 he was condemned for heresy but saved by the personal intervention of Bishop Gardiner of Winchester and the commissioner Sir Humphrey Foster. After a short term in prison he was pardoned by the King and restored to his position at Windsor. Merbecke is credited with the composition of several Latin works, but none of his English music has survived. In the last thirty-five years of life he composed no more music. He spent most of his energies as a committed Calvinist writing theological works, including *A Ripping up of the Pope's Fardel* (1581). He was the composer of the "First Communion Service" of *The Hymnal* (1940). Merbecke probably died at Windsor.

Mercer, George, School of Theology. *See* George Mercer, Jr., Memorial School of Theology.

Mercer, Samuel Alfred Browne (May 10, 1880–Jan. 10, 1969). Scholar of the OT and co-founder of the *Anglican Theological Review* (*ATR*). He was born in Bristol, England. Mercer received his B.Sc. from Bishop Field College and Central Training School, St. John's, Newfoundland, in 1900, and his B.D. from Nashotah House in 1904. He received his B.A. from Harvard University in 1908 and his Ph.D. from the University of Munich in 1910. He also studied Semitic languages at the University of Göttingen, the University of Heidelberg, and the Sorbonne in Paris. Mercer was ordained deacon on May 29, 1904, and priest on Dec. 18, 1904. From 1910 until 1922 he was professor of Hebrew and OT literature at the Western Theological Seminary in Chicago, and in 1922–1923, he was dean of Bexley Hall. From 1923 until his retirement in 1946, Mercer was Professor of Semitic Languages and Egyptology at Trinity College, Toronto. Mercer and Leicester C. Lewis co-founded the *ATR* in 1918. They served as joint editors from May 1918 through Dec. 1920. Mercer and others edited the *ATR* from Mar. 1921 until Mar. 1924. Mercer was a leading Semitic scholar. He died in Toronto.

Merton, Thomas (Brother Louis) (Jan. 31, 1915–Dec. 10, 1968). Spiritual writer and Trappist monk. He was born in Prades, France. Merton studied at Cambridge University, 1933–1934. He received his B.A. in 1938 and his M.A. in 1939, both from Columbia University. He was a nominal Anglican in his younger years but converted to Roman Catholicism in 1938. In 1940–1941, Merton taught English at St. Bonaventure College. In 1941 he joined the Order of Cistercians of the Strict Observance, or Trappists, and entered Our Lady of Gethsemani Abbey near Bardstown, Kentucky. He took the name Brother Louis in the order. He wrote extensively on the monastic life and spirituality. Especially notable are *The Seven Storey Mountain* (1948), *The Sign of Jonus* (1953), *New Seeds of Contemplation* (1961), and *Contemplative Prayer* (1969). His writings also show a keen and critical awareness of the issues of his time. Merton became a fierce opponent of nuclear weapons. He is also known for an extensive correspondence of spiritual advice and direction. Author of over 140 books, Merton influenced the renewal of interest in spirituality which has been felt in the Episcopal Church. In later years, Merton was given permission to live as a hermit. He also became interested in Buddhism, and published books such as *Zen and the Birds of the Appetite* (1968). Merton traveled in Asia, and visited the Dalai Lama. While attending a world conference of contemplatives in Bangkok, Thailand, he was accidentally electrocuted.

Messiah. From the Hebrew, "anointed" or "anointed one," indicating a person who has been anointed with oil. Messiah is translated in Greek as *christos*, and the title "Christ" is derived from it. The one who is ceremonially anointed is understood to be set apart by God with special powers and functions. In the OT, the anointed one most frequently refers to the king of Israel (1 Sm 10:1, 26:9, 11, 16, 23; 2 Sm 1:14, 16). Priests were also anointed (Ex 28:41; Lv 4:3, 5, 16).

After Samuel anointed David king over Israel, the spirit of God came mightily upon David from that day (1 Sm 16:1, 13). The prophet Nathan declared God's promise to make the throne of David's offspring an everlasting kingdom (2 Sm 711b–17; see 2 Sm 22:51, Ps 89:20–37). The messiah came to mean the idealized Davidic king whose coming was hoped for by Israel. This understanding reflects the influence of the "royal" psalms concerning God's anointed, such as Psalms 2, 18, 20, 45, and 132. The prophet Isaiah states the hope and expectation for the king who would establish the throne of David and his kingdom and "uphold it with justice and with righteousness from this time onward and forevermore" (Is 9:7; see Is 11). Similarly, the prophet Jeremiah declares the coming of the days when God "will raise up for David a righteous Branch, and he shall reign as king and deal wisely, and shall execute justice and righteousness in the land" (Jer 23:5). And Ezekiel prophesies concerning the time when David will be the king and one shepherd of the people of Israel, and "David shall be their prince forever" (Ez 37:24–25). Christians believe Jesus Christ to be the fulfillment of the messianic expectation of the OT. The Davidic ancestry of Jesus is established in the NT (Mt 1, Lk 1). Jesus is explicitly identified as the Messiah in the NT (Mt 1:1, 1:18, 11:2; Lk 2:11). Jesus' identity as the Messiah is recognized by Simeon (Lk 2:25–35), and by Peter (Mt 16:16, Mk 8:29). In the Gospel of John (1:40–41), Andrew says to his brother Simon Peter, "We have found the Messiah." Jesus identifies himself as the Messiah in his conversation with the Samaritan woman at the well (Jn 4:25–26). Jesus is the suffering messiah who rose from the dead, who reigns in heaven, and who will come again in power and glory (Mk 8:31; Lk 24:26; Acts 2:36, 3:18, 3:20–21, 5:31, 26:23). Jesus is understood in the NT to be the Messiah, the Christ, and "Christ" is used as a name for him in the letters of Paul (see Rom 1:1, 5:8; 1 Thes 1:1). The Prayer Book Catechism affirms that Jesus is the Messiah, the one "sent by God to free us from the power of sin, so that with the help of God we may live in harmony with God, within ourselves, with our neighbors, and with all creation" (p. 849). The Messiah who comes "to take away transgression, and rule in equity" is celebrated by the hymn "Hail to the Lord's Anointed" (Hymn 616). An important theme in the season of Advent is the victorious return of the Messiah, when "every eye shall now behold him, robed in dreadful majesty" ("Lo! he comes, with clouds descending," Hymn 57). *See* Jesus Christ.

Methodists, Methodism. A group of Protestant churches founded in England in the eighteenth century on the principles and practices of John Wesley, a priest of the Church of England. Methodism spread from England to the American colonies. It became an important expression of religious life and thought in the New World. Methodism was marked from the outset by its acceptance of the doctrines of historic Christianity. It did not insist strongly on conformity nor did it display a great interest in theological speculation. It emphasized the power of the Holy Spirit to confirm the faith and transform the personal life of the believer. Methodism asserts that the heart of true religion lies in the believer's relationship with God. One of its strong characteristics is its concern for the underprivileged and the improvement of social conditions. Methodism had its origins in the work of John and Charles Wesley. They were members of a group of earnest students at Oxford University who were pledged to frequent attendance at Holy Communion, serious study of scripture, and regular visitation of Oxford prisons. Members of this group were called Methodists. Methodism came to the American colonies around 1760. It was a part of the Great Awakening. Since Methodist "societies" were part of the Church of England in the American colonies, they were not persecuted like the Baptists. In Sept. 1784 John Wesley and Thomas Coke ordained Thomas Vasey and Richard Whatcoat as the first Methodist ministers for America. At the "Christmas Conference" of 1784 at Lovely Lane Chapel, Baltimore, the Methodist societies were organized as the Methodist Episcopal Church. Many evangelical members of the Episcopal Church joined the Methodist Church. The Episcopal Church is in official dialogue with three African American Methodist bodies and participates with the United Methodist Church in the Consultation on Church Union. *See* Great Awakening; *see* Wesley, Charles; *see* Wesley, John.

Methodius. *See* Cyril and Methodius.

Metrical Index of Tunes. *The Hymnal 1982 Accompaniment Edition, Vol. 2* (pp. 1039–1044) contains a Metrical Index to hymns in *The Hymnal 1982*. This tool enables use of texts which otherwise might not be usable because the tune linked with the text is unfamiliar or too difficult, or is not suitable for the available instruments, or is beyond the abilities of the instrumentalists. Tunes in this index are categorized according to the number of syllables in each line. The metrical pattern of each hymn is printed under it on the right-hand side of the page in the hymnal. A person searching for a more useful tune finds the metrical pattern printed under the hymn and then turns to the same category in the Metrical Index. However, each pairing must be tested to see if accents are right and if the mood of text and tune are compatible.

Metrical Psalter. A publication in which the psalms are written in regular poetic meters and intended for singing to musical settings in stanzas. The earliest important metrical psalter in English is the "Old Version" or "Sternhold and Hopkins." The first version of nineteen metrical psalms was published about 1547, followed by a complete version that was published in London in 1562. They were authorized for use before and after services and sermons. *The Hymnal 1982* contains William Kethe's version of Ps 100, "All people that on earth do dwell" from the 1562 edition (Hymns 377–378). The "Old Version" was used in England into the eighteenth century. It was generally replaced by the "New Version" of Nicholas Brady and Nahum Tate, which was first published in London in 1696. *The Hymnal 1982* contains three texts in altered versions from this collection (Hymns 364, 658, 666). The "New Version" was used by English colonists in America before the Revolution and was bound with the first BCP for publication in 1789. The 1832 General Convention substituted selections from the psalms for the whole Psalter. Most of these were from the "New Version," but sixteen were from other sources. The BCP allows use of metrical versions of the invitatory psalms and of the canticles after the readings at Morning and Evening Prayer (BCP, p. 141).

Mexican Missionary Society. A society organized in the United States which did missionary work in Mexico from 1857 until 1877. It aided several large reformed bodies such as "The Mexican Catholic Apostolic Society." Through the society an American Episcopal priest was maintained in Mexico for a while.

Mexico, Diocese of. Henry Chauncey Riley (1835–1904) was consecrated the Bishop of the Valley of Mexico on June 24, 1879. He served in that position until he resigned on Apr. 24, 1884. The General Convention of 1904 established the Missionary District of Mexico and elected a Missionary Bishop. In 1972 the House of Bishops divided the Missionary District of Mexico into the Missionary District of Central and South Mexico, the Missionary District of Western Mexico, and the Missionary District of Northern Mexico. All three of these Missionary Districts became dioceses on Jan. 1, 1980. In 1988 the House of Bishops divided the Diocese of Central and South Mexico into the Diocese of Mexico, the Diocese of Cuernavaca, and the Diocese of Southeastern Mexico. It continues the Diocese of Central and South Mexico. The 1994 General Convention granted the five Mexican dioceses permission to withdraw from the Episcopal Church and form an autonomous province. The Anglican Church of Mexico came into existence on Jan. 1, 1995.

Michael the Archangel, Saint. Archangel honored as the "captain of the heavenly host." Michael is described as guardian over Israel in Dn 10:13 and 12:1. In Jude 9 he refrains from pronouncing a reviling judgment of Satan. The Book of Revelation (12:7–9) describes Michael as the leader of the angels in victory over the dragon (identified with Satan) and the dragon's angels. Michael is often portrayed with a sword fighting or standing over a dragon. Observance of a day in honor of Michael dates from the fifth century. The feast of St. Michael the Archangel is traditionally celebrated on Sept. 29. In the 1549 BCP the feast was expanded to include all angels. The feast of St. Michael and All Angels is one of the major feasts of the church year in the Episcopal Church. *See* Angel.

Michigan City, Diocese of. The Diocese of Northern Indiana was known as the Diocese of Michigan City from Apr. 25, 1899, until May 20, 1919. *See* Northern Indiana, Diocese of.

Michigan, Diocese of. The primary convention of the Diocese of Michigan met at St. Paul's Church, Detroit, on Sept. 8–10, 1832. The diocese was divided by the General Conventions of 1874, 1892, and 1994. The Diocese of Michigan includes the following counties: Hillsdale, Ingham, Jackson, Lenawee, Livingston, Macomb, Monroe, Oakland (except for Holly Township), Washtenaw, Wayne, and that portion of Clinton County south of Price Road. On Jan. 8, 1907, Bishop Charles David Williams named St. Paul's Church, Detroit, St. Paul's Cathedral. It was dedicated on May 17, 1911.

Micks, Marianne Hoffman (Apr. 30, 1923–Nov. 4, 1997). Theologian and seminary professor. She was born in Seneca Falls, New York. Micks received her A.B. from Smith College in 1945, and her M.R.E. from Columbia University in 1948. In 1957 she and a classmate were the first two women to earn a degree from an Episcopal seminary. They received the B.D. from the Church Divinity School of the Pacific. In 1960 Micks received her Ph.D. from Yale University. From 1960 until 1974 she was professor of religion and dean at Western College, Oxford, Ohio. In 1974 Micks joined the faculty of Virginia Theological Seminary as Professor of Theology. She held this position until her retirement in 1988. Micks also taught occasional courses at the General Theological Seminary, Episcopal Theological Seminary of the Southwest, and Berea College. She was a member of the American Academy of Religion, the American Theological Society, and the Joint Commission on Ecumenical Relations. She was a participant in Lutheran-Episcopal Dialogue III, and was president of the Conference of Anglican Theologians, 1987–1988. Micks was the author of eight books, including *Introduction to Theology* (1964, revised 1983), *Loving the Questions: Reflections on the Nicene Creed* (1993), and *Deep Waters: An Introduction to Baptism* (1996).

Micou, Richard Wilde (June 12, 1848–June 4, 1912). Theologian and seminary professor. He was born in New Orleans, Louisiana. Micou studied at the Universities of Georgia, Alabama, Erlangen, Bavaria, Edinburgh, and the General Theological Seminary. He was ordained deacon on June 12, 1870, and priest on Nov. 16, 1872. Micou was assistant minister at St. John's Church, Montgomery, Alabama, 1870–1871; rector of St. Mary's Church, Franklin, Louisiana, 1871–1874; and rector of St. Paul's Church, Kittanning, Pennsylvania, 1874–1877. From 1877 until 1892, he was rector of Trinity Church, Waterbury, Connecticut. Micou was Professor of Systematic Theology at the Philadelphia Divinity School, 1892–1898. His major position was Professor of Fundamental Theology and Systematic

Divinity at the Virginia Theological Seminary from 1898 until his death. His two major books are *Manual of Fundamental Theology and Christian Apologetics* (1907), and *Basic Ideas in Religion, or Apologetic Theism* (1916). This last volume was edited by his son Paul Micou. Micou died in Alexandria, Virginia.

Micronesia, Episcopal Church in. This small Episcopal Church is under the jurisdiction of the Presiding Bishop, who appoints another bishop to exercise the episcopate there. Bishops appointed by the Presiding Bishop have been the Bishops of Hawaii, Okinawa, and Bishops for the Armed Forces.

Miles, James Warley (Nov. 24, 1818–Sept. 14, 1875). Priest and theologian. Miles was the leading intellectual figure of the Episcopal Church in the South in the mid-nineteenth century. He was born on his family's plantation in St. Matthew's Parish, Orangeburg District, South Carolina. He attended South Carolina College (now the University of South Carolina) and General Theological Seminary. He was ordained deacon on July 23, 1841, and served several small missions in South Carolina. He was ordained priest on Aug. 4, 1843. After a period as a missionary in the Near East between 1843 and 1847, Miles returned to parish work in Charleston, South Carolina. In Feb. 1850 he joined the faculty of the College of Charleston. He remained on the faculty of the College until 1871, despite periods of absence caused by ill heath and the threat of invasion during the Civil War. Miles published an extensive number of theological and philosophical works, including *Philosophic Theology; or, Ultimate Ground of all Religious Belief Based on Reason* (1849). He was a theological modernist who believed in God's progressive self-revelation through the course of history. Even biblical truths, he thought, could be judged by human reason and the historical process. Miles served briefly as rector of Grace Church, Camden, South Carolina, prior to his death.

Millenarianism. The belief that the second coming of Christ will bring a thousand-year reign of justice, happiness, and peace. It is also known as Chiliasm. The term is from the Latin *mille*, "a thousand." Millenarianism is based on the description in Revelation, Chapters 20–21. Christ and his saints are to rule for a thousand years while Satan is bound in chains and history is incomplete. Satan is to be unbound at the end of the millennium. Christ will win the final victory, the last judgment will separate the elect, and God will create for them a new heaven and a new earth. Millenarianism is often used in a general sense of an urgent expectation of a time of joy in the near future. Historically, this hope has been especially keen at times of distress or suffering. During the Great Awakening in America, millenarianism took the form of an expectation of the second coming of Christ after a thousand-year period of Christian progress. This was known as postmillennialism. In contrast, those expecting the return of Christ to precede the thousand-year rule may be termed "premillennialists." Various groups of Christians have believed (incorrectly) that they knew in advance the time of Christ's second coming, including the followers of the American William Miller who expected the millennium in 1843 or 1844. The Christian hope is "to await the coming of Christ in glory, and the completion of God's purpose for the world" (BCP, p. 861). *See* Eschatology. However, we do not know when this time will come (see Mk 13:32–37).

Milnor, James (June 20, 1773–Apr. 8, 1844). A leading evangelical and an opponent of the Oxford Movement. He was born in Philadelphia and studied law and theology at the University of Pennsylvania. From 1811 to 1813 he was a member of the U.S. House of Representatives from Pennsylvania. He was ordained deacon on Aug. 14, 1814, and priest on Aug. 27, 1815. He was assistant to Bishop William White at St. Peter's Church, Philadelphia, 1814–1816, where he was a leader in the Sunday School movement. From Sept. 30, 1816, until his death he was rector of St. George's Church, New York City. He believed that the Oxford Movement had abandoned justification by faith.

Milwaukee, Diocese of. The clergy in the territory of Wisconsin requested on Apr. 30, 1836, that Wisconsin be put under the jurisdiction of Missionary Bishop Jackson Kemper. The House of Bishops granted this request on Sept. 12, 1838. The Diocese of Wisconsin was organized at St. Paul's Church, Milwaukee, on June 24–25, 1847. On Oct. 8, 1859, Bishop Kemper resigned his missionary jurisdiction and became the first Bishop of Wisconsin. On Oct. 27, 1874, the General Convention divided the Diocese of Wisconsin and established the Diocese of Fond du Lac. On June 16, 1886, the Diocese of Wisconsin was changed to the Diocese of Milwaukee. The 1928 General Convention voted to create the Diocese of Eau Claire from the dioceses of Fond du Lac and Milwaukee. The Diocese of Milwaukee includes the following counties: Columbia, Crawford, Dane, Dodge, Grant, Green, Iowa, Jefferson, Kenosha, Lafayette, Milwaukee, Ozaukee, Racine, Richland, Rock, Sauk, Walworth, Washington, and Waukesha. In June 1867 Bishop William Armitage established All Saints' Church, Milwaukee, as the pro-cathedral of Wisconsin. On June 1, 1873, All Saints' Cathedral formally opened.

Minister. One who shares in the ministry of the church. The ministers of the church are lay people, bishops, priests, and deacons (BCP, p. 855). Christian ministry is based in baptism, and the promises of the baptismal covenant (BCP, pp. 304–305). All Christian ministers are to represent Christ and his church. Each order of ministry has a distinctive role in the church's ministry. Each minister of the church is called to use his or her own distinctive gifts to share in the work of ministry. In the Prayer Book rubrics, the term indicates a person who leads liturgical prayer. A liturgical minister in the Episcopal Church may be a lay person or a member of the clergy. For example, in the Ash Wednesday service, "the Celebrant or Minister appointed" reads the exhortation inviting the people to the observance of a holy Lent (BCP, p. 264). At the Holy Eucharist, after the bidding to confession is said by the deacon or celebrant, and after a period of silence, the "Minister and People" say the general confession (BCP, p. 360). In both of these examples, the minister may be a lay person or a member of the clergy. In many Protestant denominations, the term is applied exclusively to members of the clergy.

Ministration at the Time of Death. The BCP provides prayers and forms for Ministration at the Time of Death (pp. 462–467). When a person is near death, the minister of the congregation should be notified so the ministrations of the church may be provided. The BCP includes a prayer for a person near death, a Litany at the Time of Death, a commendation at the time of death, a commendatory prayer, prayers for a vigil, and a form for the reception of the body. Suitable psalms, lessons, and collects (such as those in the burial service) may be used at a Vigil before the burial (p. 465).

Ministration to the Sick. A pastoral office of the church. In its basic form the service is an abbreviated eucharist, including a rite for laying on of hands and anointing. The priest may suggest the making of a special confession if the sick person's conscience is troubled. The form for the Reconciliation of a Penitent is used. The BCP also includes various "Prayers for the Sick" (pp. 458–460) and "Prayers for use by a Sick Person" (p. 461) after the form for Ministration to the Sick. If one or more of the "Prayers for the Sick" are used in the service, they may follow the reading and precede the confession (p. 454). The service emphasizes the healing power of Christ and the connection between the worshiping community and the sick person. Communion may be administered from the reserved Sacrament, using the form beginning on p. 398 of the BCP. In many places, lay eucharistic ministers bring communion directly from the Sunday service to the sick or shut-in.

Ministry. From the Latin *mini*, "lesser." The term has the same form as the Latin *magister*, from *magis*, "greater," meaning "master" or "teacher." Ministry appears in the Vulgate translation of Mt 20:26, "he who would be great [Latin, *maior*] among you, let him be your minister," translating the underlying Greek *diakonos*, "servant," as "minister." Thus ministry entered the Christian vocabulary referring to the Christian vocation to serve. Ministry refers to the work and office of the one who ministers.

In the NT, all the Corinthians ministered (Greek *diakonein*) to the saints in Jerusalem by their collection of the free-will offering (2 Cor 8–9). In the English language, from pre-Reformation times until the mid-twentieth century, ministry in an ecclesiastical context meant ordained ministry in its three orders. The movement of liturgical renewal and reform in the second half of the twentieth century reclaimed the earlier sense of the word, so that ministry once more denotes the life of service of all baptized persons. The Prayer Book Catechism states, "The ministers of the Church are lay persons, bishops, priests and deacons" (p. 855).

Ministry Development, Standing Commission on. The 1997 General convention established this commission. The duties of the commission include: recommending policies and strategies for the development, affirmation, and exercise of the ministry of all the baptized; encouraging those engaged in education, training, deployment, and formation for ministry; and studying the trends of theological education. The commission consists of twenty-four members. Nine members are appointed on the nomination of the nine provincial presidents, and the remaining fifteen include three bishops, four presbyters, and eight lay persons.

Ministry for Tomorrow. The title of the Report of the Special Committee on Theological Education which was chaired by Nathan M. Pusey. *Ministry for Tomorrow* was published by the Episcopal Church Foundation. It was informally referred to as "the Pusey Report." The 1967 General Convention of the Episcopal Church accepted this report which recommended a consolidation of the seminaries of the Episcopal Church in ecumenical urban centers. It also recommended that the church should have a Board for Theological Education (BTE). The report resulted in the canonical requirement for the BTE. After this report, Bexley Hall moved to join the Colgate complex of schools in Rochester, New York, and the Episcopal Divinity School in Philadelphia combined with the Episcopal Theological School of Cambridge, Massachusetts, to become the Episcopal Divinity School in Cambridge. *See* Board for Theological Education (BTE).

Ministry in Higher Education. A program area of the Episcopal Church on the national level. It coordinates the ministries of the church in university and college settings.

Ministry of the Word. *See* Liturgy of the Word.

Minnesota, Diocese of. The Diocese of Minnesota was organized on Sept. 16, 1857, at Christ Church, St. Paul. On July 16, 1862, Bishop Henry Benjamin Whipple laid the cornerstone of the Cathedral of Our Merciful Saviour at Faribault. This was the first Episcopal cathedral built in the United States. It was consecrated on June 24, 1869. The 1895 General Convention voted to divide the Diocese of Minnesota and established the Missionary District of Duluth in 1907. On Jan. 14, 1944, the Diocese of Duluth reunited with the Diocese of Minnesota.

Minor Orders. Ministries such as porter (doorkeeper), lector, exorcist, and acolyte which were transitory steps that led to the major orders of deacon, priest, and bishop. The minor orders date from at least the third century. Ordination to minor orders in the early church included a commission to exercise the office and the handing over of instruments appropriate to the office. For example, a doorkeeper would be given keys to the church, and a lector would be given a book. The subdiaconate was considered a minor order until it was included among the major orders by Pope Innocent III in 1207. The subdiaconate was suppressed in the Roman Catholic Church in 1972. Pope Paul VI also abolished the orders of porter and exorcist in 1972. Lay people, candidates for the diaconate, and candidates for the priesthood can now be installed in the ministries of lector and acolyte in the Roman Catholic Church. These lectors and acolytes are not ordained or in holy orders. A few Episcopal churches continue to allow a liturgical role for a "subdeacon" at the eucharist. Lay servers at the altar in many Episcopal parishes are known as acolytes. The Anglican Ordinal of 1550 made no mention of the minor orders, and Article XXXVI of the Articles of Religion, "Of Consecration of Bishops and Ministers," mentions only the consecration of bishops, priests, and deacons. *See* Major Orders.

Miracles. Described in the NT as powers, signs, portents, and strange things. A miracle is an event in time that is perceived by the senses of those who witness it. Miracles reflect the direct activity of God which transcends the usual order of nature for a religious purpose. In NT times, miracles were not considered to be breaches of the natural law. Jesus' miracles were "deed events" of the coming Kingdom of God. The NT includes accounts of Jesus' healing miracles, nature miracles in which he exercises power over the forces of nature, exorcisms, and occasions in which a miracle illustrates an important saying or pronouncement by Jesus. The Sunday gospels of the BCP lectionary use miracle stories from Jesus' ministry to proclaim the saving message of the gospel made present in word and sacrament. They are especially featured in the Sundays after Epiphany in Year B. In this context the miracles are understood as epiphanies or manifestations of the divine Christ.

Miriam, Song of. One of the oldest fragments of Hebrew poetry. Miriam, the sister of Moses and Aaron (Nm 26:59), was a prophetess who celebrated the deliverance of Israel from the Egyptians with a victory dance (Ex 15:20–21). She sang, "Sing to the Lord, for he has/ triumphed gloriously;/ horse and rider he has thrown into/ the sea." The Song of Moses (see Canticle 8, *Cantemus Domino*, BCP, p. 85) may be a later elaboration of the Song of Miriam.

Misericord. A ledge or rest on the underside of a hinged seat in a choir stall. It was designed to provide "merciful" support for monks or others needing help to stand during long periods of worship. The term is from the Latin for "mercy." A misericord may be carved or decorated. The term is also used to describe a room set apart in a monastery for those whose age or infirmity requires some relaxation of the community rule.

Missal. An altar book that provides all the textual materials needed for celebration of the Holy Eucharist. It includes liturgical texts and directions, readings, additional prayers, hymns, and musical notations. This single volume is used by the celebrant who presides at the eucharist. Use of the missal dates from the tenth century. The Roman Missal was used by mendicant friars and officials of the Roman Curia who traveled through Europe. The Roman Missal came to be used or imitated in many places. In 1570 Pope Pius V published a revised edition of the Roman Missal that reflected the directives of the Council of Trent. This edition of the Roman Missal was required for all dioceses, churches, and religious communities that did not have a missal of their own which they had used for at least 200 years. Use of a missal has never been required in the Anglican liturgical tradition. The 1549 Prayer Book provided liturgical texts and prayers for the eucharist, including introits, collects, epistles and gospels for the church year. It also included the contents of the breviary, the missal, priests' manuals, and a revised form of the English litany of 1544 which had replaced the book of litanies and processions. The Ordinal (ordination rites) continued to be printed separately until the 1662 Prayer Book. Although there is no official missal in the Episcopal Church, an Altar Book with eucharistic texts, prayers, and music from the BCP and *The Hymnal 1982* is published by Church Publishing Incorporated. Anglo-catholic missals, such as the American Missal that was first published in 1931, included a variety of additional materials and devotions that were not in the BCP. *See* Missal Mass.

"Missal Mass." The use of a missal has never been required in the Anglican liturgical tradition. However, unofficial missals have been privately published. These missals combine liturgical texts from the Prayer Book with supplementary materials such as prayers, ceremonial directions, and scripture lessons for various occasions that may not be included in the Prayer Book. Although these supplementary materials may be drawn from a variety of sources, the Latin Rite is typically the primary source. The *American Missal* was first published by Morehouse Publishing in Milwaukee, Wisconsin, in 1931. The *American Missal* drew upon the *English Missal*, the *Anglican Missal* (published by the Society of Saints Peter and Paul), and the *People's Missal*, all of which had been published in England. The ceremonial directions of the *American Missal* were not intended to contradict the Prayer Book rubrics, but the directions of the *American Missal* conformed the liturgy to "the common tradition of Western Catholic Christendom" when no definite provision was required, or when alternate usage was allowed. A revised edition of the *American Missal* was published in 1951 by Earle Hewitt Maddux of the Society of Saint John the Evangelist in Cambridge, Massachusetts. It also drew on English, Scottish, Irish, and South African Prayer Books for supplementary materials. An American Edition of the *Anglican Missal* was published in 1943 by the Frank Gavin Liturgical Foundation of Mount Sinai, New York. Missals have typically been used by parishes with an Anglo-catholic piety. A eucharistic celebration guided by the celebrant's use of a missal may be known as a "Missal Mass." *See* Missal.

Mission. From the Latin "to send." Christian mission is the sending forth to proclaim the gospel of Jesus Christ. The authority for Christian mission is based in Christ and known through the power of the Holy Spirit. Christian mission is understood to be a response to Jesus' command for his disciples to "go and make disciples of all nations" (Mt 28:19) and to St. Paul's question, how are people to proclaim Jesus "unless they are sent?" (Rom 10:15). The Catechism notes that the mission of the church is "to restore all people to unity with God and each other in Christ." The church pursues its mission "as it prays and worships, proclaims the gospel, and promotes justice, peace, and love." This mission is carried out through all members of the church (BCP, p. 855). In 1835 the General Convention of the Episcopal Church recognized that all members of the church are called to be missionaries, although this identity has not yet been fulfilled in practice.

"Mission Services" or "Third Services." Simplified forms of the Daily Offices of the BCP. These simplified forms, also known as "Third Services," began to be used in the mid-nineteenth century in pastoral contexts that were not considered appropriate for the BCP forms of the Daily Offices. For example, the Protestant Episcopal Society for the Promotion of Evangelical Knowledge was organized in 1847 and subsequently published *The Mission Service*. It was used in the Army, the Navy, prisons, and new settlements. Bishops were authorized by the 1856 General Convention to provide simplified services for congregations that could not use the Daily Offices of the

Prayer Book. The 1892 BCP permitted a third daily service drawn from the Prayer Book and used at the discretion of the diocesan bishop. Similarly, the directions "Concerning the Service of the Church" in the 1928 BCP allowed the use of "other devotions" taken from the Prayer Book, or set forth by lawful authority in the church, or from scripture. These services could take the place of the Prayer Book forms for Morning or Evening Prayer "when the edification of the Congregation so requires." This substitution was to be done under the direction of the diocesan bishop in the case of mission churches or chapels, and with the express authorization of the bishop in cathedral or parish churches and other places. Use of these simplified services reflected a desire to encourage wider participation in the worship of the church, including those who might have struggled with some of the liturgical forms of the Prayer Book.

Mission and Ministry. Journal published by Trinity Episcopal School for Ministry, formerly *Kerygma. Mission and Ministry* began publication in Advent 1982. It combines "theological reflection and pastoral instruction on issues important to biblical Christians."

Missionary. One sent to proclaim the good news of Christ. The term is from the Latin "to send." All Christians by baptism are called to "proclaim by word and example the Good News of God in Christ" (BCP, p. 305). The church seeks to restore all people to unity with God and each other in Christ. The church carries out its mission through the ministry of all its members (BCP, p. 855). The Domestic and Foreign Missionary Society of the Protestant Episcopal Church includes all members of the Episcopal Church.

After the resurrection, Jesus commanded the 11 remaining disciples to proclaim the good news to the whole creation (Mk 16:15; see Mt 28:19–20). He promised the apostles that they would receive power when the Holy Spirit had come upon them and that they would be his witnesses "in Jerusalem, in all Judea and Samaria, and to the ends of the earth" (Acts 1:8). Christians were scattered during the persecution of the church that followed Stephen's martyrdom. Those who were scattered went from place to place, proclaiming the word (Acts 8:4; see Acts 11:19). After his conversion to Christianity, Paul undertook three missionary journeys (see Acts 13–14, 15:36–18:21, 18:23–21:16). Paul's missionary work was shared with other missionaries such as Timothy and Silvanus (2 Cor 1:19) and Titus (2 Cor 8:23). In the following centuries, the Christian faith spread widely through the work of missionaries. Noted Christian missionaries have included Augustine of Canterbury in England, Patrick in Ireland, Boniface in Germany, Cyril and Methodius among the Slavic peoples, Gregory the Illuminator in Armenia, and Anskar in Denmark and Sweden. Jackson Kemper was chosen the first missionary bishop of the Episcopal Church at the 1835 General Convention. Many missionaries have paid with their lives for their calling. Martyred missionaries include Boniface and his companions in Frisia (754), James Hannington and his companions in Eastern Equatorial Africa (1885), John Coleridge Patteson and his companions in Melanesia (1871), and the martyrs of Lyons (177), Japan (1597), and New Guinea (1942).

Missionary. This periodical was published at Burlington, New Jersey, under the patronage and editorship of Bishop George Washington Doane. The first issue was dated Sept. 20, 1835, and it ceased publication in Dec. 1837. It called itself a "Soldier of the Cross." It is very valuable for the information it provides about the 1835 General Convention, which recognized that all members of the Episcopal Church are called to be missionaries and provided for missionary bishops.

Missionary Bishops. A bishop sent by the church to lead the organization and development of the church in a new mission field. The 1835 General Convention, the Missionary Convention, passed the canon, "of Missionary Bishops." This canon provided that the House of Deputies may, on nomination by the House of Bishops, elect a person to be a bishop to exercise episcopal functions in states and territories not organized into dioceses. Prior to 1835 there was no canonical provision made for extending beyond the organized dioceses. The Episcopal Church was rather passive in its mission strategy for the newly settled territories of the United States. Jackson Kemper was the first domestic missionary bishop, and William Jones Boone was the first foreign missionary bishop. *See* Kemper, Jackson; *see* Boone, William Jones.

Missionary College of St. Augustine, Benicia, California. *See* St. Augustine, Missionary College of, Benicia, California.

Missions and Church Extension, Department of. On Nov. 25, 1919, the Presiding Bishop and the newly formed National

Council of the Episcopal Church held its initial meeting and organized five departments, one of which was the Department of Missions and Church Extension. It succeeded the Board of Missions, which held its last meeting on Dec. 10, 1919, and went out of existence on Dec. 31, 1919. The Department had an executive secretary, a domestic secretary, a secretary for Latin America, an educational secretary, and a secretary for work among foreign-born Americans. In Apr. 1931 the National Council divided the work of Missions and Church Extension into separate departments for Domestic Missions and Foreign Missions.

Mississippi, Diocese of. This diocese was organized at Trinity Church, Natchez, on May 17–18, 1826. It includes the entire state of Mississippi. On Jan. 19, 1966, St. Andrew's Church, Jackson, became the Cathedral Parish of St. Andrew.

Mississippi Conference on Church Music and Liturgy. Started in 1975 by Leslie N. Casaday, parish musician at St. Philip's Church, Jackson, Mississippi, it began as a weekend workshop for the St. Philip's choir. It provides an opportunity for spiritual renewal and professional development for the church's musicians and clergy. Most participants serve smaller churches on a part-time basis.

Missouri, Diocese of. Jackson Kemper was consecrated the Missionary Bishop of Missouri and Indiana on Sept. 1, 1835. On Nov. 16, 1840, the Diocese of Missouri was organized at Christ Church, St. Louis, which became Christ Church Cathedral on May 22, 1888. The General Convention of 1889 voted to divide the Diocese of Missouri. The Diocese of Missouri includes the following counties: Adair, Audrain, Bollinger, Boone, Butler, Callaway, Cape Girardeau, Carter, Clark, Cole, Crawford, Dent, Dunkin, Franklin, Gasconade, Iron, Jefferson, Knox, Lewis, Lincoln, Macon, Madison, Maries, Marion, Miller, Mississippi, Monroe, Montgomery, New Madrid, Oregon, Osage, Pemiscot, Perry, Phelps, Pike, Pulaski, Ralls, Randolph, Reynolds, Ripley, St. Charles, St. Francois, St. Genevieve, St. Louis, Schuyler, Scotland, Scott, Shannon, Shelby, Stoddard, Texas, Warren, Washington, and Wayne.

"Mite Box." *See* Blue Box (UTO).

Miter, or Mitre. Liturgical headgear and insignia of bishops and other prelates. It is typically worn by bishops in procession and when pronouncing episcopal blessings. It is removed during prayer, including the eucharistic canon. The term is from the Greek for "turban." The miter is shield-shaped and pointed at the top. It may be made of silk or linen and ornamented with gold embroidery. Two lappets (pendant bands or flaps) hang down the back of the miter. It is often said to represent the tongues of fire that rested on the apostles at Pentecost (Acts 2). The miter may be derived from the headgear of civil officials of the late Roman empire.

Mixed Chalice. The practice of mixing a little water with the wine that will be consecrated at the eucharist. The BCP states that this practice "is customary" (p. 407). It probably is derived from ancient Jewish custom. It was likely observed by Jesus at the Last Supper. It was the invariable practice of the early church, and it is referred to in the Apostolic Constitutions. However, it was rejected by Luther at the Reformation and not practiced in the Calvinist tradition. It was directed by the 1549 BCP but not mentioned in the 1552 Prayer Book. It is widely practiced now. It has been described as a sign of union of Christ with his people, a sign of the flow of blood and water from Jesus' side at the crucifixion, and a sign of the union of Christ's divine and human natures. In the eastern tradition, hot water is added to the chalice after the breaking of the bread to symbolize the descent of the Spirit and the vibrant energy of faith. This practice is known as the *zeon*.

Mizeki, Bernard (c. 1861–June 1896). Catechist and martyr in Rhodesia. He was born on the coast of Mozambique, and moved to Capetown, South Africa, in search of employment when he was a teenager. In Capetown he met Frederick Puller, a member of the Society of St. John the Evangelist. Puller baptized Mizeki on Mar. 9, 1886, and trained him as a catechist. Puller gave Mizeki charge over St. Columba's Home for Africans, a boarding hostel on the outskirts of Capetown. Eventually, Mizeki moved to what is now Zimbabwe and established a small mission to the people of Chief Mangwende. As Mizeki made converts, he also made enemies. Since he was a Christian, some Africans saw him as an ally of the unwelcome western colonizers. In June 1896, during an uprising of the native people against the Europeans and their African friends, two men dragged Mizeki out of his hut and attacked him with spears. He was wounded and crawled into the protection of the night's darkness. Later that night, when his wife and another woman looked for him, they saw a bright light in the direction where Mizeki had gone, and they heard a sound "like many wings of great birds." His body was never found. The site of the hut and chapel he built near Marondera is now a shrine where an annual festival is held. This annual event is an occasion for testifying, preaching, praying, singing, and healing. Mizeki is commemorated in the Episcopal calendar of the church year on June 18.

Modalism. Modalism, or modalistic monarchianism, is a pre-Nicene teaching about the relation of Christ to God. First taught by Noetus of Smyrna at the end of the second century, modalism was also taught at Rome by Praxeas, Sabellius, and others. Modalism took several forms. Praxeas taught that Word and Spirit were simply names (or modes) of God, applicable at different times. Praxeas also taught that the Father himself was born of Mary, suffered, died, and rose again. This form of modalism is therefore sometimes called *patripassianism*. Sabellius understood Father, Son, and Holy Spirit to be nothing more than aspects or modes of the one divine Person. Modalist teaching held that Father, Son, and Spirit were successive manifestations or modes—at one time in the OT world, then in the world of the gospels and then the church. The questions raised by modalism marked a significant stage on the way to a developed doctrine of the Trinity. *See* Monarchianism; *see* Patripassianism; *see* Trinity.

Modernism. The term for the thought of some late nineteenth- and early twentieth-century Roman Catholic scholars who sought to embrace the results of recent advances in history, science, and philosophy. They trusted catholic tradition but mistrusted scholastic theology. They insisted on the complete freedom of scholarly research from ecclesiastical interference. Extreme modernists asserted that it was possible to hold in faith to the truth of Christian dogma while allowing its factual contradiction on the historical level. Roman Catholic modernists best known among Anglicans are Alfred Loisy, George Tyrrell, and Friedrich von Hügel. Extreme modernist positions were condemned by Pope Pius X in the encyclical *Pascendi* (1907). Roman Catholic modernists exerted considerable influence on Anglican liberalism, particularly on the synthesis between broad church and high church represented by Charles Gore and expressed in *Lux Mundi*, a collection of essays which Gore edited and published in 1889. An Anglican modernist association, the Modern Churchman's Union, disseminated Anglican versions of modernist views for half a century through its annual

conferences and quarterly journal, *The Modern Churchman*. Among the well-known Anglican modernists were A. E. J. Rawlinson, W. R. Matthews, and H. D. A. Major. The modernist movement in England is the counterpart of liberal evangelicalism in the United States. *See* Gore, Charles; *see* Liberal Evangelicalism.

Modeste, Leon Edgar (b. Aug. 19, 1926). Director of General Convention Special Program. He was born in Brooklyn, New York. Modeste received his B.A. in 1950 from Long Island University and his M.S.W. in 1953 from the Columbia University School of Social Work. He also studied at the Graduate School of Business at Columbia University. Modeste taught at New York University, the University of Southern Mississippi, the University of Kentucky, the State University of New York, Medgar Evers College, and Syracuse University. Modeste belonged to numerous civic and political organizations. He was the Executive Director of the Brooklyn Urban League. When Presiding Bishop John E. Hines toured the Bedford-Stuyvesant area of New York City to study the poverty of the inner city, he asked Modeste to accompany him. Hines reported to the General Convention of 1967, which created the General Convention Special Program. Hines named Modeste the director of the Program. This was a controversial program, and the 1973 General Convention removed it from the budget. Modeste and his staff were terminated effective Dec. 31, 1973.

Mollegen, Albert Theodore (Feb. 17, 1906–Jan. 22, 1984). Seminary professor and theologian. He held the chair of New Testament Language and Literature and later the Clinton S. Quin Chair of Christian Ethics at Virginia Theological Seminary from 1936 until his retirement in 1974. As one of Paul Tillich's first American students, Mollegen became one of Tillich's most sympathetic and effective interpreters. He served as deputy to six General Conventions and on the Standing Commission on Ecumenical Relations for ten years. He was most noted as an apologist for liberal evangelicalism, and in 1947 he founded an association called Christianity and Modern Man. This association anticipated modern theological education for laity by many years. Mollegen wrote *Christianity and Modern Man* (1961), *The Christianity of St. Paul* (1956), and *The Faith of Christians* (1954).

Monarchianism. From the Greek *monos*, "one," and *arche*, "source" or "principle," monarchianism is a teaching about

God which flourished in the second and third centuries. It stressed the unity (or monarchy) of God rather than the three persons, Father, Son, and Spirit. Monarchianism occurred in two forms. Dynamic monarchianism, more properly called adoptionism, held that God was a single Person (Greek, *prosopon*) and Christ a "mere man" on whom the power (Greek, *dynamis*) of God descended. Modalistic monarchianism presented the unity of God as an underlying essence and the three persons as successive manifestations. *See* Modalism.

Monastery. A place where members of religious orders live in community, usually under the monastic vows of poverty, chastity, and obedience. The orderly life of prayer, work, and study is carried out in the context of the "hours of the day" or "divine offices" and the daily eucharist. The brothers in a monastery or sisters in a convent live in individual cells (rooms). They eat and worship in community. They may devote themselves to prayer and study. Members of some religious orders may participate in works of charity, service, or spiritual programs for churches or other persons. There are a number of monasteries affiliated with the Episcopal Church, including monasteries for men, for women, and a few for men and women together.

Monastic. A person who devotes his or her life to religious vows and who lives in community (in or associated with a monastery) or as a solitary. Monastic communities lead a life devoted to God in a monastery, in relative isolation from the world. Although monastic vows differ from tradition to tradition, they normally include poverty, chastity, and obedience. A monastic's schedule may be divided into prayer, study, and work. Eastern monks follow the rule of St. Basil, and most western monks follow the rule of St. Benedict. Monks are bound by solemn vows. They live in relatively independent abbeys ruled by an elected abbot, with the highest authority residing in a general chapter. The general chapter includes all the professed members of the order. Monastic and canonical orders were discontinued in England by Henry VIII but restored in the Anglican Communion during the nineteenth century.

A renewal of Anglican monasticism was encouraged by the Oxford Movement. In England, E. B. Pusey heard the vows of two women who started a religious community in 1845. Other religious communities formed in England in the mid-nineteenth century. Episcopal monasticism began

with sisterhoods formed in the mid-nineteenth century and was strengthened when the Community of St. Mary (CSM) was founded by Mother Harriet and her companions in 1865 on Feb. 2, the Feast of the Presentation. The Rev. Charles C. Grafton, a native of Boston and later Bishop of Fond du Lac, was one of the founders of the first Anglican monastic orders for men after the Reformation, the Society of St. John the Evangelist (SSJE) in England in 1866. Grafton returned to the United States and the Episcopal Church in 1872 to serve as rector of the Church of the Advent, Boston, and to lead the work of the SSJE in the United States. The first indigenous monastic order for men in the Episcopal Church was the Order of the Holy Cross (OHC), founded by the Rev. James O. S. Huntington in New York in 1884. Today the Episcopal Church includes a variety of religious orders and other Christian communities. According to the canon on Religious Orders and Other Christian Communities, a religious order is a society of Christians in communion with the See of Canterbury who voluntarily commit themselves for life or a term of years to holding their possessions in common or in trust, to celibate life in community, and to obedience to their rule and constitution.

Monica, or Monnica (c. 331–387). Mother of Augustine of Hippo. She was probably born in Tagaste, North Africa. Monica married Patricius, who may have been a nominal Christian. She was the mother of three children: Augustine, Navigius, and Perpetus. Most of the information about her is in Augustine's *Confessions* (Book IX). She was deeply committed to Augustine's conversion to Christianity. He did convert to Christianity in 386. Monica died in Ostia, Italy. In 1430 her remains were moved from Ostia to the Church of St. Augustine in Rome. Because of her influence on Augustine to become a Christian, she is recognized as a model for Christian mothers. Monica is commemorated on May 4 in the Episcopal calendar of the church year on the day before Augustine's conversion, May 5, 386.

Monk. A member of a male monastic community. *See* Monastic.

Monk, William Henry (Mar. 16, 1823–Mar. 1, 1889). British music educator, composer, and organist. He was born in London. Much of Monk's life was spent as an organist and choirmaster in London parishes. He served as musical editor for the important British hymnal, *Hymns*

Ancient & Modern. It is said that the title of this hymnal came from his suggestion. The 1861 edition contained sixty of his arrangements and fifteen original tunes. He was also musical editor of the *Parish Choir* and *The Scottish Hymnal*. *The Hymnal 1982* uses his arrangements or original tunes in twenty-one hymns, including his arrangement of *Victory* in "The strife is o'er" (Hymn 208), his arrangement of *Darwall's 148th* in "Ye holy angels bright" (Hymn 625), and his original tune, *Unde et memores*, in "And now, O Father, mindful of the love" (Hymn 337). He died in London.

Monophysitism. A christological teaching that the person of Christ consisted of a single divine nature or a united divine and human nature in which the human was absorbed by the divine. The full humanity of Christ was not upheld. The term comes from the Greek *monos*, "one," and *physis*, "nature." The teaching is associated with Eutyches, who denied that Jesus' human nature existed without confusion together with the divine nature in Christ. Monophysitism was condemned by the Council of Chalcedon (451), which acknowledged that Christ's divine and human natures exist without confusion or division. Coptic and Ethiopian churches refused to subscribe to the Chalcedonian Definition and are still known as monophysite churches. Monophysite tendencies may refer to any devaluation of the human reality in the relationship of God and humanity. *See* Incarnation.

Monothelitism. From the Greek *monos*, "one," and *thelema*, "will." A seventh-century christological teaching advocated by Sergius of Constantinople, Cyrus of Alexandria, and others. It presented the Person of Christ as having one divine will under which his human will was subsumed. Monothelitism was consistent with the Chalcedonian Definition concerning the two natures of the Person of Christ. But monothelitism upset the balance between Christ's divinity and his humanity by upholding only one independent *divine* will. It was declared heretical at the Sixth Ecumenical Council (III Constantinople) in 680–681, which held " . . .there are two natures unconfusedly, unchangeably, undividedly, and two natural wills and two natural operations. . . ." *See* Chalcedonian Definition; *see* Ecumenical Councils; *see* Christology.

Monstrance. A frame or vessel, typically made of gold or silver, used to display the consecrated bread of the eucharist for veneration or Benediction of the Blessed Sacrament. Also known as an ostensorium. The term is from the Latin "to show or display." The monstrance has a round, flat window in which the consecrated bread is placed for viewing. The holder for the consecrated host is known as the luna or lunette. The frame beyond the luna traditionally has a design of rays that seem to emanate from the center of the monstrance where the eucharistic host is placed. Modern versions of the monstrance may be simpler in design. Monstrances are seen in some Episcopal parishes with Anglo-catholic piety that practice eucharistic devotions. *See* Benediction of the Blessed Sacrament; *see* Luna.

Montana, Diocese of. On Oct. 15, 1880, the House of Bishops established the Missionary District of Montana. It has had its own bishop from that time to the present. It was preceded by two larger jurisdictions. On Oct. 19, 1865, the House of Bishops resolved "That all those portions of our country, North of a line running along the Northern boundary of the Cherokee country and New Mexico, until it reaches the Diocese of California, not yet organized into Dioceses, or included within Missionary districts, be within the jurisdiction of the Missionary Bishop of the North West." This included the present state of Montana. Two days later they created the Missionary District of Colorado and Parts Adjacent, with jurisdiction in Montana. On Oct. 4, 1866, the House of Bishops established the Missionary District of Montana, Idaho, and Utah. The primary convention of the Diocese of Montana was held at St. Mark's Church, Anaconda, on June 19–22, 1904. On Dec. 13, 1971, St. Peter's Church, Helena, became St. Peter's Cathedral.

Montanism. A charismatic Christian sect which appeared in Phrygia in Asia Minor during the closing years of the second century. Montanism was founded by Montanus and his assistants, Priscilla and Maximilla, who considered themselves to be inspired by the Holy Spirit. Their "revelations" carried the adherents of the new sect to extreme and unorthodox claims. All members of the sect, clerical or lay, were encouraged to prophesy in the power of the Spirit. They made a new call for moral rigor in the face of the rampant immorality of the surrounding secular society. They proclaimed the imminent end of the world. The movement spread rapidly through the Christian world, but it disappeared in less than a century. Tertullian became a Montanist near the end of his life because of the moral rigor of its teaching. *See* Millenarianism.

Montgomery, James (Nov. 4, 1771–Apr. 30, 1854). British newspaper editor and hymn writer. Montgomery was born in Irvine, Ayrshire, England. He was the son of Moravian missionary parents who intended that he become a minister. However, he was dismissed from seminary in 1792 because of his preoccupation with writing poetry. He became assistant to the editor and owner of the Sheffield *Register*, a radical newspaper. After the owner fled because of political persecution, Montgomery took over the paper. He renamed it *The Iris*, continued its liberal editorial policy, and used it for the occasional publication of his hymns. Imprisoned twice because of his political leanings, he became an outspoken and well-known opponent of the slave trade, child labor, and state lotteries. He supported foreign missions and the Bible Society. Although he was associated with Wesleyan Methodists, Montgomery became a supporter of Thomas Cotterill, rector of St. Paul's, Sheffield. Cotterill was attempting to popularize the singing of hymns in the Anglican Church. Montgomery was the author of over four hundred hymns. *The Hymnal 1982* contains nine of his texts, including "Shepherd of souls, refresh and bless" (Hymn 343), "When Jesus left his Father's throne" (Hymn 480), and "Hail to the Lord's Anointed" (Hymn 616). He died in Sheffield.

Moore, Clement Clarke (July 15, 1779–July 10, 1863). Seminary professor and renowned poet. He was born in Chelsea in New York City. Moore graduated from Columbia College in 1798. He studied for the ordained ministry but was never ordained. In 1809 he published *A Compendious Lexicon of the Hebrew Language: In Two Vols.* It was a major publication that made him the pioneer in the United States of Hebrew lexicography. In Feb. 1819 he donated sixty lots in New York City, including Chelsea Square, on the condition that a theological seminary be built there. This is now the General Theological Seminary. Moore was Professor of Hebrew and Greek Literature at General Seminary from 1821 until 1850. In 1822 Moore composed for his children the poem *A Visit From St. Nicholas*, popularly known as "'Twas the night before Christmas." Moore died in Newport, Rhode Island.

Moore, Richard Channing (Aug. 21, 1762–Nov. 12, 1841). A leading evangelical bishop who was known for his prayer meetings and informal services. He was born in New York City. Moore studied medicine. After practicing medicine for a while, he studied for the ordained ministry under Bishop Samuel Provoost of New York. He was ordained deacon on July 15, 1787, and priest on Sept. 19, 1787. For two years, 1787–1789, he was in charge of Christ Church, Rye, New York. From 1789 until 1809 he was rector of St. Andrew's Church, Staten Island. In 1809 Moore became the rector of St. Stephen's Church, New York. From 1814 until his death he was rector of Monumental Church, Richmond, Virginia. On May 18, 1814, he was consecrated the second Bishop of Virginia and served there until his death. Moore began the work that revived the Episcopal Church in Virginia from the disorganization that followed the American Revolution. While he was bishop, the Virginia Theological Seminary was established. Moore died in Lynchburg, Virginia.

Moral Theology. Theology that focuses on development of moral principles and norms and their application to human actions in general and to particular situations. Moral theology provides a systematic framework for casuistry and has reflected the concerns of casuistry. Traditional moral theologies broadly assumed the theology of Thomas Aquinas (1225–1274). Roman Catholic texts began with a consideration of the ends of human action, considered how we come to know and do the good, focused on the principles and norms of action, addressed particular cases, and placed decision-making in the larger context of the sacramental life of the church (especially sacramental confession). The content of moral theology was shaped by an understanding of the end of human life as the beatific vision. Union with God was understood to be realized in the cardinal and theological virtues. The principles and norms of action were developed in terms of the Ten Commandments or the virtues themselves. Contemporary Roman Catholic moral theologies address the same questions but with a traditional focus on sacramental confession. Without the requirement of sacramental confession, Anglicans never developed a clearly accepted body of teaching that could be called a system of Anglican moral theology. Significant contributions to Anglican moral theology date from the period of the English Reformation, most notably Richard Hooker and Jeremy Taylor. Anglican moral theology was renewed in the wake of the Oxford Movement, most notably by Kenneth Kirk. *See* Beatific Vision; *see* Cardinal Virtues; *see* Casuistry; *see* Theological Virtues.

Moreau, Jules Laurence (Dec. 9, 1917–June 12, 1971). Historian and editor. He was born in Irvington, New Jersey. Moreau received his B.A. from Lehigh University in 1940;

his S.T.B. in 1947 and his S.T.M. in 1953 from the General Theological Seminary; and his M.A. in 1953 and his Ph.D. in 1960 from Northwestern University. He was ordained deacon on Apr. 8, 1947, and priest on Oct. 9, 1947. Moreau began his ministry as deacon-in-charge of St. Paul's Church, Morris Plains, New Jersey, 1946–1947. He was vicar of Christ Chapel, Wortendyke, New Jersey, 1947–1948. In 1948 he went to Seabury-Western Theological Seminary to teach New Testament. From 1950 until 1960, Moreau was Librarian at Seabury-Western. Moreau taught church history at Seabury-Western from 1960 until his death. He was editor of the *Anglican Theological Review* from Jan. 1970 until his death. Moreau died in Evanston, Illinois.

Morehouse, Clifford Phelps (Apr. 18, 1904–Feb. 17, 1977). Editor, author, publisher, and ecumenist. He was born in Milwaukee, Wisconsin. Morehouse received his B.A. in 1925 from Harvard University and his M.A. from Marquette University in 1937. He was secretary of the Morehouse-Barlow Publishing Company, 1925–1939, vice-president, 1932–1964, and president, 1964–1968. Morehouse was managing editor of *The Living Church*, 1926–1932, and editor, 1932–1952. From 1968 until 1973, he was senior warden, a vestryman, and historiographer of Trinity Church, New York. He also served as a trustee of the Cathedral of St. John the Divine, New York, 1948–1952. Morehouse was deeply involved in the ecumenical movement and served as a delegate to the Assembly of the World Council of Churches at Evanston, Illinois, 1954; New Delhi, India, 1961; and Uppsala, Sweden, 1968. He was a lay deputy to the General Convention from 1934 until 1967. From 1961 until 1967, he was president of the House of Deputies. From 1967 until 1973, he was a member of the Executive Council of the Episcopal Church. Among his many books are *A Layman Looks at the Church* (1964), and *Trinity: Mother of Churches, An Informal History of Trinity Parish in the City of New York* (1973). Morehouse died in Sarasota, Florida.

Morehouse, Frederic Cook (Mar. 19, 1868–June 25, 1932). Editor, author, publisher, and ecumenist. He was born in Milwaukee, and educated privately. In 1885 he assisted his father, Linden Husted Morehouse, in establishing The Young Churchman Company, the name of which was changed in 1918 to Morehouse Publishing Company. From 1896 to 1900, Morehouse edited *The*

Church Eclectic, and from 1899 until his death he was editor of *The Living Church* and *The Living Church Annual* (now *The Episcopal Church Annual*). He was a lay deputy to every General Convention from 1910 to 1931, though he was unable to attend the 1931 convention. For many years he was a member of the National Council of the Episcopal Church, and he served on the Commission on Evangelism which inaugurated the "Bishops' Crusade," a nationwide effort to rouse the people of the church to a sense of their responsibilities as Christians. In 1927 he was a representative of the Episcopal Church to the World Conference on Faith and Order, at Lausanne, Switzerland, where he took a firm stand for the frank recognition of the differences among various Christian groups. Morehouse served on many civic boards in Milwaukee, received numerous honorary degrees, and wrote several books, including *Some American Churchmen* (1892). He died in Milwaukee. *See* Bishops' Crusade; *see* Living Church, The.

Morehouse Group, The. Morehouse Publishing was established in 1884 by Linden H. Morehouse to publish and distribute Sunday School lesson materials. The company has been known variously over the years as the Young Churchmen, Morehouse-Gorham, Morehouse-Barlow, and Morehouse Publishing. It publishes and distributes books, educational materials, and church supplies for the Episcopal Church and other churches. It published the first Church's Teaching Series. Its most recent church school curriculum, the *Episcopal Children's Curriculum* and the *Episcopal Curriculum for Youth*, was developed and published in collaboration with Virginia Theological Seminary. In recent years Morehouse has expanded the scope of its ministries through several acquisitions. In the mid-1990s Morehouse Publishing became a part of the publishing division of the Morehouse Group. In 1995, Living the Good News, a Denver-based company that publishes a lectionary-based curriculum and related books, became part of the Morehouse Group. In 1996, Trinity Press International, a publisher of academic/theological books located in Valley Forge, Pennsylvania, joined the Morehouse Group. In recent years the Morehouse Group has become a publisher for the Anglican Communion Office in London, publishing all the official documents for the 1998 Lambeth Conference. It also provides communications services to several offices of the Church Center in New York and operates Episcopal Parish Services for the Church Center.

More Hymns and Spiritual Songs. A 1971 hymnal supplement, prepared by the Joint Commission on Church Music of the Episcopal Church and published in a loose-leaf format. It has a wide variety of musical resources, including traditional hymns, folk songs, and ancient melodies. The first section of the collection, "Songs for Liturgy," contained settings of music for the offices and the eucharist. Norman Mealy served as general editor for this section. The second section of the collection, "More Hymns and Spiritual Songs," contained 71 hymns. Lee. H. Bristol was general editor for the second section. A second, paperback edition of this part of the original collection contained ten additional hymns. It was published by the Joint Commission in 1977. This 1971 publication and its 1977 edition provided many musical settings of service music and hymns found in *The Hymnal 1982.* It also established the form of notation used in the plainsong settings of canticles found in *The Book of Canticles* and *The Hymnal 1982.*

Morgan, Emily Malbone (Dec. 10, 1862–Feb. 27, 1937). Founder of the Society of the Companions of the Holy Cross. She was born in Hartford, Connecticut, the youngest child of a wealthy family. As early as 1889 she established a number of summer vacation homes for urban working women in rural Connecticut and Massachusetts. She financed these homes by lectures and children's books which she wrote and published. Morgan founded the Society of the Companions of the Holy Cross in 1884 in response to a request for a group of friends to gather regularly for prayer. This request was made by Adelyn Howard, a childhood friend of Morgan's. Howard was stricken with an incurable disease. The Society of the Companions of the Holy Cross had simple rules calling for communal intercessory prayer and thanksgiving. Eventually Morgan established Adelynrood, near Byfield, Massachusetts, as a meeting place and summer respite for the Companions. By 1920 the Companionship had spread all over the world. It includes women who hold a wide range of positions on the relationship between Christian faith and social activism. Morgan died in Boston, Massachusetts.

Morning Prayer. In many times and places, daybreak has been a time of prayer. Jews prayed in their synagogues at sunrise as well as at other times each day. This Jewish pattern of prayer formed the basis of the Christian monastic Daily Office, with its prayers or "hours" at seven times in each day. Thomas Cranmer's revision of the Daily Office for the first English Prayer Book (1549) reduced the number of services to two—one for morning (Matins) and one for evening (Evensong or vespers). In the Second English Prayer Book (1552), the morning service was given its present name, Morning Prayer.

Many elements of Morning Prayer come from the monastic hours of matins (e.g., *Venite* and *Te Deum*), lauds (e.g., *Benedicte, omnia opera Domini*, a "chapter" of scripture, *Benedictus Dominus Deus*, collect of the day), and Prime (e.g., a second "chapter" of scripture and the Apostles' Creed). Psalms were recited at every one of the offices, with the whole Psalter recited once a week. In the 1549 BCP, psalms were read at both Morning and Evening Prayer, with the whole Psalter read "in course" once each month. In subsequent Prayer Book revisions, psalms have come to be used more selectively, although a monthly cycle of psalms read "in course" is still provided as an option. In the 1549 Prayer Book, the very short monastic "chapters" were lengthened to full chapters of both the OT and NT at both Morning Prayer and Evening Prayer. In the 1979 BCP, only one lesson must be read, and the appointed lessons are not so long.

Morning Prayer once was the chief Sunday service in most Anglican churches on three out of four Sundays, the First Sunday usually being a celebration of Holy Communion. This practice has not continued because the eucharist has been recognized as the "principal act of Christian worship on the Lord's Day" in most parishes (see BCP, p. 13), However, Morning Prayer is clearly designated as a daily service for the worship of the church. This usage reflects the ancient tradition of the Daily Office.

Moscow Agreed Statement. This statement was issued in Aug. 1976 by the Anglican-Orthodox Joint Doctrinal Commission. Subjects treated were: 1) the knowledge of God, 2) the inspiration and authority of Holy Scripture, 3) scripture and tradition, 4) the authority of councils, 5) the *Filioque* clause, 6) the church as the eucharistic community, and 7) the invocation of the Holy Spirit in the eucharist. Some differences as well as agreements were noted in the Statement. The Anglicans agreed with the Orthodox that the *filioque* clause should be omitted from the Nicene Creed. The Episcopal Church resolved at the 1994 General Convention to remove the *filioque* clause from the Nicene Creed in the next edition of the Prayer Book. *See* Filioque.

Most Reverend. *See* Reverend, The.

Motet. A composition based on a sacred Latin text, sung by two or more voices. It was traditionally unaccompanied. The text sung by the upper part was a paraphrase of the plainchant text sung by the tenor or lower part. The motet was polyphonic (multiple tones) and polytextual (multiple texts). Additional parts add additional paraphrased texts and tones. The motet dates from the thirteenth century, when words were added to the upper part of two-part compositions. The upper parts of these compositions had previously been vocalized without words. The term is from the French *mot*, "word." Motets were first popular in France and then spread to other European countries during the fifteenth century. The motet is considered to be one of the most important forms of polyphonic music in the middle ages and Renaissance. It came to be used at royal courts and for secular entertainment as well as in church. Some later motets were accompanied by musical instruments, with voice parts sung by choruses or choirs. Noted composers of motets include Giovanni Pierluigi da Palestrina (c. 1525–1594), Thomas Tallis (c. 1505–1585), William Byrd (c. 1543–1623), and Johann Sebastian Bach (1685–1750). Motets continue to enrich the worship of churches with musicians who can perform polyphonic compositions.

Mother House. Traditionally, it is the headquarters for a community where the superior lives. It is distinguished from branch houses or dependent foundations of the community.

"Mothering Sunday." The fourth Sunday in Lent, also known as Refreshment Sunday and Laetare Sunday. It was the traditional mid-Lent Sunday. It was a time of refreshment and relaxing the penitential discipline of Lent. Rose-pink vestments were allowed to take the place of the purple vestments of Lent. The traditional epistle for the fourth Sunday in Lent states that the heavenly Jerusalem "is the mother of us all" (Gal 4:26). "Mothering Sunday" was a popular name in England for the fourth Sunday in Lent. It was customary in some places to visit the mother church of one's diocese or chapel on this day. In other places it was customary to visit one's mother on "Mothering Sunday." Apprentices visiting their parents on this day often took home a "mothering cake." *See* Laetare Sunday.

Movable Feast. A feast of the church year that is not celebrated on a fixed date. The date of the movable feast's celebration in each year is determined by other liturgical rules. The church year has two cycles of feasts and holy days, one dependent on the movable date of Easter Day and the other dependent on the fixed date of Christmas, Dec. 25 (BCP, p. 15). Easter Day is the first Sunday after the first full moon after the spring equinox on Mar. 21. This date is fixed in accordance with an ancient ecclesiological computation, and may not correspond to the astronomical equinox (BCP, p. 880). Easter cannot be earlier than Mar. 22, and it cannot be later than Apr. 25. The BCP provides tables and rules for finding the date of Easter Day (pp. 880–883).

The date of Easter determines the date for many feasts (and fasts) of the church year. The date of Easter will determine the number of Sundays in the church year after Epiphany, the dates of Ash Wednesday and the Sundays in Lent, the date of the Feast of the Ascension on a Thursday forty days after Easter, the dates of the Sundays of Easter including Pentecost, and the dates of the Sundays after Pentecost.

The Sundays of Advent are always the four Sundays before Christmas Day, whether Christmas occurs on a Sunday or a weekday (BCP, p. 15). Since Christmas is celebrated on different days of the week, the dates of the four Sundays of Advent preceding Christmas will vary from year to year. The First Sunday of Advent is never earlier than Nov. 27 and never later than Dec. 3. The BCP provides a table to find movable feasts and holy days (pp. 884–885). *See* Calendar of the Church Year, The.

Mozarabic Rite. The ancient liturgy of the Christian church in Spain. Its center was at Toledo. The term is derived from Arabic, "a would-be Arab." Its use stems from the centuries when Spain was under Arab or Moslem rule. Elements from eastern rites found their way into the liturgy of the church in Spain. The Mozarabic Rite continued the use of three lessons at the eucharist, the weekly singing of the Creed, and the use of other canticles. Contrary to eastern use, the phrase "and the Son" was found in the Creed in the Mozarabic Rite. Some elements of the BCP are drawn from the Mozarabic Rite. These elements include the prayer for the sanctification of the water at baptism (p. 307), the third Prayer for Light in the Order of Worship for the Evening (pp. 110–111), and the use of the *Trisagion* (p. 356). Mozarabic chant from the Mozarabic Rite is represented in *The Hymnal 1982*, including a setting of the *Sanctus* (S 123).

Mozetta, or Mozzetta. A short cape that covers the shoulders. It is fastened at the neck, and it may have a hood. It is traditionally worn by bishops and other ecclesiastical dignitaries.

M.R.E. Master of Religious Education. The degree presupposes a baccalaureate degree and is designed to train persons for leadership in educational ministry.

M.S.M. Master of Sacred Music. The degree presupposes a bachelor's degree and is designed to develop leaders of musical activities in the church.

M.T.S. Master of Theological Studies. The degree requires a bachelor's degree and can be either a research program or a general academic program.

Muhlenberg, John Peter Gabriel (Oct. 1, 1746–Oct. 1, 1807). An eighteenth-century Anglican priest who served Lutheran congregations. He was born in Trappe, Montgomery County, Pennsylvania. He went to Halle, Germany, for his education. After several years he returned to America. He studied for the Lutheran ministry with Carl Magnus von Wrangel, Provost of the Swedish churches on the Delaware. In Feb. 1769 Muhlenberg took charge of the Lutheran churches at Bedminster and New Germantown, New Jersey. In 1771 he was called to be the pastor of the German Lutheran congregation at Woodstock, Virginia. He went to England for ordination because the Church of England was established in Virginia. Muhlenberg was ordained priest on Apr. 23, 1772, by the Bishop of London. He returned to Woodstock as the pastor of the Lutheran congregation. There is no evidence that he was ever ordained a Lutheran pastor. In Jan. 1776 he preached his farewell sermon on Ecclesiastes 3, which mentions "a time for war, and a time for peace." At the end of the service he removed his clerical gown, revealing under it his military uniform. He was a successful soldier in the Revolutionary War. Afterwards he served in a variety of political positions. Muhlenberg died in Gray's Ferry, Pennsylvania.

Muhlenberg Memorial. Statement presented by William Augustus Muhlenberg, rector of the Church of the Holy Communion, New York City, and others to the House of Bishops of the Episcopal Church at the 1853 General Convention. It reflected Muhlenberg's ecumenical vision of a church both catholic and reformed that could include all Christians. It proposed "some ecclesiastical system, broader and more comprehensive than that which you now administer, surrounding and including the Protestant Episcopal Church as it now is, leaving that Church untouched, identical with that Church in all its great principles, yet providing for as much freedom in opinion, discipline, and worship as is compatible with the essential faith and order of the Gospel." The Memorial upheld the traditional catholic teaching of the Episcopal Church concerning the Creeds, the eucharist, and episcopal ordination. It urged that Episcopal bishops should ordain qualified Protestant clergy who could accept the basic teachings of the Episcopal Church. These clergy would continue to serve in their own denominations. The apostolic succession was thus to be shared more widely through the Episcopal Church for a comprehensive Protestant Church. The Memorial also urged that the Episcopal Church should relax "somewhat the rigidity of her Liturgical services." Although the immediate results of the Memorial were small, it heralded the beginning of significant ecumenical activity in the Episcopal Church and later movements for liturgical reform. It is seen as the precursor of the Chicago-Lambeth Quadrilateral (1886–1888), and the Commission on Church Unity of the House of Bishops (1856). The Commission on Church Unity eventually became the Standing Commission on Ecumenical Relations of the General Convention. *See* Muhlenberg, William Augustus.

Muhlenberg, William Augustus (Sept. 16, 1796–Apr. 8, 1877). A leading Episcopal priest of the nineteenth century. He was born in Philadelphia and baptized in the Lutheran Church. When the vestry of St. James' Episcopal Church gave his widowed mother a free pew, she attended that church and William grew up an Episcopalian. He graduated from the University of Pennsylvania in 1815 and then studied theology with Bishop William White and Jackson Kemper. Muhlenberg was ordained deacon on Sept. 21, 1817, and served as Bishop White's assistant at St. Peter's and Christ Church in Philadelphia. He was ordained priest on Oct. 22, 1820. He went to Lancaster, Pennsylvania, where he served as co-rector with Joseph Clarkson of St. James' Church. Muhlenberg's chief early interest was education, and in 1828 he founded and served as headmaster of Flushing Institute, a boys' school in Flushing, New York.

In 1838 he established St. Paul's College on Long Island Sound. Although neither institution survived very long, they were both influential models of Christian schools which others copied. The Church of the Holy Communion was built at the corner of Sixth Avenue and 20th Street, New York, by his sister, Mrs. Mary A. Rogers. Muhlenberg became the rector of this church in 1846. In 1851 he founded a monthly church journal, *The Evangelical Catholic*, which reflected his desire for ecumenical union with the Protestant bodies of Christendom. *The Evangelical Catholic* was published for two years. In 1852 Muhlenberg and Anne Ayres founded the Sisterhood of the Holy Communion. The greatest of his philanthropies was the founding of St. Luke's Hospital in New York City, which opened in 1858. In 1853 he was the leader in presenting a memorial to the House of Bishops asking for certain reforms in the liturgy and for extension of episcopal ordination. He sought to relax the liturgical rigidity of Episcopal services and to provide the apostolic succession through the Episcopal Church for a comprehensive Protestant church. The document became known as the Muhlenberg Memorial. In 1870 Muhlenberg incorporated St. Johnsland on Long Island, which was an experiment in Christian communal living. He died at St. Johnsland. His ministry is commemorated in the Episcopal calendar of the church year on Apr. 8. *See* Muhlenberg Memorial.

Mulford, Elisha (Nov. 19, 1833–Dec. 9, 1885). Social Gospel leader. He was born in Montrose, Pennsylvania. Mulford graduated from Yale in 1855. He studied theology at Union Theological Seminary, New York, and Andover Theological Seminary. He traveled in Europe and studied in Berlin, Heidelberg, and Halle. Mulford was ordained deacon on Apr. 20, 1861, and priest on Mar. 19, 1862. He began his ordained ministry at Darien, Connecticut. From 1861 until 1864, he served in South Orange, New Jersey. He retired from active ministry in 1864 because of a hearing impairment. He moved to Lakeside, Pennsylvania, where he studied and wrote. In 1881 Mulford moved to Cambridge and lectured in Apologetics at the Episcopal Theological School. In 1870 he published *The Nation, the Foundation of Civil Order and Political Life in the United States*, in which he argued that the nation is a divine institution like the church. *The Republic of God, an Institute of Theology* (1881), was a study of the Nicene Creed in which he described God as the "ground of being," and Christ as the "man for others." He advocated the coming of the kingdom of God in America. Mulford died in Cambridge.

Muller, James Arthur (Dec. 23, 1884–Sept. 5, 1945). Historian and theologian. He was born in Philadelphia. Muller received his B.A. in 1907 and his Ph.D. in 1915, both from Princeton University. He received his M.A. from Harvard in 1910 and his B.D. from the Episcopal Theological School in 1910. Muller was ordained deacon on June 5, 1910, and priest on Dec. 24, 1911. He began his ministry as curate at Trinity Church, Princeton. From 1912 until 1914 he studied abroad. Muller was Minister-in-Charge of the Church of the Redeemer, Lexington, Massachusetts, 1914–1917; Instructor at the Episcopal Theological School, 1915–1917; Professor at Boone University, Wuchang, China, 1917–1919; assistant minister at the Church of the Epiphany, New York, 1920–1921; and Professor at Stephens College, 1921–1923. From 1923 until his death, Muller was professor of church history at the Episcopal Theological School. He was a member of the Liturgical Commission of the Episcopal Church, 1933–1940. Muller wrote seven books and published numerous articles. Two of his most significant books are *Apostle of China, Samuel Isaac Joseph Schereschewsky, 1831–1906* (1937), and *The Episcopal Theological School, 1867–1943* (1943). He was an associate editor of the *Historical Magazine of the Protestant Episcopal Church* from its founding in 1932 until his death. Muller died in Cambridge, Massachusetts.

Murphy, Edgar Gardner (Aug. 31, 1869–June 23, 1913). Social Gospel theologian and southern liberal. He was born in Fort Smith, Arkansas, and studied at the University of the South, where he was deeply influenced by William Porcher DuBose. He also studied at the General Theological Seminary, but he received no degree from either school. He was ordained deacon on Aug. 31, 1890, and priest on Sept. 3, 1893. Murphy served Christ Church, Laredo, Texas; St. Paul's Church, Chillicothe, Ohio; and St. John's Church, Kingston, New York. His most significant ministry was as rector of St. John's Church, Montgomery, one of the oldest and most important congregations in Alabama. He served there from Nov. 1898 until 1901, when he resigned to devote himself to social work on a full-time basis. Murphy renounced the ordained ministry so that he could devote all his time to public education in the South. He was deposed on Mar. 30, 1903. He spent the remainder of his life working for improved child-labor laws, public education, and race relations. Murphy was an organizer and secretary of the Southern Society for the Promotion of the Study of Race Conditions and Programs in the South, a member of the Alabama Child

Labor Commission, executive secretary of the Southern Education Board, and an organizer and first secretary of the National Child Labor Commission. His major books include *Words for the Church* (1897), *The Larger Life* (1897), and *Problems of the Present South* (1904). Murphy died in New York City.

Murray, John Gardner (Aug. 31, 1857–Oct. 3, 1929). The first elected Presiding Bishop. He was born in Lonaconing, Maryland, and educated at Wyoming Seminary, near Wilkes-Barre, Pennsylvania. In 1879 he entered Drew Theological Seminary, Madison, New Jersey, to study for the Methodist ministry, but he had to withdraw to help support his family when his father died. While in Brierfield, Alabama, he joined the Episcopal Church. Murray was ordained deacon on Apr. 3, 1893, and priest on Apr. 16, 1894. He began his ministry as a missionary in Alabama and from 1896 to 1903 was rector of the Church of the Advent, Birmingham. From 1903 to 1909 he was rector of the Church of St. Michael and All Angels, Baltimore. He was elected Bishop Coadjutor of Maryland and consecrated on Sept. 29, 1909. On Jan. 18, 1911, Murray became the seventh Bishop of Maryland. At the 1925 General Convention he was elected Presiding Bishop. He served as the sixteenth Presiding Bishop from Jan. 1, 1926, until his death.

Murray, Pauli (Nov. 20, 1910–July 1, 1985). First African American woman priest. She was born in Baltimore, Maryland, and raised in Durham, North Carolina. Murray graduated from Hunter College in 1933, and from Howard University Law School in 1944. Her senior thesis at Howard challenged the separate-but-equal principle behind segregation. It was used by lawyers in the 1954 U. S. Supreme Court case, *Brown v. Board of Education*. She also earned a master's degree at the University of California School of Law in 1945. After teaching at the University of Ghana Law School in West Africa, she returned to the United States where she earned a Doctor of Juridical Science degree from the Yale Law School in 1965. Murray joined the faculty of Brandeis University in 1968. She resigned to matriculate at the General Theological Seminary in 1973, where she earned a Master of Divinity degree in 1976. She was ordained deacon on June 9, 1976. On Jan. 8, 1977, Murray was ordained the first African American woman priest. The story of her struggles against racial and gender injustice are described in *Proud Shoes: The Story of an American Family* (1956) and *Song in a Weary*

Throat: An American Pilgrimage (1987). The latter was reprinted as *Pauli Murray: The Autobiography of a Black Activist, Feminist, Lawyer, Priest, and Poet* (1989). Murray died in Pittsburgh, Pennsylvania.

Musical Settings. A term commonly used for music provided for prose texts from the BCP that cannot be used with metrical tunes. *The Hymnal 1982* provides such music (the items whose numbers are preceded by the letter S). Volume VI of the *Church Hymnal Series* provides musical settings for the Gradual Psalms, Alleluia Verses, and Tracts. The altar edition of the eucharistic rite provides musical settings for the Proper Prefaces, the Exsultet, the Blessing of the Water at Baptisms, and other occasions.

Mutual Ministry. A term given to the concept of shared ministry and leadership in a congregation. Mutual ministry is an approach to Christian ministry that is lived out of the promises made in baptism. It sees the ministry of the whole congregation as the primary ministry. All members of the congregation are doers of ministry. Deacons and priests serve as resource and support persons to the congregation, and perform the other duties appropriate to their orders. The work of Roland Allen (1868–1947), an English missionary and parish priest, is the background of mutual ministry. Allen emphasized the training and empowerment of local leadership in the church, the importance of the laity, and the use of voluntary clergy. Leaders in mutual ministry in the Episcopal Church were Wesley Frensdorff, William Gordon, Charles Long, and H. Boone Porter. The dioceses of Nevada and Northern Michigan were forerunners in mutual ministry. The dioceses of Nebraska, Iowa, Minnesota, and North Dakota used it in certain areas. *See* Allen, Roland.

Mutual Responsibility and Interdependence in the Body of Christ (MRI). This manifesto was issued by the Pan Anglican Congress in Aug. 13–23, 1963, in Toronto, Canada. It pointed to three central truths: 1) the church's mission is to respond to the living God; 2) we are united in Christ; 3) it is time to find a new level of expression and corporate obedience. The manifesto was a call to mission which sought training for lay and clergy leadership, construction of church facilities throughout the world, and improved communications among Anglicans throughout the world. The manifesto also sought the funding to realize these goals. The authors felt that their call was radical and nothing less than "asking (for) the rebirth of the Anglican Communion."

My Angelus-Rosary Yeomen (M.A.R.Y.). In Dec. 1976 Sister Althea Jackson founded this organization to promote devotion to Mary, the Mother of the Lord, through the Rosary and the Angelus. Jackson was a member of the Episcopal Church who had grown to appreciate the Rosary and the Angelus at an Episcopal convent near Boston, Massachusetts. Beginning in 1979, the *Episcopal Church Annual* listed M.A.R.Y. as a devotional organization. On Dec. 25, 1979, Jackson was received into the Roman Catholic Church. In 1986 she took private Life Vows in the Roman Catholic Church. M.A.R.Y. is still an Episcopal organization.

Myers, Chauncie Kilmer (Feb. 14, 1916–June 27, 1981). Bishop and leader in urban mission. He was born in Schuylerville, New York. Myers received his B.A. from Rutgers in 1937 and his S.T.B. from the Berkeley Divinity School in 1940. He was ordained deacon on May 27, 1940, and priest on Dec. 21, 1940. Myers served as a Resident Fellow and then as an Instructor at Berkeley, 1940–1943. He was rector of St. Mark's Church, Buffalo, 1943–1944, and then Chaplain in the United States Navy, 1944–1946. From 1946 until 1949, he was an Instructor at General Theological Seminary, and from 1949–1952, he was Lecturer in Pastoral Theology at General Seminary. Myers was vicar of St. Augustine and Christ Church, New York, 1952–1960, and vicar of the Church of the Intercession, 1960–1963. During 1963–1964, he was Director of the Urban Training Center in Chicago. On Sept. 29, 1964, Myers was consecrated Suffragan Bishop of Michigan. He became the sixth Bishop of California on Dec. 13, 1966. He retired on Dec. 31, 1979. His two major publications were *Light the Dark Streets* (1957) and *Beyond the Church* (1958). Myers died in San Francisco.

Mystagogy. From the Greek *mystagogos*, the term refers to a process of initiation into "mysteries." It may take place after baptism at the Easter Vigil, lasting throughout the Great Fifty Days of the Easter season. It involves the integration of adult neophytes into the life of the church. It is less strictly defined than the catechumenate. Members of the Christian community continue to help and instruct the new Christians. The *BOS* notes that "This period is devoted to such activities, formal and informal, as will assist the newly baptized to experience the fullness of the corporate life of the Church and to gain a deeper understanding of the meaning of the Sacraments." In the broadest sense, Christians live in *mystagogia* for the rest of their lives as they continue to enter into the mystery of Christ's death and resurrection.

Myth. The term has been used in many different ways over the centuries. Its most common use refers to a story or explanation which is unhistorical or fictional. In the past it referred to stories about gods from other religious traditions or about human heroes or heroines. Myth is used to communicate ideas or values that are difficult to state in a rational or scientific way. Myth provides a way to express faith and to communicate experience, intuition, or recognition of truth that seems beyond other forms of expression. Through myth, the limitations of our own time and cultural context can be overcome with sacred stories. In this respect, a myth is in the deepest sense "true."

N

Narrative Criticism. A new method of interpretation of scripture. "Narrative" refers to a story which has a plot and moves from a beginning to an end. It is applicable to the gospels of the NT and many stories in the OT. Its primary focus is the attempt to recognize the "world of the narrative" instead of pursuing a historical search for the world of the author at the time when the story was written. The terms "narrative" and "literary" have been used in a number of different ways, and a general agreement is not yet available. A narrative-critical study does not raise historical questions but seeks to understand the specific meaning of words or characters based on the way they are used or presented in the story under consideration. The major difference between narrative critics is their use of the term "implied reader." Some narrative critics use the term to refer to those readers the author or editor had in mind in composing the story, making narrative criticism basically the same as redaction criticism. Other narrative critics use the term "implied reader" to refer to a hypothetically constructed reader based on the specific information in the story itself, not on the possible thoughts of the presumed author or editor. This style of narrative criticism focuses primarily on the narrative world of the story. There is no basic agreement about the specifics of the method of narrative analysis.

Narthex. An entry space, foyer, or anteroom of a church between the door and the nave. The term is from the Greek for a "small case." Historically, the narthex was an enclosed vestibule or porch of a basilica. Catechumens and penitents stood in the narthex during the service. It also may serve as a place for the gathering and formation of processions and a place for people to wait before services begin.

Nashotah House, Nashotah, Wisconsin. A theological seminary of the Episcopal Church in the catholic tradition. It was founded on Aug. 30, 1842, by three young deacons, James Lloyd Breck, William Adams, and John Henry Hobart, Jr., who answered the call of Missionary Bishop Jackson Kemper to serve on the western frontier. At first they lived a monastic life, but this did not continue. The original idea was to establish in Wisconsin an associate mission from which to evangelize the surrounding region and prepare candidates for holy orders. The seminary is still known as "The Mission." In 1847 Nashotah House was chartered as a college of learning and piety. A collegiate department, usually called the preparatory department, was at St. John's Hall, Delafield. St. John's Hall merged with Racine College in 1859, and in 1873 Nashotah House and Racine College terminated their cooperative effort. A preparatory department continued at Nashotah House until 1933. The work of theological education became the primary concern at the seminary, with daily worship and manual labor still prominent features of community life. The Board of Trustees stated in 1991 that "until such time as Catholic Christendom decides the issue of female ordination, only ordained men will function sacerdotally at Nashotah House."

Nashotah Quarterly Review. This journal first appeared in the Fall of 1960. It was published by Nashotah House. With the Fall 1970 issue the name was changed to *Nashotah Review.* It ceased publication with the Fall 1976 issue.

Nashotah Scholiast. A publication of the Bishop Welles Brotherhood at Nashotah House from Dec. 1883 until July/Aug. 1885. With the next issue, the name was changed to the *Church Scholiast.*

National Altar Guild Association. A national association of individuals who share the common task of caring and providing for the altars, sanctuaries, and other worship centers of their churches. It began as the National Altar Committee with the permission of the 1922 General Convention, and continued as the National Association of Diocesan Altar Guilds. In 1987 it became the National Altar Guild Association, under the aegis of the Presiding Bishop. At the membership meetings during each General Convention, the Presiding Bishop installs the new officers, celebrates the corporate communion, and addresses the members. The purpose of the Association is to unite all altar guilds. It seeks to encourage and deepen the spiritual life of all members so that worship may be offered in the beauty of holiness. The Association also seeks to assist in the continuing organization of diocesan and provincial altar guilds. The Association publishes a newsletter, *The Epistle.*

National Association for Episcopal Christian Education Directors (NAECED). This organization was formed on Jan. 25, 1997, at the Celebration and Re-creation Conference for Professional Educators held in San Antonio, Texas. Its purpose is to provide professional support and development for Episcopal Directors of Christian Education.

National Association of Episcopal Church Business Administrators. The National Association of Church Business Administration (NACBA) is an interdenominational American organization. The Episcopal group of NACBA began meeting in the mid-1980s. On July 18, 1988, the National Association of Episcopal Church Business Administrators adopted its constitution and by-laws. The purpose of the organization is to increase the effectiveness of church business administrators as they participate in the mission of the Episcopal Church. It works to improve the relationship of the church business administrators, the clergy, other staff and church leaders. The Association holds an annual conference and business meeting.

National Association of Episcopal Interim Ministry Specialists (NAEIMS). NAEIMS was organized on Feb. 10, 1995, at a training event sponsored by the Interim Ministry Network. Its purpose is to advance understanding and recognition of intentional interim ministry as a vital and specialized area of work in the Episcopal Church.

National Association of Episcopal Schools (NAES). Incorporated on May 28, 1965, NAES took the place of the Episcopal Schools Association, which had its origins in the 1950s. The Episcopal Schools Association was the descendant of the informal Church School Headmasters and Headmistresses Association, which began meeting in the 1920s and 1930s. An Episcopal school is one owned or operated by a parish, cathedral, diocese, religious community, or other recognized Episcopal Church organization. It is a school under the jurisdiction of the bishop of the diocese in which it is located, or a school that practices the faith and worship of the Episcopal Church. NAES supports the schools and serves as an advocate for them. It publishes a *Directory of Episcopal Schools*. It began the publication of *National Association of Episcopal Schools Journal* in Spring, 1984.

National Association for the Self-Supporting Active Ministry (NASSAM). NASSAM had its beginnings in Dec. 1971, when the Rev. Dr. H. Boone Porter convened a conference at Roanridge Institute to recognize the self-supporting ministry as a model for renewal of the church. The meeting established an organization called NON-STOP (Non-Stipendiary Training and Operations Program). The third annual meeting at Roanridge, Missouri, Nov. 29–Dec. 1, 1973, changed the name to NASSAM. It is a group of bishops, priests, deacons, and lay persons who have what is called a "tent-making ministry." This term refers to St. Paul and his work of making tents to earn his living while proclaiming the gospel at no charge. Those who are priests are called worker priests. NASSAM promotes the movement of self-supporting active ministry as a complement to the traditional parish ministry. It stresses the idea of "one ministry, two jobs"—one in the church and one in the world.

"National Cathedral." *See* Cathedral Church of Saint Peter and Saint Paul in the City and Diocese of Washington, The.

National Cathedral Association. Begun in 1898 by friends of Washington National Cathedral to help maintain its work and worship, the Association was instrumental in the beginnings and completion of the Cathedral. It was incorporated on Oct. 11, 1933, in the District of Columbia to assist the Protestant Episcopal Cathedral Foundation of the District of Columbia in the establishment and maintenance of the Cathedral for the promotion of religion, education, and charity. In 1947 the Women's Committee merged with the Association to form the present fellowship. The Association is financed by the dues of the members.

Membership is open to all. It publishes *Cathedral Age*, which began in 1925.

National Coalition for the Ordination of Women to the Priesthood and Episcopacy. Organized in Dayton, Ohio, in Oct. 1974, the Coalition held its first meeting in Jan. 1975 and decided to focus on getting the 1976 General Convention to vote for the canonical changes necessary for women to be ordained priests and bishops. The General Convention subsequently voted to change Title III, Canon 9 on Ministry to read: "The provisions of these canons for the admission of Candidates, and for the Ordination to the three Orders: Bishops, Priests and Deacons, shall be equally applicable to men and women." The Coalition had accomplished its objective and went out of existence.

National Concerns, Standing Commission on. The 1997 General Convention established this commission to consider issues relevant to the ministries of the church, to strive for justice and peace among all peoples, and to recommend to the General Convention applicable policies. It has as its purview some aspects of discontinued commissions such as Human Affairs, Health, and Peace with Justice. The commission consists of two bishops, six presbyters, and eight lay persons.

National Conference of Social Service Workers of the Episcopal Church. The inaugural meeting of this group was held in Milwaukee, Wisconsin, June 20–22, 1921. It was established by the Department of Social Service of the National Council of the Episcopal Church. The Conference was to coordinate and stimulate the social service forces of the church. The Conference merged its 21st annual meeting with the program of the Church Conference of Social Work of the Federal Council of Churches in 1942.

National Council. Predecessor to the Executive Council of the Episcopal Church. By 1910 there were three independent boards of the General Convention: the General Board of Religious Education, the Board of Missions, and the Joint Commission on Social Service. On Feb. 12, 1919, the General Board of Religious Education brought before the Board of Missions a proposal to create "an Executive Board for the General Convention." A new canon was adopted at the 1919 General Convention. It was "Of the Presiding Bishop and Council," which called for an executive board of 24 members. The first sentence of the canon stated that the Presiding Bishop and Council shall administer and carry on the missionary, educational and social work of the church. The Presiding Bishop was identified as the executive head of this work. The General Board of Religious Education, the Board of Missions, and the Joint Commission on Social Service went out of existence on Dec. 31, 1919, and the Presiding Bishop and Council took over on Jan. 1, 1920. The 1919 General Convention also voted to have the Presiding Bishop elected rather than use the principle of seniority. Since a Presiding Bishop had not yet been elected, the bishops elected a president of the Council. They elected Bishop Thomas Frank Gailor of Tennessee, who served as president until Dec. 31, 1925. The first elected Presiding Bishop was John Gardner Murray of Maryland, who took office on Jan. 1, 1926. The Presiding Bishop and Council had five departments: Mission and Church Extension, Religious Education, Christian Social Service, Finance, and Publicity. The 1922 General Convention changed the name to the National Council. The 1964 General Convention changed the name to the Executive Council.

National Council of the Churches of Christ in the U.S.A. (NCCCUSA). This ecumenical organization was formed in Cleveland, Ohio, Nov. 28–Dec. 1, 1950. It was the successor organization to the Federal Council of Churches. NCCCUSA was formed by 25 Protestant groups, four Orthodox groups, and 12 interdenominational agencies. The Episcopal Church was one of the Protestant groups. The NCCCUSA is a cooperative agency which seeks to fulfill the unity and mission of the church. Member communions must confess Jesus, the incarnate Son of God, as Savior and Lord. It works to promote Christian unity and interfaith relations. It also seeks to serve the churches and the world in areas such as international disaster relief, refugee assistance and development aid, educational and worship resources, Bible translation, and efforts to address poverty, racism, and other injustices. Episcopal leaders of the Council have included Presiding Bishop Henry Knox Sherrill and Cynthia Wedel. On Nov. 12, 1997, Craig B. Anderson, resigned Bishop of South Dakota, was installed as president of the NCCCUSA on Nov. 12, 1997.

National Episcopal AIDS Coalition (NEAC). NEAC was founded on Oct. 11, 1988, at St. John's Church, Lafayette Square, Washington. Its primary purpose is to educate Episcopalians about HIV/AIDS issues and to empower them to act on that information. It serves as an advocate for the physical, emotional, and spiritual health of all people infected with or affected by HIV/AIDS, and promotes pastoral care for all persons affected by HIV/ AIDS. It publishes *Neaction Report*, which began publication in Feb. 1989.

National Episcopal Coalition on Alcohol and Drugs. *See* Recovery Ministries of the Episcopal Church.

National Episcopal Health Ministries. This organization was formed on June 11, 1996, by Episcopalians who believed that the church, at the local level, needs to live out Jesus' command to heal and to make whole in body, mind and spirit. It is comprised of nurses, clergy, hospital chaplains, social workers, teachers, health educators and others committed to this belief. The mission of this ministry is to assist local congregations in reclaiming the gospel mission of health and healing. It works to combine the ancient traditions of the Christian community with the knowledge and tools of modern health care. It also supports a program of parish nurses. A parish nurse is an experienced registered nurse whose nursing and spiritual commitment is utilized in a healing ministry within a congregation. National Episcopal Health Ministries is located at St. Paul's Church, Indianapolis. It was headed by the Rev. Jean Denton, a deacon and a registered nurse.

National Episcopal Historians and Archivists. The first conference of historiographers was held at the University of the South, Aug. 18–19, 1961. The meeting was called by Arthur Ben Chitty, historiographer of the University of the South. This conference led to the formation of the National Episcopal Historians and Archivists. It was first known as the Association of Episcopal Historiographers and then as the Conference of American Historiographers. At the annual meeting in 1980 it was decided to include archivists, registrars, and parish historians. At the 1982 meeting the name was changed to the National Episcopal Historians' Association. Its purposes were: 1) to encourage the preservation of church records according to accepted principles of archival practice, 2) to promote the writing of diocesan and parish history, and 3) to identify areas of greater cooperation among dioceses and parishes for the pursuit of these goals. On July 15, 1994, the name was changed to the National Episcopal Historians and Archivists. In Sept. 1961 the organization began publishing the *Historiographical Newsletter*, which is now known as *The Historiographer*.

National Federation of Episcopal Young People. Organized on Aug. 29, 1925, to stimulate and extend young people's work in the church through the ideas of worship, study, fellowship, and service. The Federation sponsored triennial conferences until it went out of existence in 1940.

National Guild of Churchmen. "The National Council of Churchmen," an entirely lay movement, was organized on Feb. 27, 1946, in New York City. On June 10, 1946, the name was changed to the National Guild of Churchmen. It was "organized to maintain, defend, and propagate the historic doctrine, practice and teaching of the Anglican Communion as held by the Episcopal Church and contained in the Book of Common Prayer." The objective was to unite Episcopalians for the defense and propagation of the Catholic Faith within the Episcopal Church through lay apostleship. Printed material was a prominent feature of the Guild's work. In 1964 the Order of the Holy Cross took over the Guild. Later the Guild was transferred to the Society of St. Paul. Its work expanded under the leadership of René Malcolm Roscoe Ernest Bozarth (1923–1982). It was last listed in the 1990 edition of *The Episcopal Church Annual*.

National Network of Episcopal Clergy Associations (NNECA). Founded in 1970 by a group of clergy who wanted to take responsibility for their ministries and support each other as colleagues across the country. NNECA seeks, serves, and proclaims Christ by leading clergy in the Episcopal Church to a collegial relationship for education, advocacy, self-care, and spiritual growth. Initially, local clergy associations had formed on each coast. By 1998 over thirty associations spanned the country. Representatives of the associations and individual members come together at the annual conference of NNECA to elect officers and board members and to make decisions about the direction of NNECA. The board, led by the president, does the business of NNECA between conferences, particularly working with the Church Pension Group and the National Church Ministry Cluster. NNECA publishes a newsletter, *Leaven*.

National Network of Lay Professionals in the Episcopal Church. Founded on Mar. 28, 1984, at a meeting of eight lay professionals who met at Berkeley, California, to discuss issues and concerns surrounding career ministry. The meeting was called by Barry Menuez, then coordinator for the Office of Ministry Development. At this meeting five primary issues surfaced: identity, employment, education and training, accessibility, and support. At a smaller steering committee meeting on May 31, 1985, the group decided to continue as the Lay Professional Task Force and to write a position paper. In 1985 Harry Griffith, executive director of the Anglican Fellowship of Prayer, was appointed coordinator of the Lay Professional Task Force, a position he held until 1989. A National Gathering of Lay Professionals occurred on Mar. 21–22, 1986, at Canterbury Center, Oviedo, Florida, and adopted the position paper. The Lay Professional Task Force became the National Network of Lay Professionals, and Ruth Schmidt began to serve as executive director in 1989. The network publishes *Callings*. It exists to develop a national support system for lay professionals employed in the ministry of the Episcopal Church, and it defines lay professionals as lay persons employed in the ministry of the Episcopal Church who regard their work as a vocation, who have acquired appropriate preparation and training, are committed to continuing education, and who hold themselves accountable to the particular institutional structure in which they work.

National Organization of Episcopalians for Life (NOEL). NOEL was founded in 1966 by Bishop Joseph Meakin Harte of Arizona as Episcopalians for Life. In 1982 the name was changed to National Organization of Episcopalians for Life, and on Jan. 22, 1984, the board of directors organized the National Organization of Episcopalians for Life: Research and Education Foundation. It "promotes the biblical view of the sanctity of human life at every stage of biological development and seeks to influence our Church and culture to embrace this biblical attitude morally, legally and in practice." Since 1984 it has published *Noel News*.

National Student Council of the Episcopal Church. This student organization was created by the Conference of College Workers which met at Howe School, Indiana, May 21–24, 1918, at the call of the General Board of Religious Education. The Conference created a Council which unified the church's college work in its missionary, educational, and social service phases. The Council also acted as a board of strategy in planning methods of work. Its purpose was to be the agency through which matters of policy were to be communicated to college workers and students. It recognized and promoted groups of Episcopal students on college campuses as "Units" which carried out an active program of worship, religious education, church extension, and service. The Council held its first meeting at Kenyon College, Sept. 10–12, 1918. It published *The National Student Council Bulletin* and a vocational bulletin for young people called *Guide Posts*. Its work was taken over in 1939 by the Division of College Work and Youth.

Nation-Wide Campaign. A movement launched by the 1919 General Convention "designed to bring the spiritual and material resources of the Church to bear most effectively and adequately upon her whole task as witness to the Master." It involved a survey of the church's needs and a plan of action to address those needs. It also involved a national every member canvass for the first time in the history of the Episcopal Church. The evolution of the every member canvass replaced the old pew rent system with a program of individual pledging, putting the entire church on a more stable financial basis and enabling it to do budgetary planning.

Nativity of Our Lord Jesus Christ, The. *See* Christmas, or Christ's Mass.

Nativity of St. John the Baptist, The. This feast of our Lord is celebrated on June 24 in the Episcopal calendar of the church year. Luke's gospel (Chapter 1) records that John was miraculously born to Zechariah and Elizabeth. They were childless and advanced in age when John was conceived. The angel Gabriel told Zechariah that Elizabeth would bear him a son who would be named John. Zechariah received this startling announcement with disbelief, and he was struck speechless. Zechariah's speech was restored on the eighth day after John's birth, when John was named and circumcised. At this time, Zechariah uttered the canticle known as the *Benedictus Dominus Deus* (Lk 1:67–79), which is one of the canticles for the Daily Office (see Canticles 4 and 16, BCP, pp. 50–51, 92–93). Elizabeth was in the sixth month of her pregnancy when Gabriel appeared to Mary at the Annunciation. Mary was related to Elizabeth, and Gabriel told Mary that Elizabeth had conceived a son in her old age. The feast of the Nativity of John the Baptist was originally associated with the Epiphany, but its observance was moved to June 24 in the west and June 25 in the east. This feast is celebrated about six months before Christmas, as Elizabeth was in the sixth month of her

pregnancy at the time of Jesus' conception. Propers for celebration of the Nativity of John the Baptist were included in the Leonine, Gelasian, and Gregorian sacramentaries. The feast was included in the 1549 BCP.

As an adult, John lived an ascetic life in the Judean wilderness. His life and appearance recalled the prophetic tradition of the OT. He was clothed with camel's hair and wore a leather belt. He ate locusts and wild honey. The word of God came to him, and he went into the region around the Jordan River to preach a baptism of repentance for the forgiveness of sins. John called the people to prepare for the coming of the kingdom of God and the advent of the Messiah. Many people came to John to receive his baptism, including Jesus. John exhorted the people to live righteously (see Lk 3:10–14). He told them to share clothes and food with the needy. He urged tax collectors to collect no more than was appointed for them, and he told soldiers to rob no one by violence or false accusation. John stated that he was not the Christ (Jn 1:20). John acknowledged that his influence would decrease as Christ's influence increased (Jn 3:30). He had many followers, some of whom later became disciples of Jesus (Jn 1:35–37). John criticized Herod the tetrarch for his incestuous marriage to Herodias, and for other evil deeds. John was imprisoned, and later executed at the urging of Herodias (Mt 14:1–12). John is ranked second only to the Virgin Mary among the saints in the eastern church. The collect for the Nativity of Saint John the Baptist prays that we may "follow his teaching and holy life" and "truly repent according to his preaching" so that we may "constantly speak the truth, boldly rebuke vice, and patiently suffer for the truth's sake" (BCP, p. 241). *See* John the Baptist.

Natural Law. Universal moral law that is given by God and knowable by human reason. It has been understood in terms of ethics that can be derived from reflection on ordinary human experience and contrasted with law that is divinely revealed. These universal standards provide norms of right conduct that may serve as the basis for moral choices in particular situations and the statutes of civil law. Our ability to discern the natural law may be diminished by sin. St. Paul states that although the Gentiles do not have the Mosaic law, they "show that what the law requires is written on their hearts, to which their own conscience also bears witness" when they "do instinctively what the law requires" (Rom 2:14-15). Thomas Aquinas holds in the *Summa Theologica* that the rational creature "has a share of the Eternal Reason, whereby it has a natural inclination to its proper act and end," and that natural law is the rational creature's participation in the eternal law by which the divine providence governs creation. Natural law may be understood as a rule of action that is implicit in the very nature of things. The specific content of the universal moral laws and their application has been subject to disagreement. However, natural law principles have been used as a basis for contemporary legislation in several countries. *See* Enlightenment, The.

Navajoland Area Mission. Article VI of the Episcopal Church Constitution provides for the establishment of an area mission of the church for territory not included within a diocese. The 1976 General Convention authorized all territory in the dioceses of Utah and Arizona lying within the boundaries of the Navajo Indian Nation to be organized as an area mission. In 1979 the Diocese of Rio Grande ceded all of the Navajoland Reservation in New Mexico to the new jurisdiction. The first bishop of the whole Navajo Nation chosen by the House of Bishops was the Rt. Rev. Frederick Putnam, who was enthroned in Jan. 1979. The Rt. Rev. Steven T. Plummer was consecrated in 1990. He was the first bishop of the mission of Navajo descent. The area mission is divided into three regions, each supervised by a regional vicar.

Nave. The place in the church building for the congregation. It is between the sanctuary and the narthex or entry of the church building. The term may be derived from the Latin *navis*, "ship," which was an early symbol of the church.

Neal, Emily Gardiner (Oct. 22, 1910–Sept. 23, 1989). Leader of the healing movement in the Episcopal Church. She was born in New York. She was educated at Brearly School and David Mannes College of Music, where she trained as a violinist. She married David Neal, who died in 1961. She was a writer, teacher, and "converted skeptic." In 1956 she published her first book, *A Reporter Finds God Through Spiritual Healing*. From then until her death, Neal was noted as a lecturer, counselor, and leader of healing services. She was appointed to the Joint Commission on the Ministry of Healing by the 1961 General Convention. After twenty years of ministry as a lay person, Neal was ordained deacon on Jan. 31, 1978. Two of her most significant books on healing are *The Healing Ministry: A Personal Journey* (1982), and *Celebration of Healing* (1992). Neal served on the staff of St. Thomas Church, Terrace Park, Ohio, and made her home in latter years at the Convent of the Transfiguration, Glendale, Ohio. The Episcopal Healing Ministry Foundation was founded in 1987 in her honor, and she served as its first president. Neal died at the Convent of the Transfiguration.

Neale, John Mason (Jan. 24, 1818–Aug. 6, 1866). British cleric, hymn writer, and translator. He was born in London. Neale was caught up with the ideals of the Oxford Movement while he was at Trinity College, Cambridge. In 1839 Neale and Benjamin Webb founded the Cambridge Camden Society. After 1845 it was known as the Ecclesiological Society. The Society's goals focused on church architecture and traditional catholic worship. Neale was ordained deacon in 1841 and priest in 1842. His early ordained ministry was limited by poor health. After a period of rest, Neale was appointed warden of Sackville College, East Grinstead, in 1846. He also devoted himself to literary work and the Society of St. Margaret, a religious order for women, which he founded in 1855. The Bishop of Chichester inhibited Neale from 1847 to 1863 because of his ritualistic practices. Today Neale is primarily remembered as a translator of ancient Greek and Latin hymns. His two major publications, *Medieval Hymns and Sequences* (1851) and *Hymns of the Eastern Church* (1862), had a major impact on English language hymnals published in the second half of the nineteenth century. Neale contributed nearly an eighth of the texts of the original edition of *Hymns Ancient and Modern* (1859). His translations continue in use today. *The Hymnal 1982* contains twenty-seven texts or portions of texts that were translated by Neale, including such classics as, "All glory, laud, and honor" (Hymns 154/155), "Come, ye faithful, raise the strain" (Hymns 199/200), and "Of the Father's love begotten" (Hymn 82). *The Hymnal* also has two original texts by Neale, including "Good Christian friends, rejoice" (Hymn 107). Neale died in East Grinstead on the Feast of the Transfiguration, 1866. He is commemorated in the Episcopal calendar of the church year on Aug. 7.

Neau, Elias (1662–Sept. 7, 1722). A successful "missionary vestryman" in colonial New York. He was born in France to Huguenot parents. He fled the country in 1679 and became an English citizen. He then came to the colony of New York. In 1692 his ship was seized by the French. He was made a slave and placed in a chain gang.

When he was freed in 1698, he raised money in Europe for the Huguenots before returning to New York. While still a Presbyterian, he was licensed by the Society for the Propagation of the Gospel in Foreign Parts (SPG) on Aug. 4, 1704, as a catechist and became a missionary to the slaves in New York. In Oct. 1704 he resigned as an elder with the Huguenots and joined Trinity Church, New York City. From 1705 until 1714 he was a member of the vestry of Trinity Church. The chief factor in his becoming an Episcopalian was his regard for the Prayer Book. Neau's school for slaves met in the belfry of Trinity Church and later on the third floor of his house. After ten years he had 154 slave pupils, 44 of whom he presented for baptism. Neau died in New York City.

Nebraska College and Divinity School, Nebraska City, Nebraska. Nebraska College and Divinity School was started at Nebraska City in 1861, the second year of the episcopate of the Rt. Rev. Joseph Cruikshank Talbot (1816–1883), Missionary Bishop of the Northwest. Bishop Robert Harper Clarkson (1826–1884) of Nebraska provided leadership for the school, and called it Talbot Hall in memory of Bishop Talbot. The school trained over 24 persons for ordained ministry in the Episcopal Church. The trustees voted to close the school on Apr. 21, 1885.

Nebraska, Diocese of. The territory of Nebraska was first under the jurisdiction of Jackson Kemper, Missionary Bishop of Missouri and Indiana. In 1859 it became a part of the jurisdiction of the Missionary Bishop of the Northwest, Joseph Cruikshank Talbot. The 1865 General Convention created the Missionary District of Nebraska and Dakota. The primary convention of the Diocese of Nebraska was held at Trinity Pro-Cathedral, Omaha, Sept. 9–10, 1868. On Sept. 5, 1872, the pro-cathedral became Trinity Cathedral. The Diocese of Nebraska was divided in 1889 and reunited in 1946. In 1918 George A. Beecher, Missionary Bishop of Western Nebraska, designated St. Mark's Church, Hastings, the pro-cathedral. Nebraska has both a cathedral and a pro-cathedral. *See* Kearney, Missionary District of; *see* Laramie, Missionary District of; *see* Northwest, Missionary District of the; *see* The Platte, Missionary District of; *see* Western Nebraska, Missionary District of.

Neo-Pentecostal. *See* Charismatic Renewal, or Neo-Pentecostalism.

Nestorianism. A heretical teaching that understood Christ to be two persons, one human and one divine. It also held that Mary was not the Mother of God ("*Theotokos*"), but only the mother of the human Christ. It was named for Nestorius (c. 381–c. 451), who was Patriarch of Constantinople (428–431). Nestorianism was condemned at the Council at Ephesus (431), under the presidency of St. Cyril of Alexandria. The Council also upheld Mary's title *Theotokos*, acknowledging Jesus Christ to be "one and the same" divine person. The Chalcedonian Definition (451) subsequently affirmed that Jesus Christ is at once truly God and truly man in two natures "without separation, without division" (see BCP, p. 864). Nestorius was condemned, deposed, and banished to a monastery. His works were burned by imperial order in 436. Although Nestorius clearly opposed the use of Mary's title *Theotokos*, it is debatable how much he actually believed of the condemned heresies of Nestorianism. *See* Chalcedonian Definition.

Network of Seminarians with Lay Vocations. Organized in 1980, the Network is committed to providing an environment and structure for the mutual support of seminarians with lay vocations. It promotes the ministry of the laity, along with broader and more inclusive definitions of ministry. The Network stresses a mutuality in ministry and recognizes the variety of ministries to which persons are called. It receives staff support from the Office for Ministry Development. For a while it sponsored a conference for seminarians with lay vocations every two years. A major conference was held in Jan. 1984 at the College of Preachers in Washington, with the theme "A Celebration of the Ministry of the Laity."

Nevada, Diocese of. The diocese includes the entire state of Nevada. It was preceded by a number of missionary districts. On Oct. 21, 1865, the House of Bishops established the Missionary District of Nevada and parts adjacent with jurisdiction in Nevada, Utah, Arizona, and New Mexico. In 1868 the Bishops changed it to the Missionary District of Nevada and Arizona, and then the General Convention of 1874 changed it to the Missionary District of Nevada. The House of Bishops in 1886 changed it yet again to the Missionary District of Nevada and Utah. At the 1898 General Convention, the House of Bishops created the Missionary District of Salt Lake which included Nevada. In 1907 the House of Bishops created the

Missionary District of Nevada. The primary convention of the Diocese of Nevada was held on Apr. 14–17, 1971, at Christ Church, Las Vegas. It does not have a cathedral.

***New American Bible, The* (1970).** The first Roman Catholic Bible translated into English from the original Hebrew and Greek. The work was done by members of the Catholic Biblical Association of America. It was commissioned by the Bishops' Committee of the Confraternity of Christian Doctrine. It is authorized by the Episcopal Church for use in worship.

New American Church Monthly, The. This periodical continued *The American Church Monthly* from Jan. 1938 until Jan. 1939. *See* American Church Monthly, The.

New Beginnings. A weekend retreat for youth aged twelve to fifteen designed to address spiritual and social needs in this age group. It was developed in the Diocese of Central Florida in the late 1980s. The aim is for those who attend to discover new things about themselves, their relationships, God, and the church. The weekend is designed to provide an atmosphere of openness where participants can ask questions and have the freedom to explore answers without fear of judgment. Another focus of New Beginnings is to provide some experiential training for adults who work with youth. A team of adults and teens plan and run the weekend. There are two adults who are called "Lead Adults," and at least one priest who is called the "Spiritual Director." Music and games are a very important part of the weekend. It is now in use in some other denominations. *See* Happening; *see* Vocare.

New Covenant. The new relationship with God given by Jesus Christ. The new covenant comes with Christ's promise to bring humanity into the kingdom of God and share the fullness of life with us. In response, we are to believe in Christ and keep his commandments. Love is to be at the heart of our participation in the new covenant. Jesus taught the summary of the law and the new commandment. The summary of the law is that we are to love God with all our hearts, souls, and minds; and we are to love our neighbor as ourselves. The new commandment is that we are to love one another as Christ loved us. The new covenant was given by Christ to the apostles and through them to all who believe in Christ (BCP, pp. 850–851).

The new covenant may be contrasted with the old covenant of God and the people of Israel. The old covenant was associated with law. However, Jeremiah (31:31–34) prophesied a coming time when God would "make a new covenant with the house of Israel and the house of Judah." This prophecy was recalled in the NT (Heb 8:6–13). The new covenant is associated with the gospel and the love of Christ that we are to share. The old covenant may be understood as preparing for or prefiguring the new covenant. God's covenant with Abraham was understood by Christians to be fulfilled in Jesus Christ (Gal 3:16–18). A collect at the Easter Vigil (following the reading from Ez 36:24–28) recalls that God "established the new covenant of reconciliation" in the Paschal mystery (BCP, p. 290). At the Last Supper, Jesus identified the cup of wine with "the new covenant in my blood" (1 Cor 11:25; see Mt 26:28; Mk 14:24; Lk 22:20). This identification of the wine, Jesus' self-offering of his life, and the new covenant is reflected in the institution narratives of Eucharistic Prayers A, B, C, and D in Rite 2, as well as Eucharistic Prayer II of Rite 1 (see BCP, pp. 363, 368, 371, 374, 342). Bishops are called to celebrate and provide for the administration of the sacraments of the new covenant (BCP, p. 517). Similarly, priests are to minister the sacraments of the new covenant so that the reconciling love of Christ may be known and received (BCP, p. 532). The term "new covenant" has occasionally been used to indicate the New Testament.

New Directions Ministries, Inc. This program began in 1973 when the Joint Committee on Non-Metropolitan Work of the General Convention formed the Leadership Academy for New Directions (LAND). New Directions Ministries was incorporated in 1981 with an elected board of directors and a part-time trainer/program coordinator. New Directions affirms the basic principle that the church is the body of Christ. It also recognizes the ministry of all baptized persons and that each faith community is responsible for its own life, ministry, and mission. It stresses a shared leadership model which uses the gifts of locally ordained deacons and priests. New Directions is convinced that the church must develop a viable alternative to the one priest/one parish model. Regional leadership must be developed since many small churches cannot have a full-time priest. The principal training tool of New Directions is LAND. It also works with Rural Social Science Education, a program developed at Texas A&M,

which provides training in rural sociology by extension. *See* Leadership Academy for New Directions (LAND).

***New English Bible with the Apocrypha* (1970).** A completely new translation of the Bible, unlike such translations as the Revised Standard Version which stands in the tradition of the King James (Authorized) Bible. Sponsored by the various Protestant communions of the British Isles, it was produced by biblical scholars who were aided by authorities in English literature. Its purpose was to render the original into contemporary English, avoiding all archaic words and expressions. The translation was under the direction of the noted NT scholar, C. H. Dodd. It is authorized by the Episcopal Church for use in worship.

New Fire. The fire that is kindled at the opening of the Easter Vigil service. This rite typically begins in darkness. The lighting of the new fire often takes place outdoors for reasons of safety. The new fire is kindled before anything is said. The historic practice of kindling the new fire from a kindling stone or steel has been continued by some. The celebrant may then say a prayer of blessing over the new fire before it is used to light the Paschal candle (BCP, p. 285). As fire is a source of warmth and light, the new fire of the Easter Vigil represents the victory in Christ of light and life over darkness and death. The Paschal candle, lighted with the new fire, symbolizes the risen Christ. After the lighting of the Paschal candle, the deacon or celebrant bears it and leads the procession to the chancel. Candles carried by the people and other lights may be lit from the Paschal candle. The Exsultet is sung or said after the Paschal candle is placed in its stand. The ceremony for blessing the new fire and the Paschal candle is derived from the primitive *Lucernarium*, or blessing of light, which is derived from Jewish ritual. The lighting of the new fire as a Christian ceremony may be of Celtic origin. It is mentioned in seventh-century documents concerning legends of St. Patrick. It was probably added to the Easter Vigil rite in Gaul in the eighth century through the influence of Irish monks. It was included in the Roman liturgy by the twelfth century.

New Hampshire, Diocese of. This diocese was organized on Aug. 25, 1802, at Concord. On May 29, 1810, representatives from the Diocese of New Hampshire participated in the organization of the Eastern Diocese. The Eastern Diocese was not a diocese in the usual sense, but an arrangement whereby several weak dioceses could

work together. New Hampshire remained a part of the Eastern Diocese until it withdrew on June 26, 1839. The first Bishop of New Hampshire, Charlton Chase, was consecrated on Oct. 20, 1844. The Diocese of New Hampshire does not have a cathedral. *See* Eastern Diocese.

New Jersey, Diocese of. Founded on July 6, 1785, at Christ Church, New Brunswick. The 1874 General Convention voted to divide the diocese. The Diocese of New Jersey includes the following counties: Atlantic, Burlington, Camden, Cape May, Cumberland, Gloucester, Hunterdon, Mercer, Middlesex, Monmouth, Ocean, Salem, Somerset, and Union (except Summit Township). On Nov. 1, 1930, Trinity Church, Trenton, was set apart as Trinity Cathedral and dedicated on Jan. 24, 1954.

New Jerusalem Bible, The. The first English edition of *The Jerusalem Bible* was published in 1966. It was a translation of the French *Bible de Jérusalem*, done by the École Biblique, the biblical studies institute at Jerusalem. In 1973 a new edition of the *Bible de Jérusalem* was published, and *The New Jerusalem Bible* (1987) is the English translation of it. It is one of the versions of the Bible authorized by the Episcopal Church for use in worship.

New Mexico and Southwest Texas, Diocese of. The name of the Missionary District of New Mexico was changed to the Missionary District of New Mexico and Southwest Texas on Feb. 6, 1932. The primary convention of the Diocese was held at St. Andrew's Church, Boswell, New Mexico, Feb. 10–12, 1953. On Apr. 28, 1973, the name was changed to the Diocese of the Rio Grande.

New Revised Standard Version Bible (NRSV). The latest revision of the Revised Standard Version (RSV) Bible. It was published in 1989 under the authority of the National Council of Churches of Christ in the USA (NCCCUSA). It was the work of committees of scholars drawn mainly from Protestant churches, but also including Roman Catholic and Orthodox scholars, and a Jewish representative for the OT. The committees operated under certain principles laid down by the NCC: 1) to continue in the tradition of the King James Version; 2) to depart from that tradition only when required for accuracy, clarity, euphony, and current (American) English usage, with the result to be "as literal as possible, as free as necessary"; 3) to eliminate masculine-oriented language where the original texts were intended to be inclusive. The NRSV is authorized by the Episcopal Church for use in worship.

New Testament. The collection of 27 early Christian writings accepted as canonical by all Christian confessions and denominations. These writings reveal the witness of the early church to the Christ event as the saving act of God. They include four gospels (accounts of Jesus' life, death, and resurrection), the Acts of the Apostles, 13 letters ascribed to the Apostle Paul, the Letter to the Hebrews, seven "catholic" or general letters, and the Revelation (Apocalypse) of John. The Catechism notes that "The New Testament consists of books written by the people of the New Covenant, under the inspiration of the Holy Spirit, to set forth the life and teachings of Jesus and to proclaim the Good News of the Kingdom for all people" (BCP, p. 853). *See* Bible, The.

New Year's Eve, Service for. The *BOS* provides a vigil for New Year's Eve, which is the eve of the Feast of the Holy Name (Jan. 1). It begins with the Service of Light from an Order of Worship for the Evening (BCP, p. 109), using the collect for the First Sunday after Christmas as the Prayer for Light. After the *Phos hilaron*, at least two lessons are read. Each lesson is followed by a psalm, canticle, or hymn; and a prayer. The form provides eight scripture readings, three of which are from the NT. The last reading in the service is always from the NT. A homily, sermon, or instruction may follow the readings. An act of self-dedication may also follow. The vigil may conclude with the Great Litany, or another form of intercession; or with the singing of the *Te Deum laudamus* or another hymn of praise, followed by the Lord's Prayer, the collect for Holy Name, and a blessing and/or dismissal; or with the eucharist, beginning with the *Gloria in excelsis* or another song of praise. The proper for the Feast of the Holy Name is used if the eucharist is celebrated at this service.

New York Bible and Common Prayer Book Society. This society (known at first as the Bible and Common Prayer Book Society) was founded early in 1809 by John Henry Hobart. At this meeting a constitution was adopted, Bishop Benjamin Moore was chosen president, and a Board of Managers was elected. The first meeting of the board was held in Trinity Church, New York, on Apr. 14, 1809. It distributed Bibles, New Testaments, and Prayer Books. It was incorporated on Apr. 21, 1841, as the New York Bible and Common Prayer Book Society. It is no longer in existence.

New York, Diocese of. Organized on June 22, 1785, at St. Paul's Chapel, New York City. In 1838 it was divided when the Diocese of Western New York was established. It was the first diocese in the Episcopal Church to be divided. The Diocese of New York was divided again in 1868 when the Diocese of Long Island was established. The Diocese of New York includes the following counties: Bronx, Duchess, New York, Orange, Putnam, Richmond, Rockland, Sullivan, Ulster, and Westchester. The Cathedral of St. John the Divine, New York, was incorporated on Apr. 16, 1873, and the cornerstone of the building was laid on Dec. 27, 1892.

New York Ecclesiological Society. A society that sought to improve the standards of church architecture, furnishings, decorations, and music in the Episcopal Church. It reflected the influence of the Oxford Movement and nineteenth-century romanticism. The society helped to popularize gothic architecture. It was modeled after the Cambridge Camden Society in England. The New York Ecclesiological Society was formed in 1848, and continued until 1855. It published the *New York Ecclesiologist* from 1848 to 1853. The society later became "a mere church building association."

New York Protestant Episcopal Theological Society. Founded in 1806 by John Henry Hobart, later the third Bishop of New York, its purpose was to assist ministerial candidates and encourage younger clergy to continue their theological studies. It provided background organization for the General Theological Seminary in New York City.

New York Training School for Deaconesses (NYTSD). Founded on May 9, 1891, by William Reed Huntington and Mary Abbot Emery Twing, it provided a two-year residential course for women interested in becoming deaconesses, serving as missionaries, or working in Christian education. Shortly after it was founded, a woman's anonymous gift provided a house for the school. This gift was called an "act of Faith to a work of Faith." The house served as a residence for the deaconesses being trained. It was named St. Faith's House and sometimes the school was called St. Faith's Deaconess Training School. One of the leading female deans of the school was Susan Trevor Knapp. The courses included Old Testament, New Testament, church history, and theology, which were usually taught by local priests. There were also practical courses in household management, ecclesiastical embroidery, missionary instruction, and the cutting and making of wearing apparel. The school offered summer internships in hospitals or city ministries. In 1910 it moved to a new building constructed on the grounds of the Cathedral of St. John the Divine. The school closed in 1942. It reopened again in 1944, but closed permanently in 1948. *See* Knapp, Susan Trevor.

Newark, Diocese of. On Oct. 10, 1874, the General Convention voted to divide the Diocese of New Jersey and form a new diocese. This diocese included the counties of Bergen, Essex, Hudson, Morris, Passaic, Sussex and Warren, and the township of Summit in Union County. The primary convention met at Grace Church, Newark, New Jersey, on Nov. 12, 1874, and chose the name the Diocese of Northern New Jersey. On May 19, 1886, the name was changed to the Diocese of Newark. Bishop Edwin Stevens Lines named Trinity Church, Newark, the Cathedral on Oct. 23, 1917. It was formally established as Trinity Cathedral, Newark, by the diocesan convention on May 9, 1944.

Newman, John Henry (Feb. 21, 1801–Aug. 11, 1890). One of the original leaders of the Oxford Movement in the nineteenth-century Church of England and subsequently a convert to Roman Catholicism. He entered Trinity College, Oxford, in June 1817 and received a B.A. in 1820. Newman became a fellow of Oriel College in 1822. He was ordained deacon in 1824 and priest in 1825. He began his ministry in 1825 as vice-principal of Alban Hall, and became vicar of St. Mary's, Oxford, in 1828. Newman wrote 24 of the *Tracts for the Times*, including *Tract 90* (1841). In *Tract 90* he attempted to reconcile the Thirty-Nine Articles with the teachings of the Council of Trent. He resigned as vicar of St. Mary's on Sept. 18, 1843. His growing doubts about the Church of England led to his becoming a Roman Catholic on Oct. 9, 1845. Pope Leo XIII made him a cardinal of the Roman Catholic Church in 1879.

Newman has been recognized as a major theological figure, especially in the latter part of the twentieth century. His *Essay on the Development of Christian Doctrine*, written shortly after he became a Roman Catholic, and *Apologia pro Vita Sua* (1864) set forth his reasons for becoming a Roman Catholic. Newman's *Grammar of Assent* (1870) developed his theological thought about religious belief. His text "Praise to the Holiest in the height" appears as Hymns 445–446 in *The Hymnal 1982*. *The Hymnal* (1940) also included his text "Lead, kindly Light, amid the encircling gloom." He died in Rednal, near Birmingham, England. *See* Oxford Movement, The.

Newton, John (July 24, 1725–Dec. 21, 1807). A leading Anglican evangelical and hymn-writer. He was born in London and attended school at Stratford, Essex. Newton went to sea as a midshipman in the English navy. He was later the captain of a slave ship. After his conversion, Newton read for orders and was ordained in 1764 for the cure at Olney. He and William Cowper produced the *Olney Hymns* (1779), a famous hymn collection that included 280 texts by Newton. In 1780 Newton became rector of St. Mary's Woolnoth, in London. He was active in the anti-slavery movement in the later years of his life. He received the D.D. degree in 1792 from the College of New Jersey, which is now Princeton University. Newton's texts in *The Hymnal 1982* are "May the grace of Christ our Savior" (Hymn 351), "Glorious things of thee are spoken" (Hymns 522/523), "How sweet the Name of Jesus sounds" (Hymn 644), and "Amazing grace! how sweet the sound" (Hymn 671). Newton's epitaph states that although he was "once an Infidel and Libertine," he "was by the rich mercy of our Lord and Saviour/ Jesus Christ/ Preserved, restored, pardoned/ And appointed to preach the Faith/ He had long laboured to destroy." He died in London.

Newton, Joseph Fort (July 21, 1876–Jan. 24, 1950). Outstanding preacher and broad church leader. He was born in Decatur, Texas. Newton was ordained to the Baptist ministry on Apr. 20, 1895. He then became the pastor of a small Baptist church in Rose Hill, Texas. In the fall of 1895 he entered the Southern Baptist Theological Seminary in Louisville, Kentucky. He left it in 1897 to become the Pastor of First Baptist Church, Paris, Texas where he served until 1898. Newton left Texas and the Baptists, and went to St. Louis, Missouri, where he was associate minister of the non-sectarian People's Church, 1900–1903. In 1903 he went to Dixon, Illinois, and founded the People's Church, where he served as Pastor until 1908. From 1908 until 1916, Newton was Pastor of the Liberal Christian Church (Universalist), Cedar Rapids, Iowa. Many of his sermons were published and their circulation in England brought him the invitation to be the Minister of the City Temple in London, the "Cathedral of British Nonconformity." He was there from 1916 until 1919. From 1919 until 1925, he was Minister of the Church of the Divine Paternity (Universalist), New York City. Newton was ordained deacon in the Episcopal Church on Jan. 16, 1926, and priest on

Oct. 28, 1926. He served the Memorial Church of St. Paul, Overbrook, Pennsylvania, 1925–1930, and from 1930 until 1935, he was co-rector of St. James' Church, Philadelphia. Newton was Special Preacher to the Associated Churches of Philadelphia, 1935–1938, and rector of the Church of St. Luke and the Epiphany, Philadelphia, 1938–1950. In 1939 a poll of 25,000 clergy named him one of the five most prominent ordained ministers in the United States. Newton was a widely published author, an associate editor of *The Christian Century*, a popular preacher, and a leader of the Masonic Order. He died in Philadelphia.

Newton, Richard Heber (Oct. 31, 1840–Dec. 19, 1914). A major figure in the broad church movement and a leading Episcopal Social Gospel writer. He was born in Philadelphia. Newton received his B.A. from the University of Pennsylvania in 1861. In 1862–1863 he studied at the Philadelphia Divinity School. He was ordained deacon on Jan. 19, 1862, and priest on July 15, 1866. In 1862–1863 he was assistant minister at St. Paul's Church, Philadelphia, where his father was rector. In 1863–1864 he was assistant minister at the Church of the Epiphany, Philadelphia. From 1864 until 1866, he was rector of the Church of the Epiphany, Philadelphia; and from 1866 until 1869 he was rector of St. Paul's Church, Philadelphia. His most significant ministry was as rector of All Souls' Church, New York, from 1869 until 1902, where he gained the reputation as a leading liberal preacher in the Episcopal Church. He was also called "the prince of preachers to children." In 1903 he became the preacher at Stanford University in California. William Wilberforce Newton was his son. He died in East Hampton, Long Island, New York. *See* Newton, William Wilberforce.

Newton, William Wilberforce (Nov. 4, 1843–June 25, 1914). Broad church theologian. He was born in Philadelphia. Newton graduated from the University of Pennsylvania in 1865 and from the Philadelphia Divinity School in 1868. He was ordained deacon on June 19, 1868, and priest on Feb. 19, 1869. He served for a year as assistant to his father at the Church of the Epiphany, Philadelphia, and then as rector of St. Paul's Church, Brookline, Massachusetts, 1870–1875, Trinity Church, Newark, 1875–1877, St. Paul's Church, Boston, 1877–1881, and St. Stephen's Church, Pittsfield, Massachusetts, 1881–1900. In 1903–1904 he was chaplain of the English Church at Dinan, Brittany, and in 1905–1906 he was rector of the Church of the Ascension, Wakefield, Rhode Island. Newton was one of the organizers of the American Congress of Churches in 1884. This was an effort to promote inter-denominational cooperation among the churches, which met at Hartford, Connecticut, in 1885, and at Cleveland, Ohio, in 1886. Newton's father, Richard Newton, was called "the prince of preachers to children," and William continued that tradition. He published six volumes of sermons for children in the *Pilgrim Series of Sermons for Children* (1877–1890). As a broad churchman, he was committed to the unity of the church and was opposed to any expression of dogmatic sectarianism. He called for the church to be open to the intellectual and social trends of the day and to appropriate the truths of evolution and science. Newton died in Boston. *See* Newton, Richard Heber.

Nicaragua, Diocese of. The House of Bishops in 1967 created the Missionary District of Nicaragua and placed it under the jurisdiction of the Bishop of Costa Rica. In 1968 the House of Bishops elected George Edward Haynsworth Missionary Bishop of Nicaragua. It became a diocese on Jan. 1, 1980.

Nicene Creed. It was first issued by the Council of Nicaea in 325, but in the form used today it is frequently thought to have been perfected at the Council of Constantinople in 381. There is no doubt that it was passed on to the church through the Council of Chalcedon in 451. It is commonly held to be based on the baptismal creed of Jerusalem, and it is often referred to as the Niceno-Constantinopolitan Creed. It states the full divinity of the Son, the second Person of the Trinity, in opposition to Arius. It also states the full divinity of the Holy Spirit, as denied by Macedonius. The use of the Nicene Creed in the eucharist (right after the gospel), in contrast to the use of the Apostles' Creed in baptism, began in the fifth century in Antioch and became the universal practice in the church. The Nicene Creed is expressed in its original form of "We believe" in the Rite 2 eucharistic liturgy of the 1979 BCP, and this communal expression of faith is also presented as the first option in the Rite 1 eucharistic liturgy. The Rite 1 eucharistic liturgy also offers the "I believe" form as a second option (see BCP, pp. 326–327, 358).

Nicholas, Bishop of Myra (fourth century). Very little is known about the life of Nicholas. He became Bishop of Myra on the southwest coast of Asia Minor. He may have been imprisoned for his faith in the persecution (303–311) that began under the Emperor Diocletian, and he may have attended the Council of Nicaea in 325. Nicholas is the traditional patron of seafarers and sailors. He is also known as a patron of children, based on his reputation as a bearer of gifts to children. The Dutch brought his name to New York. He is popularly known as Santa Claus. Nicholas is commemorated in the Episcopal calendar of the church year on Dec. 6.

Nightingale, Florence (1820–1910). Founder of modern nursing. She was born in Florence, Italy, and baptized in the Church of England on July 4, 1820. In 1849–1850 she studied the nursing system of the Sisters of Charity of St. Vincent dePaul at Alexandria, Egypt. She also trained for several months with the deaconesses in 1851 in Kaiserswerth in the Rhineland. In her early 30s, she became Superintendent of the Institution for the Care of Sick Gentlewomen in Distressed Circumstances in London. In this position she improved the standard of nursing care and administration. At the request of the British government, she agreed to be Superintendent of Female Nurses in Turkey to organize medical care for the British soldiers injured or ill during the Crimean War, 1854–1856. While in Crimea she became ill with Crimean Fever and was an invalid from 1858 until 1888. Today her illness is recognized as chronic brucellosis. Nightingale worked to improve the health of British soldiers and she promoted sanitation reform in England and India. She is recognized for her progressive thinking about nursing and hospital organization and serves as a model of compassion against physical suffering. Her major writing, *Notes on Nursing: What It Is and What It Is Not* (1859), went through many editions. She is also noted for her deeply mystical and pragmatic sense of spirituality. Nightingale described nurses as "handmaidens of the Lord." She died in London. She was proposed for inclusion in the Episcopal calendar of the church year.

Ninian (c. 360–c. 430/432). Missionary to the Britons and the Picts. A Briton, he received his theological education at Rome, where he was consecrated bishop in 394. He went to Scotland as a missionary to convert the Britons and the Picts. Ninian founded a church which he dedicated to St. Martin of Tours and named Candida Casa ("White House"), probably from the color of the stones. This church and monastery in Galloway became the base from which Ninian and his monks did their missionary work. His life is commemorated in the Episcopal calendar of the church year on Sept. 16.

Niobrara Convocation. The Convocation includes American Indian clergy, clergy serving American Indians, and American Indian congregations in the Diocese of South Dakota. It first met in 1870. It takes its name from the Niobrara River near the Santee Reservation where the first Convocation was held. The Convocation is the meeting of all clergy and congregations which make up the Niobrara Deanery, formerly the Niobrara Missionary District, now incorporated into the Diocese of South Dakota. The Convocation meets the fourth weekend of each June.

Niobrara, Missionary District of. The 1871 General Convention established this Missionary District. It had the following boundaries: on the east by the Missouri River; on the south by the State of Nebraska; on the west by the 104th meridian, the territories of Wyoming and Nebraska; on the north by the 46th degree of north latitude, including the several Indian Reservations on the left bank of the Missouri River, north and east of the Missouri river. In 1883 the Missionary District of Niobrara was incorporated into the Missionary District of South Dakota. *See* Niobrara Convocation.

Nippon Sei Ko Kai. The Japanese name for the Holy Catholic Church in Japan. It is sometimes written as *Nippon Seikokai*. It was organized in 1887 by uniting the work of the Church Missionary Society, the Society for the Propagation of the Gospel, and the Episcopal Church.

Noble, Thomas Tertius (May 5, 1867–May 4, 1953). Choirmaster, composer and teacher. He was born in Bath, England. In 1886 Noble won a scholarship at the Royal College of Music where he studied under Frank Bridge, Walter Parratt, and Charles Villiers Stanford. He became a Fellow of the College in 1905. In 1890 Noble was appointed assistant to Stanford at Trinity College, Cambridge. He served there until 1892 when he became organist and choirmaster at Ely Cathedral. In 1898 he became organist and choirmaster at York Minster. At York he founded a symphony orchestra, directed the York Musical Society and in 1909 was master of the music and conductor of the York Pageant. In 1912 he revived the York Musical Festival after a lapse of seventy-five years. Noble became organist and choirmaster of St. Thomas Church, New York, in 1913. In 1919 he established its choir school and developed a choral program in the English cathedral tradition. He was a member of the Joint Commission on the Hymnal in 1916, the Joint Commission on Church Music until 1943, and the Musical Committee of *The Hymnal* (1940). He exerted a major influence on church musicians in the United States. Noble retired as organist and choirmaster of St. Thomas at the age of seventy-five, but he continued to compose until his death eleven years later. He died in Rockport, Massachusetts. He was a prolific composer. *The Hymnal 1982* contains his well-known tune, "*Ora Labora*," used with the text "Come, labor on" (Hymn 541), an arrangement of "*St. Elizabeth*," used with the text "Fairest Lord Jesus" (Hymn 383), and one of his many Anglican chants (S 38).

Nocturn. A part of the traditional night office of matins, which was said at midnight or at the end of the night before dawn. The term is from the Latin for "nocturnal" or "happening at night." The nocturn included sets of antiphons and psalms, a versicle, the Lord's Prayer, a short prayer known as the "Absolutio," and three lessons, each preceded by a benediction. There were three nocturns at matins on Sundays, feasts above the rank of simple feast, and in the Office of the Dead. At these times, the lessons for the first nocturn were from scripture, the lessons for the second nocturn were from patristic or historical sources, and the lessons for the third nocturn were from a homily on the day's gospel. In the Roman Catholic Church, the number of sets of antiphons and psalms for these nocturns was set at three in 1912. There was only one nocturn at matins on simple feasts and ferial days. It had 12 psalms (later reduced to nine by Pius X), and three lessons (one from scripture, one from patristic or historical sources, and a homily). During the octaves of Easter and Pentecost, the one nocturn at matins had three psalms and three lessons.

The medieval service of matins was one of the sources for the Prayer Book service of Morning Prayer. There are no nocturns in the Prayer Book. However, three nocturns are the first part of the service of Tenebrae in the *BOS*. Each of the three nocturns includes three sets of antiphons and psalms; a versicle and response; a time for silent prayer; and three lessons, each followed by a responsory. *See* Matins; *see* Tenebrae.

Nominations, Joint Standing Committee on. The Committee submits nominations to General Convention for the election of trustees of the Church Pension Fund, members of the Executive Council, the secretary and treasurer of General Convention, the trustees of General Theological Seminary, and the General Board of Examining Chaplains. It was established by the 1973 General Convention and is composed of three bishops, three presbyters, and six lay persons.

Nonconformists. In a technical sense, the term refers to English Protestants who do not conform to the discipline, doctrines, or practices of the established Church of England. In this sense the word was first used in the penal acts following the Restoration in 1660 and the Act of Uniformity of 1662 to describe the places of worship (the "conventicles") of the congregations which separated from the Church of England at that time. Nonconformists are also called "Dissenters," a word first used to describe the "Dissenting Brethren" at the time of the Westminster Assembly of Divines (1643–1647). Nonconformists of different denominations joined together in the Free Church Federal Council and became known as "Free Churchmen."

In common usage the term "Nonconformist" describes all Protestants in England who dissent from Anglicanism—Baptists, Congregationalists, Presbyterians, Methodists, and Unitarians, as well as such independent groups as Quakers, Plymouth Brethren, and the Salvation Army. In Scotland, where the established church is Presbyterian, members of other sects, including Anglicans, are considered Nonconformists.

Nonjurors. Clergy of England and Scotland who refused to take the oath of allegiance to William of Orange and his wife, Mary Stuart, when they succeeded to the English throne in 1688. After the abdication of James II, Archbishop Sancroft and five other bishops, along with several hundred clergy, refused to take the oath of allegiance to the new monarchs on the ground that their oath to James was irrevocable. They were joined in this action by the entire bench of Scottish bishops and a few Scottish clergy. The episcopate was imposed on the Scottish church by James I and Charles I, and the bishops were intensely loyal to the Stuart line. They would not acknowledge William and Mary as legitimate rulers of Scotland. The Church of Scotland was re-established in 1690 as Presbyterian. Both the English and Scottish groups who refused to take the oath were called nonjurors.

English nonjurors were deprived of their livings and gradually declined in number and influence. The last nonjuring bishop was Charles Booth, who died in 1805. Bishop Thomas Ken (1637–1711), one of the original five nonjurors, wrote the famous doxology, "Praise God, from whom all blessings flow." William Law (1686–1761), a nonjuring priest, wrote the devotional manual, *A Serious Call to a Devout and Holy Life* (1728).

Samuel Seabury, the first bishop of the Episcopal Church, was consecrated by nonjuring bishops of the Episcopal Church in Scotland on Nov. 14, 1784, in Aberdeen, Scotland. Seabury had been denied episcopal orders in England because he could not swear allegiance to the crown. The Scottish Episcopal Church is a nonjuring church to this day.

None. *See* Terce, Sext, None.

Noonday, An Order of Service for. This service of noonday prayers includes an opening versicle, a selection from the psalms, a lesson, and prayers (BCP, 103–107). It is based on the "little offices" of terce, sext, and none in Christian monasticism. These "little offices" were said at 9 A.M., 12 noon, and 3 P.M., which were known as the third, sixth, and ninth hours of the day. Private devotions at these hours associated with the events of the Passion have been observed by Christians since the second century. Although these hours of prayer were included in the Primers of Henry VIII and Elizabeth, these offices were not included in any Prayer Books before the twentieth century. The 1979 BCP is the first American Prayer Book to include this office.

The BCP Order of Service for Noonday may be used for terce, sext, or none. A hymn may follow the opening versicle. The BCP provides suggested options for the selections for the psalm and the lesson. A silent or spoken meditation may follow the lesson. The Prayers include the Kyrie, the Lord's Prayer, the versicle "Lord, hear our prayer," with the response "And let our cry come to you," and a collect, which may be one of four provided in the office or the collect of the day. The office concludes with the *Benedicamus Domino*, "Let us bless the Lord," and the people's response, "Thanks be to God." Musical settings for An Order of Service for Noonday are found in *The Hymnal 1982 Accompaniment Edition, Vol. 1* (S 296–S 304). *See* Little Hours of the Divine Office.

North American Association for the Diaconate (NAAD). NAAD promotes the diaconate, educates the church, and supports deacons in the Episcopal Church and Anglican Church of Canada. Membership includes deacons and synods in the Evangelical Lutheran Church in America. The organization dates from 1953, when the Central House for Deaconesses was established with a house in Evanston, Illinois. The name was changed in 1974 to the National Center for the Diaconate, and in 1986 to the North American Association for the Diaconate. An office in Providence, Rhode Island, is called the Center for the Diaconate. NAAD publishes a newsletter, sells materials, and hosts conferences.

North American Missionary Society (NAMS). Incorporated on Sept. 12, 1994, NAMS plants churches which will make disciples in the Anglican tradition, by which they mean fully within the tradition of the BCP and guided by the Chicago-Lambeth Quadrilateral. A NAMS church is to be "mission oriented, not maintenance dominated." The founding board of directors were the Rt. Rev. Alex Dickson, the Rt. Rev. Alden Hathaway, the Rt. Rev. James M. Stanton, the Rev. Bill Atwood, and the Rev. Jon C. Shuler.

North Carolina, Diocese of. This diocese was organized at New Bern on Apr. 24, 1817. It joined the Protestant Episcopal Church in the Confederate States of America on May 16, 1862, and rejoined the Episcopal Church on Sept. 15, 1865. It was divided by the General Conventions of 1883 and 1895. It includes the following counties: Alamance, Anson, Cabarrus, Caswell, Chatham, Davidson, Davie, Durham, Edgecombe, Forsyth, Franklin, Granville, Guilford, Halifax, Harnett, Iredell, Johnston, Lee, Mecklenberg, Montgomery, Moore, Nash, Northampton, Orange, Person, Rockingham, Rowan, Scotland, Stanly, Stokes, Surrey, Union, Vance, Wake, Warren, and Yadkin.

North Central Philippines, Diocese of. The 1901 General Convention established the Missionary District of the Philippines. In 1973 the Missionary District of the Philippines was divided into three missionary districts. One of these was the Central Missionary District. In 1985 it became the Diocese of Central Philippines. On July 7, 1988, the House of Bishops voted to divide the Diocese of Central Philippines and established the Diocese of North Central Philippines. At this same meeting, the House of Bishops voted to release the Philippine Episcopal Church to form a new province. On May 1, 1990, the Philippine Episcopal Church became autonomous as the Twenty-Eighth Province of the Anglican Communion.

North Conway Institute, The (NCI). Founded by the Rev. Dr. David A. Works in Sept. 1951 to encourage the Episcopal Church and all faith communities to take action against alcoholism and the abuse of alcohol and other drugs. It was an outgrowth of the Yale University School of Alcohol Studies. NCI is an ecumenical, interdisciplinary, non-profit association that is concerned with alcohol problems and drug dependency. It also seeks improvement of treatment and rehabilitation for the addicted, continued research, and the development of responsible personal decision-making concerning use or non-use of alcoholic beverages. NCI has convened assemblies and conferences since 1955. These gatherings have included religious leaders, educators, and representatives of government and law enforcement, social welfare organizations, industry, and medicine. NCI publications include *Responsible Decisions on the Use and Non-Use of Alcohol* and *Pastoral Care of Families: Including Alcoholics and Problem Drinkers.*

North Dakota, Diocese of. On Oct. 19, 1859, the House of Bishops created the Missionary District of the Northwest, including North Dakota. The Missionary District of Nebraska and Dakota was established at the 1865 General Convention. On Oct. 28, 1868, the House of Bishops created the Missionary District of Dakota. On Oct. 11, 1883, the House of Bishops divided the Missionary District of Dakota and created the Missionary District of North Dakota. The primary convocation of the Missionary District of North Dakota met at Gethsemane Church, Fargo, on Sept. 24–25, 1884. On Sept. 24–26, 1971, the primary convention of the Diocese of North Dakota met at All Saints' Church, Valley City. Gethsemane Church, Fargo, was set apart as Gethsemane Cathedral on Sept. 2, 1900.

North Kwanto, Missionary District of. The name of the Missionary District of North Tokyo was changed to the Missionary District of North Kwanto in 1938. In Apr. 1941 the Missionary District of North Kwanto became a diocese in the Holy Catholic Church in Japan.

North Texas, Missionary District of. The Diocese of Northwest Texas was the Missionary District of North Texas from Oct., 1910, until Oct. 31, 1958. *See* Northwest Texas, Diocese of.

North Tokyo, Missionary District of. The name of the Missionary District of Tokyo was changed to the Missionary District of North Tokyo on Oct. 15, 1925. In 1938 the name was changed again to the Missionary District of North Kwanto.

Northern California, Diocese of. The 1874 General Convention voted to divide the Diocese of California. The new missionary district included of the following counties: Amador, Butte, Colusa, Del Norte, El Dorado, Glenn, Humboldt, Lake, Lassen, Mendocino, Modoc, Napa, Nevada, Placer, Plumas, Sacramento, Shasta, Sierra, Siskiyou, Solano, Sonoma, Sutter, Tehama, Trinity, Yolo, and Yuba. The primary convocation of the Missionary District of Northern California met at Grace Church, Sacramento, May 6–7, 1875. On Oct. 12, 1898, the House of Bishops voted that the bounds of this missionary district be changed to include the California counties plus that portion of Nevada west of the west lines of the counties of Elko, White, Pine, Eureka, Lincoln, Lander, and Nye, and that it be called the Missionary District of Sacramento. The primary convocation of the Missionary District of Sacramento met at St. Paul's Church, Sacramento, Oct. 17–18, 1899. On Oct. 10, 1907, the House of Bishops formed the Missionary District of Nevada. The Nevada counties were detached from the Missionary District of Sacramento, which then consisted of the original California counties. The first annual convention of the Diocese of Sacramento met at St. Paul's Church, Sacramento, Oct. 30–31, 1911. On Apr. 22, 1961, the name was changed to the Diocese of Northern California. Trinity Church, Sacramento, became Trinity Cathedral on May 21, 1913.

Northern Indiana, Diocese of. The 1898 General Convention voted to divide the Diocese of Indiana. The new diocese included the following counties: Adams, Allen, Benton, Blackford, Carroll, Cass, DeKalb, Elkhart, Fulton, Grant, Howard, Huntington, Jasper, Jay, Kosciusko, LaGrange, Lake, LaPorte, Marshall, Miami, Newton, Noble, Porter, Pulaski, St. Joseph, Starke, Steuben, Wabash, Wells, White, and Whitby. The primary convention of the new diocese met at Trinity Cathedral, Michigan City, Apr. 25–26, 1899. It chose the name Diocese of Michigan City. On Apr. 25, 1899, Trinity Church, Michigan City, became Trinity Cathedral. It ceased to be the cathedral on Nov. 4, 1917. On May 20, 1919, the name was changed to the Diocese of Northern Indiana. On Jan. 30, 1957, St. James Church, South Bend, became St. James Cathedral.

Northern Luzon, Diocese of. The 1901 General Convention established the Missionary District of the Philippines. In 1973 the Missionary District of the Philippines was divided into three missionary districts. One of these was the Northern Philippines Missionary District. In 1985 it became the Diocese of the Northern Philippines. On Sept. 9, 1984, the House of Bishops voted to divide the Missionary District of the Northern Philippines and established the Missionary District of Northern Luzon. It became the Diocese of Northern Luzon in 1985. In July 1988 the House of Bishops voted to release the Philippine Episcopal Church to form a new province. On May 1, 1990, the Philippine Episcopal Church became autonomous as the Twenty-Eighth Province of the Anglican Communion.

Northern Mexico, Diocese of. The General Convention of 1904 established the Missionary District of Mexico. The 1972 General Convention divided the Missionary District of Mexico into the Missionary District of Central and South Mexico, the Missionary District of Western Mexico, and the Missionary District of Northern Mexico. All three of these Missionary Districts became dioceses on Jan. 1, 1980. The 1994 General Convention granted the Mexican dioceses permission to withdraw from the Episcopal Church and form an autonomous province. The Anglican Church of Mexico came into being on Jan. 1, 1995.

Northern Michigan, Diocese of. The General Convention of 1892 voted to divide the Diocese of Michigan. The primary convocation of the Missionary District of Northern Michigan met at Grace Church, Ishpeming, on May 31, 1893. The 1895 General Convention received the Missionary District as the Diocese of Northern Michigan. The primary convention of the diocese met at St. Paul's Church, Marquette. It chose the name Diocese of Marquette. This convention also accepted the offer of St. Paul's Church, Marquette, to be the pro-cathedral. On June 2, 1937, the name was changed to the Diocese of Northern Michigan. On Nov. 9, 1939, St. Paul's, Marquette, ceased to be the pro-cathedral. The diocese does not have a cathedral. The diocese includes the following counties: Alger, Baraga, Chippewa, Delta, Dickinson, Gogebic, Houghton, Iron, Keeweenaw, Luce, Mackinac, Marquette, Menominee, Ontonagon, and Schoolcraft.

Northern New Jersey, Diocese of. The Diocese of Newark was named the Diocese of Northern New Jersey from Nov. 12, 1874, until May 19, 1886. *See* Newark, Diocese of.

Northern Philippines, Diocese of. The 1901 General Convention established the Missionary District of the Philippines. In 1973 the Missionary District of the Philippines was divided into three missionary districts.

One of these was the Northern Philippines Missionary District. In 1985 it became the Diocese of the Northern Philippines. In July 1988 the House of Bishops voted to release the Philippine Episcopal Church to form a new province. On May 1, 1990, the Philippine Episcopal Church became autonomous as the Twenty-Eighth Province of the Anglican Communion.

Northwest, Missionary District of the. The 1859 General Convention passed "That all those portions of our country, North of a line running along the Northern boundary of the Cherokee country and New Mexico, until it reaches the Diocese of California, not yet organized into Dioceses, or included in Missionary districts, be within the Jurisdiction of the Missionary Bishop of the Northwest." It was composed of the following states: Nebraska, North Dakota, South Dakota, Colorado, Utah, Nevada, Idaho, Montana, and Wyoming. Joseph Cruikshank Talbot was consecrated missionary bishop on Oct. 21, 1859. He served until Aug. 23, 1865, when he resigned to become Assistant Bishop of Indiana. Talbot was the only Missionary Bishop of the Northwest. He referred to himself as the "Bishop of All Outdoors." *See* Talbot, Joseph Cruikshank.

Northwest Texas, Diocese of. The 1910 General Convention created the Missionary District of North Texas from territories ceded by the Diocese of Dallas and the Diocese of West Texas. The Missionary District of North Texas became the Diocese of Northwest Texas when the primary council met at the Episcopal Conference Center, Amarillo, on Oct. 31, 1958. The diocese includes the following counties: Andrews, Armstrong, Bailey, Baylor, Borden, Briscoe, Callahan, Carson, Castro, Childress, Cochran, Coke, Coleman, Collingsworth, Cottle, Crane, Crosby, Dallas, Dawson, Deaf Smith, Dickens, Donley, Ector, Fisher, Floyd, Foard, Gaines, Garza, Glasscock, Gray, Hale, Hall, Hansford, Hardeman, Hartley, Haskell, Hemphill, Hockley, Howard, Hutchinson, Irion, Jones, Kent, King, Knox, Lamb, Lipscoomb, Loving, Lubbock, Lynn, Martin, Midland, Mitchell, Moore, Motley, Nolan, Ochiltree, Oldham, Parmer, Potter, Randall, Reagan, Roberts, Runnels, Scurry, Shackelford, Sherman, Sterling, Stonewall, Swisher, Taylor, Terry, Throckmorton, Tom Green, Upton, Ward, Wheeler, Wilbarger, Winkler, and Yoakum. The diocese does not have a cathedral.

Northwestern Pennsylvania, Diocese of. The 1910 General Convention voted to divide the Diocese of Pittsburgh.

The primary convention of the new diocese met at St. Paul's Church, Erie, on Nov. 16, 1910. It chose the name Diocese of Erie. It includes the following counties: Cameron, Clarion, Clearfield, Crawford, Elk, Erie, Forest, Jefferson, Lawrence, McKean, Mercer, Venango, and Warren. On Nov. 14, 1981, the name was changed to the Diocese of Northwestern Pennsylvania. St. Paul's Church, Erie, was set apart as St. Paul's Cathedral on Feb. 21, 1915.

Norwich University. It opened on Sept. 4, 1820, as a military academy at Norwich, Vermont. In 1834 it became Norwich University, and in 1866 moved to Northfield, Vermont. It had an Episcopal connection from 1850 to about 1880. Four Episcopal priests served as president: Edward Bourns (1801–1871), 1850–1865; Roger Strong Howard (1807–1880), 1869–1871; Malcolm Douglass (1825–1887), 1871–1875; and Josiah Swett (1814–1890), 1875–1876. The university is no longer in existence.

Notes of the Church. The Nicene Creed describes the church as one, holy, catholic, and apostolic (see BCP, pp. 358–359). These four characteristics are the notes, or marks, of the church. The church is to be "notable" or distinguishable by its unity, holiness, catholicity, and apostolicity. The Prayer Book Catechism discusses the meaning of the notes of the church (see BCP, p. 854). The church is described as one because it is one body, under one head, Jesus Christ. The church is described as holy because the Holy Spirit dwells in it, consecrating the members of the church and guiding them to do God's work. The church is described as catholic because it proclaims the whole Christian faith to all people until the end of time. The church is described as apostolic because it continues the teaching and fellowship of the apostles, and because it is sent to carry out Christ's mission to all people.

Catholicity has also been understood in terms of the "Vincentian Canon" of Vincent of Lérins (d. before 450), who understood catholicity in terms of what has been believed everywhere, always, by all. In this regard, catholicity is understood in terms of universality, antiquity, and consent. Many Protestants have not considered the apostolic succession of bishops, passed on with ordination by laying on of hands, to be a necessary condition for catholicity and apostolicity. Many Lutherans have understood apostolicity in terms of continuity with the witness of the apostles to the gospel, rather than a succession of bishops. Other churches, including the Anglican, Orthodox, Roman Catholic, and some Lutheran churches, have upheld the necessity of an apostolic succession of bishops ordained with the laying on of hands (see the Chicago-Lambeth Quadrilateral 1886, 1888, BCP, pp. 876–878).

During the sixteenth century, the notes of the church were used polemically by Roman Catholic theologians who claimed their church to be the "true" church. The notes of the church were also appealed to by the Tractarians to uphold the catholicity of the Church of England. In more recent times, the notes of the church have been understood to be both the present characteristics and the future goal of the church. In the present, the church's unity, holiness, catholicity, and apostolicity are not yet fulfilled or perfect. But the notes of the church are already present and visible in an imperfect way. The notes of the church may become increasingly visible as the church grows in faithfulness to Christ, and manifests the authentic Christian faith more completely. The fulfillment and perfection of the notes of the church may be hoped for in terms of the eschatological coming of the kingdom of God.

Notitia Parochialis. "Parish Reports" sent by clergy in colonial America of the Society for the Propagation of the Gospel in Foreign Parts (SPG) to the secretary of the society. These reports gave statistical information concerning their missionary work. Despite possible inaccuracies, these reports provide useful statistical evidence of the size and growth of the Church of England in the colonies.

Novice. A trainee in a religious community. After being a postulant, aspirant, or candidate (the vocabulary varies), the novice is prepared for the religious life according to the rules, constitutions, and customs of the community. Novices use this time to deepen their spiritual life and to test whether the community fits their own sense of vocation. This time is known as the novitiate. It is typically supervised by a member of the community who may be known as the novice guardian or master (mistress). *See* Novitiate.

Novice Guardian or Novice Master or Novice Mistress. Director of the process of discernment and formation that leads to the incorporation of new members in a religious order or community. The title refers to the novice guardian's responsibility for training the novices in the novitiate of the religious order or community. The novice guardian also may handle inquiries from prospective members and direct the training of postulants before they enter the novitiate. The novice guardian is seen to be a role model for those who will become members of the religious order or community. The novice guardian represents the superior in the process of discernment and formation for novices and is accountable to the superior. The novice guardian should be mature, thoroughly acquainted with the rule, constitutions, and customs of the community, gifted with spiritual experience and discernment, and knowledgeable in the theology of the spiritual life.

Novitiate. The period of training of novices in a monastery or religious community. It may lead to temporary vows of poverty, celibacy, and obedience that, in most communities, will be replaced later by final or perpetual vows. It is a time of mutual testing. The community discerns the novice's personal call and capacities, while the novice seeks to discern if he or she is called to the community and willing to follow its rules and customs. Novices may leave the novitiate at any time.

Nun. A woman who is a full member of a religious order. The term may be seen as the female equivalent of a monk. The term may be distinguished from a "sister," who is a member of a religious order with an active or mixed expression of community life. *See* Monastic.

Nunc dimittis. Canticle based on the words of Simeon, who recognized the infant Jesus to be the Messiah at the Presentation of Jesus in the temple by Mary and Joseph (Lk 2:29–32). It had been revealed to Simeon by the Holy Spirit that he would not die before he had seen the Messiah. When Simeon saw the child Jesus he took him up in his arms, blessed God, and said, "Lord, you now have set your servant free to go in peace as you have promised." Simeon was peaceful and ready to face death because he had seen the long-expected Messiah. The canticle is also known as the Song of Simeon. The term *Nunc dimittis* is from the initial words of the Song of Simeon in Latin, which mean "now let depart." The canticle is identified as the canticle for Evening Office by the Apostolic Constitutions of the late fourth century. In the seventh century, Pope Sergius (d. 701) introduced in Rome a procession with candles and the singing of the *Nunc dimittis* to celebrate the Presentation of our Lord Jesus Christ in the Temple. The day came to be known as "Candlemas." The *Nunc*

dimittis became the canticle for use at Compline in the west. It was also used as the canticle following the second lesson at Evensong in the 1549 BCP. It has appeared in this place in every subsequent Prayer Book except the 1789 BCP. The 1979 BCP uses the *Nunc dimittis* after the second lesson at Evening Prayer (p. 120) and near the conclusion of Compline (p. 135). At the Burial of the Dead, the *Nunc dimittis* may be used as an anthem as the body is borne from the church after the commendation. The *Nunc dimittis* also appears as Canticles 5 and 17 for optional use at Morning Prayer (pp. 51, 93). *The Hymnal 1982* provides musical settings of the *Nunc dimittis* (S 196–S 200, S 254–S 260). *The Hymnal 1982 Accompaniment Edition, Vol. 1* also provides musical settings of the *Nunc dimittis* (S 395, S 405).

Nuptial. Concerning a marriage. The term is from Latin words for "wedding" and "to take a husband." A nuptial blessing is the blessing of the husband and wife at the marriage (BCP, pp. 430–431).

Nuptial Mass, or Nuptial Eucharist. Eucharist celebrated at a marriage. The service for the Celebration and Blessing of a Marriage is the liturgy of the word. The eucharist begins with the offertory. Any authorized liturgy for the eucharist may be used (BCP, p. 437). At the offertory, the bride and groom may present the bread and wine for the eucharist. They may remain before the altar and receive communion before other members of the congregation (BCP, p. 438). The BCP provides a proper preface and a special postcommunion prayer for this service (pp. 381, 432). *See* Celebration and Blessing of a Marriage.

O

Oakerhater, David Pendleton (d. Aug. 31, 1931). The only American Indian listed in the Episcopal calendar of the church year. He was born between 1844 and 1851 on a Cheyenne reservation in Western Oklahoma. Oakerhater, whose name means "Making Medicine," was imprisoned in Florida for his alleged role in the Battle of Adobe Walls in 1874. He was befriended by Ohio Senator George Pendleton and his wife, who arranged for his education in Syracuse, New York. Oakerhater was ordained deacon on June 7, 1881, and spent the rest of his life as a missionary to the Cheyenne Nation of Oklahoma. Oakerhater is commemorated in the Episcopal calendar of the church year on Sept. 1.

O Antiphons. *See* Great O Antiphons of Advent.

Oath. A swearing that asserts the truth of a statement or promise, typically in the name of God. An oath is often made formally and solemnly. For example, a witness at a trial may swear that his or her testimony will be the full truth. Similarly, one who takes an oath of office swears to fulfill the duties and responsibilities of the office. The taking of oaths was criticized by Jesus, who urged in the Sermon on the Mount, "Do not swear at all," not by heaven or the earth or Jerusalem or by one's own head (Mt 5:33–37). This teaching is repeated in Jas 5:12. Since early Christian times, some have interpreted this teaching literally and refused to take oaths. A rigorist refusal to swear oaths was the predominant Christian attitude in the early centuries of the church. This position against oaths has been continued in modern times by Christian groups such as the Mennonites and Quakers. In many courts today, those with scruples against taking an oath are allowed to affirm (without swearing) that they will tell the truth.

Others have understood the teaching against swearing to criticize the excessive or casual taking of oaths that was common when Jesus lived. Certainly, a Christian should speak the truth at all times, whether or not an oath is involved. A Christian's word should not require an oath to be believed. An oath should be a superfluous addition to a Christian's word. However, since the early centuries of the church, some Christians have allowed the taking of oaths in certain circumstances. Paul calls on God as his witness in several contexts (2 Cor 1:23, Gal 1:20, Phil 1:8). Augustine would allow a Christian to take an oath for a reason of great necessity, if the oath was in the interest of a great good. Article XXXIX of the Articles of Religion states that "vain and rash Swearing is forbidden Christian men by our Lord Jesus Christ, and James his Apostle," but Christian religion does not prohibit one to swear "when the Magistrate requireth, in a cause of faith and charity, so it be done according to the Prophet's teaching in justice, judgment, and truth" (BCP, p. 876).

Oath of Allegiance. In 1604 Parliament passed an act requiring all clergy of the Church of England to take an Oath of Allegiance at their ordination to the diaconate or priesthood in which they acknowledged the King (or Queen) of England as supreme governor of the church in all spiritual and temporal matters. Those who refused to take this oath at the accession of William and Mary, or later George I, were known as "Nonjurors." This oath was a conscientious stumbling block for some clergy who felt obliged to remain loyal to the crown at the time of the American Revolution. The requirement for this oath also caused Samuel Seabury to seek consecration from Scottish nonjuring bishops when he was bishop-elect of Connecticut. In 1787 Parliament passed legislation permitting the Archbishop of Canterbury to consecrate bishops for the Episcopal Church without their taking the required oath of loyalty to the English crown.

Oblate. The term is from the Latin for "offered." Historically, in medieval times, oblates were children who were "given to God" in a monastery by their parents. The child would be educated in the monastery with a view to becoming a member of the religious community. This practice was endorsed by the Rule of St. Benedict. It was the origin of Benedictine schools and colleges. The practice was criticized because the children lacked freedom of choice at the time of entering the monastery. This practice was eventually abandoned. The term was later applied to laity who lived in a monastery or who maintained a close committed relationship with a religious community without taking full religious vows.

Oblation. 1) Prayer of self-offering. Oblation is "an offering of ourselves, our lives and labors, in union with Christ, for the purposes of God" (BCP, p. 857). Christian oblation is based in Christ's one offering of himself for our salvation. The BCP states that oblation is one of the principal kinds of prayer.

2) In reference to the eucharist, oblation has a broad and generic meaning as well as a narrow and technical meaning. In both cases, oblation is a kind of offering. In the broad sense, oblation refers to any offering—money, bread and wine, self, soul and body—made at the eucharist. The people's offerings are presented to the deacon or celebrant and placed on the altar for consecration (BCP, p. 361). The elements of bread and wine, consecrated at the eucharist, are identified with Christ's self-oblation. At the Last Supper, Christ identified the bread with his body and the wine with his blood of the new covenant. Christ's sacrifice is made present in the eucharist, uniting us in his one offering of himself (BCP, p. 859). The term "oblations" has at times been applied to money (alms) or other gifts that are presented at the eucharist. However, the Prayer Book rubrics distinguish

the oblations of bread and wine from such other gifts. The "oblations of bread and wine" may be presented by the newly baptized or their godparents at the baptismal eucharist (BCP, p. 313), and by the persons newly confirmed at the eucharist in a service of Confirmation (BCP, p. 412). One of the offertory sentences provided by the BCP is the bidding, "Let us with gladness present the offerings and oblations of our life and labor to the Lord" (p. 377). In its more technical usage, the term refers to the section of the eucharistic prayer dealing with offering. The oblation comes after the memorial (*anamnesis*) and before the invocation of the Spirit (*epiclesis*) in eucharistic prayers A, B, and D of the 1979 BCP. For example, eucharistic Prayer D prays to God the Father, "offering to you, from the gifts you have given us, this bread and this cup, we praise you and we bless you." This prayer of oblation immediately follows the memorial prayer, "Recalling Christ's death and his descent among the dead, proclaiming his resurrection and ascension to your right hand, awaiting his coming in glory . . ." (p. 374). *See* Eucharistic Sacrifice.

Obsecrations. The term comes from a Latin word which means earnest entreaty or supplication made in the name of a deity or some sacred thing. The word has often been used to designate those petitions in the Great Litany which begin with the word "By" (see BCP, p. 149).

Obsequies. Funeral rites or ceremonies for the burial of the dead.

"OC." *See* Oil, Holy.

Occasional Offices. *See* Pastoral Offices.

Occasional Papers of the Standing Liturgical Commission, The. These were originally issued beginning in 1982 as a series of papers by the Standing Liturgical Commission with the authorization of the General Convention. In 1987 those published during the 1982–85 triennium were published in book form with this title. In 1994 the title of the series was changed to *Liturgical Studies*, and two additional volumes appeared.

Occurrence. The coincidence of two scheduled feasts or observances of the calendar of the church year on the same day. For example, feasts celebrated on fixed dates such as All Saints' Day (Nov. 1) or the feast of Saint Andrew

the Apostle (Nov. 30) might occur on Sundays. The calendar of the church year provides rules of precedence concerning principal feasts, Sundays, holy days, days of special devotion, and days of optional observance (BCP, pp. 15–18). These rules determine which feast or observance has priority. Since All Saints' Day is a principal feast, it takes priority over a Sunday observance. But the Sunday observance takes priority over all feasts of apostles such as Saint Andrew the Apostle. When a feast of our Lord or other major feast appointed on a fixed day in the calendar cannot be observed because it occurs on a Sunday, the feast is normally transferred to the first convenient open day in the following week. *See* Precedence, Rules of.

Octave. Celebration of a feast over an eight-day period, beginning with the feast day itself as the first day. The term is from Latin for "eighth." The term may indicate the entire eight-day celebration or the eighth day of the celebration (also known as the octave day). Celebration of saints' days with octaves were numerous during the middle ages, but the observance of octaves is very limited in current liturgical practice. The term "octave" is not used in the Prayer Book. Proper collects and readings for the weekdays in Easter Week are provided by the Prayer Book. The celebration of Easter Week may be likened to the observance of an octave.

Odium Theologicum. The term is from the Latin, "theological hatred," and indicates the bitterness and hostility that may accompany theological controversy.

Oertel, Johannes Adam Simon (Nov. 3, 1823–Dec. 9, 1909). Priest and artist. He was born in Furth, near Nuremberg, in Bavaria, Germany. Oertel studied art in Nuremberg and Munich and spent much of his time engraving until 1848, when he came to the United States. He lived in Newark and then Madison, New Jersey. In 1861 he moved to Westerly, Rhode Island. Oertel was ordained deacon on June 7, 1867, and priest on Aug. 13, 1871. He served a rural church near Lenoir, North Carolina, until 1876. He moved to Morganton, North Carolina, where he served a church for 18 months. He lived for various periods in Washington, D. C., Sewanee, Tennessee, Nashville, Tennessee, and St. Louis, Missouri. He taught art at the University of the South. In 1889–1891, he was instructor in fine arts at Washington University, St. Louis.

Painting and ecclesiastical wood carving were his art forms. Among his more famous paintings are "The Dispensation of the Promise and the Law," "Walk to Emmaus," "The Walk to Gethsemane," "Easter Morning," "Magdalen at the Sepulchre," "The Rock of Ages," and "It Is Finished." Many of his works are at the University of the South. Oertel died in Vienna, Virginia.

Offering, Offerings. Gifts presented at a church service or other gathering. At the offertory, prior to the eucharistic prayer, representatives of the congregation bring the people's offerings of bread and wine, and money or other gifts, to the deacon or celebrant (BCP, p. 361). An offering (typically of money) may be presented at the offices of Morning and Evening Prayer (BCP, p. 142). The couple may present the offerings of bread and wine when the eucharist is part of the celebration and blessing of a marriage (BCP, p. 432). At times, those who attend a church program or presentation may be invited to make an offering to support the program, a needy cause, or the sponsoring parish. Offerings are made as an expression of faith and generosity and ultimately identified with Christ's self-offering for our salvation. *See* Alms; *see* Oblation; *see* Offertory, Offertory Procession, Offertory Sentence.

Offertory, Offertory Procession, Offertory Sentence. The first action of the second part of the Holy Eucharist—the liturgy of the table, called The Holy Communion by the BCP (pp. 333, 361). It consists of bread and wine, along with money and other gifts, which are presented to the deacon (or celebrant) who then sets the table for the feast. The procession of lay people carrying the gifts is called the offertory procession. The celebrant may begin the offertory by reciting an offertory sentence from scripture (BCP, pp. 343f, 376f). This sentence was sung by the choir as an anthem in the first Prayer Book of 1549, but it has been recited by the celebrant since 1552. Earlier editions of the Prayer Book directed that the priest offer the bread and wine at the offertory, but it is not mentioned in the 1979 BCP. The proper offering of the gifts by the priest occurs at the oblation in the Great Thanksgiving, which says, "We offer you these gifts" (BCP, p. 363; see pp. 335, 342, 369, 371, 374). *See* Oblation; *see* Preparation of the Table and Presentation of the Offerings.

Office Hymn. An office hymn has formed a part of the Daily Offices of western Christians since the time of St. Ambrose in the fourth century. Ambrose is credited with beginning the practice of singing hymns in his cathedral, and the earliest surviving Latin office hymns are attributed to him. The office hymns at noonday and compline are chosen for the time of day (see the headings Noonday and Compline in *The Hymnal 1982*), as are those for Morning and Evening Prayer on ordinary weekdays. Proper hymns are used during the major seasons of the liturgical year and on festivals. In the Prayer Book offices of Morning and Evening Prayer, the office hymn is typically sung after the collects, where the rubrics permit the singing of a hymn or anthem (BCP, pp. 58, 71, 101, 125). A suitable office hymn may also be substituted for the *Phos hilaron* at Evening Prayer (BCP, pp. 64, 118). In An Order for Service for Noonday, the office hymn immediately follows the opening preces (BCP, p. 103). At Compline the office hymn follows the short lesson (BCP, p. 132).

Office of Institution. American Prayer Books preceding the 1979 BCP included "An Office of Institution of Ministers into Parishes or Churches." After the 1844 revision, this rite only provided for the induction of the rector of a parish. Prior to the 1928 BCP, the service included Morning Prayer with proper lessons and psalms appointed, the ceremony of induction, the sermon, and the Holy Eucharist. Morning Prayer and the Eucharist were made optional for this service by the 1928 BCP. The rite for the institution of ministers in the 1979 BCP is the Celebration of a New Ministry (p. 559). It may be used in a greater variety of contexts than the Office of Institution. In addition to the induction of rectors of parishes, the 1979 rite may be used or adapted for the induction of deans and canons of cathedrals, vicars of missions, assisting priests, chaplains of institutions, and non-stipendiary clergy. It may also be used for the induction of deacons or members of the laity with pastoral responsibilities.

Officiant. The person who leads the Daily Office or another church service. The term may indicate a member of the clergy or a lay person. The BCP uses the term to identify the person who leads the Daily Offices of Morning Prayer, Noonday Prayer, Order of Worship for the Evening, Evening Prayer, and Compline; the Great Litany, including the supplication; and Ministration at the Time of Death, including the prayers for a vigil.

Oglethorpe, James Edward (Dec. 22, 1696–July 1, 1785). Social reformer and founder of Georgia. He was born in London. After education at Eton and Corpus Christi

College, Oxford, he entered the army in 1712. In 1729 Oglethorpe presided over a committee which brought about much-needed reforms in the prison system. From this experience came the idea of founding a new colony in North America. This new colony was to be a place where poor and unemployed debtors could start afresh, and where persecuted Protestant groups could find refuge. In 1732 Oglethorpe and 19 associates received a charter naming them "Trustees for establishing the colony of Georgia in America." The colony was named for King George II. The next year, 1733, Oglethorpe brought 116 debtors to Georgia, and founded Savannah. In 1738, with the outbreak of war with Spain, he conducted a vigorous defense of the colony. His campaign to capture the Spanish settlement of St. Augustine was unsuccessful. In 1743 Oglethorpe returned to England and resumed his parliamentary career as a social reformer. The Church of England was established in Georgia in 1758.

Ohio, Diocese of. The diocese was first organized on Jan. 5, 1818. The 1874 General Convention voted to divide the diocese and establish the Diocese of Southern Ohio. The Diocese of Ohio includes the following counties: Allen, Ashland, Ashtabula, Auglaize, Carroll, Columbia, Coshocton, Crawford, Cuyahoga, Defiance, Erie, Fulton, Geauga, Hancock, Hardin, Harrison, Henry, Holmes, Huron, Jefferson, Knox, Lake, Logan, Loraine, Lucas, Mahoning, Marion, Medina, Mercer, Morrow, Ottowa, Paulding, Portage, Putnam, Richland, Sandusky, Seneca, Shelby, Starke, Summit, Trumbull, Tuscarawas, Union, Van Wert, Wayne, Williams, Wood, and Wyandot. Trinity Church, Cleveland, became Trinity Cathedral on Mar. 2, 1890.

"OI." *See* Oil, Holy.

Oil, Holy. Olive oil that has been blessed is used sacramentally in the liturgical and pastoral ministries of the church. Holy oil is usually applied by the minister of the sacrament or sacramental rite to the forehead of the one who is anointed. The minister often applies the oil with the thumb, making the sign of the cross with the oil. Historically, three types of oil have been identified for use in liturgical anointing. Chrism, a mixture of olive oil and fragrant balsam, is used for the anointing after baptism. It has been abbreviated "SC," *sanctum chrisma*. Chrism may also be used at Confirmation. It has also been used to anoint newly consecrated bishops. The oil of catechumens was pure olive oil. It was used for the exorcistic anointing prior to baptism. It has also been used at the ordination of priests and the anointing of kings. It was abbreviated "OC," *oleum catechumenorum*. The oil of the sick was also pure olive oil. It was used for anointing the sick. It was abbreviated "OI," *oleum infirmorum*.

In the OT, oil was used for anointing kings and priests (see 1 Sm 10:1 and 16:1, 13; Ex 29:7). The use of oil in Christian baptism dates from at least the second century. The title "Christ" means the "anointed one." Oil is used as a symbol of baptism in the NT (see Lk 4:18, Acts 4:27, 1 Jn 2:20, 27). The NT also records the practice of anointing with oil for healing (see Mk 6:13, Jas 5:14). The *Apostolic Tradition* of Hippolytus (c. 215) included a form for the blessing of oil for the sick. The *Apostolic Tradition* also noted that anointing with oil was not required for baptism if oil were unavailable. By the fourth or early fifth century, it was required that chrism be consecrated by a bishop. The 1979 BCP (p. 307) calls for chrism to be consecrated by the bishop. This may be done when the bishop is present in the parish for Confirmation (BCP, p. 419). The *BOS* provides a form for Consecration of Chrism apart from Baptism. This rite takes place immediately after the postcommunion prayer and before the bishop's blessing and the dismissal. In many dioceses, the consecration of chrism by the bishop may be done at a service of reaffirmation of ordination vows during Holy Week. The BCP allows oil for the anointing of the sick to be blessed by a priest or bishop (p. 455). The Prayer Book does not mention the Oil of Catechumens.

The use of oil was rejected by many churches at the time of the Reformation. The 1549 BCP included a post-baptismal anointing, but this anointing was not present in the 1552 Prayer Book. The 1549 Prayer Book allowed the use of oil if the sick person desired to be anointed. But the 1549 BCP did not provide a form for setting apart the oil for this use. This use of oil was also eliminated in the 1552 BCP. The 1928 BCP restored the practice of anointing. It provided a form for "Unction of the Sick." The 1928 Prayer Book did not provide a form for blessing the oil, and it allowed no use of oil in addition to the anointing of the sick. The 1979 BCP includes the rite of chrismation at baptism (p. 308). The Prayer Book directs that the bishop or priest will mark the sign of the cross on the forehead of the newly baptized person, using chrism if desired (BCP, p. 308). The Prayer Book Catechism states that unction is the rite of anointing the sick with oil, or the laying on of hands, by which God's grace is given for the healing of spirit, mind, and body (BCP, p. 861). The Prayer Book service for Ministration to the Sick includes Part I, ministry of the word, Part II, laying on of hands and anointing, and Part III, Holy Communion (BCP, pp. 453–457). If the sick person is to be anointed, the priest dips a thumb in the holy oil and makes the sign of the cross on the sick person's forehead (BCP, p. 456). In cases of necessity, a deacon or lay person may perform the anointing with oil blessed by a bishop or priest. The *BOS* also provides a form for a Public Service of Healing. At this service the celebrant lays hands on the people, and may anoint the people with oil of the sick. Olive oil may be one of the gifts presented to the new minister at the Celebration of a New Ministry. When the oil is presented, the new minister is urged to be among the members of the congregation "as a healer and reconciler" (BCP, p. 561).

Oil Stock. Small container for oil that has been blessed for use as chrism or for anointing the sick. The oil stock is typically made of metal, and it may be decorated with a cross.

Okalona College. Okalona Industrial School, Okalona, Mississippi, was founded in 1902 by Wallace A. Battle as a high school and junior college for African American students to prepare for vocations in manual work. In 1920 the Diocese of Mississippi took over the school to "develop it along church lines." In 1921 it joined the American Church Institute for Negroes. It was later named Okalona College, but in 1965 the trustees had to close the school because of financial difficulties. The buildings and land were sold later and the proceeds went to the Okalona College Endowment Fund, which annually provides about $22,000 in educational assistance for African American students.

Okinawa, Missionary District of. The House of Bishops established the Missionary District of Okinawa on Sept. 18, 1967. The first and only Missionary Bishop of Okinawa was the Rt. Rev. Edmond L. Browning. On Jan. 1, 1972, it was transferred to the Holy Catholic Church in Japan (*Nippon Sei Ko Kai*).

Oklahoma, Diocese of. The House of Bishops in 1859 established the Missionary District of the Southwest. This included Oklahoma. The 1892 General Convention established the Missionary District of Oklahoma. In 1910 the General Convention voted to divide the Missionary

District of Oklahoma and established the Missionary District of Eastern Oklahoma. The 1919 General Convention voted to reunite the Missionary Districts of Eastern Oklahoma and Oklahoma. On Aug. 28, 1927, St. Paul's Church, Oklahoma City, became St. Paul's Cathedral. The primary convention of the Diocese of Oklahoma was held at St. Paul's Cathedral on Jan. 16–17, 1938.

Old Catholic Churches. The Old Catholic churches of the Union of Utrecht were formed in opposition to the dogma of the Roman Catholic Church in 1870 on Papal Infallibility. The Church of Utrecht in the Netherlands became the metropolitan see for these churches in many countries of western Europe, and later for the Polish National Catholic Church in America and Poland. These autonomous national churches who subscribe to the Declaration of Utrecht (1889), are in communion with the archbishop of Utrecht, who is *ex officio* president of their International Bishops' Conference. Obvious similarities eventually led these churches to intercommunion with the Anglican Communion, established by the Bonn Agreement of 1931. It provided that "Each Communion recognizes the catholicity and independence of the other and maintains its own." This meant the official opening of eucharistic fellowship and mutual participation in episcopal consecrations. The agreement was first ratified by the Old Catholics with the Church of England, and subsequently with most other churches of the Anglican Communion, and in 1948 by the Lambeth Conference. Ratification for the Episcopal Church came at the General Conventions of 1934, 1940, and 1943. Sacramental intercommunion was terminated in the U.S. by the General Synod of the Polish National Catholic Church in 1978 because of the Episcopal Church's decision to ordain women. Since 1983 there have been several meetings of a working group between the two churches in the U.S., as well as a small but official ecumenical dialogue. In the meantime, intercommunion continues between the Episcopal Church and the Old Catholic churches in Europe. The Old Catholic churches have moved steadily toward women's ordination. Several other churches style themselves "Old Catholic," but they are not recognized by the Utrecht Union.

Old Episcopal Church. This group was organized in 1972 by the Rev. Jack Capers Adams, a former Episcopal priest who had been deposed. Adams was consecrated a bishop on Feb. 6, 1972. It has several parishes in Arizona and New Mexico.

Old North Church, Boston. It was in the tower of this church on Apr. 18, 1775, that the sexton, Robert Newman, displayed the two lanterns which warned Paul Revere and his fellow riders that the British were marching toward Lexington and Concord. Its official name is Christ Church. It was founded in 1723, when the number of Episcopalians became too many for King's Chapel. The first service was held on Dec. 29, 1723. Its first rector was Timothy Cutler, the former Congregationalist who converted to the Church of England in 1722 while president of Yale. The tower of Old North houses America's first ring of bells.

Old Swede's Church, Wilmington, Delaware. Officially named Holy Trinity from its consecration on Trinity Sunday, July 4, 1699, it was the oldest of the Swedish Lutheran churches. The congregation existed from the establishment of the first Swedish settlement at Fort Christina in 1638. Gradually the Church of Sweden withdrew its support and the members began to speak English. On Feb. 7, 1795, the church's colonial charter was changed. The new charter stated that the name of the corporation was changed from "the Swedes Lutheran Church, called Trinity Church in the Borough of Wilmington" to "the vestry-men and church wardens of the Swedish Lutheran Church called Trinity Church in the Borough of Wilmington." Under the provisions of this amended charter, the vestry was elected on Mar. 2, 1795. A few days later they elected the Rev. Joseph Clarkson, an Episcopal priest, the first rector, and the congregation became an Episcopal church. It continues as an Episcopal congregation.

Old Testament. The name traditionally given to the first thirty-nine books of the Christian Bible, i.e., Genesis through Malachi in Protestant versions. Roman Catholic versions and those of the various Orthodox churches have additional books, called the Apocrypha or the Deutero-canonical books. Other versions include the apocryphal books in a separate section of the Bible. In recent years the term "Hebrew Scriptures" has been used frequently for the first part of the Bible. The practice presumably reflects the concern that the adjective "old" might seem pejorative and imply that the NT has invalidated the OT, which would be offensive to Jewish people. The Hebrew Bible itself consists of the thirty-nine books of the Protestant Bible but in a different order. It has three divisions: 1) the Pentateuch (or Torah); 2) the Prophets (or *Nebiim*), divided into the Former and the Latter Prophets; and 3) the Writings (*Kethubim*). This seems to be the order in which the three were accepted as authoritative by the Jewish community. The term "testament" comes from the Latin translation of the Hebrew word *berith*, which means "covenant." Thus the two parts of the Christian Bible refer basically to the two covenants of biblical times, the first with the Hebrew people and the second with the Christian community. *See* Apocrypha.

Olney Hymns. A 1779 collection of sixty-eight texts by William Cowper (1731–1800) and 280 texts by John Newton (1725–1807). Some of the texts were previously published. Most current hymnals include some texts from this work. Cowper was a widely acclaimed poet. His hymns reflect the melancholy which oppressed him for much of his life. Cowper moved to Olney, Buckinghamshire, in 1767. He lived there with Mary Unwin, the widow of a clergyman, and worked with Newton. Newton, a leading Anglican evangelical, was an ex-slave ship captain. After his conversion, Newton read for orders and was ordained in 1764 for the cure at Olney. In Newton's later years he was active in the anti-slavery movement. *See* Cowper, William; *see* Newton, John.

Olympia, Diocese of. On Oct. 13, 1853, the General Convention established the Missionary District of the Oregon and Washington Territory. On Oct. 15, 1880, the General Convention divided this Missionary District into the Missionary District of Oregon and the Missionary District of Washington. The 1892 General Convention then divided Washington into the Missionary District of Olympia and the Missionary District of Spokane. A special convocation met on Sept. 14, 1910, to organize the Diocese of Olympia. The diocese held its first convention at St. Paul's Church, Seattle, on May 30–31, 1911. The diocese includes the following counties: Clallam, Clark, Cowlitz, Grays Harbor, Island, Jefferson, King, Kitsap, Lewis, Mason, Pacific, Pierce, San Juan, Skagit, Skamania, Snohomish, Thurston, Whatcom, and Wahkiakum. In 1926 St. Mark's Church, Seattle, became St. Mark's Cathedral. The Cathedral was dedicated on Apr. 26, 1931.

Onderdonk, Benjamin Tredwell (July 15, 1791–Apr. 30, 1861). Controversial Bishop of New York. He was born in New York City. Onderdonk graduated from Columbia College in 1809. He studied theology under Bishop John Henry Hobart of New York, where he learned high church principles. He was ordained deacon on Aug. 2, 1812, and priest on July 26, 1815. Onderdonk served as assistant minister at Trinity Church, New York, from 1814 until 1835. He served as professor of ecclesiastical history, 1821–1822, and as professor of ecclesiastical polity and law, 1821–1861, at the General Theological Seminary. On Nov. 26, 1830, Onderdonk was consecrated the fourth Bishop of New York. He was an aggressive supporter of the Oxford Movement. In Nov., 1844, he was brought to trial by the House of Bishops on charges of "immorality and impurity." To some extent, his disciplinary trial reflected the larger controversy in the Episcopal Church over the Oxford Movement and its supporters. On Jan. 3, 1845, he was suspended from the office of bishop and from all the functions of the sacred ministry. William Manross notes in *A History of the American Episcopal Church* (1935) that the verdict against Onderdonk reflects "the bitter party feeling which prevailed at the time, especially as the voting throughout the trial was pretty much along party lines, all of the evangelicals voting to condemn Bishop Onderdonk and most, though not all, of the High Churchmen voting to acquit him." Onderdonk tried until his death to have the suspension remitted but never succeeded. Onderdonk died in New York City. Henry Ustick Onderdonk was his brother.

Onderdonk, Henry Ustick (Mar. 16, 1789–Dec. 6, 1858). Controversial Bishop of Pennsylvania. He was born in New York City. Onderdonk graduated from Columbia College in 1805, and then studied medicine in London and Edinburgh. He received his M.D. from the University of Edinburgh. After a few years of medical practice, he studied theology under Bishop John Henry Hobart of New York. Onderdonk was ordained deacon on Dec. 8, 1815, and priest on Apr. 11, 1816. He began his ministry as a missionary in Canandaigua, New York. In 1820 he became rector of St. Anne's Church, Brooklyn. On Oct. 25, 1827, he was consecrated Assistant Bishop of Pennsylvania. He became the second Bishop of Pennsylvania on July 17, 1836. The House of Bishops suspended him from office on Oct. 21, 1844, because of his abuse of alcohol. On Oct. 21, 1865, the House of Bishops lifted his suspension. He never resumed his jurisdiction. Onderdonk was friendly to the Oxford Movement, and the handling of his case reflected the partisan bitterness that divided evangelical and high church Episcopalians at the time. Onderdonk was a poet, and *The Hymnal 1982* includes his hymn text, "How wondrous and great thy works, God of praise" (Hymns 532–533). Onderdonk died in Philadelphia. Benjamin Tredwell Onderdonk was his brother.

Ontology. Deriving from the present participle of the Greek verb "to be," it is the study of being. Ontology studies being in its general, common nature rather than in its particular types and instances. It is also known as the study of first principles or metaphysics.

Open. See Associated Parishes for Liturgy and Music.

Open Communion. An invitation extended to baptized communicants in good standing of one church to receive the Holy Eucharist of another church. The practice is to be distinguished from "free communion" in which "all who love the Lord Jesus" are invited to communion.

Open Pulpit. This policy allows sermons to be delivered at public worship by persons who are not ordained or specially licensed to preach. In the Episcopal Church, sermons are normally given by a member of the clergy. The canons provide that a confirmed lay person with appropriate training and demonstrated competency may be licensed by the bishop or ecclesiastical authority of the diocese as a lay preacher. *See* Lay Preacher.

Open Pulpit, Canon on. From as early as 1792, members of the Episcopal Church were concerned about clergy from other Christian traditions speaking in Episcopal churches. The canon, "Of persons Not Ministers in this Church Officiating in any Congregation Thereof," forbade this. The 1907 General Convention amended this canon to allow Episcopal clergy to invite clergy from other churches to speak in Episcopal churches. Part of the canon stated that nothing should "prevent the Bishop of any Diocese or Missionary District from giving permission to Christian men, who are not Ministers of the Church, to make addresses in the Church, or special occasions." It became known as the "open pulpit" canon and caused considerable controversy in the church. In reaction to this canon, William McGarvey, one of the founders of the Companions of the Holy Saviour, renounced his Episcopal orders and joined the Roman Catholic Church along with some other priests and Nashotah House students.

Opening Acclamation. In the Holy Eucharist the opening acclamation is the greeting of the people by the presider and their response, which begins the service (BCP, pp. 323, 355). Its purpose is to bring the congregation corporately into dialogue with the presider and set a tone for the celebration.

Opening Preces. These versicles and responses occur at the beginning of the Daily Offices: "Lord open our lips" at Morning Prayer (BCP, pp. 42, 80; *The Hymnal 1982*, S 1, S 33) and "O God make speed to save us" at the other offices (BCP, pp. 63, 103, 117, 128; *The Hymnal 1982*, S 26, S 33). Although they are the traditional opening of the office, they may follow the opening sentences and the confession of sin. They always follow the confession at Compline. The term is from the Latin for "prayers."

Opening Sentences. *See* Sentences (Opening).

Operation Pass Along. *See* Society for Promoting and Encouraging Arts and Knowledge (SPEAK).

Orans Position. The traditional posture of early Christian prayer involved one standing with the arms raised and extended like the letter "Y" with the palms uplifted. In the early church the entire congregation prayed in this position. Today, except among charismatics, it is usually only the presider who uses the orans position for prayer. The position is frequently modified by bending the elbows so that the hands are approximately at eye level.

Oratory. A place of worship other than a parish church or cathedral. The term is from Latin, "place of prayer." It is a place of prayer set apart for the use of a particular group or individual or for worship in a specific context or situation. For example, the term may be applied to a cemetery chapel, a chapel on a ship, the chapel of a religious house, or a private chapel in a home.

Order. 1) Concerning the form or structure of a liturgical service. The BCP provides "orders" for services at noonday (pp. 103–107) and in the evening (pp. 109–114). The BCP also provides orders for eucharist (pp. 400–405), marriage (pp. 435–436), and burial (pp. 506–507). These "orders" are often used as alternate services for pastoral reasons or special occasions instead of other liturgical forms. For example, "An Order for Celebrating the Holy Eucharist" (known by some as "Rite 3") is "not intended for use at the principal Sunday or weekly celebration of the Holy Eucharist" (BCP, p. 400). These orders insure the basic form of the church's liturgy in these services, while allowing enhanced flexibility to those who plan and participate in the service.

2) Concerning the forms of ministry in the church. The ministers of the church are lay persons, bishops, priests, and deacons (BCP, p. 855). In a "vote by orders" in the House of Deputies of the General Convention, or in a diocesan convention, the votes of clergy and lay orders are counted separately. All baptized persons are members of the church and called to ministry. Some members of the church are ordained as bishops, priests, and deacons. These members of the church are in "holy orders."

3) A religious order is a society whose members voluntarily commit themselves for life or a term of years to holding their possessions in common or in trust and to living a celibate life in community in obedience to the rule and constitution of the religious order. *See* Vows.

Order of the Fleur de Lis. A church club for girls and young women founded in 1914. Its purpose was to build religious life and character through observance of the Vow of the Fleur de Lis. The vow consisted of three pledges: purity within ourselves, loyalty to our church, and service to others. The head of the order was called the Sovereign Queen. The secretary was the Sovereign Mistress of the Records, and the treasurer was the Sovereign Mistress of the Treasury. Fleur de Lis means "flower of the lily." The order went out of existence in 1967.

Order of St. Aidan. A religious order which aims to restore the memory, landmarks, witness, and experience of the Celtic Church in ways that relate to God's purposes today. Its motto is "for the healing of the land through men, women and children who draw their inspiration from the Celtic saints." In the United States the first group of aspirants of this order took its "trial" or aspirancy vows on Aug. 31, 1994. In England this group is called "The Community of Aidan and Hilda." *See* Aidan.

Order of Service for Noonday, An. *See* Noonday, An Order of Service for.

Order of Worship for the Evening, An. A form of evening service or vespers for use in the late afternoon or evening. It may be used as a complete rite instead of Evening Prayer, or as the introduction to Evening Prayer or another service, or as the prelude to an evening meal or other activity. It may also be used in private homes (BCP, p. 108). The historic roots of this service may be traced to the ritual blessing of light by Jews at the evening meal. This Jewish custom was continued in the ancient evening services of early Christians. This evening service included a blessing of light (*lucernarium*), a selection from the Psalter, and prayers. It could also include an *agapē* meal. Although this service continued in Eastern Orthodoxy, it disappeared in much of western Christianity as the monastic hours of prayer replaced the ancient congregational daily services (also known as cathedral offices). The 1979 BCP is the first Prayer Book to include this service.

At the opening of An Order of Worship for the Evening, the ministers enter a darkened church. The ministers may be preceded by one or two lighted candles. During Easter season, the Paschal candle is burning as the service begins. The officiant approaches the lighted Paschal candle and begins the service by its light. A short lesson of scripture may follow the opening acclamation. This lesson is optional. The officiant then says the Prayer for Light, using one of the forms in the rite or another suitable prayer. After the Prayer for Light, the altar candles are lighted, along with other candles and lamps. In Easter season, the candles are lighted from the Paschal candle. An appropriate anthem or psalm may be sung during the candle-lighting, or silence may be kept. The *BOS* provides a variety of anthems (*lucernaria*) for optional use at the candle-lighting. After the candle-lighting, there follows the singing of the *Phos hilaron*, or a metrical version of it, or another hymn. Incense may be used after the candle-lighting and while the *Phos hilaron* is sung (BCP, p. 143). The service may then continue with Evening Prayer, or the Holy Eucharist, or another office or devotion. The BCP directs that the Service of Light of this liturgy is to begin a Vigil of Pentecost (p. 227). In the *BOS*, this Service of Light is also used to begin a Vigil for Christmas Eve, a Service for New Year's Eve, a Vigil for the Eve of the Baptism of Our Lord, a Vigil for the Eve of All Saints' Day or the Sunday after All Saints' Day, a Service for All Hallows' Eve, and a Vigil on the Eve of Baptism. The Service of Light may also be used to introduce Advent and Christmas Festivals of Lessons and Music if these festivals take place in the evening. The service may be followed by a meal or other activity, with the *Phos hilaron* followed by the Lord's Prayer and a grace or blessing.

The service may also continue as a complete evening office. The *Phos hilaron* is then followed by a selection from the Psalter; a Bible reading which may be followed by a sermon or homily, a passage from Christian literature, or a brief silence; a canticle (which may be the *Magnificat*, the traditional evening canticle, or another canticle) or hymn of praise; prayers, including the Lord's Prayer and

possibly the collect of the day, or a collect proper to the season, or one of the prayers included in the rite, or one of the collects from Evening Prayer or Compline, or a litany; and a blessing or dismissal, or both. The Aaronic blessing in a threefold form (based on Nm 6:24–26) is provided in the rite as an option for the concluding blessing. A blessing over food may conclude the service when a meal is to follow.

Orders, Holy. *See* Order (2).

Ordinal, The. Since the sixteenth century the word "Ordinal" has been used in Anglicanism to refer to the texts of the rites for ordination. The 1549 BCP did not include the ordination rites. These were printed separately in 1550 with the title "The Form and Manner of Making and Consecrating of Archbishops, Bishops, Priests, and Deacons." These forms were printed in the BCP beginning with the 1552 revision. In medieval times an ordinal was a book that gave the *ordo* (ritual and rubrics) for liturgies.

Ordinand. One who is ordained at the ordination of a bishop, priest, or deacon.

Ordinary (of a diocese). A diocesan bishop, as distinct from a suffragan, assistant, or coadjutor bishop. The term apparently springs from the understanding of "ordinary jurisdiction" which is held in canon law to be the jurisdiction "permanently and irremovably annexed to" the office of bishop.

"Ordinary Time." This term is used in the Roman Catholic Church to indicate the parts of the liturgical year that are not included in the major seasons of the church calendar. Ordinary time includes the Monday after the Feast of the Baptism of our Lord through the Tuesday before Ash Wednesday, and the Monday after Pentecost through the Saturday before the First Sunday of Advent. A vigil or other service anticipating the First Sunday of Advent on the Saturday before that Sunday would also be included in the season of Advent. Ordinary time can be understood in terms of the living out of Christian faith and the meaning of Christ's resurrection in ordinary life. The term "ordinary time" is not used in the Prayer Book, but the season after Pentecost can be considered ordinary time. It may be referred to as the "green season," because green is the usual liturgical color for this period of the church year. The BCP provides numbered propers with collects and lectionary readings for the Sundays of the Season after Pentecost. The Epiphany season includes the Epiphany, the First Sunday after the Epiphany: the Baptism of our Lord Jesus Christ, and the Second Sunday through the Last Sunday after the Epiphany (BCP, p. 31). In view of the Epiphany themes that are presented throughout the Epiphany season, it should not be considered ordinary time. However, many parishes use green as the liturgical color for the Second Sunday through the Sunday prior to the Last Sunday after the Epiphany, and sometimes the Last Sunday after the Epiphany. Epiphany season and the season after Pentecost vary in length depending on the date of Easter (see BCP, pp. 884–885).

Ordination. A sacramental rite of the church by which God gives authority and the grace of the Holy Spirit through prayer and the laying on of hands by bishops to those being made bishops, priests, and deacons (BCP, pp. 860–861). The three distinct orders of bishops, priests, and deacons have been characteristic of Christ's holy catholic church. Bishops carry on the apostolic work of leading, supervising, and uniting the church. Presbyters (often known as priests) are associated with bishops in the ministry of church governance, along with the church's ministry of missionary and pastoral work, in preaching of the Word of God, and in the administration of the sacraments. Deacons assist bishops and priests in all of this work, and have special responsibility to minister in Christ's name to the poor, the sick, the suffering, and the helpless (BCP, p. 510). The BCP provides rites for the ordination of bishops (p. 512), priests (p. 525), and deacons (p. 537). The earliest known text of ordination rites is in the *Apostolic Tradition* of Hippolytus (c. 215). The 1549 BCP did not include ordination rites. "The Form and Manner of Making and Consecrating of Archbishops, Bishops, Priests, and Deacons" was published in 1550. Rites for ordination were included in many subsequent revisions of the Prayer Book. The Preface to the Ordination Rites of the Prayer Book notes that the church intends to maintain and continue the three orders of bishops, priests, and deacons. The ordination services are therefore appointed by the church. No person is to exercise the office of bishop, priest, or deacon unless he or she has been ordained. The manner of ordination in the Episcopal Church has been generally recognized by Christian people as suitable for conferring the sacred orders of bishop, priest, and deacon.

The services of ordination include a presentation of the ordinand to the ordaining bishop or bishops; the

ordinand's Declaration of Consent that states his or her belief in the scriptures and conformity to the doctrine, discipline, and worship of the Episcopal Church; the people's consent to the ordination and their promise to uphold the ordinand in the new ministry; the Litany for Ordinations (BCP, pp. 548–551); lessons and sermon; the examination of the candidate; the singing of the hymn "*Veni Creator Spiritus*" or "*Veni Sancte Spiritus*"; a period of silent prayer; the prayer of consecration and laying on of hands by the ordaining bishop or bishops; vesting of the newly ordained person according to the new order of ministry; and participation in the eucharist by the newly ordained person in ways that are appropriate to his or her order of ministry. At the ordination of a bishop, the Presiding Bishop and at least two other bishops lay their hands on the ordinand's head. At the ordination of a priest, the bishop is joined by priests in the laying on of hands. Only the bishop lays hands on the head of the ordinand at the ordination of a deacon. The bishop-elect leads the Creed at the ordination of a bishop after the Examination. The Creed precedes the Examination at the ordination of a priest or a deacon. The newly ordained bishop is the chief celebrant at the eucharist. The newly ordained priest joins in the celebration of the eucharist with the bishop and other presbyters. The newly ordained deacon may prepare the Lord's table and dismiss the people at the eucharist.

In the Episcopal Church the ordained ministry is normally seen as a life-long vocation. Careful selection, discernment, and preparation are required before ordination takes place. The canons call for theological instruction in the Holy Scriptures; church history, including the ecumenical movement; Christian theology; Christian ethics and moral theology; studies in contemporary society, including racial and minority groups; liturgics and church music; and theory and practice of ministry. The requirements and standards of learning may be modified in the ordination of local priests and deacons. The *BOS* provides a form for the Reaffirmation of Ordination Vows.

Ordination of Women. In 1976 the General Convention approved the ordination of women to the priesthood and the episcopate in the Episcopal Church and stated that such ordinations might begin on Jan. 1, 1977. Similar resolutions had been narrowly defeated at the 1970 and 1973 General Conventions. A 1967 General Convention resolution had opened the diaconate to women and recognized that women currently serving as deaconesses were members of the diaconate. On July 29, 1974, three bishops, claiming that "obedience to the Spirit" justified their action, ordained eleven women deacons to the priesthood. The ensuing controversy surrounding these irregular ordinations highlighted divisions evident in the church over this issue. After the 1976 vote, most dioceses accepted the ordination of women, and ordinations of women proceeded at a rapid rate. The 1997 General Convention revised the canons to prevent any diocese from denying access to the ordination process, or refusing to license a member of the clergy to officiate, solely on the grounds of gender. *See* Philadelphia Eleven, The.

Oregon, Diocese of. On Oct. 13, 1853, the General Convention created the Missionary District of Oregon and Washington Territory. On Oct. 15, 1880, the General Convention divided it into the Missionary District of Washington and the Missionary District of Oregon. The primary convention of the Diocese of Oregon met at Trinity Church, Portland, Sept. 11–13, 1889. The General Convention of 1907 divided the Diocese of Oregon and created the Missionary District of Eastern Oregon. The Diocese of Oregon includes the following counties: Benton, Clackamas, Clatsop, Columbia, Coos, Curry, Douglas, Jackson, Josephine, Lane, Lincoln, Linn, Marion, Multnomah, Polk, Tillamook, Washington, and Yamhill. On Jan. 23, 1929, the Diocesan Convention set apart St. Stephen's Church, Portland, as St. Stephen's Cathedral. On Nov. 10, 1973, St. Stephen's Cathedral became St. Stephen's Church. On that same day St. John the Baptist Church, Portland, became the Cathedral of St. John the Baptist.

Oregon and Washington, Missionary District of. The 1853 General Convention created the Missionary District of Oregon and Washington Territory. The 1880 General Convention divided this Missionary District into the Missionary District of Oregon and the Missionary District of Washington. *See* Oregon, Diocese of; *see* Olympia, Diocese of; *see* Spokane, Diocese of.

Oriental Churches. This term is used to refer to the pre-Chalcedonian or non-Chalcedonian Orthodox churches of the east who separated from the other Orthodox primarily because they did not accept the christological definition of the fourth ecumenical Council of Chalcedon (451) (BCP, p. 864). Following this council they came to be called "monophysite," because they held that Christ is of one nature (*mono-physis)* rather than two as stated by the

Council of Chalcedon. They believe that to say Christ has two natures, one divine and one human, is to compromise the unity of his person. However, they are willing to speak of a single nature that is both divine and human. They are therefore not monophysite in the classical, and heretical, sense which held that Christ was of a single divine nature. Most of them today dislike the name "monophysite," which they regard as pejorative. In Anglican terminology, they have been called the "Oriental (Orthodox) Churches" since the 1968 Lambeth Conference. In communion with one another and yet independent of each other, these churches include the Armenians, Syrians, Copts, and Ethiopians, as well as the Malankara Church in India. The Anglican tradition has enjoyed a long and friendly relationship with these churches and has not condemned them for their non-acceptance of Chalcedon (451). The head of the Coptic Church signed a statement of christological agreement with the Archbishop of Canterbury in 1987. There is an International Anglican-Oriental Orthodox Forum that has had several meetings. There is also an embryonic dialogue of the Episcopal Church with these churches in the U.S. In Roman Catholic usage, the term "Oriental Churches" is also sometimes applied to the Eastern Catholic churches, or "Uniates," which retain practices characteristic of the eastern churches but are united to the Roman Catholic Church.

Original Sin. The shared sinful condition of all humanity. This Christian doctrine is drawn from the Pauline writings, such as Rom 5:12–19 and 1 Cor 15:21–22, which suggest that humanity shares by nature in the fall of Adam described in Gn 3. Paul likewise urges that the consequences for humanity of Adam's fall are to be reversed through saving participation in Christ's victory over sin and death.

Original sin has been described as "hereditary sin." Augustine understood original sin to be transmitted through sexual intercourse leading to conception. This understanding contributed to negative attitudes concerning human sexuality on the part of some Christians.

Luther's understanding of original sin led him to emphasize humanity's utter dependence on God's grace and the need for faith. Calvinism came to emphasize humanity's total depravity relative to original sin. Although the consequences of original sin have not been emphasized as strongly in Anglicanism as in other Protestant traditions, Article IX of the Articles of Religion, "Of Original or Birth-Sin," states that "man is very far gone from original righteousness, and is of his own nature inclined to evil" (BCP, p. 869). Roman Catholics likewise identify the consequence of original sin as a fall from grace or a wounded human nature rather than a corrupt nature.

Original sin may be understood as humanity's innate self-centeredness. A consequence of this condition is human weakness and fallibility relative to sin. Another consequence is the influence of human sinfulness in our history and environment, to which we are subjected from birth. These influences all serve to restrict the actual freedom of moral choices, requiring us to look to God for hope and salvation.

Orison. A prayer, an address to God. The term is from the Latin, "oration."

Ornaments, Church. Items of symbolic or decorative value in church, such as an altar cross, a processional cross, and altar candles. There was considerable controversy in the Episcopal Church during the latter part of the nineteenth century concerning the use of church ornaments and other ritual or ceremonial practices such as genuflections and the use of incense. Canons on ritual were debated at the 1871 and 1874 General Conventions. James DeKoven was a delegate to the 1871 and 1874 General Conventions and a leading defender of ritualism. He argued that practices such as altar lights, genuflections, and the use of incense symbolize the real, spiritual presence of Christ. DeKoven believed that these practices do not symbolize the doctrine of transubstantiation, as feared by the opponents of ritualism. At the 1874 General Convention, DeKoven was an advocate for comprehensiveness and tolerance in worship. Although a canon on ritual was ultimately passed, it was seldom enforced. In many respects, DeKoven's comprehensive vision of worship was the view that prevailed in the Episcopal Church. Church ornaments such as altar crosses and altar candles are present in virtually all Episcopal churches. The Prayer Book form for the Dedication and Consecration of a Church includes a general prayer of dedication for ornaments or furnishings (BCP, p. 573). The *BOS* provides specific forms for the dedication of a variety of church furnishings and ornaments, including forms for a cross, candlesticks and lamps, a service book, pictures and statues, a vessel for incense, and any church ornament.

Ornaments Rubric, The. The common name for a rubric inserted in the 1559 BCP just before Morning Prayer: "And here is to be noted that the minister at the time of the communion, and at all other times in his ministration, shall use such ornaments in the church as were in use by authority of Parliament in the second year of the reign of King Edward the Sixth according to the Act of Parliament set in the beginning of this book." The only explicit directions about ornaments (furnishings, vessels, vestments, etc.) from the early reign of Edward are in the 1549 Prayer Book, but that book was enacted in the third rather than the second year of his reign, though the Act of Uniformity establishing the 1552 BCP spoke of the 1549 BCP as being from the second year of Edward's reign. There has therefore been great controversy as to whether the rubric was an attempt to restore the ornaments of the 1549 book or the ornaments of an earlier time. This rubric is still retained in the 1662 English book but has not been included in any American Prayer Book.

Orphrey. An ornamental band of contrasting material on a vestment or altar hanging.

Orthodox. The term has a broad application and also refers to a particular group of churches usually associated with Christendom in the east and distinct from the Roman Catholic Church. The word originates in the Greek, "correct glory" or "right belief." It is a way of indicating the appropriate or right side of a debate or issue in question. To be orthodox in a religious sense means acceptance of traditional and established statements of faith. The term came to be attached to churches in the eastern tradition who described themselves as "orthodox" or correct in belief, in distinction from other religious bodies—especially the western or Roman Catholic Church. *See* Orthodox Churches.

Orthodox and Anglican Fellowship. An organization for members of the Orthodox and Anglican churches in America who are interested in encouraging mutual understanding and friendly relations between their churches, and who seek to develop further mutual knowledge and fellowship between the Orthodox and Anglican churches. It sought to promote its purposes by holding meetings and conferences; the arrangement of special services, either Orthodox or Anglican, and the attendance of groups at regular services; the issuing of publications; and the provision of speakers before churches and other groups. The fellowship was instituted at Wellesley, Massachusetts, in Nov. 1934, and its constitution was adopted in New York City in May 1937. It was not listed in *The Episcopal Church Annual 1998.*

Orthodox Churches. The word "orthodox" means literally "correct glory" or "right belief." In the later fifth century, it first came to be applied to, and claimed by, those churches that held to the "correct doctrine" of the third and fourth ecumenical councils of Ephesus (431) and Chalcedon (451). Although they consider themselves to be really one church or communion, today the Orthodox exist in a great many independent national churches. These national churches include those of Constantinople, Alexandria, Antioch, Jerusalem, Russia, Serbia, Romania, Bulgaria, Georgia, Cyprus, Greece, Poland, Albania, and elsewhere. The Orthodox are sometimes called Eastern Orthodox because they are situated mainly in eastern Europe. They have also been called Greco-Russian because of the predominant cultural influences that shaped them. All these Orthodox churches accept the first seven ecumenical councils (unlike the Oriental Orthodox, or non-Chalcedonians, who accept only the first three). They all acknowledge the honorary primacy of the Patriarch of Constantinople as "first among equals" and their symbolic center. They all practice the veneration of icons. They all reject the primacy of the Pope and the use of *filioque* in the creed. The formal breach, or separation, of these churches with the Roman/Latin church of the west came in 1054. Since the fall of Constantinople to the Turks in 1453, the largest and most influential Orthodox church has been the Russian Orthodox Church. The Orthodox have had long and friendly relations with Anglicans. They participate in the international dialogue called the Anglican-Orthodox Joint Doctrinal Commission. Its counterpart in the United States is the Anglican-Orthodox Theological Consultation. Anglican-Orthodox relations in the United States date from 1862. Many Orthodox liturgical elements are used in the BCP, including eucharistic prayer "D" (p. 372) and the anthem "Give rest, O Christ, to your servant(s) with your saints" at the commendation in the Burial Office (p. 499). *See* Byzantine Rite; *see* Oriental Churches.

Osculatorium. See Peace, The.

Ostensorium. See Monstrance.

Otey, James Hervey (Jan. 27, 1800–Apr. 23, 1863). Bishop and educator. He was born in Liberty in Bedford County, Virginia. Otey graduated from the University of North Carolina in 1820 and then served there as a tutor for a year. In 1821 he became the principal of Harpeth Academy in Maury County, Tennessee. From 1823 until 1825, he was the principal of the Warrenton Academy, Warrenton, North Carolina. Otey studied for the ordained ministry under Bishop John Stark Ravenscroft of North Carolina. He was ordained deacon on Oct. 16, 1825, and priest on June 17, 1827. From 1827 until 1834, he was rector of St. Paul's Church, Franklin, Tennessee, and held services in Columbia and Nashville. He helped to organize the Diocese of Tennessee and was consecrated its first bishop on Jan. 14, 1834. He served in that position until his death. During his episcopate he served as Provisional Bishop of Mississippi and of Florida. He also served as Missionary Bishop of Arkansas, Louisiana, and the Indian Territory. Otey founded numerous schools in Tennessee. He was one of the founders of the University of the South and its first chancellor, serving from July 4, 1857, until his death. Otey's churchmanship was in the high church tradition of Bishop Ravenscroft. He stressed that the Episcopal Church was the American branch of the catholic church. He died in Memphis, Tennessee.

Outline of the Faith, An. *See* Catechism.

Oxford Movement, The. A nineteenth-century movement which reasserted the apostolic and catholic heritage of Anglicanism. The Oxford Movement is also known as the Catholic Revival. It emphasized the church's identity as the divine society and the sacramental character of the church's corporate life. It also sought to uphold the BCP as the rule of faith. It began when several priests of the Church of England, most notably Edward Pusey, John Henry Newman, and John Keble, became convinced that the Church of England had abandoned its heritage as a catholic and apostolic church. They feared that the Church of England was in danger of apostasy. The immediate beginning of the Oxford Movement was a sermon preached by Keble in 1833 in which he denied the authority of the British Parliament to abolish several dioceses in Ireland.

Keble, Pusey, Newman, and others began to publish a series known as *Tracts for the Times*, which called the Church of England to return to the ways of the ancient and undivided church in matters of doctrine, liturgy and devotion. The Tracts were a powerful and influential expression of the principles of the Oxford Movement, and the Oxford Movement has also been known as the Tractarian Movement. The writers of the Tracts and their supporters have been known as Tractarians. The Tracts were strongly opposed to the abuses which they saw in the Roman Catholic Church, but they were attacked as "papist" and rejected by many. However, many others were convinced by the Tracts, and the Oxford Movement became a major force in the Church of England. The leaders of the Oxford Movement taught that the Church of England and the larger Anglican Communion are part of the one, holy, catholic, and apostolic church. The last Tract was Newman's *Tract 90* (1841), which generally sought to interpret the Thirty-Nine Articles as consistent with the decrees of the Roman Catholic Council of Trent (1545–1563). This prompted considerable criticism and ended the publication of Tracts. The movement faced a crisis when Newman and others subsequently left the Church of England to become Roman Catholics. The Oxford Movement survived this crisis through the work of Pusey, Keble, Robert Wilberforce, and a second generation of priests, known as the ritualists, who worked among the poor in the large cities of Britain.

The Oxford Movement encouraged a recovery of the beauty of the church's worship in the external forms of liturgical ceremonies, vestments, and music. It led to a renewed appreciation for the church's catholic heritage and tradition, the importance of the apostolic ministry and the sacraments, the recovery of Anglican spiritual life, the revival of monastic life in the Anglican Communion, and appreciation for the ancient doctrines, discipline, and devotional practices of the church. It inspired the *Library of the Fathers*, which included English translations of patristic works. The first volume was Pusey's translation of Augustine's *Confessions* (1838), with a preface by Pusey on the significance of patristic study. The movement also led to the liberal catholic movement at the end of the nineteenth century.

In the United States, the Oxford Movement had considerable impact, although many of its theological principles had been earlier anticipated. Many Tractarian parishes were established throughout the United States, especially in the midwest where Nashotah House in Wisconsin was influential. As in England, the movement led to many controversies in the Episcopal Church. There was an investigation of the General Theological Seminary in New York. General Convention passed an anti-ritualist canon. James DeKoven was denied episcopal election, and a few people followed Newman to the Roman Catholic Church. But the controversies eventually quieted down in the United States as in England, and many of the principles of the Oxford Movement have become widely accepted in the Episcopal Church. *See* Tracts for the Times; *see* DeKoven, James.

Oxon. Pertaining or belonging to Oxford, England. (From *Oxoniensis*, a latinized form of the Middle English *Oxenford*). Usages include reference to degrees and diplomas conferred by the University of Oxford and the ecclesiastical, titular surname of the Bishop of the Diocese of Oxford in the Church of England.

P

Pacifism. The renunciation of the use of violent force that would take the life of another person. The early Christian community was of two minds whether a Christian could be a soldier. On the one hand, Jesus' positive appraisal of the faith of the centurion (Lk 7:9) and the acceptance of civil authority, specifically the military, in Romans (13:4) and in 1 Peter (2:14), served as warrant for the just use of force. This came to be developed as the just war theory. On the other hand, Jesus was believed to have rejected the use of force in his teaching. This was seen, for example, in Jesus' teaching to "turn the other cheek" (Lk 6:29; Mt 5:39). Jesus' opposition to the use of force was also seen in his life, in the rebuke of Peter's drawing of the sword (Jn 18:10–11), and in his willing acceptance of his own crucifixion. By the fourth century, with the spread of Christianity throughout the Roman Empire, the end of Christian persecution, and the establishment of Christianity as the state religion, pacifism was assumed largely by the monastic movements. The renunciation of force was believed to be a higher way of life. The Reformation gave rise to pacifist Anabaptist groups which have continued to the present. These include, most notably, the historic "peace churches"—Quakers, Mennonites, and Brethren. While Christian pacifism has historically been grounded in an absolute prohibition against the use of force, three other kinds of pacifism have developed: pragmatic, technological, and vocational. Pragmatic pacifists believe that non-violent suffering can bring about the end of violence. Technological pacifists believe that pacifism is required in opposing modern war because of the threat such war poses to all creation. Vocational pacifists believe that the renunciation of violence is not a universal obligation but a specific calling that bears witness to the larger ends of God. In Anglicanism, pacifism has generally been rejected except as vocational witness. *See* Episcopal Peace Fellowship, The (EPF).

Packard, Joseph (Dec. 23, 1812–May 3, 1902). Biblical scholar, seminary professor, and dean. He was born in Wiscasset, Maine. Packard graduated from Bowdoin College in 1831. He taught for several years and was head of Brattleboro Academy in Vermont. In 1833 he entered Andover Theological Seminary, and there decided to join the Episcopal Church. In 1834 Packard became professor of Hebrew and Latin at Bristol College. In 1836 he was chosen professor of sacred literature at the Virginia Theological Seminary, where he remained until his retirement in 1895. He was ordained deacon on July 17, 1836, and priest on Sept. 29, 1837. From 1874 until 1895 Packard was dean of Virginia Seminary. He was an evangelical. He had been influenced by Calvinism at Andover. Packard wrote "The Book of Malachi," which was published in J. P. Lange's *Commentary on the Holy Scriptures* (1874). He was a member of the American Committee for the revision of the English Version of the OT. Packard died in Alexandria, Virginia.

Page, Ann Randolph Meade (Dec. 3, 1781–Mar. 28, 1838). Anti-slavery advocate. She was born at "Chatham," Stafford County, Virginia, and was the sister of Bishop William Meade of Virginia. On Mar. 23, 1799, she married Matthew Page, a wealthy planter. He built a stately manor and named it "Annfield" in her honor. Matthew Page had about 200 slaves on a plantation of 2,000 acres, outside of Berryville, Virginia. Ann was raised in a Christian family. She had an evangelical faith combined with concern for the welfare of slaves. She believed that God had given her a sacred calling to be an emancipator, which she termed "this holy work." Her constant prayer was "O that slavery's curse might cease." She and her brother were supporters of the American Colonization Society, which transported freed slaves to Liberia. When her husband died in 1826, Ann worked almost ceaselessly for the emancipation of slaves and for the evangelization of Africa. She died at "Annfield."

Palanca. Prayers and sacrifices made on behalf of the participants at Cursillo, so that the entire weekend is permeated by prayer. The term is from the Spanish for "lever" or "leverage." Gifts are sent to the participants as visible expressions of the prayers and support that are offered. The hope is that the candidates will be touched by God in a special way on the weekend.

Pall. 1) A square, stiffened white linen cloth that is used to cover the chalice at the eucharist. There may be a design on the side of the pall that does not touch the chalice. 2) A cloth used to cover the coffin at the Burial of the Dead. The BCP states that the coffin is to be closed before the burial service. The coffin may be covered with a pall or other suitable covering (p. 468). The colors of white or gold, associated with Easter and resurrection, are especially appropriate for the pall.

Palm Sunday (The Sunday of the Passion). The Sunday before Easter at which Jesus' triumphal entry into Jerusalem (Mt 21:1–11, Mk 11:1–11a, Lk 19:29–40) and Jesus' Passion on the cross (Mt 26:36—27:66, Mk 14:32—15:47, Lk 22:39—23:56) are recalled. It is also known as the Sunday of the Passion. Palm Sunday is the first day of Holy Week. Red is the liturgical color for the day. The observance of Palm Sunday in Jerusalem was witnessed by the pilgrim Egeria in about 381–384. During this observance there was a procession of people down the Mount of Olives into Jerusalem. The people waved branches of palms or olive trees as they walked. They sang psalms, including Ps 118, and shouted the antiphon, "Blessed is he who comes in the name of the Lord!" The Palm Sunday observance was generally accepted throughout the church by the twelfth century. However, the day was identified in the 1549 BCP as simply "The Sunday next before Easter." The blessing of branches and the procession were not included. The 1928 BCP added the phrase "commonly called Palm Sunday" to the title of the day. A form for blessing palms was provided by the Book of Offices (1960). The 1979 BCP presents the full title for the day, "The Sunday of the Passion: Palm Sunday" (BCP, p. 270). The liturgy of the palms is the entrance rite for the service. The congregation may gather at a place apart from the church and process to the church after the blessing of the branches of palm or other trees (BCP, p. 270). The liturgy of the palms includes a reading of one of the gospel accounts of Jesus' entrance into Jerusalem. The branches may be distributed to the people before the service or after the prayer of blessing. All the people hold branches in their hands during the procession. Appropriate hymns, psalms, or anthems are sung. The Prayer Book notes that the hymn "All glory, laud, and honor" (Hymns 154–155) and Ps 118:19–29 may be used (BCP, p. 271). *The Hymnal 1982* also provides "Ride on! ride on in majesty!" (Hymn 156) and "Hosanna in the highest" (Hymn 157) for the procession at the liturgy of the palms. *The Hymnal*

1982 provides musical settings for the opening anthem, the blessing over the branches, and the bidding for the procession (Hymn 153). The procession may halt for a station at an appropriate place such as the church door. The BCP provides a stational collect which may be used (p. 272). The palm liturgy may be led by a deacon or lay reader if a bishop or priest is unavailable.

When the service includes the eucharist, the liturgy of the palms is followed by the salutation and the collect of the day. The service changes focus abruptly from the triumphal entry into Jerusalem to the solemnity of the Passion. In the 1979 BCP, the Passion gospel is drawn from one of the three synoptic accounts of the Passion, one of which is appointed for each of the three years in the eucharistic lectionary. The Passion gospel is announced simply, "The Passion of our Lord Jesus Christ according to _____." The customary responses before and after the gospel are omitted (BCP, p. 272). The Passion gospel may be read or chanted by lay persons. Specific roles may be assigned to different persons, with the congregation taking the part of the crowd (BCP, p. 273). It is customary to observe a brief time of silence when the moment of Jesus' death is described by the narrator. *The Hymnal 1982* provides a variety of hymns concerning the Passion, including "Sing, my tongue, the glorious battle" (Hymns 165–166), "O sacred head, sore wounded" (Hymns 168–169), and "Were you there when they crucified my Lord?" (Hymn 172).

Panagia or *panaghia* or *panhagia*. A Greek term meaning "all holy one." It is a title of the Virgin Mary in the eastern church. The term also refers to a small folding case with an image of the Virgin Mary that is worn by prelates in the eastern church. This case is worn on the breast suspended by a chain. The term also refers to bread which is solemnly blessed by Greek monks in honor of the Virgin Mary and the Trinity. It is eaten during morning meal prayers.

Pan-Anglican. This journal was published from Lent 1950 until 1970. It was published irregularly in fifteen volumes over twenty years. The normal rate of publication was two issues per year. The subtitle was "A Review of the World-Wide Episcopal Church." The editor was the Rt. Rev. Walter H. Gray, Bishop of Connecticut, 1951–1969.

Pan-Anglican Congress. This congress met at London, June 15–24, 1908, to discuss a variety of issues facing the church. An average of 17,000 persons attended each day.

While the congress had no legislative authority, its reports were published by the Society for Promoting Christian Knowledge (SPCK) in eight volumes. Most dioceses of the United States were represented.

Panama, Diocese of. The House of Bishops placed the Canal Zone under the jurisdiction of the Presiding Bishop on Oct. 17, 1904. The 1919 General Convention established the Missionary District of the Panama Canal Zone and elected James Craik Morris (1867–1944) the missionary bishop. This missionary district included the Canal Zone, and the Republics of Panama, Colombia, Costa Rica, and Nicaragua. In 1956 the House of Bishops created the Missionary District of Central America. The House of Bishops determined that the Missionary District of Panama and the Canal Zone would include the Canal Zone and the Republics of Panama and Colombia. In 1963 the House of Bishops detached the Republic of Colombia from the Missionary District of the Panama Canal Zone. It became a missionary diocese in 1971. In 1981 it was called the Missionary Diocese of Panama. In 1985 it became the Diocese of Panama.

Pange Lingua. Title for two well known Latin chant hymns, Venantius Fortunatus's passiontide hymn, "Sing my tongue the glorious battle" (Hymns 165, 166), and the *Corpus Christi* (now eucharistic) hymn, "Now, my tongue, the mystery telling" (Hymns 329–331), attributed to Thomas Aquinas. Fortunatus's hymn was written in the sixth century. It is considered to be the most famous of the passiontide hymns, and it has been used in the Good Friday ceremony for veneration of the cross since the ninth century. The BCP calls for use of this hymn, or another hymn extolling the glory of the cross, near the end of the Good Friday service (p. 282). "Now, my tongue, the mystery telling" was derived from Fortunatus's hymn in the thirteenth century. It was used with the same melody as its model. It was traditionally sung on Maundy Thursday and the feast of *Corpus Christi. The Hymnal 1982* includes it in the section of hymns for the Holy Eucharist. The fifth and sixth verses of this hymn, known as the *Tantum Ergo*, are traditionally sung at Benediction of the Blessed Sacrament. The *Tantum Ergo*, which begins "Therefore we, before him bending," is printed separately in *The Hymnal 1982* as Hymn 330.

Pantheism. Belief that God is all creation and that all creation is God. From the Greek *pan*, "all," and *theos*, "god." Pantheism is inconsistent with orthodox Christianity because it ignores God's transcendence and God's distinctness from creation. This extreme identification of creator with creation emphasizes the universal immanence of God. In some forms of pantheism, God is seen to be identical with nature and contained entirely by nature. Christianity affirms that God is both immanent and transcendent relative to creation.

Papal Infallibility. *See* Infallibility, Papal.

Parable. The term is from the Greek for "something placed by the side of something else." NT parables are sayings of Jesus in which he uses metaphors or similes, brief or extended, to challenge people to a decision about his message. The parables of Jesus are "word events" in which the Kingdom of God breaks through in power. Parables may be understood as elaborated comparisons. For example, the Gospel of Matthew (20:1–16) records Jesus' parable that likens the kingdom of heaven to a householder who hired workers for his vineyard at different hours in the day, and then paid all the workers the full day's wage that he promised to the workers who were hired in the early morning.

Paraclete, Community of the. A religious order for men and women, ordained and lay, single and married. When it was first organized, it was named the Company of the Paraclete. They are also known as Paracletians. It was founded in 1971, in Philadelphia, Pennsylvania, by two Episcopal priests, Robert H. Harvey and José Edwardo Chiovarou. It is now located at St. Stephen's Priory, Seattle, Washington. Its purpose is to help bring healing by being present to those broken in body, mind, and spirit. The community reorganized itself in 1991 and changed its name to the Order of the Community of the Paraclete.

Paraclete, Company of the. *See* Paraclete, Community of the.

Paraeschatology. The study of what happens between death and the ultimate state of a person.

Paraments. Cloth or tapestry hangings used to adorn the space for worship, especially those hangings at the altar, pulpit, and lectern. The term is derived from the Latin, "to decorate" or "prepare."

Parents of the Blessed Virgin Mary, The. *See* Anne and Joachim.

Parish. The term is used in the 1979 BCP and earlier editions, and means a self-supporting congregation under a rector, as opposed to a mission or other congregation under a vicar. Some state laws provide for the incorporation of Episcopal parishes, and the election of rectors, wardens, and vestry members. Many diocesan canons distinguish between a fully self-supporting congregation with a full-time priest and one which is not, calling the former "parishes" and the latter "missions." However, other Episcopal dioceses call all congregations "parishes," or simply "congregations." In English canon law, a parish is an area under the spiritual care of a priest. The term is used without any specific definition other than a "Congregation of this Church" in the canons of the Episcopal Church.

Parish House. A church building or house that may provide space for the parish office, clergy and staff offices, classrooms, choir rehearsal room, and meeting rooms. It may also include a chapel, a nursery, a kitchen, a library, or storage space. The parish house is typically a separate building from the church that is near the church.

Parish Life Conference. During the 1950s the national church staff responsible for Christian education sought to work with groups and parishes so that the entire community could become a learning environment. The church led group life laboratories between 1953 and 1959 and also designed conferences with special emphasis on the parish. These conferences were for the laity and were known as "Parish Life Conferences." Their intent was to provide nurture through worship and through the ongoing life of the congregation. They were first known as "intensive weekend conferences." They were held widely throughout the church. An alternative was also developed, "Parish Life Missions," which were held on successive evenings for those laity who could not participate in a weekend conference.

Parish Meeting. A meeting of the members of a parish. The by-laws of the parish generally require an annual parish meeting and state the qualifications to be a voting member of the parish. Diocesan canons may state requirements concerning parish meetings. The annual parish meeting typically elects vestry members, and it may elect vestry officers. Delegates to diocesan convention and representatives to other diocesan, deanery, or parish entities may also be elected by the parish meeting. The budget of the parish may be presented and approved. The rector, vestry officers, music director, Christian education director, and other parish or program leaders may make presentations at the annual parish meeting. The parish by-laws may allow the rector or a majority of the vestry to call a special parish meeting at any time. The by-laws may specify the requirements for a special parish meeting, including the requirements for notice to the members of the parish.

Parish Nurse. A registered nurse (RN) who provides health care in a pastoral setting. The program was founded in 1983 by the Rev. Granger Westberg, a Lutheran pastor and chaplain at Lutheran General Hospital, Park Ridge, Illinois. It has now spread to many denominations, including the Episcopal Church. Parish nurses seek to provide care and promote wellness for the whole person, taking into account both the physical and spiritual needs of the patient. They recognize that illnesses and symptoms may result from adverse circumstances in the patient's life. They identify and assess the health needs of people in a parish or other setting of pastoral ministry and seek to enhance wholeness of body, mind, and spirit. Parish nurses often provide blood pressure screenings. They may be available for office hours to consult concerning health problems and possibilities for healthier living. Parish nurses provide information and advice for better health. They may visit people who are homebound or hospitalized, and serve as advocates in the parish for the needs of those who are sick or elderly.

Parish Profile. An instrument that provides important information concerning a parish, including information about the parish's services and programs, budget, parish life and goals, and previous clergy. The standardized form that is typically used for parish profiles is provided by the Church Deployment Office of the Episcopal Church Center. The preparation of the parish profile may be part of the congregation's work to clarify goals and needs in beginning the search process for a member of the clergy. The work of preparing the parish profile may involve parish meetings, small group discussions, questionnaires answered by parishioners, the leadership of the vestry and wardens, and possibly the help of a facilitator who guides the congregation through the process. The completed parish profile is made available to clergy who may be interested in a call to a position in the parish. The parish profile may be matched with personal profiles of clergy to identify potential candidates for a vacant position.

Parish Register. The formal record of the various official acts in a parish church. Canon 15 of the Constitution and Canons of 1789 required every minister of the church to keep a register of baptisms, marriages, and funerals within his cure. The Canon Law of the Church of England also required that the clergy keep a register of baptisms, confirmations, marriages, and burials. These records from the colonial period are a primary source of historical and demographic data for the early days of this country. Other data to be kept in the parish register are a list of all baptized members, a list of all communicants, a list of all confirmands, a list of all persons who have died in the last year, and a list of those persons who have been received, and all who have been removed by letter of transfer. There should also be a list of those whose domicile is unknown and those who are inactive but whose domicile is known.

Parker, Matthew (Aug. 6, 1504–May 17, 1575). The first Archbishop of Canterbury under Queen Elizabeth. Parker was responsible for enacting and enforcing the Elizabethan Settlement. He studied at St. Mary's Hostel, Cambridge University. He received his B.A. in 1527, his M.A. in 1528, his B.D. in 1535, and his D.D. in 1537, all from Corpus Christi College, Cambridge University. He was ordained deacon on Apr. 20, 1527, and priest on June 15, 1527. While at Cambridge he belonged to a group called the "Cambridge Reformers," who helped to bring the Reformation to England. At first Parker was attracted to the teachings of Martin Luther, but then moved away from Luther as he studied more deeply the patristic literature. He supported the publication of *The Institute of a Christian Man* (1537), known as the *Bishops' Book*, which was a commentary on the Ten Articles. The Ten Articles were Henry VIII's greatest concessions to the Protestants. Martin Bucer, the reformer at Strasburg, was regius professor of divinity at Cambridge, 1549–1551, and had a great influence on Parker. Bucer represented a moderating position between Ulrich Zwingli and Martin Luther.

Parker was chaplain to Anne Boleyn, 1535–1536. He served as dean of the College of St. John the Baptist, Stoke-by-Clare, Suffolk, 1535–1547. He was rector of Ashen (Ashdon), 1542–1544. Parker was master and vice-chancellor, Corpus Christi College, 1544–1552. He was dean of Lincoln Cathedral, 1552–1553.

On Dec. 17, 1559, Parker was consecrated Archbishop of Canterbury and served in that position until his death. His primacy was one of the most important in the history of the English Church. He had to work between the extremes of the Marian party, which wanted to restore the Church of England to Roman obedience and medieval theology, and the extreme reforming party, at first called "precisianists," and then Puritans, who wanted aggressive reforms in the Church of England with regard to ceremonial and theology. Parker's great success was to steer the Church of England between these two extremes, and it has been suggested that he originated the *via media*, which is the primary characteristic of Anglicanism. He was evangelical but conservative, and catholic but reformed. He applied the broad principles of the Reformation to the Church of England without betraying the catholicity of the church.

Under Parker's leadership, the "42 Articles" were revised and issued in 1563, and published in 1571 as the "39 Articles." He supervised the translation of the "Bishops' Bible," which was published in 1568, and which superseded Tyndale's translation and the "Geneva Bible" of 1560. It remained the official English version until the publication of the Authorized Version in 1611. Parker died in London.

Parochial. Concerning a parish. For example, parochial clergy serve in parishes.

Parochial Mission. A mission that is supported by a parish. The supporting parish may provide the aided congregation with staff and program assistance in addition to financial support.

Parochial Report (Annual Report). This report is the official data-gathering instrument of the Episcopal Church. Each parish or congregation files this report annually with the diocesan bishop. A copy of each Parochial Report is sent to the Executive Council of the Episcopal Church. The Parochial Report includes information concerning the number of baptisms, confirmations, marriages, and burials during the preceding calendar year; the total number of adult baptized members, baptized members under sixteen years of age, and total number of baptized members; and the total number of confirmed adult communicants in good standing, the total number of confirmed communicants in good standing under sixteen years of age, and the total

number of confirmed communicants in good standing. The Parochial Report also provides a summary of all the receipts and expenditures of the parish; a statement of all real or personal property held by the parish, with an appraisal of its value; a statement of the parish's indebtedness, if any; and a statement of the amount of insurance carried. Preparation and delivery of the Parochial Report is the joint duty of the rector and vestry of the parish. In other congregations, preparation and delivery of the report is the duty of the member of the clergy-in-charge. The Parochial Report provides important information for the use of parishes, dioceses, and the whole Episcopal Church.

Parousia. A Greek word meaning "presence" or "arrival," *parousia* is often translated as "second coming." It is part of the area of theology called eschatology, the study of the last things or ultimate end of creation. The *parousia* is understood as the completion of God's gift of salvation, which will not take place until Jesus' return to earth. Jesus' *parousia* or second coming refers to his return to earth at a future time when he will act as judge. Jesus' second coming is the completion of history, when evil will cease to exist and God's purposes for creation will be fulfilled. The *parousia* is also related to the "new age" which Jesus' return will initiate or bring to its highest level.

Parson. The member of the clergy, typically a priest or presbyter, with pastoral responsibility for a parish. In medieval times, the rector of a parish was the parson, or legal "person" who held the legal property rights of the parish. The rector could sue and be sued as the parson of the parish. The term is from the Latin *persona*. It may now be used to indicate any member of the clergy.

Parsons, Edward Lambe (May 18, 1868–July 19, 1960). Bishop and liturgist. He was born in New York City. Parsons received his B.A. in 1889 from Yale, and graduated from Union Theological Seminary, New York, in 1892. In 1892–1893, he was a fellow at the University of Berlin. He graduated from Episcopal Theological School in 1894. Parsons was ordained deacon on Dec. 23, 1894, and priest on June 9, 1895. He was assistant at Grace Church, New York, 1894–1895, and rector of three churches in California: Trinity Church, Menlo Park, 1896–1900; St. Matthew's Church, San Mateo, 1900–1904; and St. Mark's Church, Berkeley, 1904–1919. On Nov. 5, 1919, Parsons was consecrated Bishop Coadjutor of California. On June 5,

1924, he became the third Bishop of the diocese. He retired on Dec. 31, 1940. During many of his years in California, Parsons was lecturer in liturgics at the Church Divinity School of the Pacific. He served on the Standing Liturgical Commission from 1930 until 1946. Parsons was a member of numerous ecumenical, welfare, and social service agencies. He published a number of books, articles and sermons. One of his most significant books is *The American Prayer Book: Its Origins and Principles* (1937), which he wrote with Bayard Hale Jones. Parsons followed the tradition of Phillips Brooks and the liberal evangelicals, who stressed the critical study of the scriptures and a personal relationship with Jesus Christ. Parsons died in San Francisco. *See* Jones, Bayard Hale.

Partners in Mission. A process of international consultation was first devised by the Anglican Consultative Council in 1973 and 1976 and by the Lambeth Conference of 1978. The purpose of the consultation is to examine the mission and health of a particular Anglican province in dialogue with representatives of other provinces of the Anglican Communion and of other Christian churches and communions. It is recommended that each autonomous province of the Anglican Communion have a Partners in Mission consultation each three to five years.

Pasch. This term for Easter is from the Latin and Greek *Pascha*, which transliterated the Hebrew *pesach*, "Passover." It was used both for the Jewish Passover and the Christian Easter. The Latin *Pascha* is sometimes used in English to distinguish the full celebration of the passion and resurrection of Christ in the early church from the separate celebrations of Good Friday and Easter. The adjective *paschal* is regularly used to mean pertaining to Easter, as in Paschal candle.

***Pascha nostrum* (Christ our Passover).** The term literally means "our passover" in Latin. It has two distinguishable meanings in the BCP. 1) Canticle based on 1 Cor 5:7–8, Rom 6:9–11, and 1 Cor 15:20–22. It is used as an invitatory anthem in Easter Week at Morning Prayer. It may be used daily in the Easter season until Pentecost (BCP, pp. 46, 83). This canticle is one of three that may be chosen as the song of praise to begin the eucharist at the Easter Vigil (BCP, p. 294). It is also one of three that may be chosen as the canticle that is sung or said in the Burial Office as the body is borne from the church at the end of the commendation (BCP, p. 500). It is an appropriate choice for use as the song of praise at the beginning of the eucharist during the Easter season (BCP, p. 356). This canticle was the initial song of praise in the Anglican rite for Easter Day in the 1549 BCP. Musical settings of this canticle are found in *The Hymnal 1982* at S 16–S 20, S 46–S 50. 2) Fraction anthem based on 1 Cor 5:7–8. This anthem may be sung or said as the bread is broken for distribution and chalices are filled with wine. It may be sung or said as a versicle and response. Its use is optional. The Alleluias are omitted during Lent, and may be omitted at other times except during the Easter season (BCP, p. 364). Musical settings of this fraction anthem are found in *The Hymnal 1982* at S 151–S 156.

Paschal Candle. A large candle that symbolizes the risen Christ. It is often decorated with a cross, symbols of the resurrection, the Greek letters Alpha and Omega, and the year. The term "Paschal" concerns Easter or Passover. At the Easter Vigil, the Paschal candle is lit from the new fire. It is carried by the deacon, who pauses three times and sings or says, "The light of Christ," and the people respond, "Thanks be to God." The Paschal candle is carried by the celebrant if there is no deacon. After it is carried to the chancel, its flame may be used to light candles held by members of the congregation. This symbolizes the spreading of the light of Christ into the congregation and the world. The *Exsultet* is sung or said after the Paschal candle is placed in its stand. It is customary for the Paschal candle to burn at all services from Easter through Pentecost (BCP, pp. 285–287).

After the Easter season, the Paschal candle is typically placed near the font. It should burn at baptisms, representing the new life in Christ that we share in baptism. The newly baptized person may be given a small baptismal candle that is lit from the Paschal candle. It may also be carried in procession at burials and placed near the coffin as a symbol of resurrection life.

Paschal Mystery. In this context, the word "mystery" means a transcendent purpose of God. It exceeds human understanding, but we have some knowledge and experience of it. Paschal means pertaining to Easter (the Pascha) and to its antecedent the Hebrew Passover. The Passover has the promise of redemption and the gift of freedom at the Red Sea. In the NT, the Paschal concept includes Jesus' death and resurrection, the ascension and gift of the Holy Spirit, baptism, the calling of a new people from every nation and language, and participation in the mystery through eating and drinking with our Risen Lord. The creation enhances our sense of the Paschal Mystery with the gift of light (including the Paschal full moon), with the beauty and wonder of nature, and our own creation in God's image (and in the northern hemisphere, the arrival of Spring). These meanings are drawn together in the Great Vigil of Easter, the most comprehensive and dramatic liturgy of the church (BCP, pp. 284–295). Baptism and Eucharist, and the other rites of the church, celebrate the Paschal Mystery more briefly in all times and seasons.

Passion. The redemptive suffering of Jesus Christ in the events surrounding his death. The term is from the Latin *passio*, "suffering." A gospel narrative of the Passion is called the Passion. It may also be called the Passion gospel or the Passion narrative. It is read liturgically during Holy Week. The accounts of Matthew, Mark, or Luke are read on the Sunday of the Passion, also called Palm Sunday (BCP, p. 273), in different years of the three-year eucharistic lectionary. St. John's Passion is read every year on Good Friday (BCP, p. 277). The narratives are often read dramatically with different readers taking the parts of various participants.

Passion Gospel, Passion Narrative. *See* Passion.

Passion Sunday. *See* Palm Sunday (The Sunday of the Passion).

Passover. A Jewish festival of eight days that celebrates the events leading to the Jewish Exodus from Egypt. According to the accounts of the Book of Exodus, a lamb was sacrificed by each household. Its blood was sprinkled on the lintel and door posts so that the Lord would pass over houses which bore these markings when the first-born in Egypt were slain. Jewish families customarily celebrate a meal on the first night of Passover. There exists a relationship between the origins of this meal and the eucharist, which was instituted during the period of the Passover celebration. The celebration of Easter continues to be dated by the Passover feast. Both are tied to a lunar calendar which has agricultural connotations. Some scholars believe that there is a linkage between the spring agricultural festivals and the Passover. *See* Easter Vigil.

Pastor, Pastoral Ministry. The word "pastor" derives from the work of tending sheep: a pastor is one who cares for

sheep. The term came into the Christian understanding of the ordained ministry because of the frequent references in Holy Scripture to God as a shepherd of the people of Israel and Jesus as the Good Shepherd. A priest is a pastor for his or her congregation in the sense that he or she cares for the people, protects them and directs them, and feeds them with spiritual food in the Holy Eucharist. Similarly, a bishop is a chief pastor because she or he has oversight of all those pastors who care for the people committed to their care. There are certain ambiguities in the term now that the church is much less agrarian and rural than in previous times. But the term "pastor" and the related work of pastoral ministry are deeply important for the Christian tradition of ordained ministry.

The work of pastoral care has always been deeply important in Anglicanism. It has been seen as the first work of the parish priest and of the bishop in a diocese. There have been times when pastoral care has been neglected on a wide scale. Those times have in turn provoked a demand among Christian people for a revival of pastoral care, as in the Wesleyan and evangelical revivals of the eighteenth century and the catholic revival of the nineteenth century. Each of those revivals has resulted from a sense that the church and the ordained ministry of the church have the care of God's people as their first responsibility, even while the form of that care may vary in time and place.

In the church today pastoral care takes many different forms. For example, spiritual direction and pastoral counseling are both specialized forms of pastoral care that require specific training and responsibility. In the Episcopal Church there is great interest in enhancing the pastoral work of the bishops of the church for both the clergy and lay people of their dioceses. There is also great interest in developing the ministry of the laity for pastoral care.

Pastoral Care. The ministry of caring at the heart of the church's life. It may include hospital visitation, counseling, and ministries of shared presence, listening, and support. Pastoral care can refer to the ministries of hospital chaplains, pastoral counselors and therapists, social workers, and other professionals who serve in the name of the church. It also includes parish ministries of clergy and laity who respond to human need.

Pastoral Leader. A lay person licensed under special circumstances to exercise pastoral or administrative responsibility in a congregation. A pastoral leader may be licensed to lead regularly the offices authorized by the Prayer Book. This ministry is licensed under the provisions of the canon for licensed lay persons. A pastoral leader must be a confirmed adult communicant in good standing. Guidelines for training and selection of pastoral leaders are established by the bishop. A pastoral leader is to be trained, examined, and found competent in the Holy Scriptures, the BCP and *Hymnal*, the conduct of public worship, use of the voice, church history, the church's doctrine as set forth in the Creeds and An Outline of the Faith (the Catechism) (BCP, pp. 845–862), parish administration, appropriate canons, and pastoral care. A pastoral leader is not to be licensed if the bishop or ecclesiastical authority determines that the congregation is able and has had reasonable opportunity to secure a resident clergy person in charge. A pastoral leader may be commissioned for this ministry with a form adapted from the Commissioning for Lay Ministries in the Church of the *BOS*.

Pastoral Letter. From the Latin *littera pastoral*, the original definition was an official letter addressed by a bishop to all members of the diocese. Pastoral letters may be issued in the Episcopal Church by the Presiding Bishop, the House of Bishops, or any diocesan bishop. The canons require that pastoral letters of the House of Bishops and diocesan bishops be read or otherwise distributed to the people. While the canons do not define a pastoral letter, one issued by a diocesan bishop is to address "points of Christian doctrine, worship, or manners."

Pastoral Offices. Prayer Book services that are done on an occasional basis according to pastoral need at significant moments in the lives of church members. The pastoral offices are also known as occasional offices. These services include the sacramental rites of Confirmation, Holy Matrimony, Reconciliation of a Penitent, and Unction. These sacramental rites are means of grace, but "they are not necessary for all persons in the same way that Baptism and the Eucharist are" (BCP, p. 860). The pastoral offices of the BCP also include forms for Commitment to Christian Service, Thanksgiving for the Birth or Adoption of a Child, Ministration at the Time of Death, and the Burial of the Dead. Baptism is not presented as an occasional or pastoral office in the 1979 BCP. The BCP calls for baptism to be done in the context of the regular worship of the church, within the Holy Eucharist as the chief service on a Sunday or other feast (p. 298).

Pastoral Staff. *See* Crozier, or Crosier.

Paten. A shallow dish or small plate for the bread at the eucharist. The bread is placed on the paten for consecration and distribution. It typically matches the chalice. The paten should be large enough to hold all the wafers or pieces of bread that will be distributed at communion.

Pater Noster. *See* Lord's Prayer, The.

Patrick (c. 390–c. 460). Bishop and missionary of Ireland. He was born into a Christian family somewhere on the northwest coast of Britain. Patrick was the son of a local town councilman and deacon of the church. When Patrick was about sixteen, he was captured by Irish pirates and forced to serve as a slave for six years. Patrick either escaped or was freed. He eventually returned to Britain. He was ordained deacon, priest, and bishop. Around 435, he returned to Ireland. The exaggerated popular view of Patrick maintains that he converted the whole country by himself. As a missionary bishop, Patrick established his see at Armagh. He promoted monasticism, established schools, and evangelized some of the people. His major writing is an autobiographical *Confession*. "St. Patrick's Breastplate," Hymn 370 in *The Hymnal 1982*, is attributed to Patrick. Patrick is commemorated in the Episcopal calendar of the church year on Mar. 17. *See* Breastplate of St. Patrick.

Patripassianism. From the Latin *pater*, "father," and *passio*, "suffering," it is a form of modalism chiefly associated with a third-century Roman Christian teacher, Praxeas, whose work is known to us chiefly through Tertullian's treatise, *Against Praxeas*. Praxeas regarded Word and Spirit as mere names or modes of being of the one God. Praxeas held that the Father himself was born of Mary, crucified and raised from the dead. Tertullian jibed, "He put to flight the Paraclete, and he crucified the Father" (*Against Praxeas* 1). This form of modalism has been named *patripassianism*. *Patripassianism* is excluded from orthodox Christian teaching by the doctrine of the Trinity and the traditional teaching of God's impassibility (see Art. I, Articles of Religion, BCP, p. 867). Nevertheless, the question of the suffering of God is of continuing interest in modern theology. Unless God can *somehow* be said to suffer, God is remote and imperfectly shares the human situation.

Patristics. The term is from the Latin and Greek for "father." It is the study of the lives and writings of the "Fathers" of the first centuries of the church. It now usually includes the study of the contributions of the "Mothers" of this period as well, when their history and works can be discovered. The patristic age is described as including the first five to eight centuries of the church. It was the time of the great debates concerning the church's faith and theology, including the christological and trinitarian controversies. Patristic sources provide the basis for the fundamental orthodoxy of Christian belief. The patristic period was the time of many of the great Doctors of the Church, who have been recognized for their theological significance and personal holiness. These Doctors of the Church in the patristic age included Basil the Great, Gregory of Nazianzus, John Chrysostom, and Athanasius in the east; and Ambrose, Augustine, Jerome, and Gregory the Great in the west. Traditional Anglican reverence for the patristic age was renewed by the Oxford Movement in the nineteenth century. John Keble, John Henry Newman, and Edward Pusey began work on the *Library of the Fathers* in 1836. This was a series of English translations of selected patristic sources. The first volume in this series was the *Confessions of St. Augustine*, edited by Pusey, and published in 1838. The catechumenate in the Episcopal Church reflects the use of patristic sources for traditions of Christian formation and preparation for baptism.

Patronal Feast. The feast of the patron saint or title of a church, school, religious order, or other organization. The custom of having a patron saint can be traced to the practice of building churches over the tombs of martyrs. Patron saints may be chosen for a variety of reasons. For example, a church that was founded on a saint's day might have that saint as patron. Some patron saints are associated with particular countries, regional or ethnic backgrounds, or forms of ministry. St. David is the patron saint of Wales, and St. Luke is the patron saint of physicians. The patronal festival is usually the feast of the church or organization's title, but in some cases the patron is not mentioned in the title of the church or organization. The feast of a church's patron or title may be observed on or transferred to a Sunday, taking precedence over the usual Sunday observance in the calendar of the church year. This substitution may not be made in the seasons of Advent, Lent, or Easter (BCP, p. 16). The proper readings for a patronal feast may be used at the Consecration of a Church (BCP, p. 571).

Patteson, John Coleridge (Apr. 1, 1827–Sept. 21, 1871). Bishop and martyr. Born in London, Patteson graduated from Balliol College, Oxford, in 1849, and in 1852 became a fellow at Merton College. He was ordained deacon on Sept. 14, 1853, and priest on Sept. 24, 1854. After a brief ministry at Alfington, Devonshire, he was persuaded by George Augustus Selwyn, Church of England Bishop of New Zealand, to go to Melanesia as a missionary. Patteson's missionary work in Melanesia was very successful. On Feb. 24, 1861, he was consecrated the first Missionary Bishop of the Church of England in Melanesia. On Sept. 21, 1871, on a visit to the island of Nukapu, he and several of his companions were speared to death. Patteson and his companion martyrs are commemorated in the Episcopal calendar of the church year on Sept. 20.

Paul, Saint (d. c. 64). Apostle to the Gentiles, author of several NT epistles, preeminent Christian missionary. He was originally named Saul. He was a Jew of the Diaspora, a member of the tribe of Benjamin, and a native of Tarsus in Cilicia. He spoke and wrote in Greek. Saul held Roman citizenship from birth, and his trade was tent-making. He was trained in rhetoric and educated in Jerusalem at the feet of Gamaliel, a Pharisaic member of the Jewish Sanhedrin (Acts 22:3).

Saul was a zealous Pharisee and a persecutor of the Christian church (Gal 1:13, 1 Cor 15:9, Phil 3:6). He was present and approving when Stephen was martyred (Acts 7:58). After Stephen's death, Saul "ravaged" the church, dragging off men and women whom he committed to prison (Acts 8:3). He went to Damascus with authority from the Sanhedrin to persecute the Christian church, but he was converted to Christ on the way (Acts 9:1–22). His conversion has been dated at about 34 A.D. A light from heaven flashed around Saul and he heard the voice of Jesus asking "Why do you persecute me?" He subsequently recalled that Jesus had appeared to him (1 Cor 9:1, 15:8), and he viewed this experience as authority for his apostolic ministry (Gal 1:15–17). Saul was without sight for a time after this vision, and he was led to Damascus by those who were with him. The disciple Ananias was directed by a vision to baptize him. Ananias was reluctant to baptize Saul, but the Lord told him that he had chosen Saul to bring his name "before Gentiles and kings and before the people of Israel." The Conversion of St. Paul the Apostle is celebrated on Jan. 25 in the Episcopal calendar of the church year.

After baptism, Saul confounded the Jews in Damascus by proving that Jesus was the Messiah. Saul attempted to join the disciples in Jerusalem, but they were afraid of him because they did not believe he was a disciple. Barnabas brought him to the apostles, and described Saul's conversion experience (Acts 9:26–27). Saul was accepted as a Christian disciple. Saul and Barnabas were subsequently commissioned by the church at Antioch for missionary work. Barnabas and Saul set off upon what was to be the first of Paul's three missionary journeys. It was from the time of this first missionary journey that Saul was known as Paul. He founded churches in Asia Minor and Greece, and he wrote public letters or epistles to these churches. Paul made three missionary journeys (Acts 13–14, 15:40—18:22, 18:23—21:17). Paul was accompanied on his second missionary journey by Silas (Silvanus), and later Timothy. Paul and Barnabas went separate ways because Barnabas wanted to take John (Mark) with them, but Paul felt that Mark had deserted them in Pamphylia on the first missionary journey (Acts 15:36–40, 16:3). When the Jews at Corinth opposed and reviled Paul on his second missionary journey, he declared that "From now on I will go to the Gentiles" (Acts 18:6). He also collected money for the Christians in Jerusalem (see Acts 11:29–30; 1 Cor 16:1–4).

Paul went to Jerusalem at the end of his third missionary journey despite warnings about what might happen to him. Paul was arrested by the Roman tribune after a riot broke out over Paul's presence in Jerusalem. He was transferred to Caesarea, where he was held for two years. When a new governor was going to return Paul to Jerusalem for trial, he appealed to the emperor and was transferred to Rome. He was shipwrecked at Malta, but finally arrived safely in Rome. Paul was allowed to live by himself for two years with the soldier who was guarding him. Paul explained the Christian faith to the Jews at Rome. Some were convinced by him, but others refused to believe. Paul proclaimed to them that the salvation of God has been sent to the Gentiles (Acts 28:17–30). There is no mention of Paul's death in Acts. Paul is believed to have been martyred in Rome under the Emperor Nero around A.D. 64.

Paul's epistles to Christian communities represent a significant portion of the NT. His letters are primary sources for understanding his career, along with the secondary source provided by the Book of Acts. These letters dealt with theological, ethical, and pastoral problems that the Christian communities were facing. Most scholars acknowledge that Paul authored Romans, 1 and 2 Corinthians, Galatians, 1 Thessalonians, Philippians, Colossians, and Philemon. Others also acknowledge that Paul authored 2 Thessalonians, Ephesians, 1 and 2 Timothy, and Titus. Some variations in style may be explained by the fact that secretaries assisted Paul in composing these epistles. Paul's theology emphasized the importance of salvation through faith in Christ rather than works of the law. Paul, the Apostle to the Gentiles, resisted the requirement that Gentile converts be conformed to the Jewish law (see Phil 3:2–11). Paul and Barnabas influenced the apostles and elders in Jerusalem not to require circumcision of Gentile converts to Christianity (Acts 15:1–29; Gal 2:1–10). Paul even rebuked Peter when Peter would not eat with Gentiles (Gal 2:11–14). Paul urged, "We know that a person is justified not by the works of the law but through faith in Jesus Christ" (Gal 2:16). Paul provoked the outrage of Jewish authorities against him, and his teaching influenced the early separation of the Christian church from Judaism.

Paul's writings have been foundational for Christian theology of salvation, the Christ, the church, the Spirit, and the end times. Paul emphasized the reality of salvation in Christ, whose life, death, and resurrection we may share in the church through baptism (see Rom 6:3–5). As all die in Adam, so all will be made alive in Christ (1 Cor 15:22; see Rom 5:18). God has reconciled us to himself in Christ. Anyone who is in Christ is a new creation (2 Cor 5:17–18). The new age has been inaugurated by Jesus' resurrection. Christ is the "first fruits" of the resurrection from the dead, which all who are in Christ will share when he comes (1 Cor 15:23). Although the Kingdom of God is not yet fulfilled in us, God gives us his Spirit in our hearts as a "first installment" (2 Cor 1:22, 5:5). God's love has been poured into our hearts through the Holy Spirit which has been given to us (Rom 5:5). All Christians are individual members of the one body of Christ in the church. In the one Spirit there are a variety of gifts, ministries, and members (1 Cor 12:12–13, 27–28; Rom 12:4–12:6). In Christ there are no distinctions between Jew and Greek, slave and free, or male and female, because all are one in Christ (Gal 3:28). Paul's influence is visible throughout the tradition of the Christian church, including Augustine, Aquinas, Martin Luther, and John Calvin. The Episcopal theologian William Porcher DuBose was deeply influenced by Pauline theology, and he wrote *The Gospel According to Saint*

Paul (1907). The feast of Saint Peter and Saint Paul, Apostles, is celebrated on June 29 in the Episcopal calendar of the church year.

Pavement Lights. Candles in long holders or poles in stands that rest on the floor (or pavement) of the church. Pavement lights are free-standing. They may be placed near an ambo or the altar and lighted during church services.

Pax Board. *See* Peace, The.

Pax Brede. *See* Peace, The.

Pax, The. *See* Peace, The.

Payne, John (Jan. 9, 1815–Oct. 23, 1874). First Missionary Bishop sent to Africa by the Episcopal Church. He was born in Westmoreland County, Virginia. Payne graduated from the College of William and Mary in 1833 and from Virginia Theological Seminary in 1836. He was ordained deacon on July 17, 1836. Payne sailed at once for Africa, where he worked for five years. He returned to the United States and was ordained priest on July 18, 1841. He returned to Liberia to work. Payne was consecrated Missionary Bishop of Cape Palmas and Parts Adjacent on July 11, 1851. This jurisdiction later became the Missionary District of Liberia. He resigned as bishop on Oct. 21, 1871, because of ill health. He returned to the United States and died at his home, "Cavalla," in Westmoreland County. The Bishop Payne Divinity School in Petersburg, Virginia, was named in his honor.

Peace, The. A liturgical exchange of greeting through word and gesture. It is a sign of reconciliation, love, and renewed relationships in the Christian community. It is initiated by the celebrant, who says, "The peace of the Lord be always with you." The people respond, "And also with you." The ministers and people may greet one another in the name of the Lord (BCP, pp. 332, 360). Any appropriate words of greeting may be used in the exchange of peace that follows between individuals (BCP, p. 407). The gesture of greeting has been expressed in a variety of ways, including a kiss on the cheek, an embrace, a handclasp, or a bow. The peace is also known as the kiss of peace and the Pax (from the Latin, "peace").

The peace is an ancient Christian practice. It has been associated with Rom 16:16, "Greet one another with a holy kiss," and similar passages such as 1 Cor 16:20, 2 Cor 13:12, 1 Thes 5:26, and 1 Pt 5:14. The earliest references to the peace may be found in writings concerning the baptismal liturgies. After the baptism and the laying on of hands and anointing by the bishop, the newly baptized were included in the exchange of the peace for the first time. Justin Martyr indicates that during the second century the peace took place before the presentation of the gifts at the eucharist. It appears that the peace originally concluded the liturgy of the word. However, the peace was moved to the end of the eucharistic prayer in the Roman rite during the fifth century. The peace was exchanged at the time of the breaking of the bread prior to communion. The peace was exchanged at this time in the eucharistic liturgy of the 1549 BCP, and it continues in this position in the Roman rite. The peace was deleted in the 1552 BCP. The 1979 BCP restored the peace at the eucharist to its ancient position at the end of the liturgy of the word. The BCP still allows the peace to be exchanged at the time of the administration of communion, before or after the sentence of invitation (p. 407).

At baptism, the peace follows the baptism and the welcome for the newly baptized by the celebrant and people (BCP, p. 308). At Confirmation, Reception, or Reaffirmation, it follows the bishop's concluding prayer and precedes the prayers of the people or the offertory (BCP, pp. 310, 419). The peace concludes the service for the Celebration and Blessing of a Marriage, although communion may follow (BCP, p. 431). The new minister's first action at the Celebration of a New Ministry is to initiate the peace (BCP, p. 563). The bishop initiates the peace at the end of the liturgy for the Consecration and Dedication of a Church, prior to the eucharist (BCP, p. 574). In the Order for Celebrating the Holy Eucharist, the peace may be exchanged after the prayers for the world and the church and before preparing the table, "or elsewhere in the service" (BCP, p. 401). Depending on the pastoral needs of the situation, it might be more appropriate to exchange the peace at the end or the beginning of this more informal eucharistic liturgy. The peace may be intoned by the celebrant and the people. *The Hymnal 1982* provides musical settings for the peace (S 110–111).

In the late middle ages, a wooden plaque or plate with a projecting handle was used to pass the peace without direct personal contact. It had an image of the crucifixion or another religious subject on the face. It was known as a Pax Board, Pax Brede, or Osculatorium. It was first kissed by the celebrant, and then passed to other ministers and members of the congregation who also kissed it. The custom of passing the peace by use of a Pax Board is now obsolete.

Peace with Justice, Standing Commission on. The 1979 General Convention established a Joint Commission on Peace. Its mandate was to present to the 1982 General Convention a comprehensive program for implementing a recent Pastoral Letter of the House of Bishops as it pertained to peace and war. It was thought that the "quest for peace was too important to be delegated to a special staff person, group, or program." Rather it was to emphasize peacemaking "in all the structures of the Episcopal Church, so as to bring the issue of war and peace directly and actively into the central life of the Church." While this ambition was never fully realized, the commission succeeded in bringing the issues of peace and war more to the attention of the church than had previously been done. The success in persuading General Convention to establish the commission was in part due to the efforts of the Episcopal Peace Fellowship which had for years called the attention of the church to its own peace and war resolutions, especially in its publication, "Cross before Flag." The Joint Commission on Peace became the Standing Commission on Peace with Justice. The 1997 General Convention discontinued this commission and created the Standing Commission on Anglican and International Peace with Justice Concerns. *See* Anglican and International Peace with Justice Concerns, Standing Commission on; *see* Episcopal Peace Fellowship, The (EPF).

Pectoral Cross. A cross, typically of silver or gold, suspended by a chain around the neck. The cross hangs at about the breastbone or pectoral muscles of the wearer. It may be adorned with jewels. It was used by the Pope in the thirteenth century and came into general use by bishops and certain other prelates in the sixteenth century. Bishops now often wear an ornate pectoral cross as an episcopal insignia. Some priests wear a simple pectoral cross.

Pedilavium. See Foot Washing.

Pelagianism. A heresy taking its name from Pelagius, a lay monk from either Britain or Ireland, who came to Rome in the early fifth century. Pelagius denied that infants were born in a state of original sin and taught that Christ came merely to give humankind a good example to counteract the bad example of Adam. Pelagius held that human beings alone were responsible for their good or evil actions. Pelagianism held that each person can take the first steps toward salvation without the help of grace. Pelagius and his followers were vigorously attacked by Augustine.

Penance. In the sacramental rite of Reconciliation of a Penitent, penance is a task assigned by the priest to the person who has confessed his or her sins. It is something to be said or done as a sign of penitence and an act of thanksgiving for God's forgiveness (BCP, p. 446). The penitent may be assigned a psalm, prayer, or hymn to say, or an act of reparation to make. It may be assigned in light of the sins confessed and their context in the life of the penitent. It is assigned to the penitent before the priest or bishop pronounces absolution. Although a penance is not required in the rite of Reconciliation of a Penitent, it may be assigned as part of the "advice and counsel" given by the priest after the penitent's confession (BCP, p. 446). *See* Penitent; *see* Reconciliation of a Penitent.

Penitence. Prayer in which we confess our sins and make restitution where possible, with the intention to amend our lives (BCP, p. 857). The Prayer Book Catechism identifies penitence as one of the seven principal kinds of prayer (p. 856). In the sacramental rite of Reconciliation of a Penitent, those who repent of their sins may confess them to God in the presence of a priest and receive the assurance of pardon and the grace of absolution (p. 861). The BCP provides two forms for the Reconciliation of a Penitent (pp. 447–452). The season of Lent is a penitential season of preparation for the Easter celebration of Jesus' resurrection. Ash Wednesday is the first day of Lent. At the Ash Wednesday service, the celebrant invites the people to the observance of a holy Lent "by self-examination and repentance; by prayer, fasting, and self-denial; and by reading and meditating on God's holy Word" (pp. 264–265). The Ash Wednesday service includes a Litany of Penitence (pp. 267–269). Many Prayer Book liturgies also include a confession of sin. The confession of sin and absolution follow the prayers of the people and precede the peace at the eucharist (BCP, pp. 331, 360). Another option is for the eucharist to begin with a Penitential Order (pp. 319–321, 351–353). The Penitential Order includes an acclamation and the confession of sin and absolution. It may also include the decalogue and one or more appropriate sentences of scripture. Compline includes a confession of sin and prayer for absolution (BCP, pp. 127–128). Morning Prayer and Evening Prayer may include a confession of sin and absolution (pp. 41–42, 62–63, 79–80, 116–117).

Penitent. A person seeking the church's ministry of reconciliation by making a confession to a confessor. The Reconciliation of a Penitent is one of the sacramental rites of the Episcopal Church (BCP, p. 860). Through reconciliation, penitents are restored to full fellowship in the Christian community and may receive "the assurance of pardon and the grace of absolution" (BCP, p. 861). The BCP provides two forms for the Reconciliation of a Penitent (pp. 447–452). After the penitent has confessed all serious sins and given evidence of contrition, the priest gives counsel and encouragement and pronounces absolution. Prior to giving absolution, the priest may assign a penance which is to be said or done by the penitent as a sign of penitence and an act of thanksgiving for God's forgiveness (BCP, p. 446). For example, the penitent may be assigned a psalm, prayer, or hymn to say or an act of reparation to make. Sacramental reconciliation is available to all. Confessions may be heard at any appropriate time or place. The secrecy of a confession is morally absolute for the confessor (BCP, p. 446).

Penitential Order. The eucharist may begin with a penitential order (BCP, pp. 319–321, 351–353). The Penitential Order includes an acclamation and the confession of sin and absolution. It may also include the decalogue, and one or more appropriate sentences of scripture. These sentences of scripture include the Summary of the Law, Mt 22:37–40 or Mark 12:29–31; 1 Jn 1:8–9; and Heb 4:14, 16. The Penitential Order may be used as an entrance rite during Lent or other times to emphasize the penitential aspect of the eucharist. The Penitential Order may be used as a separate service. When used separately, it concludes with suitable prayers and the grace or a blessing. When the Penitential Order is used to begin the eucharist, the service continues with the *Gloria in excelsis*, the *Kyrie eleison*, or the *Trisagion*. The confession and absolution are not repeated later in the service. A deacon or lay person who leads the Penitential Order uses a modified form for the absolution, praying "Almighty God have mercy on us, forgive us all

our sins through our Lord Jesus Christ, strengthen us in all goodness, and by the power of the Holy Spirit keep us in eternal life" (BCP, p. 321, 353). The Penitential Order is presented by the BCP in both traditional and contemporary language. The Rite 1 (traditional language) version of the Penitential Order includes both the general confession from the eucharistic rite, and the general confession from Rite 1 Morning Prayer (pp. 320–321).

Penitential Psalms. In the Christian liturgical tradition seven psalms have been singled out as penitential psalms: 6, 32, 38, 51, 102, 130, 143. They express human penitence for sin before God and are particularly appropriate for the penitential season of Lent. For example, Ps 51 begins "Have mercy on me, O God, according to your loving-kindness; in your great compassion blot out my offenses."

Penitentials (Penitential Books). Manuals or guides for confessors, including prayers, lists of questions to be asked by the confessor, and penances to be assigned for various sins. The practice of private penance, or reconciliation of a penitent, began in the Celtic Church and later spread through Europe with the Celtic and Anglo-Saxon missions. Penitentials for use by confessors in private penance appeared in the sixth through ninth centuries. These books were not decreed by episcopal synods. Their authority rested on the reputation of their compiler or editor. Public penances were assigned for public sins that caused scandal for the church. Private penances were assigned for private sins or matters of conscience. The penitentials were generally more flexible than the church's ancient penitential system which they largely replaced. Later penitentials tended to provide guidance for the confessor instead of rigid rules and penalties. *See* Penance; *see* Penitent.

Penniman, Charles Frederic (July 14, 1893–Aug. 16, 1963). Priest and educator. He was born in Asheville, North Carolina, and studied at Virginia Polytechnic Institute and Harvard University. He received his Master in Engineering from Lehigh University in 1914 and his B.D. from the Virginia Theological Seminary in 1924. Penniman was ordained deacon on June 6, 1924, and priest on June 5, 1925. He served churches in Brandy Station, Virginia; Meridian, Mississippi; and Wilmington, Delaware. He became director of the Educational Center in St. Louis in 1945. Its endowment was originally established for the care of orphans, but in time the courts were persuaded to change the terms of the bequest to provide for "spiritual orphans" whose need was for Christian nurture in all things "which a Christian ought to know and believe to his soul's health." He used this position to produce Christian education programs and teacher training methods that reflected on life experience in light of the gospel. Penniman was a pioneer in research and development of educational programs based on faith development. In time his work embraced a large number of parishes throughout the United States. He served on the boards of many social agencies and diocesan commissions and as an arbitrator of labor disputes. He became eastern representative of the center in 1958 and retired in 1961. He died in West Chester, Pennsylvania.

Pennington, Edgar Legare (Jan. 15, 1891–Dec. 10, 1951). Historian of the Episcopal Church. He was born in Madison, Georgia. Pennington received his B.A. in 1911 and his LL.B. in 1914, both from the University of Georgia. He was an ensign in the U.S. Navy during World War I. He gave up the practice of law for the ordained ministry. Pennington was ordained deacon on Feb. 2, 1921, and priest on Jan. 2, 1922. He began his ordained ministry in the Diocese of Central New York in 1921. In 1922–1923 he was general missionary for the diocese. From 1923 until 1925 Pennington was rector of St. John's Church, Marianna, and priest-in-charge of St. Andrew's Church, Panama City, Florida. He was rector of St. Andrew's Church, Jacksonville, 1925–1930, rector of Grace Church, Ocala, 1930–1936, and rector of the Church of the Holy Cross, Miami, 1936–1943. From 1943 until 1946, he was a chaplain in the Navy, and from 1946 until his death, he was rector of St. John's Church, Mobile, Alabama. During these years in parish ministry, Pennington was also a church historian with an emphasis on the Church of England in the American colonies. He was one of the founders of the *Historical Magazine of the Protestant Episcopal Church*. He served as its associate editor from 1932–1951 and as the historiographer of the Episcopal Church, 1949–1951. He published over fifty articles and pamphlets. Pennington died in Mobile, Alabama.

Pennsylvania, Diocese of. Organized at Christ Church, Philadelphia, on May 24, 1784, the diocese was divided in 1865 and again in 1871. The Diocese of Pennsylvania includes the following counties: Bucks, Chester, Delaware,

Montgomery and Philadelphia. On Jan. 1, 1992, the Church of the Saviour, Philadelphia, was designated the Cathedral Church of the Saviour.

Pentateuch. The biblical books of Genesis, Exodus, Leviticus, Numbers, and Deuteronomy. The term is from the Greek for "five" and "book." The Pentateuch is traditionally called the Five Books of Moses. The Hebrew term *Torah* is also used to indicate the Pentateuch. It recounts the history of ancient Israel from Creation to the death of Moses in Moab just before the entrance of the Hebrew people into the promised land under Joshua. The traditional view has been that is was written by Moses at the command of God. After the Enlightenment, a Documentary Theory was developed by scholars that the Pentateuch consists of four different documents concerning Israel's early life. According to this theory, the four documents were gradually combined over a period of several centuries to reach the Pentateuch's present form around 400 B.C. The documents were termed the Yahwist epic, the Elohist epic, the Priestly Writing, and Deuteronomy. In more recent years this Documentary Theory has been challenged by various scholars, but no one view has proved itself sufficiently convincing to replace it.

Perhaps no part of the OT is more important for both Jews and Christians than the Pentateuch, or Torah, as it is frequently called. A portion of it is always read in the regular liturgy of the Synagogue. For Christians it provides the foundation of many basic theological understandings, such as Creation.

Pentecost. The term means "the fiftieth day." It is used in both the OT and the NT. In the OT it refers to a feast of seven weeks known as the Feast of Weeks. It was apparently an agricultural event that focused on the harvesting of first fruits. Josephus referred to Pentecost as the fiftieth day after the first day of Passover. The term is used in the NT to refer to the coming of the Spirit on the day of Pentecost (Acts 2:1), shortly after Jesus' death, resurrection, and ascension. Christians came to understand the meaning of Pentecost in terms of the gift of the Spirit. The Pentecost event was the fulfillment of a promise which Jesus gave concerning the return of the Holy Spirit. The speaking in tongues, which was a major effect of having received the Spirit, is interpreted by some to symbolize the church's worldwide preaching. In the Christian tradition, Pentecost is now the seventh Sunday after Easter. It emphasizes that the church is understood as the body of Christ which is drawn together and given life by the Holy Spirit. Some understand Pentecost to be the origin and sending out of the church into the world. The Day of Pentecost is one of the seven principal feasts of the church year in the Episcopal Church (BCP, p. 15). The Day of Pentecost is identified by the BCP as one of the feasts that is "especially appropriate" for baptism (p. 312). The liturgical color for the feast is red. Pentecost has also been known as Whitsun or Whitsunday, a corruption of "White Sunday." This term reflects the custom by which those who were baptized at the Vigil of Pentecost would wear their white baptismal garments to church on the Day of Pentecost. The BCP provides directions for observance of a Vigil of Pentecost, which begins with the Service of Light (p. 227). *The Hymnal 1982* provides a variety of hymns for Pentecost (Hymns 223–230) and the Holy Spirit (Hymns 500–516).

Pentecost (Season). The season *after* Pentecost, according to the calendar of the church year (BCP, p. 32). It begins on the Monday following Pentecost, and continues through most of the summer and autumn. It may include as many as twenty-eight Sundays, depending on the date of Easter. This includes Trinity Sunday which is the First Sunday after Pentecost. The BCP provides proper collects and readings for the other Sundays of the season. These propers are numbered and designated for use on the Sundays which are closest to specific days in the monthly calendar, whether before or after. For example, Proper 3 is designated for use, if needed, on the Sunday closest to May 25. Proper 29 is designated for use on the Sunday closest to Nov. 23. Prior to the 1979 BCP, Sundays in this long period of the church year were identified and counted in terms of the number of Sundays after Trinity Sunday instead of the number of Sundays after Pentecost. This period is also understood by some as "ordinary time," a period of the church year not dedicated to a particular season or observance, as in the Roman Rite adapted after Vatican II. *See* Ordinary Time.

Pentecostalism. The term refers to a wide variety of churches and movements that claim to re-experience the spiritual gifts associated with the outpouring of the Holy Spirit at Pentecost, most notably the gift of tongues (see Acts 2:1–11). The experience is usually referred to as "Baptism in the Holy Spirit." Although instances of these gifts recur throughout church history, the roots of the modern movement lie in the Wesleyan holiness movement of Methodism. In 1901 a Methodist evangelist, Charles Parham, began a Bible school in Topeka, Kansas. In 1906 a controversial African American Pentecostal preacher, William Seymour, began a series of revival meetings on Azusa Street in Los Angeles. Most modern Pentecostal denominations derive from these two sources. Since most of the converts were from conservative evangelical or holiness roots, the fundamentalist theology of these bodies became typical of Pentecostalism. However, there is no necessary connection between the experience of the spiritual gifts and fundamentalist theology. *See* Charismatic Renewal, or Neo-Pentecostalism.

Perichoresis. This term means interpenetration and mutual indwelling of the three Persons of the Trinity. This understanding maintains the distinction and unity of the divine Persons. It avoids the trinitarian heresies of modalism and tritheism. *See* Trinity.

Pericope. This Greek word used by scripture scholars refers to a certain portion of a text. The word literally means "cut around." A *pericope* is a section of text that, if removed from the writing, could be recognized as a tradition that could stand on its own. It may have circulated orally before it was included in a gospel or letter. A synopsis of the gospels is divided into numbered *pericopes*.

Perkins, Frances (Apr. 10, 1880–May 14, 1965). First woman cabinet member in the United States. She was born Fannie Coralie Perkins in Boston, Massachusetts. She received her B.A. at Mount Holyoke College in 1902. While a student at Mount Holyoke College, Perkins heard a speaker vividly describe the nation's growing urban and industrial problems. She was deeply moved. When she was living in Lake Forest, Illinois, and working in Chicago, she was attracted to the Episcopal Church. Perkins was confirmed at the Church of the Holy Spirit, Lake Forest, on June 11, 1905. She remained a life-long Episcopalian. While working at a Chicago settlement house, she determined to "do something about unnecessary hazards to life, unnecessary poverty" because "our Lord has directed all those who thought they were following in His path to visit the widows, the orphans, the fatherless, the prisoners and so forth." Perkins earned an M.A. at Columbia University in 1910. She witnessed the 1911 Triangle Shirtwaist fire in New York in which 146 factory workers died. She took up industrial safety work for the City of New York. Perkins continued her work in industrial relations, serving at the state level with Al Smith and Franklin D. Roosevelt during their respective terms as Governor of New York. In 1933 President Franklin D. Roosevelt appointed her Secretary of Labor, the first woman cabinet member in United States history. Before accepting the job, she consulted with her friend, Suffragan Bishop Charles K. Gilbert of New York. As Secretary of Labor, she was instrumental in helping draft and implement Roosevelt's New Deal legislation. Perkins resigned her post shortly after Roosevelt's death in 1945. An associate of All Saints' Sisters of the Poor, she spent one day a month in silent retreat at their Catonsville, Maryland convent throughout her twelve years in the cabinet. In 1955 she joined the faculty of the Cornell University School of Industrial and Labor Relations. She remained active in teaching and lecturing until her death in New York City.

Perpetua and her Companions (d. c. 202). Catechumen and martyr. Perpetua and her companions Felicitas, Revocatus, Saturninus, Secundulus, and Saturus were Christians imprisoned in Carthage under Emperor Septimius Severus. All of them may have been catechumens. Some accounts indicate that Saturus was their catechist or a priest. Felicitas and Revocatus were slaves. Perpetua was a young woman, about twenty-two, with an infant son. Her father was a pagan who tried to turn her away from Christianity. The *Passion of Perpetua and Felicitas* recalls the trial, prison experiences, visions, and execution of Perpetua and her companions. In addition to recounting their faithful sacrifice, it also provides one of the earliest records of Christian women. Perpetua's prison diary represented the largest portion of this work. Perpetua and her companions were martyred in the arena at Carthage, c. 202. Their martyrdom is commemorated on Mar. 7 in the episcopal calendar of the church year. *See* Felicitas, or St. Felicity.

Perquisite, Perquisites. Payment or benefits in addition to a regular salary. They are known informally as "perks." The term may be applied to benefits in the compensation package for a member of the clergy or other paid members of the church staff, including provided housing or a housing allowance, life and health insurance, retirement benefits, travel or car allowance, paid vacation time, allowance for continuing education, and other benefits.

Perry, James DeWolf (Oct. 3, 1871–Mar. 20, 1947). Eighteenth Presiding Bishop of the Episcopal Church. He was born in Germantown, Pennsylvania. Perry received his B.A. from the University of Pennsylvania in 1891 and then received another B.A. from Harvard University in 1892. He received his B.D. from the Episcopal Theological School in 1895. Perry was ordained deacon on June 9, 1895. He began his ministry as an assistant at Christ Church, Springfield, Massachusetts. He was ordained priest on Feb. 18, 1896. From 1897 until 1904 he was rector of Christ Church, Fitchburg, Massachusetts. His last parochial ministry was as rector of St. Paul's Church, New Haven, Connecticut, 1904–1911. Perry was consecrated the seventh Bishop of Rhode Island on Jan. 6, 1911. He was elected Presiding Bishop by the House of Bishops on Mar. 26, 1930. Perry was reelected at the General Convention of 1931. He served until his retirement on Dec. 31, 1937. He was the last Presiding Bishop who retained his diocesan jurisdiction while serving in the national post.

Perry was especially interested in foreign missions. In 1932 the Report of the Commission of Appraisal of the Laymen's Foreign Missions Enquiry was published with the title *Rethinking Missions: A Layman's Enquiry after One Hundred Years*. This independent commission was chaired by William Ernest Hocking. It was very critical of the missionary work of the Protestant churches. The National Council of the Episcopal Church asked Presiding Bishop Perry to make an independent study of the Episcopal Church's foreign missions. He and Mrs. Perry spent five months visiting mission stations in the Philippine Islands, China, Japan, and Hawaii. Upon his return to the United States, Perry announced his disagreement with the conclusions of *Rethinking Missions*. Perry died in Summerville, South Carolina.

Perry, William Stevens (Jan. 22, 1832–May 13, 1898). Bishop and church historian. He was born in Providence, Rhode Island. Perry graduated from Harvard College in 1854 and then studied for a while at the Virginia Theological Seminary. He was ordained deacon on Mar. 29, 1857, and priest on Apr. 7, 1858. From 1858 until 1861 Perry was rector of St. Luke's Church, Nashua, New Hampshire, and from 1861 until 1863 he was rector of St. Stephen's Church, Portland, Maine. He served as rector of St. Michael's Church, Litchfield, Connecticut, 1864–1869, and of Trinity Church, Geneva, New York, 1869–1876. From 1871 until 1874, Perry was professor of history at Hobart College in

Geneva, and in 1876 for several months he was president of the college. He was secretary of the House of Deputies from Oct. 24, 1865, until Oct. 3, 1877, and from Oct. 23, 1868, until his death, he was the third historiographer of the Episcopal Church. On Sept. 10, 1876, he was consecrated the second Bishop of Iowa and served in that position until his death. Among his many publications are *Journals of the General Convention of the Protestant Episcopal Church in the United States of America* (1861), *Documentary History of the Protestant Episcopal Church in Connecticut, 1701–1789* (1863–1864), *Historical Collections Relating to the American Colonial Church*, 5 vols. (1870–1878), *Historical Notes and Documents Illustrating the Organization of the Protestant Episcopal Church in the United States of America* (1874), and *The History of the American Episcopal Church, 1587–1883*, 2 vols. (1885). Perry died in Davenport, Iowa.

***Per Saltum* (Ordination).** *See* Direct Ordination.

Personal Profile. *See* CDO Personal Profile.

Peter, Saint (d. c. 64). Apostle and leader of the early church. He was first named Simon, but Jesus named him Cephas, or Peter, which means "rock." He was also known as Simon Peter. Peter and his brother Andrew were fishermen on the Sea of Galilee. Jesus invited them to follow him and fish for people (Mt 4:18–20, Mk 1:16–18). In the Gospel of Luke, Jesus tells Peter to go into the deep water and let down his nets for a catch. Peter and his partners James and John then have a miraculous catch of fish. Jesus promises that from now on they will be catching people (Lk 5:4–11). The Gospel of John records that Andrew brought Peter to Jesus, and told him that Jesus was the Messiah. Jesus tells Simon that he will be called Cephas, which is translated Peter (Jn 1:40–42). Peter was married, and his wife accompanied him on his missionary journeys (1 Cor 9:5). Peter is named first and included in all lists of the twelve disciples (see Mk 3:16, Acts 1:13).

The NT records many vivid events and discussions involving Peter and Jesus. Peter offered to walk to Jesus on the water, and he began to walk on the water. But Peter became frightened and began to sink. Jesus reached out his hand and caught him (Mt 14:28–33). Peter asked Jesus if he should forgive his brother as many as seven times. Jesus answered that he should forgive seventy-seven times (Mt 18:21–22). Peter asked Jesus what the disciples would have for following him. Jesus promised that when the Son of Man is seated on the throne of glory they would also sit on twelve thrones and judge the twelve tribes of Israel (Mt 19:27–28). Jesus asked his disciples "Who do you say that I am?" Peter answered that Jesus was the Messiah, the Son of the living God (Mt 16:15–16). In the Gospel of Matthew, Jesus then names Peter and states that on this rock Jesus will build his church, and the gates of Hades will not prevail against it. The "rock" has been interpreted to mean either Peter or the faith in Christ that Peter expressed. Jesus also states that he will give Peter the keys of the kingdom, so that whatever he binds on earth is bound in heaven, and whatever he looses on earth is loosed in heaven (Mt 16:18–19). However, Peter's confession of faith is followed by his rebuke of Jesus, who told the disciples about the great suffering that he would face in Jerusalem. Jesus sharply rebukes Peter, saying "Get behind me, Satan!" (Mt 16:21–23). Peter was always included in the "inner group" of disciples who were present with Jesus for times such as the healing of Jairus's daughter (Mk 5:21–43), the Transfiguration of Jesus (Mt 17:1–8), and Jesus' agony in the Garden of Gethsemane (Mt 26:36–46). On the night of Jesus' betrayal, Peter boasts that he will never deny Jesus. But Jesus correctly predicts that Peter will deny him three times that night (Mt 26:33–35, 69–75). Jesus charges Peter to strengthen the other disciples after they have been scattered (Lk 22:31–32). Peter cuts off the ear of the high priest's slave at the time of Jesus' arrest (Jn 18:10). Peter was the first disciple to witness Jesus' resurrection (Lk 24:34, 1 Cor 15:5).

Peter was at the heart of the organization of the Christian church after Jesus' resurrection. The Gospel of John records a post-resurrection appearance in which Jesus charges Peter to feed his lambs and tend his sheep. Jesus also predicts Peter's martyrdom (Jn 21:15–19). Peter urged the selection of a twelfth witness to the resurrection to take the place of Judas Iscariot (Acts 1:15–22). Peter preached to the multitude on Pentecost, and some 3,000 people were converted (Acts 2:14–41). Peter often served as spokesman for the church. He denounced the deceit of Ananias and Sapphira who were holding back money from the church (Acts 5:1–11), and he rejected an offer from a man named Simon who wanted to pay for the power to confer the Holy Spirit (Acts 8:18–24). Paul says that Peter was entrusted with the gospel for the circumcised (Gal 2:7). Peter also opened the church to Gentiles after seeing a vision of ritually unclean food descending from heaven and being told not to call profane what God had made clean. Peter ordered the baptism of the Gentile Cornelius along with his relatives and close friends (Acts 10:1–48). Peter was involved in miraculous healings. He healed a man who was crippled from birth (Acts 3:1–10), a man who had been bedridden for eight years (Acts 9:32–35), and a woman who had died (Acts 9:36–42). The sick were even placed on cots and mats in the streets so that Peter's shadow might fall on some of them as he passed by (Acts 5:15). Peter ate with Gentiles at Antioch until certain people came from James. Peter then drew back and kept himself separate from the Gentiles. Paul opposed Peter to his face for this hypocrisy. Paul urged that we are justified by faith in Christ and not by doing the works of the law (Gal 2:11–21). The NT witness presents Peter to be a person with notable strengths and weaknesses. He was fallible and impetuous. He was also a strong leader of the disciples and the church, and a devoted witness to Christ. Although the NT is silent concerning his death, Peter was probably martyred in Rome during the persecution of the church by the Roman Emperor Nero. According to Origen, Peter was crucified head down at his own request. The Confession of Saint Peter the Apostle is celebrated on Jan. 18, and the feast of Saint Peter and Saint Paul, Apostles, is celebrated on June 29.

Peters, John Punnet (Dec. 16, 1852–Nov. 10, 1921). Leading biblical and archeological scholar. He was born in New York City. He received his B.A. from Yale in 1873 and his Ph.D. from Yale in 1876. He was ordained deacon on Nov. 24, 1876, and priest on Dec. 23, 1878. From 1876 to 1879 he was a tutor at Yale College, and from 1879 to 1883 he studied Semitic languages and served churches in Germany. Peters was professor of OT languages and literature at the Protestant Episcopal Divinity School in Philadelphia, 1884–1891, and professor of Hebrew at the University of Pennsylvania, 1886–1893. From 1893 to 1919 he was rector of St. Michael's Church, New York. In 1919 he became professor of NT at the School of Theology, the University of the South. He was a widely published writer and the author of *The Old Testament and the New Scholarship* (1901). Peters died in New York City.

Petition. The form of prayer in which one asks God for divine grace or assistance. Petition addresses God as divine Providence who lovingly watches over the needs of human creatures. It is an elementary form of prayer, but it should not be discouraged as long as it is not prompted by selfish motives. It expresses the fundamental powerlessness and need for help of creatures in contrast with God's greatness and generosity.

Pettigrew, Charles (Mar. 20, 1744–Apr. 8, 1807). First priest elected to serve as Bishop of North Carolina and a leading eighteenth-century evangelical. He was born near Chambersburg, Pennsylvania. Pettigrew moved to Virginia and then in 1760 to North Carolina. Around 1773 he joined the Church of England. He became a lay reader at St. Paul's Church, Edenton, North Carolina. In 1775 he went to England, where he was ordained deacon and priest. He was licensed by the Bishop of London as a missionary for the Society for the Propagation of the Gospel. He returned to North Carolina as the rector of St. Paul's Church, Edenton. Bishop William White of Pennsylvania suggested that Pettigrew call a meeting of the six Episcopal clergy in the state to organize the diocese. Two clergy and two laymen met at Tarboro on June 5, 1790, and elected deputies to the 1792 General Convention. At a convention held in Tarboro on May 31, 1794, Pettigrew was elected bishop. He was never consecrated for reasons of health. He was instrumental in founding the University of North Carolina in 1789. Pettigrew was one of the few Church of England clergy to participate in the Great Awakening and was an eighteenth-century evangelical and revivalist. Pettigrew died at his family estate, "Bonarva" in Tyrrell County, North Carolina.

Pew. A long bench, typically with a back, for congregational seating in church. Seats were not provided for the congregation in the early church, and this practice continues today in the Eastern Orthodox Church. The use of pews in the naves of churches has been dated from the thirteenth century. Some pews have been elaborately carved, and some have served to separate the occupants from others in the church. Chairs are now used for seating in some churches because chairs allow greater flexibility in the arrangement of liturgical space. Chairs also may present less of an obstacle than pews for the gathering and uniting of the community for worship.

Pew Rents. The renting of pews was the primary way that churches in many denominations collected funds prior to the twentieth century. Most of the time families were seated in separate pews. The closer a family sat to the altar or pulpit, the higher its social or economic position. *See* Free Pew.

PEWSACTION. An association of Episcopal Church-related fellowships called together to plan and serve in specific undertakings based on prayer, evangelism, worship, and study and expressed in action within and beyond the church. The idea for PEWSACTION was first discussed at the 1970 General Convention and later considered at the Feb. 1972 meeting of the Brotherhood of St. Andrew in New Orleans. The organization began to take shape at a meeting in Aug. 1972 at the home of Helen Shoemaker in Pittsburgh. At this meeting Fred Gore was elected the first president of PEWSACTION. It is believed that Gore suggested the name PEWSACTION: Prayer, Evangelism, Worship, Study, and Action. The organizations represented at the Aug. 1972 meeting were the Anglican Fellowship of Prayer, the Brotherhood of St. Andrew, the Daughters of the King, the Episcopal Center for Evangelism, and Faith Alive. One of PEWSACTION's major works is sponsoring a national Conference on Evangelism and Renewal every three years. This conference is sometimes called "The Ridgecrest Conference" since it frequently meets at the Ridgecrest Conference Center in North Carolina. The first one was held at St. Philip's Cathedral, Atlanta, Georgia, in 1974. In 1998 PEWSACTION included the following groups: Adventures in Ministry (AIM), Anglican Fellowship of Prayer, Anglican Frontiers Mission, Bible Reading Fellowship, Brotherhood of St. Andrew, Celebration, Church Army, Church Periodical Club, Committee to Assist the Episcopal Diocese of Honduras, Episcopal Church Missionary Community, Evangelical Fellowship in the Anglican Communion, Faith Alive, Happening National, Inc., National Organization of Episcopalians for Life (NOEL), Order of the Daughters of the King, Rock the World Youth Mission Alliance, Sharing of Ministries Abroad (SOMA), Shoresh Ministries, South American Missionary Society of the Episcopal Church, Trinity Episcopal Extension Ministries, and VOCARE National. PEWSACTION dissolved in 1999.

Ph.D. The Doctor of Philosophy degree. A Ph.D. in theology does not necessarily presuppose a first theological degree and is to equip persons for teaching and research in theological seminaries, colleges, and universities.

Philadelphia Divinity School. This school was founded in 1857 by Bishop Alonzo Potter of Pennsylvania. On June 6, 1974, it merged with the Episcopal Theological School at Cambridge, Massachusetts, to create the Episcopal Divinity School.

"Philadelphia Eleven, The." The eleven women who were ordained priests at the Church of the Advocate, Philadelphia, on the feast of St. Mary and St. Martha, July 29, 1974, two years before General Convention authorized the ordination of women. The women ordained were Merrill Bittner, Alla Bozarth-Campbell, Alison Cheek, Emily Hewitt, Carter Heyward, Suzanne Hiatt, Marie Moorefield, Jeanette Piccard, Betty Schiess, Katrina Swanson, and Nancy Wittig. The bishops who presided at the service were Daniel Corrigan, Robert DeWitt, and Edward Welles II. These ordinations, and the ordinations of four more women in Sept. 1975 in Washington, D.C., were widely criticized as irregular because the Episcopal Church had not yet authorized the ordination of women to the priesthood. In 1976 the House of Bishops affirmed the validity of the ordinations by requiring of the fifteen women only "an act of completion" that would be "a liturgical incorporation of what was done on those two occasions" in Philadelphia and Washington, D.C. All of the "Philadelphia Eleven" participated in public events of "completion" within the following year, with the exception of Marie Moorefield who left the Episcopal Church to join the United Methodist Church. *See* Ordination of Women.

Philadelphia Recorder. See Episcopal Recorder, The.

Philip, Saint. One of the twelve apostles. Philip was from Bethsaida in Galilee. He seems to have belonged to a small group who were under the influence of John the Baptist. In the synoptic gospels there is no mention of Philip except in the lists of apostles. In the Gospel According to John he is mentioned several times. Philip said to Nathanael, "We have found him of whom Moses in the law and also the prophets wrote, Jesus of Nazareth, the son of Joseph." When Nathanael wondered whether anything good could come out of Nazareth, Philip answered, "Come and see." (Jn 1:45–46). Eusebius and other early church writers contend that Philip preached the gospel in Phrygia and died in Hierapolis. Philip is commemorated in the Episcopal calendar of the church year on May 1, along with St. James the Less.

Philippine Independent Church. At the end of the Spanish-American War in 1901, a number of Roman Catholic clergy in the Philippines wanted to be independent of the Roman Catholic bishops of Spain. On Aug. 3, 1902, they established an independent Catholic Church and elected Gregorio Aglipay their first Supreme Bishop. On Apr. 7,

1948, three bishops of the Episcopal Church consecrated three priests as bishops of the Philippine Independent Church. The General Convention of 1961 approved full intercommunion with the Philippine Independent Church.

Philippines, Diocese of the. The 1901 General Convention established the Missionary District of the Philippines, sometimes called the Philippine Islands. In 1972 it became the Missionary Diocese of the Philippines. The Cathedral Church of St. Mary and St. John was consecrated in 1902. In July 1988 the House of Bishops voted to release the Philippine Episcopal Church to form a new province. On May 1, 1990, the Philippine Episcopal Church became autonomous as the twenty-eighth Province of the Anglican Communion.

Phos hilaron. The traditional candle-lighting hymn, which begins "O gracious Light, pure brightness of the ever living Father in heaven." It appears in the BCP at Evening Prayer before the selection from the Psalter and in the Order of Worship for the Evening after the candle lighting (BCP, pp. 64, 112, 118). It was an ancient hymn of the Byzantine liturgy. Its name means "gladdening light" in Greek. Basil the Great (329?–379) spoke of the singing of the *Phos hilaron* as a cherished tradition of the church. If incense is used in the Order of Worship for the Evening, it is appropriately used after the lighting of the candles and during the singing of the *Phos hilaron. The Hymnal 1982* includes settings and paraphrases of the *Phos hilaron* (S 27, S 59–S 61, Hymns 25, 26, 36, 37). *See* Lucinaria, Lucernarium.

Phyletism. The principle of autonomy for national churches in Eastern Orthodoxy. It arose after the destruction of Constantinople in 1453 and gave autonomy to the various churches of the Byzantine Rite. Each national church was to be independent of the ecclesiastical control of the Patriarchate of Constantinople. *See* Byzantine Rite.

Piccard, Jeanette Ridlon (Jan. 5, 1895–May 17, 1981). First woman ordained priest in the Episcopal Church. She was born in Chicago. Piccard received her B.A. in Philosophy and Psychology from Bryn Mawr College in 1918, her M.S. in Organic Chemistry from the University of Chicago in 1919, and her Ph.D. in Education from the University of Minnesota in 1942. In 1919 she married Jean Piccard. She and her husband were balloonists. In 1934 she obtained a pilot's license. With her husband, she piloted their balloon to 57,559 feet over Lake Erie in Oct. 1934. She was the first woman to reach such heights. Piccard studied at the General Theological Seminary. She was ordained deacon on June 29, 1971. She was the first woman ordained in the July 29, 1974, "irregular" ordinations of eleven women deacons to the priesthood at the Church of the Advocate, Philadelphia. Following her ordination to the priesthood, Piccard served as associate rector at St. Philip's Church, St. Paul, Minnesota. On May 14, 1981, she was installed as an honorary canon of the Cathedral of St. Mark in Minneapolis. The ceremony was held in her hospital room. Piccard died in Minneapolis.

Pike, James Albert (Feb. 14, 1913–c. Sept. 3–7, 1969). Controversial theologian and bishop. He was born in Oklahoma City, Oklahoma. Pike received his B.A. in 1934 and his LL.B. in 1936, both from the University of California at Los Angeles. In 1938 he received his J.S.D. from Yale University. After a law career in Washington, D. C., and service in the U. S. Navy, Pike decided to enter the ordained ministry. He studied at both Union Theological Seminary and the General Theological Seminary. Pike was ordained deacon on Dec. 21, 1944. He began his ordained ministry as curate at St. John's Church, Washington. He was ordained priest on Nov. 1, 1946. From 1947 until 1949 he was rector of Christ Church, Poughkeepsie, New York, and Episcopal chaplain at Vassar College. In 1949 Pike became chaplain at Columbia University and chair of the religion department. In 1952 he became the dean of the Cathedral of St. John the Divine in New York City. On May 15, 1958, he was consecrated Bishop Coadjutor of California, and on Sept. 20, 1958, he became the fifth Bishop of California. He resigned this position on Sept. 15, 1966, to become Theologian-in-Residence at the Center for the Study of Democratic Institutions, Santa Barbara, California.

Pike's controversial reputation was due to his passion and persistence in public issues such as birth control, women's rights, the racial crisis, McCarthyism, abortion, fair housing, the rights of homosexuals, censorship, civil liberties, and the Vietnam War. He was also critical of the church and its theology. His departure from orthodoxy began with an article in *The Christian Century*, Dec. 21, 1960, entitled "Three-pronged Synthesis." He denied the historical virgin birth and claimed that Joseph was the human father of Jesus. He challenged the historical development of the doctrine of the Trinity, and called it "excess baggage." He also experimented with the occult. In 1966 Bishop Henry Louttit of Florida presented five charges against Pike in the House of Bishops. One accusation was that Pike publicly taught doctrine contrary to that held by the Episcopal Church. The House of Bishops censured Pike and stated: "His writing and speaking on profound realities with which Christian faith and worship are concerned are too often marred by caricatures of treasured symbols and at the worst, by cheap vulgarizations of great expressions of the faith." Pike was a prolific writer. His views are best stated in *A Time for Christian Candor* (1964), *What Is This Treasure* (1966), and *If This Be Heresy* (1967). He died in the Israeli desert some time between Sept. 3 and 7, 1969.

Pilgrim. A pilgrim is one who goes on a pilgrimage or journey with a religious or devotional intention. *See* Pilgrimage.

Pilgrimage. A journey taken with a religious or devotional intention. Pilgrimages are typically made to shrines, holy places, or locations of religious significance. They may be made as prayers of thanksgiving, penitence, intercession, or petition. Pilgrimages have been practiced in many religious traditions, including Hinduism, Islam, Judaism, and Christianity. Lk 2:41 records that Jesus' parents went to Jerusalem every year at the feast of the Passover. There are records of Christian pilgrimages dating from the second and third centuries. Christian pilgrims often journeyed to Jerusalem and Rome. Egeria, a fourth-century pilgrim to Jerusalem, described the Holy Week celebration that she witnessed. Shrines of the Blessed Virgin Mary, such as Lourdes in France and Walsingham in England, have been popular places of pilgrimage. Geoffrey Chaucer's *Canterbury Tales* is a fictional account of stories told by pilgrims on their way to the shrine of Thomas Becket at Canterbury Cathedral. This shrine was one of the most popular places of pilgrimage until its destruction under Henry VIII. In modern times some penitential practices traditionally associated with pilgrimages are no longer encouraged by the church. Pilgrimage centers continue to provide an opportunity for retreat, renewal, and a journey of the heart.

Pilmore, or Pilmoor, Joseph (Oct. 31, 1739–July 24, 1825). A leading early evangelical preacher. He was born in Tadmouth, England. Pilmore was educated in John Wesley's school at Kingswood and was a Methodist lay missionary in Great Britain, 1767–1769. In 1769 he came to the American colonies. He served as a lay missionary from 1769 until 1774, when he returned to England. He and Richard Boardman were the first two authorized Methodist preachers sent to America by John Wesley. Pilmore separated from John Wesley when Wesley issued the "Deed of Declaration" in 1784, which provided for the continuance of the Methodist movement and laid the foundation for the separation of the Methodists from the Church of England. He was ordained deacon on Nov. 27, 1785, and priest on Nov. 29, 1785. Pilmore was rector of the United Parishes in Philadelphia, 1786–1789, and assistant minister of St. Paul's Church, Philadelphia, 1789–1793. From 1793 until 1804 he was rector of Christ Church, New York City. From 1804 until his death he was rector of St. Paul's Church, Philadelphia. He died in Philadelphia.

Piscina. A small sink, basin, or niche that empties into the earth instead of a sewer. It is typically located in the sacristy or in the wall of the sanctuary. It may be used for the reverent disposal of consecrated wine from the eucharist, blessed water from baptism, and water used in washing vessels that have been used for a sacred purpose.

Pittenger, W. Norman (July 23, 1905–June 19, 1997). Leading process theologian. He was born in Bogota, New Jersey. Pittenger received his S.T.B. from the General Theological Seminary in 1936. He was ordained deacon on June 11, 1936, and priest on Feb. 24, 1937. He began teaching at General Seminary while still a student in 1935. He taught apologetics at General Seminary until his retirement in 1966. Pittenger was made an honorary senior member of King's College, Cambridge, in 1964. He was a senior resident at King's College from 1966 until 1970. He was vice president of the American Church Congress, 1942–1948, lecturer in doctrine, liturgics and ethics at the New York Training School for Deaconesses, 1944–1947, president of the American Theological Society, 1948–1949, and chairman of the North American Section of the Theological Commission of the World Council of Churches, 1962–1966. Pittenger was a visiting professor at universities around the world. As a scholar he produced an extensive bibliography. Many of his books were popular in the sense that they were "designed to bring the truth of Christianity out of the cloister or the study and give it currency in the living thought of men and women today." At the same time, his book, *The Incarnate Word* (1959), has been counted among the foremost studies in Christology in modern times. Pittenger was influenced by the theology of William Porcher DuBose, and he edited a collection of essays by DuBose which was published as *Unity in the Faith* (1957). He had a special interest in human sexuality and was supportive of gay and lesbian Christians. A festschrift, *Lux in Lumine: Essays to Honor W. Norman Pittenger* (1966), was presented to him at the time of his retirement. Pittenger died in Cambridge, England.

Pittsburgh, Diocese of. The 1865 General Convention voted "that all that portion of the State of Pennsylvania lying west of the eastern lines of the counties of McKean, Cameron, Clearfield, Cambria, and Somerset . . . be separated from the Diocese of Pennsylvania, and formed into a new Diocese." The primary convention of this new diocese met at Trinity Church, Pittsburgh, Nov. 15–16, 1865. The 1910 General Convention voted to divide the Diocese of Pittsburgh. The Diocese of Pittsburgh includes the following counties: Allegheny, Armstrong, Beaver, Butler, Cambria, Fayette, Greene, Indiana, Somerset, Washington, and Westmoreland. On June 3, 1928, Trinity Church, Pittsburgh, was set apart as Trinity Cathedral.

Pix. *See* Pyx.

Plainchant. *See* Plainsong.

Plainsong. Sacred unison (monophonic) chant. Plainsong dates from the earliest centuries of Christianity. It has one melody (monodic). The plainsong melody is traditionally sung without musical accompaniment, although it is now at times accompanied by organ harmonies. Plainsong was most frequently based on the psalms. It is also used for canticles, antiphons, other sung liturgical texts, and hymns. For example, *The Hymnal 1982* uses plainsong melodies with a variety of hymn texts, including "Creator of the stars of night" (Hymn 60), "Sing, my tongue, the glorious battle" (Hymn 166), and "Come, Holy Ghost, our souls inspire" (Hymn 504). The rhythm of plainsong is free and based on the words of the text rather than meter. Plainsong is not structured by musical bars or time. Since plainsong follows the rhythm of a text, its pulse falls irregularly.

Plainsong may have been influenced by the musical tradition of the Jewish synagogue and the Greek modal system. A musical mode provides a scale or pattern of intervals for the arrangement of tones and semitones. At the end of the fourth century, Ambrose (c. 339–397), Bishop of Milan, ordered plainsong into four modes. Four more modes were added to the system of plainsong during the papacy of Gregory the Great (c. 540–604). This work was attributed to Gregory, and Gregorian Chant was named for him. There has been controversy concerning the extent of Gregory's personal responsibility for this work. Other "dialects" of plainsong include Ambrosian, Mozarabic, Gallican, and Byzantine. The system of eight ecclesiastical or church modes for plainsong has continued to the present day. The plainsong repertory divides into chants for the Mass and chants for the Daily Offices.

Gregorian Chant was taken to England by Augustine in 597. Augustine's party were singing plainsong as they first approached King Ethelbert in the Isle of Thanet. The court of Ethelbert and the See of Augustine at Canterbury soon became a center for Gregorian plainsong. Charlemagne (c. 742–814) had a strong influence on the development of plainsong during the late eighth and early ninth centuries. He invited singers from Rome to his court at Aix-la-Chapelle, and he founded a school of song. The earliest manuscripts of plainsong and treatises on plainsong date from the ninth century. Around the year 1000 there began a period of decline for plainsong which continued into the sixteenth, seventeenth, and eighteenth centuries. Renewed interest in liturgy and the monastic life in the Roman Catholic Church during the nineteenth century was accompanied by a revival of plainsong. The Benedictine Abbey of Solesmes in France was a center for study of plainsong and the editing of choral books. Much of this work took place under the leadership of Dom Joseph Pothier (1835–1923).

After publication of the 1549 BCP, John Merbecke (or Marbeck) (c. 1510–c. 1585) set the English liturgy to plainsong in his *The booke of Common praier noted* (1550). He sought to create a distinctly English chant and used the new English liturgical texts as the starting point for his work. He simplified the older chant to fit the vernacular English text and also composed his own settings. However, Merbecke's book was made obsolete by the 1552 BCP, and a revised edition of his work was not published. Plainsong came to disappear from the English Church until the Oxford Movement. However, plainsong did provide the basis for Anglican Chant, which dates from the seventeenth century. Anglican chant uses a harmonized melody without intonation for singing unmetrical texts such as psalms and canticles.

There has been growing interest in plainsong since the Oxford Movement. Thomas Helmore published the first English plainsong Psalter that was widely used, *The Psalter Noted* (1849), followed by *The Canticles Noted*. These collections were published together as *A Manual of*

Plainsong after 1850. H. B. Briggs and W. H. Frere revised *A Manual of Plainsong* in 1902. Charles Winfred Douglas published the *Plainsong Psalter* (1932), and Healey Willan published *The Canadian Psalter—Plainsong Edition* (1963). *The Hymnal 1982 Accompaniment Edition, Vol. 1*, includes the plainsong psalm tones (S 446). *The Plainsong Psalter*, edited by James Litton, was published by the Church Hymnal Corporation in 1988. Through these resources the ancient beauty of plainsong has been returned more fully to the life of the Episcopal Church. *See* Psalm Tone.

Plainsong Psalter, The. This volume, edited by James Litton and published by the Church Hymnal Corporation in 1988, includes the entire Psalter of the BCP, plus the antiphons which were compiled by Howard E. Galley, Jr., and published in his *The Prayer Book Office* (1980). *See* Plainsong.

Planeta. *See* Chasuble.

Planning and Arrangements, Joint Standing Committee on. The General Convention of 1976 changed the name of the Committee on Agenda and Arrangements to the Committee on Planning and Arrangements. It became the Joint Standing Committee in 1981. It is composed of the executive officer of the General Convention, the vice presidents, secretaries, and chairs of the Committee on the Dispatch of Business of the two houses of General Convention, the treasurer of General Convention, the president and first vice president of the Episcopal Church Women, the General Convention Manager, and one presbyter or deacon and one lay person appointed by the president of the House of Deputies. In the case of a General Convention for which a meeting site has been selected, the committee also includes the bishop and the general chair of arrangements of the local committee of the diocese in which the General Convention will be held. The committee consults with the presidents of the two houses, the chairmen of the Joint and Standing Committees and Commissions, Boards and Agencies of the General Convention, the Executive Council, and such other representative bodies about issues of arrangement and agenda prior to any meeting of the General Convention. The committee also participates in the selection of sites for meetings of General Convention.

Plate (Offering). Undesignated or "loose" offering of money that is among the gifts presented at the offertory (BCP, pp. 333, 361). The term may be used to distinguish the loose offering of money from pledge payments or gifts of money designated for specific purposes. The term is associated with the practice of putting the money in an offering plate or basin for presentation.

Platte, Missionary District of The. The 1889 General Convention voted to divide the Diocese of Nebraska and create the Missionary District of The Platte. This Missionary District, under several different names, existed until 1946. It was known as the Missionary District of The Platte from Oct. 23, 1889, until Oct. 13, 1898.

Pledge. A commitment to give one's time, talents, and money as an expression of faith and a personal response to God's generosity. Parish members are encouraged to make an annual stewardship pledge. This pledge represents their specific Christian commitment to "work, pray, and give for the spread of the kingdom of God" (BCP, p. 856). Parish budgets are prepared in light of the pledges received from the members. A pledge is a statement of intent, not a legal obligation. It can be changed at any time.

Plenary Inspiration. The belief that the entire Bible comes from authors whose hearts and minds were inspired by God. Their mental processes were sharpened and elevated for the task. Although all were inspired, the writers had different personalities and literary styles which are reflected in the various biblical books. The stress, therefore, is on the writers rather than the text itself. *See* Verbal Inspiration.

Plene esse. *See* Esse, Bene Esse, Plene Esse.

Plumbline. Quarterly journal of the Episcopal Society for Ministry in Higher Education (ESMHE). The journal and its title are inspired by the image of Amos and other prophets who confronted Israel as a religious community and a nation. It first appeared in Mar. 1973.

Pneumatology. From the Greek *pneuma* (wind, breath, spirit) and *logia* (doctrine), indicating that branch of Christian theology which deals with the Holy Spirit. Three aspects of the received doctrine are especially important: 1) The recognition by the Council of Constantinople in 381 that God is one Being in three Persons. This recognition acknowledges the full divinity of the Spirit, "who with the Father and the Son together is worshiped and glorified" (Nicene Creed, BCP, pp. 327, 328, 359). The decision represents the triumph of the Cappadocian Fathers over the *pneumatomachians* or Macedonians, who denied the full divinity of the Holy Spirit. 2) The definition of the difference between the Son and the Spirit. As the Council of Nicaea declared the Son to be "begotten, not made" (Nicene Creed, BCP, p. 326), the Council of Constantinople declared that the Spirit "proceeds from the Father" (see BCP, p. 327; Jn 15:26). 3) The addition to the Creed of the so-called "*filioque*" clause during the sixth century, perhaps at the Council of Toledo in 589 (or earlier). The clause asserts that the Spirit proceeds from "the Father and the Son." This "addition" came to be universally accepted in the west but rejected by Eastern Orthodox churches. The 1988 Lambeth Conference recommended that the phrase be dropped from the Nicene Creed in Anglican churches. The 1994 General Convention of the Episcopal Church resolved to delete the *filioque* from the Nicene Creed in the next edition of the Prayer Book. *See* Holy Spirit.

Pocahontas (c. 1595–1617). Daughter of the powerful Indian chief Powhatan. While being held hostage at Jamestown, Virginia, in 1613, she was converted to Christianity and baptized as Rebecca by Alexander Whitaker. In 1614 she married John Rolfe. She may have saved the life of Captain John Smith in 1607.

Pohick Church, Lorton, Virginia. George Washington's parish church. A place of worship was first established near Lewis Heights, Fort Belvoir, in the seventeenth century. Some time prior to 1730 it was relocated near the Occoquan River. This second church was about two miles southeast of the present church. In 1732 this second church became the parish church of Truro Parish which was established that year by the Virginia Assembly. It was known as Pohick Church, the name derived from a Dogue Indian word meaning "hickory," and was also referred to as the "church above Occoquan Ferry." Among Pohick vestry members were George Washington, George Mason, and George William Fairfax. The present structure was ordered by the vestry in 1767, and the site and building plans were selected mainly by George Washington. The building was completed in 1774, but the parish went into decline during the revolution and was abandoned. The Civil War brought further devastation, but the building was again fitted for services in 1874. It continues as a parish today.

Pointing. A method of marking the syllables of a psalm for chanting. It is used for Anglican Chant and Plainchant. *See* Anglican Chant; *see* Plainsong.

Polish National Catholic Church of America. An autonomous Old Catholic church in the U.S., Canada, and Poland. It was constituted between 1897 and 1907 by Polish immigrant clergy and laity who were dissatisfied with their subordination to the Irish and German hierarchy of the Roman Catholic Church in America. They insisted upon call of pastors and control of church property by congregations as well as the use of the Polish language in church services. It was founded in Scranton, Pennsylvania, on Mar. 14, 1897, and spread to other cities with Polish immigrant populations. The church later undertook a mission in Poland itself in 1923. Its founder and first Prime Bishop was Francis Hodur, who was consecrated in 1907 by the Old Catholic Archbishop of Utrecht in the Netherlands. Since that time the Polish church has accepted the Declaration of Utrecht (1889). It has been counted as one of the Old Catholic churches in communion with the Archbishop of Utrecht. Intercommunion with the Episcopal Church was established over the years 1943–1946 on the basis of the Bonn Concordat (1931) with other Old Catholic churches. The General Synod of the Polish National Catholic Church voted to enter into intercommunion with the Episcopal Church on Oct. 18, 1946. This led to some mutual consecrations of bishops and other activities, as well as a joint commission which did not meet often. Intercommunion in the U.S. was terminated on Oct. 5, 1978, by the General Synod of the Polish National Catholic Church because of the Episcopal Church's ordination of women. Since 1983 there have been several meetings of a working group between the two churches in the U.S., and a small but official ecumenical dialogue.

Polity. The term is derived from the Greek word for "city." In general English usage, polity refers to the form of government in a city or nation and the body of laws which govern a political entity. In ecclesiastical use polity has come to refer also to the form of government for an organized church. In Anglicanism the term "polity" became common through its use by Richard Hooker who wrote *Laws of Ecclesiastical Polity* (1594). Hooker defended the episcopal government of the Church of England against the Puritans. He argued that the polity of the church and the state should express the rational nature of God as shown in the Natural Law. The church, as a political society, must be governed by law. But the form of polity which operates in the church may change at any given time. Thus Hooker was able to accept the polity of those protestant churches which did not have episcopal government.

Episcopal polity describes a church in which the source of authority is the college of bishops, typically bishops within the historic episcopate. Presbyterian polity describes a church in which the source of authority is considered to be a synod of presbyters. In Anglican churches, bishops share power with presbyters and laity under a constitution. Eastern Orthodox churches exemplify episcopal polity in its purest form because their source of ecclesial power is a synod of bishops.

Polk, Leonidas (Apr. 10, 1806–June 14, 1864). Bishop and Confederate general. He was born in Raleigh, North Carolina. In 1821 he matriculated at the University of North Carolina, Chapel Hill. In 1823 he received an appointment to the United States Military Academy at West Point and graduated in 1827. He then studied at Virginia Theological Seminary and was ordained deacon on Apr. 11, 1830. As a deacon he was an assistant minister at Monumental Church, Richmond, Virginia. Polk was ordained priest on May 22, 1831. After traveling in Europe, he settled on a plantation in Tennessee. In 1834 he became the rector of St. Peter's Church, Columbia, Tennessee. On Dec. 8, 1838, he was consecrated Missionary Bishop of Arkansas and the Indian Territory. Polk served in that capacity until he was elected the Bishop of Louisiana on Oct. 16, 1841. On June 25, 1861, he was commissioned a Major General in the Confederate Army. He became known as "the fighting Bishop." Polk, Bishop James Hervey Otey and Bishop Stephen Elliott were the founders of the University of the South. Polk laid the cornerstone of the University on Oct. 9, 1860. He was the second chancellor of the University, and served from Apr. 23, 1863–June 14, 1864. Polk was killed in battle during the Civil War at Pine Mountain, Georgia.

Polly Bond Awards. Awards established in the mid-1970s by the Episcopal Communicators to acknowledge excellence and achievement in the ministry of church communications. They are named in honor of Polly Bond (1914–1979), one-time director of communications in the Diocese of Ohio. Bond was a skilled writer and a pioneer in the use of electronic media in the church.

Polycarp (d. Feb. 23, 156). Bishop and martyr. He was born in the second half of the first century and became the Bishop of Smyrna in Asia Minor (Turkey). Polycarp is listed among the "Apostolic Fathers." Writings related to him include a letter of Polycarp to the Philippians and the *Martyrdom of Polycarp*. The letter reveals that Polycarp is in the tradition of the Fourth Gospel and Ignatius of Antioch. The *Martyrdom* is a letter written by the Church of Smyrna to the Church of Philomelium, describing Polycarp's heroic martyrdom. It is the oldest "martyrdom" (account of martyrdom) that has been preserved. It contains the oldest allusion to the custom of preserving relics of martyrs. His witness is commemorated in the Episcopal calendar of the church year on Feb. 23.

Polyphony, Choral. Contrapuntal, or "many voiced," choral compositions in which the vocal lines are conceived as independent melodies that are woven together into a complex whole. This style of music is "linear" in contrast to vocal settings (including hymns) which are conceived chordally with a melody in the upper voice and with an accompaniment provided by the lower voices.

Poor Clares of Reparation, Order of. An order of semi-cloistered contemplative sisters devoted to the life and work of prayer. It was founded on Sept. 15, 1922, the Feast of our Lady's Sorrows (Roman Catholic calendar), when the first sister was clothed in the Holy Habit of St. Clare and began living the life of reparation, adoration and intercession in Merrill, Wisconsin. It sponsors the St. Clare's Fellowship of Prayer (for associates); publishes *St. Clare's Monstrance*, which began publication in Spring 1928; and manages the Grace Dieu Press, which produces devotional cards and other religious articles. They are now located at Mt. Sinai, New York.

Pope, Clarence Cullam, Jr. (b. Oct. 26, 1929). Leading traditionalist bishop. He was born in Lafayette, Louisiana. Pope received his B.A. from Centenary College in 1950, and his B.D. from the University of the South in 1954. He was ordained deacon on June 29, 1954, and priest on May 9, 1955. Pope began his ordained ministry as curate at Trinity Church, Baton Rouge, in 1954, and he was priest-in-charge of St. George's Church, Bossier City, Louisiana, from 1956 until 1958. He was rector of St. George's, 1958–1963. From 1963 until 1985, Pope was rector of St. Luke's Church, Baton Rouge. He was consecrated Bishop Coadjutor of Fort Worth on Jan. 5, 1985, and became Bishop on Jan. 1, 1986. Pope was president of the Episcopal Synod of America, 1989–1993. He retired as Bishop on Dec. 31, 1994. Before he retired, on Oct. 25, 1994, Pope announced that he was leaving the Episcopal Church to enter the Roman Catholic Church. On Feb. 1, 1995, he was received into the Roman Catholic Church by Cardinal Bernard Law of Boston and the Rt. Rev. Joseph Delaney, Archbishop of Fort Worth, at the Anglican Rite Catholic Church of St. Mary the Virgin in Arlington, Texas. On Aug. 19, 1995, Pope returned to the Episcopal Church. This was before the House of Bishops had time to act on his resignation as a Bishop of the Episcopal Church.

Porter. *See* Minor Orders.

Porter, Harry Boone (Jan. 10, 1923–June 5, 1999). Priest, liturgical scholar, professor, editor, and missioner. He was born in Louisville, Kentucky. He received his B.A. from Yale University in 1947 and his S.T.B. from the Berkeley Divinity School in 1950. From 1950 until 1952 Porter was a fellow/tutor at the General Theological Seminary, and in 1952 he received his S.T.M. from General Seminary. He earned his D.Phil. from Oxford University in 1954. In 1996 he received a master's degree in Environmental Studies from the Yale School of Forestry. Porter was ordained deacon on Apr. 12, 1950, and priest on Apr. 16, 1952. He taught Ecclesiastical History at Nashotah House, 1954–1960, and he was Professor of Liturgics at General Seminary from 1960 until 1970. He left General Seminary in 1970 to become the Director of the National Town and Country Church Institute (Roanridge). He remained at the Institute until 1977, when he became Editor of *The Living Church*. He retired from that position in 1990. Porter served on the Standing Liturgical Commission, 1961–1976, the General Board of Examining Chaplains, 1970–1982, and was president of the Episcopal Church Army, 1970–1975. He was president of New Directions Ministries from 1977 until 1985. Among his books are *The Day of Light* (1960), *Growth and Life in the Local Church* (1968), *Keeping the Church Year* (1977), and *A Song of Creation* (1986). Porter died in Bridgeport, Connecticut.

Position Paper. A paper issued by the House of Bishops which expresses the position of the House on any given subject or issue. The House of Bishops may require the dissemination of a position paper on the same basis as a pastoral letter.

Postcommunion Prayer. A prayer of thanksgiving after communion that also seeks God's help for Christian service. The eucharistic community is sent "into the world in peace" to love and serve God as witnesses of Christ (BCP, pp. 365–366). This prayer expresses the transition of the Christian's attention from the mystery of sacramental participation to the engagement of Christian ministry. The prayer follows the administration of communion to the people, and it precedes the blessing and dismissal. A hymn may be sung before or after the postcommunion prayer (BCP, p. 409). Postcommunion prayers have been dated from the fourth century. The 1549 Prayer Book provided one postcommunion prayer, and two options were included in the 1552 BCP. The Rite 1 Eucharist in the 1979 BCP provides one postcommunion prayer (p. 339), with two options for the postcommunion prayer in the Rite 2 Eucharist (pp. 365–366). The Rite 1 postcommunion prayer may be said or sung by the celebrant alone, or the people may join in saying the prayer. The Rite 2 postcommunion prayer is always said by the celebrant and people together. The 1979 BCP provides special postcommunion prayers for Communion under Special Circumstances, Communion in the Ministration to the Sick, the Celebration and Blessing of a Marriage, the Burial of the Dead, and for ordinations and the Celebration of a New Ministry.

Post-modernism. A relativistic movement that denies the existence of absolute meaning and the possibility of objective knowledge of reality. It contradicts the attempt of the Enlightenment to reach absolute truth through pure human reason. Post-modernism denies the possibility of objective theological truth. Faith is reduced to a way of speaking used by a given community rather than a means of knowing objective reality and the actual nature of God. Post-modernism as a movement is not well defined.

Postulant (Holy Orders, Monastic). One who tests a vocation such as a vocation to an ordained ministry or the religious life. Postulants for holy orders seek ordination as deacon or priest. The length of postulancy varies. The time involves meeting with the bishop of the diocese, examination by the Commission on Ministry, along with physical and mental examinations, and in some cases attending discernment conferences or weekends. Postulancy is an initial time of preparation and testing for ordained ministry. Candidacy is the next stage in the ordination process.

In religious orders, postulancy is the time of pre-novitiate discernment and preparation. Postulants may live as guests in the religious community for a period of time to become acquainted with the religious life and to allow the community and superior to observe their suitability for the religious life.

Potter, Alonzo (July 6, 1800–July 4, 1865). Bishop and educator. He was born in Beekman (La Grange), Dutchess County, New York. He graduated from Union College, Schenectady, New York, in 1818. In 1819 he returned to Union College as a tutor and in 1822 was made professor of mathematics and natural philosophy. At the same time he studied for the ordained ministry and was ordained deacon on May 1, 1822, and priest on Sept. 16, 1824. In 1826 Potter became rector of St. Paul's Church, Boston, and remained there until 1831, when he returned to Union College as professor of moral philosophy. He was consecrated the third Bishop of Pennsylvania on Sept. 25, 1845. While bishop he revived the Protestant Episcopal Academy at Philadelphia in 1860, and he founded the Divinity School of the Protestant Episcopal Church in Philadelphia in 1863. Over a period of fourteen years he delivered some sixty lectures to large audiences at the Lowell Institute in Boston. Notes from these lectures were edited and published as *Religious Philosophy; or Nature, Man, and the Bible Witnessing to God and to Religious Truth* (1872). As Bishop of Pennsylvania, Potter helped the diocese to become known for its tolerance and comprehensiveness. His generosity of spirit discouraged party strife within the church. He died on shipboard in the harbor of San Francisco. Horatio Potter was his brother.

Potter, Henry Codman (May 25, 1835–July 21, 1908). Bishop and advocate of social justice. He was born in Schenectady, New York, and was the son of Alonzo Potter, the third Bishop of Pennsylvania. In 1845 the family moved to Philadelphia, and he attended the Episcopal Academy in that city. He was a student at the Virginia Theological Seminary from 1854 to 1857. Potter was ordained deacon on May 27, 1857. His father placed him in charge of Christ Church, Greensburg, Pennsylvania. He was ordained priest on Oct. 15, 1858. In May 1859 he became the rector of St. John's Church, Troy, New York. He served there until Apr. 1866 when he was called to be assistant minister at Trinity Church, Boston. On Oct. 3, 1866, Potter was elected the seventeenth secretary of the House of Bishops. He was re-elected five times. He served until Oct. 23, 1883, when he

had to step down after he became a bishop. After two years at Trinity Church, he was called to be the rector of Grace Church, New York. Potter was consecrated Assistant Bishop of New York on Oct. 20, 1883. He became the seventh Bishop of New York when his predecessor died on Jan. 2, 1887. He served in that position until his death. On Nov. 25, 1884, he heard the profession of James Otis Sargent Huntington as a monk. This was the beginning of the Order of the Holy Cross, the first monastic order for men in the Episcopal Church that was founded in the United States. Potter was one of the leaders of the Church Association for the Advancement of the Interests of Labor and a leading social gospel advocate in the Episcopal Church. He has been called "A Prophet of Social Reform." He died in Cooperstown, New York.

Potter, Horatio (Feb. 9, 1802–Jan. 2, 1887). Bishop and educator. He was born in Beekman (La Grange), Dutchess County, New York. He received his B.A. from Union College, Schenectady, New York, in 1826. He was ordained deacon on July 15, 1827, and priest on Dec. 14, 1828. His diaconate was spent at Trinity Church, Saco, Maine, and in 1828 he became professor of mathematics and natural philosophy at Washington College, Hartford, Connecticut. Potter became rector of St. Peter's Church, Albany, New York, in 1833, and on Nov. 22, 1854, he was consecrated the sixth Bishop of New York. Since Bishop Benjamin T. Onderdonk was still alive but suspended from office, Potter served as "provisional bishop" until Onderdonk's death on Apr. 30, 1861, when he became Bishop of New York. St. Stephen's College at Annandale-on-Hudson, New York, was established in 1860 under Potter's leadership. It was subsequently renamed Bard College. The Diocese of New York grew rapidly during Potter's episcopate. In 1868 the new dioceses of Albany, Central New York, and Long Island were created from the Diocese of New York. Potter died in New York City. Alonzo Potter was his brother. *See* Bard College, Annandale-on-Hudson, New York.

Praise (Prayer). Loving worship of God in prayer. We may respond with praise for God's mighty deeds throughout salvation history. The Canticle *Te Deum laudamus* (Canticle 21, BCP, pp. 95–96), begins, "You are God: we praise you." It recalls that Christ "became man to set us free," he "did not shun the Virgin's womb," he "overcame the sting of death," and he "opened the kingdom of heaven to all believers." The people's response to the proclamation of the gospel is, "Praise to you, Lord

Christ" (BCP, p. 358). The Prayer Book Catechism identifies praise as one of the seven principal kinds of prayer (p. 856). The Catechism notes that "We praise God, not to obtain anything, but because God's Being draws praise from us" (p. 857). Except during Advent and Lent, the *Gloria in excelsis* or another song of praise precedes the salutation and collect in the entrance rite of the eucharist (p. 356). *The Hymnal 1982* includes a section of hymns of Praise to God (Hymns 372–433).

Prayer. The experience of corporate or individual nearness with God, through words, acts, or silence. Any act or activity offered to God in a spirit of dedication may be prayerful. This nearness may take the form of addressing God, as in prayers of petition, praise, and thanksgiving; or the form of listening, as in contemplative and meditative prayer. Both forms assume a relationship between God and the one who prays. Prayer is the opening of the direct relationship between God and humanity. The Catechism states, "Christian prayer is response to God the Father, through Jesus Christ, in the power of the Holy Spirit" (BCP, p. 856).

Prayer Book. *See* Book of Common Prayer, The ("BCP").

Prayer Book Commentary. A comprehensive study of the liturgical and theological background of a Prayer Book. During the Puritan Commonwealth in England, when the BCP was outlawed, two systematic commentaries were published: Anthony Sparrow's *A Rationale or Practical Exposition upon the Book of Common Prayer* (1655) and Hamon L'Estrange's *The Alliance of Divine Offices* (1659). Thomas Comber published seven volumes entitled *A Companion to the Temple and Closet* (1672–76) in an attempt to reconcile dissenters. Two commentaries were published in 1710: William Nicholls's *A Comment on the Book of Common Prayer* and Charles Wheatly's *A Rational Illustration of the Book of Common Prayer*. Wheatly's book was reprinted as late as 1890. It was listed in the "Course of Ecclesiastical Studies, Established by the House of Bishops" in 1804 and reprinted in journals of General Convention through 1889. Also listed was John Reeves's *Book of Common Prayer with Introduction and Commentary* (1801). With the list was the Bishop of Lincoln's "Library of a Parish Ministry" which contained Wheatly's book and *A Critical and Practical Elucidation of the Book of Common Prayer* (1797) by Nicholls and John Shepherd. Commentaries on the 1789 American Prayer Book include Andrew Fowler's *An Exposition of the Book of Common Prayer* (1805) and T. C. Brownell's *Family Prayer Book* (1823). Substantial, often reprinted commentaries on the 1662 English Prayer Book include Francis Procter's *A History of the Book of Common Prayer, with a Rationale of Its Offices* (1855) (revised by W. H. Frere [1900]), John Henry Blunt's *The Annotated Book of Common Prayer* (1866), Evan Daniel's *The Prayer-Book: Its History, Language, and Contents* (1877), Alfred Barry's *The Teacher's Prayer Book* (1882) (an American edition based on the 1892 revision was published in 1898), *Prayer-Book Commentary for Teachers and Students* (1883), and Charles Neil and J.M. Willoughby's *The Tutorial Prayer Book* (1912). Massey H. Shepherd, Jr., produced *The Oxford American Prayer Book Commentary* (1950) as a companion to the 1928 revision. Marion Hatchett produced *Commentary on the American Prayer Book* (1980) for the 1979 revision.

Prayer Book Concordance, The. An examination of word usage in the 1979 BCP. This volume was published in 1988 by the Church Hymnal Corporation. It was edited by Galen Bushey. There are 6,423 separate and distinct words which appear at least once in the 1979 BCP. The first section of this book is a concordance (alphabetical index of words with their contexts) of all the spoken words in the BCP, and the second section is a concordance of all the word references for the rubrics, notes, and historical documents in the BCP. The second section concerns those parts of the BCP which are never used aloud in a service of worship. There is also a glossary which lists all the words and the number of their occurrences in the BCP.

Prayer Book Preface. The Preface printed in every edition of the American BCP is an abbreviated form of the Preface prepared for the Proposed BCP of 1786 by the Rev. Dr. William Smith, then rector at Chestertown, Maryland, and founder of Washington College in that town. The second and third paragraphs and a portion of the fourth are largely a paraphrase of the Preface to the English revision of 1662. The Preface to the American BCP is heavily dependent upon an anonymous volume arguing for Prayer Book revision, *Free and Candid Disquisitions*, which was published in London in 1749. The Preface states the principle that the worship of the church may be altered for the edification of the people and sets forth the aims of Prayer Book revision: preservation of peace and unity in the church, procuring of reverence, exciting of piety and devotion, and elimination of elements which provide occasion for "cavil or quarrel" against the Prayer Book liturgy.

Prayer Book Society. Organization which advocates continued use of the 1928 BCP and opposes women's ordination. It was founded in May 1971 in Sewanee, Tennessee, by John M. Aden, Harold L. Weatherby, Walter Sullivan, John Glass, Andrew Lytle, and the Revs. William Ralston, Howard Rhys, and James Law. The original name was the Society for the Preservation of the Book of Common Prayer. Its stated purpose at the time was to preserve the 1928 BCP "from sudden and injudicious revision and more specifically, to defeat the adoption of trial liturgies because they were poorly written, ill-conceived, and in some particulars contrary to the faith." Since the adoption of the 1979 BCP, the society has worked to continue the use of the 1928 BCP as one of the fully authorized liturgies of the Episcopal Church. This would allow use of the 1928 BCP without permission from diocesan bishops. It has also raised questions about *The Hymnal 1982*. It is opposed to the ordination of women, the blessing of homosexual and lesbian unions, and the ordination of practicing homosexuals and lesbians. In Nov. 1981 it began publishing a magazine. This issue did not have a title, but announced a contest for a name. The Jan. 1982 issue had the name *Mandate*. On Mar. 4, 1987, the name of the organization was changed from the Society for the Preservation of the Book of Common Prayer to the Prayer Book Society of the Episcopal Church.

Prayer Book for Soldiers and Sailors, A. This small volume of ninety-one pages was published by the Army and Navy Commission of the Protestant Episcopal Church in 1941. It was sent as a gift to those serving in the army and navy as a "reminder that the Church follows you into the Service with deep interest." It contained An Order of Worship, The Holy Communion, Prayers, Psalms, readings from the Bible, and thirty-eight hymns.

Prayer Book Studies. A series of booklets issued by the Standing Liturgical Commission beginning in 1950 making proposals for the revision of the BCP. *Prayer Book Studies* 16 proposed the method adopted to produce the 1979 revision of the BCP. *Prayer Book Studies* 17–28 were drafts of services for that revision. In 1975–76 several unnumbered *Studies* containing additional services for the revision were issued. *Prayer Book Studies* 29 was an introduction to the proposed new Prayer Book by Charles Price. *Prayer Book*

Studies 30 (1989) contained supplemental liturgical texts in non-exclusive language drafted in response to resolutions of General Convention in 1985 and 1988. *See* Liturgy of the Lord's Supper, The (1966).

Prayer Desk. *See* Litany Desk; *see* Prie-Dieu.

Prayer, Principal Kinds of. The principal kinds of prayer include adoration, praise, thanksgiving, penitence, oblation, intercession, and petition. (see BCP, pp. 856–857, and individual entries for each of the principal kinds of prayer).

Prayers of the People. The BCP uses the title "Prayers of the People" for the *oratio fidelium* or general intercessions in the eucharist. Such prayers have a long and venerable history. Their existence was first mentioned by Justin Martyr about the year 150, and for centuries they formed a vital part of the Daily Office and eucharistic liturgy. In the early church they usually included a long series of biddings that were chanted by a deacon, to each of which the people responded with *"Kyrie eleison"* ("Lord, have mercy") or with silent prayer. Audible intercession virtually disappeared from the Mass in the west during the middle ages, until Cranmer revived it in his "prayer for the whole state of Christ's Church." In Cranmer's 1549 and 1552 versions of the BCP, however, intercession retained its medieval character as a responsibility of the priest. Modern liturgical revisers restored general intercessions to the people and made them more diverse and suitable for modern congregations. The BCP provides several forms of intercession, especially for Rite 2. The BCP also allows parishes to adapt and change these forms and to create new prayers. General intercessions include six categories of those in need: the church, the world, the nation, the community, the suffering, and the dead (BCP, p. 383).

Prayers We Have in Common. *See* International Consultation on English Texts (ICET) (1969).

Preacher. The one who preaches the sermon. In some Protestant churches, the term is used as a title for a member of the clergy. *See* Preaching.

Preaching. The event and act of proclaiming the Word of God through a sermon or homily. Preaching interprets the gospel tradition in light of faith and in the context of the liturgical and pastoral occasion of the service. The sermon draws together the life of the parish community, the life of the preacher, and the lives of those who hear the sermon. Preaching is to reflect God's presence, love, and guidance in a particular moment of the church's life. The sermon is not an abstract statement of truth, and it is not just a personalized commentary on scripture. The sermon must engage the faith and understanding of the one who preaches and the ones who hear. The Christian story, the congregation's story, and the preacher's story can be the one story of God's love that is proclaimed in the sermon. Preaching in the Episcopal Church is typically liturgical preaching. The BCP calls for the sermon to follow the gospel at the Holy Eucharist, Confirmation, Ordination, and the Celebration of a New Ministry. A sermon or address follows the gospel at the Consecration of a Church. The sermon follows the gospel or the peace at a baptism. A homily may follow the gospel at the Celebration and Blessing of a Marriage and at the Burial of the Dead. At Morning and Evening Prayer, a sermon may be preached after the Office or after the readings or at the time of the hymn or anthem after the collects.

Preaching Bands. *See* Preaching Tabs.

Preaching Gown. A long, flowing black garment that may be worn by the preacher with cassock and preaching tabs. It may have full, bell-shaped sleeves, and velvet bands.

Preaching Scarf. *See* Tippet.

Preaching Station. A location where worship services occur. These services may take place on a regular or an irregular basis. The place of meeting may or may not be set apart for church services on a permanent basis. Preaching stations are frequently located in areas of mission development. They may be served by one or more members of the clergy with pastoral responsibility for a region of mission development. Historically, preaching stations have been used in both domestic and overseas missions.

Preaching Tabs. White starched tabs that may be worn over the neck of the cassock, making an inverted "V" shape. They are also known as preaching bands. They may be worn by a preacher who is not the celebrant at the eucharist.

Prebend. A cathedral benefice, defined in English canon law as an endowment in land or pension in money, was given to a cathedral for maintenance of a secular priest or regular canon. Since the nineteenth century, incomes of prebends have been transferred to the Ecclesiastical Commission of the Church of England. The income is no longer paid to a holder of the prebend.

Prebendary. Unknown in America, a prebendary in the Church of England is basically an honorary title given to the holder of a prebend. The income of a prebend is now paid to the Ecclesiastical Commission for the benefit of all the clergy. Prior to the nineteenth century the income was paid to the prebendary.

Precedence, Rules of. The calendar of the church year provides rules of precedence concerning principal feasts, Sundays, holy days, days of special devotion, and days of optional observance (BCP, pp. 15–18). These rules determine which feast or observance has priority. The seven principal feasts (Easter Day, Ascension Day, the Day of Pentecost, Trinity Sunday, All Saints' Day, Christmas Day, and the Epiphany) take precedence over any other day or observance. In addition to the seven principal feasts, the feasts of the Holy Name, the Presentation, and the Transfiguration also take precedence over the Sunday observance. Sunday takes precedence over all other feasts and observances of the church year. When a feast of our Lord or other major feast appointed cannot be observed because it occurs on a Sunday, the feast is normally transferred to the first convenient open day in the following week. Major feasts falling in Holy Week or Easter Week are transferred to the week following the Second Sunday of Easter, in the order of their occurrence. When a Feast of our Lord or another major feast occurs on a Sunday but does not take precedence, the collect, preface, and one or more of the lessons appointed for the feast may be substituted for those of the Sunday. However, this substitution may not be done from the Last Sunday after Pentecost through the First Sunday after the Epiphany, nor from the Last Sunday after the Epiphany through Trinity Sunday. The feast of the dedication of a church, and the feast of its patron or title, may be observed on or transferred to a Sunday, except in the seasons of Advent, Lent, and Easter. A special occasion may be observed on a Sunday "for urgent and sufficient reason," with the express permission of the bishop.

Precentor. 1) The music director of a cathedral, monastic, or collegiate church. 2) The cantor or singer who introduces a chant. The term is from the Latin, "to sing before."

Preces. Brief responsive prayers which are often based on verses of scripture, especially the Psalter. The BCP includes such versicles and responses after the Lord's Prayer in Morning Prayer (pp. 55, 97–98) and Evening Prayer (pp. 67–68, 121–122), which are also known as suffrages. The BCP offices also have opening *preces* (see S 33, S 58 in *The Hymnal 1982*.)

Predella. A raised platform or footpace for the altar.

Preface (Eucharistic). Introductory section of the eucharistic prayer, including the salutation, the *Sursum Corda* and ending with the *Sanctus*. Eastern eucharistic liturgies typically have prefaces with a fixed text that recalls salvation history. This tradition is reflected in Eucharistic Prayer D, based on the liturgy of St. Basil, and Eucharistic Prayer C, both of which have a fixed preface (BCP, pp. 372–373, 369–371). Western eucharistic liturgies for certain major observances in the church year have typically included a variable portion of the preface which is included in the fixed or common portion of the preface. This variable preface reflects the theme or occasion of the day, and it is known as the proper preface. The Leonine Sacramentary, which is the oldest surviving Roman sacramentary, provided a separate preface for each Mass. The Gelasian Sacramentary had more than fifty proper prefaces, and the Sarum Missal had ten proper prefaces. The 1549 BCP provided five proper prefaces, including Christmas, Easter, Ascension, Pentecost, and Trinity Sunday. The 1552 BCP allowed the use of the Christmas, Easter, and Ascension prefaces through the octaves of those feasts, and permitted the Pentecost preface to be used until Trinity Sunday. The 1979 BCP includes twenty-two proper prefaces (pp. 377–382). There are three proper prefaces of the Lord's Day, "Of God the Father," "Of God the Son," and "Of God the Holy Spirit." There are nine proper prefaces for seasons, including Advent, Incarnation, Epiphany, two proper prefaces for Lent, Holy Week, Easter, Ascension, and Pentecost. There are ten proper prefaces for other occasions: Trinity Sunday, All Saints, Apostles and Ordinations, Dedication of a Church, Baptism, Marriage, Commemoration of the Dead, and three different options to commemorate a saint. Traditional language versions of the proper prefaces (BCP, pp. 344–349) are for use with both Rite 1 eucharistic prayers. Contemporary language versions of the proper prefaces are for use with Eucharistic Prayers A and B of Rite 2. The 1979 BCP provides a proper preface for all days of the church year, except weekdays after Pentecost that are neither saints' days nor an occasion for use of the propers for various occasions. Many of the proper prefaces are appointed for use in several different observances. For example, the proper preface for Trinity Sunday is used on Trinity Sunday, Independence Day, Saint Michael and All Angels, Thanksgiving Day, and the observances "Of the Holy Trinity," "Of the Holy Angels," and "For the Nation." It may also be used for the observances "Of a Theologian and Teacher" and "For the Unity of the Church." *The Altar Book* provides music in simple and solemn tone versions for all the proper prefaces. *See* Salutation; *see* Sanctus, The; *see* Sursum Corda.

Prelate. In the Anglican tradition, the term indicates a bishop. The term "prelacy" has been used pejoratively to describe ecclesiastical governance by bishops. In Roman Catholicism, "prelate" has been applied to other ecclesiastical officials such as higher officials of the Roman curia, abbots, cardinals, and popes. Prelates with episcopal authority have been referred to as major prelates, and prelates with quasi-episcopal authority (such as abbots) have been referred to as minor prelates. The term is seldom used in the Episcopal Church.

Pre-Lenten Season. The observance of a period of a few weeks in preparation for Lent. Septuagesima Sunday was the first Sunday of the Pre-Lenten season. It was the third Sunday before Lent and the ninth Sunday before Easter. The name literally indicated seventy days before Easter. This was inaccurate since this Sunday fell sixty-four days before Easter. The second Sunday of the Pre-Lenten season was Sexagesima Sunday. It was the second Sunday before Lent and the eighth Sunday before Easter. Its name indicated sixty days before Easter, although it was fifty-seven days before Easter. Septuagesima Sunday and Sexagesima Sunday may have been reckoned from Quinquagesima Sunday, which was exactly fifty days before Easter. It was the last Sunday before Lent and the seventh Sunday before Easter. Similarly, the forty-day season of Lent and the first Sunday of Lent have been known as Quadragesima.

Observance of the Pre-Lenten season dates from fifth- or sixth-century Roman practice. The Sundays of the Pre-Lenten season last appeared in the 1928 BCP of the Episcopal Church. The themes of Epiphany are now emphasized by the Episcopal calendar of the church year and BCP lectionaries, from the Feast of the Epiphany until the season of Lent begins on Ash Wednesday.

Prelude. An event or action that precedes another event or action. For example, An Order of Worship for the Evening may serve "as the introduction to Evening Prayer or some other service, or as the prelude to an evening meal or other activity" (BCP, p. 108). In the Episcopal Church, the term typically refers to a piece of music that is played immediately before the beginning of a service. A musical prelude is often played by an organist or other instrumentalists. The prelude may reflect the theme, liturgical season, or occasion of the day. Many musical preludes have been based on hymn tunes.

Preparation of the Table and Presentation of the Offerings. It is the function of the deacon to prepare the altar for the celebration of the eucharist, preparing and placing upon it the bread and cup of wine (BCP, p. 407). The deacon may be assisted by other ministers in preparing the table. Although a corporal (small white cloth) is not required by the BCP, in most parishes it is placed on the fair linen at the preparation of the table, with the paten, chalice, and any other vessels. A sufficient quantity of bread for the celebration may be placed on the paten, or the bread may be placed on the corporal in the vessel in which it was presented. It is customary to add a little water to the wine in preparing the table. There may also be a flagon on the altar from which additional chalices may be filled after the breaking of the consecrated bread. In order to express the symbolism of the one cup, it is appropriate that there be only one chalice on the altar during the Great Thanksgiving. Depending on the local custom of the congregation, the Altar Book may be placed on the altar at this time. The preparation of the table immediately precedes the eucharistic prayer and serves to draw the congregation's attention from the pulpit to the altar in preparation for celebrating the Great Thanksgiving.

The deacon's function in preparing the table and placing the bread and wine upon it has been traced from the second century. At times the deacon brought a small table into the room or into the center of the congregation after the catechumens were dismissed and the prayers of the people were concluded. A white cloth was placed on the table. Offerings of bread and wine were brought to the table by the people, or the deacons moved among the people to receive the offerings. Bread and wine in sufficient quantity

were put out for the sacrament, with the rest set aside for the clergy and the poor. In subsequent years the altar was prepared before the liturgy in some places. This change has been associated with the development of low Mass, in which the altar served as both pulpit and table. The 1979 BCP states that at the presentation of the offerings, representatives of the congregation will bring the people's offerings of bread and wine, and money or other gifts, to the deacon or celebrant (pp. 333, 361). The BCP also directs that at the ordination of a deacon, the newly ordained deacon prepares the bread, pours sufficient wine (and a little water) into the chalice, and places the vessels on the table before the eucharist (p. 546). The BCP clearly identifies the deacon's function in preparing the table and receiving the offerings at the eucharist. *See* Corporal; *see* Deacon; *see* Offertory, Offertory Procession, Offertory Sentence.

Pre-Sanctified, Mass of the. Celebration of communion with previously consecrated eucharistic elements, in a eucharistic liturgy without a prayer of consecration. It makes possible eucharistic sharing on days of fasting when the eucharist is not celebrated. In the Byzantine Rite, the liturgy of the pre-sanctified is used on weekdays during Lent (usually on Wednesdays and Fridays) when the eucharist is not celebrated. The liturgy of the pre-sanctified is celebrated in the west only on Good Friday. The use of the liturgy of the pre-sanctified on Good Friday dates from the early sacramentaries of the western church. The 1979 BCP allows Holy Communion to be administered from the reserved sacrament on Good Friday. The eucharistic elements that will be administered on Good Friday are consecrated at the Maundy Thursday service (p. 275). The administration of communion on Good Friday follows the solemn collects and devotions before the cross. A simple order of service is used, with a confession of sin and the Lord's Prayer preceding the communion (BCP, p. 282). A final prayer concludes the Good Friday service. The term "Mass (or liturgy) of the pre-sanctified" is not used in Anglican Prayer Books.

Presbyter, Presbyterate. From the Greek *presbyteros*, "elder" or "old man." In the NT, "presbyter" indicates a leader of the church. The presbyterate refers to the collegial leadership of the presbyters of the church. A member of the Jewish Sanhedrin was said to belong to the *presbyteron*, which was the council of the elders of the people (see Lk 22:66). In Christian usage, the presbyters were at first indistinguishable from "overseers," or bishops. The term "presbyter" was used interchangeably with *episcopos*, or bishop (see Ti 1: 5–7). By the second century, the presbyters joined with the bishop in an advisory council that was presided over by the bishop. The presbyters were associated with the bishop in the bishop's ministry of pastoral oversight, administration, and liturgical leadership. However, the bishop was distinguished from the presbyters, who derived their authority from the bishop. By the third century the bishop came to delegate primary daily pastoral responsibility in a congregation or area to a presbyter. The presbyter would then be responsible for teaching and preaching, administration, and sacramental ministry in that place, under the oversight of the bishop. The English word "priest" is derived from "presbyter," and used as a synonym for presbyter. After the Reformation, some churches began to use the term "presbyter" for the minister who preaches the word and administers the sacraments. The Anglican Church used the term "priest" for the second order of ministry. The 1979 BCP uses both terms. For example, directions for the Ordination of a Priest require that "at least two presbyters must be present" (p. 524). The Catechism notes that "the ministry of a priest or presbyter" is "to represent Christ and his Church, particularly as pastor to the people; to share with the bishop in the overseeing of the Church; to proclaim the gospel; to administer the sacraments; and to bless and declare pardon in the name of God" (BCP, p. 856). Some have favored use of "presbyter" because of historic association of the term "priest" with a narrow eucharistic piety, or with OT sacrifice. The term has also been favored in ecumenical discussions. The priests of a diocese or their meetings may be referred to as a "College of Presbyters." *See* Priest.

Prescott, Oliver Sherman (Mar. 24, 1824–Nov. 17, 1903). Ritualist priest and monk. He was born in New Haven, Connecticut, and raised in Trinity Church, New Haven, where the rector was the Rev. Harry Croswell, a leading Tractarian priest. Prescott attended Washington College, 1840–1842, and then studied for a year at Yale. He attended the General Theological Seminary and was ordained deacon on Sept. 16, 1847. Later in 1847, Prescott and William Glenny French made their monastic professions before Bishop Levi S. Ives of North Carolina at St. Luke's Church, New York. They were the first two members of Bishop Ives's Society of the Holy Cross. Prescott then immediately went to North Carolina. He worked in Rowan,

Iredell, and Davis counties, but never went to Valle Crucis, the center of the society. In 1849 he went to Boston, Massachusetts, where he was assistant at the Church of the Advent. He heard confessions and pronounced private absolutions at the Church of the Advent. Bishop Manton Eastburn of Massachusetts brought him to trial for these practices. Prescott was acquitted and moved to Westminster, Maryland, where he served the Church of the Ascension. After several other moves, Prescott went to England in 1869. He joined the Society of St. John the Evangelist as the fourth member and second American professed in the society. In 1876 he returned to the United States and became the rector of St. Clement's Church, Philadelphia, a leading ritualist parish. The vestry of St. Clement's had invited the society to take charge of the parish. He served there until 1881. He left the society in 1882. Prescott spent the remaining years of his life as rector of St. Peter's Church, Ripon, Wisconsin, and rector of St. Luke's Church, New Haven. He died in Verbank, New York.

Presentation of the Gifts. At the offertory, the people's offerings of bread and wine and money or other gifts are presented to the deacon or celebrant by representatives of the congregation (BCP, p. 361). The people stand as the offerings are presented and placed on the altar. The 1662 BCP restored the historic role of the deacon in the gathering of the people's offerings. Prior to this change the offerings were presented to the wardens. A sentence that was apparently intended for use at the presentation, "All things come of thee, O Lord, and of thine own have we given thee," was added in the 1892 BCP. The 1979 BCP has no presentation sentence, but the BCP rubric does allow a hymn, psalm, or anthem to be sung during the offertory. A presentation sentence may be considered redundant and superfluous because the gifts are offered during the prayer of oblation of the eucharistic prayer. *See* Oblation; *see* Offertory, Offertory Procession, Offertory Sentence.

Presentation of our Lord Jesus Christ in the Temple, The. A feast of our Lord celebrated on Feb. 2, also known as Candlemas and the Feast of the Purification. It commemorates the presentation of Jesus and the purification of Mary in the Jerusalem Temple forty days after Jesus' birth, in accordance with the requirements of Jewish law (Lv 12:2–8). The feast is celebrated about forty days after Christmas. According to the account of Lk 2:22–39, the presentation of Jesus was also the occasion of the meeting of Jesus with Simeon and Anna. Simeon's prayer of blessing is the basis for the canticle *Nunc dimittis* (see BCP, p. 120). Celebration of the feast dates from the fourth century in Jerusalem. It was introduced in Rome in the seventh century, where it included a procession with candles and the singing of the *Nunc dimittis.* The celebration came to include the lighting and blessing of candles which were carried in procession. This feast was known as "Candlemas." *See* Nunc dimittis.

Presentment. This is a formal allegation of a canonical offense by an ordained person. The presentment alleges that a triable offense has been committed and that there are reasonable grounds to believe the offense was committed by the person named in the presentment. The presentment is submitted by a standing committee or board of inquiry to an ecclesiastical trial court.

President, Presider (liturgical). The BCP uses the word "celebrant" to describe the priest or bishop who presides at the Holy Eucharist. The word "officiant" is used to describe the minister, lay or ordained, who presides at the Daily Offices. Most contemporary liturgical books use "president" or "presider" for both. "President" is used by the English Alternative Service Book, but it was felt to be too political to be used in the United States. Some feel that the word "celebrant" is inappropriate for the presider at the eucharist, since the entire congregation shares in the celebration. *See* Officiant.

Presiding Bishop. Chief Pastor and Primate of the Episcopal Church. The office evolved originally from a rule of the House of Bishops in 1789 making its presiding officer the senior member in terms of date of consecration. As a result of increased duties, the office was incorporated into the Constitution of the Church in 1901 and styled Presiding Bishop of the Church. In 1919 the office was made elective and invested with executive responsibility for all departments of the church's work. The first election of a Presiding Bishop by General Convention took place in 1925. Since 1943 the Presiding Bishop has been required to resign diocesan jurisdiction upon election. In 1967 the duties of the office were significantly enhanced. As "Chief Pastor," the Presiding Bishop is charged with initiating and developing church policy and strategy, speaking God's Word to the church and the world, and visiting every diocese of the church. The title "Primate" was added in 1982. The Cathedral of Saint Peter and Saint Paul in Washington, D. C., is the official seat of the Presiding Bishop. The office of the Presiding Bishop is located at the Episcopal Church Center in New York City. The present term of office for the Presiding Bishop is nine years.

Presiding Bishop and Council. *See* National Council.

Presiding Bishop's Council of Advice. *See* Council of Advice, House of Bishops.

Presiding Bishop's Diploma in Church Music Program. The original name of the Leadership Program for Musicians Serving Small Churches. *See* Leadership Program for Musicians Serving Small Churches.

Presiding Bishop's Fund for World Relief. The fund is a major response by the Episcopal Church to God's call to serve Christ in all persons, to love our neighbors, and to respect the dignity of every human being. The fund raises, receives, and uses monies for the relief of human suffering. It provides emergency relief in times of disaster; it assists in the rehabilitation of lives, property, and organizations; and it joins in partnership with those who identify and address root causes of suffering. At the 1940 General Convention, Presiding Bishop Henry St. George Tucker noted in his opening address the suffering caused by the war, and said, "I trust that this General Convention will call upon our people to take their full part in relief activities, wherever they are practicable under the conditions of war, not only as an obligation, but still more as a Christian privilege." The General Convention passed a resolution that asked the Presiding Bishop to designate the Department of Christian Social Relations of the National Council as the agency to manage these relief efforts. The fund is managed by the Presiding Bishop and a board of directors of twenty persons appointed by the Presiding Bishop. The Society of Anchor, the major donor organization for the fund, was established in 1991. The fund publishes *Lifeline*.

Prevenient Grace. The aspect of God's grace that is understood to precede the free determination of the will. The term "prevenient" is derived from the Latin meaning "to come before" or "to anticipate." The human response in faith to God is always a response to God's initiative and invitation communicated by the Holy Spirit. This faithful response is made possible by prevenient grace. It must be freely made by the person, and is never compelled by God.

Price, Charles Philip (Oct. 4, 1920–Oct. 13, 1999). Priest, theologian, and seminary professor. He was born in Pittsburgh, Pennsylvania. Price received his B.A. from Harvard University in 1941, his M.Div. from the Virginia Theological Seminary in 1949, and his Th.D. from Union Theological Seminary in 1962. He was ordained deacon on Feb. 24, 1949, and priest on Oct. 15, 1949. He began his ordained ministry in 1949 as priest-in-charge of St. Michael's Church, Valley Ligonier, Pennsylvania, where he served as rector, 1952–1954. From 1954 until 1956, he was assistant at St. James' Church, New York City. Most of his teaching career was at Virginia Theological Seminary, where he served as assistant professor of systematic theology, 1956–1959, and associate professor, 1959–1963. From 1963 until 1972 Price was preacher to the university and chairman of the Board of Preachers at Harvard University. In 1972 he returned to Virginia Theological Seminary as William Meade Professor of Systematic Theology. He held this position until his retirement in 1989. Price was a member of the Board for Theological Education, 1968–1976, the Standing Liturgical Commission, 1968–1985, and a deputy to General Convention, 1977–1985. He was chaplain of the House of Deputies, 1979–1985. Price also was a member of the Anglican-Roman Catholic Commission (USA), the Standing Commission on Church Music, and the General Board of Examining Chaplains. He served on the Committee on Texts for *The Hymnal 1982*, 1976–1982. Among his numerous writings are *Introduction to the Proposed Book of Common Prayer* (1976), *Principles of Faith and Practice* (1977), *A Matter of Faith* (1983), and *Liturgy for Living* (1979), which he wrote with Louis Weil. Hymn texts by Price in *The Hymnal 1982* include "The golden sun lights up the sky" (Hymns 12–13) and "The fleeting day is nearly gone" (Hymn 23). He died in Alexandria, Virginia.

Price, Roger (Dec. 6, 1696–Dec. 8, 1762). Commissary to New England. He was born in Whitefield, England. Price graduated from Balliol College, Oxford on Feb. 21, 1717. He was ordained deacon and priest around 1720. On Apr. 22, 1725, he was given the living at Leigh in Essex County, England, which he retained throughout his life. Price was inducted as rector of King's Chapel, Boston, on July 25, 1729. In 1730 the Bishop of London appointed him "the Bishop's Commissary over all Episcopal Churches in New England." He served in that position until Sept. 6, 1748. On Apr. 15, 1734, Price laid the cornerstone of Trinity Church, Boston. He resigned as rector of King's Chapel in Apr. 1747, and returned to England. In 1748 he came back to America and served St. Paul's Church, Hopkinton, Massachusetts, which he founded in 1735. In 1753 Price and his family returned to England. He became incumbent of his parish in Leigh, where he died. He was the only commissary to New England. The Church of England grew rapidly there under his leadership.

Prie-Dieu. A small prayer desk. The term is from the French, "pray God." It has space for one to kneel in prayer. It may have a sloping ledge above a shelf for books. It also may be known as a litany desk, a faldstool, or a kneeling desk.

Priest. Derived from the Greek *presbyteros*, "elder," or "old man," the term is used as a synonym for presbyter. Presbyters constituted a collegiate ruling body of institutions in Judaism. The Catechism notes that "the ministry of a priest or presbyter" is "to represent Christ and his Church, particularly as pastor to the people; to share with the bishop in the overseeing of the Church; to proclaim the gospel; to administer the sacraments; and to bless and declare pardon in the name of God" (BCP, p. 856). The term "priest" is more frequently used than "presbyter" in the Episcopal Church. The ordination service for this order of ministry is titled "The Ordination of a Priest" (BCP, p. 525). After the Reformation, the Anglican Church used the term "priest" for the second order of ministry. Some Protestant churches began to use the term "presbyter" for the minister who preaches the Word and administers the sacraments. The 1979 BCP uses both terms. Some members of the Episcopal Church have favored use of "presbyter" because of historic association of the term "priest" with a narrow eucharistic piety or with OT sacrifice. *See* Presbyter, Presbyterate.

"Priest's Host." *See* Host (Eucharistic).

Priesthood of All Believers. Fundamental doctrine which affirms that all baptized Christians share the eternal priesthood of Jesus. Christ's high priesthood is unique and his atoning sacrifice was offered once for all. The royal priesthood of the people of God consists in the offering of ourselves repeatedly in daily obedience in the world (1 Pt 2:5; Rom 12:1). The redemptive work of Christ makes it possible for the people of God to offer their priestly sacrifice of obedient living (Rv 1:6, 5:10). The recovery of this doctrine at the Reformation led to the recovering of the ministry of the laity. The whole church is described by the Catechism as "a royal priesthood" (BCP, p. 854).

Primacy. In ecclesiastical terms, primacy is the status of being first, or presiding, among other bishops. In the early church, primacy was often accorded to the bishop of the chief city or metropolis of a geographical region. This primate was often called a metropolitan. The Archbishop of Canterbury held a regional primacy by the middle ages, and in 1353 it was finally agreed that he would be known as Primate of All England. There are many regional primates in the worldwide Anglican Communion today. They are variously known as primate, metropolitan, archbishop, or primus. In the Anglican Communion, the place of honor (but not of jurisdiction) is always given to the See of Canterbury. The Presiding Bishop of the Episcopal Church in the U.S. has, since the 1982 General Convention, been known as "Chief Pastor and Primate." Regular meetings of the primates of all the Anglican provinces have been held since 1979, as requested by the Lambeth Conference of 1978. From the later fourth century the Bishop of Rome began to claim and exercise primacy over all the other churches of the western world. By the later eleventh century the Bishop of Rome began to claim and exercise a universal primacy over the entire church. Claims of universal primacy by the Bishop of Rome have been resisted by many who are not members of the Roman Catholic Church. The issue of universal primacy has been a stumbling block in ecumenical discussions involving the Roman Catholic Church.

Primate. The chief bishop in an Anglican Province is called a primate. In the United States, the Presiding Bishop serves as "Chief Pastor and Primate." The 1978 Lambeth Conference requested that primates' meetings should be established to enable regular consultation among the primates of the Anglican Communion. These meetings have taken place throughout the Anglican Communion. The primates' meeting provides opportunities for collegiality and enables the primates to provide support for the Archbishop of Canterbury.

Prime. The second office of the seven canonical hours. It was usually recited at about 6 A.M., which was known as the first hour. Prime along with terce, sext, and none constituted the Little Hours of the Divine Office. Material from the office of Prime was included in the 1549 Prayer Book service of Matins, which was later known as Morning Prayer. *See* Little Hours of the Divine Office; *see* Matins; *see* Morning Prayer.

Principal Feasts. The seven greatest feasts of the church year. The principal feasts of the Episcopal Church are Easter Day, Ascension Day, the Day of Pentecost, Trinity Sunday, All Saints' Day (Nov. 1), Christmas Day (Dec. 25), and the Epiphany (Jan. 6) (BCP, p. 15). The principal feasts take precedence over any other day or observance. All Saints' Day may be observed on the Sunday following Nov. 1 in addition to its observance on the fixed date.

Prior. A man who is head of a religious house known as a priory, or the second person in authority of an abbey. An abbot is a man who is the head of an abbey. In an abbey, the prior may be selected by the abbot, elected by the community, or named by the general chapter of the religious order.

Prioress. A woman who is head of a religious house known as a priory, or the second person in authority of an abbey. An abbess is a woman who is the head of an abbey. In an abbey, the prioress may be selected by the abbess, elected by the community, or named by the general chapter of the religious order.

Priory. A religious house that has a prior or prioress as superior.

Pro-anaphora. *See* Liturgy of the Word.

Pro-Cathedral. A church named by a diocesan bishop to serve as a cathedral but which remains under the governance of the vestry and dean. It is used as a cathedral for diocesan purposes, but without the formation of a legal cathedral organization and without a cathedral chapter. It is not the official cathedral of the diocese. The church's status as pro-cathedral ends when the bishop no longer holds the diocesan jurisdiction, and the pro-cathedral's status may or may not be extended by the next bishop.

Process Theology. A theological approach that understands ultimate reality in terms of a dynamic process of becoming and ongoing change. This processive understanding may be contrasted with static notions of being that are based in Aristotelian and scholastic categories. Existence is understood in terms of the mutual interaction of entities, through which change occurs. Process theology is derived from the process philosophy of Alfred North Whitehead, whose Gifford Lectures were published as *Process and*

Reality (1929). Not all process theologies are alike, but God tends to be understood in ways that differ from classic theism. God is understood as a participant in a larger creative process, so that God influences and is influenced by other entities. God is understood to participate in development through intercourse with a changing world, and may be seen to be subordinate to a larger creative process. God's power to create change in the world is persuasive rather than coercive, and exercised within the limits of the creative process. This limitation of God's power resolves questions about God's responsibility for evil in the world. But process theology tends to contradict the traditional Christian understanding of God's transcendence and perfection. Process thought has been developed by Charles Hartshorne, John B. Cobb, Jr., David R. Griffin, and Schubert Ogden. W. Norman Pittenger was the most prominent Anglican process theologian. *See* Pittenger, W. Norman.

Procession (Liturgical). A movement of participants in a liturgy from one place to another. The use of processions at the eucharist followed the legalization of Christianity by Constantine in the fourth century. Church services became more formalized with increased participation in Christian liturgies and larger buildings for Christian worship. Services included entrance rites with a procession of clergy and readers in which the gospel book was carried in procession.

Processions typically lead to the altar at the beginning of the service. A festal procession on a major feast may use the side aisles and main aisle of the church. This extended procession may pause for a station or special prayers to commemorate the occasion. Torches, banners, and incense may be carried in procession to add to the solemnity and excitement of the celebration. The entrance procession at the eucharist typically involves the ministers who will serve at the altar, including acolytes or servers, deacons or priests who will serve as assisting clergy, and the celebrant. The entrance procession may also include the choir. The gospel procession may lead to the midst of the congregation for the singing or reading of the gospel. Representatives of the congregation may bring the people's offerings of bread and wine and money or other gifts to the deacon or celebrant at the offertory procession.

Many liturgies of the Episcopal Church may include processions. For example, there may be a procession to the font at a baptism, the bride and groom and wedding party may process to the sanctuary at the Celebration and

Blessing of a Marriage, and the body may be borne from the church in procession at the Burial of the Dead. At the liturgy of the palms on Palm Sunday, and at the Dedication and Consecration of a Church, the clergy and people may gather at a place apart from the church to enter the church in procession. At the Easter Vigil, the deacon or celebrant bears the lighted Paschal candle and leads the congregation in procession to the chancel. The Great Litany may be said or sung in procession. The *BOS* provides forms for a Candlemas Procession for use immediately before the eucharist on the Feast of the Presentation of Our Lord in the Temple and for a Rogation Procession.

Processional Cross. A cross or crucifix mounted on a pole that is carried in procession by an acolyte or server.

Processions (Trinitarian). The divine processions of the Son and the Spirit in the immanent (internal) life of God are at the heart of the distinctions of the persons of the Trinity. Christian theology affirms that the Son proceeds from the Father (see Jn 8:42). Western theology has affirmed that the Spirit proceeds from the Father and the Son (see Jn 15:26). This double procession was expressed by the addition of the *filioque* clause to the Nicene Creed, which states that the Spirit "proceeds from the Father and the Son" (see BCP, p. 359). Eastern theology affirms that the Spirit proceeds from the Father through the Son. Eastern theology therefore denies the double procession of the Spirit and rejects the addition of the *filioque* clause to the Nicene Creed. Some apply the term "procession" only to the Spirit, thereby distinguishing the Spirit from the Son who is "eternally begotten of the Father" (see BCP, pp. 358–359). The trinitarian processions concern the dynamic internal life of God with respect to the Son and Spirit, who are uncreated and co-eternal with God the Father. The internal processions of the "immanent Trinity" are distinguished from God's activity in creation, which is described in terms of the "economic Trinity."

Profane. Expressing contempt or blasphemous disrespect for God or the sacred. For example, vandalism or desecration of a church is a profane act. The *BOS* provides a form for the Restoration of Things Profaned. It may be used for the restoration to sacred use of a church building, altar, font, or other consecrated objects that have been profaned. It may be used before the first church service after an act of profanation. The term may also indicate the secular or nonreligious, without indicating contempt for God or the sacred.

Professed Member of a Monastic Order. A member of a monastic or religious community who has taken vows. This person has a voice in the chapter (legislative gathering) of the community. Some communities distinguish between the rights of members in temporary vows and those in final vows.

Profession (Monastic). The commitment by which one becomes a full member of a monastic or religious community. This is usually through the three vows of poverty, chastity, and obedience. Temporary vows, or "junior profession," typically follows the novitiate and precedes life profession and full membership in the community.

Professional Ministry Development Cluster. The cluster of offices at the Episcopal Church Center which supports clergy and lay professionals. Its concerns include deployment, theological education, pastoral development, and the development of ministry. It was organized after the 1991 General Convention. At that Convention, the National Network of Episcopal Clergy Associations presented a resolution asking for a clergy desk at the Episcopal Church Center. The resolution was amended and the result was the formation of the Professional Ministry Development Cluster.

Program, Budget & Finance, Joint Standing Committee on. The committee which proposes budgets for the operation of national church programs between General Conventions. The 1973 General Convention merged the Joint Committee on Program and Budget and the Joint Committee on Finances to create the Joint Standing Committee on Program, Budget, and Finance. It consists of twenty-seven members of the General Convention who are appointed not later than the fifteenth day of Dec. following each General Convention. There is one bishop and two members of the House of Deputies, either clerical or lay, from each of the nine provinces. The bishops are appointed by the Presiding Bishop. The deputies are appointed by the president of the House of Deputies. The committee is divided into four sections: on the expenses of the General Convention, the general church program, funding, and audit. Prior to the adjournment of each regular meeting of the General Convention, the Joint Standing Committee must report to the House of Deputies a proposed budget for the contingent expenses of the General Convention for the ensuing period until the next convention. The committee must also report to a Joint Session of the General Convention a proposed budget for the general church program for the ensuing convention period.

Proper. Variable parts of the eucharistic liturgy and the Daily Office which are appointed for a particular day according to the season or occasion. These parts of the liturgy may be contrasted with the fixed portions and options of the liturgy which do not vary with the season or occasion. The proper for the eucharist includes the collect, the lessons, the selection from the Psalter, and the proper preface. The BCP collects for the church year are presented in both traditional and contemporary language versions (pp. 159–261). The Lectionary provides readings and psalms for the eucharist (BCP, pp. 889–931). The Daily Office Lectionary provides readings and psalms for Morning and Evening Prayer (BCP, pp. 936–1001). Propers for the Sundays in the Season after Pentecost are numbered one through twenty-nine. The BCP includes propers for holy days, such as "Saint Andrew" and "The Annunciation"; the Common of Saints, such as "Of a Martyr" and "Of a Monastic"; and Various Occasions, such as "Of the Holy Trinity" and "Of the Incarnation." The Proper Prefaces of the BCP include three prefaces of the Lord's Day, prefaces for seasons, and prefaces for other occasions, such as baptism and marriage (pp. 377–382). The BCP also has a section of proper liturgies for special days, such as Ash Wednesday and the Easter Vigil (pp. 264–295). The service for Morning Prayer includes proper opening sentences (pp. 37–41, 75–78) and antiphons (pp. 43–44, 80–82).

Proper Liturgies for Special Days. The BCP provides a section of forms for services on special days in Lent and Holy Week. These proper liturgies for special days include Ash Wednesday (p. 264), The Sunday of the Passion: Palm Sunday (p. 270), Maundy Thursday (p. 274), Good Friday (p. 276), Holy Saturday (p. 283), and The Great Vigil of Easter (p. 285).

Proper Preface. *See* Preface (Eucharistic).

Prophet, Prophecy. A prophet in the OT was called a messenger to proclaim the word of the God of the covenant to the people of the covenant. Prophecy refers to the message or work of a prophet.

The prophetic movement in Israel developed over a period of time, from the eleventh century B.C. with ecstatic prophetic groups, through the tenth century with court prophets such as Nathan, into the ninth century with Elijah and Elisha, reaching its full flower in the eighth, beginning with Amos, and eventually flowing to the fifth with the incomparable author of Isaiah, chs. 40–55, known as "Deutero-Isaiah." After that it gradually faded from Israel's scene.

Under a righteous and compassionate God, the prophets called for righteousness and compassion in society, stressing one or the other, depending on the historical situation. They spoke to their times but always with an eye to the future.

The NT regards John the Baptist as the last of the OT prophets. Among his various offices, Jesus is also called a prophet (Lk 13:33). In the early church the office of prophet was recognized along with other offices such as apostle, teacher, and worker of miracles (1 Cor 12:28).

Propitiation. The appeasement of divine wrath through sacrifice or its substitute in prayer. The term is not in current usage. It was used in older versions of the BCP. It appears three times in the *Authorized Version* (King James) of the Bible and four times in the *Revised Version*. The death of Jesus Christ has been presented among Christians as a propitiatory sacrifice to God the Father on behalf of the sins of the world. It is understood that this sacrificial act proceeds from divine love. *See* Atonement.

Proposed Book. *The Book of Common Prayer, . . . As Revised and Proposed to the Use of the Protestant Episcopal Church* (1786) incorporated recommendations from Connecticut and from the other New England states and revisions of a convention of states south of New England. The book was edited by William White of Philadelphia, William Smith of Maryland, and Charles H. Wharton of Delaware. The language was slightly modernized and some repetitiousness eliminated. The Psalter and metrical psalter were abridged to omit troublesome passages. Proper lessons were appointed for some days that lacked them, and proper NT lessons were appointed for Sundays. Some OT passages and most lessons from the Apocrypha were omitted. Black Letter Days were eliminated. "Minister" replaced "Priest." "He descended into hell" was omitted from the Apostles' Creed,

and the Nicene and Athanasian Creeds deleted. There were abridgements and changes in all rites and in the Catechism and Articles of Religion. The book contained fifty-one hymns, several times the number in earlier metrical psalters. This book was the basis for the first American BCP (1789). The 1789 revision restored some elements from the 1662 BCP but made even more radical changes, including deleting mention of confession from Visitation of the Sick and omitting the *Magnificat* and *Nunc dimittis*. *See* Book of Common Prayer, The ("BCP").

Proposed Book of Common Prayer. Proposals for revision of the 1928 BCP were first published by the Standing Liturgical Commission in a series of *Prayer Book Studies*, the first of which was published in 1950. When trial use of a revision of the eucharistic rite was authorized by the 1967 General Convention, pew copies were printed in a book titled *The Liturgy of the Lord's Supper*. A revision of the eucharistic rite, a new eucharistic lectionary, and revisions of the Daily Office, the pastoral offices, and the ordination rites were authorized for trial use by the 1970 General Convention and published in *Services for Trial Use*. It was known as the "Green Book" because of its green cover. Additional changes authorized in 1973 were published in *Authorized Services 1973*, known as the "Zebra Book" because of its striped cover. Further revisions were incorporated in a complete Prayer Book, *The Draft Proposed Book of Common Prayer*, which was essentially a workbook for the use of bishops and deputies to the 1976 General Convention. The book authorized by that convention was published as the *Proposed Book of Common Prayer*. That Prayer Book was ratified by the 1979 General Convention, making it the authorized BCP of the Episcopal Church.

Prostration. Lying full length and face down on the floor or ground as a gesture of humility and devotion. This posture may also express adoration or submission. Historically, prostrations have been made in some churches by the celebrant and assisting ministers at the beginning of the Good Friday service and during litanies at the Easter Vigil service. Prostrations have also been made by ordinands during the Litany for Ordinations. Prostration is never required by the BCP.

Protestant Churchman, The. This weekly magazine began publication on Aug. 12, 1843, in New York City. In 1862 its name was changed to *Christian Times*. In 1866 the title was changed to the *Episcopalian*. The *Episcopalian* was published simultaneously in New York, Philadelphia, and Baltimore until 1869. It was mainly a news magazine. With the first issue of 1872 the name was changed to *Church and State.*

Protestant Episcopal Church in the Confederate States of America. When the southern states seceded from the Union and planned to form a new nation, many southern Episcopal bishops and others believed they needed a new national, southern Episcopal Church. On May 23, 1861, Bishop Leonidas Polk of Louisiana and Bishop Stephen Elliott of Georgia issued a call for a meeting to be held at St. John's Church, Montgomery, Alabama, to begin on July 3, 1861. The first preliminary meeting of dioceses of the Confederate States met July 3–6, 1861. It named a committee to draw up a constitution and canons. Four southern bishops attended this meeting as well as representatives from six dioceses. The second preliminary meeting was held at Christ Church, Columbia, South Carolina, Oct. 16–23, 1861. It adopted a constitution and canons. They changed the word "convention" to "council." When seven dioceses ratified the constitution, the Protestant Episcopal Church in the Confederate States of America would come into being. On Sept. 19, 1862, the seventh diocese ratified the constitution. The first General Council of the Protestant Episcopal Church in the Confederate States met at St. Paul's Church, Augusta, Georgia, Nov. 12–22, 1862. It made some necessary revisions in the Prayer Book. They insisted that the separation had nothing to do with doctrine, discipline, or worship. The 1862 General Convention of the Protestant Episcopal Church in the United States refused to acknowledge that there was a division of the church. The next General Convention after the Civil War was at Philadelphia in 1865. Two southern bishops, Henry Lay of Arkansas and Thomas Atkinson of North Carolina, attended and were welcomed. The second General Council met at St. Paul's Church, Augusta, on Nov. 8–10, 1865. It recognized that the need for a separate church no longer existed. Within one year all the southern dioceses had reunited with the Protestant Episcopal Church in the United States.

Protestant Episcopal Church in the United States of America (PECUSA). *See* Episcopal Church, The.

Protestant Episcopal Church in the United States of America, Incorporated, The. A group of conservative bishops in the Episcopal Church formed this non-profit organization in 1996. Its goal was to provide a place for traditionalist Episcopalians in the church. They sought to use the old name of the Episcopal Church to indicate the faith shared by traditionalists. The incorporation papers, first chartered in the state of Wisconsin in Aug. 1996 stated that the corporation's purpose is "to engage in religious, educational and charitable activities and particularly the executive, administrative and financial administration of the Protestant Episcopal Church in the United States of America, otherwise known as the Episcopal Church. It shall have charge of the church pension fund and the church's program. . . ." The founding directors of the new corporation were Bishops William Wantland of Eau Claire, John Howe of Central Florida, and John-David Schofield of San Joaquin. Bishop Howe resigned from the board of directors in Dec. 1997. Presiding Bishop Edmond Browning said this was "an unauthorized and misleading effort in the name of the church," which "violates the church's right and need to protect its name from misleading and unfair use." The Board of Trustees of the organization subsequently changed its name to the Anglican Province of the United States, making its name and corporate structure available to groups concerned about the status of the Episcopal Church.

Protestant Episcopal Evangelical Society. This society, no longer in existence, was organized in Philadelphia in 1813. Its purpose was to improve religious knowledge, invigorate pious affections, promote a spirit of Christian fellowship, and enjoy the pleasures and advantages of social worship. The society promoted the reading of scripture, prayers, and religious conversation. It was an evangelical organization.

Protestant Episcopal Quarterly Review and Church Register. A low church publication critical of Roman Catholicism that was published in New York from Jan. 1854 until Oct. 1861, by the Rev. Herman Dyer.

Protestant Episcopal Review. A journal which claimed to be conservative and yet progressive, liberal and yet reverent, critical and yet constructive, scholarly and popular, catholic and protestant. It was an outgrowth of two previous publications of the Virginia Theological Seminary. The earlier ancestor was *The Seminarian*, which was published monthly from Nov. 1878, until July 1887. The second ancestor was *The Virginia Seminary Magazine*, which began publication in Dec. 1887. It continued as a nine-issue-per-annum journal until July 1892. In 1892 the *Protestant Episcopal Review* began publication. It was published ten times a year until it went out of existence in 1900.

Protestant Episcopal Society for the Advancement of Christianity in South Carolina. The society was formed on June 10, 1810, for the promotion of Christian knowledge, learning, and piety in South Carolina. The leader of the organization was Theodore Dehon, later the second Bishop of South Carolina. It was the first organization in the Episcopal Church for the extension of the gospel. It was modeled after the Society for the Propagation of the Gospel. It was responsible for the establishment of more than forty missions and parishes in South Carolina during the nineteenth century.

Protestant Episcopal Society for Promoting the Extension of the Church Among Colored People. This society was founded in 1856 by the Rev. James Theodore Holly, rector of St. Luke's Church, New Haven, Connecticut, and later the first Episcopal Bishop of Haiti. The original membership consisted of four African American clergy and seven congregations. The female auxiliary was called the Good Angels. The society worked to get African Americans into Episcopal seminaries. The society also took a stand against slavery. After Holly went to Haiti, a remnant existed for a few years under the leadership of Samuel V. Berry of St. Philip's Church, Buffalo, New York.

Protestant Episcopal Society for Promoting Religion and Learning in the State of New York. This organization was formed on Aug. 16, 1802, to publish and distribute Christian literature. It also supported diocesan missions and theological students. It was liberally supported by Trinity Parish in New York City.

Protestant Episcopal Society for the Promotion of Evangelical Knowledge (E.K.S.). Established by evangelicals in 1848 in reaction to the Oxford Movement and its influence in the United States, it eventually became known as the Evangelical Knowledge Society (E.K.S.). Its object was "To maintain and set forth the principles and doctrines of the gospel embodied in the Articles, Liturgy and Homilies of the Protestant Episcopal Church, by the publication of tracts, Sunday School and other books." Its abbreviated service from the BCP, "The Mission Service," was widely used. E.K.S. published two journals,

The Parish Visitor and *The Standard Bearer*, the latter for use in Sunday Schools. It promoted the evangelical cause in controversies with the high church party.

Protestant Episcopal Sunday School and Tract Society. Low and high churchmen cooperated in the organization of this society in 1826. It was to be inclusive of the diversity of opinion among the clergy. Eventually, the evangelicals became disturbed by the character of some of the publications, especially the *Hobart Catechism*. Bishop William Meade of Virginia became convinced that some of the society's publications were similar to the writings of the Tractarians. He published *Two Letters* in 1847 voicing his objections. They were addressed to the board of managers of the society. After 1847, the evangelicals withdrew support from the society.

Protestant Episcopal Theological Seminary in Virginia, The; Alexandria, Virginia (VTS). This school, also called the Virginia Theological Seminary, was formed by the Society for the Education of Pious Young Men for the Ministry of the Protestant Episcopal Church in Maryland and Virginia. It opened on Oct. 15, 1823, in a room in St. Paul's Church, Alexandria, with two professors and fourteen students. In 1827 the school was moved to eighty acres of land, then outside of Alexandria, but now a part of the city. During the Civil War, the seminary was used to house wounded Union soldiers. The property was used as a burial ground for some 500 soldiers. In 1878 VTS opened a branch seminary for African Americans in connection with St. Stephen's Normal and Industrial School in Petersburg, Virginia. In 1884 it was named the Bishop Payne Divinity School in honor of John Payne, the first Bishop of Liberia and a VTS graduate. It closed in 1949, and in 1953 it was merged with Virginia Seminary. The library at Virginia is the Bishop Payne Library. VTS has a Center for the Ministry of Teaching, a Center for Continuing Education, a Lay School of Theology, and an Institute in School Ministry. The seminary is a part of the Washington Theological Consortium, which is an association of Episcopal, Roman Catholic, Methodist, Lutheran, and interdenominational seminaries.

Protestant Episcopal Theological Society. Founded in New York in 1806 by John Henry Hobart, its purpose was to bring clergy of the diocese together for weekly meetings, which included devotional services and the reading of sermons and essays. It assisted ministerial students and encouraged younger clergy to continue their theological studies. The society was part of the process that led to the establishment of General Theological Seminary.

Protestant Episcopal Tract Society. It was founded by John Henry Hobart, rector of Trinity Church, New York, in 1809, to distribute free religious literature such as tracts and pamphlets. The tracts defended the faith held by the Episcopal Church, as a branch of the One Holy Catholic and Apostolic Church. Hobart met with John Henry Newman in England in 1824. It is possible that Hobart's extensive use of tracts may have influenced Newman and the subsequent publication of the *Tracts for the Times* of the Oxford Movement.

Protestantism. Western Christianity that is not subject to papal authority. The term is from the *protestatio* at the Diet of Speyer of 1529 by Lutheran princes against the policies of Charles V that would have practically eliminated the Lutheran territorial churches. The term has positive connotations in the sense of witness and testimony to the truth. It is not just negative in the sense of protest against something. Historically, there have been a variety of Protestant expressions of faith and many Protestant churches or denominations. Protestant thought can be traced to John Huss (c. 1369–1415) of Bohemia. Huss questioned the authority of the Pope, as well as neglect of the Bible and the doctrine of grace. Huss was influenced by John Wycliffe (c. 1329–1384) of England, who upheld the superior authority of the Bible over the papacy.

The Protestant schism came in the sixteenth century. Martin Luther (1483–1546) was a professor in the faculty of theology at the University of Wittenberg and vicar of the Augustinian order. On Oct. 31, 1517, Luther challenged the sale and abuse of indulgences by posting his Ninety-Five Theses on the door of the castle church at Wittenberg. Luther denied the primacy of the Pope and the infallibility of general councils in 1519 at the Leipzig Disputation. In 1520 Luther urged the civil rulers to reform the church. The Roman Catholic Church excommunicated Luther and condemned his teachings in 1521. After Luther's condemnation by the Diet of Worms (1521), the Elector of Saxony protected Luther at Wartburg castle. Luther translated the NT into German while he was at Wartburg. The Diet of Speyer of 1526 granted princes the right to organize national churches. Lutheranism spread through many parts of Germany and Scandinavia. In the sixteenth century, "Protestant" meant Lutheran.

Luther urged that Christians are justified only through God's grace, which is received through faith. Christians are not justified or made righteous through their works or merits that result from their works. The Christian can therefore be described as "at once justified and a sinner" (*simul justus et peccator*). The righteousness of Christ is imputed to us by God and received by faith. We are thus justified by a righteousness that is extrinsic and alien to us personally. Although we are pronounced righteous by God in Christ, we continue to be sinners. Luther's theology of the cross (*Theologia Crucis*) held that the saving and merciful God is known only as hidden in Christ crucified (see 1 Cor 1:17–31). Luther upheld the priesthood of all believers. He rejected purgatory, the veneration of saints, relics, monasticism, celibacy of the clergy, and Masses for the dead. Lutheranism has included several confessional statements that provide written summaries of doctrine. Luther's Large and Small Catechisms appeared in 1529, and he prepared the Schmalkaldic Articles in 1536. Luther supported the Augsburg Confession (1530), which was drafted by Philipp Melanchthon (1497–1560). Melanchthon also prepared the *Apology* for the Augsburg Confession (1531). Lutheranism may be summarized in terms of belief in justification by faith alone (*sola fides*), justification by God's grace alone (*sola gratia*), and the Bible as the only authoritative rule of faith (*sola scriptura*). Lutheran Churches in North America include the Evangelical Lutheran Church in America (ELCA), the Lutheran Church-Missouri Synod, and the Lutheran Church-Wisconsin Synod.

The Reformed Protestant tradition is associated with John Calvin (1509–1564). He was the leading figure in the sixteenth-century movement of reform in Switzerland. Calvin's reform is especially associated with the city of Geneva, Switzerland. In July 1536, Guillaume Farel (1489–1565) convinced Calvin to stay in Geneva to organize the reform. Calvin and Farel were expelled from Geneva in 1538, but the city council invited Calvin to return in 1541. Calvin worked to establish a theocracy in Geneva, and Calvinism came to dominate the Protestant movement of reform. Another leader of reform in Switzerland was Ulrich Zwingli (1484–1531). He initiated the Swiss Reformation in Zurich in 1519. Zwingli was killed in battle in 1531 during the civil war between Zurich and Roman Catholic cantons. Zwingli was succeeded in Zurich by Heinrich Bullinger (1504–1575). In May 1549, differences between the reformed churches in Zurich and Geneva were resolved by the Zurich Consensus (*Consensus Tigurinus*), which was agreed to by Calvin,

Farel, and Bullinger. The Reformed Church movement in Switzerland was consolidated by their agreement.

Calvin published the first edition of his *Institutes of the Christian Religion* in 1536. The last edition of the *Institutes* was published in 1559. His teaching emphasized the sovereignty of God, scripture as the supreme rule of faith and life, the total depravity of humanity after the Fall, the predestination of the elect to salvation and the reprobate to damnation, and the importance of the church as an ordered and disciplined community. The ministers or officers of the Reformed Church included pastors, teachers, elders, and deacons. The Dutch Reformed theologian Jacob Arminius (1560–1609) sought to moderate Calvinist teaching concerning predestination and the importance of free human will relative to divine sovereignty. The Synod of Dort (1618–1619) of the Dutch Reformed Church responded to Arminianism by upholding strict Calvinist principles concerning total depravity, unconditional election, limited atonement, irresistibility of grace, and the perseverance of the saints. The Reformed Church in Switzerland influenced the French Huguenots, the Scottish Church reforms of John Knox (c. 1513–1572), the Puritans in England, and the reformed churches in the Netherlands. Calvin's influence is seen in the American Reformed, Congregational, and Presbyterian churches.

The Anabaptists were radical Protestants who held that only believing adults should be baptized. They called for the rebaptism of those who were baptized as infants. Anabaptists also stressed the importance of inner religious experience and held that believers should not be involved with or subject to the civil authority. Military service was rejected. Anabaptist groups tended to support nonresistance and pacifism. There were Anabaptist groups in Germany, Switzerland, Moravia, and the Low Countries. Noted Anabaptist leaders included the Zwickau Prophets Nicholas Storch (d. c. 1530) and Thomas Müntzer (c. 1489–1525), Jacob Hutter (d. 1536), Melchior Hoffmann (c. 1500–c. 1543), and Menno Simons (c. 1496–1561). Anabaptists were persecuted by both Roman Catholics and other Protestants. The Anabaptist tradition continues in the Mennonites, the Hutterites, the Amish, the Quakers, and some Baptists.

Anglicans are categorized as Protestants by many Roman Catholics, Protestants, and some Anglicans. Article XIX of the Articles of Religion clearly states that "the Church of Rome hath erred, not only in their living and manner of Ceremonies, but also in matters of Faith" (BCP, p. 871). However, some Anglicans are ambivalent about being categorized as Protestants because of the importance of the catholic tradition in Anglicanism. In this regard, catholicity is understood in terms of what has been believed everywhere, always, and by all in the church rather than submission to papal authority and Roman Catholic doctrine. The Anglican, Orthodox, and Roman Catholic churches are understood by some Anglicans to be branches of the one holy catholic and apostolic church. When a confirmed member of the Roman Catholic or Orthodox churches is received into the Episcopal Church, the bishop says, "we recognize you as a member of the one holy catholic and apostolic Church, and we receive you into the fellowship of this Communion" (BCP, p. 418). Anglicanism reflects both catholic and Protestant influences in liturgy, polity, and doctrine.

John Wesley (1703–1791) was the founder of Methodism within the Church of England during the eighteenth century. Methodism was a movement of pietistic revivalism. Wesley was a student at Oxford when he organized a "Holy Club" that included his brother Charles Wesley (1707–1788), George Whitefield (1714–1770), and several other students. They were "methodical" in their devotion to disciplines such as Bible study and visiting the needy. They came to be known as Methodists. John Wesley had a conversion experience at a Moravian meeting in Aldersgate Street, London, in 1738. He recalled that his heart was "strangely warmed." Charles also had an experience of inner conversion in 1738. The Methodist revival emphasized personalized faith and conversion of the heart. Methodist theology has been characterized as Arminian. John and Charles both engaged in an itinerant ministry of preaching. Charles wrote over 5,000 hymn texts, including "Come, thou long expected Jesus" (Hymn 66), "O for a thousand tongues to sing my dear Redeemer's Praise" (Hymn 493), and "Love divine, all loves excelling" (Hymn 657). Hymn singing has an important role in Methodist worship. John organized and extended the Methodist Movement. Lay preachers were used to proclaim the gospel. Conferences of lay preachers were held in England from 1744. In 1784 John ordained Thomas Coke (1747–1814) as Superintendent for the Methodists in America. John also instructed Coke to ordain Francis Asbury (1745–1816) as a Superintendent. Coke and Asbury became joint superintendents of Methodist work in America. The title superintendent was changed to bishop in 1787. Preachers were elected and ordained at the Christmas Conference in 1784 in Baltimore, Maryland. The Methodist Episcopal Church in America was begun. Charles opposed the ordinations by John, who was a priest of the Church of England. Charles also opposed separation from the Church of England. Although John performed more than twenty ordinations of English Methodists before he died, the schism of the Methodists from the Church of England followed his death. John and Charles Wesley are commemorated in the Episcopal calendar of the church year on Mar. 3. The United Methodist Church is one of the largest Protestant denominations in the United States and the largest Methodist body in the world. There are also smaller Methodist churches in the United States, such as the African Methodist Episcopal Church.

The twentieth-century Pentecostal movement in the United States is associated with the ministry of Charles Parham (1873–1937) in the early 1900s. Parham connected baptism in the Spirit with glossolalia. In 1901 Parham led the Apostolic Faith movement in Kansas, Missouri, and Texas. Parham's ministry was continued in 1906 in Zion City, Illinois. A significant expansion of the Pentecostal movement came with the Azusa Street revival in Los Angeles, 1906–1909, under the African American pastor William J. Seymour. Pentecostalism upholds a continuing Pentecost in which baptism in the Spirit is accompanied by speaking in tongues and divine healing. Pentecostals are usually fundamentalists. Pentecostals have not generally been engaged in the ecumenical movement. The Charismatic Movement is considered by some to be a continuation or second wave of Pentecostalism. Participants in the Charismatic Movement believe in the availability of personal pentecostal experience in the Spirit, which may often be accompanied by speaking in tongues and spiritual gifts (charisms or charismata; see 1 Cor 12:8–10). Some Episcopal congregations reflect the influence of the Charismatic Movement.

Although there are many Protestant traditions and denominations, there are also many shared concerns and beliefs within Protestantism. Protestant churches generally emphasize the proclamation of the Word of God. Preaching and study of the Bible have an important role in Protestantism. The individual life of faith by grace is central, including personal morality with the Bible as the ultimate standard of belief and conduct. Many Protestant denominations showed interest in the ecumenical movement during the twentieth century, and some churches merged. There has been Protestant support for conciliar movements such as the World Council of Churches. Protestants were also active in social issues during the nineteenth and twentieth century, such as emancipation, suffrage, temperance, desegregation, and opposition to warfare and domestic violence.

Province. 1) An internal division of an autonomous national (or multi-national) church of the Anglican Communion. The churches of England and Ireland, the Anglican Church of Canada, the Anglican Church of Australia, and the Episcopal Church are all divided into internal provinces. There are two each in England and Ireland, four in Canada, five in Australia, and nine in the Episcopal Church, including overseas jurisdictions. Article VII of the Episcopal Church Constitution provides for internal provinces. 2) An autonomous national church member of the Anglican Communion.

Provincial Synod. The Episcopal Church is divided into nine provinces. Each province has a synod consisting of a House of Bishops and a House of Deputies. These houses sit and deliberate either separately or together. The synod meets on a regular basis as determined by each province. Every bishop having jurisdiction within the province, every bishop coadjutor, suffragan bishop, and assistant bishop, and every bishop whose episcopal work has been within the province, but who by reason of advanced age or bodily infirmity has resigned, has a seat and vote in the House of Bishops of the province. Each diocese and area mission within the province is entitled to representation in the provincial House of Deputies. Each province determines the number of deputies, and each diocese and area mission determines the manner in which its deputies shall be chosen. The president of the province may be one of the bishops, presbyters, deacons, or lay persons of the province. The provincial synod elects the president.

Provoost, Samuel (Feb. 26, 1742–Sept. 6, 1815). First Bishop of New York. He was born in New York City and graduated from King's College (Columbia) in 1758. Later he studied at St. Peter's College, Cambridge. He was ordained deacon on Feb. 3, 1766, and priest on Mar. 25, 1766. Provoost became rector of Trinity Church, New York, where he served for 16 years. He was consecrated Bishop of New York on Feb. 4, 1787. In 1801 he sought to resign as Bishop of New York, but the House of Bishops refused to accept his resignation and gave permission for the election of an assistant bishop. Provoost retired in 1801 and left the diocese in charge of Assistant Bishop Benjamin Moore. He died in New York City.

Provost. In the Episcopal Church the title has been used to indicate a priest in charge of a cathedral when the bishop is the dean. Historically, the provost was the official next in dignity to the abbot of a monastery. A provost may also be an administrative officer of a college or university.

Psalm, Psalmody, Psalter. Psalm is the name given to the hymns of the OT. The psalms are found in the Psalter, a collection of songs, prayers, and other types of poetic compositions. The Book of Psalms has traditionally been attributed to David because he seems to have composed hymns. Some hymns of ancient Israel were certainly composed before David, such as the brief Song of Miriam (Ex 15:21). The dates of the various hymns of the Psalter are usually impossible to determine, but they come from virtually every period of Israel's history. They were finally compiled for use in the Second Temple, which was completed c. 515 B.C. This hymnal of the Second Temple was divided into five parts (1–41; 42–72; 73–89; 90–106; 107–150), presumably following the fivefold division of the Pentateuch. The psalms were composed for both individual and community use. Psalms would have been used in various liturgical settings. The most common literary types of psalms were the hymn, the thanksgiving and the lament. Some can be related to specific festivals, such as Covenant Renewal (81) or Royal-Zion (132). Others call for reflection on the Torah, e.g. Pss. 1, 119. The psalms of the OT have been used through the centuries in both Jewish and Christian worship. This has given rise to psalmody, i.e., the art of singing the psalms. The Psalter is included in the BCP (pp. 585–808). The Prayer Book lectionaries appoint a selection from the Psalter for all services of the eucharist and the Daily Office.

Psalm Tone. A melodic formula for the unison singing of psalm texts. The tones correspond to the eight medieval modes. A ninth psalm tone, the *Tonus Peregrinus*, is also used for the singing of the psalms. Each psalm tone consists of two parts. The first part has an intonation, a reciting note and a mediation or cadence. The second part has a reciting note and an ending or final cadence. The first half of a psalm verse up to the asterisk ("*") is sung to the first half of the chant, and the second half of the text is sung to the second half of the chant. A Psalm Tone chart is found in *The Hymnal 1982 Accompaniment Edition, Vol. 1*, at S 446. *See* Plainsong.

Psalter. *See* Psalm, Psalmody, Psalter.

Puerto Rico, Diocese of. The Puerto Rican ministry of the Diocese of Antigua was transferred to the Episcopal Church on Oct. 5, 1891. The General Convention of 1901 established the Missionary District of Puerto Rico. On Jan. 1, 1980, the Diocese of Puerto Rico became an Extra-Provincial Diocese related to Province Nine of the Episcopal Church.

Pulkingham, William Graham (Sept. 14, 1926– Apr. 16, 1993). Charismatic leader. He was born in Alliance, Ohio. Pulkingham received his B.A. from the University of Western Ontario and his M.Div. from the Episcopal Theological Seminary of the Southwest in 1957. He was ordained deacon on June 20, 1957, and priest on June 13, 1958. In 1957–1958 he was deacon-in-charge at St. John's, Hitchcock, and St. Mark's, Alta Loma, Texas. From 1958 until 1960 he was a chaplain at the University of Texas Medical School. From 1960 until 1963 he was assistant minister at St. David's Church, Austin, Texas. From 1963 until 1974 Pulkingham was rector of the Church of the Redeemer, Houston, Texas, where he rose to fame as the parish became a showplace of charismatic renewal and social action. In 1974 he moved to Scotland where he established the Community of Celebration on Cumbrae Island. Its extension ministry, the Fisherfolk, traveled extensively to teach new hymns and liturgical settings for contemporary worship. His wife, Betty Jane Carr Pulkingham, was also a leader in this music ministry. While in Scotland, he was provost of the Cathedral of Isles and rector of St. Andrew's, Cumbrae. In 1980 Pulkingham returned to the United States and was associate rector of the Church of the Redeemer, Houston, 1980–1982. In 1982–1983 he was priest-in-charge of St. David's Church, Woodland Park, Colorado. In 1985 the Community of Celebration moved to Aliquippa, Pennsylvania. Pulkingham's last position was general convenor of the Community of Celebration. He wrote *Gathered for Power* (1972), and *They Left Their Nets* (1973). Pulkingham died in Burlington, North Carolina.

Pulpit. An elevated platform, usually enclosed with a railing or waist-high paneling and equipped with a reading desk. The pulpit is set prominently in the front of the church building to be the place where sermons are delivered. However, the altar rather than the pulpit typically occupies the central place at the front of the church. The term is from the Latin *pulpitum*, a wooden platform for dramatic performances. Medieval pulpits were often made of stone and elaborately decorated. In the middle ages the term came to replace "ambo." In the early church, an ambo was an elevated structure with steps at both ends. It was often longer than the typical modern pulpit. All liturgical readings were done from the ambo. In many cases it is virtually impossible to distinguish between pulpits and ambos. The terms are sometimes used as synonyms. The term "pulpit" may also refer metaphorically to those who preach, or it may refer to what is preached.

Purcell, Henry (1659–Nov. 21, 1695). Outstanding English composer. He was born in London. At age eight Purcell was a chorister in the Chapel Royal. He was appointed an unpaid assistant to the Keeper of the King's Instruments in 1673, after his voice changed. From 1674 to 1678 he tuned the organ of Westminster Abbey. In 1677 Purcell was appointed composer-in-ordinary of the royal violins, and in 1679 he became organist of Westminster Abbey. In 1682 he was made one of the organists of the Chapel Royal. Purcell was appointed Keeper of the King's Instruments in 1685 by Charles II, and he was reappointed to the position in the same year by James II. A most prolific composer for both voices and instruments, Purcell composed primarily for the theater in the later years of his life. His sacred compositions include about seventy anthems and forty-six other sacred vocal works of various kinds. The hymn tune, *Westminster Abbey*, is derived from the concluding Alleluias of his verse anthem, "O God, Thou art my God." It is used in *The Hymnal 1982* with the text "Christ is made the sure foundation" (Hymn 518). *The Hymnal 1982* also contains one Anglican chant credited to Purcell (S 221). He died in Westminster, London.

Purgatory. A doctrine traceable to patristic times of a temporary, intermediate state between heaven and hell. As developed in the Roman Catholic Church, purgatory is a state or place of hope and anticipation. Venial sins are cleansed, and temporal punishment is completed for forgiven sins. Article XXII of the Articles of Religion states that the "Romish Doctrine concerning Purgatory" is "grounded upon no warranty of Scripture, but rather repugnant to the Word of God" (BCP, p. 872). Purgatory is seldom mentioned in Anglican descriptions or speculations concerning life after death, although many Anglicans believe in a continuing process of growth and development after death. A vivid literary description of purgatory is provided by Dante in *The Divine Comedy. See* Eschatology.

Purification, Feast of the. *See* Presentation of our Lord Jesus Christ in the Temple, The.

Purification of Women (after childbirth). The title given in the 1549 BCP to the rite commonly called the Churching of Women. It is derived from the Sarum rite. Its ultimate source is the Jewish rite of purification, and the Purification of the Blessed Virgin Mary (Lk 2:22–39). St. Augustine of Canterbury mentions the existence of this Christian rite. In the 1552 BCP the title of the service was changed to "The Thanksgiving of Women after Childbirth, commonly called the Churching of Women." In the 1979 BCP the service was replaced by "A Thanksgiving for the Birth or Adoption of a Child." The text of the Prayer Book service has always stressed thanksgiving for the mother's preservation through "the great danger of childbirth." The service itself includes a psalm and prayers. The churching was originally the occasion for the return of the child's white baptismal robe to the parish. The present rite includes both parents and gives thanks for the birth (or adoption) of the child. All suggestions of ritual impurity have been removed.

Purificator. A small square of white linen, usually with an embroidered cross and folded in thirds, used to wipe the chalice after use at the eucharist.

Puritanism. The term has become an epithet without precise meaning. At one time it described a reform movement in the Church of England during the late sixteenth and seventeenth centuries. It sought to carry the English Reformation beyond the stage reached in the reign of Elizabeth I. In this sense the term was first applied to those who wished to "purify" the church from the remnants of "popery." Puritanism included representatives of a wide range of doctrines, from Presbyterians, independents, and separatists, through levellers and millenarians. Within English Puritan ranks there was much lively debate. Puritan literature of the seventeenth century was thus by definition polemic.

By the 1640s, in an overheated atmosphere complicated by new ideas of political, economic, and institutional reform, radical Puritanism could no longer be fitted into the constitutional structure of the English state.

Radical Puritans turned against the conservative element in Protestantism—against Presbyterianism, against the rule of elders, and finally against every form of authority in society, the state, or the law. The Puritan recognized only human experience—the authority derived from direct religious revelation, the "trying of the spirit." In the Puritan view, the only true Christian person is the person who knows God. All that mattered was salvation and God's light, wherever they might appear. Any person could find salvation. By the late 1640s radical Puritanism had spawned political radicalism in England and America.

Puritanism was an important force in England. It contributed to the idea of political liberty and democracy and to the development of the "nonconformist conscience." However, in matters of religious life it spent its energies in sharpening distinctions with respect to questions of concern chiefly to students of political theory. In America, Puritans did not spend their energies debating with each other. They marked off the boundaries of new towns, enforced criminal laws, and fought Indians undistracted by theology or metaphysics. Allowing no dissent, they moved single-mindedly to the task of overcoming the unpredictable perils of the wilderness. If English Puritans were the precursors of modern democracy, those in America helped to found a nation.

Pusey, Edward Bouverie (Aug. 22, 1800–Sept. 16, 1882). Tractarian leader. He was born at Pusey, Berkshire, England, and received his B.A. in 1822 and his M.A. in 1825 from Christ Church College, Oxford. In 1824 he became a fellow at Oriel College, Oxford, where he became closely associated with John Henry Newman and John Keble. Pusey was ordained deacon on June 1, 1828, and priest on Nov. 23, 1828. Late in 1828 he was named Regius Professor of Hebrew at Oxford and Canon of Christ Church, positions he held until his death. In 1833 the *Tracts for the Times* began to appear and the Tractarian movement commenced. Pusey wrote Tract 18, *Thoughts on the Benefits of the System of Fasting enjoined by our Church*, and thus became a part of the movement. His most famous tract was *Scriptural Views of Holy Baptism*, which was actually three tracts (Nos. 67, 68, and 69), published in 1835. Pusey became the leader of the Tractarian or Oxford movement when Newman joined the Roman Catholic Church in 1845. Pusey established the first Anglican sisterhood since the Reformation, the Sisterhood of the Holy Cross, in 1845. He died at the convent at Ascot Priory in Berkshire. His ministry is commemorated in the Episcopal calendar of the church year on Sept. 18.

"Puseyism." *See* Tracts for the Times.

Pusey Report. *See* Ministry for Tomorrow; *see* Board for Theological Education (BTE).

Pyx (or Pix). A small round container or box for consecrated bread that is taken to those who cannot be present for the eucharist at church. During the first centuries of the church, Christians carried home portions of the consecrated bread from the Sunday Eucharist to communicate themselves. They carried the consecrated bread in small boxes of wood, ivory, or metal. These boxes were known as *arcae* or *arculae*. They were carried by a cord suspended around the neck. Some modern pyxes are relatively flat and still carried in this way. Somewhat larger pyxes may be carried in a pocket or purse. Pyxes may be made of gold or silver and may be decorated with a cross or other Christian religious symbols. The term has also been applied to a vessel for reservation of the sacrament that was suspended over the high altar. It was known as a "hanging pyx." The first monstrances were pyxes with openings on the sides which were mounted upon a stem and foot.

Q

Quadragesima. Archaic term for the forty days of Lent or the First Sunday in Lent. *See* Pre-Lent season.

Quaerite Dominum. Canticle 10 of the BCP (pp. 86–87), also known as the Second Song of Isaiah, based on Is 55:6–11. Many OT scholars identify the author of this canticle to be Deutero-Isaiah, or Second Isaiah, who lived some 150 years after Isaiah of Jerusalem during the Babylonian exile. This canticle begins, "Seek the Lord while he wills to be found; call upon him when he draws near." This canticle urges the wicked to forsake their ways, and turn to the Lord who will have compassion and richly pardon. The BCP suggests its use at Morning Prayer on Fridays after the OT reading, except in Lent, and at Evening Prayer after the OT reading on Tuesdays (pp. 144–145). *The Hymnal 1982* provides six musical settings for the *Quaerite Dominum* (S 217–S 222).

Quest International. The official worldwide online network of the Anglican Communion. It is a network of people providing economical and effective communication for dioceses, ministry groups, organizations, and individuals. It is enabled by a computer system called Ecunet, a nonprofit organization dedicated to serving communities of faith. Quest International is the conferencing and business meeting connection of the Inter-Anglican Information Network.

Quicunque Vult. *See* Athanasian Creed.

Quincy, Diocese of. The 1877 General Convention voted to divide the Diocese of Illinois into three dioceses. The three dioceses are Quincy, Springfield, and Chicago. The Diocese of Quincy includes the following counties: Adams, Brown, Bureau, Fulton, Hancock, Henry, Knox, McDonough, Mercer, Peoria, Pike, Schuyler, Stark, Warren, and Woodford. The primary convention of the Diocese met at St. John's Cathedral, Quincy, Dec. 11, 1877. On Sept. 15, 1877, even before the official creation of the new diocese, St. John's Church, Quincy, was given to the diocese as St. John's Cathedral. On May 7, 1962, St. John's Cathedral became St. John's Parish, and St. Paul's Church, Peoria, became the Cathedral Church of St. Paul.

Quinquagesima Sunday. *See* Pre-Lenten Season.

Quintard, Charles Todd (Dec. 22, 1824–Feb. 15, 1898). Bishop and Educator. He was born in Stamford, Connecticut, and attended Trinity School in New York. In 1847 Quintard received his M.D. degree from University Medical College, New York University. For a year he worked at Bellevue Hospital. He moved to Athens, Georgia, where he practiced medicine. In 1851 he became professor of physiology and pathological anatomy at the Memphis Medical College and one of the editors of the *Memphis Medical Recorder.* While in Memphis he became friends with Bishop James Otey and began to study for the ordained ministry. Quintard was ordained deacon on Jan. 1, 1855, and priest on Jan. 6, 1856. He served as rector of the Church of the Advent, Nashville, until he was consecrated Bishop of Tennessee on Oct. 11, 1865. He served as bishop until his death.

Quintard was instrumental in the revival of the church in Tennessee. He supported missions to the freed African Americans. He was a supporter of the Oxford Movement and was deeply interested in the educational mission of the church. Quintard was the second founder of the University of the South after the devastation of the Civil War. In Mar. 1866 he went to Sewanee, selected locations for the buildings, and planted a cross. He was the first vice-chancellor of the University, Feb. 14, 1867–July 12, 1872, and presided at its official opening on Sept. 18,

1868. He made several trips to England to raise money for the University. On one of those trips he convinced a woman to give the money for a theological building. This resulted in the construction of St. Luke's Hall, so named because Quintard was a physician. Quintard died in Darien, Georgia.

Quire. *See* Choir.

R

"R." *See* Response.

Rabat. A vest or shirtfront worn by clergy. It is usually black, and often worn over a white shirt with long sleeves. The clerical collar is attached to the rabat.

Racine College, Racine, Wisconsin. The Episcopal Diocesan Council of Milwaukee, Wisconsin, in 1851, felt the need for an Episcopal college in southeastern Wisconsin, to prepare young men for the seminary at Nashotah House, as well as to prepare others for professional and business careers. The Rev. Joseph H. Nichols, rector of St. Luke's Episcopal Church in Racine, with other Episcopal priests and local businessmen, became the moving spirit of the project, and raised donations of $10,000 and ten acres of land, which established the location of the college in Racine.

During the years of its existence the institution's educational offerings changed. It originally offered a preparatory course, probably equivalent to high school studies, and two college courses. In 1859 a grammar school curriculum was added when it consolidated with St. John's Hall of Delafield, Wisconsin. St. John's headmaster, James DeKoven, became president of the consolidated schools. Under his leadership and reorganization the college enjoyed its greatest period of vitality and prosperity. During this time, students and faculty established several missions which became parishes. Military drill was part of the curriculum during part of the time. In the final days of the school, a military academy flourished briefly.

After DeKoven's death in 1879, the school continued with varying degrees of success. The long depression of the early thirties and declining enrollment finally brought about the closing of the school in 1933. Among its graduates over the years were many prominent community and national leaders, including General Billy Mitchell and Bishop Thomas Gailor of Tennessee.

After the school closed, the property was purchased by the Episcopal Community of St. Mary. The Sisters of St. Mary established the DeKoven Foundation for Church Work, which is still an active force in the Episcopal community. The property is on the National Register of Historic Places. *See* DeKoven Center, The.

Rainsford, William Stephen (Oct. 30, 1850–Dec. 17, 1933). Priest and social reformer. He was born near Dublin, Ireland. Rainsford received his B.A. from St. John's College, Cambridge, in 1872. He was ordained deacon on Dec. 21, 1873, and priest on Dec. 20, 1874. He began his ministry at St. Giles's Church, Norwich, and came to the United States in 1876. He was a mission preacher in America for two years. Rainsford was assistant rector at St. James' Cathedral, Toronto, 1878–1882. In Jan. 1883 he became the rector of St. George's Church, Stuyvesant Square, New York. He reorganized St. George's as a free church with no pew rents. Rainsford turned it into an "institutional church," that is, an urban church organized to provide not only worship and Christian education but a full program of social services. Under his leadership, St. George's was turned "into a giant hive of activity." Rainsford was an active social reformer and a defender of the rights of labor. He even permitted dancing in the parish house. After several physical breakdowns, he resigned from the parish in 1906. On May 3, 1912, he was deposed from the priesthood at his own request. Rainsford was a part of the broad church movement, sharing its liberal theology and commitment to social action. He described his ministry in *The Story of a Varied Life: An Autobiography* (1922). Rainsford died in New York City.

Rakestraw, Caroline Leiding (June 28, 1912–Oct. 29, 1993). Broadcast media pioneer for the Episcopal Church. She was a native of Atlanta, Georgia, and served as executive secretary to the Bishop of Atlanta and produced his radio talks. In 1954 she founded and became the first executive director of the Episcopal Radio-TV Foundation. She won awards for her television work and retired in 1980. *See* Episcopal Radio-TV Foundation. She died in Atlanta.

Ramsey, Michael (Nov. 14, 1904–Apr. 23, 1988). A significant Anglican theologian and Archbishop of Canterbury from 1961 to 1974. His work as a theologian began with *The Gospel and the Catholic Church* (1936), an ecumenical and biblical study which established his reputation as a major voice in Anglicanism. His later works included *The Glory of God and the Transfiguration of Christ* (1949), *An Era in Anglican Theology: The Development of Anglican Theology between* Lux Mundi *and the Second World War* (1960), and numerous smaller books on various pastoral and theological themes. He was closely involved in ecumenical work between Anglicanism and the Orthodox churches, the Roman Catholic Church, and various Protestant churches through the World Council of Churches. In 1966, while Archbishop of Canterbury, he met with Pope Paul VI. It was through their mutual efforts that the Anglican/Roman Catholic International Commission began its work.

As Archbishop of Canterbury, Ramsey presided over especially turbulent years for the Church of England and the Anglican Communion. He wrote extensively about political and theological questions, and he visited all of the provinces of the Anglican Communion. After his retirement from Canterbury, he frequently visited the United States and taught for several years at Nashotah House in Wisconsin. *See* Anglican-Roman Catholic International Commission (ARCIC).

Ratcliffe, Robert (1657–1700). First rector of King's Chapel, Boston. He was a graduate of Exeter College, Oxford University, and appointed by the Bishop of London to minister in Boston. Ratcliffe arrived in Boston on May 15, 1686, and on June 15, 1686, King's Chapel parish was organized with Ratcliffe as the rector. This was the first Church of England parish organized in New England. Ratcliffe presided at the opening of King's Chapel on June 30, 1689, which seems to have been his last official act.

Rationalism. In Christian theology, rationalism (from the Latin *ratio*, meaning "reason") indicates a mode of thought in which human reason is the ultimate authority in establishing religious truth. In normative Anglican theology, reason is treated as one of three related sources of authority, along with scripture and tradition. In Anglican theology, reason allows itself to be corrected by scripture and tradition as it interprets them. In a rationalistic theology, on the other hand, reason is not corrected by anything else. *See* Authority, Sources of (in Anglicanism); *see* Deism; *see* Reason.

Ravenscroft, John Stark (May 17, 1772–Mar. 5, 1830). Bishop and high churchman. He was born in Blandford in Prince George's County, Maryland. Ravenscroft studied law at the College of William and Mary, but he never practiced law. He settled in Lunenburg County, Virginia, where for eighteen years he exhibited no interest in religion. Around 1810 he had a conversion experience, joined the Republican Methodists, and became a lay preacher. After a short while, he was confirmed in the Episcopal Church. In 1817 Ravenscroft became the rector of St. James' Church, Mecklenburg County, some months before his ordination. He was ordained deacon on Apr. 25, 1817, and priest on May 6, 1817. He was consecrated the first Bishop of North Carolina on May 22, 1823. While he was bishop, he served as rector of Christ Church, Raleigh, and then as rector of St. John's Church, Williamsborough. He was a high churchman in the tradition of Bishop John Henry Hobart. He held a high view of episcopacy and apostolic succession. He insisted on strict adherence to the liturgy and offices of the BCP. At times he could be brusque and blunt. Some called him "mad Jack." He died in Raleigh.

Reader. *See* Lector; *see* Lay Reader.

Reading Desk. *See* Reading Pew.

Reading Pew. A small pew used by the officiant who led Morning or Evening Prayer. It was also known as the reading desk. Historically, it was also used for reading the litany, and the decalogue, the epistle, and the gospel at the eucharist. It was typically located in the nave so that the people could hear the officiant at Morning and Evening Prayer, as called for by Prayer Book rubrics after 1552. The reading pew was combined in various ways with the clerk's pew and the pulpit in different churches. One arrangement was the well-known "three–Decker" pulpit, in which the clerk's pew was on the lowest level, the reading pew was on the middle level, and the pulpit was on the highest level. The "three–Decker" pulpit came into use in England and America during the eighteenth century.

Reaffirmation of Baptismal Vows. The BCP refers to those persons already baptized who are presented to the bishop in the context of a service of Baptism or Confirmation to reaffirm their baptismal vows. These might be persons returning to the church after a period of unbelief or those who have entered a new level of spiritual life. The BCP does not specify who these persons are, and a variety of interpretation exists. The BCP provides a form to be used for reaffirmation of baptismal vows instead of the confirmation formula (BCP, p. 419). The word "renewal" rather than "reaffirmation" is used to describe the reaffirming of the baptismal covenant by the entire congregation at Baptism, Confirmation, or the Easter Vigil (BCP, p. 292).

Real Presence. The presence of Christ in the sacrament of the Holy Eucharist. The 1991 statement of the Anglican-Roman Catholic International Commission notes, "The elements are not mere signs; Christ's body and blood become really present and are really given. But they are really present and given in order that, receiving them, believers may be united in communion with Christ the Lord." A classic Anglican statement attributed to John Donne (or to Queen Elizabeth I) and included in *The Hymnal 1982* (Hymn 322) is "He was the Word that spake it, he took the bread and brake it, and what that Word did make it, I do believe and take it." In Eucharistic Prayer A of Rite 2, the celebrant prays that God the Father will sanctify the gifts of bread and wine "by your Holy Spirit to be for your people the Body and Blood of your Son, the holy food and drink of new and unending life in him" (BCP, p. 363). The Catechism notes that the inward and spiritual grace in the eucharist is "the Body and Blood of Christ given to his people and received by faith" (BCP, p. 859). Belief in the real presence does not imply a claim to know how Christ is present in the eucharistic elements. Belief in the real presence does not imply belief that the consecrated eucharistic elements cease to be bread and wine. *See* Transubstantiation; *see* Receptionism.

Realized Eschatology. *See* Eschatology.

Reason. One of the three sources of authority in Anglicanism, along with scripture and tradition. Reason interprets scripture and tradition and allows itself to be corrected and enlarged by them. Reason is considered in Anglican thought to be more than calculation and logic, and it draws upon the entirety of human understanding and experience. Reason makes it possible to evaluate and determine what is good to be done in a particular situation. *See* Authority, Sources of (in Anglicanism); *see* Hooker, Richard.

Recant. To retract. Used especially in regard to a charge of ecclesiastical misdoing or heresy, the word meant to repent of a prohibited or heretical act. The word is no longer found in the canons, but the concept is found in the canon, "Of the Abandonment of the Communion of this Church," whereby a member of the clergy guilty of acts of abandonment may make "a good faith retraction" of acts or words constituting abandonment and avoid being deposed.

Recapitulation. This theological term indicates that fallen humanity has been "reheaded" and reconstituted in Christ. The term is from the Greek *anacephalaeosis*, "summing up" or "summary." It is found in the statement of Eph 1:10 that God set forth in Christ "to unite (recapitulate) all things in him, things in heaven and things on earth." This concept of salvation history was used by patristic sources, especially St. Irenaeus of Lyons (c. 130–c. 200).

Reception of the Body (At Time of Death). The BCP provides a form of prayers for use when the body is brought to the church prior to the burial service (pp. 466–467). The form includes prayers for the deceased and the bereaved.

Reception (Christian Commitment). Baptized persons who have been members of another Christian fellowship and who wish to be affiliated with the Episcopal Church may make a public affirmation of their faith and commitment to the responsibilities of their baptism in the presence of a bishop. The bishop lays hands on each candidate for reception and says, "We recognize you as a member of the one holy catholic and apostolic Church, and we receive you into the fellowship of this Communion" (BCP, p. 418). Candidates for reception normally have made a mature commitment in another Christian fellowship. Some dioceses have reserved reception for those candidates who have previously received sacramental confirmation with laying on of hands by a bishop in apostolic succession.

Reception (of Doctrine). Consent of the faithful to statements of the church's faith. An ancient view states that the truth of a doctrine is known by the universality of its reception or acceptance in the church. Under the guidance of the Holy Spirit, the entire church can receive and recognize God's truth in Christ. Whenever an attempt is made to define the faith of the church, it is necessary for the community of believers to recognize the truth of the

faith statement made on their behalf. This recognition and consent is the reception of the doctrine by the church. *See* Infallibility, Papal.

Receptionism. The belief that the eucharistic elements of bread and wine are unchanged during the prayer of consecration but that the faithful believer receives the body and blood of Christ in receiving communion. This was the prevailing eucharistic theology in the Reformation era of Anglicanism. The Articles of Religion state that the bread and wine of the eucharist are the body and blood of Christ "to such as rightly, worthily, and with faith, receive the same. . . ." Article XXVIII, Of the Lord's Supper (BCP, p. 873). Thomas Cranmer held a receptionist understanding of the eucharist, which informed his work on the 1549 and 1552 Prayer Books. This historic receptionistic language is still retained in Eucharistic Prayer I of Rite 1. However, Anglican eucharistic theology has tended to hold in balance both an objective change of some kind in the eucharistic elements to become the body and blood of Christ and the subjective faith of the believer who receives the sacrament. The words of administration of the 1559 Prayer Book joined language from the 1549 BCP that identified the sacrament as the body and blood of Christ with more receptionistic language from the 1552 BCP that urged the communicant to receive the sacrament "in remembrance" of Christ's sacrifice. This combination was continued in the 1662 BCP, and in subsequent American Prayer Books (see BCP, p. 338). The balance of objective and subjective theologies of the eucharist is also presented by the Catechism, which states that "The inward and spiritual grace in the Holy Communion is the Body and Blood of Christ given to his people, and received by faith" (BCP, p. 859). The receptionistic language of Eucharistic Prayer I in Rite 1 is not found in the other eucharistic prayers of the BCP. *See* Real Presence; *see* Transubstantiation.

Recitation. The traditional methods of psalmody, whether spoken or sung, are direct recitation, antiphonal recitation, and responsorial recitation. Direct recitation means the reading or singing of the entire psalm or portion of the psalm in unison. It is frequently used to recite or chant the psalm following the first lesson at the eucharist and the canticles at the Daily Offices. Antiphonal recitation is the alternation of verses of the psalm between two groups of singers or readers, e.g., the sides of the congregation, men and women, choir and congregation. An antiphon said or sung in unison may begin and conclude antiphonal recitation. It is the traditional monastic method of reciting the psalms at the Daily Offices. Responsorial recitation assigns the verses to a single voice, with the congregation responding with a refrain after each verse or group of verses. This is the traditional method of singing the invitatory psalm at Morning Prayer and the psalm between the readings, often called the responsorial psalm.

Reciting Note. A note found in each half of a psalm tone on which much of the text is sung. Its duration is determined by the length of the text to which it is sung.

Recognition and Investiture of a Diocesan Bishop. This is one of the "Episcopal Services" in the *BOS*. It is designed for the recognition, investiture, and seating of a bishop who has already been ordained and consecrated. The Presiding Bishop presides at this service, but another bishop may be deputized for the occasion. The service takes place in the context of a eucharist. The rubrics envisage that this service will take place in the cathedral church. However, it may be held in another suitable place, and the service may be adapted when necessary. At the Recognition, the Presiding Bishop is escorted to a chair placed at the entrance to the chancel, facing the people. The new bishop is escorted by the welcoming procession to a place before the Presiding Bishop. Ps 23 appropriately follows with the antiphon "I will give you a shepherd after my own heart, who will feed you with knowledge and understanding." The new bishop petitions for recognition and investiture. A representative of the diocese states that the new bishop was duly elected and that consents to the election have been received. The people recognize and receive the new bishop and promise to uphold the new bishop in this ministry. After the Litany for Ordinations or another litany, the Presiding Bishop says the collect of the day or the collect for ordination. The liturgy of the word continues in the usual manner. After the sermon and the creed, the new bishop may reaffirm the commitments of episcopal ordination. At the Investiture, the Presiding Bishop invests the new bishop with all temporal and spiritual rights and responsibilities of the bishop's new office. If the pastoral staff is given to the new bishop, it is presented by the former bishop of the diocese, or it is brought from the altar and presented by the representative of the diocese. The new bishop lays a hand upon a Bible that is brought from the altar, and takes the oath of office. If the bishop is to be seated in the *cathedra*, the seating

follows the taking of the oath. The new bishop is escorted by the Presiding Bishop and the representative of the diocese to the chair designated for the diocesan bishop. The new bishop may be seated in the *cathedra* by the dean of the cathedral. After the bishop sits, the people may offer their acclamations and applause. Bells may be rung and trumpets sounded. The new bishop is the chief celebrant at the eucharist. Other bishops and representative presbyters of the diocese may concelebrate the eucharist with the new bishop. The postcommunion prayer for this service is the prayer used after communion at ordinations. At the end of the service, the new bishop blesses the people, and the people are dismissed by a deacon.

Reconciliation of a Penitent. Sacramental rite in which those who repent may confess their sins to God in the presence of a priest and receive the assurance of pardon and the grace of absolution (BCP, p. 861). It is also called penance and confession. The church's ministry of reconciliation is from God, "who reconciled us to himself through Christ, and has given us the ministry of reconciliation" (2 Cor 5:18). The ministry of reconciliation has been committed by Christ to the church. It is exercised through the care each Christian has for others, through the common prayer of Christians assembled for public worship, and through the priesthood of the church and its ministers declaring absolution (BCP, p. 446). The Reconciliation of a Penitent is not limited to times of sickness. Confessions may be heard at any time and any place.

The BCP provides two forms of service for the Reconciliation of a Penitent. Only a bishop or priest may pronounce absolution. A declaration of forgiveness may be used by a deacon or lay person who hears a confession. When a confession is heard in a church building, the confessor may sit inside the altar rails while the penitent kneels nearby. The confession may be heard in a place set aside for greater privacy. It is also appropriate for the confessor and penitent to sit face to face for a spiritual conference that leads to absolution or a declaration of forgiveness. After the penitent has confessed all serious sins troubling the conscience and given evidence of contrition, the priest offers counsel and encouragement before pronouncing absolution. Before pronouncing absolution, the priest may assign a psalm, prayer, or hymn to be said, or something to be done, as a sign or penitence and act of thanksgiving.

The 1979 BCP is the first American Prayer Book to provide forms for the Reconciliation of a Penitent as a separate office. Form One (p. 447) is shorter and less elaborate than Form Two (p. 449), which includes material similar to the Byzantine form for confession. Form Two begins with verses from Psalm 51 and the *Trisagion*, and it includes scriptural words of comfort. A rubric in Form Two also directs that the priest lay a hand upon the penitent's head or extend a hand over the penitent at the absolution. This gesture also may be used at the absolution in Form One. The secrecy of the confession is morally absolute for the confessor and must not be broken (BCP, p. 446).

Recorder (of Ordinations). A person or incorporated organization of the Episcopal Church is elected by the House of Deputies upon nomination of the House of Bishops "to continue the List of Ordinations and to keep a list of the Clergy in regular standing." Each diocese must report annually to the recorder all persons ordained, the names of all clergy who have died, all clergy received from another jurisdiction or transferred to another jurisdiction, and those suspended, removed, deposed, and restored.

Recovered Alcoholic Clergy Association (RACA). Founded on Oct. 24, 1968, in San Francisco by the Rev. James T. Golder and five others who were recovering alcoholic priests. It promotes mutual self-help, fellowship, and pastoral concern for recovering alcoholic clergy. Members are committed to support fellow members and to respond to calls from clergy or members of clergy families who seek and need help. It maintains a hot line for persons in trouble with alcohol and drugs. RACA sponsors educational conferences, retreats, and clergy seminars.

Recovery Ministries of the Episcopal Church. The Episcopal Church passed its first resolution on alcohol and drug abuse at the 1979 General Convention. The National Episcopal Coalition on Alcohol and Drugs (NECAD) was founded on Apr. 29, 1982, to provide information about alcohol and drug abuse and support for families, parishes, and dioceses. On May 11, 1995, the name was changed to Recovery Ministries of the Episcopal Church. It is an independent, nationwide network of Episcopal clergy and laity, dioceses and parishes, schools, agencies, and other institutions with a common commitment to address the use and abuse of alcohol and other drugs. It established an annual Alcohol-Drug

Awareness Sunday and provides parishes and missions with related materials. It supports intervention and treatment resources for church employees and their families. It recognizes leaders in education, prevention, and treatment of alcohol and drug addiction. It annually presents the Samuel Shoemaker Award in memory of this early pioneer in the formation of Alcoholics Anonymous.

Rector. The priest in charge of a parish. Typically, a rector is the priest in charge of a self-supporting parish, and a vicar is the priest in charge of a supported mission. The rector is the ecclesiastical authority of the parish. The term is derived from the Latin for "rule." The rector has authority and responsibility for worship and the spiritual jurisdiction of the parish, subject to the rubrics of the BCP, the constitution and canons of the church, and pastoral direction of the bishop. The rector is responsible for selection of all assistant clergy, and they serve at the discretion of the rector. The church and parish buildings and furnishings are under the rector's control. The rector or a member of the vestry designated by the rector presides at all vestry meetings.

Rectory. A house owned by the parish and provided for the rector's home. Such provided housing has been known as "the parsonage" and "the manse" in other traditions.

Redaction Criticism. The German word "redaction" is best translated as editing. The main point of this exegetical method is to find an understanding of the techniques and thoughts used by the redactor or final editor of a gospel. We have no specific information about who the gospel editors were, or when the editing was done, or where the editing was completed. Redaction criticism seeks to determine the theological emphases of the editor that can be based on an examination of the details of a specific gospel. Redaction critics seek to explain the reason for the changes that have been made by the editor. They consider how specific sources were altered, modified, or rewritten. Redaction critics also evaluate how the stories were combined and arranged and the use of words, phrases, or styles by the editor. The social and environmental context of the editor is also considered in redaction criticism.

Redeemer. Savior. One who pays a price to buy back something, to liberate a person or a people from bondage, or to save a life that was legally forfeit. In the OT, the Lord God is the redeemer of Israel (see Ex 6:6; 2 Sm 7:23; Ps 130:7;

Is 44:6, 54:5). God delivered Israel from bondage in Egypt and from the Babylonian exile. The OT also includes a messianic expectation of the redeemer who will come (see Is 7:14–17, 9:1–7, 11, 40:1–11). Christians identify Jesus Christ as the expected messiah and redeemer. Jesus is the redeemer of fallen humanity (see Rom 3:24; Gal 3:13, 4:4–5; Ti 2:14). The NT uses a variety of images and metaphors to present Jesus as our redeemer. The sacrifice of Jesus' life is described as "a ransom for many" (Mk 10:45; Mt 20:28). Jesus predicted that he would draw all to himself when he was lifted up from the earth (Jn 12:32). Jesus was "handed over to death for our trespasses and was raised for our justification" (Rom 4:25). He is the "Second Adam," who restores humanity to righteousness and right relationship with God (see Rom 5:19). St. Paul states that "as all die in Adam, so all will be made alive in Christ" (1 Cor 15:22). The Letter to the Hebrews (2:17) states that Jesus was "a merciful and faithful high priest in the service of God" who made "a sacrifice of atonement for the sins of the people."

Jesus' role as our redeemer is at the heart of Christian theology. This theme is powerfully expressed in the worship of the Episcopal Church. The collect for the Second Sunday of Advent prays that "we may greet with joy the coming of Jesus Christ our Redeemer (BCP, pp. 159, 211). The first collect for Easter Day states that God gave his only-begotten Son to death on the cross for our redemption and that Jesus delivered us from the power of our enemy by his glorious resurrection (BCP, pp. 170, 222, 295). Eucharistic Prayer B recalls that in these last days God the Father sent Jesus "to be incarnate from the Virgin Mary, to be the Savior and Redeemer of the world" (BCP, p. 368). *The Hymnal 1982* includes "Redeemer of the nations, come" as a hymn for Advent (Hymn 55).

Redemption may be understood in terms of atonement, forgiveness of sins, justification, deliverance from the power of death, righteousness, and the doing away with human alienation from God. Christians affirm that we may share the saving benefits of Christ's life, death, and resurrection through baptism and participation in the life of the church (see Col 2:12; Rom 6:4–5).

Redemption. *See* Redeemer.

Red-letter Days. Major feasts of the church year, including the principal feasts, feasts of our Lord, feasts of all apostles, evangelists, and other major saints' days and festivals. The term reflects the early practice of printing Prayer Book calendars in red. These major feasts were included in the Prayer Book calendar and printed with red letters. The term is applied to those feasts for which the BCP provides full propers, including collect, OT lesson, psalm, NT epistle, and gospel. Red-letter days are distinguished from the lesser feasts of the calendar of the church year, which are also known as black-letter days and printed with black letters. In Prayer Books with single-color printing, major feasts are printed in bold type, and lesser feasts are printed in lightface type. See The Calendar of the Church year (BCP, pp. 19–30).

Refectory. A room where meals are shared. The term is from the Latin, "to restore" or "refresh." This term has been applied to the room used for meals in monasteries or other religious houses. It may indicate a separate building. The term has also been used to indicate the room or building for meals on a seminary campus.

Reformed. *See* Protestantism.

Reformed Episcopal Church. This denomination emerged out of the high church–low church controversy of the mid-nineteenth century. Assistant Bishop David Cummins of Kentucky and Charles Edward Cheney, rector of Christ Church, Chicago, were both opposed to the high church party and especially to the doctrine of baptismal regeneration. Bishop Cummins was criticized for participating in an ecumenical communion service at the Fifth Avenue Presbyterian Church, New York, in connection with the sixth General Convention of the Evangelical Alliance. He decided to leave the Episcopal Church. On Dec. 2, 1873, Cummins met with eight clergy and twenty laymen of the Episcopal Church at the YMCA building in New York and organized the Reformed Episcopal Church. This body rejects baptismal regeneration, any sacerdotalism associated with the Lord's Supper, apostolic succession in the historic episcopate, and does not participate in the ecumenical movement.

Regina Coeli. Latin for "Queen of Heaven," the phrase refers to the Blessed Virgin Mary. *Regina Coeli* is also the beginning of a devotion, common in some Anglo-catholic circles, used during the Easter season in place of the *Angelus.* The customary bell-ringing sequence for *Regina Coeli*, at morning, noon, and evening, consists of four sets of two strokes, with pauses between each set, followed by eight peals. The *Regina Coeli* begins "O Queen of heaven, be joyful, alleluia; Because he whom so meetly thou barest, alleluia, Hath arisen, as he promised, alleluia; Pray for us to the Father, alleluia."

Registrar (of the General Convention). The Registrar maintains all journals and other records of the General Convention, and maintains records of all ordinations and consecrations of bishops in the Episcopal Church. The Registrar is a presbyter elected by the House of Deputies upon the nomination of the House of Bishops.

Regular Clergy (Regulars). Historically, priests who have taken solemn vows and live in a religious community under a rule of life. The term "regular" is from the Latin, "rule." These priests may be distinguished from secular priests who do not live in a religious community.

Relations of Capital and Labor, Joint Commission on the. The 1901 General Convention appointed this Joint Commission to study the aims and purposes of the labor organizations of the United States. The commission was to investigate the causes of industrial disturbances and to act as arbitrators between labor and employers if needed. Their services as arbitrators were never requested. The appointment of the commission indicated that the Episcopal Church supported the work of labor unions and union labor. It was replaced by the Joint Commission on Social Service by the 1910 General Convention.

Relics. The material remains of the body of a saint or martyr after death, such as bones, teeth, or hair. Relics may also include objects that have been in direct contact with the body of a saint or martyr in life, such as clothing, items used by the saint or martyr, or even instruments of torture. Relics may be placed in a reliquary for protection and display. The veneration of relics has been an ancient and at times controversial practice in Christianity. Some have believed that religious relics have miraculous powers. Supporters of the veneration of relics have noted the powers associated with Elijah's mantle (2 Kgs 2:14), the bones of Elisha (2 Kgs 13:21), and the handkerchiefs or aprons that had touched Paul's skin (Acts 19:12). The bodies of early Christian martyrs were venerated by the church, including the remains of Ignatius and Polycarp, who were martyred in the second century. The eucharist was celebrated over the tombs of Christian martyrs in the catacombs of Rome in the fourth century. The Second Council of Nicaea (787) and the Council of Constantinople

(1084) were supportive of the veneration of religious relics. However, icons came to exercise a more important role than relics in the spirituality of the eastern church. The veneration of religious relics increased during the middle ages, especially as the crusaders brought back to Europe a variety of objects from the Holy Land. Relics were often placed as close as possible to the altar in a church or chapel. Abuses were associated with religious relics, including bogus claims, superstitious practices, competing shrines, and the marketing of religious relics. Protestant reformers such as John Huss (c. 1372–1415) and Martin Luther (1483–1546) opposed the cult of relics. Religious relics may be understood as a tangible reminder and connection with the life of a holy Christian person. The veneration given to saints and their relics (*dulia*) is distinguished from the worship that is offered only to God (*latria*). See Reliquary; *see* Martyrium.

Religious. 1) Concerning religion or belief in the divine. 2) A technical term indicating a religious order or congregation in which the members voluntarily commit themselves by vows for life, or a term of years, to holding their possessions in common or in trust, to living a celibate life in community, and to obedience to their rule and constitution. The term may also indicate a member of such a religious order or congregation. *See* Conference on the Religious Life in the Anglican Communion in the Americas, The.

Religious Education, Department of. The National Council of the Episcopal Church established this Department in 1920. It did most of its work through commissions that included the Commission on Student Work, the Commission to Survey Church Colleges, the Commission on Ministry, the Commission to Advance the Church's Interest Among Boarding Schools, the Commission on Teacher Training, the Commission for the Development of Primary Courses of the Christian Nurture Series, the Commission on Senior Lesson Courses, the Commission on Provincial Boards of Religious Education, the Commission on Vocation and Recruiting of Young People, the Commission on Registration and Reference of Church Workers, the Commission on Cooperation with Public Schools for Week Day Religious Education, the Commission on the Church School Service League, the Commission on Daily Vacation Bible Schools, and the Commission on Bible Reading. At the meeting of the National Council in Dec. 1938, the name was changed to the Department of Christian Education. It operated until 1968.

Religious House. A place of residence for a religious community or a branch house operated by or for a religious order. The term may be used as a synonym for a monastery or convent, but it normally denotes a place of prayer or retreat which may or may not be administered by a religious community. The House of the Redeemer in New York City and the DeKoven Center in Racine, Wisconsin, are religious houses under "secular" or diocesan oversight.

Religious Life. The life that is lived under the obligation of the traditional vows in a religious community. In a broad sense it may designate the life of any person that is lived in awareness of God. *See* Conference on the Religious Life in the Anglican Communion in the Americas, The; *see* Monastic.

Religious Order. A society of Christians who voluntarily commit themselves for life or a term of years to living a celibate life in community, holding possessions in common with other community members, and obeying the rule or constitution of the community. A religious order must have at least six professed members to be officially recognized in the Episcopal Church, according to the canon on religious orders and other Christian communities. The superior is the head or presider of a religious order. A novice guardian typically guides the formation of prospective new members. Religious orders in the Episcopal Church must have an episcopal visitor who serves as guardian of the rule or constitution of the community and as final arbiter of unresolved issues in the community. The rule or constitution reflects and shapes the community's mission and spirituality. It also defines the duties and responsibilities of the community's members and leaders. The Episcopal Church includes a variety of religious orders for women, for men, and for mixed communities. There are religious orders with active, contemplative, and mixed expressions of community life. A variety of spiritualities are represented in Episcopal religious orders, including Benedictine, Franciscan, and Augustinian. Recognized religious orders of the Episcopal Church belong to the Conference on the Religious Life in the Anglican Communion in the Americas. The Conference on the Religious Life publishes a Directory which includes descriptions and addresses for its members. *See*

Conference on the Religious Life in the Anglican Communion in the Americas, The; *see* Monastic.

Reliquary. A container for religious relics. It is used to protect and exhibit the relic. Reliquaries have often been made of precious metals or other costly materials or glass. Some reliquaries have been elaborately decorated with enamel, jewels, or paintings. Reliquaries have been made in a variety of shapes, including caskets, boxes, churches, gabled buildings, crosses, amulets, ampullae, capsules, rings, small tables, the shape of the relic contained, or the symbol of the saint whose relic is contained in the reliquary. *See* Relics.

Remigius of Reims (c. 438–c. 533). "Apostle of the Franks." He was born in Laon, France. At the age of twenty-two he was consecrated the Bishop of Reims. Remigius is remembered for converting Clovis, King of the Franks, to Christianity. Through Remigius's efforts, the Franks were converted to Nicene Christianity rather than Arian Christianity. Remigius baptized Clovis and about 3000 of his followers on Christmas Day, 496. He was also known as "Remi." Remigius is remembered for saying to Clovis, "Worship what you have burned, and burn what you have worshiped." He is commemorated in the Episcopal calendar of the church year on Oct. 1.

Remission of Sins. To remit is to refrain from enforcing a punishment. Remission of sins generally means forgiveness and absolution of sins. However, the suggestion of remitted punishment recalls a juridical understanding of sin and forgiveness that is no longer emphasized in the Episcopal Church. The "absolution and remission" of sins is pronounced after the general confession of the congregation in the Penitential Order of Rite 1 and after the confession of sin in the Rite 1 versions of Morning and Evening Prayer (BCP, pp. 321, 42, 63). One version of the Nicene Creed in Rite 1 mentions belief in baptism for the remission of sins. But the more contemporary Rite 1 version and the Rite 2 version of the Nicene Creed substitute "forgiveness" for "remission," and make no mention of the remission of sins (BCP, pp. 327–328, 359).

Renewal of Baptismal Vows. When there are no candidates for baptism or Confirmation at the Easter Vigil, the celebrant leads the people in the Renewal of Baptismal Vows (BCP, pp. 292–294). The Renewal of Baptismal Vows traditionally follows the Easter Vigil readings. It may also follow the gospel and a sermon or homily. The celebrant invites the people to the Renewal of Baptismal Vows with a bidding that recalls the Easter theme of death and rebirth with Christ by baptism. This address notes that the Lenten observance is ended and invites the people to renew the solemn promises and vows of baptism (BCP, p. 292). The Renewal of Baptismal Vows includes nine questions by the celebrant with responses by the people. The people's response to the first question reaffirms their renunciation of evil and renews their commitment to Jesus Christ. This recalls the threefold renunciation of Satan, evil, and sin and the threefold commitment to Christ of the baptismal service (BCP, pp. 302–303). The remaining eight questions and responses are the same as the baptismal covenant (see BCP, pp. 304–305). The affirmations of the Apostles' Creed (the Baptismal Creed) are made by the people in response to the second, third, and fourth questions by the celebrant. These questions and responses correspond to the three sections of the Apostles' Creed (see BCP, p. 96). The baptismal covenant then continues with five additional questions and responses concerning how the people will live the Christian life. This form for the Renewal of Baptismal Vows may also be used at the other baptismal feasts (Pentecost, All Saints' Day or the Sunday after All Saints' Day, and the Feast of the Baptism of our Lord) when there is no candidate for baptism. The Renewal of Baptismal Vows takes the place of the Nicene Creed at the Easter Vigil and the other baptismal feasts (BCP, pp. 295, 312).

Renewal Movement. The enlivening and spiritual reawakening of the church through prayer and a variety of ministries and programs. These programs seek to revitalize the church by increasing Christian faith, devotion, and commitment. Many participants in the renewal movement attribute its success to the active presence of the Holy Spirit. The renewal movement has included a diversity of expressions and movements within the Episcopal Church. Catholic renewal has brought liturgical renewal, the recovery of classical spirituality, and Cursillo. Evangelical renewal has placed a new emphasis on shared Bible study, personal conversion, and world mission. Charismatic renewal has emphasized the availability of the gifts of the Holy Spirit for the church. The broad church has encouraged renewal of commitment to issues of justice and peace. All these movements manifest the nature of the church as always being reformed and always in need of renewal. The renewal movement gained strength and participation in the Episcopal Church in the later decades of the twentieth century.

Renunciation (of orders). A member of the clergy not under presentment for a canonical offense may renounce his or her orders and be removed from the active exercise of the ordained ministry. Removal upon renunciation means that the person is deprived of the right to exercise ordained ministry.

Repose, Altar of. See Altar of Repose.

Reproaches, The. The reproaches are a traditional anthem based on OT prophetic passages (see Mi 6:3–4) and the *Trisagion*. It is sung at the Good Friday liturgy during the veneration of the cross. It is also called *Improperia*. It begins, "O my people, what have I done unto thee? or wherein have I wearied thee? Testify against me." In this anthem the crucified Christ recalls God's mighty acts for the salvation of humanity and reproaches humanity for unfaithfulness. The text was included in *The Draft Proposed Book of Common Prayer*, but was rejected by the 1976 General Convention as capable of an anti-Semitic interpretation. In 1979 a revised version of the reproaches which avoided the possible misinterpretation appeared in the Methodist *From Ashes to Fire*, and was subsequently included in *The Book of Alternative Services* of the Anglican Church of Canada (1985). In this version Christ reproaches humanity for making his "chosen Israel" the "scapegoats for your own guilt." The BCP allows "appropriate devotions" at the time of the veneration of the cross, which may include the Reproaches (p. 281). None of the biblical accounts of the crucifixion describe words of reproach for humanity by Christ on the cross.

Requiem. A Mass or eucharist offered on behalf of the dead. It contains prayers appropriate to a funeral. If the Mass is immediately followed by burial it concludes with the prayer of commendation. The title originates from the first words for this rite in the Roman tradition, *requiem aeternam dona eis, Domine* ("Give them eternal rest, O Lord").

Reredos. Decorations behind or above the altar. The reredos is typically a wooden screen, hanging, or panel. It may consist of stone, wood, jeweled metalwork, or drapery. The reredos may contain biblical scenes, scenes from the lives of the martyrs, statues of apostles and saints, panels inscribed with the Lord's Prayer and the Ten Commandments, or other Christian symbols.

Reservation of the Sacrament. Following ancient custom, the BCP provides that the consecrated bread and wine may be reserved for the communion of the sick or others who for "weighty cause" could not be present at the celebration or for administration of communion by a deacon to a congregation when a priest is unavailable (pp. 408–409). The sacrament may also be reserved on Maundy Thursday for communion on Good Friday. It is customary to keep the consecrated elements in a tabernacle or an aumbry or covered with a veil on a table or altar. A lamp or candle burns nearby to announce the presence of the reserved sacrament. This light is known as a sanctuary lamp if the reservation is near the altar. Although not provided for by the BCP, the reserved sacrament is used for benediction and private devotions in some parishes with an Anglo-catholic piety. *See* Altar of Repose; *see* Benediction of the Blessed Sacrament; *see* Deacon's Mass.

Resolution. A proposed action or decision that is to be considered by a legislative body such as the House of Bishops or the House of Deputies at General Convention, or at a diocesan convention, or at the gathering of another representative legislative body. The legislative vote is taken only on the substance of the resolution, which follows the word "Resolved" in the working of the resolution. Reasons, intentions, and justifications for resolutions may be included in a statement of explanation that follows the resolution. This information provides legislative history for future interpretation, but it is not included in the formal resolution. The procedural rules of each legislative body control which persons and entities are entitled to introduce resolutions and the technical requirements concerning resolutions. *See* Memorial (to General Convention).

Response. A liturgical answer or statement that responds to a prayer, bidding, or reading. The response may be paired with and follow a versicle. For example, Suffrages A and B in Morning Prayer each contain a series of versicles and responses (BCP, pp. 97–98). The initial letter "R" indicates the responses in these suffrages and in other pairs of versicles and responses (see, e.g., BCP, p. 569). Noonday Office and Evening Prayer begin with the versicle, "O God, make speed to save us," and the response, "O

Lord, make haste to help us" (BCP, pp. 103, 117). This versicle and response, which is based on Ps 70:1, also follows the confession of sin at the beginning of Compline (BCP, p. 128).

The readings from scripture at Noonday Office and Compline are followed by the people's response, "Thanks be to God." After each lesson at Morning Prayer, Evening Prayer, and the eucharist, the reader may say, "The Word of the Lord," and the people answer, "Thanks be to God." The reader may also say, "Here ends the Lesson (or reading)," to which no verbal response is made by the people. After the deacon or priest announces the gospel at the eucharist, the people answer, "Glory to you, Lord Christ." After the gospel is read or sung, the reader says, "The Gospel of the Lord," and the people answer, "Praise to you, Lord Christ." The customary responses before and after the gospel are omitted on Palm Sunday and Good Friday (BCP, pp. 272, 277).

Intercessions and other prayers may also have a response. For example, the biddings of the prayers of the people, Form V, are followed by the people's response, "Lord, have mercy" (BCP, p. 389). At the Ordination of a Bishop, the people respond to questions by the Presiding Bishop, answering that it is their will that the bishop-elect be ordained a bishop and that they will uphold the bishop-elect as bishop (BCP, p. 514).

In addition to fixed liturgical responses, there are also occasions when a response may be a personal statement. A response to the scripture readings may follow the gospel at a Marriage (BCP, p. 426). Responses may be made to the sermon at a Celebration of New Ministry (BCP, p. 560). At the Dedication and Consecration of a Church, the bishop may respond to the plans of the congregation for witness to the gospel by indicating the place of the congregation within the life of the diocese (BCP, p. 576).

Responsive Recitation (Psalmody). A method of psalmody in which the minister alternates verse by verse with the congregation. This method of recitation has been most frequently used in Episcopal churches (see BCP, p. 582).

Responsorial Recitation (Psalmody). A method of psalmody in which the verses are sung by a solo voice, and a refrain is sung by the choir and congregation after each verse or group of verses. Responsorial recitation was the traditional method of singing the *Venite*. It was also a traditional manner of chanting the psalms between the lessons at the eucharist (BCP, p. 582).

Responsory. A prayer with responses. For example, Suffrages A and B in Morning Prayer each contain a series of versicles and responses (BCP, pp. 55, 97–98).

Restoration (Ministry). A member of the clergy who has been suspended, removed, or deposed may be restored to active exercise of the ordained ministry under certain conditions. The technical term used is "remission of sentence." Bishops may be restored only by action of the House of Bishops. Priests and deacons may be restored by action of the bishop of the diocese where the sentence was imposed, subject to certain conditions. Termination or remission of a sentence of removal or deposition requires consent of two-thirds of the Standing Committees and at least four of the five diocesan bishops nearest the diocese where the sentence was imposed. The person who desires to be restored must subscribe to the declaration required of ordinands concerning belief that the Holy Scriptures of the OT and NT are the Word of God containing all things necessary to salvation, and solemnly engaging to conform to the doctrine, discipline, and worship of the Episcopal Church.

Restoration, The. The reinstatement in 1660 of the English monarchy under Charles II of the House of Stuart after the interregnum of the Commonwealth and Protectorate. On May 8, 1660, Charles II was proclaimed king by Parliament. He returned to England from the continent on May 25. With his return, the Church of England was restored, and the Clarendon Code was passed. The Clarendon Code placed severe restrictions on those who did not subscribe to the doctrines of the Church of England and to the 1662 BCP. In the colony of Massachusetts, where the Congregational Church was established and the Anglicans were repressed, the Restoration revived an Anglican desire for freedom of worship. A number of Bostonians petitioned the king "That a Church might be allowed in that City, for the Exercise of Religion according to the Church of England." Although King Charles II moved slowly, King's Chapel, Boston, was founded in 1686.

Restoring of Things Profaned. A form in the *BOS* for restoring to sacred use a church building, an altar, or other consecrated objects that have been profaned. It may precede the first church service after an act of vandalism or desecration. Portions of the prayer may be repeated for pastoral reasons at subsequent services on that day. The bishop or the parish priest may be the celebrant. Ps 118 and an antiphon may be sung or said in procession at the beginning of this rite. After the procession, each profaned object may be symbolically cleansed by use of signs of purification such as water or incense. The celebrant may touch, or extend a hand toward each object, declaring it "restored to the use for which it has been dedicated and consecrated."

Resurrection of Jesus. The belief that Jesus was raised bodily from the dead by God on the third day after Jesus' crucifixion and burial, exalting him to the near presence of God in eternal glory. The resurrection of Jesus is at the heart of Christianity (Acts 2:22–36). Christian faith would be meaningless without the resurrection of Jesus (1 Cor 15:14). The reality of Jesus' resurrection was experienced by chosen witnesses and proclaimed by the early Christian community. Easter is the day of Jesus' resurrection. Jesus is understood to have been raised on the Sunday following the Friday of his crucifixion. The resurrection is to be distinguished both from resuscitation (restoration to the prior mode of human existence) and the immortality of the soul. Jesus' resurrection began the transformation and glorification of the whole cosmos, including the redeemed Christian community. Christ was raised as the "first fruits of those who have fallen asleep" (1 Cor 15:20). By Christ's resurrection, this same new mode of existence is made available to all. The Catechism notes that "By his resurrection, Jesus overcame death and opened for us the way of eternal life" (BCP, p. 850). Jesus' resurrection is celebrated by Christians at all times, especially at Easter and throughout the Great Fifty Days of the Easter season, and on Sunday, which is the Lord's Day and the day of resurrection.

Retable. The term may refer to a raised shelf or ledge behind the altar. This shelf is also called a gradine. The altar cross, altar lights, and vases of flowers may be placed on it. The tabernacle may also be placed on it. The term may also refer to a frame above and behind the altar for decorated panels or to a framework for panels, paintings, or sculpture. This framework is also known as a reredos.

Retreat. A period of time, in a "place apart" from daily life and work, which normally includes silence, reflection, and may include some form of still, meditative prayer which may be combined with brief periods of activity and study. Retreats often focus on particular themes of the church year. Retreats may be communal, though they can also be individual and undirected or unstructured. The concept of retreat has its roots in the scriptural injunction to withdraw to a quiet, lonely place as Christ did periodically. The practice of making retreats is also based in the monastic tradition of structured time for silence and contemplation to balance the spiritual life between the contemplative way of life and the active way of life. The retreat movement reached a twentieth-century high point after World War II in the 1940s and 1950s. It became popular again in the 1990s with the growing interest in meditation, spirituality and the holistic health movements. Many religious orders sponsor retreats, as do diocesan retreat and conference centers.

Reverence. 1) Great respect, honor, or veneration. It may be associated with awe, devotion, and love. For example, the BCP notes the "Hebrew reverence and reticence with regard to the Name of God" (p. 583). The Preface to the 1789 BCP states that "the procuring of reverence, and the exciting of piety and devotion in the worship of God" are among the reasons for revisions to the forms of Prayer Book worship (BCP, p. 10). 2) Ceremonial gestures to express reverence. In some parishes, it is customary to reverence the altar or the consecrated elements of the eucharist with a genuflection or a solemn bow. A gesture of reverence may be made as one approaches or departs from the altar or at other times. A gesture of reverence may also be made by the celebrant at the conclusion of the eucharistic prayer. These gestures are not required by the BCP.

Reverend, The. An adjective used in formally addressing a member of the clergy. It is from the Latin *reverendus*, "worthy of reverence." It is intended to be descriptive. The term is incorrectly used as a noun title (like bishop or sister) to refer to a member of the clergy. For example, it is appropriate to say "the bishops are at the meeting," but it is *not* appropriate to say "the reverends are at the meeting." It is applied without further qualification to priests and deacons in the Episcopal Church and to clergy in other denominations. It is also used by abbesses, prioresses, and other nuns with the title "Mother." Hierarchical churches (such as the Episcopal Church and the Roman Catholic Church) further modify the term to indicate varying degrees of respect that are due. "The Very Reverend" indicates a dean of a deanery, a seminary, or a cathedral. "The Right Reverend" indicates a bishop, an abbot or abbess, or other prelate. "The Most Reverend" indicates an archbishop or primate.

Revised English Bible. A 1989 revision of the New English Bible (1970) that was intended to make it more suitable for public worship. "You" is used instead of "thou" in addressing God. The Revised English Bible also opted for inclusive language for people. The Roman Catholic Church joined the Protestant communions of the British Isles in sponsoring the effort.

Revised Standard Version Bible (RSV). The RSV is a revision of the American Standard Version (ASV) of the Holy Scriptures (1901), which was an American modification of the British revised version of 1881–1885. In 1937 the project of revising the ASV was authorized by the National Council of Religious Education. The RSV was completed in 1952 and published by the successor to the International Council, the National Council of Churches. The Apocrypha was subsequently added in 1957 at the request of the Episcopal Church, which was involved in the project from the beginning. A second edition of the NT was published in 1971, reflecting later textual and linguistic discoveries. The RSV is authorized by the Episcopal Church for use in worship.

Revised Standard Version of the Bible, an Ecumenical Edition, The ("RSV Common Bible"). A 1973 revision of the Revised Standard Version that was completed with the cooperation of members of the Protestant, Roman Catholic, and Eastern Orthodox churches. The inclusion of the Apocrypha or Deutero-canonical books with the thirty-nine books of the Protestant canon make it acceptable to Roman Catholics. The addition of 3 and 4 Maccabees and Ps 151 of the Septuagint give it the stamp of approval of the Eastern Orthodox communion. Thus it is ecumenical.

Revised Version of the Bible, The. In 1870 the Convocation of Canterbury appointed a commission to revise the King James Version of the Bible. The intention was not to make a new translation but to make necessary changes called for by Hebrew and Greek manuscripts not available at the time of the Authorized Versions, and also to clarify some of the ambiguities and archaic language of the seventeenth-century version. The style of the older version, however, was to be followed as closely as possible. The Revised

Version of the NT was published in 1881, the OT in 1885, and the Apocrypha in 1895. This was the first revision of the King James Version after two hundred and sixty years. It was subsequently followed in 1901 by a somewhat revised American version of the same translation, called the American Standard Version.

Revival. Christian worship characterized by intense and personal emotional experiences, fervent preaching, and extemporaneous prayer. It has served as a primary technique for evangelism in much of American Protestant Christianity. Several periods of revivalism swept through the American churches, beginning with the Great Awakening in the eighteenth century. Revival spread through the denominations under the leadership of Theodore Frelinghuysen, a Dutch Reformed pastor; William and Gilbert Tennent, Presbyterian pastors; and Jonathan Edwards, a Congregationalist. Church of England authorities viewed the Great Awakening with suspicion because of its Calvinist doctrine, religious enthusiasm, and emotionalism. John and Charles Wesley and George Whitefield, clergy of the Church of England, supported and participated in the revival during the Great Awakening. The majority of Church of England clergy in the colonial period did not support revivalism. The Church of England suffered significant numerical losses when the Methodists withdrew from the Church of England. Some nineteenth-century evangelical Episcopalians used and supported the revival method.

Rhode Island, Diocese of. Organized at Newport on Nov. 18, 1790, it voted to declare Bishop Samuel Seabury of Connecticut "Bishop of the Church in this State." From July 20, 1798, until Sept. 10, 1803, Rhode Island was under the jurisdiction of Bishop Edward Bass of Massachusetts. On May 29, 1810, Rhode Island participated in the organization of the Eastern Diocese. It was part of this diocese until the death of Bishop Alexander Griswold on Feb. 13, 1843. Since that time the diocese has had its own bishop. St. John's Church, Providence, was set apart as St. John's Cathedral on May 21, 1929. Geralyn Wolf was elected Bishop of Rhode Island on Sept. 30, 1995, the second female diocesan bishop in the Episcopal Church.

Richard, Bishop of Chichester (c. 1197–Apr. 2 or 3, 1253). Bishop and clerical reformer. He studied at Oxford, Paris, and Bologna. Richard became university chancellor at Oxford around 1235. He was later appointed chancellor by the Archbishop of Canterbury, Edmund of Abingdon. Richard also served as chancellor of Canterbury under Boniface of Savoy. Richard was ordained priest in 1243, after study at the Dominican house at Orléans. He was elected Bishop of Chichester in 1244, even though King Henry III favored another candidate. Pope Innocent IV consecrated Richard at Lyons in 1245. Henry III excluded Richard from the temporalities of the See of Chichester. During this time, Richard traveled through his diocese on foot. Henry eventually acknowledged Richard in 1246 under a papal threat of excommunication. Richard was known for his humility and ascetic life. He was concerned for the poor. He sought to reform clerical discipline and standards. Richard was a patron of the Dominicans, and he supported the crusades. He contracted an illness and died while campaigning for a new crusade. Richard's life is commemorated on Apr. 3 in the calendar of the church year. The collect for this observance in *Lesser Feasts and Fasts* reflects a well-known prayer attributed to Richard, asking that "we may see Christ more clearly, love him more dearly, and follow him more nearly." This prayer also provides the text for "Day by day," Hymn 654 in *The Hymnal 1982*.

Ridley, Nicholas (c. 1500–Oct. 16, 1555). Bishop and Protestant martyr. He was born in Willimoteswick, Northumberland. Ridley attended Pembroke Hall, Cambridge, where he later became a fellow. In 1527 he was ordained priest. He then studied at the Sorbonne in Paris and at Louvain. He returned to Cambridge and in 1540 was appointed the king's chaplain and master of Pembroke Hall. In 1541 he was made a canon of Canterbury and in 1545 a canon of Westminster. He was an outstanding preacher and very effective in preaching the themes of the Reformation. Ridley was consecrated Bishop of Rochester on Sept. 25, 1547, and on Apr. 1, 1550, he was made the Bishop of London. When Mary became Queen of England in 1553, his Protestant views were opposed and he was deposed in July 1553. Ridley, Thomas Cranmer, and Hugh Latimer were the foremost leaders of English Protestantism. Ridley and Latimer were burned at the stake in Oxford. Ridley said before he died, "So long as breath is in my body, I will never deny my Lord Christ and his known truth." The witness and martyrdom of Ridley, Cranmer, and Latimer are commemorated in the Episcopal calendar of the church year on Oct. 16.

Right of Sanctuary. *See* Sanctuary (2).

Righteousness. Living in right relationship with God and others. Unrighteous behavior would tend to undermine right relationship with God. For example, the disobedience of Adam and Eve in the Garden of Eden (Gn 3) was unrighteous because it distorted relationship with God. In the OT, righteousness was understood in terms of the demands of God's covenant with Israel. Righteous behavior upheld the covenant relationship. The NT acknowledges human incapacity to fulfill the demands of righteousness. Paul states that "all have sinned and fall short of the glory of God" (Rom 3:23). We share by nature in the tendency to turn away from God and the demands of righteousness (see Art. IX, Articles of Religion, BCP, p. 869). But human righteousness is made possible through faith in Christ and participation in Christ's life by the Holy Spirit (see Rom 1:17, 5:5, 9:30). Paul states that "as all die in Adam, so all will be made alive in Christ" (1 Cor 15:22). The "many will be made righteous" by Christ's obedience (Rom 5:19), which enables us to "walk in newness of life" (Rom 6:4). In Christ, we may live in righteousness with God and each other. Christ is the "Sun of Righteousness," as noted by Charles Wesley in "Christ, whose glory fills the skies" (Hymns 6–7 in *The Hymnal 1982*).

Righteousness is understood in terms of right relationship with God and others and not primarily in ethical or legal terms. But our right relationship with God and others is expressed through a moral and generous life. The righteous will feed the hungry, give drink to the thirsty, welcome the stranger, clothe the naked, care for the sick, and visit those in prison (see Mt 25:31–46). Protestant theology has tended to emphasize that God pronounces us righteous even while we remain sinners. According to this view, our righteousness is understood to be alien and extrinsic. Our justification takes place through God's righteousness, not our own merit. Catholic, Orthodox, and some Anglican theologians have urged that we may participate in a process of being made holy in Christ through the Holy Spirit. This view emphasizes the actual transformation of the one who accepts the grace of God in faith. *See* Original Sin; *see* Justification; *see* Simul justus et peccator.

Righter, Walter Cameron (b. Oct. 23, 1923). Bishop brought to trial for ordaining a homosexual. He was born in Philadelphia, Pennsylvania. Righter received his B.A. from the University of Pittsburgh in 1948 and his S.T.B. from the Berkeley Divinity School in 1951. He was ordained deacon on Apr. 7, 1951, and priest on Oct. 6, 1951. He began his ministry in Pennsylvania. From 1954 until 1972, he was the rector of the Church of the Good Shepherd, Nashua, New Hampshire. Righter was consecrated the seventh Bishop of Iowa on Jan. 12, 1972. He served in that position until his retirement on Dec. 31, 1988. From 1989 until 1991 he was Assistant Bishop in the Diocese of Newark. On Sept. 30, 1990, Righter ordained Barry Lee Stopfel, a non-celibate homosexual, to the diaconate. Ten bishops brought a presentment against Righter, charging that he violated the doctrine of the church and his ordination vows by ordaining Stopfel. The Court for the Trial of a Bishop met in Hartford, Connecticut, and Wilmington, Delaware. The court issued its verdict on May 15, 1996. It stated that the Episcopal Church "has no doctrine prohibiting the ordination of homosexuals," and that Bishop Righter did not contradict the "core doctrine" of the church. Righter reflected on the trial and his life in his book *A Pilgrim's Way* (1998).

Rightmyer, Nelson Waite (July 19, 1911–Sept. 29, 1983). Historian and seminary professor. He was born in Chester, Pennsylvania. Rightmyer received his M.A. from the University of Pennsylvania in 1935, his Th.B. from the Philadelphia Divinity School in 1935, his Ed.D. from Temple University in 1945, his Ed.M. from Loyola College (Baltimore) in 1961, and his Ph.D. from International University in 1977. He was ordained deacon on June 7, 1934, and priest on July 17, 1935. Rightmyer was curate at St. Luke and Epiphany Church, Philadelphia, 1934–1937, and rector of St. Peter's Church, Lewes, and All Saints' Church, Rehoboth, Delaware, 1937–1947. He was lecturer at the Philadelphia Divinity School, 1945–1947, and then professor of ecclesiastical history there from 1947 until 1952. After several parochial responsibilities, Rightmyer was professor of church history at the Ecumenical Institute of St. Mary's Seminary, Baltimore, from 1968 until his retirement in 1973. While at St. Mary's, Rightmyer was rector of St. George's Church, Baltimore. He was a long time member of the Board of Managers of the Historical Society of the Episcopal Church, and historiographer of the Diocese of Maryland, 1952–1973. He wrote *The Anglican Church in Delaware* (1947), and *Maryland's Established Church* (1957). He contributed numerous articles to the *Historical Magazine of the Protestant Episcopal Church*. Rightmyer died in Shelby, North Carolina.

Right Reverend, The. *See* Reverend, The.

Rikkyo University. *See* St. Paul's University, Tokyo.

Rings. Christians have apparently worn finger-rings with Christian symbols since the third or fourth centuries. Rings have been associated with fidelity. There are several specific Christian uses of rings.

Wedding Rings. It was a Roman custom for the man to give the woman a ring at the time of betrothal. The use of wedding rings by Christians is derived from this custom. Wedding rings may be exchanged by the husband and wife at the Celebration and Blessing of a Marriage (BCP, p. 427). These rings are signs of the vows by which the husband and wife bind themselves to each other. The rings are blessed by the priest at the marriage before they are exchanged by the man and woman. A ring may be given by the husband, the wife, or both. The giver of the ring places the ring on the ring-finger of the other's hand, addresses the other by name, and says, "I give you this ring as a symbol of my vow, and with all that I am, and all that I have, I honor you, in the Name of the Father, and of the Son, and of the Holy Spirit" (BCP, p. 427). The BCP allows an alternative ending, "in the Name of God," for the trinitarian conclusion to the statement that is made when the ring is given. Another suitable symbol of the vows may be used instead of rings (BCP, p. 437). The BCP service for the Blessing of a Civil Marriage also includes a blessing of rings (p. 434).

Episcopal Rings. In the late middle ages, the rite for the ordination of bishops came to include the delivery of instruments of office. An episcopal ring was given to the newly ordained bishop, along with staff and miter. The episcopal ring was a signet ring. It may have been used as an official seal. Some episcopal rings contained relics. The use of episcopal rings has been dated to the seventh century. At the ordination of a bishop in the Episcopal Church, a ring, staff, and miter, or other suitable insignia of office may be presented to the newly-ordained bishop. This follows the presentation of the Bible and the formula of presentation (BCP, p. 553). Modern episcopal rings are often made of gold and ornamented with an amethyst. The episcopal ring is usually worn on the ring-finger of the bishop's right hand. Similar rings are worn by abbots and some abbesses.

Rings are also worn by professed members of religious orders. Some Christians wear rings with Christian symbols as an expression of devotion. Rosary rings have ten small knobs which are used in saying the rosary.

Rio Grande, Diocese of. The 1892 General Convention established the Missionary District of New Mexico. The 1895 General Convention voted to take the counties of El Paso, Reeves, Culberson, Jeff Davis, Presidio, Brewster, Terrell, Hudspeth, and Pecos from the Missionary District of Western Texas and add them to the Missionary District of New Mexico. On Feb. 6, 1923, the name was changed to the Missionary District of New Mexico and Southwest Texas. In 1927 St. John's Church, Albuquerque, was made St. John's Cathedral. A new building was constructed and dedicated on Nov. 11, 1952, and consecrated on Apr. 23, 1963. The primary convention of the diocese was held at St. Andrew's Church, Roswell, New Mexico, Feb. 10–12, 1953. On Apr. 28, 1973, the name was changed to the Diocese of the Rio Grande. On Nov. 26, 1978, St. Clement's Church, El Paso, became the Pro-Cathedral Church of St. Clement. The diocese has a cathedral and a pro-cathedral.

Ritchie, Arthur (June 22, 1849–July 9, 1921). Anglo-catholic leader. He was born in Philadelphia, and received his B.A. from the University of Pennsylvania in 1867. After teaching at the Episcopal Academy, Philadelphia, 1867–1868, he entered the General Theological Seminary. He received his S.T.B. in 1871. He was ordained deacon on July 2, 1871, and priest on June 22, 1873. He served brief ministries at the Church of the Advent, Boston, St. Clement's, Philadelphia, and Mount Calvary, Baltimore. He was rector of the Church of the Ascension, Chicago, from 1875 to 1884. From 1884 until 1914 Ritchie was the rector of St. Ignatius' Church, New York, where he introduced incense, holy water, confessionals, non-communicating high mass—the so-called "Shortened Mass"—and Benediction of the Blessed Sacrament, possibly for the first time in the Episcopal Church. From Dec. 1, 1888 to Nov. 1, 1904, he edited *The Catholic Champion*, and he was a founder of The Clerical Union for the Maintenance and Defense of Catholic Principles. He died in Nyack, New York.

Rite. A form for religious ceremony. It includes both what is said and what is done in the religious observance. Rite expresses the church's relationship with God through words, actions, and symbols. It orders the church's common worship. Rite enables the community to share its faith and experience God's presence in a particular liturgical and pastoral context. Divine transcendence is to be known through participation in the specific and finite realities of rite.

Rites are prescribed for various sacraments, offices, and occasions in liturgical churches such as the Episcopal Church. The rites of the Episcopal Church are found in the BCP. Authorized services and texts for optional use are found in the *BOS*. Other rites may be approved for trial use prior to full approval for use in the worship of the church. The term may also designate a particular collection of liturgies. In the 1979 BCP, Rite 1 liturgies are traditional language services and Rite 2 liturgies are contemporary language services.

"Rite" may also identify a church or denomination that uses a particular rite or rites, such as "Byzantine Rite." The term "rite" may also indicate the form for any solemn ceremony or practice.

Rite 1, Rite 2. The 1979 BCP provides the services of Morning and Evening Prayer, the Holy Eucharist, and the Burial Office in both traditional language and contemporary language rites. The traditional language rites are known as Rite 1, and the contemporary language rites are known as Rite 2. The BCP also presents the collects for the church year in both traditional and contemporary language. The Rite 1 liturgies reflect the language and piety of the Elizabethan era and the first BCP, although the structure of these liturgies also reflects the influence of modern liturgical scholarship. The Rite 2 liturgies reflect more fully the influence of the liturgical movement and contemporary theology. Rite 2 liturgies tend to reflect greater sensitivity for inclusive language issues. The proper liturgies for special days (such as Ash Wednesday and Palm Sunday), pastoral offices (such as the Celebration and Blessing of a Marriage), and episcopal services (such as ordinations) are printed in contemporary language in the BCP. When these services are celebrated in the context of a Rite 1 Eucharist, the contemporary idiom may be conformed to traditional language (BCP, p. 14). *The Hymnal 1982* and *The Hymnal 1982 Accompaniment Edition, Vol. 1*, provide service music settings that are designated for Rite 1 and Rite 2 services of Morning and Evening Prayer and the Eucharist.

Although the structure of Rite 1 and Rite 2 liturgies are essentially the same, the options and requirements of the rites differ in certain respects. For example, the Rite 1 Eucharist requires the collect for purity in the entrance rite (BCP, p. 323), but the collect for purity may be omitted in Rite 2 (BCP, p. 355). The summary of the Law is optional in the Rite 1 Eucharist, but it is not included as an option in the Rite 2 Eucharist. The prayer for the whole state of Christ's Church and the world (BCP, pp. 328–330) is presented as an option in the Rite 1 Eucharist, but this prayer is not included in the Rite 2 service. The BCP also provides six forms for the prayers of the people which may be done in traditional or contemporary language. The Rite 1 Eucharist includes two biddings to confession, the first of which dates to 1548. This bidding begins, "Ye who do truly and earnestly repent you of your sins" (BCP, p. 330). It is not found in the Rite 2 Eucharist. The Rite 1 Eucharist allows one or more of four sentences of scripture to be said after the confession and absolution. These sentences, previously known as the "comfortable words," do not appear in the Rite 2 Eucharist. The *Agnus Dei* and the prayer of humble access may be said after the breaking of the bread in the Rite 1 Eucharist (BCP, p. 337). These prayers are not presented as options in the Rite 2 Eucharist, although a suitable anthem may be used after the breaking of the bread. A blessing by the bishop or priest is required after the postcommunion prayer in the Rite 1 Eucharist, but this blessing is optional in the Rite 2 Eucharist (BCP, pp. 339, 366).

"Rite 3." The nickname given to "An Order for Celebrating the Holy Eucharist" (BCP, pp. 400–405). This rite is in the form of an outline that allows the participants to prepare many of the liturgical texts that will be used in the eucharistic celebration while maintaining the same basic structure of the eucharistic liturgy that is found in other rites. The other eucharistic liturgies are designated "Rite 1" (traditional) or "Rite 2" (contemporary). "Rite 3" liturgies are "not intended for use at the principal Sunday or weekly celebration of the Holy Eucharist" (BCP, p. 400). The outline format of the rite allows flexibility that may be very appropriate for special occasions such as small weekday celebrations of the eucharist, and liturgies with a particular thematic emphasis or concern. The BCP provides two forms for the Great Thanksgiving in the Order for Eucharist. The BCP also allows flexibility in the services for marriage and burial. Outlines for these services are provided by "An Order for Marriage" (p. 435) and "An Order for Burial" (p. 506).

Ritual. Liturgical texts and ceremonies of divine worship. The term originally indicated the prescribed words of worship, but it came to include the entire liturgical action and presentation of the rite. The nineteenth-century ritualist controversy in the Episcopal Church included disputes over such practices as the use of processional crosses, altar lights, eucharistic vestments, incense, genuflection before the Blessed Sacrament, and elevation of the consecrated elements at the eucharist. In *The Law of Ritualism* (1866), Presiding Bishop John Henry Hopkins urged that a wide variety of ritual usage is permissible in the church. James DeKoven also appealed for comprehensiveness and tolerance in worship. He defended the ritualist cause at the 1871 and 1874 General Conventions. He urged that such practices as altar lights, genuflections, and the use of incense do not symbolize the doctrine of transubstantiation. Although DeKoven's position was not upheld in the canonical battle at the 1874 General Convention, his vision of a comprehensive approach to ritual prevailed in the Episcopal Church. *See* Hopkins, John Henry; *see* DeKoven, James; *see* Ritualism.

Ritual Controversy. *See* Ritualism.

Ritualism. Ritual refers to the prescribed form of words of an act of worship and also has been used to indicate the ceremonial of worship. The term "ritualism" was applied to the ceremonial enrichment of public worship by re-introducing pre-Reformation ceremonial practices into Anglicanism. These included practices at the eucharist such as the use of vestments, a processional cross, altar lights, incense, the mixed chalice, and liturgical actions such as genuflection and the elevation of the host for adoration. Those who supported the advance of ritualism were known as "ritualists."

The early stages of the Oxford Movement emphasized the recovery of catholic beliefs and ideas rather than ceremonial. But the renewed emphasis on catholic theology led to an expanding use of catholic practices and forms in the mid-nineteenth century. The advance of ritualism became intensely controversial in the Episcopal Church. Some opponents of ritualism believed the changes were introducing Roman Catholic practices and beliefs into a Protestant Church. Evangelicals were often strong and vocal opponents of ritualism. For many years, Bishop Manton Eastburn of Massachusetts refused to visit the Church of the Advent, Boston, because of the parish's ritual practices. This dispute eventually led to a canon passed by the 1856 General Convention requiring a bishop to visit every parish in the bishop's jurisdiction at least once every three years. The controversy over ritualism led John Henry Hopkins, Presiding Bishop of the Episcopal Church, to publish *The Law of Ritualism* (1866). Hopkins urged that a wide variety of ritual uses were canonically permitted in the Episcopal Church. He

predicted that many of the controverted practices would eventually be accepted.

Proposed canons on ritual were considered at the General Conventions of 1868 and 1871, but no canons on ritual were enacted. However, resolutions condemning ceremonies expressing doctrines foreign to the church were adopted at the 1871 General Convention, and the pastoral letter of the House of Bishops condemned the new ritualism. Ritualism was one of the issues that led some radical evangelicals into schism from the Episcopal Church in 1873. George David Cummins, Assistant Bishop of Kentucky, and others organized the Reformed Episcopal Church. The General Convention of 1874 did pass a canon on ritual. Many hoped this would satisfy the evangelicals, and prevent further departures from the Episcopal Church. This canon called for a bishop to investigate any use of ceremonies or practices in the bishop's jurisdiction symbolizing "false or doubtful doctrine." The bishop was empowered first to admonish and then bring to trial any member of the clergy who persisted in these practices. However, this canon did virtually nothing to slow the expansion of ritual practices in the Episcopal Church. Only one trial for ritualism took place. In 1877 Oliver Prescott received episcopal admonishment for his ritual practices. The canon on ritual was quietly repealed at the 1904 General Convention.

James DeKoven was a distinguished defender of ritual practices and a strong advocate for ritualism at the 1871 and 1874 General Conventions. At the 1871 General Convention, he argued that ritual practices do not symbolize the doctrine of transubstantiation. He noted that such practices preceded the doctrine of transubstantiation. These practices were shared by Orthodox and Lutheran churches that denied transubstantiation. At the 1874 General Convention, DeKoven urged the church to adopt a comprehensive approach to worship. The canon on ritual was passed despite DeKoven's plea for comprehensiveness. His defense of ritualism led his opponents to question his theology of the eucharist and block his election as Bishop of Illinois. However, DeKoven's vision of comprehensiveness in worship ultimately prevailed in the Episcopal Church. His life and ministry are commemorated on Mar. 22 in the Episcopal calendar of the church year. Many of the ritualist practices and actions that were controversial in the nineteenth century are now generally accepted. *See* DeKoven, James; *see* Oxford Movement; *see* Transubstantiation.

Roanridge Training Conference Center. Wilbur Cochel, a deputy from West Missouri to the 1940 General Convention, believed that a good rural priest needed to know about farming. In 1942 he and his wife offered their 320-acre demonstration farm, twenty miles north of Kansas City, to the Episcopal Church. It was called Roanridge Farm because of the mixed red and white cattle known as Shorthorns. Later the Roanridge Rural Training Foundation was established. Roanridge was for years the location of the Town and Country Institute. In 1969 the site was named the Roanridge Conference Center. The Rev. Dr. H. Boone Porter became the director in 1970. Later Roanridge was the Leadership Academy for New Directions (LAND). Roanridge closed on Feb. 28, 1977. The property was sold and the endowment used to support the continuation of LAND, also known as New Directions Ministries, as well as St. Luke's Hospital and Grace Cathedral, both in Kansas City. Roanridge's major contribution was the training of people for town and country ministries.

Robbins, Harold Chandler (Dec. 11, 1876–Mar. 20, 1952). Cathedral dean, preacher, and writer. He was born in Philadelphia. Robbins received his B.A. from Yale University in 1899 and graduated from the Episcopal Theological School in 1903. He was ordained deacon on May 17, 1903, and priest on May 29, 1904. Robbins was rector of St. Paul's Church, Englewood, New Jersey, 1904–1911. He was rector of the Church of the Incarnation, New York, from 1911 until 1917. He was the second dean of the Cathedral of St. John the Divine, 1917–1929. While dean, he made the Cathedral a center for Christian unity and civic activities. From 1929 until 1941 he was Eugene Augustus Hoffman Professor of Pastoral Theology at the General Theological Seminary. Robbins was a delegate to the World Conference on Faith and Order at Edinburgh, Scotland, in 1937. He was a member of the administrative committee of the Federal Council of the Churches of Christ in America. He was also a member of the American Bible Society and the Church Peace Union. Robbins wrote numerous books, most notably *Cathedral Sermons* (1927), *Charles Lewis Slattery* (1931), and *Preaching the Gospel* (1939). Robbins died in Washington, D.C.

Roberts, Owen Josephus (May 2, 1875–May 17, 1955). First lay president of the House of Deputies, and associate justice of the United States Supreme Court. He was born in Philadelphia. Roberts received his B.A. in 1895 and his LL.B. in 1898, both from the University of Pennsylvania.

He was admitted to the Pennsylvania bar in 1898. He was successively instructor, assistant professor, and professor of law at the University of Pennsylvania, 1898–1918. From 1918 until 1930, Roberts practiced law and served on a number of government boards and agencies. From 1930 until his retirement in 1945, he was an Associate Justice of the United States Supreme Court. On Sept. 10, 1946, Roberts was elected the first lay president of the House of Deputies. He served until the 1949 General Convention. Roberts died in Philadelphia.

Robertson, John J. (1796–Oct. 5, 1881). Missionary to Greece. He was born in New York City. After study at the Virginia Theological Seminary, Robertson was ordained deacon on Dec. 10, 1820. He was ordained priest the next year, and then became president of Middlebury College in Middlebury, Vermont. Robertson later became the president of Oglethorpe University in Atlanta, Georgia. On Dec. 31, 1828, he sailed for Greece on his own initiative. He had convinced the Domestic and Foreign Missionary Society to appoint him as an agent to inquire into the state of religion in Greece and to see if the people there might be interested in receiving Episcopal missionaries. He returned to the United States in Dec. 1829 and persuaded the Board of the Domestic and Foreign Missionary Society to send a mission to Greece. This mission was not to convert the Greeks but to provide opportunities for education which subjection under the Turks and poverty had prevented. The society appointed Robertson and his wife; the Rev. John H. Hill and his wife, Frances Maria; and Solomon Bingham, a printer, as missionaries to Greece. Robertson served as missionary to Greece until 1842, when he returned to the United States and became rector of St. Luke's Church, Matteawan, New York. In 1858 he became the rector of Trinity Church, Saugerties, New York, where he remained until his retirement in 1879. Robertson died in Saugerties. *See* Hill, Frances Maria Mulligan.

Rochester, Diocese of. The 1931 General Convention voted to divide the Diocese of Western New York. The primary convention of the Diocese of Rochester met at Trinity Church, Geneva, New York, Dec. 15–16, 1931. The diocese includes the following counties: Allegany, Livingston, Monroe, Ontario, Schuyler, Steuben, Wayne, and Yates. The diocese does not have a cathedral.

Rochet. A vestment of white linen or similar material which replaced the alb and which in time came to be used only by bishops. Early American bishops found the huge balloon sleeves difficult both to launder and to carry, so the rochet was sleeveless, and the sleeves were tacked lightly to the chimere. Styles have changed in recent years, and many rochets now resemble albs.

Rodenmayer, Alice Elizabeth "Betsy" Midworth (June 11, 1909–Jan. 14, 1985). Christian educator. She was born in Detroit, Michigan. Rodenmayer received her B.A. from the University of Michigan, her M.R.E. from Columbia Teachers College, and her B.D. from Union Theological Seminary, New York. She married the Rev. Robert Rodenmayer on July 8, 1935. She was director of Christian Education, Christ Church, Glendale, Ohio, 1933–1935; and professor of Christian Education at St. Margaret's House, Berkeley, California, 1953–1962. Her last two positions were with the national church. She served as associate director of the Division of Christian Ministries of the Executive Council, 1962–1967, and director of the Department of Professional Leadership Development of the Executive Council, 1968–1973. She was a founding member and a board member of the Episcopal Women's History Project, 1980–1985. Rodenmayer died in New York City.

Rogation Days. Traditionally, these are the three days before Ascension Day on which the litany is sung (or recited) in procession as an act of intercession. They originated in Vienne, France, in the fifth century when Bishop Mamertus introduced days of fasting and prayer to ward off a threatened disaster. In England they were associated with the blessing of the fields at planting. The vicar "beat the bounds" of the parish, processing around the fields reciting psalms and the litany. In the United States they have been associated with rural life and with agriculture and fishing. The propers in the BCP (pp. 207–208, 258–259, 930) have widened their scope to include commerce and industry and the stewardship of creation. The BCP also permits their celebration at other times to accommodate different regional growing seasons. The *BOS* contains material for a Rogation procession, including petitions to be added to the Great Litany and the prayers of the people. The term is from the Latin *rogatio*, "asking."

Rollo. At Cursillo, one of the fifteen talks on Christian faith and life. The person assigned to give the *rollo* is called a "*rollista.*"

Romanticism. The term is applied to an intellectual and cultural development which flourished in western Europe and North America in the late-eighteenth and nineteenth centuries. It was largely a reaction against the Enlightenment and the neo-classicism which accompanied the Enlightenment. In place of the earlier emphasis on reason, order, and mechanism there came to be an emphasis on feeling, mystery, the transcendent, vitality, the individual, and the brooding power of nature. Romantic religion upheld the continuity of tradition and community.

The movement takes its name from a new appreciation of medieval romances, a literary genre involving tales of chivalric adventure. This turn to the culture of the middle ages can be seen in the beginnings of the liturgical movement. A revival of plainsong took place under Prosper Guéranger at the monastery of Solesmes. Romanticism influenced the theologians of the Oxford Movement and the Cambridge ecclesiologists. Its influence was also felt in the Episcopal Church. It lay behind the Ritual Controversy and the eventual recovery of certain aspects of catholic worship in the BCP.

James DeKoven, a priest and warden of Racine College, has been identified as a representative of romantic religion in the Episcopal Church. DeKoven's religion was a faith of the heart which was not limited to rationality. His romantic religion led him to seek fullness of beauty and mystery in worship. He was dedicated to liturgy, sacraments, and ceremonial. DeKoven was a forceful advocate for comprehensiveness and tolerance in worship at the 1871 and 1874 General Conventions. DeKoven urged a personal conversion of heart and devotion to God that pointed beyond the reasonable and enlightened self-interest that he found in the world around him. *See* DeKoven, James.

Rood Screen. The term "rood," from Old English, means cross. Rood screens were used as early as the twelfth century to separate the chancel or choir from the nave. The rood screen was surmounted with a rood beam on which was placed a crucifix or Christus Rex. Candles and other figures such as the Virgin Mary and St. John might also be placed on the rood screen. The rood screen was at times used to separate the monastic chapter in the chancel from the laity in the nave. Such divisions of the congregation have not been encouraged in modern liturgical practice, and rood screens are seldom used today.

Roosevelt, Franklin Delano (Jan. 30, 1882–Apr. 12, 1945). Thirty-second President of the United States, 1933–1945. He was the leader of the United States in the face of the Great Depression and World War II. Roosevelt was baptized at St. James' Episcopal Church, Hyde Park, New York, and later served as senior warden of St. James'. He graduated from Groton School and Harvard. He attended Columbia University School of Law, but discontinued his schooling after he was admitted to the New York bar. He was elected to the New York State Senate in 1910 and appointed Assistant Secretary of the Navy in 1913. Roosevelt was stricken with poliomyelitis in 1921, but his illness did not prevent his career of public service. He was elected governor of New York in 1928, and reelected in 1930. Roosevelt sought to give tax relief for farmers. He sought to use the resources of the state government to help the economy. He established state relief agencies and sought to provide cheaper public utilities for consumers. He was elected president in 1932 and inaugurated in 1933. In his first inauguration address as president he urged that "the only thing we have to fear is fear itself." He sought to counter the ravages of the Depression with a sweeping economic program known as the New Deal. The programs of the New Deal sought to restore farm prosperity and restore business enterprise, along with providing relief, loans, and jobs through a variety of federal agencies. Federal agencies established during this time included the Securities and Exchange Commission, the Tennessee Valley Authority, the National Recovery Administration, and the Agricultural Adjustment Administration. Roosevelt was also the first president to appoint a woman, Frances Perkins, as a member of the Cabinet. Before the United States entered World War II, Roosevelt provided assistance to Great Britain and its allies through the Lend-Lease Act. He also denied war supplies to Japan. As President of the United States during World War II, Roosevelt played a leading role in creating the alliance with Great Britain and the Soviet Union. He was reelected president in 1936, 1940, and 1944. He died in Warm Springs, Georgia.

Rosary. A Marian devotion that leads to Jesus. It combines repetitions of familiar prayers with meditation on fifteen mysteries of faith. Meditation on each mystery is accompanied by recitation of the Lord's Prayer, ten (a "decade") Hail Marys, and the *Gloria Patri*. The mysteries are divided into three sets of five, which are known as chaplets. Each chaplet or third of the rosary may be done separately. The terms "rosary" and "chaplet" may also be applied to the string of beads that is often used to aid the memory and count the prayers of this devotion. The three chaplets are the joyful mysteries which focus on the Incarnation, the sorrowful mysteries which focus on Christ's sufferings, and the glorious mysteries which focus on Christ's glorification. The five joyful mysteries are the Annunciation, the Visitation, Christ's Nativity, the Presentation of Christ in the Temple, and the finding of the child Jesus in the Temple. The five sorrowful mysteries are Christ's agony in the garden at Gethsemane, Christ's scourging, the crowning with thorns, the carrying of the cross, and the crucifixion. The five glorious mysteries are Christ's Resurrection, the Ascension, the coming of the Holy Spirit at Pentecost, the assumption of the Blessed Virgin Mary, and the coronation of the Blessed Virgin Mary.

Pious belief that the rosary was founded by St. Dominic (1170–1221) dates from the fifteenth century. This belief has not been proven by historical evidence. The rosary developed from christological and marian devotions from the twelfth to sixteenth centuries when its current form became standardized. Dominicans have encouraged the popularization of the rosary, and it is also known as the Dominican rosary. Use of this devotion is much more widespread and traditional in the Roman Catholic Church than in the Episcopal Church.

Rose Gates College, Okolona, Mississippi. This school opened at Okolona, Mississippi, in 1859. Bishop William Mercer Green was president of the board of trustees. It was named after Rose Gates, the daughter of Col. Charles Gates, who bought the property. The headmaster was the Rev. William S. Lacey (d. 1867), who served until the school closed in 1862.

Rose, Lawrence (Nov. 2, 1905–Oct. 17, 1987). Priest and educator. He was born in Monterey, Mexico, and received his B.A. from Harvard in 1923 and his S.T.B. from the General Theological Seminary in 1928. He was ordained deacon on June 2, 1926, and priest on May 24, 1927. After ministries in Brooklyn, New York, and Phillipsburg, Montana, he became professor of Christian apologetics and religious education at Central Theological College, Tokyo, Japan, 1934–1941. He was dean of the Berkeley Divinity School, New Haven, Connecticut, 1942–1947, and dean of General Seminary, 1947–1966. He retired in 1966. Rose died at his home in Kent, Connecticut.

"Rose Sunday." *See* Laetare Sunday; *see* Gaudete Sunday.

Rose Window. A circular stained glass window with radiating tracery in the form of a rose. The rose window is usually placed on the west façade of the church. This window may be quite large, dominating the west end of the nave. A rose window may also appear in the triangular ends of transepts. Undecorated circular windows were a feature of Roman architecture. Rose or wheel windows came to be seen in Romanesque and gothic churches. Wheel windows were formed by straight bars which intersected like the spokes of a wheel to form geometric patterns. The design of these bars eventually became more delicate, with the tracery resembling an open rose. Rose windows may reflect the influence of the decorated circular forms of Muslim architecture that were seen by crusaders. Rose windows are characteristic of gothic cathedrals. A beautiful rose window may be seen at the Cathedral Church of Saint Peter and Saint Paul in Washington, D.C.

Rota. A rotating service schedule that identifies who will serve in a particular ministry (such as acolytes or lectors) at scheduled services throughout a given period.

Round (Musical). *See* Canon (5).

Routley, Erik (1917–1982). A British Reformed Church minister, composer, hymn writer, hymnal editor, and teacher. He was born in Brighton, Sussex, England, and educated at Lancing College and Mansfield College, Oxford. He was one of the most influential hymnodists of his time. He served as minister of Congregational and reformed churches in England and Scotland. At various times from 1948 to 1959, he served as tutor in church history, Mackennal Lecturer in Church History, chaplain, librarian and director of music at Mansfield College. His involvement in the Dunblane Consultations (1961–1969) was very influential in starting the movement that changed the face of contemporary English hymnody. Routley moved to the United States in 1975 to be visiting lecturer and director of music at Princeton Theological Seminary, Princeton, New Jersey. In 1976 he became professor of church music at Westminster Choir College, Princeton. Throughout his adult life he was involved as a committee member or as an editor of several important hymnals in both England and the United States. Routley was also a prolific author of church music and theology. He served

as a reader consultant of texts being proposed for inclusion in *The Hymnal 1982*. Routley died in Nashville in 1982. He is the author of two hymn texts in *The Hymnal 1982*, "New songs of celebration render" (413) and "All who love and serve your city" (570–571). He is also the composer of four hymn tunes, including *Augustine*, used with "Let all the world in every corner sing" (402) and *Sharpthorne*, used with "What does the Lord require" (605).

Rowson, Susanna Haswell (c. 1762–Mar. 2, 1824). Novelist and educator. She was born in Portsmouth, England. When she was seven her family settled in Nantasket, Massachusetts. Her first novel, published in 1786, was *Victoria*. It received good reviews. In 1791 she published *Charlotte, a Tale of Truth*, which was also known as *Charlotte Temple*. It was the leading "best seller" in America before *Uncle Tom's Cabin* (1852), and it made her famous. From 1792 until 1797 she worked as an actress. In 1797 she opened a school for girls in Newton, Massachusetts. Rowson later opened a school for girls in Boston, where she worked until her retirement in 1822. During this period she continued to write. She was a contributor to *The Boston Magazine* and *The Monthly Anthology and Boston Review*. Rowson was editor of the *Boston Weekly Magazine*, 1802–1805. She also wrote textbooks to be used in girls' schools. She served for a while as president of the Boston Fatherless and Widows Society. Rowson was a communicant of Trinity Church, Boston. She died in Boston.

Ruach. *See* Episcopal Women's Caucus.

Rubric. A ceremonial or other direction given in the BCP, now typically printed in italics. Rubrics were printed in red in medieval service books. The term "rubric" is derived from the Latin word for "red." *See* Black Rubric, The.

Rule of Faith. A term designating a summary of orthodox faith (*regula fidei*) in the first Christian centuries. It was a confession of faith in the three divine Persons that included a confession of faith in the Incarnation of the Word. It eventually designated three traditional creeds: the Apostles' Creed, which grew out of the confessions of faith that took place during baptism; the Nicene Creed, formulated by the Council of Nicaea (325) and completed by the first Council of Constantinople (381); and the *Quicunque Vult*, or Athanasian Creed, a western document of the fifth century directed against the Arian heresy (BCP, pp. 864–865). Article VIII of the Thirty-Nine Articles of 1571 affirmed that the three creeds "ought thoroughly to be received and believed: for they may be proved by most certain warrants of Holy Scripture." Later forms of the Articles of Religion omit the Athanasian Creed, including the form adopted by the Episcopal Church in 1801 (BCP, pp. 867–876).

Rule of Life. 1) A set of guidelines and commitments directing one's life. The rule usually includes set times of daily prayer and meditation, study (such as reading the Bible), and acts of charity. It can also include regular attendance at the Holy Eucharist, making retreats, placing oneself under a spiritual director or confessor, and fasting or other acts of self denial. A rule may be worked out with a spiritual director, or one may follow a shortened or modified version of the rule of a particular religious order. Some people commit to a rule that is basically a resolve to live with a certain disposition of prayer, study, and charity. Participation in the Daily Office is at the heart of Anglican spirituality, and included in many rules of life. 2) The document in which a religious community has formulated its fundamental understanding of religious life. The early model was the Rule of St. Augustine, in which spiritual principles are accompanied by simple regulations. It inspired the more elaborate Rule of St. Benedict and other monastic rules. *See* Daily Office; *see* Monastic.

Rural and Small Community Ministries Office. This office does its work in conjunction with the Standing Commission on the Church in Small Communities. Its major objectives are to identify, prepare, and support the ministry of the baptized in small congregations; to advocate policies which suggest and encourage clergy to do ministry in small communities; to engage dioceses and seminaries in development of leadership programs for the baptized in churches in small communities; and to address issues of economic and environmental issues which affect rural and small-town America. It publishes *Jottings*.

Rural Messenger, The. *See* Rural Workers' Fellowship.

Rural Workers' Fellowship. An organization whose purpose is to promote the interest of the whole ministry of the church in rural communities, increase the fellowship among those interested in such services, and to aid the national church in its service to the rural field and workers.

By 1921 the Department of Christian Social Service of the National Council was involved in rural work and ministry. In 1924 the first secretary of the Division of Rural Work was employed. The informal contact with the University of Wisconsin's Rural Pastors' Conference, established in 1922, developed into an official National Episcopal Conference of Rural Workers. On July 9, 1924, when the National Episcopal Conference was held at Madison, Wisconsin, the Rural Workers' Fellowship was established. The fellowship holds an annual conference on rural ministry. In Sept. 1925 the fellowship began publishing a monthly journal called *The Rural Messenger.* In 1949 the title was changed to *Crossroads: A Magazine of Town and Country Life.* It describes itself as "The Journal of the Rural Workers' Fellowship of the Episcopal Church."

Rusch, Paul. *See* KEEP (Kiyosato Educational Experiment Project), American Committee for.

Russo-Greek Committee. A committee established by the 1862 General Convention to consider the expediency of opening communications with the Russo-Greek Church. The immediate question of some sort of closer relations with the Russian Orthodox was raised at this General Convention by the Rev. Dr. Stephen Thrall, a deputy from California and rector of Holy Trinity Church in San Francisco. The question was raised in light of the influx of members of both churches to that city in the wake of the California gold rush. Early leaders of the Russo-Greek Committee included John Freeman Young and Milo Mahan. Young was secretary of the committee, assistant minister of Trinity Church, Wall Street, and later Bishop of Florida. Mahan was St. Mark's Professor of Ecclesiastical History at the General Theological Seminary from 1851–1864. The founding of this committee preceded by a year and directly influenced the establishment of a similar committee for closer relations with the Orthodox churches by the Convocation of the Province of Canterbury in the Church of England. On Mar. 2, 1865, Trinity Chapel of Trinity Parish was the location for what has been called the first public celebration of the Orthodox liturgy in New York. This was done at Young's instigation and with the full approval of Bishop Horatio Potter. The Committee sponsored several visits of its members to the Orthodox Church of Russia. It published at least three series of papers related to its work. The 1874 General Convention recommended that its work would better be done by the bishops of the church as occasion might arise, rather than by a committee. The work of this committee is generally regarded as heralding a new, official, and more intense era of Anglican-Orthodox relations, led by the Episcopal Church.

S

Sabbatarian. A person who observes Saturday as the Sabbath, as in Judaism, some Puritan groups, and some sect groups in Christianity such as Seventh Day Adventists. It also means a person who believes in a strict observance of the Sabbath, whether observed on Saturday or Sunday, including the OT prohibitions against work on the Sabbath. *See* Sabbath.

Sabbath. The seventh day of the Jewish week, our Saturday. It was marked by a total prohibition of work (Ex 23:12). In Christian liturgical usage, Holy Saturday is called the Great or Holy Sabbath, the day when Christ rested in the tomb. Early Christians rejected the celebration of the Jewish Sabbath and the restrictions on activity associated with it in the OT. It was considered as part of the ceremonial law which was abolished in Christ. Instead they kept the Lord's Day, the first day of the week, the day of the Resurrection, as their day of worship. Seventh Day Adventists and a few other Christian groups continue to worship on the sabbath. Sabbatarians are those Christians, usually Scottish or English Calvinists, who apply the OT prohibitions against work to Sunday, deeming it the Christian sabbath. This was a point of conflict between Anglicans and Puritans in the seventeenth century. The "blue laws" in many localities forbidding various activities on Sunday are inherited from Puritan sabbath-keeping. Some Christian groups also forbid various forms of recreation on Sunday in order to keep the sabbath.

Sabbatical. This term comes from the word "sabbath," and means seven or seventh. It means a period of rest and an intermission in labor. A sabbatical year is the seventh year. It is a time when persons are relieved from their duties for study and travel. It is now used for a period of leave that is not necessarily every seven years. Sometimes it is called a "sabbatical leave."

Sabellianism. Trinitarian theology of Sabellius, a teacher in Rome before his condemnation by Pope Callistus (217–222). Sabellius believed that the Creator (Father) is not personally distinguished from the Redeemer (Son) or the Sanctifier (Spirit), but rather exists and acts according to three modes of being and action. Already repudiated by the Church Fathers, this theology was also rejected explicitly in the Lutheran *Formula of Concord* and in Calvin's *Institutio Christiana*, and implicitly in Article I of the Thirty-Nine Articles (see BCP, p. 867). *See* Modalism.

Sacerdotal, Sacerdotalism. From the Latin *sacerdos*, "priest." It means of or pertaining to the order of priests or the role, identity, or function of priests. A ministry reserved to the ordained priesthood is a sacerdotal ministry. Sacerdotal ministries include celebrating the eucharist and granting absolution in the Reconciliation of a Penitent.

Sacramental Rites. The sacramental rites of the Episcopal Church include Confirmation, Ordination, Holy Matrimony, Reconciliation of a Penitent, and Unction (BCP, pp. 860–861). These rites are distinguished from the sacraments of Baptism and Eucharist, which were given by Christ and are understood to be necessary for the Christian life of all persons. The Roman Catholic Church recognizes seven sacraments, including Baptism, Eucharist, and the five other sacramental rites. Peter Lombard (c. 1095–1160) identified these seven rites as sacraments of the church. This position was affirmed by the Council of Florence (1439) and the Council of Trent (1545–1563). The Orthodox Church also accepts seven sacraments. Martin Luther (1483–1546) was willing to identify Reconciliation of a Penitent as a sacrament, in addition to Baptism and Eucharist. In 1521 Henry VIII was awarded the title "Defender of the Faith" by Pope Leo X in recognition of Henry's treatise *Assertio Septem Sacramentorum* (Assertion of the Seven Sacraments) which defended the doctrine of the seven sacraments against Luther. After the English Reformation, Marriage or the Reconciliation of a Penitent are presented as sacraments by some Elizabethan homilies and formularies. Article XXV of the Articles of Religion acknowledged Baptism and the Lord's Supper as the two sacraments ordained by Christ in the gospel. Article XXV states that the five other sacramental rites "have not like nature of Sacraments with Baptism, and the Lord's Supper, for that they have not any visible sign or ceremony ordained of God" (BCP, p. 872). The five sacramental rites are not understood to be necessary for all Christians.

Sacramentalists. This term is commonly applied to priests ordained according to the provisions of the canons which allow "communities which are small, isolated, remote, or distinct in respect of ethnic composition, language, or culture" to identify someone from their own community for ordination. Preparation for ordained ministry under this provision does not assume a seminary education as the norm. Most dioceses provide a formation process that does not require the candidate to move away from his or her home. It is assumed that such a priest, trained in the local community, will remain in that community for the duration of his or her ministry. Such a priest might not be charged with preaching or pastoral care, if someone else has been identified for these functions. Sacramentalists are also known as local priests, or Canon 9 priests—based on the canon which allows their ordination. This provision allows flexibility for sacramental ministry in a variety of circumstances in which this ministry would not otherwise be available.

Sacramentals. The Prayer Book Catechism notes that the sacramental rites of Confirmation, Ordination, Holy Matrimony, Reconciliation of a Penitent, and Unction evolved in the church under the guidance of the Holy Spirit (BCP, pp. 860–861). These other sacramental rites, or sacramentals, are distinguished from Baptism and the Eucharist, the two great sacraments of the gospel. Baptism and Eucharist are known as "dominical" sacraments because they were commanded by the Lord Jesus Christ. The five other sacramental rites are means of grace. However, unlike Baptism and Eucharist, they are not necessary for all persons.

The term has at times been applied to various other outward signs and expressions of faith, such as grace at meals, the sign of the cross, the Angelus, the rosary, imposition of ashes on Ash Wednesday, and distribution of palms on Palm Sunday. *See* Sacramental Rites.

Sacramentary. A liturgical book containing prayers used by the celebrant at the eucharist throughout the year, along with other liturgical prayers. The celebrant's prayer at the eucharist was mainly extemporaneous during the first three centuries of the Christian church. By the third and fourth centuries, the celebrant's prayer was in written form. These prayers appeared in booklets known as *libelli*. Each booklet might contain only the prayers for one Mass. *Libelli* were later collected into sacramentaries for the entire liturgical year. The Leonine Sacramentary was a sixth-century collection of *libelli*. It is the earliest known book of prayers for the eucharist according to the Roman Rite. Sacramentaries came to include the eucharistic prayer, proper collects, prefaces, and other prayers. Sacramentaries did not include the epistle, the gospel, or the gradual of the Mass. Sacramentaries came to be replaced by the missal, which provided all the texts and directions needed for the eucharist in one book. The missal began to be used in the tenth century. Sacramentaries continued in use until the thirteenth century. Many BCP collects are drawn from the Leonine Sacramentary, including the collect for the Second Sunday after Christmas Day (p. 214) and the collect for Thursday in Easter Week (pp. 172, 223).

Sacramento, Diocese of. The 1898 General Convention voted that the bounds of the Missionary District of Northern California be changed to include the original counties in California plus all that portion of Nevada west of the west lines of the counties of Elko, White, Pine, Eureka, Lincoln, Lander, and Nye. It was called the Missionary District of Sacramento. On Oct. 30–31, 1911, the First Annual Convention of the Diocese of Sacramento met at St. Paul's Church, Sacramento. The name was changed to the Diocese of Northern California on Apr. 22, 1961.

Sacraments. Outward and visible signs of inward and spiritual grace, given by Christ as sure and certain means for receiving God's grace. Baptism and Eucharist are the two great sacraments given by Christ to his church. (BCP, pp. 857–858). The Episcopal Church recognizes that five other sacramental rites evolved in the church under the guidance of the Holy Spirit, including Confirmation, Ordination, Holy Matrimony, Reconciliation of a Penitent, and Unction (the anointing of the sick with oil, or the laying on of hands) (BCP, pp. 860–861).

Sacrifice (Eucharistic). *See* Eucharistic Sacrifice.

Sacristan. A person who works in the sacristy, the room for storing and working with the various items needed for the liturgies and worship of the church. Such items may include the vessels, vestments, books, bread and wine, and candles. Individual members of a parish's altar guild might be called sacristans.

Sacristy. The room adjoining a church where vestments, altar hangings and linens, sacred vessels, and liturgical books are kept until needed for use in worship. Clergy typically vest in the sacristy.

Saint. A holy person, a faithful Christian, one who shares life in Christ. The term may also indicate one who has been formally canonized or recognized as a saint by church authority. In the NT, the term is applied to all faithful Christians (see Acts 9:32, 26:10). Paul addresses the saints or those called to be saints who are the members of Christian communities that receive his letters (see Rom 1:7, 1 Cor 1:2, 2 Cor 1:1, Eph 1:1, Phil 1:1, Col 1:2). Christ makes it possible for us to be saints as we share his life. We are washed, sanctified, and justified "in the name of the Lord Jesus Christ and in the Spirit of our God" (1 Cor 6:11).

The term later came to be applied to "elite" Christians whose lives were distinguished and exemplary because of their self-sacrifice, witness, virtue, or accomplishments. Special recognition was given to the martyrs of the early church. A feast of All Martyrs dates from at least the third century. The saints were the heroes of the church. The identification of saints as exceptional Christians has been associated with the legalization of Christianity and the growth of the church to include members who were not fervently committed to Christian faith. The celebration of All Saints' Day in the west dates from at least the ninth century. In the western church, the requirement for papal approval for canonization of a saint dates from the twelfth century. An elaborate and complicated process for canonization developed in the Roman Catholic Church. A multiplication of saints' days followed the establishment of Christianity in the Roman world. This may reflect a need to provide a Christian alternative to days of celebration for pagan gods and heroes. The saints came to be seen as protectors and intercessors rather than witnesses for the Christian faith. Saints' days proliferated in the western church during the middle ages. Churches and institutions were named for saints. Many faithful people made pilgrimages to shrines of saints, such as the shrine of Thomas Becket at Canterbury.

Lutheran church orders restricted holy days to feasts of our Lord, the days of apostles and evangelists, St. Stephen, the Holy Innocents, St. John the Baptist, St. Michael the Archangel, and All Saints. The BCP followed the example of the German church orders, although other observances were later added. The calendar of the church year of the 1979 BCP includes the names of saints and many others whose lives are commemorated with feasts (pp. 15–33). The BCP provides collects, psalms, and lessons for holy days, including apostles such as St. Andrew (Nov. 30) and evangelists such as St. Mark (Apr. 25). The BCP also provides collects, psalms, and lessons for the Common of Saints for commemoration of saints listed in the calendar for which no proper is provided in the BCP (pp. 246–250, 925–927), including propers such as "Of a Martyr" and "Of a Missionary." *Lesser Feasts and Fasts* provides collects, psalms, and lessons for commemorations in the calendar that do not have propers appointed by the Prayer Book, such as Nicholas Ferrar (Dec. 1) and John Henry Hobart (Sept. 12). *Lesser Feasts and Fasts* also includes a short biographical sketch for each person commemorated. New commemorations may be added to the calendar with the approval of two General Conventions.

St. Andrew, Brotherhood of. *See* Brotherhood of St. Andrew.

St. Andrew's College, Jackson, Mississippi. St. Andrew's College opened on Jan. 1, 1852, with the Rev. Meyer Lewin (1816–1886) as president. It was under the jurisdiction of the Diocese of Mississippi. It received its charter on Oct. 16, 1852, and was the first college with its own grounds and buildings to be established in Jackson. It closed on Feb. 1, 1856, because of several severe outbreaks of yellow fever in the area.

St. Andrew's Divinity School, Syracuse, New York. Founded by Bishop Frederic Dan Huntington of Central New York, it opened on Sept. 16, 1876, and closed in 1905. The school's principal scholar was the Rev. Dr. William Dexter Wilson, who was dean, 1880–1900.

St. Andrew's-Sewanee School, Sewanee, Tennessee (SAS). Successor to several late nineteenth-/early twentieth-century schools. St. Andrew's Industrial and Training School for Boys opened on Sept. 21, 1905, near Gibson's Switch, Tennessee, near Sewanee. Later in 1905 the Order of the Holy Cross took over the school. In Apr. 1906 it officially adopted the school as a "work of the Order." In 1888 St. Mary's-on-the-Mountain, a convent of the Community of St. Mary, opened near Sewanee. In the fall of 1896 St. Mary's-on-the-Mountain opened its Mountain Training School for Girls. It evolved into St. Mary's Preparatory School for Girls. It closed at the end of the 1967–1968 academic year. Sixty-eight of the girls transferred to the previously all-male Sewanee Military Academy. The Sewanee Military School began as the

Sewanee Grammar School. It was a preparatory school for the University of the South. In 1902 it became the Sewanee Grammar Academy. In 1908 it became the Sewanee Military Academy. In 1971 the Academy demilitarized and became the Sewanee Academy. The St. Andrew's Industrial and Training School for Boys evolved into St. Andrew's School. St. Andrew's School and the Sewanee Academy merged and opened on the St. Andrew's campus in the fall of 1981 as St. Andrew's-Sewanee School (SAS).

St. Andrew's Theological Seminary, Mexico City. The oldest Anglican institution of theological education in the Spanish-speaking world. It was founded in 1894, by the Rev. Henry Forrester. The seminary is accredited by ALIET (*Asociasion Latinoamericana Internacional de Escuelas Teologicas*, Latin American Association of Theological Schools). It participates in a consortium of seminaries called the Comunidad Teologica. It was a seminary of the Episcopal Church as long as Mexico was part of the Episcopal Church. In 1994 the General Convention granted the five Mexican dioceses permission to withdraw from the Episcopal Church and constitute themselves an autonomous province. The Anglican Church of Mexico came into existence on Jan. 1, 1995. The seminary is now called St. Andrew's Anglican Seminary.

St. Anne, Order of. This order for women was founded on Nov. 22, 1910, in Arlington Heights, Massachusetts. In 1901 the Rev. Frederick Cecil Powell of the Society of St. John the Evangelist was sent from England to join the staff at the Church of St. John the Evangelist in Boston. Etheldred Barry, a St. John's parishioner who had inherited a property in Arlington Heights when her father died, built a small frame chapel in the garden in back of the house, where she had a Sunday School for children in the neighborhood. In 1909 Barry offered her house to Powell, who was looking for a home for neglected children. On Nov. 22, 1910, Sister Etheldred, Sister Monica, and Sister Anne received the habit, and the order was begun. On that same day, four women were admitted as associates. Sister Etheldred became the first Mother of the order. The rule of the order is a modified Benedictine Rule. There are two divisions in the community: first and second sisters. Sisters of the second order may be employed in work outside the convent. An enclosed and contemplative life is also possible. Those in the second order do not wear a traditional habit but wear grey dresses and a white veil while in the convent. Sisters of the first order wear a light grey habit with a white collar and black veil. Women in the world may become tertiaries and live the rule of a third order. Both men and women may become associates and assist the sisters with prayer, works, and alms. Houses of the order have included Bethany Convent in Arlington, Massachusetts, the Convent of St. Anne in Chicago, and St. Anne Convent in Denver.

St. Ann's Church for the Deaf. The idea of a church for the deaf came to the Rev. Thomas Gallaudet while he was ministering to a deaf teenager who was a student at the New York School for the Deaf, New York City. Gallaudet, with the support of the Bishop of New York, established St. Ann's Church for the Deaf. The first service performed in sign language was held on Oct. 3, 1852. Gallaudet was its vicar, and he was its rector from Oct. 1, 1858, until his retirement in 1892. St. Ann's Church was incorporated on Sept. 11, 1854, and received into union with the Diocese of New York on Oct. 28, 1854. It is the mother church for hearing impaired Episcopalians in the United States.

St. Augustine College, Chicago, Illinois. A bilingual institution of higher education created to make the American system of higher education accessible to a non-traditional student population with an emphasis on those of Hispanic descent. It was granted operating authority by the Illinois State Board of Higher Education on Oct. 7, 1980. It is a coeducational, two-year college with an emphasis on technological and vocational training. It was founded by the Rev. Carlos Alberto Plazas, and it is a member of the Association of Episcopal Colleges.

St. Augustine, Missionary College of, Benicia, California. One of several schools founded by James Lloyd Breck. In Dec. 1867, he bought the twenty-acre tract and buildings which belonged to the recently closed Benicia Collegiate Institute and Law School at Benicia, California. Breck opened his Missionary College in 1868. Breck also established St. Mary's School for girls on the same campus. St. Mary's closed in 1885 and St. Augustine's closed in 1889.

St. Augustine, Order of. This religious order for men was established in Marion, North Carolina, in 1943. Later it moved to Good Shepherd Island off the coast of South Carolina. They then moved to Orange City, Florida, and established the Good Shepherd Monastery. It was a contemplative community. The daily life was spent in study, prayer, and manual labor. Friends were affiliated with the order as lay associates (men and women), seminarian associates, priest associates, and the oblates of St. Monica (women), and the oblates of St. Augustine (men). The order is no longer in existence.

St. Augustine's College, Raleigh, North Carolina. A historically African American, coeducational institution, offering the bachelor's degree. The leader in its founding was Joseph Brinton Smith, executive director of the Freedman's Commission of the Episcopal Church. It was chartered on July 19, 1867, at St. Augustine's Normal School and Collegiate Institute and received its first four students on Jan. 13, 1868. From 1896 to 1959, St. Agnes' Hospital and Nursing Home was part of the college. It also operated the Bishop Tuttle School for religious and social workers, 1925–1941. In 1921 the name was changed to St. Augustine's College, and in 1931 the first twelve B.A. degrees were awarded. In 1934 it was accredited by the Southern Association of Schools and Colleges.

St. Barnabas Brotherhood. A religious order of laymen which worked with convalescent and incurable men and boys. It operated St. Barnabas Free Home, Gibsonia, Pennsylvania, and St. Barnabas House-By-The-Lake, North East, Pennsylvania. Gouverneur Provoost Hance (d. 1954) joined the Church Army on Jan. 25, 1897, at Trinity Church, Pittsburgh, and in 1900 opened a convalescent home in downtown Pittsburgh. In 1901 he moved the home to the south side of Pittsburgh and named it St. Barnabas Home. In 1902, with a fellow novice, Hance began to live the religious life under a secular priest. The Rule of the Brotherhood was formulated in 1910. On June 11, 1913, St. Barnabas' Day, Hance and three others made their annual vows before Bishop Cortlandt Whitehead. On July 11, 1919, Hance and two other brothers took life vows before Bishop Whitehead. Beginning in 1903 the Brotherhood published *Faith and Work*. It was last listed as the Society of St. Barnabas in the 1985 edition of *The Episcopal Church Annual*. It is no longer in existence.

St. Barnabas Center. A spiritually based, ecumenical, hospital-based mental and addictions treatment program for church professionals. It was located on the grounds of Rogers Hospital, a psychiatric hospital, on land leased from Nashotah House at Oconomowoc, Wisconsin. It brought together the insights and disciplines of spirituality and psychotherapy to provide a program designed to meet the needs of people whose personal and professional lives were centered in the church. The concept for the center was developed by Donald Raymond Hands, Wayne L. Fehr, and Michael Joseph Stolpman (1939–1990), three priests of the Episcopal Church. Bishop Roger White of Milwaukee supported the project. It opened on Jan. 1, 1988, and closed on Apr. 30, 1993. Some four hundred persons were treated. Hands and Fehr wrote *Spiritual Wholeness for Clergy, A New Psychology of Intimacy with God, Self and Others* (1993), which was based on their experiences at the St. Barnabas Center.

St. Benedict, Order of (OSB). A religious order for men whose primary purpose is to experience and express the saving power of Christ within a body of believers, and to use that power in interceding for the church and the world. In 1935 a group of Episcopalians, led by Dom Paul Severance, traveled to England to be trained by the Anglican Benedictines of Nashdom Abbey at Burnham in Buckinghamshire. After training, they returned to the United States. Some of these men became life professed monks. On Mar. 12, 1939, St. Gregory's House in Valparaiso, Indiana, was selected to be the first residence. Later it became St. Gregory's Priory. On Apr. 21, 1939, the community celebrated its first Mass. Dom Paul and Dom Francis made their life professions on Mar. 21, 1941. On Apr. 17, 1946, the community moved to Three Rivers, Michigan, and began to accept postulants. Thus the nickname "Three Rivers." In 1969 St. Gregory's Priory, Three Rivers, became independent of Nashdom Abbey in England. The principal work of the community is prayer, which is based in the Divine Office and the private prayers of the monks. A Conventual (Family) Eucharist is at the center of each day's activities. Each member of the community is expected to engage in regular study. *See* Benedictine Spirituality.

St. Clement's Church, Philadelphia. On Sept. 13, 1855, a charter was granted to "The rector, Church Wardens, and Vestrymen of St. Clement's Church in the City of Philadelphia." The cornerstone of the new church was laid on May 12, 1856, by Bishop Alonzo Potter. The church was consecrated on Apr. 12, 1864. The influence of the Catholic Revival, sometimes called Ritualism, on the parish began in 1869, when Hermon Batterson became the rector. From 1874 until 1891 the parish was served by brothers and priests of the Society of St. John the Evangelist. On Apr. 10, 1944, it was designated the Shrine of our Lady of

Clemency. Over the years continuous novenas have been said at the Shrine. Upon request, petitions and thanksgivings are remembered at the Shrine for nine consecutive days, and a votive candle is lit on the ninth day. In 1943 a Shrine to the Virgin Mary was erected and dedicated on the Feast of the Annunciation, Mar. 25. Liturgically, St. Clement's uses the BCP "as arranged in the 1928 American version," traditional hymnody as found in *The Hymnal* (1940) and the New English Hymnal, and the Authorized Version of the Bible. The mission statement of the parish declares that the final arbiter of doctrine is the Catechism of the Council of Trent, and that the parish rejects the "errors" of the Episcopal Church of the last thirty years: "the so-called 'ordination of women,' feminist theology, the new permissive marriage canons, the 'revised liturgies,' and so on."

St. Faith's Deaconess Training School, New York. *See* New York Training School for Deaconesses (NYTSD).

St. Francis Academy, Salina, Kansas. A national, not-for-profit behavioral health care organization serving children, adolescents, and their families. The Rt. Rev. Robert Herbert "Father Bob" Mize (1870–1956), founded St. Francis Academy (originally the St. Francis Boys' Home) in 1945. At that time he was the retired Bishop of Western Kansas. The first residential facility was located in Ellsworth, Kansas, and opened on Sept. 15, 1945. In 1948 a second residential facility was established in Salina, Kansas. These homes provide a caring environment for boys. The healing process is termed "therapy in Christ." It has four basic principles: unconditional love, forgiveness, honesty, and starting and ending the day with God. Beginning in 1951, additional treatment programs were added to the Academy through counseling, psychiatric, psychological, and social services staff. The Lake Placid, New York, campus was established in 1965; the campus in Atchison, Kansas, opened in 1991; the former St. Michael's Farm for Boys in Picayune, Mississippi, merged with St. Francis in 1992; community services and case management programs were established in Santa Fe, Española, and Taos, New Mexico, in 1995; a girls' residential facility was opened in 1995 in Philadelphia, Pennsylvania; and the Building Families family preservation program began in 1996 in western Kansas. Programs include residential treatment centers for boys and girls, an emergency shelter for temporary care, secure living facilities for chronic runaway boys and girls, independent living skills transitional programs, a residential program for dually diagnosed developmentally disabled/behavior disordered boys, outpatient services for boys and girls, early-intervention programs, case management and community services, family preservation programs, and team-building programs. All St. Francis residential treatment centers are accredited by the Joint Commission on Accreditation of Healthcare Organizations.

St. Francis, Community of (CSF). This community of Franciscan Sisters is the oldest of the existing Franciscan communities in the Anglican Communion. CSF was founded in London in 1905 by Sister Rosina Rice. On Feb. 27, 1974, four sisters arrived in San Francisco from England to found the first CSF house in the United States. St. Francis' House, San Francisco, was blessed on Sept. 7, 1975. The purpose of the order is to be a link of praying and loving concern between the "still point" and the "turning world." It is involved in Christian education, parish work, peace and justice ministries, hospital chaplaincy, and spiritual nurture. *See* Franciscan Spirituality.

St. Francis, Society of (SSF). Franciscan friars who live under the vows of poverty, obedience, and chastity. They practice the three ways of service: devotion, sacred study and active works of service. It is a community of men, lay and ordained. The society publishes *The Little Chronicle*. The American Congregation of Franciscans began on the Feast of the Sacred Heart of Jesus, a Roman Catholic observance, June 15, 1917, when fifteen or more men and women met in the Convent of the Poor Clares in Cincinnati, Ohio. They wanted to restore the Franciscan life in the Episcopal Church. Among them were the men and women who afterwards became the first members of the three orders in the American Congregation. On that same day, June 15, 1917, the "House of Our Lady, Help of Christians," Cincinnati, was blessed. Among the early members was the Rev. Claude Crookston (1889–1979). On Feb. 2, 1917, Crookston dedicated himself to a Franciscan vocation and took the name Father Joseph. In May 1918 Father Joseph went to the Bishop of Fond du Lac to find a location for the developing Franciscan communities. On Holy Cross Day, Sept. 14, 1919, Bishop Reginald Heber Weller received Father Joseph and several others as postulants. The First Order of Franciscans began at Merrill, Wisconsin. On June 15, 1928, the Order of St. Francis moved to Little Portion Friary on Long Island. In 1968 the Order of St. Francis united with the Society of St. Francis. This community is called the Society of St. Francis. The former Society of St.

Francis came into being in 1937 from the joining of the Brotherhood of St. Francis and the Brotherhood of the Love of Christ, which was the English branch of the Indian Franciscan Community Christa Prema Seva Sangha. *See* Franciscan Spirituality.

St. Francis, Society of, Third Order, American Province. The Society of St. Francis is a worldwide religious community of the Anglican Communion. Its patron is St. Francis of Assisi. The society is composed of three orders: First Order brothers and sisters, who live a community life under vows and practice outward service to the world; Second Order sisters, generally known as the Order of Poor Clares, who live under vows and live an austere life of enclosure with an emphasis on penitence, poverty, and prayer; and Third Order brothers and sisters, who are married or single, lay or ordained, and live a life of renunciation, simplicity, and discipline even though continuing to live in their own homes and earning their own living. Third Order brothers and sisters are also called tertiaries. The formation process for a tertiary consists of a postulancy of no less than six months and a novitiate of no less than two years. Tertiaries concentrate on prayer, study, and work. *See* Franciscan Spirituality.

St. Francis, Third Order of Divine Compassion. Brother John Charles (the Rt. Rev. John Charles Vockler) left the American Province of the Society of St. Francis on July 25, 1990. He later established the Third Order of the Divine Compassion of St. Francis at Rock Island, Illinois. The Third Order of the Divine Compassion is for clerics and lay people, married and celibate, who want to follow the Franciscan life but cannot enter a friary or convent because of personal commitments. The order was established to preserve the historic catholic faith as received by the Anglican Church and to follow the teachings and ministry of St. Francis. Vockler was Bishop of Polynesia from 1962 until 1969. The Order was last listed in *The Episcopal Church Annual 1994*. *See* Franciscan Spirituality.

St. Gregory, Brotherhood of. *See* Brotherhood of St. Gregory (BSG).

St. Gregory, Companion Sisterhood of. *See* Companion Sisterhood of St. Gregory (CSSG).

St. Gregory and St. Augustine, Fellowship of. An international communion of prayer, work, and study dedicated to the organic reunion of the Anglican and Roman Catholic churches. It was organized in June 1977. It is sponsored by the Camaldolese Order (Roman Catholic), the Order of the Holy Cross (Anglican), the Order of St. Helena (Anglican), and the Camaldolese Nuns' communities (Roman Catholic). The fellowship seeks to be a source of spiritual, pastoral, and theological support for existing Anglican and Roman Catholic organizations that are interested in Anglican-Roman Catholic reunion. The fellowship publishes a newsletter, *The Cross and Dove*, whose name is drawn from the traditional symbols for St. Gregory (dove) and St. Augustine (cross).

St. Gregory's Abbey. *See* St. Benedict, Order of (OSB).

St. Helena, Order of (OSH). A women's religious order which seeks to witness to a contemporary version of traditional monasticism. On Nov. 8, 1945, nine sisters of the Order of St. Anne at Margaret Hall School, Versailles, Kentucky, led by mother superior Rachel Hosmer, organized a new order, the Order of St. Helena. Under the guidance of Fr. Alan Griffith Whittemore (1890–1960), superior of the Order of the Holy Cross, the sisters began to live according to the Rule of the Order of the Holy Cross. The superior of Holy Cross was also the superior of the Order of St. Helena. In 1975 the two orders became administratively separate. The mother house is at Vails Gate, New York, and branches are in Augusta, Georgia; Seattle, Washington; and New York City. Since 1980 it has published *Saint Helena*. *See* Hosmer, Rachel Elizabeth.

St. Hilda's & St. Hugh's. An independent Episcopal School for Children founded in 1950 in New York City by the Community of the Holy Spirit. It is named in honor of two educators. St. Hilda was a seventh-century saint and a member of the nobility. She founded the Abbey at Whitby in Yorkshire, England, where both men and women were educated in the academic disciplines and in the arts. St. Hilda founded this co-educational institution centuries before women were considered capable of education. St. Hugh of Lincoln was a twelfth-century bishop known for his personal courage and kindness. Both are in the Episcopal calendar of the church year. St. Hilda's & St. Hugh's is a day school for children of all faiths, from toddlers to grade eight. The Bishop of New York is the honorary chairman of the Board of Trustees. *See* Holy Spirit, Community of the.

St. Ives, Guild of. A group of lawyers and priests who study legal issues of importance to the church. It was founded on Feb. 24, St. Matthias Day, 1967. The guild's major publication is *Churches and Taxation Revisited*, which was first published in *The St. Luke's Journal of Theology* (June 1974). Suffragan Bishop Walter Decoster Dennis of New York was a co-founder and the primary leader of the group. St. Ives or Ivo of Brittany (c. 1235–1303) was a lawyer and the patron of lawyers and judges.

St. James College, Fountain Rock, Hagerstown, Maryland. St. James College was founded by the Rt. Rev. William Rollinson Whittingham, the fourth Bishop of Maryland, and the Rev. Theodore Benedict Lyman (1815–1893), rector of St. John's Church, Hagerstown. St. James was to be patterned after St. Paul's School, College Point, New York. Bishop Whittingham arranged for the Rev. John Barrett Kerfoot (1816–1881) to leave St. Paul's School and to head the new school. On Oct. 2, 1842, St. James College opened in Claggett Hall, named after Thomas John Claggett, the first Bishop of Maryland. The final commencement was held on July 12, 1864. On Sept. 1, 1864, an announcement was made that "The College of St. James is forced by the perils of war to suspend its work." It continues as St. James School.

St. James of Jerusalem, Fellowship of. An organization of Anglicans, Orthodox, and Old Catholics concerned about Christian people and places in the Holy Land. It promotes understanding among individual members of these communions, common prayer, united effort and correspondence. It works with the Jerusalem and the Middle East Church Association of the Church of England. Its theme is "neither 'Eastern' nor 'Western,' but the whole Church, true orthodoxy, real catholicity, beginning at Jerusalem." It was founded in 1951.

St. John Baptist, Community of (CSJB). Community of women founded in Windsor, England, in 1852, under the guidance of Thomas Thellusson Carter, Canon of Christ Cathedral, Oxford, and Harriet Monsell, an Irish widow. Monsell became the first superior. On Feb. 5, 1874, three sisters from Clewer, England, landed in New York City to begin work with German immigrants on the Lower East Side. They founded Holy Cross Episcopal Church in New York. In Nov. 1881 the Community of St. John the Baptist became an autonomous American community. In 1884 the Rev. James Otis Sargent Huntington, who had been working with the community, made his religious profession before the altar of St. John Baptist House and founded the Order of the Holy Cross. The Community seeks to cultivate the interior life through prayer and the sacraments, and the vows of poverty, obedience, and chastity. The sisters live by an Augustinian Rule. They combine a life of prayer and worship with service to people in need. The oblates of the Community make an annual commitment to a personal rule, which includes prayer and service in the church. The associates of the community support the sisters with their prayers. In 1913 the sisters sold the property in New York and moved the Mother House to Mendham, New Jersey.

St. John the Evangelist, College of, Denver and Greeley, Colorado. The goals for the College of St. John the Evangelist were never fully realized. Jarvis Hall for boys, Wolfe Hall for girls, and Matthews Hall for theological students operated sporadically from 1879 to 1937. No degrees were ever awarded.

St. John the Evangelist, Sisterhood of. Bishop Abram Newkirk Littlejohn (1824–1901) of Long Island founded this deaconess society in 1872. In 1888 it was formed into a religious community, the Sisters of the Community of St. John the Evangelist. Their primary work was in the Church Charity Foundation, which included St. John's Hospital, homes for the aged and blind, and other social service work. The order went out of existence in 1970.

St. Johnland. A Christian community for poor people established by William Augustus Muhlenberg. Around 1864 he purchased 425 acres of land on the north shore of Long Island, about forty-five miles from New York City. The underlying motivation was to transplant families and individuals from the urban squalor of New York to the countryside. On this property Muhlenberg built homes for families and old men, a home for crippled and destitute children, a school, and shops for baking and making clothes. At the center of the community was the Church of the Testimony of Jesus. The community did not develop as Muhlenberg hoped. Gradually the projects at St. Johnland were taken over by other institutions, and only the orphanage was left. In 1955 the orphanage was discontinued and it became a retirement home. St. Johnland has been called the church's answer to socialism. Muhlenberg is buried there.

St. John's Church, Richmond, Virginia. Historic seat of Henrico Parish, one of the oldest parishes in the United States. The plantation parish of Henrico began in 1611 with the Rev. Alexander Whitaker as its first rector. In 1617 plans were made for the "University and Colledge" of Henrico, and in 1619 ten thousand acres were granted for the college. In 1622 this effort was destroyed by the Indians. Whitaker baptized Pocahontas, the first Indian convert to Christianity. On Mar. 23, 1775, at the second convention of the church in Virginia at St. John's Church, Patrick Henry made his famous speech in which he said, "Give me liberty . . . or give me death." The Rev. William F. Lee, the rector, started calling the church St. John's in 1828. The present church building is the fourth or possibly the fifth built for the parish. It was constructed in 1741 on land given by Colonel William Byrd, Jr., founder of the city of Richmond. About thirty of the pews and the pulpit remain from the colonial interior. St. John's is still an active parish.

St. John's College, Annapolis, Maryland. In 1696 "King William's School" opened as a free school at Annapolis "to instruct youth in Arithmetick, Navigation and all useful learning, but chiefly for the fitting such as are disposed to study divinity." Governor Nicholson gave the land for a school building which was completed in 1701. In Nov. 1784 the Maryland legislature passed a bill with the following title: "An act for founding a college on the Western Shore of this state and constituting the same, together with Washington College on the Eastern Shore, into one university by the name of the University of Maryland." The first meeting of the Board of Governors of St. John's College was held on Feb. 28, 1786. One member of the Board of Governors was the Rev. Thomas John Claggett, later the first Bishop of Maryland. On Mar. 2, 1786, King William's School was amalgamated with the proposed St. John's College, which opened on Nov. 11, 1789. St. John's College is no longer affiliated with the Episcopal Church.

St. John's College, Spartanburg, South Carolina. St. John's College opened in Jan. 1852 as St. John's School for Boys, under the leadership of the Rev. John DeWitt McCollough (1822–1902). It was never really a college, and it closed in 1862 because of the Civil War. In Oct. 1866 the Theological Seminary of South Carolina reopened St. John's campus but closed on May 16, 1868. The property was sold to Converse College in 1889.

St. John's Hall. A preparatory school for boys in Delafield, Wisconsin, founded by James DeKoven in 1858. DeKoven was the warden of the school. It exemplified DeKoven's belief that students should live as a family in one building. The depression of 1859 caused it to merge with Racine College. DeKoven served as the warden of Racine College until his death. *See* DeKoven, James.

St. John's University, Shanghai. The Episcopal Church began an institution for boys in Shanghai around 1851. It was the foundation for St. John's. The school was founded by the Rt. Rev. Samuel Isaac Joseph Schereschewsky, Bishop of Shanghai, 1877–1883. The cornerstone of the building was laid on Easter Monday, Apr. 14, 1879, and a house for the bishop was completed in June 1879. St. John's College opened on Sept. 1, 1879. Instruction in theology began on Oct. 28, 1879. In Oct. 1880 a medical school with nine students was opened. St. Mary's Hall, a boarding school for women, opened in June 1881. It was separated from the college by a brick wall. In 1905 the college was incorporated as St. John's University. It was recognized as the foremost Christian institution in China.

St. Joseph, Brothers of. This religious order was founded in 1935 by Brother Francis Anthony in Peekskill, New York. It was also known as the Working Brothers of St. Joseph. It was a lay brotherhood devoted to prayer and manual labor. The rule was based on the Benedictine Rule. The community, following the example of their patron St. Joseph, made church furniture and repaired churches and chapels. It moved to Sayville, Long Island, and then to East Moriches, Long Island. It went out of existence around 1958.

St. Louis Congress. The sixty-fifth General Convention met at Minneapolis, Sept. 11–22, 1976, and approved the ordination of women to the priesthood and episcopate and the *Draft Proposed Book of Common Prayer.* The Fellowship of Concerned Churchmen met at Nashville, Nov. 4–5, 1976, to respond to the actions of General Convention. The fellowship passed a resolution calling for a Church Congress to meet in St. Louis, Sept. 14–16, 1977, "for the purpose of presenting the spiritual principles and ecclesiastical structure of the continuing Episcopal Church." When the congress met it had 1,746 registrations, three of whom were bishops. It adopted guidelines for a new ecclesiastical structure, called "The Affirmation of St. Louis," which became the basis for a number of new churches. It also adopted a provisional title for the proposed new structure, the "Anglican Church in North America."

St. Luke's Church, Smithfield, Virginia. This church, also known as Old Brick Church, is near Smithfield in Isle of Wight County. It claims the distinction of being the oldest Episcopal Church in Virginia and the oldest building of English origin still standing in the United States. Historians think it was built in 1632 because three bricks were found imprinted with the year 1632 when the east wall fell in 1887. It is a gothic style building with buttresses, stepped gables, and the original brick traceried windows. It has a Jacobean interior and a rood screen. The building is fully restored and is now a National Historic Shrine.

St. Luke's Hospital, New York. William Augustus Muhlenberg wanted to have a church hospital linked with the Sisterhood of the Holy Communion. The sisters were to serve as nurses. In 1853 a 17-bed infirmary with an outpatient clinic and dispensary opened. On May 13, 1858, the hospital opened for patients. Its purpose was to afford "medical or surgical aid, and nursing, to sick or disabled persons; and also to provide them, while inmates of the hospital, with the ministrations of the Gospel, agreeably to the doctrines and forms of the Protestant Episcopal Church." A further object of the hospital was "the instructing and training of suitable persons in the art of nursing and attending the sick." Muhlenberg gave the hospital the motto, *Corpus sanare, animam salvare,* "to cure the body, to save the soul." This motto is on the hospital's seal. When the hospital opened, Muhlenberg left the Church of the Holy Communion to live in the hospital as the house father and to attend to the spiritual needs of the patients. In 1888 the Sisters opened St. Luke's Hospital Training School for Nurses. The hospital is now St. Luke's-Roosevelt Hospital. It is still affiliated with the Episcopal Church.

St. Luke's Journal of Theology. See Sewanee Theological Review.

St. Luke the Physician, The International Order of. The purpose of this order is the restoration of the healing ministry of Christ in the church. It is an outgrowth of the Fellowship of St. Luke, begun in 1932 by the Rev. John Gayner Banks (1886–1953). In 1947 the Fellowship of St. Luke became the International Order of St. Luke the

Physician. Professional people in all phases of medical work, clergy in the ministry of the Roman, Orthodox, Anglican, and Protestant churches, and lay people from all walks of life comprise the membership. The order promotes the restoration of the apostolic practice of healing as taught and demonstrated by Jesus and encourages healing services in every church. Local chapters work to promote healing missions, workshops, and prayer groups in the parishes. The order is dedicated to healing the whole person (body, soul, and mind), the healing of the situations of the nations, and the healing of God's creation. Members of the order subscribe to a rule which stresses praying for the sick and the daily reading of the gospels. The Latin motto of the order is *Jesu Esto Mihi Jesus Dux Lux Rex Lex,* which roughly translates as *O Jesus, be to me my Saviour (Healer), my Leader, my Light, my King and my Law.* The Order publishes *Sharing,* a journal of Christian healing. It began in 1934 as a newsletter and in 1937 became a regular periodical.

St. Margaret's House (School for Christian Service and Deaconess Training School of the Pacific). Anita Adela Hodgkin was received as a candidate for the office of deaconess by Bishop William F. Nichols of California on Apr. 3, 1907. May Bostick Mott was received as a prospective deaconess by Bishop Nichols on May 18, 1908. Both women were members of St. Mark's Church, Berkeley, where Edward Lambe Parsons was the rector. Since there was no school for deaconesses in the west, Parsons organized a school in his parish. It was named St. Mark's Deaconess School. Bishop Nichols wanted the school to be larger than St. Mark's parish. In 1908 the Deaconess Training School of the Pacific was established and officially recognized as an agency of the Diocese of California. The rented place in which the school began was called St. Ann's House. One of the members of the Board of Managers was Mary Robertson. When she died she left the school a bequest. The money was used to buy an estate. It was named St. Margaret's House. Miss Robertson's sister was named Margaret. On Oct. 10, 1909, Hodgkin and Mott were set apart by Bishop Nichols as deaconesses. St. Margaret, Queen of Scotland, was later adopted as the patron saint. From the beginning, St. Margaret's House was closely associated with the Church Divinity School of the Pacific. Gradually the faculty of the divinity school became the faculty of the Deaconess Training School. St. Margaret's closed in 1966.

St. Margaret, Society of (SSM). This religious order for women was founded in England by the Rev. John Mason Neale, warden of Sackville College in East Grinstead, Sussex, England in 1855. It was not until July 20, 1865, that the cornerstone of the convent was laid. July 20 was the feast of St. Margaret of Antioch, the patron saint of the society. In 1871 three sisters were sent to the United States to take charge of the Boston Children's Hospital, a nine-bed hospital on Washington Street. On Sept. 13, 1873, Mother Louisa Mary was installed as the mother superior of St. Margaret's Convent. The Rev. Charles Grafton, a member of the Society of St. John the Evangelist, was named the first chaplain of the American branch of the order. The members today live a "mixed" life of active work and contemplative prayer. At one time the society operated St. Monica's Home in Roxbury, Massachusetts, a nursing home for African American patients, and St. Anne's House in Lexington, Kentucky, a shelter for out-patients having treatment at the University of Kentucky Hospital. The society has a mission in Port-au-Prince, Haiti. The mother house is in Roxbury, Massachusetts. In 1920 the society began publishing *St. Margaret's Quarterly*.

St. Mark's College, Grand Rapids, Michigan. In 1850 a charter was obtained for the establishment of an institution for academic, collegiate, and theological learning to be known as St. Mark's College. The only president was the Rev. Charles C. Taylor (d. 1855). St. Mark's College was abandoned in 1851.

St. Mary, Community of (CSM). William Augustus Muhlenberg and Anne Ayres established the Sisterhood of the Holy Communion in 1845. It was formally organized in 1852. On Apr. 9, 1863, Sister Harriet Starr Cannon, Sister Mary B. Heartt (d. 1903), Sister Jane C. Haight (d. 1868), and Sister Sarah C. Bridge (d. 1899) left the Sisterhood of the Holy Communion with plans to form a more traditional monastic order. On Feb. 2, 1865, Sisters Harriett, Mary, Jane, and Sarah, along with Amelia W. Asten (d. 1898), were received into the Sisterhood of St. Mary. Bishop Horatio Potter of New York presided over their religious profession service at St. Michael's Church, Manhattan. The sisterhood was incorporated in May 1865. In Sept. 1865 Sister Harriett was elected mother superior. On Apr. 4, 1866, the Rev. Morgan Dix, rector of Trinity Church, New York, and chaplain to the sisters, presented the sisterhood its first rule. The great work of the sisterhood was in the education of young women. At first the sisters

had to defend themselves against accusations of "Romanism," but they were gradually accepted by the church. The Sisterhood of St. Mary was the first official religious community in the Episcopal Church. The order is now called the Community of St. Mary. The Eastern Province of the community is in Peekskill, New York, the Southern Province is in Sewanee, Tennessee, and the Western Province is based in Mukwonago, Wisconsin. The community also has houses in Los Angeles, California, and Sagada Mountain Province in the Philippines.

St. Mary's College, Dallas, Texas. The Rt. Rev. Alexander Charles Garrett, the first Bishop of Dallas, founded this school for women. A cornerstone was laid on July 4, 1876, but classes did not begin until Sept. 10, 1889. By 1900 the school offered a four-year program leading to a Bachelor of Arts degree. With the exception of Bishop Garrett, the faculty was female. The school closed in June 1930.

St. Mary's College, Raleigh, North Carolina. This school opened on May 12, 1842. In 1954 the name was changed to St. Mary's Junior College. It is now called St. Mary's College. It is a two-year school with a liberal arts curriculum for women.

St. Mary's Hall, Burlington, New Jersey. In 1836 Bishop George Washington Doane of New Jersey bought an existing school for girls in Burlington and renamed it St. Mary's Hall. The new school opened on May 1, 1837, with fifty-two students. In 1849 the assets of St. Mary's Hall were transferred to the Trustees of Burlington College, which Doane had founded in 1846 for boys. The corporate name of the school became Trustees of Burlington College (St. Mary's Hall). In 1933 the charter was amended, and St. Mary's was governed directly by the Diocese of New Jersey. As a result of the dissolution of the official connection between the diocese and the school in 1955, it returned to its status as a private independent school. In 1966 Doane Academy for boys was established as a coordinate school on the same campus. In 1974 the two schools were completely united with the name St. Mary's Hall-Doane Academy, A College Preparatory School. In 1989 Doane Academy was dropped from the name.

St. Michael's Church, Charleston, South Carolina. Historic seat of St. Michael's parish. By an act of the South Carolina General Assembly on June 14, 1751, the parish of

St. Philip's was divided and the parish of St. Michael established. Construction of the building took about a decade. The building is an important example of colonial architecture and is largely unchanged after revolution, civil war, fire, earthquake, hurricanes, and tornadoes. Three Bishops of South Carolina have served as rectors. A long-time assistant minister was Frederick Dalcho, the diocesan historian. Members of the church included Thomas Lynch and Thomas Heyward, Jr., who were signers of the Declaration of Independence.

St. Monica Sisterhood. This religious order was founded in 1886 as an order for widows. It was based first in Fond du Lac, Wisconsin, where it had charge of St. Monica's School. It was sometimes called the Order of St. Monica. It moved to Springfield, Illinois, in 1897 and was called St. Monica Sisters. In Springfield it was concerned primarily with intercessory prayer and operated the Orphanage of the Holy Child. It is no longer in existence.

St. Patrick's Breastplate. *See* Breastplate of St. Patrick.

St. Paul, Brothers of. Founded in 1928 by Brother Robert Paul Allan in Kingston, New York, it was a society for laymen only. The Brothers of St. Paul sought to help working men with little education. Its special work was running homes for working men. Later it moved to Roxbury, Massachusetts. It is no longer in existence.

St. Paul, Society of (SSP). A monastic community of priests and brothers. It was founded on July 1, 1958, in Gresham, Oregon, by the Rev. René Malcolm Roscoe Ernest Bozarth (1923–1982). The monks are dedicated to a life of prayer and the showing forth of God's love in works of mercy, charity, and evangelism. In 1977 the community moved the monastery to Palm Desert, California. The ministry of St. Jude's Home Corporation and St. Paul's Press, both founded in 1958, continue in operation. The press publishes *St. Paul's Printer*. The vows and rule are Benedictine. Private prayer, the Divine Offices, and the daily eucharist are central to the life of the community. The community engages in study, daily chores of the common life, preaching, retreats, counseling, and spiritual direction. The Fellowship of St. Paul is the extended family of the community. It is comprised of men and women who are friends, associates, companions and oblates. The brothers wear a brown tunic and scapular with hood and black belt. *See* Benedictine Spirituality.

St. Paul's College, College Point (Flushing), New York. The cornerstone of St. Paul's College was laid on Oct. 15, 1836, by the Rev. William Augustus Muhlenberg. The Christian religion was the center of education for Muhlenberg, and the school was to train missionaries and teachers. It closed in 1848.

St. Paul's College, Lawrenceville, Virginia. St. Paul's Normal and Industrial School was founded on Sept. 24, 1888, by the Rev. James Solomon Russell (1857–1935). In 1906 it became a part of the American Church Institute for Negroes. On Dec. 30, 1941, the name was changed to St. Paul's Polytechnic Institute, and on Feb. 27, 1957, to St. Paul's College. St. Paul's is a four-year, historically African American college, and is a member of the Association of Episcopal Colleges.

St. Paul's College, Palmyra, Missouri. The Governor Clark Mission was established in Feb. 1848 on fifty-seven acres of land in Marion County which was purchased by the Rt. Rev. Cicero Stephens Hawks, the second Bishop of Missouri. On Feb. 24, 1853, the legislature incorporated the school as St. Paul's College. In June 1889 St. Paul's graduated its last class, and the school did not reopen because of inadequate funding.

St. Paul's College, Texas. The Rev. Charles Gillette (1813–Mar. 6, 1869) founded St. Paul's College. It opened on Jan. 5, 1852, at Anderson, as the Anderson Female Institute and Texas Diocesan School. It received a charter on Feb. 4, 1853, as St. Paul's College. On Apr. 5, 1855, the board of trustees voted to move the school to Austin, but it closed in 1856. It was re-established at Brenham and opened on Jan. 1, 1868. St. Paul's closed in 1870. Plans to re-open the school at Hempstead were never realized.

St. Paul's School, Concord, New Hampshire. A leading co-educational college preparatory school in the United States. It was founded on Apr. 3, 1856, by a Boston physician, George Cheyne Shattuck, Jr. Dr. Shattuck wanted to educate his sons in a place where natural beauty could play a part in the boys' education. St. Paul's was influenced by two other schools. The Round Hill School in Northampton, Massachusetts, where Shattuck went to school, provided a progressive education model, and the Flushing Institute, Flushing, Long Island, provided the model of an intense religious life. The first rector, the Rev. Henry Augustus Coit, attended the Flushing Institute.

St. Paul's University, Tokyo. Founded in 1874 by Bishop Channing Moore Williams, it officially became St. Paul's College in 1907. Native Japanese leadership assumed administration in 1920 and it acquired university status in 1922. It was reorganized and became co-educational in 1949. The graduate school was established in 1951.

St. Philip's Church, Charleston, South Carolina. Oldest religious congregation in South Carolina. It was formed around 1670, when a colony of settlers disembarked in Apr. at "Albemarle Point." By 1679 the settlers had moved to the peninsula between the Ashley and Cooper Rivers to form Charles Town, named after Charles II, King of England at the time. The first permanent church edifice, built of cypress wood, was completed about 1681–1682. It was usually called "the English Church," but its official name was St. Philip's. By 1710 an act provided for the building of a new brick church on Church Street, three blocks away. The work began that year and was completed in 1727, when the first building was taken down. This second building burned on Feb. 15, 1835. The cornerstone of a new and third St. Philip's Church was laid on Nov. 12, 1835. The new church was built on the foundation of the old one. John Wesley preached in the church and George Washington worshiped there. It is still in use.

St. Philip's Church, New York. This African American congregation was founded in 1818. It was the second African American Episcopal congregation in the United States after St. Thomas African Episcopal Church, Philadelphia. The first members of St. Philip's had been members of Trinity Parish, New York. The leader of the parish was Peter Williams, Jr., a lay reader, "Absalom Jones's New York counterpart," and later the first rector. The Union of Black Clergy and Laity, now the Union of Black Episcopalians, was organized at St. Philip's Church on Feb. 8, 1968.

St. Philip's College, San Antonio, Texas. St. Philip's College was founded in 1898 by the Rt. Rev. James Steptoe Johnston (1843–1924), the second Bishop of West Texas, as St. Philip's Normal and Industrial School, to prepare African American people for the responsibilities of citizenship. In Sept. 1902 Artemisia Bowden (1884–1969) took charge of the school, and in 1927 it became St. Philip's Junior College and Vocational Institute. By 1940 the diocese had relinquished all ties with the school. In Aug.

1942 St. Philip's ceased to function as a private institution and became a municipal junior college affiliated with San Antonio College.

St. Saviour, Community of. An order for women founded in San Francisco in 1901 by Mrs. Gertrude Ames, who took the name Mother Gertrude Paula. It was founded for the promotion of the honor and worship due to God, for the cultivation of the life of the evangelical counsels, for service in corporal works of mercy, and for parochial mission work. It also sponsored private retreats. The community made altar breads and sold religious cards. The rule was based on the Benedictine Rule. It is no longer in existence.

St. Stephen's College. *See* Bard College, Annandale-on-Hudson, New York.

St. Stephen's College Theological Department. St. Stephen's College (now Bard) was established on Mar. 20, 1860. Under its second warden, the Rev. Thomas Richey, a theology department with a three-year course was established. Three young men began the course, but soon decided "that they could accomplish their objectives more satisfactorily in some of the older seminaries."

St. Thomas African Episcopal Church, Philadelphia. *See* Free African Society.

St. Thomas Choir School, New York City. A boarding school for boys in fifth through eighth grades who sing in the choir of St. Thomas Church on Fifth Avenue in New York City. It was founded in 1919 under the direction of Dr. T. Tertius Noble, organist and choirmaster at St. Thomas Church. It is one of the few remaining choir schools of the type associated with English cathedrals. The school seeks to provide opportunities for religious preparation and growth in a caring, Christian community. The Choir School is owned by St. Thomas Church, and directed by a Board of Trustees including the rector, wardens, and vestry of the church. The operation of the school is supervised by the Choir School Committee. Gordon Roland-Adams joined the Choir School as headmaster in the fall of 1997.

St. Thomas Church, New York. This parish was organized on Dec. 25, 1823. The first church building was constructed in 1824–1825, at the corner of Broadway and Houston Street.

The present building, erected in 1868–1870, and designed by Richard Upjohn, is at the northwest corner of Fifth Avenue and 53rd Street. The cornerstone of this building was laid on Oct. 14, 1868. The first worship service was on Oct. 6, 1870. The building was consecrated on May 15, 1883. Upjohn considered this building his masterpiece.

St. Vincent, International Order of. An order of men, women, boys, and girls who have been called, trained, and authorized to perform one or several lay ministries associated with liturgies. It is a worldwide fellowship of lay ministers associated with sanctuary service such as acolyte, usher, lay reader, lay eucharistic minister, sacristan, chorister, verger, catechist, and acolyte warden. The first Guild of St. Vincent was formed in 1882 at St. Clement's Church in Philadelphia, where the acolytes joined together in prayer, study, and training. The order was officially founded on the Feast of St. Vincent of Saragossa, Jan. 22, 1915, at the Church of the Advent, Boston. In 1939 the order affiliated with the Scottish and British acolyte guilds. In 1970 the order opened membership to girls and women. The Council of Governors voted in 1984 to continue affiliation with the "continuing" Anglican bodies, and to call all Catholic communions to visible and comprehensive unity. The order encourages regular attendance at the eucharist and more careful preparation for its reception. The motto of the order is *Amori Christi et Ecclesiae* (For the love of Christ and His Church).

St. Willibrord, Society of. This organization, also known as the Society of St. Willibrord (Old Catholic Section-USA), was founded in 1908 to promote solidarity between the Old Catholic and Anglican communions, including the fullest use of intercommunion between them.

Salina, Missionary District of. This jurisdiction existed from Oct. 17, 1901, until Nov. 14, 1960. *See* Western Kansas, Diocese of.

Salomon, Richard Georg (Apr. 20, 1884–Feb. 3, 1966). Church historian. He was born in Berlin, Germany. Salomon received his doctoral degree in history from the University of Berlin in 1907, and then served as research assistant for the Monumenta Germaniae Historica. From 1919 until 1934, he was professor of history at the University of Hamburg, but he was dismissed from that position by the Nazis. He was a foe of Adolf Hitler, and left Hamburg for the United

States in 1937. He lectured at the University of Pennsylvania, Swarthmore College, and Bryn Mawr College, before he joined the faculty of Bexley Hall in 1939 as the Cooke Professor of Ecclesiastical History. He remained in this position until he retired in 1961. He was also professor of history at Kenyon College. He served as the official historiographer of the Diocese of Ohio and as unofficial historiographer of Kenyon College. One of his major publications was his editing of William White's *The Case of the Episcopal Churches in the United States Considered* (1953). This book included an introduction and the criticisms of *The Case* which had been previously published. He died in Gambier, Ohio.

Salt Lake, Missionary District of. This jurisdiction existed from Oct. 13, 1898, until Oct. 10, 1907. *See* Utah, Diocese of.

Salutation. A liturgical dialogue of mutual greeting: "The Lord be with you. And also with you." The salutation calls the people back to attention and adds emphasis to important moments in the liturgy. This dialogue of greeting and response is based on Boaz's greeting to the reapers and their answer in Ru 2:4. At the Holy Eucharist, a salutation precedes the collect of the day at the beginning of the liturgy of the word (BCP, p. 357). A second salutation precedes the *sursum corda* at the beginning of the liturgy of the table (BCP, p. 361). A salutation also begins the thanksgiving over the water at Baptism (BCP, p. 306). It precedes the collect at Confirmation (BCP, p. 413), Burial (BCP, p. 493), and Ordination (BCP, p. 515), and begins the ministry of the word at Marriage (BCP, p. 425). A salutation precedes the Lord's Prayer at Morning Prayer (BCP, p. 97) and Evening Prayer (BCP, p. 121). A salutation is also included at the blessing of the palms on Palm Sunday (BCP, p. 271), in the *Exsultet* at the Easter Vigil (BCP, p. 286), and at the consecration of the font in the Consecration of a Church (BCP, p. 570).

Salvation. Eternal life in the fullness of God's love. Salvation is deliverance from anything that threatens to prevent fulfillment and enjoyment of our relationship with God. In the OT, God was experienced as the savior who delivered Israel from bondage in Egypt (Ex 14–15; See Canticle 8, The Song of Moses, BCP, p. 85; Dt 6:21–23). Salvation history is the ongoing story of God's activity and initiative for salvation. The OT records how God reached out to save the people of Israel through the law and the prophets. God's saving deeds in OT history are celebrated in the liturgy of the word at the Easter Vigil (BCP, pp. 288–291).

Christians affirm that the life, death, and resurrection of Jesus constitute the climax of salvation history. Jesus is our savior who redeems us from sin and death. As we share Christ's life, we are restored to right relationship with God and one another. Despite our sins and insufficiency, we are made righteous and justified in Christ. We share the saving benefits of Jesus' victory over sin and death. Without God's help for our salvation, we die with Adam. But we live in Christ as we share his life by faith (1 Cor 15:22). Christ has "brought us out of sin into righteousness, out of death into life" (BCP, p. 368).

Salvation in Christ is made available to us through the Spirit, especially in the life and sacraments of the church. By the water of baptism, we are buried with Christ in his death and share his resurrection (BCP, p. 306; see Rom 6:3–4). The consecrated elements of the eucharist are for God's people "the bread of life and the cup of salvation," by which we share the body and blood of Christ (BCP, pp. 363, 375; see Jn 6:53–56; 1 Cor 10:16–17).

The gospel proclaims the good news of salvation in Christ (see Jn 3:16–17). We may participate in a saving process of sanctification by which the saving life of Christ is increasingly the reality of our own lives. This process is completed and revealed in Christ, and it is begun in us through faith in him. Completed union with God is the end of this saving process. In Christ, we come to be at one with God. This union with God is not yet completed, and the eschatological Kingdom of God is not yet fulfilled. But the coming of the Kingdom of God has been inaugurated by Christ. The Kingdom of God was revealed in Jesus, who ate with outcasts, forgave sinners, healed the sick, and raised the dead (see Lk 5:17–32; Jn 11:1–44).

We are now in the "in between times." We can know the present reality of salvation in Christ, even though the Kingdom of God is not yet complete in our world, our church, or our hearts. The fulfillment of the Kingdom of God is associated with Jesus' second coming in power and glory. Our hope is that all humanity and all creation will be united in God's love in the fullness of time, and that "nothing, not even death, shall separate us from the love of God which is in Christ Jesus our Lord" (BCP, p. 862; see Rom 8:38–39). *See* Atonement; *see* Eschatology; *see* Heaven; *see* Redeemer; *see* Righteousness; *see* Soteriology.

Salvation History. The study of salvation history identifies the theological elements and influences in historical narratives. God's offer of salvation and humanity's response to that offer are expressed and visible in history. The importance of the biblical narratives of salvation history is reflected in the scripture readings for the Easter Vigil of the BCP (pp. 288–291), including the story of creation, the flood, Abraham's sacrifice of Isaac, Israel's deliverance at the Red Sea, and other stories of redemption and renewal. The celebrant may introduce the scripture readings at the Easter Vigil with the invitation, "Let us hear the record of God's saving deeds in history, how he saved his people in ages past; and let us pray that our God will bring each of us to the fullness of redemption." The concept is based on the German term *Heilsgeschichte* (history of salvation, or redemptive history). It was used by J. C. von Hofmann (1810–1877), who urged that all sacred history can be deduced from the fact of personal conversion.

Sancta sanctis. As early as the fourth century, eastern liturgies contained the *Sancta sanctis*, "the holy for the holy" or "holy things for holy people," at a showing of the sacrament to the people immediately before the administration of communion. A typical response of the people was "One is holy, one is Lord, Jesus Christ, to the glory of God the Father." This text, translated "The Gifts of God for the People of God," entered the BCP at the 1979 revision. Its use is optional in Rite 1, but required in Rite 2 (BCP, p. 364). This acclamation may be followed by a sentence based on the Words of Administration of the Bread of the 1552 BCP, "Take them in remembrance that Christ died for you, and feed on him in your hearts by faith, with thanksgiving" (BCP, p. 365).

Sanctification. A theological term which derives from the Latin *sanctus*, "holy." In its proper sense "holy" refers to the holiness of God, but in a derived sense it applies to all those who are made holy. By extension it thus refers to all those who, in Christ, participate in the holiness of God through baptism. In the western or Latin theological tradition sanctification refers to the process of becoming holy through the transforming power of the Holy Spirit. At the time of the Reformation controversy arose about whether sanctification was to be considered a change made in a person, a process begun and continuing on through the sanctifying grace of the Holy Spirit, or whether sanctifying grace was to be limited to the grace received at initial justification. Lutherans have tended to limit sanctification to the work of justification, while Calvinists have been willing to speak of sanctification in terms of obedience.

Anglican formularies have tended to speak of sanctification as the process of God's work within us by means of which we grow into the fullness of the redeemed life. In the 1979 BCP, sanctification has been closely associated with the Holy Eucharist, as in the prayer of thanksgiving: "Sanctify us also that we may faithfully receive this holy Sacrament, and serve you in unity, constancy, and peace; and at the last day bring us with all your saints into the joy of your eternal kingdom" (Eucharistic Prayer A, BCP, p. 363); and: "We pray you, gracious God, to send your Holy Spirit upon these gifts that they may be the Sacrament of the Body of Christ and his Blood of the new Covenant. Unite us to your Son in his sacrifice, that we may be acceptable through him, being sanctified by the Holy Spirit" (Eucharistic Prayer B, BCP, p. 369).

Sanctorale. The section of a service book such as a missal or breviary that provided the variable portions of services for the fixed dates of the church calendar. The propers for the fixed holy days appeared in the *Sanctorale*, with the exception of those in the Christmas season which were in the *Temporale*. The propers for the seasons of the church year that were centered on the date of Christmas or Easter also appeared in the *Temporale*.

Sanctuary. 1) Holy place, usually the worship space of a church. Sanctuary may mean the area around the altar, especially in liturgical churches. It may be separated from the rest of the church by an altar rail. It may refer to the entire chancel area, including the choir and/or the space reserved for the clergy. It may also refer to the entire interior of the church where worship takes place. 2) Historically, a sanctuary would be a place of safe refuge for criminals or fugitives. This is also known as the right of sanctuary. It is based on the understanding that holy places such as churches are not subject to the powers of this world. In modern times, churches have provided sanctuary for refugees and illegal aliens. The right of sanctuary in cities of refuge was available in OT times for one who killed a person without intent (Nm 35:9–15; Ex 21:13).

Sanctuary Lamp. A lamp or candle which burns near the reserved sacrament when the reservation is near the altar. *See* Reservation of the Sacrament.

Sanctus, The. From the Latin for "holy," a hymn of adoration and praise which begins, "Holy, holy, holy, Lord God of Hosts." It typically follows the preface in the eucharistic prayer (BCP, pp. 334, 341, 362, 367, 371, 373, 402, 404). It is sung or said by the celebrant and people. The *Sanctus* is based on the song of the seraphim as recorded in Isaiah's vision of the Lord in the year King Uzziah died (Is 6:1–3; see Rv 4:8). The congregation may be said to share in the praise of God that is continually offered by the whole company of heaven. The *Sanctus* has been accompanied by bells since the fifteenth century in some places.

Sanctus Bell. A bell rung by a server during the eucharist to emphasize and call attention to particular moments in the liturgy. The bell may be a small hand bell or set of bells, or a gong rung with a clapper, or the tower bell of the church. The term is based on the practice of ringing the bell three times during the *Sanctus*. The practice of accompanying the *Sanctus* with bells dates from the fifteenth century. It is also traditionally rung during the institution narrative when the celebrant elevates the elements of bread and wine, especially in parishes with an Anglo-catholic piety. Since the practice emphasizes certain elements of the eucharistic prayer more than others, some prefer to ring the bell only after the conclusion of the eucharistic prayer, including the great Amen. *See* Bells and Smells.

San Diego, Diocese of. The 1973 General Convention voted to divide the Diocese of Los Angeles. The primary convention of the Diocese of San Diego met at St. Paul's Church, San Diego, Dec. 7–8, 1973. It includes the following counties: Imperial, a portion of Riverside, and San Diego. On Jan. 25, 1985, St. Paul's Church, San Diego, became St. Paul's Cathedral.

San Joaquin, Diocese of. The 1910 General Convention voted to divide the Diocese of California, and establish the Missionary District of San Joaquin. It includes the following counties: Alpine, Calaveras, Fresno, Inyo, Kern, Kings, Madera, Mariposa, Merced, Mono, San Joaquin, Stanislaus, Tulare, and Tuolumne. The primary convocation of the Missionary District met at St. James' Church, Fresno, May 9, 1911. On Jan. 28, 1925, St. Paul's Pro-Cathedral, Fresno, was set apart as St. James' Cathedral. The primary convention of the Diocese of San Joaquin met at St. James' Cathedral, Fresno, Nov. 4, 1961.

Sarcophagus. Ancient ornamented coffin in the form of a chest and lid. The term is from Latin words that mean "flesh-eating." This refers to the belief that a sarcophagus lined with caustic limestone would cause the body of the deceased to dissolve within forty days. Sarcophagi were made of stone, terra-cotta, wood, marble, alabaster, or metal. Etruscan sarcophagi have been dated from the sixth century B.C., and often had an image of the deceased person on the lid. The deceased might be portrayed as reclining on a bed. The "anthropoid" sarcophagus was shaped like a human being, and crowned with a mask. It spread from Egypt in the fifth century B.C. Greek sarcophagi date from the fourth century. They were decorated with ornamentation and figures. The earliest Christian sarcophagi have been dated from the end of the first century to the early third century. Sarcophagi were used by both Christians and pagans during this time. Sarcophagi with Christian designs have been dated from the fourth century. Christian sarcophagi often displayed biblical scenes, such as Jonah and the whale or the raising of Lazarus. Sarcophagi provide a significant record of the early illustration of Christian ideas and historical documentation of art in the late Roman empire.

Sarum Rite. Liturgy based on practices at the cathedral of Salisbury, England. Sarum is the Latin name for Salisbury. The Synod of Whitby (664) decided for Roman rather than Celtic liturgical usage, but British books still contained non-Roman elements. Secular cathedrals were strengthened after the Norman Conquest, and stronger centers influenced surrounding areas. The 1549 BCP mentions uses of Salisbury, Hereford, Bangor, York, and Lincoln. These were not different rites but variations in words or actions or placement within the Roman rite. *Consuetudinarium*, or the book of customs, of Salisbury was earlier attributed to Osmund, Bishop of Sarum, 1078–1099, and founder of the cathedral at Old Sarum. The Salisbury use was therefore called Sarum Rite. It is now associated with Richard le Poore, bishop 1217–1228, who moved the see to Salisbury and initiated construction of a new cathedral. Later books (*Ordinal, Customary*, and *"New" Ordinal*) gave greater definition to the use. Because of the convenience of these books and the reputation of Salisbury as a model, this use spread over much of the British Isles. In Mar. 1543 the Salisbury Breviary was imposed upon the whole Province of Canterbury. It is generally the use of Salisbury that is the source of medieval materials retained in the 1549 BCP.

Satterlee, Henry Yates (Jan. 11, 1843–Feb. 22, 1908). Bishop and founder of the Washington Cathedral. He was born in New York City. Satterlee received his B.A. from Columbia College in 1863 and studied for the ordained ministry at the General Theological Seminary. He was ordained deacon on Nov. 21, 1865, and priest on Jan. 11, 1867. He began his ministry as an assistant at Zion Parish, Wappinger Falls, New York, and later became the rector. In 1882 Satterlee became the rector of Calvary Church, New York, and served there until he was consecrated the first Bishop of Washington on Mar. 25, 1896. He served as Bishop of Washington until his death. Under his leadership the Cathedral of St. Peter and St. Paul was founded, and the cornerstone was laid on Sept. 29, 1907. He saw it as a cathedral for the whole nation. Satterlee believed that a cathedral was the bishop's church, where the bishop could exercise pastoral ministry. The cathedral would be the mother church of the diocese and would be the center of the diocese's missionary and educational work. The most important of his books is *A Creedless Gospel and the Gospel Creed* (1895), in which he stressed the revelation of God in Jesus Christ. Satterlee died in Washington. *See* Cathedral Church of Saint Peter and Saint Paul in the City and Diocese of Washington, The.

Savage, Thomas Staughton (June 7, 1804–Dec. 29, 1880). The first medical missionary sent out by the Episcopal Church. He was born in Middletown (now Cromwell), Connecticut, and graduated from Yale in 1825. He received his M.D. from the Yale Medical School in 1833 and graduated from the Virginia Theological Seminary in 1836. Savage was ordained deacon on July 17, 1836, and priest on Oct. 23, 1836. On Nov. 1, 1836, he sailed for Africa as a missionary of the Domestic and Foreign Missionary Society and reached Cape Palmas, Liberia, on Dec. 25, 1836. He resigned his missionary work in Dec. 1846. In 1848–1849 he was the rector of St. James' Church, Livingston, Alabama, and from 1849 to 1857 he was the rector of Trinity Church, Pass Christian, Mississippi. From 1857 to 1868 he lived in Pass Christian and worked in education. In 1869 he became the associate secretary of the Foreign Committee of the Board of Missions, and from 1871 until his death he was rector of the Church of the Ascension, Rhinecliff, New York. While in Africa, Savage studied the bones and skulls of an animal that proved to be the gorilla, which was previously unknown. He also published scientific articles. He died in Rhinecliff.

Sayre, John Nevin (Feb. 4, 1884–Sept. 13, 1977). Founder of the Episcopal Peace Fellowship. He was born in Bethlehem, Pennsylvania. Sayre received his B.A. from Princeton in 1907 and his B.D. from Union Theological Seminary, New York, in 1910. He was ordained deacon on Oct. 31, 1911, and priest on Nov. 7, 1912. In 1911–1912 and 1914–1915, Sayre was an instructor at Princeton. In 1913 he was a missionary in the Missionary District of Kankow, China. From 1915 until 1916 he was assistant minister, and from 1916 until 1919 he was rector of Christ Church, Suffern, New York. Sayre was a founding member of the American branch of the Fellowship of Reconciliation in 1915. He then served as its director from 1924 until 1935. In 1939 Sayre convened a meeting of like-minded members of the Episcopal Church which led to the formal establishment of the Episcopal Pacifist (now Peace) Fellowship. He served as its national chair, 1962–1967. His commitment to peace and active non-violent alternatives to war shaped the EPF. Sayre was chairman of the International Fellowship of Witness, 1935–1955, and president of the National Peace Conference, 1935–1938. In recognition of Sayre's life and work in the cause of peace, the Episcopal Peace Fellowship established the John Nevin Sayre peacemakers' award. Its first presentation was made during the General Convention on Sept. 13, 1979, the second anniversary of Sayre's death. He died in South Nyack, New York. *See* Fellowship of Reconciliation, The (FOR); *see* Episcopal Peace Fellowship, The (EPF); *see* Pacifism.

"SC." *See* Oil, Holy.

Scapular. A sleeveless garment that hangs from the shoulders to the ankles. The term is derived from the Latin for "shoulder-blades." The scapular is a wide band of material, usually black, with an opening for the head. It forms part of the regular monastic habit for many religious orders. It is typically worn over a cassock or other similar garment. In some churches, a scapular is worn by servers or members of the choir.

Scarf. *See* Tippet.

Schereschewsky, Samuel Isaac Joseph (May 6, 1831–Oct. 15, 1906). Missionary bishop and translator. He was born in Tauroggen, Russian Lithuania, to Jewish parents. He became convinced that he should become a Christian and in 1854 came to the United States. He decided to enter the Presbyterian ministry and studied at Western Theological Seminary, Allegheny, Pennsylvania, 1855–1858. He then joined the Episcopal Church and studied at the General Theological Seminary, Oct. 1858–May 1859. At General Seminary he decided to devote his whole life to the China mission. He was ordained deacon on July 7, 1859, sailed for China on July 13, and was ordained priest on Oct. 28, 1860. His greatest work was translating Christian writings for the Chinese and the founding of St. John's College, which opened on Sept. 1, 1879. The House of Bishops elected him "Missionary Bishop of Shanghai, having Episcopal jurisdiction in China" on Oct. 13, 1876, and he was consecrated at Grace Church, New York, by Bishop Benjamin B. Smith on Oct. 31, 1877. In 1881 he became ill and almost died. He resigned as bishop on Sept. 30, 1883. He spent the rest of his life translating, even though he could write only by pressing the keys of the typewriter with one finger of one hand. He died in Tokyo. His life and ministry are commemorated in the Episcopal calendar of the church year on Oct. 14.

Schism. This word of Greek origin means a rip, tear, split, or division. In ecclesiastical terms, it is a formal and willful separation from the unity of the church. The term is used in the NT for any kind of quarrel or division. Its meaning was later restricted to divisions of the church having a non-doctrinal basis, such as divisions over disciplinary or organizational matters. Heresy is separation for doctrinal reasons. In the middle ages, the major schisms were that between east and west, which began in 1054, and that within the western (Roman) church from 1378–1417, when there were two Popes and then three. In the Eastern Orthodox Church, the major schism has been that of the Old Believers in later seventeenth-century Russia. Today the term is generally used by the Roman Catholic and Orthodox churches to refer to separations from themselves. In the Episcopal/Anglican and Protestant churches, the term is typically used to designate schisms within the church as a whole. In the Episcopal Church it is often said that the unity of the church was sundered by schisms that have separated the Orthodox, Roman, Anglican, and Protestant churches from one another in various ways. The earliest significant schism from the Episcopal Church was that of the Reformed Episcopal Church, which began in 1873. There were also some smaller schisms from it in the later twentieth century over Prayer Book revision and the ordination of women.

Schola Cantorum. A school for church singers. The first Roman *schola cantorum* has been dated from the fourth century. It provided music for papal masses. The Roman *schola cantorum* was reorganized by Gregory the Great (c. 540–604), who served as Pope from 590 to 604. Gregorian Chant developed in the Roman *schola cantorum* during the seventh and eighth centuries. The Roman *schola cantorum* was a center that provided instructors in chant for other churches and institutions. The use of Gregorian Chant spread in the western church. The Roman *schola cantorum* served as a model for other schools that were established in the west. These schools of singers diminished in importance in the later middle ages as secular musicians became increasingly involved in church music. The term *schola cantorum* may still be used to indicate a choir school, a school for church singers, or a place where chant is taught.

Scholarly Engagement with Anglican Doctrine (SEAD). SEAD was organized in 1989 at the Virginia Theological Seminary to insure persistent, widespread, thoughtful engagement with the theological heritage of historic Anglicanism, along with sustained reflection upon the content, form, and implications of its contemporary reinterpretation. SEAD's purpose is to affirm the tradition of history and engage the challenges of modernity. It seeks to promote a creative engagement between the "faith once delivered to the saints" and the modern world. While affirming the principle of comprehensiveness, SEAD is concerned to insure that Anglican comprehensiveness does not degenerate into theological incoherence. SEAD has seven study groups: Anglican Studies, Biblical Studies, Ethics, Evangelism, Pastoralia, Theology, and Worship & Spirituality. Its first newsletter was called *SEAD* and began publication in June 1991. With vol. 3, number 4 (Oct./Nov. 1993), the name was changed to *The Harvest.*

Scholasticism. A movement or approach to theology in Christianity which developed during the middle ages. It flourished from the time of Anselm of Canterbury (1033–1109) until the beginning of the "modern" period in the philosophy of Descartes (1596–1650). It included such noted theologians and philosophers as Anselm, Peter Lombard, Abelard, Bonaventure, Thomas Aquinas, Duns Scotus, and William of Ockham.

The name derives from the development in the middle ages of the great centers of learning, first in the monasteries and cathedrals, and later in the emerging universities. The medieval period was a time of considerable intellectual ferment, and the various "schools" of theology and philosophy debated and analyzed Christian faith in light of the emerging new learning.

Scholasticism was especially important in two areas: the development of the science of logic and the analysis of the relationships between faith and reason, grace and nature, theology and philosophy. The schools differed in their analyses, but all shared a common conviction that the relationship of human beings to God needed systematic analysis. Among the Scholastics, Thomas Aquinas and Bonaventure have been the most important for the development of subsequent theology.

The theological and philosophical work of Thomas Aquinas was of considerable importance for the Anglican Richard Hooker in his *Laws of Ecclesiastical Polity.* Hooker followed Aquinas's basic teaching that reason is fulfilled in faith, the natural order in grace, and human law in the divine law. *See* Aquinas, Thomas; *see* Hooker, Richard.

School of Theology of the Diocese of Arkansas. *See* Arkansas Theological Chautauqua School.

School of Theology, University of the South. One of the recognized, accredited seminaries of the Episcopal Church. The first meeting of the trustees of the University of the South was held at Lookout Mountain, Tennessee, on July 4, 1857. The cornerstone was laid at Sewanee, Tennessee, on Oct. 10, 1860, but the Civil War delayed the construction of buildings. A school of theology was to be at the center of the university. The university finally opened on Sept. 18, 1868, with four professors and nine students. After William Porcher DuBose came to the university as chaplain in 1871, students began studying for the ordained ministry with him. The first dean of the Theological Department was elected on July 29, 1878. The new building for the Theological Department, St. Luke's Memorial Hall, was opened on Mar. 25, 1879. In that same year the Theological Department faculty was separated from the faculty of the College of Arts and Sciences. In 1948 the name was changed from the Theological Department to the School of Theology. *See* DuBose, William Porcher.

SCOM. *See* Seminary Consultation on Mission (SCOM).

Scott, Thomas Fielding (Mar. 12, 1808–July 14, 1867). First Missionary Bishop of Oregon and Washington Territory. He was born in Iredell County, North Carolina. Scott graduated from Franklin College, now the University of Georgia, Athens, Georgia, in 1829. He was licensed to preach in the Presbyterian Church and served in Georgia and Tennessee. In 1842 Scott met Bishops James Hervey Otey and Leonidas Polk. He decided to enter the Episcopal Church. He was ordained deacon on Mar. 12, 1843, and priest on Feb. 24, 1844. Scott was the rector of St. James Church, Marietta, Georgia, and then rector of Trinity Church, Columbus, Georgia. On Jan. 8, 1854, he was consecrated the first Missionary Bishop of Oregon and Washington Territory. This area is now divided into four dioceses. Scott died in New York City.

Scripture. This word comes from the Latin for "writings" and refers to a collection of the most important documents in a given religious community. Many different religions have scriptures. The term "canon," which means a rule or listing, refers to the list of items included in a scripture.

The word "Bible" is used by Christians to refer to the OT and NT, the two parts of scripture. Other books, called the Apocrypha, are often included in the Bible (BCP, p. 853). In the Jewish tradition the OT is called Hebrew Scripture. When early Christians began to select writings for their scripture, they wanted to keep the Hebrew scripture and therefore chose to use the titles Old Testament (or covenant) for the Jewish writings and New Testament for the normative Christian writings. The Apocrypha is a collection of books written by people of the old covenant. The Articles of Religion note that these books may be read "for example of life and instruction of manners," but are not used to establish any doctrine (Art. VI, BCP, p. 868). Selections from the Apocrypha are included in the BCP lectionaries for the Holy Eucharist and the Daily Office.

The selection of writings to be included in the NT was not final until about 360 A.D. Some Christians did not want to include the Gospel of John or the Second Letter of Peter. After a long period of time, the currently accepted canon of scripture was determined on the basis of apostolic authorship or attribution and widespread acceptance of the texts included in the canon.

All persons ordained as bishops, priests, or deacons in the Episcopal Church must solemnly declare at their ordination that they "do believe the Holy Scriptures of the Old and New Testaments to be the Word of God, and

to contain all things necessary to salvation. . . ." (BCP, pp. 513, 526, 538). Scripture, along with tradition and reason, is one of the sources of authority in Anglicanism. Selections from scripture for the Episcopal Church's services of the Holy Eucharist and the Daily Offices are provided by the lectionaries of the BCP (pp. 889–1001).

Scudder, Vida Dutton (Dec. 15, 1861–Oct. 9, 1954). Educator and Christian Socialist. She was born in Madura, India, and was initially named Julia Davida. Her father was a Congregationalist missionary. She and her mother returned to Auburndale, Massachusetts after he died. When she was a teenager, she and her mother joined the Episcopal Church. Scudder received her B.A. in 1884 and her M.A. in 1889, both from Smith College. In 1884–1885, she studied at Oxford University. In 1887 she joined the English Department of Wellesley College and remained there until her retirement in 1927. At Wellesley she combined her love of letters with a concern for social reform. In 1889 Scudder joined the Society of the Companions of the Holy Cross, a devotional order. In 1890 she joined the Society of Christian Socialists in Boston, which was founded by W. D. P. Bliss. She was also a member of the Brotherhood of the Carpenter and was active in the Christian Social Union. In 1911 Scudder helped to found the Episcopal Church Socialist League, and in 1919 she helped to establish the Church League for Industrial Democracy. After World War I she became a pacifist and in 1923 she joined the Fellowship of Reconciliation. During her retirement years she studied the Franciscans. In 1931 she published *The Franciscan Adventure*, which made her a leading Franciscan scholar. Among her many books were *Social Ideals in English Letters* (1898), *The Social Teachings of the Christian Year* (1921), and her autobiography, *On Journey* (1937). Scudder died in Wellesley, Massachusetts. *See* Society of Christian Socialists.

Seabury Divinity School, Faribault, Minnesota. *See* Seabury-Western Theological Seminary.

Seabury Press. A church-owned publishing house that was sold in 1984. Lewis Bliss Whittemore (1885–1965), Bishop of Western Michigan, called attention to the lack of progress in Christian education throughout the Episcopal Church in 1946. The result of his action was a revitalized, reorganized Department of Christian Education, which began a project called the "New Curriculum," now known as the Seabury Series. As the project developed, an agency was needed to produce and publish the books and pamphlets. In 1951 the National Council (now the Executive Council), established the Seabury Press. On Sept. 1, 1951, Leon McCauley was appointed the first Manager of Seabury Press, named after Samuel Seabury, the first American Episcopal bishop. It officially opened for business on Jan. 2, 1952. Seabury Press was incorporated in Feb. 1952 with the Presiding Bishop as Chairman. Although responsible to the Department of Christian Education, it received no funds from the church's budget. Beginning in 1953, Seabury Press published Prayer Books and Prayer Book/Hymnal combinations. Seabury Press was a publishing house, not a printing plant. It designed books and book jackets as well as getting manuscripts ready for publication. Seabury Press went out of business in 1984. Winston Press acquired its publishing assets. *See* Seabury, Samuel.

Seabury, Samuel (Nov. 30, 1729–Feb. 25, 1796). First bishop in the Episcopal Church. He was born in Groton, Connecticut, and graduated from Yale College in 1748. He read theology under his father and then studied medicine at the University of Edinburgh, 1752–1753. Seabury was ordained deacon on Dec. 21, 1753, and priest on Dec. 23, 1753, in England. He was a missionary of the Society for the Propagation of the Gospel at New Brunswick, New Jersey, 1754–1757, and rector at Jamaica, New York, 1757–1766. From 1766 to 1776 he served as rector of St. Peter's Church, Westchester, New York, and from 1776 to 1783 he was in private medical practice and chaplain to British troops at Staten Island and New York. He wrote forceful pamphlets in defense of loyalty to the British Crown. On Mar. 25, 1783, he was elected Bishop of Connecticut and was consecrated at Aberdeen, Scotland, Nov. 14, 1784, by three nonjuring bishops of the Scottish Episcopal Church. He also served as Bishop of Rhode Island, 1790–1796. Seabury served as Presiding Bishop, Oct. 5, 1789–Sept. 8, 1792. He was a high churchman in the tradition of the Nonjurors and the Caroline Divines. A valid episcopacy and the threefold orders of clergy were central concerns for him. He died in New London, Connecticut. Seabury and the passing of the episcopate to the Episcopal Church are commemorated on Nov. 14 in the Episcopal calendar of the church year. *See* Loyalty Oath to the English Sovereign.

Seabury, Samuel (June 9, 1801–Oct. 10, 1872). Priest, educator, and editor. The grandson and namesake of the first bishop of the Episcopal Church, he was born in New

London, Connecticut. Although he was unable to obtain a formal college education, he pursued classical and theological studies privately. He was ordained deacon on Apr. 12, 1826, and priest on July 7, 1828. He served in the Diocese of New York for his entire ministry. Seabury was rector of the Church of the Annunciation, New York, from 1838 to 1868. He also served at the General Theological Seminary, New York, as professor of evidences, 1835–1838, and as professor of biblical learning, 1862–1872. Seabury edited *The Churchman* from Sept. 1, 1833, until Feb. 1849. During his tenure as editor, he championed high church theology and welcomed the influence of the Oxford Movement on American church life. Seabury was the author of a number of books, the most notable being *American Slavery . . . Justified by the Law of Nature*. This defense of slavery in the South was published in 1861 at the beginning of the Civil War. It caused serious scandal both inside and outside the Episcopal Church. Seabury died in New York City.

Seabury Series, The. A comprehensive parish education program of the Episcopal Church that was published between 1948 and 1970. The program included a series of six basic books, *The Church's Teaching Series*, which became the foundational subject matter resource of the adult materials and of the publications for Sunday church school. These materials were published by the Seabury Press, and known as "The Seabury Series." An essential part of the total program was leadership training, which included basic training courses for clergy and lay leaders at the College of Preachers (Washington Cathedral), mobile training teams that visited dioceses for eight years, weekend parish life conferences providing basic training for parish leaders, and a two-week laboratory training program that enrolled more than 2,600 clergy and lay leaders, including a special lab for bishops.

Seabury-Western Theological Seminary. An accredited seminary of the Episcopal Church, located in Evanston, Illinois. Seabury-Western was the result of the merger of Seabury Divinity School, Faribault, Minnesota, and the Western Theological Seminary, Chicago, on July 1, 1933. Seabury Divinity School was founded in 1858 by James Lloyd Breck. It was first called Seabury Divinity Hall. Western Theological Seminary opened on Sept. 29, 1885, under the leadership of Bishop William Edward McLaren (1831–1905) of Chicago. *See* Breck, James Lloyd; *see* Bishop Seabury University.

SEAD. *See* Scholarly Engagement with Anglican Doctrine (SEAD).

Seal of Baptism. After baptism, the bishop or priest places a hand on the head of the newly baptized person, marking the forehead with the sign of the cross, addressing each one by name and saying, "You are sealed by the Holy Spirit in Baptism and marked as Christ's own for ever" (BCP, p. 308). This marking of the newly baptized with the sign of the cross is also known as signation or consignation. Chrism may be used, but it is not required. The signation may be done immediately after the administration of the water at baptism, or it may follow the prayer for the gift of the Spirit after baptism (BCP, p. 308). This action is not performed by a deacon or lay person who administers baptism. If a deacon or lay person administers baptism in an emergency, the signation may be performed by a bishop or priest at the next public baptism.

In Judaism, the newly baptized person was marked on the forehead with the Taw (T), the last letter of the alphabet, indicating the name of God. The newly baptized person was "branded" as God's sheep, slave, and soldier. A similar post-baptismal practice continued in the Christian church with the sign of the cross on the forehead by which we are "marked as Christ's own for ever." The use of chrism is associated with incorporation into Christ, the "Anointed One." It is also associated with the historic anointing of kings and priests, and the cleansing of a bath. The *Apostolic Tradition* of Hippolytus, dated about 215, indicates that the newly baptized were anointed and signed with a cross on their foreheads. The post-baptismal anointing was almost universal practice in the church by the late fourth or early fifth century. The 1549 Prayer Book included a post-baptismal anointing, but this was not continued in the 1552 BCP. A sign of the cross on the forehead replaced the post-baptismal anointing in the 1552 Prayer Book. The signation was made optional by the 1789 BCP, but it was once again required by the 1928 BCP. The 1979 BCP restored the rite of chrismation at baptism. The baptismal service includes a form for the consecration of the chrism by the bishop (BCP, p. 307). *See* Chrism.

Seal of Confession. A penitent may seek a priest for listening to his or her confession of sins, declaring genuine sorrow and promising amendment of life together with restitution, where possible, to those wronged. The priest in turn gives counsel, penance, and absolution. It is understood by both that the confession is under the "seal." Under no circumstances may the information given be revealed by the priest, unless the penitent gives permission. The penitent may rely on this implicitly. In some states, the priest may be asked by a court of law to divulge information but must refuse even though this may lead to imprisonment. It would be prudent for those hearing confessions to discover what provisions are legally in force for the protection of such privileged information.

Seal of the Episcopal Church. *See* Episcopal Church Flag and Seal.

Seamen's Church Institute of New York and New Jersey. Founded in 1834 as the Young Men's Church Missionary Society, its forty-two charter members were drawn from Episcopal parishes in Manhattan, Brooklyn, and Staten Island. The society sought to improve the treatment of merchant seamen entering the Port of New York. At this time there were many bad influences and violent threats along the waterfront of the port. The society brought the church to the seamen by building and mooring floating chapels in New York Harbor. The first floating chapel, the Church of Our Savior, was seventy feet long and thirty feet wide. It continued to serve seamen in the port until 1866. The second floating chapel, the Church of the Holy Comforter, was built by the Institute in 1846. It was used until 1869. The third floating chapel, Church of Our Savior, was completed in 1869. It remained in service for forty-one years. This chapel was first opened for services on Jan. 9, 1870, with Horatio Potter, Bishop of New York, officiating.

The Seamen's Church Institute is now an ecumenical, voluntary agency. Its three program divisions are the Center for Maritime Education, the Center for Seafarers' Rights, and the Center for Seafarers' Services. The headquarters of the Institute is in Lower Manhattan. It operates three seafarers' centers in New York and New Jersey, and a training facility in Paducah, Kentucky, that serves mariners on America's inland waterways.

Seamen's Church Institute of Philadelphia. The Episcopal Church's involvement in maritime ministry began in New York City. On Nov. 3, 1847, three members of Christ Church, Philadelphia, Joseph E. Hover, James E. Booth, and William C. Kent agreed to organize a "Church Mission for Seamen," select a suitable clergyman, and erect "a Floating Church." On Dec. 7, 1847, they adopted the constitution of the Churchmen's Missionary Association for Seamen of the

Port of Philadelphia. The Floating Church of the Redeemer was dedicated on Jan. 11, 1849. In 1908 it was named the Seamen's Church Institute of Philadelphia. It is an ecumenical agency closely associated with the Episcopal Church. The institute serves U.S. and international merchant and cruise ship seafarers on a fifty-mile stretch of the Delaware River from the Port of Philadelphia to the Port of Camden, New Jersey. Its main activity is a ministry of hospitality and justice.

Search Committee. A group charged to identify candidates for the position of bishop, rector, or other ministry in the life of the church. It may be the responsibility of the search committee to clarify the job description and identify the qualifications that are needed for the job. It is often the responsibility of the search committee to advertise the position or otherwise seek applications and nominations; to review applications, supporting documents, and references; to interview applicants; and to recommend one or more "finalists" to the body or group charged with final responsibility for the selection or appointment.

Seasonal Blessings. The *BOS* provides seasonal blessings for Advent, Christmas season, Epiphany, Easter season, the Day of Pentecost, the First Sunday after Pentecost: Trinity Sunday, and All Saints. In place of a seasonal blessing in Lent, a solemn Prayer over the People (*Super Populum*) is used. The seasonal blessings may be used by a bishop or priest whenever a blessing is appropriate. The *BOS* provides two forms for each seasonal blessing. There is a threefold form with an Amen at the end of each sentence, leading into a trinitarian blessing, and a single-sentence formula leading directly into the blessing. The *BOS* also provides forms for Blessing of Homes at Epiphany and Easter. These services may conclude with appropriate seasonal blessings.

Seasons of the Church Year. *See* Church Year.

Second Song of Isaiah, The. *See* Quaerite Dominum.

Secularizing a Consecrated Building. This service is used to deconsecrate and secularize a consecrated building that is to be taken down or used for other purposes. The form for this service is provided by the *BOS*. The presiding minister may be the bishop or a deputy appointed by the bishop. The altar and all consecrated and dedicated objects that are to be preserved are removed from the building before the service begins. The service begins with an address by the presiding minister. This statement acknowledges that for many the building has been "hallowed by cherished memories." The address prays that those who suffer a sense of loss will be comforted by knowledge that the presence of God is not tied to any place or building. The presiding minister also states the intention of the diocese that the congregation will not be deprived of the ministry of Word and sacrament. The bishop's Declaration of Secularization is then read. It revokes the Sentence of Consecration, and remits the building and all objects in it for any lawful and reputable use in accordance with the laws of the land. After the Declaration of Secularization is read, the presiding minister and people say the Lord's Prayer. The presiding minister says the concluding prayers. The peace may be exchanged at the end of the service.

Seder Meal. At this traditional Jewish Passover meal the story of the Exodus (*haggadah*) is read and ritual actions are performed. The seder today consists of fourteen elements: 1) *Kiddush*, the blessing of wine and the day, 2) *Urehatz*, washing of hands, 3) *Karpas*, eating green herbs, 4) *Yachatz*, breaking the middle matzo, 5) *Maggid*, the Passover story, 6) *Rahatz*, washing of hands, 7) *Motzee-Matzo*, blessing the unleavened bread, 8) *Maror*, eating bitter herb, 9) *Korekh*, eating bitter herb and matzo together, 10) *Shulhan Orekh*, the Passover meal, 11) *Tzafun*, the afikomen (finding a piece of matzo hidden for the children), 12) *Berakah*, grace after the meal, 13) *Hallel*, recital of the Hallelujah psalms, and 14) *Neertza*, the conclusion of the seder. It is unclear how much of this order was in place in the first century, but it was at a meal similar to this that Jesus celebrated the Passover. Because of its apparent connection with the institution of the eucharist, Christians have sometimes celebrated Christian Seders. These have sometimes been offensive to Jews. The celebration of a Christian Seder during Holy Week is considered inappropriate because it is a festal celebration.

Sedilia. This triple seat in the sanctuary of a church is for the celebrant, deacon, and sub-deacon at solemn Mass. It is usually a bench with a back divided into thirds. In some stone churches the sedilia are incorporated into the north wall of the sanctuary. Today, the use of a single seat for the presider with chairs or benches for assisting ministers and acolytes is more typical.

See. The bishop's throne or chair. The term is from the Latin, "seat." The episcopal throne is a symbol of the bishop's authority and jurisdiction. It is typically located in the cathedral of the diocese. By extension, the location of the cathedral or church with the bishop's throne is known as the bishop's see. For example, New Orleans is the see city of the Diocese of Louisiana.

Seed & Harvest. A newsletter for the friends of Trinity Episcopal School for Ministry. It began publication in July 1980.

Seedlings, Inc. A ministry providing Christian Education materials. It has a special concern to address the needs of very small churches. The Rev. Betty Works Fuller began publishing a Sunday School curriculum in 1977 for St. James Church, La Grange, Texas. Other churches joined her in the effort. By 1979 the material, now called *Seedlings*, was being used in a number of small rural churches. Initial publications were produced with the help of the Resource Center for Small Churches, and funded by grants from the Episcopal Church Foundation and the United Thank Offering. Seedlings was incorporated in 1982. It produces a four-year curriculum for elementary level Sunday Schools as well as a variety of catechetical aids for children and adults. Seedlings retains a focus on serving small congregations by designing lessons for use with open classrooms for children of all ages, developing materials not available from other publishers, and keeping costs at a minimum. However, materials from Seedlings have been used widely in churches of all sizes in the United States and overseas.

Selwyn, George Augustus (Apr. 5, 1809–Apr. 11, 1878). First Church of England Bishop of New Zealand. He was born in Hempstead, London, England. Selwyn was educated at Eton and St. John's College, Cambridge. He was ordained priest in 1833. After parish work at Windsor and tutoring at Eton, he was consecrated the first Church of England Bishop in New Zealand. In 1842 he reached Auckland, which later became the see city. He encouraged churches in the English colonies to be independent of the Church of England. Selwyn was named the Bishop of Lichfield in England in 1868. He remained there until his death. He preached at the 1874 General Convention. His ministry is commemorated in the Episcopal calendar of the church year on Apr. 11. Selwyn died in Lichfield.

Seminarian. A seminary student. *See* Seminary.

Seminary. Theological school for training ordained and lay leaders of the church. Those seeking to be ordained typically participate in a three-year course of studies leading to the Master of Divinity degree. First-year students are called "juniors," second-year students are called "middlers," and third-year students are called "seniors." In addition to providing theological instruction and assisting with vocational formation, the seminary faculty evaluate the suitability of those seeking ordination for the ministries they seek. Some seminary students who do not intend to be ordained seek theological education for vocations such as work in Christian education or other forms of service. Many seminaries have also developed specialized programs in such areas as Christian education, congregational development, and Christian spirituality. These expanded programs are attended by clergy and laity seeking training for ministry and continuing education. The scope of these offerings varies from weekend seminars to extension courses to graduate-level degree programs. The accredited seminaries of the Episcopal Church are the General Theological Seminary, New York City; the Berkeley Divinity School, Yale University, New Haven, Connecticut; Bexley Hall at Colgate-Rochester Divinity School, Rochester, New York; the Church Divinity School of the Pacific, Berkeley, California; the Episcopal Divinity School, Cambridge, Massachusetts; the Episcopal Theological Seminary of the Southwest, Austin, Texas; Nashotah House, Nashotah, Wisconsin; the Protestant Episcopal Theological Seminary in Virginia, Alexandria, Virginia; School of Theology, the School of Theology, the University of the South, Sewanee, Tennessee; Seabury-Western Theological Seminary, Evanston, Illinois; and Trinity Episcopal School for Ministry, Ambridge, Pennsylvania. All Episcopal seminaries are accredited by the Association of Theological Schools (A.T.S.).

Seminary Consultation On Mission (SCOM). A cooperative effort of Episcopal seminaries to draw together theological reflection and the work of mission. A preliminary meeting was convened at Seabury House, Greenwich, Connecticut, Oct. 20–22, 1978, by Charles Halsey Clark. He was a former missionary in the Philippines and at that time dean of the Berkeley Divinity School at Yale. The meeting sought "to give serious if preliminary consideration to where the seminaries are and ought to be today as centers of education for mission in the light of the church's programs and needs." Participants included twenty-one faculty and students from nine Episcopal seminaries, together with staff from the Episcopal Church Center. At a follow-up meeting at the General Theological Seminary on May 5–6, 1979, attended by one representative from each of the accredited seminaries of the Episcopal Church, Professor Roland Foster was asked to serve for three years as coordinator of a Seminary Consultation on Mission (SCOM). SCOM seeks to understand current Anglican Communion trends, to assess the state of theological understanding of mission, and to recover a place for mission in the life and work of the seminaries. One of its major accomplishments has been a series of theological consultations bringing together American Episcopal seminary faculty with other Anglican counterparts. Theological consultations were held in Hong Kong for Asia in 1990, in Zimbabwe for Africa in 1991, and in several sites for Latin America in 1992. SCOM has met annually since 1979. Its income is derived chiefly from a Venture in Mission Trust Fund, and it functions under the supervision of the Council of Deans of the Episcopal seminaries.

Seminary of the Streets. A ministry of Trinity Parish, New York City, which integrated traditional academic work with an involvement in the issues, struggles, and experiences of actual ministry. It operated from 1970 until 1973. The Rev. John Swanson was the dean. It operated out of Trinity Parish's St. Christopher's Chapel in a low-income section of the Lower East Side in New York City.

Senior Warden. *See* Wardens of a Parish.

Sentences (Opening). Sentences of scripture that may be used at the beginning of Morning and Evening Prayer. These sentences may relate the office to the season, day, or time of worship. The opening sentences may also recall a general theme of Christian worship, and draw the congregation together for prayer as the office begins. The BCP service of Morning Prayer provides opening sentences for the seasons of the church year; for Trinity Sunday and All Saints and other Major Saints' Days; for occasions of thanksgiving; and general sentences for use at any time (pp. 75–78). The opening sentences for Evening Prayer may be used at any time. Several of these sentences relate faith to the context of darkness or night. One of the opening sentences for Evening Prayer, based on Ps 139:10–

11, includes the statement, "darkness is not dark to you, O Lord; the night is as bright as the day" (BCP, p. 116). Use of the opening sentences is optional.

There were no opening sentences in the 1549 Prayer Book. Opening sentences preceded the confession of sin at Morning and Evening Prayer in the 1552 BCP. These sentences were penitential. Subsequent revisions of the Prayer Book came to include general sentences, and sentences appropriate for particular seasons, days, or occasions.

Septuagesima Sunday. *See* Pre-Lenten Season.

Septuagint. Name given to the Greek version of the OT. The word "Septuagint," meaning seventy, comes from the early legend that seventy-two (rounded down to seventy) Jewish scholars translated the Pentateuch into Greek during the reign of Ptolemy II Philadelphus (282–246 B.C.) in Alexandria, Egypt. This translation of the Hebrew Bible is often designated by the Roman numerals LXX, which mean "seventy." The term originally applied only to the translation of the Pentateuch. It was subsequently extended to include the rest of the Hebrew Bible. In spite of some of its fanciful details, most scholars agree that the legend preserves the authentic memory of the translation of the Pentateuch in Alexandria in the third century B.C. for Greek-speaking Jews. During the next two centuries in Egypt or elsewhere the Prophets and Writings were translated and the rest of the sacred books were composed. All were finished before the time of Christ.

The Septuagint was used by writers of the NT, particularly the authors of Luke and Hebrews. It provided a bridge of language and ideas between the two testaments. Christian Bibles follow the order of books in the LXX rather than the Hebrew Bible. Since it apparently used a different and earlier version of the Hebrew Bible than the traditional Hebrew Masoretic Text (MT) used today, the LXX can frequently aid in interpreting difficult readings in the MT.

Sequence. A hymn sung after the second lesson and before the gospel acclamation at the eucharist. Many sequences were composed in the middle ages, but the Council of Trent (1545–1563) sought to streamline the liturgy and reduced the number of sequences to those for Easter, Pentecost, Corpus Christi, and the Mass for the Dead. The sequence *Stabat Mater* was reinstated by the Roman Catholic Church in 1727 for the Feast of the Seven Sorrows of the Virgin Mary, which was celebrated on Sept. 15. The historic sequences for Easter, Pentecost, Corpus Christi, and the Seven Sorrows of the Virgin Mary continue to be used in the Episcopal Church, although the feasts of Corpus Christi and the Seven Sorrows are not included in the Episcopal calendar of the church year. Those four sequences in *The Hymnal 1982* include: for Easter, *Victimae Paschali laudes*, "Christians to the Paschal victim" (Hymn 183); for Pentecost, *Veni Sancte Spiritus*, "Come, thou Holy Spirit bright" (also known as "the Golden Sequence") (Hymn 226); for Corpus Christi, *Lauda Sion Salvatorem*, "Zion, praise thy Savior, singing" (Hymn 320); and for the Feast of the Seven Sorrows of the Virgin Mary, *Stabat Mater Dolorosa*, "At the cross her vigil keeping" (Hymn 159). *The Hymnal 1982* also provides a contemporary tune for "Come, thou Holy Spirit bright," Arbor Street (Hymn 227). The medieval sequence *Dies Irae* ("Day of Wrath") is not included in *The Hymnal 1982*. *See* "Golden Sequence, The."

Seraph (s.), Seraphim (pl.). Supernatural creatures which have six wings and stand in attendance above the throne of the Lord, according to the vision of Isaiah (6:2–7). In this vision, a seraph said "Holy, holy, holy is the Lord of Hosts; the whole earth is full of his glory." A seraph flew to Isaiah and touched his mouth with a burning coal to take away his guilt and forgive his sin. The term has been associated with burning. Seraphim have been understood to be angels who "burn" with love for God. They have been ranked highest in the nine orders of angels. Seraphim are mentioned in the canticle *Te Deum laudamus* (BCP, pp. 95–96), and the hymn "Ye watchers and ye holy ones" (Hymn 618). They are among the angels celebrated on the feast of Saint Michael and All Angels (Sept. 29). *See* Angel; *see* Cherubim.

Sergius I (d. 701). Pope from 687. He was Syrian and spoke Greek. Sergius brought several liturgical innovations to the Roman Church. He introduced the *Agnus Dei* ("O Lamb of God, that takest away the sins of the world, have mercy upon us"; see BCP, p. 337) to the fraction (breaking of the bread) in the Roman rite. The *Agnus Dei* originated in the east. It was based on Jn 1:29. Sergius also introduced in Rome the celebration of the feast of the Annunciation on Mar. 25. Celebration of this feast has been traced to the fifth century in the east. He introduced the use of a procession with candles and the singing of the *Nunc dimittis* for the Presentation of Our Lord Jesus Christ in the Temple on Feb. 2. The feast of the Presentation came to be known as "Candlemas." Sergius also introduced a litany that had been used for private devotions in the east. This litany included only one intercession, with the response, "We beseech thee to hear us." Its influence may be seen in the intercessions and responses of the Great Litany (see BCP, pp. 150–152).

Sergius of Radonezh (1314–1392). Abbot, mystic, and a patron saint of Russia. Sergius is considered the most popular Russian saint. In 1334 Sergius and his brother went to the forests near Radonezh, north of Moscow, to live in monastic solitude. They were joined by others. A chapel in honor of the Trinity was built in 1334. A community rule was adopted in 1354, and the Monastery of the Holy Trinity developed. Sergius served as abbot. Holy Trinity Monastery became the center for the renewal of Christianity in Russia, and the spiritual heart of Russian Orthodoxy. Holy Trinity became a model for Russian monasticism and a center for pilgrimage. Sergius founded forty monasteries. He refused election to the Patriarchate of Moscow in 1378. Sergius supported and inspired Prince Dmitri Donskoi's victory against the Tartars at the Battle of Kulikovo in 1380. Sergius also stopped four civil wars between Russian princes. Sergius was known for his gentle spirit, his mystical temperament, and his concern for serving the needs of others. His shrine at the monastery of Zagorsk is a center of pilgrimage. Sergius's life is commemorated on Sept. 25 in the Episcopal calendar of the church year.

Sermon. Religious address in a worship service. The sermon is to "break open" the Word of God and proclaim the gospel in the context of the readings from scripture, the liturgical occasion, the congregation gathered, and the pastoral needs of the situation. The Christian story, the congregation's story, and the preacher's story can be the one story of God's love that is proclaimed in the sermon. A short sermon is often called a "homily."

The sermon was a regular part of the eucharist in the early centuries of the church. However, preaching had become infrequent by the late middle ages. Luther's Latin rite of 1523 called for a sermon to be preached at every eucharist. Sermons were preached in the churches of the Reformation on Sundays and during the week. But the integral connection of the sermon to the liturgy was obscured in many Protestant churches. The 1549 BCP required a sermon or the reading of a homily at each eucharist on a Sunday or holy day. The 1552 BCP made no exception to the requirement of a sermon on weekdays. The sermon came to be emphasized in seventeenth- and eighteenth-century Anglicanism. Many colonial Anglican churches in North America were built with prominent pulpits. The ministry of preaching has at times been given special emphasis by evangelicals. The importance of the sermon was not emphasized by the nineteenth century liturgical revival in Anglicanism. However, the twentieth-century liturgical movement has tended to reclaim the sermon as an integral part of the liturgical celebration.

The 1979 BCP requires a sermon after the gospel at the eucharist. At a baptism, the sermon may follow the gospel or the peace. A sermon may be preached at the Daily Offices of Morning Prayer and Evening Prayer. The sermon may follow the readings at the Daily Office, or it may be preached at the time of the hymn or anthem after the collects, or it may follow the office.

Sermon on the Mount. A collection of the teachings of Jesus in the Gospel of Matthew (Chapters 5–7). It is the first of five special speeches in Matthew and takes place at the beginning of Jesus' ministry. Many of the sayings in the Sermon on the Mount are also found in the Gospel of Luke. Scholars agree that this material probably comes from the Q source, even though the sayings are not in the same order or sequence. As a result, historical critics suggest that Matthew and Luke have two different ways of presenting Jesus' teaching to their intended audience. Although the Sermon is addressed to the disciples, at the conclusion of the speech Matthew remarks that the crowd was amazed at Jesus' teaching. Beginning with the beatitudes and followed by two metaphors, the main thesis is stated in 5:17–20. Jesus affirms the importance of the law but emphasizes the higher demands of a disciple: "Unless you show yourselves far better than the scribes and Pharisees, you can never enter the Kingdom of Heaven" (Mt 5:20). In this way Jesus describes the requirements of his followers at the beginning of his ministry. *See* Sermon on the Plain.

Sermon on the Plain. This is a less widely used term to refer to the portion of Luke's gospel which is parallel to Matthew's Sermon on the Mount. Lk 6:17 states that after Jesus chose the twelve, he stood on a "level place." The "sermon" begins at 6:20 and ends at 6:49. It contains some of the material that is found in the Sermon on the Mount. It is not exactly the same. Because there is nothing similar in Mark, it is assumed to be from the Q source. Both the Sermon on the Mount and the Sermon on the Plain are addressed to the disciples and are close to the beginning of Jesus' ministry. They both begin with beatitudes, but Luke's four beatitudes are simpler in form and are followed by four woes. The rest of the speech has a heavy emphasis on love. *See* Sermon on the Mount.

Servants of Christ the King, Order of (SCK). A devotional fellowship founded in 1938. SCK was based on the common keeping of a rule of life. It was open to young men and women who were communicants of the church, thirty-three years of age and under. Its object was to form in its members the habits of prayer and frequenting the sacraments. It was last listed in *The Episcopal Church Annual 1994*.

Servants of Christ Priory, Order of St. Benedict. A religious order of male clergy and laymen who live in community under the Rule of St. Benedict dedicated to prayer, study, and works of mercy. It was formed as a community on Nov. 14, 1968. Companions and Associates are part of the extended family of the Servants of Christ. The community says four Offices a day and has a daily eucharist. It is located in Phoenix, Arizona.

Servants of Jesus, Community of. A community of monks in Lexington, Kentucky. It was founded on Aug. 29, 1981. The monks lived a life centered in prayer, study, worship, service, and community living while under the traditional three monastic vows. Its primary service was to the street people and the extreme poor of the Lexington area. It is no longer in existence.

Service Music. "Service Music" is the term used in *The Hymnal* (1940) and *The Hymnal 1982* for musical settings of prose texts from the BCP and other liturgical sources. The numbers which refer to items in this portion of *The Hymnal 1982* are preceded by the letter "S."

Service of Light. The Service of Light may be traced to the ritual blessing of light by Jews at the evening meal. This custom was continued by early Christians. Evening services at the dinner table were introduced by a blessing of light (*Lucernarium*). This candle-lighting ceremony was later a part of Christian worship in church. It is still reflected in the service of vespers in Eastern Orthodox churches. The *Lucernarium* largely died out in the west as the congregational or cathedral daily services were replaced by the monastic hours of prayer. However, the *Lucernarium* has been revived in recent liturgical use. The 1979 BCP provides two forms of the Service of Light.

The term may indicate the opening section of An Order of Worship for the Evening (BCP, pp. 109–114). This Service of Light includes the entrance of the ministers into the darkened church, the opening acclamation or greeting, a short lesson of scripture, a prayer for light, the lighting of the candles, and the singing of the *Phos hilaron* (O Gracious Light). The *Phos hilaron* is the ancient candle-lighting hymn of the church. It has been associated with the use of incense. An appropriate anthem or psalm may be sung during the candle-lighting, or silence may be kept (BCP, p. 112). *The Hymnal 1982 Accompaniment Edition, Vol. 1*, provides a variety of candle-lighting anthems (*Lucernaria*) (S 305–S 320). The *BOS* also provides responsive texts for candle-lighting anthems. When the *BOS Lucernaria* are used, it is appropriate to omit the short lesson which precedes the prayer for light.

The Service of Light from An Order of Worship for the Evening may introduce a variety of liturgies. The Service of Light may serve as a festal introduction to Evening Prayer, with the selection from the Psalter at Evening Prayer following the *Phos hilaron*. The Service of Light may also begin an evening eucharist, with the salutation and collect of the day following the *Phos hilaron*. This order of service is used for a eucharist on the Vigil of Pentecost (BCP, p. 227). The *BOS* also calls for this order of service to be used at a Vigil Eucharist for the Eve of the Baptism of our Lord, the Eve of All Saints' Day or All Saints' Sunday, or the Eve of Baptism. The *BOS* notes that the Service of Light introduces services for New Year's Eve and All Hallows' Eve. It also may introduce Advent and Christmas Festivals of Lessons and Music. The short lesson of scripture may be omitted when one or more scripture lessons are to be read later in the service (BCP, p. 143).

The term also indicates the first part of the Great Vigil of Easter. This Service of Light includes the kindling of the new fire in the darkness, the opening collect, the lighting of the Paschal candle from the newly kindled fire, the procession to the chancel, and the *Exsultet* (BCP, pp. 285–287). The procession to the chancel is led by the deacon who bears the Paschal candle. This procession is led by the celebrant if there is no deacon. Candles held by members of the congregation may be lighted from the Paschal candle before it is placed in its stand. Other candles and lamps in the church, except for those at the altar, may

also be lighted. *The Altar Book* provides music for the *Exsultet*, and the people's responses are in *The Hymnal 1982* (S 69).

Services for Trial Use (1970). *See* Proposed Book of Common Prayer.

Seven Deadly Sins. These are traditionally pride, covetousness, lust, envy, gluttony, anger, and sloth. Since sin is faithlessness—the opposite of faith—it may be said that all sin is deadly rebellion against God. But it is difficult to conceive any sinful act that is not defined by one of these terms. In some sense this list is a categorization of sinful behavior described or implied by the decalogue (Ex 20:1–17 and Dt 5:6–21; see BCP, pp. 847–848) and by the great commandment given by Jesus in Matthew (22:34–40) concerning love for God and neighbor (see BCP, pp. 850–851). Pride has often been considered the chief and original sin since it beclouds all subsequent moral judgment. Covetousness, lust, envy, and gluttony may be considered self-destructive attempts to grasp what one seems to lack in order to achieve self-defined wholeness. In this the creature usurps the place of creator to become the author of one's own creation. Anger and sloth are thus the final terms of such fruitlessness—fury or despair at the failure of rebellion against God.

Seven Gifts of the Holy Spirit. The gifts are 1) wisdom, 2) understanding, 3) counsel, 4) fortitude, 5) knowledge, 6) piety, and 7) fear of the Lord. This list is based on Is 11:2. The imparting of the gifts of the Spirit is associated with baptism, as well as Confirmation and Ordination. The "sevenfold" gift of the Holy Spirit is mentioned in the hymns *Veni Sancte Spiritus*, "Come, thou Holy Spirit bright" (Hymns 226–227) and *Veni Creator Spiritus*, "Come, Holy Ghost, our souls inspire" (Hymns 503–504). One of these hymns precedes the period of silent prayer and the prayer of consecration at each ordination. *See* Gifts of the Spirit.

Sewanee Theological Review. This periodical began publication on St. Luke's Day, Oct. 18, 1957, as the *St. Luke's Journal of Theology.* It was founded by the Very Rev. George M. Alexander, dean of the School of Theology at the University of the South, for the continuing education of clergy. It was edited by students in the School of Theology from its founding until Sept. 1976, when Dr. John M. Gessell became the first faculty editor. Gessell retired as editor in Dec. 1990 and several changes were made in the journal. On Feb. 19, 1991, the Board of Regents of the University approved changing the name to the *Sewanee Theological Review*, giving it symmetry in name with the University's *Sewanee Review*. A new editor took over on Jan. 1, 1991, a thematic approach was adopted, complimentary subscriptions were reduced, and the purpose of the journal was changed to read "Anglican journal of theological reflection."

Sexagesima Sunday. *See* Pre-Lenten Season.

Sext. *See* Terce, Sext, None.

Sexton. A custodian who cleans and takes care of the church and any other parish buildings. Sextons are typically responsible for maintenance of the buildings and grounds of the parish. Traditionally, the sexton's duties included ringing the church bell, cleaning church fabric, and digging graves.

Sexual Ethics. A field of study focusing on the nature, practices, and purposes of human sexuality. Since Augustine human sexuality has been understood primarily in light of marriage and family by Christian ethics. The ends of human sexuality were understood thus in terms of procreation, mutual society, and the remedy of sin. Protestant reformers generally raised mutual society or companionship as the primary end of sexuality rather than procreation. Contemporary moralists have emphasized the positive end of pleasure rather than seeing pleasure as the occasion for sin and therefore in need of remedy. In addition to understandings formed by scripture and the moral tradition, contemporary sexual ethics are more broadly informed by historical studies as well as the natural and social sciences. Central questions in sexual ethics now include the nature of sexuality, sexual orientation, sexual identity, and gender identity; the historic and social diversity of sexual practices and relationships; and the effects of patriarchy and the need for justice, equality, and intimacy.

Shanghai, Missionary District of. William Jones Boone was consecrated the first Missionary Bishop of China on Oct. 26, 1844. The 1874 General Convention changed the title from China to the "Missionary Bishop of Shanghai, having Episcopal jurisdiction in China." The 1901 General Convention divided China into the Missionary Districts of Shanghai and Hankow. On Apr. 26, 1912, the Chung Hua Sheng Kung Hui, the Holy Catholic Church in China, was formed by the merger of American, Canadian and English missionary districts. In 1949 it became the Diocese of Kiangsu in the Holy Catholic Church in China.

Shape-Note Hymnody. William Little and William Smith's *Easy Instructor* (1801) introduced a system for teaching music by shapes of notes rather than by lines and spaces. A triangle represented "fa," a circle "sol," a square "la," and a diamond "mi." Many shape-note books followed. As early as John Wyeth's *Wyeth's Repository of Sacred Music, Part Second* (1813) shape-note books included folk hymns transcribed from oral tradition. Eventually a seven-shape system, generally in the form of Jesse B. Aiken's *Christian Minstrel* (1846), superseded the earlier four-shape system. Northern musicians, such as Lowell Mason and Thomas Hastings, influenced by current European music, opposed the "dunce notes" and succeeded in displacing most early American tunes in later nineteenth-century books with tunes in the current European style. Five older shape-note books, however, remain in use in "singings": William Walker's *Southern Harmony* and B. F. White and E. J. King's *Sacred Harp*, which are four-shape books, and Joseph Funk's *Harmonia Sacra*, M. L. Swan's *New Harp of Columbia*, and William Walker's *Christian Harmony*, which are seven-shape books. Appreciation for early American folk hymns has grown in recent decades and newer hymnals have included a number of these tunes. *The Hymnal 1982* includes seventeen tunes first published in four-shape shape-note books: *Bourbon, Detroit, Dunlap's Creek, Foundation, Holy Manna, Land of Rest, Middlebury, Morning Song, Nettleton, New Britain, Resignation, Restoration, Salvation, Tender Thought, The Church's Desolation, Vernon,* and *Wondrous Love*. It also includes other early American tunes frequently printed in shape-note books: *Charleston, Coronation, Kedron, Light, Pleading Savior,* and *Star in the East*.

Shaping Our Future, Inc. At the Dec. 1991 convention of the Diocese of East Tennessee, the Rev. Stephen Freeman presented a resolution on the structure of the church, which called for the reduction of the size of the national church and for the General Convention to meet only once a decade. Bishop Robert Tharp named a committee, chaired by the Rev. Jon Shuler, to handle the resolution. Freeman next wrote an article, which was published in *The*

Living Church, June 7, 1992, entitled "Structural Reform Needed." This article attracted considerable attention and it was decided to hold a national symposium. The resolution and the desire to hold a national meeting became known as the East Tennessee Initiative. A Shaping Our Future Symposium was held Aug. 12–15, 1993, in St. Louis, Missouri, attended by over one thousand people from ninety-three dioceses and five nations. Most of the papers from the symposium were published in a book, *Shaping Our Future* (1994). The mission of "Shaping Our Future: A Grassroots Forum on Episcopal Structures" was to work for the biblical reform of the Episcopal Church for effective mission and ministry in the twenty-first century. When a resolution to restructure the Episcopal Church was not adopted at the 1994 General Convention, Shaping Our Future, Inc., decided to end its ministry.

Sharer's. *See* Associated Parishes for Liturgy and Music.

Sharing of Ministries Abroad U. S. A. (SOMA). A Christian mission agency in the Anglican Communion dedicated to fostering renewal in the Holy Spirit throughout the world. SOMA was founded in 1978 in the aftermath of the Anglican International Renewal Conference at Canterbury Cathedral. SOMA USA was formally founded in 1985 at the International Renewal Conference on the campus of the University of Southern California in Los Angeles. SOMA seeks to enable the church to fulfill the Great Commission by ministering in the power of the Holy Spirit and changing the world for Jesus Christ. It publishes the *SOMA Newsletter*. SOMA prepares and sends short-term mission teams across national and cultural boundaries at the invitation of the diocesan bishop.

Shattuck-St. Mary's School, Faribault, Minnesota. Shattuck-St. Mary's School is a coeducational Episcopal boarding school for grades six through twelve. It was founded in 1858 by the Rev. James Lloyd Breck, who organized the school in conjunction with the formation of the Diocese of Minnesota. He created it as a mission for children of Native Americans and white settlers in the area. It included both a primary and a secondary school and a seminary. Breck's creation eventually developed into four related but separate institutions: Shattuck Grammar School, a boys' high school named after benefactor George Shattuck of Boston; St. Mary's Hall, which Henry Whipple, Bishop of Minnesota, opened in 1866 for the daughters of Episcopal clergy; St. James

School, which Shattuck's headmaster James Dobbins founded in 1901 for grade-school boys; and Seabury Divinity School. Seabury moved in 1933 and merged with Western Theological Seminary in Chicago to become Seabury-Western Theological Seminary. The three other schools joined in 1972 and became a single institution. Shattuck-St. Mary's School is now the oldest school of its kind west of the Alleghenies.

Shekinah. The term comes from a Hebrew word which means "to dwell." It refers to the visible dwelling of God among the people of God on earth. It does not appear in the Bible as such but comes from Jewish tradition during the period of the Second Temple, i.e., after 515 B.C. The same phenomenon appears in the Bible as the glory of God, which is particularly associated with the Tabernacle (Ex 40:34–35) and the Temple (1 Kgs 8:10–11) in the OT, and with the Incarnation (Jn 1:14) in the NT.

Shelby College. No longer in existence, Shelby College operated at Shelbyville, Kentucky, with interruptions, from 1840 to around 1868. Bishop Benjamin B. Smith of Kentucky wanted a "Literary institution of an elevated character under the auspices of the Church in this Diocese." In 1840 the Diocese of Kentucky took charge of Shelby College, which was founded four years earlier. The Episcopal Theological Seminary in Kentucky operated as a department of Shelby College for a while in the 1840s.

Shell, Baptismal. A shell used to pour water over the head of candidates for baptism. The celebrant may use the shell instead of his or her hand to pour the water. The shell may be made of silver or other precious metal or pottery.

Shema. Summary of Jewish belief and statement of faith. Dt 6:4–9, "Hear O Israel: The Lord (Yahweh) our God is one God; and you shall love the Lord your God with all your heart, with all your soul, and with all your might. And these words which I command you this day shall be upon your heart; and you shall teach them diligently to your children." It emphasizes the oneness of God against the divine pluralism of other religions.

Shepherd, Massey Hamilton, Jr. (Mar. 14, 1913–Feb. 18, 1990). Liturgist and educator. He was born in Wilmington, North Carolina. Shepherd received his B.A. in 1932, and his M.A. in 1933, both from the University of South

Carolina. In 1937 he received his Ph.D. from the University of Chicago and in 1941 his B.D. from the Berkeley Divinity School. Shepherd was ordained deacon on Mar. 5, 1941, and priest on Sept. 17, 1941. From 1937 until 1940, he was an instructor at the University of Chicago, and from 1940 until 1954, he was professor of church history at the Episcopal Theological School. While at the Episcopal Theological School, he served as an assistant at St. John's Church, Roxbury, Massachusetts. He taught frequently in the Graduate School of Theology of the University of the South, and was its director from 1952 until 1970. From 1954 until 1981, when he retired, Shepherd was professor of liturgics at the Church Divinity School of the Pacific. He was president of the American Church History Society in 1949, and president of the Historical Society of the Episcopal Church from 1961 until 1974. Shepherd served on numerous worship and ecumenical boards and commissions, most notably the Standing Liturgical Commission from 1947 until 1976. Of his many publications, *The Oxford American Prayer Book Commentary* (1950) is one of the most important. He was a major architect of the 1979 BCP. Shepherd died in Sacramento, California.

Sherrill, Henry Knox (Nov. 6, 1890–May 11, 1980). Twentieth Presiding Bishop. He was born in Brooklyn, New York. Sherrill received his B.A. from Yale University in 1911 and his M. Div. from the Episcopal Theological School in 1914. He was ordained deacon on June 7, 1914, and priest on May 9, 1915. He began his ministry as assistant minister at Trinity Church, Boston. He remained there until 1917, when he became Red Cross chaplain of the Massachusetts General Hospital, later known as Base Hospital Six. In that same year he and others from the hospital were sent to Europe where they assumed responsibility for a hospital in Talence, France. In 1919 he was discharged from the Army. He became rector of the Church of Our Saviour, Brookline, Massachusetts, where he remained until 1923. In 1923 he became the twelfth rector of Trinity Church, Boston, and stayed there until 1930. While at Trinity Church he taught pastoral care and homiletics at the Episcopal Theological School, and he taught pastoral care in the Boston University School of Theology.

On Oct. 14, 1930, Sherrill was consecrated the ninth Bishop of Massachusetts. He served in that position until June 1, 1947, when he resigned to become Presiding Bishop. From Jan. 1, 1947, until Nov. 14, 1958, he was Presiding Bishop of the Episcopal Church. At the General Convention of 1943, a canon was passed which required the Presiding Bishop to tender to the House of Bishops the resignation of his previous jurisdiction to take effect on the date of assuming the office of Presiding Bishop or no later than six months thereafter. Sherrill was the first Presiding Bishop chosen after this canon was passed. While Presiding Bishop he led in the organization of the Episcopal Church Foundation and the establishment of the Seabury Press. Sherrill was one of the presidents of the World Council of Churches from 1954 until 1961. He was the first president of the National Council of Churches from 1950 until 1952. He resigned as Presiding Bishop in 1958 for reasons of health. Sherrill died in Boxford, Massachusetts.

Shimer College. A school that was once an Episcopal college, located in Waukegan, Illinois. It was established in 1853 by Frances Ann Wood Shimer. Under the influence of William Rainey Harper, first president of the University of Chicago, it became a Baptist institution known as the Frances Shimer Academy of the University of Chicago. In 1957 the board of trustees severed the relationship with the Baptists, and on June 30, 1959, the dioceses of Chicago, Eau Claire, Fond du Lac, Indianapolis, Iowa, Milwaukee, Quincy, and Northern Indiana recognized it as an Episcopal college. It became a member of the Association of Episcopal Colleges, but the relationship with the Episcopal Church ended in 1973.

Shoemaker, Helen Smith (Mar. 16, 1903–Jan. 29, 1993). Co-founder of the Anglican Fellowship of Prayer. She was born in New York City. Shoemaker was educated privately and then studied art in New York City. She was attracted to the Moral Rearmament Movement (MRA) in the 1920s in New York. She worked and resided with an MRA group at Calvary Church, New York, and there met the Rev. Sam Shoemaker. After their marriage, she sought to help her clergyman husband by a ministry of hospitality and entertaining. She was a founder of the Anglican Fellowship of Prayer, an international prayer movement. It was begun by small groups of people meeting in church basements and homes to pray for soldiers during World War II. It expanded in 1958 into a nationwide organization whose mission is to intercede continually for the national church and beyond, following the Anglican Cycle of Prayer. After the death of her husband, she wrote a memoir of him, *I Stand By the Door: The Life of Sam Shoemaker* (1967). She published a number of books on prayer including

Prayer and You (1948), and *The Secret Effect of Prayer* (1967). She died in Brooklandville, Maryland. *See* Anglican Fellowship of Prayer; *see* Shoemaker, Samuel Moor.

Shoemaker, Samuel Moor (Dec. 27, 1893–Jan. 31, 1963). Episcopal priest and one of the founders of Alcoholics Anonymous (AA). He was born in Baltimore, Maryland. In the summers of 1911 and 1912, he attended conferences in Northfield, Massachusetts, where he was exposed to such evangelical leaders as John R. Mott, Robert E. Speer, and Sherwood Eddy. He called them "spiritual giants." Shoemaker received his B.A. in 1916 from Princeton University. From 1917 until 1919 he worked for the YMCA in China. He studied at the General Theological Seminary and received his M.Div. from Union Theological Seminary in 1921. Shoemaker was ordained deacon on June 20, 1920, and priest on June 11, 1921. He began his ordained ministry as a curate at Grace Church, New York. On May 15, 1925, he accepted the call to be rector of Calvary Church, New York, and served there until 1952. He used his imagination, evangelical preaching, and concern for the needy to revitalize and strengthen Calvary Church. He assisted in the organization of Alcoholics Anonymous and helped to write the "Twelve Steps." In 1952 Shoemaker became the rector of Calvary Church, Pittsburgh, and served there until his retirement in 1962. While there he developed the "Pittsburgh Experiment," a program in which lay people met in small groups to discuss how to bring Christianity into their daily lives and their business relationships. Shoemaker's emphasis on empowering the laity led him and his wife to hold "schools of prayer." These grew into what is now known as the Anglican Fellowship of Prayer. He was the founder of *Faith at Work* magazine and wrote twenty-three books. Shoemaker died in Pittsburgh. *See* Anglican Fellowship of Prayer (AFP); *see* Shoemaker, Helen Smith.

Shoresh/USA. This organization was formerly Christian Ministry among Jewish People/USA. Shoresh's focus is on the Jewish roots ("shoresh" in Hebrew) of Christian faith. It encourages Jewish people to recognize Jesus as the Messiah. Shoresh also sponsors study tours to Israel in cooperation with Trinity Episcopal School for Ministry.

Shoup, Francis Asbury (Mar. 22, 1834–Sept. 4, 1896). Priest and seminary professor. He was born in Laurel, Indiana. He attended DePauw University in Greencastle, Indiana. He later entered the United States Military Academy at West Point, New York, where he graduated in 1855. In 1860 he resigned from the Army, studied law, and was admitted to the bar in Indianapolis. Shoup moved to St. Augustine to practice law. When the Civil War began, he entered the Confederate Army. During the war he met some Episcopalians and was baptized and confirmed on the battlefield by Bishop Stephen Elliott. After teaching mathematics at the University of Mississippi, he was ordained deacon on Dec. 20, 1868, and priest on May 2, 1869. From 1869 until 1875 he was professor of mathematics at the University of the South, and from 1869 until 1871 he was acting chaplain of the university. From 1871 until 1875 Shoup was the professor of ecclesiastical history and polity at the university, and from 1870 until 1875 he was the rector of St.-Paul's-on-the-Mountain, Sewanee. After serving parishes in Waterford, New York, Nashville, Tennessee, and New Orleans, he returned to the University of the South as professor of engineering and physics. Shoup died in Columbia, Tennessee.

Shrine. A holy place that commemorates a person or event of religious significance. Shrines may include a reliquary, statue, or other sacred image. There are many shrines of the Blessed Virgin Mary, such as Lourdes in France and Walsingham in England. Shrines are often places of pilgrimage. The shrine of St. Thomas Becket at Canterbury Cathedral was a popular place of pilgrimage until it was destroyed under Henry VIII. Visitation of shrines is part of the devotional piety of some members of the Episcopal Church, especially Anglo-catholics. *See* Pilgrimage.

Shrine of Our Lady of Clemency, Philadelphia. *See* St. Clement's Church, Philadelphia.

Shrove Tuesday. The Tuesday before Ash Wednesday. The term is derived from shriving, which means confessing and absolving. The Tuesday before the beginning of Lent was a traditional day for hearing confessions. The three days before Ash Wednesday have been known as Shrove Sunday, Shrove Monday, and Shrove Tuesday, with these three days collectively known as "Shrovetide." The Tuesday before Ash Wednesday is also commonly known as "Mardi Gras" or "Fat Tuesday." Because of the Lenten fast, the day before Ash Wednesday was a day to consume animal fat. In some places it was a day of celebration and indulgence before the discipline of Lent. The Tuesday before Ash Wednesday is also known as "Carnival," which literally means the removal or putting away of flesh (meat).

Some Episcopal churches observe Shrove Tuesday with a parish supper, or the burning of palms from Palm Sunday to provide ashes for Ash Wednesday.

Side Altar. An altar that is not the main or high altar of a church and therefore located to the side of the main or high altar. It may be located in a niche or chapel of the church. The early Christian practice was for there to be only one altar in each church, with only one celebration of the eucharist in each church on any day. This practice has continued in the eastern church. However, there was a multiplication of altars in many churches of the west during the middle ages. The proliferation of altars in churches has been associated with the celebration of private Masses and the multiplication of Masses for special intentions. Depending on the architectural design of the church, the symbolic power and focus of the main altar may be weakened by the presence of side altars. In many Episcopal parishes, a side altar is used for weekday celebrations of the eucharist that are usually attended by small congregations.

Sign of the Cross. This ancient Christian gesture traces the cross on oneself, on objects, or other people. Depending on the context, the gesture may express personal Christian devotion or identity, blessing, absolution, exorcism, consecration to holy use, or the conclusion of something done to the honor of God. The sign of the cross may be traced with a hand, as when the sign of the cross is made over an object or when one signs the cross on oneself from forehead to lower chest and from shoulder to shoulder. In the Christian west, this gesture customarily moves from the left shoulder to the right shoulder, while in the Christian east this gesture moves from right to left. Signing of the forehead alone, or of the forehead, lips, and heart at the gospel in the eucharist, is customarily done with the thumb. The sign of the cross is a customary gesture in a variety of liturgical contexts. For example, it may be used at the beginning or ending of one of the Daily Offices, at the reading of the gospel in the eucharist, or at the absolution following the confession in the eucharist. The BCP directs that the celebrant at baptism will make the sign of the cross on the forehead of the candidate for baptism (using chrism if desired), saying "You are sealed by the Holy Spirit in Baptism and marked as Christ's own for ever" (BCP, p. 308). In the form for Ministration to the Sick, the BCP directs that if the sick person is to be anointed, the priest dips a thumb in the holy oil and makes the sign of the cross on the sick person's forehead (BCP, p. 456). The *BOS* provides that at the admission of catechumens, each catechumen is presented by name to the celebrant who marks a cross on the forehead of each with a thumb, saying, "Receive the sign of the Cross on your forehead and in your heart, in the Name of the Father, and of the Son, and of the Holy Spirit." Although use of the sign of the cross is widespread throughout the Episcopal Church by celebrants, officiants, and parishioners, its use is typically a matter of custom and personal piety. The BCP does not require the gesture to be made by members of the congregation at any time.

Signation. *See* Seal of Baptism.

Silent Missionary, The. This newsletter was first published in Philadelphia in 1886 on behalf of the missions to the deaf in the Diocese of Pennsylvania, Central Pennsylvania, New Jersey, Delaware, and Maryland. It was edited by Henry Winter Syle. When Syle died in 1890, the Rev. Jacob Michael Koehler (1860–1932) became the editor. It appears to have ceased publication in 1892.

Silver Eagles Episcopal Clergy Association. An association for retired Episcopal clergy and surviving spouses of deceased clergy. It is an affiliate of the National Network of Episcopal Clergy Associations. The idea for the Silver Eagles emerged in June 1994. The association was incorporated on Mar. 29, 1996. The goals of the association are to provide support, fellowship, and information to retired Episcopal clergy and surviving spouses and to provide a voice on issues affecting them. It publishes a newsletter called *Soaring*. The association's guiding biblical text is Is 40:31: "They will soar as on eagle wings, run and not grow weary, walk and not be faint."

Simeon, Charles (Sept. 24, 1759–Nov. 13, 1836). Leading eighteenth-century evangelical. He was born in Reading, England. Simeon was educated at Eton and King's College, Cambridge, where he became a fellow in 1782. He was ordained a deacon in 1782. Even before Simeon was a priest he was named the rector of Holy Trinity Church, Cambridge, where he remained his entire life. While at Cambridge he was closely associated with King's College, where he lived and was very popular with undergraduate students. He was one of the founders of the Church Missionary Society (CMS) in 1799. He supported the British and Foreign Bible Society. Simeon was a leading evangelical in the Church of England and was known as "the Evangelical of Evangelicals." At the same time he was loyal to the Church of England. He had a high view of the ordained ministry and a deep devotion to the eucharist. Simeon's primary fame was as a preacher. His major publication was *Horae Homileticae*, a commentary on the entire Bible. It was first published in 1796. He described the three great aims of all his preaching: "To humble the sinner, To exalt the Saviour, To promote holiness." Simeon died in Cambridge. He is commemorated in the Episcopal calendar of the church year on Nov. 12.

Simon and Jude, Saints and Apostles. Two of the apostles. Very little is known about them. Simon is known as Simon the Cananaean and Simon the Zealot. He was probably a member of the political sect known as the Zealots, which was violently opposed to the domination of Palestine by Rome. Tradition claims that he carried the Christian faith to Egypt, Cyrene, Mauritania, Armenia, and Persia, and that he died in Persia by being sawed in half. Jude, also known as Thaddeus and Lebbaeus, was probably the author of the epistle of Jude. By the twentieth century Jude had become popular as the "patron of hopeless causes." According to tradition, Simon and Jude labored and died together. They are commemorated in the Episcopal calendar of the church year on Oct. 28.

Simul justus et peccator. Latin phrase meaning "at once justified and a sinner." It is associated with Martin Luther and Protestant thought concerning salvation. The righteousness of Christ is imputed to us by God and received by faith. We are thus justified by a righteousness that is extrinsic and alien to us personally. Although we are pronounced righteous by God in Christ, we continue to be sinners. In contrast, other views of salvation have emphasized that the righteousness of Christ is actually imparted and transformative for the one who receives God's grace in faith. Justification is thereby understood to involve a real change in the life of the believer through participation in an ongoing process of sanctification. In the sixteenth century the Roman Catholic Council of Trent upheld the transformation of the believer in the saving process, and contradicted *simul justus et peccator*. Contemporary theologians have moved beyond the polemics and caricatures of the sixteenth century. Many affirm the reality of a saving process involving participation in the unmerited gift of God's grace for salvation that is received by faith,

and assert the ongoing need for human repentance. *See* Justification; *see* Salvation; *see* Sanctification.

Sin. Following our own will instead of following the will of God, thereby being centered on ourselves instead of God and distorting our relationships with God, other people, and creation (see BCP, p. 848). Sin is intentional disobedience and rebellion against God. It alienates us from our true selves. Sin is a misuse of human free will by one who is capable of choice (see BCP, p. 845). St. Paul states clearly that all have sinned and fallen short of the glory of God (Rom 3:23; see 1 Jn 1:8). The harm of sin is ultimately not in the bad act itself but in the damage caused by sin to one's relationships with God and others. Sin is identified with death, as our life-giving relationship with God is impaired by sin (see Rom 6:23). Distortion of our relationship with God results in our loss of liberty as sin gains power over us (see BCP, p. 849). We may recognize our sin and need for redemption more clearly through the Ten Commandments and the biblical law (see BCP, p. 848). St. Paul also notes that the law can provide the occasion for sin, although the law is holy (see Rom 7:7–12). Roman Catholic thought has distinguished mortal (deadly) sins from venial (slight) sins, but Protestants have generally rejected this distinction.

We participate in redemption from the power of evil, sin, and death through Jesus Christ who came into the world to save sinners (1 Tm 1:15; see BCP, p. 849). Jesus is the Lamb of God who takes away the sin of the world (Jn 1:29). He is our advocate with God the Father and the atoning sacrifice for our sins and the sins of the whole world (1 Jn 2:1). As we share in the death of Adam's original sin, in Christ we may share in the victory of life over sin and death (1 Cor 15:22). The practice of Christian faith is concerned with receiving the grace of God's forgiveness and new life in Christ. The BCP services for the Holy Eucharist and the Daily Offices all include forms for confession of sins (pp. 41–42, 62–63, 79–80, 116–117, 330–332, 360). Reconciliation of a Penitent is a sacramental rite of the Episcopal Church, and the BCP provides two forms for this rite (pp. 447–452). Forgiveness of sins concerns not just the removal of guilt but the restoration of personal relationships with God and others. *See* Original Sin; *see* Redeemer.

Sindicators. This organization came into being in the fall of 1976 at a meeting in Reno, Nevada, hosted by Bishop Wesley Frensdorff, Bishop of Nevada. He called together representatives of dioceses and regions which used the canonical provisions for local ordained ministry. Sindicators supports the ideas of total or mutual ministry. It supports theological education by extension and works for the renewal of the diaconate. It also stresses the primacy of baptism as the foundational sacrament for ministry. Sindicators works with Coalition 14 and the Living Stones Diocesan Partnership.

Sisco, Curtis Winfield, Jr. (May 1, 1958–Nov. 23, 1992). Priest and liturgical editor. He was born in Philadelphia. Sisco was a graduate of Temple University and General Theological Seminary. He was ordained priest in 1987. He served as a consultant to the National Council of Churches in New York, 1985–1986, diocesan intern, St. Simons', Philadelphia, 1986–1987, and rector, St. Luke's Church, New Orleans, 1987–1992. He served until his death as liturgical editor and member of the committee that produced the hymnal supplement, *Lift Every Voice and Sing, II* (1993). The volume is dedicated to his memory. He died in New Orleans.

Sister. The term has been applied to female Christians since the earliest NT times. The language of family kinship recalls the closeness of the bond that is shared by those who live in Christ. For example, the Gospel of Mk (3:35) records Jesus' statement that "Whoever does the will of God is my brother and sister and mother." The term has been used more specifically to indicate a woman who is a member of a religious order or community. Historically, the term indicates a laywoman, but it is now also used by some priests in religious orders or communities as an expression of equality and community.

Sisterhood of the Good Shepherd, Baltimore. Religious order founded in 1855 in Baltimore, Maryland, by Catherine Minard, with the support of Bishop William R. Whittingham. The sisters dispersed at the beginning of the Civil War. They reassembled in 1863 at St. Luke's Church, Baltimore, under the direction of the Rev. Charles W. Rankin, where they conducted schools and did nursing. In 1866 they operated a church home and an infirmary. In 1872 the Sisterhood moved to St. Louis. It is no longer in existence.

Sisterhood of the Good Shepherd, New York. A late nineteenth-century religious order which ministered to the poor, the sick, the homeless, and the outcast. They also cared for young children. The Sisterhood ran the School of the Good Shepherd and the Summer Home for Church Workers in Asbury Park, New Jersey; the Buttercup Cottage in Philadelphia as a summer home for working girls; and a clothing bureau in New York City. The order had its origins in work undertaken by the Community of St. Mary, which operated Sheltering Arms and St. Barnabas House in New York City. When some persons from the low church party visited St. Barnabas House, they found the oratory and proclaimed it a "Roman extravagance" and "mawkish Mariolatry." The Sisters of St. Mary left St. Barnabas House, and a lay woman, Ellen Hume, took charge of it. On Apr. 6, 1869, she and Bishop Horatio Potter founded the Sisterhood of the Good Shepherd at St. Ann's Church, New York. The Sisterhood went out of existence around 1902.

Sisterhood of St. John, The. Organized by the Rev. John Vaughan Lewis, rector of St. John's Church, Washington, in Dec. 1867, the order was devoted to works of mercy among children, the sick, and the destitute. The sisterhood included Sisters, Probationers, and Associates. It went out of existence in 1876.

Sisterhood of St. Joseph of Nazareth. Founded in Bronxville, New York, in 1892, it was sometimes called the Society of St. Joseph of Nazareth. It operated St. Martha's Training Home for Girls in New York City and the Nazareth Industrial School in Bronxville. It went out of existence around 1920.

Sisterhood of St. Martha. After the Sisterhood of the Good Shepherd in Baltimore, Maryland, disbanded, one of the Sisters moved to Louisville, Kentucky, and established the Orphanage of the Good Shepherd in 1869. Others joined her and they founded the Sisterhood of St. Martha on June 29, 1875. This diocesan Sisterhood assumed charge of the orphanage. The sisterhood is no longer in existence.

Sisters of the Annunciation of the Blessed Virgin Mary. Religious order founded in 1893 in New York City. By 1900 it was operating the House of the Annunciation in New York to care for physically disabled children and St. Elizabeth's House, a summer retreat, in Riverbank, Connecticut. It went out of existence around 1935.

Sisters of Bethany. Bishop Joseph Pere Bell Wilmer (1812–1878) of Louisiana founded the Order of the Sisters of St.

Philip and St. James on Nov. 7, 1871, to care for the children in the Children's Home in New Orleans. In 1896 the name was changed to the Sisters of Bethany. The order went out of existence when the last Sister, Mary Louisa Fitch, died on Feb. 3, 1932.

Sisters of Charity. This monastic order was founded in 1869 in England by the Rev. Arthur Hawkins Ward and Miss Elizabeth Lloyd. Ward was guided by the Rule of St. Vincent de Paul developed for the first Sisters of Charity in France in the seventeenth century. On July 1, 1967, the Sisters came to the United States to answer a call from the Rev. Jack Adams to staff St. Jude's Ranch for abused and neglected children in Boulder City, Nevada. In 1977 the sisters purchased the old Boulder City hospital and converted it into a convent for the sisters in the United States and a retreat center. On Apr. 5, 1981, Wellspring Convent and Retreat Center was dedicated by Bishop Wesley Frensdorff. The sisters left St. Jude's Ranch in 1982. Their primary ministry is to visit the sick, the elderly, and those in prison. Their life is centered around the Holy Eucharist and recitation of the Daily Office. The mother house is in Plymouth, England.

Sisters of St. Gregory. *See* Companion Sisters of St. Gregory (CSSG).

Situation Ethics. Moral decision-making understood as highly specific to the situation or context. Situation ethics is often contrasted with a focus on moral principles or duties which are seen as leading to formalism and legalism. A variety of reasons may be used to support a situational ethic. Most combine an existentialist emphasis on the uniqueness of each situation with an emphasis on the will of the person making decisions. Situation ethics often are dispositional ethics in which the right orientation of the will is important. Examples of such an ethic include Augustine's dictum "Love God and do what you will," Luther's understanding of the freedom of the Christian given in faith active in love, and Karl Barth's emphasis on the uniqueness of the concrete command of God given anew in each situation and moment in time. Situation ethics also includes consequentialism in which judgments are made based upon the consequences that follow from the actions taken in a situation. Anglican ethicist Joseph Fletcher popularized situation ethics by combining an emphasis on love and a focus on consequences.

Skiles, William West (Oct. 12, 1807–Dec. 8, 1862). Missionary deacon and pioneer monastic in Southern Appalachia. He was born in Hertford, North Carolina. When Bishop Levi S. Ives of North Carolina decided to establish a mission in the Watauga region of North Carolina in 1844, he invited Skiles to be the manager of the farm and the teacher of agriculture. The mission was named Valle Crucis. Within a year at the mission, Skiles decided to enter the ordained ministry so that he could better serve those who had been placed in his charge. On Aug. 1, 1845, he was ordained deacon. Skiles practiced medicine among the mountain people and worked in the missions. In 1847 Bishop Ives founded a secret Episcopal monastic order, the Order of the Holy Cross. The community was controversial because of its monastic character. It disbanded in 1849. "Brother" Skiles, as he had come to be known, decided to remain in the region and continue his missionary work. In the inscription on the altar in the Church of the Holy Cross, Valle Crucis, Skiles is memorialized as the "first person in the Anglican Communion since Reformation Days to persevere in the life of Poverty, Chastity and Obedience under Vows." The education and parish hall wing of the Church of the Holy Cross is named "Skiles Hall." Skiles died in Mitchell County, North Carolina. *See* Valle Crucis, North Carolina.

Smart, Christopher (Apr. 11, 1722–May 20, 1771). English religious poet. He was born in Shipbourne, Kent, England. Smart was educated at Durham Grammar School and Pembroke Hall, Cambridge. He was elected a scholar of Cambridge University in 1742, and a fellow of Pembroke Hall in 1745. Emotional instability soon became evident, and in 1749 he lost his university appointment. He moved to London and tried to make his way as a journalist. Every year from 1750 to 1755 he won the Seatonian Prize of Cambridge for a poem on a religious subject. He won the friendship of many of the artistic and literary "greats" of his day. In 1756 he was confined to an asylum for the first time. He was in and out of asylums from 1756 until his death in a debtor's prison. During lucid periods, however, he was able to work creatively. Smart produced several collections of poetry which provide the sources of texts found in contemporary hymnals. *The Hymnal 1982* uses four texts by Smart, including "Awake, arise, lift up your voice" (Hymn 212) and "Where is this stupendous stranger?" (Hymn 491). His poetry also provides the text for Benjamin Britten's "Rejoice in the Lamb" (1958). Smart died in London.

Smith, Benjamin Bosworth (June 13, 1794–May 31, 1884). Bishop of Kentucky and ninth Presiding Bishop. He was born in Bristol, Rhode Island. Smith graduated from Brown University in 1816. He was ordained deacon on Apr. 23, 1817, and priest on June 24, 1818. He began his ordained ministry at St. Michael's Church, Marblehead, Massachusetts, and then moved to Virginia to be rector of St. George's Church, Accomack County. About two years later Smith became the rector of Zion Church, Charlestown, Virginia (now West Virginia). In 1823 he became the rector of St. Stephen's Church, Middlebury, Vermont. In 1828 he took charge of Grace Church Mission, Philadelphia, and on Oct. 8, 1830, he became the rector of Christ Church, Lexington, Kentucky. On Oct. 31, 1832, Smith was consecrated the first Bishop of Kentucky and served in that position until his death. Under his leadership, the Episcopal Theological Seminary in Kentucky was established in 1834. It was the fourth seminary to be established in the Episcopal Church. A controversy arose in the diocese about Smith's ability to function as bishop, rector, and head of the seminary at the same time, and over Smith's management of funds collected for the seminary. In Sept. 1837 a formal trial was held and Smith was cleared of the charges against him. He resigned as rector of Christ Church on Oct. 22, 1838. From 1839 until 1842 Smith was superintendent of public instruction for the State of Kentucky. He served as Presiding Bishop from Jan. 9, 1868 to May 31, 1884. Smith died in New York City.

Smith, Captain John (Jan. 1579–June 21, 1631). An organizer of the Virginia Company of London. Smith was born in Willoughby, Lincolnshire, England. He promoted the Virginia Company's plan to found a colony in America. In 1606 he and 143 other colonists sailed to Virginia. They landed at Jamestown on May 24, 1607. Legend claims that he was rescued by Pocahontas, the daughter of Chief Powhatan, after he was taken prisoner by the Indians in 1607. Smith was Governor of Virginia in 1608–1609. His pamphlet, *A True Relation* (1608), provides the earliest description of the settlement at Jamestown. In 1612 Smith published *A Map of Virginia*. It was a primary contribution to cartography. In 1614 he explored the coast of New England. He published *A Description of New England* (1616), which fixed the name of that region. He died in London.

Smith, John Cotton (Aug. 4, 1826–Jan. 9, 1882). Nineteenth-century broad churchman. He was born in

Andover, Massachusetts. Smith attended Phillips Academy, Andover, and graduated from Bowdoin College in 1847. After studying theology at Kenyon College, he was ordained deacon on May 6, 1849, and priest on Aug. 4, 1850. He began his ministry as rector of St. John's Church, Bangor, Maine, where he served from 1850 until 1852. He then served as assistant minister of Trinity Church, Boston. In 1860 he became the rector of the Church of the Ascension, New York City, where he served until his death. Smith became associate editor of *The Protestant Churchman* in 1867, and later became the editor. He was committed to the church's mission of social service and was active in ecumenical activities. His book, *Improvements of the Tenement House System in New York* (1879), was most significant in bringing this issue to the attention of the city's leaders. He taught that the Episcopal Church "offered the best available basis for the unifying of American religion." Smith was a promoter of the Church Congress, one of the major expressions of the broad church movement. He died in New York City.

Smith, Robert (Aug. 25, 1732–Oct. 28, 1801). First Bishop of South Carolina. He was born in the County of Norfolk, England. Smith studied at Caius College and Gonville College, Cambridge University, and received his B.A. in 1753. Smith was ordained deacon on Mar. 7, 1756, and priest on Dec. 21, 1756. He emigrated to America. Smith became assistant minister at St. Philip's Church, Charleston, South Carolina, in 1757, and rector in 1759. He supported the American Revolution. When the British occupied Charleston in 1780 he fled to Maryland and became priest-in-charge of St. Paul's Parish in Queen Anne County. Smith returned to St. Philip's, Charleston, in 1783. He helped to found the College of Charleston, where he served as president until 1797. On Sept. 13, 1795, he was consecrated Bishop of South Carolina. He served in that position until his death. He also continued as rector of St. Philip's Church. He died in Charleston.

Smith, William (Sept. 7, 1727–May 14, 1803). Educator and priest. Born in Aberdeen, Scotland, Smith received his M.A. degree from the University of Aberdeen in 1747. He lived in London after graduation and served as an agent for the Society for the Education of Parochial Schoolmasters and then for the Society for the Propagation of the Gospel. In 1751 he sailed to the United States to be a tutor to a family on Long Island. In Aug. 1753 Smith published *A General Idea of the College of Mirania*, which was a description of the ideal university. He returned to England. Smith was ordained deacon on Dec. 21, 1753, and on Dec. 23, 1753, he was ordained priest. Upon his return to Philadelphia, Smith taught at the Academy and Charitable School. When a college was added in 1754 he became Provost of the College, Academy and Charitable School of Philadelphia. He served in that position until 1779. While provost he also served as rector of Trinity Church, Oxford, Pennsylvania, 1766–1777. In 1779 the Pennsylvania Assembly passed an act which made void the charter of the College and created a new institution called the Trustees of the University of the State of Pennsylvania. Smith moved to Maryland. He became the principal of Kent County Free School, which had been founded around 1729. In 1782 Kent School became Washington College. While there he was also rector of Kent Parish. During the American Revolution he supported the Loyalist position. Smith played a leading role in the organization of the Episcopal Church and in adapting the BCP to the Episcopal Church. He was elected the first Bishop of Maryland in 1783, but his election was not confirmed by the General Convention. Smith died in Philadelphia.

Smith, William (1754–Apr. 6, 1821). Leading priest and musician. He was born probably at Aberdeen, Scotland, and possibly attended the University of Aberdeen. Smith came to the American colonies in 1785 as a priest in the Scottish Nonjuring Episcopal Church. He served from Jan. until July 1785 as minister at Trinity Church, Oxford, and All Saints, Pequestan, Pennsylvania. From July 1785 until 1787 he was rector of Stepney Parish, Maryland. From 1787 until 1790, he was rector of St. Paul's Church, Narragansett, Rhode Island. From 1790 until 1797, he was rector of Trinity Church, Newport. He was a leader in the organization of the Diocese of Rhode Island in 1790. From 1797 until 1800 Smith was rector of St. Paul's Church, Norwalk, Connecticut. In 1800 he went to New York City, where he opened a grammar school and gained a reputation as a teacher.

In Apr. 1802 Smith became the second Principal of the Episcopal Academy at Cheshire, Connecticut. However, he was unsuccessful and forced to resign on June 5, 1806. Later he returned to Connecticut but never again had a permanent ecclesiastical position. He influenced the development of church music in the Episcopal Church when he published *The Churchman's Choral Companion to His Prayer Book* (1809). In 1814 he published *The*

Reasonableness of Setting Forth the Most Worthy Praise of Almighty God, According to the Usage of the Primitive Church; With Historical Views of the Nature, Origin, and Progress of Metre Psalmody, which criticized the practice of singing metrical psalms and argued for chanting. Possibly Smith's greatest contribution was writing the "Office of Institution of Ministers." It was adopted by the Diocese of Connecticut and then sent to the 1804 General Convention, which approved it. The 1808 General Convention made slight alternations to it and included it in the BCP where it has remained with modifications until the present. He died in New York City.

Sobornost. 1) A Russian theological term indicating a conciliar and ecumenical ideal of the church, based on a spiritual unity of freedom and love. This interior communion of the church is contrasted with Protestant individualism and the external ordering of the Roman Catholic Church. The term is a neologism, or new word, based on the Russian for catholic, assembly. It is associated with the nineteenth-century Slavophile movement and the writings of Alexis S. Khomyakov (1806–1860). Russian Orthodox claim *sobornost* as a special attribute of their church. The term does not have an exact English translation. 2) Title of the journal of the Anglican-Orthodox Fellowship of St. Alban and St. Sergius. This ecumenical fellowship was founded in 1928, and its journal was renamed *Sobornost* in 1935. The title reflects the ecumenical ideals of the fellowship.

Social Gospel. The Social Gospel movement, which began towards the end of the nineteenth century and continued until World War I, was chiefly a response to the failure of mainline Protestant churches to address the social realities of poverty and industrialization. Their tendency had been to concern themselves exclusively with individual salvation and economic prosperity. As a theological movement, it found its chief exponent in Walter Rauschenbusch (1861–1918). Rauschenbusch argued in *A Theology for the Social Gospel* (1917), a series of lectures given at Yale, that sin is more than individual. He understood sin to be the consequence of forces of evil in human society so that salvation must involve the redemption of the social order as well as the redemption of the individual. In this redemptive process, he argued, the churches have a critical role to play. The churches must exercise a prophetic commitment to redeeming the social order and show forth the presence of the Kingdom of

God, which he understood as "a fellowship of righteousness."

While it could be said that the movement itself died, its continuing impact upon Protestant churches can be seen in the social action programs which have characterized much of mainline Protestantism since World War II. Its continuing importance lies in its emphasis upon the social dimension of Christian faith over against the individualism of much American religion.

Social Justice. Justice indicates what is right or fair. Social justice is concerned with the fairness of transactions and distribution. What is called commutative justice considers such matters as contracts and due process of law. Commutative justice is focused on civil law, but it includes matters of criminal law in the case of punishment for theft. Distributive justice considers the distribution of goods and burdens for the sake of the individual and the society as a whole. Social justice has most often focused on questions of distributive justice and the common good. The central question of social justice is, "On what basis are goods and burdens distributed fairly?" In fact, several bases or principles of justice indicate what is fair, depending upon what is being distributed. This includes individual need, merit or deserving effort, and benefit to the society as a whole. Justice is often complex since goods and services such as education or taxes are distributed on the basis of several principles. The Christian tradition has emphasized the intrinsic value or worth of the individual person. It has thereby claimed that justice requires meeting the basic needs of the individual and insuring that person's participation in society. However, disagreement is great over what constitutes basic justice and how individual needs and the benefit of the whole of society may be best achieved.

Social Service, Joint Commission on. The 1910 General Convention discharged the Joint Commission on the Relations of Capital and Labor and appointed a Joint Commission on Social Service. Its purpose was to study and report upon social and industrial conditions; to coordinate the activities of the various organizations in the church in the interests of social service; to cooperate with similar bodies in other communions; to encourage sympathetic relations between capital and labor; and to deal according to their discretion with these and kindred matters. It consisted of five bishops, five presbyters, and five laymen. The work of this commission made the Episcopal Church a leader in the Social Gospel movement. In 1919 the Joint Commission was replaced by the Department of Christian Social Service.

Society for the Advancement of Christianity in Pennsylvania. One of several predecessors to the Domestic and Foreign Missionary Society. It was organized in 1812. The society's purpose was to support missionary work in western Pennsylvania. It used its funds to support young men studying for the ordained ministry, to buy them books, and to send missionaries to the western areas of Pennsylvania. Two of its earliest missionaries were Joseph Pilmore and Jackson Kemper. William Augustus Muhlenberg also served as a missionary for the society. After the General Conventions of 1820 and 1821 established the Domestic and Foreign Missionary Society, most dioceses folded their Advancement of Christianity Societies into it.

Society of Anglican and Lutheran Theologians (SALT). A professional society of scholars and theologians from the Episcopal Church and the Evangelical Lutheran Church in America. The Conference of Anglican Theologians, formed in the early 1960s, met at the Lutheran Theological Seminary in Gettysburg, Pennsylvania, on Sept. 26–28, 1997, the first meeting to include Lutheran theologians and the first on a Lutheran seminary campus. On Sept. 28, the Conference voted to change its name to the Society of Anglican and Lutheran Theologians to encourage the ecumenical relationship of the two churches resulting from the Lutheran-Episcopal dialogues. *See* Conference of Anglican Theologians.

Society of the Atonement. The society was founded on Oct. 7, 1898, by the Rev. Lewis Thomas Wattson and Mother Lurana Mary White (1870–1935) at Graymoor, near Garrison, New York. It was to work and pray for the reunion of a divided Christianity. On Oct. 30, 1909, at the Chapel of Our Lady of the Angels, Graymoor, Bishop Joseph Conroy, Vicar General of the Diocese of Ogdenberg, received into the Roman Catholic Church Wattson, Mother Lurana, and fifteen of their followers. The society published *The Lamp*.

Society of Christian Socialists. Ecumenical socialist organization founded in Feb. 1889 by William Dwight Porter Bliss, Vida Dutton Scudder, and other Boston clergy. Bliss was its leader. On May 15, 1889, it adopted a "Declaration of Principles," which stated its purpose: "To awaken members of Christian churches to the fact that the teachings of Jesus Christ lead directly to some specific form or forms of Socialism." It sought to encourage the church to apply itself to the realization of the social principles of Christianity. The society began publication of a monthly journal, *The Dawn*, on May 15, 1889. The society went out of existence in 1896 when Bliss became a traveling secretary of the Christian Social Union. *See* Bliss, William Dwight Porter; *see* Scudder, Vida Dutton.

Society of the Companions of the Holy Cross. A society of church women founded on May 3, 1884, the Feast of the Invention of the Cross on the Roman Catholic calendar, for the purposes of intercession, thanksgiving, simplicity of life, Christian unity and social justice. It was founded by Emily Malbone Morgan and Harriet Hastings (d. 1915), who were inspired by the desire of the young invalid Adelyn Howard to offer prayers for a wider circle of people and her expressed need for spiritual companionship. The two women drew up rules and aims and selected an ancient prayer for daily use for a group of women envisioned as "Companions of the Cross." The society's first annual conference was held at Beulahland in Blandford, Massachusetts, which had been established as a summer vacation home for working women, girls, and children. In the summer of 1901 the society rented a farmhouse on the grounds of Governor Dummer Academy in Byfield, Massachusetts, so that the women might live a corporate life together. This was the first Adelynrood. The name of this place combines Adelyn Howard's name with the word "rood," which means cross. Conferences and retreats for companions and their guests were held here each summer until 1914, when a new Adelynrood was built. The members of the society are women of the Episcopal Church. They are devoted to intercession, thanksgiving, and simplicity. The society continues to host summer conferences and retreats at Adelynrood.

Society for the Education of Pious Young Men for the Ministry of the Protestant Episcopal Church in Maryland and Virginia. This society, usually called the Education Society, was founded in June 1818 in Washington, D.C., by William Holland Wilmer, William Meade, Oliver Norris, Reuel Keith, and others to raise funds to enable candidates for the ministry to prepare themselves under competent tutors. It supported Reuel Keith at the College of William and Mary where he taught theology students. Keith was at William and Mary from 1820 until 1823. However, he had

only one or two students, and the experiment was abandoned in 1823. The society, which was called "the Seminary in embryo," worked with the Diocese of Virginia to establish the Protestant Episcopal Theological Seminary at Alexandria, Virginia.

Society of the Epiphany. Religious order for women founded in 1897 in Washington, D.C., by Bishop Henry Satterlee and a former member of the Community of St. Mary. It was also known as the Sisterhood of the Epiphany. It operated a Retreat House and a school for girls in Washington. The order is no longer in existence.

Society for the Increase of the Ministry. This organization was founded on Oct. 2, 1857, at Hartford, Connecticut, by the Revs. Edward A. Washburn, Alonzo B. Chapin, Charles R. Fisher, A. B. Goodrich, Samuel F. Jarvis, David R. Goodwin, F. R. Pynchon, and Mr. Samuel Eliot. Its purpose was to find young men for the ordained ministry "and to aid them in acquiring a thorough education." On June 9, 1859, it was incorporated by the legislature of the State of Connecticut. The society is governed by an executive committee of nine persons. Business operations are handled by an executive director. In the past the society provided financial assistance only to postulants and candidates enrolled on a full-time basis in one of the eleven accredited Episcopal seminaries. The society later recognized the growing need of the church to support alternative measures for education leading to ordination. It expanded its award criteria to provide funding to students in part-time educational programs or seminaries outside the Episcopal Church. Students in such alternative educational programs must remain postulants or candidates within the Episcopal Church to receive financial assistance from the society.

Society for the Preservation of the Book of Common Prayer. *See* Prayer Book Society.

Society for Promoting Christian Knowledge (SPCK). The oldest Anglican missionary society. It is sometimes called the Society for the Promotion of Christian Knowledge. It was organized in 1698 by the Rev. Thomas Bray and four laymen "to promote and encourage the erection of charity schools in all parts of England and Wales; to disperse, both at home and abroad, Bibles and tracts of religion; and in general to advance the honor of God and the good of mankind, by promoting Christian knowledge at home and in the other parts of the world by the best methods that should offer." The first meeting of the society was held on Mar. 9, 1699. It established libraries for the colonies. It supports Anglican churches and schools and publishes materials in many languages for worldwide distribution. SPCK Publishing is one of the largest and most active publishers in Britain. Branches of SPCK exist in England, India, Australia, and the United States. *See* Society for the Propagation of the Gospel; *see* Society for Promoting Christian Knowledge/United States of America (SPCK/USA).

Society for Promoting Christian Knowledge/United States of America (SPCK/USA). Sister society of the SPCK in England. SPCK/USA was established on Nov. 1, 1983, at the University of the South, Sewanee, Tennessee. It was housed in Hamilton Hall, the building of the School of Theology. SPCK/USA is a part of the cooperating network of the societies in England, India, New Zealand, and Ireland. It sends Sunday Church School materials around the world, prepares book translations, supports seminarians and seminaries in impoverished lands, keeps Christian printing presses running, and sends Bibles, theological works, commentaries, and other books to the church in more than fifty countries. The Archbishop of Canterbury is the society's patron and the Presiding Bishop is its honorary president. *See* Society for Promoting Christian Knowledge (SPCK).

Society for Promoting and Encouraging Arts and Knowledge (SPEAK). A fivefold ministry to help all who want to learn more about the Episcopal Church. This ministry includes the Episcopal Book Club (EBC), founded in 1953 to provide carefully selected books on the Anglican tradition to subscribers; *The Anglican Digest* (TAD), a journal; The Anglican Bookstore (TAB), which offers selected current and classic books and tapes covering a wide range of Christian interests; Operation Pass Along, which solicits used and new books about the church so they can be passed on to others; and the Howard Lane Foland Library, started in 1980, which provides a library for scholars who wish to study a particular church-related topic. Since 1960 SPEAK has been located at Hillspeak, Arkansas. *See* Anglican Digest, The; *see* Episcopal Book Club (EBC); *see* Hillspeak.

Society for the Promotion of Church Work Among the Colored People. This society was organized in Baltimore by a group of African American Episcopalians in 1876. It was organized in the same year that the Protestant Episcopal Freedman's Commission to Colored People disbanded. The society worked for a national program of education and evangelism among African Americans. The society went out of existence in a few years.

Society for the Promotion of Evangelical Knowledge. This organization, sometimes known as the Evangelical Knowledge Society, was founded in 1847 to counteract the influence of the Oxford Movement's *Tracts for the Times*. By "evangelical" it meant the leading and fundamental doctrines of the Reformation. Its professed object was to maintain and set forth the principles and doctrines of the gospel as embodied in the BCP and the Thirty-Nine Articles. The society taught that scripture is the sole rule of faith, that we are utterly lost and helpless sinners, that Jesus is a sufficient Savior, and that justification is a gracious act of God, received by faith without works. The society is no longer in existence.

Society for the Propagation of the Gospel in Foreign Parts (SPG). This Anglican missionary society was organized in the early eighteenth century by Thomas Bray to achieve two objectives: 1) to provide an educated and effective ordained ministry for Church of England parishes in the English colonies; and 2) to Christianize the non-Christians of the world, especially the Native Americans. It was to assist the work of the Society for the Promotion of Christian Knowledge, which had been founded previously. The SPG was granted a charter by King William III on June 16, 1701, and held its first meeting on June 27, 1701. The society sent 353 missionaries to the American colonies. In the eighteenth century most of its work was done in the American colonies, Canada, and the West Indies. In the nineteenth century its sphere of influence was increased to include India, South and West Africa, Australia, and the Far East. On Jan. 1, 1965, the SPG merged with the Universities' Mission to Central Africa, which was founded in 1857, to form the United Society for the Propagation of the Gospel.

Society of St. John the Evangelist, The (SSJE) (Cowley Fathers). The Society of St. John the Evangelist, popularly known as the Cowley Fathers, is an Anglican monastic order whose American headquarters is located in Cambridge, Massachusetts. On Dec. 27, 1866, Richard Meux Benson, vicar of the village of Cowley (near Oxford),

England, established an order of missionary priests who took vows of celibacy, poverty, and obedience. Also involved in the founding of SSJE were Simeon Wilberforce O'Neill and Charles C. Grafton, an Episcopal priest who was living in England. Benson had been strongly influenced by the Oxford Movement, the revival of catholic theology and practice within the mid-nineteenth century Church of England. He came to the United States with two other priests in Nov. 1870 and established a residence house in Boston. In 1877 the society also assumed control of a church in a rundown part of the city. There the Cowley Fathers combined a life of prayer with an active social ministry. In the early twentieth century, members of the society began a ministry among students at Harvard University. With the financial support of Isabella Stewart Gardner, a wealthy devotee of Anglo-catholicism, the society erected a medieval-style monastery near Harvard Square in the 1920s.

The ministries of the society today are essentially those of hospitality, spiritual direction, preaching, and the conducting of individual and private retreats. Members of the society are encouraged to respond individually to the call of the gospel by participating in local programs which care for the sick, feed and shelter the homeless, or serve the poor and disadvantaged. Another ministry of the society is Cowley Publications, which publishes a variety of books and other resources for ongoing theological exploration and spiritual development. *See* Benson, Richard Meux; *see* Grafton, Charles Chapman.

Sodality. A pious fellowship or guild that promotes the Christian life of its members and may include other religious purposes such as evangelism or outreach to the needy. Although the term has been associated with Roman Catholic laity, there have been Anglican and Episcopal sodalities. *See* Living Rosary of Our Lady and S. Dominic.

Solemn Collects. Biddings and collects used in the Good Friday service (BCP, pp. 277–280). It includes biddings for the church throughout the world, for all nations and peoples of the earth, for those who suffer in body or mind, and for those who have not received the gospel of Christ. The biddings of the solemn collects may be read by a deacon or other person appointed. After a period of silence, each bidding is concluded by the celebrant with a collect. The biddings may be adapted at the discretion of the celebrant. *The Altar Book* provides musical settings for the biddings.

The solemn collects are derived from the most ancient western form of the prayers of the people. The biddings date from the third or fourth century, and the collects date from the fifth century. The ancient solemn collects appear in the Gelasian and Gregorian sacramentaries. The practice of kneeling for the bidding and standing for the collect dates from the sixth century. The BCP states that the people may be directed to stand or kneel for the solemn collects. The 1549 BCP included two collects that were derived from the ancient solemn collects. The 1979 BCP is the first Prayer Book to restore the solemn collects to the Good Friday liturgy.

Solemn Eucharist. Eucharist celebrated with a full ceremonial style, typically including ministers (lay and ordained) in vestments, the chanting of all or part of the liturgy of the word and the eucharistic prayer, sung responses, a vested choir, and (usually) incense. Such a full celebration is often reserved for a major feast or the main Sunday service of a congregation. The elaborate ceremonial emphasizes the significance of the occasion. *See* High Mass; *see* Anglo-Catholic Movement, Anglo-Catholicism.

Solemn Evensong. The Evening Office done with full ceremonial, usually including processional(s), chanting of the officiant's parts with chanted responses by the people, singing of the canticles by choir or congregation, and the use of incense at the *Phos Hilaron* and/or the *Magnificat*. *See* Evensong; *see* Evening Prayer.

Solemn Procession. A procession undertaken with full ceremonial, usually at the beginning of a festive liturgy or on some penitential occasions. The procession ordinarily includes all the participating ministers, lay and ordained. The route of the procession takes them around the inside of the church. In some customaries, the procession begins and ends at the altar. Often the procession involves the use of incense. It is customary for many parishes to say or sing the Great Litany (BCP, pp. 148–54) in conjunction with a solemn procession during Lent and on Rogation Days.

Solitary. *See* Eremitic; *see* Hermit, Hermitess.

SOMA. *See* Sharing of Ministries Abroad U.S.A. (SOMA).

Song of Mary, The. *See Magnificat*.

Song of Moses, The. Canticle based on an OT text celebrating the crossing of the Red Sea by the people of Israel, as recorded in Ex 15:1–6, 11–13, 17–18. It may be a later elaboration of the song of Miriam, Ex 15:19–21. This canticle, also known as *"Cantemus Domino,"* appears as Canticle 8 in the BCP (p. 85). The Song of Moses is used at the Easter Vigil after the reading of Israel's deliverance at the Red Sea (Ex 14:10–15:1). It is especially suitable for use in the Easter season and is suggested for use by the Table of Canticles after the OT reading at Morning Prayer on Sundays during the Easter season. It is also suggested for use after the OT reading on Thursdays at Morning Prayer throughout the year and at Evening Prayer on Mondays except during Lent. The 1979 BCP was the first to include this canticle.

Song of Praise. 1) *Gloria in excelsis* or another song of praise is sung or said prior to the collect of the day at the eucharist from Christmas Day through the Feast of the Epiphany; on Sundays from Easter Day through the Day of Pentecost, on all the days of Easter Week, and on Ascension Day. It may be used at other times, and it is traditionally used on major feasts. It is not used on the Sundays or ordinary weekdays of Advent or Lent (BCP, pp. 356, 406). *The Hymnal 1982* provides a section of hymns of Praise to God (Hymns 372–433). Other hymns of praise may be used. Canticles of praise from the Daily Office may also be used in place of *Gloria in excelsis. The Hymnal 1982 Accompaniment Edition, Vol. 1*, includes a chart with canticles for use in place of *Gloria in excelsis* (S 355). *The Hymnal 1982* provides musical settings for the canticles (S 177–S 288). A listing of hymns based on the canticles (metrical settings) is provided by *The Hymnal 1982 Accompaniment Edition, Vol. 1* (pp. 680–681). Marion J. Hatchett notes in his *Commentary on the American Prayer Book* (p. 322) that the alternative song of praise should be a canticle from the Daily Office, based on the traditional Gallican use and the options listed for use at the Easter Vigil (BCP, p. 294). A song of praise may be used instead of the *Te Deum laudamus* at the conclusion of the All Hallows' Eve Service. A song of praise may also be used instead of the *Te Deum laudamus* or the *Gloria in excelsis* after the seating of the bishop at the Welcoming and Seating of a Bishop in the Cathedral. These services are found in the *BOS*. 2) Canticles 2 and 13, *Benedictus es, Domine*, are also known as A Song of Praise (BCP, pp. 49, 90). These canticles are based on the

Song of the Three Young Men, 29–34. *Benedictus es, Domine* may have been a hymn of praise for the restoration of temple worship. Canticles 2 and 13 may be used at Morning and Evening Prayer. The BCP suggests use of *Benedictus es, Domine* after the OT reading at Morning Prayer on Tuesday, and after the OT reading at Evening Prayer on Friday (pp. 144–145).

Song of the Redeemed. *See* Magna et mirabilia.

Songs for Celebration. This 1980 hymnal supplement was intended to broaden the forms of musical expression available to the church. It was produced under the direction of the Standing Commission on Church Music as No. IV in the *Church Hymnal Series.* George E. Mims served as music editor. This hymnal supplement includes canticles, canons, hymns, and folk songs.

Songs for Liturgy and More Hymns and Spiritual Songs. This supplement to *The Hymnal* (1940) was prepared by the Joint Commission on Church Music and approved by the 1970 General Convention. It was published in 1971. The general editor was Norman C. Mealy.

Soteriology. Theology of salvation. Theological reflection on the meaning of salvation in Christ and how we may share salvation by faith. Salvation is eternal life in the fullness of God's love. In Christ, we are redeemed from sin and death and restored to right relationship with God. We are made righteous and justified in Christ, despite the inadequacy of our works for salvation. Salvation is deliverance from anything that threatens to prevent fulfillment and enjoyment of our relationship with God. Through the Spirit, especially in the life and sacraments of the church, we may share in Christ's life, death, and resurrection. We may participate in a saving process of sanctification by which the saving life of Christ becomes increasingly our own reality. This process is completed and revealed in Christ, and it is begun in us through faith in him. Completed union with God is the end of this saving process. In Christ, we come to be at one with God. Although this saving process is not yet completed, we look with hope for its fulfillment in the final coming of the kingdom of God. The Episcopal theologian William Porcher DuBose wrote *The Soteriology of the New Testament* (1892), which is a significant presentation of soteriology. *See* Atonement; *see* Heaven; *see* Redeemer; *see* Righteousness.

Soul. The spiritual nature of a human being, as distinguished from the bodily or physical nature. This distinction is reflected in Eucharistic Prayer I, which states, "here we offer and present unto thee, O Lord, our selves, our souls and bodies. . . ." (BCP, p. 336). Scriptural sources and Christian teaching have not always been clear or consistent concerning the soul. Aquinas, following Aristotle, identifies the soul as the metaphysical "form" of the body, which is its "matter." Soul and body thus act jointly as co-principles of being and together constitute the human unity. The soul is understood to be directly created by God and immortal. It is meant to be united with a body. The soul is separated from the body at death, but understood to be capable of separate existence until reunited with a body at the resurrection of the dead. The BCP Catechism states that the resurrection of the body means that "God will raise us from death in the fullness of our being. . . ." (BCP, p. 862). In scholastic terms, this fullness of being is understood to include both the soul and a bodily nature. The modern understanding prefers to see body and soul as a substantive unity in which previous distinctions are blurred.

Source Criticism. Critical study of the sources of the NT gospels. Given the similarity yet individuality of the synoptic gospels, nineteenth-century scholars sought to find a way to determine the gospels' historical connection to each other. They sought to determine the sources that were used by the authors of the gospels to produce the three distinct but similar stories of Jesus. Because we have no specific historical information about the author, time, or place of composition, the criticism is based on the texts of the gospels themselves. Therefore the solutions about the sources are suggested possibilities. There are two major accepted solutions: 1) *Two Source Theory*. Because much of Mark's material is found in Matthew and Luke, in the same basic sequence, and because Mark is much shorter than Matthew and Luke, it is argued that Mark was one of their sources. The second source identifies some other material in Matthew and Luke which is very similar but not found at all in Mark. It is called "Q," from the German word for source, "*Quelle*." Since both Matthew and Luke have material that is unique in each gospel, this theory also refers to sources "M" and "L." The great majority of NT scholars accept the Two Source Theory. 2) *Griesbach hypothesis*. Because the "Q" source has never been found as a document, Matthew would be the earliest, used as a source by Luke. This view holds that Mark is the latest gospel, a condensed, compacted version of Matthew and Luke. *See* Synoptic Gospels.

South American Missionary Society of the Episcopal Church, Inc. (SAMS). A voluntary missionary society whose missionaries work in evangelism, church planting and a wide range of social ministries. It was founded on Dec. 3, 1976, when a group of Episcopalians met at Christ Church in Hamilton, Massachusetts. The rector of Christ Church, the Rev. James Hampson, wanted to see what might be done to help the church meet more fully its global responsibilities regarding the proclamation of the gospel. It was decided that an independent sending agency should be formed to supplement the work already being done. The focus of the work was Latin America, and the new society worked closely with the British South American Missionary Society, which was founded in 1844. The first SAMS-USA missionaries were John and Susan Harvard, who went to Peru. In 1979 the society established its headquarters in Union Mills, North Carolina. In Apr. 1988 SAMS moved to Ambridge, Pennsylvania, across the street from Trinity Episcopal School for Ministry.

South Carolina, Diocese of. The first convention of this diocese was held on May 12, 1785, at the State House in Charles Town. The 1922 General Convention voted to divide the diocese. The Diocese of South Carolina includes the following counties: Allendale, Bamberg, Barnwell, Beaufort, Berkeley, Calhoun, Charleston, Chesterfield, Clarendon, Colleton, Darlington, Dillon, Dorchester, Florence, Georgetown, Hampton, Horry, Jasper, Lee, Marion, Marlboro, Orangeburg, Sumter, and Williamsburg. On Sept. 20, 1963, the Church of St. Luke and St. Paul, Charleston, became the Cathedral of St. Luke and St. Paul.

South Dakota, Diocese of. The House of Bishops established the Missionary District of Dakota in 1868, and in 1871 it established the Missionary District of Niobrara. On Oct. 11, 1883, the House of Bishops divided the Missionary District of Dakota into the Missionary District of North Dakota and the Missionary District of South Dakota. The Missionary District of Niobrara was incorporated into the Missionary District of South Dakota. On Dec. 18, 1889, the Church of St. Augusta, Sioux Falls, was dedicated. It is now known as Calvary Cathedral. The Missionary District of South Dakota did not become a diocese until 1971. The primary convention of the Diocese of South Dakota was held at Trinity Church, Pierre, Sept.

23–26, 1971. *See* Niobrara Convocation; *see* Niobrara, Missionary District of.

South Florida, Diocese of. The 1892 General Convention voted to divide the Diocese of Florida. The Missionary Jurisdiction of Southern Florida included all the counties in Florida south of the counties of Leon, Alachua, Putman and St. John's. The first convocation of the Missionary District was held Feb. 21–22, 1893, at the Church of the Holy Cross, Sanford. On Mar. 31, 1902, St. Luke's Church, Orlando, was designated the Cathedral Church of St. Luke. The first convention of the Diocese of South Florida was held Jan. 16–18, 1923, at St. Luke's Cathedral, Orlando. The name was also changed to the Diocese of South Florida at this convention. The 1969 General Convention voted to divide the Diocese of South Florida into three dioceses, which are now the dioceses of Central Florida, Southeast Florida, and Southwest Florida.

Southeast Florida, Diocese of. The 1969 General Convention voted to divide the Diocese of South Florida into three dioceses. One of the three dioceses had the temporary name of the East Coast Diocese of Florida, but at the primary convention at Holy Trinity Church, West Palm Beach, Oct. 8, 1969, the name was changed to the Diocese of Southeast Florida. It includes five counties: Briarwood, Dade, Martin, Monroe, Palm Beach, and one parish in Hendry County. On Mar. 29, 1970, Trinity Church, Miami, was set apart as Trinity Cathedral.

Southeastern Mexico, Diocese of. The 1904 General Convention established the Missionary District of Mexico. The 1972 General Convention divided the Missionary District of Mexico into the Missionary District of Central and South Mexico, the Missionary District of Western Mexico, and the Missionary District of Northern Mexico. All three of these Missionary Districts became dioceses. In 1988 the House of Bishops divided the Diocese of Central and South Mexico into the Diocese of Mexico, the Diocese of Cuernavaca, and the Diocese of Southeastern Mexico. The 1994 General Convention granted the five Mexican dioceses permission to withdraw from the Episcopal Church and form an autonomous province. The Anglican Church of Mexico came into existence on Jan. 1, 1995.

Southern Brazil, Missionary District of. The mission to Brazil began on Aug. 31, 1889, when James Watson Morris (1859–1954) and Lucien Lee Kinsolving (1862–1929) sailed for Brazil as missionaries. On Oct. 20, 1898, the House of Bishops elected Kinsolving Bishop for the United States of Brazil. The 1907 General Convention established the Missionary District of Brazil, and elected Kinsolving Missionary Bishop. The same General Convention also changed the name to the Missionary District of Southern Brazil. On Sept. 30, 1949, the House of Bishops divided the Missionary District of Southern Brazil into three missionary districts—Southern Brazil, Southwestern Brazil, and Central Brazil. On Oct. 20, 1964, the House of Bishops voted for an independent Brazilian Church, and in 1965 the Episcopal Church of Brazil, became an independent Province of the Anglican Communion.

Southern Churchman. This journal began publication on Jan. 2, 1835, at Richmond, Virginia. It was published weekly, and had the motto: "Catholic For Every Truth of God. Protestant For Every Error of Man." On July 12, 1947, it absorbed *The Chronicle*, which was published at Poughkeepsie, New York. On Jan. 2, 1952, it was continued by *Episcopal Churchnews*.

Southern Episcopal Church. This body was founded late in 1962 in Nashville, Tennessee, by ten families from All Saints Episcopal Church who were dissatisfied with the Episcopal Church. The leader of the group was Burnice Hoyle Webster, a medical doctor, who became the Presiding Bishop of the Southern Episcopal Church. The group uses the 1928 BCP, and is conservative by definition. It publishes *The Southern Episcopalian*.

Southern Episcopalian. 1) This journal was published irregularly at Charleston, South Carolina, in 1854–1855, 1858–1859, and 1863. The first issue appeared on Apr. 1, 1854, and the last issue was dated Mar. 7, 1863. 2) A publication of the Southern Episcopal Church, a conservative church that was founded in 1962.

Southern Florida, Missionary District of. The General Convention of 1892 voted to divide the Diocese of Florida. The Missionary District of Southern Florida existed until 1923, when it became the Diocese of South Florida. *See* South Florida, Diocese of.

Southern Harmony. This four-shape shape-note tunebook was compiled by William Walker (1809–1875). Walker was a bookstore proprietor and singing-school teacher in Spartanburg, South Carolina. *Southern Harmony* was first published in New Haven in 1835. Several editions were published 1835–1854. It had the widest circulation of the shape-note tunebooks of its time. More than 600,000 copies were published in Walker's lifetime. It is one of five old shape-note tunebooks still in use in shape-note singings. It contained the first printings of *Restoration* (*The Hymnal 1982*, Hymn 550) (1835 edition) and of *Wondrous Love* (*The Hymnal 1982*, Hymn 439) (1840 printing). The 1835 edition also printed one tune for the first time under the name *New Britain* and used it with the text "Amazing grace! how sweet the sound" (*The Hymnal 1982*, Hymn 671). The tune can be traced back to 1829 but under other names and in association with other texts. Seventeen of the twenty-four early American tunes in *The Hymnal 1982* were in the 1854 last edition of *Southern Harmony*. It is a source of the arrangement of several of these, including *Star in the East*, used with the text "Brightest and best of the stars of the morning" (*The Hymnal 1982*, Hymn 118). "Southern Harmony" is sometimes used loosely as a term for this general type of early American music.

Southern Ohio, Diocese of. The 1874 General Convention voted to divide the Diocese of Ohio. The primary convention of the Diocese of Southern Ohio was held at Trinity Church, Columbus, Jan. 13, 1875. It includes the following counties: Adams, Athens, Belmont, Brown, Butler, Champaign, Clark, Clermont, Clinton, Drake, Delaware, Fairfield, Fayette, Franklin, Gallia, Greene, Guernsey, Hamilton, Highland, Hocking, Jackson, Lawrence, Licking, Madison, Meigs, Miami, Monroe, Montgomery, Morgan, Muskingum, Noble, Perry, Pickaway, Pike, Preble, Ross, Scioto, Vinton, Warren, and Washington. On Apr. 4, 1904, St. Paul's Church, Cincinnati, became St. Paul's Cathedral. On May 22, 1940, the diocesan convention declared St. Paul's Cathedral to be "defunct and extinct." Christ Church, Cincinnati, was set apart as Christ Church Cathedral on Feb. 24, 1993, and it was dedicated on May 29, 1993.

Southern Philippines, Diocese of. The 1901 General Convention established the Missionary District of the Philippines. In 1973 the Missionary District of the Philippines was divided into three missionary districts. One of these was the Southern Philippines Missionary District. In 1985 it became the Diocese of the Southern Philippines. In July 1988 the House of Bishops voted to

release the Philippine Episcopal Church to form a new province. On May 1, 1990, the Philippine Episcopal Church became autonomous as the Twenty-Eighth Province of the Anglican Communion.

Southern Virginia, Diocese of. The 1892 General Convention voted to divide the Diocese of Virginia. The new diocese was the Diocese of Southern Virginia. It held its primary convention at St. Paul's Church, Lynchburg. The 1919 General Convention voted to divide the Diocese of Southern Virginia. It includes the following counties: Accomac, Amelia, Appomattox, Brunswick, Buckingham, Charlotte, Chesterfield, Craig, Cumberland, Dinwiddie, Elizabeth City, Greeneville, Halifax, Henry, Highland, Isle of Wight, James City, Lunenberg, Mecklenberg, Nansemond, Northampton, Norfolk, Nottaway, Pittsylvania, Powhatan, Prince Edward, Prince George, Princess Anne, Southampton, Surry, Sussex, Warwick, and York. The Diocese does not have a cathedral.

Southgate, Horatio (July 5, 1812–Apr. 12, 1894). Missionary Bishop to Greece. He was born in Portland, Maine. Southgate graduated from Bowdoin College in 1832. He then entered Andover Theological Seminary to study for the Congregational ministry. While at Andover he joined the Episcopal Church and was confirmed on Oct. 26, 1834. He was ordained deacon on July 12, 1835. Southgate was appointed by the Committee of Foreign Missions of the Domestic and Foreign Missionary Society to investigate the state of Islam in Turkey and Persia. He sailed from New York on Apr. 24, 1836, and returned in Dec. 1838. On Oct. 3, 1839, Southgate was ordained priest. In May 1840 he sailed as a missionary to Constantinople. He was consecrated Missionary Bishop of the Dominions and Dependencies of the Sultan of Turkey on Oct. 26, 1844. He resigned this position on Oct. 12, 1850. Southgate returned to Portland, Maine, where he established St. Luke's Church in 1851. From 1852 until 1858 he was rector of the Church of the Advent, Boston. From 1859 until his retirement on Sept. 1, 1872, he was rector of Zion Church, New York City. Southgate died in Astoria, Long Island, New York.

Southwest Florida, Diocese of. The General Convention of 1969 voted to divide the Diocese of Florida into three dioceses. One of the new dioceses was known as the Gulf Coast Diocese of Florida. It included the following counties: Charlotte, Collier, DeSoto, Glades, Hernando,

Hillsborough, Lee, Manatee, Pasco, Pinellas, Sarasota, and part of Hendry. The primary convention of this diocese was held at North Redington Beach, Oct. 16, 1969. At that convention the name was changed to the Diocese of Southwest Florida. On Nov. 18, 1969, St. Peter's Church, St. Petersburg, was set apart as St. Peter's Cathedral.

Southwest, Missionary District of the. The 1835 General Convention nominated the Rev. Francis Lister Hawks to exercise episcopal functions in the State of Louisiana and in the Territories of Arkansas and Florida. Hawks declined the election and was never consecrated. On Dec. 9, 1838, Leonidas Polk was consecrated Missionary Bishop of Arkansas and the Indian Territory with Provisional Charge in Alabama, Mississippi, and the Republic of Texas. This carried on the work in the Southwest, until Polk was elected Bishop of Louisiana in 1841. The 1859 General Convention created the Missionary District of the Southwest, which included all parts of the country not yet organized in dioceses or included in missionary districts, south of the northern border of Cherokee Country and New Mexico, as far as the eastern border of California. Henry Chaplin Lay was consecrated Bishop of the Southwest on Oct. 23, 1859, and served until Apr. 1, 1869, when he was translated to the Diocese of Easton.

Southwestern Brazil, Missionary District of. On Sept. 30, 1949, the House of Bishops divided the Missionary District of Southern Brazil into three missionary districts—Southwestern Brazil, Southern Brazil, and Central Brazil. On Oct. 20, 1964, the House of Bishops voted for an independent Brazilian Church, and in 1965 the Episcopal Church of Brazil became an independent Province of the Anglican Communion. *See* Southern Brazil, Missionary District of.

Southwestern Diocese. The 1832 General Convention voted that the dioceses of Mississippi and Alabama, and the clergy and churches in the State of Louisiana could associate and join in the election of a bishop. Delegations from these three areas met at Christ Church, New Orleans, on Mar. 4–5, 1835, and formed the Southwestern Diocese. They elected Francis Lister Hawks their bishop. However, he declined the election. The plans for the Southwestern Diocese were never realized. The Southwestern Diocese was unrelated to the Missionary District of the Southwest, which was established by the 1859 General Convention and which included different territory.

Southwestern Virginia, Diocese of. The 1919 General Convention voted to divide the Diocese of Southern Virginia. The primary convention of the Diocese of Southwestern Virginia was held at St. John's Church, Roanoke, Dec. 10–11, 1919. The Diocese is composed of the following counties: Alleghany, Amherst, Augusta, Bath, Bedford, Bland, Botetourt, Buchanan, Campbell, Carroll, Craig, Dickinson, Floyd, Franklin, Giles, Grayson, Henry, Highland, Lee, Montgomery, Nelson, Patrick, Pulaski, Roanoke, Rockbridge, Russell, Scott, Smythe, Tazewell, Washington, Wise, and Wythe. The Diocese does not have a cathedral.

Spalding, Franklin Spencer (Mar. 13, 1865–Sept. 25, 1914). A leading advocate of the Social Gospel, known as the "socialist bishop." He was born in Erie, Pennsylvania. He graduated from Princeton in 1887 and from the General Theological Seminary in 1901. He was ordained deacon on June 3, 1891, and began his ministry as pastor of All Saints' Church, Denver, Colorado. Spalding was ordained priest on June 1, 1892, and immediately began his duties as head master of Jarvis Hall, Denver, the diocesan school for boys, and remained there until 1896. From 1897 to 1904 he was rector of St. Paul's Church, Erie. The 1904 General Convention chose him to be the Missionary Bishop of the District of Salt Lake, which included all of Utah and parts of Colorado, Nevada, and Wyoming. He was consecrated on Dec. 14, 1904, at St. Paul's Church, Erie. His jurisdiction became the Missionary District of Utah on Oct. 10, 1907. Spalding served until his death in Salt Lake City.

Sparrow, William (Mar. 12, 1801–Jan. 17, 1874). Leading evangelical theologian and opponent of Tractarianism. He was born in Charlestown, Massachusetts. His family moved to Huron County, Ohio, and Sparrow became involved with the educational enterprises of Bishop Philander Chase. He taught at a school in Worthington, Ohio, administered by Bishop Chase's son, and then at Cincinnati College, where the Bishop was president. In 1824 Sparrow became the professor of languages at the newly opened Miami University, but within about a year he returned to assist Bishop Chase in establishing a theological seminary at Worthington. Sparrow was the principal and main teacher at this school, which evolved into Kenyon College and Bexley Hall Theological Seminary. He was ordained deacon on June 7, 1826, and priest on June 11, 1826. In 1841 he moved to the Virginia Theological Seminary, where he taught for the rest of his life. His primary areas of teaching were church history, theology, and Christian evidences. He served also for a while as dean. He is known for the advice he gave his students, "Seek the truth; come whence it may, cost what it will." Sparrow died in Alexandria, Virginia.

SPCK/USA. *See* Society for Promoting Christian Knowledge/United States of America (SPCK/USA).

SPEAK. *See* Society for Promoting and Encouraging Arts and Knowledge (SPEAK).

Specialized Ministries Fellowship. A support group of clergy and missioners who served in ministries where there were significant numbers of working class and poor communicants. It was organized in the late 1980s. It went out of existence around 1994.

Species, Eucharistic. *See* Eucharistic Elements.

Spirit of Missions, The. This monthly journal was published by the Board of Missions of the Episcopal Church. The first issue appeared in Jan. 1836, and the last issue appeared in Dec. 1939. It was continued by *Forth. The Spirit of Missions* is one of the major primary sources for the history of the Episcopal Church.

Spiritual Director. A person, lay or ordained, with whom one communicates concerning the spiritual life may also be known as a soul-friend, soul-mate, or spiritual companion. A director listens and, when appropriate, responds by giving "direction" which may include spiritual advice, help with discernment, suggested reading or action, or a question to ponder. Different directors have different styles. Most understand their roles as companions and listeners along the way. Spiritual directors seek to be available for open and honest sharing concerning the spiritual life. They are found throughout religious experiences and history in both eastern and western traditions. Some spiritual directors use highly structured techniques. Others respond intuitively to the present conversation. Kenneth Leech, Margaret Guenther, Alan Jones, and Tilden Edwards are among the best known Anglican and Episcopal writers who have discussed spiritual direction. The Shalem Institute in Washington, D.C., has a ministry of training spiritual directors.

Spiritual Gifts. Also called charisms, and partially listed in 1 Cor 12:4–11, these are graces granted by the Holy Spirit to empower the faithful to perform specific tasks. Called *gratiae gratis datae* (freely given graces) by the scholastics, they are at the service of charity (1 Cor 13:13). Given over and above the fundamental gift of faith and friendship with God (or, *gratia sanctificans*, sanctifying grace) they are neither necessary nor sufficient to salvation, but they characterize the specific call of God to each believer. *See* Gifts of the Spirit.

Spirituality. An interest and intentional participation in the spiritual life, providing a context for open and direct experience of God and the entire spiritual realm at an intensely personal level. Spirituality concerns the whole of life in the context of faith. Resources for spirituality include participation in retreats, quiet days, spiritual direction, and use of books, journals, tapes, and other materials that provide a point of reference for personal prayer and religious experience, including periods of darkness and doubt as well as moments of joy and ecstasy. *See* Rule of Life.

Spokane, Diocese of. On Oct. 13, 1853, the General Convention created the Missionary District of Oregon and Washington Territory. On Oct. 15, 1880, the General Convention divided it into the Missionary District of Oregon and the Missionary District of Washington. On Oct. 20, 1892, the General Convention divided the Missionary District of Washington into the Missionary District of Olympia and the Missionary District of Spokane. The primary convention of the Missionary District of Spokane met June 7, 1893, at All Saints Church, Spokane. The 1898 General Convention added that portion of Idaho lying north of the south line of the County of Idaho to the Missionary District of Spokane. The 1907 General Convention removed all portions of Idaho from the Missionary District of Spokane. The 1935 General Convention added that portion of Idaho known as the Panhandle to the Missionary District of Spokane. On Oct. 20, 1929, three Spokane parishes, All Saints Cathedral, St. Peter's, and St. James', merged to form the Cathedral of St. John the Evangelist. The primary convention of the Diocese of Spokane met at the Cathedral of St. John the Evangelist on Nov. 1, 1964. The diocese includes nineteen counties in Washington: Adams, Asotin, Benton, Chelan, Columbia, Douglas, Ferry, Franklin, Garfield, Grant, Kittitas, Lincoln, Okanagan, Pend Oreille, Spokane, Stevens, Walla Walla, Whitman, and Yakima; and ten counties in Idaho: Benewah,

Bonner, Boundary, Clear Water, Idaho, Kootenai, Latah, Lewis, Nez Perce, and Shosone.

Sponsor (at Baptism). A baptized Christian who presents a candidate for baptism, thereby endorsing the candidate and signifying an intention to support the new Christian by prayer and example. Each candidate for baptism is to have one or more baptized sponsors. There is no longer a requirement for a particular number of sponsors, nor is there a requirement concerning their gender. Sponsors may present the candidate by name to the celebrant or to an assisting priest or deacon at the time of baptism. A sponsor of an infant or younger child is known as a godparent. The BCP notes that it is "fitting" that parents be included among the godparents of their children. The BCP emphasizes the seriousness and importance of the sponsors' responsibilities. (pp. 298, 301–303). Parents and godparents make promises in their own names and in the name of the candidate. They speak for the candidate in the renunciation of Satan, the evil powers of this world, and all sinful desires; and they promise that the candidate will turn to Christ, trust in Christ, and follow Christ. They are to be involved in helping the new Christian grow in the knowledge and love of God and fulfill the responsibilities of a church member. They also promise to help the child grow into the full stature of Christ by their prayers and witness. Parents and godparents are to be instructed in the meaning of baptism and their responsibilities. At the baptismal eucharist the sponsors may appropriately read the lessons preceding the gospel, read the Prayers for the Candidates, and present the oblations of bread and wine.

Springfield, Diocese of. The 1877 General Convention voted to divide the Diocese of Illinois into the dioceses of Illinois, Quincy and Springfield. The primary convention of the Diocese of Springfield met at St. Paul's Church, Springfield, Dec. 18–19, 1877. It includes the following counties: Carr, Champaign, Christian, Clark, Coles, Cumberland, De Witt, Douglass, Edgar, Greene, Jersey, Logan, Macon, Macoupin, Mason, McLean, Menard, Montgomery, Morgan, Moultrie, Platt, Sangamon, Scott, Shelby, Tazewell, and Vermillion. As early as 1906, St. Paul's Church, Springfield, was recognized as the "Cathedral of St. Paul," but there was some confusion within the diocese with regard to its status. The status of St. Paul's was clarified on Dec. 11, 1979, when a constitution and by-laws were adopted establishing the Cathedral Church of St. Paul.

S.S.C. *See* Holy Cross, Society of the.

Stabat Mater. This text, Hymn 159 in *The Hymnal 1982*, was probably composed by a Franciscan in the first half of the thirteenth century. In the fourteenth century it was sung by the flagellants as they scourged themselves in their processions. During the fifteenth century it made its way into a few missals as a sequence hymn. Its use in the Roman Catholic Church was suppressed at the Council of Trent. But *Stabat Mater* entered the Roman missal in 1727 as the sequence for the Feast of the Seven Sorrows of the Virgin Mary, observed on Sept. 15. *Stabat Mater* has also frequently been used as part of the liturgy of the Way of the Cross. A translation from *Hymns Ancient and Modern*, an amended form of that of Edward Caswall in his *Lyra Catholica* (1849), entered the American Episcopal Hymnal at the 1892 revision. The *BOS* suggests that at the Way of the Cross selected stanzas may be sung at the entrance of the ministers and as the procession approaches the first station. *See* Sequence.

Stalls. Fixed rows of seats for choir members, clergy, and assistants. These long rows may be located on both sides of the chancel, sanctuary, or choir of cathedrals, chapels of religious houses, or other churches. A book rest may stand in front of each row of the stalls. Arm rests may divide individual seats along the rows. Stalls may be elaborately carved. Some stalls are covered by a canopy. Stalls used by choir members may be known as choir stalls.

Standard of the Cross. This weekly periodical continued the *Western Episcopalian*. It began publication on Aug. 22, 1868, at Gambier, Ohio, and was published until June 16, 1887. It merged with *The Church*, which was published at Philadelphia, and continued from July 2, 1887, until May 7, 1892.

Standing Commissions. *See* Commissions of the General Convention; *See* Standing Commissions alphabetized by subject.

Standing Committee. The ecclesiastical authority of the diocese in the absence of a bishop. The Canons of 1789 made four references to an organization known as the Standing Committee. It formed its duties over the next forty-three years. In 1832 the General Convention brought all the functions of the Standing Committee under Canon Four, adding that where there was no bishop the Standing Committee was the ecclesiastical authority. In 1901 the role of the Standing Committee was added to the Constitution of the Episcopal Church. The Standing Committee is elected by the diocesan convention. Half of its members are clerical, half lay. It serves as the bishop's council of advice. The Standing Committee is requested to give consent for all bishops elected in the Episcopal Church. It recommends persons for ordination. It gives the bishop advice and consent on the purchase, sale, or encumbrance of any property held by a congregation or the diocese. It gives the bishop advice and consent as to any judicial sentence given to a clergy person or concurs in allowing a clergy person to cease functioning as a member of the clergy. It investigates and reports to the bishop on the charge that a deacon or priest has abandoned the Episcopal Church. It also receives the bishop's resignation.

Standing Liturgical Commission. Predecessor to the Standing Commission on Common Worship. The 1928 General Convention, which adopted the 1928 BCP, discharged the Joint Commission on the Revision and Enrichment of the Book of Common Prayer. It appointed a Standing Liturgical Commission of eight bishops, eight priests, and eight laymen. This commission was charged with the functions of preserving and studying "all matters relating to the Book of Common Prayer with the idea of developing and conserving for some possible further use the liturgical experience and scholarship of the Church." The 1940 General Convention clarified the purpose and structure of the commission. The commission consisted of three bishops, three priests, and three laymen. It was to "collect and collate material bearing upon future revisions of the Book of Common Prayer." The Standing Liturgical Commission became the designated instrument for revising the Prayer Book. The commission consists of nine members, including at least two bishops, two presbyters or deacons, and two lay persons. The Custodian of the Standard Book of Common Prayer is a member *ex officio* of the commission. The Standing Liturgical Commission produced the *Prayer Book Studies*, and the proposed drafts for the 1979 BCP. The 1997 General Convention discontinued the Standing Liturgical Commission and consolidated it into a new Standing Commission on Common Worship.

Stanley, Clifford Leland (Mar. 16, 1902–Oct. 11, 1994). Theologian and professor. He was born in Williamsport,

Pennsylvania. Stanley received his B.A. in 1924 and his M.A. in 1925, both from the University of Virginia. He received his B.D. in 1928 from the Virginia Theological Seminary. Stanley was ordained deacon on June 5, 1928, and priest on Dec. 19, 1928. Stanley began his ordained ministry as rector of Trinity Church, Tyrone, Pennsylvania, 1928–1931. From 1931 until 1935, he was associate professor of the history of religions and philosophy at the Virginia Theological Seminary. He then studied at Union Theological Seminary, New York, and received his Th.D. in 1938. Stanley was rector of Christ Church, Cape Girardeau, Missouri, 1939–1942, and rector of St. Peter's Church, St. Louis, Missouri, 1942–1946. He returned to Virginia Theological Seminary in 1946 as professor of theology and remained in that position until his retirement in 1970. A major essay he wrote, "The Church, in but not of the World," was published in *Christian Faith and Social Action*, edited by John A. Hutchinson (1953). Stanley was a scholar of both Kierkegaard and Tillich. In 1978 he was theologian-in-residence at St. Bartholomew's Church, Corpus Christi, Texas. Stanley died in Stafford, Virginia.

Stanton, Elizabeth Cady (Nov. 12, 1815–Oct. 26, 1902). Women's rights leader. She was born in Johnstown, New York. Stanton graduated from Emma Willard's Female Seminary in Troy, New York, in 1832. She had an early interest in the abolition of slavery and the temperance movement. Stanton attended the World's Anti-Slavery Convention in London with her husband, Henry Stanton, in 1840, where the exclusion of female delegates inspired a friendship with Lucretia Mott, a Quaker minister. In 1846 the family moved from Boston to Seneca Falls, New York. On July 19–20, 1848, she held a women's rights conference at the Wesleyan Methodist Church in Seneca Falls. Stanton met Susan B. Anthony in 1851, and from then until her death they worked together for women's rights. During the Civil War, Stanton founded the Women's Loyal National League, which supported the Union and gathered 300,000 signatures demanding the immediate abolition of slavery by constitutional amendment. When the American Woman Suffrage Association was founded in May 1869, she was chosen president and served in that capacity for twenty-one years. She moved to New York City after her husband's death in 1887. Stanton was the primary author of the *Woman's Bible*, published in two parts in 1895 and 1898. Her major writing, with Susan B. Anthony and Matilda Joslyn Gage, was the three-volume *History of Woman*

Suffrage (1881–1886). Her memoirs, *Eighty Years and More*, was published in 1898. Stanton died in New York City. Stanton is commemorated in the Episcopal calendar of the church year on July 20. *See* Bloomer, Amelia Jenks; *see* Truth, Sojourner; *see* Tubman, Harriet Ross.

Station. A place where a solemn liturgical procession pauses for a versicle, a response, and a collect. A "stational collect" is the collect that is sung or said at this time. The BCP provides a collect for a station at the Palm Sunday service (p. 271–272). This may be done at the entrance to the church. The *BOS* also provides forms for a Station at a Christmas Crèche, a Station at a Candlemas Procession, and for the fourteen stations in the Way of the Cross (also known as "Stations of the Cross").

Station at a Christmas Crèche. *See* Station.

Stations of the Cross. *See* Way of the Cross (Stations of the Cross).

S.T.B. The Bachelor of Sacred Theology degree presupposes a first bachelor's degree and was designed to prepare persons for ministry in the church. It is no longer used.

S.T.D. The Doctor of Sacred Theology degree presupposes a first theological degree and is to equip persons for teaching and research in theological seminaries, colleges, and universities.

Stephen, Saint, Deacon and Martyr. First Christian martyr. He was a Hellenist, a Greek-speaking Jew born and reared outside Palestine. His name is Greek, meaning "crown." He was one of the seven chosen by the Jerusalem congregation to see that the Hellenistic Jewish Christians got their fair share of the contributions. Stephen's preaching caused a revolution in the attitude of some of the Jewish people toward the young Christian church. There was a period of persecution which scattered Christians into many parts of the world outside Jerusalem. The young Pharisee, Saul of Tarsus, witnessed Stephen's stoning and heard the martyr's prayer for his enemies. Saul eventually took up the work cut short by Stephen's death. Tradition says that Stephen's burial place was discovered on Dec. 5, 415, and that his bones were moved to Jerusalem on Dec. 26. Some scholars say that Dec. 26 was chosen as St. Stephen's Day because he was the first

martyr for Christ and that he appropriately appears first in the procession of saints who surround the cradle of Christ. Stephen is commemorated in the Episcopal calendar of the church year on Dec. 26.

Stewardship. Our personal response to God's generosity in the way we share our resources of time, talent, and money. Stewardship reflects our commitment to making God's love known through the realities of human life and our use of all that God has given us. It is also our service to God's world and our care of creation. Parish members are encouraged to make an annual stewardship pledge. This pledge represents their specific Christian commitment to "work, pray, and give for the spread of the kingdom of God" (BCP, p. 856).

Stewardship and Development, Standing Commission on. The 1979 General Convention established this Standing Commission whose purpose is to hold up before the church the responsibility of faithful stewardship and to recommend strategy for stewardship education throughout the church. It is also to encourage a joint strategy for the various church agencies in their fund-raising efforts. It has twelve members: two bishops, two presbyters or deacons, and eight lay persons. The Presiding Bishop appoints the bishop members and the president of the House of Deputies appoints the clerical and lay members. All members serve a term of six years.

Stewart, Marshall Boyer (Sept. 4, 1880–July 28, 1956). Educator and theologian. He was born in Galveston, Texas. He received his B.A. in 1902 and his M.A. in 1907, both from Trinity College, Hartford, Connecticut. He received his B.D. from the General Theological Seminary in 1906. Stewart was ordained deacon on June 18, 1905, and priest on Dec. 21, 1905. He was minister-in-charge of St. John's Parish, Prince George and Prince Charles Counties, Maryland, 1905, and rector, 1906–1907. From 1907 until 1909, he was fellow and instructor at General Seminary. In 1909 he went to Western Theological Seminary as professor of ecclesiastical history. He remained there until 1913, when he became principal of St. John's Military Academy, Salina, Kansas. In 1914 he was called to Nashotah House where he was instructor, 1914–1916, and professor of dogmatic and moral theology, 1916–1928. From 1929 until 1951, Stewart was professor of dogmatic theology at General Seminary. He retired to Sewanee, Tennessee, in 1952. In 1952–1953, he was visiting lecturer in theology at the School of Theology of the University of the South, at Sewanee. From 1953 until his death, Stewart was acting professor of dogmatic theology and instructor in church music at the School of Theology. He served as director of the Graduate School of Theology at Sewanee from 1948 until 1951. His major writings are *God and Reality* (1926) and *In Other Words: Reflections on Christian Theology* (1952). Stewart died in Sewanee.

Stigmata. Wounds, like those of Christ's, imprinted on the body of a believer by a special act of divine grace or by an involuntary psychosomatic process. Actual self-inflicted wounds are not stigmata. St. Francis of Assisi is said to have received the stigmata in the thirteenth century. The attitude of the church towards stigmata is guarded.

"Stir-up Sunday." A term often used for the day referred to as "the Sunday next before Advent" by a rubric in the 1662 BCP. This phrase was then used in the 1892 and 1928 American Prayer Books as a title for the day which had previously been designated simply as "The Twenty-fifth Sunday after Trinity," which was the last Sunday before the season of Advent. The term comes from the opening words of the collect of the day in the 1549 and later Prayer Books, "Stir-up, we beseech thee, O Lord, the wills of thy faithful people; that they, plenteously bringing forth the fruit of good works, may of thee be plenteously rewarded; through Jesus Christ our Lord. Amen." The Latin word translated "stir-up" is *excita*. In the Sarum Missal the collects of the first, second, and fourth Sundays of Advent also began with this word. These collects date back to the Gregorian Sacramentary, a manuscript from the late eighth century which purports to be the liturgy of the time of Gregory the Great, Bishop of Rome, 590–604.

The emphasis for the last Sunday before Advent is different in the 1979 BCP. Although Christ the King Sunday is not officially celebrated in the Episcopal Church, the collect for the last Sunday of the liturgical year (Proper 29) in the 1979 BCP prays that all the peoples of the earth may be brought together under the "most gracious rule" of Christ, "the King of kings and Lord of lords" (BCP, p. 236). However, the collect for the third Sunday of Advent begins with the prayer "Stir up your power, O Lord, and with great might come among us. . . ." (BCP, p. 212). *See* Christ the King Sunday.

S.T.M. The Master of Sacred Theology degree presupposes the M. Div. degree and is an academic program stressing fuller mastery of resources in one of the theological disciplines.

Stokes, Olivia Egleston Phelps (Jan. 11, 1847–Dec. 14, 1927), and Caroline Phelps Stokes (Dec. 4, 1854–Apr. 26, 1909). Benefactors to African Americans. Both sisters were born in New York City and never married. The family was Presbyterian, but the sisters in later years joined the Episcopal Church. They are primarily known for their philanthropy to charitable and religious enterprises. They gave generously to the public baths in New York, St. Paul's Chapel at Columbia University, a new building for the Peabody Home for Aged and Infirm Women in Ansonia, Connecticut, and a library in Ansonia. They donated Woodbridge Hall, an administration building at Yale University. The sisters provided an open-air pulpit for the Cathedral of St. John the Divine in New York and a chapel for Berea College in Kentucky. They also supported missionary causes. However, they are best known for their benefaction and recognition of the plight of African Americans. Upon her death, Caroline's bequests included a chapel for Tuskegee Institute, the Calhoun Colored School in Alabama, and an endowment fund for the education of Negroes and Indians at Hampton Institute in Virginia. The remainder of her estate went to establish the Phelps-Stokes Fund for tenement housing in New York and to educate Negroes and Indians. In 1901 the sisters financed a "model" tenement for African American housing in New York with the help of their nephew, I. N. Phelps Stokes, an architect with special interest in tenement housing. Olivia published several inspirational writings, including *Pine and Cedar: Bible Verses* (1885), *Forward in the Better Life* (1915), and *Saturday Nights in Lent* (1922). Olivia died in Washington, D. C., and Caroline died in Redlands, California.

Stole. A long narrow strip of material that is the distinctive vestment and insignia of the clergy. Its use may be derived from the ancient practice of wearing a ceremonial garland at a festival and from use as an insignia of rank by Roman officials such as senators and consuls. It is typically worn with other vestments. Its color usually reflects the liturgical color of the day. It may match the design and material of other vestments and altar hangings, and it may be decorated. It is worn over an alb or surplice, and may be worn under or over a chasuble or dalmatic. An underlay stole is a stole worn under a chasuble or dalmatic, and an overlay stole is a stole worn over a chasuble or dalmatic.

Bishops and priests wear the stole around the back of the neck, with equal ends hanging down in front. Some priests cross the ends of the stole in the front. If a cincture is worn, the ends of the stole are usually placed through it. Deacons wear the stole over the left shoulder, with the ends of the stole falling diagonally across the front and back of the body. The deacon's stole is tied near the right hip. Historically, the deacon's stole simply hung over the left shoulder, with the ends of the stole hanging down in front and back. In the east, and occasionally in the west, the deacon's stole may be worn under the right arm, with the ends of the stole crossing over the left shoulder and hanging down in the front and back. Stoles are not worn by candidates for ordination. The BCP calls for newly ordained priests and deacons to be vested according to their order after ordination (pp. 534, 545). The stole, worn according to the new order, or other insignia of office, is placed on newly ordained priests and deacons after the entire prayer of consecration is completed and before presentation of the Bible (BCP, p. 553–554). The BCP form for Celebration of a New Ministry calls for a stole or other symbol to be presented to the new minister at the Induction (p. 561).

Stole Fee. Payment to clergy for officiating at a church service, usually a baptism, a marriage, or a funeral. The term is derived from the stole typically worn by the member of the clergy person while officiating.

Stoup. The term is from the Old English for "vessel." It is a small basin or container for holy water. It is placed near an entrance of the church. Those who enter the church may touch the water to their foreheads while making the sign of the cross. This gesture of personal piety may be done to recall baptism and the baptismal promises and as a sign of blessing. Historically, a fountain was in the atrium of certain basilicas. Some would wash their hands and faces in the fountain before entering the basilica. Making the sign of the cross with water from a stoup likely derived from this practice. The practice of sprinkling the people in church with holy water dates from the ninth century. Holy water was left in the church for the use of those who were unable to be present at the eucharist.

Stowe's Clerical Directory of the American Church. In 1916 Frederick Ebenezer John Lloyd sold his *Lloyd's Clerical Directory* to the Rev. Andrew David Stowe (1851–1925). It became *Stowe's Clerical Directory*. It was published under that title in 1917, 1920, 1924, 1926, 1929, 1932, 1935, and 1938. In 1941 it became *Stowe's Clerical Directory of the Protestant Episcopal Church in the United States of America*. It was published under that title in 1941, 1947, 1950, and 1953. In 1956 it became *The Clerical Directory of the Protestant Episcopal Church in the United States of America*.

Stowe, Walter Herbert (Jan. 22, 1895–Jan. 2, 1989). Historian and writer. He was born in Waterville, Minnesota. Stowe received his B.A. in 1915 from the University of Minnesota and his B.D. in 1918 from Seabury Hall Divinity School. He was ordained deacon on Dec. 16, 1917, and priest on Feb. 2, 1919. Stowe was master of Shattuck School, 1918–1919, and priest-in-charge of Trinity Church, Woodbridge, New Jersey, 1919–1921. While at Woodbridge he was a fellow at the General Theological Seminary. Stowe was rector of St. Luke's Church, Willmar, Minnesota, 1921–1925; rector of St. Mark's Church, Denver, 1925–1929; and then rector of Christ Church, New Brunswick, New Jersey, from 1929 until his retirement in 1966. He was managing editor of the *Historical Magazine of the Protestant Episcopal Church*, 1934–1949, and editor, 1949–1961. He contributed numerous articles to the *Historical Magazine*. Stowe was historiographer of the Diocese of New Jersey, 1936–1967, and historiographer of the Episcopal Church, 1952–1967. One of his major books is *The Life and Letters of Bishop William White; together with the services and addresses commemorating the one hundred fiftieth anniversary of his consecration to the episcopate* (1937). Stowe died in Bound Brook, New Jersey.

Stringfellow, William (Apr. 26, 1928–Mar. 2, 1985). Theologian, activist, and Episcopal layman. He was born in Cranston, Rhode Island. He attended Bates College and the London School of Economics. He graduated from Harvard Law School in 1956. He then began a private legal practice in Harlem, where he lived. He defended the legal rights of poor African American people. Stringfellow utilized a theological perspective to attack racism, the war in Vietnam, and other social ills. He perceived the powers and principalities of death to be active in the social evils of his day and in the idolatries of contemporary culture. Stringfellow urged that intercession and eucharistic praise are well suited to political resistance. Stringfellow moved to Block Island (New Shoreham), Rhode Island, in 1968 because of his failing health. He lived there with his friend Anthony Towne in the household they named "Eschaton."

They were charged with harboring Daniel Berrigan as a fugitive. Berrigan, a Jesuit priest, was arrested at the home of Stringfellow and Towne after Berrigan's conviction for burning draft records. Stringfellow supported Berrigan's protest against American involvement in the war in Vietnam. The charges against Stringfellow and Towne were eventually dismissed. Stringfellow was a prolific writer, despite the limitations of his health. He was an advocate for Bishop James Pike, and the co-author with Towne of two books that were supportive of the controversial bishop. Stringfellow's many theological books included *Free in Obedience* (1964), *Dissenter in a Great Society* (1966), *Count It All Joy* (1967), *A Second Birthday* (1970), *An Ethic for Christians and Other Aliens in a Strange Land* (1973), *Instead of Death, New and Expanded Edition* (1976), *Conscience & Obedience* (1977), *A Simplicity of Faith: My Experience of Mourning* (1982), and *The Politics of Spirituality* (1984). His writings were direct and accessible to a wide audience. He encountered the evils of his society with a profound Christian spirituality. Stringfellow died in Providence, Rhode Island.

Stripping of the Altar. Ritual removal of the vessels, hangings, worship books, linens, and other movable items from the altar and the area around the altar after the Maundy Thursday liturgy. This ceremony may be accompanied by the recitation of Ps 22.

Structure of the Church, Standing Commission on the. The 1958 General Convention established the Joint Committee on Committees and Commissions to make evaluations and recommendations with regard to the creation, continuation, or discontinuing of joint and standing committees and commissions. The 1967 General Convention established the Standing Commission on the Structure of the Church to study and make recommendations concerning the structure of the General Convention and the church. It is also to review the operation of the several committees and commissions to determine the need for their continuance and their effectiveness. The commission consists of twelve members. The three bishop members are appointed by the Presiding Bishop, and the three presbyters or deacons and the six lay persons are appointed by the president of the House of Deputies. The creation of a new committee or commission is to be referred to this Standing Commission for its consideration and advice.

Stuck, Hudson (Nov. 11, 1863–Oct. 10, 1920). Missionary to Alaska. He was born in Paddington, London, England. Stuck was educated at King's College, London. In 1885 he came to the United States and became an acting principal in the public schools of San Angelo, Texas. In 1889 he entered the Theological Department of the University of the South. He was ordained deacon on Aug. 7, 1892, and priest on Nov. 30, 1892. Stuck served as rector of Grace Church, Cuero, Texas, from 1892 to 1894, and as dean of St. Matthew's Cathedral, Dallas, from 1894 to 1904. After his resignation from St. Matthew's, Stuck became Archdeacon of the Yukon in the Missionary District of Alaska. During his ministry in Alaska he explored the territory extensively and published several articles and books describing his journeys. These publications included *A Winter Circuit of Our Arctic Coast* (1920), which described the first ascent of Mount McKinley, and *The Alaskan Missions of the Episcopal Church* (1920). Also noted as a defender of the region's indigenous people, Stuck emphasized the value of education for integrating native Alaskans into the emerging culture of the territory. He died in Fort Yukon, Alaska.

Subdeacon. *See* Major Orders; *see* Minor Orders.

Sub-Dean. The first assistant of the dean. The sub-dean may act with the authority of the dean in the dean's absence. *See* Dean (Cathedral, Seminary, College, Deanery).

Suffragan Bishop. A suffragan bishop is an assisting bishop who does not automatically succeed a diocesan bishop. A suffragan bishop may be elected bishop or bishop coadjutor. In 1814 James Kemp was consecrated Suffragan Bishop of Maryland, even though the office was not authorized by the Episcopal Church's Constitution. From 1829 until 1910, different General Conventions discussed proposals for electing and consecrating suffragan bishops. The 1910 General Convention enacted "Of Suffragan Bishops." A diocese may elect a suffragan bishop, but no diocese may have more than two suffragan bishops except with the special consent of a General Convention.

Suffrages. These petitionary versicles and responses precede the collects in the Daily Offices (see, e.g., BCP pp. 97–98, 121–122). The suffrages in the BCP are based on those in the Sarum offices, although Suffrages B for Evening Prayer are from a Byzantine evening litany. They are responsive prayers of petition which are usually concluded with a collect.

Sullivan, Arthur Seymour (May 13, 1842–Nov. 22, 1900). English composer. He was born in London. Sullivan was educated as a chorister in the Chapel Royal (1854–1858), the Royal Academy of Music, and at Leipzig Conservatory. Sullivan was best known for his famous Savoy Operas, with texts by William S. Gilbert. Sullivan was also highly respected as a church musician, hymnal editor, and composer of orchestral and choral music and songs. Between 1861 and 1871 he was organist of two London parishes. Sullivan was music editor of *Church Hymns with Tunes* (1874). Sullivan's *Hymn Tunes* (London, 1902) was a collection of original tunes and arrangements. He was knighted in 1883. Although his tunes were very popular in their day, their use has diminished in more recent decades. His original tunes in *The Hymnal 1982* include *Fortunatus*, used with the text "'Welcome, happy morning!' age to age shall say" (Hymn 179), *St. Kevin*, used with the text "Come, ye faithful, raise the strain of triumphant gladness!" (Hymn 199), and *St. Gertrude*, used with the text "Onward, Christian soldiers" (Hymn 562). He was also the arranger for *Noel*, used with the texts "It came upon the midnight clear" (Hymn 90) and "Praise God for John, evangelist" (Hymn 245). Sullivan died in London.

Summary of the Law, The. The Summary of the Law includes the two commandments that call for the love of God and the love of neighbor. These commandments appear separately in the OT (Dt 6:5; Lv 19:18). Although there is some precedent in pre-Christian Judaism for bringing these two commandments together, Jesus was apparently the first to formulate them precisely in this way as a summary of all the requirements of the Law (Mk 12:29–31). The Summary of the Law was first introduced as a substitute for the decalogue in the Nonjurors' liturgy of 1718. It was taken into the Scottish liturgy of 1764, and from there it was adopted by the first American Prayer Book of 1789 as an alternative to the decalogue. It is retained in Rite 1 of the BCP and it is an option in the Penitential Order of both Rites I and II. The Summary of the Law is stated in the Catechism relative to the New Covenant (BCP, p. 851).

Sunday. The Lord's Day, the first day of the biblical week. The NT specifies that on this day Jesus rose from the dead and appeared to his disciples. At an early date Sunday—rather than the Sabbath (Saturday)—became the occasion for Christians to meet together and celebrate the eucharist. Its meaning was enriched by reference to the creation of light and the work of the Holy Spirit (Gn 1:1–5). Pentecost has generally been considered to have fallen on the "First Day." Under Christian emperors, Sunday became a public holiday. Attendance at the eucharist and at vespers on Saturday and/or Sunday evening became normative for many centuries. After the Reformation, Puritans sought to impose austere regulations reflecting the biblical Sabbath, whereas Anglicans have regarded social gatherings, sports, and other entertainments appropriate after church. The Holy Eucharist is "the principal act of Christian worship on the Lord's Day and other major feasts" (BCP, p. 13). Collects for Saturday evening and Sunday, and Sunday eucharistic prefaces, articulate the themes of creation, the Resurrection, and new life in the Spirit appropriate for Sunday as the day of the eucharist. In *The Hymnal 1982*, Hymns 47–52 express these classic Sunday themes, including "O day of radiant gladness" (Hymn 48).

Sunday Church School. Robert Raikes (1735–1811) began the first Sunday School in England in 1780 as a charity school to teach poor children to read and write. The Sunday Church Schools were gradually freed to engage in religious instruction by the spread of general public education. Their moralistic educational models were inherited from Reformation and eighteenth-century learning theory. However, as new developments occurred in the field of general education, church leaders called for catechetical instruction in Sunday Church School teaching.

The first Episcopal Sunday Church School was opened in 1790 by James Milnor and Jackson Kemper at the United Parish of Christ Church and St. Peter's, Philadelphia. William White was rector of the United Parish at that time. The Sunday School in the Episcopal Church became a conscious instrument for religious education in 1826 with the organization of the General Protestant Episcopal Sunday School Union. Its focus was catechetical, and its energy arose from the nineteenth-century evangelical impulse. The 1946 General Convention provided funding to undertake a complete overhaul of Sunday Church School programs. The Department of Christian Education developed a "new curriculum" under the leadership of the Rev. John Heuss. This new curriculum called on the Sunday Church Schools to encourage faith development.

Sunday Church Schools continue to have an important place in the life of many Episcopal parishes.

Sunday Letter. One of the first seven letters of the alphabet, "A" through "g," is assigned to each date in the calendar year (except Feb. 29) in rotation in the Prayer Book calendar (pp. 19–30). The letter "A" is assigned to Jan. 1, Jan. 8, Jan. 15, etc. The letter "b" is assigned to Jan. 2, Jan. 9, Jan. 16, etc. The Sunday Letter can be used to determine all the dates of the Sundays in a calendar year. For example, if Jan. 1 is a Sunday, "A" is the Sunday Letter. All dates in the table with the letter "A" will be Sundays. Leap Year presents the one exception to this rule. In a Leap Year, the letter corresponding to the date of the first Sunday in Jan. will be the Sunday Letter for the months of Jan. and Feb. However, the Sunday Letter for Mar. through Dec. in a Leap Year will be the letter preceding the Sunday Letter for Jan. and Feb. For example, if "g" is the Sunday Letter in Jan. and Feb. of a Leap Year, "f" will be the Sunday Letter in Mar. through Dec. of that Leap Year. This change results from the additional day (Feb. 29) in a Leap Year. The BCP provides a table for ready reference to the Sunday Letter of any year between A.D. 1900 and A.D. 2099 (pp. 880–881). It is possible to determine the date of Easter Day for any particular year in the calendar (pp. 21–22) by using the Golden Number and the Sunday Letter for that year (see Tables and Rules for Finding the Date of Easter Day, BCP, pp. 880–881). The Sunday Letter is also known as the Dominical Letter. Clergy and parishioners usually determine the dates of Sundays by consulting a printed calendar.

Sunday of the Passion. *See* Palm Sunday (The Sunday of the Passion).

Sunday Visitant. This periodical was the second weekly publication in the Episcopal Church. It began publication on Jan. 3, 1818, at Charleston, South Carolina. Its full title was *Sunday Visitant; or Weekly Repository of Christian Knowledge.* It was edited by the Rev. Andrew Fowler (1760–1850), and published until Dec. 25, 1819.

Super Populum. A prayer of blessing said over the people by the celebrant at the conclusion of the liturgy. The term means "over the people" in Latin. In Lent, this solemn prayer over the people is used in place of a seasonal blessing. The *BOS* provides six forms for this prayer during Lent. It also provides one form for use from Palm Sunday through Maundy Thursday. Before this solemn Prayer over the People, the deacon or celebrant directs the people to "Bow down before the Lord." This ancient form of blessing prayer was used after the postcommunion at every Mass in the Leonine sacramentary. This seventh-century book is the oldest surviving book of prayers for the eucharist according to the Roman rite. The *super populum* was used only on the weekdays of Lent in the Gregorian sacramentary. The prayer became a blessing of public penitents. It came to be associated with Lent as public penitential discipline was discontinued and Lent became a penitential season for the whole church. The 1549 BCP did not include the Lenten *super populum.* Use of this prayer is not required by the Prayer Book. *See* Seasonal Blessings.

Superfrontal. *See* Frontal.

Superior. The person who has been designated as the head or presider of a religious community. The superior is typically elected for a term of years by the members of the community. The superior of an abbey is an abbot or abbess. The term may be used as a title.

Supplemental Liturgical Materials (SLM). A booklet prepared by the Standing Liturgical Commission and published by Church Hymnal Corporation in 1991 to supplement the existing Rite 2 liturgies of the BCP. It includes materials for Morning and Evening Prayer, complete eucharistic prayers, and forms for the eucharistic prayer for use with the Order for Celebrating the Holy Eucharist (BCP, pp. 400–401). These texts reflect awareness of the power of words and images in worship to shape our understanding of and relationship with God. The Preface for *SLM* identifies three stages in the evolution in awareness and understanding of liturgical language. The first stage of this process called for the use of "non-sexist" terms, in which gender specific words such as "he" and "man" were replaced with terms such as "God" and "humanity." This stage was documented in *Liturgical Texts for Evaluation* (1987). The second stage involved the use of balanced language, including both masculine and feminine words, images, and metaphors. This stage was reflected in *Supplemental Liturgical Texts, Prayer Book Studies 30* (1989). The third stage was seeking to challenge the church "to hear and use familiar and new passages and prayers in a different way." In this stage, the language of liturgy was to be opened to new interpretation and the hearer opened to deeper meaning.

Supplemental Liturgical Texts, Prayer Book Studies 30. *See* Prayer Book Studies; *see* Supplemental Liturgical Materials (SLM).

Supplementary Consecration. Consecration of additional bread or wine, or both, when there is not enough for all communicants. The celebrant may use the brief prayer for supplementary consecration provided by the BCP in the Additional Directions for the Eucharist (p. 408). In this trinitarian prayer, God the Father, the Word, and the Holy Spirit are asked to bless and sanctify the bread (or wine) that it also may be the sacrament of the precious Body (or Blood) of Jesus Christ. The celebrant may also say again the words of the eucharistic prayer instead of using the brief prayer for supplementary consecration (BCP, p. 408). The celebrant begins with the words following the *Sanctus*, and ends with the Invocation of the Holy Spirit (*epiclesis*) (see BCP, pp. 362–363). If Eucharistic Prayer C is used, the celebrant begins with the invocation of the Holy Spirit which follows the *Sanctus*, and continues through the narrative of the institution (see BCP, p. 371). In many parishes, consecrated bread and wine are reserved in a tabernacle and available for use if additional consecrated elements are needed.

Supplication. A prayer that seeks God's help. The term is used in the BCP for additional petitions to be inserted into the Great Litany which may follow the Lord's Prayer at the Great Litany or at the end of Morning or Evening Prayer, or be used as a separate devotion, "especially in time of war, or of national anxiety, or of disaster" (BCP, p. 154). These petitions formed a part of the first English litany of 1544, issued by Henry VIII to pray for the success of his army in war with France. They are derived from the petitions *in tempore belli* in the *Manuale Sarum*. They ask for protection from our enemies, without avoiding recognition that we ourselves may be responsible for our difficulties. In contemporary eucharistic theology, supplication and thanksgiving are considered the two essential elements of a eucharistic prayer.

Surge, illuminare. Canticle 11 in the BCP (p. 87), also known as the Third Song of Isaiah, based on Is 60:1–3, 11a, 14c, 18–19. It is named for the opening words of the canticle in Latin, which begins with the phrase "Arise, shine, for your light has come." It celebrates the glorious restoration of Jerusalem and the rebuilding of the Jerusalem temple. Imagery for the new Jerusalem in Rv 21 is based

on this passage. The BCP Table of Canticles suggests use of Canticle 11 after the OT reading at Morning Prayer on Sunday and Wednesday and after the OT reading at Evening Prayer on Thursday (pp. 144–145).

Surplice. A full white vestment with wide sleeves. It has an opening for the head at the top and typically reaches to the knees or beyond. The term is from the Latin *superpelliceum*, meaning "over a fur garment." It was an oversized alb that was worn as a choir vestment over a fur coat in the drafty and cold churches of northern Europe. It is usually worn over a cassock by clergy at non-eucharistic services such as the Daily Office. It may also be worn by lay people with particular liturgical ministries at worship such as lectors or choir members. Acolytes often wear a shorter version of the surplice, a cotta, which reaches to the hips and has narrower sleeves than the surplice. The academic dress of clergy may include cassock, surplice, and tippet, with or without an academic hood. The surplice may be worn with a stole by a member of the clergy assisting at the eucharist or by a member of the clergy who preaches. Surplice and stole may also be worn by a member of the clergy who presides at a eucharist or baptism. However, eucharistic vestments are typically worn by the celebrant at the eucharist instead of surplice and stole. Use of the surplice was a cause of dispute during the nineteenth-century controversies over ritual in the United States and in England. It came to be widely accepted as the standard vestment for Daily Office.

Surpliced Choir. *See* Vested Choir.

Sursum corda. The Latin term for the versicle and response of celebrant and congregation, "Lift up your hearts. We lift them to the Lord" (BCP, p. 361). It follows the salutation in the dialogue at the beginning of the Great Thanksgiving of the eucharist. It is a universal element of the eucharistic liturgy, and appears in all BCP eucharistic prayers. It calls for the people to stand. The celebrant's hands may be raised up as a gesture to give emphasis to this moment in the liturgy. The response of the people in Rite 1 eucharistic liturgies is slightly different from the Rite 2 response, stating, "We lift them up unto the Lord" (BCP, p. 333). *The Hymnal 1982* provides musical settings for the Rite 1 and Rite 2 versions of the *Sursum corda* (S 112, S 120).

Suspension. By this sentence a member of the clergy is directed to refrain temporarily from the exercise of ordained ministry. A sentence of suspension shall specify on what terms, on what conditions, and at what time the suspension shall cease.

Suter, John Wallace (Dec. 1, 1859–Apr. 11, 1942). Priest and liturgist. He was born in Boston, Massachusetts. Suter received his B.A. from Harvard University in 1881 and his B.D. from the Episcopal Theological School in 1885. He was ordained deacon on June 17, 1885, and priest on June 8, 1886. From 1885 until 1912 he was the rector of the Church of the Epiphany, Winchester, Massachusetts. While there he also served other churches in Massachusetts, including the Church of the Redeemer, Lexington, Trinity Church, Woburn, and St. James Church, Somerville. He retired in 1912 to devote full time to writing and lecturing. From 1913 until his death, he was a member of the Commission on Revision and Enrichment of the Prayer Book, and from 1932 until 1942, he was the fifth Custodian of the Standard Book of Common Prayer. He published several books on liturgy with the Rev. Dr. Charles Morris Addison, including the *People's Book of Worship* (1919). It was a story of the BCP. Suter has been described as a "devotional liturgist." He died in Boston, Massachusetts. His son, John Wallace Suter, Jr., succeeded him as Custodian of the Standard Book of Common Prayer. *See* Suter, John Wallace, Jr.

Suter, John Wallace, Jr. (June 18, 1890–Nov. 27, 1977). He was born in Winchester, Massachusetts. Suter received his B.A. from Harvard University in 1912 and his B.D. from the Episcopal Theological School in 1914. He was ordained deacon on June 7, 1914, and priest on Apr. 25, 1915. Suter was assistant minister and director of Christian Education at Christ Church, Springfield, Massachusetts, 1916–1917; rector of Christ Church, Boston, 1917–1920; and a member of the clergy staff of St. Paul's Cathedral, Boston, 1920–1925. From 1925 until 1933, he was executive secretary of the Department of Religious Education of the National Council of the Episcopal Church. Suter was rector of the Church of the Epiphany, New York, 1933–1944, and dean of the Cathedral of St. Peter and St. Paul, Washington, D.C., 1944–1950. From 1951 until his retirement in 1957, Suter taught at St. Paul's School, Concord, New Hampshire. During some of that time he served St. Andrew's Church, Hopkinton, New Hampshire. He was an advocate for an increased role for women in the church and for the revision of the Prayer Book. He succeeded his father, John Wallace Suter, as Custodian of the Standard Book of Common

Prayer. He served in that position from 1942 until 1963. Suter died in Concord, New Hampshire. *See* Suter, John Wallace.

SWEEP, SWEEPS. A process of congregational self-evaluation for mission and ministry. The name is an acronym for five aspects of church mission as expressed in "The Next Step in Mission": service, worship, evangelism, education, and pastoral care. The Next Step was adopted by General Convention in 1982 at the suggestion of Presiding Bishop John M. Allin. It followed the "Venture in Mission" program, which was begun in 1976. It continued in use in the church in the 1990s. Some clergy and lay leaders added stewardship as a sixth aspect of church mission, resulting in the modified acronym "SWEEPS."

Syle, Henry Winter (Nov. 9, 1846–Jan. 6, 1890). First hearing-impaired person ordained in the Episcopal Church. He was born in Shanghai, China, and lost his hearing as a result of scarlet fever. He studied at Trinity College, Hartford, Connecticut, St. John's College, Cambridge, and in 1872 received his M.A. from Yale University. While teaching at the New York Institution for Deaf-Mutes, he was active in St. Ann's Church for the Deaf. He came under the influence of Thomas Gallaudet, a pioneer in ministry among the deaf in the Episcopal Church. In 1875 he moved to Philadelphia, where he prepared for ordained ministry. He was encouraged by Gallaudet and supported by Bishop William Bacon Stevens of Pennsylvania, against the opposition of many who believed that the impairment of one of the senses was an impediment to ordination. He was ordained deacon on Oct. 8, 1876, and priest on Oct. 14, 1883. In 1888 he built All Souls' Church for the Deaf, Philadelphia, the first Episcopal church constructed especially for hearing-impaired persons. The ministry of Syle and Thomas Gallaudet is commemorated in the Episcopal calendar of the church year on Aug. 27.

Symbol. Object, image, or action that embodies and expresses a meaning beyond itself. For example, the crucifix is a symbol of Christ's passion, sacrifice, and atonement. Some symbols are drawn from scripture. The winged ox is a symbol for St. Luke's gospel, which begins with Zechariah sacrificing in the temple and which describes the sacrifice of Christ. The sacraments may be understood as symbols that represent God's activity for the salvation of humanity. Other symbols are drawn from legends or pre-Christian myths. Symbols may evoke conscious and unconscious responses. They sometimes convey both information and emotion. The meaning of symbols is often open-ended and not subject to exact definition, allowing the possibility of differing interpretations.

Synagogy. A community of people who live in, worship in, and work with small congregations. It is more a process than a program. It had its beginning at a meeting in Sewanee, Tennessee, over Pentecost weekend, May 12–14, 1989. Twenty-six persons representing twenty dioceses in eighteen states attended this meeting. These participants felt strongly that there should be another, larger gathering of people involved in small congregations. They decided to call it Synagogy. The first meeting under that name was held at the St. Francis Center in Cincinnati, Sept. 13–16, 1990. This meeting was sponsored by the Standing Commission on the Church in Small Communities and the Diocese of Southern Ohio. Synagogy stresses the baptismal ministry of every Christian.

Synaxis. The liturgy of the word, or *Pro-anaphora*, at the eucharist. The term is from the Greek for a meeting or assembly. It is related to the word "synagogue," which was the place of gathering for Jewish worship. The basic elements of reading from scripture, psalmody, and prayer were included in the synagogue service. Christians in the early church continued to participate in worship at synagogue and celebrated the eucharist at home. After Christians were expelled from synagogue worship, the main elements of the synagogue service came to precede the eucharist in a single Christian service. These elements are still present in the *synaxis* at the eucharist. The term has also been used in the Christian tradition for any meeting for public worship.

Synderesis. *See* Syneidesis.

Syneidesis. The function of conscience as a guide to conduct. The term may be derived from the Greek, "consciousness," hence our term conscience. Because of a scribal error, it is often called *synderesis* or *synteresis*. Contemporary usage in moral theology concerns the capacity for deciding right or wrong in a particular case in light of general moral principles. It is a judgment of practical reason, reflecting the capacity for the human mind to make moral judgments. *See* Moral Theology.

Synod. This term comes from the Greek *synodos*, "a meeting" or "a coming together." It means an assembly of bishops or a meeting of church people. Before the Council of Nicaea (325), synod and council were used interchangeably. After the Council of Nicaea, the term "council" was used for an ecumenical council and the term "synod" was used for a meeting of bishops. The Episcopal Church is divided into nine provinces. Each province has a Provincial Synod or a Synod of the Province. Each synod consists of a House of Bishops and a House of Deputies, which meets on a regular basis as determined by the province. Every bishop having jurisdiction within the province has a seat and voice in the House of Bishops of the province. The House of Deputies of a province consists of presbyters, deacons, and lay persons from each diocese and area mission in the province. The president of the province may be a bishop, presbyter, deacon, or lay person elected by the synod. In Oct. 1984 the Synod of Province VII elected Dixie Hutchinson president, the first lay person and first woman to be president of a province. Each province elects one bishop or presbyter or deacon and one lay person to the Executive Council of the Episcopal Church. Each Provincial Synod has the power to elect judges of the Provincial Court of Review. The convention of a missionary diocese may, in lieu of electing a bishop, request that the election of a bishop be made on its behalf by the Synod of the Province, or by the House of Bishops of the province subject to confirmation by the Provincial Synod. Lutherans and Presbyterians use the term "synod" for geographical districts.

Synoptic Gospels. The word "synoptic" means "to see or view together." Scholars use the term to refer to three of the four gospels—Matthew, Mark, and Luke. The synoptic gospels are very similar but not exactly the same. They are quite different from the fourth gospel, John. The three synoptic gospels have similar structure, language, basic perspective, and basic contents. They have different beginnings and endings, distinctive events, some individual teachings, and their own emphases. In source criticism, scholars seek to determine if one gospel is the earliest and the source of the others. The great majority of NT scholars accept the Two Source Theory which proposes that Mark is the earliest gospel. This conclusion is based on the language and forms of Mark. *See* Source Criticism.

Synteresis. See Syneidesis.

Systematic Theology. An approach to theology that integrates revealed truths and theological reflection into a coherent whole. For example, systematic theology may be applied to consider how salvation in Christ is made available to humanity through the church. The relationships between truths of faith and Christian doctrines are synthesized and arranged in terms of various ordering principles so that Christian faith will be intelligible to those outside the Christian community as well as to those who believe. Systematic theology may integrate philosophical, historical, scientific, economic, and humanistic studies. Although Anglicanism has not produced many comprehensive "systems" of theology, there have been notable exceptions. The Episcopal theologian William Porcher DuBose has been described as one of the few and one of the best systematic theologians in Anglicanism. DuBose's theology was rooted in the "turning points" of his life experience, and he described that relationship in his autobiographical and theological work *Turning Points in My Life* (1912). John Macquarrie's *Principles of Christian Theology* (2d ed., 1977) takes as its philosophical grounding the existential philosophy of Martin Heidegger. *See* DuBose, William Porcher.

T

Tabernacle. According to Ex 25–30, 35–40, the Tabernacle was a portable sanctuary of the Israelites. It was constructed at Sinai in connection with the making of the covenant. It was to be a place of sacrifice and worship. Rectangular in shape, the Tabernacle had a wooden framework and was covered with curtains. Its two main sections were the "holy place" and the "holy of holies." The holy of holies contained the Ark of the Covenant. The table of incense, the seven-branched lampstand, and the table for the bread of the presence stood in the holy place.

The description of the Tabernacle in Exodus comes from the fifth century B.C. Priestly source of the Pentateuch. In some respects this description probably reflects the structure and furnishings of the Solomonic Temple. The shrine of the time of Moses may have been a somewhat simpler tent, which appears in Ex 33:7–11 and elsewhere as the Tent of Meeting.

In the NT the Letter to the Hebrews sees the true Tabernacle as the one in heaven where Christ is the high priest (see Heb 8:1–6, 9:24).

Taiwan, Diocese of. The Missionary District of Taiwan (Formosa) was transferred to the Episcopal Church from the Nippon Seikokai on July 6, 1960. It is now a Diocese of the Episcopal Church.

Taizé Chant. This form of contemporary liturgical song was first developed for use by the ecumenical Christian community at Taizé, France. It uses repetitive structures that can easily be memorized, along with other parts for solo voices, choirs, and instruments. Jacques Berthier prepared the musical settings for Taizé chant. In recent years it has gained acceptance and is used in many denominations. Latin is now used for singing Taizé Chant at Taizé because of the international nature of the community. However, settings of Taizé Chant are edited for use in other languages, including English. *Wonder, Love, and Praise* has a variety of hymns that use Taizé chant, such as "O Lord hear my pray'r" (Hymn 827) and "Laudate omnes gentes" (Hymn 830).

Talbot, Ethelbert (Oct. 9, 1848–Feb. 27, 1928). Fifteenth Presiding Bishop and ecumenist. He was born in Fayette, Missouri. Talbot graduated from Dartmouth College in 1870 and from the General Theological Seminary in 1873. He was ordained deacon on June 29, 1873, and priest on Nov. 4, 1874. From 1873 until 1887, he was rector of St. James' Church, Macon, Missouri. Talbot was consecrated the first Missionary Bishop of Wyoming and Idaho on May 27, 1887. He served as Bishop of Central Pennsylvania from Feb. 2, 1898, until his death. When the Presiding Bishop died, Talbot, by seniority of consecration, became the Presiding Bishop on Feb. 18, 1924. He was committed to the ecumenical movement, and urged the immediate organic union of American Protestant groups. Talbot died in Tuchanoe, New York.

Talbot, John (1645–Nov. 29, 1727). Leading advocate for a bishop for the American colonies. He was born in Wymondham, Norfolk, England. Talbot studied at Christ's College, Cambridge, where he received his B.A. in 1664 and his M.A. in 1671. He was a fellow of Peterhouse, 1664 to 1668, and was rector of a church in Icklingham, Suffolk, 1673 to 1689. From 1695 until 1701 he was rector of the church at Fretherne, Gloucestershire. On Apr. 28, 1701, he sailed from Clowes, England, to Boston as Chaplain of the *Centurion*. On the ship were George Keith and Patrick Gordon, the first missionaries sent to the American colonies by the newly organized Society for the Propagation of the Gospel in Foreign Parts. Talbot became an assistant to Keith after they arrived in Boston. On Sept. 18, 1702, Talbot was named a missionary for the Society for the Propagation of the Gospel. Talbot and Keith made an extended missionary journey of the American colonies, which lasted two years and stretched from the Piscataway River in New England to Caratuck in North Carolina. By Oct. 1702 they had moved their missionary work into New Jersey. On Mar. 25, 1703, the Feast of the Annunciation, Talbot laid the foundation stone of St. Mary's Church at Burlington. He and Keith continued missionary work in the area until Apr. 2, 1704, when Talbot became the rector of St. Mary's, where he remained off and on until his death. From 1720 until 1723 he was in England trying to convince the society to send a bishop. Talbot, known as the "apostle to New Jersey," died in Burlington.

Talbot, Joseph Cruikshank (Sept. 5, 1816–Jan. 15, 1883). Missionary Bishop of the Northwest. He was born in Alexandria, Virginia. In 1835 Talbot moved to Louisville, Kentucky, and in 1837 was confirmed in the Episcopal Church. He studied for ordination under Bishop Benjamin B. Smith. Talbot was ordained deacon on Sept. 5, 1846, and priest on Sept. 6, 1848. While in deacon's orders he organized St. John's Church, Louisville, and he became the rector upon his ordination to the priesthood. In 1853 he moved to Indianapolis and became the rector of Christ Church. He was consecrated Missionary Bishop of the Northwest on Feb. 15, 1860. The Missionary District of the Northwest included New Mexico, Dakota, Wyoming, Colorado, Arizona, Utah, Montana, and Idaho, covering nearly nine hundred thousand square miles. Talbot referred to himself as "Bishop of All Outdoors." On Aug. 23, 1865, he was elected Assistant Bishop of Indianapolis, and became the Bishop on Aug. 26, 1872. He served in this capacity until his death. He died in Indianapolis. *See* Northwest, Missionary District of the.

Tallis, Thomas (c. 1505–1585). Musician and composer, often called the "father of English Church music." Tallis was possibly born in Kent, England. His early years as a musician were spent in the service of the Roman Catholic Church, primarily at Waltham Abbey from 1538 to 1540

when the monasteries were dissolved. He was subsequently a lay clerk at Canterbury Cathedral and a gentleman of the Chapel Royal until his death. In 1571 Queen Elizabeth I granted Tallis and William Byrd a 21-year monopoly in music printing. Tallis was best known as a composer of choral music for both the Latin and reformed rites, but he also wrote prolifically for solo voice, strings, and keyboard. Tallis wrote nine tunes for Archbishop Parker's Psalter of 1567–1578. *The Hymnal 1982* contains three of these tunes: *The Eighth Tune*, better known as *Tallis' Canon*, used for Hymns 25 and 43; *The Third Tune*, used for Hymns 170 and 692, and *Tallis' Ordinal*, used for Hymns 260 and 489. *The Third Tune* is the basis for Ralph Vaughan Williams's orchestral composition, "A Fantasia on a Theme of Tallis." Tallis died in Greenwich, Kent.

Tantum Ergo. See Pange Lingua.

Taylor, Jeremy (Aug. 15, 1613–Aug. 13, 1667). Leader among the "Caroline Divines." He was born in Cambridge, England. Taylor studied at Gonville and Gaius College, Cambridge. He was ordained in 1633. He was a fellow at All Souls' College, Oxford, and in 1638 he became rector of Uppingham. Taylor was a zealous supporter of the royal cause. During the Commonwealth period he was deprived of all his preferments. After the Restoration, he was consecrated the Bishop of Down and Connor in Ireland on Jan. 27, 1661. Taylor was one of the leading devotional writers in English history. Among his most popular writings are *A Discourse of the Liberty of Prophesying* (1647), *Rule and Exercises of Holy Living* (1650), *Rule and Exercises of Holy Dying* (1651), and *Ductor Dubitantium or the Rule of Conscience* (1660). He was a popular preacher and has been called "the Chrysostom of England." Taylor died in Lisburn, Ireland. He is commemorated in the Episcopal calendar of the church year on Aug. 13.

Teachers of the Children of God. Religious order with an educational vocation. The order began its work in Providence, Rhode Island, where the community was founded on Dec. 1, 1934. It was at this site that the first postulants and novices were trained and the first sisters took their vows. The founder was Dr. Abbie Loveland Tuller, who became Mother Abbie, the first mother superior of the order. She had a Ph.D. from Harvard University and was the originator of the Tuller Method of education. The purpose of the order is to develop through the gifts of the Holy Spirit the fruits of the Spirit, especially faith, love, and joy. The order seeks to provide a Christian community in which sisters and children may live together, learning to know, love, and serve God and neighbor. The order establishes and conducts day and boarding schools. It also offers teacher training courses for women interested in Sunday Church School or other phases of educational work within the church. A permanent member of the order is given a white veil and a gold wedding band, a symbol of her marriage to Christ. The order operates the Tuller School in Tucson, Arizona, and the Tuller School in Fairfield, Connecticut.

Team Ministry. A cooperative approach to parish ministry in which the entire ministry team shares responsibility for formulating the overall vision of ministry. The ministry team may include youth ministers, Christian education directors, secretaries, musicians, and others, along with the parish clergy. Team ministry emphasizes the importance of each member's perspective and contribution. Maintaining the integrity of the group and open sharing within the group are priorities for team ministry.

Te Deum laudamus. Canticle of praise named for its opening words in Latin. It appears as Canticles 7 and 21 in the BCP (pp. 52–53, 95–96). The traditional language Canticle 7 is also known as "We Praise Thee," and the contemporary language Canticle 21 is also known as "You are God." This hymn of praise dates from the fourth century. Unlike most canticles, it is not based on scripture. It is usually attributed to Niceta (c. 392–414), Bishop of Remesiana in Dacia. It is mentioned in the Rule of Caesarius and the Rule of Benedict as the canticle at matins. The Sarum Breviary used it after the last lesson at Sunday matins except during Advent, Pre-Lent, Lent, and certain other days. The 1549 BCP called for its use after the OT reading at matins except during Lent. The 1979 BCP lists the *Te Deum laudamus* as one of three songs of praise which may begin the first eucharist of Easter (p. 294). The Table of Canticles suggests its use at Morning Prayer after the NT reading on Sunday, except during Advent and Lent, and after the NT reading on Feasts of our Lord and other major feasts (p. 144). It is traditionally used as the hymn of praise following the pontifical blessing and dismissal at the ordination of a bishop. The *BOS* calls for the *Te Deum laudamus* or other song of praise after the seating of a bishop in the cathedra of the diocese in the service for the Welcoming and Seating of a Bishop in the Cathedral. The *BOS* also suggests its use in other seasonal services such as a Vigil for All Hallows' Eve and a Vigil for New Year's Eve. It has also been traditional to sing the *Te Deum laudamus* at other times of celebration outside the context of a liturgy, such as the election of a bishop at diocesan convention or a military victory. *The Hymnal 1982* provides a variety of musical settings for both the traditional and contemporary versions of the *Te Deum laudamus* (S 205–S 207, S 282–S 288). *The Hymnal 1982 Accompaniment Edition, Vol. 1*, also provides a musical setting for the contemporary version of the *Te Deum laudamus* (S 407).

Temple, William (Oct. 15, 1881–Oct. 26, 1944). The only son of an Archbishop of Canterbury to become the Archbishop of Canterbury. He was born in Exeter, England. Temple was educated at Rugby and then at Balliol College, Oxford. In 1904 he became a fellow at Queen's College, Oxford. In 1906 he was refused ordination by Bishop Francis Baget of Oxford, who had doubts about Temple's theology of the Virgin Birth and the Resurrection. Temple was ordained priest in 1908. In 1910 he became the headmaster of Repton. In 1914 Temple became the rector of St. James' Church, Piccadilly. During the war years he was secretary of the Mission of Repentance and Hope. He was later the leader of the Life and Liberty Movement. On Jan. 25, 1921, he was consecrated Bishop of Manchester. He served in that position until he became Archbishop of York on Jan. 2, 1929. On Apr. 1, 1942, Temple became the ninety-eighth Archbishop of Canterbury. He served in that position until his death. He was a leader in the ecumenical movement and a strong advocate of educational and labor reform. His chief publications were *Mens Creatrix* (1917) and his Gifford Lectures, *Nature, Man and God* (1934). His sympathetic attitude toward the working-class movement led him to membership in the Labor Party in 1918. His influential *Christianity and Social Order* (1944) is sometimes described as a twentieth-century adaptation of Christian Socialism and one of the underpinnings of the welfare state. He was chairman of an interdenominational and international Conference on Christian Politics, Economics, and Citizenship in 1924, an Anglican delegate to the Faith and Order Conference at Lausanne in 1927, and chairman of the Faith and Order Conference at Edinburgh in 1937. He was largely responsible for the British Council of Churches and the formation of the World Council of Churches. Temple was an incarnational theologian and a leader in the social application of the gospel. He was noted for his ability to express complicated ideas clearly and persuasively.

Temporale. The section of a service book such as a missal or breviary that provided the variable portions of services for seasons of the church year that were centered on the date of Christmas or Easter, and not the fixed dates of the church calendar. The propers for the fixed holy days appeared in the *Sanctorale*, with the exception of those in the Christmas season.

Ten Commandments, The. The commands, also known as the decalogue or Ten Words, given by God at Sinai in connection with the making of the covenant (Ex 20:1–17). Another slightly different version appears in the extended homily Moses delivers shortly before the entrance of the Hebrews into the Promised Land (Dt. 5:6–21). The Sinai version precedes the large collection of laws also associated with the Mosaic covenant. The Ten Commandments form the fundamental law of God for Israel and concern the cult (no other gods, no images, no misuse of God's name, observance of the Sabbath) as well as social relations (honor of parents, no killing, no adultery, no false witness, no coveting). Unlike the case law of the OT, where an offense is followed by its punishment, the Ten Commandments are categorical. Some religious communities differ from the numbering of the Ten Commandments in Anglican and reformed traditions, but agree in the content. In the NT both Jesus (Mk 10:17–22 and parallel passages) and Paul (Rom 13:8–10) affirm their continuing validity.

Tenebrae. This form of the monastic office (matins and lauds) is commonly adapted for congregational use during Holy Week. The office is structured around psalms, readings, and responsories. A distinguishing characteristic of this service is the series of readings from Lamentations which appear early in the office. The distinctive ceremonial of *Tenebrae* includes use of fifteen lighted candles, often set on a special, triangular stand. One candle is extinguished as each of the fourteen appointed psalms is completed. The fifteenth candle, symbolic of Christ, is left lighted at the end of the final psalm. But it is carried away to be hidden, which signifies the apparent victory of the forces of evil. A sudden loud noise is made at the end of the service, symbolizing the earthquake at Christ's death. The lighted candle is then restored to its place, suggesting Christ's eventual triumph. The *BOS* includes *Tenebrae* as an option for use on Wednesday in Holy Week.

Tennessee, Diocese of. The primary convention of the Diocese of Tennessee was held in Nashville on July 1–2, 1829. The 1982 General Convention voted to divide the Diocese of Tennessee into the dioceses of Tennessee, East Tennessee, and West Tennessee. The Diocese of Tennessee includes the following counties: Bedford, Canon, Cheatham, Clay, Coffee, Davidson, DeKalb, Dickson, Fentress, Franklin, Giles, Grundy, Hickman, Houston, Humphreys, Jackson, Lawrence, Lewis, Lincoln, Macon, Marshall, Maury, Montgomery, Moore, Overton, Perry, Pickett, Putnam, Robertson, Rutherford, Smith, Stewart, Sumner, Trousdale, Van Buren, Warren, Wayne, White, Williamson, and Wilson. On Jan. 27, 1995, Christ Church, Nashville, was set apart as Christ Church Cathedral.

Terce, Sext, None. Traditional monastic offices that were recited at 9 A.M., "the third hour" (terce), 12 noon, "the sixth hour" (sext), and 3 P.M., "the ninth hour" (none). These canonical hours of the breviary office were known as little hours or little offices. The early Christian church followed the Jewish custom of community prayers at sunrise and sunset, with private devotions at the third, sixth, and ninth hours (9 A.M., 12 noon, and 3 P.M.). These little hours of prayer were associated with the Passion. Jesus' dying on the cross was recalled in the sixth hour, and his burial was recalled in the ninth hour. The custom of daily prayer is evidenced by Acts 3:1, which records that Peter and John "were going up to the temple at the hour of prayer, at three o'clock in the afternoon." Acts 10:9 also states that Peter went to pray at noon on the day when the men sent by Cornelius arrived.

As monasticism developed, the private devotions at the third, sixth, and ninth hours became the little offices of terce, sext, and none. These little offices had a common structure. Development of the full round of canonical hours—including matins and lauds, prime, terce, sext, none, vespers, and compline—has been dated from the late fifth century. terce, sext, and none were not included in early Anglican Prayer Books. The Order of Service for Noonday in the 1979 BCP (p. 103) is based on the traditional structure of the little offices. The Order of Service for Noonday may be used (with appropriate choices from the options for lessons and collects) for terce, sext, or none. *See* Little Hours of the Divine Office.

Teresa of Avila (Mar. 28, 1515–Oct. 4, 1582). Monastic reformer. She was born in Avila, Spain. In 1534 Teresa entered the monastery of the Incarnation of the Carmelite nuns in Avila. While a nun she had numerous visions. In 1559 Teresa had a vision in which she was convinced that Christ was present to her in bodily form, though invisible. Teresa was very much concerned about the laxity in the Carmelite monasteries and resolved to reform them. In 1562 she established the monastery of St. Joseph in Avila, and there she wrote the first of her mystical treatises, *The Way of Perfection*. Under her leadership a number of reform convents were founded in Spain. St. John of the Cross was encouraged by Teresa to seek the reform of the Carmelite friars. Teresa is known for her mystical contemplative spiritual writings, especially *The Interior Castle*. She died in Alba de Tormes, and was canonized in 1622. Teresa was declared a Doctor of the Church by the Roman Catholic Church. She is commemorated in the Episcopal calendar of the church year on Oct. 15.

Tertiary. A member of a third order of a religious community. *See* Third Order.

Terwilliger, Robert Elwin (Aug. 28, 1917–June 3, 1991). Bishop and founding director of Trinity Institute, New York. He was born in Cortland, New York. He received his B.A. from Syracuse University in 1939, his B.D. from the Episcopal Theological School in 1943, his Ph.D. from Yale University in 1948, and his S.T.M. from General Theological Seminary in 1949. Terwilliger was ordained deacon on Dec. 7, 1942, and priest on June 29, 1943. He was curate at All Saints Church, Worcester, Massachusetts, 1942–1944; assistant at Christ Church Cathedral, Hartford, Connecticut, 1944–1949; fellow and tutor at the General Theological Seminary, 1947–1949; rector of Christ Church, Poughkeepsie, New York, 1949–1960; rector of St. James Church, Los Angeles, 1960–1962; and associate pastor at All Saints Church, New York, 1963–1967. In 1967 Terwilliger founded Trinity Institute in New York City. He served as its first director until he was consecrated Suffragan Bishop of Dallas on Dec. 29, 1975. He served in that position until he retired on Apr. 30, 1986. Terwilliger wrote several books and was on the board of trustees of several schools. He was a member of the Anglican-Orthodox International

Dialogue. Terwilliger died in Huntington, New York. *See* Trinity Institute.

Tetragrammaton. A word from Greek meaning "four letters." It refers to the four consonants of the biblical name of God, Yahweh, *YHWH*. From ancient times it was considered too sacred to be pronounced, and *Adonai* was substituted for it. The Prayer Book Psalter and the King James OT rendered the name of God "Lord," and the 1979 BCP continues this usage with *YHWH* rendered in capital and small capital letters: Lord (BCP, p. 583).

Texas, Diocese of. From Dec. 8, 1838, until Oct. 16, 1841, the Republic of Texas was under the episcopal jurisdiction of Leonidas Polk, Missionary Bishop of Arkansas and the Indian Territory. Texas was at that time a foreign mission. Polk also served Texas when he was Bishop of Louisiana. On Oct. 26, 1844, George Washington Freeman was consecrated the Missionary Bishop of Arkansas and the Indian Territory and was "to exercise Episcopal functions over the missions of this Church in the Republic of Texas." The Diocese of Texas was organized at Christ Church, Matagorda, on Jan. 1, 1849, and Freeman served it as bishop until his death. On Oct. 26, 1874, the General Convention divided Texas into the Diocese of Texas and the Missionary Districts of Northern Texas and Western Texas. The Diocese of Texas includes the following counties: Anderson, Angelina, Austin, Bastrop, Bell, Brazoria, Brazos, Burleson, Burnet, Chambers, Cherokee, Colorado, Coryell, Falls, Fayette, Fort Bend, Freestone, Galveston, Gregg, Grimes, Hardin, Harris, Harrison, Houston, Jasper, Jefferson, Orange, Lampasas, Lee, Leon, Liberty, Limestone, Madison, Marion, Matagorda, McLennan, Milam, Montgomery, Nacagdoches, Newton, Orange, Panola, Polk, Robertson, Rusk, Sabine, San Augustine, San Jacinto, Shelby, Smith, Travis, Trinity, Tyler, Walker, Waller, Washington, Wharton and Williamson. On Jan. 24, 1949, Christ Church, Houston, was set apart as Christ Cathedral.

Thanksgiving for the Birth or Adoption of a Child. The BCP (p. 439) states that after the birth or adoption of a child, the parents and other family members should come to the church to be welcomed by the congregation and give thanks to God. It is desirable that this be done at a Sunday service. The BCP provides a form for A Thanksgiving for the Birth or Adoption of a Child (pp.

440–445). It may follow the prayers of the people preceding the offertory at the eucharist. At Morning or Evening Prayer, it may take place before the close of the office. At the proper time, the celebrant invites the parents and other family members to present themselves before the altar. The BCP provides forms of address for the celebrant that are appropriate for the birth of a child or for an adoption. The form for an adoption also includes a formal inauguration of the new relationship. In response to a question by the celebrant, the parents take the child for their own. If the child is old enough to answer, the child accepts the woman and man as mother and father. The service continues with an Act of Thanksgiving, which includes the *Magnificat*, or Ps 116, or Ps 23. After a prayer of thanksgiving for the blessing bestowed on the family in the gift of a child (BCP, p. 443), the celebrant may add one or more additional prayers, including a prayer of thanks for a safe delivery, a prayer for the parents, a prayer for a child not yet baptized, or a prayer for a child already baptized. This form concludes with a threefold blessing of the family. This trinitarian blessing recalls that God the Father adopts us as his children by baptism, that God the Son sanctified a home at Nazareth, and that God the Holy Spirit has made the church one family (BCP, p. 445). A shorter form of this service may be used, especially in a hospital or at home. If the shorter form is used, the celebrant may begin with the Act of Thanksgiving, or with the prayer of thanksgiving for the blessing bestowed on the family in the gift of a child. A passage of scripture may first be read. The BCP identifies Lk 2:41–51 and Lk 18:15–17 as appropriate readings for this service. The service also includes a rubric that calls upon the minister of the congregation to instruct the people concerning the duty of Christian parents to provide for the well-being of their families and for all persons to make wills to arrange for the disposal of their temporal goods, including bequests for religious and charitable uses if possible (BCP, p. 445).

Historically, there were prayers of ritual purification for women who had been through childbirth. This purification was also known as the "churching" of women. The service of purification was done at the entrance of the church in the Sarum rite. Similarly, the 1549 Prayer Book included "The Order of the Purification of Women." This rite was known as "The Thanksgiving of Women after Childbirth, commonly called the Churching of Women" in the 1552 BCP, and in subsequent Prayer Books through the 1928 BCP. The 1979 BCP focuses on thanksgiving for the gift of a child, and suggests no ritual impurity associated with childbirth.

Thanksgiving Day. A national holiday and day of thanks. Thanksgiving Day is celebrated in the United States on the fourth Thursday in Nov. This custom is based on the celebration of three days of prayer and feasting by the Plymouth, Massachusetts, colonists in 1621. There was also a Thanksgiving celebration with prayer by members of the Berkeley plantation, near what is now Charles City, Virginia, in 1619. The first national Thanksgiving Day was celebrated in 1789. Under President Abraham Lincoln, Thanksgiving Day came to be celebrated annually on the last Thursday of Nov. Thanksgiving Day was celebrated on the third Thursday of Nov. in the three years 1939–1941 under President Franklin D. Roosevelt. However, the Thanksgiving Day commemoration was moved back to the fourth Thursday in Nov. by Congress in 1941.

Thanksgiving Day is a major holy day and a national day in the Prayer Book calendar of the church year (pp. 16–17, 33). The Proposed Prayer Book of 1786 included "A Form of Prayer and Thanksgiving to Almighty God, for the Fruits of the Earth, and all the other Blessings of his merciful Providence." The first American Prayer Book (1789) replaced the four national days of the 1662 English book with propers for Thanksgiving Day. The collect for Thanksgiving Day gives thanks to God the Father for the fruits of the earth in their season and for the labors of those who harvest them. It asks that we may be faithful stewards of God's great bounty, providing for our own necessities and the relief of all who are in need (BCP, p. 246). Hymns for Thanksgiving Day in *The Hymnal 1982* include "Praise to God, immortal praise" (Hymn 288), "Come, ye thankful people, come" (Hymn 290), and "We plow the fields, and scatter" (Hymn 291). *The Hymnal 1982 Accompaniment Edition, Vol. 1*, provides musical settings for a Litany of Thanksgiving for a Church (S 391; see BCP, pp. 578–579) and a Litany of Thanksgiving (S 392; see BCP, pp. 836–837). The Litany of Thanksgiving may be used on Thanksgiving Day in place of the prayers of the people at the eucharist, or at any time after the collects at Morning or Evening Prayer, or separately.

Thanksgiving, Great. Prayer of consecration said over bread and wine at the eucharist. The BCP uses the title "The Great Thanksgiving" as a major subheading in bold typeface for both eucharistic rites (BCP, pp. 333, 361), thus recovering one of the ancient designations for the eucharistic prayer. *See* Eucharistic Prayer.

Thanksgiving (Prayer). The Catechism identifies thanksgiving as one of the seven principal kinds of prayer (BCP, p. 856). We offer thanksgiving to God "for all the blessings of this life, for our redemption, and for whatever draws us closer to God" (p. 857). The eucharistic prayer, from the *Sursum corda* through the people's Amen, is known as the Great Thanksgiving (see BCP, p. 361). The BCP provides a variety of thanksgivings, including general thanksgivings, and thanksgivings for the church, national life, the social order, the natural order, and for family and personal life (pp. 836–841).

Th.D. The Doctor of Theology degree presupposes a first theological degree and is to equip persons for teaching and research in theological seminaries, colleges, and universities.

The Episcopal Network for Stewardship (TENS). *See* Episcopal Network for Stewardship, The (TENS).

Theodicy. A defense of the existence of God despite the presence of evil and suffering in the world. The term was coined by Gottfried W. Leibniz (1646–1716). It is drawn from Greek words meaning God and justice, and it justifies God's omnipotence, omniscience, and benevolence in the face of evil. Theodicies often emphasize the importance of human free will and moral responsibility, which allow the possibility of evil through destructive choices. Human virtue can also be understood to have meaning in terms of a choice for virtue despite possible failure and painful consequences—i.e., in the face of and in opposition to real evil. Human moral and spiritual development would be deprived of meaning if moral choices or favorable outcomes were somehow predetermined by God. The reality of free will allows us to choose to accept the offer of God's saving love. This response to the invitation of God's love would be meaningless if it were forced or unfree. Thomas Aquinas has been associated with the free will defense to the problem of evil. Leibniz believed this world to be the best of all possible worlds and held that evil provides a necessary contrast to disclose beauty and harmony. The term has also been applied to natural theology, which is the knowledge of God that can be attained by human reason.

Theodore of Tarsus (602–Sept. 19, 690). Scholar and reformer. He was born in Tarsus, Cilicia, in Asia Minor. Theodore was a lay monk when he was chosen by Pope Vitalian to become Archbishop of Canterbury. After he was ordained a subdeacon, Theodore was consecrated the seventh Archbishop of Canterbury on Mar. 26, 668, where he served until his death. Theodore was very effective in using synods to unify the church in England. A canon that called for uniformity in the observance of Easter was adopted by a synod of bishops held by Theodore in 672. At the Council of Hatfield in 680 all the English bishops attested to their orthodoxy by affirming the Nicene faith. A collection of Theodore's judgments concerning penance were collected and called a *Penitentiale.* The Venerable Bede said Theodore was the "first to whom the whole English church made submission." Theodore died at Canterbury. He is commemorated in the Episcopal calendar of the church year on Sept. 19.

Theologian. A person who is knowledgeable concerning theology. Theologians may be members of the clergy or lay people. For example, William Stringfellow (1928–1985) was one of the best known Episcopal theologians of the twentieth century. He was a lay person without advanced academic training in theology. Stringfellow identified the power of death with the forces of injustice and oppression in society. William Porcher DuBose, an Episcopal priest who taught for many years at the School of Theology of the University of the South, is commemorated on Aug. 18 in the Episcopal calendar of the church year. DuBose's emphasis on the role of experience in the process of salvation is reflected in his spiritual autobiography, *Turning Points in My Life.* The Anglican theologian Richard Hooker is also commemorated in the calendar of the church year. Hooker was a priest who was Master of the Temple in London. He later served English country parishes. He wrote *Laws of Ecclesiastical Polity*, a comprehensive defense of the Elizabethan Settlement. The collect in *Lesser Feasts and Fasts* for Hooker's commemoration recalls that God raised him up "in a day of bitter controversy to defend with sound reasoning and great charity the catholic and reformed religion." Theologians reflect the diversity of backgrounds and perspectives of the church. *See* Stringfellow, William; *see* DuBose, William Porcher; *see* Hooker, Richard.

Theological Seminary of the Protestant Episcopal Church of the Diocese of South Carolina. The 1858 Convention of the Diocese of South Carolina authorized a diocesan seminary and elected a board of trustees. It was located in Camden where Bishop Thomas Davis resided. It opened on Jan. 18, 1859, with three students and four faculty members. In Oct. 1859 William Porcher DuBose entered this seminary. It closed on June 30, 1862, because of the Civil War. It reopened in Oct. 1866 in Spartanburg, on the campus of what had been St. John's College. It suspended operation in Oct. 1868. The seminary trained about twelve men for the ordained ministry.

Theological Virtues. A virtue is the perfection of a human power or capacity. As distinct from the cardinal virtues which we can develop, the theological virtues are the perfection of human powers given by the grace of God. Cited first in 1 Cor 13:13, faith, hope, and love are described as theological virtues by Augustine. This tradition reaches its culmination in the thought of Thomas Aquinas. In his *Summa Theologica*, Thomas places faith, hope, and love at the center of his understanding of grace and sanctification or the deepening of the person's relationship with God. Faith is a matter of knowledge of God which perfects the intellect. Faith thereby perfects all human powers by orienting them to the final end or purpose of life. Hope is a matter of the perfection of the will. What is known in terms of hope is not narrowly an object of knowledge but a power that animates and sustains human willing. Love is a matter of perfection itself as love is the perfection of all powers. Richard Hooker, Jeremy Taylor, and other Anglican divines of the seventeenth century assumed this framework in terms of the theological virtues. Kenneth Kirk also used this understanding in seeking the renewal of Anglo-catholic moral theology in the twentieth century.

Theology. The term is derived from two Greek words meaning, respectively, "God" and "the study of" or "the knowledge of." It was used prior to the Christian era in Greek philosophy to mean the study of the gods. It became an important term in Christian usage in two senses. First, in the writings of the Greek Fathers it referred to that knowledge of God which human beings have through contemplation, mystical ascesis, and prayer, as opposed to the knowledge which we have through the created order. Second, in the western tradition during the medieval period of Scholasticism, it replaced the more common term "*sacra doctrina*," the study of scripture, as Christian thinkers became concerned with the rational, scientific analysis of Christian belief, especially with the kind of knowledge of God which derived from the study of the natural, created order. But theology never lost its deeper meaning of the knowledge of God derived from contemplation of the mystery of God which lies beyond all human knowing.

Theophany. The term is from two Greek words meaning "God" and "appearance." A theophany is a manifestation of God, usually with both visual and audible elements. For example, God appears to Moses in a burning bush and commissions him to lead the Hebrew people out of slavery in Egypt (Ex 3:1–12). Later at Sinai there are both visual (cloud, lightning) and audible (thunder, voice) indications of God's presence in connection with the making of the covenant (Ex 19). Subsequently in the OT there are many passages recounting theophanies, especially in connection with the calls of the prophets. In the NT the theophanies are usually associated with God's visual and audible revelation in Christ, for example, the Transfiguration (Mk 9:2–8 and parallels). When it refers to Christ, it is termed a Christophany.

Theosis. A term used in the tradition of Orthodox theology to refer to the participation of the human person in the life of God. It is also known as deification or divinization. It means "being made God" and reflects the dominant Orthodox understanding of salvation in Christ. Athanasius urged that God became man so that we might become divine. Humanity and God are understood to be infinitely distant from each other, but finite humanity and the infinite God are fully joined in Christ. As stated by Cyril of Alexandria, "We are made partakers of the divine nature and are said to be sons of God. . . not only because we are exalted by grace to supernatural glory, but also because we have God dwelling in us." The saving benefit of *theosis* is rooted in the Incarnation and the activity of divine grace. The active presence of the Holy Spirit brings us into communion with God. A central image for *theosis* is Christ's transfiguration (Mk 9:2–8 and parallels). *Theosis* is associated with the gift of divine glory (Jn 17:5, 22–24), adoption as children of God by the indwelling Spirit (Rom 8), and participation in the divine nature (2 Pt 1:4).

Although *theosis* has not been emphasized in Anglican theology of salvation, it is compatible with William Porcher DuBose's understanding of humanity's destined union with God through the saving process of divine grace. Richard Hooker emphasized the theological significance of sacramental participation in Book V of the *Laws of Ecclesiastical Polity*. An understanding of *theosis* is also implicit in the collect for the Second Sunday after Christmas Day, which prays, "Grant that we may share the divine life of him who humbled himself to share our humanity, your Son Jesus Christ. . . ." (BCP, p. 214). *See* DuBose, William Porcher; *see* Hooker, Richard; *see* Orthodox Churches.

Third Order. An association of those who live in the secular world while affiliated with a religious order. Although the members of the third order do not live in a religious community, they share the spirit and some of the practices of the order. The members of the third order, known as tertiaries, may have a distinctive rule of life.

Tertiaries originated among Franciscans in the early thirteenth century. The Franciscans (men, friars, founded by St. Francis) were the first order, and the Poor Clares (women, enclosed nuns, founded by St. Clare) were the second order. A Franciscan third order was created as an association of lay persons remaining in the secular world. They were admitted to participate in the spiritual life of the communities. Subsequently other religious orders created their own third orders. The Society of St. Francis in the Episcopal Church includes a third order. *See* Franciscan Spirituality; *see* St. Francis, Society of, Third Order, American Province.

"Third Services." *See* Mission Services (Third Services).

Thirty-Nine Articles, or Articles of Religion. The Thirty-Nine Articles were the result of a long process in which the Church of England attempted to provide a theological foundation for its existence during the doctrinal conflicts of the sixteenth century. The conflicts arose from the competing views between Protestants and Roman Catholics as well as controversy within the Church of England itself. The Articles are not a creed nor are they a confessional statement such as those produced by the churches of the Reformation. They seek only to provide a basic consensus on disputed points and to separate the Church of England from certain Roman Catholic doctrines which were regarded as medieval abuses or superstitions. At the same time, however, they affirmed other aspects of Christian belief which were held in the Roman Catholic Church.

The Articles have always been subjected to a variety of interpretations by those who emphasized their Reformation heritage and by those who interpreted the Articles in a more catholic manner. The most controversial interpretation of them was made by John Henry Newman in his *Tract 90.*

He was at that time a leader of the Oxford Movement. Newman interpreted the Articles virtually in accordance with the teaching of the Council of Trent. Shortly after writing *Tract 90*, Newman joined the Roman Catholic Church.

The Church of England required the clergy to subscribe to the Articles until the last century. Subscription to the Articles is now required only in a general sense in the Church of England. The Episcopal Church has never required subscription to the Articles. They now appear in a section called "Historical Documents" in the back of the BCP (pp. 867–876). The status and authority of the Articles has often been a subject of debate among Anglicans. The Articles have also been a source of confusion for those non-Anglicans who want to know what may be the authoritative teaching of the Anglican Church.

Th.M. The Master of Theology degree presupposes the M. Div. degree and is an academic program stressing fuller mastery of resources in one of the theological disciplines.

Thomas à Kempis (c. 1380–1471). Monastic, priest, and spiritual writer. He was born in Kempen near Koln, Germany. Kempis was educated in the school at Deventer, the Netherlands. It was run by the Brethren of the Common Life, who stressed the necessity of imitating the life of Christ by loving one's neighbor as oneself. He entered the Augustinian Convent of Mt. Saint Agnes near Zwolle, the Netherlands, in 1399. Kempis took his vows in 1407, and was ordained priest in 1413. In 1429 he became subprior of this community and spent the rest of his life there. He is renowned chiefly as the probable author of the *Imitatio Christi*, the *Imitation of Christ.* It is a manual of devotion to instruct the Christian in seeking perfection by following Christ as one's model. The book first appeared anonymously in 1418. It stresses asceticism rather than mysticism, and moderate rather than extreme austerity. Kempis died at the Convent of Mt. Saint Agnes. He is commemorated in the Episcopal calendar of the church year on July 24.

Thomas the Apostle, Saint. Also called Didymus, the twin, Thomas is identified as an apostle in all the lists of the apostles (Mt 10:3, Mk 3:18, Lk 6:15, Acts 1:13), and he has an important role in John's gospel. Thomas boldly urges his fellow disciples to go with Jesus to Bethany in Judea, despite the dangers they will face. Thomas says, "Let us also go, that we may die with him" (Jn 11:16). At the Last

Supper, Thomas tells Jesus that he does not know where Jesus is going, and asks, "How can we know the way?" (Jn 14:5). Thomas was absent at the time of Jesus' first appearance to the disciples after the resurrection. Thomas did not believe the other disciples when they told him they had seen the Lord. He has been known as "doubting Thomas" because of his disbelief that Jesus had appeared to the disciples. Thomas needed proof to believe. He did believe when Jesus appeared to him and the other disciples a week later. Thomas responds to Jesus' appearance by clearly proclaiming his faith, "My Lord and my God!" (Jn 20:28). Jesus said, "Blessed are those who have not seen and yet have come to believe" (Jn 20:29). Several apocryphal works have been attributed to Thomas, including the *Gospel of Thomas*. He is associated with the Christian mission to Parthia and India. Thomas's willingness to express his doubts and his faith in Jesus has provided a helpful example for many Christians. The BCP collect for Saint Thomas the Apostle prays that "our faith may never be found wanting" (BCP, p. 237). His life is commemorated on Dec. 21 in the Episcopal calendar of the church year.

Thomism. The theological system of St. Thomas Aquinas (1224/25–1275), embodied in his *Summa Theologica.* Adapting Aristotle's philosophy to Christian revelation, Thomas defined God as Primary Being, in whom alone essence and existence are one. The Three Persons subsist in the divine Essence, with which each is identical. Creation is a going out of the creature from God. The Incarnation of the Word, the institution of the church, the sacraments, the theological virtues of faith, hope, and charity, and the moral virtues are the normal means of the creature's return to God. Salvation is entirely God's gift. Eternal beatitude is given in a face-to-face vision of God in heaven. The English theologian Richard Hooker made use of Thomism. In 1879 Pope Leo XIII made Thomism the chief instrument of theological education in Roman Catholic seminaries.

Thompson, Hugh Miller (June 5, 1830–Nov. 18, 1902). Bishop and theologian. He was born in Londonderry, Ireland. Thompson came to the United States when he was six years old and later studied at Nashotah House. He was ordained deacon on June 6, 1852, and priest on Aug. 31, 1856. His early ministry was spent as a missionary in Wisconsin and Illinois. While in Wisconsin he served as professor of ecclesiastical history at Nashotah House, 1860–1870. During those same years he was editor of the

American Churchman. He also founded Kemper Hall, a school for girls. In 1871–1872, Thompson was rector of St. James' Church, Chicago, and from 1872 until 1875, he was the rector of Christ Church, New York. From 1876 until his election as bishop, he was rector of Trinity Church, New Orleans. On Feb. 24, 1883, Thompson was consecrated Assistant Bishop of Mississippi. He became the second Bishop of the diocese on Feb. 13, 1887. He served as bishop until his death. Many of the editorials he wrote for the *American Churchman* were collected and published in books. He wrote a number of books, including *The World and the Logos* (1886) and *The World and the Kingdom* (1888), which won him a significant reputation as a theologian. He was in the high church tradition but was an opponent of extreme ritualism. His editorials expressed concern for the oppressed and the disenfranchised. Thompson died in Jackson, Mississippi.

Thomson, Elizabeth Mars Johnson (Nov. 1807–Apr. 26, 1864). One of the first Episcopal foreign missionaries. She was born in Connecticut to former slave parents. She was a member of the Charitable Society in the African Sunday School at Hartford. In 1830 Mars volunteered to serve as a teacher in Liberia. Though church authorities initially refused her support, she and her new husband, William Johnson, entered Liberia in 1834. He died soon after their arrival. Elizabeth married James Madison Thomson, who had migrated to Liberia in 1832. They established a Sunday School in Monrovia. In 1835 they were appointed teachers in the Cape Palmas School by the Domestic and Foreign Missionary Society. James Thomson died in 1838, but Elizabeth continued teaching at the Cape Palmas School until 1845. After a U.S. furlough, she returned to Liberia where she served until her death. She died in Cape Palmas, Liberia.

Thousandfold, Order of the. A devotional society founded in Jan. 1920. The purpose of the order is to increase the power and usefulness of Christians. It seeks to inspire them to prayer and faith to draw upon the resources placed at their disposal by Jesus Christ. The rule of the order is to pray every day to be a thousand times more useful than ever before. The order does not have a regular organization.

"Three-Decker" Pulpit. A structure in which the clerk's pew was on the lowest level, the officiant's reading pew was on the middle level, and the pulpit was on the highest level. It was typically located in the nave. With this arrangement, the sermon was preached from the highest level of the structure. The "three-Decker" pulpit came into use in England and America during the eighteenth century. *See* Reading Pew.

"Three Rivers." *See* St. Benedict, Order of (OSB).

Throne, Episcopal. The bishop's official and ceremonial seat. It is also known as the *cathedra*, from the Latin for chair. It is typically located in the cathedral of the diocese. The term "cathedral" is derived from *cathedra*, in that the cathedral is the church where the bishop's chair is located. The episcopal throne is a symbol of the bishop's authority and jurisdiction. Some parishes reserve a distinctive chair for the bishop. This chair may be known as the bishop's throne.

Thurible. A small metal pot on chains in which incense is burned during the eucharist and other liturgies. The thurible is also known as a censer. The term is derived from the Latin for "incense." Fragrant smoke is produced when incense is spooned onto hot charcoals inside the thurible. The smoke escapes through holes in the thurible, especially when it is swung. The thurible is carried in procession by the thurifer. The apocalyptic vision recorded in Revelation mentions use of a censer by an angel (Rv 8:3, 5). *See* Incense; *see* Thurifer.

Thurifer. The server or acolyte who carries and swings the thurible in which incense is burned during the eucharist and other liturgies. The thurifer, the celebrant, the deacon, or other ministers may use the thurible in the ceremonial censing of people or objects such as the gospel book or altar. The thurifer may be assisted by another minister, a "boat person," who carries the incense boat or container which holds the incense that will be used during the service. *See* Incense; *see* Thurible.

Tiffany, Charles Comfort (Oct. 5, 1829–Aug. 20, 1907). Episcopal Church historian. He was born in Baltimore, Maryland. Tiffany received his M.A. from Dickinson College in 1853. He studied at the Andover Theological Seminary. He also studied at the Universities of Halle, Heidelberg, and Berlin. Tiffany was ordained deacon on July 15, 1866, and priest on Nov. 11, 1866. He was rector of St. James' Church, Fordham, New York, 1867–1871;

assistant on the Green Foundation, Trinity Church, Boston, 1871–1874; rector of the Church of the Atonement, New York, 1874–1880; and rector of Zion Church, New York, 1880–1890. In 1893 Tiffany became Archdeacon of New York. His major contribution to the Episcopal Church was his book, *A History of the Protestant Episcopal Church in the United States of America* (1895). It was a volume in the "American Church History" series. This series is the beginning of serious historiography with regard to American denominations. Tiffany died in North East Harbor, Maine.

Tiffany Window. A stained glass window by the American artist Louis Comfort Tiffany (1848–1933). Tiffany was a native of New York City. He used an original process for making opalescent glass which was called "favrile." Tiffany built a factory at Cirona, New York, in 1878 to produce this glass. These stained glass windows are highly prized for use in churches.

Timothy. Timothy was described by Paul as his "brother and co-worker for God" (1 Thes 3:2; see also Rom 16:21). He is credited by Paul with co-authoring Paul's Second Letter to the Corinthians, and Paul's Letters to the Philippians, the Colossians, and to Philemon. Timothy and Silvanus are identified as co-authors of Paul's First and Second Letters to the Thessalonians. Timothy's mother was a Jewish Christian, and his father was a Greek. Timothy and his family lived in Lystra, in Asia Minor, where Paul found him. Timothy was well-regarded by the believers in Lystra and Iconium. Paul wanted Timothy to accompany him on his missionary journeys. Paul had Timothy circumcised because the Jews knew Timothy's father was a Greek (Acts 16:1–3). Timothy shared with Paul and Silvanus in proclaiming Christ among the Corinthians (2 Cor 1:19). Paul sent Timothy as his representative to Corinth (1 Cor 4:17) and Thessalonica (1 Thes 3:2), and hoped to send Timothy to Philippi (Phil 2:19). Timothy is also identified as the recipient of two letters from Paul that are included in the NT (1 and 2 Tm). However, Paul's role in authoring these letters is disputed by scholars. In the First Letter of Paul to Timothy, Paul states that he told Timothy to remain in Ephesus to give right instruction to certain people (1 Tm 1:3–4). Timothy is believed to have become the first Bishop of Ephesus. Timothy and Titus are commemorated on Jan. 26 in the Episcopal calendar of the church year.

Tindal, William. *See* Tyndale, or Tindal, William.

Tippet. A large black scarf worn by clergy over surplice and cassock at the Daily Offices. It resembles a stole and is worn around the neck with the ends hanging down the front. It may be ornamented by emblems such as the Episcopal Church seal or the insignia of the wearer's seminary.

Tithe. A tenth of a person's income, usually mandated for sacred purposes. Tithing was a practice in Israel but not unique to Israel. It was well known throughout the ancient Near East from at least the fourteenth century B.C., particularly in Mesopotamia. The first reference to a tithe in the OT is the one that Abraham vows to the priest-king Melchizedek (Gn 14:20). Jacob also promised a tithe to God at Bethel (Gn 28:18–22). Various laws concerning the tithe appear in the legislation said to have been given with the covenant at Sinai, e.g., Lv 27:30–33 for the fifth-century priestly code and Dt 14:22–29 from the earlier Deuteronomic Code. The laws differ somewhat in terms of the content of the tithe (produce, animals, money); the recipients (priests, Levites, needy people, king); and the precise use, depending on the time and circumstance of their enactment. While not criticizing the tithe as such, a prophet like Amos criticizes those who pay tithes (4:4) but do not exercise justice (5:24), a sentiment which Jesus himself shared (Mt 23:23).

Titus. Companion of St. Paul. Titus was described by Paul as his "partner and co-worker" (2 Cor 8:23). Titus and Barnabas went with Paul to Jerusalem at the time of the apostolic council (c. 50) (Gal 2:1). This council decided to accept Gentiles as full members of the church. Although Titus was a Greek, he was not compelled to be circumcised (Gal 2:3). Paul sent Titus as his representative to Corinth, and he was comforted by the news that Titus brought him (2 Cor 7:6–16). Titus shared Paul's eagerness for the spiritual welfare of the Corinthians (2 Cor 8:16). Titus is identified as the recipient of a letter from Paul that is included in the NT. However, Paul's role in authoring this letter is disputed by scholars. In this letter, Paul states that he left Titus in Crete to "put in order what remained to be done" for the church, and to "appoint elders in every town" (Ti 1:5). Titus is believed to have become the first Bishop of Crete. Timothy and Titus are commemorated on Jan. 26 in the Episcopal calendar of the church year.

Tohuku, Missionary District of. The House of Bishops voted on Oct. 27, 1920, to divide the Missionary District of Tokyo and establish the Missionary District of Tohoku. In Apr. 1941 the Missionary District of Tohoku became a diocese in the Holy Catholic Church in Japan.

Tokyo, Missionary District of. The 1872 General Convention established the Missionary District of Yedo in Japan. In 1893 the name was changed to the Missionary District of Tokyo. On Oct. 15, 1925, the name was changed to the Missionary District of North Tokyo. In 1938 the name was changed again to the Missionary District of North Kwanto. It became a diocese in the Holy Catholic Church in Japan in Apr. 1941.

Tonsure. A traditional shaving of the head for monks and diocesan clergy. The tonsure was a point of friction between Celtic and Latin monks in the British Isles of the seventh and eighth centuries. The Celtic monks shaved the fore part of the head; Latin monks shaved the center part of the head, leaving a crown of hair. The Celtic practice disappeared progressively as more monks adopted the Rule of St. Benedict. The smaller tonsure of diocesan clergy marked admittance to clerical privileges. The practice of clerical tonsure was abandoned by the Reformers. It was abolished in the Roman Catholic Church in 1972 by Paul VI. The monastic tonsure is itself becoming rare as monks become more involved in outside activities.

Tonus Peregrinus. A Latin title for a medieval psalm tone. In translation it means a foreign or wandering tone. In the psalm tone, *Tonus peregrinus*, there is a different pitch for the reciting tone for each half of the chant. Historically it is associated with the singing of Ps. 114, which triumphantly recalls "when Israel came out of Egypt" and began its forty years of wandering.

Torah. A Hebrew noun coming from the verb "to teach." It has the basic meaning of teaching or instruction, but it is usually translated law. Although in the OT it can refer to teaching, it most commonly indicates that which comes from God. It first seems to have been used for a single commandment (e.g., Ex 13:9). Gradually it was extended to larger collections, such as the Book of Deuteronomy (e.g., Dt. 1:5). Finally, in the period of the Second Temple it was extended to the entire Pentateuch (Ps. 119). The Torah came to be the most important part of the biblical canon for the Jews. In Jewish tradition the term usually refers to the Pentateuch. In the NT the expression "the law and the prophets" almost certainly refers to the first two sections of the Hebrew Scriptures, i.e., the Torah/Pentateuch and the prophets. At times Paul means the Pentateuch when he refers to the law (Greek, *nomos*), e.g., Rom 2:15. However, the term has a number of other meanings for him, depending on its context.

Torch Bearer. An acolyte or server who carries a torch in procession, including the gospel procession. *See* Torches.

Torches. Candles mounted on poles for use in the liturgy. Lighted torches may be carried by acolytes or servers in procession, including the gospel procession. Torches may be placed near the altar and the ambo or lectern. Torches are used to enhance the solemnity and festivity of worship. *See* Pavement Lights.

Tory. *See* Loyalists.

Total Ministry. A model of pastoral oversight based on the development of the ministry of the whole church, lay and ordained. This model seeks to provide a comprehensive program for the education of the laity for ministry. It also seeks to insure that the laity are able to exercise their ministry by sharing fully in the power and authority of the church. The term came into official use in the Episcopal Church at the 1976 General Convention through various reports and resolutions. In Sept. 1978 forty-five lay and clergy participants met in Cincinnati, Ohio, as members of the informal support network for the Office of Lay Ministries of the Episcopal Church Center. They noted that Total Ministry is the ministry of all God's people in all areas of life, carried out through the interdependent and mutually affirming ministries of laity and clergy. Total Ministry is, therefore, correctly understood as Mutual Ministry. The drafters of this outline recognized that the local parish has the primary responsibility to develop Total Ministry.

Tract. 1) (Liturgical) Psalm verses that were sung or recited without antiphon or refrain before the gospel. Historically, the Tract took the place of the Alleluia during the penitential seasons of Pre-Lent and Lent and at Masses for the dead. The festal character of Easter was expressed when the Alleluia replaced the relatively plain Tract. The BCP simply states that a psalm, hymn, or anthem may

follow each reading prior to the gospel at the eucharist (BCP, p. 357). Alleluias are omitted during Lent.

2) (Educational or controversial) Pamphlet or booklet intended to educate the reader or to persuade the reader to a particular viewpoint. Some parishes make a variety of tracts available to parishioners in a "tract rack" that may be located near the entry to the church or a parish building. These tracts may be devoted to particular topics of interest, such as prayer or stewardship. Other tracts may provide a general introduction to the beliefs, practices, history, and customs of the Episcopal Church. Historically, tracts have been used to advance a perspective at a time of controversy. For example, "Tractarians" such as John Henry Newman, Edward B. Pusey, and John Keble published tracts to recall and uphold the catholic tradition of the Church of England.

Tractarian Movement. *See* Oxford Movement; *see* Tracts for the Times.

Tracts for the Times. Ninety publications issued by the leaders of the Oxford Movement in England. The first tract, *Thoughts on the Ministerial Commission, Respectfully Addressed to the Clergy*, was written by John Henry Newman and appeared on Sept. 9, 1833. Tract 90, *Remarks on Certain Passages in the Thirty-Nine Articles*, was issued on Jan. 25, 1841, and was also written by Newman. The later tracts were more extensive in scope than the first tracts. Controversy over Newman's Tract 90 led to the end of the publication of new tracts. The Oxford Movement is also called Tractarianism, and the writers and their supporters are called Tractarians. The *Tracts* emphasized high church doctrines, such as the authority of the ordained ministry derived from ordination at the hands of a bishop in the historic episcopate, the real presence of Christ in the eucharist, baptismal regeneration, and the church as a divine institution. In addition to Newman, the Tractarians included Edward Bouverie Pusey, John Keble, Arthur P. Perceval, Richard H. Froude, and Isaac Williams. The Tractarian Movement was also known as "Puseyism." Pusey put his initials on *Tract 18* (1833), which concerned the benefits of the church's system of fasting. Earlier *Tracts* had been published anonymously. Pusey's name provided another name for this movement, although at times "Puseyism" was used pejoratively. The *Tracts* were first published in the United States in 1839, and were especially popular at the General Theological Seminary. The *Tracts* contributed to the rise of an Anglo-catholic party in the

Episcopal Church. *See* Keble, John; *see* Newman, John Henry; *see* Pusey, Edward Bouverie.

Tradition. In Christian theology, tradition originally referred simply to that which had been handed down to the church from the prophets and the apostles concerning belief in God and God's redemptive work in Christ. Before the development of an authorized canon of Hebrew and Christian scriptures, the oral teaching of the Apostles and their successors formed the Christian tradition. Gradually, however, the term took on different meanings to include, for example, the authorized teaching of church councils and commonly accepted credal formulations. By the time of the middle ages it had taken on the sense of an authentic body of teaching in addition to scripture. Such an understanding of tradition was rejected by the Reformers, who appealed only to the authority of scripture itself. Article XXXIV of the Articles of Religion took a mediating position, admitting the authority of traditions so long as they were not "repugnant to the Word of God, and be ordained and approved by common authority." Anglicanism reflects balance in its devotion to scripture, tradition, and reason as sources of authority. *See* Authority, Sources of (in Anglicanism).

Transept. In a cruciform or cross-shaped church building, the parts of the building which are the two lateral arms of the cross. The transepts extend from the nave and chancel.

Transfiguration, Community of the (CT). This community was established by Eva Lee Matthews and Beatrice Henderson (1877–1963) on Aug. 6, 1898. They made their profession in St. Luke's Church, Cincinnati, before Assistant Bishop Boyd Vincent of Southern Ohio. In 1896 they had established Bethany Mission House in Cincinnati and began to live by a rule and wear a distinctive dress. Sister Eva's vision was to pattern the life of the community after Mary and Martha of Bethany. Since there was already a community named after these sisters, she chose the name Transfiguration. In the summer of 1898 they moved to Glendale, Ohio. On Aug. 6, 1903, Mother Eva Mary made life vows, and on Mar. 8, 1904, Sister Beatrice Martha made life vows. This was the first American Episcopal community to undertake foreign mission work. In 1914 the sisters founded St. Lioba's Girls' School in Wuhu, China. In 1918 they established St. Andrew's Priory School in Honolulu. The motto of the order is *Benignitas, Simplicitas, Hilaritas,* "Kindness, Simplicity, Joy." The sisters live a mixed life of daily prayer and work, especially works of mercy and missionary work. The community publishes *The Transfiguration Quarterly. See* Matthews, Sister Eva Mary.

Transfiguration of Our Lord Jesus Christ, The. Feast that celebrates Jesus' radical change of appearance while in the presence of Peter, James, and John, on a high mountain (Mt 17:1–8; Mk 9:2–8; Lk 9:28–36). The Gospel of Matthew records that "he was transfigured before them, and his face shone like the sun, and his garments became white as light." At this moment Moses and Elijah appeared, and they were talking with Jesus. Peter, misunderstanding the meaning of this manifestation, offered to "make three booths" for Jesus, Moses, and Elijah. A bright cloud overshadowed them and a voice from the cloud stated, "This is my beloved Son, with whom I am well pleased; listen to him." The disciples fell on their faces in awe, but Jesus encouraged them to arise and "have no fear." They saw only Jesus. This event is alluded to in 2 Pt 1:16–18, which records that "we were eyewitnesses of his majesty" and "we were with him on the holy mountain." The Transfiguration revealed Christ's glory prior to the crucifixion, and it anticipated his resurrection and ascension. It may have given strength and comfort to his disciples in the difficult times that followed. It also prefigures the glorification of human nature in Christ.

Celebration of the Transfiguration began in the eastern church in the late fourth century. The feast is celebrated on Aug. 6. This was the date of the dedication of the first church built on Mount Tabor, which is traditionally considered to be the "high mountain" of the Transfiguration. Others locate the Transfiguration on Mount Hermon or the Mount of Olives. Celebration of the feast was not common in the western church until the ninth century. It was declared a universal feast of the western church by Pope Callistus III in 1457. The feast was first included in the English Prayer Book as a black letter day in the 1561 revision of the calendar of the church year. It was included as a red letter day with proper collect and readings in the American Prayer Book of 1892. Its inclusion reflects the efforts of William Reed Huntington, who wrote the BCP collect for the Transfiguration. This collect prays, "O God, who on the holy mount revealed to chosen witnesses your well-beloved Son, wonderfully transfigured, in raiment white and glistening: Mercifully grant that we, being delivered from the disquietude of this world, may by faith behold the king in his beauty...." (BCP, p. 243). The Transfiguration is listed among the holy days of the church year as a Feast of our Lord. Other provinces of the Anglican Communion followed the lead of the Episcopal Church in celebrating the Transfiguration as a major feast. The Transfiguration gospel is used on the Last Sunday after the Epiphany in all three years of the BCP eucharistic lectionary. As an Epiphany story, the Transfiguration provides one of the most distinctive and dramatic showings of Jesus' divinity. *The Hymnal 1982* provides several hymns for the Transfiguration, including "Christ upon the mountain peak" (Hymns 129–130) and "O wondrous type! O vision fair" (Hymns 136–137). *See* Theosis.

Transfiguration Retreat Monastery. A small, semi-eremitic community that had a few cottages on forty acres of land at Pulaski, Wisconsin. They were Antonian monks, both men and women, who lived a simple life and included Native American spirituality in their formation. The group was founded on June 21, 1968. It was last listed in *The Episcopal Church Annual 1995*.

Transubstantiation. The belief that the substance (essence) of Christ's body and blood *replaces* the substance of the eucharistic bread and wine, although the appearances (known as "accidents" or "species") of the bread and wine continue outwardly unchanged. This eucharistic theology is based on the philosophical categories of Aristotle, elaborated at length by medieval Latin theologians, and regarded as definitive in the Roman Catholic tradition. The term is derived from the Latin *trans* "across" or "over," and *substantia*, "substance." The classical explanation of transubstantiation was presented by Thomas Aquinas in the *Summa Theologica.* Transubstantiation was also defended by the Fourth Lateran Council (1215) and the Council of Trent (1545–1563). Article XXVIII of the Articles of Religion rejected transubstantiation as "repugnant" and unscriptural, asserting instead that Christ is present in the eucharist in a "heavenly and spiritual manner" (BCP, p. 873). The English Test Act of 1673 required a Declaration Against Transubstantiation by all persons holding civil or military office. Some nineteenth-century Tractarians, such as John Henry Newman, found transubstantiation to be compatible with their understanding of the eucharist. But the concept of transubstantiation has generally been avoided and excluded from Anglican theologies of the Real Presence of Christ's body and blood in the eucharist. *See* Real Presence; *see* Receptionism.

Trial Use. The process of Prayer Book revision has been ongoing since the sixteenth century. The first Episcopal Prayer Book began with a process of trial use. The 1786 Proposed Prayer Book was the basis for the 1789 BCP, which was the first official Prayer Book in the Episcopal Church. During the twentieth century in the Episcopal Church proposed revisions of the Prayer Book were used on a trial basis prior to final approval. The Standing Liturgical Commission was established by the 1928 General Convention and given significant responsibility for preparing materials needed for Prayer Book revision. In 1950 the Standing Liturgical Commission began publishing a series of Prayer Book Studies. A revised eucharistic rite was presented by the Standing Liturgical Commission to the 1967 General Convention. This proposed revision was approved for trial use. A series of rites was published as *Services for Trial Use* and authorized for use by the 1970 General Convention. It was known as the "Green Book" because of its green cover. Additional rites were authorized at the 1973 General Convention, and revised eucharistic rites, rites of initiation, orders for the Daily Office, and a complete revision of the Psalter were subsequently published as *Authorized Services 1973*. It was known as the "Zebra Book" because of its striped cover. The 1976 General Convention approved the full report of the Standing Liturgical Commission, known as the Draft Proposed Book of Common Prayer. This became the Proposed Book of Common Prayer. It was approved as the Standard Prayer Book by the 1979 General Convention. The process of trial use for Prayer Book revision continued after the 1979 BCP. The 1985 General Convention resolved that the Standing Liturgical Commission should prepare inclusive language liturgies for the regular services of the church. This process of study, development, and evaluation of inclusive language texts was continued by the 1988 General Convention, ultimately resulting in the publication of *Prayer Book Studies 30—Supplemental Liturgical Texts* (1989). The use of these texts was authorized by General Convention, with use limited by the direction of the diocesan bishop or ecclesiastical authority.

Tridentine. Concerning the Council of Trent. This general council was called by Paul III to give a Catholic answer to the Reformation. It met intermittently from 1545 to 1563. In twenty-five sessions it dealt concurrently with doctrinal questions and church reform. Its doctrinal decrees explained scripture and tradition (1546), justification (1547), sacraments (1547, 1551, 1562, 1563), and purgatory (1563).

Most decrees included anathemas on those who denied the doctrines, but the Reformers were not condemned by name. Tridentine church reforms obliged bishops to reside in their dioceses, created seminaries to train the clergy, outlawed clandestine marriages, initiated a moderate liturgical reform, and inspired the *Roman Catechism* (1566) and a revision of the text of the Latin Vulgate Bible (1592). Theologians of the counter-reformation followed Tridentine doctrine closely.

Triduum. A period of three days of preparation for a feast day. The term is most frequently used for Maundy Thursday, Good Friday, and Holy Saturday, the three days prior to Easter Sunday that are the concluding days of Holy Week, also known as the Easter *Triduum*. Other usage for the Easter *Triduum* reckons the days from the evening of Maundy Thursday through the evening of Easter Day. The term may indicate any three-day period of preparation for a feast.

Triennial, The. A national meeting of Episcopal Church Women which occurs at the time of General Convention, sometimes called the "Women's Triennial," because it meets every three years. The 1871 General Convention discussed the role of women in the missionary and educational work of the church, and concluded that women needed a national organization. At the meeting of the Board of Missions in Oct. 1872, the Woman's Auxiliary to the Board of Missions was organized. At the 1874 General Convention, the first general meeting of the Woman's Auxiliary was held. It met annually for the next four years. Beginning with the General Convention of 1880, the Woman's Auxiliary met every three years when the General Convention met. This meeting was called the Triennial. It was called the "Third House" of the General Convention, along with the House of Deputies and the House of Bishops, although it had no canonical basis or authority. The United Offering, now called the United Thank Offering, was established at the 1889 General Convention. When the 1919 General Convention reorganized the Episcopal Church, the Woman's Auxiliary to the Board of Missions became the Woman's Auxiliary to the National Council, now called the Executive Council. In 1958 the Woman's Auxiliary transformed itself into the General Division of Women's Work of the National Council. Local units were encouraged to call themselves Episcopal Church Women. *See* Episcopal Church Women (ECW).

Trinity. The Trinity is one God: Father, Son, and Holy Spirit (BCP, p. 852). The term is from the Latin *tri*, "three," and *unitas*, "unity." The term was devised by Tertullian to express the mystery of the unity-in-diversity of God. Trinity means "threefold unity." The corresponding word in Greek is *ho trias*, which means "the Triad." The Trinity is a perfect relationship of love in which neither unity nor distinctness of the divine persons is compromised. God's life is understood to be dynamic, loving, and available to be shared in relationship with humanity for salvation. The term "economic Trinity" has been applied to the life of the Trinity in time and space, in the "economy" of salvation; as distinguished from the "immanent Trinity" which refers to the inner life of God beyond the limits of time and space. It may be said that our experience of the economic Trinity leads us to know the immanent Trinity and that God's self-revelation corresponds to God's essential nature. However, the helpfulness of this distinction should not be overemphasized because there is only one divine trinitarian life. Karl Rahner states, "The economic Trinity is the immanent Trinity, and vice versa."

Christian theology is the heir of both uncompromising biblical monotheism and the Platonic, Aristotelian, and Stoic emphases on the unity and simplicity of God. However, the NT ascribed a place of equality with God to the Word of God who became incarnate in Jesus of Nazareth (e.g., Jn 1:1–18, Col 1:15–20). The Spirit of God was also included in the divine life (1 Cor 2:10–13). The church took several centuries to work out a reasonably acceptable way to express the complex relation of Father, Son, and Spirit. The nearly complete doctrine of the Trinity announced at Constantinople in 381 held that God is one Being (*ousia*) in three equal and consubstantial persons or hypostases: the Father uncreated, the Son uncreated but begotten, the Spirit proceeding from the Father (and, in the western version of the Creed, the Son). The Athanasian Creed states that "we worship one God in Trinity, and Trinity in Unity, neither confounding the Persons, nor dividing the Substance" (BCP, p. 864). Article I of the Articles of Religion affirms that in the unity of God "there be three Persons, of one substance, power, and eternity; the "Father, the Son and the Holy Ghost" (BCP, p. 867). *See* Filioque; *see* Homoousios; *see* Perichoresis; *see* Trinity Sunday.

Trinity Church, Boston, Massachusetts. The third Episcopal parish in Boston, it was founded on Oct. 17,

1733, by a group of fourteen men who met in a tavern. In 1829 a stone Gothic Revival building was erected on the original site of the church. Phillips Brooks, Trinity's most famous pastor, became the rector in 1869. A new church was built under Brooks's leadership. It was consecrated on Feb. 9, 1877. Henry Hudson Richardson was the architect for this building. It is considered by many to be a masterpiece of church architecture in the United States. The chancel was dedicated on Dec. 18, 1938. A statue of Brooks by Augustus Saint Gaudens stands outside the North Transept of the church. *See* Brooks, Phillips.

Trinity Church, New Orleans. In Apr. 1835 the Rev. James Angell Fox established an Episcopal congregation in New Orleans with the name Trinity Church. It was the second Episcopal church in New Orleans. It was dissolved when Fox returned to Mississippi. On July 8, 1847, Trinity Church was incorporated, and on May 3, 1848, it was admitted into union with the Diocese of Louisiana. Bishop Leonidas Polk of Louisiana was rector of Trinity Church from 1855 until 1860. Six of Trinity's rectors have become bishops and it has the nickname the "Bishops' Church." The Rev. John Stone Jenkins was the rector from 1971 until 1984. While he was at Trinity he developed a program for lay theological education, Disciples of Christ ("DOC"). This program is now known as Disciples of Christ in Community ("DOCC"), and used in a variety of Episcopal parishes. Training and administration for the program is based at the School of Theology, University of the South.

Trinity Church, New York. Sometimes called Trinity Church, Wall Street. In 1696 Governor Benjamin Fletcher of New York granted his approval for the Anglicans in Manhattan to purchase land for a new church. On Nov. 2, 1696, the vestry of the new Trinity Church called William Vesey to be the rector. King William III of England granted a charter and a land grant for Trinity Church. The annual rent was "one peppercorne" to be sent to the king. On Mar. 13, 1698, the first Trinity Church building, a modest rectangular structure, opened for worship. In 1705 Queen Anne and Lord Cornbury, governor of New York, gave Trinity Church a tract of land known variously as "Duke's Farm," "King's Farm," and "Queen's Farm." This increased Trinity's holdings to 215 acres. Trinity later divested most of this land to establish and endow other churches and institutions, including what is now Columbia University. It also provided Trinity Church with a large endowment. In 1709 it founded the Charity School, now known as Trinity

School. In Sept. 1776 the original church structure and the Charity School were destroyed by fire. The second building was consecrated in 1790. Heavy snows in the winter of 1838/1839 weakened this second structure and it was torn down. On Ascension Day, May 21, 1846, the third and current church structure was consecrated. Designed by Richard Upjohn, it is considered one of the finest examples of Gothic Revival architecture in the United States. In 1950 Trinity Church published the first issue of *Trinity News*. On July 9, 1976, Queen Elizabeth II was presented with the symbolic "back rent" of 279 peppercorns. Trinity Church is one of the largest commercial landlords in New York City.

Trinity College, Hartford, Connecticut. Trinity College began as Washington College. The charter was granted on May 16, 1823. On Sept. 23, 1824, Washington College opened with nine students. The founder and first president, 1823–1831, was Bishop Thomas Church Brownell of Connecticut. In 1845 the name was changed to Trinity College. In 1968 the trustees voted to withdraw from the Association of Episcopal Colleges.

Trinity College of Quezon City, Philippines. Trinity College was founded in 1963 by the Philippine Episcopal Church and the Philippine Independent Church. It was named after Trinity College, Hartford, Connecticut, where Remsen Brinckerhoff Ogilby served as president, 1920–1943. His son, Lyman Cunningham Ogilby, was Bishop of the Philippines, 1957–1967.

Trinity Episcopal School for Ministry. In the early 1970s a group of Episcopal lay people and clergy sensed the need for a new seminary to emphasize biblical faith and train lay persons and clergy for parish ministry in light of faith. The Fellowship of Witness led the effort. On Apr. 15, 1975, Trinity Episcopal School for Ministry was incorporated. The Rt. Rev. Alfred Stanway of Melbourne, Australia, became the first dean and president of the school on Sept. 1, 1975. The school opened on Sept. 25, 1976, on the campus of Robert Morris College in Coraopolis, Pennsylvania. In Aug. 1978 the school moved to its present location in Ambridge, Pennsylvania. Trinity stresses the biblical foundations of Christian faith, practical evangelism, training in the devotional life, and the training of the laity for ministry in the church and world. The school adheres to the "Statement of Faith" of the Fellowship of Witness. It is accredited by the Association of Theological Schools.

See Evangelical Fellowship in the Anglican Communion–USA (EFAC–USA); *see* Fellowship of Witness (FOW).

Trinity Institute. Inaugurated in Trinity Church, New York, on Sept. 30, 1967, it was founded by Robert Elwin Terwilliger, then a priest at the Church of the Ascension, New York. Terwilliger was director from June 1, 1967, until Jan. 31, 1976. Trinity Institute offers various programs, consultations, publications, audio-visual material, and an annual conference to promote theological renewal in the Episcopal Church. It is sponsored by Trinity Church. *See* Terwilliger, Robert Elwin.

Trinity Sunday. Feast that celebrates "the one and equal glory" of Father, Son, and Holy Spirit, "in Trinity of Persons and in Unity of Being" (BCP, p. 380). It is celebrated on the first Sunday after Pentecost. Trinity Sunday is one of the seven principal feasts of the church year (BCP, p. 15). The proper readings and collect for Trinity Sunday are used only on the feast, not on the weekdays following. The numbered proper which corresponds most closely to the date of Trinity Sunday is used (BCP, p. 228). The BCP also provides the proper "Of the Holy Trinity" for optional use at other times, subject to the rules of the calendar of the church year (see BCP, pp. 251, 927). *The Hymnal 1982* presents ten hymns in a section on The Holy Trinity (Hymns 362–371), including "Holy, holy, holy! Lord God Almighty!" (Hymn 362), "Come, thou almighty King" (Hymn 365), and "Holy Father, great Creator" (Hymn 368).

Celebration of Trinity Sunday was approved for the western church by Pope John XXII in 1334. This feast is associated with Thomas Becket (c. 1118–1170), who was consecrated bishop on Trinity Sunday, 1162. His martyrdom may have influenced the popularity of the feast in England and the custom of naming the remaining Sundays of the church year "Sundays after Trinity." The Sarum Missal and editions of the Prayer Book through the 1928 BCP named these Sundays the Sundays after Trinity. The 1979 BCP identifies this portion of the church year as the season after Pentecost, and names these Sundays the Sundays after Pentecost (see BCP, p. 32).

Trisagion. An ancient hymn of the eastern church. "Holy God, Holy and Mighty, Holy Immortal One, Have mercy upon us" (BCP, p. 356). The term is from the Greek, meaning "thrice holy." It is mentioned in the acts of the Council of Chalcedon (451). This hymn was used at the opening of the eucharistic rite in the east and in Gallican liturgies. It came to be used in the Roman rite as part of the reproaches on Good Friday. A paraphrase of the *Trisagion* was used in the anthem "In the midst of life," which was included in the Burial Office of the 1549 BCP and all subsequent Prayer Books (see BCP, pp. 484–485, 492). This anthem is also used on Holy Saturday, after the gospel (and homily) (p. 283). *The Hymnal 1982 Accompaniment Edition, Vol. 1*, provides musical settings for this anthem (S 379, S 382). The 1979 BCP is the first Prayer Book to use the *Trisagion* as an alternative for the *Kyrie* at the opening of the eucharistic rite (p. 356). The *Kyrie* or *Trisagion* are normally used at the opening of the rite in Advent and Lent, when the *Gloria in excelsis* is not used. They may be used on other occasions. The *Trisagion* may be sung or said three times, or antiphonally (BCP, p. 406). Musical settings for the *Trisagion* are provided by *The Hymnal 1982* (S 99–S 102), and the *Accompaniment Edition, Vol. 1* (S 360). The *Trisagion* is also used at the beginning of the Reconciliation of a Penitent, Form Two (BCP, p. 449). The *BOS* recommends use of the *Trisagion* in the Way of the Cross as the procession goes from station to station. The *Trisagion* may also be used to conclude each station in the Way of the Cross.

Trope. A textual insertion into the authorized liturgical texts. Tropes varied from a few words to lengthy sentences. Used with traditional plainchant, the extra words were matched to the notes of a long melisma (a series of notes assigned to one syllable of the text). For example, the setting for the *Kyrie eleison* at S 356 in *The Hymnal 1982 Accompaniment Edition, Vol. 1*, once included the trope *cunctipotens Genitor Deus* inserted after the word *Kyrie*. The practice of including tropes was popular in the ninth to thirteenth centuries.

True Catholic, The. This journal's full title was *The True Catholic: Reformed, Protestant and Free. Edited by Members of the Protestant Episcopal Church, with the Approbation of the Bishop of Maryland.* It was published from May 1843 until Dec. 1856 and edited by the layman and lawyer Hugh Davey Evans. It published news about the church in England and the United States, and dealt with a number of doctrinal issues. In 1857 it was merged with *The American Church Monthly.*

Truth, Sojourner (c. 1797/98–Nov. 26, 1883). Antislavery reformer. She was born a slave in Ulster County, New York, and named Isabella Baumfree. She purchased her freedom when she was twenty-eight. After one of her many religious visions, on June 1, 1843, she took the name Sojourner Truth. She moved to New York City and became a member of the African Methodist Episcopal Zion Church. She was a traveling preacher, an advocate of woman's rights, and an abolitionist. She was a leading suffrage speaker, and her brief classic speech, "Ain't I a Woman," criticizes men and white women for neglect of the plight of African American women. She was also known as "Miriam of the Last Exodus." She died in Battle Creek, Michigan. She is commemorated in the Episcopal calendar of the church year on July 20. *See* Bloomer, Amelia Jenks; *see* Stanton, Elizabeth Cady; *see* Tubman, Harriet Ross.

Tubman, Harriet Ross (c. 1821–Mar. 10, 1913). Abolitionist. She was born a slave in Dorcester County, Maryland. She was first named Araminta, but later changed her name to Harriet. Tubman was a member of the African Methodist Episcopal Zion Church. In 1849 she escaped from slavery and was a fugitive slave. Tubman became one of the leaders in the work of the Underground Railroad. She was given the name "Moses." John Brown, the abolitionist who seized the U.S. arsenal at Harper's Ferry, West Virginia, called her "General Tubman." She helped more than 300 slaves to freedom as a major "conductor" of the Underground Railroad. When the Civil War broke out, she attached herself to the Union Army and worked as a cook, laundress, and nurse. Tubman also worked as a spy within the Confederate lines. After the war she lived in Auburn, New York, where she housed children and poor older people. Her story is told in *Harriet the Moses of Her People* (1886). The Harriet Tubman Home for indigent aged African Americans existed for a number of years after her death. Tubman died in Auburn, New York. She is commemorated in the Episcopal calendar of the church year on July 20. *See* Bloomer, Amelia Jenks; *see* Stanton, Elizabeth Cady; *see* Truth, Sojourner.

Tucker, Francis Bland (Jan. 6, 1895–Jan. 1, 1984). Priest and hymn composer. He was born in Norfolk, Virginia, the son of Beverley Dandridge Tucker, later Bishop of Southern Virginia, and Anna Maria (Washington) Tucker, who had been born in Mount Vernon. He was educated at the University of Virginia and Virginia Theological Seminary. Tucker was ordained deacon on July 21, 1918, and priest on Jan. 13, 1920. He served Grammar Parish, Brunswick County, Virginia, 1920–1925, St. John's, Georgetown, District of Columbia, 1925–1945, and Christ Church, Savannah, Georgia, 1945–1967. He served on the Joint Commission on the Hymnal for *The Hymnal* (1940) and on the text committee for *The Hymnal 1982*. Tucker contributed six original hymns, translations, or metrical paraphrases to *The Hymnal* (1940). *The Hymnal 1982* has seventeen contributions from Tucker, including his translations of the texts "O gracious light" (Hymns 25–26), "Father, we thank thee who hast planted" (Hymns 302–303), and "The great Creator of the worlds" (Hymn 489), and his original text "Our Father, by whose Name" (Hymn 587). Only John Mason Neale is credited with more items in *The Hymnal 1982*. Several of his hymns are included in other current hymnals, both in this country and abroad. He died in Savannah.

Tucker, Henry St. George (July 16, 1874–Aug. 8, 1959). Nineteenth Presiding Bishop. He was born in Warsaw, Virginia. Tucker received his M.A. from the University of Virginia in 1895 and his B.D. from the Virginia Theological Seminary in 1899. He was ordained deacon on June 23, 1899, and priest on July 30, 1900. Tucker began his ordained ministry as a missionary in Japan, and from 1903 until 1912 he was president of St. Paul's College, Tokyo. On Mar. 25, 1912, Tucker was consecrated the second Missionary Bishop of Kyoto, Japan. He served in that capacity until he resigned on Nov. 14, 1923. From 1923 until 1926, he was professor of pastoral theology at the Virginia Theological Seminary. On Sept. 21, 1926, he became Bishop Coadjutor of Virginia, and on June 25, 1927, he became the eighth Bishop of Virginia. He served as Presiding Bishop from Jan. 1, 1938, until Dec. 31, 1946, when he retired. He resigned as Bishop of Virginia on June 1, 1944. He was the first Presiding Bishop to resign his diocesan jurisdiction. From 1942 until 1944 Tucker was president of the Federal Council of the Churches of Christ in the United States. He died in Richmond, Virginia.

Tucker, Irwin St. John (Jan. 10, 1886–Jan. 8, 1982). Priest and social activist. He was born in Mobile, Alabama. Tucker received his B.D. from the General Theological Seminary in 1913. He was ordained deacon on June 2, 1912, and priest on May 18, 1913. In 1914 Tucker left New York for Chicago where he became managing editor of the *Christian Socialist*, the organ of the Christian Socialist Fellowship. He served as a non-parochial priest. In 1917 he opposed American involvement in World War I and became a leading antiwar propagandist. From 1927 until 1954 Tucker was priest-in-charge of St. Stephen's Church,

Chicago. In 1954 he converted to Roman Catholicism. Tucker was deposed from the ordained ministry of the Episcopal Church on Nov. 30, 1954. He was a layman until he was reinstated as an Episcopal priest on June 5, 1970, at the age of eighty-four. During much of his time in Chicago he worked for the *Chicago Herald American*, a newspaper. He stressed that Christianity and socialism share the ideal of economic and social justice and an emphasis on the unity of humanity. Tucker insisted that "Socialism without Christianity is a corpse and Christianity without Socialism is little better than a ghost." Tucker died in Chicago.

Tune-Book, The. A collection of tunes for use in the Episcopal Church. The 1856 General Convention resolved to appoint a committee to prepare a book of psalm and hymn tunes, chants, and anthems. The committee included William Augustus Muhlenberg, Gregory Thurston Bedell, George J. Geer, and James A. Johnson. The committee presented their book of tunes to the 1859 General Convention. The book also included chants for the canticles and the communion service. The book was never given official status by the General Convention. It was published in 1859, with a subsequent printing in 1860. *The Hymnal 1982* includes twenty-nine tunes from *The Tune-Book*, including *Adeste fideles* (Hymn 83), *Duke Street* (Hymn 544), *Dundee* (Hymns 126, 526, and 709), *Leoni* (Hymns 372, 401), *Wareham* (Hymns 20, 137, 353), and *Winchester New* (Hymns 76, 391).

Tunicle. Once the distinctive vestment of subdeacons in the western church, the tunicle is now obsolete. The term is from the Latin *tunicula*, which is the diminutive of *tunica*, "tunic." The tunic was a long, loose-fitting garment that was worn by men and women in ancient Greece and Rome. The tunicle was originally a white tunic with narrow sleeves. In the middle ages it evolved to resemble the dalmatic, with only one horizontal orphrey. Anglicans abolished the subdiaconate in the sixteenth century, and Roman Catholics "suppressed" it after Vatican II. Parishes of the Episcopal Church that use a "subdeacon" in the liturgy sometimes dress this person (who may be of any order) in a tunicle. The similar tunic worn by crucifers in some places is not properly a tunicle.

Tunnell, William Victor (d. Dec. 23, 1943). African American theological educator. He received his B.A. from Howard University. Tunnell was the second African American student to be admitted to the General

Theological Seminary and received his B.D. in 1887. He was ordained deacon on June 5, 1887, and priest on Dec. 18, 1887. From 1888 until 1890 he was minister-in-charge of St. Augustine's Mission, Brooklyn, New York. From 1891 until 1892 he was rector of St. Augustine's Church, Brooklyn. In 1892 he became professor of history at Howard University. From 1893 until 1907 Tunnell was warden of King Hall, Howard University. King Hall had been established in 1889 to train African American clergy for the Episcopal Church. It operated until 1908. From 1908 until 1928 he was priest-in-charge of St. Philip's Chapel, Washington, D.C. Some time after 1928 Tunnell moved to Toronto, Ontario, where he lived in retirement. He died in Toronto.

Turner, Samuel Hulbeart (Jan. 23, 1790–Dec. 21, 1861). Priest and biblical scholar. He was born in Philadelphia, Pennsylvania. He graduated from the University of Pennsylvania in 1807 and then studied for the ministry under Bishop William White. Turner was ordained deacon on Jan. 27, 1811, and priest on Jan. 23, 1814. From 1814 to 1817 he was rector of the church in Chestertown, Maryland, and in 1817 he moved to Philadelphia. The following year he became superintendent of theological students in the Diocese of Pennsylvania. On Oct. 8, 1818 he was named professor of historic theology at the newly established General Theological Seminary in New York City. In 1821 he was named professor of biblical learning and served in that position until his death. He was an irenic low churchman, a biblical scholar, and the author of *A Companion to the Book of Genesis* (1846). He died in New York City.

Tutor. A person who gives private instruction or additional and remedial instruction. In some universities and colleges, a tutor is a teacher or teaching assistant with a rank below that of an instructor. The General Theological Seminary has used graduate students as tutors for students in the Master of Divinity program.

Tuttle, Daniel Sylvester (Jan. 26, 1837–Apr. 17, 1923). Thirteenth Presiding Bishop. He was born in Windham, New York. He graduated from Columbia in 1857 and from the General Theological Seminary in 1862. Tuttle was ordained deacon on June 29, 1862, and priest on July 19, 1863. He began his ordained ministry as curate at Zion Church, Morris, New York, and succeeded to the rectorship of the parish shortly afterward upon the death of the rector.

On Oct. 5, 1866, the House of Bishops elected him Missionary Bishop of Montana with jurisdiction in Utah and Idaho. He was consecrated on May 1, 1867, after he had turned thirty, the canonical age requirement for consecration of a bishop. On Oct. 15, 1880, the House of Bishops formed the Missionary District of Utah and Idaho, and Tuttle served as its Missionary Bishop. On May 26, 1886, he was elected Bishop of Missouri. He served in that capacity from Aug. 10, 1886, until his death. From Dec. 3, 1903, until Dec. 14, 1904, he was acting Bishop of the Missionary District of Salt Lake, which included all of Utah and portions of Nevada and Wyoming. Tuttle served as Presiding Bishop from Sept. 7, 1903, until his death. He died in St. Louis. *See* Utah, Diocese of.

Twing, Mrs. A.T. *See* Emery, Mary Abbot (Mrs. Alvi Tabor Twing).

Two-penny Act. Two acts passed by the Virginia Assembly concerning the payment of public officials, including clergy. In the Virginia colony the primary means of payment was in tobacco. In 1758 there was a "prodigious diminution" of this staple crop because of the "unseasonableness" of the weather. The legislature voted to pay public officials, including clergy, with money. A similar act in 1755 had caused very little protest, but the 1758 act caused considerable trouble. The clergy protested the most because they would receive less compensation. There were a number of court actions, of which the so-called "parson's cause" was the most famous.

Tyndale, or Tindal, William (c. 1495–Oct. 6, 1536). Translator of the scriptures. He was born in Slymbridge, "about the borders of Wales." Tyndale received his B.A. and M.A. from Magdalen College, Oxford, and then studied at Cambridge. He was ordained priest around 1521 and soon determined to translate the scriptures into English. He was not free to do his translating in England. Tyndale went to Hamburg, Germany, in 1524, visited Martin Luther at Wittenberg, and began printing the NT at Cologne. King Henry VIII of England and others tried to destroy his work and kill him, but Tyndale eluded them. In 1533 he fled to Antwerp in the Netherlands and remained there the rest of his life. He was joined by John Rogers in 1534, who assisted him in translating the OT. Tyndale was able to translate only the Pentateuch and the Book of Jonah from the OT. In 1535 he was betrayed by a man named Henry Phillips. Tyndale was arrested, imprisoned, tried for heresy, and condemned to death. He was strangled and then burned at the stake on Oct. 6, 1536. Tyndale was an apostle of liberty and a promoter of the Reformation in England. His life is commemorated in the Episcopal calendar of the church year on Oct. 6.

Tyng, Stephen Higginson (Mar. 1, 1800–Sept. 3, 1885). Leading evangelical. He was born in Newburyport, Massachusetts. Tyng graduated from Harvard College in 1817. He then studied for the ordained ministry under Bishop Alexander V. Griswold. He was ordained deacon on Mar. 4, 1821, and priest on Jan. 28, 1824. Tyng began his ministry as rector of St. John's Church, Georgetown, in Washington, D.C., 1821–1823. From 1823 to 1829 he was rector of Queen Anne's Parish, Prince George County, Maryland. He then moved to Philadelphia, where he was rector of St. Paul's Church, 1829–1834, and then rector of the Church of the Epiphany, 1834–1845. He was rector of St. George's Church, New York, 1845–1878.

Tyng was recognized as one of the great preachers in the Episcopal Church in the nineteenth century. St. Paul's Church, Philadelphia, was nicknamed "Tyng's Theatre." He was a supporter of the Sunday Church School movement. He used the Sunday Schools to teach the Bible and to prepare people for conversion. Tyng was a militant evangelical, opposed to both the high church party and the broad church movement. He made St. George's Church a pioneer parish in missionary work among the poor. Tyng supported the founding of the Virginia Theological Seminary. He stressed that revivals were the primary way to bring people to Christ. He was editor of the *Episcopal Recorder* in Philadelphia and the *Protestant Churchman* in New York. Even though he was a leading evangelical, he opposed the schism of the Reformed Episcopal Church in 1873. Tyng died in Irving-on-Hudson, New York.

Tyng, Stephen Higginson, Jr. (June 28, 1839–Nov. 17, 1898). Leading evangelical. He was born in Philadelphia. Tyng graduated from Williams College in 1858. He studied for the ordained ministry at the Virginia Theological Seminary. He was ordained deacon on May 8, 1861, and served for two years as his father's assistant at St. George's Church, New York City. Tyng was ordained priest on Sept. 11, 1863. He then became rector of the Church of the Mediator in New York. He served as a chaplain in the United States Army in 1864. In 1865 Tyng founded Holy Trinity Church, New York. He served the remainder of his active ministry there. He resigned in Apr. 1881. Tyng was an ecumenical evangelical who participated in the services of other denominations. In 1867 he conducted a service in St. James' Methodist Church in New Brunswick, New Jersey, without the permission of the local Episcopal clergy. This was contrary to canon law and custom in the Episcopal Church. The "intrusion" canon stated that no member of the clergy should officiate in another's parish without the express permission of the resident clergy. The two New Brunswick rectors from that parish, Alfred Stubbs and Edward Boggs, made a formal complaint to Bishop Horatio Potter of New York. A court of five New York clergy found Tyng guilty of "intrusion" and recommended public admonition. The decision was not a severe penalty, but it created a furor in the Episcopal Church. It became a cause in the Ritual Controversy of the period. On Mar. 14, 1868, Bishop Potter carried out the admonition of Tyng in the high church parish of the Church of the Transfiguration, New York. Several years later Bishop George D. Cummins left the Episcopal Church and formed the Reformed Episcopal Church. Tyng was persuaded by his father not to leave the Episcopal Church. Tyng remained an Episcopal priest, but after 1881 he worked mainly in the insurance business in New York and Paris. He died in Paris.

U

Ubiquitarianism. This eucharistic theology is based on the understanding that Christ is present in all places. The term is derived from the Latin *ubique*, "everywhere." Christ's presence in the bread and wine of the eucharist is understood to be an intensification or an amplification of his all-pervasive presence. Ubiquitarianism can be traced to the work of Martin Luther, and it continues to be important in Lutheranism.

Ultramontanism. From the Italian, meaning "beyond the mountains," referring to the Italian Alps. The term indicates a tendency in the Roman Catholic Church to favor a strong papacy and the power of the curia instead of encouraging a sense of independence on national or diocesan bases. The term originated in the middle ages and denoted ecclesiastical opposition to anti-church movements which culminated in the French Revolution of 1789.

In the nineteenth century the Ultramontane position triumphed in a series of events which began with the revival of the Jesuit order in 1814, the rejection of liberalism by Pope Pius IX in 1864, and the 1870 declaration by the first Vatican Council that asserted the infallibility of the Pope when making pronouncements by virtue of his office concerning faith and morals.

Ultreya. A regular gathering of cursillistas for prayer and fellowship outside the three-day Cursillo weekend. Ultreya is a colloquial Spanish term that means "to persevere" or "to be persistent."

Unction. *See* Anointing.

Undercroft. A large room or area beneath a church building. It may be used as a space for prayer, church meetings, Christian education classes, or other church purposes. Some cathedrals or other large church buildings have vaulted crypts in a subterranean room. Some modern church buildings have a columbarium or chapel in the undercroft.

Underhill, Evelyn (Dec. 6, 1875–June 15, 1941). Renowned spiritual writer. She was born in Wolverhampton, England. Underhill studied at King's College for Women, London, and was made an honorary fellow in 1913. She was raised in the Church of England, but went through a period when she thought seriously about converting to Roman Catholicism. In 1911 she published *Mysticism: A Study of the Nature and Development of Man's Spiritual Consciousness*. It brought her international fame. She continued to publish many books, the most significant being *Worship* (1936), which was reprinted numerous times. She was a very popular lecturer, retreat leader, and spiritual director. Underhill insisted that the mystical life is available to all and not reserved to a spiritual elite. She said, "The mystic is not a person who has queer experiences, but a person for whom God is the one reality; he is a religious realist." She died in London. Underhill is commemorated in the Episcopal calendar of the church year on June 15.

Uniate (or Uniat) Churches. *See* Eastern Catholic Churches.

Union of Black Episcopalians, The (UBE). The UBE was formerly the Union of Black Clergy and Laity, an unofficial organization of the Episcopal Church. The union was formed on Feb. 8, 1968, by a group of African American clergy who met in St. Philip's Church, New York, to identify the church with the growing black power movement in their communities. The desire to articulate the problems of minority populations had been expressed by the Episcopal Society for Cultural and Racial Unity. However, it was felt that its agenda was influenced largely by white liberals and did not necessarily express the aspirations of African American people. The organization meets annually, and includes clergy and laity, men and women, without distinction. Chapters are organized by dioceses and are joined in regional groups to express local concerns more effectively. The goals of the union are to help the church eradicate racism within its structure, to indicate the importance of an authentic African American voice in the decisions of diocesan and national governing bodies, to develop liturgical styles in worship, and to encourage and participate in the political and religious concerns of the African American community.

United Congregations of Christ Church and St. Peter's in the City of Philadelphia. *See* Christ Church, Philadelphia.

United Episcopal Charities (UEC). No longer in existence, UEC was a national network of diocesan charities, foundations and community services committed to the building of the Kingdom of God through social justice ministries of the Episcopal Church. It was founded with the support of the National Commission on Social and Specialized Ministries at the 1985 General Convention and was recognized and endorsed by the Executive Council of the Episcopal Church at its meeting on Nov. 12–14, 1986. It worked to assist dioceses in creating and/or strengthening Episcopal charities, foundations, and diocesan social service agencies through conferences and consultative services to dioceses. It went out of existence on Oct. 1, 1998.

United Episcopal Church of America. An independent Episcopal Church was started in 1970 in Columbia, South Carolina, by some persons who thought the Episcopal Church was too liberal. In Oct. 1970, Richard C. Acker was called to be rector. On Jan. 3, 1971, Acker was installed as rector of St. James Church by Bishop Anthony F. Clavier of the American Episcopal Church. The parish became a part of the American Episcopal Church. On Mar. 9, 1973, the congregation voted to withdraw from the American Episcopal Church. It became an independent parish. On Jan. 30, 1976, Acker was elected a bishop of the United Episcopal Church. On May 1, 1976, Acker was consecrated bishop. The United Episcopal Church had no connection with the Episcopal Church. This body was subsequently called the United Episcopal Church of America.

United Episcopal Church of the United States of America. This body was founded on Dec. 7, 1980, at Coshocton, Ohio. At the third Provincial Synod of the Anglican Catholic Church, Oct. 22–25, 1980, Bishop C. Dale Doren of the Mid-Atlantic States announced that he was leaving the Anglican Catholic Church because it was too "high church." At the time Doren was rector of Holy Trinity Church, Pittsburgh, Pennsylvania. On Dec. 7, 1980, St. Paul's Church, Coshocton, and Holy Trinity Church, Pittsburgh, united to found the United Episcopal Church of the United States. On that day, Doren was elected archbishop. This church was the only group recently separated from the Episcopal Church that stressed the Thirty-Nine Articles. It used the 1928 BCP.

United Thank Offering (UTO). Nationwide fund-raising and grant-making program which focuses on compelling human needs and mission expansion. Such programs must be closely connected to the Episcopal Church or the worldwide Anglican Communion. Grant applications are reviewed by the UTO Committee which includes representatives of each province. The Triennial Meeting of the Women of the Episcopal Church allocates the grants for the year it meets. In the interim years, the UTO Committee makes the awards. The program is administered by the UTO Coordinator whose office is at the Episcopal Church Center. It was established in 1889 as the United Offering by the Women's Auxiliary to the Board of Missions. The United Thank Offering continues to be collected annually by UTO coordinators in parishes and dioceses throughout the Episcopal Church. Historically, the UTO was primarily used to support the work of women missionaries and missionary endeavors among women and children. That emphasis broadened in the 1960s to include all areas of the church's work.

Unity. *See* Notes of the Church.

University of the South, Sewanee, Tennessee. A university owned by twenty-eight southern dioceses. Bishops James Hervey Otey of Tennessee, Leonidas Polk of Louisiana, and Stephen Elliott of Georgia were the principal founders of this school. The first meeting of the trustees of the proposed school was held at Lookout Mountain, Tennessee, on July 4, 1857. The cornerstone was laid on

Oct. 10, 1860, but the Civil War delayed any construction of buildings. The university finally opened on Sept. 18, 1868, at Sewanee, Tennessee, with four professors and nine students. For most of its history, the university was all male. Women were admitted in 1969. For many years the university also operated the Sewanee Military Academy, which changed its name to the Sewanee Academy when it admitted women. At one time the university had a law school and a medical school. It now has a College of Arts and Sciences and a School of Theology.

Upjohn, Richard (Jan. 22, 1802–Aug. 17, 1878). Major church architect. He was born in Shaftesbury, Dorsetshire, England. Intent on becoming a draftsman, he was apprenticed to a cabinetmaker. At twenty-two he was a master craftsman and established his own business. Upjohn came to America in 1829 and settled in New Bedford, Massachusetts, where he worked as a draftsman and opened an evening school of drawing. He later advertised as an architect. In 1834 he moved to Boston. In 1837 he completed his first gothic church, St. John's, Bangor, Maine. He was hired by Trinity Church, New York, in 1839 as architect for a new building, which was begun in 1841. He moved to New York after he was hired by Trinity. Upjohn designed many notable churches, residences, and civil buildings. At least as early as 1852 he began to publish books of plans for small wooden churches in the gothic style. Churches were built throughout the country according to these plans. Upjohn was a principal founder and the president of the American Institute of Architects from its beginning in 1857 until his resignation in 1876. He died in Garrison, New York.

Upper South Carolina, Diocese of. The 1922 General Convention voted to divide the Diocese of South Carolina. The primary convention of the Diocese of Upper South Carolina was held at Trinity Church, Columbia, Oct. 10–11, 1922. The diocese includes the following counties: Abbeville, Aiken, Anderson, Cherokee, Chester, Edgefield, Fairfield, Greenville, Greenwood, Kershaw, Lancaster, Laurens, Lexington, McCormick, Newberry, Oconee, Pickens, Richland, Saluda, Spartanburg, Union, and York. On Jan. 19, 1977, Trinity Church, Columbia, became Trinity Cathedral.

Urban Bishops' Coalition. It was organized at the 1976 General Convention in Minneapolis, when the urban bishops held a press conference and issued a statement of concern about the cities of the nation. In June 1977, twenty urban bishops met in Chicago and decided to hold a series of public hearings in locations representative of the various manifestations of crisis in urban life. The bishops felt a need not only to be better informed about urban issues but also a need to act in concert in some specific ways. They were convinced that the life of the Episcopal Church was inextricably interwoven with the life of the cities, and that its membership in those cities included both many of those who were making basic decisions about the future of the cities and many of those who suffered from the decisions which were made. Bishop John T. Walker of Washington was the chairman of the steering committee. The Coalition published *To Hear and To Heed: The Episcopal Church Listens and Acts in the Cities* (1978). The Coalition is no longer in existence.

Urban Caucus. *See* Episcopal Urban Caucus (EUC).

Urn. A container for the ashes of the cremated body of a deceased person.

Usher. A lay person who greets and assists people as they enter the church. Ushers may hand out service bulletins, answer questions of visitors and newcomers, count the number of people in the congregation, collect and present the offering at the offertory, assist parishioners during the administration of communion, and clean the pews and church building after the service. In some churches, ushers may bring the people's offerings of bread and wine, and money or other gifts, to the deacon or celebrant at the presentation of the gifts.

Utah, Diocese of. On Oct. 19, 1859, the House of Bishops resolved "That all those portions of our country, North of a line running along the Northern boundary of the Cherokee country and New Mexico, until it reaches the Diocese of California, not yet organized into Dioceses, or included within Missionary districts, be within the jurisdiction of the Missionary Bishop of the North West." This included the present state of Utah. On Oct. 4, 1866, the House of Bishops formed the Missionary District of Montana, Utah and Idaho, and on Oct. 15, 1880, the House formed the Missionary District of Utah and Idaho. The Bishops formed the Missionary District of Nevada and Utah on Oct. 16, 1886, and on Oct. 13, 1898, they formed the Missionary District of Salt Lake, which included all of

Utah, with all that portion of Nevada lying east of the west lines of the counties of Elko, White Pine, Eureka, Lincoln, Lander, and Nye, together with that portion of the county of Uintah, in Wyoming, lying south of the 41½ degree of latitude, and the Missionary District of Western Colorado. The House of Bishops formed the Missionary District of Utah on Oct. 10, 1907, and on Jan. 1, 1971, it became the Diocese of Utah. St. Mark's Cathedral, Salt Lake City, was consecrated on May 14, 1874.

UTO. *See* United Thank Offering (UTO).

Utrecht, Declaration of. A profession of faith promulgating the doctrinal foundation of the Old Catholic Church. It was compiled at a synod of Old Catholic bishops at Utrecht on Sept. 24, 1889. The document claims adherence to the beliefs of the primitive church, including the decrees of the first seven Ecumenical Councils. Much of the document contains refutations of various Roman Catholic dogmas, including papal infallibility and the Immaculate Conception. The Old Catholic Church has been in full communion with the churches of the Anglican Communion since the Bonn Agreement in 1932. *See* Bonn Agreement; *see* Old Catholic Churches.

V

"V." *See* Versicles and Responses.

Vail, Thomas Hubbard (Oct. 21, 1812–Oct. 6, 1889). Bishop and ecumenist. He was born in Richmond, Virginia. Vail graduated from Washington (now Trinity) College in 1831 and from the General Theological Seminary in 1835. He was ordained deacon on June 29, 1835, and priest on Jan. 6, 1837. While a deacon he officiated at St. James' Church, Philadelphia, and then served as an assistant at St. Paul's church, Boston. While in Boston he organized All Saints' Church, Worcester, Massachusetts. From 1837 until 1839, Vail was rector of Christ Church, Cambridge, and he was rector of St. John's Church, Essex, Connecticut, from 1839 until 1844. In 1844 he moved to Westerly, Rhode Island, where he was rector of Christ Church. In 1857 he returned to Massachusetts, where he was rector of St. Thomas' Church, Taunton. In 1863 Vail moved to Muscatine, Iowa, where he was rector of Trinity Church. On Dec. 15, 1864, he was consecrated the first Bishop of Kansas. The Episcopal Female Seminary of Topeka had been established in 1861, and in 1872 Vail obtained a new charter which changed the name to the College of the Sisters of Bethany. In 1841 he published *The Comprehensive Church; or, Christian Unity and Ecclesiastical Union in the Protestant Episcopal Church*, which anticipated the Chicago-Lambeth Quadrilateral. Vail died in Bryn Mawr, Pennsylvania.

Validity (Sacramental). A sacrament is recognized by the church to be genuine and true when certain minimum requirements are met. These requirements concern proper form, matter, minister, and intent. The form means the words of prayer that are used in the sacramental rite, and the matter concerns the material or gesture constituting the outward and visible sign of a sacrament. The matter in baptism is water; bread and wine are the matter in the eucharist. The minister must be properly qualified and intend to do what the church intends in celebrating the sacrament. The minister at the eucharist is the celebrant, who must be a bishop or priest. The minimum form for a valid sacrament does not require the entire BCP liturgy. For example, an emergency baptism may be administered according to the form, "I baptize you in the Name of the Father, and of the Son, and of the Holy Spirit" (BCP, p. 313). In the situation of an emergency baptism, any baptized person can be a qualified minister of the sacrament. This minister would need to baptize with water, and intend to do what the church does in baptism. The concept of sacramental validity dates from the third century, when the Church of Rome held that schismatics and heretics could administer valid baptism. This contradicted the position of Cyprian, Bishop of Carthage, that the church's sacraments could not be administered by anyone outside the church. Augustine of Hippo subsequently insisted in his controversy with Donatism that the personal unworthiness of the minister does not impair the validity of sacraments celebrated by the minister (see Art. XXVI, Articles of Religion, BCP, p. 873). *See* Augustine of Hippo.

Valle Crucis, North Carolina. In 1842 Bishop Levi S. Ives of North Carolina decided to form a religious community in North Carolina on the model of the one that was beginning in Nashotah, Wisconsin. It was established in western North Carolina, near the Tennessee border, where three streams make their junction and thus form the shape of a cross. Valle Crucis (from the Latin "Valley of the Cross") was also the name of a pre-Reformation monastery in the mountains of Wales. It was to be a place for an agricultural mission and a school for training clergy. The bishop intended it to be modeled after the Society of Jesus (Jesuits). He planned to serve as the general of the community. The first missionary there was the Rev. Henry H. Prout, who began his work late in 1842. In 1845 a training school for the ministry was opened, along with a classical and agricultural school for boys. The school opened with thirty boys and seven candidates for the ordained ministry. The first head of the school was the Rev. William Thurston. William West Skiles joined the community as a missionary and worked as a deacon in the area until 1862. Skiles practiced medicine among the mountain people and worked in the missions. The religious community which formed there was called the Order of the Holy Cross. The first members were professed in 1847 at St. Luke's Chapel, New York, while Bishop Ives attended the General Convention in New York. The first superior of the community was the Rev. William Glenny French. At first the Associate Mission and Training School for the Ministry was successful. Controversy plagued the community because of its monastic character. It disbanded in 1849. Valle Crucis closed when Bishop Ives resigned in 1852. Bishop Joseph Blount Chesire revived the school in the 1890s, but it closed in 1943. In the 1960s the property and facilities were converted into the Episcopal Church Conference Center. *See* Skiles, William West.

Vaughan Williams, Ralph (Oct. 12, 1872–Aug. 26, 1958). English composer, hymn writer, and editor. He was born in Down Ampney, Gloucestershire. Williams was educated at Charterhouse, The Royal College of Music, and Trinity College, Cambridge. He studied music with several of the most prominent musicians and composers of the day in England and Europe. His musical roots were the music of the Tudor period, Purcell, and most especially, English folk song. Williams was a prolific composer. His catalogue includes nine symphonies, as well as concertos, opera, ballet, music for films, songs, part songs, chamber music, and cantatas. Although never a professing Christian, he wrote several anthems, canticle settings and a Mass for two choirs. Williams left his greatest mark on church music as the editor of *The English Hymnal* (1906, revised 1933), *Songs of Praise* (1925, enlarged 1931), and *The Oxford Book of Carols* (1928). He was a proponent of unison singing by the congregation, and many of his own tunes and arrangements are for this medium. To hymnal repertoires he introduced British and Irish folk tunes and carols, Welsh hymn tunes, arrangements of historic German, French and Swiss tunes, tunes by Orlando Gibbons and Thomas Tallis, and English and Scottish Psalter tunes in their original forms. Most English language hymnals published since 1930 have been strongly influenced by his work as a hymnal editor, composer, and arranger. *The Hymnal 1982* contains five of his original tunes, including *Salve festa dies*, used with "Hail thee, festival day!" (Hymns 175, 216, 225), *The Call*, used with "Come, my Way" (Hymn 487), and *Down Ampney*, used with "Come down, O Love divine" (Hymn 516), and seventeen of his arrangements. He died in London.

Veil. 1) A square cloth that covers the paten and chalice until preparation of the altar for communion. The veil usually matches the vestments and altar hangings in the liturgical color of the season. It is draped over the pall, which is a white square placed on top of the paten, purificator, and chalice. The burse, which usually contains the corporal and purificators, is placed on top of the veil. After the ablutions following communion, the veil may once again be placed over the paten and chalice. The term has also indicated a linen covering that was placed over the unconsumed elements of the eucharist after communion.

2) Material used to cover the crosses in church after the stripping of the altar on Maundy Thursday. In some parishes, the processional cross, pictures, and statues are also veiled. Customs have varied for the veiling of crosses. Crosses have been veiled throughout Lent or during Passiontide, which was the last two weeks of Lent. This veiling has also been associated with Holy Week. Veils have been black, violet, or white. This veiling is not required in the Episcopal Church.

3) Veils are part of the religious habit worn by members of women's religious orders. The veil drapes over the top and back of the head to the shoulders, and possibly as far as the back, depending on the length of the veil. The veil of a professed sister may be black or another color. The veil worn by a novice is distinguishable from the veil worn by professed members of the community. A novice's veil may be white, and it may be shorter than the veil worn by professed sisters. In the early church, Christian women wore veils to indicate their religious vocation or status. Veils were worn by virgins who rejected marriage and by widows who would not marry again. *See* Humeral Veil; *see* Veil of the Temple.

Veil of the Temple. In the Jerusalem Temple, the veil or curtain of the temple was at the entrance to the most holy place (see Ex 26:33, 35:12, 39:34; 2 Chr 3:14). It has also been known as the holy of holies. This inner room contained the ark of the covenant, which was covered with the veil when the tabernacle was moved (Nm 4:5). At first only the Levitical priests could enter the most holy place (Nm 18:7). Eventually only the high priest could pass through the veil to enter the most holy place and only on the Day of Atonement (see Lv 16). The veil of the temple was torn when Jesus died on the cross (Mk 15:38). This has been associated with the removal of the barriers to right relationship between God and humanity through Jesus' death. The Letter to the Hebrews notes that in Christ we have "a hope that enters the inner shrine behind the curtain, where Jesus, a forerunner on our behalf, has entered" (Heb 6:19–20; see Heb 10:19–20). This imagery of entering the most holy place through the veil is reflected in the hymn, "Humbly I adore thee, Verity unseen," which states that faith "pierces through the veil" (Hymn 314). It also appears in the hymn, "Alleluia! sing to Jesus!", which states, "thou within the veil hast entered, robed in flesh, our great High Priest" (Hymns 460–461).

Venerable. 1) The title of address for an archdeacon. It is abbreviated The Ven. 2) In the Roman Catholic Church, a deceased person may be declared venerable in the first main stage of the process of beatification. This process may eventually lead to canonization as a saint in the Roman Catholic Church.

"Venerable Society, The." *See* Society for the Propagation of the Gospel in Foreign Parts (SPG).

Veneration. The reverence or honor paid by Christians to saints, crosses, altars, images, etc. Veneration is distinguished from the absolute worship that is due to God alone. Various Puritans and iconoclasts have failed to make this distinction and wrongly accused others of idolatry.

Veneration of the Cross. The earliest description of this ceremony is found in the late fourth century treatise "The Pilgrimage of Egeria." In this diary she describes the Good Friday ceremonies in Jerusalem. During that service, fragments that were believed to be of the true cross were placed on a table in front of the bishop. The people came forward, bowed toward the table, and kissed the sacred wood. Variations of the ceremony developed throughout Christianity. The custom was restored in the 1979 BCP (p. 281), in which a wooden cross may be brought into the church and placed in the sight of the people. Following this the people may sing the Good Friday anthems and the hymn "Sing, my tongue, the glorious battle" (Hymns 165–166). *See* Veneration.

Veneration of Saints. Christians began to honor their departed heroes of the faith as early as the second century. After Polycarp, Bishop of Smyrna, was martyred in about 155, his ashes were gathered up by the faithful and laid in a suitable place. The cult concerning the relics of saints began at the same time. Memorial buildings came to be built over the graves of saints or martyrs, and the eucharist was celebrated on the anniversaries of their deaths. Christian teaching about the communion of the saints is the foundation for the custom of the veneration of the saints.

Veni Creator Spiritus. The opening line of a medieval Latin hymn, "Come, Creator Spirit," usually ascribed to Rabanus Maurus (776–856). It appears in *The Hymnal 1982* in three different translations (Hymns 500–504). It was used in the middle ages as an office hymn at terce on Pentecost. It was later used in the Sarum ordination rites, and it passed from the Sarum rites into the Anglican Ordinal. It appeared in the first Ordinal of 1550 in a translation by Thomas Cranmer, "Come holy ghost eternall god Proceeding from above." This was superseded in 1662 by John Cosin's translation, "Come, Holy Ghost our souls inspire." In 1928 the American Prayer book replaced Cranmer's translation with one from *Hymns Ancient and Modern* by Edward Caswell. The 1979 BCP does not contain a text, but it requires either the hymn *Veni Creator Spiritus* or the hymn *Veni Sancte Spiritus* before the prayer of consecration and laying on of hands in the ordination of bishops, priests, and deacons (pp. 520, 533, 544). In this position the hymn is an invocation of the Holy Spirit by the assembly. In addition to Cosin's translation (Hymns 503, 504), *The Hymnal 1982* contains John Dryden's "Creator Spirit, by whose aid" (Hymn 500) and John Webster Grant's "O Holy Spirit, by whose breath" (Hymns 501–502). *See* Veni Sancte Spiritus.

Veni Sancte Spiritus. The opening words of the medieval Latin Golden Sequence, "Come Holy Spirit," sung before the gospel on Pentecost. It is considered a masterpiece of Latin sacred poetry and has been ascribed to various authors, including Archbishop Stephen Langton and Pope

Innocent III. It was probably written in the twelfth century. It appears in *The Hymnal 1982* in two translations, "Come, thou Holy Spirit bright," by Charles P. Price (Hymns 226–227) and "Holy Spirit, font of light," by John Webster Grant (Hymn 228). The translation of Edward Caswell from *Hymns Ancient and Modern* appeared in *The Hymnal* (1940). The BCP permits this hymn, without specifying any particular version thereof, as an alternative to *Veni Creator Spiritus* in the ordination rites (pp. 520, 533, 544). It serves there as a congregational invocation of the Holy Spirit before the prayer of consecration and laying on of hands. *See* Sequence; *see* Veni Creator Spiritus.

Venice Statement. This agreed statement on Authority was finalized by the Anglican-Roman Catholic International Commission (ARCIC) at Venice in 1976. It was eventually included within the ARCIC *Final Report* (1982). It said the church can be described as "indefectible" because human "failures cannot destroy the Church's ability to proclaim the Gospel and to show forth the Christian life; for we believe that Christ will not desert his Church and that the Holy Spirit will lead it into all truth." On conciliar authority, it said that ecumenical councils "are authoritative when they express the common faith and mind of the Church" and are thus "binding upon the whole church" and, therefore, "When the Church meets in ecumenical council its decisions on fundamental matters of faith exclude what is erroneous" so long as they are "faithful to Scripture and consistent with Tradition" and "formulate the central truths of salvation." On primacy, after setting forth an ideal, the statement deemed it "appropriate that in any future union a universal primacy such as has been described should be held by [the Roman see]." An "Elucidation" issued by the commission (1981) explained that "much Anglican objection has been directed against the manner of the exercise and particular claims of the Roman primacy rather than against universal primacy as such." The 1985 General Convention of the Episcopal Church resolved that the Venice Statement "represents a theological model of convergence towards which both of our Churches may grow and, in that sense, is sufficiently consonant in substance with the faith of this Church to justify further conversations and to offer a basis for taking further steps." The official response of the 1988 Lambeth Conference welcomed it "as a firm basis for the direction and agenda of the continuing dialogue." However, the Vatican's definitive response to the *Final Report*, finally released in 1991, raised a number of unresolved objections.

Venite, The. Invitatory psalm based on Ps 95:1–7. It begins, "Come, let us sing to the Lord; let us shout for joy to the Rock of our salvation" (BCP, p. 44–45, 82). *See* Invitatory Psalm.

Venture in Mission (VIM). The 1976 General Convention resolved to issue a call to the church to work and pray for a "Venture in Mission" to provide mission development funding for the national church. Most dioceses participated, joining their efforts for Venture in Mission with their own fund-raising efforts to contact every congregation for support. The 1979 and 1982 General Conventions continued this largely successful fund-raising program with resolutions of commendation and appreciation.

Verbal Inspiration. The belief that the individual words and even verbal relationships of the Bible were inspired by God. Some would make a distinction between the words themselves and the ideas expressed by the words, holding that only the latter were inspired. This theory, therefore, stressed the inspiration of the biblical text itself rather than the inspiration of the hearts and minds of the human authors. It has traditionally been espoused by those who view the Bible as inerrant. *See* Fundamentalism; *see* Plenary Inspiration.

Verge. *See* Verger; *see* Virge.

Verger. A lay minister who assists the clergy in the conduct of public worship, especially in the marshaling of processions. Vergers may be full-time or part-time, paid or volunteer. The history of the verger dates back to the middle ages when the verger was the "Protector of the Procession." He would lead the way, making room for the procession to enter the church from the town square, and with his virge (mace) in hand would literally clear the way if necessary. The basic vestment of the verger is a black cassock. The ministry of vergers is supported and encouraged by the Vergers' Guild of the Episcopal Church.

Vergers' Guild of the Episcopal Church. This guild was founded as an informal association in 1988 and formally organized on Nov. 30, 1989, at an inaugural conference at St. George's Church, Nashville, Tennessee. Its primary purpose is to promote communication among members of the guild. It holds an annual conference, and publishes *The President's Virge: A Newsletter* and *On the Verge:*

Vermont, Diocese of. On Sept. 20, 1790, the Diocese of Vermont was organized at Arlington. On May 29, 1810, representatives from Vermont and four other New England dioceses met in Boston and organized the Eastern Diocese. The Diocese of Vermont withdrew from the Eastern Diocese on May 30, 1832, and elected its own bishop, John Henry Hopkins. St. Paul's Church, Burlington, was set apart as St. Paul's Cathedral on May 6, 1966, and the new building was consecrated on Nov. 11, 1973. The Diocese of Vermont was the first diocese to elect a woman diocesan bishop. Mary Adelia Rosamond McLeod was elected Bishop of Vermont on June 5, 1993.

Vernacular. A language that is commonly spoken in a locality, the native language of a place. In the early church, the vernacular was used as the language for Christian liturgy. However, language that was once vernacular may in time become archaic or disused as a common language of the people. For example, Latin became the vernacular in the areas of Roman imperial conquest in the west. As the vernacular language, Latin was also used as the language of liturgy. Other languages such as Italian, French, Spanish, and Portuguese eventually replaced Latin as the vernacular language in Italy, France, Spain, and Portugal. But Latin remained the language of liturgy in the Roman Catholic Church until the liturgical reforms of the Second Vatican Council (1963). At times there has been reluctance to change the language of liturgy, even when it has ceased to be vernacular. Some have associated an archaic or dead language with the mystery or transcendence of God. Others have found archaic or commonly disused language to hinder liturgical participation and understanding. Use of liturgical language that was often not understood by the laity tended to foster the clericalization of the liturgy. Vernacular language was used for worship by the churches of the Protestant Reformation. The 1549 BCP used sixteenth-century English. The Preface to the First Book of Common Prayer (1549) recalls that St. Paul urged the use of language in church that would be understandable and profitable for the people. However, "the Service in the Church of England (these many years) hath been read in Latin to the people, which they understood not; so that they have heard with their ears only; and their hearts, spirit, and mind, have not been edified thereby" (BCP, p.

866; See 1 Cor 14:9). The use of vernacular language was a distinguishing feature of the first Prayer Book. This commitment to the use of contemporary and understandable language has also been reflected in the Prayer Book revision process of the twentieth century.

Versicles and Responses. Short sentences, often drawn from the Psalter, that are said or sung antiphonally in worship. Typically the versicle is said or sung by the officiant or celebrant, with the response made by the congregation. The versicles and responses may also be made between sections of the choir, or between the choir or cantor and the congregation. Examples of versicles and responses include the fraction anthem "Christ our Passover" at the eucharist (BCP, pp. 337, 364) and the suffrages following the Lord's Prayer in Morning Prayer and Evening Prayer (BCP, pp. 55, 97–98, 67–68, 121–122). *See* Preces.

Very Reverend, The. *See* Reverend, The.

Vesey, William (c. Aug. 10 or Oct. 10, 1674–July 11, 1746). Early leader of New York Anglicanism. He was born in Braintree, Massachusetts, and graduated from Harvard College in 1693. He served as lay reader at Hempstead, New York, 1695–1696, and studied for ordained ministry. Merton College, Oxford, awarded him the M.A. on July 8, 1697. The Bishop of London ordained him deacon on July 25, 1697, and priest on Aug. 2, 1697. Upon his return to New York, he was inducted as rector of Trinity Church on Dec. 25, 1697, and served in that position until his death. Around 1715 the Bishop of London named him Commissary for New York. Vesey worked with the Society for the Propagation of the Gospel and helped the Church of England grow in New York. He died in New York City.

Vespers. The early evening office of prayer in the church. The term is from the Latin word for "evening." *Lucernarium* (lamp or lamp-lighting time) was an early name for vespers. Early Christians continued the Jewish custom of prayer at the time when daylight faded and the lamps were lit. The practice of Christian evening prayer dates from the third century. It is mentioned by Tertullian and in the *Apostolic Tradition* of Hippolytus. During the fourth to sixth centuries the evening service came to take the form of vespers. Lauds and vespers, the two most important of the canonical day hours of prayer, were said at dawn and sunset. Vespers has also been called the "evening sacrifice" of prayer. Ps 141:2, "Let my prayer be set forth in your sight as incense, the lifting up of my hands as the evening sacrifice," has been traditionally associated with vespers.

Archbishop Cranmer combined vespers with other offices for the BCP office of Evening Prayer. In addition to Evening Prayer, the 1979 BCP provides a form of evening service or vespers for use in the late afternoon or evening (p. 109). This vespers service, An Order of Worship for the Evening, may be used in place of Evening Prayer or it may serve as the introduction to Evening Prayer (BCP, p. 108). It may include a candle-lighting (BCP, p. 112). The *BOS* provides anthems (*Lucernaria)* for optional use at the candle-lighting of this service.

Vessels, Sacred. Vessels used in the eucharist, such as the paten and chalice. The term has also indicated the pyx, used to take communion to those unable to attend the eucharist, and items such as the monstrance and luna that are used in Benediction or exposition of the Blessed Sacrament. Sacred vessels have been distinguished from other liturgical vessels that do not come in contact with the consecrated elements of the eucharist, such as the lavabo bowl. *See* Benediction of the Blessed Sacrament.

Vested Choir. A choir vested in cassock and surplice. A vested choir was often associated with a choral or sung service. The use of the surplice by choir members was one of the issues of dispute in the nineteenth-century controversy over ritual in the Episcopal Church. The introduction of the surpliced choir in England has been associated with the Cambridge Camden Society. In the Episcopal Church, by 1865 there was a vested choir at Racine College in Racine, Wisconsin, under the leadership of James DeKoven. William Augustus Muhlenberg introduced the first vested boys' choir in New York City at the Church of the Holy Communion. However, Bishop Charles P. McIlvaine of Ohio brought canonical proceedings against the Rev. Colin Tate of Columbus who vested his choir with surplices, and used processional and recessional hymns. In *The Law of Ritualism* (1866), Presiding Bishop John Henry Hopkins urged that a wide variety of ritual usage was permissible in the church. A vested choir of men and boys was present when Bishop Hopkins consecrated Bishops Henry Adams Neeley and Daniel Sylvester Tuttle in New York City in 1867. DeKoven defended the ritualist cause at the General Conventions of 1871 and 1874. He appealed for comprehensiveness

and tolerance in worship. DeKoven's vision of a comprehensive approach to ritual eventually prevailed in the Episcopal Church. Although the use of choir vestments is not required, many Episcopal parishes have a vested choir. *See* DeKoven, James.

Vestibule. *See* Narthex.

Vesting Room. A room near the sanctuary of a church where clergy and lay people vest. Ordained and lay ministers use this room to put on and take off vestments that are worn in the liturgy. Vestments are usually kept in this room, along with liturgical books and vessels, altar furnishings, and other items needed throughout the year for the worship of the church. This room may also be known as the sacristy or the vestry.

Vestments. The distinctive garments worn by leaders of the church's worship. Many of the church's vestments are descended from the ordinary dress of the imperial Roman society in which the early church came into being.

Vestments worn by the celebrant at the eucharist typically include a stole and chasuble. These vestments usually reflect the liturgical color of the day or season of the celebration. The celebrant also usually wears an alb and may wear a girdle and amice. The officiant at the Daily Office or other non-eucharistic services may wear a cassock and surplice. A tippet may also be worn. A stole indicates that the wearer is an ordained person. Bishops and priests wear the stole over both shoulders, and deacons typically wear the stole over the left shoulder. Bishops may wear distinctive episcopal vestments, including the rochet and chimere, and the miter. A purple shirt with a clerical collar usually indicates that the wearer is a bishop, and a black shirt with a clerical collar usually indicates that the wearer is a member of the clergy.

Lay servers, acolytes, lectors, and choir members may also wear vestments at worship. According to local custom, they may wear an alb, or a cassock with surplice or cotta.

Vestry. In England the annual election of churchwardens took place in Easter week. The parishioners gathered at the church to hear the outgoing wardens render their accounts and elect their successors. The parishioners assembled in the vestry, the room off the chancel where the clergy vested. The assembled parishioners came to be known as the vestry. These were open vestries in that all adult male parishioners could participate. It was like a modern annual congregational meeting. In Virginia the parishes were very large and it was difficult to get all the male parishioners together. So they would meet only once and elect twelve of their number to serve for life. This was known as a closed vestry. The transition to a closed vestry was completed by 1633 or 1634, when a Vestry Act was passed. It provided that "there be a vestrie held in each parish." The current vestry evolved from this colonial pattern.

The vestry is the legal representative of the parish with regard to all matters pertaining to its corporate property. The number of vestry members and the term of office varies from parish to parish. Vestry members are usually elected at the annual parish meeting. The presiding officer of the vestry is the rector. There are usually two wardens. The senior warden leads the parish between rectors and is a support person for the rector. The junior warden often has responsibility for church property and buildings. A treasurer and a secretary or clerk may be chosen. These officers may or may not be vestry members. The basic responsibilities of the vestry are to help define and articulate the mission of the congregation; to support the church's mission by word and deed, to select the rector, to ensure effective organization and planning, and to manage resources and finances.

Vesture. Another word for vestments, the distinctive garments worn by leaders of the church's worship. *See* Vestments.

Via Media. Latin phrase translated as "middle way" or the "way between two extremes." It is from the philosophy of Aristotle. In his *Nicomachean Ethics*, he found the virtues such as justice and courage to be the middle way between the extremes of either side. "Courage" was thus the *via media* between foolhardiness and cowardice. The *via media* came into religious usage when Anglicans began to refer to the Church of England as a middle way between the extremes of Roman Catholicism and Puritanism. Under Queen Elizabeth I, the *via media* of the Elizabethan Settlement retained much of the traditional catholic practice but without submission to papal authority. Uniformity of worship was required, but considerable latitude was allowed for individual conscience. Richard Hooker was the great apologist for the Elizabethan Settlement against both Puritanism and Roman Catholicism.

Via media is often misunderstood in a negative way to mean compromise or unwillingness to take a firm position.

However, for Aristotle and those Anglicans who have used it, the term refers to the "golden mean" which is recognized as a more adequate expression of truth between the weaknesses of extreme positions. *See* Elizabethan Settlement; *see* Hooker, Richard.

Viaticum. The administration of communion to a dying person. It was given as sustenance for a journey. The practice of *viaticum* as a meal for the dead was a pagan burial custom from pre-Christian times. Communion was substituted as *viaticum* by the early Christians. The Christian practice of *viaticum* was apparently regarded as an ancient custom by the fourth century. The BCP provides a form for Communion under Special Circumstances (pp. 396–399), with communion administered from the reserved sacrament. A postcommunion prayer is included in the BCP rite for ministration to the sick (p. 457). The benefits of communion are understood to be received by a person who desires to receive the eucharist but cannot eat and drink the bread and wine because of sickness or physical disability. *See* Last Rites.

Vicar. In the Episcopal Church, the title generally applies to the priest in charge of a mission congregation. The diocesan bishop is the rector, and the priest representing the bishop is the vicar. The term is derived from the Latin *vicarius*, "substitute." Historically, as early as the twelfth century in England, clergy known as vicars were appointed to act as substitutes or vicarious representatives of the bishop to serve congregations. The use of terms such as vicar, priest in charge, and rector is not consistent in the dioceses of the Episcopal Church.

Vicarage. The vicar's residence. The vicarage may or may not be provided by the congregation served by the vicar.

Victimae Paschali. Latin *incipit* (opening words) of the traditional Easter sequence, "Christians, to the Paschal victim" (Hymn 183 in *The Hymnal 1982)*. This plainsong chant hymn is ascribed to Wigbert (Wipo of Burgundy) in the eleventh century. It provides a dramatic celebration of Christ's victory over death in the context of a dialogue between Mary Magdalene and a narrator. It was well known in the middle ages and at times performed as part of a traditional extraliturgical Easter drama. Adaptations of this sequence include Luther's "Christ Jesus lay in death's strong bands" (Hymn 185) and the twelfth-century German adaptation "Christ the Lord is risen again!" (Hymn 184).

The chant hymn tune for "Christians, to the Paschal victim" (Hymn 183) is named *Victimae Paschali laudes. See* Sequence.

Vigil. 1) A service at night prior to a major feast or other important observance. The vigil anticipates and begins the commemoration of the following day. It may allow the participants an opportunity to reflect on the meaning of the next day's service. Scripture texts that will be used at the service on the following day may be introduced at a vigil. Christian vigils have been observed since the early years of the church. The Easter Vigil dates from at least the second century, and it is described in Hippolytus's *Apostolic Tradition.* The candidates for baptism spent the night in vigil, where they listened to readings and instructions. At cockcrow, the baptismal water was blessed and the candidates were baptized. The pilgrim Egeria mentions a vigil at the tomb in Jerusalem on Good Friday in the fourth century. Ancient sacramentaries provide evidence of a Pentecost vigil. The 1662 BCP lists sixteen feasts that were preceded by a vigil. Although the Easter Vigil was not retained as a vigil by the 1549 Prayer Book, the 1979 BCP includes a rite for the Great Vigil of Easter (pp. 285–295). The 1979 BCP also provides for a Vigil of Pentecost (BCP, p. 227), which resembles the Easter Vigil in a simplified form. The BCP also includes prayers for a vigil prior to burial of the dead (BCP, pp. 465–466). Psalms, lessons, and collects from the burial service may be used at this vigil. The Litany at the Time of Death may also be used. The *BOS* provides vigils for Christmas Eve, the Eve of the Baptism of our Lord, and the Eve of All Saints' Day or the Sunday after All Saints' Day. The *BOS* also includes a Vigil on the Eve of Baptism and a vigil Service for New Year's Eve (Eve of Holy Name). 2) The term may also indicate a watch in the presence of the body of a deceased person prior to burial. *See* Wake.

Vincent of Lérins. *See* Vincentian Canon.

Vincent of Saragossa (d. 304). He was probably born in Osca, the modern Huesca, in Spain. Vincent is known as the Deacon of Saragossa. He was martyred during the persecutions of Diocletian and Maximian. He was apparently subjected to torture and starvation before he died as a result of his sufferings. There are six ancient churches dedicated to him in England. Vincent is commemorated in the Episcopal calendar of the church year on Jan. 22.

Vincentian Canon. The canonical threefold test of catholicity is found in the fifth-century *Commonitorium* of Vincent of Lérins (d. c. 445). Vincent was a monk on the island of Lérins in Gaul. He may have written the *Commonitorium* around 434. It defines the catholic faith as "what has been believed everywhere, always, and by all." It was often misquoted by nineteenth-century English writers who put "antiquity" first. It is often used by Anglican scholars as a patristic source for Hooker's "three legged stool" of scripture, tradition, and reason as sources of authority in Anglicanism. The *Commonitorium*, written by Vincent under the pseudonym "Peregrinus," is a guide to the catholic faith and the source of the Vincentian Canon. The *Commonitorium* emphasizes the primacy of scripture as the ground of truth. It also places significant emphasis on tradition and allows for development of doctrine as scripture is more fully explicated.

Virge. The virge is the staff which a verger carries in procession. The name comes from the Latin *virga,* "rod" or "staff." It goes back to the ceremonial mace carried before civic and ecclesiastical dignitaries. It was originally a weapon used to clear the way for processions and to control unruly choristers. One end has a cross or other Christian symbol on it. A longer variation of the virge is called the beadle, originally used to lead academic processions.

Virgin Birth. This term describes the birth of Jesus. Jesus' mother was Mary, and he was conceived through the power of the Holy Spirit, without a human father. Mary's virginity at the time of Jesus' birth is mentioned specifically in the gospels of Matthew (Ch. 1) and Luke (Ch. 1). Although Matthew and Luke have two very different stories about the origin of Jesus, they both clearly state that he was born of a virgin. The prologue to the Gospel of John has a statement that could be interpreted as a virgin birth (Jn 1:12–13), but the term is not used. The Virgin Birth is a way of describing Jesus as the Son of God. It is a way of verifying Jesus' true humanity and divinity. Although Jesus is a human being, he is believed to be truly distinct from all other human beings. There is some indication in Christian writings that the term "Virgin Birth" can be understood as a way of helping to understand Jesus' humanity and divinity. Belief in the Virgin Birth was not completely accepted by all early Christians. Some Christians today question it as a historical fact. The Virgin

Birth is affirmed by the Nicene Creed and the Apostles' Creed. The Catechism states that "by God's own act his divine Son received our human nature from the Virgin Mary, his mother" (BCP, p. 849). Belief in the Virgin Birth does not imply belief in the Roman Catholic doctrine of the Immaculate Conception, which holds that Mary was free of all sin, including original sin, from her conception. *See* Mary the Virgin, Mother of our Lord Jesus Christ, Saint.

Virgin Islands, Diocese of. The Virgin Islands became a part of the Missionary District of Puerto Rico in 1919. The House of Bishops established the Missionary District of the Virgin Islands in 1947, but it was still under the care of the Missionary Bishop of Puerto Rico. The first Missionary Bishop of the Virgin Islands, Cedric Earl Mills, was consecrated on Apr. 9, 1963. On Jan. 1, 1971, it became the Missionary Diocese of the Virgin Islands, and in 1985 it became the Diocese of the Virgin Islands.

Virginia Company of London. On Apr. 10, 1606, King James I of England chartered two companies to settle, respectively, the southern and northern portions of the land claimed by England in America. The Virginia Company was to settle the south and the Plymouth Company was to settle the north. In 1607 the Virginia Company founded and settled at Jamestown, Virginia. One of the petitioners for the charter of the Virginia Company was the Rev. Robert Hunt. He was the first chaplain of the Jamestown colony. The Virginia Company created parishes in each of its settlements and set aside glebe lands to provide income. It provided for churches to be built and appointed clergy for the churches. The company was torn by dissension and dissolved on May 24, 1624. The Virginia colony became a royal colony subject to the King.

Virginia, Diocese of. Organized in Richmond on May 18, 1785. The 1892 General Convention divided the diocese and today it includes the following counties: Albemarle, Arlington, Caroline, Charles City, Clark, Culpeper, Essex, Fairfax, Fauquier, Fluvanna, Frederick, Gloucester, Goochland, Greene, Hanover, Henrico, King and Queen, King George, King William, Lancaster, Loudoun, Louisa, Madison, Mathews, Middlesex, New Kent, Northumberland, Orange, Page, Prince William, Rappahannock, Richmond, Rockingham, Shenandoah, Spotsylvania, Stafford, Warren, Westmoreland, and that part of the city of Richmond north of the James River.

While not officially a cathedral, the Cathedral Shrine of the Transfiguration at Shrine Mont, the diocesan conference center, was consecrated on Aug. 6, 1925.

Virginia Theological Seminary. *See* Protestant Episcopal Theological Seminary in Virginia, The, Alexandria, Virginia (VTS).

Virgin Mary. *See* Mary the Virgin, Mother of our Lord Jesus Christ, Saint.

Vision Interfaith Satellite Network (VISN). This coalition works to arrange the broadcasting of religious programs via satellite. VISN is owned by the National Interfaith Coalition. It was formed in 1987 at Trinity Episcopal Church, New York City. The VISN center for the Episcopal Church is located in facilities owned by Trinity Church.

Visitation of the Blessed Virgin Mary, The. The Gospel of Luke, Chapter 1, records that at the time of the Annunciation, Mary learned her relative Elizabeth was miraculously pregnant. Mary went to visit Elizabeth and greeted her. At this greeting the child leaped in Elizabeth's womb. Her child was John the Baptist. Elizabeth was filled with the Holy Spirit. She greeted Mary as the mother of the Lord and exclaimed that Mary and the child in her womb were blessed. Mary responded with the song of praise known as the *Magnificat*, "My soul magnifies the Lord, and my spirit rejoices in God my Savior."

Liturgical celebration of the Visitation dates from the fourteenth century. This feast was included on July 2 as a black-letter day in the 1662 BCP. The Visitation is now celebrated as a Feast of our Lord on May 31.

Visitation, Episcopal. *See* Episcopal Visitation.

Visitation of the Sick. Traditional term for the pastoral office of Ministration to the Sick (BCP, p. 453). It may include one or more of the following: ministry of the word, laying on of hands and anointing, and Holy Communion. These parts are used in the order indicated if two or more are used together. The Lord's Prayer is always included. The BCP also provides a variety of Prayers for the Sick and Prayers for use by a Sick Person. *See* Ministration to the Sick.

Vocare. *Vocare* is a form of the Latin word meaning "to call." The Vocare weekend is a renewal weekend for young adults, ages nineteen to thirty. At this time they face many serious decisions which set the direction for much of their adult life. The focus of the weekend is "Let yourself hear Christ's call." Its aim is to concentrate closely on the person and teachings of Jesus Christ. The weekend includes talks and discussions. The talks include: "Identity," "What Is A Christian?", "Reconciliation," "Response to Christ," "Spiritual Journey," "Community," "Vocation," "Empowerment," and "Tomorrow." Vocare came into existence in Sept. 1980 when a number of Happening graduates met in Dallas, Texas, to plan the first Vocare weekend. The name of the ministry and the format of the Vocare weekend was chosen at a meeting in Dallas in Dec. 1980. Vocare National was established in Feb. 1989. *See* Happening; *see* New Beginnings.

Vocation. From the Latin *vocare*, "to call," vocation is the "calling" one infers from the external and internal signs which evolve over time. Vocation may involve a task or job, but it also concerns a way of life. All Christian vocations—lay or ordained, single or married or religious—are specific expressions of Christian identity rooted in the baptismal covenant.

Volunteers for Mission. This national program was mandated by the 1978 General Convention to place volunteers—lay and clergy—in both overseas and domestic missionary projects. Volunteers are sent in response to requests for skilled personnel from provinces and dioceses throughout the Anglican Communion. These volunteers serve for terms ranging from six months to two years. They are expected to raise some of their own support and are provided with minimal living allowances at their assigned positions. The program is administered by the office of Mission Personnel at the Episcopal Church Center.

von Wied, Hermann. *See* Hermann von Wied of Cologne.

Voorhees College, Denmark, South Carolina. A historically African American, coeducational, liberal arts college affiliated with the Episcopal Church. Voorhees was founded by Elizabeth Evelyn Wright (1872–1906) as the Denmark Industrial School. It opened on Apr. 14, 1897. In 1902 the name was changed to Voorhees Industrial School in honor of Ralph Voorhees, a generous benefactor. The name was changed in 1916 to Voorhees Normal and Industrial School, and in 1924 the dioceses of South

Carolina and Upper South Carolina began supporting the school. In 1947 the name was changed to Voorhees School and Junior College, and in 1963 it became Voorhees College.

Votive. Eucharistic celebration in which the proper collect, psalms, and readings concern a particular devotion. A votive may be chosen for pastoral reasons when no other celebration is required by the calendar of the church year. The BCP provides twenty-five propers for Various Occasions, including "Of the Holy Trinity," "Of the Incarnation," "For the Departed," "For the Unity of the Church," and "For Vocation in Daily Work" (pp. 927–931).

Votive Lights. These are short thick candles inserted into small glass cups which worshipers may light as an act of devotion. They may be placed on shelves or stands in front of the Blessed Sacrament, or in front of pictures or statues of Our Lord or saints. Votive lights may also be used in the home, especially with a small crèche at Christmas time.

Vows. Formal pledges or promises. All Christian vows are ultimately based in the promises made in the baptismal covenant (BCP, pp. 304–305). Vows may give form and particularity to the baptismal covenant in the person's life. In the Christian tradition, vows often reflect a life commitment to a specific Christian vocation or manner of life. Such vows include the promises by an ordinand at the ordination of a bishop, priest, or deacon, the promises a man and woman make to each other in marriage, and the promises of a person making a life commitment to membership in a monastic or religious community. Monastic or religious vows typically include a commitment to poverty, obedience, and chastity. Vows of life commitment are often preceded by formal or informal vows that are temporary in nature. A man and woman may go through a period of engagement prior to making the vows of marriage. A member of a monastic or religious community may make temporary vows for a period of years before making vows of life commitment or solemn profession. Temporary or informal vows provide an opportunity for the person to test vocation and the appropriateness of a particular commitment. A vow may be made privately or publicly to express any formal intention, resolve, or purpose. A private vow may be expressed confidentially to a spiritual director or confessor, or it may be expressed only in prayer to God.

W

Wainwright, Jonathan Mayhew (Feb. 24, 1792–Sept. 21, 1854). Bishop and music editor. He was born in Liverpool, England, and came to the United States in 1803. He graduated from Harvard in 1812. Wainwright was ordained deacon on Apr. 13, 1817, and priest on May 29, 1818. He was assistant minister, Trinity Church, New York, 1819–1821; rector, Grace Church, New York, 1821–1834; rector, Trinity Church, Boston, 1834–1836; and assistant minister, Trinity Church, New York, 1836–1852. While at Grace Church, New York, he edited *Music of the Church: A Collection of Psalms, Hymns and Chant Tunes adapted to the Worship of the Protestant Episcopal Church in the United States* (1823). This collection went through at least ten editions, the last one published in 1849. When Bishop Benjamin T. Onderdonk of New York was suspended from office on Jan. 3, 1845, Wainwright was elected provisional bishop. Wainwright was consecrated on Nov. 10, 1852, and served as the fourth Bishop of New York until his death.

Wake. A vigil or watch in the presence of the body of a deceased person prior to burial. It may be in the church, a funeral parlor, or a home. The observance of this funeral custom is separate from the funeral or burial liturgy. Prayers may be offered for the deceased and the grieving. The wake may also include shared food and drink and may involve festivity. The BCP states that it is appropriate for the family and friends of the deceased to come together for prayers prior to the funeral. Psalms, lessons, and collects from the burial service or other suitable psalms, lessons, and collects may be used. Prayers for a vigil or the Litany at the Time of Death may be said (BCP, pp. 465–466).

Walker, John Thomas (July 27, 1925–Sept. 30, 1989). Bishop and first African American to graduate from the Virginia Theological Seminary. He was born in Barnesville, Georgia. He received his B.A. from Wayne State University in 1951 and his B.D. from the Virginia Theological Seminary in 1954. Walker was ordained deacon on July 18, 1954, and priest on Feb. 19, 1955. He was rector of St. Mary's Church, Detroit, from 1955 until 1957, and he taught at St. Paul's School, Concord, New Hampshire, from 1957 until 1966. While there, he took a leave of absence to teach at the Bishop Tucker Theological College in Mukono, Uganda. From 1966 until 1971, Walker was canon of the Cathedral of St. Peter and St. Paul, Washington. He was consecrated Suffragan Bishop of Washington on June 29, 1971, and served in that position until he was elected Bishop Coadjutor on June 12, 1976. On July 1, 1977, Walker became the Bishop of Washington, a position he held until his death. In 1978 he assumed the additional responsibility of dean of the Cathedral. He died in Washington, D.C.

Ward, Vesper Ottmer (July 22, 1890–Oct. 17, 1968). Priest and leading educator in the Episcopal Church. He was born in Pleasant Retreat, West Virginia. He received his B.A. from Ohio Wesleyan University in 1913 and his S.T.B. from Boston University School of Theology in 1916. He was a Methodist minister for 15 years and then joined the Episcopal Church. He was ordained deacon on Nov. 24, 1931, and priest on May 27, 1932. Ward served as dean of the Cathedral of Our Merciful Saviour, Faribault, Minnesota, from 1933 to 1941, rector of St. Mary's-by-the-Sea in Pacific Grove, California, from 1941 to 1944, and canon chancellor, Grace Cathedral, San Francisco, from 1944 to 1948. He was editor-in-chief of the Division of Curriculum Development of the Department of Christian Education of the National Council (now Executive Council) of the Episcopal Church from 1948 to 1953, and editor of the "Church's Teaching Series" from 1949 to 1952. Ward served as professor of Christian education and homiletics at the School of Theology of the University of the South, Sewanee, Tennessee, from 1953 until his retirement in 1963. In that position he developed an innovative teaching program in both disciplines. His work in education later became one of the major influences in the revision of the theological curriculum at Sewanee. In 1952 he received the D.D. from Ohio Wesleyan University. Ward died in Seal Beach, California.

Wardens of a Parish. Officers of a parish. Two wardens are typically selected to serve with members of the vestry. The wardens are generally ranked "senior" and "junior." The mode of selection and duties of the wardens are determined by state law, diocesan canon, or parish by-laws. The senior warden is usually the primary elected lay leader of the congregation, and serves as a principal liaison between the parish and the rector. The junior warden is often given responsibility for the upkeep of the parish buildings and grounds. The senior warden typically presides at vestry meetings in the absence of the rector, and the junior warden presides at vestry meetings if both the rector and the senior warden are absent. In case of clerical vacancy, the senior warden may be the ecclesiastical authority of the parish for certain purposes. In the BCP service for the Celebration of a New Ministry (p. 559), the wardens begin the institution at the beginning of the service by addressing the bishop. They express the congregation's intent to welcome the new minister and state that the new minister has been selected in a prayerful and lawful manner. If the new minister is the rector or vicar of the congregation, a warden may present the keys of the church to the new minister during the induction ceremony. In some parishes, the senior warden is known as the "priest's warden," and the junior warden is known as the "people's warden." Historically, in the Church of England, one warden was named by the priest and the other chosen by the congregation.

Washburn, Henry Bradford (Dec. 2, 1869–Apr. 25, 1962). Priest and seminary professor. He was born in Worcester, Massachusetts. Washburn received his B.A. from Harvard in 1891 and his B.D. from the Episcopal Theological School in 1894. He was ordained deacon on June 20, 1894, and priest on Sept. 29, 1896. Washburn began his ordained ministry as assistant at St. John's Church, Providence, Rhode Island. From 1898 until 1908 he was the rector of St. Mark's Church, Worcester. From 1908 until 1940 Washburn was the professor of ecclesiastical history at the Episcopal Theological School, and dean of that school from 1920 until 1940. He served on numerous boards and commissions of the church and wrote several books. He died in Cambridge, Massachusetts.

Washing of the Altar. It is customary for the altar to be stripped after the Maundy Thursday liturgy. The *BOS* appoints Ps 22 and an antiphon for use if the stripping of the altar is observed as a public ceremony. Stripping the altar may be followed by the washing of the altar. Historically, the stripping and washing of altars took place on Good Friday in Gallican churches, and on Maundy Thursday in Rome. Neither the stripping nor the washing of the altar is mentioned by the BCP. The washing of the altar is also not mentioned by the *BOS*.

Washing of Feet. *See* Foot Washing.

Washington College, Chestertown, Maryland. College formerly associated with the Episcopal Church. In early 1780 the Rev. William Smith became the principal of Kent County Free School, Chestertown, Maryland, which began instruction around 1729–1730. Kent School became

Washington College on May 24, 1782, by virtue of a charter granted by the Maryland General Assembly "in honorable and perpetual memory of his *Excellency George Washington* the illustrious and virtuous commander-in-chief of the armies of the U.S." The college held its first commencement on May 14, 1783. Smith was succeeded by the Rev. Colin Ferguson (1751–1806), who served as principal from 1789 to 1806. Two other Episcopal principals were the Rev. Jacob Goldsmith Cooper (deposed in 1820), 1816–1817, and the Rev. Timothy Clowes, 1823–1827. The school is no longer associated with the Episcopal Church.

Washington College, Hartford, Connecticut. *See* Trinity College, Hartford, Connecticut.

Washington, Diocese of. The 1895 General Convention voted to divide the Diocese of Maryland and form the Diocese of Washington. The new diocese includes the District of Columbia and four Maryland counties: Charles, Prince George's, Montgomery, and St. Mary's. The primary convention of the Diocese was held at St. Andrew's Church, Washington, on Dec. 4–6, 1895. On Sept. 29, 1907, President Theodore Roosevelt laid the cornerstone for the Cathedral of St. Peter and St. Paul. On Sept. 30, 1990, the cathedral was consecrated. It is also called Washington Cathedral or the National Cathedral. This cathedral is the seat of the Bishop of Washington as well as the seat of the Presiding Bishop of the Episcopal Church. *See* Cathedral Church of Saint Peter and Saint Paul in the City and Diocese of Washington, The.

Washington, George (Feb. 22, 1732–Dec. 14, 1799). First President of the United States and Episcopal vestryman. He was born on the family estate "Wakefield" in Westmoreland County, Virginia. Washington was baptized on Apr. 5, 1732, "according to conformity of the Church of England." He served in the Virginia House of Burgesses, 1759–1774, and was a delegate to the Continental Congress. He was a leader of Virginia's opposition to British control. On June 15, 1775, he was named commander in chief of the Continental forces. He resigned from the army in 1783, and retired to Mount Vernon. Washington presided at the Federal Constitutional Convention in 1787, and in 1789 the unanimous vote of the electors made him the first President of the United States. He served as president until 1797, the end of his second term. He refused to run for a third term and returned to Mount Vernon.

Washington attended Pope's Creek Church in Westmoreland County. He was married in the Anglican Church in Virginia, presumably at St. Peter's Church in Kent. He attended services at the Pohick Church regularly, and served on its vestry. The Rev. Lee Massey, the rector, stated, "I never knew so constant an attendant on church as Washington." Washington owned two pews in the Pohick Church and one in Christ Church, Alexandria. He was an active member of the Truro vestry from 1763 until 1784. On three occasions he also served as one of the church wardens. Washington probably attended church about once a month while president. There are no records substantiating that he was a communicant. He bequeathed his Bible to his friend, the Rev. Brian Lord Fairfax, Episcopal clergyman of Fairfax County, Virginia. The Bible had been given to him by the Rev. Thomas Wilson, the only son of the Rt. Rev. Thomas Wilson, Bishop of Sodor and Man, England. Washington died at Mount Vernon, Virginia.

Washington National Cathedral. *See* Cathedral Church of Saint Peter and Saint Paul in the City and Diocese of Washington, The.

Washington Theological Repertory. This monthly journal first appeared in Aug. 1819 and was founded and edited by William Holland Wilmer. Any profits were to go to the Society for the Education of Pious Young Men for the Ministry, and the American Colonization Society. With the Aug. 1823 issue the title was extended to the *Washington Theological Repertory and Churchman's Guide*, and the new editor was William Hawley. It ceased publication with the Dec. 1830 issue and was merged with the *Philadelphia Recorder*.

Watch. A period of "staying awake" for spiritual reasons. Traditionally, watches have been kept before the Blessed Sacrament on the night of Maundy Thursday at the "Altar of Repose." Watches may also be kept to provide prayer and comfort for the sick or the dying. The term derives in part from Christ's question to his disciples at Gethsemane, "Could you not watch with me for an hour?" (Mt 26:40). In the seventeenth century, Deacon Nicholas Ferrar instituted a "Night Watch" at Little Gidding in Huntingdonshire, England. During these watches one or more members of the extended Ferrar family recited the whole Psalter while kneeling.

Watchman, The. This periodical appeared in Mar. 1819 and was published in New Haven, Connecticut. There was probably only one issue since no trace of any other issue has appeared.

Water. Water is a major element in religious rituals. It is a natural symbol of birth, fertility, life, and cleansing. To emerge from the waters is to be clean and fresh and new. To wash the body, or even the hands, is symbolically to become clean in an interior sense. Ritually, water is a symbol of purity and washing is a symbol of purifying. Ritual immersion renews life and power. It is a reappropriation of the energy of the first creation so that what is immersed is made new. Water is necessary to all animal and vegetable life. It is a part of their physical being. It is also part of the structure of many minerals. Water is characterized by fluidity, formlessness, and an almost endless ability to adapt itself to shapes and temperatures. Genesis describes the formless waste at the beginning of creation as "the waters" (Gn 1:2). Everything is born out of the primeval waters of chaos. The earth itself takes form when it emerges from the waters.

The principal use of water in Christian worship is to immerse the candidate in baptism. It is a sign not only of cleansing but of ritual death and rebirth in Jesus Christ. Water is the sacramental matter of baptism. The use of "holy water" for blessing, or for signing oneself with the cross, is intended to renew baptism and the baptismal covenant in the believer. Water is also mixed with wine in the chalice at the eucharist, recalling the general custom in the ancient world of mixing water with wine before drinking it. It was given a symbolic interpretation during the Monophysite controversy. The mixture of water and wine was seen as symbolic of the union of humanity and deity in the person of Christ. The monophysites refused to add water, symbolizing their belief in one nature of the Incarnate Word. *See* Matter (Sacramental).

Watts, Isaac (July 17, 1674–Nov. 25, 1748). Nonconformist clergyman. He was born in Southampton, England. He served from 1699 to 1702 as assistant and from 1702 until 1712 as pastor of an independent church in Mark Lane, London. Watts was never robust, and he went into semi-retirement in 1712 at the home of Sir Thomas Abney, where he lived until his death. There he devoted himself to writing theological and philosophical works, as well as hymns and metrical psalms. He is often considered "the father of English hymnody." His *Hymns and Spiritual Songs* was published in 1707 and his metrical psalter in 1719. His metrical psalms are not strict paraphrases but

Christianized versions of the psalms, as the title of his collection indicates, *The Psalms of David, Imitated in the Language of the New Testament* (London, 1719). Seventeen of his hymns or metrical psalms are used in *The Hymnal 1982*, including "Joy to the world! the Lord is come" (Hymn 100), "Come, let us join our cheerful songs with angels round the throne" (Hymn 374), "When I survey the wondrous cross" (Hymn 474), "Jesus shall reign where'er the sun" (Hymn 544), and "O God, our help in ages past" (Hymn 680).

Wattson, Paul James Francis (Jan. 16, 1863–Feb. 8, 1940). Founder of the Church Unity Octave, which was a precursor of the Week of Prayer for Christian Unity. He was born in Millington, Maryland, and baptized Lewis Thomas Wattson. He received his B.A. (1882) and his M.A. (1885) from St. Stephen's (Bard) College and his B.D. from the General Theological Seminary in 1887. He was ordained deacon on June 5, 1885, and priest on Dec. 12, 1886. He began his ordained ministry in Port Deposit, Maryland, and then became rector of St. John's Church, Kingston, New York. In 1894 he began publishing *The Pulpit of the Cross*, an Anglo-catholic parish bulletin. In 1895 he became the superior of an Episcopal mission in Omaha. In Dec. 1898 he and Lurana Mary White founded the Society of the Atonement, an order which was to work for the unity of the church. On July 27, 1900, he made his monastic profession before Bishop Leighton Coleman of Delaware and took the name Paul James Francis. In 1903 he began publishing *The Lamp*, which stressed the reunion of the Anglican Communion and the Church of Rome. Wattson founded the Church Unity Octave in 1909, an eight-day period of prayer for Christian unity. He began to doubt the validity of Anglican orders, and on Oct. 30, 1909, he, Mother Lurana, and fifteen others were received into the Roman Catholic Church. Wattson was ordained a Roman Catholic priest on July 16, 1910. He died in Garrison, New York. *See* Society of the Atonement; *see* Week of Prayer for Christian Unity; *see* White, Lurana Mary.

Way of the Cross, Community of the. The beginnings of this group, located in Buffalo, New York, go back to Mar. 17, 1939, when several women began to live under a definite discipline and rule while remaining in secular professions. Mother Pattie Ellis and Sister Gwendolyn Morgan were employed in the business world when they organized themselves as the Community of the Way of the Cross in 1940. They adopted St. Catherine of Siena as the patroness of the community, and on Mar. 28, 1940, the convent chapel bearing her name was dedicated. Their purpose was "So to live in God as through His Incarnate Son's Way of the Cross to create a community of persons who desire to live realistically on the social frontier of the world as it is and at the same time to live in the reality of the world as it ought to be." The community is no longer in existence.

Way of the Cross, Fellowship of the. A community of Episcopal clergy and candidates for holy orders who seek to integrate prayer and action in ministry. It was founded in Oct. 1882 as the Brotherhood of the Way of the Cross by ten clergy who belonged to a group called the Merrimack Valley Clericus in northeastern Massachusetts and southern New Hampshire. Although they do not live in community, they are bound together by a rule of life, daily prayer for each other, quarterly days of reflection, and an annual silent retreat. It works to provide parish clergy with a supportive community of colleagues. The community is headed by a superior, who is elected for a three-year term. Its primary purpose is to nurture the spiritual life of the members of the fellowship. It seeks to encourage Christlike love among all people, especially among the clergy. It describes itself as a unique group that is between a religious order and a devotional society. The Latin name of the group is *Fraternitas Viae Crucis*.

Way of the Cross (Stations of the Cross). A devotion to the Passion of Christ which recalls a series of events at the end of Jesus' life from his condemnation to his burial. The Way of the Cross imitates the practice of visiting the places of Jesus' Passion in the Holy Land by early Christian pilgrims. The first stations outside Palestine were built in Bologna in the fifth century. This devotion was encouraged by the Franciscans, and it became common in the fifteenth century. The number of stations for prayer and meditation in the Way of the Cross has varied, but it typically includes fourteen stations. Each station may have a cross and an artistic representation of the scene. The stations may be erected inside a church or outdoors. The *BOS* includes the following stations in the Way of the Cross: 1) Jesus is condemned to death; 2) Jesus takes up his cross; 3) Jesus falls the first time; 4) Jesus meets his afflicted mother; 5) the cross is laid on Simon of Cyrene; 6) a woman wipes the face of Jesus; 7) Jesus falls a second time; 8) Jesus meets the women of Jerusalem; 9) Jesus falls a third time; 10) Jesus is stripped of his garments; 11) Jesus is nailed to the cross; 12) Jesus dies on the cross;

13) the body of Jesus is placed in the arms of his mother; 14) Jesus is laid in the tomb. The *BOS* notes that eight of the stations are based on events that are recorded in the gospels. The remaining six (stations 3, 4, 6, 7, 9, 13) are based on inferences from the gospels or pious legends. The *BOS* allows these six stations to be omitted from the Way of the Cross. The *BOS* provides opening devotions and the Lord's Prayer. There is a versicle and response, a reading, a prayer, and a collect for each of the fourteen stations. Concluding prayers before the altar follow the fourteenth station in the *BOS* service. The hymn *Stabat Mater* has been associated with the Way of the Cross. Verses of this hymn traditionally have been sung between each of the stations when the devotion is done by a congregation. The *Stabat Mater* appears as "At the cross her vigil keeping," Hymn 159 in *The Hymnal 1982*. The *BOS* suggests that verses of this hymn be sung as the ministers enter for the Way of the Cross and as they approach the first station. The *BOS* also suggests that the *Trisagion* be chanted as the procession goes from station to station. The Way of the Cross is a popular devotion that is often done on Fridays during Lent. However, it should not displace the Proper Liturgy for Good Friday. Some have questioned its disassociation of Jesus' death from his resurrection.

"Wayside Cathedral." Founded in 1941 by Bishop Henry Wise Hobson of Southern Ohio, this program provided a "church on wheels" to minister in areas with no Episcopal parish. Its inspiration was a portable office used by Standard Oil. The name "Wayside Cathedral" was suggested by the decision to demolish and not replace the badly dilapidated St. Paul's Cathedral in Cincinnati. Sale of the cathedral property helped to support the new venture. Hobson went to Detroit and had a trailer built which he pulled behind his automobile. Bishop Hobson himself often accompanied the "Wayside Cathedral." This program emphasized evangelism and spiritual growth, reflecting two particular emphases in his diocese. A correspondence Sunday School was started in connection with the "Wayside Cathedral." At one time, more than one thousand children were reached by this ministry.

Wedding Ring. *See* Rings.

Wedel, Cynthia Clark (Aug. 26, 1908–Aug. 24, 1986). First woman to serve as president of the National Council of Churches. Cynthia Clark was born in Dearborn,

Michigan. She grew up in Evanston, Illinois. She earned a B.A. and M.A. from Northwestern University and a Ph.D. from George Washington University in 1957. She served as a youth worker in the Episcopal Church's national office. In 1939 she married the Rev. Theodore O. Wedel. She moved with him to Washington, D.C., where he was warden of the College of Preachers. She taught religion at the National Cathedral School for Girls from 1939 to 1948. She served on the national executive board of the Episcopal Women's Auxiliary from 1946 to 1952 and as a member of the National Council of the Episcopal Church from 1955 to 1962. She served from 1955 to 1958 as president of United Church Women. She was associate general secretary for Christian union (1965–69), president of the National Council of Churches (1969–75), and president of the World Council of Churches (1975–83). She was appointed by President Kennedy to his Commission on the Status of Women (1961–63). She served on the national boards of the Girl Scouts and the Red Cross. She was the author of several books including *Employed Women and the Church*, and *Citizenship, Our Christian Concern*. She was an official observer at the Second Vatican Council, 1962–1965, and one of three women consultants at the Lambeth Conference of 1978. She died in Alexandria, Virginia.

Wedel, Theodore Otto (Feb. 19, 1892–July 20, 1970). Preacher, lecturer, and educator. He was born in Halstead, Kansas. Wedel received his B.A. from Oberlin College in 1914, his M.A. from Harvard in 1915, and his Ph.D. from Yale University in 1918. He was instructor in English at Yale, 1919–1922, professor of English at Carleton College, Northfield, Minnesota, 1922–1930, and professor of biography at Carleton, 1930–1934. He studied theology at Marburg University. Wedel was ordained deacon on Sept. 24, 1929, and priest on May 31, 1930. Wedel began his ordained ministry as secretary for college work of the National Council of the Episcopal Church. In 1939 he became director of studies at the College of Preachers and canon chancellor of Washington Cathedral. From 1943 until 1960 he was warden of the College of Preachers. Wedel was president of the House of Deputies at the 1952, 1955, and 1958 General Conventions. He was a very popular lecturer and preacher. Among his many books were *The Christianity of Main Street* (1950) and *The Coming Great Church* (1945). He also wrote the exposition of Ephesians in *The Interpreter's Bible* (1953). Wedel died in Alexandria, Virginia.

"Wee Bookies." Booklets printed for Scottish nonjuring Episcopalians that contained the liturgy of the table portion of the eucharistic rite. The first (1722) reproduced that of the 1637 Scottish BCP. Its eucharistic prayer contained elements from the eucharistic prayer of the 1549 BCP that were missing in later English Prayer Books. Significant changes were made in later printings. In 1735 a prayer of oblation, "which we now offer unto thee," was inserted. Bishop Thomas Rattray's reconstruction *The Ancient Liturgy of the Church of Jerusalem* (1744) led to the invocation of the Holy Spirit upon the elements being moved to a West Syrian position—following the *anamnesis* rather than preceding the institution narrative—in a 1755 printing. In the 1764 "Wee Bookie" the *epiclesis* was abbreviated and reworded, "that they may become the body and blood of thy most dearly beloved Son," and the eucharistic prayer was linked to the *Sanctus* by the insertion of "All glory be to thee." The first American Prayer Book picked up this phrase. Its prayer, however, was based on the 1755 "Wee Bookie" with its fuller form of *epiclesis*, except that "may be to us the body and blood of thy most dearly beloved Son" was omitted.

Week of Prayer for Christian Unity. This observance began on St. Peter's Day, June 29, 1900, when Spencer Jones, a Church of England priest, preached a sermon on closer relations with the Church of Rome. Jones urged that sermons be preached on St. Peter's Day emphasizing Rome as the center of unity. Paul James Wattson, an Episcopal priest, suggested that the Octave from the Feast of St. Peter's Chair (Jan. 18) to the Feast of the Conversion of St. Paul (Jan. 25) be a time of prayer for Christian unity on a papal basis. Church Unity Week was first observed in 1908, and later the name was changed to the Church Unity Octave by Wattson. In the 1930s, it was suggested by Abbé Paul Couturier, a Roman Catholic priest in France, that the basis for prayer be broadened to include all who desired unity in Jesus Christ, without reference to the Pope. Also in the 1930s, Wattson changed the name to the Chair of Unity Octave. Since 1966 the Faith and Order Commission of the World Council of Churches and the Vatican Secretariat for Promoting Christian Unity have worked together on common international texts for the Week of Prayer for Christian Unity. *See* Wattson, Paul James Francis.

Weems, Mason Locke (Oct. 11, 1759–May 23, 1825). First person ordained by the Church of England for the Episcopal Church after the American Revolution. Weems was born near Herring Creek, Anne Arundel, Maryland. He studied medicine in London and at the University of Edinburgh but never practiced. Weems was ordained deacon on Sept. 5, 1784, and priest on Sept. 12, 1784. This was made possible when Parliament passed the Enabling Act on Aug. 13, 1784, which enabled English bishops to ordain clergy for the American Church without requiring the loyalty oath to the English sovereign. He was rector of All Hallows' Parish, Anne Arundel County, 1784–1789, and of Westminister Parish in the same county, 1790–1792. For about two decades Weems preached at different Virginia parishes, notably at Pohick Church, where George Washington worshiped before the Revolution. This enabled him later to refer to himself as "Formerly rector of Mt. Vernon Parish." Weems was a book peddler and writer from 1791 until his death. His most famous book was *The Life and Memorable Actions of George Washington* (*1800*). In the fifth edition, published in 1806, there appeared for the first time the anecdote of Washington and the cherry tree. He also published biographies of General Francis Marion, Benjamin Franklin, and William Penn, as well as numerous tracts designed to inculcate morality in the reader. He died in Beaufort, South Carolina. *See* Loyalty Oath to the English Sovereign.

Wendt, William Andrew (b. Jan. 18, 1920). Leading advocate for the ordination of women in the Episcopal Church. He was born in Mitchell, South Dakota. Wendt received his B.A. from George Washington University in 1948 and his S.T.B. from the General Theological Seminary in 1951. Wendt was ordained deacon on June 16, 1951, and priest on Dec. 21, 1951. From 1951 until 1954 he was an assistant at Trinity Church, New York, and from 1954 until 1960 he was priest-in-charge of St. Stephen's Church, New York. He was rector of St. Stephen and the Incarnation, Washington, 1960–1978. In 1978 Wendt founded the St. Francis Center in Washington and was its director until 1990. He served as an assistant at St. Thomas' Church, 1978–1987, and at St. Margaret's Church, 1988–1990, both in Washington. Wendt retired in 1990. While he was rector of St. Stephen's and the Incarnation, Wendt permitted some of the women irregularly ordained on June 29, 1974, to preside at the eucharist. At a ceremony at the Cathedral of St. Peter and St. Paul in Washington, D.C., Wendt stood before his bishop, the Rt. Rev. William Creighton, and was formally admonished for his disobedience. Twenty-four years later, on June 7, 1999, a ceremony in the Washington

Cathedral celebrated his life and praised him for his influence for justice. *See* "Philadelphia Eleven, The."

We Sing of God: A Hymnal for Children. This hymnal, edited by Robert N. Roth and Nancy L. Roth, consists of 108 hymns or selections of service music from *The Hymnal 1982* which were chosen with children's understanding of texts and their vocal abilities in mind. A *Teacher's Guide*, also edited by the Roths, provides commentaries, teaching ideas, and simplified accompaniments. It includes a Christmas pageant which makes use of a number of hymns. Keyed to this hymnal is another volume by the Roths, entitled *Rudiments of Music Worksheets*, which has worksheets for children. All the volumes were published by Church Hymnal Corporation in 1989. A cassette recording of twenty-eight of these selections is also available. It is a recording by a choir of boys and girls from St. Paul's Church, Akron, Ohio. This book is unique among hymn collections for children because it introduces children to texts and tunes from the church's official hymnal rather than to texts and tunes which they will soon outgrow.

Wesley, Charles (Dec. 18, 1708–Mar. 29, 1788). English hymn writer, priest, and missionary to colonial America. He was born in Epworth, England, the eighteenth child of Samuel and Susannah Wesley. Wesley graduated from St. Peter's College, Westminster, London, in 1721 and from Christ Church, Oxford, in 1726. At Oxford he, along with his brother John, was a member of the "Holy Club," and lived a very disciplined religious life. They were nicknamed the "Methodists." In 1735 he was ordained priest and went to Georgia with John as a missionary for the Society for the Propagation of the Gospel. Charles returned to England in 1736. On May 21, 1738, he "experienced the witness of adoption," that is, an experience of conversion. He had an itinerant ministry and eventually settled in London. He wrote more than 5,500 hymns. Twenty of these are in *The Hymnal 1982*, including "Christ, whose glory fills the skies" (Hymns 6–7); "Lo! He comes, with clouds descending" (Hymns 57–58); "Come, thou long expected Jesus" (Hymn 66); "Hark! the herald angels sing" (Hymn 87); "Love's redeeming work is done" (Hymn 188–189); "Jesus Christ is risen today" (Hymn 207); "Hail the day that sees him rise" (Hymn 214); "Rejoice, the Lord is King!" (Hymn 481); "O for a thousand tongues" (Hymn 493); "Let saints on earth in concert sing" (Hymn 526); "Ye servants of God" (Hymn 535); "Come, O thou Traveler unknown" (Hymn 638–639); and "Love divine, all loves excelling" (Hymn 657). He died in London. Charles and his brother John are commemorated in the Episcopal calendar of the church year on Mar. 3.

Wesley, John (June 17, 1703–Mar. 2, 1791). Generally considered the founder of Methodism. He was born in Epworth, England, the fifteenth of nineteen children born to Samuel and Susannah Wesley. He entered Christ Church College, Oxford, in 1720 and was ordained deacon in 1725. After serving as a curate to his father, he was ordained priest in 1728. He returned to Oxford to be a fellow at Lincoln College. Wesley and others formed the "Holy Club" at Oxford. They were derisively called "Methodists" because of their methodical religious practices. In 1735 Wesley went to the colony of Georgia as a missionary for the Society for the Propagation of the Gospel. His preaching against slavery and gin and his inexperience alienated him from the colonists. After two years he returned to England. On May 24, 1738, he had a conversion experience during a meeting at Aldersgate Street when his "heart was strangely warmed." Wesley died a priest of the Church of England, but his followers separated from the Church of England and organized the Wesleyan Methodists. His life and ministry, along with that of his brother Charles, is commemorated in the Episcopal calendar of the church year on Mar. 3.

Wesley, Samuel Sebastian (Aug. 14, 1810–Apr. 19, 1876). English church musician and composer. He was born in London, the grandson of Charles Wesley. Wesley studied music at Oxford University and was organist at Hereford Cathedral, 1832–1835; Exeter Cathedral, 1835–1842; Leeds Parish Church, 1842–1849; Winchester Cathedral, 1849–1865; and Gloucester Cathedral, 1865–1876. He has five hymn tunes in *The Hymnal 1982*, including *Alleluia*, used with the text "Alleluia! sing to Jesus!" (Hymn 461), and *Aurelia*, used with the text "The Church's one foundation" (Hymn 525). He also wrote S 251, an Anglican chant setting for "The Song of Zechariah." Wesley died in Gloucester.

West, Edward Nason (Nov. 5, 1909–Jan. 3, 1990). Leading theologian and liturgist. He was born in Boston. West received his B.S. from Boston University in 1931 and his B.D. from the General Theological Seminary in 1934. He was ordained deacon on June 13, 1934, and priest on May 31, 1935. After seven years of ministry at Trinity Church, Ossining, New York, West joined the staff of the Cathedral of St. John the Divine, New York City, where he held numerous positions until he retired in 1981. He joined the cathedral staff as canon sacrist in 1941. He was master of ceremonies when he retired. West was a leading spokesman about liturgy and ceremony around the world. West was a member of a number of honorary organizations, including the Order of the British Empire. He was an honorary chaplain to the Archbishop of Canterbury, a theological consultant for the *American Heritage Dictionary* and the *Funk and Wagnall Encyclopedia*, and a member of the Commission for Anglican/Orthodox Doctrinal Discussions. West designed the Compass Rose that became the emblem of the Anglican Communion. It was dedicated by the Archbishop of Canterbury, Robert Runcie, at the 1988 Lambeth Conference. West died in New York City. *See* Compass Rose.

West Missouri, Diocese of. The 1889 General Convention divided the Diocese of Missouri. The primary convention of the new diocese met at Grace Church, Kansas City, on June 3–4, 1890. It chose the name Diocese of West Missouri. It includes the following counties: Andrew, Atchison, Barry, Barton, Bates, Benton, Buchanan, Caldwell, Camden, Carroll, Cass, Cedar, Chariton, Christian, Clay, Clinton, Cooper, Dade, Dallas, Davies, DeKalb, Douglass, Gentry, Greene, Grundy, Harrison, Henry, Hickory, Holt, Howard, Howell, Jackson, Jasper, Johnson, Laclede, Lafayette, Lawrence, Linn, Livingston, McDonald, Mercer, Moniteau, Morgan, Newton, Nodaway, Ozark, Pettis, Platte, Polk, Putnam, Ray, St. Clair, Saline, Stone, Sullivan, Taney, Vernon, Webster, Worth, and Wright. On June 17, 1904, the name was changed to the Diocese of Kansas City, and on May 13, 1914, it was changed back to the Diocese of West Missouri. On May 15, 1935, Grace and Holy Trinity Parish, Kansas City, became Grace and Holy Trinity Cathedral.

West Tennessee, Diocese of. The 1982 General Convention voted to divide the Diocese of Tennessee into three dioceses—Tennessee, East Tennessee, and West Tennessee. The Diocese of West Tennessee includes the following counties: Benton, Carroll, Chester, Crockett, Decatur, Dyer, Fayette, Gibson, Hardeman, Hardin, Haywood, Henderson, Henry, Lake, Lauderdale, Madison, McNairy, Obion, Shelby, Tipton, and Weakley. The primary convention of the diocese was held at St. Mary's Cathedral, Memphis, on Oct. 21–22, 1982. St. Mary's became the cathedral of the Diocese of Tennessee on Jan. 1, 1871, and continues as the cathedral of the Diocese of West Tennessee.

West Texas, Diocese of. On Oct. 26, 1874, the General Convention voted to divide the Diocese of Texas and form the Missionary District of Northern Texas and the Missionary District of Western Texas. The primary convention of the Missionary District of Western Texas met at St. Mark's Church, San Antonio, on May 6–8, 1875. The primary convention of the Diocese of West Texas met at St. Mark's Church, San Antonio, on May 10–15, 1904. The 1910 General Convention formed the Missionary District of North Texas from the Diocese of Dallas and West Texas. The Diocese of West Texas includes the following counties: Aransas, Atascosa, Bandera, Bee, Bexar, Blanco, Brooks, Caldwell, Calhoun, Cameron, Comal, Concho, Crockett, DeWitt, Dimmit, Duval, Edwards, Frio, Gillespie, Goliad, Gonzales, Guadelupe, Hay, Hidalgo, Jackson, Jim Hogg, Jim Wells, Karnes, Kendall, Kenedy, Kerr, Kimble, Kinney, Kleberg, Lavaca, LaSalle, Live Oak, Llano, Mason, Maverick, McCullough, McMullen, Medina, Menard, Nueces, Real, Refugio, San Patricio, San Saba, Schleicher, Starr, Sutton, Uvalde, Val Verde, Victoria, Webb, Willacy, Wilson, Zapata, and Zavala. The diocese does not have a cathedral.

West Virginia, Diocese of. West Virginia was part of the Diocese of Virginia until 1877. The General Convention of 1877 created the Diocese of West Virginia, which held its primary convention at St. John's Church, Charleston, on Dec. 5–7, 1877. The diocese does not have a cathedral. It includes the entire state.

Western Colorado, Missionary District of. The 1892 General Convention voted to divide the Diocese of Colorado and establish the Missionary District of Western Colorado. The Missionary District of Western Colorado included the following counties: Archuleta, Delta, Dolores, Eagle, Garfield, Grand, Gunnison, Hinsdale, La Plata, Mesa, Montezuma, Montrose, Ouray, Pitkin, Rio Blanca, Routt, San Juan, San Miguel, and Summit. The primary convocation of the Missionary District met at the Church of the Good Shepherd, Gunnison, on Sept. 19–21, 1893. In 1895 the General Convention placed the Missionary District of Western Colorado under the jurisdiction of the Missionary Bishop of Nevada and Utah, and changed the name to the Missionary District of Nevada, Utah, and Western Colorado. In 1907 the House of Bishops voted to revive the Missionary District of Western Colorado. The 1919 General Convention voted that the Missionary District of Western Colorado be retroceded to the Diocese of Colorado, which now includes the entire state of Colorado.

Western Episcopal Observer. *See* Gambier Observer.

Western Episcopalian. This journal was published from Aug. 11, 1853, until June 25, 1868. It had various changes in ownership, editorship, name, and frequency of publication. It was succeeded and continued by the *Standard of the Cross.*

Western Kansas, Diocese of. The 1901 General Convention voted to divide the Diocese of Kansas and form a Missionary District in the western part of the state. It was named the Missionary District of Salina and includes the following counties: Barber, Barton, Cheyenne, Clark, Cloud, Comanche, Decatur, Edwards, Ellis, Ellsworth, Finney, Ford, Gove, Graham, Grant, Gray, Greeley, Hamilton, Harper, Haskell, Hodgeman, Jewell, Kearny, Kingman, Kiowa, Lane, Lincoln, Logan, McPherson, Meade, Mitchell, Morton, Ness, Norton, Osborne, Ottawa, Pawnee, Phillips, Pratt, Rawlins, Reno, Republic, Rice, Rooks, Rush, Russell, Saline, Scott, Seward, Sheridan, Sherman, Smith, Stanton, Stevens, St. John, Thomas, Trego, Wallace, and Wichita. On Nov. 14, 1960, the House of Bishops changed the name to the Missionary District of Western Kansas, and on Oct. 15, 1970, the General Convention made it the Diocese of Western Kansas. On July 13, 1903, Christ Church, Salina, became Christ Cathedral.

Western Louisiana, Diocese of. The 1979 General Convention voted to divide the Diocese of Louisiana and establish a new diocese. The primary convention of the new diocese met at St. James Church, Alexandria, on Oct. 10–11, 1979. It voted to call itself the Western Diocese of Louisiana. It includes the following civil parishes (counties): Acadia, Allen, Avoyelles, Beauregard, Bienville, Bossier, Caddo, Calcasieu, Caldwell, Cameron, Catahoula, Claiborne, Concordia, Desoto, East Carroll, Evangeline, Franklin, Grant, Iberia, Jackson, Jefferson Davis, Lafayette, Lasalle, Lincoln, Madison, Morehouse, Natchitoches, Ouachita, Rapides, Red River, Richland, Sabine, St. Landry, St. Martin (northeast portion lying west of Iberville Parish and north of Iberia Parish), Tensas, Union, Vermilion, Vernon, Webster, West Carroll, and Winn. On Feb. 3, 1984, the name was changed to the Diocese of Western

Louisiana. St. Mark's Church, Shreveport, was set apart as St. Mark's Cathedral on July 7, 1990.

Western Massachusetts, Diocese of. The 1901 General Convention voted to divide the Diocese of Massachusetts and create the Diocese of Western Massachusetts. The Diocese of Western Massachusetts includes the four counties of Berkshire, Franklin-Hampshire, Hampden, and Worcester. The primary convention of the Diocese met at Christ Church, Springfield, on Nov. 19, 1901. On Feb. 7, 1929, Christ Church, Springfield, was set apart as Christ Church Cathedral.

Western Mexico, Diocese of. The General Convention of 1904 established the Missionary District of Mexico. The 1972 General Convention divided the Missionary District of Mexico into the Missionary District of Central and South Mexico, the Missionary District of Western Mexico, and the Missionary District of Northern Mexico. In 1986 all three of these missionary districts became dioceses. The 1994 General Convention granted the Mexican dioceses permission to withdraw from the Episcopal Church and form an autonomous province. The Anglican Church of Mexico came into being on Jan. 1, 1995.

Western Michigan, Diocese of. The 1874 General Convention voted to divide the Diocese of Michigan and establish a new diocese. The primary convention of the new diocese met at St. Mark's Church, Grand Rapids, on Dec. 2, 1874. It chose the name the Diocese of Western Michigan. It includes the following counties: Allegan, Antrim, Barry, Benzie, Berrien, Branch, Calhoun, Cass, Charleviox, Clare, Eaton, Emmett, Grand Traverse, Iona, Isabella, Kalamazoo, Kalkaska, Kent, Lake, Leelenau, Manistee, Mason, Mecosta, Missaukee, Montcalm, Muskegon, Newaygo, Oceana, Osceola, Ottawa, St. Joseph, Van Buren, and Wexford. On Dec. 15, 1942, St. Mark's Church, Grand Rapids, was set apart as St. Mark's Cathedral, and on May 19, 1964, it reverted to being St. Mark's Church. The Cathedral Church of Christ the King, Kalamazoo, opened on May 4, 1969, and it was dedicated on Oct. 26, 1969.

Western Nebraska, Missionary District of. The 1889 General Convention voted to divide the Diocese of Nebraska and create the Missionary District of The Platte. The name was changed to the Missionary District of

Laramie in 1898 and to the Missionary District of Kearney in 1907. From Oct. 14, 1913, until Sept. 14, 1946, when the General Convention voted to retrocede it to the Diocese of Nebraska, it was known as the Missionary District of Western Nebraska.

Western New York, Diocese of. The 1838 General Convention of voted to divide the Diocese of New York. This was the first division of a diocese and the first diocese that did not follow state lines. The primary convention of the Diocese of Western New York met at Trinity Church, Geneva. The 1868 General Convention divided the diocese as did the 1931 General Convention. The present Diocese of Western New York includes the following counties: Cattaraugus, Chautauqua, Erie, Genesee, Niagara, Orleans, and Wyoming. Bishop Arthur Cleveland Coxe named St. Paul's Church, Buffalo, the Cathedral, and the diocesan convention made this official on May 20, 1930.

Western North Carolina, Diocese of. The diocese was created in Oct. 1895 when the General Convention voted to divide the Diocese of North Carolina. It was first called the Missionary District of Asheville and held its primary convention at Trinity Church, Asheville, Nov. 12–13, 1895. On Apr. 26, 1922, the convention voted to change the name to the Diocese of Western North Carolina. On Oct. 18–19, 1922, the primary convention of the diocese met at the Church of the Ascension, Hickory. It consists of the following counties: Alexander, Alleghany, Ashe, Avery, Buncombe, Burke, Caldwell, Catawba, Cherokee, Clay, Cleveland, Gaston, Graham, Haywood, Henderson, Jackson, Lincoln, Macon, Madison, McDowell, Mitchell, Polk, Rutherford, Swain, Transylvania, Watauga, Wilkes, and Yancey. On Jan. 1, 1995, All Soul's Church, Asheville, became All Soul's Cathedral.

Western Texas, Missionary District of. On Oct. 26, 1874, the General Convention divided Texas into the Diocese of Texas and the Missionary Districts of Northern Texas and Western Texas. The primary convention of the Missionary District of Western Texas met at St. Mark's Church, San Antonio, May 6–8, 1875. The Missionary District became the Diocese of West Texas at the primary convention, May 10–15, 1904, at St. Mark's Church, San Antonio. *See* West Texas, Diocese of.

Western Theological Seminary, Chicago. *See* Seabury-Western Theological Seminary.

Wetmore, James (Dec. 25, 1695–May 15, 1760). One of the Yale Converts. He was born in Middletown, Connecticut. Wetmore graduated from Yale College in 1714, and was ordained a Congregational minister in Nov. 1718. In Sept. 1722, while pastor of the First Congregational Church in New Haven, Connecticut, he and several other Congregational ministers announced that they had converted to the Church of England. On Mar. 2, 1723, Wetmore was appointed assistant minister, catechist, and schoolmaster at Trinity Church, New York. Accordingly, he sailed for England and arrived in London on July 4, 1723, where he was ordained deacon and priest, both on July 25, 1723, by the Bishop of London. On Dec. 30, 1726, he was named the rector of the church at Rye, New York, where he served until his death. Wetmore died in Rye. *See* Yale Converts.

Wharton, Charles Henry (May 25, 1748–July 23, 1833). An organizer of the Episcopal Church. He was born in St. Mary's County, Maryland. Wharton was raised a Roman Catholic, and in 1760 he entered the Jesuit college at Saint-Omer, France. He was ordained a Roman Catholic priest on Sept. 19, 1772, and then became a chaplain to the Roman Catholics at Worcester, England. Wharton returned to America in 1783 after his conversion to Anglicanism. He became the rector of Immanuel Church, New Castle, Delaware. He was a deputy to the first General Convention in 1785 and named a member of the committee that prepared the constitution of the new church. In 1798 he became the rector of St. Mary's Church, Burlington, New Jersey, where he remained until his death. Wharton died in Burlington.

Wharton College, Austin, Texas. It was founded in 1858 by the Rev. Charles Gillette (1813–Mar. 6, 1869), and named after his wife, Mary Ann Wharton. The school received its charter on Feb. 11, 1860, and closed in 1865.

Wharton, Francis (Mar. 7, 1820–Feb. 21, 1889). Lawyer, priest, and government official. He was born in Philadelphia. Wharton graduated from Yale College in 1839 and then studied law. He was admitted to the Pennsylvania bar in 1843. Wharton became active in the Episcopal Church after the death of his wife in 1854. For a while he edited the *Episcopal Recorder*. In 1856 he accepted a teaching position at Kenyon College. He was ordained deacon on Apr. 11, 1862, and priest on Dec. 10, 1862. From 1863 until 1871 Wharton was rector of St. Paul's Church, Brookline, Massachusetts. He was one of the founders of the Episcopal Theological School and served there as the first dean, Apr. 19, 1867–July 3, 1867. Wharton taught various subjects at the Episcopal Theological School from 1867 until 1881. During the last years of his life Wharton was an official in the administration of President Grover Cleveland. He continued to write books on law and government. Wharton died in Washington, D. C.

Whipple, Henry Benjamin (Feb. 15, 1822–Sept. 16, 1901). Bishop and missionary to American Indians. He was born in Adams, Jefferson County, New York. Whipple studied at the Oberlin Collegiate Institute but did not receive a degree. He was raised a Presbyterian, but he decided to study for ordained ministry in the Episcopal Church. He was ordained deacon on Aug. 17, 1849, and priest on July 16, 1850. After seven years as rector of Zion Church, Rome, New York, he became the rector of the Church of the Holy Communion, Chicago, in 1857. He remained there until elected to the episcopate. Whipple was consecrated the first Bishop of Minnesota on Oct. 13, 1859, and served in that position until his death. He did extensive missionary work among the Indians, which earned him the title the "Apostle to the Red Men." He made Faribault his diocesan headquarters. He assisted in the founding of St. Mary's Hall, Shattuck Military School, and Seabury Hall, which was to be a theological seminary for students west of the Mississippi River. In 1899 he published *Lights and Shadows of a Long Episcopate*, which is his autobiography and a description of his work with the Indians. He died in Faribault.

Whitaker, Alexander (1585–Mar. 1617). The "Apostle of Virginia." He was born in Cambridge, England. Whitaker received his B.A. in 1604/1605 and his M.A. from Cambridge University in 1608. He was ordained a priest in the Church of England. After serving several years in England, he came to the Virginia colony in 1611. Whitaker began his ministry in Virginia at Henrico and then extended it to Bermuda Hundreds. In 1613 he instructed and baptized the Indian princess, Pocahontas. Also in 1613 the London Company published a sermon written by him, entitled *Good Newes from Virginia*. In this sermon he stated the reasons for converting the Indians to Christianity and he urged people in England to support the colony. He drowned in Henrico County.

White, Edwin Augustine (Dec. 27, 1854–July 6, 1925). Priest and noted canon lawyer. He was engaged in law before studying theology. He was ordained deacon on Dec. 18, 1887, and priest on Oct. 31, 1888. He taught canon law at the General Theological Seminary, Bexley Hall, and Western Theological Seminary. White was a deputy to eight General Conventions, from 1901 to 1922, and he served as chair of the Committee on Canons of Convention from 1913 until his death. He wrote a number of books on canon law, the most significant being *Constitution and Canons for the Government of the Protestant Episcopal Church in the United States of America, Adopted in General Conventions, 1789–1922, Annotated, with an Exposition of the Same, and Reports of Such Cases as Have Arisen and Been Decided Thereunder*, published by order of the House of Deputies (1924). In 1954 it was edited by Jackson Arman Dykman (1887–1974), and titled *Annotated Constitution and Canons for the Government of the Protestant Episcopal Church in the United States of America, Adopted in General Conventions, 1789–1952*, 2d ed., 2 vols.

White, Lurana Mary (Apr. 12, 1870–Apr. 15, 1935). Member of an Anglican religious order and co-founder of the Society of the Atonement. She was born in New York City. On Oct. 17, 1894, she became a postulant in the Community of the Sisters of the Holy Child. On Sept. 25, 1896, she took the vows of poverty, obedience, and chastity. In 1896 she began corresponding with Lewis Thomas Wattson, later named Paul James Francis. They acquired property at Graymoor, near Garrison, New York, and established the Society of the Atonement. On Dec. 15, 1909, Father Paul, Mother Lurana, and fifteen other members of the Society of the Atonement became Roman Catholics. *See* Society of the Atonement; *see* Wattson, Paul James.

White, William (Apr. 4, 1748–July 17, 1836). First Bishop of Pennsylvania and one of the chief architects of the newly independent church. He was born in Philadelphia. White graduated from the College of Philadelphia in 1765 and then studied theology under Richard Peters and Jacob Duche. He was ordained deacon on Dec. 23, 1770, and priest on June 25, 1772. White was assistant minister at the United Parishes of St. Peter's and Christ Church in Philadelphia, 1772–1779, and rector of the United Parishes from 1779 until his death. He was a chaplain to the Continental and Constitutional Congresses and the United States Senate from 1777 until 1801. On Aug. 6, 1782, White published *The Case of the Episcopal Churches*

Considered, in which he argued for the temporary ordination of deacons and presbyters by presbyters until the episcopate could be obtained. Despite his argument in *The Case*, the church maintained an episcopal polity. Many of his other ideas in *The Case*, such as lay representation in the church's legislative bodies, were adopted in the Constitution of the Episcopal Church. He was consecrated Bishop of Pennsylvania on Feb. 4, 1787, and served in that position until his death. White was Presiding Bishop from July 28, 1789, until Oct. 3, 1789, and from Sept. 8, 1795, until his death. He died in Philadelphia.

Whitefield, George (Dec. 16, 1714–Sept. 30, 1770). Leading figure in the "Great Awakening" in eighteenth-century America. He was born in Gloucester, England. Whitefield attended Pembroke College, Oxford University, 1733 until 1736, where he came under the influence of Charles and John Wesley. He was ordained deacon in 1736. In 1738 he came with the Wesleys to Georgia. In 1739 he returned to England, was ordained priest, and began to preach outside of church buildings. In 1740 he returned to Georgia and established an orphanage at Savannah called Bethesda. In 1741 he and John Wesley split over the issue of predestination, with Whitefield supporting the Calvinist position. Whitefield was the leader of the English Calvinist Methodists from that time until his death. He made seven trips to the American colonies. He preached the evangelical message up and down the eastern seaboard. He was a leader of the Evangelical Revival in England and of the Great Awakening in the American colonies. Whitefield is recognized as one of the great preachers in the history of the church. He died in Newburyport, Massachusetts. *See* Great Awakening.

Whitsunday. A traditional English name for the Feast of Pentecost. The term is a corruption of "White Sunday." It is associated with the white robes of baptism which were worn by the newly baptized at the Pentecost service. The liturgical color for the Feast of Pentecost is red.

Whittingham, William Rollinson (Dec. 2, 1805–Oct. 17, 1879). Bishop and influential early catholic. He was born in New York City. Whittingham graduated from the General Theological Seminary in 1825 and became its librarian. He was ordained deacon on Mar. 11, 1827, and priest on Dec. 17, 1829. Whittingham began his ordained ministry as chaplain at the Charity School of Trinity Church, New York. From 1829 until 1830 he was rector of St. Mark's Church, Orange, New Jersey. From 1831 until 1835 he was rector of St. Luke's Church, New York. In 1835 he traveled in Europe for his health. From 1836 until 1840 he was professor of ecclesiastical history at General Seminary. He taught the principles of the high church party and insisted on the highest standards of scholarship. Whittingham was consecrated the fourth Bishop of Maryland on Sept. 17, 1840, and served in that capacity until his death. While he was bishop, he helped to found St. James' College in Hagerstown. He established an order of deaconesses, probably the first in the Episcopal Church. He also founded the Sisterhood of St. John in Washington. During the Civil War, he was a leading advocate for the Union cause. Whittingham published a number of scholarly books and had a library of over 17,000 volumes. He gave his library to the Diocese of Maryland. It became the nucleus of the Maryland Diocesan Library, one of the best diocesan libraries in the Episcopal Church. Whittingham upheld the doctrine of apostolic succession and the sacramental system of the church. He died in Orange, New Jersey.

Wider Episcopal Fellowship. The 1948 Lambeth Conference recommended that bishops of the Anglican Communion and bishops of other churches which are, or may be, in communion with them should meet together from time to time as an episcopal conference. These conferences were to be advisory in character, for counsel and encouragement. This recommendation was reaffirmed and elaborated by the 1958 Lambeth Conference. It recommended that the Archbishop of Canterbury invite representative bishops from each Province of the Anglican Communion and representative bishops from each church possessing the historic episcopate with which the churches and provinces of the Anglican Communion are in full communion or in a relation of inter-communion. A conference was held in Canterbury in Apr. 1964, and the Wider Episcopal Fellowship was created. This conference was attended by some forty archbishops and bishops, half of whom were Anglicans and half from other churches with episcopal polities. Before it went out of existence, the fellowship included seven national churches, six Old Catholic churches, the Polish National Catholic Church of America, and representatives from Yugoslavia. The seven national churches were: Church of Finland, Lusitanian Church (Portugal), Mar Thoma Syrian Church of Malabar, Philippine Independent Church, Church of South India,

Spanish Reformed Church, and Church of Sweden. The six Old Catholic churches were from Holland, Austria, Czechoslovakia, Germany, Poland, and Switzerland.

Widow. A woman who has remained unmarried since the death of her husband. In biblical times, women were very much dependent on male relatives for their welfare. A woman could find herself in a vulnerable and defenseless position when her husband died. An untimely and early death of the husband could be seen as judgment for sin, which could also mean disgrace for the widow (see Is 54:4). After the death of her husband and sons, Ruth lamented that God had dealt harshly with her and brought calamity on her (Ru 1:20–21). The OT calls for the care and protection of widows (see Dt 10:18, 14:28–29, 24:19, 26:12). The plight of widows was at times associated with orphans. The Lord upholds the orphan and widow (Ps 146:9), and they are not to be abused (Ex 22:22). In the NT, Jesus warns that those who devour widows' houses and say long prayers for the sake of appearance will receive the greater condemnation (Lk 20:47). The Letter of James (1:27) describes pure and undefiled religion in terms of caring for orphans and widows in their distress. Seven members of the Christian community were appointed to the task of waiting on tables after the Hellenists complained that their widows were being neglected in the daily distribution of food (Acts 6:1–7). A widow's family should contribute to her support (1 Tm 5:4, 16). There was a distinct order or society of "real widows" in the early church (see 1 Tm 5:3–16). Real widows set their hope on God, and continued night and day in supplications and prayers. In order to be placed on the church's list, a widow had to be sixty years old, married only once, and well attested for good works, such as bringing up children, showing hospitality, washing the saints' feet, and helping the afflicted. Concern that younger widows would want to marry again led to advice that they should not be put on the list of widows (1 Tm 5:11). Enrolled widows constituted a charitable organization or ministry for the church. Their duties included nursing the sick, giving alms, and evangelizing pagan women. The order of widows had declined by the fourth century, and their work was done by deaconesses. In the church, widowhood came to be associated with honor and service rather than shame. *See* Foot Washing.

Wilberforce, William (Aug. 24, 1759–July 29, 1833). English philanthropist, reformer, orator, and evangelical layman. He was born in Hull, Yorkshire. Wilberforce studied at St. John's College, Cambridge University, 1776–1779. In 1780 he was elected to the House of Commons representing Hull. It was in the House of Commons that he worked against slavery and the slave trade. Wilberforce became active in the abolition effort as early as 1787 through his association with the Quaker-founded Society for the Abolition of the Slave Trade. His first political success occurred on May 9, 1788, when legislation was passed that reduced the number of slaves carried aboard a slave vessel. Because of overcrowding, the mortality rate in slave vessels was quite high. Under Wilberforce's leadership, Parliament passed the bill for the abolition of the slave trade in 1807. From then until his death, Wilberforce worked for the abolition of slavery in the British Empire. On Aug. 28, 1833, a month after his death, the bill of Parliament abolishing slavery throughout the British dominions received the King's consent and became law. In 1797 Wilberforce published his major reform volume, *A Practical View of the Prevailing Religious System of Professed Christians in the Higher and Middle Classes in the Country, Contrasted with Real Christianity*. The chief point of the book was to distinguish between two types of Christians, the nominal or lukewarm and the real or vital. The vital Christian knows that conversion and the transformation of life are at the heart of Christianity. Wilberforce died in London. His life and work are commemorated in the Episcopal calendar of the church year on July 30.

Wilkinson, Christopher (d. Apr. 15, 1729). Second Commissary to Maryland. Bishop of London John Robinson appointed Wilkinson Commissary of the Eastern Shore of Maryland in 1716. He served until his death.

Willan, Healey (Oct. 12, 1880–Feb. 16, 1968). Renowned composer of church music. He was born in Balham, in Surrey, England. He trained at St. Saviour's, Eastbourne. After advanced study in organ and piano, he served several churches in and near London. In 1913 he came to Toronto, Ontario, Canada, as head of the music theory department at the University of Toronto and organist and choirmaster at St. Paul's Church. From 1921 until his death he was precentor at the Church of St. Mary Magdalene. He wrote adaptations of ancient service music, hymn tunes, faux-bourdons, newly composed service music, motets, symphonies, operas, cantatas, organ works, chamber music, songs, and incidental music for plays. *The Hymnal 1982* includes the *Kyrie, Sanctus, Agnus*

Dei, and *Gloria in excelsis* (S 91, S 114, S 158, and S 202) from his *Missa de Sancta Maria Magdalena.* He died in Toronto.

William and Mary, College of. First Anglican college in the American colonies. It was founded by James Blair, the first Commissary to Virginia. On Feb. 8, 1693, King William III and Queen Mary II granted a charter. On Dec. 20, 1693, 330 acres were purchased at "Middle Plantation," now Williamsburg, for the school. The cornerstone of the first building was laid on Aug. 8, 1695. One of its main purposes was to be a "nursery of pious ministers" for the church in Virginia. On Dec. 4, 1779, under the leadership of Thomas Jefferson, the Governor of Virginia, the college became a university and the Divinity School was discontinued. In 1820 a chair of theology was established, but no students came. The presidents of William and Mary were Episcopal clergy for most of its first 160 years. It became a state institution on Mar. 5, 1860.

William Smith College. William Smith, a nurseryman in Geneva, New York, wanted to establish a college for women in Geneva. Though his family were members of the Episcopal Church, Smith had moved towards spiritualism. President Langdon Cheves Stewardson of Hobart College, Geneva, suggested to Smith a women's college. The new college was to be associated with Hobart, sharing equipment and staff. The deed for the land for the new school was signed on Dec. 13, 1906. Hobart's trustees feared the outrage of students and alumni if their college became co-educational. Separate classes for men and women were held, often in the same building, but not on the Hobart campus. The Hobart campus was off-limits for women, but they were permitted to use the library and chapel. Women had to walk on public sidewalks and not on campus paths. William Smith College opened in 1908. Smith died, at the age of ninety-four, just before the first graduation in 1912. *See* Hobart College, Geneva, New York.

Williams, Channing Moore (July 18, 1829–Dec. 2, 1910). Missionary Bishop to China and Japan. He was born in Richmond, Virginia. Williams received the M.A. degree from the College of William and Mary in 1852. He graduated from the Virginia Theological Seminary in 1855, and was ordained deacon on July 1, 1855. In Nov. 1855 he sailed for Shanghai to do missionary work. He was ordained priest on Jan. 11, 1857. On Feb. 14, 1859, Williams and John Liggins were appointed the first Episcopal missionaries to Japan, and Williams reached Nagasaki on July 1, 1859. On Oct. 3, 1866, he was consecrated the second Missionary Bishop of China with jurisdiction over Japan. On Oct. 23, 1874, the House of Bishops constituted Japan a missionary district and named it the Missionary District of Yedo. On that same day Williams relinquished China and became Missionary Bishop of Yedo. He resigned this position on Oct. 18, 1889, but continued to work in Japan until 1908. He died in Richmond, Virginia. His work and ministry is commemorated in the Episcopal calendar of the church year on Dec. 2.

Williams, Charles David (July 30, 1860–Feb. 14, 1923). Bishop, theologian, and social gospel advocate. He was born in Bellevue, Ohio. Williams received his B.A. in 1880 and his M.A. in 1893 from Kenyon College. He studied for the ordained ministry at Bexley Hall. Williams was ordained deacon on June 17, 1883, and priest on Oct. 30, 1884. He was rector of the Church of the Resurrection, Fernbank, Ohio, and the Church of the Atonement, Riverside, Ohio, 1884–1889. From 1889 until 1893 he was rector of St. Paul's Church, Steubenville, Ohio. In 1893 Williams became the dean of Trinity Cathedral, Cleveland, where he remained until 1906. He was consecrated the fourth Bishop of Michigan on Feb. 7, 1906, and continued in that position until his death. Williams supported the Inter-Church World Movement and was president of the Church League for Industrial Democracy. His social views were articulated in *A Valid Christianity for Today* (1909), *The Christian Ministry and Social Problems* (1917), and *The Gospel of Fellowship* (1923). In 1920–1921 he delivered the Lyman Beecher Lectures on Preaching at the Yale Divinity School. These lectures were published as *The Prophetic Ministry for Today* (1921). Williams died in Detroit.

Williams, David McKinley (1887–1978). American church musician, composer, and teacher. He was born in Carnarvonshire, Wales. Williams began his career in church music as a chorister in the choir of the Cathedral of St. John, Denver. At the age of thirteen he became the organist of St. Peter's Church, Denver. In 1908 he went to New York to serve as the organist of Grace Church Chapel. He moved to Paris in 1911 for study with some of the best known French organists of the time. Upon his return, he served as organist of the Church of the Holy Communion in New York. Williams served in the Royal Canadian Artillery in World War I and returned to his New York position in 1920. After only six months, he was appointed organist and choirmaster of St. Bartholomew's Church, New York. He held this position until his retirement in 1947. Williams developed one of the most outstanding music programs in the country at St. Bartholomew's. He was head of the organ department of the Juilliard School of Music and a member of the faculty of the School of Sacred Music, Union Theological Seminary. He also served as a member of the Joint Commission on Church Music and the Joint Commission on the Revision of the Hymnal that produced *The Hymnal* (1940). *The Hymnal 1982* uses five of his tunes, including *Malabar*, used with "Strengthen for Service" (Hymn 312), *Canticum refectionis*, used with "This is the hour of banquet and of song" (Hymn 316), and *Georgetown*, used with "They cast their nets in Galilee" (Hymn 661). Williams died in Oakland, California.

Williams, John (Aug. 30, 1817–Feb. 7, 1899). Founder of Berkeley Divinity School and eleventh Presiding Bishop. He was born in Deerfield, Massachusetts. In 1831 he began his studies at Harvard College. He became an Episcopalian, and at the end of his sophomore year he transferred to Washington College, Hartford, Connecticut, where he graduated in 1835. From 1837 until 1840 he was a tutor at the college. Williams was ordained deacon on Sept. 2, 1838, and priest on Sept. 26, 1841. He was assistant minister at Christ Church, Middletown, Connecticut, 1841–1842, and rector of St. George's Church, Schenectady, New York, 1842–1848. On Aug. 3, 1848, he was elected the fourth president of Trinity College, Hartford, Connecticut, which had been Washington College. He served in that position until 1853. Williams was consecrated Assistant Bishop of Connecticut on Oct. 29, 1851, and he became the fourth Bishop of Connecticut on Jan. 13, 1865. He founded the Berkeley Divinity School at Middletown in 1854 and served as its dean and professor of theology and liturgics until his death. From Apr. 12, 1887, until his death he was the Presiding Bishop of the Episcopal Church. Williams died in Middletown.

Williams, Peter, Jr. (c. 1780–Oct. 17, 1840). The second African American ordained to the Episcopal priesthood. He was born in New Brunswick, New Jersey. Williams's father, Peter Williams, Sr., was one of the founders of the African Methodist Episcopal Zion Church in New York City. Williams, Jr., became associated with a congregation of African American Episcopalians who worshiped at Trinity Church, New York, on Sunday afternoons. Under Williams's leadership this group organized itself in 1818

as a separate congregation and erected a church building. On July 3, 1819, the church for this Episcopal congregation was consecrated as St. Philip's African Church. Williams was ordained deacon on Oct. 20, 1820, and priest on July 10, 1826. He was a leader in the abolition movement and committed to the education of African Americans. Williams died in New York City.

Williams, Ralph Vaughan. *See* Vaughan Williams, Ralph.

Willibrord (658–Nov. 7, 739). He was born in Northumbria, England. He was educated in the monastery at Ripon, where he became a monk. After study in Ireland, he decided he wanted to become a missionary. In 690 he and eleven companions crossed the English Channel to Frisia (Holland). He was consecrated Bishop on Nov. 22, 695. King Pepin III of France designated Utrecht (Wiltaburg) as his seat. Willibrord established a monastery at Echternach in Luxembourg. He was so successful in his missionary work that he is known as the "Apostle of Frisia." His work is commemorated in the Episcopal calendar of the church year on Nov. 7.

Wilmer, Richard Hooker (Mar. 15, 1816–June 14, 1900). The only bishop consecrated by the Protestant Episcopal Church in the Confederate States. He was born in Alexandria, Virginia. His father was William Holland Wilmer, a founder and one of the original members of the faculty of the Virginia Theological Seminary. Richard Wilmer graduated from Yale College in 1836 and from Virginia Seminary in 1839. He was ordained deacon on Mar. 31, 1839, and priest on Apr. 19, 1840. He served parishes in Goochland and Fluvanna counties in Virginia prior to becoming rector of St. James Church in Wilmington, North Carolina. Wilmer returned to Virginia where he continued his ministry in Clarke, Loudon, and Fauquier counties. He also ministered in Bedford County, Virginia, from 1853–1858. In 1858 Wilmer started a mission in Henrico County, Virginia, and that mission grew into Emmanuel Church. He served there until his consecration as the second Bishop of Alabama. He was elected bishop on Nov. 21, 1862. This occurred a little over three months after the Diocese of Alabama decided that the Episcopal Church in Alabama would secede from the Protestant Episcopal Church in the United States. He was consecrated without a majority vote of the House of Bishops and the Standing Committees of the Episcopal Church. A majority of the bishops of the Protestant Episcopal Church in the Confederate States consented to Wilmer's consecration. He was consecrated on Mar. 6, 1862, at St. Paul's Church in Richmond, Virginia. During his episcopate, a Home for Orphans was opened in Tuscaloosa, Alabama, a diocesan Board of Missions was established, a diocesan newspaper was published, attempts were made to organize missionary work, and the financial affairs of the diocese were systematized. After the reunion of the southern dioceses with the Episcopal Church following the Civil War, Wilmer's ordination as a bishop was recognized and accepted by the Episcopal Church. He died in Mobile, Alabama.

Wilmer, William Holland (Oct. 29, 1782–July 24, 1827). Founder and one of the two original members of the faculty of the Virginia Theological Seminary. He was born in Kent County, Maryland, and educated at Washington College, Kent County. He was ordained deacon on Feb. 19, 1808, and began his ordained ministry at Chester Parish, Chestertown, Maryland. On June 16, 1810, he was ordained priest, and from 1812 to 1826 was rector of St. Paul's Church, Alexandria, Virginia. From 1813 to 1814 he was also rector of St. John's Church, Washington. He taught at Virginia Seminary from 1823 to 1826. In 1826 Wilmer became the president of the College of William and Mary and rector of Bruton Parish, Williamsburg. He was a leader in reviving the church in Virginia, and a deputy to the General Conventions of 1814, 1817, 1820, 1821, 1823, and 1826. He served as president of the House of Deputies for five successive General Conventions, 1817–1826. He helped to establish the Society for the Education of Pious Young Men for the Ministry of the Protestant Episcopal Church, and was an editor and principal founder of the *Washington Theological Repertory*, 1819–1823. In 1815 he published *The Episcopal Manual*, which was one of the earliest statements of evangelical doctrines. Richard Hooker Wilmer was his son.

Wilson, Bird (Jan. 8, 1777–Apr. 14, 1859). Professor of theology and priest. He was born in Carlisle, Pennsylvania. Wilson graduated from the University of Pennsylvania in 1792, and was admitted to the bar in 1797. He was president judge of the Court of Common Pleas, Seventh Circuit, Pennsylvania, 1802–1818. Wilson studied for the ordained ministry under Bishop William White. He was ordained deacon on Mar. 12, 1819, and priest in 1820. In 1820–1821, he was rector of St. John's Church, Norristown, and St. Thomas' Church, Whitemarsh, Pennsylvania. Wilson was professor of systematic divinity at the General Theological

Seminary from 1821 until he retired 1850. He was secretary of the House of Bishops from Aug. 12, 1829, until Oct. 6, 1841. Wilson's major publication was *Memoir of the Life of the Rt. Rev. William White* (1839). Wilson died in New York City.

Wilson, William Dexter (Feb. 28, 1816–July 30, 1900). Widely published writer in mathematics, philosophy, and church history. He was born in Stoddard, New Hampshire, and graduated from Harvard Divinity School in 1838. After four years as a Unitarian minister, he joined the Episcopal Church. Wilson was ordained deacon on Apr. 7, 1842, and priest on Sept. 21, 1847. From 1842 to 1850 he served a church in Sherborne, New York, and in 1850 became an instructor in moral and intellectual philosophy in Geneva (later Hobart) College. In 1868 he became professor of moral and intellectual philosophy at the newly founded Cornell University. In 1887 he became the dean of St. Andrew's Divinity School, Syracuse, New York, where he lived until his death. He was the author of *The Church Identified* (1848) and *The Foundations of Religious Belief* (1883).

Windham House, New York City. National graduate training center for women workers in the Episcopal Church. It was purchased by the Woman's Auxiliary as a memorial to Bishop Daniel S. Tuttle. The house was named for Windham, New York, which was Tuttle's birthplace. It opened in 1928. It served as a residential center for furloughed missionaries or women who were training for church work at Columbia University, Teachers' College, Union Theological Seminary, or the New York School of Social Work. The house offered regular worship and special courses, often taught by General Theological Seminary faculty. By 1945 the program had evolved into a two-year training course which included supervised field education. Most Windham House residents enrolled in the Masters of Religious Education program at Union Theological Seminary when that program began in 1954. There was a declining enrollment at Windham House after Episcopal seminaries were opened to women in the 1960s. United Thank Offering support also decreased at this time. Windham House closed on June 30, 1967.

Windsor Statement. This agreed statement on eucharistic doctrine was finalized by the Anglican-Roman Catholic International Commission (ARCIC) at Windsor in 1971. It was eventually included within the ARCIC *Final Report*

(1982). The commission reached consensus on the eucharist as sacrifice and the real presence. An "Elucidation" issued by the commission in 1979 explained that it had reached "unanimous agreement 'on essential matters where it considers that doctrine admits no divergence,'" although it believed that there could still be "a divergence in matters of practice and in theological judgments relating to them." The 1979 General Convention of the Episcopal Church went on to affirm that the Windsor Statement "provide[s] a statement of the faith of this Church in the matters concerned and form[s] a basis upon which to proceed in furthering the growth towards unity of the Episcopal Church with the Roman Catholic Church." Likewise the official response of the 1988 Lambeth Conference found the Windsor Statement, together with the Elucidation, to be "consonant in substance with the faith of Anglicans and . . . a sufficient basis for taking the next step forward towards the reconciliation of our Churches grounded in agreement in faith." However, the Vatican's definitive response to the *Final Report*, finally released in 1991, raised a number of unresolved objections. These objections were answered in the United States by ARC-USA on Jan. 7, 1994, in five "Affirmations on the Eucharist as Sacrifice," agreed to unanimously.

Wine. Alcoholic beverage made from the fermented juice of grapes. Wine and bread are the essential elements of the eucharist. Wine is associated with celebration, fellowship, and joy. In Judaism, bread and wine were used in household worship such as the Sabbath meal and the Passover meal. The synoptic gospels identify Jesus' Last Supper with his disciples on the night before his death as a Passover meal. At this meal Jesus identified the cup of wine with his blood of the new covenant and foretold that he would not again drink "the fruit of the vine" with his disciples until drinking it new with them in the kingdom of God (Mt 26:26–29, Mk 14:22–25, Lk 22:14–20). This identification of Christ's blood of the new covenant with the wine is continued in the institution narratives of the eucharistic prayers of the BCP (pp. 342, 363, 368, 371, 374). Rite 1, Prayer I identifies the wine with Christ's blood of the New Testament (BCP, p. 335). However, the doctrine of concomitance upholds the truth of sacramental theology that Christ's body and blood are both present in each of the eucharistic elements of bread and wine. Christ is understood to be "really present" in a special way in the consecrated elements of bread and wine. The bread and wine constitute the sacramental matter of the eucharist.

It is customary to add a little water to the wine in preparing the altar for the eucharistic prayer. This custom is known as the "mixed chalice." Wine of any color may be used at the eucharist. There is to be only one chalice on the altar during the prayer of consecration. Additional chalices may be filled from a flagon containing consecrated wine after the eucharistic prayer is completed. If there is insufficient wine to distribute to the people, additional wine may be consecrated by the celebrant. Any consecrated wine that is not administered at communion may be consumed by the ministers, reserved, or disposed of in a reverent manner. Some Protestant churches substitute grape juice for wine and substitute individual small cups for the common chalice or cup at their celebrations of communion. *See* Concomitance; *see* Elements, Eucharistic; *see* Matter (Sacramental); *see* Mixed Chalice; *see* Real Presence.

Winkworth, Catherine (Sept. 13, 1827–July 1, 1878). Hymn translator. She was born in London. She was interested in educational and social problems and became secretary of an association for the promotion of higher education for women in 1870, governor of Red Maids' School, Bristol, promoter of Clifton High School for Girls, and a member of the Cheltenham Ladies' College. She was a delegate to the German conference on women's work at Darmstadt in 1872. She is considered one of the best of the translators from German. Her *Lyra Germanica* (1855) was published in two series. The first series went into twenty-three editions and the second into twelve. She also published *Chorale Book for England* (1862). Her *Christian Singers of Germany* (1869) contained biographies of German hymnwriters. A number of her translations were included in *Hymns Ancient and Modern*. *The Hymnal 1982* uses nine of her translations, including "Once he came in blessing" (53), "Comfort, comfort ye my people" (67), and "Deck thyself, my soul, with gladness" (339). She died in Monnetier in Savoy, France.

Wisconsin, Diocese of. In 1836 Wisconsin was organized as a Missionary territory under the jurisdiction of Bishop Samuel A. McCroskey of Michigan. On Sept. 12, 1838, the House of Bishops voted to give jurisdiction over Wisconsin to Jackson Kemper, Missionary Bishop of Indiana and Missouri. On June 24–25, 1847, the Diocese of Wisconsin was organized at St. Paul's Church, Milwaukee. Bishop Kemper resigned his missionary jurisdiction on Oct. 8, 1859, to become the first Bishop of

Wisconsin. The 1874 General Convention divided the Diocese of Wisconsin and created the Diocese of Fond du Lac. On June 16, 1886, the Diocese of Wisconsin was changed to the Diocese of Milwaukee. In 1928 the General Convention created a new diocese, the Diocese of Eau Claire, from the dioceses of Milwaukee and Fond du Lac. The state of Wisconsin now includes the dioceses of Milwaukee, Fond du Lac, and Eau Claire.

Wisdom Literature. The wisdom literature of the OT consists of the books of Proverbs, Job, and Ecclesiastes (Qoheleth). Among the books of the Apocrypha, Ecclesiasticus (The Wisdom of Jesus the son of Sirach) and the Wisdom of Solomon also belong to this wisdom category. In contrast to other parts of the OT, such as the Pentateuch and the former and latter prophets, which stress God's initiative in revealing the divine nature and will for his people, Israel's earliest wisdom literature stressed the human search for order in society and nature. In Israel the main roots of the wisdom movement were 1) the family and clan, as suggested by many of the Proverbs where the parent admonishes the child; and 2) the royal court in Jerusalem where Solomon reigned and is said to have been a source of wisdom (1 Kgs 4:29–34). It was presumably for this reason that the authorship of Proverbs and Ecclesiastes are attributed to him. The wisdom movement continued through the intertestamental period when God was clearly identified as the author of order, termed wisdom. According to Ecclesiasticus (1:4), wisdom (a feminine noun) was God's first creation. Eventually wisdom was personified, attributed a heavenly status and even viewed as God's first-born. St. Paul identifies Christ with the wisdom of God (1 Cor 1:24).

Witness, The. Monthly journal published by the Episcopal Church Publishing Company. It was founded in 1917 as an organization financially independent from the Episcopal Church. The first issue appeared on Jan. 6, 1917. At first it was edited by Bishop Irving Peake Johnson (1866–1947) of Colorado. It was a weekly publication until June 10, 1937. Johnson envisioned a publication that was accessible to the working class. In the earlier years, *The Witness* combined traditional church news and advertising with impassioned editorials concerning workers' rights and other issues of religious and social consequence. Under the Rev. William Benjamin Spofford (1892–1972), who succeeded Johnson as editor, the periodical became embroiled in the Industrial Democracy movement. The activist nature of *The Witness* was thus established. Although it has undergone changes in frequency of publication and appearance, it retains its emphasis on social action and justice in light of the gospel. Its roots remain Episcopal, but its readership is ecumenical.

Woman's Auxiliary to the Board of Missions; Woman's Auxiliary to the National Council. It was founded in 1872 to enlist women in the church's missionary efforts. The Woman's Auxiliary grew to include chapters in every domestic and missionary district and became the church's largest missionary organization. The auxiliary raised funds, publicized the missionary program, provisioned mission stations, and recruited and trained women missionaries. In 1889 it began the United Offering (renamed United Thank Offering in 1919) which provided funds for a wide range of innovative missionary projects. Beginning in 1874 the auxiliary's program was set at triennial meetings held in conjunction with the General Convention. Its program was administered through diocesan and local chapters. In 1919 the organization's name was changed to Woman's Auxiliary to the National Council. In 1958 it became Women of the Protestant Episcopal Church with local groups called Episcopal Church Women (ECW). Corresponding to the enlarged mandate of the National Council, the Woman's Auxiliary also enlarged its work to include departments of Christian Education and Christian Social Relations along with its longstanding department of Missions. The Auxiliary was not represented on the National Council until 1934 when four women were added to the twenty-eight member board. However, auxiliary members did serve on the boards of the various departments. *See* Episcopal Church Women (ECW).

Women in Mission and Ministry (W!MM). Since 1985, primary responsibility for women's concerns has been vested in the WIMM office at the Episcopal Church Center. Its program includes a leadership development program consisting of three areas: 1) Women of Vision/Unidas En Liderazgo, Gaining Authority through Training, Education and Service, and the Creative Journey—designed to empower women to minister in all areas of their lives—self, family, church and world; 2) the Council for Women's Ministries, a body made up of representatives of over twenty women's organizations within the Episcopal Church which facilitates cooperative programming among the members; and 3) an international initiative that has worked to strengthen ties with worldwide religious networks, particularly the Anglican Women's Network.

Women's Ordination Now (WON). U.S. advocates of women's ordination to the priesthood and episcopate formed WON in Feb. 1975 as a support group for the women who were ordained priests in Philadelphia the previous year and to lobby for general church acceptance of women's ordination. In the campaign for national church approval of women's ordination, WON's strategy was to concentrate on supporting the priestly ministry of the women ordained in Philadelphia and Washington, D.C. and supporting those clergy who invited the women to celebrate the eucharist in their parishes. WON's chief concern at the 1976 General Convention was to see that those fifteen women priests were recognized as priests and allowed to function as priests without penalties. With that goal accomplished, WON's organizational structure disintegrated shortly after the 1976 General Convention. *See* Philadelphia Eleven, The.

Women's Triennial. The Triennial Meeting of the Women of the Episcopal Church has been held in conjunction with General Convention since 1874. The women's organization has been known by several different names during this period: The Woman's Auxiliary to the Board of Missions, the Women's Auxiliary to the National Council, the Women of the Episcopal Church, and the Episcopal Church Women (ECW). Including representatives of each diocesan ECW and other specified women's organizations, the Triennial Meeting combines inspiration, education, program development, and political organization. The national board of Episcopal Church Women is responsible for administering the Triennial.

Wonder, Love, And Praise: A Supplement to The Hymnal 1982. An eclectic collection of two hundred hymns, songs, and spiritual songs with a selection of service music and devotional pieces, published by Church Publishing Incorporated in 1997. It is a resource for parish functions, home use, and Sunday worship. It includes twelve bilingual hymns, and twenty-nine selections of music for table graces, rounds, and acclamations. It also includes selections from *Music from Taizé*. It includes a *Leader's Guide* in a separate volume, which provides full accompaniments and background information on each musical selection.

Wood Bridge Newsletter, The. Published by members of the Anglo-Orthodox Society in the Diocese of Albany to bring the society to the attention of Episcopalians. The Anglo-Orthodox Society was founded in England. Its purpose is the "revival of Orthodoxy within the Anglican Communion, and the promotion of unity in truth." Its members "affirm the true Faith of Anglicans is the Faith of the One Church before the division between east and west, defined by the Seven Ecumenical Councils. They recognize that this same Faith is professed by the Orthodox Churches of the East in communion with Constantinople." The society promotes the restoration of unity according to the canon of truth taught by St. Vincent of Lérins, "That which has been believed everywhere, always and by all." The newsletter began publication in Aug. 1992. *See* Vincentian Canon.

Worcester, Elwood (May 16, 1862–July 19, 1940). Founder of the Emmanuel Movement. He was born in Massillon, Ohio, and grew up in Rochester, New York. Worcester graduated from Columbia College in 1887 and then studied at General Theological Seminary. From 1888 until 1890 he was superintendent of the Sunday School at St. Ann's, Brooklyn. He was ordained deacon on Feb. 6, 1890, and priest on May 23, 1891. Worcester also studied at the University of Leipzig, where he focused on experimental psychology and psychosomatic relationships. He received his Ph.D. from Leipzig in 1889. From 1890 until 1896 he was chaplain and professor of philosophy, psychology, and Christian evidences at Lehigh University in Bethlehem, Pennsylvania. In 1896 he became the rector of St. Stephen's Church, Philadelphia. From 1904 until his retirement in 1929 he was the rector of Emmanuel Church, Boston. While at Emmanuel he sought to combine Christianity and medicine in ministry. This healing ministry became known as the "Emmanuel Movement." It was noted for the Christian application of psychotherapy to nervous disorders and was one of the major healing ministries in the history of the Episcopal Church. Among his numerous publications were *Religion and Medicine* (1908), and *The Christian Religion as a Healing Power* (1909). Worcester died in Kennebunkport, Maine. *See* Emmanuel Movement.

Word of God, The. This phrase can indicate the effective and creative verbal expression of God's power; or the Holy Scriptures that were written under God's inspiration; or Jesus Christ, the *Logos*, the eternal Son of God, the Word made flesh (Jn 1:1–14). The power of God's creative word is shown in Genesis (1:3) when God said "'let there be light'; and there was light." The heavens and all the heavenly hosts were made by the word of God (Ps 33:6). God's word is also communicated in the OT through the law and the prophets. The decalogue is literally the ten words of God, and the law is identified with the word of God in the OT (see Dt 4:13, 5:6–21; Ex 20:2–17, 34:28). The prophets proclaimed the word of God with power, making known God's righteous will. The word of God was like fire (Jer 20:9, 23:29), and effective (Is 55:11). As stated in Hebrews (4:12), "the word of God is living and active, sharper than any two-edged sword, piercing until it divides soul from spirit, joints from marrow; it is able to judge the thoughts and intentions of the heart." As the word of God conveyed revelation, the term also was applied to the gospel of Jesus (see Lk 5:1, 8:1, 11:28, Jn 3:34) and the gospel as preached by the apostles (see Acts 4:31; 13:44, 48; 16:32). The scriptures were inspired by God (see 2 Tm 3:16, 2 Pt 1:21), and are termed the word of God. The Catechism notes that we call the scriptures the Word of God "because God inspired their human authors and because God still speaks to us through the Bible" (BCP, p. 853). After the lessons at Morning and Evening Prayer and at the eucharist, the reader may say, "The Word of the Lord" (see BCP, pp. 84, 119, 357). A literalistic view holds that the Bible contains God's actual words which were dictated to inspired scribes who put the words on paper. Few Anglicans would endorse this literalistic view. Others have suggested that the authors or editors of biblical material communicated their faith in their own words after being inspired by God. The ultimate expression of God's word was not in law, prophecy, or scripture, but in Jesus Christ, the incarnate Word of God. *See* Scripture; *see* Logos.

Words of Administration (of Communion). Ministers of the sacrament say these words as the bread and wine are given to the communicants. In a Rite 2 Eucharist, the ministers may say "The Body (Blood) of our Lord Jesus Christ keep you in everlasting life" or "The Body of Christ, the bread of heaven/The Blood of Christ, the cup of salvation" (BCP, p. 365). In a Rite 1 Eucharist, the ministers also may use the historic words of administration derived from the 1559 Prayer Book, which identified the sacrament as the body and blood of Christ and urged the communicant to receive the sacrament "in remembrance" of Christ's sacrifice (BCP, p. 338).

Words of Institution. *See* Institution Narrative.

Wordsworth, Christopher (Oct. 30, 1807–Mar. 21, 1885). Hymn writer and bishop. A nephew of the poet William Wordsworth, he was born at Lambeth, where his father was rector. He was educated at Winchester School and Trinity College, Cambridge, where he served as a fellow from 1830 to 1836. Wordsworth was headmaster at Harrow School, 1836–1844. He was canon of Westminster, 1844–1869, and was also vicar of Stanford-in-the-Vale-cum-Goosey, Berkshire. Wordsworth was the Hulsean lecturer at Cambridge from 1848 until 1849. He was rural dean from 1850–1869, and Archdeacon of Westminster, 1865–1869. He was Bishop of Lincoln, 1869–1885. He was a celebrated Greek scholar and published in several fields. Wordsworth frequently visited and corresponded with William Wordsworth, and began hymn writing after the poet's death in 1850. He continued to write hymns until he became Bishop of Lincoln in 1869. Wordsworth believed hymns to be "one of the most efficacious instruments for correcting error and for disseminating truth, as well as for ministering comfort and edification." His *The Holy Year; or Hymns for Sundays and Holy Days throughout the Year*, came out in 1862. *The Hymnal 1982* uses eight of his hymns, including "O day of radiant gladness" (Hymn 48), "Songs of thankfulness and praise" (Hymn 135, stanzas 1–3), and "See the conqueror mounts in triumph" (Hymn 215). He died in Lincoln shortly after he resigned as Bishop of Lincoln.

Worker Sisters of the Holy Spirit, The (WSHS)/Worker Brothers of the Holy Spirit, The (WBHS). International Covenant Community which was founded in Kansas City, Missouri, by Sister Angela Blackburn on Dec. 1, 1972. The Worker Brothers were started in 1979. The Community was officially recognized by the Standing Committee on Religious Orders of the House of Bishops on Oct. 3, 1984. The Community is open to all women and men, regardless of marital status. It is Benedictine in orientation, but the members do not live together. There are five categories of membership: First Order—the Worker Sisters of the Holy Spirit (lay workers and lay sisters); Second Order—The Worker Brothers of the Holy Spirit (lay workers and lay brothers); Third Order—clergy sisters and clergy brothers; Companions—lay and clergy persons; Friends—lay and clergy persons. The first three orders are bound together under a life commitment to a rule of life. To become a Lay Worker requires a year of preparation, and three years are required for Sisters and Brothers. Companions make a commitment to pray for the community and are encouraged to live under a rule of life. Friends can share their spiritual journey in the community.

World Conference on Faith and Order. Charles Henry Brent was the Episcopal leader in the Faith and Order Movement. He persuaded the 1910 General Convention to request an international meeting to discuss the unity of the church. The 1910 General Convention passed a resolution "that a joint commission be appointed to bring about a conference for the consideration of questions touching on Faith and Order." Under his leadership a preparatory meeting was held at Geneva to plan a world conference on Faith and Order. The first World Conference on Faith and Order met at Lausanne, Switzerland, Aug. 3–21, 1927. The second World Conference on Faith and Order met at Edinburgh, Scotland, Aug. 3–18, 1937. The World Conference on Faith and Order and the World Conference on Life and Work merged at a meeting in Amsterdam on Aug. 23, 1948, to create the World Council of Churches. The World Council of Churches continues to have a Commission on Faith and Order. *See* World Council of Churches (WCC).

World Council of Churches (WCC). The WCC was officially organized at Amsterdam, Aug. 22–Sept. 4, 1948. Its roots go back to the early 1900s and the World Missionary Conference at Edinburgh in 1910. The Faith and Order Movement and the Life and Work Movement were the two major streams that created the WCC. The 1937 General Convention endorsed the proposed WCC and named three representatives, Bishop James DeWolfe Perry, Bishop George Craig Stewart, and Mrs. Henry Hill Pierce, to attend the conference at Utrecht, Holland, May 9–12, 1938. The conference adopted a constitution which stated the basis of the WCC: "The World Council of Churches is a fellowship of Churches which accept our Lord Jesus Christ as God and Saviour." The 1940 General Convention officially accepted the invitation to become a constituent member of the WCC. Delayed by World War II, the First Assembly of the World Council of Churches met at Amsterdam, Aug. 22–Sept. 4, 1948. The Episcopal Church was represented by Bishop Angus Dun, Bishop Henry Knox Sherrill, the Very Rev. William Hamilton Nels, and Mr. Charles Phelps Taft. In 1993 the WCC had 326 member churches, including almost every Province of the Anglican Communion.

World Mission, Standing Commission on. The 1979 General Convention established this commission. Its purpose is to review, evaluate, plan, and propose policy on overseas mission to the General Convention. It includes twelve members: three bishops, three presbyters or deacons, and six lay persons. Half of the members must come from jurisdictions outside the continental United States.

Worship. The term, from the Anglo Saxon, means to pay someone what is their due. It was used in the sixteenth century relative to God and human beings. In the Sarum and English Prayer Book marriage rites, the groom said to the bride, " . . . with my body I thee worship." Certain British magistrates are still addressed as "Your Worship." Today, it refers to the paying of divine honor to God. It is both a verb and a noun, used to translate the Latin verb *adorare* and the noun *cultus* and their equivalents in other languages. It was defined by Evelyn Underhill as "the response of the creature to the Eternal." It is a very broad term concerning acts of adoration, which may be as diverse as private prayer and meditation, public corporate liturgies, prayer services, or cultic sacrifices. Christian worship, both individual and corporate, is offered through and in the name of Jesus Christ.

Worthington College, Worthington, Ohio. Former church-related college. In the summer of 1817 the Rev. Philander Chase moved to Worthington and soon became principal of the academy there. On Feb. 8, 1819, the legislature gave the academy a college charter and Chase became president. In 1821 Chase moved to Cincinnati, and in 1828 the teachers and students moved to Kenyon College. In 1830 the college became the "Reformed Medical College" with no Episcopal connection.

Wright, Elizabeth Evelyn (Lizzie) (Apr. 3, 1872–Dec. 14, 1906). Pioneer educator among African Americans. She was born in Talbotton, Georgia. Wright was the seventh child of an African American carpenter and former slave, John Wesley Wright, and a full-blooded Cherokee Indian mother, Virginia Rolfe. Wright graduated from Tuskegee Industrial School in 1894. She was determined to open schools for the training of African American men and women. After numerous setbacks, she founded the Denmark Industrial School for Colored Youth at Denmark, South Carolina. It opened in Apr. 1897. Wright served as principal until her death. In 1902 the name was changed to Voorhees Industrial School in honor of the generosity of

Ralph and Elizabeth Rodman Voorhees. Wright died in Denmark, South Carolina. *See* Voorhees College, Denmark, South Carolina.

Wuhu, Missionary District of. On Oct. 11, 1910, the House of Bishops voted to divide the Missionary District of Hankow in China and create the Missionary District of Wuhu. It was known as the Missionary District of Wuhu until Oct. 17, 1913, when the name was changed to the Missionary District of Anking. It became a part of the Holy Catholic Church in China in 1949.

Wulfstan (c. 1008–Jan. 18, 1095). Bishop of Worcester during the Norman Conquest. He was born in Long Itchington, near Warwick, England, and educated at the monastic schools at Evesham and Peterborough. Wulfstan was ordained between 1033 and 1038. He became a monk at Worcester, where he later became prior. On Sept. 8, 1062, he was consecrated Bishop of Worcester and served there until his death. He submitted to William the Conqueror at Berkhamstead in 1066, and thus was able to retain his see. As a supporter of William the Conqueror and William II, he helped the church in England in its transition from Anglo-Saxon Christianity to Anglo-Norman Christianity. Wulfstan was canonized in 1203. He is commemorated in the Episcopal calendar of the church year on Jan. 19.

Wycliffe, John (c. 1330–1384). English reformer of the fourteenth century. Wycliffe was born in Ipreswell (now Hipswell) in Yorkshire, England. He entered Oxford University around 1345 and received his doctorate in theology around 1372. Wycliffe was appointed rector of Fillingham, Lincolnshire, in 1361, warden of Canterbury Hall in 1365, rector of Ludgershall in 1368, and finally rector of Lutterworth in 1374, where he remained until his death. He was a critic of the worldly papacy of the fourteenth century and an opponent of monasticism. He argued that monasticism placed one class of Christians above another, and he called for the dissolution of all the monasteries. His primary criticism was of the doctrine of transubstantiation. He insisted that the bread and wine remain bread and wine after the consecration. He taught that the church is not centered in the Pope and the Cardinals but that the church is the whole company of the elect and its only head is Christ. Wycliffe claimed that the Bible is the only standard for Christian faith and practice and that it should be read in English. He and others translated the Bible from the Vulgate into English. This was his major achievement as a reformer. His published treatises included *De Dominio Divino* (1375), *De Civili Dominio* (1376), *De Ecclesia* (1378), and *De Potestate Papae* (1379). On May 22, 1377, Pope Gregory XI issued five bulls condemning the work of Wycliffe. He died in Lutterworth. The Council of Constance in 1415 condemned 267 errors in his teaching, ordered that his books be burned and that his bones be dug up and burned. Wycliffe's followers were called Lollards. He has been called the "Morning Star of the Reformation."

Wyoming, Diocese of. Wyoming was part of the Missionary District of the Northwest from Oct. 19, 1859, until Oct. 21, 1865, when it came under the jurisdiction of the Missionary District of Colorado and Parts Adjacent. From Oct. 4, 1866, until Oct. 30, 1874, it was part of the Missionary District of Colorado, New Mexico and Wyoming. On Oct. 30, 1874, the House of Bishops changed it to the Missionary District of Colorado with jurisdiction in Wyoming. On Oct. 14, 1886, the Bishops formed the Missionary District of Wyoming and Idaho, and the 1898 General Convention changed it to the Missionary District of Boise. On Oct. 10, 1907, the House of Bishops formed the Missionary District of Wyoming. The 1967 General Convention made it the Diocese of Wyoming. The primary convention of the diocese was held at St. Matthew's Cathedral, Laramie, on Jan. 30, 1968. The cornerstone of St. Matthew's Cathedral was laid on Sept. 21, 1892, and it was dedicated on Dec. 17, 1896. The Cathedral was consecrated on Aug. 11, 1901. The Diocese of Wyoming includes the entire state of Wyoming.

Y

Yahwist, or Jahwist, The. Name given to one of the four sources of the Pentateuch by scholars who accept the Documentary Theory of the Pentateuch's composition. It is called the Yahwist because it uses the name Yahweh for God from the time of creation (Gn 2). It is found in the books of Genesis, Exodus, Numbers, and perhaps Judges 1:1–2:5. It tells of the creation and the primeval history, the ancestors, the oppression of the Hebrew people and the call of Moses, the Exodus, the covenant at Sinai, and the wilderness wanderings. Thus it provided the basic outline for the entire Pentateuch. It may have been written in Jerusalem around 950 B.C.

Yale Converts. On Sept. 13, 1722, the day after commencement at Yale College, seven Congregationalist clergy from Connecticut met with the Yale trustees and announced that they questioned the validity of their ordinations. The seven were Timothy Cutler, rector of Yale College, Daniel Brown, tutor at Yale College, Samuel Johnson, minister at Stratford, James Wetmore, minister at North Haven, John Hart, minister at East Guilford, Jared Eliot, minister at Killingworth, and Samuel Whittlesey, minister at Wallingford. This has been called the "Great Apostasy," and "the dark day." Brown, Cutler, Johnson, and Wetmore sailed to England, where they were ordained deacons and then priests. Brown died abroad, but Cutler, Johnson, and Wetmore returned to America and served as Anglican clergy. Cutler began a long ministry in Boston. Wetmore went to Rye, New York, and Johnson went to Stratford, Connecticut. Johnson completed the first Anglican church building in Connecticut and acted as "dean" of the Society for the Propagation of the Gospel (SPG) missionaries in Connecticut for some twenty years. Johnson was also the first president of King's College (later Columbia) where he began to serve in 1754.

Yedo, Missionary District of. The General Convention of 1874 constituted Japan a missionary district and named it the Missionary District of Yedo. Its name was changed to the Missionary District of Tokyo in 1893.

York College, York, Pennsylvania. York College traces its origins to an academy founded in 1787 by the Rev. John Andrews (1746–1813), rector of St. John's Church. The Diocese of Central Pennsylvania took over the school in 1873. The first two principals were the Rev. Octavius Perinchief (d. 1877), and the Rev. Henry Lafayette Phillips (1830–1906). It no longer has any connection with the Episcopal Church.

Young Christian Soldier, The. Periodical for youth published by the Domestic and Foreign Missionary Society from 1867 to 1911. Its editors included Marie H. Bullfinch 1867–71, Susan Lavinia Emery, 1871–74, and Julia Chester Emery, 1874–76. The magazine was published monthly until 1873 when it absorbed another journal, *Carrier Dove*, and became a weekly magazine. Seeking to involve children in the church's missionary endeavor, the magazine enrolled each young subscriber in the "missionary army." The missionary army was organized into platoons with a current missionary bishop leading each platoon. Current news from the mission field was presented along with edifying tales and pious poetry.

Young Churchman Company, The. A publishing company founded in 1885. In 1918 its name was changed to Morehouse Publishing Company. Young Churchman published hundreds of books during its existence.

Young Churchman's Miscellany, The. This monthly magazine had the subtitle "A Magazine of Religious and Entertaining Knowledge." It was published at New York from Jan. 1846 until Dec. 1848. The editor and proprietor was Jesse Ames Spencer (1816–1898), an Episcopal priest.

Young, John Freeman (Oct. 30, 1820–Nov. 15, 1885). Teacher of liturgics and church music, and Bishop of Florida. He was born in Pittston, Maine. Young attended Wesleyan University, Middletown, Connecticut. He graduated from the Virginia Theological Seminary in 1845. He was ordained deacon on Apr. 20, 1845, and priest on Jan. 11, 1846. Young began his ministry as rector of St. John's Church, Jacksonville, Florida. In 1846 he moved to Texas, where he was a missionary in Brazoria County. He then did missionary work in Livingston, Madison County, Mississippi. In 1852 he moved to Napoleonville, Louisiana, where he was rector of Assumption Parish. In 1860 Young became the assistant rector at Trinity Church, New York City. He was secretary of the Russo-Greek Committee of the General Convention. In 1864 he edited the papers of that committee, which encouraged intercommunion of the eastern, English, and American churches. Young was consecrated the second Bishop of Florida on July 25, 1867, and served in that position until his death. In 1882–1883 the Department of Liturgics and Ecclesiastical Music was added to the School of Theology, University of the South. Young was named lecturer in that department. He served there as lecturer until his death. Among his publications were *Papers on Liturgical Enrichment* (1883) and *Great Hymns of the Church* (1887). Young died in New York.

Young People's Fellowship (YPF). *See* Episcopal Young Church People (EYC).

Youth Quest. This independent organization is dedicated to the revitalization of the Episcopal Church through youth ministry in the areas of education, research, evangelism, social action, spiritual formation, networking, and publication. Youth Quest assists parishes with programs for young people (junior age through college age). Its program includes the Josiah Project which trains and places teams of students in summer ministries of evangelism and service to the poor.

YouthVision. The vision for this training network began through the work of the Rev. John Palarine in his role as canon for youth and education in the Diocese of Central Florida. In 1991 Palarine combined with the Rev. Timothy Sexton, then canon for youth and young adult ministries in the Diocese of Utah, to form YouthVision. A primary goal of YouthVision is to develop and implement "Youth Growth," a program of outreach and evangelism throughout the church. Youth Growth focuses on the growth and development of a church's youth ministry through a two-year training and support program. It also offers a method for building community and developing strong teenage leaders. YouthVision serves as a referral source for the networking of youth leaders, and it offers leadership training programs for young people.

Z

Zabriskie, Alexander Clinton (Jan. 21, 1898–June 24, 1956). Priest and educator. He was born in New York City. Zabriskie received his B.A. in 1920 from Princeton University and his B.D. in 1924 from the Virginia Theological Seminary. He was ordained deacon on June 15, 1924, and served at St. John's Church, New York. He was ordained priest on Dec. 20, 1924. He soon joined the faculty at Virginia Seminary, where he taught church history. From 1931 until 1940 he was professor of medieval and modern church history. From 1940 until 1950 he was the dean of Virginia Seminary. Under his leadership the parish of Immanuel Church-on-the-Hill was organized in May 1941, and Zabriskie served as its first rector. In 1946

the seminary gave a parcel of its land to the parish on which to build a rectory, a parish hall, and later a chapel, named Zabriskie Chapel. Zabriskie resigned as dean in 1950 and returned to teaching church history. He edited and contributed to *Anglican Evangelicalism* (1943). Zabriskie died in Alexandria.

Zebra Book. *See* Authorized Services (1973), or the "Zebra Book".

Zeon. In the eastern liturgical tradition, hot water is added to the chalice after the breaking of the bread to symbolize the descent of the Spirit and the vibrant energy of faith. This practice is known as the *zeon*. The term is from the Greek for "boiling."

Zuchetto. A skullcap worn by clerics. It is small, round, and its color may reflect the order of ministry of the wearer. It may be worn at the eucharist, but it is removed during the eucharistic canon.

Zurich Consensus. *See* Protestantism.

Zwingli, Huldreich (Ulrich) (Jan. 1, 1484–Oct. 11, 1531). The leading Protestant Reformer in German-speaking Switzerland. His receptionist understanding of the eucharist may have had some influence on Thomas Cranmer and subsequent Anglican theology. He was born in Wildhaus, Switzerland. Zwingli received his B.A. in 1504 and his M.A. in 1506, both from the University of Basel. He was ordained to the priesthood in 1506 and for the next ten years was the pastor at Glarus. In 1516 Zwingli became the parish priest at Einseideln. On Jan. 1, 1519, he became the priest in the Great Minster in Zurich, where he remained the rest of his life. He died in a military battle at Kappel. *See* Protestantism.

Contributors

Don S. Armentrout has taught church history at the School of Theology, the University of the South, since 1967. He is professor of church history and historical theology and associate dean of academic affairs at the School of Theology. He is the co-editor of *Documents of Witness, A History of the Episcopal Church, 1782–1985* and editor of *A DuBose Reader*.

Edward Oscar de Bary is director of the Education for Ministry program at the School of Theology, the University of the South. He is an associate faculty member at the School of Theology and was on the Board of Theological Education, 1991–1997. He served parishes in the Diocese of Mississippi.

Sandra Hughes Boyd is a member of the adjunct faculty of Regis University, 1992–. She was also a member of the adjunct faculty and reference librarian at Episcopal Divinity School, 1978–1986. She was editor of the Episcopal Women's History Project Newsletter, 1988–1995, vice president of the Episcopal Women's History Project, 1981–1988, and director of the Deaconess History Project, 1983–1985. She received the Whitely Award for Excellence in Sociology of Religion, Iliff School of Theology, 1996. She is the co-editor of *Women in American Religious History: An Annotated Bibliography and Guide to Sources* and editor of *Cultivating Our Roots: A Guide to Gathering Church Women's History*.

Mary Sudman Donovan has served as substitute assistant professor, Hunter College of the City University of New York, 1994–. She was a lecturer in history, University of Arkansas at Little Rock, 1981–1993, and lecturer in history, Drew University, Madison, New Jersey, 1978–1980. She has served as a visiting sabbatical professor, the General Theological Seminary, and a visiting lecturer in church history, the Virginia Theological Seminary. She served as president of the Historical Society of the Episcopal Church, 1991–, and as a member of the Board of Trustees of General Seminary, 1990–1996. She is the author of *Women Priests in the Episcopal Church: The Experience of the First Decade* and *A Different Call: Women's Ministries in the Episcopal Church, 1850–1920*.

Travis Talmadge Du Priest is director of the DeKoven Center and warden of the shrine of Blessed James DeKoven in Racine, Wisconsin. He also teaches literature and non-fiction writing classes as a member of the faculty of Carthage College in Kenosha, Wisconsin, and serves as book editor of *The Living Church* magazine. He is chaplain for the Community of St. Mary (Western Province).

Richard A. Edwards is associate professor in the Department of Theology at Marquette University, where he has served since 1978. He has also been an assistant and an associate professor at Virginia Tech, 1972–1978, and at Thiel College, 1968–1972. He is the author of *Matthew's Narrative Portrait of Disciples: How the Text-Connoted Reader is Informed* and *Matthew's Story of Jesus*.

James C. Fenhagen was dean and president of the General Theological Seminary, 1978–1992, and director of the Cornerstone Project of the Episcopal Church Foundation, 1992–1994. He was also director of the Church and Ministry Program, Hartford Seminary, 1973–1978. He served parishes in Maryland, South Carolina, and Washington, D.C. His publications include *Invitation to Holiness* and *Ministry for a New Time*.

Reginald H. Fuller was Molly Laird Downs Professor of New Testament at the Virginia Theological Seminary, 1972–1985. He also served as Baldwin Professor of Sacred Literature at Union Theological Seminary, New York, 1966–1972, professor of New Testament languages and literature, Seabury-Western Theological Seminary, 1955–1966, and professor of theology, St. David's College, Lampeter, Wales, 1950–1955. He participated in the national Lutheran-Episcopal dialogues (I-II), and the international Anglican-Lutheran dialogue. He is the author of *Foundations of New Testament Christology* and *Preaching the Lectionary*.

John M. Gessell served on the faculty of the School of Theology of the University of the South from 1961 to 1984. He was professor of Christian education, assistant to the dean, and professor of Christian ethics. He was editor of *St. Luke's Journal of Theology*, 1972–1990. He received the John Nevin Sayre peacemaker's award from the Episcopal Peace Fellowship in 1994.

Joanna Bowen Gillespie has served as adjunct professor of church and society at Bangor Theological Seminary, Hanover, New Hampshire. She was an associate professor at Drew University, 1972–1978, and visiting professor, 1984–1990. She was a co-founder of the Episcopal Women's History Project, a founding member of the Council of Women Ministers, and coordinator for Twentieth Century Episcopal Women in the Lilly Mainstream Protestant Study, 1987–1991. She is the author of *Women Speak: of God, Congregations, and Change.*

Raymond F. Glover is professor of music and chapel organist at the Virginia Theological Seminary. He was general editor of *The Hymnal 1982*, and editor of *The Hymnal 1982 Companion*. He was president of the Association of Diocesan Liturgical and Music Commissions and the Association of Anglican Musicians. He was a member of the Standing Commission on Church Music of the Episcopal Church, 1970–1980. He served as organist and choirmaster of the episcopal cathedrals in Buffalo, New York, and Hartford, Connecticut, and of St. Paul's Church, Richmond, Virginia. He taught at Berkeley Divinity School, 1964–1970, and was head of the music department, St. Catherine's School, Richmond, Virginia, 1976–1980. He is the author of *A Commentary on New Hymns*.

James E. Griffiss is editor of the *Anglican Theological Review*, and theological consultant to the Presiding Bishop. He has served as visiting professor of theology at Seabury-Western since 1995. He was William Adams Professor of Philosophical and Systematic Theology at Nashotah House, 1971–1990. He also taught at the Seminary of the Caribbean, 1961–1971, and the Church Divinity School of the Pacific, 1990–1991. He has participated in various ecumenical conversations. His publications include *The Anglican Vision* and *Naming the Mystery*. He is general editor of The New Church's Teaching Series.

Marion J. Hatchett was professor of liturgics and church music at the School of Theology, the University of the South, where he taught, 1969–1999. He served parishes in South Carolina. He was chair of the Text Committee for *The Hymnal 1982* and chair of the Committee for *The Book of Occasional Services*. He served on the Standing Liturgical Commission, 1977–1982. He is the author of *Sanctifying Life, Time, and Space*, and *Commentary on the American Prayer Book*.

Charles R. Henery is professor of church history and homiletics at Nashotah House, 1996–, where he has taught since 1983. He is also priest-in-charge of St. John Chrysostom, Delafield, Wisconsin. He served parishes in New Hampshire and New York. He was a fellow and tutor at the General Theological Seminary. He is editor of *Beyond the Horizon: Frontiers for Mission.*

William Lawrence Hicks served parishes in North Carolina, Kentucky, South Carolina, and Arizona. He was rector of Resurrection, Greenwood, South Carolina, 1964–1983, and rector of St. Francis in the Valley, Green Valley, Arizona, 1983–1991. He retired in 1991.

Maurice Fred Himmerich was rector, St. Paul's, Watertown, Wisconsin, 1965–1995, and an adjunct instructor at Nashotah House at various times from 1970–1990. He retired in 1995. He was interim dean, All Saints Cathedral, Milwaukee, 1997–1998.

Robert D. Hughes is professor of systematic theology at the School of Theology, the University of the South, 1992–. He has taught at the School of Theology since 1977. He was a fellow of the Episcopal Church Foundation.

Sr. Brigit Carol Lay, S.D., is a solitary religious under vows to the bishop of the Diocese of West Texas. She took James DeKoven as her patron, so she is known as a Solitary of DeKoven. She currently lives as a hermit in a rural area of south central Texas, and spends a regular time in residence yearly at the DeKoven Center in Racine, Wisconsin. She previously served as a psychotherapist and mental health consultant.

Leonel Lake Mitchell has served parishes in New York and Indiana. He was professor of liturgics, Seabury-Western Theological Seminary, 1978–1995. He also served as assistant professor, Department of Theology, University of Notre Dame, 1971–1978, as well as director of M.A. program, 1974–1978, and summer session chairman, 1975–

1980, at Notre Dame. He was a lecturer in church history and liturgics, Berkeley Divinity School, 1969–1971. He has served on the Standing Commission on Liturgy and Music of the Episcopal Church. He is the author of *Lent Holy Week Easter, and the Great Fifty Days* and *Pastoral and Occasional Liturgies*.

Rodger Lindsay Patience is coordinator of development services for the Field Museum, Chicago, Illinois. He serves as deacon at the Church of the Holy Communion, Lake Geneva, Wisconsin. He was editor of *The Covenant,* the newspaper for the Diocese of Milwaukee.

Ormonde Plater is archdeacon of the Diocese of Louisiana and serves as a deacon at Grace Episcopal Church in New Orleans. He has been active for many years in the renewal of the diaconate. He is a member of the Council of Associated Parishes, an Anglican group advocating liturgical renewal. In 1997 he was appointed to the Standing Commission on Ministry Development, serving on a task group charged with drafting a theology of ministry for the Episcopal Church. He is the author of several books on ministry and worship, including *Many Servants: An Introduction to the Diaconate* and *Intercession: A Theological and Practical Guide*.

H. Boone Porter was editor of *The Living Church* magazine, 1977–1991. He founded the Leadership Academy for New Directions (LAND), and was director of Roanridge, the national town and country church institute in Kansas City, Missouri. He taught church history at Nashotah House, 1954–1960, and was professor of liturgics at the General Theological Seminary, 1960–1970. He was a member of the Standing Liturgical Commission during the period of Prayer Book revision. He served as priest-in-charge of St. Peter's, North Lake, Wisconsin, 1979–1990. He is the author of *The Day of Light, Keeping the Church Year*, and *A Song of Creation.*

Charles P. Price was on the faculty of the Virginia Theological Seminary from 1956 to 1963. He served as preacher to the university and chairman of the board of preachers at Harvard from 1963 to 1972, and he was appointed Plummer Professor of Christian Morals in 1968. After 1972 he taught theology and liturgics at Virginia Seminary, where he held the William Meade chair in Systematic Theology. He retired in 1989. He is the author of *A Matter of Faith*, and co-author of *Liturgy for Living.*

Fred D. Schneider was professor of commonwealth history at Vanderbilt University, where he taught, 1955–1986. He was also instructor in history, Stanford University, 1950–1955. He served parishes in Tennessee. He served as president of the Southern Conference of British Studies.

Timothy F. Sedgwick is professor of Christian ethics at the Virginia Theological Seminary. He served as professor of Christian ethics and moral theology at Seabury-Western Theological Seminary, 1978–1997. He is a participant in the steering committee for the College of Bishops, and a member of the Episcopal Church's Committee on Sexual Exploitation. His publications include *The Christian Moral Life: Practices of Piety* and *The Making of Ministry.*

Gardiner H. Shattuck, Jr., has served parishes in Massachusetts and Rhode Island. He has taught church history courses in the School for Deacons and in the School for Ministries of the Diocese of Rhode Island, and has served on the governing board of both schools. He also works as an editor at Cowley Publications in Boston. He is author of *A Shield and Hiding Place: The Religious Life of the Civil War Armies* and co-author of *The Encyclopedia of American Religious History.*

Robert Boak Slocum is rector of the Church of the Holy Communion, Lake Geneva, Wisconsin, and a lecturer in theology at Marquette University. He also served parishes in Louisiana. He is co-editor of *Documents of Witness, A History of the Episcopal Church, 1782–1985*, and editor of *Prophet of Justice, Prophet of Life, Essays on William Stringfellow* and *A New Conversation, Essays on the Future of Theology and the Episcopal Church.* He is the author of the forthcoming *Life, Movement, and Being, An Introduction to the Theology of William Porcher DuBose.*

George Wayne Smith is rector of St. Andrew's, Des Moines, Iowa, 1989–. He has served parishes in Texas and Michigan. He is the author of *Admirable Simplicity.*

George H. Tavard is professor emeritus of theology, Methodist Theological School in Ohio. He was "peritus" at Vatican Council II and has been involved in the ecumenical dialogues of the Roman Catholic Church with Anglicans, Lutherans, and Methodists. He is the author of *The Church, Community of Salvation, An Ecumenical Ecclesiology*, and *The Thousand Faces of the Virgin Mary.*

Arthur A Vogel was bishop of the Diocese of West Missouri, 1973–1989, and bishop coadjutor of the Diocese of West Missouri, 1971–1972. He taught at Nashotah House, 1952–1971, where he was sub-dean and William Adams Professor of Philosophical and Systematic Theology, 1965–1971. He served on the first Anglican-Roman Catholic International Commission (ARCIC), 1969–1982, and the second ARCIC, 1983–1990. He also served on the Anglican-Roman Catholic Commission (USA), 1964–1984, of which he was co-chairman, 1973–1983. He is the author of *God, Prayer, and Healing: Living with God in a World Like Ours* and *Radical Christianity and the Flesh of Jesus*.

William C. Wantland was the bishop of the Diocese of Eau Claire, 1980–1999. He also served as interim bishop of Navajoland, 1993–1994. He served as canon law advisor and episcopal visitor for the Anglo-Catholic Studies Program at Duquesne University, Pittsburgh, Pennsylvania, and taught canon law at Nashotah House.

His publications include *Canon Law in the Episcopal Church* and *The Prayer Book and the Catholic Faith*.

John Robert Wright is the St. Mark's Church-in-the-Bowerie Professor of Ecclesiastical History at the General Theological Seminary, where he has taught since 1968. He was also an instructor in church history at the Episcopal Divinity School from 1966 to 1968. He has served Episcopal/Anglican parishes both in England and in America. He has been a member of or consultant to the Anglican-Roman Catholic Consultation (USA), and he serves as theological consultant to the ecumenical office of the Episcopal Church. He has been a visiting professor at Nashotah House, Philadelphia Divinity School, Claremont School of Theology in California, Union Theological Seminary in New York City, Trinity College in Toronto, and St. George's College in Jerusalem. He is editor of *On Being a Bishop: Papers on Episcopacy from the Moscow Consultation 1992* and *They Still Speak: Readings for the Lesser Feasts*.

Bibliography

Addison, James Thayer. *The Episcopal Church in the United States, 1789–1931*. New York: Charles Scribner's Sons, 1951.

Ahlstrom, Sydney E. *A Religious History of the American People*. New Haven: Yale University Press, 1972.

Albright, Raymond W. *A History of the Protestant Episcopal Church*. New York: Macmillan Company, 1964.

Apel, Willi. *Harvard Dictionary of Music*. Cambridge, Massachusetts: Harvard University Press, 1965.

Armentrout, Don S. and Robert Boak Slocum. *A Documentary History of the Episcopal Church, 1782–1985*. New York: Church Publishing Incorporated, 1994.

Armentrout, Don S., ed. *A DuBose Reader, Selections from the Writings of William Porcher DuBose*. Sewanee, Tennessee: The University of the South, 1984.

Bainton, Roland H. *Christendom, A Short History of Christianity and Its Impact on Western Civilization, Vol. I, From the Birth of Christ to the Reformation*. New York: Harper Torchbooks, 1964.

Bainton, Roland H. *Christendom, A Short History of Christianity and Its Impact on Western Civilization, Vol. II, From the Reformation to the Present*. New York: Harper Torchbooks, 1964.

Borsch, Frederick Houk, ed. *Anglicanism and the Bible*. Wilton, Connecticut: Morehouse Barlow, 1984.

Brauer, Jerald C., ed. *The Westminster Dictionary of Church History*. Philadelphia: Westminster Press, 1971.

Brown, Raymond E., S.S., Joseph A. Fitzmyer, S.J., and Roland E. Murphy, O. Carm., *The Jerome Biblical Commentary*. Englewood Cliffs, New Jersey: Prentice-Hall Inc., 1968.

Buttrick, George Arthur, ed. *The Interpreter's Dictionary of the Bible* (4 vols.). Nashville: Abingdon Press, 1962.

Cairncross, Henry, E. C. R. Lamburn, and G. A. C. Whatton. *Ritual Notes, A Comprehensive Guide to the Rites and Ceremonies of the Book of Common Prayer of the English Church Interpreted in Accordance with the Recently Revised "Western Use."* London: W. Knott & Son, Ltd., 1935.

Chadwick, Henry. *The Early Church* [Vol. 1, *The Pelican History of the Church*]. Harmondsworth, Middlesex, England: Penguin Books, 1967.

Chadwick, Owen, ed. *The Mind of the Oxford Movement*. Stanford, California: Stanford University Press, 1961.

Chadwick, Owen. *The Reformation* [Vol. 3, *The Pelican History of the Church*]. Harmondsworth, Middlesex, England: Penguin Books, Ltd., 1972.

Chorley, E. Clowes. *Men and Movements in the American Episcopal Church*. New York: Charles Scribner's Sons, 1946.

Cragg, Gerald R. *The Church and the Age of Reason, 1648–1789* [Vol. 4, *The Pelican History of the Church*]. Harmondsworth, Middlesex, England: Penguin Books, 1970.

Cross, F. L., and E. A. Livingstone. *The Oxford Dictionary of the Christian Church, Third Edition*. New York: Oxford University Press, 1997.

Davies, J. G., ed. *The Westminster Dictionary of Worship*. Philadelphia: Westminster Press, 1972.

Dawley, Powel Mills. *Chapters in Church History*. New York: Seabury Press, 1950.

Dickens, A. G. *The English Reformation*. New York: Schocken Books, 1964.

Dix, Gregory. *The Shape of the Liturgy*. Westminster: Dacre Press, 1945.

Edwards, Richard A. *Matthew's Narrative Portrait of Disciples: How the Text-Connoted Reader is Informed*. Harrisburg, Pennsylvania: Trinity Press International, 1997.

Edwards, Richard A. *Matthew's Story of Jesus*. Philadelphia: Fortress Press, 1985.

Elmen, Paul. *The Anglican Moral Choice*. Wilton, Connecticut: Morehouse-Barlow, 1983.

Evans, G. R. and J. Robert Wright. *The Anglican Tradition: A Handbook of Sources*. London: SPCK, 1991.

Ferguson, Everett, ed. *Encyclopedia of Early Christianity, Second Edition* (2 vols.). New York: Garland Publishing, Inc., 1997.

Fuller, Reginald C., Leonard Johnston, and Conleth Kearns, eds. *A New Catholic Commentary on Holy Scripture*. Nashville: Thomas Nelson Publishers, 1969.

Fuller, Reginald H. *A Critical Introduction to the New Testament*. London: Duckworth, 1966.

Fuller, Reginald H. *Preaching the Lectionary: The Word of God for the Church Today*. Collegeville, Minnesota: Liturgical Press, 1984.

Glazier, Michael and Monika K. Hellwig. *The Modern Catholic Encyclopedia*. Collegeville, Minnesota: Michael Glazier, 1994.

Glover, Raymond F. *A Commentary on New Hymns* [*Hymnal Studies Six*]. New York: Church Publishing Incorporated, 1987.

Glover, Raymond F., ed. *The Hymnal 1982 Companion, Vol. 1*. New York: Church Publishing Incorporated, 1990.

Glover, Raymond F., ed. *The Hymnal 1982 Companion, Vol. 2,* Service Music and Biographies. New York: Church Publishing Incorporated, 1994.

Glover, Raymond F., ed. *The Hymnal 1982 Companion, Vol. 3A*, Hymns 1–384. New York: Church Publishing Incorporated, 1994.

Glover, Raymond F., ed. *The Hymnal 1982 Companion, Vol. 3B*, Hymns 385–720. New York: Church Publishing Incorporated, 1994.

González, Justo L. *A History of Christian Thought, Vol. I, Revised Edition, From the Beginnings to the Council of Chalcedon*. Nashville: Abingdon Press, 1970.

González, Justo L. *A History of Christian Thought, Vol. II, Revised Edition, From Augustine to the Eve of the Reformation*. Nashville: Abingdon Press, 1971.

González, Justo L. *A History of Christian Thought, Vol. III, Revised Edition, From the Protestant Reformation to the Twentieth Century*. Nashville: Abingdon Press, 1975.

Griffiss, James E., ed. *Anglican Theology and Pastoral Care*. Wilton, Connecticut: Morehouse-Barlow, 1985.

Griffiss, James E. *The Anglican Vision*. Cambridge, Massachusetts: Cowley Publications, 1997.

Griffiss, James E. *Church, Ministry and Unity*. Oxford: Basil Blackwell, 1983.

Griffiss, James E. *A Silent Path to God*. Philadelphia: Fortress, 1980.

Guilbert, Charles Mortimer, ed. *Words of our Worship*. New York: Church Publishing Incorporated, 1988.

Hatchett, Marion J. *Commentary on the American Prayer Book*. New York: Seabury, 1981.

Hatchett, Marion J. *A Manual for Clergy and Church Musicians.* New York: Church Publishing Incorporated, 1980.

Hatchett, Marion J. *Sanctifying Life, Time, and Space: An Introduction to Liturgical Study*. New York: Seabury Press, 1976.

Henery, Charles R., ed. *Beyond the Horizon: Frontiers for Mission*. Cincinnati, Ohio: Forward Movement, 1986.

Hodges, George. *Three Hundred Years of the Episcopal Church in America*. Philadelphia: George W. Jacobs & Co., 1906.

Holmes, David L. *A Brief History of the Episcopal Church*. Valley Forge, Pennsylvania: Trinity Press International, 1993.

Holmes, Urban T., III. *Ministry and Imagination*. New York: Seabury Press, 1981.

Holmes, Urban T., III. *What is Anglicanism?* Wilton, Connecticut: Morehouse-Barlow Co., Inc., 1982.

Jones, Cheslyn, Geoffrey Wainwright, and Edward Yarnold, S.J., eds. *The Study of Liturgy*. New York: Oxford University Press, 1978.

Jungmann, J. A. *The Mass of the Roman Rite: Its Origins and Development*, Trans. F. X. Brunner (2 vols.). New York: Benziger Brothers, 1950.

Kavanagh, Aidan. *The Shape of Baptism: The Rite of Christian Initiation*. New York: Pueblo Press, 1978.

Kelly, J. N. D. *Early Christian Creeds*. London: Longmans, Green, 1950.

Lossky, Nicholas, José Míguez Bonino, John Pobee, Tom Stransky, Geoffrey Wainwright, and Pauline Webb, eds. *Dictionary of the Ecumenical Movement*. Grand Rapids, Michigan: William B. Eerdmans, 1991.

Macquarrie, John, ed. *Dictionary of Christian Ethics*. Philadelphia: Westminster Press, 1967.

Macquarrie, John. *Principles of Christian Theology, Second Edition*. New York: Charles Scribner's Sons, 1977.

Manross, William Wilson. *A History of the American Episcopal Church*. New York: Morehouse Publishing Co., 1935.

Marty, Martin E. *A Short History of Christianity*. New York: Meridian Books, 1959.

McBrien, Richard P., ed. *The HarperCollins Encyclopedia of Catholicism*. San Francisco: HarperCollins, 1995.

McDonald, William J., ed. *The New Catholic Encyclopedia* (18 vols.). New York: McGraw-Hill Book Company, 1967.

Meagher, Paul Kevin, OP, Thomas C. O'Brien, and Consuelo Maria Aherne, SSJ, *Encyclopedic Dictionary of Religion* (3 vols.). Washington, D.C.: Corpus Publications, 1979.

Merriman, Michael W, ed. *The Baptismal Mystery and the Catechumenate*. New York: Church Publishing Incorporated, 1990.

Meyers, Ruth A., ed. *Baptism and Ministry*. New York: Church Publishing Incorporated, 1994.

Meyers, Ruth A. *Continuing the Reformation: Re-Visioning Baptism in the Episcopal Church*. New York: Church Publishing Incorporated, 1997.

Mitchell, Leonel L. *Pastoral and Occasional Liturgies*. Cambridge, Massachusetts: Cowley Publications, 1998.

Mitchell, Leonel L. *Lent Holy Week Easter, and the Great Fifty Days*. Cambridge, Massachusetts: Cowley Publications, 1996.

Mitchell, Leonel L. *Praying Shapes Believing: A Theological Commentary on the Book of Common Prayer*. San Francisco: Harper & Row, 1985.

Moorman, J. R. H. *The Anglican Spiritual Tradition*. London: Darton, Longman and Todd, 1983.

Moorman, J. R. H. *A History of the Church in England*. London: Adam and Charles Black, 1958.

More, Paul Elmer and Frank Leslie Cross, eds. *Anglicanism, The Thought and Practice of the Church of England, Illustrated from the Religious Literature of the Seventeenth Century*. London: SPCK, 1951.

Neill, Stephen. *Anglicanism, Fourth Edition*. New York: Oxford University Press, 1977.

Neill, Stephen. *A History of Christian Missions* [Vol. 6, *The Pelican History of the Church*]. Harmondsworth, Middlesex, England: Penguin Books, Ltd., 1964.

Norris, Richard A. *Understanding the Faith of the Church.* New York: Seabury Press, 1979.

O'Brien, T. C. *The Encyclopedic Dictionary of the Western Churches.* Washington, D.C.: Corpus Publications, 1970.

O'Collins, Gerald, S.J., and Edward G. Farrugia, S.J. *A Concise Dictionary of Theology.* New York: Paulist Press, 1991.

Pelikan, Jaroslav. *The Christian Tradition, A History of the Development of Doctrine, Vol. 1, The Emergence of the Catholic Tradition (100–600).* Chicago: University of Chicago Press, 1971.

Pelikan, Jaroslav. *The Christian Tradition, A History of the Development of Doctrine, Vol. 2, The Spirit of Eastern Christendom (600–1700).* Chicago: University of Chicago Press, 1974.

Pelikan, Jaroslav. *The Christian Tradition, A History of the Development of Doctrine, Vol. 3, The Growth of Medieval Theology (600–1300).* Chicago: University of Chicago Press, 1978.

Pelikan, Jaroslav. *The Christian Tradition, A History of the Development of Doctrine, Vol. 4, Reformation of Church and Dogma (1300–1700).* Chicago: University of Chicago Press, 1984.

Pelikan, Jaroslav. *The Christian Tradition, A History of the Development of Doctrine, Vol. 5, Christian Doctrine and Modern Culture (since 1700).* Chicago: University of Chicago Press, 1989.

Pelikan, Jaroslav. *The Melody of Theology, A Philosophical Dictionary.* Cambridge, Massachusetts: Harvard University Press, 1988.

Pittenger, W. Norman. *The Episcopalian Way of Life.* Englewood Cliffs, New Jersey: Prentice-Hall, Inc., 1957.

Plater, Ormonde. *The Deacon in the Liturgy.* Boston: National Center for the Diaconate, 1981.

Plater, Ormonde. *Intercession: A Theological and Practical Guide.* Cambridge, Massachusetts: Cowley Publications, 1995.

Plater, Ormonde. *Many Servants: An Introduction to Deacons.* Cambridge, Massachusetts: Cowley Publications, 1991.

Porter, Harry Boone, Jr. *The Day of Light: The Biblical and Liturgical Meaning of Sunday.* Greenwich, Connecticut: Seabury Press, 1960.

Porter, Harry Boone, Jr. *Keeping the Church Year.* New York: Seabury Press, 1977.

Price, Charles P. and Louis Weil. *Liturgy for Living.* New York: Seabury Press, 1979.

Price, Charles P. *A Matter of Faith.* Wilton, Connecticut: Morehouse-Barlow Company, 1983.

Prichard, Robert W. *A History of the Episcopal Church. Revised Edition.* Harrisburg, Pennsylvania: Morehouse Publishing, 1999.

Prichard, Robert W., ed. *Readings from the History of the Episcopal Church.* Wilton, Connecticut: Morehouse-Barlow, 1986.

Rahner, Karl, ed. *Encyclopedia of Theology, The Concise Sacramentum Mundi.* New York: Crossroad, 1984.

Rahner, Karl, and Herbert Vorgrimler. *Dictionary of Theology, Second Edition.* New York: Crossroad, 1981.

Ramsey, Arthur Michael. *An Era in Anglican Theology, From Gore to Temple.* New York: Charles Scribner's Sons, 1960.

Rowell, Geoffrey. *The Vision Glorious, Themes and Personalities of the Catholic Revival in Anglicanism.* New York: Oxford University Press, 1983.

Sedgwick, Timothy F. *The Christian Moral Life: Practices of Piety.* Grand Rapids, Michigan: W. B. Eerdmans, 1999.

Sedgwick, Timothy F. *The Making of Ministry.* Cambridge, Massachusetts: Cowley Publications, 1993.

Shattuck, Gardiner H., Jr. *A Shield and Hiding Place: The Religious Life of the Civil War Armies*. Macon, Georgia: Mercer University Press, 1987.

Shepherd, M. H., Jr. *The Oxford American Prayer Book Commentary*. New York: Oxford University Press, 1950.

Slocum, Robert Boak, ed. *A New Conversation, Essays on the Future of Theology and the Episcopal Church*. New York: Church Publishing Incorporated, 1999.

Slocum, Robert Boak, ed. *Prophet of Justice, Prophet of Life, Essays on William Stringfellow*. New York: Church Publishing Incorporated, 1997.

Smith, George Wayne. *Admirable Simplicity: Principles for Worship Planning in the Anglican Tradition*. New York: Church Publishing Incorporated, 1996.

Southern, R. W. *Western Society and the Church in the middle ages* [Vol. 2, *The Pelican History of the Church*]. Harmondsworth, Middlesex, England: Penguin Books, 1970.

Spencer, Bonnell, O.H.C. *Ye Are the Body, A People's History of the Church, Revised Edition*. West Park, New York: Holy Cross Publications, 1965.

Stevick, Daniel B. *Baptismal Moments; Baptismal Meanings*. New York: Church Publishing Incorporated, 1987.

Stuhlman, Byron D. *Eucharistic Celebration, 1789–1979*. New York: Church Publishing Incorporated, 1988.

Stuhlman, Byron D. *Prayer Book Rubrics Expanded*. New York: Church Publishing Incorporated, 1987.

Sumner, David E. *The Episcopal Church's History: 1945–1985*. Wilton, Connecticut: Morehouse-Barlow, 1987.

Sykes, Stephen W. *The Integrity of Anglicanism*. New York: Seabury Press, 1978.

Talley, Thomas J. *The Origins of the Liturgical Year*. New York: Pueblo Publishing Company, 1986.

Tavard, George H. *The Church, Community of Salvation, An Ecumenical Ecclesiology* [Vol. 1, *New Theology Studies*]. Collegeville, Minnesota: Liturgical Press, 1992.

Terwilliger, Robert E. and Urban T. Holmes, III, eds. *To Be a Priest, Perspectives on Vocation and Ordination*. New York: Seabury Press, 1975.

Tiffany, Charles C. *A History of the Protestant Episcopal Church in the United States of America*. New York: Christian Literature Company, 1895.

Vidler, Alec R. *The Church in an Age of Revolution* [Vol. 5, *The Pelican History of the Church*]. Harmondsworth, Middlesex, England: Penguin Books, 1974.

Vogel, Arthur A. *Radical Christianity and the Flesh of Jesus: The Roots of Eucharistic Living*. Grand Rapids, Michigan: W. B. Eerdmans, 1995.

Vogel, Arthur A., ed. *Theology in Anglicanism*. Wilton, Connecticut: Morehouse-Barlow, 1984.

Wainwright, G. *Doxology: The Praise of God in Worship, Doctrine and Life: A Systematic Theology*. New York: Oxford University Press, 1980.

Wall, John N., Jr. *A New Dictionary for Episcopalians*. San Francisco: HarperCollins, 1985.

Wantland, William C. *Canon Law in the Episcopal Church*. Chicago: Evangelical and Catholic Mission, 1984.

Weil, Louis. *Gathered to Pray: Understanding Liturgical Prayer*. Parish Life Source Books. Cambridge, Massachusetts: Cowley Publications, 1986.

Weil, Louis. *Sacraments & Liturgy, The Outward Signs*. Oxford: Basil Blackwell, 1983.

Witmer, Joseph W. and J. Robert Wright. *Called to Full Unity: Documents on Anglican-Roman Catholic Relations, 1966–1983*. Washington, D.C.: United States Catholic Conference, 1986.

Wolf, William J, ed. *Anglican Spirituality*. Wilton, Connecticut: Morehouse-Barlow, 1982.

Wolf, William J., ed. *The Spirit of Anglicanism*. Wilton, Connecticut: Morehouse-Barlow, 1979.

Wright, J. Robert, ed. *On Being a Bishop: Papers on Episcopacy from the Moscow Consultation, 1992*. New York: Church Publishing Incorporated, 1993.

Wright, J. Robert, ed. *A Communion of Communions: One Eucharistic Fellowship, The Detroit Report and Papers of the Triennial Ecumenical Study of the Episcopal Church, 1976–1979*. New York: Seabury Press, 1979.

Wright, J. Robert. *Prayer Book Spirituality*. New York: Church Publishing Incorporated, 1989.

Wright, J. Robert, ed. *They Still Speak: Readings for the Lesser Feasts*. New York: Church Publishing Incorporated, 1993.

Yarnold, Edward J. *The Awe-Inspiring Rites of Initiation, Baptismal Homilies of the Fourth Century*. Middlegreen, Slough, Great Britain: St. Paul Publications, 1972.